Gleim Publications, Inc., offers five university-level study systems:

Auditing & Systems Exam Questions and Explanations with Test Prep Software
Business Law/Legal Studies Exam Questions and Explanations with Test Prep Software
Federal Tax Exam Questions and Explanations with Test Prep Software
Financial Accounting Exam Questions and Explanations with Test Prep Software
Cost/Managerial Accounting Exam Questions and Explanations with Test Prep Software

The following is a list of Gleim examination review systems:

CIA Review: Part 1, The Internal Audit Activity's Role in Governance, Risk, and Control
CIA Review: Part 2, Conducting the Internal Audit Engagement
CIA Review: Part 3, Business Analysis and Information Technology
CIA Review: Part 4, Business Management Skills
CIA Review: A System for Success

CMA Review: Part 1, Financial Planning, Performance, and Control
CMA Review: Part 2, Financial Decision Making
CMA Review: A System for Success

CPA Review: Financial
CPA Review: Auditing
CPA Review: Business
CPA Review: Regulation
CPA Review: A System for Success

EA Review: Part 1, Individuals
EA Review: Part 2, Businesses
EA Review: Part 3, Representation, Practices, and Procedures
EA Review: A System for Success

D1611584

Use the order form provided at the back of this book or contact us at www.gleim.com or (800) 874-5346.

Visit www.gleim.com for the latest updates and information on all of our products.

ii

REVIEWERS AND CONTRIBUTORS

Garrett W. Gleim, B.S., CPA (not in public practice), received a Bachelor of Science degree from The Wharton School at the University of Pennsylvania. Mr. Gleim coordinated the production staff, reviewed the manuscript, and provided production assistance throughout the project.

Grady M. Irwin, J.D., is a graduate of the University of Florida College of Law, and he has taught in the University of Florida College of Business. Mr. Irwin provided substantial editorial assistance throughout the project.

Michael Kustanovich, M.A., CPA, Israeli CPA, is a graduate of Ben-Gurion University of the Negev, Israel. He has worked in the audit department of KPMG, Israel, and as a financial accounting lecturer in the department of Economics of Ben-Gurion University of the Negev. Mr. Kustanovich provided substantial editorial assistance throughout the project.

John F. Rebstock, B.S.A., is a graduate of the Fisher School of Accounting at the University of Florida. He has passed the CPA and CIA exams. Mr. Rebstock reviewed portions of the manuscript.

Kristina M. Rivet, CPA, CIA, graduated *cum laude* from Florida International University. She has extensive public accounting experience in the areas of financial accounting, tax, and consulting. Ms. Rivet provided substantial editorial assistance throughout the project.

Stewart B. White, CIA, is a graduate of the School of Business at Virginia Commonwealth University. He has passed the CPA and CISA exams and has worked in the fields of retail management, financial audit, IT audit, COBOL programming, and data warehouse management. Mr. White provided substantial editorial assistance throughout the project.

A PERSONAL THANKS

This manual would not have been possible without the extraordinary effort and dedication of Jacob Brunny, Julie Cutlip, Eileen Nickl, Teresa Soard, Joanne Strong, Candace Van Doren, Jennifer Vann, and Eleanor Wilson, who typed the entire manuscript and all revisions, and drafted and laid out the diagrams and illustrations in this book.

The authors also appreciate the production and editorial assistance of Melissa Del Valle, Chris Hawley, Katie Larson, Cary Marcous, Shane Rapp, Drew Sheppard, Katie Wassink, and Martha Willis.

The authors also appreciate the critical reading assistance of Ellen Buhl, Reed Daines, Stephanie Garrison, Devin Grief, Daniela Guanipa, Alyssa Hagerty, and Jerry Mathis.

Finally, we appreciate the encouragement, support, and tolerance of our families throughout this project.

Financial

by

Irvin N. Gleim, Ph.D., CPA, CIA, CMA, CFM, RTRP

with the assistance of
Grady M. Irwin, J.D.

The AICPA title of this section is *Financial Accounting and Reporting*, and the AICPA acronym is FAR.

ABOUT THE AUTHOR

Irvin N. Gleim is Professor Emeritus in the Fisher School of Accounting at the University of Florida and is a member of the American Accounting Association, Academy of Legal Studies in Business, American Institute of Certified Public Accountants, Association of Government Accountants, Florida Institute of Certified Public Accountants, The Institute of Internal Auditors, and the Institute of Management Accountants. He has had articles published in the *Journal of Accountancy*, *The Accounting Review*, and *The American Business Law Journal* and is author/coauthor of numerous accounting books, aviation books, and CPE courses.

Gleim Publications, Inc.
P.O. Box 12848
University Station
Gainesville, Florida 32604
(800) 87-GLEIM or (800) 874-5346
(352) 375-0772
Fax: (352) 375-6940
Internet: www.gleim.com
Email: admin@gleim.com

For updates to this 2013 printing of
CPA Review: Financial

Go To: www.gleim.com/updates

Or: Email update@gleim.com with
CPA FAR 2013-1 in the subject line.
You will receive our current update
as a reply.

Updates are available until the next edition is
published.

ISSN: 1547-8025

ISBN: 978-1-58194-266-8 *CPA Review: Auditing*
ISBN: 978-1-58194-271-2 *CPA Review: Business*
ISBN: 978-1-58194-272-9 *CPA Review: Financial*
ISBN: 978-1-58194-273-6 *CPA Review: Regulation*
ISBN: 978-1-58194-292-7 *CPA Review: A System for Success*

ACKNOWLEDGMENTS

Material from *Uniform CPA Examination, Selected Questions and Unofficial Answers*, Copyright
© 1974-2012 by the American Institute of Certified Public Accountants, Inc., is reprinted and/or adapted
with permission. Visit the AICPA's website at www.aicpa.org for more information.

The author is indebted to the Institute of Certified Management Accountants for permission to use
problem materials from past CMA examinations. Questions and unofficial answers from the Certified
Management Accountant Examinations, copyright by the Institute of Certified Management
Accountants, are reprinted and/or adapted with permission.

The author is grateful for permission to reproduce Certified Internal Auditor Examination
Questions, Copyright © 1991-2008 by The Institute of Internal Auditors, Inc.

This publication was printed and bound by Corley Printing Company, St. Louis, MO, a registered
ISO-9002 company. More information about Corley Printing Company is available at
www.corleyprinting.com or by calling (314) 739-3777.

TABLE OF CONTENTS

	Page
Detailed Table of Contents	vi
Preface for CPA Candidates	viii
Optimizing Your Financial Score	1
Study Unit 1. The Financial Reporting Environment	19
Study Unit 2. Financial Statements	59
Study Unit 3. Statement of Cash Flows	95
Study Unit 4. Income Statement Items	123
Study Unit 5. Financial Statement Disclosure	163
Study Unit 6. Cash and Investments	197
Study Unit 7. Receivables	231
Study Unit 8. Inventories	261
Study Unit 9. Property, Plant, Equipment, and Depletable Resources	303
Study Unit 10. Intangible Assets and Other Capitalization Issues	347
Study Unit 11. Payables and Taxes	381
Study Unit 12. Employee Benefits	419
Study Unit 13. Noncurrent Liabilities	457
Study Unit 14. Leases and Contingencies	495
Study Unit 15. Equity	527
Study Unit 16. Business Combinations and Consolidated Financial Reporting	571
Study Unit 17. Derivatives, Hedging, and Other Topics	607
Study Unit 18. Governmental Accounting	643
Study Unit 19. Governmental Reporting	687
Study Unit 20. Not-for-Profit Concepts	729
Appendix: IFRS Differences	767
Index	779
Order Form	791

DETAILED TABLE OF CONTENTS

Page

Study Unit 1. The Financial Reporting Environment
1.1. Standard Setting for Financial Accounting 19
1.2. The Objective of General-Purpose Financial Reporting 22
1.3. Objectives of Financial Reporting -- Not-for-Profit (Nongovernmental) Entities 23
1.4. Objectives of Financial Reporting -- Governmental Entities 24
1.5. Assumptions, Principles, and Constraints 26
1.6. Qualitative Characteristics of Useful Financial Information 28
1.7. Elements of Financial Statements 30
1.8. Recognition and Measurement Concepts 33
1.9. Cash Flow Information and Present Value 36
1.10. SEC Reporting 37
1.11. Practice Simulation 52

Study Unit 2. Financial Statements
2.1. Balance Sheet 59
2.2. Statements of Income, Retained Earnings, and Changes in Equity 63
2.3. Comprehensive Income 69
2.4. Other Financial Statement Presentations 71
2.5. First-Time Adoption of IFRS 73
2.6. Practice Simulation 87

Study Unit 3. Statement of Cash Flows
3.1. Statement of Cash Flows -- Classifications 95
3.2. Statement of Cash Flows -- Calculations 98
3.3. Direct and Indirect Methods -- Classifications 98
3.4. Direct and Indirect Methods -- Calculations 104
3.5. Practice Simulation 114

Study Unit 4. Income Statement Items
4.1. Discontinued Operations 123
4.2. Extraordinary Items 125
4.3. Accounting Changes and Error Corrections 126
4.4. Earnings per Share (EPS) 129
4.5. Long-Term Construction Contracts 135
4.6. Revenue Recognition after Delivery 138
4.7. Fair Value Measurements 140
4.8. Practice Simulation 152

Study Unit 5. Financial Statement Disclosure
5.1. Significant Accounting Policies 163
5.2. Segment Reporting 164
5.3. Interim Financial Reporting 168
5.4. Related Party Disclosures 173
5.5. Unconditional Purchase Obligations 174
5.6. Significant Risks and Uncertainties 175
5.7. Subsequent Events 177
5.8. Financial Statement Disclosures 178
5.9. Practice Simulation 190

Study Unit 6. Cash and Investments
6.1. Cash 197
6.2. Fair Value Option (FVO) 201
6.3. Classification of Investments 203
6.4. Equity Method 207
6.5. Investments in Bonds 211
6.6. Cash Surrender Value 213
6.7. Practice Simulation 224

Page

Study Unit 7. Receivables
7.1. Accounts Receivable -- Fundamentals 231
7.2. Accounts Receivable -- Measurement 234
7.3. Transfers of Receivables and Other Financial Assets 237
7.4. Notes Receivable -- Recognition 242
7.5. Notes Receivable -- Discounting 244
7.6. Practice Simulation 254

Study Unit 8. Inventories
8.1. Inventory Fundamentals 261
8.2. Consignment Accounting 267
8.3. Cost Flow Methods -- Application 268
8.4. Cost Flow Methods -- Comparison 274
8.5. Dollar-Value LIFO 274
8.6. Lower of Cost or Market (LCM) 277
8.7. Special Topics in Inventory Accounting 279
8.8. Estimating Inventory 281
8.9. Practice Simulation 297

Study Unit 9. Property, Plant, Equipment, and Depletable Resources
9.1. Initial Measurement of Property, Plant, and Equipment (PPE) 303
9.2. Special Measurement Issue -- Internally Constructed Assets (ICAs) 307
9.3. Subsequent Expenditures for PPE 310
9.4. Depreciation Methods -- Calculations 312
9.5. Depreciation Methods -- Changes and Comparison 316
9.6. Exchanges of Nonmonetary Assets 317
9.7. Disposals Other than by Exchange 319
9.8. Impairment of Long-Lived Assets 320
9.9. Depletion 323
9.10. Practice Simulation 337

Study Unit 10. Intangible Assets and Other Capitalization Issues
10.1. Intangible Assets Distinct from Goodwill -- Initial Recognition 347
10.2. Intangible Assets Distinct from Goodwill -- Accounting Subsequent to Acquisition 348
10.3. Franchise Accounting 352
10.4. Goodwill 353
10.5. Research and Development 356
10.6. Prepayments 359
10.7. Computer Software 359
10.8. Special Issues 361
10.9. Practice Simulation 373

Study Unit 11. Payables and Taxes
11.1. Accounts Payable 381
11.2. Accrued Expenses 382
11.3. Certain Taxes Payable 384
11.4. Deposits and Other Advances 384
11.5. Coupons and Premiums 385
11.6. Warranties 386
11.7. Income Tax Accounting -- Overview 387
11.8. Income Tax Accounting -- Temporary and Permanent Differences 389
11.9. Income Tax Accounting -- Applicable Tax Rate 392

Page

Study Unit 11. Payables and Taxes (continued)
11.10. Income Tax Accounting -- Recognition of Tax Expense 392
11.11. Income Tax Accounting -- Other Issues 394
11.12. Practice Simulation 410

Study Unit 12. Employee Benefits
12.1. Components of Pension Expense 419
12.2. Funded Status of Pension Plans 426
12.3. Pension Disclosures and Other Issues 429
12.4. Postretirement Benefits Other than Pensions .. 430
12.5. Compensated Absences and Postemployment Benefits 432
12.6. Share-Based Payment 434
12.7. Practice Simulation 449

Study Unit 13. Noncurrent Liabilities
13.1. Types of Bond Liabilities 457
13.2. Time Value of Money 458
13.3. Bonds Payable -- Initial Measurement 460
13.4. Bonds Payable -- Subsequent Measurement .. 462
13.5. Debt Issue Costs 463
13.6. Securities with Characteristics of Liabilities and Equity 464
13.7. Extinguishment of Debt 466
13.8. Refinancing of Current Obligations 467
13.9. Noncurrent Notes Payable 468
13.10. Troubled Debt Restructurings 469
13.11. Asset Retirement Obligations 472
13.12. Costs Associated with Exit or Disposal Activities 473
13.13. Practice Simulation 488

Study Unit 14. Leases and Contingencies
14.1. Lease Classification 495
14.2. Lessee Accounting for Capital Leases -- Initial Measurement 496
14.3. Lessee Accounting for Capital Leases -- Subsequent Measurement 498
14.4. Lessee Accounting for Capital Leases -- Other Considerations 499
14.5. Lessor Accounting for Capital Leases 500
14.6. Operating Leases 504
14.7. Sale-Leaseback Transactions 504
14.8. Contingencies -- Recognition and Reporting ... 506
14.9. Contingencies -- Amounts Recognized 508
14.10. Practice Simulation 519

Study Unit 15. Equity
15.1. Classes of Equity 527
15.2. Issuance of Stock 530
15.3. Stock Warrants and Stock Rights 533
15.4. Treasury Stock -- Acquisition 534
15.5. Treasury Stock -- Reissue 535
15.6. Retirement of Stock 536
15.7. Cash Dividends 537
15.8. Property Dividends and Liquidating Dividends . 538
15.9. Stock Dividends and Stock Splits 539
15.10. Partnerships -- Formation and Allocation 540
15.11. Partnerships -- Changes and Liquidation 543
15.12. Quasi-Reorganization 549
15.13. Practice Simulation 563

Page

Study Unit 16. Business Combinations and Consolidated Financial Reporting
16.1. Accounting for Business Combinations -- Overview 571
16.2. Consolidated Financial Reporting -- Acquisition Method 575
16.3. Consolidated Financial Reporting -- Acquisition-Date Balance Sheet 577
16.4. Consolidated Financial Reporting -- Net Income and Changes in Equity 579
16.5. Consolidated Financial Reporting -- Intraentity Eliminations 581
16.6. Other Aspects of Business Combinations 584
16.7. Combined Financial Statements 586
16.8. Practice Simulation 598

Study Unit 17. Derivatives, Hedging, and Other Topics
17.1. Derivatives and Hedging 607
17.2. Foreign Currency Issues 616
17.3. Financial Statement Analysis -- Liquidity 619
17.4. Financial Statement Analysis -- Activity 621
17.5. Financial Statement Analysis -- Solvency, Valuation, and Comparative Analysis 624
17.6. Practice Simulation 636

Study Unit 18. Governmental Accounting
18.1. Fund Accounting Concepts and Reporting 643
18.2. Budgetary Accounting and Encumbrances 649
18.3. Governmental Sources of Financing 654
18.4. Characteristic Transactions of Governmental Entities 661
18.5. Practice Simulation 678

Study Unit 19. Governmental Reporting
19.1. The Reporting Entity and the CAFR 687
19.2. MD&A and the Government-Wide Financial Statements 691
19.3. Governmental Funds Reporting 697
19.4. Proprietary Funds Reporting 702
19.5. Fiduciary Funds Reporting and Interfund Activity 705
19.6. Practice Simulation 720

Study Unit 20. Not-for-Profit Concepts
20.1. The Not-for-Profit Environment 729
20.2. Financial Statements of NFPs 731
20.3. Revenues of NFPs 739
20.4. Investments Held by NFPs 744
20.5. Healthcare Entities (HCEs) 745
20.6. Practice Simulation 758

PREFACE FOR CPA CANDIDATES

The purpose of this Gleim *CPA Review* study book is to help YOU prepare to pass the 2013 Financial Accounting and Reporting (referred to throughout the rest of this text as Financial) section of the CPA examination. Our overriding consideration is to provide an inexpensive, effective, and easy-to-use study program. This book

1. Explains how to optimize your grade by focusing on the Financial section of the CPA exam.

2. Defines the subject matter tested on the Financial section of the CPA exam.

3. Outlines all of the subject matter tested on the Financial section in 20 easy-to-use-and-complete study units.

4. Presents multiple-choice questions from recent CPA examinations to prepare you for questions in future CPA exams. Our answer explanations are presented to the immediate right of each question for your convenience. Use a piece of paper to cover our answer explanations as you study the questions.

5. Presents several task-based simulations in each study unit to acquaint you with simulation task formats. Answer the simulations in your book. The answers and grading instructions follow each simulation.

The outline format, the spacing, and the question and answer formats in this book are designed to facilitate readability, learning, understanding, and success on the CPA exam. Our most successful candidates use the entire Gleim CPA Review System*, which includes books, Test Prep Online, Audio Review, Gleim Online, Simulation Wizard, Practice Exam, and access to a Personal Counselor; or a group study CPA review program. (Check our website for live courses we recommend.) This review book and all Gleim *CPA Review* materials are compatible with other CPA review materials and courses that follow the AICPA Content and Skill Specification Outlines (CSOs/SSOs).

To maximize the efficiency and effectiveness of your CPA review program, augment your studying with *CPA Review: A System for Success*. This booklet has been carefully written and organized to provide important information to assist you in passing the CPA examination.

Thank you for your interest in the Gleim *CPA Review* materials. We deeply appreciate the thousands of letters and suggestions received from CIA, CMA, EA, RTRP, and CPA candidates during the past 5 decades.

If you use the Gleim materials, we want YOUR feedback immediately after the exam and as soon as you have received your grades. The CPA exam is NONDISCLOSED, and you will sign an attestation including, "I hereby agree that I will maintain the confidentiality of the Uniform CPA Examination. In addition, I agree that I will not divulge the nature or content of any Uniform CPA Examination question or answer under any circumstance..." We ask only for information about our materials, i.e., the topics that need to be added, expanded, etc. Our approach has AICPA approval.

Please go to www.gleim.com/feedbackFAR to share your suggestions on how we can improve this edition.

Good Luck on the Exam,

Irvin N. Gleim

December 2012

OPTIMIZING YOUR FINANCIAL SCORE

Allow Gleim to Guide You through the Study Process and PASS the Exam 2
Overview of Financial 3
AICPA Content Specification Outlines (CSOs) 4
AICPA Skill Specification Outlines (SSOs) 8
References 8
Steps to Become a CPA 9
How to Study a Financial Study Unit Using the Gleim CPA Review System 10
CPA Final Review 11
CPA Gleim Online 11
Gleim Simulation Wizard for Auditing, Financial, and Regulation 12
Gleim Books 12
CPA Test Prep Online 13
Studying with Book and Test Prep Online 13
Gleim Audio Reviews 14
Time Budgeting and Question-Answering Techniques for Financial 14
Multiple-Choice Questions 14
Task-Based Simulations 16
If You Have Questions 17
How to Be In Control 17
AICPA's Nondisclosure Agreement 17
Citations to Authoritative Pronouncements 17

CBT-e Exam

Gleim Section Title	Auditing	Business	Financial	Regulation
AICPA Formal Title	Auditing & Attestation	Business Environment & Concepts	Financial Accounting & Reporting	Regulation
Acronym	AUD	BEC	FAR	REG
Exam Length	4 hours	3 hours	4 hours	3 hours
Testlets:				
Multiple-Choice	3, 30 questions each	3, 24 questions each	3, 30 questions each	3, 24 questions each
Simulations	1 with 7 tasks	0	1 with 7 tasks	1 with 6 tasks
Written Communication	0	1 with 3 tasks	0	0

ALLOW GLEIM TO GUIDE YOU THROUGH THE STUDY PROCESS AND PASS THE EXAM

1. Read this **Introduction** to familiarize yourself with the content and structure of the Financial section of the exam. In the following pages, you will find

    a. An **overview of the Financial section** and what it generally tests, including

        1) The AICPA's Content Specification Outlines (CSOs) for Financial, cross-referenced with the Gleim study units that contain each topic
        2) The AICPA's Skill Specification Outlines (SSOs) for Financial
        3) The AICPA's suggested references for Financial

    b. A detailed plan with **steps to obtain your CPA license**, including

        1) The order in which you should apply, register, and schedule your exam
        2) The studying tactics on which you should focus
        3) How to organize your study schedule to make the most out of each resource in the Gleim CPA Review System (i.e., books, Test Prep Online, Audio Review, Gleim Online, Simulation Wizard, etc.)

    c. Tactics for your **actual test day**, including

        1) Time budgeting so you complete each testlet with time to review
        2) Question-answering techniques to obtain every point you can in both the multiple-choice and simulation testlets
        3) An explanation of how to be in control of your CPA exam

2. Scan the Gleim *CPA Review: A System for Success* booklet and note where to revisit later in your studying process to obtain a deeper understanding of the of the CPA exam.

    a. *CPA Review: A System for Success* has seven study units:

        Study Unit 1: The CPA Examination: An Overview and Preparation Introduction
        Study Unit 2: AICPA Content Specification Outlines and Skill Specification Outlines
        Study Unit 3: Content Preparation, Test Administration, and Performance Grading
        Study Unit 4: Multiple-Choice Questions
        Study Unit 5: Task-Based Simulations and Written Communication Questions
        Study Unit 6: Preparing to Pass the CPA Exam
        Study Unit 7: How to Take the CPA Exam

    b. If you feel that you need even more details on the test-taking experience, watch our **Free Tutorial** at www.gleim.com/accounting/cpa/basics.php.

        1) This tutorial is best for candidates who have little or no experience with the basic computer skills required for the CPA exam (e.g., copy/paste, search, etc.).

    c. Additionally, the AICPA requires that all candidates review the tutorial and sample tests at www.aicpa.org.

3. Before you begin studying, take a **Diagnostic Quiz** at www.gleim.com/cpadiagnosticquiz or use our Gleim Diagnostic Quiz App for iPhone, iPod Touch, and Android.

    a. The Diagnostic Quiz includes a representative sample of 40 multiple-choice questions and will determine your weakest areas in Financial.

    b. When you are finished, one of our **Personal Counselors** will consult with you to better focus your review on any areas in which you have less confidence.

4. Follow the steps outlined on page 10, "How to Study a Financial Study Unit Using the Gleim CPA Review System." This is the **study plan** that our most successful candidates adhere to. Study until you have reached your **desired proficiency level** (e.g., 75%) for each study unit in Financial.

   a. As you proceed, be sure to check any **Updates** that may have been released.

      1) Gleim Online, Simulation Wizard, and Test Prep Online are updated automatically.

      2) Book updates can be viewed at www.gleim.com/updates, or you can have them emailed to you. See the information box in the top right corner of page iv for details.

   b. **Review the *CPA Review: A System for Success* booklet** and become completely comfortable with what will be expected from you on test day.

5. Shortly before your test date, take a **Practice Exam** (complimentary with the CPA Review System) at www.gleim.com/cpapracticeexam.

   a. The Gleim Practice Exam is designed to exactly emulate the CPA test-taking experience at Prometric.

   b. This timed, scored exam tests you not only on the content you have studied, but also on the question-answering and time-management techniques you have learned throughout the Gleim study process.

   c. When you have completed the exam, consult with your Personal Counselor to discuss where you should **focus your review during the final days before your exam** (question-answering techniques, time management, specific content areas, etc.).

6. **Take and PASS** the Financial section of the CPA exam!

   a. When you have completed the exam, please contact Gleim with your **suggestions, comments, and corrections**. We want to know how well we prepared you for your testing experience.

OVERVIEW OF FINANCIAL

Financial is scheduled for 4 hours (240 minutes).

AICPA title:	Financial Accounting and Reporting
AICPA acronym:	FAR
Gleim title/acronym:	Financial/FAR
Question format:	90 multiple-choice questions in three testlets of 30 questions each
	One testlet with seven Task-Based Simulations
Areas covered:	I. (20%) Conceptual Framework, Standards, Standard Setting, and Presentation of Financial Statements
	II. (30%) Financial Statement Accounts: Recognition, Measurement, Valuation, Calculation, Presentation, and Disclosures
	III. (30%) Specific Transactions, Events, and Disclosures: Recognition, Measurement, Valuation, Calculation, Presentation, and Disclosures
	IV. (10%) Governmental Accounting and Reporting
	V. (10%) Not-for-Profit (Nongovernmental) Accounting and Reporting

The Financial section tests knowledge and understanding of the financial reporting framework used by business, not-for-profit, and governmental entities. The financial reporting frameworks that are included are those issued by the Financial Accounting Standards Board, the International Accounting Standards Board, the U.S. Securities and Exchange Commission, and the Governmental Accounting Standards Board.

In addition to demonstrating knowledge and understanding of accounting principles, candidates are required to demonstrate the skills required to apply that knowledge in performing financial reporting and other tasks as certified public accountants.

According to the AICPA, candidates will be expected to perform the following inclusive list of tasks to demonstrate such knowledge and skills:

- Identify and understand the differences between financial statements prepared on the basis of accounting principles generally accepted in the United States of America (U.S. GAAP) and International Financial Reporting Standards (IFRS).
- Prepare and/or review source documents, including account classification, and enter data into subsidiary and general ledgers.
- Calculate amounts for financial statement components.
- Reconcile the general ledger to the subsidiary ledgers or underlying account details.
- Prepare account reconciliation and related schedules; analyze accounts for unusual fluctuations and make necessary adjustments.
- Prepare consolidating and eliminating entries for the period.
- Identify financial accounting and reporting methods and select those that are appropriate.
- Prepare consolidated financial statements, including balance sheets, income statements, and statements of retained earnings, equity, comprehensive income, and cash flows.
- Prepare appropriate notes to the financial statements.
- Analyze financial statements, including analysis of accounts, variances, trends, and ratios.
- Exercise judgment in the application of accounting principles.
- Apply judgment to evaluate assumptions and methods underlying estimates, including fair value measures of financial statement components.
- Produce required financial statement filings in order to meet regulatory or reporting requirements (e.g., Form 10-Q, 10-K, Annual Report).
- Determine appropriate accounting treatment for new or unusual transactions and evaluate the economic substance of transactions in making the determinations.
- Research relevant professional literature.

AICPA CONTENT SPECIFICATION OUTLINES (CSOs)

In the Uniform CPA Examination Alert newsletter of Spring 2009, when it was first unveiling the new CBT-e exam, the AICPA indicated that the content specification outlines have several purposes, including

1. *Ensure that the testing of entry-level knowledge and skills that are important to the protection of the public interest is consistent across examination administrations*
2. *Determine what kinds of questions should be included on the CPA Examination so that every version of the examination reflects the required distribution and balance of knowledge and skill components*
3. *Provide candidates preparing for the examination with information about the subject matter that is eligible to be tested*

For your convenience, we have reproduced verbatim the AICPA's Financial CSOs. We also have provided cross-references to the study units and subunits in this book that correspond to the CSOs' coverage. If one entry appears above a list, it applies to all items.

AICPA CONTENT SPECIFICATION OUTLINE

Financial Accounting and Reporting

I. **Conceptual Framework, Standards, Standard Setting, and Presentation of Financial Statements (20%)**

    A.   Process by which Accounting Standards are Set and Roles of Accounting Standard-Setting Bodies - 1.1

        1.   U.S. Securities and Exchange Commission (SEC)
        2.   Financial Accounting Standards Board (FASB)
        3.   International Accounting Standards Board (IASB)
        4.   Governmental Accounting Standards Board (GASB)

    B.   Conceptual Framework - 1.2-1.9

        1.   Financial reporting by business entities - 1.2
        2.   Financial reporting by not-for-profit (nongovernmental) entities - 1.3
        3.   Financial reporting by state and local governmental entities - 1.4

    C.   Financial Reporting, Presentation, and Disclosures in General-Purpose Financial Statements

        1.   Balance sheet - 2.1
        2.   Income statement - 2.2
        3.   Statement of comprehensive income - 2.3
        4.   Statement of changes in equity - 2.2
        5.   Statement of cash flows - SU 3
        6.   Notes to financial statements - 1.7
        7.   Consolidated and combined financial statements - 2.4
        8.   First-time adoption of IFRS - 2.5

    D.   SEC Reporting Requirements (e.g., Form 10-Q, 10-K) - 1.10

    E.   Other Financial Statement Presentations, including Other Comprehensive Bases of Accounting (OCBOA)

        1.   Cash basis - 2.4
        2.   Modified cash basis - 2.4
        3.   Income tax basis - 2.4
        4.   Personal financial statements - 2.4
        5.   Financial statements of employee benefit plans/trusts - SU 2

II. **Financial Statement Accounts: Recognition, Measurement, Valuation, Calculation, Presentation, and Disclosures (30%)**

    A.   Cash and Cash Equivalents - 6.1

    B.   Receivables - SU 7

    C.   Inventory - SU 8

    D.   Property, Plant, and Equipment - SU 9

    E.   Investments

        1.   Financial assets at fair value through profit or loss - 6.2, 6.3
        2.   Available for sale financial assets - 6.3
        3.   Held-to-maturity investments - 6.3
        4.   Joint ventures - 5.4
        5.   Equity method investments (investments in associates) - 6.4
        6.   Investment property - 6.5

    F.   Intangible Assets – Goodwill and Other - 10.1, 10.2

    G.   Payables and Accrued Liabilities - 11.1-11.6

    H.   Deferred Revenue - 11.4

    I.   Long-Term Debt (Financial Liabilities)

        1.   Notes payable - 13.9
        2.   Bonds payable - 13.1-13.5
        3.   Debt with conversion features and other options - 13.6
        4.   Modifications and extinguishments - 13.7, 13.8
        5.   Troubled debt restructurings by debtors - 13.10
        6.   Debt covenant compliance - 6.5, 13.1, 15.1

    J.   Equity - SU 15

    K.   Revenue Recognition - 4.5, 4.6

    L.   Costs and Expenses - 2.2

    M. Compensation and Benefits

        1.   Compensated absences - 12.5
        2.   Deferred compensation arrangements - 12.1-12.3
        3.   Nonretirement postemployment benefits - 12.5
        4.   Retirement benefits - 12.4
        5.   Stock compensation (share-based payments) - 12.6

    N.   Income Taxes - 11.7-11.11

III. **Specific Transactions, Events, and Disclosures: Recognition, Measurement, Valuation, Calculation, Presentation, and Disclosures (30%)**

    A.   Accounting Changes and Error Corrections - 4.3

    B.   Asset Retirement and Environmental Obligations - 9.7, 13.11

    C.   Business Combinations - 16.1

    D.   Consolidation (including Off-Balance Sheet Transactions, Variable-Interest Entities, and Noncontrolling Interests) - 16.2-16.6

    E.   Contingencies, Commitments, and Guarantees (Provisions) - 14.8, 14.9

    F.   Earnings Per Share - 4.4

    G.   Exit or Disposal Activities and Discontinued Operations - 4.1

    H.   Extraordinary and Unusual Items - 4.2

    I.   Fair Value Measurements, Disclosures, and Reporting - 4.7

    J.   Derivatives and Hedge Accounting - 5.8, 17.1

    K.   Foreign Currency Transactions and Translation - 17.2

    L.   Impairment - 9.8

    M. Interim Financial Reporting - 5.3

    N.   Leases - 14.1-14.7

    O.   Distinguishing Liabilities from Equity - 13.6

    P.   Nonmonetary Transactions (Barter Transactions) - 9.6

    Q.   Related Parties and Related Party Transactions - 5.4

    R.   Research and Development Costs - 10.5

    S.   Risks and Uncertainties - 5.6

    T.   Segment Reporting - 5.2

    U.   Software Costs - 10.7

    V.   Subsequent Events - 5.7

    W. Transfers and Servicing of Financial Assets and Derecognition - 7.3

IV. Governmental Accounting and Reporting (10%)

    A. Governmental Accounting Concepts

        1. Measurement focus and basis of accounting - 18.1
        2. Fund accounting concepts and applications - 18.1
        3. Budgetary accounting - 18.2

    B. Format and Content of Comprehensive Annual Financial Report (CAFR)

        1. Government-wide financial statements - 19.2
        2. Governmental funds financial statements - 19.3
        3. Proprietary funds financial statements - 19.4
        4. Fiduciary funds financial statements - 19.5
        5. Notes to financial statements - 19.1
        6. Management's discussion and analysis - 19.2
        7. Required supplementary information (RSI) other than Management's Discussion and Analysis - 19.1
        8. Combining statements and individual fund statements and schedules - 19.1
        9. Deriving government-wide financial statements and reconciliation requirements - 19.3

    C. Financial Reporting Entity, Including Blended and Discrete Component Units - 19.1

    D. Typical Items and Specific Types of Transactions and Events: Recognition, Measurement, Valuation, Calculation, and Presentation in Governmental Entity Financial Statements

        1. Net assets and components thereof - 19.2
        2. Fund balances and components thereof - 18.1
        3. Capital assets and infrastructure assets - 18.1, 18.4
        4. General long-term liabilities - 18.1
        5. Interfund activity, including transfers - 19.5
        6. Nonexchange revenue transactions - 18.3
        7. Expenditures - 18.1
        8. Special items - 18.1, 18.2
        9. Encumbrances - 18.2

    E. Accounting and Reporting for Governmental Not-for-Profit Organizations - SU 18, SU 19

V. Not-for-Profit (Nongovernmental) Accounting and Reporting (10%)

    A. Financial Statements - 20.2

        1. Statement of financial position
        2. Statement of activities
        3. Statement of cash flows
        4. Statement of functional expenses

    B. Typical Items and Specific Types of Transactions and Events: Recognition, Measurement, Valuation, Calculation, and Presentation in Financial Statements of Not-for-Profit Organizations

        1. Support, revenues, and contributions - 20.3
        2. Types of restrictions on resources - 20.2, 20.3
        3. Types of net assets - 20.2
        4. Expenses, including depreciation and functional expenses - 20.2
        5. Investments - 20.4

AICPA SKILL SPECIFICATION OUTLINES (SSOs)

The SSOs identify the skills that will be tested on the CPA exam. The following table explains the skills tested, the weight range assigned to each skill category (approximate percentage of CPA exam that will use skills in the category) in Financial, the question format that will be used to test the skill in Financial, and the resources that will be available to the candidates to demonstrate proficiency in each skill.

Skills Category	Weight	Question Format	Resource(s)
Knowledge and Understanding	60%	Multiple-choice questions	Calculator
Application of the Body of Knowledge	40%	Task-based simulations	Authoritative literature, calculator, spreadsheets, etc.
Written Communication*	--	--	--

*The Written Communication category is tested through essays, which are not present in the Financial section of the CPA exam.

REFERENCES

The AICPA suggests that the following publications will be sources of questions for Financial. Our outlines and answer explanations are based on these publications and are organized into meaningful, easy-to-use, common-sense study units to facilitate your exam preparation via the Gleim Knowledge Transfer System.

1. Financial Accounting Standards Board (FASB) Accounting Standards Codification
2. Governmental Accounting Standards Board (GASB) Codification of Governmental Accounting and Financial Reporting Standards
3. Standards issued by the U.S. Securities and Exchange Commission (SEC):
   - Regulation S-X of the Code of Federal Regulations (17 CFR Part 210)
   - Financial Reporting Releases (FRR)/Accounting Series Releases (ASR)
   - Interpretive Releases (IR)
   - SEC Staff Guidance in Staff Accounting Bulletins (SAB)
   - SEC Staff Guidance in EITF Topic D and SEC Staff Observer Comments
   - Regulation S-K of the Code of Federal Regulations
4. International Accounting Standards Board (IASB) International Financial Reporting Standards (IFRS), International Accounting Standards (IASs), and Interpretations
5. AICPA Auditing and Accounting Guides
6. Codification of Statements on Auditing Standards
   - AU Section 623, *Special Reports*
7. Current textbooks on accounting for business, not-for-profit, and governmental entities
8. FASB Concept Statements
9. GASB Concept Statements
10. IFRS Framework

STEPS TO BECOME A CPA

1. Become knowledgeable about the exam, and decide which section you will take first.

2. Purchase the Gleim CPA Review System to thoroughly prepare for the CPA exam. Commit to our systematic preparation for the exam as described in our review materials, including *CPA Review: A System for Success*.

3. Communicate with your Personal Counselor to design a study plan that meets your needs. Call (800) 874-5346 or email CPA@gleim.com.

4. Determine the board of accountancy (i.e., state) to which you will apply to sit for the CPA exam.

5. Obtain, complete, and submit your application form, including transcripts, fees, etc., to your State Board or NASBA. You should receive a Notice To Schedule (NTS) from NASBA in 4 to 6 weeks.

    a. Do not apply for a section of the exam until you are ready to take it. An NTS is valid for a specific period established by the boards of accountancy, and you will forfeit any fees you paid for sections not taken.

    b. Remember, the following testing windows are available for test taking: January/February, April/May, July/August, and October/November.

6. Schedule your test with Prometric (online or by calling your local Prometric testing site). Schedule at least 45 days before the date you plan to sit for the exam.

7. Work systematically through the study units in each section of the Gleim CPA Review System (Auditing, Business, Financial, and Regulation).

8. Use the Gleim CPA Test Prep Online: thousands of questions, all updated to current tax law, Accounting Standards Codification, etc. Listen to CPA Audio Review as a supplement.

9. Sit for and PASS the CPA exam while you are in control.

10. Enjoy your career and pursue multiple certifications (CIA, CMA, EA, RTRP, etc.), recommend Gleim to others who are also taking these exams, and stay up-to-date on your continuing professional education with Gleim CPE.

More specifically, you should focus on the following **system for success** on the Financial section of the CPA exam:

1. **Understand the exam, including its purpose, coverage, preparation, format, administration, grading, and pass rates.**

    a. The better you understand the examination process from beginning to end, the better you will perform.

    b. Study the Gleim *CPA Review: A System for Success*. Please be sure you have a copy of this useful booklet. (*CPA Review: A System for Success* is also available online at www.gleim.com/sfs.)

2. **Learn and understand the subject matter tested.** The AICPA's CSOs and SSOs for the Financial section are the basis for the study outlines that are presented in each of the 20 study units that make up this book.* You will also learn and understand the Financial material tested on the CPA exam by answering numerous multiple-choice questions from recent CPA exams. Multiple-choice questions with the answer explanations to the immediate right of each question are a major component of each study unit.

---

*Please fill out our online feedback form (www.gleim.com/feedbackFAR) IMMEDIATELY after you take the CPA exam so we can adapt to changes in the exam. Our approach has been approved by the AICPA.

3. **Practice answering actual exam questions to perfect your question-answering techniques.** Answering recent exam questions helps you understand the standards to which you will be held. This motivates you to learn and understand while studying (rather than reading) the outlines in each of the 20 study units.

   a. Question-answering techniques are suggested for multiple-choice questions and task-based simulations in Study Units 4 and 5 of *CPA Review: A System for Success*.

   b. Our **CPA Test Prep Online** contains thousands of additional multiple-choice questions that are not offered in our books. Additionally, CPA Test Prep Online has many useful features, including documentation of your performance and the ability to simulate the CBT-e exam environment.

   c. Our **CPA Gleim Online** is a powerful Internet-based program that allows CPA candidates to learn in an interactive environment and provides feedback to candidates to encourage learning. It includes multiple-choice questions and task-based simulations in Prometric's format. Each CPA Gleim Online user has access to a Personal Counselor, who helps organize study plans that work with busy schedules.

   d. Additionally, all candidates are required by the AICPA to review the tutorial and sample tests at www.aicpa.org. According to the AICPA, failure to follow the directions provided in the tutorial and sample tests, including the directions on how to respond, may adversely affect your scores.

4. **Plan and practice exam execution.** Anticipate the exam environment and prepare yourself with a plan: When to arrive? How to dress? What exam supplies to bring? How many questions and what format? Order of answering questions? How much time to spend on each question? See Study Unit 7 in *CPA Review: A System for Success*.

   a. Expect the unexpected and adjust! Remember, your sole objective when taking an examination is to maximize your score. You must outperform your peers, and being as comfortable and relaxed as possible gives you an advantage!

5. **Be in control.** Develop confidence and ensure success with a controlled preparation program followed by confident execution during the examination.

HOW TO STUDY A FINANCIAL STUDY UNIT USING THE GLEIM CPA REVIEW SYSTEM

To ensure that you are using your time effectively, we recommend that you follow the steps listed below when using all of the CPA Review System materials together (books, Test Prep Online, Audio Review, Gleim Online, and Simulation Wizard). Before you begin the steps, take the **Gleim CPA Diagnostic Quiz**. The Gleim CPA Diagnostic Quiz provides a representative sample of 40 multiple-choice questions for each exam part to identify your preliminary strengths and any weaknesses before you start preparing in earnest for the CPA exam.

1. (30 minutes, plus 10 minutes for review) In the **CPA Gleim Online** course, complete Multiple-Choice Quiz #1 in 30 minutes. It is expected that your scores will be lower on the first quiz in each study unit than on subsequent quizzes.

   a. Immediately following the quiz, you will be prompted to review questions you flagged and/or answered incorrectly. For each question, analyze and understand why you were unsure or answered it incorrectly. This step is an essential learning activity.

2. (30 minutes) Use the online audiovisual presentation for an overview of the study unit. **CPA Audio Review** can be substituted for audiovisual presentations and can be used while driving to work, exercising, etc.

3. (45 minutes) Complete the 30-question online True/False quiz. It is interactive and most effective if used prior to studying the Knowledge Transfer Outline.

4. (60 minutes) Study the Knowledge Transfer Outline, particularly the troublesome areas identified from the multiple-choice questions in the Gleim Online course. The Knowledge Transfer Outline can be studied either online or from the books.

5. (30 minutes, plus 10 minutes for review) Complete Multiple-Choice Quiz #2 in the Gleim Online course.

    a. Immediately following the quiz, you will be prompted to review questions you flagged and/or answered incorrectly. For each question, analyze and understand why you were unsure or answered it incorrectly. This step is an essential learning activity.

6. (60 minutes) Complete two 20-question quizzes while in Test Mode from the **CPA Test Prep Online**. Review as needed.

7. (90 minutes) Complete and review the simulation section of the Gleim Online course.

When following these steps, you will complete all 20 study units in about 120 hours. Then spend about 10-20 hours taking customized tests in the CPA Test Prep Online until you approach your desired proficiency level, e.g., 75%+. To get immediate feedback on questions in your problem areas, use Study Sessions. You should also complete all of the simulation tasks in the Simulation Wizard for extra practice on this difficult aspect of the exam.

CPA FINAL REVIEW

Final review is the culmination of all your studies and topics and should occur one week prior to when you sit for your exam. All study units in Gleim Online should be completed by this time.

Step 1: Take the CPA Practice Exam at the beginning of your final review stage. The Practice Exam is 4 hours (240 minutes) long and contains three testlets with 30 multiple-choice questions each and one testlet with seven task-based simulations, just like the CPA exam. This will help you identify any weak areas for more practice. Discuss your results with your Personal Counselor for additional guidance.

Step 2: Work in Gleim CPA Test Prep Online, focusing on your weak areas identified from your Practice Exam. Also, be sure to focus on all the material as a whole to refresh yourself with topics you learned at the beginning of your studies. View your performance chart to make sure you are scoring 70% or higher.

CPA GLEIM ONLINE

CPA Gleim Online is a versatile, interactive, self-study review program delivered via the Internet. It is divided into four courses (one for each section of the CPA exam).

Each course is broken down into 20 individual, manageable study units. Completion time per study unit will average out to 5 hours. Each study unit in the course contains an audiovisual presentation, 30 true/false study questions, 10-20 pages of Knowledge Transfer Outlines, and two 20-question multiple-choice quizzes. Task-based simulations are also included with each study unit in Auditing, Financial, and Regulation, while written communication tasks are in each study unit of Business. Downloadable PDFs with additional information, such as Core Concepts, are also included with each study unit.

CPA Gleim Online provides you with access to a Personal Counselor, a real person who will provide support to ensure your competitive edge. CPA Gleim Online is a great way to get confidence as you prepare with Gleim. This confidence will continue during and after the exam.

GLEIM SIMULATION WIZARD FOR AUDITING, FINANCIAL, AND REGULATION

The Gleim Simulation Wizard for Financial is a training program that focuses on the task-based simulations that appear in the Auditing, Financial, and Regulation sections of the CPA exam. This online course provides one simulation per study unit, as well as test-taking tips from Dr. Gleim to help you stay in control.

GLEIM BOOKS

This edition of the CPA Financial Review book has the following six features to make studying easier:

1. **Examples:** Illustrative examples, both hypothetical and those drawn from actual events, are set off in shaded, bordered boxes.

EXAMPLE

The accuracy of an unobservable price cannot be determined. But the entity can disclose that the estimate is in fact an estimate. It can also explain the estimation process and its limits. Given this disclosure and explanation, if no errors have been made in choosing and performing the process, the representation is faithful.

---

2. **Backgrounds:** In certain instances, we have provided historical background or supplemental information. This information is intended to illuminate the topic under discussion and is set off in bordered boxes with shaded headings. This material does not need to be memorized for the exam.

Background

The FASB's Accounting Standards Codification became effective on July 1, 2009. It is the sole source of non-SEC authoritative accounting and reporting standards. In the Codification, the FASB combined the many pronouncements that formerly constituted U.S. GAAP into a consistent, searchable format available through the Internet.

---

3. **Gleim Success Tips:** These tips supplement the core exam material by suggesting how certain topics might be presented on the exam or how you should prepare for an issue.

Over the years, the topic of earnings per share has been continually tested on CPA exams, often through calculations. Expect to see one or two questions testing earnings per share on your exam.

---

4. **Memory Aids:** These mnemonics are designed to assist you in memorizing important concepts. See the example below.

   Memory aid: **Owners bargain** for **life** and **fair value**

5. **Financial Review Checklist:** This appendix to the 20 study units contains a complete listing of all study units and subunits in the Gleim Financial Review for 2013. Use this list as a study aid to mark off your progress and to provide jumping-off points for review.

6. **IFRS Differences:** The CPA exam began testing international standards for the first time in 2011. When international standards diverge significantly from U.S. GAAP, the differences are highlighted. If there is no specification between GAAP and IFRS, use GAAP.

IFRS Difference

The **elements** of financial statements are (1) assets, (2) liabilities, (3) equity, (4) income (including revenues and gains), and (5) expenses (including losses).

CPA TEST PREP ONLINE

Twenty-question tests in the **CPA Test Prep Online** will help you to focus on your weaker areas. Make it a game: How much can you improve?

Our CPA Test Prep Online (in Test Mode) forces you to commit to your answer choice before looking at answer explanations; thus, you are preparing under true exam conditions. It also keeps track of your time and performance history for each study unit, which is available in either a table or graphical format.

STUDYING WITH BOOK AND TEST PREP ONLINE*

Simplify the exam preparation process by following our suggested steps listed below. DO NOT omit the step in which you diagnose the reasons for answering questions incorrectly; i.e., learn from your mistakes while studying so you avoid making similar mistakes on the CPA exam.

1. In test mode of CPA Test Prep Online, answer a 20-question diagnostic test before studying any other information.

2. Study the Knowledge Transfer Outline for the corresponding study unit in your Gleim book.

    a. Place special emphasis on the weaker areas that you identified with the initial diagnostic quiz in Step 1.

3. Take two or three 20-question tests in test mode after you have studied the Knowledge Transfer Outline.

4. Immediately following each test, you will be prompted to review the questions you flagged and/or answered incorrectly. For each question, analyze and understand why you were unsure or answered it incorrectly. This step is an essential learning activity.

5. Continue this process until you approach a predetermined proficiency level, e.g., 75%+.

6. Modify this process to suit your individual learning process.

    a. Learning from questions you answer incorrectly is very important. Each question you answer incorrectly is an **opportunity** to avoid missing actual test questions on your CPA exam. Thus, you should carefully study the answer explanations provided until you understand why the original answer you chose is wrong as well as why the correct answer indicated is correct. This learning technique is clearly the difference between passing and failing for many CPA candidates.

    b. Also, you **must** determine why you answered questions incorrectly and learn how to avoid the same error in the future. Reasons for missing questions include

        1) Misreading the requirement (stem)
        2) Not understanding what is required
        3) Making a math error
        4) Applying the wrong rule or concept
        5) Being distracted by one or more of the answers
        6) Incorrectly eliminating answers from consideration
        7) Not having any knowledge of the topic tested
        8) Using a poor educated guessing strategy

    c. It is also important to verify that you answered correctly for the right reasons (i.e., read the discussion provided for the correct answers). Otherwise, if the material is tested on the CPA exam in a different manner, you may not answer it correctly.

---

*Gleim does not recommend studying for Auditing using only this book and Test Prep Online. Candidates need to practice the task-based simulations in an exam environment, which means on a computer. Use CPA Gleim Online and CPA Simulation Wizard to become an expert on task-based simulations.

d.   It is imperative that you complete the predetermined number of study units per week so you can review your progress and realize how attainable a comprehensive CPA review program is when using the Gleim CPA Review System. Remember to meet or beat your schedule to give yourself confidence.

GLEIM AUDIO REVIEWS

Gleim **CPA Audio Reviews** provide an average of 30 minutes of quality review for each study unit. Each review provides an overview of the Knowledge Transfer Outline in the *CPA Review* book. The purpose is to get candidates started so they can relate to the questions they will answer before reading the study outlines in each study unit.

The audios get to the point, as does the entire **Gleim System for Success**. We are working to get you through the CPA exam with minimum time, cost, and frustration. You can listen to two short sample audio reviews on our website at www.gleim.com/accounting/demos.

TIME BUDGETING AND QUESTION-ANSWERING TECHNIQUES FOR FINANCIAL

Expect three testlets of 30 multiple-choice questions each and one task-based simulation testlet with seven tasks on the Financial section with a 240-minute time allocation. See Study Units 4 and 5 in *CPA Review: A System for Success* for additional discussion of how to maximize your score on multiple-choice questions and simulations.

MULTIPLE-CHOICE QUESTIONS

1.   **Budget your time.** We make this point with emphasis. Just as you would fill up your gas tank prior to reaching empty, so too would you finish your exam before time expires.

a.   Here is our suggested time allocation for Financial:

	Minutes	Start Time	
Testlet 1 (MC)	45	4 hours	00 minutes
Testlet 2 (MC)	45	3 hours	15 minutes
Testlet 3 (MC)	45	2 hours	30 minutes
Testlet 4 (TBS)	90	1 hour	45 minutes
***Extra time	15	0 hours	15 minutes

b.   Before beginning your first testlet of multiple-choice questions, prepare a Gleim Time Management Sheet as recommended in Study Unit 7 of *CPA Review: A System for Success*.

c.   As you work through the individual items, monitor your time. In Financial, we suggest 45 minutes for each testlet of 30 questions. If you answer five items in 7 minutes, you are fine, but if you spend 10 minutes on five items, you need to speed up.

***Remember to allocate your budgeted extra time, as needed, to each testlet. Your goal is to answer all of the items and achieve the maximum score possible.

2.   **Answer the questions in consecutive order.**

a.   Do **not** agonize over any one item. Stay within your time budget.

b.   Flag for review any questions you are unsure of and return to them later as time allows.

1)   Once you have selected either the Continue or Quit option, you will no longer be able to review or change any answers in the completed testlet.

c.   Never leave a multiple-choice question unanswered. **Make your best educated guess in the time allowed.** Remember that your score is based on the number of correct responses. You will not be penalized for guessing incorrectly.

3. **For each multiple-choice question,**

    a. **Try to ignore the answer choices.** Do not allow the answer choices to affect your reading of the question.

        1) If four answer choices are presented, three of them are incorrect. These choices are called **distractors** for good reason. Often, distractors are written to appear correct at first glance until further analysis.

        2) In computational items, the distractors are carefully calculated such that they are the result of making common mistakes. Be careful, and double-check your computations if time permits.

    b. **Read the question** carefully to determine the precise requirement.

        1) Focusing on what is required enables you to ignore extraneous information, to focus on the relevant facts, and to proceed directly to determining the correct answer.

            a) Be especially careful to note when the requirement is an **exception**; e.g., "Which of the following is **not** a required disclosure?"

    c. **Determine the correct answer** before looking at the answer choices.

    d. **Read the answer choices carefully.**

        1) Even if the first answer appears to be the correct choice, do **not** skip the remaining answer choices. Questions often ask for the "best" of the choices provided. Thus, each choice requires your consideration.

        2) Treat each answer choice as a true/false question as you analyze it.

    e. **Click on the best answer.**

        1) You have a 25% chance of answering the question correctly by guessing blindly; improve your odds with educated guessing.

        2) For many multiple-choice questions, two answer choices can be eliminated with minimal effort, thereby increasing your educated guess to a 50-50 proposition.

4. After you have answered all the items in a testlet, consult the question status list at the bottom of each multiple-choice question screen **before** clicking the "Exit" button, which permanently ends the testlet.

    a. Go back to the flagged questions and finalize your answer choices.

    b. Verify that all questions have been answered.

5. **If you don't know the answer,**

    a. Again, guess; but make it an educated guess, which means select the best possible answer. First, rule out answers that you think are incorrect. Second, speculate on what the AICPA is looking for and/or the rationale behind the question. Third, select the best answer or guess between equally appealing answers. Your first guess is usually the most intuitive. If you cannot make an educated guess, read the stem and each answer and pick the best or most intuitive answer. It's just a guess!

    b. Make sure you accomplish this step within your predetermined time budget per testlet.

TASK-BASED SIMULATIONS

In Financial, Testlet 4 consists of seven short task-based simulations. The following information and toolbar icons are located at the top of the testlet screen.

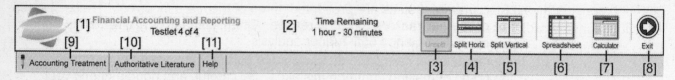

1. **Exam Section and Testlet Number:** For Financial, this part of the toolbar will always show Financial as the Exam Section and Testlet 4 of 4 as the Testlet Number.
2. **Time Remaining:** This information box displays to the examinee how long (s)he has remaining in the entire exam. Consistently check the amount of time remaining in order to stay on schedule.
3. **Unsplit:** This icon, when selected, will unsplit the screen between two tabs.
4. **Split Horiz:** This icon, when selected, will split the screen horizontally between two tabs, enabling you to see, for example, both the simulation question and the help tab at the same time.
5. **Split Vertical:** This icon, when selected, will split the screen vertically between two tabs, enabling you to see, for example, both the simulation question and the help tab at the same time.
6. **Spreadsheet:** This icon opens a spreadsheet that operates like most others and is provided as a tool available for complex calculations. You may enter and execute formulas as well as enter text and numbers.
7. **Calculator:** The calculator provided is a basic tool for simple computations. It is similar to calculators used in common software programs.
8. **Exit:** There are three options when you choose this icon.
    *   You may choose Review Testlet to return to the beginning of the testlet to review your answers. You will be able to change your answers.
    *   You may choose Continue Exam to close the current testlet and go on to the next testlet. Once you have chosen Continue, you may not return to that testlet. For Financial, the choice to Continue will only be relevant after each multiple-choice testlet, since the simulation is the last testlet.
    *   Finally, you may choose Quit Exam, which means either that you have completed the exam or that you chose not to complete it. Your exam will end and you will not be able to return to any testlet. If you chose to quit your exam before you have completed it, there are security measures in place to determine that you are intentionally not completing the exam.
9. **Work Tabs:** A work tab requires the test taker to respond to given information. Each task will have at least one work tab (distinguished by a pencil icon), and each work tab will have specific directions that you must read in order to complete the tab correctly. There are different varieties of work tabs; the one in the toolbar above is just an example. You may encounter work tabs that require you to complete forms, fill in spreadsheets, or select an option from multiple choices.
10. **Information Tabs:** An information tab gives the test taker information to aid in responding to work tabs. Each task will have at least one information tab (the Authoritative Literature, as shown in the example above). If your task has additional information tabs, go through each to familiarize yourself with the task's content.
11. **Help:** This tab, when selected, provides a quick review of certain functions and tool buttons specific to the type of task you are working on. It will also provide directions and general information but will not include information related specifically to the test content.

Task-Based Simulation Grading

Remember, on the real exam, you will need to complete seven different tasks, all of which will count toward your final grade. Your score on all of the tasks together will make up **40%** of your total grade. The other **60%** of your grade will be your total score on the multiple-choice testlets.

IF YOU HAVE QUESTIONS

Content-specific questions about our materials will be answered most rapidly if they are sent to us via email to accounting@gleim.com. Our team of accounting experts will give your correspondence thorough consideration and a prompt response.

Questions regarding the information in this Introduction (study suggestions, studying plans, exam specifics) should be emailed to personalcounselor@gleim.com.

Questions concerning orders, prices, shipments, or payments should be sent via email to customerservice@gleim.com and will be promptly handled by our competent and courteous customer service staff.

For technical support, you may use our automated technical support service at www.gleim.com/support, email us at support@gleim.com, or call us at (800) 874-5346.

HOW TO BE IN CONTROL

Remember, you must be in control to be successful during exam preparation and execution. Perhaps more importantly, control can also contribute greatly to your personal and other professional goals. Control is the process whereby you

1. Develop expectations, standards, budgets, and plans
2. Undertake activity, production, study, and learning
3. Measure the activity, production, output, and knowledge
4. Compare actual activity with expected and budgeted activity
5. Modify the activity, behavior, or study to better achieve the expected or desired outcome
6. Revise expectations and standards in light of actual experience
7. Continue the process or restart the process in the future

Exercising control will ultimately develop the confidence you need to outperform most other CPA candidates and PASS the CPA exam! Obtain our *CPA Review: A System for Success* booklet for a more detailed discussion of control and other exam tactics.

AICPA's NONDISCLOSURE AGREEMENT

The following is taken verbatim from the AICPA's Candidate Bulletin dated June 2012. It is reproduced here to remind all CPA candidates about the AICPA's strict policy of nondisclosure, which Gleim consistently supports and upholds.

Policy Statement and Agreement Regarding Exam Confidentiality and the Taking of Breaks

I hereby agree that I will maintain the confidentiality of the Uniform CPA Examination. In addition, I agree that I will not:

- *Divulge the nature or content of any Uniform CPA Examination question or answer under any circumstance*
- *Engage in any unauthorized communication during testing*
- *Refer to unauthorized materials or use unauthorized equipment during testing; or*
- *Remove or attempt to remove any Uniform CPA Examination materials, notes, or any other items from the examination room*

I understand and agree that liability for test administration activities, including but not limited to the adequacy or accuracy of test materials and equipment, and the accuracy of scoring and score reporting, will be limited to score correction or test retake at no additional fee. I waive any and all right to all other claims.

I further agree to report to the AICPA any examination question disclosures, or solicitations for disclosure of which I become aware.

I affirm that I have had the opportunity to read the Candidate Bulletin and I agree to all of its terms and conditions.

I understand that breaks are only allowed between testlets. I understand that I will be asked to complete any open testlet before leaving the testing room for a break.

In addition, I understand that failure to comply with this Policy Statement and Agreement may result in invalidation of my grades, disqualification from future examinations, expulsion from the testing facility and possible civil or criminal penalties.

CITATIONS TO AUTHORITATIVE PRONOUNCEMENTS

Throughout the book, we refer to certain authoritative accounting pronouncements by the following abbreviations:

GAAP – The sources of authoritative U.S. generally accepted accounting principles (GAAP) recognized by the FASB as applicable by nongovernmental entities are (1) the FASB's Accounting Standards Codification (ASC) and (2) (for SEC registrants only) pronouncements of the SEC. All guidance in the Codification is equally authoritative. SEC pronouncements must be followed by registrants regardless of whether they are reflected in the codification.

IFRS and IASs – International Financial Reporting Standards (IFRS) are issued by the current standard-setter, the International Accounting Standards Board (IASB). International Accounting Standards (IASs), related Interpretations, and the framework for the preparation and presentation of financial statements were issued by the predecessor entity. IFRS also is the collective term for IASs.

GASB Statements – The Governmental Accounting Standards Board issues statements that apply to state and local governments.

SFAC – FASB Statements of Financial Accounting Concepts establish financial accounting and reporting objectives and concepts. SFACs are other accounting literature. They are considered only in the absence of applicable authoritative guidance (the FASB Accounting Standards Codification or SEC pronouncements). They were designed for use by the FASB in developing their other authoritative pronouncements.

ASC – The FASB's Accounting Standards Codification is "the single source of authoritative nongovernmental U.S. generally accepted accounting principles." The Codification organizes the many pronouncements that constitute U.S. GAAP into a consistent, searchable format accessible through the Internet.

Update Service

Visit the GLEIM® website for free updates,
which are available until the next edition is published.

gleim.com/updates

STUDY UNIT ONE
THE FINANCIAL REPORTING ENVIRONMENT

(22 pages of outline)

1.1	Standard Setting for Financial Accounting	19
1.2	The Objective of General-Purpose Financial Reporting	22
1.3	Objectives of Financial Reporting -- Not-for-Profit (Nongovernmental) Entities	23
1.4	Objectives of Financial Reporting -- Governmental Entities	24
1.5	Assumptions, Principles, and Constraints	26
1.6	Qualitative Characteristics of Useful Financial Information	28
1.7	Elements of Financial Statements	30
1.8	Recognition and Measurement Concepts	33
1.9	Cash Flow Information and Present Value	36
1.10	SEC Reporting	37
1.11	Practice Simulation	52

The first major subject area in this study unit describes the domestic and international bodies that set accounting and reporting standards. The second major area concerns the financial reporting objectives for the three reporting environments: general-purpose entities, not-for-profit entities, and governments. The third major area is the conceptual framework for accounting and reporting. The fourth subject area addresses the reporting requirements of the Securities and Exchange Commission.

1.1 STANDARD SETTING FOR FINANCIAL ACCOUNTING

1. **Nature of Financial Accounting**

   a. Financial accounting addresses accounting for an entity's assets, liabilities, revenues, expenses, and other elements of financial statements.

      1) Financial statements are the primary method of communicating to external parties information about the entity's results of operations, financial position, and cash flows.

      2) For general-purpose financial statements to be useful to external parties, they must be prepared in conformity with accounting principles that are generally accepted in the United States (GAAP).

   b. Financial accounting is contrasted with managerial accounting.

      1) Managerial accounting assists management decision making, planning, and control. Managerial accounting information is therefore primarily directed to specific internal users, and it ordinarily need not follow GAAP.

2. **U.S. Securities and Exchange Commission (SEC)**

   a. The SEC has been empowered by Congress to establish principles for financial reporting by publicly traded companies (called issuers) in the United States.

      1) The SEC delegated this authority to the Financial Accounting Standards Board (FASB).

   b. While allowing the accounting profession (through the FASB) to establish principles, the SEC enforces those principles by ensuring that issuers meet certain periodic reporting requirements.

      1) This approach allows investors to evaluate investments for themselves.

   c. In addition to overseeing financial reporting requirements, the SEC's Division of Enforcement investigates possible violations of securities laws and prosecutes them in federal court.

3. **Financial Accounting Standards Board (FASB)**

   a. The Financial Accounting Foundation (FAF), a fully independent body established by the accounting profession in 1973, oversees two other bodies.

      1) The FASB establishes **generally accepted accounting principles (GAAP)** for U.S. businesses.

      2) The Financial Accounting Standards Advisory Council (FASAC) advises the FASB on priorities and proposed standards and evaluates the FASB's performance.

   b. The FASB follows a due process procedure before issuing final pronouncements.

      1) After discussing the issues and considering input from interested parties (e.g., business, academia, and the profession), the FASB then votes on a final draft proposal. If a majority of the seven board members approves, an Accounting Standards Update (ASU) is issued.

      2) Once an ASU has been incorporated into the FASB's Accounting Standards Codification (ASC), it has the status of U.S. GAAP.

         a) The Codification is one of two sources of authoritative guidance for nongovernmental entities in the United States. The other source of mandatory guidance consists of SEC pronouncements. These apply only to SEC registrants.

Background

The FASB's Accounting Standards Codification became effective on July 1, 2009. It is the sole source of non-SEC authoritative accounting and reporting standards. In the Codification, the FASB combined the many pronouncements that formerly constituted U.S. GAAP into a consistent, searchable format available through the Internet.

---

4. **International Accounting Standards Board (IASB)**

   a. The Board's mission is summarized as follows:

      The IASB is committed to developing, in the public interest, a single set of high quality, understandable and enforceable global accounting standards that require transparent and comparable information in general purpose financial statements.

      1) The principal benefit of a single set of global standards is that multinational corporations do not have to rewrite their statements in (or perform a complex reconciliation to) the local GAAP to trade their stock on a foreign exchange.

         a) Foreign investment is thereby made much easier, and the cost of capital is lowered.

Background

In the early 1970s, financial reporting and the accounting profession worldwide were in a period of substantial change. In 1973, the same year the FASB was formed in the U.S., the International Accounting Standards Committee (IASC) was established with the goal of preparing a set of global accounting standards. During its existence, the IASC issued 41 International Accounting Standards (IASs).

Disagreements among accountants over the source of the IASC's authority and the direction of its standards led to the creation in 2001 of the IFRS (formerly IASC) Foundation, a not-for-profit, private sector organization governed by 22 trustees. These trustees select the members of the IASB.

---

   b. The IASB issues authoritative pronouncements in the form of International Financial Reporting Standards (IFRS).

      1) The IASB's approach to standard setting recognizes a need to publish standards that will have worldwide acceptance. Accordingly, IFRS are principles-based.

    2)   IFRS tend to be less detailed than U.S. GAAP, with few exceptions and less interpretive and implementation guidance.

        a)   Thus, they require a greater exercise of professional judgment regarding their application to the economic substance of transactions.

    3)   In contrast, U.S. GAAP are sometimes criticized as stressing adherence to the letter of accounting rules rather than to the economic substance of a transaction.

        a)   For this reason and as part of its convergence initiatives, the FASB is considering a more principles-based approach to standard setting.

  c.   The IASB estimates that 95% of all businesses around the world are small- or medium-sized.

    1)   In response to objections that such firms lack the resources to implement a large, complex basis of accounting like IFRS, the IASB has issued the 230-page **IFRS for Small- and Medium-Sized Entities** (IFRS for SMEs).

        a)   It is not necessary for a jurisdiction to adopt full IFRS for it to adopt IFRS for SMEs. However, issuers and financial institutions may not use it.

    2)   The following are some differences between the two sets of principles:

        a)   Certain topics do not apply to nonissuers (e.g., earnings per share, interim reporting, segment reporting).

        b)   Where full IFRS may offer a choice of accounting principles in a given situation, IFRS for SMEs only allows the simplest choice.

        c)   Required disclosures are reduced by about 90%.

  d.   Pronouncements of the IASB are not binding. Their authority is restricted to the willingness of national authorities to adopt them. IFRS was recognized by the European Union as of January 1, 2005.

  e.   In September 2002, the FASB and the IASB pledged

... to use their best efforts to (1) make their existing financial reporting standards fully compatible as soon as is practicable and (2) to coordinate their future work programs to ensure that once achieved, compatibility is maintained.

    1)   This agreement began the convergence project, an effort to harmonize U.S. GAAP and IFRS.

        a)   As of the fall of 2012, the SEC still has not committed to requiring the adoption of either IFRS or the converged standards for U.S. issuers.

5.   **Governmental Accounting Standards Board (GASB)**

  a.   The GASB, established in 1984, is the primary standard setter for state and local governmental entities (the GASB does not establish GAAP for the federal government).

    1)   The GASB was formed to address the problem of comparability of governmental financial statements with those of private enterprises. GASB Statements have the status of GAAP for state and local governments (governmental accounting will be covered in Study Units 18 and 19).

6.   **Federal Accounting Standards Advisory Board (FASAB)**

a.   Accounting principles for the federal government are established by the FASAB, which issues Statements of Federal Accounting Standards.

b.   The FASB, IASB, GASB, and FASAB are designated by the AICPA Council as bodies that issue GAAP for the purpose of compliance with Conduct Rule 203, Accounting Principles. A member of the AICPA ordinarily may not express an unmodified opinion on statements that contain a material departure from GAAP issued by the appropriate standard setter.

Stop and review! You have completed the outline for this subunit. Study multiple-choice questions 1 through 4 beginning on page 40.

1.2 THE OBJECTIVE OF GENERAL-PURPOSE FINANCIAL REPORTING

Background
In 1973, the FASB developed a conceptual framework designed as a coherent set of interrelated objectives and fundamental concepts. This framework is stated in the **Statements of Financial Accounting Concepts (SFACs)**. However, SFACs are not authoritative and are not included in the Codification. Instead, they are intended to influence the development and application of GAAP. This subunit is based on SFAC No. 8, Chapter 1, *The Objective of General Purpose Financial Reporting*, and Chapter 3, *Qualitative Characteristics of Useful Financial Information*.

1.   The objective is to report financial information that is **useful** in making decisions about providing resources to the reporting entity.

a.   **Primary users** of financial information are current or prospective investors and creditors who cannot obtain it directly.

1)   Their decisions depend on expected returns.

a)   Accordingly, primary users need information that helps them assess the entity's future net cash inflows.

2)   Primary users cannot obtain all necessary information solely from general-purpose financial reports. These reports are

a)   Insufficient to determine the value of the entity and
b)   Based significantly on estimates, judgments, and models.

b.   The information reported relates to the entity's **economic resources and claims** to them (financial position) and to **changes** in those resources and claims.

1)   Information about economic resources and claims helps to evaluate liquidity, solvency, financing needs, and the probability of obtaining financing.

c.   Users need to differentiate between changes in economic resources and claims arising from (1) the entity's performance and (2) other events and transactions (e.g., issuing debt and equity). Information about financial performance is useful for

1)   Understanding the return on economic resources, its variability, and its components;
2)   Evaluating management; and
3)   Predicting future returns.

d.   The **accrual basis of accounting** reports the effects of transactions and other events and circumstances on the entity's resources and claims when they occur, not necessarily when the cash flows occur. Thus, accrual-basis information is preferable to the cash basis for evaluating past performance and predicting future performance.

       1)   An entity should be able to increase its economic resources **other than by obtaining resources from investors and creditors**.

          a)   Information about this performance is useful in evaluating potential operating net cash inflows.

       2)   Information about financial performance is useful in determining how external factors (e.g., interest rate changes) affected economic resources and claims.

   e.   Information about **cash flows** is helpful in

       1)   Understanding operations;
       2)   Evaluating financing and investing activities, liquidity, and solvency;
       3)   Interpreting other financial information; and
       4)   Assessing the potential for net cash inflows.

Stop and review! You have completed the outline for this subunit. Study multiple-choice questions 5 through 8 beginning on page 41.

1.3 OBJECTIVES OF FINANCIAL REPORTING -- NOT-FOR-PROFIT (NONGOVERNMENTAL) ENTITIES

Background
The not-for-profit sector of the U.S. economy is significant. According to *The Nonprofit Almanac 2011*, the number of not-for-profit organizations registered with the IRS grew by 19% from 1999 to 2009. Public charities and private foundations had combined revenues of $1.87 trillion and reported assets of $4.3 trillion for 2009. This subunit is based on SFAC No. 4, *Objectives of Financial Reporting by Nonbusiness Organizations*.

1.   **Aspects of Not-for-Profit Reporting**

   a.   **Distinguishing Characteristics of Not-for-Profit Entities**

       1)   They receive significant resources from providers who do not expect to receive repayment or proportionate economic benefits.

          a)   Not-for-profit entities have transactions that are infrequent in businesses, such as grants and contributions.

       2)   They have operating purposes other than to provide goods or services at a profit.

       3)   Not-for-profit entities have no single indicator of performance like net income. Thus, other performance indicators are needed.

       4)   They lack defined ownership interests that (a) can be sold, transferred, or redeemed or (b) entitle an owner to distributions upon liquidation of the entity.

          a)   Not-for-profit entities report net assets rather than equity.

          b)   Investor-owned entities that provide economic benefits directly to owners, members, or participants (e.g., credit unions or employee benefit plans) are not not-for-profit entities.

          c)   An entity may possess some of the characteristics of a not-for-profit entity but not others. Examples include private not-for-profit hospitals and schools that receive small amounts of contributions but are essentially dependent on debt issues and user fees. For such entities, the reporting objectives of business entities may be more appropriate.

b.   **Users and Their Reporting Needs**

   1)   The FASB identified four key stakeholder groups that are interested in financial reporting by nonbusiness entities:

   a)   Resource providers
   b)   Constituents
   c)   Governing and oversight bodies
   d)   Managers

   2)   Stakeholders of for-profit entities are primarily concerned about financial return. By contrast, stakeholders of not-for-profit entities are primarily concerned about the services rendered and the entity's continuing ability to render those services.

2.   **Objectives include providing information**

   a.   Useful in making resource allocation decisions
   b.   Useful in assessing services and ability to provide services
   c.   Useful in assessing management stewardship and performance
   d.   About economic resources, obligations, net resources, and changes in them
   e.   About the performance of an organization during a period
   f.   About factors that may affect an organization's liquidity
   g.   Consisting of explanations and interpretations to help users understand financial information presented

Stop and review! You have completed the outline for this subunit. Study multiple-choice questions 9 through 12 beginning on page 43.

1.4 OBJECTIVES OF FINANCIAL REPORTING -- GOVERNMENTAL ENTITIES

Background
The United States has 50 state governments and thousands of local governments. The United States Census Bureau reported that these entities had combined revenues of $2.6 trillion during the 2010 calendar year.
The GASB's conceptual framework project provides a basis for the development and application of accounting standards for state and local governments. This subunit is based on GASB Concepts Statement No. 1, *Objectives of Financial Reporting*.

1.   **Governmental-Type Activities**

   a.   **The Governmental Environment**

   1)   Three primary characteristics of the governmental environment distinguish it from the business and not-for-profit environments:

   a)   The representative form of government and the separation of powers
   b)   The federal system of government, with its hierarchy of national, state, county, and city governments, along with the significant flow of revenues among them
   c)   The expectations of taxpayers, who provide government with revenue, about the services they receive

   2)   The structure of government has two inherent control characteristics:

   a)   The budget as the embodiment of policy decisions and a legally binding control tool
   b)   The use of fund accounting

    3) The following are other characteristics of the governmental environment:

      a) Governments at the same level of the hierarchy may be vested with dissimilar functions.

      b) Resources are heavily invested in nonrevenue-producing assets, such as highways and bridges.

      c) Citizens want the maximum level of services to be provided for the minimum amount of taxes.

  b. **Users and Uses of Governmental Reporting**

    1) The following are users of financial reporting for governmental-type activities:

      a) Citizens (those to whom the governmental body is directly accountable)
      b) Legislative and oversight bodies (those who represent the citizenry)
      c) Investors and creditors (those who provide financing)

    2) The following are uses of governmental reporting:

      a) Comparing actual results with budgeted amounts
      b) Assessing financial condition and operating results
      c) Determining compliance with laws, rules, and regulations
      d) Evaluating efficiency and effectiveness

2. **Business-Type Activities**

  a. The business-type activities of a government differ from its governmental activities. They

    1) Involve a direct exchange of money in return for goods delivered or services rendered.

    2) Have large investments in revenue-producing capital assets (e.g., toll roads, manufacturing facilities for prison industries).

    3) Often perform only a single function. Thus, they are more easily compared between governments than are governmental activities.

    4) May still be influenced by the political process (e.g., direct subsidies, rate setting).

    5) Adopt budgets that often lack the legal force of the budget for governmental activities despite raising most of their revenues from service delivery.

3. **Accountability and Interperiod Equity**

  a. **Accountability**

    1) Accountability is the essence of governmental reporting. Accountability requires that a government justify how it spends the resources it collects in pursuit of the goals citizens have set for it.

  b. **Interperiod Equity**

    1) Interperiod equity implies that current citizens should treat future citizens with equity; i.e., later generations should not have to pay for services received by prior generations. This principle implies that current-year revenues should be sufficient to cover current-year services.

4. **Characteristics of Information in Financial Reporting**

  a. The GASB defines the following characteristics of governmental financial reporting: understandability, reliability, relevance, timeliness, consistency, and comparability.

    1) These characteristics should be compared with those defined by the FASB for reporting by business entities (covered later in this study unit).

5.   **Objectives**

a.   The GASB states that no major differences exist between the objectives of governmental financial reporting of governmental activities and business-type activities.

b.   **Public Accountability.** The entity should provide information

1)   About whether current-year revenues were sufficient to pay for current-year services

2)   About whether the governmental body adhered to its legally enacted budget and complied with laws and regulations

3)   For assessing service efforts, costs, and accomplishments

c.   **Evaluating Operating Results.** The entity should provide information

1)   About sources and uses of financial resources

2)   About how government financed its activities and met its cash requirements

3)   To determine whether financial condition strengthened or weakened

d.   **Assessing Services Provided.** The entity should provide information

1)   About the financial position and condition of the governmental body

2)   About the governmental body's long-lived assets

3)   That discloses legal or contractual restrictions and potential risks

Stop and review! You have completed the outline for this subunit. Study multiple-choice questions 13 through 16 beginning on page 44.

1.5 ASSUMPTIONS, PRINCIPLES, AND CONSTRAINTS

The AICPA has used definitional questions to test the assumptions, principles, and constraints of the financial accounting structure.

1.   **Assumptions**

a.   Certain assumptions underlie the environment in which the reporting entity operates. They have developed over time and are generally recognized by the accounting profession.

b.   **Economic-Entity Assumption**

1)   The reporting entity is separately identified for the purpose of economic and financial accountability. Thus, the economic affairs of owners and managers are kept separate from those of the reporting entity. Also, the legal entity and the economic entity are not necessarily the same, as in the case of a parent and its subsidiary.

c.   **Going-Concern (Business Continuity) Assumption**

1)   Unless stated otherwise, every business is assumed to be a going concern that will continue operating indefinitely. As a result, liquidation values are not important. It is assumed that the entity is not going to be liquidated in the near future.

d.   **Monetary-Unit (Unit-of-Money) Assumption**

1)   Accounting records are kept in terms of money. The changing purchasing power of the monetary unit is assumed not to be significant.

e.   **Periodicity (Time Period) Assumption**

1)   Economic activity can be divided into distinct time periods. This assumption requires reporting estimates in the financial statements. It sacrifices some degree of faithful representation of information for increased relevance.

2.   **Principles**

a.   Certain principles provide guidelines for recording financial information. The **revenue recognition** and **matching principles** have been formally incorporated into the conceptual framework as recognition and measurement concepts (discussed later in this study unit). Two additional principles are described below.

b.   **Historical Cost Principle**

1)   Transactions are recorded initially at cost because that is the most objective determination of fair value. It is a reliable measure. However, the trend is toward more extensive reporting of fair value information (fair value measurement is discussed in detail in Study Unit 4).

c.   **Full-Disclosure Principle**

1)   Financial statement users should be able to assume that financial information that could influence users' judgment is reported in the financial statements.

a)   **Notes** present information to explain financial statement amounts, for example, by describing the accounting policies used.

b)   **Supplementary information**, such as management's discussion and analysis or the effects of changing prices, provides information additional to that in the statements and notes. It may include relevant information that does not meet all recognition criteria.

c)   Full disclosure is not a substitute for reporting in accordance with GAAP.

3.   **Constraints**

a.   The **cost constraint** is a limit on reporting (discussed in the next subunit).

b.   **Industry Practices Constraint**

1)   Occasionally, GAAP are not followed in an industry because adherence to them would generate misleading or unnecessary information.

a)   For example, banks and insurers typically measured marketable equity securities at fair value even before this treatment became generally accepted. Fair value and liquidity are most important to these industries.

c.   **Conservatism Constraint**

1)   The conservatism constraint is a response to uncertainty. When alternative accounting methods are appropriate, the one having the less favorable effect on net income and total assets is preferable.

a)   However, conservatism does not permit a deliberate understatement of total assets and net income.

2)   Furthermore, SFAC 5 describes "a general tendency to emphasize purchase and sale transactions and to apply conservative procedures in accounting recognition."

3)   The application of the lower-of-cost-or-market rule (lower of cost or NRV under IFRS) to inventories is an example of conservatism.

Stop and review! You have completed the outline for this subunit. Study multiple-choice questions 17 through 20 beginning on page 45.

1.6 QUALITATIVE CHARACTERISTICS OF USEFUL FINANCIAL INFORMATION

Background

The characteristics described in this subunit make accounting information useful for decision making. They apply to both for-profit and not-for-profit nongovernmental entities.

This subunit is based on SFAC No. 8.

---

1. **Fundamental Qualitative Characteristics**

   a. **Relevance.** Information is relevant if it can make a difference in user decisions. To do so, it must have predictive value, confirmatory value, or both.

      1) Something has **predictive value** if it can be used as an input in a predictive process.

      2) Something has **confirmatory value** with respect to prior evaluations if it provides feedback that confirms or changes (corrects) them.

      3) Predictive value and confirmatory value are interrelated. For example, current revenue may confirm a prior prediction and also be used to predict the next period's revenue.

      4) Information is **material** if its omission or misstatement can influence user decisions based on a specific entity's financial information. Thus, it is an **entity-specific** aspect of relevance.

   b. **Faithful representation.** Useful information faithfully represents economic events.

      1) A representation is perfectly faithful if it is **complete** (containing what is needed for user understanding), **neutral** (unbiased in its selection and presentation), and **free from error**.

      2) A representation is free from error if it has no errors or omissions in (a) the descriptions of the phenomena and (b) the selection and application of the reporting process.

EXAMPLE

The accuracy of an unobservable price cannot be determined. But the entity can disclose that the estimate is in fact an estimate. It can also explain the estimation process and its limits. Given this disclosure and explanation, if no errors have been made in choosing and performing the process, the representation is faithful.

---

      3) The concept of **substance over form** guides accountants to present the financial reality of a transaction over its legal form. An example is the consolidation of a legally separate subsidiary by a parent. Presenting a parent and a separate entity that it controls as one reporting entity is faithfully representational.

   c. To be useful, information must be relevant and faithfully represented. The process for applying these characteristics is to

      1) Identify what may be useful to users of the financial reports,
      2) Identify the relevant information, and
      3) Determine whether the information is available and can be faithfully represented.

    d.   The following memory aids are helpful for learning the fundamental qualitative characteristics:

R = Relevance	Relevance
P = Predictive value	Prepares
C = Confirmatory value	Candidates
M = Materiality	Most
F = Faithful representation	Faithful
C = Complete	CPAs
N = Neutral	Now
F = Free from error	Flourish

2.   **Enhancing Qualitative Characteristics**

    a.   The following enhance the usefulness of relevant and faithfully represented information:

        1)   **Comparability.** Information should be comparable with similar information for (a) other entities and (b) the same entity for another period or date. Thus, comparability allows users to understand similarities and differences.

            a)   Consistency is a means of achieving comparability. It is the use of the same methods, for example, accounting principles, for the same items.

        2)   **Verifiability.** Information is verifiable (directly or indirectly) if knowledgeable and independent observers can reach a consensus (not necessarily unanimity) that it is faithfully represented.

        3)   **Timeliness.** Information is timely when it is available in time to influence decisions.

        4)   **Understandability.** Understandable information is clearly and concisely classified, characterized, and presented.

            a)   Information should be readily understandable by reasonably knowledgeable and diligent users but should not be excluded because of its complexity.

    b.   The following memory aid is helpful for learning the enhancing qualitative characteristics:

E = Enhancing	Enhancing
C = Comparability	Can
V = Verifiability	Validate
T = Timeliness	The
U = Understandability	User

Do not confuse the fundamental qualitative characteristics and the enhancing characteristics. Also, be aware of the aspects of each fundamental characteristic.

3.   **Cost Constraint**

    a.   This constraint affects all financial reporting. It states that the costs of reporting should be justified by its benefits.

        1)   Provider costs (collection, processing, verification, and distribution) ultimately are incurred by users as reduced returns.

        2)   Other user costs include those to analyze and interpret the information provided or to obtain or estimate information not provided.

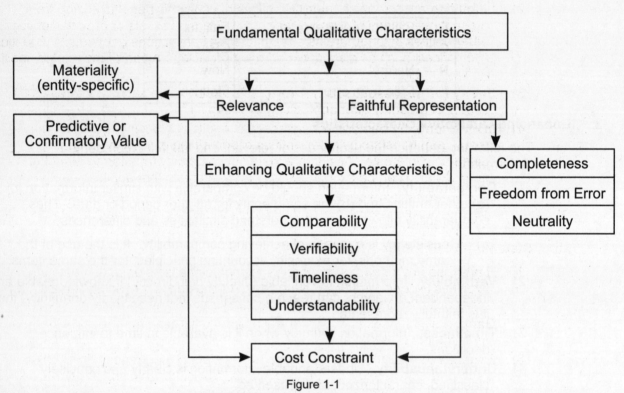

Figure 1-1

Stop and review! You have completed the outline for this subunit. Study multiple-choice questions 21 through 24 beginning on page 46.

1.7 ELEMENTS OF FINANCIAL STATEMENTS

Background
Elements are the essential building blocks used to construct financial statements.
This subunit is based on SFAC No. 6, *Elements of Financial Statements*.

1.   **Financial Statements**

    a.   Financial statements are the primary means of communicating financial information to external parties. Additional information is provided by financial statement notes, supplementary information, and other disclosures. Information typically disclosed in notes is essential to understanding the financial statements.

    b.   A full set of financial statements should show the following:

        1)   Financial position at the end of the period
        2)   Earnings for the period
        3)   Comprehensive income for the period
        4)   Cash flows during the period
        5)   Investments by and distributions to owners during the period

2. The elements are distributed as follows among the **financial statements** other than the statement of cash flows:

    a. **Statement of Financial Position (Balance Sheet)**

        1) **Assets** are "probable future economic benefits obtained or controlled by a particular entity as a result of past transactions or events." Valuation allowances, such as premiums on notes receivable, are part of the related assets and are not assets or liabilities.

        2) **Liabilities** are "probable future sacrifices of economic benefits arising from present obligations of a particular entity to transfer assets or provide services to other entities in the future as a result of past transactions or events." Valuation allowances, such as discounts on bonds payable, are part of the related liability and are not liabilities or assets.

        3) **Equity (or net assets of a not-for-profit entity)** is the residual interest in the assets of an entity after subtracting liabilities.

        4) **Investments by owners** are increases in equity of a business entity. They result from transfers by other entities of something of value to increase ownership interests. Assets are the most commonly transferred item, but services also can be exchanged for equity interests (not applicable to NFPs).

        5) **Distributions to owners** are decreases in equity. They result from transferring assets, providing services, or incurring liabilities. A distribution to owners decreases the ownership interest (not applicable to NFPs).

    b. **Statement of Earnings (Net Income)**

        1) **Revenues** are inflows or other enhancements of assets or settlements of liabilities (or both) from delivering or producing goods, providing services, or other activities that qualify as ongoing major or central operations.

        2) **Gains** are increases in equity (or net assets) other than from revenues or investments by owners.

        3) **Expenses** are outflows or other usage of assets or incurrences of liabilities (or both) from delivering or producing goods, providing services, or other activities that qualify as ongoing major or central operations.

        4) **Losses** are decreases in equity (or net assets) other than from expenses or distributions to owners.

    c. **Statement of Comprehensive Income**

        1) **Comprehensive income** is the periodic change in equity of a business entity from nonowner sources. It excludes the effects of investments by owners and distributions to owners (not applicable to NFPs).

            a) Comprehensive income is based on a financial (not physical) **capital maintenance concept** that distinguishes return **on** capital from a return **of** capital.

                i) Under this concept, the effects of any recognized price changes on assets and liabilities are holding gains and losses. These are included in return on capital.

    d. **Statement of Investments by and Distributions to Owners**

        1) **Investments by owners** (see above)

        2) **Distributions to owners** (see above)

IFRS Difference

The **elements** of financial statements are (1) assets, (2) liabilities, (3) equity, (4) income (including revenues and gains), and (5) expenses (including losses).

3.   **Transactions and Other Events and Circumstances Affecting a Business Entity**

   a.   **Changes in Assets and Liabilities with No Change in Equity**

      1)   Asset exchanges
      2)   Liability exchanges
      3)   Receipt of goods or services with incurrence of payables
      4)   Settlement of payables with assets

   b.   **Changes in Assets and Liabilities with Change in Equity**

      1)   Comprehensive Income

         a)   Revenues
         b)   Expenses
         c)   Gains
         d)   Losses

      2)   Transfers between Entity and Owners

         a)   Investments by owners
         b)   Distributions to owners

   c.   **Changes in Equity with No Change in Assets or Liabilities**

      1)   Declaration and distribution of stock dividends
      2)   Conversion of preferred stock

4.   **Accrual Accounting**

   a.   Accrual accounting involves recording the financial effects of transactions and other events and circumstances when they occur rather than when their direct cash consequences occur. Accrual accounting embraces the following concepts:

   b.   **Accruals**

      1)   Accruals anticipate future cash flows. They recognize assets or liabilities and the related liabilities, assets, revenues, expenses, gains, or losses. Sales or purchases on account, interest, and taxes are common accruals.

   c.   **Deferrals**

      1)   Deferrals reflect past cash flows. They recognize liabilities (for receipts) and assets (for payments), with deferral of the related revenues, expenses, gains, and losses. The deferral ends when the obligation is satisfied or the future economic benefit is used up. Prepaid insurance is a typical deferral.

   d.   **Allocation**

      1)   Systematic and rational allocation is the assignment or distribution of an amount according to a plan or formula. Examples are the apportionment of a lump-sum purchase price among the assets acquired and the assignment of manufacturing costs to products.

   e.   **Amortization**

      1)   Amortization is a form of allocation. It decreases an amount by periodic payments or write-downs. More specifically, it is an allocation process for deferrals. It involves reducing a liability (asset) recorded as a result of a cash receipt (payment) by recognizing revenues (expenses). Examples are depreciation and depletion expenses and the recognition of earned subscriptions revenue.

f.   **Recognition and Realization**

1)   Recognition is the formal incorporation of an item in the financial statements.
2)   Realization is the conversion of noncash resources into money. These concepts are explained more fully in the next subunit.

Stop and review! You have completed the outline for this subunit. Study multiple-choice questions 25 through 28 beginning on page 47.

1.8 RECOGNITION AND MEASUREMENT CONCEPTS

Background
Recognition and measurement concepts provide guidance on what information should be included in the financial statements of a business entity and when.
This subunit is based on SFAC No. 5, *Recognition and Measurement in Financial Statements of Business Enterprises*.

1.   **Recognition Criteria**

a.   Recognition criteria determine whether and when items should be incorporated into the financial statements, either initially or as changes in existing items.

b.   Four fundamental recognition criteria apply to all recognition issues.

1)   The item must meet the **definition** of an element of financial statements.
2)   It must have a relevant attribute **measurable** with sufficient reliability.
3)   The information about it must be **relevant**, i.e., capable of making a difference in user decisions.
4)   The information must be **reliable**, i.e., representationally faithful, verifiable, and neutral.

c.   Incorporation of any item is subject to the pervasive cost constraint and the materiality threshold.

d.   The following memory aid is helpful for learning the recognition criteria:

R = Recognition criteria	Recognizing
D = Definition	Danger
M = Measurable	May
R = Relevant	Repel
R = Reliable	Remorse

2.   **Revenue Recognition**

a.   According to the revenue recognition principle, revenues and gains should be recognized **when (1) realized or realizable and (2) earned.**

1)   Revenues and gains are realized when goods or services have been exchanged for cash or claims to cash. Revenues and gains are realizable when goods or services have been exchanged for assets that are readily convertible into cash or claims to cash.
2)   Revenues are earned when the earning process has been substantially completed, and the entity is entitled to the resulting benefits or revenues.

IFRS Difference

For a **sale of goods**, revenue is recognized when **five conditions** are met. (1) The entity has transferred the significant **risks and rewards** of ownership, (2) the entity has neither continuing **managerial involvement** to an extent associated with ownership nor effective **control** over the goods, (3) the revenue (measured at the fair value of the consideration received or receivable) can be reliably measured, (4) it is probable that the **economic benefits** will flow to the entity, and (5) **transaction costs** can be reliably measured.

For the rendering of a service, if the outcome can be reliably estimated, revenue (measured as described above) is recognized based on the stage of completion (the **percentage-of-completion** method.) The outcome can be reliably estimated when (1) revenue can be **reliably measured**, (2) it is probable that the **economic benefits** will flow to the entity, (3) the **stage of completion** can be reliably measured, and (4) the **costs incurred** and the **costs to complete** can be reliably measured.

Revenue from interest, royalties, and dividends must meet the economic benefits and reliability criteria described above. The bases of recognition are (1) the effective interest method, (2) the accrual basis in accordance with an agreement, and (3) establishment of the right to receive, respectively.

The revenue recognition principle under U.S. GAAP states that revenues and gains should be recognized when (1) realized or realizable and (2) earned. Under IFRS, the conditions for revenue recognition are different. This difference may be tested.

3.   **Expense Recognition**

    a.   As a reflection of the profession's conservatism, expenses and losses have historically been subject to less strict recognition criteria than revenues and gains. Also, expenses and losses are not subject to the realization criterion.

        1)   Rather, expenses and losses are recognized when (a) a **consumption of economic benefits** occurs in connection with the entity's primary activities or (b) an **impairment** of the ability of existing assets to provide future benefits has occurred.

            a)   An expense or loss also may be recognized when a liability has been incurred or increased without the receipt of corresponding benefits. A probable and reasonably estimable contingent loss is an example.

    b.   The **expense recognition principles** are associating cause and effect, systematic and rational allocation, and immediate recognition.

        1)   **Matching** is essentially synonymous with **associating cause and effect**. Such a direct relationship is found when the cost of goods sold is recognized in the same period as the revenue from the sale of the goods.

        2)   **Systematic and rational allocation** procedures do not directly relate costs and revenues but are applied when a causal relationship is "generally, but not specifically, identified." The most common example is depreciation.

        3)   **Immediate recognition** applies when costs cannot be directly or feasibly related to specific revenues. The benefits of certain of these costs are used up in the period in which they are incurred. Utilities expense is a common example. But other costs are immediately recognized because the period(s) to which they relate may not be feasibly determinable.

4. **Measurement Attributes**

    a. **Historical cost** is the acquisition price of an asset. It is ordinarily adjusted subsequently for amortization (which includes depreciation) or other allocations. It is the relevant attribute for plant assets and most inventories.

    b. **Current (replacement) cost** is the amount of cash that would have to be paid for a current acquisition of the same or an equivalent asset.

    c. **Current market value (exit value)** is the cash or equivalent realizable by selling an asset in an orderly liquidation (not in a forced sale). It is used to measure some marketable securities, e.g., those held by investment entities or assets expected to be sold at below their carrying amount.

    d. **Net realizable value** is the cash or equivalent expected to be received for an asset in the due course of business, minus the costs of completion and sale. It is used to measure short-term receivables and some inventories, for example, damaged inventories. Net realizable value is distinct from liquidation value, the appropriate measure of assets and liabilities when the going-concern assumption no longer holds.

    e. **Present value** is in theory the most relevant method of measurement because it incorporates time value of money concepts.

        1) Determination of the present value of an asset or liability requires discounting at an appropriate interest rate the related future cash flows expected to occur in the due course of business. In practice, it is currently used only for noncurrent receivables and payables (explained in detail in Study Unit 13).

5. **Summary**

    a. The following table summarizes the components of the FASB's conceptual framework:

Objective of Financial Reporting
Provide information • Useful in investment and credit decisions • Useful in assessing cash-flow prospects • About entity resources, claims to those resources, and changes in them

Qualitative Characteristics	Elements of Financial Statements
Fundamental	Assets
Relevance	Liabilities
Materiality (entity-specific)	Equity or net assets
Predictive or confirmatory value	Investments by owners
Faithful representation	Distributions to owners
Completeness	Comprehensive income
Freedom from error	Revenues
Neutrality	Expenses
Enhancing	Gains
Comparability	Losses
Verifiability	
Timeliness	
Understandability	
Cost constraint	

Recognition and Measurement Concepts	
Financial statements	Expense recognition
Revenue recognition	Measurement attributes

Assumptions	Principles	Constraints
Economic entity	Historical cost	Industry practice
Going concern	Revenue recognition	Conservatism
Monetary unit	Matching	
Periodicity	Full disclosure	

Stop and review! You have completed the outline for this subunit. Study multiple-choice questions 29 through 32 beginning on page 48.

1.9 CASH FLOW INFORMATION AND PRESENT VALUE

Background
In most present value measurements used in U.S. financial reporting, a single interest rate is used to discount all future cash flows. This method may not always be adequate to reflect the uncertainties inherent in any particular set of cash flows. To address this deficiency, the FASB incorporated the expected cash flow method into its conceptual framework.
This subunit is based on SFAC No. 7, *Using Cash Flow Information and Present Value in Accounting Measurements*.

1. **Overview**

   a. Accounting measurements ordinarily use an observable amount determined by market forces. Absent such an amount, estimated cash flows often serve as a measure of an asset or a liability. Thus, the conceptual framework uses cash flows for

      1) Measurements at initial recognition,
      2) Fresh-start measurements, and
      3) Applications of the interest method of allocation.

2. **Objective**

   a. The objective is to estimate fair value by distinguishing the economic differences between sets of future cash flows that may vary in amount, timing, and uncertainty. For example, a series of $1,000 payments due at the end of each of the next 5 years has the same undiscounted value as a single $5,000 payment due in 5 years.

3. **Elements**

   a. Estimates of future cash flows
   b. Expected variability of their amount and timing
   c. The time value of money based on the risk-free interest rate
   d. The price of uncertainty inherent in an asset or liability
   e. Other factors, such as lack of liquidity or market imperfections

4. **Calculations**

   a. The **traditional approach** to calculating present value uses one set of estimated cash flows and one interest rate. Uncertainty is reflected solely in the choice of an interest rate. This approach is expected to continue to be used in many cases, for example, when contractual cash flows are involved.

   b. The **expected cash flow (ECF)** approach is applicable in more complex circumstances, such as when no market or no comparable item exists for an asset or liability.

      1) The ECF results from multiplying each possible estimated amount by its probability and adding the products. The ECF approach emphasizes explicit assumptions about the possible estimated cash flows and their probabilities.
      2) By allowing for a range of possibilities, the ECF approach permits the use of expected present value when the timing of cash flows is uncertain.
      3) Expected present value is the sum of present values of estimated cash flows discounted using the same interest rate and weighted according to their probabilities.

5. **Liabilities**

   a. The purpose of a present value measurement of the fair value of a liability is to estimate the assets required currently to (1) settle it or (2) transfer it to an entity of comparable credit standing.

6. **Changes**

 a. Changes in estimated cash flows may result in a fresh-start measurement or in a change in the plan of amortization. If remeasurement is not done, a change in the scheme may be effected by

 1) Prospectively determining a new effective rate given the carrying amount and the remaining cash flows

 2) Retrospectively determining a new effective rate given the original carrying amount, actual cash flows, and the newly estimated cash flows and using it to adjust the current carrying amount

 3) Using a catch-up approach to adjust the carrying amount to the present value of the remaining cash flows discounted at the original rate (the FASB's preferred method)

Stop and review! You have completed the outline for this subunit. Study multiple-choice questions 33 through 35 beginning on page 49.

1.10 SEC REPORTING

Background

The Securities and Exchange Commission (SEC) was created by the Securities Exchange Act of 1934 to regulate the trading of securities and to otherwise enforce securities legislation. The basic purposes of the securities laws are to prevent fraud and misrepresentation and to require full and fair disclosure so investors can evaluate investments on their own.

Under the Securities Act of 1933, disclosure is made before the initial issuance of securities by registering with the SEC (initial filing) and providing a prospectus to potential investors. Under the Securities Exchange Act of 1934, disclosures regarding subsequent trading of securities are made by filing periodic reports that are available to the public for review.

1. **SEC Regulations**

 a. **Regulation S-X** governs the reporting of financial statements, including notes and schedules.

 b. **Regulation S-K** provides disclosure standards, including many of a nonfinancial nature. Regulation S-K also covers certain aspects of corporate annual reports to shareholders.

 c. **Regulation S-B** applies to small business issuers. It reduces the disclosure requirements for a small business when it files a registration statement under the 1933 act or reports under the 1934 act.

 d. **Financial Reporting Releases (FRRs)** announce accounting and auditing matters of general interest.

 e. **Staff Accounting Bulletins (SABs)** are issued as interpretations to be followed by the SEC staff in administering disclosure requirements.

 1) Because they are merely the views of the staff, SABs are not legally required to be followed by registrants, but a company should have a good reason not to comply.

2. **Integrated Disclosure System**

 a. Standardizes the financial statements

 b. Uses a basic information package (BIP) common to most of the filings

 c. Allows incorporation by reference from the annual shareholders' report to the annual SEC report (Form 10-K)

3.   **Standardized Financial Statements**

    a.   Annual statements must be audited and include

        1)   Balance sheets for the 2 most recent fiscal year ends

        2)   Statements of income, cash flows, and changes in equity for the 3 most recent fiscal years

    b.   They are required in the annual shareholders' report as well as in forms filed with the SEC.

    c.   The accountant certifying the financial statements must be independent of the management of the filing company. The accountant is not required to be a CPA, but (s)he must be registered with a state.

4.   **Contents of Basic Information Package (BIP)**

    a.   Standardized financial statements

    b.   Selected financial information

        1)   Columnar format for the preceding 5 fiscal years

        2)   Presentation of financial trends through comparison of key information from year to year

    c.   Management's discussion and analysis of financial condition and results of operations

        1)   This information addresses such matters as liquidity (including cash flow trends), capital resources, results of operations (including trends in sales and expenses), effects of tax legislation, and the impact of changing prices. Management must also discuss the firm's outlook and the significant effects of known trends, events, and uncertainties.

            a)   Management should discuss discontinued operations, extraordinary items, and items that are unusual or infrequent with material implications for financial condition or results of operations.

            b)   Management must disclose certain information about segments: need for cash, contribution to revenues or profits, and restriction on funds flows among segments.

        2)   Forward-looking information (a forecast) is encouraged but not required.

    d.   Market price of securities and dividends

    e.   Description of business

    f.   Locations and descriptions of physical properties

    g.   Pending litigation, e.g., principal parties, allegations, and relief sought

    h.   Management

        1)   General data for each director and officer

        2)   Financial transactions with the company involving amounts in excess of $60,000

        3)   Remuneration for the five highest-paid directors and officers whose compensation exceeds $50,000 (including personal benefits)

    i.   Security holdings of directors, officers, and those owning 5% or more of the security

    j.   Matters submitted to shareholders for approval

    k.   Description of certain business relationships, such as those with related parties

5. **Initial Filing under the Securities Act of 1933 (Registration)**

   a. The issuer must register new issuances of securities with the SEC.

      1) **Form S-1** is used for the registration statement for companies that have never registered securities.

      2) **Form S-3** is a simplified form used for shelf registrations (described in item 9. on the next page).

      3) **Form S-4** is a simplified form for business combinations.

Background

Initial and other filings become public information. They can be accessed at sec.gov/edgar.shtml in the SEC's EDGAR (electronic data gathering, analysis, and retrieval) database.

---

   b. The registration statement has two parts.

      1) Part I is the prospectus. Its purpose is to provide investors with information to make an informed investment decision. It must be given to persons to whom the securities are offered or sold.

      2) Part II contains agreements relevant to the securities, the articles of incorporation, major contracts, legal opinions, and agreements with underwriters.

   c. Securities may not be offered to the public until the registration is effective.

      1) The registration statement is examined by the Division of Corporation Finance. Registration becomes effective 20 days after filing unless an amendment is filed or the SEC issues a stop order.

      2) A preliminary prospectus is allowed that contains the same information as a regular prospectus (prices are omitted) but is clearly marked in red. Thus, it is called a red herring prospectus.

6. **Form 10-K** is the annual report to the SEC.

   a. It must be filed within 60 days of the last day of the fiscal year for large accelerated filers ($700 million or more in public float), 75 days for accelerated filers ($75 million to $700 million), and 90 days for nonaccelerated filers (less than $75 million).

   b. It is certified by an independent accountant and signed by the following:

      1) Principal executive, financial, and accounting officers
      2) Majority of the board of directors

   c. Form 10-K is presented with the basic information package.

7. **Form 10-Q** is the quarterly report to the SEC.

   a. It must be filed within 40 days of the last day of the first three fiscal quarters for both large accelerated filers ($700 million or more in public float) and accelerated filers ($75 million to $700 million) and within 45 days for nonaccelerated filers (less than $75 million).

   b. Interim financial information must be reviewed (not audited) by an independent accountant.

   c. Also required are changes during the quarter, for example,

      1) Legal proceedings
      2) Increases, decreases, or changes in securities or indebtedness
      3) Matters submitted to shareholders for a vote
      4) Exhibits and reports on Form 8-K
      5) Other material events not reported on Form 8-K

   d. Form 10-QSB is filed by small businesses.

8. **Form 8-K** is a current report to disclose material events.

    a. It must be filed within 4 business days after the material event occurs.

    b. Material events include

        1) A change in control
        2) Acquisition or disposition of a significant amount of assets not in the ordinary course of business
        3) Bankruptcy or receivership
        4) Resignation of directors
        5) A change in the registrant's certifying accountant

    c. Under the Sarbanes-Oxley Act of 2002, issuers must make real-time disclosure on a rapid and current basis of material changes in financial condition or operations.

9. **Shelf Registration**

    a. Corporations may file registration statements covering a stipulated amount of securities that may be issued over the 2-year effective period of the statement. The securities are placed on the shelf and issued at an opportune moment without the necessity of filing a new registration statement, observing a 20-day waiting period, or preparing a new prospectus.

    b. The issuer is required only to provide updating amendments or to refer investors to quarterly and annual statements filed with the SEC. It is most advantageous to large corporations that frequently offer securities to the public.

Stop and review! You have completed the outline for this subunit. Study multiple-choice questions 36 through 39 beginning on page 50.

QUESTIONS

1.1 Standard Setting for Financial Accounting

1. Which of the following is true regarding the comparison of managerial and financial accounting?

A. Managerial accounting is generally more precise.

B. Managerial accounting has a past focus, and financial accounting has a future focus.

C. The emphasis on managerial accounting is relevance, and the emphasis on financial accounting is timeliness.

D. Managerial accounting need **not** follow generally accepted accounting principles (GAAP), while financial accounting must follow them.

Answer (D) is correct.
   REQUIRED: The true comparison of managerial and financial accounting.
   DISCUSSION: Managerial accounting assists management decision making, planning, and control. Financial accounting addresses accounting for an entity's assets, liabilities, revenues, expenses, and other elements of financial statements. Financial statements are the primary method of communicating to external parties information about the entity's results of operations, financial position, and cash flows. For general-purpose financial statements to be useful to external parties, they must be prepared in conformity with accounting principles that are generally accepted in the United States (GAAP). However, managerial accounting information is primarily directed to specific internal users. Hence, it ordinarily need not follow GAAP.
   Answer (A) is incorrect. Managerial accounting may be no more precise than financial accounting. For example, it relies on allocations of certain product costs (e.g., overhead) that are based on assumptions rather than on cause-and-effect relationships. Answer (B) is incorrect. Neither managerial accounting nor financial accounting is forward-looking. Both essentially record what has already occurred. Answer (C) is incorrect. Choices of financial accounting information to be reported must balance relevance (including timeliness) and reliability. External parties will not find financial accounting information useful if it is timely but unreliable.

2. Congress empowered which of the following bodies with the authority to set accounting standards for publicly traded companies in the U.S.?

A. The Securities and Exchange Commission (SEC).

B. The American Institute of Certified Public Accountants (AICPA).

C. The Financial Accounting Standards Board (FASB).

D. The International Accounting Standards Board (IASB).

Answer (A) is correct.
   REQUIRED: The body empowered by Congress to establish U.S. GAAP.
   DISCUSSION: The SEC has been empowered by Congress to establish rules for financial reporting by publicly traded companies (called issuers) in the United States. The SEC has in turn delegated the authority for detailed rule making to the Financial Accounting Standards Board (FASB).
   Answer (B) is incorrect. The SEC, not the AICPA, was empowered by Congress to establish rules for financial reporting by publicly traded companies. Answer (C) is incorrect. The FASB's rule-making authority was delegated to it by the SEC. Only the SEC has been empowered by Congress with the authority to set U.S. accounting standards. Answer (D) is incorrect. The IASB does not operate under the auspices of Congress.

3. Arpco, Inc., a for-profit provider of healthcare services, recently purchased two smaller companies and is researching accounting issues arising from the two business combinations. Which of the following accounting pronouncements are the most authoritative?

A. FASB Accounting Standards Updates.

B. FASB Statements of Financial Accounting Concepts.

C. FASB Statements of Financial Accounting Standards.

D. The Accounting Standards Codification.

Answer (D) is correct.
   REQUIRED: The most authoritative pronouncements.
   DISCUSSION: The FASB's Accounting Standards Codification is the only source of authoritative guidance for nongovernmental entities in the U.S. All other sources of guidance are nonauthoritative.
   Answer (A) is incorrect. Accounting Standards Updates are authoritative only to the extent they have been incorporated in the Accounting Standards Codification. Answer (B) is incorrect. Statements of Financial Accounting Concepts are nonauthoritative. Answer (C) is incorrect. Statements of Financial Accounting Standards are no longer issued. Existing SFASs are authoritative only to the extent they have been incorporated in the Accounting Standards Codification.

4. The principal benefit of a single set of global financial reporting standards is

A. The harmonization of world financial reporting.

B. Increased ease of capital flow.

C. Simplified enforcement for local and national regulatory bodies.

D. Minimization of the amount of professional judgment required to implement them.

Answer (B) is correct.
   REQUIRED: The principal benefit of a single set of global financial reporting standards.
   DISCUSSION: The principal advantage of a single set of global financial reporting standards is that multinational companies do not have to rewrite their statements in (or perform a complex reconciliation to) the local GAAP in order to trade their stock on the local exchange. Foreign investment is thereby made much easier, and the cost of capital is lowered.
   Answer (A) is incorrect. The harmonization of world financial reporting is a means to an end, not an end in itself. Answer (C) is incorrect. While simplified enforcement for local and national regulatory bodies is a secondary benefit, it is not the principal benefit of having a single set of global financial reporting standards. Answer (D) is incorrect. A single set of global standards does not necessarily minimize the amount of professional judgment required to implement them.

1.2 The Objective of General-Purpose Financial Reporting

5. According to the FASB's conceptual framework, the objective of general-purpose financial reporting is most likely based on

A. Generally accepted accounting principles.

B. Reporting on how well management has discharged its responsibilities.

C. The need for conservatism.

D. The needs of the users of the information.

Answer (D) is correct.
   REQUIRED: The objectives of financial reporting for business enterprises.
   DISCUSSION: The objective of general-purpose financial reporting is to provide information that is useful to existing and potential investors, lenders, and other creditors in making decisions about providing resources to the entity.
   Answer (A) is incorrect. GAAP govern how to account for items in the financial statements. Answer (B) is incorrect. Financial reporting provides information that is helpful, among other things, in evaluating how well management has discharged its responsibilities to make effective and efficient use of entity resources. Answer (C) is incorrect. Conservatism is a constraint on recognition in the statements.

6. Which basis of accounting is most likely to provide the best assessment of an entity's past and future ability to generate net cash inflows?

    A. Cash basis of accounting.

    B. Modified cash basis of accounting.

    C. Accrual basis of accounting.

    D. Tax basis of accounting.

Answer (C) is correct.
    REQUIRED: The basis that best indicates an entity's ability to generate net cash inflows.
    DISCUSSION: Accrual accounting reports the effects of transactions and other events and circumstances on the reporting entity's economic resources and claims when those effects occur, even if the resulting cash flows occur in a different period. The advantage of accrual accounting is that information about an entity's economic resources and claims and changes in them during a period provides a better basis for assessing past and future performance than information solely about cash flows (SFAC 8).
    Answer (A) is incorrect. The cash basis is inadequate to depict the financial performance of businesses because their activities are largely based on credit and often involve long and complex financial arrangements or production or marketing processes. The accrual and deferral of costs and benefits better reflects the current-period effects on economic resources and claims. Answer (B) is incorrect. A modified cash basis does not adequately depict the long and complex financial arrangements or production or marketing processes and extensive use of credit employed by modern businesses. Answer (D) is incorrect. The basis of accounting specified in the federal income tax code has objectives other than those that users of financial statements seek to satisfy (usefulness in investment and credit decisions, etc.). The tax code has social and fiscal policy objectives, which are distinct from the goals of investors and grantors of credit.

7. Which of the following is a true statement about the objective of general-purpose financial reporting?

    A. Financial reporting is ordinarily focused on industries rather than individual entities.

    B. The objective applies only to information that is useful for investment professionals.

    C. Financial reporting directly measures management performance.

    D. The information provided relates to the entity's economic resources and claims.

Answer (D) is correct.
    REQUIRED: The true statement about the objective of general-purpose financial reporting.
    DISCUSSION: The information reported relates to the entity's economic resources and claims to them (financial position) and to changes in those resources and claims.
    Answer (A) is incorrect. Financial reporting is focused on individual entities. Answer (B) is incorrect. The objectives apply to information that is useful for current and potential investors, creditors, and other users in making rational investment, credit, and other decisions. Answer (C) is incorrect. Entity performance is affected by many factors other than management.

8. What are the Statements of Financial Accounting Concepts intended to establish?

    A. Generally accepted accounting principles in financial reporting by business enterprises.

    B. The meaning of "present fairly in accordance with generally accepted accounting principles."

    C. The objectives and concepts for use in developing standards of financial accounting and reporting.

    D. The hierarchy of sources of generally accepted accounting principles.

Answer (C) is correct.
    REQUIRED: The purpose of the SFACs.
    DISCUSSION: SFACs do not establish accounting and reporting requirements. They are nonauthoritative guidance for nongovernmental entities. SFACs describe the objectives, qualitative characteristics, and other fundamental concepts that guide the FASB in developing sound accounting principles.
    Answer (A) is incorrect. SFACs are intended to guide the development of accounting standards by the FASB. Answer (B) is incorrect. This language is from a Statement on Auditing Standards. Answer (D) is incorrect. The ASC contains the only authoritative guidance issued by the FASB.

1.3 Objectives of Financial Reporting -- Not-for-Profit (Nongovernmental) Entities

9. Which of the following is ordinarily **not** considered one of the major distinguishing characteristics of nonbusiness entities?

   A. Significant amounts of resources are provided by donors in nonreciprocal transactions.

   B. There is an absence of defined, transferable ownership interests.

   C. Performance indicators similar to a business enterprise's profit are readily available.

   D. The primary operating purpose is not to provide goods or services at a profit.

Answer (C) is correct.
   REQUIRED: The statement not ordinarily considered a major characteristic of nonbusiness entities.
   DISCUSSION: The objectives of financial reporting are derived from the common interests of those who provide the resources to nonbusiness entities. Such entities ordinarily have no single indicator of performance comparable to a business enterprise's profit. Thus, nonbusiness entity performance is usually evaluated in terms of management stewardship.

10. The resource providers of not-for-profit entities have which of the following as their primary concerns?

I. Financial return on investment

II. Services rendered by the not-for-profit entity

III. The continuing ability of the not-for-profit entity to render services

IV. The avoidance of fraud or embezzlement

   A. I and IV.

   B. II, III, and IV.

   C. I, II, and III.

   D. II and III.

Answer (D) is correct.
   REQUIRED: The primary concerns of resource providers of not-for-profit entities.
   DISCUSSION: Resource providers of not-for-profit entities have as their primary concerns the services rendered by the entity and the continuing ability of the entity to render those services. These needs differ from the needs of resource providers for business enterprises, whose primary concern is financial return.

11. All of the following are objectives of financial reporting by nonbusiness entities **except**

   A. To provide information that is useful to current and potential resource providers in making resource allocation decisions.

   B. To provide information that concerns the sources and uses of cash and other liquid assets, borrowing and repayment activities, and other factors affecting liquidity.

   C. To provide information that concerns performance, including a single indicator comparable to a business enterprise's net income, that permits resource providers to assess how effectively the entity is competing with others.

   D. To provide information that concerns economic resources, liabilities, net resources, and the effects of changes in resources and interests.

Answer (C) is correct.
   REQUIRED: The objectives of financial reporting by nonbusiness entities.
   DISCUSSION: Nonbusiness entities often have no single indicator of performance comparable to a business enterprise's net income. Accordingly, other performance indicators are needed, with the most useful being information measuring the changes in the amount and nature of net resources that is combined with information about service efforts and accomplishments.
   Answer (A) is incorrect. Among the objectives of financial reporting by nonbusiness entities is to provide information that is useful to current and potential resource providers in making resource allocation decisions. Answer (B) is incorrect. Among the objectives of financial reporting by nonbusiness entities is to provide information that concerns the sources and uses of cash and other liquid assets, borrowing and repayment activities, and other factors affecting liquidity. Answer (D) is incorrect. Among the objectives of financial reporting by nonbusiness entities is to provide information that concerns economic resources, liabilities, net resources, and the effects of changes in resources and interests.

12. The reporting model described in the guidance on not-for-profit financial statements applies to

A. Business entities and governmental not-for-profit entities.

B. Business entities and nongovernmental not-for-profit entities.

C. Nongovernmental not-for-profit entities.

D. Governmental not-for-profit entities that also use proprietary fund accounting.

Answer (C) is correct.
 REQUIRED: The entities that use the net assets reporting model.
 DISCUSSION: The reporting model for financial accounting and reporting by nongovernmental not-for-profit entities (NFPs) recognizes that the information needs of resource providers of NFPs differ from those of resource providers of business entities. The latter are primarily concerned about financial return, whereas the former are primarily concerned about the services rendered by the NFP and its continuing ability to render those services.

1.4 Objectives of Financial Reporting -- Governmental Entities

13. Which of the following objectives of financial reporting is applicable to business entities, **not** to governmental entities? Provide information to

A. Assist in public accountability.

B. Assist in evaluating operating results.

C. Assist in assessing services provided.

D. Assist in assessing cash flow prospects.

Answer (D) is correct.
 REQUIRED: The reporting objective applicable to business entities.
 DISCUSSION: Current and potential investors and creditors of a business entity want to assess their likelihood of receiving cash from dividends or interest or from the proceeds from the sale, redemption, or maturity of securities or loans.

14. Which of the following objectives of financial reporting is applicable to governmental entities? Provide information

A. Useful in making resource allocation decisions.

B. For assessing service efforts and accomplishments.

C. Useful in assessing management stewardship and performance.

D. About economic resources, obligations, net resources, and changes in them.

Answer (B) is correct.
 REQUIRED: The reporting objective applicable to governmental entities.
 DISCUSSION: Providing information for assessing service efforts and accomplishments is one of the objectives that serves to assist in evaluating the operating results of a governmental entity.
 Answer (A) is incorrect. Providing information useful in making resource allocation decisions is a reporting objective of not-for-profit entities. Answer (C) is incorrect. Providing information useful in assessing management stewardship and performance is a reporting objective of not-for-profit entities. Answer (D) is incorrect. Providing information about economic resources, obligations, net resources, and changes in them is a reporting objective of not-for-profit entities.

15. Which of the following does **not** describe a difference between the business-type activities and the governmental-type activities of a governmental entity?

A. Business-type activities have heavy investments in revenue-producing capital assets.

B. Business-type activities adopt budgets, but they often lack the legal force of the budget for governmental-type activities.

C. Business-type activities involve a direct exchange of money in return for goods delivered or services rendered.

D. Business-type activities often perform multiple functions and are thus more easily compared between governments than are governmental-type activities.

Answer (D) is correct.
 REQUIRED: The item that does not describe a difference between governmental-type activities and business-type activities.
 DISCUSSION: Business-type activities often perform only a single function and are thus more easily compared between governments than are governmental-type activities.
 Answer (A) is incorrect. Business-type activities have heavy investments in revenue-producing capital assets (e.g., toll roads, manufacturing facilities for prison industries). Answer (B) is incorrect. Business-type activities adopt budgets, but they often lack the legal force of the budget for governmental-type activities. Answer (C) is incorrect. Business-type activities of governmental bodies involve a direct exchange of money in return for goods delivered or services rendered.

16. Which of the following is **not** a characteristic of the governmental reporting environment?

   A. Interperiod equity.

   B. Balance sheet equity.

   C. Legally binding budget.

   D. Accountability.

Answer (B) is correct.
    REQUIRED: The item not a characteristic of the governmental reporting environment.
    DISCUSSION: Governmental bodies report fund balance or net position, not equity.
    Answer (A) is incorrect. Interperiod equity implies that current citizens should treat future citizens with equity; i.e., later generations should not have to pay for services received by prior generations. This principle implies that current-year revenues should be sufficient to cover current-year services. Answer (C) is incorrect. A legally binding budget is one of the control characteristics inherent in the structure of government. Answer (D) is incorrect. Accountability is the essence of governmental reporting. Accountability requires that a governmental body justify how it spends the monies it collects in pursuit of the goals the citizens have set for it.

1.5 Assumptions, Principles, and Constraints

17. Reporting inventory at the lower of cost or market (LCM) is a departure from the accounting principle of

   A. Historical cost.

   B. Consistency.

   C. Conservatism.

   D. Full disclosure.

Answer (A) is correct.
    REQUIRED: The principle from which reporting inventory at the lower of cost or market is a departure.
    DISCUSSION: Historical cost is the amount of cash, or its equivalent, paid to acquire an asset. Thus, the LCM rule departs from the historical cost principle when the utility of the inventory is judged no longer to be as great as its cost.
    Answer (B) is incorrect. LCM does not violate the consistency characteristic if it is consistently applied. Answer (C) is incorrect. LCM yields a conservative inventory valuation. Answer (D) is incorrect. As long as the basis of stating inventories is disclosed, LCM does not violate the full disclosure principle.

18. Which of the following is a generally accepted accounting principle that illustrates the practice of conservatism during a particular reporting period?

   A. Capitalization of research and development costs.

   B. Accrual of a contingency deemed to be reasonably possible.

   C. Reporting investments with appreciated market values at market value.

   D. Reporting inventory at the lower of cost or market value.

Answer (D) is correct.
    REQUIRED: The generally accepted accounting principle that illustrates conservatism.
    DISCUSSION: Under the conservatism constraint, when alternative accounting methods are appropriate, the one having the less favorable effect on net income and total assets is preferable. An understatement of assets is to be avoided so that earnings are not overstated when the assets are realized. Accordingly, the market measurement under the LCM rule is subject to a ceiling of net realizable value and a floor of NRV minus a normal profit. Reporting inventory above NRV will result in a loss on sale. Reporting inventory below NRV minus a normal profit will result in an overstatement of profit. Thus, the LCM rule results in a conservative balance sheet without an unduly conservative measurement that will overstate earnings and retained earnings.
    Answer (A) is incorrect. R&D costs normally are expensed as incurred. Answer (B) is incorrect. Most contingent losses are recognized only if probable and capable of being reasonably estimated. However, the fair value of a guarantee is accrued even if the payment is not probable. Answer (C) is incorrect. Recognizing unrealized holding gains on investments, e.g., trading securities, does not result in a conservative balance sheet or earnings amount.

19. What is the underlying concept governing the generally accepted accounting principles pertaining to recording gain contingencies?

    A. Conservatism.

    B. Relevance.

    C. Consistency.

    D. Faithful representation.

Answer (A) is correct.
    REQUIRED: The underlying concept governing the GAAP relating to gain contingencies.
    DISCUSSION: Under the conservatism constraint, when alternative accounting methods are appropriate, the one having the less favorable effect on net income and total assets is preferable. However, conservatism does not permit a deliberate understatement of total assets and net income. Furthermore, SFAC 5 describes "a general tendency to emphasize purchase and sale transactions and to apply conservative procedures in accounting recognition." This tendency is a response to uncertainty. Thus, a loss, not a gain, contingency is recorded in the financial statements. If the probability of realization of a gain is high, the contingency is disclosed in the notes.
    Answer (B) is incorrect. Relevance relates to the capacity of information to affect a decision. Answer (C) is incorrect. Consistency requires the application of the same accounting principles to the same items. Answer (D) is incorrect. Faithful representation is a fundamental qualitative characteristic. Useful information faithfully represents the economic events that it purports to represent.

20. The information provided by financial reporting pertains to

    A. Individual business enterprises rather than to industries or an economy as a whole, or members of society as consumers.

    B. Individual business enterprises and industries rather than to an economy as a whole or to members of society as consumers.

    C. Individual business enterprises and an economy as a whole rather than to industries or to members of society as consumers.

    D. Individual business enterprises, industries, and an economy as a whole rather than to members of society as consumers.

Answer (A) is correct.
    REQUIRED: The economic level(s) to which the information provided by financial reporting pertains.
    DISCUSSION: Financial reporting pertains essentially to individual economic entities. Information about industries and economies in which an industry operates is usually provided only to the extent necessary for understanding the individual business enterprise.
    Answer (B) is incorrect. Financial reporting does not pertain to industries. Answer (C) is incorrect. Financial reporting does not pertain to the economy as a whole. Answer (D) is incorrect. Financial reporting does not pertain to industries or the economy as a whole.

1.6 Qualitative Characteristics of Useful Financial Information

21. According to *Statements of Financial Accounting Concepts*, predictive value relates to

	Relevance	Faithful Representation
A.	No	No
B.	Yes	Yes
C.	No	Yes
D.	Yes	No

Answer (D) is correct.
    REQUIRED: The primary quality of which predictive value is an aspect.
    DISCUSSION: Relevance is a fundamental qualitative characteristic of useful financial information. It is the capacity of information to make a difference in a decision. It must have (1) predictive value, (2) confirmatory value, or both. Moreover, materiality is an entity-specific aspect of relevance. Something has predictive value if it can be used in a predictive process. Something has confirmatory value with respect to prior evaluations if it provides feedback that confirms or changes (corrects) them.

22. According to the FASB's conceptual framework, what does the concept of faithful representation in financial reporting include?

A. Predictive value.

B. Certainty.

C. Perfect accuracy.

D. Neutrality.

Answer (D) is correct.

REQUIRED: The item included in the concept of faithful representation.

DISCUSSION: Faithful representation and relevance are the fundamental qualitative characteristics of accounting information. A perfectly faithful representation is complete, neutral, and free from error. Faithfully represented information is neutral if it is unbiased in its selection or presentation of information.

Answer (A) is incorrect. Relevant information has predictive value, confirmatory value, or both. Faithfully represented information is not necessarily relevant. Answer (B) is incorrect. Certainty and perfect accuracy are not implied by faithful representation. The financial statements are a model of the reporting entity. This model may be representationally faithful for its intended purposes without corresponding precisely to the real-world original. Thus, uncertainty that does not reach the materiality threshold does not impair faithful representation. Answer (C) is incorrect. The concept of faithful representation includes the concept of perfect faithfulness, not perfect accuracy.

23. According to the FASB's conceptual framework, the usefulness of providing information in financial statements is subject to the constraint of

A. Consistency.

B. Cost.

C. Relevance.

D. Representational faithfulness.

Answer (B) is correct.

REQUIRED: The constraint on financial reporting.

DISCUSSION: Cost is a pervasive constraint on the information provided by financial reporting. The benefits of financial information should exceed the costs of reporting.

Answer (A) is incorrect. Consistency is a means of achieving comparability, an enhancing qualitative characteristic. It is the use of the same methods, for example, accounting principles, for the same items. Answer (C) is incorrect. Relevance is a fundamental qualitative characteristic of useful information, not a constraint. Answer (D) is incorrect. Representational faithfulness is a fundamental qualitative characteristic of useful information, not a constraint.

24. Under SFAC 8, the ability, through consensus among measurers, to ensure that information represents what it purports to represent is an example of the concept of

A. Relevance.

B. Verifiability.

C. Comparability.

D. Predictive value.

Answer (B) is correct.

REQUIRED: The term that describes the ability to ensure that information represents what it purports to represent.

DISCUSSION: Verifiability is a qualitative characteristic that enhances relevance and faithful representation. Information is verifiable (directly or indirectly) if knowledgeable and independent observers can reach a consensus (not necessarily unanimity) that it is faithfully represented.

Answer (A) is incorrect. Relevance (a fundamental qualitative characteristic) is the capacity of information to make a difference in a decision. Answer (C) is incorrect. Comparability (an enhancing qualitative characteristic) is the quality of information that enables users to identify similarities and differences among items. Answer (D) is incorrect. Relevant information is able to make a difference in user decisions. To do so, it must have predictive value, confirmatory value, or both. Something has predictive value if it can be used as an input in a predictive process.

1.7 Elements of Financial Statements

25. According to the FASB's conceptual framework, asset valuation accounts are

A. Assets.

B. Neither assets **nor** liabilities.

C. Part of equity.

D. Liabilities.

Answer (B) is correct.

REQUIRED: The conceptual framework's definition of asset valuation accounts.

DISCUSSION: Asset valuation accounts are separate items sometimes found in financial statements that reduce or increase the carrying amount of an asset. The conceptual framework considers asset valuation accounts to be part of the related asset account. They are not considered to be assets or liabilities in their own right.

Answer (A) is incorrect. Asset valuation accounts are not assets. Answer (C) is incorrect. An asset valuation account is part of the related asset account. Answer (D) is incorrect. Asset valuation accounts are not liabilities.

26. According to the FASB's conceptual framework, which of the following is an essential characteristic of an asset?

A. The claims to an asset's benefits are legally enforceable.

B. An asset is tangible.

C. An asset is obtained at a cost.

D. An asset provides future benefits.

Answer (D) is correct.
REQUIRED: The essential characteristic of an asset.
DISCUSSION: One of the three essential characteristics of an asset is that the transaction or event giving rise to the entity's right to or control of its assets has already occurred; i.e., it is not expected to occur in the future. A second essential characteristic of an asset is that an entity can obtain the benefits of and control others' access to the asset. The third essential characteristic is that an asset must embody a probable future benefit that involves a capacity to contribute to future net cash inflows.
Answer (A) is incorrect. Claims to an asset's benefits may not be legally enforceable. Goodwill is an example. Answer (B) is incorrect. Some assets are intangible. Answer (C) is incorrect. Assets may be obtained through donations or investments by owners.

27. Under SFAC 6, *Elements of Financial Statements*, interrelated elements of financial statements that are directly related to measuring the performance and status of a business enterprise include

	Distributions to Owners	Notes to Financial Statements
A.	Yes	Yes
B.	Yes	No
C.	No	Yes
D.	No	No

Answer (B) is correct.
REQUIRED: The interrelated elements directly related to measuring performance and status.
DISCUSSION: The elements of financial statements directly related to measuring the performance and status of business enterprises and not-for-profit entities are assets, liabilities, equity of a business or net assets of a not-for-profit entity, revenues, expenses, gains, and losses. The elements of investments by owners, distributions to owners, and comprehensive income relate only to business enterprises. Information disclosed in notes or parenthetically on the face of financial statements amplifies or explains information recognized in the financial statements.

28. According to the FASB's conceptual framework, which of the following decreases shareholder equity?

A. Investments by owners.

B. Distributions to owners.

C. Issuance of stock.

D. Acquisition of assets in a cash transaction.

Answer (B) is correct.
REQUIRED: The item that decreases equity.
DISCUSSION: Equity equals assets minus liabilities. Accordingly, transactions that decrease assets without affecting liabilities also decrease equity. Distributions to owners, such as payments of dividends (debit retained earnings and credit dividends payable, then debit dividends payable and credit cash), are such transactions.
Answer (A) is incorrect. Investments by owners increase assets and equity. Answer (C) is incorrect. An issuance of stock results either in no change in equity (e.g., a stock split or stock dividend) or an increase. Answer (D) is incorrect. Acquisition of assets in a cash transaction has no effect on equity.

1.8 Recognition and Measurement Concepts

29. What is the purpose of information presented in notes to the financial statements?

A. To provide disclosures required by generally accepted accounting principles.

B. To correct improper presentation in the financial statements.

C. To provide recognition of amounts **not** included in the totals of the financial statements.

D. To present management's responses to auditor comments.

Answer (A) is correct.
REQUIRED: The purpose of information presented in notes to the financial statements.
DISCUSSION: Notes are an integral part of the basic financial statements. Notes provide information essential to understanding the financial statements, including disclosures required by GAAP.
Answer (B) is incorrect. Notes may not be used to rectify an improper presentation. Answer (C) is incorrect. Disclosure in notes is not a substitute for recognition in financial statements for items that meet recognition criteria. Answer (D) is incorrect. Management's responses to auditor comments are not an appropriate subject of financial reporting.

30. According to the FASB's conceptual framework, which of the following attributes should **not** be used to measure inventory?

A. Historical cost.

B. Replacement cost.

C. Net realizable value.

D. Present value of future cash flows.

Answer (D) is correct.
REQUIRED: The attribute not used to measure inventory.
DISCUSSION: The present value of future cash flows is not an acceptable measure of inventory. Present value is typically used for long-term receivables and payables.

31. On December 31, Year 1, Brook Co. decided to end operations and dispose of its assets within 3 months. At December 31, Year 1, the net realizable value of the equipment was below historical cost. What is the appropriate measurement basis for equipment included in Brook's December 31, Year 1, balance sheet?

A. Historical cost.

B. Current reproduction cost.

C. Liquidation value.

D. Current replacement cost.

Answer (C) is correct.
REQUIRED: The attribute used to measure equipment after a decision to end operations.
DISCUSSION: Financial accounting principles assume that a business entity is a going concern in the absence of evidence to the contrary. This concept justifies the use of depreciation and amortization schedules and the recording of assets and liabilities at attributes other than liquidation value. However, the going concern assumption is no longer applicable when the entity's existence will be terminated in 3 months. Accordingly, historical cost is no longer appropriate as a measurement attribute, and assets should be restated at liquidation value.
Answer (A) is incorrect. Historical cost is of little usefulness when the entity is about to discontinue operations. Answer (B) is incorrect. Current reproduction cost reflects the cost of reproducing equipment or inventories and is inconsistent with a liquidation basis of measurement. Answer (D) is incorrect. Current replacement cost reflects the cost of replacing equipment and is inconsistent with a liquidation basis of measurement.

32. Under a royalty agreement with another entity, a company will receive royalties from the assignment of a patent for 3 years. The royalties received should be reported as revenue

A. At the date of the royalty agreement.

B. In the period earned.

C. In the period received.

D. Evenly over the life of the royalty agreement.

Answer (B) is correct.
REQUIRED: The timing of recognition of royalty revenue.
DISCUSSION: Revenues should be recognized when they are realized or realizable and earned. Revenues are realized when products, merchandise, or other assets are exchanged for cash or claims to cash. Revenues are realizable when related assets received or held are readily convertible to known amounts of cash or claims to cash. Revenues are earned when the entity has substantially accomplished what it must do to be entitled to the benefits represented by the revenues. Earning embraces the activities that give rise to revenue, for example, allowing other entities to use entity assets (such as patents) or the occurrence of an event specified in a contract (such as production using the patented technology).
Answer (A) is incorrect. At the date of the royalty agreement, the contract is wholly executory. The recognition criteria have not been met, and no asset, revenue, or liability is recognized. Answer (C) is incorrect. Royalties received before they are earned are credited to a liability. Answer (D) is incorrect. Revenue is recognized evenly over the life of the royalty agreement only if earned evenly over that period.

1.9 Cash Flow Information and Present Value

33. Which of the following is(are) a necessary element(s) of present value measurement?

A. Estimates of future cash flows.

B. The price of uncertainty inherent in an asset or liability.

C. Liquidity or market imperfections.

D. All of the answers are correct.

Answer (D) is correct.
REQUIRED: The necessary elements of present value measurement.
DISCUSSION: A measurement based on present value should reflect uncertainty so that variations in risks are incorporated. Accordingly, the following are the necessary elements of a present value measurement:

1. Estimates of future cash flows,
2. Expected variability of their amount and timing,
3. The time value of money (risk-free interest rate),
4. The price of uncertainty inherent in an asset or liability, and
5. Other factors, such as liquidity or market imperfections.

34. The objective of present value when used to determine an accounting measurement for initial recognition purposes is to

A. Capture the value of an asset or liability in the context of a given entity.

B. Estimate fair value.

C. Calculate the effective-settlement amount of assets.

D. Estimate value in use.

Answer (B) is correct.
REQUIRED: The objective of present value in an initial recognition measurement.
DISCUSSION: The objective of present value measurements is to estimate fair value by distinguishing the economic differences between sets of future cash flows that may vary in amount, timing, and uncertainty. A present value measurement includes five elements: estimates of cash flows, expectations about their variability, the time value of money, the price of uncertainty inherent in an asset or liability, and other factors (e.g., liquidity or market imperfections). Fair value encompasses all these elements using the estimates and expectations of participants in the market.
Answer (A) is incorrect. Entity-specific measurements are based on the entity's assumptions. Answer (C) is incorrect. An effective-settlement measurement (the current assets needed to be invested today at a given interest rate to generate future cash inflows to match future cash outflows for a liability) excludes the price components related to uncertainty and the entity's credit standing. Parties that hold an entity's liabilities consider its credit standing when determining the prices they will pay. Answer (D) is incorrect. Value-in-use measurements are based on the entity's assumptions.

35. The objective of present value is to estimate fair value when used to determine accounting measurements for

	Initial-Recognition Purposes	Fresh-Start Purposes
A.	No	No
B.	Yes	Yes
C.	Yes	No
D.	No	Yes

Answer (B) is correct.
REQUIRED: The purposes for using present value measurement to estimate fair value.
DISCUSSION: The objective of present value in initial-recognition or fresh-start measurements is to estimate fair value. A present value measurement includes five elements: estimates of cash flows, expectations about their variability, the time value of money (the risk-free interest rate), the price of uncertainty inherent in an asset or liability, and other factors (e.g., liquidity or market imperfections). Fair value encompasses all these elements using the estimates and expectations of participants in the market.

1.10 SEC Reporting

36. Which of the following statements is correct concerning corporations subject to the reporting requirements of the Securities Exchange Act of 1934?

A. The annual report (Form 10-K) need **not** include audited financial statements.

B. The annual report (Form 10-K) must be filed with the SEC within 20 days of the end of the corporation's fiscal year.

C. A quarterly report (Form 10-Q) need only be filed with the SEC by those corporations that are also subject to the registration requirements of the Securities Act of 1933.

D. A report (Form 8-K) must be filed with the SEC after a materially important event occurs.

Answer (D) is correct.
REQUIRED: The reporting required under the Securities Exchange Act of 1934.
DISCUSSION: Current reports must be filed on Form 8-K describing specified material events: (1) changes in control of the registrant, (2) the acquisition or disposition of a significant amount of assets not in the ordinary course of business, (3) bankruptcy or receivership, (4) resignation of a director, and (5) a change in the registrant's certifying accountant.
Answer (A) is incorrect. Form 10-K must include audited financial statements: comparative balance sheets and statements of income, cash flows, and changes in equity. Answer (B) is incorrect. Form 10-K is due at least 60 days after the entity's fiscal year end. Answer (C) is incorrect. An entity required to file Form 10-K must also file Form 10-Q for each of the first three quarters.

37. Integral Corp. is subject to the reporting provisions of the Securities Exchange Act of 1934. For its current fiscal year, Integral filed the following with the SEC: quarterly reports, an annual report, and a periodic report listing newly appointed officers of the corporation. Integral did not notify the SEC of shareholder "short-swing" profits, did not report that a competitor made a tender offer to Integral's shareholders, and did not report changes in the price of its stock as sold on the New York Stock Exchange. Under the SEC reporting requirements, which of the following was Integral required to do?

A. Report the tender offer to the SEC.

B. Notify the SEC of shareholder "short-swing" profits.

C. File the periodic report listing newly appointed officers.

D. Report the changes in the market price of its stock.

Answer (C) is correct.
REQUIRED: The reporting required of a covered corporation under the 1934 act.
DISCUSSION: A covered corporation is required to file annual (10-K), quarterly (10-Q), and current events (8-K) reports with the SEC. Similar reports are sent to shareholders. The 10-K report contains information about the entity's business activities, securities, management, related parties, disagreements about accounting principles and disclosure, audited financial statements, etc. It is intended to bring the information in the registration statement up to date. Thus, newly appointed officers will be listed.
Answer (A) is incorrect. The target need only file a statement with the SEC if the tender offer is hostile (unsolicited). Answer (B) is incorrect. Insiders are liable to the corporation for short-swing profits. Insiders include directors, officers, and persons owning more than 10% of the corporation's stock. Answer (D) is incorrect. Although the annual report (Form 10-K) requires disclosure of the market price of the common stock of the registrant (including the high and low sales prices) for each quarter of the last 2 fiscal years and any subsequent interim periods, not every change in the market price of its stock need be reported.

38. An external auditor's involvement with Form 10-Q that is being prepared for filing with the SEC most likely will consist of a(n)

A. Audit of the financial statements included in Form 10-Q.

B. Compilation report on the financial statements included in Form 10-Q.

C. Comfort letter that covers stub-period financial data.

D. Review of the interim financial statements included in Form 10-Q.

Answer (D) is correct.
REQUIRED: The external auditor's most likely involvement with Form 10-Q.
DISCUSSION: Form 10-Q is the quarterly report to the SEC. It need not contain audited financial statements, but it should be prepared in accordance with GAAP. Thus, an SEC registrant must obtain a review by an independent auditor of its interim financial information that is to be included in a quarterly report to the SEC.
Answer (A) is incorrect. Audited statements are not required in quarterly reports. Answer (B) is incorrect. A compilation provides no assurance and would thus not satisfy the SEC requirement of "accurate, representative, and meaningful" quarterly information. Answer (C) is incorrect. Comfort letters are addressed to underwriters, not the SEC.

39. The management's discussion and analysis (MD&A) section of an annual report

A. Includes the company president's letter.

B. Covers three financial aspects of a firm's business: liquidity, capital resources, and results of operations.

C. Is a technical analysis of past results and a defense of those results by management.

D. Covers marketing and product line issues.

Answer (B) is correct.
REQUIRED: The item that is an aspect of MD&A.
DISCUSSION: The MD&A section is included in SEC filings. It addresses in a nonquantified manner the prospects of a company. The SEC examines it with care to determine that management has disclosed material information affecting the company's future results. Disclosures about commitments and events that may affect operations or liquidity are mandatory. Thus, the MD&A section pertains to liquidity, capital resources, and results of operations.
Answer (A) is incorrect. The MD&A section may be separate from the president's letter. Answer (C) is incorrect. A technical analysis and a defense are not required in the MD&A section; it is more forward-looking. Answer (D) is incorrect. The MD&A section does not have to include marketing and product line issues.

Use the additional questions in Gleim **CPA Test Prep Online** to create Test Sessions that emulate Prometric!

1.11 PRACTICE SIMULATION

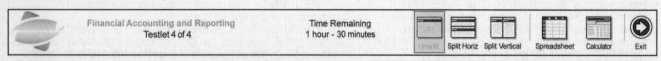

DIRECTIONS

Note: If you believe you have encountered a software malfunction, report it to the test center staff immediately.

Navigation

To navigate from task to task, use the controls at the bottom of the screen. Click on the **Next** button to advance to the next task, or the **Previous** button to go to the previous task. To go directly to any task, click on its number.

If you would like a reminder to revisit a task, or want to indicate that you are finished with it, click on the reminder flag below the task number. To clear the flag, click on it again. Reminder flags are for your use only – they do not contribute to your score.

Tabs

In this part of the examination, you will be asked to complete various tasks. Every task has one or more **Work Tabs**. Some tasks have one or more **Information Tabs**, others may have none. Every task has a **Help** tab.

If a task has **Information Tabs**, you may use the information in them to complete your responses in the **Work Tabs**.

| Work tab | Information tab | Help tab |

Work Tabs:

- **Work Tabs** are identified with a pencil icon. This is where your responses are expected.
- Each task has one or more **Work Tabs**.
- **Work Tabs** contain directions for completing the task – be sure to read these directions carefully.
- The **Work Tab** name in the example above is for illustration only – yours will differ.
- You must complete all of the **Work Tabs** in each task to receive full credit.

Information Tabs:

- The Authoritative Literature will be provided in all tasks in the AUD, FAR, and REG sections for your reference.
- Your simulation may have one or more additional **Information Tabs**. Like the Authoritative Literature tabs, **Information Tabs** do not have a pencil icon.
- If your task has additional **Information Tabs**, go through each to familiarize yourself with the task content.

Help Tab:

- The **Help Tab** provides assistance with the exam software that is used in this task. For example, if the task is to compose a memorandum, **Help** will provide information about the word processor.

The Toolbar

The toolbar at the top of the screen shows the amount of time remaining for you to complete the tasks. In addition, the following tools are available. Note that only the **Exit** button is displayed when Directions are visible - the others will appear when you begin the tasks.

 Click on these buttons to split or unsplit the screen. You can split the screen vertically or horizontally.

 Click on this button to display the calculator; click on it again to hide the calculator. To move the calculator, click on the calculator title bar and drag the calculator to the desired location.

 Click on this button to use the spreadsheet; click on it again to hide the spreadsheet. To move the spreadsheet, click on the the spreadsheet title bar and drag the spreadsheet to the desired location.

 Click on this button to go on to the next part of the examination. You must complete all of the tasks to receive full credit. Once you click on **Exit** and confirm the action, you will NOT be able to return to this testlet.

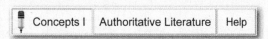

Select from the list provided the term that best matches each concept below. Each choice may be used once, more than once, or not at all.

Concept	Answer
1. Residual interest in assets	
2. The accounting process of reducing an amount by periodic payments or write-downs	
3. The change in equity during a period from transactions and other events and circumstances from nonowner sources	
4. Use of assets or incurrence of liabilities by an entity's major or central operations	
5. Assigning an amount according to a plan or formula	
6. An accounting process concerned with cash prepayments received or paid	
7. Decreases in equity resulting from transfers by the enterprise to owners	

Choices
A) Liabilities
B) Revenues
C) Gains
D) Realization
E) Assets
F) Losses
G) Accrual
H) Financial statement
I) Recognition
J) Deferral
K) Amortization
L) Earnings
M) Allocation
N) Comprehensive income
O) Dividends
P) Capital contributions
Q) Equity
R) Expenses

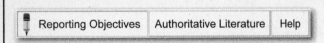

Select from the list provided the type(s) of financial reporting to which each objective most clearly applies. Each choice may be used once, more than once, or not at all.

Reporting Objective	Answer
1. Assessing management stewardship and performance	
2. Assessing services provided	
3. Entity resources, claims to those resources, and changes in them	
4. Factors that may affect an organization's liquidity	
5. Investment and credit decisions	
6. Public accountability	

Type
A) General-purpose financial reporting
B) Not-for-profit entities
C) Governmental entities

The concept of recognition requires that an item have a relevant attribute capable of being quantified in monetary units with reasonable reliability. Different measurement attributes of assets and liabilities are used in current practice. Select from the list provided the attribute that best relates to each recognition concept below. Each choice may be used once, more than once, or not at all.

Recognition Concept	Answer
1. The relevant attribute for plant assets and most inventories	
2. The relevant attribute defined as the cash or equivalent that would be paid for a current acquisition of the same or an equivalent asset	
3. The relevant attribute used to measure assets expected to be sold at below their carrying amount	
4. The relevant attribute used to measure short-term receivables	
5. The relevant attribute that incorporates time value of money concepts	

Attributes
A) Current market value
B) Net realizable value
C) Historical cost
D) Replacement cost
E) Present value

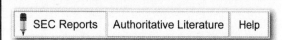

Select from the list provided the SEC term that best matches each reporting characteristic below. Each choice may be used once, more than once, or not at all.

Characteristic	Answer
1. Report of change in the certifying accountant	
2. Governs disclosures for annual reports	
3. Report of quarterly financial information	
4. Filed within 60 days by large accelerated filers	
5. Governs reporting of financial statements	
6. Contains audited financial statements	
7. Filed within 4 business days	
8. Filed within 45 days by nonaccelerated filers	
9. Contains management's discussion and analysis	

Choices
A) Form 10-K
B) Form 10-Q
C) Form 8-K
D) Regulation S-K
E) Regulation S-X

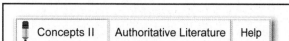

Select from the list provided the appropriate description of each accounting concept below. Each choice may be used once or more than once.

Concept	Answer
1. Cost (pervasive)	
2. Comparability	
3. Conservatism	
4. Consistency	
5. Relevance	
6. Economic entity	
7. Confirmatory value	
8. Full disclosure	
9. Going concern	
10. Historical cost	
11. Industry practices	

Description
A) Enhancing qualitative characteristic
B) Threshold for recognition
C) Relevance
D) Fundamental qualitative characteristic
E) Faithful representation
F) Constraint
G) Assumption
H) Principle

Biological Industries, Inc., an issuer, purchased manufacturing equipment in exchange for a 15-year note receivable. Biological expects the installation and setup of the equipment to take place over the next 6 months. However, payments on the note begin immediately. Which section of the authoritative guidance best outlines the treatment of interest in the historical cost of a long-lived tangible asset?

Enter your response in the answer fields below. Unless specifically requested, your response should not cite implementation guidance.

FASB ASC [   ] - [   ] - [   ] - [   ]

▼ = Reminder   Directions   1 2 3 4 5 [6]   ◀ Previous   Next ▶
                                      ▽ ▽ ▽ ▽ ▽ ▽

Unofficial Answers

1. Concepts I (7 Gradable Items)

1. Q) Equity is the "residual interest in the assets of an entity that remains after deducting its liabilities." In a business enterprise, the equity is the ownership interest.

2. K) Amortization is a form of allocation. It is "the accounting process of reducing an amount by periodic payments or write-downs." This process entails reducing a liability (asset) recorded as a result of a cash receipt (payment) by recognizing revenues (expenses).

3. N) Comprehensive income is the "change in equity of a business enterprise during a period from transactions and other events and circumstances from nonowner sources. It includes all changes in equity during a period except those resulting from investments by owners and distributions to owners."

4. R) Expenses are "outflows or other using up of assets or incurrences of liabilities (or a combination of both) from delivering or producing goods, rendering services, or carrying out other activities that constitute the entity's ongoing major or central operations."

5. M) Allocation is "the accounting process of assigning or distributing an amount according to a plan or formula." Allocation is broader than amortization. Product costing is an example of an allocation. Depreciation is a common example of amortization.

6. J) Deferral "is the accounting process of recognizing a liability resulting from a current cash receipt (or the equivalent) or an asset resulting from a current cash payment (or the equivalent) with deferred recognition of revenues, expenses, gains, or losses."

7. O) Dividends (distributions to owners) are "decreases in equity of a particular business enterprise resulting from transferring assets, rendering services, or incurring liabilities by the enterprise to owners. Distributions to owners decrease ownership interest (or equity) in an enterprise." They are sometimes called dividends; distributions of earnings, profits, or income; or capital distributions.

2. Reporting Objectives (6 Gradable Items)

1. B) Not-for-profit entities. A reporting objective of not-for-profit (nongovernmental) entities is to provide information useful in assessing management stewardship.

2. B) Not-for-profit entities and C) Governmental entities. A reporting objective of not-for-profit entities and governmental entities is to assist in assessing services provided.

3. A) General-purpose financial reporting. The objective of general-purpose financial reporting is to report financial information that is useful in making decisions about providing economic resources to the reporting entity. The information relates to entity resources, claims to those resources, and changes in them.

4. B) Not-for-profit entities. A reporting objective of not-for-profit (nongovernmental) entities is to provide information about factors that may affect an organization's liquidity.

5. A) General-purpose financial reporting. The objective of general-purpose financial reporting is to report financial information that is useful in making decisions about providing economic resources to the reporting entity. Primary users are current and prospective investors and creditors.

6. C) Governmental entities. A reporting objective of governmental entities is to assist in public accountability.

3. Measurement Attributes (5 Gradable Items)

1.   <u>C) Historical cost</u> is the relevant attribute for plant assets and most inventories. It is the cash or equivalent actually paid for an asset and is ordinarily adjusted subsequently for amortization (which includes depreciation) or other allocations.

2.   <u>D) Replacement cost</u> (current cost) is used to measure certain inventories, e.g., inventories valued at LCM. It is the cash or equivalent that would be paid for a current acquisition of the same or an equivalent asset.

3.   <u>A) Current market value</u> is used to measure some marketable securities, e.g., those held by investment companies, or assets expected to be sold at below their carrying amount.

4.   <u>B) Net realizable value</u> is used to measure short-term receivables and some inventories. It is the cash or equivalent expected to be received for an asset in the due course of business minus the costs of completion and sale.

5.   <u>E) Present value</u> is, in theory, the most relevant method of measurement because it incorporates time value of money concepts. In practice, it is currently used only for long-term receivables and payables.

4. SEC Reports (9 Gradable Items)

1.   <u>C) Form 8-K</u> is a current report to disclose material events. Material events include a change in control, an acquisition or disposition of a significant amount of assets not in the ordinary course of business, a bankruptcy or receivership, a resignation of directors, or a change in the registrant's certifying accountant. It must be filed within 4 business days after occurrence of the material event.

2.   <u>D) Regulation S-K</u> provides disclosure standards, including many of a nonfinancial nature. Regulation S-K also covers certain aspects of corporate annual reports to shareholders.

3.   <u>B) Form 10-Q</u> is the quarterly report to the SEC. It must be filed within 40 days of the last day of the first three fiscal quarters for both large accelerated filers and accelerated filers and within 45 days for non-accelerated filers.

4.   <u>A) Form 10-K</u> is the annual report to the SEC. It must be filed within 60 days of the last day of the fiscal year for large accelerated filers. The annual report contains audited financial statements and management's discussion and analysis.

5.   <u>E) Regulation S-X</u> governs the reporting of financial statements, including notes and schedules.

6.   <u>A) Form 10-K</u> is the annual report to the SEC. It must be filed within 60 days of the last day of the fiscal year for large accelerated filers. The annual report contains audited financial statements and management's discussion and analysis.

7.   <u>C) Form 8-K</u> is a current report to disclose material events. Material events include a change in control, an acquisition or disposition of a significant amount of assets not in the ordinary course of business, a bankruptcy or receivership, a resignation of directors, or a change in the registrant's certifying accountant. It must be filed within 4 business days after occurrence of the material event.

8.   <u>B) Form 10-Q</u> is the quarterly report to the SEC. It must be filed within 40 days of the last day of the first three fiscal quarters for both large accelerated filers and accelerated filers and within 45 days for non-accelerated filers.

9.   <u>A) Form 10-K</u> is the annual report to the SEC. It must be filed within 60 days of the last day of the fiscal year for large accelerated filers. The annual report contains audited financial statements and management's discussion and analysis.

5. Concepts II (11 Gradable Items)

1.   F) Constraint. Constraints are the following: cost (pervasive), industry practice, and conservatism.

2.   A) Enhancing qualitative characteristic. Qualitative characteristics of accounting information consist of fundamental characteristics (relevance and faithful representation) and enhancing characteristics (comparability, verifiability, timeliness, and understandability).

3.   F) Constraint. Constraints are the following: cost (pervasive), industry practice, and conservatism.

4.   A) Enhancing qualitative characteristic. Qualitative characteristics of accounting information consist of fundamental characteristics (relevance and faithful representation) and enhancing characteristics (comparability, verifiability, timeliness, and understandability). Consistency is a means of achieving comparability.

5.   D) Fundamental qualitative characteristic. Qualitative characteristics of accounting information consist of fundamental characteristics (relevance and faithful representation) and enhancing characteristics (comparability, verifiability, timeliness, and understandability).

6.   G) Assumption. Assumptions are the following: economic entity, going concern, monetary unit, and periodicity.

7.   C) Relevance. Fundamental qualitative characteristics include relevance and faithful representation. Relevant information has predictive value, confirmatory value, or both. Materiality is an entity-specific aspect of relevance.

8.   H) Principle. Principles are the following: historical cost, revenue recognition, matching, and full disclosure.

9.   G) Assumption. Assumptions are the following: economic entity, going concern, monetary unit, and periodicity.

10.   H) Principle. Principles are the following: historical cost, revenue recognition, matching, and full disclosure.

11.   F) Constraint. Constraints are the following: cost (pervasive), industry practice, and conservatism.

6. Research (1 Gradable Item)

Answer: FASB ASC 835-20-05-1

835-20-05-1 This Subtopic establishes standards of financial accounting and reporting for capitalizing interest cost as a part of the historical cost of acquiring certain assets. The historical cost of acquiring an asset includes the costs necessarily incurred to bring it to the condition and location necessary for its intended use. If an asset requires a period of time in which to carry out the activities necessary to bring it to that condition and location, the interest cost incurred during that period as a result of expenditures for the asset is a part of the historical cost of acquiring the asset.

Gleim Simulation Grading

Task	Correct Responses		Gradable Items		Score per Task
1	___	÷	7	=	___
2	___	÷	6	=	___
3	___	÷	5	=	___
4	___	÷	9	=	___
5	___	÷	11	=	___
Research	___	÷	1	=	___

Total of Scores per Task   ___

÷   Total Number of Tasks   6

Total Score   ___ %

Use **CPA Gleim Online** and **Simulation Wizard** to practice more task-based simulations in a realistic environment.

STUDY UNIT TWO
FINANCIAL STATEMENTS

(18 pages of outline)

2.1	Balance Sheet	59
2.2	Statements of Income, Retained Earnings, and Changes in Equity	63
2.3	Comprehensive Income	69
2.4	Other Financial Statement Presentations	71
2.5	First-Time Adoption of IFRS	73
2.6	Practice Simulation	87

This study unit covers most of the **basic financial statements**: the statements of financial position, income, retained earnings (changes in equity), and comprehensive income. The statement of cash flows is covered in Study Unit 3. However, specific names and formats for these statements are **not** specified under GAAP. Instead, the formats of these statements have evolved to fulfill the requirements of GAAP.

The accompanying **notes** are an integral part of the financial statements. The notes and statements together are a means of achieving the objectives of financial reporting. Supplementary information (e.g., on changing prices) and various other methods of financial reporting (such as management's discussion and analysis) also are useful.

Financial statements **complement** each other. They describe different aspects of the same transactions, and more than one statement will be necessary to provide information for a specific economic decision. Moreover, the **elements** of one statement **articulate** (interrelate) with those of other statements.

2.1 BALANCE SHEET

1. **Overview**

    a. The balance sheet (statement of financial position) reports assets, liabilities, equity, and their relationships at a moment in time. It helps users to assess liquidity, financial flexibility, profitability, and risk.

    b. The balance sheet is a detailed presentation of the basic accounting equation:

    ### Assets = Liabilities + Equity

    1) The left side of this equation depicts the entity's resource structure. The right side depicts the financing structure.

Background

The balance sheet equation is a fundamental component of the double-entry system of bookkeeping that keeps debits and credits constantly equal. This system was widely used by Venetian merchants during the European Renaissance and was first codified in 1494 in a mathematics textbook by the monk Luca Pacioli.

---

    c.   Assets are generally reported in order of liquidity.

        1)   Some variation of the following classifications is used by most entities:

Assets	Liabilities
Current assets:	Current liabilities:
Cash	Accounts payable
Certain investments	Current notes payable
Accounts and notes receivable	Current maturities of noncurrent liabilities
Inventories	Noncurrent liabilities:
Prepaid expenses	Noncurrent notes payable
Noncurrent assets:	Bonds payable
Certain investments and funds	
Property, plant, and equipment (PPE)	**Equity**
Intangible assets	Investments by owners
Other noncurrent assets	Retained earnings (income reinvested)
	Accumulated other comprehensive income
	Noncontrolling interest in a consolidated entity

2. **Current Assets**

    a.   Current assets consist of "cash and other assets or resources commonly identified as reasonably expected to be realized in cash or sold or consumed **during the normal operating cycle** of the business."

    b.   The operating cycle is the average time between the acquisition of resources and the final receipt of cash from their sale as the culmination of revenue generating activities. If the cycle is less than a year, 1 year is the period used for segregating current from noncurrent assets.

    c.   Current assets include (1) cash and cash equivalents; (2) certain individual trading, available-for-sale, and held-to-maturity securities; (3) receivables; (4) inventories; and (5) prepaid expenses.

3. **Noncurrent Assets**

    a.   Noncurrent assets are those not qualifying as current.

    b.   **Investments and funds** include nonoperating items intended to be held beyond the longer of 1 year or the operating cycle. The following assets are typically included:

        1)   (a) Advances or investments in securities made to control or influence another entity and (b) other noncurrent securities

            a)   Certain individual trading, available-for-sale, and held-to-maturity securities may be noncurrent.

        2)   Funds restricted as to withdrawal or use for other than current operations, for example, to (a) retire long-term debt, (b) satisfy pension obligations, or (c) pay for the acquisition or construction of noncurrent assets

        3)   Cash surrender value of life insurance policies

        4)   Capital assets not used in current operations, such as (a) idle facilities or (b) land held for a future plant site

    c.   **Property, plant, and equipment (PPE)** are tangible operating items recorded at cost and reported net of any accumulated depreciation. They include

        1)   Land and natural resources subject to depletion, e.g., oil and gas

        2)   (a) Buildings, (b) equipment, (c) furniture, (d) fixtures, (e) leasehold improvements, (f) land improvements, (g) assets held under capital leases, (h) noncurrent assets under construction, and (i) other depreciable assets

    d.   **Intangible assets** are nonfinancial assets without physical substance. Examples are patents and goodwill.

e. **Other noncurrent assets** include noncurrent assets not readily classifiable elsewhere. Examples are

1) Bond issue costs
2) Machinery rearrangement costs (also classifiable as PPE)
3) Long-term prepayments
4) Deferred tax assets arising from interperiod tax allocation
5) Long-term receivables from unusual transactions, e.g., loans to officers or employees and sales of capital assets

NOTE: The **Sarbanes-Oxley Act of 2002** generally prohibits an issuer, as defined by federal securities law, from extending personal credit to directors or officers.

f. The category **deferred charges** (long-term prepayments) appears on some balance sheets.

1) Many of these items, which involve long-term prepayments (e.g., bond issue costs and rearrangement costs), are frequently classified as other assets.

The AICPA has previously tested candidates on their knowledge of what the classification of current liabilities entails. Potentially, candidates could see a list of fixed accounts with a question on the amount of current liabilities of the firm.

---

4. **Current Liabilities**

a. Current liabilities are "obligations whose liquidation is reasonably expected to require the use of existing resources properly classifiable as current assets, or the creation of other current liabilities."

b. **Trade payables** for items entering into the operating cycle, e.g., for materials and supplies used in producing goods or services for sale.

c. **Other payables** arising from operations, such as accrued wages, salaries, rentals, royalties, and taxes.

d. **Unearned revenues** arising from collections in advance of delivering goods or performing services, e.g., ticket sales revenue.

e. Other obligations expected to be liquidated in the ordinary course of business during the longer of the next year or the operating cycle. These include

1) Short-term notes given to acquire capital assets
2) Payments required under sinking-fund provisions
3) Payments on the current portion of serial bonds
4) Agency obligations incurred by the collection of assets for third parties

f. Amounts expected to be required within a relatively short time to pay known obligations even though

1) Outlays can only be estimated, e.g., accrual of bonus payments, or
2) Specific payees have not been designated, for example, in the case of warranties for repair of products sold.

g. Obligations that, by their terms, are **due on demand** within the longer of 1 year or the operating cycle. Liquidation need not be expected.

h. **Noncurrent obligations callable** at the balance sheet date because of a violation of the debt agreement or that will become callable if the violation is not cured within a specified period.

   i.   Current liabilities **do not include**

      1)   Current obligations if an entity (a) intends to refinance them on a noncurrent basis and (b) demonstrates an ability to do so.

         a)   The ability to refinance may be demonstrated by

            i)   Entering into a **financing agreement** meeting all conditions before the balance sheet is issued.

            ii)   Issuing a noncurrent obligation or equity securities after the end of the reporting period but before issuance of the balance sheet.

      2)   Dividends not yet declared.

      3)   Debts to be paid from funds accumulated in noncurrent asset accounts. Thus, a liability for bonds payable in the next period will not be classified as current if payment is to be from a noncurrent fund.

   j.   The difference between current assets and current liabilities is working capital.

IFRS Difference

Financial liabilities due to be settled within 12 months should continue to be classified as current. This treatment applies even if (1) the original term exceeded 12 months and (2) an agreement to refinance or reschedule payments on a noncurrent basis is completed after the reporting period and before the financial statements are authorized for issue.

- An entity that expects and has discretion to refinance or roll over the liability under an existing loan agreement classifies it as noncurrent.

---

5. **Noncurrent Liabilities**

   a.   Noncurrent liabilities are those not qualifying as current. The noncurrent portions of the following items are reported in this section of the balance sheet:

      1)   Noncurrent notes and bonds
      2)   Liabilities under capital leases
      3)   Most postretirement benefit obligations
      4)   Deferred tax liabilities arising from interperiod tax allocation
      5)   Obligations under product or service warranty agreements
      6)   Advances for noncurrent commitments to provide goods or services
      7)   Advances from affiliated entities
      8)   Deferred revenue

6. **Fair Value Option (FVO)**

   a.   Assets and liabilities measured using the FVO are reported in a way that separates their fair values from the carrying amounts of similar items measured using another attribute, such as net realizable value, amortized cost, or present value (the fair value option will be described in Study Unit 6).

7. **Equity or Net Assets**

   a.   Equity (or net assets for a not-for-profit entity) is the residual after total liabilities are subtracted from total assets. Any recognized transaction that does not have equal and offsetting effects on total assets and total liabilities changes equity.

      1)   Equity consists of

         a)   Capital contributed by owners
         b)   Retained earnings (income reinvested)
         c)   Accumulated other comprehensive income (all comprehensive income items not included in net income)
         d)   The noncontrolling interest in a consolidated entity

2) Items in the contributed capital section are presented in descending order of priority in liquidation.

3) Treasury stock recorded at cost is a reduction of total equity (a debit). Treasury stock recorded at par is a direct reduction of the pertinent contributed capital balance, e.g., common stock or preferred stock.

IFRS Difference

The minimum presentation on the face of the statement of financial position includes the following line items (but no particular order or format is prescribed):

1. Property, plant, and equipment
2. Investment property
3. Intangible assets
4. Financial assets (other than 5., 8., and 9.)
5. Equity-based investments
6. Biological assets
7. Inventories
8. Trade and other receivables
9. Cash and cash equivalents
10. Trade and other payables
11. Current and deferred tax amounts
12. Provisions
13. Financial liabilities (other than 10. and 12.)
14. Noncontrolling interest
15. Issued capital and reserves
16. The total of assets classified as held for sale and assets and liabilities included in disposal groups classified as held for sale

---

Stop and review! You have completed the outline for this subunit. Study multiple-choice questions 1 through 6 beginning on page 76.

2.2 STATEMENTS OF INCOME, RETAINED EARNINGS, AND CHANGES IN EQUITY

Background

The accounts presented on the balance sheet are called real or permanent accounts -- an entity's resources and financing elements that exist from period to period. The accounts presented on the income statement, however, are termed nominal or temporary accounts -- they are emptied at the end of each period and started again from zero for the next period.

---

1. **Nature of the Income Statement**

    a. The results of operations are reported in the income statement (statement of earnings) on the **accrual basis** using an approach oriented to historical transactions.

        1) The traditional income statement reports **revenues** from, and **expenses** of, the entity's major activities and **gains** and **losses** from other activities.

        2) The sum of these income statement elements is net income (loss) for an interval of time.

    Revenues – Expenses + Gains – Losses = Net Income or Loss

b. Income statement elements are reported in temporary **(nominal)** accounts that are periodically closed to permanent **(real)** accounts. The accountant need not close each transaction directly to equity.

   1) Income or loss is **closed to retained earnings** at the end of the period.

   2) Any recognized amounts not included in continuing operations are reported in separate sections for **discontinued operations** and **extraordinary items**.

      a) The term "continuing operations" is used only when a discontinued operation is reported.

2. **All-Inclusive Approach to Income**

    a. Under the all-inclusive approach, **all transactions affecting the net change in equity** during the period are included with certain exceptions.

    b. The **transactions not included** in net income are (1) transactions with owners, (2) prior-period adjustments (error corrections), (3) items reported initially in other comprehensive income, (4) transfers to and from appropriated retained earnings, (5) adjustments made in a quasi-reorganization, and (6) effects on prior periods of accounting changes.

    c. The net income reported in this way over the life of the entity reflects the **sum of the periodic net incomes**, including nonrecurring items.

       1) An additional advantage of the all-inclusive approach is that it reduces variation caused by differences in judgment.

       2) The utility of the statement as a predictor of future income is not impaired if full disclosure of unusual, irregular, or nonrecurring items is made and an appropriate format is used.

3. **Income Statement Format**

    a. **Three formats** are commonly used for presentation of recurring items:

       1) The **single-step income statement** provides one grouping for revenues and gains and one for expenses and losses. The single step is the one subtraction necessary to arrive at net income.

EXAMPLE

Bonilla Company
Income Statement
For Year Ended December 31, Year 1

Revenues and gains:		
Net sales	$XXX	
Other revenues	XXX	
Gains	XXX	
Total revenues and gains		$ XXX
Expenses and losses:		
Costs of goods sold	$XXX	
Selling and administrative expenses	XXX	
Interest expense	XXX	
Losses	XXX	
Income tax expense	XXX	
Total expenses and losses		(XXX)
Net income		$ XXX
Earnings per common share		
(simple capital structure)		$ Y.YY

2) The **multiple-step income statement** matches operating revenues and
    expenses in a section separate from nonoperating items. It enhances
    disclosure by presenting subtotals.

EXAMPLE

Willis Company
Income Statement
For Year Ended December 31, Year 1

Revenues:			
Gross sales			$ XXX
Minus: Sales discounts		$(XXX)	
Sales returns and allowances		(XXX)	(XXX)
Net sales			$ XXX
Cost of goods sold:			
Beginning inventory		$ XXX	
Purchases	$XXX		
Minus: Purchase returns and discounts	(XXX)		
Net purchases	$XXX		
Transportation-in	XXX	XXX	
Goods available for sale		$ XXX	
Minus: Ending inventory		(XXX)	
Cost of goods sold			(XXX)
Gross profit			$ XXX
Operating expenses:			
Selling expenses:			
Sales salaries and commissions	$XXX		
Freight-out	XXX		
Travel	XXX		
Advertising	XXX		
Office supplies	XXX	$XXX	
Administrative expenses:			
Executive salaries	$XXX		
Professional salaries	XXX		
Wages of office staff	XXX		
Depreciation	XXX		
Office supplies	XXX	XXX	
Total operating expenses			(XXX)
Income from operations			$ XXX
Other revenues and gains:			
Dividend revenue		$ XXX	XXX
Other expenses and losses:			
Interest expense		$ XXX	
Loss on disposal of equipment		XXX	(XXX)
Income before taxes *			$ XXX
Income taxes			(XXX)
Net income *			$ XXX
Earnings per common share (simple capital structure)			$Y.YY

* If a discontinued operation is reported, these line items are "Income from continuing
operations before taxes" and "Income from continuing operations," respectively.

3) The **condensed income statement** includes only the section totals of the multiple-step format.

EXAMPLE

Marzullo Company
Income Statement
For Year Ended December 31, Year 1

Net sales		$ XXX
Cost of goods sold		(XXX)
Gross profit		$ XXX
Selling expenses	$XXX	
Administrative expenses	XXX	(XXX)
Income from operations		$ XXX
Other revenues and gains		XXX
Other expenses and losses		(XXX)
Income before taxes *		$ XXX
Income taxes		(XXX)
Net income *		$ XXX
Earnings per common share		$Y.YY
(simple capital structure)		

* If a discontinued operation is reported, these line items are "Income from continuing operations before taxes" and "Income from continuing operations," respectively.

---

4. Income Statement Sections

Previous CPA exams have included questions with cost and inventory information that require candidates to calculate cost of goods sold or cost of goods manufactured.

a. **Cost of goods sold** equals purchases for a retailer or cost of goods manufactured (COGM) for a manufacturer, adjusted for the change in finished goods (FG) in inventory.

>   Beginning FG inventory
> + Purchases or COGM
>   Goods available for sale
> − Ending FG inventory
>   Cost of goods sold

b. **Cost of goods manufactured** equals the period's manufacturing costs adjusted for the change in work-in-process. It also may be stated as cost of goods sold adjusted for the change in finished goods inventory.

>   Beginning work in process   Ending FG inventory
> + Sum of periodic manufacturing costs   + Cost of goods sold
> − Ending work-in-process   − Beginning FG inventory
>   Cost of goods manufactured   Cost of goods manufactured

c. **Selling expenses** are incurred in selling or marketing.

1) Examples include (a) sales representatives' salaries, commissions, and traveling expenses; (b) sales department rent, salaries, and depreciation; and (c) communications (e.g., Internet) costs. Shipping costs also are often classified as selling costs.

d. **Administrative (general) expenses** are incurred for the direction of the entity as a whole and are not related entirely to a specific function, e.g., selling or manufacturing.

   1) They include (a) accounting, legal, and other fees for professional services; (b) officers' salaries; (c) insurance; (d) wages of office staff; (e) miscellaneous supplies; and (f) office occupancy costs.

e. **Interest expense** is recognized based on the passage of time. In the case of bonds, notes, and capital leases, the effective interest method is used.

f. When an entity reports a **discontinued operation or an extraordinary item**, it must be presented in a separate section after income from continuing operations.

   1) **Intraperiod tax allocation** is required. Thus, income tax expense or benefit is allocated to (a) continuing operations, (b) discontinued operations, (c) extraordinary items, (d) other comprehensive income, and (e) items debited or credited directly to other components of equity.

   2) The following items are reported separately in the **discontinued operations** section:

      a) Income or loss from operations of the component unit (including any gain or loss on disposal)

      b) Income tax expense or benefit

   3) **Extraordinary items** arise from material transactions that are both unusual in nature and infrequent in occurrence in the environment in which the entity operates. If an item meets one but not both criteria, it should be presented separately as a component of income from continuing operations.

IFRS Difference

No items are classified as extraordinary, either on the statement of comprehensive income or in the notes.

---

   4) Appropriate earnings per share amounts must be disclosed, either on the face of the statement or in the accompanying notes.

EXAMPLE
(Dilutive PCS)

Income from continuing operations before income from discontinued operation and loss on extraordinary item		$XXX
Discontinued operations:		
Income from discontinued component unit (net of loss on disposal of $XX)	$XXX	
Income tax expense	(XXX)	XXX
Income before extraordinary item		$XXX
Extraordinary item:		
Loss from volcanic eruption (net of applicable income tax benefit of $XXX)		(XXX)
Net income		$XXX

	Basic	Diluted
Basic and diluted EPS:		
Income from continuing operations before income from discontinued operation and loss on extraordinary item	$Y.YY	$Y.YY
Income from discontinued component unit, net of tax	Y.YY	Y.YY
Income before extraordinary item	$Y.YY	$Y.YY
Extraordinary loss, net of tax	(Y.YY)	(Y.YY)
Net income	$Y.YY	$Y.YY

---

g. Specific income statement line items are discussed in Study Unit 4.

IFRS Difference

All recognized income and expense items are included in profit or loss unless a pronouncement requires otherwise. The minimum presentation on the face of the statement of comprehensive income includes the following line items:

1.   Revenue

2.   Gains (losses) on (a) derecognition of financial assets measured at amortized cost and (b) reclassification of financial assets to fair value

3.   Finance costs

4.   Share of profits and losses of associates and joint ventures accounted for under the equity method

5.   Tax expense

6.   One amount for the sum of (a) after-tax profit (loss) on discontinued operations and (b) after-tax gain (loss) on the measurement at fair value minus cost to sell or on disposal of the assets or disposal groups

7.   Profit or loss

8.   Each component of OCI classified by nature

9.   Share of OCI of associates and joint ventures accounted for under the equity method

10. Total comprehensive income

---

5.   **Statement of Retained Earnings**

   a.   The statement of retained earnings is a **basic financial statement**. The income statement and the statement of retained earnings (presented separately or combined) broadly reflect the results of operations.

   b.   The statement of retained earnings displays

      1)   Beginning balance of retained earnings;
      2)   Any prior-period adjustments (net of tax);
      3)   Adjusted beginning balance;
      4)   Net income (loss);
      5)   Dividends paid or declared;
      6)   Certain other rare items, e.g., quasi-reorganizations; and
      7)   Ending balance of retained earnings.

EXAMPLE

Statement of Retained Earnings
For Year Ended December 31, Year 1

Beginning retained earnings (originally reported)	$XXX
Overstatement of depreciation expense in prior period	XXX
Beginning retained earnings (restated)	$XXX
Net income	XXX
Cash dividends paid	(XXX)
Ending retained earnings	$XXX

---

   c.   Most entities report changes in retained earnings in a **statement of changes in equity** or a separate statement.

      1)   Disclosures of changes in equity and in the number of shares of equity securities are necessary whenever financial position and results of operations are presented. These disclosures may occur in the basic statements, in the notes, or in separate statements.

EXAMPLE

CI Company
Consolidated Statement of
Changes in Equity
Year Ended December 31, Year 1

Retained earnings	
January 1	$ XXX,XXX
Net income	XX,XXX
Dividends declared	(XX,XXX)
December 31	$ XXX,XXX
Accumulated OCI	
January 1	$ XX,XXX
OCI	XX,XXX
December 31	$ XX,XXX
Common stock	
January 1	$ XX,XXX
Shares issued	XX,XXX
December 31	$ XX,XXX
Additional paid-in capital	
January 1	$ XXX,XXX
Common shares issued	XXX,XXX
December 31	$ XXX,XXX
Total equity	$X,XXX,XXX

---

    d.   Retained earnings is sometimes **appropriated** (restricted) to a special account to disclose that earnings retained in the business (not paid out in dividends) are being used for special purposes (discussed in Study Unit 15).

    e.   **Quasi-reorganizations** are undertaken by entities with negative retained earnings (discussed in Study Unit 15).

Stop and review! You have completed the outline for this subunit. Study multiple-choice questions 6 through 9 beginning on page 78.

2.3 COMPREHENSIVE INCOME

1. **Overview**

    a.   Comprehensive income includes all changes in equity of a business during a period except those from investments by and distributions to owners. It includes all components of (1) net income and (2) **other comprehensive income (OCI)**.

    b.   OCI includes all items of comprehensive income not included in net income. Requiring these items to be included in net income may be misleading. They are usually valuation adjustments, not independent economic events. Under existing accounting standards, items of OCI include, among others,

        1)   Unrealized gains and losses on **available-for-sale securities** (except those that are hedged items in a fair value hedge).

        2)   Gains and losses on **derivatives** designated, qualifying, and effective as **cash flow hedges**.

        3)   Certain amounts associated with recognition of the **funded status of post-retirement defined benefit plans** (these will be discussed in Study Unit 12).

        4)   **Certain foreign currency items** (these will be discussed in Study Unit 17).

        5)   The following memory aid is helpful for learning the major items of OCI:

A = Available-for-sale	Always
D = Derivatives	Desire
R = Retirement	Real
F = Foreign currency	Friends

   c.   Each component of OCI must be presented **net of tax**, or one amount must be presented for the aggregate tax effect on the total of OCI. In either case, the tax effect on each component must be disclosed.

2. **Reporting**

   a.   An entity that presents a full set of financial statements but has no items of OCI need not report OCI or comprehensive income. Otherwise, an entity must present all items of comprehensive income recognized for the period either

      1)   In one continuous financial statement or
      2)   In two separate but consecutive statements.

   b.   **One continuous statement** must have two sections: net income and OCI. It must include

      1)   A total of net income with its components,
      2)   A total of OCI with its components, and
      3)   A total of comprehensive income.

   c.   **Separate but consecutive statements** must be presented as follows:

      1)   The first statement (the income statement) presents the components of net income and total net income.
      2)   The second statement (the statement of OCI) is presented immediately after the first. It presents

         a)   The components of OCI,
         b)   The total of OCI, and
         c)   A total for comprehensive income.

      3)   The entity may begin the second statement with net income.

   d.   The following is an example of the **single-statement** presentation for reporting comprehensive income of an entity with no noncontrolling interest:

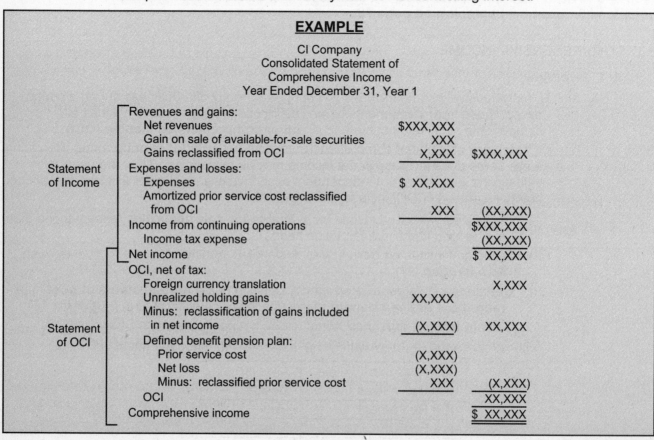

EXAMPLE

CI Company
Consolidated Statement of
Comprehensive Income
Year Ended December 31, Year 1

Statement of Income			
Revenues and gains:			
Net revenues		$XXX,XXX	
Gain on sale of available-for-sale securities		XXX	
Gains reclassified from OCI		X,XXX	$XXX,XXX
Expenses and losses:			
Expenses		$ XX,XXX	
Amortized prior service cost reclassified from OCI		XXX	(XX,XXX)
Income from continuing operations			$XXX,XXX
Income tax expense			(XX,XXX)
Net income			$ XX,XXX

Statement of OCI			
OCI, net of tax:			
Foreign currency translation			X,XXX
Unrealized holding gains		XX,XXX	
Minus: reclassification of gains included in net income		(X,XXX)	XX,XXX
Defined benefit pension plan:			
Prior service cost		(X,XXX)	
Net loss		(X,XXX)	
Minus: reclassified prior service cost		XXX	(X,XXX)
OCI			XX,XXX
Comprehensive income			$ XX,XXX

        1)   A **two-statement** presentation is easily derived from the example on the previous page.

           a)   The final component of the **statement of net income** is net income.

           b)   The first component of the **statement of OCI** is net income, and the final component is comprehensive income.

        2)   If a **noncontrolling interest** exists, amounts for net income and comprehensive income attributable to the parent and to the subsidiary must be reported in the appropriate statements (consolidations are covered in Study Unit 16).

IFRS Difference

An entity must group items of OCI as follows: (1) those that will not be reclassified to profit or loss (e.g., actuarial gains and losses on defined benefit pension plans) and (2) those that may be (e.g., exchange differences arising from foreign operations).

---

3.   **Other Aspects**

    a.   The **components of OCI** are recorded initially in a temporary (nominal) account. The total OCI for a period must be transferred to a component of equity (a permanent or real account) separate from retained earnings and additional paid-in capital. The component must have a descriptive title, e.g., accumulated OCI.

        1)   The changes in the accumulated balances for each component of OCI must be disclosed in the notes or as a reconciliation in a statement of changes in equity.

    b.   **Reclassification adjustments** must be made for each component of OCI. Their purpose is to avoid double counting when an item included in net income also was included in OCI for the same or a prior period.

        1)   For example, if a gain or loss on available-for-sale securities is realized in the current period, the prior-period recognition of an unrealized holding gain or loss must be eliminated from accumulated OCI.

        2)   Reclassification adjustments and their effects must be presented in the statement in which the components of net income and OCI are presented.

        3)   The components of net income and OCI and a total for comprehensive income must be reported in **interim-period** condensed statements

        4)   The terms "comprehensive income" and "other comprehensive income" need not be used.

Stop and review! You have completed the outline for this subunit. Study multiple-choice questions 13 through 17 beginning on page 80.

2.4 OTHER FINANCIAL STATEMENT PRESENTATIONS

1.   **Consolidated and Combined Financial Statements**

    a.   Consolidated financial statements are used when one entity holds a controlling financial interest in one or more other entities. They are required by GAAP.

        1)   Consolidated statements report the financial position, results of operations, and cash flows as if the consolidated entities were a single economic entity.

    b.   Combined financial statements are used to combine the statements of the subsidiaries without consolidating them with those of the parent. They are not an allowable substitute for consolidated statements.

        1)   Combined statements are useful when one individual owns a controlling financial interest in several entities with related operations. They also may be used to present the statements of entities under common management.

2. **Other Comprehensive Bases of Accounting**

   a. Financial statements based on a reporting system other than GAAP are prepared using an other comprehensive basis of accounting (OCBOA). Thus, an OCBOA does not conform with GAAP.

   b. Examples of OCBOAs are

      1) The cash basis and modifications of the cash basis having substantial support
      2) A basis used for tax purposes
      3) A basis used to comply with the requirements of a regulator
      4) A definite set of criteria having substantial support

   c. Statements using an OCBOA should include a summary of significant accounting policies that discusses the basis used and how it differs from GAAP.

3. **Cash Basis**

   a. Under the strict cash basis of accounting, revenues and expenses are recognized when cash is received or paid, respectively, regardless of when goods are delivered or received or when services are rendered.

      1) The cash basis ignores the revenue and expense recognition principles that are fundamental to the accrual basis.

      2) This method may be appropriate for small businesses operated as sole proprietorships.

4. **Modified Cash Basis**

   a. The modified cash basis uses the cash basis for typical operating activities with modifications having substantial support, for example, reporting inventory, accruing income taxes, and capitalizing and depreciating fixed assets.

      1) This method often is used by professional services firms, such as physicians, realtors, and architects.

5. **Income Tax Basis**

   a. This basis must be applied to calculate income tax liability.

   b. Certain doctrines underlying the federal tax code differ significantly from those in the conceptual framework. For example, the code requires use of the modified accelerated cost recovery system (MACRS), a depreciation method not recognized under GAAP.

6. **Personal Financial Statements**

   a. Personal financial statements of individuals or families are prepared to plan their financial affairs in general or for a specific purpose, e.g., tax or retirement planning.

   b. A **statement of financial condition** must be prepared. It presents assets, liabilities, estimated income taxes, and net worth (total assets – total liabilities – estimated income tax) at a given date.

      1) **Assets** should be presented at their estimated current values.

         a) The estimated current value is the amount at which a buyer and seller can exchange an item if each is well informed, willing, and not compelled to buy or sell.

      2) **Liabilities**, including payables, are presented at their estimated current amounts at the date of the statement.

         a) The estimated current amount is the discounted amount of cash to be paid.

            i) The discount rate is the debt's implicit rate.
            ii) If lower, the amount at which the debt can be discharged should be used.

3) **Estimated income taxes** are calculated as if the assets had been realized or the liabilities liquidated.

    a) Estimated income taxes are based on the differences between the carrying amounts of assets and liabilities and their tax bases.

    b) Taxes payable, including estimated taxes, are reported between liabilities and net worth.

c. A **statement of changes in net worth** and comparative financial statements may be presented.

    1) Assets and liabilities and changes in them are recognized on the accrual basis.

    2) Estimated current values (amounts) may be based on recent transactions involving similar assets and liabilities in similar circumstances.

        a) Absent such transactions, other measurement bases (e.g., discounted cash flow, appraisal value, etc.) may be used if they are consistently applied.

d. **Noncancelable commitments** to pay future sums are presented at their discounted amounts as liabilities if they are for fixed or determinable amounts, are not contingent, and do not require the future performance of service by another.

    1) Nonforfeitable rights to receive future sums are presented as assets at their discounted amounts if they meet the same criteria.

    2) The assets and liabilities of an investment in a limited business activity not conducted in a separate business entity (such as an investment in real estate and a related mortgage) are separately presented.

    3) A business interest that is a large part of an individual's total assets is presented separately as one amount equal to the estimated current value of the interest.

IFRS Difference

Personal financial statements are not specifically addressed.

Stop and review! You have completed the outline for this subunit. Study multiple-choice questions 18 through 26 beginning on page 81.

2.5 FIRST-TIME ADOPTION OF IFRS

Background

In February 2010, the SEC directed its staff to study the effect that adoption of IFRS would have on the U.S. securities market. The SEC intends to use the results of this study and the output of the convergence project between the FASB and the IASB to decide whether, and if so when and how, the converged standards would be incorporated into U.S. financial reporting. As of October 2012, the SEC had not yet decided whether to incorporate IFRS into the U.S. financial reporting system.

---

1. **Selecting Applicable Pronouncements**

a. When an IASB Standard or Interpretation specifically applies to a transaction, other event, or condition, it must be selected if the effect is material.

    1) Any Implementation Guidance also must be considered.

b. Absent such a standard or Interpretation, management considers

    1) Guidance for similar and related issues in other IASB Standards and Interpretations

    2) The content of the Framework for the Preparation and Presentation of Financial Statements

2.   **Statement of IFRS Compliance**

a.   An entity's **first IFRS financial statements** are the first annual statements in which it includes an **explicit and unreserved statement** of compliance with IFRS.

1)   This provision applies even if the entity's previous financial statements conformed to IFRS in every way but did not contain the statement of compliance.

3.   **Initial Measurement**

a.   An entity adopting IFRS must prepare and present an **opening IFRS statement of financial position** at the **date of transition**. It is the starting point for IFRS accounting.

1)   The date of transition is the beginning of the earliest period for which an entity presents full comparative information under IFRS in its first IFRS financial statements (IFRS 1).

EXAMPLE

In its annual financial statements for the reporting period ending December 31, Year 3, an entity adopts IFRS for the first time. These statements are the first IFRS statements because they include an explicit and unreserved statement of compliance with IFRS. The statements also contain full comparative information for Years 1 and 2. The date of transition is January 1, Year 1, and the entity prepared a statement of financial position as of that date to serve as the starting point for IFRS accounting. The first IFRS reporting period is Year 3 because it is the latest period covered by the first IFRS statements.

---

b.   The **accounting policies** used in the opening IFRS statement of financial position must be those in effect at the end of the first **IFRS reporting period** (the latest covered by the first IFRS statements).

c.   The policies used in the opening IFRS statement of financial position may differ from those used for the same date under prior GAAP.

1)   The resulting adjustments must be reported directly in opening retained earnings (or other appropriate equity account) at the transition date.

d.   In its opening statement of financial position, the entity

1)   Recognizes as assets and liabilities only those required by IFRS;
2)   Makes any necessary reclassifications of assets, liabilities, and components of equity; and
3)   Measures recognized assets and liabilities in accordance with IFRS.

e.   The opening statement of financial position need not comply with IFRS if certain exceptions apply:

1)   Prohibitions of retrospective application of other IFRS
2)   Elective exemptions from other IFRS

4.   **Prohibitions of Retrospective Application**

a.   Estimates made under IFRS at the transition date must be consistent with those made under prior GAAP after adjustment for any changes in accounting policy. But this prohibition does not apply if the entity has objective evidence that the estimates were in error.

1)   With certain exceptions, the following are other items for which **retrospective application** of other IFRS is prohibited:

a)   Derecognition of financial assets and liabilities,
b)   Hedges,
c)   Noncontrolling interests,
d)   Classification and measurement of financial assets, and
e)   Embedded derivatives.

5. **Examples of Elective Exemptions**

    a. **Business Combinations**

       1) The entity may continue to use the method used prior to the transition date.

    b. **Revaluation to Fair Value**

       1) The entity may remeasure any item of property, plant, and equipment to its fair value at the transition date and use that as its **deemed cost**.

          a) An entity may not revalue liabilities, but it may revalue

             i) Certain investment properties and
             ii) Intangible assets.

          b) An entity also may use an event-driven deemed cost, such as that arising from a privatization or initial public offering.

    c. **Employee Benefit Plans**

       1) The entity may elect to recognize and report all cumulative actuarial gains and losses on employee benefit plans at the transition date.

    d. **Cumulative Translation Differences**

       1) The entity may measure the cumulative differences arising from foreign currency translation at zero on the transition date rather than as a separate component of equity.

    e. **Compound Financial Instruments**

       1) The entity need not separate compound financial instruments (e.g., convertible debt) into two separate equity components if the liability component is no longer outstanding at the transition date.

    f. **Financial Instruments**

       1) Any financial liabilities meeting certain criteria may be designated as at fair value through profit or loss at the transition date.

       2) Based on the facts at the transition date, an entity may designate

          a) A financial asset as at fair value through profit or loss
          b) An equity instrument as at fair value through other comprehensive income

    g. **Share-Based Payment Transactions**

       1) First-time adopters are encouraged, but not required, to apply the provisions of IFRS to share-based payment transactions.

6. **Presentation and Disclosure**

    a. **Comparative Information**

       1) In the entity's first IFRS financial statements, it must include at least

          a) Three statements of financial position (end of current period, end of previous period, and beginning of first comparative period),
          b) Two statements of comprehensive income,
          c) Two separate income statements (if presented),
          d) Two statements of cash flows, and
          e) Two statements of changes in equity.

    b. **Historical Summaries**

       1) Historical summaries that include information before the transition date need not be restated to be in conformity with IFRS if they are clearly labeled.

          a) The nature of any adjustments necessary to bring them into conformity must be described (not necessarily quantified).

c.   **Reconciliations**

1)   The first IFRS financial statements must include the following reconciliations:

a)   Equity reported under previous GAAP to equity reported under IFRS at

i)   The transition date and

ii)   The end of the latest period presented under previous GAAP.

b)   Total comprehensive income reported under previous GAAP to total comprehensive income reported under IFRS.

d.   **Impairment Losses**

1)   The entity may have recognized or reversed impairment losses for the first time in preparing its opening IFRS statement of financial position.

a)   In this case, the first IFRS financial statements must make the disclosures required if the entity had recognized those impairment losses or reversals in the period beginning with the transition date.

Stop and review! You have completed the outline for this subunit. Study multiple-choice questions 27 through 31 beginning on page 85.

QUESTIONS

2.1 Balance Sheet

1. In analyzing a company's financial statements, which financial statement will a potential investor primarily use to assess the company's liquidity and financial flexibility?

A. Balance sheet.

B. Income statement.

C. Statement of retained earnings.

D. Statement of cash flows.

Answer (A) is correct.
REQUIRED: The statement used to assess liquidity and financial flexibility.
DISCUSSION: The balance sheet includes information that is often used in assessing liquidity and financial flexibility but should be used at minimum with a cash flow statement. Liquidity reflects nearness to cash. Financial flexibility is the ability to take action to alter cash flows so that the entity can respond to unexpected events.
Answer (B) is incorrect. The income statement is primarily concerned with profitability. Answer (C) is incorrect. The statement of retained earnings shows changes in the balance of retained earnings for the period. Answer (D) is incorrect. The statement of cash flows provides an incomplete basis for assessing future cash flows. It cannot show interperiod relationships.

2. Zinc Co.'s adjusted trial balance at December 31, Year 6, includes the following account balances:

Common stock, $3 par	$600,000
Additional paid-in capital	800,000
Treasury stock, at cost	50,000
Net unrealized holding loss on available-for-sale securities	20,000
Retained earnings: appropriated for uninsured earthquake losses	150,000
Retained earnings: unappropriated	200,000

What amount should Zinc report as total equity in its December 31, Year 6, balance sheet?

A. $1,680,000

B. $1,720,000

C. $1,780,000

D. $1,820,000

Answer (A) is correct.
REQUIRED: The total equity.
DISCUSSION: Total credits to equity equal $1,750,000 ($600,000 common stock at par + $800,000 additional paid-in capital + $350,000 retained earnings). The treasury stock recorded at cost is subtracted from (debited to) total equity, and the unrealized holding loss on available-for-sale securities is debited to other comprehensive income, a component of equity. Because total debits equal $70,000 ($50,000 cost of treasury stock + $20,000 unrealized loss on available-for-sale securities), total equity equals $1,680,000 ($1,750,000 – $70,000).
Answer (B) is incorrect. The amount of $1,720,000 treats the unrealized loss as a credit. Answer (C) is incorrect. The amount of $1,780,000 treats the treasury stock as a credit. Answer (D) is incorrect. The amount of $1,820,000 treats the treasury stock and the unrealized loss as credits.

Questions 3 and 4 are based on the following information.

The following trial balance of Trey Co. at December 31, Year 6, has been adjusted except for income tax expense.

	Dr.	Cr.
Cash	$ 550,000	
Accounts receivable, net	1,650,000	
Prepaid taxes	300,000	
Accounts payable		$ 120,000
Common stock		500,000
Additional paid-in capital		680,000
Retained earnings		630,000
Foreign currency translation adjustment	430,000	
Revenues		3,600,000
Expenses	2,600,000	
	$5,530,000	$5,530,000

Additional Information

- During Year 6, estimated tax payments of $300,000 were charged to prepaid taxes. Trey has not yet recorded income tax expense. There were no differences between financial statement and income tax income, and Trey's tax rate is 30%.
- Included in accounts receivable is $500,000 due from a customer. Special terms granted to this customer require payment in equal semiannual installments of $125,000 every April 1 and October 1.

3. In Trey's December 31, Year 6, balance sheet, what amount should be reported as total current assets?

A. $1,950,000
B. $2,200,000
C. $2,250,000
D. $2,500,000

Answer (A) is correct.
REQUIRED: The total current assets.
DISCUSSION: Trey's current assets include cash, accounts receivable, and prepaid taxes. However, income tax expense is $300,000 [($3,600,000 revenues – $2,600,000 expenses) × 30%]. After recording income tax expense, prepaid taxes equal $0. Moreover, $250,000 of the receivables is due in Year 8 and is therefore noncurrent. Thus, total current assets equal $1,950,000 [$550,000 cash + ($1,650,000 – $250,000 noncurrent A/R)].
Answer (B) is incorrect. The amount of $2,200,000 includes the noncurrent accounts receivable. Answer (C) is incorrect. The amount of $2,250,000 includes $300,000 of prepaid taxes. Answer (D) is incorrect. The amount of $2,500,000 includes $300,000 of prepaid taxes and the noncurrent accounts receivable.

4. In Trey's December 31, Year 6, balance sheet, what amount should be reported as total retained earnings?

A. $1,029,000
B. $1,200,000
C. $1,330,000
D. $1,630,000

Answer (C) is correct.
REQUIRED: The total retained earnings.
DISCUSSION: Retained earnings equal $1,330,000 {$630,000 beginning retained earnings + [($3,600,000 revenues – $2,600,000 expenses) × (1.0 – .30 tax rate)]}.
Answer (A) is incorrect. The amount of $1,029,000 results from subtracting the $430,000 foreign currency translation adjustment from retained earnings and subtracting $171,000 of taxes [($1,000,000 – $430,000) × 30%]. Answer (B) is incorrect. The amount of $1,200,000 results from subtracting the $430,000 foreign currency translation adjustment and from not subtracting the $300,000 in taxes. Answer (D) is incorrect. The amount of $1,630,000 results from not subtracting the $300,000 in taxes.

5. A company has outstanding accounts payable of $30,000 and a short-term construction loan in the amount of $100,000 at year end. The loan was refinanced through issuance of long-term bonds after year end but before issuance of financial statements. How should these liabilities be recorded in the balance sheet?

A. Noncurrent liabilities of $130,000.
B. Current liabilities of $130,000.
C. Current liabilities of $30,000, noncurrent liabilities of $100,000.
D. Current liabilities of $130,000, with required footnote disclosure of the refinancing of the loan.

Answer (C) is correct.
REQUIRED: The classification of liabilities.
DISCUSSION: Accounts payable are properly classified as current liabilities because they are for items entering into the operating cycle. Short-term debt that is refinanced by a post-balance-sheet-date issuance of long-term debt should be classified as noncurrent. (The ability to refinance on a long-term basis has been demonstrated.) Thus, the short-term construction loan is classified as noncurrent. Accordingly, the entity records current liabilities of $30,000 and noncurrent liabilities of $100,000.
Answer (A) is incorrect. Outstanding accounts payable are normally classified as current liabilities. Answer (B) is incorrect. The $100,000 that is to be refinanced on a long-term basis should be reclassified as noncurrent. Answer (D) is incorrect. The $100,000 that is to be refinanced on a long-term basis should be reclassified as noncurrent.

6. Brite Corp. had the following liabilities at December 31, Year 6:

Accounts payable	$ 55,000
Unsecured notes, 8%, due 7/1/Year 7	400,000
Accrued expenses	35,000
Contingent liability	450,000
Deferred income tax liability	25,000
Senior bonds, 7%, due 3/31/Year 7	1,000,000

The contingent liability is an accrual for possible losses on a $1 million lawsuit filed against Brite. Brite's legal counsel expects the suit to be settled in Year 8 and has estimated that Brite will be liable for damages in the range of $450,000 to $750,000. The deferred income tax liability is not related to an asset for financial reporting and is expected to reverse in Year 8. What amount should Brite report in its December 31, Year 6, balance sheet for current liabilities?

A. $515,000

B. $940,000

C. $1,490,000

D. $1,515,000

Answer (C) is correct.

REQUIRED: The amount reported for current liabilities.

DISCUSSION: The following are current liabilities: (1) Obligations that, by their terms, are or will be due on demand within 1 year (or the operating cycle if longer) and (2) obligations that are or will be callable by the creditor within 1 year because of a violation of a debt covenant. Thus, current liabilities are calculated as

Accounts payable	$ 55,000
Unsecured notes, 8%, due 7/1/Year 7	400,000
Accrued expenses	35,000
Senior bonds, 7%, due 3/31/Year 7	1,000,000
Current liabilities	$1,490,000

Answer (A) is incorrect. The amount of $515,000 excludes the senior bonds due within 1 year and includes the deferred income tax liability that will not reverse within 1 year. Whether a deferred tax asset or liability is current depends on the classification of the related asset or liability. If it is not related to an asset or liability, the expected reversal date of the temporary difference determines the classification. Answer (B) is incorrect. The amount of $940,000 includes the contingent liability not expected to be settled until Year 8 and excludes the senior bonds. Answer (D) is incorrect. The amount of $1,515,000 includes the deferred income tax liability not expected to reverse until Year 8.

2.2 Statements of Income, Retained Earnings, and Changes in Equity

7. The effect of a material transaction that is infrequent in occurrence but **not** unusual in nature should be presented separately as a component of income from continuing operations when the transaction results in a

	Gain	Loss
A.	Yes	Yes
B.	Yes	No
C.	No	No
D.	No	Yes

Answer (A) is correct.

REQUIRED: The circumstances in which an infrequent but not unusual transaction is shown as a separate component of income from continuing operations.

DISCUSSION: To be classified as an extraordinary item, a transaction must be both unusual in nature and infrequent in occurrence within the environment in which the business operates. If an item meets one but not both of these criteria, it should be presented separately as a component of income from continuing operations (but not net of tax). Whether it is a gain or a loss does not affect this presentation.

8. The changes in account balances of the Vel Corporation during Year 6 are presented below:

	Increase
Assets	$356,000
Liabilities	108,000
Capital stock	240,000
Additional paid-in capital	24,000

Vel has no items of other comprehensive income (OCI), and the only charge to retained earnings was for a dividend payment of $52,000. Thus, the net income for Year 6 is

A. $16,000

B. $36,000

C. $52,000

D. $68,000

Answer (B) is correct.

REQUIRED: The net income for the year given the increase in assets, liabilities, and paid-in capital.

DISCUSSION: Assets equal the sum of liabilities and equity (contributed capital, retained earnings, and accumulated OCI). To calculate net income, the dividend payment ($52,000) should be added to the increase in assets ($356,000). The excess of this sum ($408,000) over the increase in liabilities ($108,000) gives the total increase in equity ($300,000). Given no items of OCI, the excess of this amount over the combined increases in the capital accounts ($264,000) equals the increase in retained earnings ($36,000) arising from net income.

Answer (A) is incorrect. The amount of $16,000 is the excess of the sum of the increases in the capital accounts other than retained earnings over the increase in net assets. Answer (C) is incorrect. The amount of $52,000 is the dividend. Answer (D) is incorrect. The amount of $68,000 equals the sum of the dividend and the excess of the sum of the increases in the capital accounts other than retained earnings over the increase in net assets.

9. The correction of an error in the financial statements of a prior period should be reported, net of applicable income taxes, in the current

A. Retained earnings statement after net income but before dividends.

B. Retained earnings statement as an adjustment of the opening balance.

C. Income statement after income from continuing operations and before extraordinary items.

D. Income statement after income from continuing operations and after extraordinary items.

Answer (B) is correct.
REQUIRED: The proper recording of a prior-period adjustment (correction of an error).
DISCUSSION: Prior-period adjustments of single-period statements must be reflected net of applicable income taxes as changes in the opening balance in the statement of retained earnings of the current period. In comparative financial statements, all prior periods affected by the prior-period adjustment should be restated to reflect the adjustment.

10. The following items were among those that were reported on Lee Co.'s income statement for the year ended December 31, Year 1:

Legal and audit fees	$170,000
Rent for office space	240,000
Interest on inventory floor plan	210,000
Loss on abandoned data processing equipment used in operations	35,000

The office space is used equally by Lee's sales and accounting departments. What amount of the above-listed items should be classified as general and administrative expenses in Lee's multiple-step income statement?

A. $290,000

B. $325,000

C. $410,000

D. $500,000

Answer (A) is correct.
REQUIRED: The general and administrative expenses for the year.
DISCUSSION: The interest expense and the loss on the abandoned data processing equipment should be classified as other expenses. The legal and audit fees and one-half of the rent for the office space should be classified as general and administrative expenses. The total is $290,000 [$170,000 + ($240,000 × 50%)].
Answer (B) is incorrect. The amount of $325,000 includes the loss. Answer (C) is incorrect. The amount of $410,000 includes the legal and audit fees as well as the total rent for the office space. Answer (D) is incorrect. The amount of $500,000 includes the interest.

11. Data regarding Ball Corp.'s available-for-sale securities follow:

	Cost	Fair Value
December 31, Year 3	$150,000	$130,000
December 31, Year 4	150,000	160,000

Differences between cost and fair values are considered temporary. The decline in fair value was considered temporary and was properly accounted for at December 31, Year 3. Ball's Year 4 statement of changes in equity should report an increase of

A. $30,000

B. $20,000

C. $10,000

D. $0

Answer (A) is correct.
REQUIRED: The increase reported in the statement of changes in equity because of a change in the fair value of available-for-sale securities.
DISCUSSION: Unrealized holding gains and losses on available-for-sale securities that are deemed to be temporary are ordinarily excluded from earnings and reported in other comprehensive income. At 12/31/Year 4, the fair value was greater than the cost. Consequently, the net amount reported for these securities (an unrealized net holding gain) is a credit of $10,000 ($160,000 fair value – $150,000 cost). At 12/31/Year 3, the net amount reported (an unrealized holding loss) was a debit of $20,000 ($150,000 cost – $130,000 fair value). Thus, the change from a debit of $20,000 to a credit of $10,000 increases total equity by $30,000.
Answer (B) is incorrect. The amount of $20,000 is the excess of cost over fair value on 12/31/Year 3. Answer (C) is incorrect. The amount of $10,000 is the excess of fair value over cost on 12/31/Year 4. Answer (D) is incorrect. Equity increases when the unrealized holding gain is reported in other comprehensive income.

12. The following data were available from Mith Co.'s records on December 31:

Finished goods inventory, 1/1	$120,000
Finished goods inventory, 12/31	110,000
Cost of goods manufactured	520,000
Loss on sale of plant equipment	50,000

The cost of goods sold for the year was

- A. $510,000
- B. $520,000
- C. $530,000
- D. $580,000

Answer (C) is correct.
REQUIRED: The cost of goods sold.
DISCUSSION: Cost of goods sold equals cost of goods manufactured (or purchases for a retailer) adjusted for the change in finished goods inventory. The loss on sale of equipment is not an inventoriable cost. Thus, cost of goods sold is $530,000 ($520,000 COGM + $120,000 BI – $110,000 EI).
Answer (A) is incorrect. The amount of $510,000 results from subtracting, rather than adding, the inventory decrease. Answer (B) is incorrect. The amount of $520,000 equals the cost of goods manufactured. Answer (D) is incorrect. The amount of $580,000 includes the loss.

2.3 Comprehensive Income

13. On December 31, Year 4, the last day of its fiscal year, OCI Company purchased 2,000 shares of available-for-sale securities at a price of $10 per share. These securities had a fair value of $24,000 and $30,000 on December 31, Year 5, and December 31, Year 6, respectively. No dividends were paid, and all of the securities were sold on December 31, Year 6. OCI recognizes all holding gains and losses on available-for-sale securities before recognizing realized gain. If OCI's tax rate is 25%, the total after-tax effect on comprehensive income in Year 6 of the foregoing transactions was

- A. $10,000
- B. $7,500
- C. $4,500
- D. $3,000

Answer (C) is correct.
REQUIRED: The total after-tax effect on comprehensive income in Year 6.
DISCUSSION: OCI paid $20,000 for the shares. Thus, its after-tax holding gain in Year 5 was $3,000 [($24,000 fair value – $20,000) × (1.0 – .25 tax rate)]. Because the shares were classified as available-for-sale, the $3,000 holding gain was credited to other comprehensive income, not net income. OCI's after-tax holding gain in Year 6 was $4,500 [($30,000 – $24,000) × (1.0 – .25)]. Moreover, its realized after-tax gain in Year 6 included in net income was $7,500 [($30,000 – $20,000) × (1.0 – .25)]. The recognition of these amounts in Year 5 and Year 6 necessitates a reclassification adjustment to prevent double counting. This adjustment to other comprehensive income (a debit) is equal to the realized gain recognized in net income. Accordingly, the after-tax effect on comprehensive income in Year 6 of the sale of the available-for-sale securities is $4,500 ($7,500 realized gain + $4,500 holding gain – $7,500 reclassification adjustment).
Answer (A) is incorrect. This figure is the pretax realized gain recognized in net income in Year 6. Answer (B) is incorrect. This figure is the amount of the reclassification adjustment and the realized after-tax gain. Answer (D) is incorrect. This figure is the after-tax holding gain in Year 5.

14. Which of the following describes how comprehensive income is reported under U.S. GAAP?

- A. No specific format is required.
- B. It should be disclosed in the notes but not reported in the financial statements.
- C. It may be reported in a statement of equity.
- D. It must be reported in two separate but consecutive statements or in one continuous statement.

Answer (D) is correct.
REQUIRED: The reporting of comprehensive income.
DISCUSSION: Two reporting formats for comprehensive income are allowed: (1) two separate but consecutive statements and (2) one continuous statement. One continuous statement must have two sections: net income and other comprehensive income (OCI). It must include (1) a total of net income with its components, (2) a total of OCI with its components, and (3) a total of comprehensive income. If separate but consecutive statements are presented, the first statement (the income statement) presents the components of net income and total net income. The second statement (the statement of OCI) is presented immediately after the first. It presents (1) the components of OCI, (2) the total of OCI, and (3) a total for comprehensive income. The entity may begin the second statement with net income.
Answer (A) is incorrect. Comprehensive income must be reported in (1) one continuous financial statement or (2) two separate but consecutive financial statements. Answer (B) is incorrect. Comprehensive income and its components must be presented in a financial statement. Answer (C) is incorrect. Reporting in a statement of equity is prohibited under U.S. GAAP and IFRS.

15. Comprehensive income includes

	Net Income	Unrealized Holding Gains and Losses on Available-for-Sale Securities
A.	Yes	No
B.	Yes	Yes
C.	No	Yes
D.	No	No

Answer (B) is correct.
REQUIRED: The item(s), if any, included in comprehensive income.
DISCUSSION: Comprehensive income is divided into net income and other comprehensive income (OCI). Under existing accounting standards, OCI includes (1) unrealized holding gains and losses on available-for-sale securities (except those that are hedged items in a fair value hedge); (2) foreign currency translation adjustments; (3) gains and losses on certain derivatives or nonderivatives designated, qualifying, and effective as foreign currency hedging instruments; (4) the effective and unreclassified portion of a gain or loss on a derivative designated and qualifying as a cash flow hedge; and (5) certain amounts associated with recognition of the funded status of postretirement benefit plans.

16. A company reports the following information as of December 31:

Sales revenue	$800,000
Cost of goods sold	600,000
Operating expenses	90,000
Unrealized holding gain on available-for-sale securities, net of tax	30,000

What amount should the company report as comprehensive income as of December 31?

A. $30,000

B. $110,000

C. $140,000

D. $200,000

Answer (C) is correct.
REQUIRED: The amount to report as comprehensive income.
DISCUSSION: Comprehensive income includes net income and other comprehensive income. Net income equals $110,000 ($800,000 sales revenue – $600,000 COGS – $90,000 operating expenses). Unrealized holding gains on available-for-sale securities ($30,000) are included in other comprehensive income. Thus, comprehensive income is $140,000 ($110,000 + $30,000).
Answer (A) is incorrect. The amount of other comprehensive income is $30,000. Comprehensive income includes net income and other comprehensive income. Answer (B) is incorrect. The amount of net income is $110,000. Comprehensive income includes net income and other comprehensive income.
Answer (D) is incorrect. The excess of sales revenue over cost of goods sold is $200,000.

17. Rock Co.'s financial statements had the following balances at December 31:

Extraordinary gain	$ 50,000
Foreign currency translation gain	100,000
Net income	400,000
Unrealized gain on available-for-sale equity securities	20,000

What amount should Rock report as comprehensive income for the year ended December 31?

A. $400,000

B. $420,000

C. $520,000

D. $570,000

Answer (C) is correct.
REQUIRED: The amount to report as comprehensive income.
DISCUSSION: Comprehensive income includes all changes in equity of a business entity except those changes resulting from investments by owners and distributions to owners. Comprehensive income includes two major categories: net income and other comprehensive income (OCI). Net income includes the results of continuing and discontinued operations and extraordinary items. Components of comprehensive income not included in the determination of net income are included in OCI, for example, unrealized gains and losses on available-for-sale securities (except those that are hedged items in a fair value hedge) and certain foreign currency items, such as a translation adjustment. Thus, Rock's comprehensive income equals $520,000 ($400,000 net income + $100,000 translation gain + $20,000 unrealized gain on available-for-sale securities).
Answer (A) is incorrect. Certain foreign currency items and unrealized gains on available-for-sale equity securities are components of OCI. Answer (B) is incorrect. A foreign currency translation gain is a component of OCI. Answer (D) is incorrect. The extraordinary gain is already included in the net income amount of $400,000.

2.4 Other Financial Statement Presentations

18. Personal financial statements usually consist of

A. A statement of net worth and a statement of changes in net worth.

B. A statement of net worth, an income statement, and a statement of changes in net worth.

C. A statement of financial condition and a statement of changes in net worth.

D. A statement of financial condition, a statement of changes in net worth, and a statement of cash flows.

Answer (C) is correct.
REQUIRED: The basic financial statements that should be included in personal financial statements.
DISCUSSION: Personal financial statements must include at least a statement of financial condition. A statement of changes in net worth and comparative financial statements are recommended but not required. A personal statement of cash flows is neither required nor recommended.

19. Mrs. Taft owns a $150,000 insurance policy on her husband's life. The cash value of the policy is $125,000, and a $50,000 loan is secured by the policy. In the Tafts' personal statement of financial condition at December 31, what amount should be shown as an investment in life insurance?

A. $150,000

B. $125,000

C. $100,000

D. $75,000

Answer (D) is correct.
REQUIRED: The amount at which an investment in life insurance should be presented in a personal statement of financial condition.
DISCUSSION: Assets must be presented at their estimated current values in a personal statement of financial condition. Also, investments in life insurance must be reported at their cash values minus the amount of any outstanding loans. Thus, the amount that should be reported in Mrs. Taft's personal financial statement is $75,000 ($125,000 cash value – $50,000 loan).
Answer (A) is incorrect. The amount of $150,000 is the amount of the policy. Answer (B) is incorrect. The amount of $125,000 is the cash value. Answer (C) is incorrect. The amount of $100,000 is the amount of the policy minus the loan.

20. Quinn is preparing a personal statement of financial condition as of April 30. Included in Quinn's assets are the following:

- 50% of the voting stock of Ink Corp. A share-holders' agreement restricts the sale of the stock and, under certain circumstances, requires Ink to repurchase the stock. Quinn's tax basis for the stock is $430,000, and at April 30, the buyout value is $675,000.
- Jewelry with a fair value aggregating $70,000 based on an independent appraisal on April 30 for insurance purposes. This jewelry was acquired by purchase and gift over a 10-year period and has a total tax basis of $40,000.

What is the total amount at which the Ink stock and jewelry should be reported in Quinn's April 30 personal statement of financial condition?

A. $470,000

B. $500,000

C. $715,000

D. $745,000

Answer (D) is correct.
REQUIRED: The amount at which stock and jewelry should be reported in a personal statement of financial condition.
DISCUSSION: All assets must be reported at estimated current value. An interest in a closely held business is an asset and should be shown at its estimated current value. The buyout value is a better representation of the current value of the Ink stock than the tax basis. The appraisal value is the appropriate basis for reporting the jewelry. Thus, the stock and jewelry should be reported at $745,000 ($675,000 + $70,000).
Answer (A) is incorrect. The amount of $470,000 reports both assets at their tax basis. Answer (B) is incorrect. The amount of $500,000 includes the stock at its tax basis. Answer (C) is incorrect. The amount of $715,000 includes the jewelry's tax basis rather than its fair value.

21. On December 31, Year 4, Shane is a fully vested participant in a company-sponsored pension plan. According to the plan's administrator, Shane has at that date the nonforfeitable right to receive a lump sum of $100,000 on December 28, Year 5. The discounted amount of $100,000 is $90,000 at December 31, Year 4. The right is not contingent on Shane's life expectancy and requires no future performance on Shane's part. In Shane's December 31, Year 4, personal statement of financial condition, the vested interest in the pension plan should be reported at

A. $0

B. $90,000

C. $95,000

D. $100,000

Answer (B) is correct.
REQUIRED: The amount at which the vested interest in a pension plan should be reported in a personal statement of financial condition.
DISCUSSION: Noncancelable rights to receive future sums must be presented at their estimated current value as assets in personal financial statements if they (1) are for fixed or determinable amounts; (2) are not contingent on the holder's life expectancy or the occurrence of a particular event, such as disability or death; and (3) do not require the future performance of service by the holder. The fully vested rights in the company-sponsored pension plan therefore should be reported at their current value, which is equal to the $90,000 discounted amount.
Answer (A) is incorrect. The current value of the right should be reported. Answer (C) is incorrect. The amount of $95,000 is a nonsense amount. Answer (D) is incorrect. The amount of $100,000 is the undiscounted amount.

22. On December 31, Year 5, Mr. and Mrs. Blake owned a parcel of land held as an investment. The land was purchased for $95,000 in Year 1 and was encumbered by a mortgage with a principal balance of $60,000 at December 31, Year 5. On this date, the fair value of the land was $150,000. In the Blakes' December 31, Year 5, personal statement of financial condition, at what amount should the land investment and mortgage payable be reported?

	Land Investment	Mortgage Payable
A.	$150,000	$60,000
B.	$95,000	$60,000
C.	$90,000	$0
D.	$35,000	$0

Answer (A) is correct.
REQUIRED: The amounts at which the land investment and mortgage payable should be reported.
DISCUSSION: For an investment in a limited business activity not conducted in a separate business entity (such as an investment in real estate and a related mortgage), the assets and liabilities must not be presented as a net amount. Instead, they should be presented as separate assets at their estimated current values and separate liabilities at their estimated current amounts. This presentation is particularly important if a large portion of the liabilities may be satisfied with funds from sources unrelated to the investments. Thus, the land should be reported at its $150,000 fair value, and the mortgage principal at $60,000 (the amount at which the debt could currently be discharged).
Answer (B) is incorrect. The amount of $95,000 was the cost of the land. Answer (C) is incorrect. The asset and liability should be presented separately and not as a net amount. Answer (D) is incorrect. The amount of $35,000 equals the cost minus the mortgage balance.

23. Which of the following is **not** a comprehensive basis of accounting other than generally accepted accounting principles?

A. Cash receipts and disbursements basis of accounting.

B. Basis of accounting used by an entity to file its income tax returns.

C. Basis of accounting used by an entity to comply with the financial reporting requirements of a government regulatory agency.

D. Basis of accounting used by an entity to comply with the financial reporting requirements of a lending institution.

Answer (D) is correct.
REQUIRED: The item not a comprehensive basis of accounting other than GAAP.
DISCUSSION: A comprehensive basis of accounting other than GAAP may be (1) a basis that the reporting entity uses to comply with the requirements or financial reporting provisions of a regulatory agency; (2) a basis used for tax purposes; (3) the cash basis, and modifications of the cash basis having substantial support, such as recording depreciation on fixed assets or accruing income taxes; or (4) a definite set of criteria having substantial support that is applied to all material items, for example, the price-level basis. However, a basis of accounting used by an entity to comply with the financial reporting requirements of a lending institution does not qualify as governmentally mandated or as having substantial support.

24. On April 1, Julie began operating a service proprietorship with an initial cash investment of $1,000. The proprietorship provided $3,200 of services in April and received a payment of $2,500 in May. The proprietorship incurred expenses of $1,500 in April that were paid in June. During May, Julie drew $500 from her capital account. What was the proprietorship's income for the 2 months ended May 31 under the following methods of accounting?

	Cash-Basis	Accrual-Basis
A.	$500	$1,200
B.	$1,000	$1,700
C.	$2,000	$1,200
D.	$2,500	$1,700

Answer (D) is correct.
REQUIRED: The income for a proprietorship under the cash basis and accrual basis.
DISCUSSION: Under the cash basis, $2,500 of income is recognized for the payments received in May for the services rendered in April. The $1,500 of expenses is not recognized until June. Under the accrual basis, the $3,200 of income and the $1,500 of expenses incurred in April but not paid until June are recognized. The net income is $1,700 under the accrual basis. The cash investment and capital withdrawal are ignored because they do not affect net income.
Answer (A) is incorrect. The $500 withdrawal should not be recognized in the computation of net income under either method, and the $1,500 of expenses should not be recognized under the cash basis. Answer (B) is incorrect. The cash basis does not recognize the $1,500 in expenses until June. Answer (C) is incorrect. The $500 withdrawal should not be recognized in the computation of net income under either method.

25. Hahn Co. prepared financial statements on the cash basis of accounting. The cash basis was modified so that an accrual of income taxes was reported. Are these financial statements in accordance with the modified cash basis of accounting?

A. Yes.

B. No, because the modifications are illogical.

C. No, because there is no substantial support for recording income taxes.

D. No, because the modifications result in financial statements equivalent to those prepared under the accrual basis of accounting.

Answer (A) is correct.
REQUIRED: The true statement about whether cash-basis statements may be modified for accrual of income taxes.
DISCUSSION: A comprehensive basis of accounting other than GAAP includes the cash basis. Modifications of the cash basis having substantial support, such as accruing income taxes or recording depreciation on fixed assets, may be made when preparing financial statements on the cash basis (AU 623).
Answer (B) is incorrect. Accrual of quarterly income taxes is a logical modification of the cash basis of accounting. Answer (C) is incorrect. Substantial support exists for accrual of a reasonably estimable expense such as income taxes. Answer (D) is incorrect. A modification of the cash basis that accrues income taxes but incorporates no other accruals or deferrals will not result in financial statements equivalent to those prepared under the accrual basis.

26. Income tax-basis financial statements differ from those prepared under GAAP in that income tax-basis financial statements

A. Do not include nontaxable revenues and nondeductible expenses in determining income.

B. Include detailed information about current and deferred income tax liabilities.

C. Contain no disclosures about capital and operating lease transactions.

D. Recognize certain revenues and expenses in different reporting periods.

Answer (D) is correct.
REQUIRED: The difference between income tax-basis financial statements and those prepared under GAAP.
DISCUSSION: Income tax-basis financial statements and those prepared under GAAP differ when the tax basis of an asset or a liability and its reported amount in the GAAP-based financial statements are not the same. The result will be taxable or deductible amounts in future years when the reported amount of the asset is recovered or the liability is settled. Thus, certain revenues and expenses are recognized in different periods. An example is subscriptions revenue received in advance, which is recognized in taxable income when received and in financial income when earned in a later period. Another example is a warranty liability, which is recognized as an expense in financial income when a product is sold and in taxable income when the expenditures are made in a later period.
Answer (A) is incorrect. Even if financial statements are prepared on the income tax basis, permanent difference items, e.g., nondeductible expenses, are included as revenues or expenses in the income statement. They do not have to be presented in a special category of the income statement. Answer (B) is incorrect. Detailed information about current and deferred income tax liabilities is necessary whether financial statements are prepared on the income tax-basis or in conformity with GAAP. Temporary differences, which result in deferred tax amounts, arise under either basis of accounting. Answer (C) is incorrect. Lease disclosures are the same under either basis of accounting.

2.5 First-Time Adoption of IFRS

27. On July 1, Year 2, a company decided to adopt IFRS. The company's first IFRS reporting period is as of and for the year ended December 31, Year 2. The company will present 1 year of comparative information. What is the company's date of transition to IFRS?

A. January 1, Year 1.

B. January 1, Year 2.

C. July 1, Year 2.

D. December 31, Year 2.

Answer (A) is correct.
  REQUIRED: The date of transition to IFRS.
  DISCUSSION: The date of transition is "the beginning of the earliest period for which an entity presents full comparative information under IFRS in its first IFRS financial statements" (IFRS 1). Thus, the date of transition is January 1, Year 1. In the entity's first IFRS financial statements, it must present at least (1) three statements of financial position, (2) two statements of comprehensive income, (3) two separate income statements (if presented), (4) two statements of cash flows, and (5) two statements of changes in equity and related notes.
  Answer (B) is incorrect. January 1, Year 2, is the beginning of the entity's first IFRS reporting period. Answer (C) is incorrect. July 1, Year 2, is the date the entity decided to adopt IFRS. The transition date is the beginning of the earliest period presented. Answer (D) is incorrect. December 31, Year 2, is the end of the entity's first IFRS reporting period.

28. Which of the following may be accounted for retrospectively by first-time adopters of IFRS?

A. Hedges.

B. Estimates.

C. Employee benefit plans.

D. Noncontrolling interests.

Answer (C) is correct.
  REQUIRED: The item for which retrospective application is allowed to first-time adopters of IFRS.
  DISCUSSION: With certain exceptions, the items for which retrospective application is prohibited for first-time adopters of IFRS are (1) derecognition of financial assets and financial liabilities, (2) hedges, (3) estimates, (4) noncontrolling interests, (5) classification and measurement of financial assets, and (6) embedded derivatives.

29. Under IFRS, which of the following is the first step within the hierarchy of guidance to which management refers, and whose applicability it considers, when selecting accounting policies?

A. Consider the most recent pronouncements of other standard-setting bodies to the extent they do not conflict with the IFRS or the IASB Framework.

B. Apply a standard from IFRS if it specifically relates to the transaction, other event, or condition.

C. Consider the applicability of the definitions, recognition criteria, and measurement concepts in the IASB Framework.

D. Apply the requirements in IFRS dealing with similar and related issues.

Answer (B) is correct.
  REQUIRED: The first step in the IFRS hierarchy.
  DISCUSSION: When an IASB Standard or Interpretation specifically applies to a transaction, other event, or condition, it must be selected if the effect is material. Any Implementation Guidance also must be considered. Absent such a standard or Interpretation, management considers (1) guidance for similar and related issues in other IASB Standards and Interpretations and (2) the content of the Framework for the Preparation and Presentation of Financial Statements.
  Answer (A) is incorrect. The IFRS hierarchy does not refer to pronouncements of other standard-setters. Answer (C) is incorrect. The content of the Framework is considered only when a specific IASB Standard or Interpretation does not apply. Answer (D) is incorrect. An entity may apply the requirements in IFRS dealing with similar and related issues only when a specific IASB Standard or Interpretation does not apply.

30. Which of the following is **incorrect** regarding the financial statements of an entity adopting IFRS for the first time?

A. Business combinations may be accounted for using the method in use before the adoption of IFRS.

B. If the liability component of a compound financial instrument is no longer outstanding, the instrument need not be reported as having two separate equity components.

C. All cumulative actuarial gains and losses on employee benefit plans may be recognized as of the transition date.

D. Inventories measured using LIFO prior to the transition date may continue to be accounted for using LIFO.

Answer (D) is correct.
  REQUIRED: The incorrect statement regarding first-time adoption of IFRS.
  DISCUSSION: No exemption available to first-time adopters of IFRS permits the use of the LIFO inventory method.
  Answer (A) is incorrect. In its first IFRS financial statements, the entity may elect to employ the same method of accounting for business combinations as that used prior to the IFRS transition date. Answer (B) is incorrect. If the liability component of a compound financial instrument is no longer outstanding, the instrument need not be reported as having separate liability and equity components in an entity's first IFRS financial statements. Answer (C) is incorrect. On its first IFRS financial statements, the entity may elect to recognize all cumulative actuarial gains and losses on employee benefit plans at the transition date rather than splitting them into a recognized portion and an unrecognized portion.

31. Which of the following most likely is **not** required to be presented by first-time adopters of IFRS?

A. Reconciliation from total comprehensive income (or profit or loss if TCI was not reported) reported under previous GAAP to total comprehensive income reported under IFRS.

B. Reconciliation from extraordinary items reported under previous GAAP to extraordinary items reported under IFRS.

C. Disclosure of the amount of impairment losses recognized for the first time in preparing the first IFRS statement of financial position.

D. Reconciliation from equity reported under previous GAAP to equity reported under IFRS.

Answer (B) is correct.
  REQUIRED: The item most likely not required to be presented by first-time adopters of IFRS.
  DISCUSSION: Extraordinary items are never recognized under IFRS.
  Answer (A) is incorrect. The first IFRS financial statements must present a reconciliation of total comprehensive income reported under previous GAAP (or profit or loss if TCI was not reported) to total comprehensive income reported under IFRS. Answer (C) is incorrect. If the entity recognized or reversed any impairment losses for the first time in preparing its first IFRS statement of financial position, it must make the disclosures that IAS 36, *Impairment of Assets,* would have required if the entity had recognized those items in the period beginning with the transition date. Answer (D) is incorrect. The first IFRS financial statements must present a reconciliation of equity reported under previous GAAP to equity reported under IFRS as of (1) the transition date and (2) the end of the latest period presented under previous GAAP.

2.6 PRACTICE SIMULATION

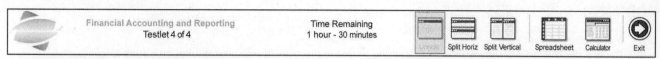

| Financial Accounting and Reporting
Testlet 4 of 4 | Time Remaining
1 hour - 30 minutes | Unsplit | Split Horiz | Split Vertical | Spreadsheet | Calculator | Exit |

DIRECTIONS

Note: If you believe you have encountered a software malfunction, report it to the test center staff immediately.

Navigation

To navigate from task to task, use the controls at the bottom of the screen. Click on the **Next** button to advance to the next task, or the **Previous** button to go to the previous task. To go directly to any task, click on its number.

| ▼ = Reminder | | Directions | 1 2 3 4 5 6 7 | | Previous Next ▶ |

If you would like a reminder to revisit a task, or want to indicate that you are finished with it, click on the reminder flag below the task number. To clear the flag, click on it again. Reminder flags are for your use only – they do not contribute to your score.

Tabs

In this part of the examination, you will be asked to complete various tasks. Every task has one or more **Work Tabs**. Some tasks have one or more **Information Tabs**, others may have none. Every task has a **Help** tab.

If a task has **Information Tabs**, you may use the information in them to complete your responses in the **Work Tabs**.

| Corporate Gain and Basis | Authoritative Literature | Help |
| Work tab | Information tab | Help tab |

Work Tabs:

- **Work Tabs** are identified with a pencil icon. This is where your responses are expected.
- Each task has one or more **Work Tabs**.
- **Work Tabs** contain directions for completing the task – be sure to read these directions carefully.
- The **Work Tab** name in the example above is for illustration only – yours will differ.
- You must complete all of the **Work Tabs** in each task to receive full credit.

Information Tabs:

- The Authoritative Literature will be provided in all tasks in the AUD, FAR, and REG sections for your reference.
- Your simulation may have one or more additional **Information Tabs**. Like the Authoritative Literature tabs, **Information Tabs** do not have a pencil icon.
- If your task has additional **Information Tabs**, go through each to familiarize yourself with the task content.

Help Tab:

- The **Help Tab** provides assistance with the exam software that is used in this task. For example, if the task is to compose a memorandum, **Help** will provide information about the word processor.

The Toolbar

The toolbar at the top of the screen shows the amount of time remaining for you to complete the tasks. In addition, the following tools are available. Note that only the **Exit** button is displayed when Directions are visible - the others will appear when you begin the tasks.

Click on these buttons to split or unsplit the screen. You can split the screen vertically or horizontally.

Click on this button to display the calculator; click on it again to hide the calculator. To move the calculator, click on the calculator title bar and drag the calculator to the desired location.

Click on this button to use the spreadsheet; click on it again to hide the spreadsheet. To move the spreadsheet, click on the the spreadsheet title bar and drag the spreadsheet to the desired location.

Click on this button to go on to the next part of the examination. You must complete all of the tasks to receive full credit. Once you click on **Exit** and confirm the action, you will NOT be able to return to this testlet.

| ▼ = Reminder | | Directions | 1 2 3 4 5 6 | | ◀ Previous Next ▶ |

Retained Earnings | Authoritative Literature | Help

Min Co. is a publicly held company whose shares are traded in the over-the-counter market. It issues single-period statements only. The equity accounts at December 31, Year 5, had the following balances:

Preferred stock, $100 par value, 6% noncumulative; 5,000 shares authorized; 2,000 issued and outstanding	$ 200,000
Common stock, $1 par value, 150,000 shares authorized; 100,000 issued and outstanding	100,000
Additional paid-in capital	800,000
Retained earnings	1,586,000
Accumulated other comprehensive income	312,000
Total equity	$2,998,000

Transactions during Year 6 and other information relating to the equity accounts were as follows:

- February 1, Year 6 -- Issued 13,000 shares of common stock to Ram Co. in exchange for land. On the date issued, the stock had a market price of $11 per share. The land had a carrying amount on Ram's books of $135,000 and an assessed value for property tax purposes of $90,000.

- March 1, Year 6 -- Purchased 5,000 shares of its own common stock to be held as treasury stock for $14 per share. Min uses the cost method to account for treasury stock. Transactions in treasury stock are legal in Min's state of incorporation.

- May 10, Year 6 -- Declared a property dividend of marketable securities to be distributed to common shareholders. The securities had a carrying amount of $600,000. Fair values on relevant dates were

Date of declaration (May 10, Year 6)	$ 720,000
Date of record (May 25, Year 6)	758,000
Date of distribution (June 1, Year 6)	736,000

- September 17, Year 6 -- Purchased 150,000 shares of Max Co. stock classified as available for sale for $12 per share.

- October 1, Year 6 -- Reissued 2,000 shares of treasury stock for $16 per share.

- November 4, Year 6 -- Declared a cash dividend of $1.50 per share to all common shareholders of record on November 15, Year 6. The dividend was paid on November 25, Year 6.

- December 20, Year 6 -- Declared the required annual cash dividend on preferred stock for Year 6. The dividend was paid on January 5, Year 7.

- January 16, Year 7 -- After issuance of the financial statements for Year 6, Min became aware that no amortization had been recorded for Year 6 for a patent purchased on July 1, Year 6. The patent was properly capitalized at $320,000 and had an estimated useful life of 8 years when purchased. Min's income tax rate is 30%.

- Adjusted net income for Year 6 was $838,000.

- Max Co. stock traded at $14 per share on December 31, Year 6.

For the following retained earnings items, enter in the shaded cells the amounts requested using the information above. These items will be reported on Min's statement of changes in equity or in a separate statement of retained earnings.

Retained Earnings Item	Amount Charged To Retained Earnings
1. Prior-period adjustment	
2. Preferred dividends	
3. Common dividends -- cash	
4. Common dividends -- property	

On January 1, Year 9, the first day of its fiscal year, Noel Company purchased 2,000 shares of available-for-sale securities at a price of $10 per share. These securities had a fair value of $24,000 and $30,000 on December 31, Year 9, and December 31, Year 10, respectively. No dividends were paid, and all of the securities were sold on December 31, Year 10. Noel recognizes all holding gains and losses on available-for-sale securities before recognizing realized gain.

Prepare the journal entries, if any, necessary for December 31, Year 9, and December 31, Year 10, that relate to these available-for-sale securities. Also prepare the journal entry to record the sale of the securities on December 31, Year 10. Ignore income tax effects.

To prepare the entries, in the Account column, select the appropriate account from the list provided. Then enter the correct amounts in the Debit or Credit columns. Each choice may be used once, more than once, or not at all.

Account	Debit	Credit
December 31, Year 9		
1.		
2.		
December 31, Year 10		
3.		
4.		
Sale of the securities		
5.		
6.		
7.		
8.		
9.		

Choices
A) No entry required
B) Unrealized holding gain–OCI
C) Unrealized holding gain–earnings
D) Unrealized holding loss–OCI
E) Unrealized holding loss–earnings
F) Securities fair value adjustment
G) Cash
H) Available-for-sale securities
I) Gain on sale of securities

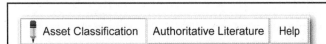

Select from the list provided the appropriate balance sheet classification for each asset below. Each choice may be used once, more than once, or not at all.

Asset	Answer
1. Land	
2. Debt sinking fund	
3. Capital lease	
4. Inventory	
5. Goodwill	

Classification
A) Property, plant, and equipment
B) Investments and funds
C) Other noncurrent assets
D) Current assets
E) Intangible assets

The following is the income statement for the period ending December 31, Year 1, for Manatee Construction Company:

Manatee Construction Company
Income Statement
FYE December 31, Year 1

Sales	$ 8,000,000
Cost of goods sold	(6,500,000)
Gross profit	1,500,000
Salaries expense	(300,000)
Other administrative expenses	(100,000)
Interest expense	(900,000)
Advertising expense	(450,000)
Total expenses	(1,750,000)
Operating loss	(250,000)
Gain from the sale of investments	100,000
Total net loss	$ (150,000)

Based on this information, perform the adjusting journal entry to close Manatee's books at the end of Year 1. If no entry is necessary, leave the cell blank. Enter all numbers as positive.

Account	Debit	Credit
1. Sales		
2. Cost of goods sold		
3. Salaries expense		
4. Other administrative expenses		
5. Interest expense		
6. Advertising expense		
7. Gain from the sale of investments		
8. Retained earnings		

Min Co. is a publicly held company whose shares are traded in the over-the-counter market. It issues single-period statements only. The equity accounts at December 31, Year 5, had the following balances:

Preferred stock, $100 par value, 6% noncumulative; 5,000 shares authorized; 2,000 issued and outstanding	$ 200,000
Common stock, $1 par value, 150,000 shares authorized; 100,000 issued and outstanding	100,000
Additional paid-in capital	800,000
Retained earnings	1,586,000
Accumulated other comprehensive income	312,000
Total equity	$2,998,000

Transactions during Year 6 and other information relating to the equity accounts were as follows:

- February 1, Year 6 -- Issued 13,000 shares of common stock to Ram Co. in exchange for land. On the date issued, the stock had a market price of $11 per share. The land had a carrying amount on Ram's books of $135,000 and an assessed value for property tax purposes of $90,000.
- March 1, Year 6 -- Purchased 5,000 shares of its own common stock to be held as treasury stock for $14 per share. Min uses the cost method to account for treasury stock. Transactions in treasury stock are legal in Min's state of incorporation.
- May 10, Year 6 -- Declared a property dividend of marketable securities to be distributed to common shareholders. The securities had a carrying amount of $600,000. Fair values on relevant dates were

Date of declaration (May 10, Year 6)	$ 720,000
Date of record (May 25, Year 6)	758,000
Date of distribution (June 1, Year 6)	736,000

- September 17, Year 6 -- Purchased 150,000 shares of Max Co. stock classified as available for sale for $12 per share.
- October 1, Year 6 -- Reissued 2,000 shares of treasury stock for $16 per share.
- November 4, Year 6 -- Declared a cash dividend of $1.50 per share to all common shareholders of record on November 15, Year 6. The dividend was paid on November 25, Year 6.
- December 20, Year 6 -- Declared the required annual cash dividend on preferred stock for Year 6. The dividend was paid on January 5, Year 7.
- January 16, Year 7 -- After issuance of the financial statements for Year 6, Min became aware that no amortization had been recorded for Year 6 for a patent purchased on July 1, Year 6. The patent was properly capitalized at $320,000 and had an estimated useful life of 8 years when purchased. Min's income tax rate is 30%.
- Adjusted net income for Year 6 was $838,000.
- Max Co. stock traded at $14 per share on December 31, Year 6.

For the following equity items, enter in the shaded cells the amounts requested using the information above. These items will be reported on Min's statement of changes in equity at December 31, Year 6.

Equity Item	Amount to Be Included in Equity
1. Number of common shares issued	
2. Dollar amount of common stock issued	
3. Additional paid-in capital, including treasury stock transactions	
4. Treasury stock	

| Research | Authoritative Literature | Help |

Monty Carlo is the CFO of Invest-a-lot, Inc., a leading investment company in Louisiana. Monty recently began preparing the financial statements for the company and, when beginning to prepare the income statement, referred to the authoritative guidance to determine how this information should be presented. Which section best outlines the requirement for presentation of net income for investment companies?

Enter your response in the answer fields below. Unless specifically requested, your response should not cite implementation guidance.

FASB ASC [   ] - [ ] - [ ] - [ ]

| ▼ = Reminder | Directions | 1 2 3 4 5 6 | ◀ Previous Next ▶ |

Unofficial Answers

1. Retained Earnings (4 Gradable Items)

1. $14,000. The prior-period adjustment to beginning retained earnings for the Year 7 fiscal year is to correct the failure to record 6 months of patent amortization for Year 6. The patent was capitalized at $320,000 and had an expected useful life of 8 years. Thus, Year 6 amortization was $20,000 [($320,000 ÷ 8) × (6 ÷ 12)], and the prior-period adjustment to beginning retained earnings (net of tax) is $14,000 [$20,000 × (1.0 – .30)].

2. $12,000. The preferred stock is 6% noncumulative. The dividend is $12,000 ($200,000 × .06). When a dividend is declared, retained earnings is debited.

3. $165,000. At the beginning of the year, 100,000 shares of common stock were outstanding. Given that 13,000 shares were issued in February, 5,000 shares were purchased as treasury stock in March, and 2,000 shares were reissued in October, 110,000 shares were outstanding at November 4 (100,000 + 13,000 – 5,000 + 2,000). The dividend is $165,000 (110,000 shares × $1.50).

4. $720,000. Most nonreciprocal transfers of nonmonetary assets to owners are recorded at the fair value of the assets transferred. Thus, on the declaration date, the property should be restated at fair value. Any gain or loss should be recognized. The entries for Min on the date of declaration are

Investment in securities	$120,000	
Gain on appreciation of securities		$120,000
Retained earnings	$720,000	
Property dividends payable		$720,000

2. Comprehensive Income (9 Gradable Items)

December 31, Year 9, journal entry:

	Account	Debit	Credit
1.	F) Securities fair value adjustment	$4,000	
2.	B) Unrealized holding gain – OCI		$4,000

A holding gain or loss on available-for-sale securities is the net change in fair value of the securities during the period. To retain historical cost in the accounts while reporting changes in the carrying amount from changes in fair value, a valuation allowance may be established. At each reporting date, the company reports the available-for-sale securities at fair value with an adjustment to an unrealized holding gain or loss account that is included in other comprehensive income (OCI). For December 31, Year 9, Noel has a holding gain of $4,000 for its available-for-sale securities ($24,000 fair value – $20,000 cost). This gain is credited to the unrealized holding gain account in OCI, with a corresponding debit to the securities valuation account.

December 31, Year 10, journal entry:

	Account	Debit	Credit
3.	F) Securities fair value adjustment	$6,000	
4.	B) Unrealized holding gain – OCI		$6,000

On December 31, Year 10, the fair value of Noel's available-for-sale securities is $30,000. This amount is compared to the fair value of the securities on December 31, Year 9 ($24,000), resulting in a holding gain of $6,000. Noel makes the same journal entry for this unrealized holding gain as it did for the December 31, Year 9, unrealized holding gain, except that the amount of the adjustment equals $6,000.

Journal entry for sale of the securities:

	Account	Debit	Credit
5.	G) Cash	$30,000	
6.	B) Unrealized holding gain – OCI	10,000	
7.	H) Available-for-sale securities		$20,000
8.	I) Gain on sale of securities		10,000
9.	F) Securities fair value adjustment		10,000

Noel's journal entry for the December 31, Year 10, sale of the available-for-sale securities must reflect both the sale and a reclassification adjustment. The sale portion of the journal entry is straightforward: Debit cash for the amount received, credit available-for-sale securities at their cost, and credit gain on the sale. The gain equals $10,000 ($30,000 selling price – $20,000 cost). Reclassification adjustments must be made for each component of OCI in order to avoid double counting when an item included in net income also was included in OCI for the same or prior period. This adjustment to OCI (a debit) is equal to the realized gain recognized in net income. Noel's unrealized holding gains on these available-for-sale securities for Year 9 and Year 10 equal $10,000, the same amount as the recognized gain on the sale of the securities. Thus, Noel debits the unrealized holding gain account in OCI, and credits the securities fair value adjustment account, for $10,000.

3. Asset Classification (5 Gradable Items)

1. A) Property, plant, and equipment. These noncurrent assets are tangible operating items recorded at cost and reported net of any accumulated depreciation. An example is land, a nondepreciable asset.

2. B) Investments and funds. These noncurrent assets include a variety of nonoperating items intended to be held beyond the longer of 1 year or the operating cycle, e.g., funds restricted to retirement of noncurrent debt.

3. A) Property, plant, and equipment. These noncurrent assets are tangible operating items recorded at cost and reported net of any accumulated depreciation. An example is a leased asset held under a capital lease.

4. D) Current assets. These assets consist of "cash and other assets or resources commonly identified as reasonably expected to be realized in cash or sold or consumed during the normal operating cycle of the business." Current assets include inventory.

5. E) Intangible assets. These assets are nonfinancial assets without physical substance. Goodwill is an intangible asset that is recorded only in a business combination. It is the excess of (a) the sum of the fair values of (1) the consideration transferred, (2) any prior equity interest in the acquiree, and (3) any noncontrolling interest over (b) the fair value of the net identifiable assets acquired.

4. End-of-Period Adjusting Entry (16 Gradable Items)

1. Debit $8,000,000. A positive sales account has a credit balance. To close the sales account to retained earnings, the entire balance should be debited.

2. Credit $6,500,000. Cost of goods sold has a debit balance. To close the cost of goods account, the entire balance should be credited.

3. Credit $300,000. Salaries expense is held with a debit balance. To close the salaries expense account, the entire balance should be credited.

4. Credit $100,000. Other administrative expenses are held with a debit balance. To close the other administrative expenses account, the entire balance should be credited.

5. Credit $900,000. Interest expense has a debit balance. To close the interest expense account, the entire balance should be credited.

6. Credit $450,000. Advertising expense has a debit balance. To close the advertising expense account, the entire balance should be credited.

7. Debit $100,000. Gains are kept on the books with a credit balance. To close the gain from sale of investments account to retained earnings, the entire balance should be debited.

8. Debit $150,000. The change in retained earnings should reflect the net income or loss earned in the current year. Since there is a net loss, the retained earnings account should be debited.

5. Equity (4 Gradable Items)

1. <u>113,000 shares.</u> Given that 100,000 shares of common stock were issued and outstanding at the beginning of the year and that 13,000 shares were issued in February, 113,000 shares had been issued as of year end. Of these, 110,000 were outstanding (113,000 shares issued – 5,000 shares repurchased + 2,000 shares reissued).

2. <u>$113,000.</u> The number of shares issued is 113,000 (100,000 beginning shares issued + 13,000 issued in February). The stock has a par value of $1. Thus, the dollar amount of common stock issued is $113,000.

3. <u>$934,000.</u> Beginning additional paid-in capital was $800,000. When 13,000 shares were issued for land, the most clearly evident basis for measuring the transaction was the fair value of the stock ($11 per share). Hence, additional paid-in capital would have been credited for $130,000 [$143,000 – (13,000 shares × $1 par)]. When 2,000 shares of treasury stock purchased at $14 per share were reissued for $16 per share, additional paid-in capital was credited for $4,000 [2,000 shares × ($16 – $14)]. Thus, additional paid-in capital is $934,000 ($800,000 + $130,000 + $4,000).

4. <u>$42,000.</u> When 5,000 shares were reacquired, treasury stock was debited for $70,000 (5,000 shares × $14). When 2,000 shares of treasury stock were reissued at $16, treasury stock was credited for $28,000 (2,000 shares × $14), and additional paid-in capital was credited for $4,000 (2,000 shares × $2). The balance in the treasury stock account is therefore $42,000 ($70,000 – $28,000).

6. Research (1 Gradable Item)

Answer: FASB ASC 225-10-45-1

225-10-45-1 Net income shall reflect all items of profit and loss recognized during the period with the sole exception of error corrections as addressed in Topic 250. However, the requirement that net income be presented as one amount does not apply to the following entities that have developed income statements with formats different from those of the typical commercial entity:

1. Investment companies
2. Insurance entities
3. Certain not-for-profit entities (NFPs)

General Note: The Other Presentation Matters Section provides guidance on other presentation matters not addressed in the Recognition, Initial Measurement, Subsequent Measurement, and Derecognition Sections. Other presentation matters may include items such as current or long-term balance sheet classification, cash flow presentation, earnings per share matters, and so forth. The FASB Codification also contains Presentation Topics, which provide guidance for general presentation and display items. See those Topics for general guidance.

S45-1 See paragraph 225-10-S99-1, Regulation S-X Rule 3-03, for the instructions to income statement requirements.

Gleim Simulation Grading

Task	Correct Responses		Gradable Items		Score per Task
1	___	÷	5	=	___
2	___	÷	4	=	___
3	___	÷	9	=	___
4	___	÷	16	=	___
5	___	÷	4	=	___
Research	___	÷	1	=	___

Total of Scores per Task ___

÷ Total Number of Tasks   6

Total Score ___%

Use **CPA Gleim Online** and **Simulation Wizard** to practice more task-based simulations in a realistic environment.

STUDY UNIT THREE
STATEMENT OF CASH FLOWS

(10 pages of outline)

3.1	Statement of Cash Flows -- Classifications	95
3.2	Statement of Cash Flows -- Calculations	98
3.3	Direct and Indirect Methods -- Classifications	98
3.4	Direct and Indirect Methods -- Calculations	104
3.5	Practice Simulation	114

This study unit covers the statement of cash flows. The first subunit explains the purposes of the statement and how cash flows are classified. The second subunit consists of questions that require the candidate to perform typical statement of cash flows calculations. The third subunit describes the direct and indirect methods of presenting operating cash flows and provides extended examples. The fourth subunit contains questions requiring calculations pertinent to the direct and indirect methods.

3.1 STATEMENT OF CASH FLOWS -- CLASSIFICATIONS

Background
In 1969, in a desperate attempt to boost sales, the department store chain W.T. Grant drastically lowered its credit standards. As a result, sales boomed. However, during the economic downturn of 1970-71, customer accounts began to turn delinquent and cash inflows dried up. The company finally collapsed in 1974. Grant's creditors were caught completely unaware because the company's accrual-basis income statement had shown consistently positive results and Grant had never stopped paying a dividend. The Grant bankruptcy made the inadequacy of the traditional income statement for assessing liquidity glaringly obvious. This incident was one of the driving forces behind the adoption of the statement of cash flows by the FASB.

1. **Purposes**

   a. The **primary purpose** of a statement of cash flows is to provide information about the cash receipts and payments of an entity during a period. A **secondary purpose** is to provide information about significant operating, investing, and financing activities.

      1) The format reconciles the cash balance at the beginning of the period with the balance at the end of the period.

      2) A statement of cash flows is required as part of a full set of financial statements of most business and not-for-profit entities.

         a) If an entity reports financial position and results of operations, it must present a statement of cash flows for any period for which results of operations are presented.

         b) Cash flow per share is not reported.

   b. The statement of cash flows classifies cash receipts and disbursements into one of three categories.

      1) The proper classification can be generalized as follows:

Classification	Source
Operating activities	Income statement
Investing activities	Investment securities and noncurrent assets
Financing activities	Noncurrent liabilities and equity

2.   **Treatment of Cash and Equivalents**

   a.   If an entity invests its cash in cash equivalents, it should use the descriptive term "cash and cash equivalents." Otherwise, the term "cash" is acceptable.

      1)   Terms such as "funds" or "quick assets" may not be used.

   b.   **Cash equivalents** are readily convertible to known amounts of cash and are so near maturity that they present insignificant risk of changes in value because of changes in interest rates.

      1)   Usually, investments with **original maturities of 3 months or less** qualify. Thus, a 3-year Treasury note meets the definition if purchased 3 months from maturity. However, if the note was purchased 3 years ago, it does not meet the definition when its remaining maturity is 3 months.

         a)   Other examples of cash equivalents are Treasury bills, commercial paper, and money market funds.

   c.   Not all qualifying investments must be classified as cash equivalents. An entity should **consistently apply a policy** for classifying cash equivalents.

      1)   For example, an entity with operations that primarily involve investing in short-term, highly liquid investments may choose not to treat them as cash equivalents.

      2)   Any change in policy is a **change in accounting principle** that requires retrospective application.

3.   **Operating Activities**

   a.   Operating activities are all transactions and other events that are **not financing or investing activities**. In general, operating activities involve the production and delivery of goods and the provision of services. Their effects are normally reported in earnings.

   b.   **Cash inflows from operating activities** include receipts from collection or sale of accounts and notes resulting from sales to customers. They also include cash receipts in the form of interest and dividends, that is, returns on loans, other debt instruments of other entities, and equity securities.

   c.   **Cash outflows from operating activities** include cash payments to buy materials for manufacture of goods for resale, including principal payments on accounts and notes payable to suppliers. They also include cash payments to

      1)   Other suppliers and employees for other goods and services
      2)   Governments for taxes, fees, and penalties
      3)   Creditors for interest

   d.   Cash flows from purchases, sales, and maturities of **trading securities** (securities bought and held primarily for sale in the near term) are classified based on the **nature and purpose** for which the securities were acquired.

   e.   Other operating cash flows result from items acquired for resale:

      1)   Certain securities and other assets carried at market value in a trading account (e.g., by banks, brokers, and dealers in securities) or
      2)   Loans carried at lower of cost or fair value.

4. **Investing Activities**

   a. Investing activities include (1) making and collecting loans; (2) acquiring and disposing of debt or equity instruments; and (3) acquiring and disposing of property, plant, and equipment and other productive assets (but not materials in inventory) held for or used in the production of goods or services.

      1) Investing activities **exclude** transactions in (a) cash equivalents and (b) certain loans or other debt or equity instruments acquired for resale.

      2) Cash flows from purchases, sales, and maturities of **available-for-sale and held-to-maturity securities** are from investing activities. They are reported gross for each classification of security in the cash flows statement.

5. **Financing Activities**

   a. Financing activities include (1) issuance of stock, (2) payment of dividends, (3) treasury stock transactions, (4) incurrence of debt, (5) repayment or other settlement of debt obligations, and (6) the exercise of share options resulting in excess tax benefits.

      1) They also include receiving restricted resources that, by donor stipulation, must be used for long-term purposes.

IFRS Difference

Cash flows from **interest and dividends** should be separately disclosed and consistently classified. Total interest paid is disclosed whether it was expensed or capitalized. A **financial institution** customarily classifies interest paid or received and dividends received as operating items. For **entities other than financial institutions**, the following are the appropriate classifications:

	Operating	Financing	Investing
Interest paid	Yes	Yes	No
Interest received	Yes	No	Yes
Dividends paid	Yes	Yes	No
Dividends received	Yes	No	Yes

Reporting cash flow per share is not prohibited.

An entity must disclose the operating, investing, and financing cash flows of a discontinued operation.

If bank overdrafts that are repayable on demand are part of an entity's cash management program, they are included in cash and cash equivalents, not in cash flows from financing activities.

---

6. **Noncash Investing and Financing Activities**

   a. Information about all **investing and financing activities** that affect recognized assets or liabilities **but not cash flows** must be disclosed. Given only a few transactions, disclosure may be on the same page as the statement of cash flows. Otherwise, they may be reported elsewhere in the statements with a clear reference to the statement of cash flows.

      1) Examples include (a) converting debt to equity, (b) obtaining assets by assuming directly related liabilities or entering into a capital lease, (c) obtaining a building or investment asset by receiving a gift, and (d) exchanging a noncash asset or liability for another.

Stop and review! You have completed the outline for this subunit. Study multiple-choice questions 1 through 7 beginning on page 104.

3.2 STATEMENT OF CASH FLOWS -- CALCULATIONS

Many questions concerning the statement of cash flows ask for the calculation of the appropriate amount. This subunit consists entirely of such questions. Please review Subunit 3.1 before answering the questions.

Stop and review! You have completed the outline for this subunit. Study multiple-choice questions 8 through 14 beginning on page 106.

3.3 DIRECT AND INDIRECT METHODS -- CLASSIFICATIONS

1. **Overview**

    a. The **direct method** is **preferable** but **not required**. However, if it is used, a **reconciliation** of net income and net operating cash flow must be reported in a separate schedule. Because the reconciliation is based on the indirect method, the **indirect method** is used most often in practice. The same net operating cash flow is reported under both methods.

    b. The **direct method** converts the accrual-basis amounts in the income statement to the cash basis. An entity using this method must, at a minimum, report the following:

        1) Cash collected from customers
        2) Interest and dividends received (unless donor-restricted for long-term purposes)
        3) Other operating cash receipts, if any
        4) Cash paid to employees and other suppliers of goods or services
        5) Interest paid
        6) Income taxes paid and the separately reported amount that would have been paid if excess tax benefits from share-based payment arrangements had not been available
        7) Other operating cash payments, if any

    c. The **indirect method** reconciles net income of a business or the change in net assets of a not-for-profit entity to net operating cash flow. It removes the effects of

        1) All **deferrals** of past operating cash flows. Examples are changes in (a) inventory, (b) deferred income, (c) prepaid expenses, and (d) amortization of premium on bonds.
        2) All **accruals** of estimated future operating cash flows. Examples are changes in receivables and payables and amortization of discount on bonds.
        3) Items included in net income that do not affect net operating cash flow. Examples are depreciation and amortization of intangible assets. This category includes items whose cash effects are **investing or financing cash flows**. Examples include gains and losses on (a) sales of property, plant, and equipment; (b) discontinued operations; and (c) debt extinguishment.

2. Indirect Presentation -- Extended Example

EXAMPLE

Dice Corp's balance sheet accounts as of December 31, Year 6 and Year 5, are presented below. Information relating to Year 6 activities is to the left.

Information Relating to Year 6 Activities

- Net income for Year 6 was $690,000.
- Cash dividends of $240,000 were declared and paid in Year 6.
- Equipment costing $400,000 and having a carrying amount of $150,000 was sold on January 1, Year 6, for $150,000 in cash.
- A noncurrent investment was sold in Year 6 for $135,000 in cash.
- 10,000 shares of common stock were issued in Year 6 for $22 a share.
- Current investments consist of Treasury bills maturing on 6/30/Year 7. They are not cash equivalents because their maturities are not 3 months or less and they are not classified as trading securities.
- The provision for Year 6 income taxes was $210,000.
- The accounts receivable balances at the beginning and end of Year 6 were net of allowances for bad debts of $50,000 and $60,000, respectively. Dice wrote off $40,000 of bad debts during Year 6. The only transactions affecting accounts receivable and the allowance were credit sales, collections, write-offs, and recognition of bad debt expense.
- During Year 6, Dice constructed a plant asset. The accumulated expenditures during the year included $11,000 of capitalized interest.
- Dice accounts for its interest in Thrice Corp. under the equity method. Its equity in Thrice's Year 6 earnings was $25,000. At the end of Year 6, Dice received a $10,000 cash dividend from Thrice.

		December 31	
Assets		Year 6	Year 5
Cash		$ 195,000	$ 100,000
Current investments		300,000	0
Accounts receivable (net)		480,000	510,000
Inventory		680,000	600,000
Prepaid expenses		15,000	20,000
Noncurrent investments		215,000	300,000
Plant assets		1,700,000	1,000,000
Accumulated depreciation		(450,000)	(450,000)
Goodwill		90,000	100,000
Total assets		$3,225,000	$2,180,000
Liabilities and Equity			
Accounts payable		$ 825,000	$ 720,000
Interest payable		15,000	10,000
Income tax payable		20,000	30,000
Current debt		325,000	0
Deferred taxes		250,000	300,000
Common stock, $10 par		800,000	700,000
Additional paid-in capital		370,000	250,000
Retained earnings		620,000	170,000
Total liabilities and equity		$3,225,000	$2,180,000

The following computations are required to determine **net cash provided by operations** ($905,000, as shown in the reconciliation on the next page).

a. **Depreciation.** Equipment costing $400,000 and having a carrying amount of $150,000 was sold on January 1, Year 6, for $150,000 in cash. Thus, the debit to accumulated depreciation must have been $250,000 ($400,000 – $150,000). In Year 6, Dice must have recognized $250,000 of depreciation [$450,000 accumulated depreciation at 12/31/Year 6 – ($450,000 accumulated depreciation at 12/31/Year 5 – $250,000 accumulated depreciation on equipment sold]). The depreciation should be added to net income because it is included in the determination of net income but had no cash effect.

Accumulated Depreciation

1/1/Year 6 (Equipment sale)	$250,000	$450,000	12/31/Year 5
		250,000	Exp. Year 6
		$450,000	12/31/Year 6

b. **Goodwill.** The $10,000 ($100,000 at 12/31/Year 5 – $90,000 at 12/31/Year 6) loss on impairment of goodwill should be added to net income because it is included in the determination of net income but had no cash effect.

-- Continued on next page --

EXAMPLE -- Continued

c.   **Inventory and accounts payable.** The adjustment from cost of goods sold (an accrual accounting amount used to calculate net income) to cash paid to suppliers requires two steps: (1) from **cost of goods sold to purchases** and (2) from **purchases to cash paid to suppliers**. The $80,000 ($680,000 – $600,000) increase in inventory is subtracted from net income. It indicates that purchases were $80,000 greater than cost of goods sold. The $105,000 ($825,000 – $720,000) increase in accounts payable is added to net income. It indicates that cash paid to suppliers was $105,000 less than purchases. Thus, the net effect of the changes in inventory and accounts payable is that cash paid to suppliers was $25,000 less than the accrual basis cost of goods sold.

d.   **Accounts receivable.** The net accounts receivable balance declined by $30,000 ($510,000 – $480,000), implying that cash collections exceeded sales. Given that sales, collections, write-offs, and recognition of bad debt expense were the only relevant transactions, $30,000 should be added to net income. Use of the change in net accounts receivable as a reconciliation adjustment is a short-cut method. It yields the same net adjustment to net income as separately including the effects of the change in gross accounts receivable [($510,000 + $50,000 bad debt allowance) – ($480,000 + $60,000 bad debt allowance) = an addition of $20,000], bad debt expense (a noncash item resulting in an addition of $50,000), and bad debt write-offs (a subtraction of $40,000 to reflect that write-offs did not result in collections).

Gross Accounts Receivable				Allowance for Bad Debts		
12/31/Year 5	$560,000	$40,000	Write-offs	Write-offs $40,000	$50,000	12/31/Year 5
($510,000 + $50,000)					50,000	Year 6 expense
	20,000				$60,000	12/31/Year 6
12/31/Year 6	$540,000					
($480,000 + $60,000)						

e.   **Prepaid expenses.** The $5,000 decrease in prepaid expenses signifies that noncash expenses were recognized and should be added back to net income.

f.   **Dividends received.** Earnings of an affiliate accounted for under the equity method are debited to the investment account and credited to net income. A cash dividend from the affiliate is debited to cash and credited to the investment account. Thus, an adjustment of $15,000 ($25,000 earnings – $10,000 cash dividend) for undistributed earnings is necessary.

g.   **Noncurrent investments.** A $100,000 ($300,000 + $25,000 equity in affiliate's earnings – $10,000 cash dividend – $215,000) decrease in the noncurrent investments balance occurred when investments were sold for $135,000. The resulting $35,000 gain was included in net income. The cash effect is classified as a cash flow from an investing activity. (Distinguishing among trading, available-for-sale, and held-to-maturity securities is not necessary because the investment in Thrice Corp. is accounted for under the equity method.) Thus, the $35,000 should be subtracted from net income to remove it from the determination of cash flows from operating activities.

h.   **Interest payable** increased by $5,000, a noncash expense and a reconciling addition to net income. The interest capitalized is ignored for reconciliation purposes because it is not reported as interest expense in the income statement or as interest paid in the statement of cash flows or in related disclosures. The $11,000 of capitalized interest is included in the capitalized cost of the plant asset constructed for Dice.

i.   **Income tax payable** decreased by $10,000, giving rise to a reconciling reduction of net income because tax expense was less than cash paid for taxes.

j.   **Deferred taxes** decreased by $50,000. This reconciling deduction from net income resulted when temporary differences reversed and cash payments for taxes exceeded tax expense.

Reconciliation of Net Income to Net Operating Cash Flow		
Net income for Year 6	$690,000	
Depreciation	250,000	a.
Loss on impairment	10,000	b.
Inventory	(80,000)	c.
Accounts payable	105,000	c.
Accounts receivable (net)	30,000	d.
Prepaid expenses	5,000	e.
Undistributed earnings of an affiliate	(15,000)	f.
Gain on sale of investments	(35,000)	g.
Interest payable	5,000	h.
Income tax payable	(10,000)	i.
Deferred taxes	(50,000)	j.
Net operating cash flow	$905,000	

-- Continued on next page --

EXAMPLE -- Continued

Net Investing Cash Flow

k. The $300,000 increase in current investments indicates that a purchase occurred.

l. The balance sheet further indicates that plant assets increased by $700,000 ($1,700,000 – $1,000,000). Moreover, plant assets (equipment) costing $400,000 were sold. The cost of constructing the plant asset thus equaled the $700,000 increase plus the $400,000 cost of the equipment sold, or $1,100,000.

m. The cash flows from investing activities include the cash effects of the sale of equipment and the noncurrent investments, the purchases of current investments (given that they are not trading securities), and the construction of a plant asset. The equipment was sold for $150,000, and the noncurrent investments were sold for $135,000. Thus, the net cash used in investing activities was $1,115,000.

Purchases:		
Current investments	$ (300,000)	k.
Plant assets	(1,100,000)	l.
Sales:		
Equipment	150,000	m.
Noncurrent investments	135,000	m.
Net investing cash flow	$(1,115,000)	

Net Financing Cash Flow

n. Dice Corp.'s Year 6 financing activities included the issuance of current debt ($325,000 – $0 = $325,000), the issuance of common stock and the recording of additional paid-in capital [($800,000 – $700,000) + ($370,000 – $250,000) = $220,000], and the payment of cash dividends ($240,000). The net cash provided by these financing activities was $305,000.

Current debt	$325,000	n.
Common stock	220,000	n.
Cash dividends	(240,000)	n.
Net financing cash flow	$305,000	

Net change in cash. According to Dice Corp.'s balance sheets, the net change in cash was an increase of $95,000 ($195,000 – $100,000). This amount reconciles with the net cash provided by (used in) operating, investing, and financing activities ($905,000 – $1,115,000 + $305,000 = $95,000).

Noncash financing and investing activities. Dice Corp. had no such transactions in Year 6 to be reported in supplemental disclosures.

Supplemental cash flow disclosures. If Dice Corp. uses the indirect method to present its statement of cash flows, the interest paid (excluding amounts capitalized) and income taxes paid must be reported in related disclosures. Calculation of interest paid requires the income statement data for Dice Corp. (See the following page.) Income taxes paid were $270,000 ($210,000 provision for income taxes + $50,000 decrease in deferred taxes + $10,000 decrease in taxes payable).

Dice Corp.
Statement of Cash Flows -- Indirect Method
for the Year Ended December 31, Year 6
Increase (Decrease) in Cash and Cash Equivalents

Cash flows from operating activities:		Cash flows from investing activities:		
Net income for Year 6	$ 690,000	Proceeds from sale of equipment	$ 150,000	
Depreciation	250,000	Proceeds from sale of noncurrent		
Loss on impairment	10,000	investments	135,000	
Inventory	(80,000)	Payments for current investments	(300,000)	
Accounts payable	105,000	Payments for plant assets	(1,100,000)	
Accounts receivable (net)	30,000	Net cash used in investing activities		$(1,115,000)
Prepaid expenses	5,000			
Undistributed earnings		Cash flows from financing activities:		
of an affiliate	(15,000)	Proceeds from current debt	$ 325,000	
Gain on sale of investments	(35,000)	Proceeds from issuing common		
Interest payable	5,000	stock	220,000	
Income tax payable	(10,000)	Dividends paid	(240,000)	
Deferred taxes	(50,000)	Net cash provided by financing		
Net cash provided by		activities		305,000
operating activities	$ 905,000	Net increase in cash		$ 95,000
		Beginning balance		100,000
		Ending balance		$ 195,000

3. Direct Presentation -- Extended Example

a. An entity may apply a method to derive information about the major classes of gross operating cash receipts and payments at the minimum specified level of detail. This method adjusts **nominal accounts** (revenues and expenses) for changes in related **real accounts** (assets and liabilities).

b. **Collections from customers** may be determined by adjusting sales for the changes in customer receivables. This calculation requires information similar to that used in an indirect presentation to reconcile net income to net operating cash flow: total operating receivables (which are usually separate from those for interest and dividends), bad debt write-offs, and any other noncash entries in customer accounts.

c. **Cash paid to employees and other suppliers** of goods and services may be determined by adjusting cost of goods sold and expenses (excluding interest, income tax, and depreciation) for the changes in inventory, prepaid expenses, and operating payables. This calculation is also similar to the process used in reconciling net income to net operating cash flow. It requires that operating payables and expenses be separated from interest and income tax payable.

EXAMPLE

Additional information. The indirect presentation analysis on the previous page and the additional facts from Dice Corp.'s income statement for the year ended December 31, Year 6, given below, are necessary to derive the amounts of the major classes of gross operating cash inflows and outflows required in a direct presentation.

Income Statement

Sales	$7,810,000	
Cost of sales	(5,500,000)	
Depreciation and impairment loss	(260,000)	
Selling, general, administrative expenses	(1,100,000)	
Interest expense	(140,000)	y.
Equity in earnings of affiliate	25,000	
Gain on sale of investments	35,000	
Interest income	30,000	x.
Income before income taxes	$ 900,000	
Income tax expense	(210,000)	z.
Net income	$ 690,000	

Cash collected from customers is derived as follows:

o. The beginning and ending balances ($510,000 and $480,000, respectively) of accounts receivable were net of $50,000 and $60,000 bad debt allowances, respectively. Hence, the beginning gross receivables balance was $560,000, and the ending balance was $540,000. If the direct presentation is used, the change in gross receivables, write-offs, and bad debt expense must be reported separately. The shortcut or net method is inappropriate because bad debt expense is not included in the determination of sales. It is included in selling, general, and administrative expenses and must be subtracted in the derivation of cash paid to employees and suppliers as calculated on the next page.

p. Subtracting write-offs eliminates noncash credits to accounts receivable.

q. An increase in receivables signifies cash collected was less than sales.

Sales		$7,810,000	
Change in balance of receivables:			
Gross receivables (12/31/Year 5)	$560,000		o.
Write-offs	(40,000)		d.
Gross receivables (12/31/Year 6)	(540,000)		o.
Increase in gross receivables		(20,000)	q.
Cash received from customers		$7,790,000	r.

-- Continued on next page --

EXAMPLE -- Continued

Cash paid to employees and suppliers is derived as follows:

s. Bad debt expense is a noncash item included in selling, general, and administrative expenses and should be deducted from them. Given that the bad debt allowance increased by $10,000 ($60,000 – $50,000) despite $40,000 of write-offs, bad debt expense must have been $50,000.

t. An increase in inventory means that purchases exceeded cost of sales.

u. An increase in accounts payable indicates that purchases exceeded cash paid to suppliers. This amount is subtracted.

v. A decrease in prepaid expenses signifies recognition of a noncash expense related to a prior-period cash payment. Accordingly, this amount is subtracted.

Cost of sales		$5,500,000
Selling, general, administrative expenses	$1,100,000	
Noncash expense (bad debts)	(50,000) s.	
Net cash expenses		1,050,000
Inventory (12/31/Year 5)	$ (600,000) c.	
Inventory (12/31/Year 6)	680,000 c.	
Net inventory increase from operations		80,000
Accounts payable (12/31/Year 5)	$ 720,000 c.	
Accounts payable (12/31/Year 6)	(825,000) c.	
Net increase in accounts payable		(105,000)
Prepaid expenses (12/31/Year 5)	$ (20,000) e.	
Prepaid expenses (12/31/Year 6)	15,000 e.	
Net decrease in prepaid expenses		(5,000)
Cash paid to employees and suppliers		$6,520,000 w.

Dice Corp.
Statement of Cash Flows -- Direct Method
for the Year Ended December 31, Year 6
Increase (Decrease) in Cash and Cash Equivalents

Cash flows from operating activities:		
Cash collected from customers	$7,790,000 r.	
Cash paid to employees and suppliers	(6,520,000) w.	
Dividend from affiliate	10,000 ff.	
Interest received	30,000 xx.	
Interest paid	(135,000) yy.	
Income taxes paid	(270,000) zz.	
Net cash provided by operating activities		$ 905,000 (a)
Cash flows from investing activities:		
Proceeds from sale of equipment	$ 150,000	
Proceeds from sale of noncurrent investments	135,000	
Payments for current investments	(300,000)	
Payments for plant assets	(1,100,000)	
Net cash used in investing activities		(1,115,000) (b)
Cash flows from financing activities:		
Proceeds from current debt	$ 325,000	
Proceeds from issuing common stock	220,000	
Dividends paid	(240,000)	
Net cash provided by financing activities		305,000 (b)
Net increase in cash		$ 95,000 (c)
Beginning balance		100,000 (c)
Ending balance		$ 195,000 (c)

The difference between the direct and indirect method is the determination of operating cash flows. Compare the direct method format presented above with the indirect method format on page 101. The only difference is in how the $905,000 of cash provided by operations is calculated.

-- Continued on next page --

EXAMPLE -- Continued

Notes:

ff. The dividend received, not the amount of equity-based earnings recognized in net income, is included.

xx. Interest income was $30,000. Given no interest receivable, cash interest collected must also have been $30,000.

yy. Interest capitalized is not considered in determining interest paid because it is included in payments for plant assets, not in interest expense ($140,000) reported in the income statement. Given that interest payable increased by $5,000, interest paid must have been $135,000. No supplemental disclosure of interest paid or of income taxes paid is necessary because the amounts are reported directly in this format.

zz. Income taxes paid equaled tax expense ($210,000), plus the decrease in deferred taxes ($50,000), plus the decrease in taxes payable ($10,000), or $270,000.

(a) This amount is the same regardless of the statement format used.

(b) These sections are the same regardless of the method of presentation.

(c) The statement of cash flows (direct or indirect method) reconciles the beginning and ending balances of cash (including cash equivalents).

Dice Corp. had no noncash investing and financing transactions to report in supplemental disclosures.

---

    d.   If the **direct method** is used, the reconciliation of net income to net operating cash flow (the operating section of the indirect method format) must be provided in a separate schedule. The FASB's example presents this schedule immediately beneath the statement.

        1)   If the **indirect method** is used, the reconciliation may be either reported in the statement of cash flows or provided in a separate schedule.

IFRS Difference

An entity must disclose comparative information for the previous period for all amounts reported in the current financial statements.

Stop and review! You have completed the outline for this subunit. Study multiple-choice questions 15 through 21 beginning on page 109.

3.4 DIRECT AND INDIRECT METHODS -- CALCULATIONS

Many questions concerning the direct and indirect methods for reporting operating cash flows ask for the calculation of the appropriate amount. This subunit consists entirely of such questions. Please review Subunit 3.3 before answering the questions.

Stop and review! You have completed the outline for this subunit. Study multiple-choice questions 22 through 29 beginning on page 111.

QUESTIONS
3.1 Statement of Cash Flows -- Classifications

1. In accordance with IFRS, in the statement of cash flows, the payment of cash dividends appears in the <List A> activities section as a <List B> of cash.

	List A	List B
A.	Operating or investing	Source
B.	Operating or financing	Use
C.	Investing or financing	Use
D.	Investing	Source

Answer (B) is correct.

    REQUIRED: The treatment of cash dividends in a statement of cash flows under IFRS.

    DISCUSSION: According to IAS 7, dividends paid may be treated as a cash outflow from financing activities because they are a cost of obtaining resources from owners. However, they also may be treated as operating items to help determine the entity's ability to pay dividends from operating cash flows.

2. The primary purpose of a statement of cash flows is to provide relevant information about

A. Differences between net income and associated cash receipts and disbursements.

B. An entity's ability to generate future positive net cash flows.

C. The cash receipts and cash disbursements of an entity during a period.

D. An entity's ability to meet cash operating needs.

Answer (C) is correct.
REQUIRED: The primary purpose of a statement of cash flows.
DISCUSSION: The primary purpose is to provide information about the cash receipts and cash payments of a business entity during a period. This information helps investors, creditors, and other users to assess the entity's ability to generate net cash inflows, meet its obligations, pay dividends, and secure external financing. It also helps assess reasons for the differences between net income and net cash flow and the effects of cash and noncash financing and investing activities.

3. Mend Co. purchased a 3-month U.S. Treasury bill. Mend's policy is to treat as cash equivalents all highly liquid investments with an original maturity of 3 months or less when purchased. How should this purchase be reported in Mend's statement of cash flows?

A. As an outflow from operating activities.

B. As an outflow from investing activities.

C. As an outflow from financing activities.

D. Not reported.

Answer (D) is correct.
REQUIRED: The effect of purchasing a 3-month T-bill.
DISCUSSION: Cash equivalents are short-term, highly liquid investments that are both readily convertible to known amounts of cash and so near maturity that they present insignificant risk of changes in value because of changes in interest rates. Moreover, cash equivalents ordinarily include only investments with original maturities to the holder of 3 months or less. The T-bill is therefore a cash equivalent and has no effect on the statement of cash flows.

4. In a statement of cash flows, interest payments to lenders and other creditors should be classified as cash outflows for

A. Operating activities.

B. Borrowing activities.

C. Lending activities.

D. Financing activities.

Answer (A) is correct.
REQUIRED: The classification of interest payments to lenders and other creditors.
DISCUSSION: Cash receipts from sales of goods and services, interest on loans, and dividends on equity securities are from operating activities. Cash payments to (1) suppliers for inventory; (2) employees for services; (3) other suppliers for other goods and services; (4) governments for taxes, duties, fines, and fees; and (5) lenders for interest are also from operating activities.
Answer (B) is incorrect. Borrowing is not among the three categories of cash flows. Answer (C) is incorrect. Lending is not among the three categories of cash flows. Answer (D) is incorrect. Financing activities include (1) issuance of stock, (2) payment of distributions to owners, (3) treasury stock transactions, (4) issuance of debt, (5) repayment or other settlement of debt obligations, and (6) receipt of resources donor-restricted for long-term purposes.

5. In accordance with IFRS, which combination below explains the effect of credit card interest incurred and paid during the period on (1) equity on the statement of financial position and (2) the statement of cash flows?

	(1) Effect on Equity on Balance Sheet	(2) Reflected on Statement of Cash Flows as a(n)
A.	Decrease	Investing outflow
B.	Decrease	Operating or financing outflow
C.	No effect	Financing or investing outflow
D.	No effect	Operating outflow

Answer (B) is correct.
REQUIRED: The effect of interest paid on the balance sheet and cash flow statement under IFRS.
DISCUSSION: Interest incurred is classified as interest expense on the income statement, which in turn reduces equity on the statement of financial position by reducing retained earnings. According to IAS 7, cash payments for interest made by an entity that is not a financial institution may be classified on the statement of cash flows as an outflow of cash from operating or financing activities.
Answer (A) is incorrect. Interest payments are classified as an operating or financing outflow on the statement of cash flows. Answer (C) is incorrect. Credit card interest charges reduce equity. Answer (D) is incorrect. Credit card interest charges reduce equity.

6. A company acquired a building, paying a portion of the purchase price in cash and issuing a mortgage note payable to the seller for the balance. In a statement of cash flows, what amount is included in investing activities for this transaction?

A. Cash payment.

B. Acquisition price.

C. Zero.

D. Mortgage amount.

Answer (A) is correct.

REQUIRED: The amount included in investing activities.

DISCUSSION: Investing activities include the lending of money; the collection of those loans; and the acquisition, sale, or other disposal of (1) loans and other securities that are not cash equivalents and that have not been acquired specifically for resale and (2) property, plant, equipment, and other productive assets. Thus, the portion of the purchase price paid in cash to acquire a building (a productive asset) should be classified as a cash flow from an investing activity. To provide the necessary information about all investing and financing activities, those not involving cash receipts or cash payments during the accounting period should be reported in a separate schedule and not in the statement of cash flows. The issuance of a mortgage as part of the acquisition price of a building does not involve cash. It is therefore classified as a noncash financing activity and is included in a separate schedule.

Answer (B) is incorrect. Only the actual cash flow is reported in the statement of cash flows. Answer (C) is incorrect. The cash paid is a cash flow from an investing activity. Answer (D) is incorrect. The repayment of the mortgage principal is a financing cash flow.

7. Which of the following items is included in the financing activities section of the statement of cash flows?

A. Cash effects of transactions involving making and collecting loans.

B. Cash effects of acquiring and disposing of investments and property, plant, and equipment.

C. Cash effects of transactions obtaining resources from owners and providing them with a return on their investment.

D. Cash effects of transactions that enter into the determination of net income.

Answer (C) is correct.

REQUIRED: The item included in the financing section of the statement of cash flows.

DISCUSSION: Financing activities include (1) issuance of stock, (2) payment of dividends, (3) treasury stock transactions, (4) issuance of debt, (5) obtaining cash from creditors and repayment or other settlement of debt obligations, (6) the exercise of share options resulting in excess tax benefits, and (7) receiving resources that are donor-restricted to long-term use.

Answer (A) is incorrect. The cash effects of making and collecting loans are reported under investing activities. Answer (B) is incorrect. The cash effects of transactions of acquiring and disposing of investments and property, plant, and equipment are reported under investing activities. Answer (D) is incorrect. The cash effects of transactions that enter into the determination of net income ordinarily are reported under operating activities.

3.2 Statement of Cash Flows -- Calculations

8. The following information is available from Sand Corp.'s accounting records for the year ended December 31, Year 6:

Cash received from customers	$870,000
Rent received	10,000
Cash paid to suppliers and employees	510,000
Taxes paid	110,000
Cash dividends paid	30,000

Net cash flow provided by operations for Year 6 was

A. $220,000

B. $230,000

C. $250,000

D. $260,000

Answer (D) is correct.

REQUIRED: The net cash flow provided by operations.

DISCUSSION: Payment of dividends is a financing activity. All other transactions listed are cash flows from operating activities. Accordingly, the net cash flow provided by operations is $260,000 ($870,000 + $10,000 − $510,000 − $110,000).

Answer (A) is incorrect. This figure includes the $30,000 dividend payment as an operating, not a financing, cash outflow and omits the rent received. Answer (B) is incorrect. This figure includes the $30,000 dividend payment as an operating, not a financing, cash outflow. Answer (C) is incorrect. This figure omits the rent received.

9. Paper Co. had net income of $70,000 during the year. Dividend payment was $10,000. The following information is available:

Mortgage repayment	$20,000
Available-for-sale securities purchased	10,000 increase
Bonds payable-issued	50,000 increase
Inventory	40,000 increase
Accounts payable	30,000 decrease

What amount should Paper report as net cash provided by operating activities in its statement of cash flows for the year?

A. $0

B. $10,000

C. $20,000

D. $30,000

Answer (A) is correct.
    REQUIRED: The net cash provided by operating activities.
    DISCUSSION: The payment of dividends, the repayment of debt (the mortgage), and the issuance of debt (the bonds) are financing activities. The purchase of debt or equity instruments the (available-for-sale securities) is an investing activity. Operating cash flows exclude these financing and investing cash flows. Moreover, these items do not affect net income. Consequently, net cash provided by operating activities can be determined by adjusting net income for the changes in inventory and accounts payable. To account for the difference between cost of goods sold (a deduction from income) and cash paid to suppliers, a two-step adjustment is necessary. The difference between cost of goods sold and purchases is the change in inventory. The difference between purchases and the amount paid to suppliers is the change in accounts payable. Accordingly, the conversion of cost of goods sold to cash paid to suppliers requires subtracting the inventory increase and the accounts payable decrease. The net cash provided by operating activities is therefore $0 ($70,000 net income – $40,000 inventory increase – $30,000 accounts payable decrease).
    Answer (B) is incorrect. The amount of $10,000 is the difference between the bond proceeds and the sum of the cash outflows for dividends paid, the mortgage repayment, and the securities purchase. Answer (C) is incorrect. The amount of $20,000 equals net income minus the bond proceeds. Answer (D) is incorrect. The amount of $30,000 equals net income minus the inventory increase.

10. New England Co. had net cash provided by operating activities of $351,000, net cash used by investing activities of $420,000, and cash provided by financing activities of $250,000. New England's cash balance was $27,000 on January 1. During the year, there was a sale of land that resulted in a gain of $25,000, and proceeds of $40,000 were received from the sale. What was New England's cash balance at the end of the year?

A. $27,000

B. $40,000

C. $208,000

D. $248,000

Answer (C) is correct.
    REQUIRED: The cash balance at year end.
    DISCUSSION: The cash balance at year end is $208,000 ($27,000 on January 1 + $351,000 provided by operations – $420,000 used by investing activities + $250,000 provided by financing activities). The proceeds from the land sale are included in the calculation of the cash used by investing activities.
    Answer (A) is incorrect. The amount of $27,000 represents the cash balance on January 1. Answer (B) is incorrect. The amount of $40,000 equals the proceeds from the sale of land. Answer (D) is incorrect. The amount of $248,000 results from double-counting the land sale proceeds.

11. Green Co. had the following equity transactions at December 31:

Cash proceeds from sale of investment in Blue Co. (carrying value - $60,000)	$75,000
Dividends received on Grey Co. stock	10,500
Common stock purchased from Brown Co.	38,000

What amount should Green recognize as net cash from investing activities in its statement of cash flows at December 31?

A. $37,000

B. $47,500

C. $75,000

D. $85,500

Answer (A) is correct.
    REQUIRED: The amount of net cash flows from investing activities.
    DISCUSSION: Assuming the investment in Blue was classified as available-for-sale, not trading, the sale proceeds ($75,000) are a cash inflow from an investing activity. Cash outflows from acquiring equity instruments ($38,000) also are from an investing activity. But cash inflows from operating activities include cash receipts in the form of dividends ($10,500). Thus, the net cash flow from investing activities is $37,000 ($75,000 – $38,000).
    Answer (B) is incorrect. Cash inflows from operating activities include cash receipts in the form of dividends ($10,500). Answer (C) is incorrect. The purchase of common stock, a cash outflow of $38,000, is an investing activity. Answer (D) is incorrect. The purchase of common stock, a cash outflow of $38,000, is an investing activity. Cash inflows from operating activities include cash receipts in the form of dividends ($10,500).

Questions 12 and 13 are based on the following information. Kollar Corp.'s transactions for the year ended December 31, Year 6, included the following:

- Purchased real estate for $550,000 cash borrowed from a bank
- Sold available-for-sale securities for $500,000
- Paid dividends of $600,000
- Issued 500 shares of common stock for $250,000

- Purchased machinery and equipment for $125,000 cash
- Paid $450,000 toward a bank loan
- Reduced accounts receivable by $100,000
- Increased accounts payable by $200,000

12. Kollar's net cash used in investing activities for Year 6 was

A. $675,000

B. $375,000

C. $175,000

D. $50,000

Answer (C) is correct.
REQUIRED: The net cash used in investing activities.
DISCUSSION: The purchases of real estate and of machinery and equipment were uses of cash in investing activities. The sale of available-for-sale securities provided cash from an investing activity. Consequently, the net cash used in investing activities was $175,000 ($550,000 – $500,000 + $125,000). The reduction in accounts receivable and the increase in accounts payable were operating activities.
Answer (A) is incorrect. The amount of $675,000 omits the sale of securities. Answer (B) is incorrect. The amount of $375,000 results from either (1) improperly including the increase in accounts payable, a noncash transaction, as a use of cash in an investing activity ($550,000 cash borrowed – $500,000 sale of securities + $125,000 purchase of machinery + $200,000 increase in accounts payable) or (2) improperly calculating the net cash used in investing activities as the difference between the $500,000 sale of securities and the $125,000 purchase of machinery. Answer (D) is incorrect. The amount of $50,000 does not include the purchase of machinery and equipment.

13. Kollar's net cash used in financing activities for Year 6 was

A. $50,000

B. $250,000

C. $450,000

D. $500,000

Answer (B) is correct.
REQUIRED: The net cash used in financing activities.
DISCUSSION: The dividend payment and the payment of the bank loan were uses of cash in financing activities. The borrowing from the bank and the issuance of stock provided cash from financing activities. Thus, the net cash used in financing activities was $250,000 ($600,000 – $550,000 – $250,000 + $450,000).
Answer (A) is incorrect. The amount of $50,000 omits the issuance of stock and the repayment of the bank loan. Answer (C) is incorrect. The amount of $450,000 results from including the increase in accounts payable, a noncash transaction, as a use of cash in a financing activity. Answer (D) is incorrect. The amount of $500,000 excludes the issuance of stock.

14. Fara Co. reported bonds payable of $47,000 on December 31, Year 1, and $50,000 on December 31, Year 2. During Year 2, Fara issued $20,000 of bonds payable in exchange for equipment. There was no amortization of bond premium or discount during the year. What amount should Fara report in its Year 2 statement of cash flows for redemption of bonds payable?

A. $3,000

B. $17,000

C. $20,000

D. $23,000

Answer (B) is correct.
REQUIRED: The amount reported in the statement of cash flows for redemption of bonds payable.
DISCUSSION: Assuming no amortization of premium or discount, the net amount of bonds payable reported was affected solely by the issuance of bonds for equipment and the redemption of bonds. Given that $20,000 of bonds were issued and that the amount reported increased by only $3,000, $17,000 of bonds must have been redeemed. This amount should be reported in the statement of cash flows as a cash outflow from a financing activity.
Answer (A) is incorrect. The amount of $3,000 equals the increase in bonds payable. Answer (C) is incorrect. The amount of bonds issued is $20,000. Answer (D) is incorrect. The amount of $23,000 is the sum of the bonds issued and the increase in bonds payable.

3.3 Direct and Indirect Methods -- Classifications

15. Payne Co. prepares its statement of cash flows using the indirect method. Payne's unamortized bond discount account decreased by $25,000 during the year. How should Payne report the change in unamortized bond discount in its statement of cash flows?

A. As a financing cash inflow.

B. As a financing cash outflow.

C. As an addition to net income in the operating activities section.

D. As a subtraction from net income in the operating activities section.

Answer (C) is correct.

REQUIRED: The reporting of a change in unamortized bond discount in a statement of cash flows.

DISCUSSION: The amortization of bond discount (debit interest expense, credit discount) is a noncash item that reduces net income. In a statement of cash flows prepared using the indirect method, net operating cash flow is determined by adjusting net income. The indirect method begins with net income and then removes the effects of (1) deferrals of past operating cash receipts and payments, (2) accruals of estimated future operating cash receipts and payments, and (3) net income items not affecting operating cash flows. Thus, bond discount amortization should be added to net income in the reconciliation to net operating cash flow.

Answer (A) is incorrect. Amortization of bond discount is not a cash flow. Answer (B) is incorrect. Amortization of bond discount is not a cash flow. Answer (D) is incorrect. The amortization of bond discount is added to net income.

16. Dee's inventory and accounts payable balances at December 31, Year 2, increased over their December 31, Year 1, balances. Should these increases be added to or deducted from cash payments to suppliers to arrive at Year 2 cost of goods sold?

	Increase in Inventory	Increase in Accounts Payable
A.	Added to	Deducted from
B.	Added to	Added to
C.	Deducted from	Deducted from
D.	Deducted from	Added to

Answer (D) is correct.

REQUIRED: The effect of increases in inventory and accounts payable on the reconciliation of cash payments to suppliers to cost of goods sold.

DISCUSSION: A two-step adjustment is needed. The first step is to adjust for the difference between cash paid to suppliers and purchases. Because accounts payable increased, purchases must have been greater than cash paid to suppliers. Thus, the increase in accounts payable is an addition. The second step adjusts for the difference between purchases and cost of goods sold. Given that inventory increased, purchases must have exceeded cost of goods sold. Hence, the increase in inventories is a subtraction.

17. How should the amortization of bond discount on long-term debt be reported in a statement of cash flows prepared using the indirect method?

A. As a financing activities inflow.

B. As a financing activities outflow.

C. In operating activities as a deduction from income.

D. In operating activities as an addition to income.

Answer (D) is correct.

REQUIRED: The reporting of bond discount amortization in a statement of cash flows prepared using the indirect method.

DISCUSSION: Amortization of bond discount on long-term debt is presented in the operating activities section as an addition to net income. It is a noncash expense.

Answer (A) is incorrect. Amortization of bond discount is a noncash item presented in operating activities as an addition to income. Answer (B) is incorrect. Amortization of bond discount is a noncash item presented in operating activities as an addition to income. Answer (C) is incorrect. Amortization of bond discount is an addition to income. It is a noncash expense.

18. The statement of cash flows may be presented in either a direct or an indirect (reconciliation) format. In which of these formats would cash collected from customers be presented as a gross amount?

	Direct	Indirect
A.	No	No
B.	No	Yes
C.	Yes	Yes
D.	Yes	No

Answer (D) is correct.

REQUIRED: The format in which cash collected from customers would be presented as a gross amount.

DISCUSSION: The statement of cash flows may report cash flows from operating activities in either an indirect (reconciliation) or a direct format. The direct format reports the major classes of operating cash receipts and cash payments as gross amounts. The indirect presentation reconciles net income to the same amount of net cash flow from operations that would be determined in accordance with the direct method. To arrive at net operating cash flow, the indirect method adjusts net income by removing the effects of (1) all deferrals of past operating cash receipts and payments, (2) all accruals of expected future operating cash receipts and payments, (3) all financing and investing activities, and (4) all noncash operating transactions.

19. With respect to the content and form of the statement of cash flows,

A. The pronouncements covering the cash flow statement encourage the use of the indirect method.

B. The indirect method adjusts ending retained earnings to reconcile it to net cash flows from operations.

C. The direct method of reporting cash flows from operating activities includes disclosing the major classes of gross cash receipts and gross cash payments.

D. The reconciliation of the net income to net operating cash flow need not be presented when using the direct method.

Answer (C) is correct.
REQUIRED: The true statement about the content and form of the statement of cash flows.
DISCUSSION: Use of the direct method of reporting major classes of operating cash receipts and payments is encouraged, but the indirect method may be used. The minimum disclosures of operating cash flows under the direct method are (1) cash collected from customers, (2) interest and dividends received (unless donor-restricted to long-term purposes), (3) other operating cash receipts, (4) cash paid to employees and other suppliers of goods or services, (5) interest paid, (6) income taxes paid (and the amount that would have been paid if excess tax benefits from share-based payment arrangements had not been available), and (7) other operating cash payments.
Answer (A) is incorrect. Use of the direct method is encouraged. Answer (B) is incorrect. The indirect method reconciles net income with the net cash flow from operations. Answer (D) is incorrect. The reconciliation is required regardless of the method used.

Question 20 is based on the following information. Royce Company had the following transactions during the fiscal year ended December 31, Year 2:

- Accounts receivable decreased from $115,000 on December 31, Year 1, to $100,000 on December 31, Year 2.
- Royce's board of directors declared dividends on December 31, Year 2, of $.05 per share on the 2.8 million shares outstanding, payable to shareholders of record on January 31, Year 3. The company did not declare or pay dividends for fiscal Year 1.

- Sold a truck with a net carrying amount of $7,000 for $5,000 cash, reporting a loss of $2,000.
- Paid interest to bondholders of $780,000.
- The cash balance was $106,000 on December 31, Year 1, and $284,000 on December 31, Year 2.

---

20. Royce Company uses the direct method to prepare its statement of cash flows at December 31, Year 2. The interest paid to bondholders is reported in the

A. Financing section, as a use or outflow of cash.

B. Operating section, as a use or outflow of cash.

C. Investing section, as a use or outflow of cash.

D. Debt section, as a use or outflow of cash.

Answer (B) is correct.
REQUIRED: The proper reporting of interest paid.
DISCUSSION: Payment of interest on debt is considered an operating activity, although repayment of debt principal is a financing activity.
Answer (A) is incorrect. Interest paid on bonds is an operating cash flow. Answer (C) is incorrect. Investing activities include the lending of money and the acquisition, sale, or other disposal of securities that are not cash equivalents and the acquisition, sale, or other disposal of long-lived productive assets. Answer (D) is incorrect. The statement does not have a debt section.

---

21. Depreciation expense is added to net income under the indirect method of preparing a statement of cash flows in order to

A. Report all assets at gross carrying amount.

B. Ensure depreciation has been properly reported.

C. Reverse noncash charges deducted from net income.

D. Calculate net carrying amount.

Answer (C) is correct.
REQUIRED: The reason depreciation expense is added to net income under the indirect method.
DISCUSSION: The indirect method begins with net income and then removes the effects of (1) deferrals of past operating cash receipts and payments, (2) accruals of estimated future operating cash receipts and payments, and (3) net income items not affecting operating cash flows (e.g., depreciation).
Answer (A) is incorrect. Assets other than cash are not shown on the statement of cash flows. Answer (B) is incorrect. Depreciation is recorded on the income statement. On the statement of cash flows, depreciation is added back to net income because it was previously deducted on the income statement. Answer (D) is incorrect. Net carrying amount of assets is shown on the balance sheet, not the statement of cash flows.

3.4 Direct and Indirect Methods -- Calculations

Questions 22 and 23 are based on the following information. Flax Corp. uses the direct method to prepare its statement of cash flows. Flax's trial balances at December 31, Year 6 and Year 5, are as follows:

	December 31		Credits	Year 6	Year 5
	Year 6	Year 5	Allowance for uncollectible accounts	$ 1,300	$ 1,100
Debits			Accumulated depreciation	16,500	15,000
Cash	$ 35,000	$ 32,000	Trade accounts payable	25,000	17,500
Accounts receivable	33,000	30,000	Income taxes payable	21,000	27,100
Inventory	31,000	47,000	Deferred income taxes	5,300	4,600
Property, plant, & equipment	100,000	95,000	8% callable bonds payable	45,000	20,000
Unamortized bond discount	4,500	5,000	Common stock	50,000	40,000
Cost of goods sold	250,000	380,000	Additional paid-in capital	9,100	7,500
Selling expenses	141,500	172,000	Retained earnings	44,700	64,600
General and administrative			Sales	538,800	778,700
expenses	137,000	151,300		$756,700	$976,100
Interest expense	4,300	2,600			
Income tax expense	20,400	61,200			
	$756,700	$976,100			

• Flax purchased $5,000 in equipment during Year 6.

• Flax allocated one-third of its depreciation expense to selling expenses and the remainder to general and administrative expenses, which include the provision for uncollectible accounts.

22. What amount should Flax report in its statement of cash flows for the year ended December 31, Year 6, for cash collected from customers?

A. $541,800
B. $541,600
C. $536,000
D. $535,800

Answer (D) is correct.
REQUIRED: The cash collected from customers.
DISCUSSION: Collections from customers equal sales minus the increase in gross accounts receivable, or $535,800 ($538,800 – $33,000 + $30,000).
Answer (A) is incorrect. The amount of $541,800 results from adding the increase in receivables. Answer (B) is incorrect. The amount of $541,600 results from adding the increase in receivables and subtracting the increase in the allowance for uncollectible accounts, that is, from adding net accounts receivable. Answer (C) is incorrect. The amount of $536,000 results from subtracting net accounts receivable, a procedure that is appropriate when reconciling net income to net operating cash flow, not sales to cash collected from customers.

23. What amount should Flax report in its statement of cash flows for the year ended December 31, Year 6, for cash paid for income taxes?

A. $25,800
B. $20,400
C. $19,700
D. $15,000

Answer (A) is correct.
REQUIRED: The cash paid for income taxes.
DISCUSSION: To reconcile income tax expense to cash paid for income taxes, a two-step adjustment is needed. The first step is to add the decrease in income taxes payable. The second step is to subtract the increase in deferred income taxes. Hence, cash paid for income taxes equals $25,800 [$20,400 + ($27,100 – $21,000) – ($5,300 – $4,600)].
Answer (B) is incorrect. Income tax expense is $20,400. Answer (C) is incorrect. Income tax expense minus the increase in deferred income taxes equals $19,700. Answer (D) is incorrect. Subtracting the decrease in income taxes payable and adding the increase in deferred taxes payable results in $15,000.

24. The net income for Cypress, Inc., was $3,000,000 for the year ended December 31. Additional information is as follows:

Depreciation on fixed assets	$1,500,000
Gain from cash sale of land	200,000
Increase in accounts payable	300,000
Dividends paid on preferred stock	400,000

The net cash provided by operating activities in the statement of cash flows for the year ended December 31 is

A. $4,200,000

B. $4,500,000

C. $4,600,000

D. $4,800,000

Answer (C) is correct.

REQUIRED: The net cash provided by operations.

DISCUSSION: Net operating cash flow may be determined by adjusting net income for items that did not affect cash (the indirect method). Depreciation is an expense not directly affecting cash flows that should be added back to net income. The increase in accounts payable is added to net income because it indicates that an expense has been recorded but not paid. The gain on the sale of land is an inflow from an investing, not an operating, activity and should be subtracted from net income. The dividends paid on preferred stock are cash outflows from financing, not operating, activities and do not require an adjustment. Thus, net cash flow from operations is $4,600,000 ($3,000,000 + $1,500,000 − $200,000 + $300,000).

Answer (A) is incorrect. The amount of $4,200,000 equals net cash provided by operating activities minus the $400,000 financing activity. Answer (B) is incorrect. The amount of $4,500,000 equals net income, plus depreciation. Answer (D) is incorrect. The amount of $4,800,000 equals net income, plus depreciation, plus the increase in accounts payable.

Questions 25 and 26 are based on the following information. Royce Company had the following transactions during the fiscal year ended December 31, Year 2:

- Accounts receivable decreased from $115,000 on December 31, Year 1, to $100,000 on December 31, Year 2.
- Royce's board of directors declared dividends on December 31, Year 2, of $.05 per share on the 2.8 million shares outstanding, payable to shareholders of record on January 31, Year 3. The company did not declare or pay dividends for fiscal Year 1.

- Sold a truck with a net carrying amount of $7,000 for $5,000 cash, reporting a loss of $2,000.
- Paid interest to bondholders of $780,000.
- The cash balance was $106,000 on December 31, Year 1, and $284,000 on December 31, Year 2.

25. Royce Company uses the indirect method to prepare its Year 2 statement of cash flows. It reports a(n)

A. Source or inflow of funds of $5,000 from the sale of the truck in the financing section.

B. Use or outflow of funds of $140,000 in the financing section, representing dividends.

C. Deduction of $15,000 in the operating section, representing the decrease in year-end accounts receivable.

D. Addition of $2,000 in the operating section for the $2,000 loss on the sale of the truck.

Answer (D) is correct.

REQUIRED: The correct presentation of an item on a statement of cash flows prepared under the indirect method.

DISCUSSION: The indirect method determines net operating cash flow by adjusting net income for items that did not affect cash. Under the indirect method, the $5,000 cash inflow from the sale of the truck is shown in the investing section. A $2,000 loss was recognized and properly subtracted to determine net income. This loss, however, did not require the use of cash and should be added to net income in the operating section.

Answer (A) is incorrect. The $5,000 inflow is reported in the investing section. Answer (B) is incorrect. No outflow of cash dividends occurred in Year 2. Answer (C) is incorrect. The decrease in receivables should be added to net income.

26. The total of cash provided (used) by operating activities plus cash provided (used) by investing activities plus cash provided (used) by financing activities is

A. Cash provided of $284,000.

B. Cash provided of $178,000.

C. Cash used of $582,000.

D. Equal to net income reported for fiscal year ended December 31, Year 2.

Answer (B) is correct.

REQUIRED: The net total of cash provided and used.

DISCUSSION: The total of cash provided (used) by the three activities (operating, investing, and financing) should equal the increase or decrease in cash for the year. During Year 2, the cash balance increased from $106,000 to $284,000. Thus, the sources of cash must have exceeded the uses by $178,000.

Answer (A) is incorrect. This figure represents the ending cash balance, not the change in the cash balance; it ignores the beginning balance. Answer (C) is incorrect. The cash balance increased during the year. Answer (D) is incorrect. Net income must be adjusted for noncash expenses and other accruals and deferrals.

27. Metro, Inc., reported net income of $150,000 for the current year. Changes occurred in several balance sheet accounts during the current year as follows:

Investment in Videogold, Inc., stock, all of which was acquired in the previous year, carried on the equity basis $5,500 increase
Accumulated depreciation, caused by major repair to projection equipment   2,100 decrease
Premium on bonds payable   1,400 decrease
Deferred income tax liability (long-term)   1,800 increase

In Metro's current year cash flow statement, the reported net cash provided by operating activities should be

A. $150,400

B. $148,300

C. $144,900

D. $142,800

Answer (C) is correct.
REQUIRED: The net cash provided by operating activities.
DISCUSSION: The increase in the equity-based investment reflects the investor's share of the investee's net income after adjustment for dividends received. Hence, it is a noncash revenue and should be subtracted in the reconciliation of net income to net operating cash inflow. A major repair provides benefits to more than one period and therefore should not be expensed. One method of accounting for a major repair is to charge accumulated depreciation if the useful life of the asset has been extended, with the offsetting credit to cash, a payable, etc. However, the cash outflow, if any, is from an investing activity. The item has no effect on net income and no adjustment is necessary. Amortization of bond premium is a noncash income statement item that reduces accrual-basis expenses and therefore must be subtracted from net income to arrive at net cash flow from operating activities. The increase in the deferred tax liability is a noncash item that reduces net income and should be added in the reconciliation. Accordingly, net cash provided by operations is $144,900 ($150,000 – $5,500 – $1,400 + $1,800).
Answer (A) is incorrect. The amount of $150,400 results from omitting the adjustment for the equity-based investment. Answer (B) is incorrect. The amount of $148,300 results from omitting the adjustment for the equity-based investment and improperly subtracting the decrease in accumulated depreciation. Answer (D) is incorrect. The amount of $142,800 results from improperly subtracting the decrease in accumulated depreciation.

28. Savor Co. had $100,000 in cash-basis pretax income for Year 2. At December 31, Year 2, accounts receivable had increased by $10,000 and accounts payable had decreased by $6,000 from their December 31, Year 1, balances. Compared to the accrual basis method of accounting, Savor's cash pretax income is

A. Higher by $4,000.

B. Lower by $4,000.

C. Higher by $16,000.

D. Lower by $16,000.

Answer (D) is correct.
REQUIRED: The relation of cash pretax income and accrual-basis pretax income.
DISCUSSION: The increase in accounts receivable indicates that cash-basis pretax income is $10,000 lower than accrual-basis pretax income. Revenues from the increase in receivables are reported as earned in an earlier period (Year 2) than the future related cash inflows. The decrease in accounts payable indicates that cash-basis pretax income is $6,000 lower than accrual-basis pretax income. The cash outflows related to the increase in payables occurred in Year 2, but the related expense was accrued in Year 1. Hence, cash pretax income is lower than accrual-basis income by $16,000.
Answer (A) is incorrect. The increase in receivables indicates that cash-basis pretax income is lower than accrual-basis pretax income. Answer (B) is incorrect. The decrease in accounts payable indicates that cash-basis pretax income is lower than accrual-basis pretax income. Answer (C) is incorrect. The increases in receivables and payables both indicate that cash-basis pretax income is lower than accrual-basis pretax income.

29. Tam Co. reported the following items in its year-end financial statements:

Capital expenditures $1,000,000
Capital lease payments   125,000
Income taxes paid   325,000
Dividends paid   200,000
Net interest payments   220,000

What amount should Tam report as supplemental disclosures in its statement of cash flows prepared using the indirect method?

A. $545,000

B. $745,000

C. $1,125,000

D. $1,870,000

Answer (A) is correct.
REQUIRED: The amount of supplemental disclosures using the indirect method.
DISCUSSION: If an entity uses the indirect method to present its statement of cash flows, the interest paid (excluding amounts capitalized) and income taxes paid must be disclosed. The sum of these amounts is $545,000 ($220,000 + $325,000).
Answer (B) is incorrect. Dividends paid ($200,000) are not required to be included in the supplemental disclosures when the indirect method is used. Answer (C) is incorrect. The total of capital expenditures and capital lease payments is $1,125,000. Answer (D) is incorrect. The sum of all listed items is $1,870,000.

3.5 PRACTICE SIMULATION

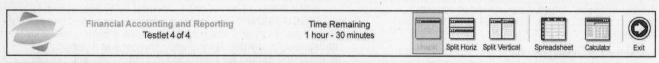

| Financial Accounting and Reporting
Testlet 4 of 4 | Time Remaining
1 hour - 30 minutes | Unsplit | Split Horiz | Split Vertical | Spreadsheet | Calculator | Exit |

DIRECTIONS

Note: If you believe you have encountered a software malfunction, report it to the test center staff immediately.

Navigation

To navigate from task to task, use the controls at the bottom of the screen. Click on the **Next** button to advance to the next task, or the **Previous** button to go to the previous task. To go directly to any task, click on its number.

| ▼ = Reminder | | Directions | 1 2 3 4 5 6 7 | | Previous Next ▶ |

If you would like a reminder to revisit a task, or want to indicate that you are finished with it, click on the reminder flag below the task number. To clear the flag, click on it again. Reminder flags are for your use only – they do not contribute to your score.

Tabs

In this part of the examination, you will be asked to complete various tasks. Every task has one or more **Work Tabs**. Some tasks have one or more **Information Tabs**, others may have none. Every task has a **Help** tab.

If a task has **Information Tabs**, you may use the information in them to complete your responses in the **Work Tabs**.

| Corporate Gain and Basis | Authoritative Literature | Help |

Work tab   Information tab   Help tab

Work Tabs:

- **Work Tabs** are identified with a pencil icon. This is where your responses are expected.
- Each task has one or more **Work Tabs**.
- **Work Tabs** contain directions for completing the task – be sure to read these directions carefully.
- The **Work Tab** name in the example above is for illustration only – yours will differ.
- You must complete all of the **Work Tabs** in each task to receive full credit.

Information Tabs:

- The Authoritative Literature will be provided in all tasks in the AUD, FAR, and REG sections for your reference.
- Your simulation may have one or more additional **Information Tabs**. Like the Authoritative Literature tabs, **Information Tabs** do not have a pencil icon.
- If your task has additional **Information Tabs**, go through each to familiarize yourself with the task content.

Help Tab:

- The **Help Tab** provides assistance with the exam software that is used in this task. For example, if the task is to compose a memorandum, **Help** will provide information about the word processor.

The Toolbar

The toolbar at the top of the screen shows the amount of time remaining for you to complete the tasks. In addition, the following tools are available. Note that only the **Exit** button is displayed when Directions are visible - the others will appear when you begin the tasks.

Click on these buttons to split or unsplit the screen. You can split the screen vertically or horizontally.

Click on this button to display the calculator; click on it again to hide the calculator. To move the calculator, click on the calculator title bar and drag the calculator to the desired location.

Click on this button to use the spreadsheet; click on it again to hide the spreadsheet. To move the spreadsheet, click on the the spreadsheet title bar and drag the spreadsheet to the desired location.

Click on this button to go on to the next part of the examination. You must complete all of the tasks to receive full credit. Once you click on **Exit** and confirm the action, you will NOT be able to return to this testlet.

| ▼ = Reminder | | Directions | 1 2 3 4 5 6 | | Previous Next ▶ |

| Classification of Cash Flows I | Authoritative Literature | Help |

The following condensed trial balance of Gator Co., a publicly held company, has been adjusted except for income tax expense.

Gator Co.
CONDENSED TRIAL BALANCE

	12/31/Year 5 Balances Dr.(Cr.)	12/31/Year 4 Balances Dr.(Cr.)	Net Change Dr.(Cr.)
Cash	$ 413,000	$ 757,000	$(344,000)
Accounts receivable, net	670,000	610,000	60,000
Property, plant, and equipment	1,070,000	995,000	75,000
Accumulated depreciation	(345,000)	(280,000)	(65,000)
Available-for-sale securities	70,000	60,000	10,000
Dividends payable	(25,000)	(10,000)	(15,000)
Income taxes payable	35,000	(150,000)	185,000
Deferred income tax liability	(42,000)	(42,000)	--
Bonds payable	(500,000)	(1,000,000)	500,000
Unamortized premium on bonds	(71,000)	(150,000)	79,000
Common stock	(350,000)	(150,000)	(200,000)
Additional paid-in capital	(430,000)	(375,000)	(55,000)
Retained earnings	(185,000)	(265,000)	80,000
Accumulated other comprehensive income	(10,000)		(10,000)
Sales	(2,420,000)		
Cost of sales	1,863,000		
Selling and administrative expenses	220,000		
Interest income	(14,000)		
Interest expense	46,000		
Depreciation	88,000		
Loss on sale of equipment	7,000		
Extraordinary gain	(90,000)		
	$ 0	$ 0	$ 300,000

Additional Information:

- During Year 5, equipment with an original cost of $50,000 was sold for cash, and equipment costing $125,000 was purchased.
- On January 1, Year 5, bonds with a par value of $500,000 and related premium of $75,000 were redeemed. The $90,000 gain met the criteria for treatment as an extraordinary item. The $1,000 face amount, 10% stated rate bonds had been issued 9 years ago to yield 8%. Interest is payable annually every December 31 for 20 years.
- Gator's tax payments during Year 5 were debited to income taxes payable. Gator recorded a deferred income tax liability of $42,000 based on temporary differences of $120,000 and an enacted tax rate of 35% at December 31, Year 4. Gator's Year 5 financial statement income before income taxes was greater than its Year 5 taxable income, due entirely to taxable temporary differences, by $60,000. Gator's cumulative net taxable temporary differences at December 31, Year 5, were $180,000. Gator's enacted tax rate for Year 5 and future years is 30%.
- The 60,000 shares of common stock, $2.50 par, were outstanding on December 31, Year 4. Gator issued an additional 80,000 shares on April 1, Year 5.
- There were no changes in retained earnings other than dividends declared.

For each of the following, select from the list provided where the specific item should be separately reported on the statement of cash flows prepared using the indirect method. A choice may be used once, more than once, or not at all.

Transaction	Answer
1. Cash paid for income taxes	
2. Cash paid for interest	
3. Redemption of bonds payable	
4. Issuance of common stock	
5. Cash dividends paid	
6. Proceeds from sale of equipment	

Choices
A) Operating
B) Investing
C) Financing
D) Supplementary information
E) Not reported on Gator's statement of cash flows

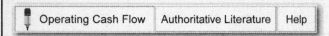

| Operating Cash Flow | Authoritative Literature | Help |

Presented below are the balance sheet accounts of Kern, Inc., as of December 31, Year 2 and Year 1, and their net changes.

	Year 2	Year 1	Net Change
Assets			
Cash	$ 471,000	$ 307,000	$ 164,000
Trading securities, at cost	150,000	250,000	(100,000)
Securities fair value adjustment (trading)	(10,000)	(25,000)	15,000
Accounts receivable, net	550,000	515,000	35,000
Inventories	810,000	890,000	(80,000)
Investments in Word Corp., at equity	420,000	390,000	30,000
Property, plant, and equipment	1,145,000	1,070,000	75,000
Accumulated depreciation	(345,000)	(280,000)	(65,000)
Patent, net	109,000	118,000	(9,000)
Total assets	$3,300,000	$3,235,000	$ 65,000
Liabilities and Shareholders' Equity			
Accounts payable and accrued liabilities	$ 845,000	$ 960,000	$ (115,000)
Note payable, noncurrent	600,000	900,000	(300,000)
Deferred income taxes	190,000	190,000	---
Common stock, $10 par value	850,000	650,000	200,000
Additional paid-in capital	230,000	170,000	60,000
Retained earnings	585,000	365,000	220,000
Total liabilities and stockholders' equity	$3,300,000	$3,235,000	$ 65,000

Additional Information:

- On January 2, Year 2, Kern sold equipment costing $45,000, with a carrying amount of $28,000, for $18,000 cash.
- On March 31, Year 2, Kern sold one of its trading security holdings for $119,000 cash. Cash flows from purchases, sales, and maturities of Kern's trading securities are from investing activities. No other transactions involved trading securities.
- On April 15, Year 2, Kern issued 20,000 shares of its common stock for cash at $13 per share.
- On July 1, Year 2, Kern purchased equipment for $120,000 cash.
- Kern's net income for Year 2 is $305,000. Kern paid a cash dividend of $85,000 on October 26, Year 2.
- Kern acquired a 20% interest in Word Corp.'s common stock during Year 1. There was no goodwill attributable to the investment, which is appropriately accounted for by the equity method. Word reported net income of $150,000 for the year ended December 31, Year 2. No dividend was paid on Word's common stock during Year 2.

For the following operating cash flow items, enter in the shaded cells the amounts that will be reported in Kern's statement of cash flows.

Cash flows from operating activities:	
Net income	$305,000
Adjustments to reconcile net income to net cash provided by operating activities:	
1. Depreciation	
2. Amortization of patent	
3. Loss on sale of equipment	
4. Equity in income of Word Corp.	
5. Gain on sale of trading securities	
6. Decrease in securities fair value adjustment	
7. Increase in accounts receivable	
8. Decrease in inventories	
9. Decrease in accounts payable and accrued liabilities	
10. Net cash provided by operating activities	

Classification of Cash Flows II | Authoritative Literature | Help

Select from the list provided the best classification for each activity below. Each choice may be used once, more than once, or not at all.

Cash Flow	Answer
1. Purchase of available-for-sale securities	
2. Purchase of land	
3. Dividends distributed to shareholders	
4. Equipment acquired through capital lease	
5. Sale of trading securities	
6. Collection of trade receivables	
7. Equipment acquired through purchase	
8. Dividends received	
9. Interest paid	
10. Interest received	
11. Retirements of bond principal	
12. Issuance of preferred shares	

Classification
A) Operating activity
B) Investing activity
C) Financing activity
D) Noncash investing and financing activities
E) Not reported on statement of cash flows
F) Depends on nature and purpose

| Cash Flows from Investing Activities | Authoritative Literature | Help |

Alaskan Travels, Inc., had the following transactions for the year ended December 31, Year 2:

- Purchased land for $150,000
- Sold trading securities for $139,000
- Purchased available-for-sale securities for $75,000
- Purchased inventory for $22,000
- Paid dividends $80,000
- Purchased treasury stock for $100,000
- Financed an airplane for $275,000, with a 10% down payment
- Settled a note payable for $325,000, which included $15,000 interest
- Converted a $1,000,000 bond payable to common stock
- Issued preferred stock for $550,000

Using the direct method, prepare the investing activities section of the statement of cash flows for Alaskan Travels, Inc., as of December 31, Year 2. In the first column, from the list provided, enter the description for cash flows that are clearly from investing activities. In the second column, enter the amounts that will be reported in the investing activities section of the statement of cash flows.

Cash flows from investing activities:	Net cash provided by (used in) investing activities:
1.	4.
2.	5.
3.	6.
	7.

Choices

A) Payment for purchase of land

B) Proceeds from sale of trading securities

C) Purchase of available-for-sale securities

D) Payment for inventory

E) Dividends paid

F) Payment for treasury stock

G) Payment for purchase of airplane

H) Payment of note payable

I) Conversion of bond to stock

J) Proceeds from issuance of preferred stock

Alaskan Travels, Inc., had the following transactions for the year ended December 31, Year 2:

- Purchased land for $150,000
- Sold trading securities for $139,000
- Purchased available-for-sale securities for $75,000
- Purchased inventory for $22,000
- Paid dividends $80,000
- Purchased treasury stock for $100,000
- Financed an airplane for $275,000, with a 10% down payment
- Settled a note payable for $325,000, which included $15,000 interest
- Converted a $1,000,000 bond payable to common stock
- Issued preferred stock for $550,000

Using the direct method, prepare the operating section of the statement of cash flows for Alaskan Travels, Inc., as of December 31, Year 2. In the first column, from the list provided, enter the description for cash flows that are clearly from financing activities. In the second column, enter the amounts that will be reported in the financing activities section of the statement of cash flows.

Cash flows from financing activities:	Net cash provided by (used in) financing activities:		Choices
1.	5.		A) Payment for purchase of land
2.	6.		B) Proceeds from sale of trading securities
3.	7.		C) Purchase of available-for-sale securities
4.	8.		D) Payment for inventory
	9.		E) Dividends paid
			F) Payment for treasury stock
			G) Payment for purchase of airplane
			H) Payment of note payable
			I) Conversion of bond to stock
			J) Proceeds from issuance of preferred stock

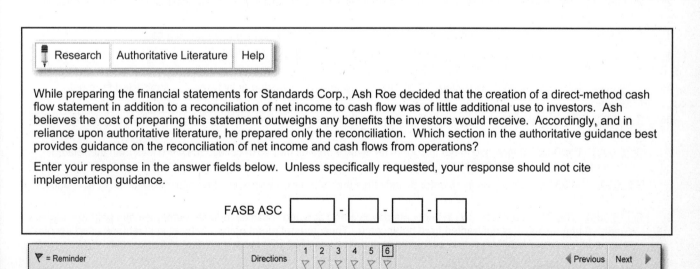

While preparing the financial statements for Standards Corp., Ash Roe decided that the creation of a direct-method cash flow statement in addition to a reconciliation of net income to cash flow was of little additional use to investors. Ash believes the cost of preparing this statement outweighs any benefits the investors would receive. Accordingly, and in reliance upon authoritative literature, he prepared only the reconciliation. Which section in the authoritative guidance best provides guidance on the reconciliation of net income and cash flows from operations?

Enter your response in the answer fields below. Unless specifically requested, your response should not cite implementation guidance.

FASB ASC ☐ - ☐ - ☐ - ☐

Unofficial Answers

1. Classification of Cash Flows I (6 Gradable Items)

1. D) Supplementary information. The indirect method of presentation is used. Thus, income taxes and interest paid must be given in disclosures related to the statement of cash flows.

2. D) Supplementary information. Given that the indirect method of presentation is used, interest paid must be provided in related disclosures. Interest expense is $46,000 (given). This amount does not include premium amortization.

3. C) Financing. Financing activities include the issuance of stock, the payment of dividends and other distributions to owners, receipt of donor-restricted resources to be used for long-term purposes, treasury stock transactions, the issuance of debt, and the repayment or other settlement of debt obligations.

4. C) Financing. The issuance of common stock is a financing activity.

5. C) Financing. The payment of cash dividends is a financing activity.

6. B) Investing. Investing activities include acquiring and disposing of productive assets.

2. Operating Cash Flow (10 Gradable Items)

Cash flows from operating activities:	
Net income	$305,000
Adjustments to reconcile net income to net cash provided by operating activities:	
1. Depreciation	82,000
2. Amortization of patent	9,000
3. Loss on sale of equipment	10,000
4. Equity in income of Word Corp.	(30,000)
5. Gain on sale of trading securities	(19,000)
6. Decrease in securities fair value adjustment	(15,000)
7. Increase in accounts receivable	(35,000)
8. Decrease in inventories	80,000
9. Decrease in accounts payable and accrued liabilities	(115,000)
10. Net cash provided by operating activities	$272,000

1. $82,000. Accumulated depreciation at the end of Year 1 was $280,000. Of this amount, $17,000 ($45,000 – $28,000) was eliminated when equipment was sold at the beginning of Year 2. Thus, the change during the year was $82,000 [$345,000 – ($280,000 – $17,000)]. This amount is the depreciation recognized for Year 2. It is added to net income because it is a noncash expense.

2. $9,000. The net change in the patent's carrying amount is a decrease of $9,000. It is added to net income because it is a noncash expense.

3. $10,000. The loss on the sale of equipment ($28,000 CA – $18,000 = $10,000) is a noncash item.

4. $(30,000). The equity in the income of the investee [($150,000 × 20%) = $30,000] is a noncash revenue item that decreases net income in the reconciliation.

5. $(19,000). The $19,000 gain ($119,000 – $100,000 CA) is from an investing activity, so it is subtracted from net income.

6. $(15,000). The unrealized holding gain ($25,000 – $10,000 year-end FV adjustment) is a noncash item subtracted from net income.

7. $(35,000). The $35,000 increase in net accounts receivable implies that cash collections were less than the related revenues. Thus, it is subtracted from net income.

8. $80,000. The $80,000 decrease in inventories indicates that purchases were less than cost of goods sold. It is added to net income.

9. $(115,000). The $115,000 decrease in accounts payable and accrued liabilities indicates that the cash paid to suppliers exceeded purchases. It is subtracted from net income. Thus, the net effect of the changes in inventories and accounts payable and accrued liabilities is that cash paid to suppliers was $35,000 more than cost of goods sold.

10. $272,000. The net provided in $272,000.

3. Classification of Cash Flows II (12 Gradable Items)

1. __B) Investing activity.__ Cash flows from purchases, sales, and maturities of available-for-sale and held-to-maturity securities are from investing activities. They are reported gross for each classification of security in the cash flows statement.

2. __B) Investing activity.__ Investing activities include (a) making and collecting loans; (b) acquiring and disposing of debt or equity instruments; and (c) acquiring and disposing of property, plant, and equipment and other productive assets (but not materials in inventory) held for or used in the production of goods or services.

3. __C) Financing activity.__ Financing activities include (a) issuance of stock, (b) payment of dividends, (c) treasury stock transactions, (d) incurrence of debt, (e) repayment or other settlement of debt obligations, and (f) the exercise of share options resulting in excess tax benefits.

4. __D) Noncash investing and financing activities.__ Some transactions affect recognized assets or liabilities but not cash flows. They are reported in related disclosures. The acquisition of equipment subject to a capital lease is such an activity.

5. __F) Depends on nature and purpose.__ Cash flows from purchases, sales, and maturities of trading securities (securities bought and held primarily for sale in the near term) are classified based on the nature and purpose for which the securities were acquired.

6. __A) Operating activity.__ Operating activities are all transactions and other events that are not financing or investing activities. In general, they involve producing and delivering goods and providing services. Their effects normally are reported in earnings.

7. __B) Investing activity.__ Investing activities include (a) making and collecting loans; (b) acquiring and disposing of debt or equity instruments; and (c) acquiring and disposing of property, plant, and equipment and other productive assets (but not materials in inventory) held for or used in the production of goods or services.

8. __A) Operating activity.__ Operating activities are all transactions and other events that are not financing or investing activities. In general, they involve producing and delivering goods and providing services. Their effects normally are reported in earnings.

9. __A) Operating activity.__ Operating activities are all transactions and other events that are not financing or investing activities. In general, they involve producing and delivering goods and providing services. Their effects normally are reported in earnings.

10. __A) Operating activity.__ Operating activities are all transactions and other events that are not financing or investing activities. In general, they involve producing and delivering goods and providing services. Their effects normally are reported in earnings.

11. __C) Financing activity.__ Financing activities include (a) issuance of stock, (b) payment of dividends, (c) treasury stock transactions, (d) incurrence of debt, (e) repayment or other settlement of debt obligations, and (f) the exercise of share options resulting in excess tax benefits.

12. __C) Financing activity.__ Financing activities include (a) issuance of stock, (b) payment of dividends, (c) treasury stock transactions, (d) incurrence of debt, (e) repayment or other settlement of debt obligations, and (f) the exercise of share options resulting in excess tax benefits.

4. Cash Flows from Investing Activities (7 Gradable Items)

1. __A) Payment for purchase of land.__ Investing activities include acquiring and disposing of productive assets, such as land.

2. __C) Purchase of available-for-sale securities.__ Cash flows from purchases, sales, and maturities of available-for-sale and held-to-maturity securities are from investing activities. They are reported gross for each classification of security in the cash flows statement.

3. __G) Payment for purchase of airplane.__ Investing activities include acquiring and disposing of productive assets, such as an airplane.

4. __$(150,000).__ The cash outflow from the purchase of land was $150,000.

5. __$(75,000).__ The cash outflow from the purchase of available-for-sale securities was $75,000.

6. __$(27,500).__ The cash outflow from the purchase of the airplane was only $27,500 ($275,000 × 10% down payment). The difference of $247,500 was financed and did not affect cash flow.

7. __$(252,500).__ The cash outflows from investing activities include the purchase of land ($150,000), the purchase of available-for-sale securities ($75,000), and the down payment for the airplane ($27,500). Cash flows from purchases, sales, and maturities of trading securities are classified based on the nature and purpose for which the securities were acquired. The nature and purpose of the trading securities are not defined. Accordingly, their sale is not clearly an investing activity. The cash outflow from the purchase of inventory is from an operating activity. The cash flows related to the payment of dividends, purchase of treasury stock, settlement of debt, and the issuance of stock are from financing activities. The conversion of a bond to common stock was a noncash activity.

5. Cash Flows from Financing Activities (9 Gradable Items)

1. E) Dividends paid. Financing activities include the payment of dividends to shareholders.

2. F) Payment for treasury stock. Financing activities include the purchase of treasury stock.

3. H) Payment of note payable. Financing activities include the repayment or other settlement of debt.

4. J) Proceeds from issuance of preferred stock. Financing activities include the issuance of equity securities.

5. $(80,000). The cash outflow from dividends paid is $80,000.

6. $(100,000). The cash outflow from the purchase of treasury stock is $100,000.

7. $(310,000). The cash outflow for the retirement of debt was $325,000. Of this amount, $310,000 was a financing outflow for payment of principal and $15,000 was an operating outflow for payment of interest.

8. $550,000. The proceeds from the issuance of preferred stock is a cash inflow of $550,000.

9. $60,000. The net cash inflow from financing activities is $60,000 ($550,000 – $80,000 – $100,000 – $310,000). The conversion of the bond payable to common stock is a noncash transaction. The classification of cash flows from purchases, sales, or maturities of trading securities is based on the nature and purpose for which they were acquired. The nature and purpose of the trading securities are not defined. Accordingly, their sale is not clearly a financing activity.

6. Research (1 Gradable Item)

Answer: FASB ASC 230-10-45-28

230-10-45-28 Entities that choose not to provide information about major classes of operating cash receipts and payments by the direct method as encouraged in paragraph 230-10-45-25 shall determine and report the same amount for net cash flow from operating activities indirectly by adjusting net income of a business entity or change in net assets of a not-for-profit entity (NFP) to reconcile it to net cash flow from operating activities (the indirect or reconciliation method). That requires adjusting net income of a business entity or change in net assets of an NFP to remove both of the following:

a. The effects of all deferrals of past operating cash receipts and payments, such as changes during the period in inventory, deferred income, and the like, and all accruals of expected future operating cash receipts and payments, such as changes during the period in receivables and payables. Adjustments to net income of a business entity or change in net assets of an NFP to determine net cash flow from operating activities shall reflect accruals for interest earned but not received and interest incurred but not paid. Those accruals may be reflected in the statement of financial position in changes in assets and liabilities that relate to investing or financing activities, such as loans or deposits. However, interest credited directly to a deposit account that has the general characteristics of cash is a cash outflow of the payor and a cash inflow of the payee when the entry is made.

b. All items that are included in net income that do not affect net cash provided from, or used for, operating activities such as depreciation of property, plant, and equipment and amortization of finite-life intangible assets. This includes all items whose cash effects are related to investing or financing cash flows, such as gains or losses on sales of property, plant, and equipment and discontinued operations (which relate to investing activities), and gains or losses on extinguishment of debt (which relate to financing activities).

Gleim Simulation Grading

Task	Correct Responses		Gradable Items		Score per Task
1	_____	÷	6	=	_____
2	_____	÷	10	=	_____
3	_____	÷	12	=	_____
4	_____	÷	7	=	_____
5	_____	÷	9	=	_____
Research	_____	÷	1	=	_____

Total of Scores per Task		_____
÷ Total Number of Tasks		6
Total Score		_____ %

STUDY UNIT FOUR
INCOME STATEMENT ITEMS

(20 pages of outline)

4.1	Discontinued Operations	123
4.2	Extraordinary Items	125
4.3	Accounting Changes and Error Corrections	126
4.4	Earnings per Share (EPS)	129
4.5	Long-Term Construction Contracts	135
4.6	Revenue Recognition after Delivery	138
4.7	Fair Value Measurements	140
4.8	Practice Simulation	152

The first four subunits of this study unit concern the presentation of certain items on the income statement. The next two subunits address various revenue recognition issues. The seventh subunit addresses the tools available for the application of fair value to financial statement items.

4.1 DISCONTINUED OPERATIONS

1. **Overview**

   a. The operating results of a **discontinued operation** are reported separately in the income statement (or statement of activities of a not-for-profit entity) if **three conditions are met**:

      1) A component of the entity has been **disposed of** or is **classified as held for sale**.

      2) Its operations and cash flows are or will be eliminated from the entity's operations.

      3) The entity will have no significant continuing involvement after disposal.

   b. A **component** of an entity has operations and cash flows that are clearly distinguishable for operating and financial reporting purposes. A component may be a(n)

      1) Reportable segment,
      2) Operating segment,
      3) Reporting unit,
      4) Subsidiary, or
      5) Asset group (a disposal group if it is to be disposed of).

   c. If a long-lived asset (or disposal group) is **not a component**, it cannot be reported as a discontinued operation. In this case, a gain or loss on its sale is included in income from continuing operations before income taxes.

2. **Adjustments**

   a. Amounts reported in discontinued operations may require adjustment. If the adjustment **directly relates** to a **prior-period disposal** of a component, it is **reported currently and separately** in discontinued operations. Its nature and amount are disclosed. Adjustments may include the following:

      1) **Contingencies** arising under the terms of the disposal transaction may be resolved, for example, by purchase price adjustments.

         a) Contingencies directly related to the pre-disposal operations of the component may be resolved. Examples are the seller's environmental and warranty obligations.

2) Employee benefit plan obligations for pensions and other postemployment benefits may be settled. Reporting in discontinued operations is required if the settlement is directly related to the component disposed of.

3. **Income Statement Presentation**

a. The operating results of a component that has been disposed of or is classified as held for sale are reported in discontinued operations. This section is presented **after continuing operations but before extraordinary items**.

b. When a component is **classified as held for sale**, it is measured at the lower of its carrying amount or fair value minus cost to sell.

1) Operating results reported in discontinued operations include any income earned or loss incurred during the reporting period.

2) Operating results also include any loss for a writedown to fair value minus cost to sell. They also include a gain arising from an increase in fair value minus cost to sell (limited to losses previously recognized).

3) Operating results do not include depreciation or amortization.

c. The results of discontinued operations are reported **minus (plus) income tax (benefit)**. The following format may be used by a business:

EXAMPLE

Each of ING Company's divisions is a component of the entity. The X Division's results are declining. Consequently, ING decided on July 15, Year 1, to commit to a plan to sell X. The sale was completed on December 1, Year 1. The operations and cash flows of X were eliminated from the ongoing operations of ING. Moreover, the entity will have no continuing post-sale involvement in X's operations. The following is ING's single-step income statement after the disposal:

ING Company
INCOME STATEMENT
For the Year Ended 12/31/Yr 1

Revenue:		
Net sales	$1,500,000	
Other revenue	40,000	
Total revenue		$1,540,000
Expenses:		
Cost of goods sold	$ 750,000	
Selling expense	75,000	
Administrative expense	90,000	
Interest expense	70,000	
Total expenses		(985,000)
Income from continuing operations before income taxes		$ 555,000
Income taxes		(206,000)
Income from continuing operations		$ 349,000
Discontinued operations (see Note Z)		
Loss from operations of component unit -- X Division		
(including gain on disposal of $200,000)	$ (340,000)	
Income tax benefit	56,000	
Loss on discontinued operations		(284,000)
Net income		$ 65,000

---

1) Any **gain or loss on disposal** must be disclosed on the face of the income statement or in the notes.

2) **Basic and diluted EPS** amounts for a discontinued operation are presented on the face of the income statement or in the notes.

3) The caption "Income from continuing operations" should be revised to "Income from continuing operations before extraordinary item" if an extraordinary item is reported. The EPS presentation also may require revision.

IFRS Difference

Net cash flows from operating, investing, and financing activities of a discontinued operation must be disclosed in the notes or the statements.

Stop and review! You have completed the outline for this subunit. Study multiple-choice questions 1 through 3 on page 143.

4.2 EXTRAORDINARY ITEMS

1. **Overview**

    a. A material transaction or event that is **unusual in nature** and **infrequent in occurrence** in the environment in which the entity operates is an extraordinary item.

       1) A transaction or event is **unusual** if it has a high degree of abnormality and is of a type clearly unrelated to, or only incidentally related to, the ordinary and typical activities of the entity.

EXAMPLE

A warehouse fire is clearly unrelated to an entity's ordinary and typical activities.

---

       2) A transaction or event is **infrequent** if it is not reasonably expected to recur in the foreseeable future.

EXAMPLE

An earthquake in Florida (but not in California) is not reasonably expected to recur.

---

    b. Sometimes a pronouncement specifically classifies an item as extraordinary even if these criteria are not met.

2. **Items Not Considered Extraordinary**

    a. The following are examples:

       1) Write-downs of receivables, inventories, intangible assets, etc.
       2) Gains and losses from exchange or translation of foreign currencies, including those resulting from major devaluations and revaluations
       3) Gains and losses on disposal of a component of an entity
       4) Other gains and losses from sale or abandonment of property, plant, and equipment used in the business
       5) Effects of a strike, including those against competitors and major suppliers
       6) Adjustments of accruals on long-term contracts

    b. However, an extraordinary event or transaction may occur that includes a gain or loss listed just above. In this rare case, gains or losses, such as those in 2.a.1) and 2.a.4) [but not 2.a.3)], may be classified as extraordinary.

       1) The gains or losses that qualify are those directly resulting from a(n)

          a) **Major casualty** (e.g., flood),
          b) **Expropriation**, or
          c) **Prohibition under a new law or regulation**.

    c. Any portion of the losses described in 2.b. that would have resulted from measurement of assets on a going-concern basis (e.g., writing down assets to fair value) is not included in the extraordinary items.

3.   **Adjustments of Estimates**

   a.   Adjustments of estimates included in extraordinary items previously reported are separately presented and disclosed in the current statements. They are classified in the same way as the original items.

4.   **Income Statement Presentation**

   a.   Extraordinary items should be reported individually in a separate section in the income statement, **net of tax**, after results of discontinued operations. However, disclosure in the notes of individual items included in this section also is acceptable.

   1)   **Basic and diluted EPS** amounts for extraordinary items are presented on the face of the income statement or in the notes.

   b.   If a material transaction or event is **unusual or infrequent but not both**, it is not an extraordinary item. Thus, it is reported as a separate component of income from continuing operations but **not net of tax**. No EPS disclosure is made on the income statement.

IFRS Difference

No items are classified as extraordinary, either on the face of the statement of comprehensive income or in the notes.

---

   c.   The following memory aid is helpful for learning the order of items on the income statement:

   I = Income from Continuing Operations   I
   D = Discontinued Operations   Do
   E = Extraordinary Items   Excel

Stop and review! You have completed the outline for this subunit. Study multiple-choice questions 4 through 6 on page 144.

4.3 ACCOUNTING CHANGES AND ERROR CORRECTIONS

 The AICPA traditionally tests candidates' knowledge of how to account for the effects of a change in accounting principle, a change in accounting estimate, and the correction of errors. Be prepared to see questions that ask how to handle each of these situations, either by describing the accounting, calculating the requested amounts, or choosing the correct journal entries.

1.   **Accounting Changes -- Overview**

   a.   If financial information is to have the qualities of comparability and consistency, entities must not make voluntary changes in accounting principles unless they can be justified as preferable.

   1)   Thus, the **general presumption** is that **a principle once adopted must be applied consistently** in preparing financial statements.

   b.   The three **types of accounting changes** are a change in accounting principle, a change in accounting estimate, and a change in reporting entity.

2.   **Change in Accounting Principle**

   a.   A change in accounting principle occurs when an entity (1) adopts a generally accepted principle different from the one previously used, (2) changes the **method** of applying a generally accepted principle, or (3) changes to a generally accepted principle when the principle previously used is no longer generally accepted.

   1)   A change in principle does not include the initial adoption of a principle because of an event or transaction occurring for the first time or that previously had an immaterial effect.

2)   It also does not include adoption of a principle to account for an event or transaction that clearly differs in substance from a previously occurring event or transaction.

b.   **Retrospective application** is required for all direct effects and the related income tax effects of a change in principle.

1)   An example of a direct effect is an adjustment of an inventory balance to implement a change in the method of measurement.

2)   Retrospective application must **not include indirect effects**. These are changes in current or future cash flows from a change in principle applied retrospectively.

a)   An example of an indirect effect is a required profit-sharing payment based on a reported amount that was directly affected (e.g., revenue).

b)   Indirect effects are recognized and reported in the period of change.

c.   The carrying amounts of (1) assets, (2) liabilities, and (3) retained earnings (or other components of equity or net assets) at the beginning of the first period reported are adjusted for the **cumulative effect (CE)** of the new principle on all periods not reported.

1)   All periods reported must be individually adjusted for the **period-specific effects (PSE)** of the new principle.

d.   It may be **impracticable** to determine the **cumulative effect** of a new principle on any prior period (for example, when the change is from FIFO to LIFO).

1)   In that case, the new principle must be applied as if the change had been made prospectively at the earliest date practicable.

e.   It may be **practicable** to determine the cumulative effect of applying the new principle to all prior periods but **not** the **period-specific effects** on all prior periods presented.

1)   In these circumstances, cumulative-effect adjustments must be made to the beginning balances for the first period to which the new principle can be applied.

IMPRACTICABILITY EXCEPTIONS

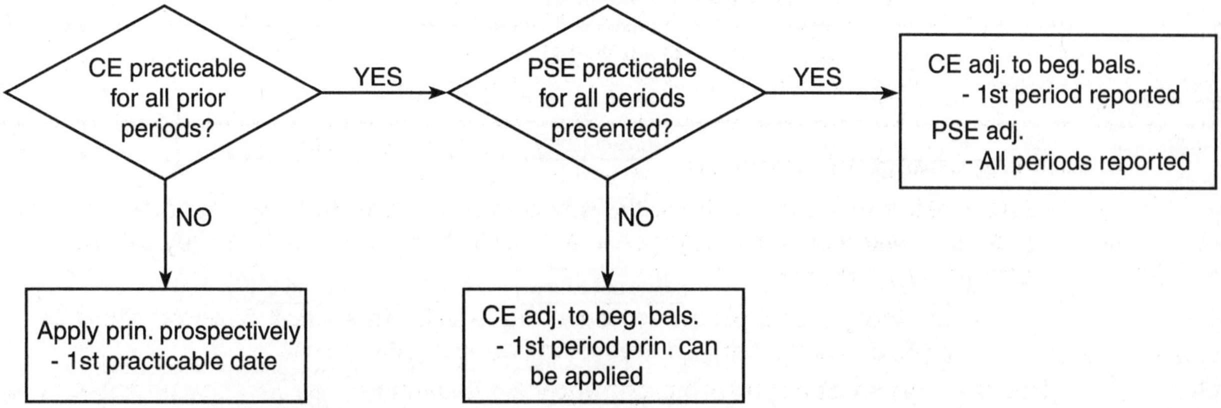

Figure 4-1

3.   **Change in Accounting Estimate**

a.   A change in accounting estimate results from new information. It is a reassessment of the future status and benefits and obligations of assets and liabilities. Its effects must be accounted for only in the period of change and any future periods affected (**prospectively**).

b.   A change in estimate inseparable from a change in principle is accounted for as a change in estimate. An example is a change in a method of depreciation, amortization, or depletion of long-lived, nonfinancial assets.

4. **Change in Reporting Entity**

   a. A change in reporting entity results in statements that are effectively those of a different entity.

      1) Most such changes occur when (a) consolidated or combined statements replace those of individual entities, (b) consolidated statements include different subsidiaries, or (c) combined statements include different entities.

      2) A change in reporting entity does not result from a **business combination** or consolidation of a variable interest entity.

      3) This change is retrospectively applied to interim and annual statements.

5. **Error Correction**

   a. An error in prior statements results from (1) a mathematical mistake, (2) a mistake in the application of GAAP, or (3) an oversight or misuse of facts existing when the statements were prepared. A change to a generally accepted accounting principle from one that is not is an error correction, **not an accounting change**.

      1) Any error related to a prior period discovered after the statements are, or are available to be, used must be reported as an error correction by restating the prior-period statements. **Restatement** requires the same adjustments as retrospective application of a new principle.

         a) However, corrections of prior-period errors must not be included in net income.

      2) Error corrections must be reported in single-period statements as adjustments of the opening balance of retained earnings.

         a) If comparative statements are presented, corresponding adjustments must be made to net income (and its components) and retained earnings (and other affected balances) for all periods reported.

6. **Error Analysis**

   a. A correcting journal entry combines the reversal of the error with the correct entry. Thus, it requires a determination of the (1) journal entry originally recorded, (2) event or transaction that occurred, and (3) correct journal entry.

EXAMPLE

If the purchase of a fixed asset on account had been debited to purchases:

Incorrect Entry	Correct Entry	Correcting Entry
Purchases	Fixed asset	Fixed asset
Payables	Payables	Purchases

If cash had been incorrectly credited:

Incorrect Entry	Correct Entry	Correcting Entry
Purchases	Fixed asset	Fixed Asset
Cash	Payables	Cash
		Purchases
		Payables

---

   b. Error analysis addresses (1) whether an error affects prior-period statements, (2) the timing of error detection, (3) whether comparative statements are presented, and (4) whether the error is counterbalancing.

   c. An error affecting **prior-period statements** may or may not affect prior-period net income. For example, misclassifying an item as a gain rather than a revenue does not affect income and is readily correctable. No prior-period adjustment to retained earnings is required.

     d.   An error that affects prior-period net income is **counterbalancing** if it self-corrects over two periods. However, despite the self-correction, the financial statements remain misstated.   They should be restated if presented comparatively in later periods. For an example, see Study Unit 8, Subunit 7.

         1)   An example of a **noncounterbalancing** error is a misstatement of depreciation. Such an error does not self-correct over two periods. Thus, a prior-period adjustment will be necessary.

IFRS Difference

A prior-period error must be corrected by restatement unless it is impracticable to do so. A change in accounting policy must be made only if it (1) is required by a new standard or interpretation or (2) results in reliable and more relevant information about transactions, financial condition, financial performance, and cash flows. The indirect effects of a change in accounting policy are not addressed by IFRS.

Stop and review! You have completed the outline for this subunit. Study multiple-choice questions 7 through 11 beginning on page 145.

4.4 EARNINGS PER SHARE (EPS)

Background
Beginning in 1969, U.S. GAAP required three earnings per share calculations for entities with capital structures other than simple. The calculation called primary EPS reported the effects of dilutive securities that were common stock equivalents. Under this reporting regimen, the figure that is now termed diluted EPS (that includes the effects of all dilutive securities, whether they are common stock equivalents or not) was called fully diluted EPS. In an effort to harmonize U.S. GAAP with international standards, the FASB dropped the calculation of primary EPS in 1997. Current GAAP is found in FASB ASC 260.

    1.   **Overview**

       a.   **Earnings per share (EPS)** is the amount of current-period earnings that can be associated with a single share of a corporation's common stock.

          1)   The guidance regarding calculation and presentation of EPS must be followed by public entities and by other entities that choose to report EPS.

       b.   EPS is calculated **only for common stock** because common shareholders are the residual owners of a corporation.

          1)   Because preferred shareholders have a superior claim to the entity's earnings, amounts associated with preferred stock must be removed during the calculation of EPS.

Over the years, the topic of earnings per share has been continually tested on CPA exams, often through calculations. Expect to see one or two questions testing earnings per share on your exam.

---

    2.   **Basic Earnings per Share (BEPS)**

       a.   All corporations must report two BEPS amounts on the face of the income statement. Their numerators are **income from continuing operations** and **net income**, respectively.

$$BEPS = \frac{Income\ available\ to\ common\ shareholders}{Weighted\text{-}average\ number\ of\ common\ shares\ outstanding}$$

EXAMPLE

At year end, an entity's capital structure consisted of 10,000,000 shares of $1 par value common stock. The entity issued no new shares during the year. Its income from continuing operations and net income for the year were $1,278,000 and $1,141,000, respectively.

BEPS calculations:

Income from continuing operations: $1,278,000 ÷ 10,000,000 = $0.128
Net income: $1,141,000 ÷ 10,000,000 = $0.114

---

3.   **Calculation of the BEPS Numerator**

a.   **Income available to common shareholders** is the BEPS numerator.

1)   Thus, neither BEPS amount (income from continuing operations or net income) is calculated directly from the amount reported for that line item on the income statement.

a)   Income in the BEPS numerator is reduced by preferred dividends **declared or accumulated in the current period**.

b)   Undistributed accumulated preferred dividends for prior years do not affect the calculation. They are included in BEPS of prior years.

2)   The following calculation is performed for net income and income from continuing operations (or other number):

	Income statement amount
Minus:	Dividends on preferred stock for the current period (cumulative or declared noncumulative)
Equals:	Income available to common shareholders

EXAMPLE

An entity has two classes of preferred stock. It declared a 4% dividend on its $100,000 of noncumulative preferred stock. The entity did not declare a dividend on its $200,000 of 6% cumulative preferred stock. Undistributed dividends for the past 4 years have accumulated on this stock. The following is an excerpt from the entity's condensed income statement for the year:

Income from continuing operations before income taxes	$1,666,667
Income taxes	(666,667)
Income from continuing operations	**$1,000,000**
Discontinued operations:	
Income from operations of component unit --	
Pipeline Division (including gain on disposal of $2,897)	$15,283
Income tax expense	(5,283) 10,000
Income before extraordinary item	$1,010,000
Loss from volcano damage, net of applicable income taxes of $52,221	(140,000)
Net income	**$ 870,000**

The numerators for income from continuing operations and for net income are calculated as follows:

	Income from continuing operations	Net income
Income statement amounts	$1,000,000	$870,000
Declared or accumulated preferred dividends:		
Dividends declared on noncumulative preferred stock in the current period	(4,000)	(4,000)
Dividends accumulated on cumulative preferred stock in the current period	(12,000)	(12,000)
Income available to common shareholders	**$ 984,000**	**$854,000**

---

b.   Given an extraordinary item but no discontinued operation, BEPS is reported for **income before extraordinary items**, not income from continuing operations.

4.   **Calculation of the BEPS Denominator**

   a.   The **weighted-average number of common shares outstanding** is determined by relating the portion of the period that the shares were outstanding to the total time in the period.

   1)   Weighting is necessary because some shares may have been issued or reacquired during the period.

EXAMPLE

In the previous example, assume the following common stock transactions during the year just ended:

Date	Stock Transactions	Shares Outstanding	Times: Portion of Year	Equals: Weighted Average
Jan 1	Beginning balance	240,000	2 ÷ 12	40,000
Mar 1	Issued 60,000 shares	300,000	5 ÷ 12	125,000
Aug 1	Repurchased 20,000 shares	280,000	3 ÷ 12	70,000
Nov 1	Issued 80,000 shares	360,000	2 ÷ 12	60,000
	Total			**295,000**

The **BEPS** amounts for income from continuing operations and net income are **$3.336** ($984,000 ÷ 295,000) and **$2.895** ($854,000 ÷ 295,000), respectively.

---

   b.   **Stock dividends and stock splits** require an adjustment to the weighted-average of common shares outstanding.

   1)   EPS amounts for all periods presented are **adjusted retroactively** to reflect the change in capital structure as if it had occurred at the beginning of the first period presented.

   2)   Adjustments are made for such changes even if they occur after the end of the current period but before issuance (or the availability for issuance) of the statements.

EXAMPLE

In the previous example, assume declaration of a 50% common stock dividend and a 2-for-1 common stock split during the year:

Date	Stock Transactions	Shares Outstanding	Times: Restate for Stock Div.	Times: Restate for Stock Split	Times: Portion of Year	Equals: Weighted Average
Jan 1	Beginning balance	240,000	1.5	2	2 ÷ 12	120,000
Mar 1	Issued 60,000 shares	300,000	1.5	2	5 ÷ 12	375,000
Jun 1	Distributed 50% stock dividend	450,000				
Aug 1	Repurchased 20,000 shares	430,000		2	3 ÷ 12	215,000
Oct 1	Distributed 2-for-1 stock split	860,000				
Nov 1	Issued 80,000 shares	940,000			2 ÷ 12	156,667
	Total					**866,667**

The **BEPS** amounts for income from continuing operations and net income are **$1.135** ($984,000 ÷ 866,667) and **$0.985** ($854,000 ÷ 866,667), respectively.

---

5.   **Diluted Earnings per Share (DEPS)**

   a.   A corporation with only common stock outstanding (a simple capital structure) need report only BEPS.

   1)   An entity that does not have a simple capital structure must report DEPS as well as BEPS. Thus, the DEPS calculation includes the effects of **dilutive potential common stock (PCS)**.

   a)   PCS is a security or other contract that may entitle the holder to obtain common stock.

b.   **Dilution** is a reduction in BEPS (or an increase in loss per share) resulting from the assumption that

1)   Convertible securities (preferred stock or debt) were converted;

2)   Options, warrants, and their equivalents were exercised; or

3)   **Contingently issuable common shares** were issued.

   a)   The conditions for contingent issuance (passage of time or a specified market price, level of earnings, etc.) may be satisfied by year end. The shares are then deemed to have been issued at the beginning of the period or date of the contingent stock agreement.

   b)   However, the conditions may not have been met at year end. In this case, the shares included in the DEPS denominator equal those that would have been issued if the end of the year were the end of the contingency interval.

EXAMPLE

The contingency may involve earnings. The contingently issuable shares equal those issuable (if any) based on the current period's earnings if the result is dilutive.

---

6.   **Calculation of DEPS**

a.   DEPS measures performance after considering the effect on the numerator and denominator of dilutive PCS. DEPS is calculated as follows:

1)   **The BEPS denominator is increased** to include the weighted-average number of additional shares of common stock that would have been outstanding if dilutive PCS had been issued.

2)   **The BEPS numerator** is adjusted to **add back** any dividends on convertible preferred stock and the after-tax interest (after amortization of discount or premium) related to any convertible debt.

   a)   The numerator also is adjusted for other changes in income or loss, such as profit-sharing expenses, that would result from the assumed issuance of PCS.

$$DEPS = \frac{BEPS\ numerator + Effect\ of\ dilutive\ PCS}{BEPS\ denominator + Effect\ of\ dilutive\ PCS}$$

b.   Amounts are based on the most advantageous conversion rate or exercise price from the perspective of the holder.

1)   Previously reported DEPS is not retroactively adjusted for subsequent conversions or changes in the market price of the common stock.

2)   The calculation of DEPS does not assume the conversion, exercise, or contingent issuance of antidilutive securities, i.e., securities that increase EPS or decrease loss per share.

3)   Dilutive securities issued during a period and dilutive convertible securities for which (a) conversion options lapse, (b) preferred stock is redeemed, or (c) debt is extinguished are included in the DEPS denominator for the period they were outstanding.

   a)   Moreover, dilutive convertible securities that were actually converted are included for the **period before conversion**. Common shares actually issued are included for the **period after conversion**.

c.   Three methods are used to determine the **dilutive effect** of PCS: (1) the if-converted method for convertible securities, (2) the treasury stock method for call options and warrants, and (3) the reverse treasury stock method for put options.

7. **The If-Converted Method**

a. The if-converted method calculates DEPS assuming the conversion of all dilutive convertible securities at the beginning of the period or at the time of issue, if later.

1) The conversion of **antidilutive** securities (those whose conversion would **increase EPS** or decrease loss per share) is **not assumed**. Thus, convertible PCS is antidilutive if the current dividend or after-tax interest per common share issuable exceeds BEPS.

b. In determining whether PCS is dilutive, each issue or series of issues is considered separately and in sequence from the most dilutive to the least dilutive.

1) The issue with the lowest earnings per incremental share is included in DEPS before issues with higher earnings per incremental share. If the issue with the lowest earnings per incremental share is found to be dilutive with respect to BEPS, it is included in a trial calculation of DEPS.

2) If the issue with the next lowest earnings per incremental share is dilutive with respect to the first trial calculation of DEPS, it is included in a new DEPS calculation that adjusts the numerator and denominator from the prior calculation.

3) This process continues until all issues of PCS have been tested.

c. If a **discontinued operation or extraordinary item** is reported, the same number of shares used to adjust the denominator for income from continuing operations (or income before extraordinary items) is used to adjust the DEPS denominator for all other reported earnings amounts. This rule applies even if the effect on the other amounts is antidilutive.

d. If a **loss from continuing operations** or a loss from continuing operations attributable to common shareholders is reported, PCS is not included in the calculation of DEPS for any reported earnings amount. Its effect on the continuing operations calculation is antidilutive.

EXAMPLE

In the continuing example, assume that the noncumulative preferred stock is convertible into 20,000 shares of common stock. Also assume that, on the first day of the year, the entity issued $2,400,000 of 8% debt, convertible into 20,000 shares of common stock. Its tax rate is 40%.

The entity has two issues of PCS: the 4% noncumulative preferred stock and the 8% convertible debt. The earnings per incremental share of the preferred stock is $.067 [($100,000 × .04) ÷ 60,000 PCS as adjusted for the stock dividend and stock split]. The earnings per incremental share of the debt is $1.92 {[($2,400,000 × .08) × (1.0 − .40)] ÷ 60,000 PCS}.

Because the $.067 incremental effect of the convertible preferred is lower, it is more dilutive. Thus, it is compared with the $1.135 BEPS amount for income from continuing operations. Because $.067 is lower than $1.135, the convertible preferred is dilutive and is included in the trial calculation of DEPS. The result is $1.066 [($984,000 + $4,000) ÷ (866,667 shares + 60,000 PCS)].

However, the $1.92 incremental effect of the convertible debt is higher than the $1.066 trial calculation. The convertible debt is therefore antidilutive. It is excluded from the DEPS calculation.

---

e. No test for dilution is performed for net income.

8. **Treasury Stock Method**

a. The second method used to determine the dilutive effect of PCS is the treasury stock method. It is used to determine the dilutive effect of outstanding **call options, warrants**, and their equivalents. They are dilutive if the average market price for the period exceeds the exercise price.

1) Equivalents include nonvested stock granted to employees, stock purchase contracts, and partially paid stock subscriptions.

b.   The options and warrants are assumed to be exercised at the beginning of the period (or time of issuance, if later). The assumed proceeds equal the weighted-average number of shares issuable upon exercise times the option or warrant price.

1)   The options or warrants may relate to unrecognized compensation cost for future services. In this case, the assumed proceeds also include (a) such cost and (b) the amount of any excess tax benefit (tax deduction in excess of compensation expense recognized for financial reporting).

a)   The excess benefit results from an increase in the fair value of the optioned shares between the measurement date and the date at which the tax deduction is calculated.

2)   The proceeds are assumed to be used to purchase common stock at the average market price during the period.

c.   To arrive at the DEPS denominator, the BEPS denominator is assumed to be increased by the excess, if any, of the shares issued over the number purchased.

EXAMPLE

Troupe Company had 100,000 shares of common stock issued and outstanding at January 1. On July 1, Troupe issued a 10% stock dividend. Unexercised call options to purchase 20,000 shares of Troupe's common stock (adjusted for the stock dividend) at $20 per share were outstanding at the beginning and end of the year. The average market price of the stock (not affected by the stock dividend) was $25 per share. Net income for the year ended December 31 was $550,000. What is DEPS for the year?

A stock dividend occurring before issuance of the financial statements requires a retroactive adjustment at the beginning of the first period presented. Hence, the 110,000 shares outstanding after the stock dividend are deemed to have been outstanding during the entire year.

The options are not antidilutive because the exercise price was less than the average market price. Accordingly, exercise of the options is assumed to have occurred at the beginning of the year at the exercise price of $20. Under the treasury stock method, the assumed proceeds of $400,000 (20,000 shares × $20) are used to repurchase 16,000 shares ($400,000 ÷ $25) at the average market price. Thus, DEPS equals $4.82 {$550,000 ÷ [110,000 shares + (20,000 assumed issued – 16,000 assumed repurchased)]}.

---

9.   **Reverse Treasury Stock Method**

a.   The third method used to determine the dilutive effect of PCS is the reverse treasury stock method. It is used when the entity has entered into contracts to repurchase its own stock, for example, when it has **written put options** held by other parties.

1)   When the contracts are **in the money** (the exercise price exceeds the average market price), the potential dilutive effect on EPS is calculated by

a)   Assuming the issuance at the beginning of the period of sufficient shares to raise the proceeds needed to satisfy the contracts,

b)   Assuming those proceeds are used to repurchase shares, and

c)   Including the excess of shares assumed to be issued over those assumed to be repurchased in the calculation of the DEPS denominator.

b.   Options held by the entity on its own stock, whether they are puts or calls, are not included in the DEPS denominator because their effect is antidilutive.

10.   **Income Statement Presentation**

a.   An entity with **only common stock outstanding** must report BEPS but not DEPS for income from continuing operations and net income on the **face of the income statement**.

1)   **All other entities** must present BEPS and DEPS for income from continuing operations and net income with equal prominence on the face of the income statement.

       2) An entity that reports a **discontinued operation**, an **extraordinary item**, or both must report BEPS and DEPS for the item(s) on the face of the income statement or in the notes.

  b. EPS disclosures are **made for all periods** for which an income statement or earnings summary is presented. For each period for which an income statement is presented, the following are disclosed:

     1) A reconciliation by individual security of the numerators and denominators of BEPS and DEPS for income from continuing operations, including income and share effects

     2) The effect of preferred dividends on the BEPS numerator

     3) PCS not included in DEPS because it would have had an antidilutive effect in the periods reported

  c. If DEPS data are **reported for at least one period**, they are **reported for all periods** shown, even if they are equal to BEPS amounts.

  d. For the latest period for which an income statement is presented, an entity must **disclose subsequent events** that would have had a material effect on common shares or PCS outstanding if the transaction had occurred prior to the balance sheet date.

     1) Subsequent events occur after the balance sheet date and prior to the issuance (or availability for issuance) of the financial statements.

  e. An entity must explain within its financial statements the rights of outstanding securities. It also must disclose the number of shares issued upon conversion, exercise, or satisfaction of conditions during the last fiscal year and any subsequent interim period presented.

     1) The equity section should disclose in the aggregate the preferences given in involuntary liquidation to senior stock that are considerably greater than par or stated value.

       a) The entity also must disclose the aggregate or per-share amounts at which preferred stock is callable and the aggregate and per-share amounts of preferred dividends in arrears.

     2) Other necessary disclosures are the redemption requirements for the next 5 years for capital stock redeemable at fixed or determinable prices and dates.

Stop and review! You have completed the outline for this subunit. Study multiple-choice questions 12 through 15 beginning on page 147.

4.5 LONG-TERM CONSTRUCTION CONTRACTS

1. **The Completed-Contract Method**

  a. The completed-contract method is used to account for a long-term project when the percentage-of-completion method is inappropriate.

     1) It **defers all contract costs** in the inventory account **construction in progress** until the project is completed. It records progress billings in the contra-inventory account **progress billings**.

     2) Revenue and gross profit are recognized only upon completion.

2.   The Percentage-of-Completion Method

a.   Percentage-of-completion is the preferable method. It records (1) all contract costs in construction in progress and (2) all amounts billed in progress billings. However, the percentage-of-completion method differs from the completed-contract method because it recognizes revenue on long-term contracts when the

1)   Extent of progress toward completion, contract revenue, and contract costs are reasonably estimable;

2)   Enforceable rights regarding goods or services to be provided, the consideration to be exchanged, and the terms of settlement are clearly specified; and

3)   Obligations of the parties are expected to be fulfilled.

b.   The **amount of gross profit recognized** in a period is calculated as follows:

1)   Calculate the estimated total gross profit on the project.

EXAMPLE

A contractor is constructing an office complex for a real estate developer. The agreed-upon contract price was $75 million. As of the close of Year 4 of the project, the contractor had incurred $44 million of costs. By its best estimates as of that date, costs remaining to finish the project were $19 million.

Contract price	$75,000,000
Minus: costs incurred to date	(44,000,000)
Minus: estimated costs to complete	(19,000,000)
Estimated total gross profit	$12,000,000

---

2)   Calculate the percentage of the project completed as of the reporting date, determined by the ratio of costs incurred thus far to estimated total costs.

EXAMPLE

Total estimated costs for the project as of the end of Year 4 are calculated as follows:

Costs incurred to date	$44,000,000
Estimated costs to complete	19,000,000
Total estimated costs	$63,000,000

The project is therefore 69.8% complete ($44,000,000 ÷ $63,000,000).

---

3)   Subtract the gross profit recognized so far.

EXAMPLE

The contractor will recognize $2,151,000 in gross profit for Year 4, calculated as follows:

Estimated total gross profit	$12,000,000
Times: percentage complete	× 69.8%
Gross profit earned to date	$ 8,376,000
Minus: gross profit recognized in prior periods (given)	(6,225,000)
Gross profit for current period	$ 2,151,000

---

c.   When estimated revenue and costs are revised, a change in accounting estimate is recognized. Recognition of the change is in

1)   The period of change if only that period is affected or
2)   The period of change and future periods if both are affected.

d.   As soon as an **estimated loss** on any project becomes apparent, it is recognized in full, under both the completed-contract and percentage-of-completion methods.

3. **Comparative Journal Entries**

EXAMPLE

A contractor agrees to build a bridge that will take 3 years to complete. The contract price is $2 million and expected total costs are $1.2 million.

	Year 1	Year 2	Year 3
Costs incurred during each year	$300,000	$600,000	$550,000
Costs expected in future	900,000	600,000	0

By the end of Year 1, 25% ($300,000 ÷ $1,200,000) of expected costs has been incurred. Using percentage-of-completion, the contractor will recognize 25% of the revenue or gross profit that will be earned on the project. The total gross profit is expected to be $800,000 ($2,000,000 – $1,200,000), so $200,000 ($800,000 × 25%) of gross profit should be recognized in Year 1.

	Percentage-of-Completion		Completed-Contract	
Year 1: Construction in progress	$300,000		$300,000	
Cash or accounts payable		$300,000		$300,000
			--	
Construction in progress	$200,000			
Construction gross profit		$200,000		--

At the end of Year 2, total costs incurred are $900,000 ($300,000 + $600,000). Given that $600,000 is expected to be incurred in the future, the total expected cost is $1,500,000 ($900,000 + $600,000), and the estimate of gross profit is $500,000 ($2,000,000 contract price – $1,500,000 costs). If the project is 60% complete ($900,000 ÷ $1,500,000), $300,000 of cumulative gross profit should be recognized for Years 1 and 2 ($500,000 × 60%) under percentage-of-completion. Because $200,000 was recognized in Year 1, $100,000 should be recognized in Year 2.

	Percentage-of-Completion		Completed-Contract	
Year 2: Construction in progress	$600,000		$600,000	
Cash or accounts payable		$600,000		$600,000
			--	
Construction in progress	$100,000			
Construction gross profit		$100,000		--

At the end of the third year, total costs are $1,450,000. Thus, the total gross profit is known to be $550,000. Because a total of $300,000 was recognized in Years 1 and 2, $250,000 should be recognized in Year 3, using percentage-of-completion.*

	Percentage-of-Completion		Completed-Contract	
Year 3: Construction in progress	$550,000		$550,000	
Cash or accounts payable		$550,000		$550,000
Cash	$2,000,000		$2,000,000	
Construction in progress		$1,750,000		$1,450,000
Construction gross profit		250,000		550,000

* This is the first recognition of gross profit under the completed-contract method.

---

4. **Progress Billings**

    a. Ordinarily, progress billings are made and payments are received during the term of the contract. The entries are

      The customer is billed:

Accounts receivable	$XXX	
Progress billings		$XXX

      The customer pays:

Cash	$XXX	
Accounts receivable		$XXX

      1) Neither billing nor the receipt of cash affects gross profit. Moreover, billing, receipt of payment, and incurrence of cost have the same effects under both accounting methods.

b. The difference between **construction in progress** (costs and recognized gross profit) and progress billings to date is reported as a **current asset** if construction in progress exceeds total billings and as a **current liability** if billings exceed construction in progress.

<u>Closing entry:</u>

Progress billings	$XXX	
Construction in progress		$XXX

c. A variation on the entries above is to credit periodic gross revenue instead of gross profit. This practice requires a debit to a cost of revenue earned account similar to cost of goods sold. The debit equals the costs incurred in the current period. For example, in Year 1, the second entry would be

Construction in progress (gross profit)	$200,000	
Construction expenses (a nominal account)	300,000	
Gross revenue		$500,000

IFRS Difference

The completed-contract method is not used. When the outcome of a long-term construction contract cannot be reliably estimated, revenue recognition is limited to recoverable costs incurred. Contract costs must be recognized as an expense in the period in which they are incurred.

Stop and review! You have completed the outline for this subunit. Study multiple-choice questions 16 through 19 beginning on page 148.

4.6 REVENUE RECOGNITION AFTER DELIVERY

1. **The Installment Method**

   a. The installment method is only acceptable when receivables are collectible over an extended period and no reasonable basis exists for estimating the degree of collectibility.

   b. The installment method recognizes a **partial profit** on a sale as each installment is collected.

      1) This approach differs from the ordinary procedure, that is, recognition of revenue when a transaction is complete. Thus, when collection problems (bad debts) can be reasonably estimated, the full profit is usually recognized in the period of sale.

   c. The amount recognized each period under the installment method is the **realized gross profit**. This amount equals the cash collected on installment sales for the period times the gross profit percentage on installment sales for the period (a separate gross profit percentage is calculated for each period).

$$\text{Gross profit percentage} = \frac{\text{Gross profit on installment sales}}{\text{Installment sales}}$$

1) In addition, interest income must be accounted for separately from the gross profit on the sale.

EXAMPLE

A TV costing $600 is the only item sold on the installment basis in Year 1. The TV was sold for a price of $1,000 on November 1, Year 1. Thus, the gross profit percentage is 40% [($1,000 – $600) ÷ $1,000]. A down payment of $100 was received, and the remainder is due in nine monthly payments of $100 each. Because all payments are due within 1 year, no interest is charged. The entry for the sale is

Cash	$100	
Installment receivable, Year 1	900	
Cost of installment sales	600	
Inventory		$ 600
Installment sales		1,000

---

d. At the end of the period, a portion of deferred gross profit is realized.

EXAMPLE

In December, when the first installment is received, the entry is

Cash	$100	
Installment receivable, Year 1		$100

At December 31, installment sales and cost of installment sales are closed, and deferred gross profit is recognized. Moreover, deferred gross profit must be adjusted to report the portion that has been earned. Given that $200 of the total price has been received, $80 of the gross profit ($200 × 40%) has been earned. The entry is

Installment sales	$1,000	
Cost of installment sales		$600
Deferred gross profit		400
Deferred gross profit (Year 1)	$80	
Realized gross profit		$80

Net income should include only the $80 realized gross profit for the period. The balance sheet should report a receivable of $800 minus the deferred gross profit of $320. Thus, the net receivable is $480.

Balance sheet:		
Installment receivable		
(net of deferred gross profit of $320)		$480

---

e. The gross profit percentage for the period of the sale continues to be applied to the realization of deferred gross profit from sales of that period.

EXAMPLE

In Year 2, the remaining $800 is received, and the $320 balance of deferred gross profit is recognized. If only $400 were received in Year 2 (if payments were extended), the December, Year 2, statements would report a $400 installment receivable and $160 of deferred gross profit.

---

f. If goods sold are repossessed due to nonpayment, their fair value, remaining deferred gross profit, and any loss are debited. The remaining receivable is credited.

EXAMPLE

Assume that the TV is repossessed because no payments other than the down payment were made. The realized gross profit at December 31 is therefore $40 ($100 × 40%). Assume also that the used TV is recorded at its fair value at the time of repossession of $400.

Inventory of used merchandise	$400	
Deferred gross profit	360	
Loss on repossession	140	
Installment receivable		$900

The loss on repossession is the difference between the $400 fair value and the $540 carrying amount [$900 remaining receivable – ($400 deferred gross profit – $40 realized gross profit)] of the receivable.

---

g.   The term **installment sale** applies not to the use of the installment method but to a
     sale in which the consideration is receivable in installments. The sale price is the
     present value of the consideration and is recognized as revenue at the time of sale.
     Interest is recognized as earned under the effective interest method.

2.   **Cost-Recovery Method**

a.   The cost-recovery method may be used only in the same circumstances as the
     installment method. However, no profit is recognized until collections exceed the cost
     of the item sold. Subsequent receipts are treated entirely as revenues.

EXAMPLE

In Year 1, Creditor made a $100,000 sale. The cost of the item sold was $70,000, and Year 1 collections equaled $50,000.
In Year 2, collections equaled $25,000, and $10,000 of the receivable was determined to be uncollectible. The net
receivable (receivable – deferred profit) was $0 at the end of Year 2. The following entries are based on the cost-recovery
method:

Year 1:	Receivable	$100,000	
	Inventory		$70,000
	Deferred gross profit		30,000
	Cash	$50,000	
	Receivable		$50,000
Year 2:	Cash	$25,000	
	Deferred gross profit	5,000	
	Receivable		$25,000
	Realized gross profit		5,000
	Deferred gross profit	$10,000	
	Receivable		$10,000

---

3.   **Deposit Method**

a.   This method is used when cash is received, but the criteria for a sale have not been
     met. Thus, the seller continues to account for the property in the same way as an
     owner. No revenue or profit is recognized because it has not been earned, e.g., by
     transferring the property. The entry is

Cash	$XXX	
Deposit liability		$XXX

**Stop and review! You have completed the outline for this subunit. Study multiple-choice
questions 20 through 23 beginning on page 149.**

4.7 FAIR VALUE MEASUREMENTS

1.   **Overview**

a.   GAAP establish a framework for fair value measurements (FVMs) required by other
     pronouncements. But they do not determine when FVMs are required. Accordingly,
     they

     1)   Define **fair value**,
     2)   Discuss **valuation techniques**,
     3)   Establish a **fair value hierarchy** of inputs to valuation techniques, and
     4)   Require expanded **disclosures** about FVMs.

b.   Practicability exceptions to FVMs stated in other pronouncements are not affected by
     this guidance. For example, it does not eliminate the exemption from the requirement
     to measure financial instruments at fair value if it is not feasible to do so.

2. **Definitions**

   a. "**Fair value** is **the price that would be received** to sell an asset or paid to transfer a liability in an **orderly transaction between market participants** at the measurement date."

   b. The FVM is for a particular asset or liability that may stand alone (e.g., a financial instrument) or constitute a group (e.g., a business). The definition also applies to instruments measured at fair value that are classified as equity.

      1) The price is an **exit price** paid or received in a hypothetical transaction considered from the perspective of a market participant.

      2) The FVM considers attributes specific to the asset or liability, e.g., restrictions on sale or use, condition, and location.

      3) The unit of account is what is measured.

         a) For example, a component of an entity may be classified as held for sale and remeasured at fair value minus cost to sell. Thus, the component is the unit of account.

   c. Market participants are **not related parties**. They are independent of the reporting entity.

      1) They are knowledgeable (i.e., they have a reasonable understanding based on all available information).

      2) They are willing and able (but not compelled) to engage in transactions involving the asset or liability.

      3) The FVM is market-based, not entity-specific.

   d. An orderly transaction is not forced, and time is assumed to be sufficient to allow for customary marketing activities.

   e. The transaction is assumed to occur in the reporting entity's principal market for the asset or liability.

      1) In the absence of such a market, it is assumed to occur in the most advantageous market. This market is the one in which the specific reporting entity can (a) maximize the amount received for selling the asset or (b) minimize the amount paid for transferring the liability, after considering transportation and transaction costs.

      2) Given a principal (or most advantageous) market, the FVM is the price in that market without adjustment for transaction costs.

         a) However, if location is an attribute of the asset or liability, the price includes transportation costs.

   f. **Assets.** The FVM is based on the **highest and best use (HBU) by market participants**.

      1) The HBU is in-use if the value-maximizing use is in combination with other assets in a group. An example is machinery in a factory.

      2) The HBU is in-exchange if the value-maximizing use is as a stand-alone asset. An example is a financial asset.

   g. **Liabilities.** The FVM assumes transfer, not settlement.

      1) The liability to the counterparty is unaffected.

      2) Nonperformance risk is unaffected and is included in the FVM.

3. **Valuation Techniques**

    a.   These should be consistently applied, appropriate in the circumstances, and based on sufficient data. Given a range, the FVM is the point most representative of fair value. All or any of the following should be used:

        1)   The **market approach** is based on information, such as multiples of prices, from market transactions involving identical or comparable items.

        2)   The **income approach** uses valuation methods based on current market expectations about future amounts, e.g., earnings or cash flows.

            a)   It converts future amounts to one present discounted amount.
            b)   Examples are present value methods and option-pricing models.

        3)   The **cost approach** is based on current replacement cost. It is the cost to buy or build a comparable asset.

    b.   Inputs to valuation techniques are the pricing assumptions of market participants.

        1)   **Observable inputs** are based on market data obtained from independent sources.

        2)   **Unobservable inputs** are based on the entity's own assumptions about the assumptions of market participants that reflect the best available information. Their use should be minimized.

4. **The Fair Value Hierarchy**

    a.   **Level 1 inputs** are the **most reliable**. They are unadjusted quoted prices in active markets for identical assets or liabilities that the entity can access at the measurement date.

        1)   If the entity has a position in a single financial instrument that is traded in an active market, the position is measured within Level 1. The FVM equals the quantity held times the instrument's quoted price.

    b.   **Level 2 inputs** are **observable**. But they exclude quoted prices included within Level 1.

        1)   Examples are quoted prices for similar items in active markets, quoted prices in markets that are not active, and observable inputs that are not quoted prices.

    c.   **Level 3 inputs** are the **least reliable**. They are unobservable inputs that are used in the absence of observable inputs. They should be based on the best available information in the circumstances.

        1)   The entity need not exhaust every effort to gain information about the assumptions of market participants.

5. **Disclosures**

    a.   One set of **quantitative disclosures** in tabular format is made for each major category of assets and liabilities measured at fair value **on a recurring basis** (e.g., trading securities).

        1)   For example, a **reconciliation** of the beginning and ending balances is required for any assets or liabilities measured at fair value on a recurring basis that use **significant unobservable inputs** (that is, Level 3) during the period.

    b.   For each major category of assets and liabilities measured at fair value **on a nonrecurring basis** (e.g., impaired assets) during the period, quantitative disclosures also must be made in tabular format.

Stop and review! You have completed the outline for this subunit. Study multiple-choice questions 24 through 27 on page 151.

QUESTIONS

4.1 Discontinued Operations

1. For the purpose of reporting discontinued operations, a component of an entity is best defined as

A. An operating segment or one level below an operating segment.

B. A set of operations and cash flows clearly distinguishable from the rest of the entity for operational and financial reporting purposes.

C. A separate major line of business or class of customer.

D. A significant disposal group.

Answer (B) is correct.
    REQUIRED: The nature of a component of an entity.
    DISCUSSION: A component of an entity is a set of operations and cash flows clearly distinguishable from the rest of the entity for operational and financial reporting purposes. A component may be a(n) (1) reportable segment, (2) operating segment, (3) reporting unit, (4) subsidiary, or (5) asset group (a disposal group if it is to be disposed of).
    Answer (A) is incorrect. The term "component of an entity" was broadly defined to improve the usefulness of information by requiring more frequent reporting of discontinued operations. Thus, a component of an entity is not restricted to a reporting unit, that is, an operating segment or one level below an operating segment. Answer (C) is incorrect. Reporting of a discontinued operation no longer is limited to a separate major line of business or class of customer. Answer (D) is incorrect. The criteria for the reporting of discontinued operations do not emphasize either the significance of a component or any quantitative threshold.

2. On January 1, Year 4, Dart, Inc., entered into an agreement to sell the assets and product line of its Jay Division, which met the criteria for classification as an operating segment. The sale was consummated on December 31, Year 4, and resulted in a gain on disposal of $400,000. The division's operations resulted in losses before income tax of $225,000 in Year 4 and $125,000 in Year 3. For both years, Dart's income tax rate is 30%, and the criteria for reporting a discontinued operation have been met. In a comparative statement of income for Year 4 and Year 3, under the caption discontinued operations, Dart should report a gain (loss) of

	Year 4	Year 3
A.	$122,500	$(87,500)
B.	$122,500	$0
C.	$(157,500)	$(87,500)
D.	$(157,500)	$0

Answer (A) is correct.
    REQUIRED: The amounts reported for discontinued operations in comparative statements.
    DISCUSSION: When a component (e.g., an operating segment) has been disposed of or is classified as held for sale, and the criteria for reporting a discontinued operation have been met, the income statements for current and prior periods (in this case, Year 3 and Year 4) must report its operating results in discontinued operations. The gain from operations of the component for Year 4 is the net of the $225,000 operating loss for Year 4 and the $400,000 gain on disposal. The pretax gain is therefore $175,000 ($400,000 – $225,000), and the after-tax amount is $122,500 [$175,000 × (1.0 – .30)]. The $125,000 pretax loss for Year 3 should be reported in the comparative statements for Years 3 and 4 as an $87,500 [$125,000 × (1.0 – .30)] loss from discontinued operations.
    Answer (B) is incorrect. The comparative statement of income for Year 4 and Year 3 should report a loss on discontinued operations for Year 3. Answer (C) is incorrect. An after-tax loss of $157,500 for Year 4 does not consider the gain on disposal. Answer (D) is incorrect. The comparative statement of income for Year 4 and Year 3 should report a loss on discontinued operations for Year 3, and an after-tax loss of $157,500 for Year 4 does not consider the gain on disposal.

3. During January of Year 6, Doe Corp. agreed to sell the assets and product line of its Hart division. The sale was completed on January 15, Year 7, and resulted in a gain on disposal of $900,000. Hart's operating losses were $600,000 for Year 6 and $50,000 for the period January 1 through January 15, Year 7. Disregarding income taxes and assuming that the criteria for reporting a discontinued operation are met, what amount of net gain (loss) should be reported in Doe's comparative Year 7 and Year 6 income statements?

	Year 7	Year 6
A.	$0	$250,000
B.	$250,000	$0
C.	$850,000	$(600,000)
D.	$900,000	$(650,000)

Answer (C) is correct.
    REQUIRED: The amounts reported in comparative statements for discontinued operations.
    DISCUSSION: The results of operations of a component classified as held for sale are reported separately in the income statement under discontinued operations in the periods when they occur. Thus, in its Year 6 income statement, Doe should recognize a $600,000 loss. For Year 7, a gain of $850,000 should be recognized ($900,000 – $50,000).
    Answer (A) is incorrect. The amount of $250,000 is the net gain for Year 6 and Year 7. However, the results for Year 7 may not be anticipated. Answer (B) is incorrect. The results for Year 6 should not be deferred. Answer (D) is incorrect. The operating loss for January Year 7 should be recognized in Year 7.

4.2 Extraordinary Items

4. Strand, Inc., incurred the following infrequent losses during the year just ended:

- A $90,000 write-down of equipment leased to others
- A $50,000 adjustment of accruals on long-term contracts
- A $75,000 write-off of obsolete inventory

In its income statement for the year, what amount should Strand report as total infrequent losses that are **not** considered extraordinary?

A. $215,000

B. $165,000

C. $140,000

D. $125,000

Answer (A) is correct.
REQUIRED: The amount to be reported as total infrequent losses not considered extraordinary.
DISCUSSION: To be classified as an extraordinary item, a material transaction or event must be both unusual in nature and infrequent in occurrence in the environment in which the entity operates. Six items are not normally considered extraordinary. These items include (1) the write-down of equipment, (2) the adjustment of accruals on long-term contracts, and (3) the write-off of obsolete inventory. Thus, Strand should report $215,000 ($90,000 + $50,000 + $75,000) of total infrequent losses as a component of income from continuing operations (not net of tax).
Answer (B) is incorrect. The amount of $165,000 improperly excludes the adjustment of accruals. Answer (C) is incorrect. The amount of $140,000 improperly excludes the write-off of inventory. Answer (D) is incorrect. The amount of $125,000 improperly excludes the write-down of equipment.

5. During the year just ended, Teller Co. incurred losses arising from its guilty plea in its first antitrust action and from a substantial increase in production costs caused when a major supplier's workers went on strike. Which of these losses should be reported as an extraordinary item?

	Antitrust Action	Production Costs
A.	No	No
B.	No	Yes
C.	Yes	No
D.	Yes	Yes

Answer (C) is correct.
REQUIRED: The loss(es), if any, reported as an extraordinary item.
DISCUSSION: The effects of a strike are not extraordinary. However, a loss from the company's first antitrust action is clearly infrequent and most likely unusual, that is, abnormal and of a type unrelated to the typical activities of the entity in the environment in which it operates.

6. An extraordinary item should be reported separately on the income statement as a component of income

	Net of Income Taxes	Before Discontinued Operations of a Component of an Entity
A.	Yes	Yes
B.	Yes	No
C.	No	No
D.	No	Yes

Answer (B) is correct.
REQUIRED: The presentation of an extraordinary item.
DISCUSSION: Extraordinary items should be reported separately in the income statement, net of tax, after results of discontinued operations.

4.3 Accounting Changes and Error Corrections

Questions 7 through 9 are based on the following information. Loire Co. has used the FIFO method since it began operations in Year 3. Loire changed to the weighted-average method for inventory measurement at the beginning of Year 6. This change was justified. In its Year 6 financial statements, Loire included comparative statements for Year 5 and Year 4. The following shows year-end inventory balances under the FIFO and weighted-average methods:

Year	FIFO	Weighted-Average
3	$ 90,000	$108,000
4	156,000	142,000
5	166,000	150,000

7. What adjustment, before taxes, should Loire make retrospectively to the balance reported for retained earnings at the beginning of Year 4?

A. $18,000 increase.

B. $18,000 decrease.

C. $4,000 increase.

D. $0.

Answer (A) is correct.

REQUIRED: The pretax retrospective adjustment to retained earnings at the beginning of the first period reported.

DISCUSSION: Retrospective application requires that the carrying amounts of assets, liabilities, and retained earnings at the beginning of the first period reported be adjusted for the cumulative effect of the new principle on periods prior to the first period reported. The pretax cumulative-effect adjustment to retained earnings at the beginning of Year 4 equals the $18,000 increase ($108,000 – $90,000) in inventory. If the weighted-average method had been applied in Year 3, cost of goods sold would have been $18,000 lower. Pretax net income and ending retained earnings for Year 3 (beginning retained earnings for Year 4) would have been $18,000 greater.

Answer (B) is incorrect. Beginning retained earnings for Year 4 is increased. Answer (C) is incorrect. The amount of $4,000 is equal to the difference at the end of Year 3 minus the difference at the end of Year 4. Answer (D) is incorrect. A cumulative-effect adjustment should be recorded.

8. What amount should Loire report as inventory in its financial statements for the year ended December 31, Year 4, presented for comparative purposes?

A. $90,000

B. $108,000

C. $142,000

D. $156,000

Answer (C) is correct.

REQUIRED: The amount to be reported as inventory at December 31, Year 4.

DISCUSSION: Retrospective application requires that all periods reported be individually adjusted for the period-specific effects of applying the new principle. Thus, the ending inventory for Year 4 following the retrospective adjustment should be reported as the weighted-average amount of $142,000.

Answer (A) is incorrect. The amount of $90,000 is the FIFO balance at December 31, Year 3. Answer (B) is incorrect. The amount of $108,000 is the weighted-average balance at December 31, Year 3. Answer (D) is incorrect. The amount of $156,000 is the FIFO balance at December 31, Year 4.

9. By what amount should Loire's cost of sales be retrospectively adjusted for the year ended December 31, Year 5?

A. $0.

B. $2,000 increase.

C. $14,000 increase.

D. $16,000 increase.

Answer (B) is correct.

REQUIRED: The retrospective adjustment to cost of sales for the year ended December 31, Year 5.

DISCUSSION: Retrospective application requires that all periods reported be individually adjusted for the period-specific effects of applying the new principle. Cost of sales equals beginning inventory, plus purchases, minus ending inventory. Purchases are the same under FIFO and weighted average. Thus, the retrospective adjustment to cost of sales equals the change in beginning inventory resulting from the change from FIFO to weighted average minus the change in ending inventory. This adjustment equals an increase in cost of sales of $2,000 [($156,000 – $142,000) – ($166,000 – $150,000)].

Answer (A) is incorrect. Period-specific adjustments are required. Answer (C) is incorrect. The amount of $14,000 is the difference between FIFO and weighted-average inventory amounts at the end of Year 4. Answer (D) is incorrect. The amount of $16,000 is the difference between FIFO and weighted-average inventory amounts at the end of Year 5.

10. Under IFRS, the impracticability exception applies to which of the following?

I.   Retrospective application of a new accounting policy

II. Retrospective application of a change in estimate

III. Retrospective restatement of a prior period error

    A. I and II only.

    B. I and III only.

    C. II and III only.

    D. I only.

Answer (B) is correct.
    REQUIRED: The item(s) to which an impracticability exception applies.
    DISCUSSION: Under IAS 8, *Accounting Policies, Changes in Accounting Estimates, and Errors*, retrospective application of a new accounting policy is not done if it is impracticable to determine period-specific effects or the cumulative effect. Impracticable means that the entity cannot apply a requirement after making every reasonable effort. Accordingly, retrospective application to a prior period is impracticable unless the cumulative effects on the opening and closing statements of financial position for the period are practically determinable. The impracticability exception also applies to retrospective restatement of a prior-period error. However, a change in estimate is applied prospectively in profit or loss. By definition, a change in estimate is not an error correction or a change in accounting policy. It is based on new information or developments. A change in estimate should be distinguished from retrospectively applying a new accounting policy or correcting a prior-period error that involves developing estimates.
    Answer (A) is incorrect. A change in estimate is applied prospectively, and retrospective restatement of a prior-period error is subject to an impracticability exception. Answer (C) is incorrect. Retrospective application of a new accounting policy is subject to an impracticability exception, and a change in estimate is applied prospectively. Answer (D) is incorrect. Retrospective restatement of a prior-period error is subject to an impracticability exception.

11. How should the effect of a change in accounting estimate be accounted for?

    A. By retrospectively applying the change to amounts reported in financial statements of prior periods.

    B. By reporting pro forma amounts for prior periods.

    C. As a prior-period adjustment to beginning retained earnings.

    D. By prospectively applying the change to current and future periods.

Answer (D) is correct.
    REQUIRED: The accounting for the effect of a change in accounting estimate.
    DISCUSSION: The effect of a change in accounting estimate is accounted for in the period of change, if the change affects that period only, or in the period of change and future periods, if the change affects both. For a change in accounting estimate, the entity may not (1) restate or retrospectively adjust prior-period statements or (2) report pro forma amounts for prior periods.

4.4 Earnings per Share (EPS)

Questions 12 through 15 are based on the following information.

Pubco is a public company that uses a calendar year and has a complex capital structure. In the computation of its basic and diluted earnings per share (BEPS and DEPS, respectively), Pubco uses income before extraordinary items as the control number. Pubco reported no discontinued operations, but it had an extraordinary loss (net of tax) of $1.2 million in the first quarter when its income before the extraordinary item was $1 million.

The average market price of Pubco's common stock for the first quarter was $25, the shares outstanding at the beginning of the period equaled 300,000, and 12,000 shares were issued on March 1.

At the beginning of the quarter, Pubco had outstanding $2 million of 5% convertible bonds, with each $1,000 bond convertible into 10 shares of common stock. No bonds were converted.

At the beginning of the quarter, Pubco also had outstanding 120,000 shares of preferred stock paying a quarterly dividend of $.10 per share and convertible to common stock on a one-to-one basis. Holders of 60,000 shares of preferred stock exercised their conversion privilege on February 1.

Throughout the first quarter, warrants to buy 50,000 shares of Pubco's common stock for $28 per share were outstanding but unexercised.

Pubco's tax rate was 30%.

12. The weighted-average number of shares used to calculate Pubco's BEPS amounts for the first quarter is

A. 444,000

B. 372,000

C. 344,000

D. 300,000

Answer (C) is correct.

REQUIRED: The weighted-average number of shares used to calculate BEPS amounts for the first quarter.

DISCUSSION: The number of shares outstanding at January 1 was 300,000, 12,000 shares were issued on March 1, and 60,000 shares of preferred stock were converted to 60,000 shares of common stock on February 1. Thus, the weighted-average number of shares used to calculate BEPS amounts for the first quarter is 344,000 {300,000 + [12,000 × (1 ÷ 3)] + [60,000 × (2 ÷ 3)]}.

Answer (A) is incorrect. The quantity of 444,000 is the adjusted weighted-average number of shares used in the diluted EPS calculation. Answer (B) is incorrect. The quantity of 372,000 is the total outstanding at March 31. Answer (D) is incorrect. The quantity of 300,000 equals the shares outstanding at January 1.

13. The control number for determining whether Pubco's potential common shares are dilutive or antidilutive for the first quarter is

A. $1,000,000

B. $994,000

C. $(206,000)

D. $(1,200,000)

Answer (B) is correct.

REQUIRED: The control number for determining whether potential common shares are dilutive or antidilutive.

DISCUSSION: If a company reports discontinued operations or extraordinary items, it uses income from continuing operations (in Pubco's case, income before extraordinary item), adjusted for preferred dividends, as the control number for determining whether potential common shares are dilutive or antidilutive. Hence, the number of potential common shares used in calculating DEPS for income from continuing operations is also used in calculating the other DEPS amounts even if the effect is antidilutive with respect to the corresponding BEPS amounts. However, if the entity has a loss from continuing operations attributable to common shareholders, no potential common shares are included in the calculation of any DEPS amount. The control number for Pubco is $994,000 {$1,000,000 income before extraordinary item − [(120,000 preferred shares − 60,000 preferred shares converted) × $.10 per share dividend]}.

Answer (A) is incorrect. The amount of $1,000,000 is unadjusted income from continuing operations. Answer (C) is incorrect. The amount of $(206,000) represents the net loss available to common shareholders after subtracting the extraordinary loss. Answer (D) is incorrect. The amount of $(1,200,000) is the extraordinary loss.

14. The BEPS amount for Pubco's net income or loss available to common shareholders for the first quarter after the extraordinary item is

A. $2.89

B. $(0.46)

C. $(0.60)

D. $(3.49)

Answer (C) is correct.

REQUIRED: The BEPS amount for the net income or loss available to common shareholders after the extraordinary item.

DISCUSSION: The weighted-average number of shares used in the BEPS denominator is 344,000 {300,000 + [12,000 × (1 ÷ 3)] + [60,000 × (2 ÷ 3)]}. The numerator equals income before extraordinary item, minus preferred dividends, minus the extraordinary loss. Thus, it equals the control number minus the extraordinary loss, or $(206,000) [$994,000 − $1,200,000]. The BEPS amount for the net income or loss available to common shareholders after the extraordinary item is $(0.60) [$(206,000) ÷ 344,000 shares].

Answer (A) is incorrect. The amount of $2.89 is the BEPS amount for income available to common shareholders before the extraordinary item. Answer (B) is incorrect. The amount of $(0.46) uses the denominator of the DEPS calculation. Answer (D) is incorrect. The amount of $(3.49) is the BEPS amount for the extraordinary loss.

15. Refer to the information on the preceding page(s). The weighted-average number of shares used to calculate Pubco's DEPS amounts for the first quarter is

A. 444,000

B. 438,000

C. 372,000

D. 344,000

Answer (A) is correct.

REQUIRED: The weighted-average number of shares used to calculate DEPS amounts for the first quarter.

DISCUSSION: The denominator of DEPS equals the weighted-average number of shares used in the BEPS calculation, 344,000 {300,000 + [12,000 × (1 ÷ 3)] + [60,000 × (2 ÷ 3)]}, plus dilutive potential common shares (assuming the control number is not a loss). The number of incremental shares from assumed conversion of warrants is zero because they are antidilutive. The $25 market price is less than the $28 exercise price. The assumed conversion of all the preferred shares at the beginning of the quarter results in 80,000 incremental shares {[120,000 shares × (3 ÷ 3)] – [60,000 shares × (2 ÷ 3)]}. The assumed conversion of all the bonds at the beginning of the quarter results in 20,000 incremental shares [10 common shares per bond × ($2,000,000 ÷ $1,000 per bond)]. Consequently, the weighted-average number of shares used to calculate DEPS amounts for the first quarter is 444,000 (344,000 + 0 + 80,000 + 20,000).

Answer (B) is incorrect. The quantity of 438,000 assumes the hypothetical exercise of all the warrants at the beginning of the period at a price of $28 and the repurchase of shares using the proceeds at a price of $25. Answer (C) is incorrect. The quantity of 372,000 is the total outstanding at March 31. Answer (D) is incorrect. The quantity of 344,000 is the denominator of the BEPS fraction.

4.5 Long-Term Construction Contracts

16. The calculation of the income recognized in the third year of a 5-year construction contract accounted for using the percentage-of-completion method includes the ratio of

A. Costs incurred in Year 3 to total billings.

B. Costs incurred in Year 3 to total estimated costs.

C. Total costs incurred to date to total billings.

D. Total costs incurred to date to total estimated costs.

Answer (D) is correct.

REQUIRED: The ratio used in calculating income under the percentage-of-completion method.

DISCUSSION: The percentage-of-completion method recognizes gross profit or revenue based on the ratio of costs to date to estimated total costs. (This relationship is the recommended but not the only basis for determining progress.)

Answer (A) is incorrect. The estimate of progress may be based on various methods, e.g., units delivered, units of work performed, efforts expended, or cost incurred. However, billings do not necessarily measure progress. Also, the elements of the ratio should be measured on the same basis, but billings are not measured in terms of costs. Moreover, the gross profit or revenue recognized to date should be based on a cumulative calculation that reflects changes in estimates. Answer (B) is incorrect. The ratio of costs in one year to total costs does not estimate progress. Answer (C) is incorrect. Billings do not necessarily measure progress, and the elements of the ratio should be measured on the same basis.

17. A company appropriately uses the completed-contract method to account for a long-term construction contract. Revenue is recognized when progress billings are

	Recorded	Collected
A.	No	Yes
B.	Yes	Yes
C.	Yes	No
D.	No	No

Answer (D) is correct.

REQUIRED: The effect of progress billings on the recognition of revenue.

DISCUSSION: GAAP require that revenue be recognized when it is realized or realizable and earned. Under the completed-contract method, revenue recognition is appropriate only at the completion of the contract. Neither the recording nor the collection of progress billings affects this recognition.

18. Haft Construction Co. has consistently used the percentage-of-completion method. On January 10, Year 3, Haft began work on a $3 million construction contract. At the inception date, the estimated cost of construction was $2,250,000. The following data relate to the progress of the contract:

Gross profit recognized at 12/31/Yr 3	$ 300,000
Costs incurred 1/10/Yr 3 through	
12/31/Yr 4	1,800,000
Estimated cost to complete at 12/31/Yr 4	600,000

In its income statement for the year ended December 31, Year 4, what amount of gross profit should Haft report?

A. $450,000

B. $300,000

C. $262,500

D. $150,000

Answer (D) is correct.
REQUIRED: The amount of gross profit reported using the percentage-of-completion method.
DISCUSSION: The percentage-of-completion method provides for the recognition of gross profit based on the relationship between the costs incurred to date and estimated total costs for the completion of the contract. The total anticipated gross profit is multiplied by the ratio of the costs incurred to date to the total estimated costs, and the product is reduced by previously recognized gross profit. The percentage-of-completion at 12/31/Yr 4 is 75% [$1,800,000 ÷ ($1,800,000 + $600,000)]. The total anticipated gross profit is $600,000 ($3,000,000 contract price – $2,400,000 expected total costs). Consequently, a gross profit of $150,000 [(($600,000 total gross profit × 75%) – $300,000 previously recognized gross profit] is recognized for Year 4.
Answer (A) is incorrect. The current year's profit equals the cumulative income minus the previously recognized gross profit. Answer (B) is incorrect. The amount of $300,000 is the previously recognized gross profit. Answer (C) is incorrect. The amount of $262,500 assumes the total estimated gross profit is $750,000 ($3,000,000 price – $2,250,000 originally estimated total cost).

19. Pell Co.'s construction jobs (described below) commenced during the year just ended.

	Project 1	Project 2
Contract price	$420,000	$300,000
Costs incurred during the year	240,000	280,000
Estimated costs to complete	120,000	40,000
Billed to customers during the		
year	150,000	270,000
Received from customers		
during the year	90,000	250,000

If Pell appropriately used the completed-contract method, what amount of gross profit (loss) should Pell report in its income statement for the year?

A. $(20,000)

B. $0

C. $340,000

D. $420,000

Answer (A) is correct.
REQUIRED: The gross profit (loss) reported under the completed-contract method.
DISCUSSION: Under the completed-contract method, gross profit is deemed to meet the revenue recognition criteria (realized or realizable and earned) when the contract is completed. Neither project will be completed by the end of the year. Hence, no gross profit is recognized for Project 1 even though estimated data predict a gross profit of $60,000 ($420,000 contract price – $240,000 costs incurred – $120,000 additional estimated costs). However, when the current estimate of total contract costs indicates a loss, an immediate provision for the entire loss should be made regardless of the method of accounting used. Thus, a $20,000 loss ($300,000 contract price – $280,000 costs incurred – $40,000 additional estimated costs) will be reported for Project 2.

4.6 Revenue Recognition after Delivery

20. For financial statement purposes, the installment method of accounting may be used if the

A. Collection period extends over more than 12 months.

B. Installments are due in different years.

C. Ultimate amount collectible is indeterminate.

D. Percentage-of-completion method is inappropriate.

Answer (C) is correct.
REQUIRED: The use of the installment method.
DISCUSSION: Profits from sales in the ordinary course of business usually should be recognized at the time of sale unless collection of the sales price is not reasonably assured. When receivables are collected over an extended period and, because of the terms of the transaction or other conditions, no reasonable basis exists for estimating the degree of collectibility, the installment method or the cost-recovery method of accounting may be used.
Answer (A) is incorrect. Regardless of the length of the collection period, sales in the ordinary course of business should usually be recognized at the time of sale unless collectibility is not reasonably assured. Answer (B) is incorrect. Even if installments are due in different years, sales should be recognized at the time of sale unless collectibility is not reasonably assured. Answer (D) is incorrect. The installment method is not an alternative to the percentage-of-completion method, which is ordinarily used to account for long-term construction contracts.

21. It is proper to recognize revenue prior to the sale of merchandise when

I.   The revenue will be reported as an installment sale.

II. The revenue will be reported under the cost-recovery method.

A. I only.

B. II only.

C. Both I and II.

D. Neither I nor II.

Answer (D) is correct.
REQUIRED: The condition(s) under which it is proper to recognize revenue prior to the sale of merchandise.
DISCUSSION: The installment method recognizes income on a sale as the related receivable is collected. Under the cost-recovery method, profit is recognized only after collections exceed the cost of the item sold.

22. Dolce Co., which began operations on January 1, Year 8, appropriately uses the installment method of accounting to record revenues. The following information is available for the years ended December 31, Year 8 and Year 9:

	Year 8	Year 9
Sales	$1,000,000	$2,000,000
Gross profit realized on sales made in:		
Year 8	150,000	90,000
Year 9	--	200,000
Gross profit percentages	30%	40%

What amount of installment accounts receivable should Dolce report in its December 31, Year 9, balance sheet?

A. $1,100,000

B. $1,300,000

C. $1,700,000

D. $1,900,000

Answer (C) is correct.
REQUIRED: The amount of installment accounts receivable.
DISCUSSION: Gross profit realized on installment sales equals the cash collected on installment sales for the period times the gross profit percentage on installment sales for the period. Hence, cash collected on Year 8 sales was $800,000 [($150,000 + $90,000) ÷ 30%], and cash collected on Year 9 sales was $500,000 ($200,000 ÷ 40%). The remaining balance of installment receivables is therefore $1,700,000 ($1,000,000 + $2,000,000 – $800,000 – $500,000).
Answer (A) is incorrect. The amount of $1,100,000 equals the total gross profit (both realized and unrealized) for Year 8 and Year 9. Answer (B) is incorrect. The amount of $1,300,000 is the total cash collected. Answer (D) is incorrect. The amount of $1,900,000 equals total sales minus total gross profit for Year 8 and Year 9.

23. Several of Fox, Inc.'s customers are having cash flow problems. Information pertaining to these customers for the years ended March 31, Year 7 and Year 8 follows:

	3/31/Yr 7	3/31/Yr 8
Sales	$10,000	$15,000
Cost of sales	8,000	9,000
Cash collections		
on Year 7 sales	7,000	3,000
on Year 8 sales	--	12,000

If the cost-recovery method is used, what amount would Fox report as gross profit from sales to these customers for the year ended March 31, Year 8?

A. $2,000

B. $3,000

C. $5,000

D. $15,000

Answer (C) is correct.
REQUIRED: The gross profit from sales if the cost-recovery method is used.
DISCUSSION: The cost-recovery method recognizes profit only after collections exceed the cost of the item sold, that is, when the full cost has been recovered. Subsequent amounts collected are treated entirely as revenue (debit cash and deferred gross profit, credit the receivable and realized gross profit). The sum of collections in excess of costs to be recognized as gross profit is $5,000 {[$3,000 Year 8 collections on Year 7 sales – ($8,000 cost – $7,000 Year 7 collections on Year 7 sales)] + ($12,000 collections on Year 8 sales – $9,000 cost)}.
Answer (A) is incorrect. The amount of $2,000 excludes the profit on Year 8 sales. Answer (B) is incorrect. The amount of $3,000 excludes the profit on Year 7 sales. Answer (D) is incorrect. The amount of $15,000 equals Year 8 sales.

4.7 Fair Value Measurements

24. For the purpose of a fair value measurement (FVM) of an asset or liability, a transaction is assumed to occur in the

A. Principal market if one exists.

B. Most advantageous market.

C. Market in which the result is optimized.

D. Principal market or most advantageous market at the election of the reporting entity.

Answer (A) is correct.
REQUIRED: The market in which a transaction is assumed to occur.
DISCUSSION: For FVM purposes, a transaction is assumed to occur in the principal market for an asset or liability if one exists. The principal market has the greatest volume or level of activity. If no such market exists, the transaction is assumed to occur in the most advantageous market.

25. Fair value measurements (FVMs) of assets and liabilities are based on transactions between market participants at the measurement date. Market participants

A. Must be specifically identified.

B. May be related parties if they are knowledgeable about the asset or liability.

C. Include parties who are forced to engage in the transactions if they are independent of the entity.

D. Are willing and able to engage in transactions involving the asset or liability.

Answer (D) is correct.
REQUIRED: The characteristic of market participants.
DISCUSSION: Market participants are not related parties. They are independent of the reporting entity. They also are knowledgeable and willing and able (but not compelled) to engage in transactions involving the asset or liability.
Answer (A) is incorrect. Market participants need not be specifically identified. Instead, the entity must identify their general characteristics, with consideration of factors specific to (1) the asset or liability, (2) the market, and (3) parties with whom the entity would deal. Answer (B) is incorrect. Market participants must be independent of the entity. Answer (C) is incorrect. Market participants do not include parties who engage in forced or liquidation sales or are otherwise compelled to act.

26. The fair value measurement (FVM) of an asset

A. Assumes transfer, not a settlement.

B. Is based on the expected use by the reporting entity.

C. Reflects the highest and best use by market participants.

D. Includes the entity's own credit risk.

Answer (C) is correct.
REQUIRED: The true statement about the FVM of an asset.
DISCUSSION: The FVM is based on the highest and best use (HBU) by market participants. This use maximizes the value of the asset. The HBU is in-use if the value-maximizing use is in combination with other assets in a group. An example is machinery. The HBU is in-exchange if the value-maximizing use is as a standalone asset. An example is a financial asset.
Answer (A) is incorrect. The FVM of a liability, not an asset, assumes transfer without settlement. Answer (B) is incorrect. The FVM assumes use by market participants. Answer (D) is incorrect. The FVM of a liability includes nonperformance risk. An element of nonperformance risk is the entity's own credit risk (credit standing).

27. Fair value measurement (FVM) of an asset or liability is based on a fair value hierarchy that establishes priorities among inputs to valuation techniques. According to the hierarchy,

A. Observable inputs are on Level 1.

B. Unobservable inputs are on Level 2.

C. Quoted prices for items similar to the asset or liability are on Level 3.

D. Unadjusted quoted prices for an identical asset or liability are on Level 1.

Answer (D) is correct.
REQUIRED: The appropriate level of the fair value hierarchy for inputs to valuation techniques.
DISCUSSION: The level of the FVM depends on the lowest level input significant to the entire FVM. Level 1 inputs are unadjusted quoted prices in active markets for identical assets (liabilities) that the entity can access at the measurement date. An adjustment for new information results in a lower level FVM.
Answer (A) is incorrect. Observable inputs that are not Level 1 quoted prices are on Level 2. Examples are quoted prices for similar items in active markets and quoted prices in markets that are not active. Answer (B) is incorrect. Level 3 inputs are unobservable. They are used in the absence of observable inputs and should be based on the best available information in the circumstances. Answer (C) is incorrect. Quoted prices for items similar (not identical) to the asset or liability are on Level 2.

Use the additional questions in Gleim **CPA Test Prep Online** to create Test Sessions that emulate Prometric!

4.8 PRACTICE SIMULATION

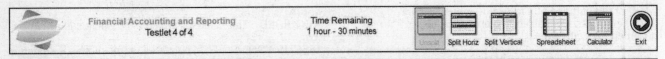

Financial Accounting and Reporting
Testlet 4 of 4

Time Remaining
1 hour - 30 minutes

Unsplit Split Horiz Split Vertical Spreadsheet Calculator Exit

DIRECTIONS

Note: If you believe you have encountered a software malfunction, report it to the test center staff immediately.

Navigation

To navigate from task to task, use the controls at the bottom of the screen. Click on the **Next** button to advance to the next task, or the **Previous** button to go to the previous task. To go directly to any task, click on its number.

▼ = Reminder   Directions 1 2 3 4 5 6 7   ◄ Previous Next ►

If you would like a reminder to revisit a task, or want to indicate that you are finished with it, click on the reminder flag below the task number. To clear the flag, click on it again. Reminder flags are for your use only – they do not contribute to your score.

Tabs

In this part of the examination, you will be asked to complete various tasks. Every task has one or more **Work Tabs**. Some tasks have one or more **Information Tabs**, others may have none. Every task has a **Help** tab.

If a task has **Information Tabs**, you may use the information in them to complete your responses in the **Work Tabs**.

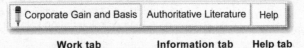

Corporate Gain and Basis   Authoritative Literature   Help

Work tab   Information tab   Help tab

Work Tabs:
- **Work Tabs** are identified with a pencil icon. This is where your responses are expected.
- Each task has one or more **Work Tabs**.
- **Work Tabs** contain directions for completing the task – be sure to read these directions carefully.
- The **Work Tab** name in the example above is for illustration only – yours will differ.
- You must complete all of the **Work Tabs** in each task to receive full credit.

Information Tabs:
- The Authoritative Literature will be provided in all tasks in the AUD, FAR, and REG sections for your reference.
- Your simulation may have one or more additional **Information Tabs**. Like the Authoritative Literature tabs, **Information Tabs** do not have a pencil icon.
- If your task has additional **Information Tabs**, go through each to familiarize yourself with the task content.

Help Tab:
- The **Help Tab** provides assistance with the exam software that is used in this task. For example, if the task is to compose a memorandum, **Help** will provide information about the word processor.

The Toolbar

The toolbar at the top of the screen shows the amount of time remaining for you to complete the tasks. In addition, the following tools are available. Note that only the **Exit** button is displayed when Directions are visible - the others will appear when you begin the tasks.

Unsplit   Split Horiz   Split Vertical

Click on these buttons to split or unsplit the screen. You can split the screen vertically or horizontally.

Calculator

Click on this button to display the calculator; click on it again to hide the calculator. To move the calculator, click on the calculator title bar and drag the calculator to the desired location.

Spreadsheet

Click on this button to use the spreadsheet; click on it again to hide the spreadsheet. To move the spreadsheet, click on the the spreadsheet title bar and drag the spreadsheet to the desired location.

Exit

Click on this button to go on to the next part of the examination. You must complete all of the tasks to receive full credit. Once you click on **Exit** and confirm the action, you will NOT be able to return to this testlet.

▼ = Reminder   Directions 1 2 3 4 5 6   ◄ Previous Next ►

Classification of Transactions | Authoritative Literature | Help

Select from the list provided the best classification for each transaction below. Each choice may be used once, more than once, or not at all.

Transaction	Answer
1. An increase in the unrealized holding loss for trading securities.	
2. An increase in the unrealized holding loss for available-for-sale securities.	
3. Income from operations of an operating segment in the segment's disposal year. The operations and cash flows of the segment can be clearly distinguished from the rest of the entity for operational and financial reporting purposes.	
4. A gain on remeasuring a foreign subsidiary's financial statements from the local currency into the functional currency.	
5. A loss on translating a foreign subsidiary's financial statements from the functional local currency into the reporting currency.	
6. A loss caused by a major earthquake in an area previously considered to be subject only to minor tremors.	
7. The probable receipt of $1 million from a pending lawsuit.	
8. The purchase of research and development services. There were no other research and development activities.	

Choices
A) Income from continuing operations, with no separate disclosure
B) Income from continuing operations, with separate disclosure
C) Extraordinary items
D) Other comprehensive income
E) None of the other categories

▼ = Reminder   Directions   [1] 2 3 4 5 6   ◀ Previous   Next ▶
                                    ▽ ▽ ▽ ▽ ▽ ▽

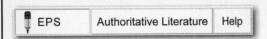

Pucket Corp. is in the process of preparing its financial statements for the year ended December 31, Year 4. Before closing the books, it prepared the following:

Condensed Trial Balance
December 31, Year 4

	Debit	Credit
Total assets	$ 7,082,500	
Total liabilities		$ 1,700,000
Common stock		1,250,000
Additional paid-in capital		2,097,500
Donated capital		90,000
Retained earnings, 1/1/Year 4		1,650,000
Net sales		6,250,000
Cost of sales	3,750,000	
Selling and administrative expenses	1,212,500	
Interest expense	122,500	
Gain on sale of long-term investments		130,000
Income tax expense	300,000	
Loss on disposition of plant assets	225,000	
Loss due to earthquake damage	475,000	
	$13,167,500	$13,167,500

Other financial data for the year ended December 31, Year 4:

- Sales returns and allowances equaled $215,000, and sales discounts taken were $95,000.
- Estimated federal income tax payments were $200,000, and accrued federal income taxes equaled $100,000. The total charged to income tax expense does not properly reflect current or deferred income tax expense or interperiod income tax allocation for income statement purposes. The enacted tax rate on all types of taxable income for the current and future years is 30%. The alternative minimum tax is less than the regular income tax.
- Interest expense includes 6% interest on 20-year bonds issued at their face amount of $1,500,000.
- A $90,000 excess of carrying amount over tax basis in depreciable assets arose from receipt of a contribution of equipment by a local government on December 31, Year 4. It is expected to be depreciated over 5 years beginning in Year 5. There were no temporary differences prior to Year 5.
- Officers' life insurance expense (not tax deductible) is $70,000.
- The earthquake damage is considered unusual and infrequent, but the disposition of plant assets is considered infrequent but not unusual. Moreover, the disposition of plant assets was not a disposal of a component of an entity.
- The shares of common stock ($5 par) traded on a national exchange:

Outstanding at 1/1/Year 4	200,000
Issued on 3/30/Year 4 as a 10% stock dividend	20,000
Issued shares for $25 per share on 6/30/Year 4	30,000
Outstanding at 12/31/Year 4	250,000

- Pucket declared a $1.25 common stock dividend on December 28, Year 4.

Using the information above, enter in the shaded cells the EPS calculations.

Basic EPS	*Answer*
1. Income before extraordinary items	
2. Extraordinary items	
3. Net income	

| Accounting Changes | Authoritative Literature | Help |

An entity is considering events that may have an effect on accounting treatments. For each event below, select from the lists provided the appropriate description and accounting treatment. Assume that all events are material in amount. A choice may be used once, more than once, or not at all.

Event	Description	Accounting Treatment
1. Change in long-term construction contract from the completed-contract method to the percentage-of-completion method		
2. Write off of uncollectible receivables under the allowance method		
3. Change in salvage value of a depreciable asset		
4. Change in the useful life of a patent		
5. Inventory costing method changed from FIFO to LIFO		
6. An increase in the estimated effective tax rate		
7. A change in depreciation method		

Descriptions
A) Change in accounting principle
B) Change in accounting estimate
C) Change in reporting entity
D) Change in estimate effected by a change in principle
E) Error correction
F) Neither an accounting change nor an error correction

Accounting Treatments
I) Retrospective application
II) Restatement
III) Current and prospective application
IV) No effect

Pucket Corp. is in the process of preparing its financial statements for the year ended December 31, Year 4. Before closing the books, it prepared the following:

Condensed Trial Balance
December 31, Year 4

	Debit	Credit
Total assets	$ 7,082,500	
Total liabilities		$ 1,700,000
Common stock		1,250,000
Additional paid-in capital		2,097,500
Donated capital		90,000
Retained earnings, 1/1/Year 4		1,650,000
Net sales		6,250,000
Cost of sales	3,750,000	
Selling and administrative expenses	1,212,500	
Interest expense	122,500	
Gain on sale of long-term investments		130,000
Income tax expense	300,000	
Loss on disposition of plant assets	225,000	
Loss due to earthquake damage	475,000	
	$13,167,500	$13,167,500

Other financial data for the year ended December 31, Year 4:

- Sales returns and allowances equaled $215,000, and sales discounts taken were $95,000.
- Estimated federal income tax payments were $200,000, and accrued federal income taxes equaled $100,000. The total charged to income tax expense does not properly reflect current or deferred income tax expense or interperiod income tax allocation for income statement purposes. The enacted tax rate on all types of taxable income for the current and future years is 30%. The alternative minimum tax is less than the regular income tax.
- Interest expense includes 6% interest on 20-year bonds issued at their face amount of $1,500,000.
- A $90,000 excess of carrying amount over tax basis in depreciable assets arose from receipt of a contribution of equipment by a local government on December 31, Year 4. It is expected to be depreciated over 5 years beginning in Year 5. There were no temporary differences prior to Year 5.
- Officers' life insurance expense (not tax deductible) is $70,000.
- The earthquake damage is considered unusual and infrequent, but the disposition of plant assets is considered infrequent but not unusual. Moreover, the disposition of plant assets was not a disposal of a component of an entity.
- The shares of common stock ($5 par) traded on a national exchange:

Outstanding at 1/1/Year 4	200,000
Issued on 3/30/Year 4 as a 10% stock dividend	20,000
Issued shares for $25 per share on 6/30/Year 4	30,000
Outstanding at 12/31/Year 4	250,000

- Pucket declared a $1.25 common stock dividend on December 28, Year 4.

-- Continued on next page --

| Income Statement | Authoritative Literature | Help | -- **Continued** |

Using the information from the previous page, enter in the shaded cells the correct amounts for Pucket Corporation's income statement.

Pucket Corporation Income Statement For the Year Ended December 31, Year 4		
Net sales		$
Cost of sales		
Gross profit		
Selling and administrative expenses		
Income from operations		
Other revenues and gains:		
Gain on sale of long-term investments		
Other expenses and losses:		
Interest expense	$	
Loss on disposition of plant assets		
Income from continuing operations before income tax		
Income tax expense:		
Current tax expense		
Deferred tax expense		
Income before extraordinary item		
Extraordinary item-loss from earthquake (net of applicable taxes)		
Net income		$

| ▼ = Reminder | | Directions | 1 ▽ | 2 ▽ | 3 ▽ | 4 ▽ | 5 ▽ | 6 ▽ | | ◀ Previous | Next ▶ |

Construction Contracts | Authoritative Literature | Help

On January 1, Year 1, a contractor began work on a $24,000 construction contract that is expected to be completed in 3 years. At the inception date, the estimated cost of construction was $21,000. The following data relate to the actual and expected construction costs and the gross profit or loss recognized each year:

	Year 1	Year 2	Year 3
Costs incurred during each year	$ 6,300	$11,300	$4,000
Costs expected in the future	14,700	C	0
Gross profit (loss) recognized each year	A	B	800

The contractor uses the percentage-of-completion method to account for this project.

Using the information above, enter in the shaded cells the missing information marked at the capital letters **A**, **B**, and **C**. Round all amounts to the nearest dollar. If the amount is zero, enter zero (0). If the amount is a loss, enter as a negative amount.

Missing Information	*Answer*
1. Gross profit (loss) recognized in Year 1 (**A**)	
2. Gross profit (loss) recognized in Year 2 (**B**)	
3. Estimate at the end of Year 2 of costs expected to be incurred during Year 3 (**C**)	

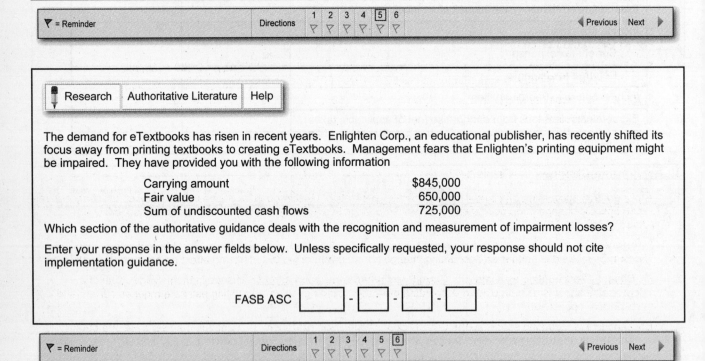

Research | Authoritative Literature | Help

The demand for eTextbooks has risen in recent years. Enlighten Corp., an educational publisher, has recently shifted its focus away from printing textbooks to creating eTextbooks. Management fears that Enlighten's printing equipment might be impaired. They have provided you with the following information

Carrying amount	$845,000
Fair value	650,000
Sum of undiscounted cash flows	725,000

Which section of the authoritative guidance deals with the recognition and measurement of impairment losses?

Enter your response in the answer fields below. Unless specifically requested, your response should not cite implementation guidance.

FASB ASC [ ] - [ ] - [ ] - [ ]

Unofficial Answers

1. Classification of Transactions (8 Gradable Items)

1. <u>B) Income from continuing operations, with separate disclosure.</u> An unrealized holding loss (a decline in fair value) on trading securities must be recognized in earnings. The change in net unrealized holding gain or loss included in earnings for the period must be disclosed.

2. <u>D) Other comprehensive income.</u> An unrealized holding loss on available-for-sale securities is excluded from earnings and reported in other comprehensive income until realized. GAAP require a variety of disclosures regarding available-for-sale securities.

3. <u>E) None of the other categories.</u> The operating segment meets the criteria for classification as a component of an entity. Thus, its operating results should be reported in discontinued operations provided that (1) its operations and cash flows will be or have been eliminated from the ongoing operations of the entity as a result of the disposal and (2) the entity will have no significant continuing involvement after the disposal.

4. <u>A) Income from continuing operations, with no separate disclosure.</u> Remeasurement gains and losses are included in income from continuing operations. GAAP are silent regarding remeasurement disclosures.

5. <u>D) Other comprehensive income.</u> Translation adjustments are reported in other comprehensive income. They are not reported in earnings until the entity is sold or liquidated.

6. <u>C) Extraordinary items.</u> Because the area has previously been subject to minor tremors only, the loss caused by the major earthquake is unusual and infrequent in the environment in which the entity operates. Hence, the loss meets the criteria of an extraordinary item.

7. <u>E) None of the other categories.</u> A gain contingency is not recognized until realized, but it should be disclosed. However, care should be taken to avoid misleading implications about the likelihood of realization.

8. <u>B) Income from continuing operations, with separate disclosure.</u> The costs of R&D contract services are included in R&D costs. These costs are reported under continuing operations with separate disclosure.

2. EPS (3 Gradable Items)

1. <u>$2.98.</u> The weighted-average number of shares outstanding is 235,000 {200,000 + 20,000 + [30,000 × (6 ÷12)]}. Basic EPS before extraordinary item is $2.98 ($701,000 income before extraordinary item ÷ 235,000 shares).

2. <u>$(1.41).</u> Basic loss per share for the extraordinary item (net of tax effect) is $(1.41) ($332,500 ÷ 235,000 shares).

3. <u>$1.57.</u> Net income is $368,500 ($701,000 − $332,500).
   Basic EPS for net income is $1.57 ($368,500 ÷ 235,000 shares).

3. Accounting Changes (7 Gradable Items)

1. <u>A) Change in accounting principle, I) Retrospective application.</u> A change in long-term construction contract accounting methods is a change in an accounting principle. A change in an accounting principle requires retrospective application.

2. <u>F) Neither an accounting change nor an error correction, IV) No effect.</u> Writing off uncollectible receivables under the allowance method is neither an accounting change nor an error correction. It has no effect on accounting treatments.

3. <u>B) Change in accounting estimate, III) Current and prospective application.</u> A change in the salvage value of a depreciable asset is a change in an accounting estimate. A change in an accounting estimate requires current and prospective application.

4. <u>B) Change in accounting estimate, III) Current and prospective application.</u> A change in the useful life of a patent is a change in an accounting estimate. A change in an accounting estimate requires current and prospective application.

5. <u>A) Change in accounting principle, I) Retrospective application.</u> Changing the inventory costing method from FIFO to LIFO is a change in an accounting principle. A change in an accounting principle requires retrospective application.

6. <u>B) Change in accounting estimate, III) Current and prospective application.</u> An increase in the estimated effective tax rate is a change in an accounting estimate. A change in an accounting estimate requires current and prospective application.

7. <u>D) Change in estimate effected by a change in principle, III) Current and prospective application.</u> A change in depreciation method is a change in an estimate effected by a change in principle. A change in an estimate effected by a change in principle requires current and prospective application.

4. Income Statement (16 Gradable Items)

Pucket Corporation Income Statement For the Year Ended December 31, Year 4		
Net sales		$6,250,000 [1]
Cost of sales		3,750,000 [2]
Gross profit		2,500,000 [3]
Selling and administrative expenses		1,212,500 [4]
Income from operations		1,287,500 [5]
Other revenues and gains:		
Gain on sale of long-term investments		130,000 [6]
Other expenses and losses:		
Interest expense	$(122,500) [7]	
Loss on disposition of plant assets	(225,000) [8]	(347,500) [9]
Income from continuing operations before income tax		1,070,000 [10]
Income tax expense:		
Current tax expense	342,000 [11]	
Deferred tax expense	27,000 [12]	369,000 [13]
Income before extraordinary item		701,000 [14]
Extraordinary item-loss from earthquake (net of applicable taxes)		332,500 [15]
Net income		$368,500 [16]

Explanation of amounts

[1] Net sales equals $6,250,000 as provided in the situation.

[2] Cost of sales equals $3,750,000 as provided in the situation.

[3] Gross profit is $2,500,000 ($6,250,000 net sales – $3,750,000 cost of sales).

[4] Selling and administrative expenses equal $1,212,500 as provided in the situation.

[5] Income from operations is $1,287,500 ($2,500,000 gross profit – $1,212,500 selling and administrative expenses).

[6] The gain on the sale of long-term investments is considered an infrequent but not unusual event. Thus, this gain must be reported in the other revenues and gains section.

[7] Interest expense equals $122,500 as provided in the situation. Interest expense is generally presented in the other expenses and losses section.

[8] The loss on the disposition of plant assets is considered an infrequent but not unusual event. Thus, this gain must be reported in the other expenses and losses section.

[9] The total of other expenses and losses is $347,500 ($122,500 interest expense + $225,000 loss on disposition of plant assets).

[10] Income from continuing operations before income tax is $1,070,000 ($1,287,500 operating income + $130,000 other revenues and gains – $347,500 other expenses and losses).

[11] Income before income taxes and extraordinary item $1,070,000
    Plus officers' life insurance expense (nondeductible)   70,000
Income subject to tax   1,140,000
   Income tax rate   ×   30%
Income taxes excluding extraordinary item $ 342,000

[12] Excess of carrying amount over tax basis in depreciable assets
    (expected to reverse equally over next 5 years) $90,000
Deferred income tax liability, 12/31/Year 4 ($90,000 × 30%) $27,000
   Minus beginning balance, 1/1/Year 4   0
Net change in deferred tax liability for Year 4 $27,000

[13]	Current tax expense	$342,000
	Plus deferred tax expense	27,000
	Total income tax expense	$369,000

[14] Income before extraordinary item is $701,000 ($1,070,000 income from continuing operations before income tax – $369,000 income tax expense).

[15]	Extraordinary loss from earthquake damage	$475,000
	Minus income tax benefit ($475,000 × 30%)	142,500
	Net of income tax effect	$332,500

[16] Net income is $368,500 ($701,000 income before extraordinary item – $332,500 extraordinary loss).

5. Construction Contracts (3 Gradable Items)

1.   Gross profit recognized in Year 1 (**A**) is $900. The percentage of completion is 30% ($6,300 ÷ $21,000). The expected profit from the project is $3,000 ($24,000 – $21,000). Thus, the gross profit recognized in Year 1 is $900 ($3,000 × 30%).
2.   Gross profit recognized in Year 2 (**B**) is $700. The total cost of the project was $21,000 ($6,300 + $11,300 +$4,000). Thus, the total gross profit recognized from the project is $2,400 ($24,000 – $21,600). The gross profits of $900 and $800 were recognized in Years 1 and 3, respectively. Thus, the gross profit recognized in Year 2 is $700 ($2,400 – $900 – $800).
3.   Estimate at the end of Year 2 of costs expected to be incurred during Year 3 (**C**) is $4,400. The gross profit recognized in Years 1 and 2 is $1,600 ($900 + $700). At the end of Year 2, total costs incurred are $17,600 ($6,300 + $11,300). The amount of total expected costs of the project as estimated at the end of Year 2 (represented by **X**) can be calculated from the following equation: ($24,000 – **X**) × ($17,600 ÷ **X**) = $1,600. Thus, **X** is equal to $22,000, and (**C**) is equal to $4,400 ($22,000 – $17,600).

6. Research (1 Gradable Item)

Answer: FASB ASC 360-10-35-17

360-10-35-17 An impairment loss shall be recognized only if the carrying amount of a long-lived asset (asset group) is not recoverable and exceeds its fair value. The carrying amount of a long-lived asset (asset group) is not recoverable if it exceeds the sum of the undiscounted cash flows expected to result from the use and eventual disposition of the asset (asset group). That assessment shall be based on the carrying amount of the asset (asset group) at the date it is tested for recoverability, whether in use (see paragraph 360-10-35-33) or under development (see paragraph 360-10-35-34). An impairment loss shall be measured as the amount by which the carrying amount of a long-lived asset (asset group) exceeds its fair value.

Gleim Simulation Grading

Task	Correct Responses		Gradable Items		Score per Task
1	_____	÷	8	=	_____
2	_____	÷	3	=	_____
3	_____	÷	7	=	_____
4	_____	÷	16	=	_____
5	_____	÷	3	=	_____
Research	_____	÷	1	=	_____

	Total of Scores per Task	_____
÷	Total Number of Tasks	6
	Total Score	_____%

Use **CPA Gleim Online** and **Simulation Wizard** to practice more task-based simulations in a realistic environment.

STUDY UNIT FIVE
FINANCIAL STATEMENT DISCLOSURE

(18 pages of outline)

5.1	Significant Accounting Policies	163
5.2	Segment Reporting	164
5.3	Interim Financial Reporting	168
5.4	Related Party Disclosures	173
5.5	Unconditional Purchase Obligations	174
5.6	Significant Risks and Uncertainties	175
5.7	Subsequent Events	177
5.8	Financial Instrument Disclosures	178
5.9	Practice Simulation	190

According to the **full disclosure principle**, understandable information capable of affecting user decisions should be reported. The financial statements are the primary means of disclosure. However, almost all accounting pronouncements require additional disclosures in the notes. Because memorizing them is virtually impossible, candidates should anticipate the disclosure requirements before reading the summary, outline, or actual pronouncement. The appropriate perspective is that of an informed creditor or investor.

The study unit begins with significant accounting policies to set the tone for the types of disclosures required by GAAP.

5.1 SIGNIFICANT ACCOUNTING POLICIES

1. **Overview**

    a. Accounting policies are the specific principles and the methods of applying them used by the reporting entity. Management selects these policies as the most appropriate for fair presentation of financial statements.

    b. Business and not-for-profit entities **must disclose** all significant accounting policies as an **integral part** of the financial statements.

        1) Disclosure of accounting policies in unaudited interim financial statements is not required when the reporting entity has not changed its policies since the end of the preceding fiscal year.

2. **Presentation and Disclosure**

    a. The preferred presentation is a **summary of accounting policies** in a separate section preceding the notes or in the initial note.

    b. The disclosure should include accounting principles adopted and the methods of applying them that materially affect the financial statements. Disclosure extends to accounting policies that involve

        1) A selection from existing acceptable alternatives,

        2) Policies unique to the industry in which the entity operates, even if they are predominantly followed in that industry, and

        3) GAAP applied in an unusual or innovative way.

    c.   Certain disclosures about policies of business entities are commonly required. These items include the following:

        1)   Basis of consolidation
        2)   Depreciation methods
        3)   Amortization of intangible assets (excluding goodwill, which is not amortizable)
        4)   Inventory pricing
        5)   Recognition of profit on long-term construction-type contracts
        6)   Recognition of revenue from franchising and leasing operations
        7)   Policy for determining which items are cash equivalents

    d.   Disclosure of accounting policies should **not duplicate details** presented elsewhere. For example, the summary of significant policies should not contain the composition of plant assets or inventories or the maturity dates of noncurrent debt.

Stop and review! You have completed the outline for this subunit. Study multiple-choice questions 1 through 3 beginning on page 180.

5.2 SEGMENT REPORTING

1.   **Overview**

    a.   Segment reporting includes interim financial reports and annual financial statements of **public** business entities. The objective is to provide information about the different business activities of the entity and the economic environments in which it operates.

        1)   Ordinarily, information is to be reported on the basis that is used internally for evaluating performance and making resource allocation decisions. This approach aligns external and internal reporting.

        2)   Disclosure of information is **not** required if it is not prepared for internal use, and reporting it would not be feasible.

    b.   Segmentation is based on internal organizational structure and the availability of separate financial information. An **operating segment** has three characteristics:

        1)   It is a business component of the entity that may earn revenues and incur expenses.

        2)   Its operating results are regularly reviewed by the entity's **chief operating decision maker** (CODM) for the purpose of resource allocation and performance assessment.

        3)   Its separate financial information is available.

    c.   Operating segments may be **aggregated** if (1) doing so is consistent with the objective; (2) they have similar economic characteristics; and (3) they have similar products and services, production processes, classes of customers, distribution methods, and regulatory environments.

2.   **Quantitative Thresholds**

    a.   **Reportable segments** are operating segments that must be separately disclosed if one of the following quantitative thresholds is met:

        1)   **Revenue test.** Reported revenue, including sales to external customers and intersegment sales or transfers, is at least 10% of the combined revenue of all operating segments.

        2)   **Asset test.** Assets are at least 10% of the combined assets of all operating segments.

3) **Profit (loss) test.** The absolute amount of reported profit or loss is at least 10% of the greater, in absolute amount, of either the combined reported **profit** of all operating segments that did **not** report a loss or the combined reported **loss** of all operating segments that **did** report a loss.

    a) GAAP do not specify how segment profit (loss) is calculated. This amount depends upon the revenues, expenses, gains, and losses included in the measure reviewed by the CODM. However, the following is the general approach:

> Sales
> (Traceable costs)
> (Allocated costs)
> Profit (loss)

b. If an operating segment does not meet any threshold, management may report it if such information would be useful.

Test Amount	Percent of Relevant Amount
Revenue	≥ 10% of all operating segments
Assets	≥ 10% of all operating segments
Absolute Profit or Loss	≥ 10% of greater of absolute sum of (1) all profitable OSs or (2) all loss-reporting OSs

---

EXAMPLE

Greque Co. operates in four industries. Which of the following operating segments should be identified as a reportable segment under the operating profit or loss test?

Segment	Operating Profit (Loss)
Rho	$ 90,000
Sigma	(100,000)
Tau	910,000
Upsilon	(420,000)

An operating segment is identified as a reportable segment if it meets the profit or loss test (among others). The segment is reportable if the absolute amount of the operating profit or loss equals at least 10% of the greater, in absolute amount, of (1) the combined operating profit of all operating segments not reporting an operating loss or (2) the combined operating loss of all operating segments reporting an operating loss.

The first step in applying the operating profit (loss) test is to classify the segments into those reporting profits and those reporting losses and summing the amounts.

Segment	Operating Profit	Operating Loss
Rho	$ 90,000	$ 0
Sigma	0	100,000
Tau	910,000	0
Upsilon	0	420,000
	$1,000,000	$520,000

The greater sum, in absolute dollars, is that of the operating profit segments. The reporting threshold is therefore $100,000 ($1,000,000 × 10%). Segments Sigma, Tau, and Upsilon report absolute amounts greater than this threshold, and they are the reportable segments.

---

c. Information about operating segments not meeting the quantitative thresholds may be combined to produce a reportable segment only if they share a **majority** of the **aggregation criteria**.

d. If the **total external revenue** of the operating segments meeting the quantitative thresholds is **less than 75%** of consolidated revenue, additional operating segments are identified as reportable until the 75% level is reached.

e. Information about nonreportable activities and segments is combined and disclosed in an **all other** category as a reconciling item.

f.   As the number of reportable segments increases above 10, the entity may decide that it has reached a practical limit.

Reportable Segments

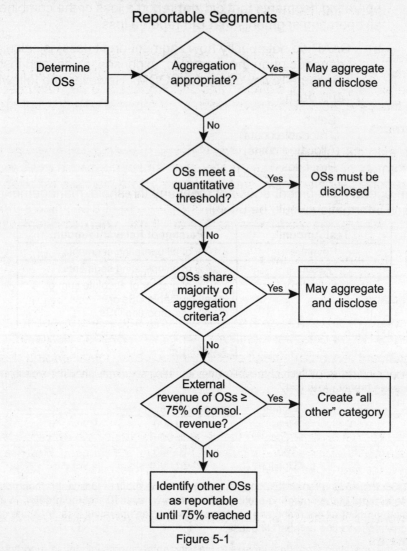

Figure 5-1

3. **Disclosures**

    a. **General information**, such as the factors used to identify the reportable segments, including the basis of organization, and the types of revenue-generating products and services for each reportable segment.

    b. A **measure of profit or loss and total assets** for each reportable segment. Moreover, if the amounts are included in the measure of profit or loss reviewed by the CODM or are otherwise regularly provided to that person, other disclosures about each reportable segment include the following:

        1) Revenues from external customers and other operating segments,
        2) Interest revenue and expense,
        3) Depreciation,
        4) Depletion,
        5) Amortization,
        6) Unusual items,
        7) Equity in the net income of equity-based investees,
        8) Income tax expense or benefit,
        9) Extraordinary items, and
        10) Other significant noncash items.

c.   The investment in **equity-based investees** and total expenditures for additions to most **long-lived assets** for each reportable segment if they are included in the segment assets reviewed by the CODM.

4.   **Interest**

a.   A segment's interest revenue and interest expense are reported separately. However, a majority of a segment's revenues may be from interest, with net interest revenue the primary basis for assessing its performance and the resources allocated to it. In this case, net interest revenue may be reported given proper disclosure.

5.   **Measurement**

a.   The external information reported is measured in the same way as the internal information used for resource allocation and performance evaluation. The amount of a reported segment item, such as assets, is the measure reported to the CODM.

1)   If the CODM uses more than one measure of a segment's profit or loss or assets, the reported measures are those most consistent with the consolidated statements.

2)   Explanations of the measurements of segment profit or loss and segment assets should be given for each reportable segment.

6.   **Reconciliations**

a.   Reconciliations to the consolidated amounts must be provided for the total reportable segments' amounts for significant items of information disclosed.

b.   Significant reconciling items should be separately identified and described. However, reconciliations of balance sheet items are required only for years in which a balance sheet is presented.

7.   **Interim Period Information**

a.   This information is disclosed for each reportable segment in condensed financial statements. Disclosures include (1) external revenues; (2) intersegment revenues; (3) a measure of segment profit or loss; (4) total assets that have materially changed since the last annual report; (5) differences from the last annual report in the basis of segmentation or of segment profit or loss; and (6) a reconciliation of the total reportable segments' profit or loss to consolidated pretax income and its components.

8.   **Restatements**

a.   Restatement of previously reported information is required if changes in internal organization cause the composition of reportable segments to change. However, an entity must restate only items of disclosure that it can feasibly restate.

b.   The entity may choose not to restate segment information for earlier periods, including interim periods. Segment information for the year of the change then must be disclosed under the old basis and the new basis of segmentation if feasible.

9.   **Entity-Wide Disclosures**

a.   Such disclosures must be provided only if they are not given in the reportable operating segment information.

b.   Revenues from external customers for each product and service (or each group of similar products and services) are reported if feasible based on the financial information used to produce the general-purpose financial statements.

c.   The following information about geographic areas is also reported if feasible:

1)   External revenues attributed to the home country and to all foreign countries,

2)   Material external revenues attributed to an individual foreign country,

3)   The basis for attributing revenues from external customers, and

4)   Certain information about assets.

d.   If 10% or more of revenue is derived from sales to any single customer, (1) that fact, (2) the amount from each such customer, and (3) the segment(s) reporting the revenues must be disclosed. Single customers include entities under common control and each federal, state, local, or foreign government.

The AICPA has tested segment reporting mainly from a conceptual standpoint but occasionally has utilized calculation questions.

Stop and review! You have completed the outline for this subunit. Study multiple-choice questions 4 through 10 beginning on page 181.

5.3 INTERIM FINANCIAL REPORTING

1.   **Overview**

   a.   Reporting of interim information is required, and minimum disclosure requirements apply when **publicly traded companies** issue summarized interim information.

      1)   For many reasons, the usefulness of interim financial information is limited. Hence, their best qualitative characteristic is **timeliness**.

   b.   Each interim period is treated primarily as an **integral part** of an annual period. Ordinarily, the results for an interim period should be based on the **same accounting principles** the entity uses in preparing annual statements, but certain principles may require modification at interim dates.

IFRS Difference

- Each interim period is viewed as a discrete reporting period.

- An interim financial report must include, at a minimum, condensed financial statements (financial position, comprehensive income, changes in equity, and cash flows) and notes.

- If the interim financial report contains a complete set of statements, their form and content must conform to those required for annual statements. If the interim financial report contains condensed statements, they must include, at a minimum, all headings and subtotals included in the most recent annual statements.

---

2.   **Revenue and Associated Costs**

   a.   **Revenue**, e.g., from long-term construction contracts, should be recognized as earned during an interim period on the same basis as followed for the full year.

   b.   **Costs associated with revenue** are treated similarly for annual and interim reporting. However, some exceptions are appropriate for inventory accounting at interim dates.

      1)   The gross profit method may be used for estimating cost of goods sold and inventory because a physical count at the interim date may not be feasible. (This will be described in Study Unit 8.)

      2)   Use of LIFO at an interim date may cause a partial liquidation of the base period inventory level. If the decline is expected to be temporary and the partial liquidation will be replaced prior to year end, no effect is given to the LIFO liquidation.

         a)   Cost of goods sold for the interim period should include the expected cost of replacing the liquidated LIFO base.

IFRS Difference

LIFO liquidation is not an issue in interim (or annual) periods because LIFO is not a permitted accounting policy.

---

      3)   An inventory loss from a market decline may be deferred if no loss is reasonably anticipated for the year.

          a)   Inventory losses from nontemporary market declines, however, must be recognized at the interim date. If the loss is recovered during the year (in another quarter), it is treated as a change in estimate. The amount recovered is limited to the losses previously recognized.

IFRS Difference

For an interim period, an inventory loss from a market decline must be recognized even if no loss is reasonably expected for the year.

---

      4)   Entities using standard costing ordinarily should follow the same procedures for reporting variances at interim dates as at year end. But planned variances are deferred if they are expected to be absorbed in subsequent interim periods of a year.

          a)   Unanticipated variances are recognized in the interim period when incurred.

3. **All Other Costs and Expenses**

    a.   Costs and expenses other than product costs are either charged to income in interim periods as incurred or allocated among interim periods.

    b.   The **allocation** is based on the (1) benefits received, (2) estimates of time expired, or (3) activities associated with the period. If an item expensed for annual reporting benefits more than one interim period, it should be allocated.

      1)   **Gains and losses** that are similar to gains and losses that would not be deferred at year end are not deferred to later interim periods. For example, an extraordinary gain is recorded in full in the quarter in which it occurs.

      2)   Some items expensed in annual statements should be allocated to the interim periods that are clearly benefited.

      3)   **Quantity discounts** based on annual sales volume should be charged to interim periods based on periodic sales.

      4)   **Interest, rent, and property taxes** may be accrued or deferred at interim dates to assign an appropriate cost to each period.

EXAMPLE

On March 15 of the current year, Chen Company paid property taxes of $120,000 on its factory building for the current calendar year. On April 1, Chen made $240,000 in unanticipated repairs to its equipment. The repairs will benefit operations for the remainder of the calendar year.

The benefit from the payment of the property taxes relates to all four quarters of the current year and should be prorated at $30,000 ($120,000 ÷ 4) per quarter. The benefit from the unanticipated repairs to plant equipment relates to the second, third, and fourth quarters. It should be spread evenly over these quarters at $80,000 ($240,000 ÷ 3) per quarter.

---

      5)   **Advertising costs** may be deferred within a fiscal year if the benefits clearly extend beyond the interim period of the expenditure.

      6)   Certain costs and expenses, such as (a) inventory shrinkage, (b) allowance for bad debts, (c) allowance for quantity discounts, and (d) discretionary bonuses, are subject to **year-end adjustment**. To the extent possible, these adjustments should be estimated and assigned to interim periods.

4. **Seasonality**

    a. If interim information is issued, certain disclosures are mandatory for businesses that have material seasonal fluctuations. These fluctuations cannot be smoothed in interim information.

    b. Accordingly, reporting entities must disclose the seasonal nature of their activities. They also should consider supplementing interim reports with information for the 12-month period that ended at the interim date for the current and preceding years.

        1) Reporting entities in industries not subject to seasonal fluctuations are required to present balance sheet information on Form 10-Q only for (a) the most recent quarter end and (b) the end of the preceding fiscal year.

5. **Interim Period Tax Expense (Benefit)**

    a. At the end of each interim period, the entity should estimate the annual effective tax rate.

    b. **Interim period tax expense (benefit)** equals the estimated annual effective tax rate, times year-to-date ordinary income (loss), minus the tax expense (benefit) recognized in previous interim periods.

        1) Ordinary in this context means excluding unusual or infrequent items, extraordinary items, and results of discontinued operations.

    c. The **estimated annual effective tax rate** is based on the statutory rate adjusted for the current year's expected conditions. These include (1) anticipated tax credits, (2) foreign tax rates, (3) capital gains rates, and (4) other tax planning alternatives.

        1) The rate also includes the effect of any expected valuation allowance at year end for deferred tax assets related to deductible temporary differences and carryforwards arising during the year.

        2) The rate is determined without regard to significant unusual or extraordinary items to be reported separately or reported net of tax effect. However, such items are recognized in the interim period when they occur. The method of intraperiod tax allocation described in Study Unit 11 is used.

    d. A **tax benefit** is recognized for a loss early in the year if the benefits are expected to be realized during the year or recognizable as a deferred tax asset at year end.

        1) A valuation allowance must be recognized if it is more likely than not that a deferred tax asset will not be fully realized. Accordingly, the tax benefit of an ordinary loss early in the year is not recognized to the extent that this criterion is met.

            a) However, no income tax expense is recognized for subsequent ordinary income until the earlier unrecognized tax benefit is used.

        2) The foregoing principles are applied in determining the estimated tax benefit of an ordinary loss for the fiscal year used to calculate (a) the annual effective tax rate and (b) the year-to-date tax benefit of a loss.

EXAMPLE

The following information was used in preparing quarterly income statements during the first half of the current year:

Quarter	Income before Income Taxes	Estimated Effective Annual Income Tax Rate
1	$80,000	45%
2	70,000	45%
3	50,000	40%

The tax expense for the third quarter equals the estimated annual effective tax rate determined at the end of the third quarter, times the cumulative year-to-date ordinary income (loss), minus the cumulative tax expense for the first two quarters. At the end of the third quarter, the year-to-date ordinary income is $200,000 ($80,000 + $70,000 + $50,000), and the cumulative tax expense is $80,000 ($200,000 × 40%). Because the cumulative tax expense at the end of the second quarter was $67,500 [($80,000 + $70,000) × 45%], $12,500 ($80,000 – $67,500) should be reported as income tax expense in the income statement for the third quarter.

e. Taxes on all items other than continuing operations are determined at incremental rates. Thus, their marginal effect on taxes is calculated.

6. **Interim Period Accounting Changes**

a. In interim as well as annual periods, a change in accounting principle is retrospectively applied unless it is impracticable to determine the cumulative or period-specific effects of the change.

1) However, the impracticability exception does not apply to prechange interim periods of the fiscal year of change.

2) When application to prechange interim periods is impracticable, the change is made at the beginning of the next annual period.

b. The **cumulative effect** of the change on periods prior to those presented is reflected in the carrying amounts of assets, liabilities, and retained earnings (or other appropriate components of equity or net assets) at the beginning of the first period presented.

1) All periods presented must be adjusted for **period-specific effects**.

EXAMPLE

The following information is applicable to a change in accounting principle made in the second quarter of the year from FIFO to LIFO. The new principle can be applied retrospectively. For all relevant periods, prices have risen. The effect of the change is limited to the effects on the inventory balance and income tax provisions (a 40% tax rate).

Period	Net Income on the Basis of FIFO	Gross Effect of Changes	Gross Effect Minus Income Taxes
Prior to 1st Qtr	$6,262,000	$300,000	$180,000
1st Qtr	1,032,400	60,000	36,000
2nd Qtr	1,282,400	60,000	36,000
3rd Qtr	1,298,600	90,000	54,000
4th Qtr	1,164,800	120,000	72,000

Given the period-specific effects for the first quarter, net income based on retrospective application is $996,400 ($1,032,400 – $36,000 gross after-tax effect of applying the new principle). Changing to LIFO when prices are rising decreases net income.

---

c. A **change in an accounting estimate**, including a change in the estimated effective annual tax rate, is accounted for prospectively in the interim period in which the change is made and in future periods. Prior-period information is not retrospectively adjusted.

1) Only material changes should be disclosed.

7. **Prior Interim Period Adjustments**

a. The following items apply to adjustment or settlement of (1) litigation, (2) income taxes (except for the effects of retroactive tax legislation), (3) renegotiation proceedings, or (4) utility revenue under rate-making processes.

b. All or part of the adjustment or settlement must relate specifically to a prior interim period of the current year. Moreover, its effect must be material, and the amount must have become reasonably estimable only in the current interim period.

c. If an **item of profit or loss** occurs in other than the first interim period and meets the criteria for an adjustment, the portion of the item allocable to the current interim period is included in net income for that period.

1) The financial statements for the **prior interim periods are restated** to include their allocable portions of the adjustment.

2) The portion of the adjustment directly related to prior fiscal years is included in net income of the first interim period of the current fiscal year.

EXAMPLE

On June 1, Year 5, a calendar-year entity settled a patent infringement lawsuit. The court awarded it $3,000,000 in damages. Of this amount, $1,000,000 related to Year 3, $1,000,000 to Year 4, and $500,000 to each of the first two quarters in Year 5. The applicable tax rate is 40%. Prior interim periods should be restated to include their allocable portions of the adjustment. Accordingly, $500,000 of the settlement should be included in earnings for the second quarter. Given a tax rate of 40%, the settlement increases net income of the second quarter by $300,000.

---

8. **Summarized Financial Information**

   a. Publicly traded companies may report **information at interim dates** that is less detailed than information in annual statements. The required **minimum disclosures** when such reports are issued include

      1) Sales or gross revenues, income tax benefit, extraordinary items (including related tax), net income, and comprehensive income
      2) Basic and diluted EPS for each period presented
      3) Seasonal revenues, costs, or expenses
      4) Significant changes in estimates or income tax amounts
      5) Disposal of a component of an entity and unusual or infrequent items
      6) Contingent items
      7) Changes in accounting principles or estimates
      8) Significant changes in financial position

         a) Reporting of balance sheet and cash flow data is encouraged. Otherwise, significant changes in liquid assets, net working capital, long-term liabilities, or equity must be disclosed.

      9) Certain information about reportable operating segments
      10) Certain information about defined benefit postretirement plans

         a) Net periodic benefit cost, with separate disclosures of its components and the gain (loss) due to settlement or curtailment
         b) Total employer's contributions paid and expected to be paid in the current year if significantly different from amounts previously disclosed

      11) Certain information about fair value measurement of assets and liabilities

   b. When summarized quarterly data are regularly reported, the information for the current quarter and the current year to date (or the last 12 months to date) should be provided along with comparable data for the preceding year.

9. **Disclosures**

   a. The following are separately disclosed, included in interim-period net income, and not prorated over the year:

      1) **Extraordinary items**
      2) Gains or losses from disposal of a **component of an entity**
      3) Material **unusual or infrequent items**

   b. Disclosures of contingencies are the same for interim and annual periods.

   c. Unusual seasonal results and business combinations also should be disclosed.

   d. If an accounting change is made in an interim period, the entity must make all disclosures in the period of change that are required for annual reporting. They include the nature of, and reason for, the change.

      1) In a postchange interim period of the fiscal year of the change, the effect on (a) income from continuing operations, (b) net income (or other appropriate captions), and (c) related per-share amounts must be disclosed for that interim period.

Expect to possibly be tested on interim financial reporting, as the AICPA has traditionally tested candidates' knowledge of this topic. Candidates could see either a conceptual question or a calculation question.

Stop and review! You have completed the outline for this subunit. Study multiple-choice questions 11 through 16 beginning on page 184.

5.4 RELATED PARTY DISCLOSURES

Background

In the early 2000s, the price of Worldcom's stock began to decline. The board of directors approved a massive loan to the CEO to keep him from having to sell his own stock holdings, which would have depressed the price even further. The company was simultaneously committing other accounting-related irregularities and was eventually forced into bankruptcy.

Disclosures about related party transactions are thus extremely important in published financial statements. Current GAAP regarding these disclosures are found in FASB ASC 850.

1. **Related Parties**
    a. Disclosure of material related party transactions is required. Parties related to the entity include
        1) Employee trusts managed by or under the trusteeship of the entity's management.
        2) Principal owners, management, or members of their immediate families. Principal owners are owners of record or known beneficial owners of more than 10% of the voting interests of the entity.
        3) Affiliates. An affiliate controls, is controlled by, or is under common control with an entity.
        4) Equity-based investees or other investees that would be accounted for by the equity method if the fair value option had not been elected (the fair value option will be explained in Study Unit 6).
        5) Any other entity if one party can significantly influence the other to the extent that one may be prevented from fully pursuing its interests.
        6) A party that can significantly influence the transacting parties or has an ownership interest in one and can significantly influence the other.
    b. Related party transactions that are eliminated in the preparation of **consolidated or combined financial statements**, such as intraentity sales or loans, are not required to be disclosed in those statements. However, they must be disclosed in the parties' separate statements.
    c. Transactions between an entity and its management, such as borrowings and lendings, must be disclosed.

NOTE: The **Sarbanes-Oxley Act of 2002** generally prohibits an issuer, as defined by federal securities law, from extending credit to its directors and officers.

2.   **Exceptions**

    a.   Exceptions are (1) compensation arrangements (officers' salaries and expenses), (2) expense allowances, and (3) other similar items in the ordinary course of business.

IFRS Difference

The entity must disclose the compensation of key management personnel in total and by components.

---

3.   **Required Disclosures**

    a.   The nature of the relationship involved

    b.   A description of the transactions for each period an income statement is presented and such other information as is deemed necessary to an understanding of the effects of the transactions

    c.   The dollar amounts of transactions for each period an income statement is presented and the effects of any change in the method of establishing their terms

    d.   Amounts due from or to related parties at the date of each balance sheet, including the terms of settlement

    e.   Certain tax information if the entity is part of a group that files a consolidated tax return, such as (1) aggregate current and deferred tax expense, (2) tax-related amounts due to or from affiliates, and (3) the method used to allocate consolidated current and deferred tax expense to group members

        1)   Disclosure of the effect on the cash flow statement for each period a cash flow statement is presented is not required.

Stop and review! You have completed the outline for this subunit. Study multiple-choice questions 17 through 20 beginning on page 185.

5.5 UNCONDITIONAL PURCHASE OBLIGATIONS

Background

To ensure a steady supply of inventory, some firms enter into unconditional purchase obligations with their supplier. To protect the supplier, the contract may be noncancelable, also called "take-or-pay." However, because neither party has performed the contract, the purchaser must not accrue a liability. To address this gray area, the FASB requires certain disclosures. Current GAAP is found in FASB ASC 440-10-50.

---

1.   **Overview**

    a.   Disclosure of commitments to transfer funds for fixed or minimum amounts of goods or services at fixed or minimum prices is required.

    b.   A **take-or-pay contract** requires one party to purchase a certain number of goods from the other party or else pay a penalty. A **throughput contract** requires one party to purchase a certain amount of services.

        1)   **Sinking-fund requirements** for the retirement of noncurrent debt also are affected by the provisions of this pronouncement.

    c.   An unconditional purchase obligation with the following characteristics must be disclosed:

        1)   It is either noncancelable or cancelable only (a) upon the happening of a remote contingency, (b) with the permission of the other party, or (c) under terms that make continuation or replacement (but not cancelation) of the agreement reasonably assured.

            a)   A purchase obligation cancelable upon the payment of a nominal penalty is not unconditional.

      2)   It was negotiated as part of the financing arrangement for facilities that will provide contracted goods or services.

      3)   It has a remaining term of more than 1 year.

2.   **Disclosure – Recorded Obligations**

   a.   Disclosure of the aggregate amount of **payments** for unconditional purchase obligations is required for recorded obligations for each of the 5 years following the date of the latest balance sheet presented.

3.   **Disclosure – Unrecorded Obligations**

   a.   If an unconditional purchase obligation is not recorded, certain disclosures are required. They include the following:

      1)   The **nature and term** of the obligation

      2)   The **variable components** of the obligation

      3)   The **amounts purchased** under the obligation for each period an income statement is presented

      4)   Amount of the **fixed and determinable portion** of the obligation at the latest balance sheet date and, if determinable, for each of the 5 succeeding fiscal years

   b.   When an unconditional purchase obligation is not recorded, the disclosure of the amount of imputed interest necessary to reduce the unconditional purchase obligation to its present value is encouraged.

      1)   If known by the purchaser, the rate should be the initial effective interest rate of the debt that financed the facilities providing the contracted goods or services.

         a)   If the rate cannot be determined by the purchaser, the purchaser's incremental borrowing rate should be used.

Stop and review! You have completed the outline for this subunit. Study multiple-choice questions 21 and 22 on page 187.

5.6 SIGNIFICANT RISKS AND UNCERTAINTIES

1.   **Overview**

   a.   Disclosures should be made at the balance sheet date about certain items that could significantly affect reported amounts in the near term, that is, within 1 year of the balance sheet date.

2.   **Nature of Operations**

   a.   One set of disclosures concerns risks and uncertainties relating to the nature of operations. Thus, entities must disclose their (1) major products or services, (2) principal markets, and (3) the locations of those markets.

   b.   They also should disclose (1) all industries in which they operate; (2) the relative importance of each; and (3) the basis for determining the relative importance, e.g., assets, revenue, or earnings. However, this set of disclosures need not be quantified.

3.   **Use of Estimates**

a.   A second type of disclosures concerns the use of estimates in the preparation of financial statements. Financial statements should explain that conformity with GAAP requires management to use numerous estimates.

b.   Disclosure concerning certain **significant estimates** used to value assets, liabilities, or contingencies is required when the estimated effects of a condition, situation, or set of circumstances at the balance sheet date are subject to a **reasonable possibility** of change in the near term and the effects will be material.

1)   The effect of using a different estimate determines materiality.

2)   The nature of the uncertainty, that it is reasonably possible, and that the estimate may change in the near term are to be disclosed.

3)   If an estimate is of a loss contingency, the disclosure should include the estimated range of loss or a statement that an estimate cannot be made.

4)   Factors making an estimate sensitive to change may be, but need not be, disclosed.

5)   If an entity is not required to make disclosures about certain significant estimates because it has employed risk-reduction techniques, it is encouraged to disclose the uncertainty and the risk-reduction techniques.

4.   **Concentrations**

a.   A third set of disclosures concerns current vulnerability due to concentrations, for example, when entities fail to diversify.

b.   Disclosure is necessary if management knows prior to issuance of the statements that

1)   The concentration **exists** at the balance sheet date,

2)   It makes the entity vulnerable to a near-term **severe impact**, and

3)   Such impact is at least **reasonably possible** in the near term.

c.   Disclosable concentrations include those in

1)   The volume of business with a given customer, supplier, lender, grantor, or contributor;

2)   Revenue from given products, services, or fund-raising events;

3)   The available suppliers of materials, labor, services, or rights (e.g., licenses) used in operations; and

4)   The market or geographic area where the entity operates.

d.   A severe impact may result from (1) loss of all or a part of a business relationship, (2) price or demand changes, (3) loss of a patent, (4) changes in the availability of a resource or right, or (5) the disruption of operations in a market or geographic area.

1)   Furthermore, it is always reasonably possible in the near term that (a) any customer, grantor, or contributor will be lost and (b) operations located in another country will be disrupted.

e.   For concentrations of labor subject to collective bargaining, disclosure should include the percentage of employees covered by a collective bargaining agreement and the percentage covered by an agreement that will expire within 1 year.

1)   For concentrations of operations in another country, disclosure should include the carrying amounts of net assets and the areas where they are located.

Stop and review! You have completed the outline for this subunit. Study multiple-choice question 23 on page 187.

5.7 SUBSEQUENT EVENTS

1. **Overview**

   a. The guidance in this outline applies to accounting and disclosure issues for subsequent events not covered by other GAAP (e.g., the principles related to contingencies).

   b. Subsequent events are events or transactions that occur **after the balance sheet date** and **prior to the issuance or availability for issuance of the financial statements**.

      1) An SEC filer evaluates subsequent events through the date the statements are issued (become widely available for general use).

      2) Other entities evaluate subsequent events through the date statements are available for issuance (are complete in accordance with GAAP and approved).

         a) The entity must disclose the date through which subsequent events have been evaluated.

2. **Recognized Subsequent Events**

   a. One type of subsequent event provides additional evidence about **conditions at the date of the balance sheet**, including the estimates inherent in statement preparation.

      1) This type of event must be recognized in the financial statements.

      2) Subsequent events affecting the realization of assets (such as receivables and inventories) or the settlement of estimated liabilities ordinarily require recognition.

         a) They usually reflect the resolution of conditions that existed over a relatively long period.

         b) Examples are (1) the settlement of litigation for an amount differing from the liability recorded in the statements and (2) a loss on a receivable resulting from a customer's bankruptcy.

3. **Unrecognized Subsequent Events**

   a. The second type of subsequent event provides evidence about **conditions that did not exist at the date of the balance sheet**. These events do not require recognition, but some of them do require disclosure.

      1) Examples of nonrecognized subsequent events requiring **disclosure only** include

         a) Sale of a bond or capital stock issue

         b) A business combination

         c) Settlement of litigation when the event resulting in the claim occurred after the balance sheet date

         d) Loss of plant or inventories as a result of a fire or natural disaster

         e) Losses on receivables resulting from conditions (e.g., a customer's major casualty) occurring after the balance sheet date

      2) Some events of the second type may be so significant that the most appropriate disclosure is to supplement the historical statements with pro forma financial data.

Stop and review! You have completed the outline for this subunit. Study multiple-choice questions 24 and 25 on page 188.

5.8 FINANCIAL INSTRUMENT DISCLOSURES

Background
Historical cost is an appropriate measurement attribute for property, plant, and equipment, which often remain in an entity's possession for years, but not for financial instruments, which are constantly turning over. The FASB thus requires all entities to either report on the face of the balance sheet or disclose in the notes the fair values of all financial instruments. Current GAAP are found in FASB ASC 825.

1. **Definition**

    a.   A financial instrument is cash, evidence of an ownership interest in an entity, or a contract that both

        1)   Imposes on one entity a **contractual obligation** to

            a)   Deliver cash or another financial instrument to a second entity or

            b)   Exchange other financial instruments on potentially unfavorable terms with the second entity, **and**

        2)   Conveys to that second entity a **contractual right** to

            a)   Receive cash or another financial instrument from the first entity or

            b)   Exchange other financial instruments on potentially favorable terms with the first entity.

2. **Disclosures**

    a.   Certain entities must disclose the **fair value** of financial instruments. This rule applies whether or not they are recognized if (1) it is feasible to estimate such fair values and (2) the aggregated fair value is material.

        1)   If estimating fair value is not feasible, disclosures include information pertinent to estimating fair value, such as the carrying amount, effective interest rate, and maturity. The reasons that estimating the fair value is not feasible also should be disclosed.

            a)   The framework for determining fair values, including approaches to measurement and a hierarchy of inputs to those approaches, will be discussed in Study Unit 4, Subunit 7.

        2)   Ordinarily, disclosures should not net the fair values of instruments even if they are of the same class or are related, e.g., by a risk management strategy.

    b.   A publicly traded company must disclose in its summarized financial information for **interim periods** the fair value of all financial instruments for which estimation is practicable.

3. **Concentration of Credit Risk**

    a.   **Credit risk** is the risk of accounting loss from a financial instrument because of the possible failure of another party to perform.

        1)   With certain exceptions, for example, (a) instruments of pension plans, (b) certain insurance contracts, (c) warranty obligations and rights, and (d) unconditional purchase obligations, an entity must disclose significant **concentrations of credit risk** arising from financial instruments, whether from one counterparty or groups.

            a)   Group concentrations arise when multiple counterparties have similar activities and economic characteristics that cause their ability to meet obligations to be similarly affected by changes in conditions.

        2)   **Disclosures** (in the body of the statements or the notes) should include

            a)   Information about the shared activity, region, or economic characteristic that identifies the concentration.

b) The **maximum loss** due to credit risk if parties failed completely to perform and the security, if any, proved to be of no value.

c) The **policy of requiring collateral** or other security, information about access to that security, and the nature and a brief description of the security.

d) The policy of entering into **master netting arrangements** to mitigate the credit risk; information about them; and a description of the terms, including the extent to which they reduce the maximum amount of loss.

4. **Market Risk**

   a. An entity is encouraged, but not required, to disclose quantitative information about the **market risks** of instruments that is consistent with the way the entity manages those risks.

5. **Derivatives and Hedging**

   a. The guidance for disclosures about derivative instruments and hedging activities applies to all entities and all derivatives and hedged items.

      1) Its objective is to help users understand (a) the reasons for using derivatives, (b) how they are used, (c) the accounting methods applied, and (d) their effect.

      2) Derivatives and hedging are explained in detail in Study Unit 17.

   b. The following are the disclosures for every reporting period for which statements of financial position and performance are issued:

      1) **Objectives** of hedging instruments; their context, including each instrument's **primary risk exposure**; and the entity's related strategies.

         a) A distinction must be made between instruments (whether or not hedges) used for (1) risk management and (2) other purposes. The entity must disclose which hedging instruments are hedges of fair value, cash flows, or the net investment in a foreign operation. If derivatives are not hedges, their purpose must be described.

      2) Information about the **volume** of derivatives.

      3) Optional qualitative disclosures in the form of discussion of **overall risk exposures** (interest rate, exchange rate, commodity price, equity price, and credit risks), even if not managed by using derivatives.

      4) **Location** and **gross fair values** of reported derivatives.

         a) These amounts are separately reported as assets and liabilities and classified as hedges and nonhedges. Within these classes, amounts are separately reported by type of derivative. The entity also must disclose the line items where the fair value amounts for the classes are reported.

      5) **Location** and amounts of **gains and losses** on derivatives and hedged items.

         a) This information includes separate disclosures for (1) fair value hedges (hedging instruments and hedged items), (2) effective portions of gains and losses on cash flow hedges and hedges of net investments that are currently recognized in OCI or reclassified from accumulated OCI, (3) ineffective portions and amounts excluded from the assessment of the effectiveness of cash flow hedges and hedges of net investments, and (4) derivatives that are not used as hedges.

         b) The information is separately reported by type of derivative, with identification of line items.

         c) An entity may include nonhedging derivatives in its trading activities. In this case, separate gain/loss disclosures for such instruments are **not** required if information about the trading activities is disclosed.

6) **Fair value hedging** instruments and hedged items. The entity discloses the net gain (loss) reported in earnings that results from

   a) Hedge ineffectiveness and the part of the derivatives' gain/loss not included in the assessment of hedge effectiveness.

   b) A hedged firm commitment no longer qualifying as a fair value hedge.

7) **Cash flow hedging** instruments and hedged transactions. The entity discloses

   a) Transactions that will result in reclassification into earnings from accumulated OCI and the net amount estimated to be reclassified in the next 12 months.

   b) The maximum period for hedging of forecasted transactions (other than those related to current payment of variable interest).

   c) Amounts reclassified into earnings because of the discontinuance of cash flow hedges of forecasted transactions when it becomes probable they will not occur within the specified period.

c. The following disclosures are made for every reporting period for which a statement of financial position is issued for derivatives (and hedging nonderivatives) with **contingent features** that are related to **credit risk**:

   1) Nature of the features, how they may be activated in derivatives that are in a net liability position, and the aggregate fair values of such instruments

   2) An aggregate fair value of posted collateral, potentially required collateral, and immediate settlement amounts

Stop and review! You have completed the outline for this subunit. Study multiple-choice questions 26 through 28 beginning on page 188.

QUESTIONS

5.1 Significant Accounting Policies

1. Which of the following items should be included in Melay, Inc.'s summary of significant accounting policies for the current year?

A. Property, plant, and equipment is recorded at cost with depreciation computed principally by the straight-line method.

B. During the current year, the Delay Segment was sold.

C. Operating segment sales for the current year are Alay $1M, Belay $2M, and Celay $3M.

D. Future common share dividends are expected to approximate 60% of earnings.

Answer (A) is correct.
   REQUIRED: The item properly disclosed in the summary of significant accounting policies.
   DISCUSSION: Certain items are commonly required disclosures in a summary of significant accounting policies: (1) the basis of consolidation, (2) depreciation methods, (3) amortization of intangible assets (excluding goodwill), (4) inventory pricing, (5) recognition of profit on long-term construction-type contracts, (6) recognition of revenue from franchising and leasing operations, and (7) policy for determining which items are cash equivalents. Hence, the summary of significant accounting policies should disclose the fact that property, plant, and equipment are depreciated principally by the straight-line method.
   Answer (B) is incorrect. The sale of a segment is a transaction, not an accounting principle. It is reflected in the discontinued operations section on the income statement. Answer (C) is incorrect. Specific segment information does not constitute an accounting policy. An accounting policy is a specific principle or a method of applying it. Answer (D) is incorrect. Future dividend policy is a financial management policy.

2. Which of the following facts concerning fixed assets should be included in the summary of significant accounting policies?

	Depreciation Method	Composition
A.	No	Yes
B.	Yes	Yes
C.	Yes	No
D.	No	No

Answer (C) is correct.
REQUIRED: The fact(s) concerning fixed assets disclosed in the summary of significant accounting policies.
DISCUSSION: Disclosure of significant accounting policies is required when (1) a selection has been made from existing acceptable alternatives; (2) a policy is unique to the industry in which the entity operates, even if the policy is predominantly followed in that industry; and (3) GAAP have been applied in an unusual or innovative way. A depreciation method is a selection from existing acceptable alternatives and should be included in the summary of significant accounting policies. Financial statement disclosure of accounting policies should not duplicate details presented elsewhere in the financial statements, such as composition of plant assets.

3. The summary of significant accounting policies should disclose the

A. Reasons that retrospective application of a change in an accounting principle is impracticable.

B. Basis of profit recognition on long-term construction contracts.

C. Adequacy of pension plan assets in relation to vested benefits.

D. Future minimum lease payments in the aggregate and for each of the 5 succeeding fiscal years.

Answer (B) is correct.
REQUIRED: The item disclosed in the summary of significant accounting policies.
DISCUSSION: Certain items are commonly required disclosures in a summary of significant accounting policies: (1) the basis of consolidation, (2) depreciation methods, (3) amortization of intangible assets (excluding goodwill), (4) inventory pricing, (5) recognition of profit on long-term construction-type contracts, (6) recognition of revenue from franchising and leasing operations, and (7) policy for determining which items are cash equivalents.
Answer (A) is incorrect. If retrospective application of a change in accounting principle is impracticable, disclosure of the reasons and the alternative method of reporting the change is required. The reasons are not policies. Answer (C) is incorrect. The adequacy of pension plan assets in relation to vested benefits is not a disclosure required by GAAP. Answer (D) is incorrect. The future minimum lease payments in the aggregate and for each of the 5 succeeding fiscal years should be disclosed but not in the summary of significant accounting policies.

5.2 Segment Reporting

4. Which of the following qualifies as a reportable operating segment?

A. Corporate headquarters, which oversees $1 billion in sales for the entire company.

B. North American segment, whose assets are 12% of the company's assets of all segments, and management reports to the chief operating officer.

C. South American segment, whose results of operations are reported directly to the chief operating officer, and has 5% of the company's assets, 9% of revenues, and 8% of the profits.

D. Eastern Europe segment, which reports its results directly to the manager of the European division, and has 20% of the company's assets, 12% of revenues, and 11% of profits.

Answer (B) is correct.
REQUIRED: The reportable operating segment.
DISCUSSION: An operating segment engages in business activities, is reviewed by the company's chief operating decision maker, and has discrete financial information available. For an operating segment to be reportable, it must meet one or more of the following quantitative thresholds: (1) Reported revenue is at least 10% of the combined revenue of all operating segments; (2) reported profit or loss is at least 10% of the greater (in absolute amount) of the combined reported profit of all operating segments that did not incur a loss, or the combined reported loss of all operating segments that did report a loss; or (3) its assets are at least 10% of the combined assets of all operating segments. North American segment holds 12% of the company's assets and reports to the chief operating officer, so it meets the requirements of an operating segment.
Answer (A) is incorrect. A corporate headquarters is not an operating segment. Any revenues it earns are incidental to the entity's activities. Answer (C) is incorrect. This segment does not meet the asset, revenue, or profit (or loss) quantitative threshold to qualify as an operating segment. Answer (D) is incorrect. This segment does not report to the chief operating decision maker.

5. In financial reporting for operating segments of a public business entity, which of the following must be included in the reported amount of a reportable operating segment's assets?

	Accumulated Depreciation	Marketable Securities Valuation Allowance
A.	No	No
B.	No	Yes
C.	Yes	Yes
D.	Yes	No

Answer (A) is correct.
REQUIRED: The items to be included in computing the assets of a reportable operating segment.
DISCUSSION: The amount of a reported segment item, such as assets, is the measure reported to the chief operating decision maker for purposes of making resource allocation and performance evaluation decisions regarding the segment. Thus, if accumulated depreciation and a marketable securities valuation allowance are not included in that measure, they need not be included in the reported amount of the operating segment's assets.

6. Terra Co.'s total revenues from its three operating segments were as follows:

Segment	Sales to External Customers	Inter-segment Sales	Total Revenues
Lion	$ 70,000	$ 30,000	$100,000
Monk	22,000	4,000	26,000
Nevi	8,000	16,000	24,000
Combined	$100,000	$ 50,000	$150,000
Elimination	--	(50,000)	(50,000)
Consolidated	$100,000	$ --	$100,000

Which operating segment(s) can be deemed reportable?

A. None.

B. Lion only.

C. Lion and Monk only.

D. Lion, Monk, and Nevi.

Answer (D) is correct.
REQUIRED: The reportable operating segments in conformity with the revenue test.
DISCUSSION: For the purpose of identifying reportable operating segments, revenue is defined to include sales to external customers and intersegment sales or transfers. In accordance with the revenue test, a reportable operating segment has revenue equal to 10% or more of the total combined revenue, internal and external, of all of the entity's operating segments. Given combined revenues of $150,000, Lion, Monk, and Nevi all qualify because their revenues are at least $15,000 ($150,000 × 10%).

7. Correy Corp. and its divisions are engaged solely in manufacturing operations. The following data (consistent with prior years' data) pertain to the industries in which operations were conducted for the year ended December 31, Year 2:

Operating Segment	Total Revenue	Profit	Assets at 12/31/Yr 2
A	$10,000,000	$1,750,000	$20,000,000
B	8,000,000	1,400,000	17,500,000
C	6,000,000	1,200,000	12,500,000
D	3,000,000	550,000	7,500,000
E	4,250,000	675,000	7,000,000
F	1,500,000	225,000	3,000,000
	$32,750,000	$5,800,000	$67,500,000

In its segment information for Year 2, how many reportable segments does Correy have?

A. Three.

B. Four.

C. Five.

D. Six.

Answer (C) is correct.
REQUIRED: The number of reportable operating segments.
DISCUSSION: Four operating segments (A, B, C, and E) have revenue equal to or greater than 10% of the $32,750,000 total revenue of all operating segments. These four segments also have profit equal to or greater than 10% of the $5,800,000 total profit. Five segments (A, B, C, D, and E) have assets greater than 10% of the $67,500,000 total assets. Because an operating segment is reportable if it meets one or more of the three tests, Correy Corp. has five reportable segments for Year 2.

8. Opto Co. is a publicly traded, consolidated entity reporting segment information. Which of the following items is a required entity-wide disclosure regarding external customers?

A. The fact that transactions with a particular external customer constitute more than 10% of the total entity revenues.

B. The identity of any external customer providing 10% or more of a particular operating segment's revenue.

C. The identity of any external customer considered to be "major" by management.

D. Information on major customers is **not** required in segment reporting.

Answer (A) is correct.
REQUIRED: The entity-wide disclosure about external customers.
DISCUSSION: Information about products and services and geographical areas is reported if it is feasible to do so. If 10% or more of revenues is derived from one external customer, (1) that fact, (2) the amount from each such customer, and (3) the segment(s) reporting the revenues must be disclosed.
Answer (B) is incorrect. The identity of the segment(s) reporting the revenues must be disclosed, not that of the customer. Answer (C) is incorrect. The identity of any external customer, regardless of whether it meets the revenue criterion or is considered to be "major" by management, does not have to be disclosed. Answer (D) is incorrect. The entity must disclose information about sales to each major customer, that is, one providing at least 10% of revenues.

9. Hyde Corp. has three manufacturing divisions, each of which has been determined to be a reportable operating segment. In Year 4, Clay division had sales of $3 million, which was 25% of Hyde's total sales, and had traceable operating costs of $1.9 million. In Year 4, Hyde incurred operating costs of $500,000 that were not directly traceable to any of the divisions. In addition, Hyde incurred interest expense of $300,000 in Year 4. The calculation of the measure of segment profit or loss reviewed by Hyde's chief operating decision maker does not include an allocation of interest expense incurred by Hyde. However, it does include traceable costs. It also includes nontraceable operating costs allocated based on the ratio of divisional sales to aggregate sales. In reporting segment information, what amount should be shown as Clay's operating profit for Year 4?

A. $875,000

B. $900,000

C. $975,000

D. $1,100,000

Answer (C) is correct.
REQUIRED: The amount to be shown as profit for a reportable operating segment.
DISCUSSION: The amount of a segment item reported, such as profit or loss, is the measure reported to the chief operating decision maker for purposes of making resource allocation and performance evaluation decisions regarding the segment. However, the FASB does not stipulate the specific items included in the calculation of that measure. Consequently, allocation of revenues, expenses, gains, and losses are included in the determination of reported segment profit or loss only if they are included in the measure of segment profit or loss reviewed by the chief operating decision maker. Given that this measure for Clay reflects traceable costs and an allocation of nontraceable operating costs, the profit is calculated by subtracting the $1,900,000 traceable costs and the $125,000 ($500,000 × 25%) of the allocated costs from the division's sales of $3,000,000. The profit for the division is $975,000.

Sales	$ 3,000,000
Traceable costs	(1,900,000)
Allocated costs (25%)	(125,000)
Profit	$ 975,000

Answer (A) is incorrect. No amount of interest expense should be included in the calculation. Answer (B) is incorrect. Clay's share of interest expense ($300,000 × 25% = $75,000) is excluded from the calculation of profit. Answer (D) is incorrect. The allocated nontraceable operating costs must also be subtracted.

10. Bean Co. included interest expense and transactions classified as extraordinary items in its determination of segment profit, which Bean's chief financial officer considered in determining the segment's operating budget. Bean is required to report the segment's financial data in accordance with GAAP. Which of the following items should Bean disclose in reporting segment data?

	Interest expense	Extraordinary items
A.	No	No
B.	No	Yes
C.	Yes	No
D.	Yes	Yes

Answer (D) is correct.
REQUIRED: The items disclosed in segment data.
DISCUSSION: The objective is to provide information about the different types of business activities of the entity and the economic environments in which it operates. Disclosures include a measure of profit or loss and total assets for each reportable segment. Other items typically disclosed include revenues from external customers and other operating segments, interest revenue and expense, depreciation, depletion, amortization, unusual items, equity in the net income of equity-based investees, income tax expense or benefit, extraordinary items, and other significant noncash items.
Answer (A) is incorrect. Items that contribute to the profit and loss of a segment should be disclosed in the segment's data. Answer (B) is incorrect. Interest expense affects the profit and loss of a business segment and should be reported. Answer (C) is incorrect. Extraordinary items affect the profit and loss of a business segment and should be reported.

5.3 Interim Financial Reporting

11. Because of a decline in market price in the second quarter, Petal Co. incurred an inventory loss, but the market price was expected to return to previous levels by the end of the year. At the end of the year, the decline had not reversed. When should the loss be reported in Petal's interim income statements?

A. Ratably over the second, third, and fourth quarters.

B. Ratably over the third and fourth quarters.

C. In the second quarter only.

D. In the fourth quarter only.

Answer (D) is correct.
REQUIRED: The true statement about reporting inventory at interim dates when a market decline is expected to reverse by year end but does not.
DISCUSSION: A market decline reasonably expected to be restored within the fiscal year may be deferred at an interim reporting date because no loss is anticipated for the year. (Inventory losses from nontemporary market declines must be recognized at the interim reporting date.) Consequently, Petal would not have reported the market decline until it determined at the end of the fourth quarter that the expected reversal would not occur.

12. Conceptually, interim financial statements can be described as emphasizing

A. Timeliness over reliability.

B. Reliability over relevance.

C. Relevance over comparability.

D. Comparability over neutrality.

Answer (A) is correct.
REQUIRED: The emphasis of interim statements.
DISCUSSION: Interim financial statements cover periods of less than 1 year. Because of (1) the seasonality of some businesses, (2) the need for increased use of estimates, (3) the need for allocations of costs and expenses among interim periods, and (4) other factors, the usefulness of the information provided by interim financial statements may be limited. Hence, they emphasize timeliness over reliability.

13. In general, an enterprise preparing interim financial statements should

A. Defer recognition of seasonal revenue.

B. Disregard permanent decreases in the market value of its inventory.

C. Allocate revenues and expenses evenly over the quarters, regardless of when they actually occurred.

D. Use the same accounting principles followed in preparing its latest annual financial statements.

Answer (D) is correct.
REQUIRED: The method of preparing interim financial statements.
DISCUSSION: Each interim period is viewed primarily as an integral part of an annual period. Ordinarily, interim results are based on the same principles applied in annual statements. Certain principles and practices used for annual reporting, however, may require modification so that interim reports may relate more closely to the results of operations for the annual period.
Answer (A) is incorrect. Seasonal revenue is not deferred. However, an entity with material seasonal fluctuations must disclose the seasonal nature of its activities and should consider making additional disclosures. Answer (B) is incorrect. Inventory losses from nontemporary market declines must be recognized at the interim date. Recovery during the fiscal year is treated as a change in estimate. Answer (C) is incorrect. Revenue is recognized as earned during an interim period on the same basis followed for the annual period.

14. Wilson Corp. experienced a $50,000 decline in the market value of its inventory in the first quarter of its fiscal year. Wilson had expected this decline to reverse in the third quarter, and the third quarter recovery exceeded the previous decline by $10,000. Wilson's inventory did not experience any other declines in market value during the fiscal year. What amounts of loss or gain should Wilson report in its interim financial statements for the first and third quarters?

	First Quarter	Third Quarter
A.	$0	$0
B.	$0	$10,000 gain
C.	$50,000 loss	$50,000 gain
D.	$50,000 loss	$60,000 gain

Answer (A) is correct.
REQUIRED: The loss or gain reported for changes in market value of inventory in interim statements.
DISCUSSION: A market decline reasonably expected to be restored within the fiscal year may be deferred at an interim reporting date because no loss is anticipated for the year. Since Wilson expected the first quarter loss to be temporary, it did not recognize the loss in the interim statements. Recoveries of market value may only be recognized to the extent of previous losses, so no gain was recognized in the third quarter.
Answer (B) is incorrect. Gains in the market value of inventory that are not recoveries of nontemporary declines are not recognized. Answer (C) is incorrect. A loss reasonably expected to be restored in a later interim period is deferred. Answer (D) is incorrect. Gains in the market value of inventory that are not recoveries of nontemporary declines are not recognized.

15. During the first quarter of Year 4, Tech Co. had income before taxes of $200,000, and its effective income tax rate was 15%. Tech's Year 3 effective annual income tax rate was 30%, but Tech expects its Year 4 effective annual income tax rate to be 25%. In its first quarter interim income statement, what amount of income tax expense should Tech report?

A. $0

B. $30,000

C. $50,000

D. $60,000

Answer (C) is correct.
REQUIRED: The provision for income taxes for the first interim period.
DISCUSSION: At the end of each interim period, the entity should estimate the annual effective tax rate. This rate is used in providing for income taxes on a current year-to-date basis. Tech's ordinary income before taxes for the first quarter is $200,000, and the estimated annual effective tax rate for Year 4 is 25%. The provision for income taxes for the first interim period is therefore $50,000 ($200,000 × 25%).
Answer (A) is incorrect. Zero excludes any income tax expense. Answer (B) is incorrect. The amount of $30,000 uses Tech's quarterly effective income tax rate. Answer (D) is incorrect. The amount of $60,000 uses Tech's Year 3 effective annual income tax rate.

16. An inventory loss from a market price decline occurred in the first quarter. The loss was not expected to be restored in the fiscal year. However, in the third quarter the inventory had a market price recovery that exceeded the market decline that occurred in the first quarter. For interim financial reporting, the dollar amount of net inventory should

A. Decrease in the first quarter by the amount of the market price decline and increase in the third quarter by the amount of the market price recovery.

B. Decrease in the first quarter by the amount of the market price decline and increase in the third quarter by the amount of decrease in the first quarter.

C. Decrease in the first quarter by the amount of the market price decline and **not** be affected in the third quarter.

D. **Not** be affected in either the first quarter or the third quarter.

Answer (B) is correct.
REQUIRED: The proper interim financial reporting of a market decline and a market price recovery.
DISCUSSION: A market price decline in inventory must be recognized in the interim period in which it occurs unless it is expected to be temporary, i.e., unless the decline is expected to be restored by the end of the fiscal year. This loss was not expected to be restored in the fiscal year, and the company should report the dollar amount of the market price decline as a loss in the first quarter. Inventory may never be written up to an amount above its original cost. Accordingly, the market price recovery recognized in the third quarter is limited to the extent of losses previously recognized, whether in a prior interim or annual period.
Answer (A) is incorrect. The recovery recognized in the third quarter is limited to the amount of the losses previously recognized. Answer (C) is incorrect. Assuming no market price decline had been recognized prior to the current year, the first quarter loss and the third quarter recovery would be offsetting. The recognized third quarter gain is limited to the amount of the first quarter loss, and the year-end results would not be affected. Answer (D) is incorrect. The inventory amount is affected in both the first and third quarters.

5.4 Related Party Disclosures

17. Dex Co. has entered into a joint venture with an affiliate to secure access to additional inventory. Under the joint venture agreement, Dex will purchase the output of the venture at prices negotiated on an arm's-length basis. Which of the following is (are) required to be disclosed about the related party transaction?

I. The amount due to the affiliate at the balance sheet date.

II. The dollar amount of the purchases during the year.

A. I only.

B. II only.

C. Both I and II.

D. Neither I nor II.

Answer (C) is correct.
REQUIRED: The disclosures for a related party transaction.
DISCUSSION: In regard to related parties, GAAP require disclosure of (1) the nature of the relationship involved; (2) a description of the transactions for each period an income statement is presented and such other information as is deemed necessary to an understanding of the effects of the transactions; (3) the dollar amounts of transactions for each period an income statement is presented and the effects of any change in the method of establishing their terms; (4) amounts due from or to related parties as of the date of each balance sheet, including the terms of settlement; and (5) certain tax information required by GAAP if the entity is part of a group that files a consolidated tax return.

18. Lemu Co. and Young Co. are under the common management of Ego Co. Ego can significantly influence the operating results of both Lemu and Young. While Lemu had no transactions with Ego during the year, Young sold merchandise to Ego under the same terms given to unrelated parties. In the notes to their respective financial statements, should Lemu and Young disclose their relationship with Ego?

	Lemu	Young
A.	Yes	Yes
B.	Yes	No
C.	No	Yes
D.	No	No

Answer (A) is correct.

REQUIRED: The disclosure(s), if any, by entities under common management regarding an entity that can significantly influence them.

DISCUSSION: Financial statements should disclose material related party transactions. A related party is essentially any party that controls or can significantly influence the management or operating policies of the reporting entity. Moreover, two or more entities may be under common ownership or management control such that the results of the reporting entity might vary significantly from those obtained if the entities were autonomous. In these circumstances, the relationship should be disclosed even though no transactions occurred between the parties.

19. Dean Co. acquired 100% of Morey Corp. prior to Year 6. Dean and Morey are not issuers. During Year 6, they included in their separate financial statements the following:

	Dean	Morey
Officers' salaries	$ 75,000	$50,000
Officers' expenses	20,000	10,000
Loans to officers	125,000	50,000
Intercompany sales	150,000	--

The amount reported as related party disclosures in the notes to Dean's Year 6 consolidated statements is

A. $150,000

B. $155,000

C. $175,000

D. $330,000

Answer (C) is correct.

REQUIRED: The amount of related party disclosures.

DISCUSSION: GAAP require the disclosure of material related party transactions other than (1) compensation arrangements, (2) expense allowances, and (3) other similar items in the ordinary course of business. Related party transactions that are eliminated in consolidated or combined statements also are not required to be disclosed in those statements. Accordingly, the compensation arrangements (officers' salaries and expenses) and the intercompany sales, which will be eliminated in the consolidated statements, need not be disclosed. However, other transactions between an entity and its management, such as borrowings and lendings, must be disclosed. Dean should therefore report as related party disclosures the $175,000 ($125,000 + $50,000) of loans to officers. The Sarbanes-Oxley Act of 2002 generally prohibits an issuer, as defined by federal securities law, from extending credit to its directors and officers.

Answer (A) is incorrect. The interentity sales equal $150,000. Answer (B) is incorrect. The officers' salaries and expenses equal $155,000. Answer (D) is incorrect. The officers' salaries and expenses plus the loans to officers equals $330,000.

20. Which of the following payments by a company should be disclosed in the notes to the financial statements as a related party transaction?

I. Royalties paid to a major shareholder as consideration for patents purchased from the shareholder.

II. Officers' salaries.

A. I only.

B. II only.

C. Both I and II.

D. Neither I nor II.

Answer (A) is correct.

REQUIRED: The payment(s), if any, disclosed as related party items.

DISCUSSION: GAAP require the disclosure of material related party transactions other than compensation arrangements (officers' salaries), expense allowances, and other similar items in the ordinary course of business. However, royalties paid to a major shareholder must be disclosed because the shareholder may have considerable influence over the corporation, and the transaction may not be made at arm's length.

5.5 Unconditional Purchase Obligations

21. GAAP pertaining to disclosure of long-term obligations do not apply to an unconditional purchase obligation that is cancelable under which of the following conditions?

A. Upon the occurrence of a remote contingency.

B. With the permission of the other party.

C. Under a replacement agreement signed by the same parties.

D. Upon payment of a nominal penalty.

Answer (D) is correct.
    REQUIRED: The circumstance in which GAAP pertaining to disclosure of an unconditional purchase obligation do not apply.
    DISCUSSION: GAAP relevant to disclosure of an unconditional purchase obligation do not apply when the obligation (1) was negotiated as part of the financing arrangement for (a) facilities that will provide contracted goods or services or (b) the related costs, (2) has a remaining term of more than 1 year, and (3) is either noncancelable or cancelable only under specific terms that make continuation or replacement (but not cancelation) of the agreement reasonably assured. A purchase obligation cancelable upon the payment of a nominal penalty is not unconditional.

22. If an unconditional purchase obligation is not presented in the balance sheet, certain disclosures are required. A disclosure that is **not** required is

A. The nature and term of the obligation.

B. The variable components of the obligation.

C. The imputed interest necessary to reduce the unconditional purchase obligation to its present value.

D. The amounts purchased under the obligation for each period an income statement is presented.

Answer (C) is correct.
    REQUIRED: The item not required to be disclosed if an unconditional purchase obligation is not recognized.
    DISCUSSION: When an unconditional purchase obligation is not recognized, an entity is encouraged, but not required, to disclose the amount of imputed interest necessary to reduce the unconditional purchase obligation to its present value. Disclosure of the other items is required when an unconditional purchase obligation is not recognized. Moreover, GAAP require disclosure of the amount of the fixed and determinable portion of the obligation in the aggregate as of the latest balance sheet date. If determinable, the amounts due in each of the next 5 years also should be disclosed.

5.6 Significant Risks and Uncertainties

23. Financial statements must disclose significant risks and uncertainties. The required disclosures include

A. Quantified comparisons of the relative importance of the different businesses in which the entity operates.

B. Information about a significant estimate used to value an asset only if it is probable that the financial statement effect of a condition existing at the balance sheet date will change materially in the near term.

C. Risk-reduction techniques that have successfully mitigated losses.

D. Vulnerability due to a concentration if a near-term severe impact is at least reasonably possible.

Answer (D) is correct.
    REQUIRED: The required disclosure.
    DISCUSSION: The current vulnerability due to concentrations must be disclosed if certain conditions are met. Disclosure is necessary if management knows prior to issuance of the statements that the concentration exists at the balance sheet date, it makes the entity vulnerable to a near-term severe impact, and such impact is at least reasonably possible in the near term. A severe impact may result from loss of all or a part of a business relationship, price or demand changes, loss of a patent, changes in the availability of a resource or right, or the disruption of operations in a market or geographic area.
    Answer (A) is incorrect. Disclosures about the nature of operations need not be quantified. Answer (B) is incorrect. A material financial statement effect need only be reasonably possible in the near term. Answer (C) is incorrect. The criteria for required disclosures about significant estimates may not be met if the entity has successfully employed risk-reduction techniques. In these circumstances, disclosure of those techniques is encouraged but not required.

5.7 Subsequent Events

24. On January 15, Year 2, before the Mapleview Co. released its financial statements for the year ended December 31, Year 1, it settled a long-standing lawsuit. A material loss resulted and no prior liability had been recorded. How should this loss be disclosed or recognized?

A. The loss should be disclosed, but the financial statements themselves need **not** be adjusted.

B. The loss should be disclosed in an explanatory paragraph in the auditor's report.

C. No disclosure or recognition is required.

D. The loss must be recognized in the financial statements.

Answer (D) is correct.
REQUIRED: The proper treatment of a material loss on an existing lawsuit after year end.
DISCUSSION: Subsequent events that provide additional evidence with the respect to conditions that existed at the balance sheet date, including the estimates inherent in preparing the financial statements, must be recognized in the current financial statements. Settlement of a lawsuit is indicative of conditions existing at year end and calls for recognition in the statements.
Answer (A) is incorrect. The loss must be recognized in the financial statements. Answer (B) is incorrect. The audit report need not be modified. Answer (C) is incorrect. Failure to recognize a material loss on an asset that existed at year end is a departure from GAAP.

25. Zero Corp. suffered a loss that would have a material effect on its financial statements on an uncollectible trade account receivable due to a customer's bankruptcy. This occurred suddenly due to a natural disaster 10 days after Zero's balance sheet date but 1 month before the issuance of the financial statements. Under these circumstances,

	The Loss Must be Recognized in the Financial Statements	The Event Requires Financial Statement Disclosure Only
A.	Yes	Yes
B.	Yes	No
C.	No	No
D.	No	Yes

Answer (D) is correct.
REQUIRED: The effect on the financial statements of a customer's bankruptcy after the balance sheet date but before the issuance of the statements.
DISCUSSION: Certain subsequent events may provide additional evidence about conditions at the date of the balance sheet, including estimates inherent in the preparation of statements. These events require recognition in the statements at year end. Other subsequent events provide evidence about conditions not existing at the date of the balance sheet but arising subsequent to that date and before the issuance of the statements or their availability for issuance. These events may require disclosure but not recognition in the statements. Thus, the loss must not be recognized in Zero's statements, but disclosure must be made.

5.8 Financial Instrument Disclosures

26. Whether recognized or unrecognized in an entity's financial statements, disclosure of the fair values of the entity's financial instruments is required when

A. It is feasible to estimate those values and aggregated fair values are material to the entity.

B. The entity maintains accurate cost records and aggregated fair values are material to the entity.

C. Aggregated fair values are material to the entity and credit risk has been appropriately hedged.

D. Individual fair values are material to the entity or any of the instruments are accounted for as derivatives.

Answer (A) is correct.
REQUIRED: The circumstance in which disclosure of the fair values of the entity's financial instruments is required.
DISCUSSION: Certain entities must disclose the fair value of financial instruments, whether or not they are recognized in the balance sheet, if it is feasible to estimate such fair values and aggregated fair values are material to the entity. If estimating fair value is not feasible, disclosures include information pertinent to estimating the fair value of the financial instrument or class of financial instruments, such as the carrying amount, effective interest rate, and maturity. The reasons that estimating the fair value is not feasible also should be disclosed.

27. Disclosure of information about significant concentrations of credit risk is required for

   A. Most financial instruments.

   B. Financial instruments with off-balance-sheet credit risk only.

   C. Financial instruments with off-balance-sheet market risk only.

   D. Financial instruments with off-balance-sheet risk of accounting loss only.

Answer (A) is correct.
   REQUIRED: The financial instruments for which disclosure of significant concentrations of credit risk is required.
   DISCUSSION: GAAP require the disclosure of information about the fair value of financial instruments, whether recognized or not (certain nonpublic entities and certain instruments, such as leases and insurance contracts, are exempt from the disclosure requirements). GAAP also require disclosure of all significant concentrations of credit risk for most financial instruments (except for obligations for deferred compensation, certain instruments of a pension plan, insurance contracts, warranty obligations and rights, and unconditional purchase obligations).

28. Where in its financial statements should a company disclose information about its concentration of credit risks?

   A. No disclosure is required.

   B. The notes to the financial statements.

   C. Supplementary information to the financial statements.

   D. Management's report to shareholders.

Answer (B) is correct.
   REQUIRED: The method of disclosure about concentration of credit risk.
   DISCUSSION: An entity must disclose significant concentrations of risk arising from most instruments. These disclosures should be made in the basic financial statements, either in the body of the statements or in the notes.
   Answer (A) is incorrect. Disclosure in the basic statements is required. Answer (C) is incorrect. Disclosure in supplementary information is normally done when certain entities are excluded from the scope of the requirements. However, the required disclosures are to be made by all entities. Answer (D) is incorrect. Management's report to shareholders is not part of the basic statements.

Use the additional questions in Gleim **CPA Test Prep Online** to create Test Sessions that emulate Prometric!

5.9 PRACTICE SIMULATION

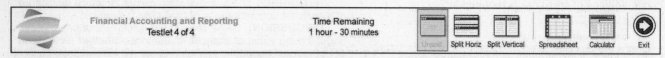

Financial Accounting and Reporting	Time Remaining		
Testlet 4 of 4	1 hour - 30 minutes	Unsplit Split Horiz Split Vertical	Spreadsheet Calculator Exit

DIRECTIONS

Note: If you believe you have encountered a software malfunction, report it to the test center staff immediately.

Navigation

To navigate from task to task, use the controls at the bottom of the screen. Click on the **Next** button to advance to the next task, or the **Previous** button to go to the previous task. To go directly to any task, click on its number.

If you would like a reminder to revisit a task, or want to indicate that you are finished with it, click on the reminder flag below the task number. To clear the flag, click on it again. Reminder flags are for your use only – they do not contribute to your score.

Tabs

In this part of the examination, you will be asked to complete various tasks. Every task has one or more **Work Tabs**. Some tasks have one or more **Information Tabs**, others may have none. Every task has a **Help** tab.

If a task has **Information Tabs**, you may use the information in them to complete your responses in the **Work Tabs**.

Work tab   Information tab   Help tab

Work Tabs:

- **Work Tabs** are identified with a pencil icon. This is where your responses are expected.
- Each task has one or more **Work Tabs**.
- **Work Tabs** contain directions for completing the task – be sure to read these directions carefully.
- The **Work Tab** name in the example above is for illustration only – yours will differ.
- You must complete all of the **Work Tabs** in each task to receive full credit.

Information Tabs:

- The Authoritative Literature will be provided in all tasks in the AUD, FAR, and REG sections for your reference.
- Your simulation may have one or more additional **Information Tabs**. Like the Authoritative Literature tabs, **Information Tabs** do not have a pencil icon.
- If your task has additional **Information Tabs**, go through each to familiarize yourself with the task content.

Help Tab:

- The **Help Tab** provides assistance with the exam software that is used in this task. For example, if the task is to compose a memorandum, **Help** will provide information about the word processor.

The Toolbar

The toolbar at the top of the screen shows the amount of time remaining for you to complete the tasks. In addition, the following tools are available. Note that only the **Exit** button is displayed when Directions are visible - the others will appear when you begin the tasks.

Click on these buttons to split or unsplit the screen. You can split the screen vertically or horizontally.

Click on this button to display the calculator; click on it again to hide the calculator. To move the calculator, click on the calculator title bar and drag the calculator to the desired location.

Click on this button to use the spreadsheet; click on it again to hide the spreadsheet. To move the spreadsheet, click on the the spreadsheet title bar and drag the spreadsheet to the desired location.

Click on this button to go on to the next part of the examination. You must complete all of the tasks to receive full credit. Once you click on **Exit** and confirm the action, you will NOT be able to return to this testlet.

| Disclosure | Authoritative Literature | Help |

Check the box beside each issue for which disclosure is required.

Disclosure Required	Accounting Issue
	1. Material related-party transactions
	2. The amount of imputed interest necessary to reduce an unconditional purchase obligation, which is not recorded in the balance sheet, to its present value
	3. The prior-interim-period adjustment effect on income from continuing operations for each prior interim period of the current year
	4. The effect of a change in accounting principle on EPS amounts for interim periods after the change is made
	5. The accounting policies reflected in unaudited interim financial statements when the policies have not changed since the end of the preceding fiscal year
	6. A reportable operating segment's carrying amounts of identifiable assets
	7. Certain information about sales to a single external customer when it accounts for 5% of revenue
	8. Segment information in interim statements of public business entities

▼ = Reminder   Directions   1 2 3 4 5 6   ◀ Previous   Next ▶

| Related Party | Authoritative Literature | Help |

Indicate by checking the appropriate box whether the following parties are related.

	Related Parties	Not Related Parties
1. A parent and its subsidiaries		
2. An entity and a 1% shareholder		
3. Subsidiaries of a common parent		
4. An entity and its vendors		
5. An entity and its customers		
6. An entity and employee trusts managed by, or under the trusteeship of, the entity's management		
7. An entity and members of the immediate families of its management		
8. Affiliates		
9. An entity and its nonmanagement employees		
10. An entity and its equity-based investees		
11. An entity and any other entity that can significantly influence it		
12. A party that can significantly influence the parties to a transaction		

▼ = Reminder   Directions   1 2 3 4 5 6   ◀ Previous   Next ▶

Company A is a publicly traded company that reports interim financial statements on a quarterly basis. For each of the following independent situations described below, enter the correct amount of revenue (profit) or expense (loss) that should be recognized in the company's interim income statements for the 3 months ended September 30, Year 3 (third quarter).

Round all amounts to the nearest dollar. If the amount is zero, enter zero (0). If the amount is an expense, enter as a negative amount.

Situation	Answer
1. On September 30, Year 3, the company determined that inventory with a cost of $80,000 has a market value of $74,000. The company estimates that the inventory's market value at the end of Year 3 will be at least $82,000.	
2. On March 31, Year 3, the company recognized a $40,000 write-down due to market decline in inventory. During the third quarter, the inventory's market value unexpectedly increased by $46,000.	
3. The company applies IFRS. On September 30, Year 3, the company determined that inventory with a cost of $60,000 has a net realizable value (NRV) of $48,000. The company estimates that the inventory's NRV at the end of Year 3 will be at least $65,000.	
4. On March 31, Year 3, the company experienced a $30,000 decline in the market value of its inventory. The company expects this decline to reverse by the end of the year. During the third quarter of Year 3, due to low demand for the company's products, the inventory's market value declined by an additional $15,000, and no reversal is expected by the end of the year.	

Check the appropriate box to indicate whether each statement is true or false.

Statement	True	False
1. An SEC filer evaluates subsequent events through the date the financial statements are complete and approved.		
2. Entities not SEC filers evaluate subsequent events through the date the financial statements are issued.		
3. An entity must disclose the date through which subsequent events have been evaluated.		
4. Entities not SEC filers evaluate subsequent events through the date the financial statements are available for issuance.		
5. Pro forma financial data must be presented when subsequent events are recognized in the financial statements.		
6. Subsequent events occur after the balance sheet date and before the financial statements are issued or available for issuance.		
7. A subsequent event must be recognized in the financial statements if it provides evidence about estimates inherent in the financial statements.		
8. A subsequent event qualifying as a business combination must be recognized.		

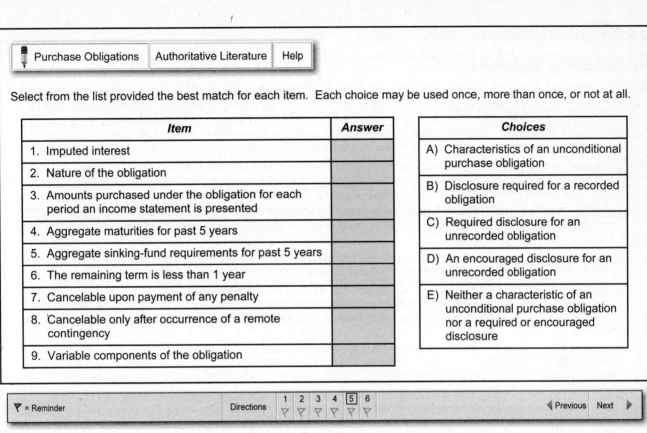

Purchase Obligations | Authoritative Literature | Help

Select from the list provided the best match for each item. Each choice may be used once, more than once, or not at all.

Item	Answer	Choices
1. Imputed interest		A) Characteristics of an unconditional purchase obligation
2. Nature of the obligation		
3. Amounts purchased under the obligation for each period an income statement is presented		B) Disclosure required for a recorded obligation
4. Aggregate maturities for past 5 years		C) Required disclosure for an unrecorded obligation
5. Aggregate sinking-fund requirements for past 5 years		D) An encouraged disclosure for an unrecorded obligation
6. The remaining term is less than 1 year		
7. Cancelable upon payment of any penalty		E) Neither a characteristic of an unconditional purchase obligation nor a required or encouraged disclosure
8. Cancelable only after occurrence of a remote contingency		
9. Variable components of the obligation		

▼ = Reminder   Directions   1 2 3 4 [5] 6   ◀ Previous   Next ▶

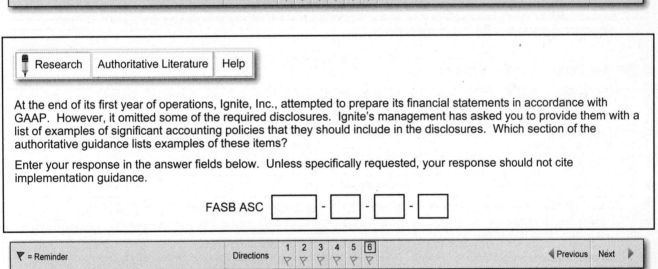

Research | Authoritative Literature | Help

At the end of its first year of operations, Ignite, Inc., attempted to prepare its financial statements in accordance with GAAP. However, it omitted some of the required disclosures. Ignite's management has asked you to provide them with a list of examples of significant accounting policies that they should include in the disclosures. Which section of the authoritative guidance lists examples of these items?

Enter your response in the answer fields below. Unless specifically requested, your response should not cite implementation guidance.

FASB ASC [ ] - [ ] - [ ] - [ ]

▼ = Reminder   Directions   1 2 3 4 5 [6]   ◀ Previous   Next ▶

Unofficial Answers

1. Disclosure (8 Gradable Items)

1. Disclosure required. GAAP require the disclosure of material related-party transactions. Exceptions are compensation arrangements, expense allowances, and similar items in the ordinary course of business. Transactions eliminated in the preparation of consolidated or combined financial statements also need not be disclosed.

2. Disclosure not required. If an unconditional purchase obligation is not recorded in the balance sheet, an entity is encouraged, but not required, to disclosure the imputed interest used to reduce the obligation to its present value.

3. Disclosure required. In the financial reports of the interim period when the adjustment occurs, disclosure of the following is required: the effect on (a) income from continuing operations, (b) net income, and (c) related per-share amounts for each prior interim period of the current year and for each prior interim period restated.

4. Disclosure required. GAAP require certain disclosures in postchange interim periods after an entity adopts a new accounting principle. These disclosures include the effect of the change on income from continuing operations, net income, and related EPS amounts.

5. Disclosure not required. GAAP require that all significant accounting policies be disclosed. However, when accounting policies have not changed, disclosure is not required for unaudited interim financial statements.

6. Disclosure not required. GAAP require disclosure of total assets for each reportable segment. Disclosure is also required of the amount of investment in equity-based investees and total expenditures for additions to most long-lived assets for each reportable segment if they are included in segment assets reviewed by the chief operating decision maker.

7. Disclosure not required. If 10% or more of revenue is derived from sales to any single customer, it must be disclosed. The amount of revenue from each such customer and the segment(s) reporting the revenues must also be disclosed. Single customers include entities under common control and each federal, state, local, or foreign government.

8. Disclosure required. Interim period information is disclosed for each reportable segment in condensed financial statements. Disclosures include external revenues, intersegment revenues, a measure of segment profit or loss, total assets that have materially changed since the last annual report, differences from the last annual report in the basis of segmentation or of segment profit or loss, and a reconciliation of the total reportable segments' profit or loss to consolidated pretax income and its components.

2. Related Party (12 Gradable Items)

1. Related parties. GAAP require disclosure. By definition, a parent can control its subsidiaries. Thus, they are affiliates.

2. Not related parties. GAAP require disclosure if the shareholder is a principal (more than 10%) owner.

3. Related parties. GAAP require disclosure. Subsidiaries of a common parent are affiliates because they are under common control.

4. Not related parties. GAAP do not require disclosure unless one party can significantly influence the other.

5. Not related parties. GAAP do not require disclosure unless one party can significantly influence the other.

6. Related parties. GAAP require disclosure. Examples of these trusts are pension and profit-sharing trusts.

7. Related parties. GAAP require disclosure of transactions between the entity and its principal owners, management, or members of their immediate families.

8. Related parties. GAAP require disclosure. An affiliate controls, is controlled by, or is under common control with an entity.

9. Not related parties. GAAP do not require disclosure. Management consists of persons responsible for achieving entity objectives (e.g., directors, the CEO, the COO, etc.).

10. Related parties. GAAP require disclosure. An equity-based investee can be significantly influenced by the investor.

11. Related parties. GAAP require disclosure of transactions between an entity and any other entity if one party can significantly influence the other to the extent that one party may be prevented from fully pursuing its interests.

12. Related parties. GAAP require disclosure. A party is a related party if it can significantly influence the management or operating policies of the transacting parties.

3. Interim Reporting (4 Gradable Items)

1. <u>$0.</u> No write-down of inventory is recognized in the interim financial statements, since no loss is reasonably anticipated for the year.

2. <u>$40,000.</u> Inventory losses from nontemporary market declines must be recognized at the interim date ($40,000 loss in the first quarter). If the loss is recovered in another quarter, it is recognized as a change in estimate. The amount recovered is limited to the loss previously recognized. Thus, the company recognized in the third quarter a gain of $40,000 as a result of the reversal of the previous inventory write-down.

3. <u>($12,000).</u> Under IFRS, each interim period is viewed as a discrete reporting period. The inventory is measured at the lower of cost or NRV regardless of its NRV at the end of the year. Thus, a loss of $12,000 ($60,000 – $48,000) must be recognized in the third quarter.

4. <u>($45,000).</u> No write-down of inventory was recognized in the first quarter, since no loss was reasonably anticipated for the year. During the third quarter, the company's estimates that the entire decline in the inventory's market value of $45,000 ($30,000 + $15,000) will not be reversed. Thus, the loss of $45,000 must be recognized in the third quarter.

4. Subsequent Events (8 Gradable Items)

1. <u>False.</u> An SEC filer evaluates subsequent events through the date the statements are issued.

2. <u>False.</u> A non-SEC filer evaluates subsequent events through the date the statements are available for issuance.

3. <u>True.</u> An entity must disclose the date through which subsequent events have been evaluated.

4. <u>True.</u> Entities that are not SEC filers evaluate subsequent events through the date the financial statements are available for issuance.

5. <u>False.</u> Pro forma financial data should supplement historical statements when a significant subsequent event provides evidence about a condition that did not exist at the date of the balance sheet.

6. <u>True.</u> Subsequent events occur after the balance sheet date and before the financial statements are issued or available for issuance.

7. <u>True.</u> A subsequent event must be recognized in the financial statements if it provides evidence about estimates inherent in the financial statements.

8. <u>False.</u> A business combination requires disclosure only.

5. Purchase Obligations (9 Gradable Items)

1. <u>D) An encouraged disclosure for an unrecorded obligation.</u> When an unconditional purchase obligation is not recorded, the disclosure of the amount of imputed interest necessary to reduce the unconditional purchase obligation to its present value is encouraged.

2. <u>C) Required disclosure for an unrecorded obligation.</u> A disclosure is required for the nature of an unrecorded obligation.

3. <u>C) Required disclosure for an unrecorded obligation.</u> A disclosure is required for the amounts purchased under an unrecorded obligation for each period an income statement is presented.

4. <u>B) Disclosure required for a recorded obligation.</u> A disclosure is required for the aggregate maturities for the past 5 years for a recorded obligation.

5. <u>B) Disclosure required for a recorded obligation.</u> A disclosure is required for aggregate sinking-fund requirements for the past 5 years for a recorded obligation.

6. <u>E) Neither a characteristic of an unconditional purchase obligation nor a required or encouraged disclosure.</u> Having a remaining term less than 1 year is neither a characteristic of an unconditional purchase obligation nor a required or encouraged disclosure.

7. <u>E) Neither a characteristic of an unconditional purchase obligation nor a required or encouraged disclosure.</u> Being cancelable upon payment of any penalty is neither a characteristic of an unconditional purchase obligation nor a required or encouraged disclosure.

8. <u>A) Characteristics of an unconditional purchase obligation.</u> A purchase is considered unconditional if it is cancelable upon the happening of a remote contingency.

9. <u>C) Required disclosure for an unrecorded obligation.</u> A disclosure is required for the variable components of an unrecorded obligation.

6. Research (1 Gradable Item)

Answer: FASB ASC 235-10-50-4

235-10-50-4 Examples of disclosures by an entity commonly required with respect to accounting policies would include, among others, those relating to the following:

a.   Basis of consolidation
b.   Depreciation methods
c.   Amortization of intangibles
d.   Inventory pricing
e.   Accounting for recognition of profit on long-term construction-type contracts
f.   Recognition of revenue from franchising and leasing operations.

Gleim Simulation Grading

Task	Correct Responses		Gradable Items		Score per Task
1	_____	÷	8	=	_____
2	_____	÷	12	=	_____
3	_____	÷	4	=	_____
4	_____	÷	8	=	_____
5	_____	÷	9	=	_____
Research	_____	÷	1	=	_____

Total of Scores per Task   _____

÷   Total Number of Tasks   6

Total Score   _____%

Use **CPA Gleim Online** and **Simulation Wizard** to practice more task-based simulations in a realistic environment.

STUDY UNIT SIX
CASH AND INVESTMENTS

(17 pages of outline)

6.1	Cash	197
6.2	Fair Value Option (FVO)	201
6.3	Classification of Investments	203
6.4	Equity Method	207
6.5	Investments in Bonds	211
6.6	Cash Surrender Value	213
6.7	Practice Simulation	224

The first subunit concerns **cash**, the most liquid of assets. It includes **cash equivalents**, a special category of assets so close to conversion to cash that they are classified with cash on the balance sheet. **Securities held as investments** are reported in three classifications on the balance sheet. Other matters, such as the **equity method** of accounting for investments in common stock and **bond** investments, also are discussed.

6.1 CASH

1. **Nature of Cash**

   a. Cash is money, the **most liquid of assets**. Because of that liquidity and the ability to transfer it electronically, internal control of cash must be strong.

   b. As the customary **medium of exchange**, it also provides the **standard of value** (the unit of measurement) of the transactions that are reported in the financial statements.

      1) Changes in the purchasing power of money are not recognized in standard financial statements. **Nominal units of money** provide the measurement scale.

      2) Cash is the standard medium of exchange. Thus, its effective management is vital. Economic entities must hold sufficient cash (have adequate liquidity) to execute transactions. However, the amount held should be limited because cash usually does not increase in value (appreciate) unless invested.

   c. Cash is a **current asset** unless it is used in the near term for such purposes as payments to sinking funds.

2. **Readily Available**

   a. To be classified as cash, an asset must be readily available for use. The use should not be restricted. The cash account on the balance sheet should consist of

      1) Coin and currency on hand, including petty cash and change funds
      2) Demand deposits (checking accounts)
      3) Time deposits (savings accounts)

         a) Although technically subject to a bank's right to demand notice before withdrawal, savings accounts are treated as cash because the right is seldom exercised.

4) Near-cash assets

    a) They include many negotiable instruments, such as money orders, bank drafts, certified checks, cashiers' checks, and personal checks.

    b) They are usually in the process of being deposited (deposits in transit).

    c) They must be depositable. They exclude unsigned or postdated checks.

    d) Checks written to creditors but not mailed or delivered at the balance sheet date should be included in the payor's cash account (not considered cash payments at year end).

3. Restricted Cash

a. Restricted cash is not actually set aside in special accounts. However, it is designated for special uses and should be separately presented and disclosed in the notes.

    1) Examples are bond sinking funds and new building funds.

    2) The nature of the use determines whether cash is current or noncurrent.

        a) A bond sinking fund to redeem noncurrent bond debt is noncurrent, but a fund to be used to redeem bonds currently redeemable is a current asset.

    3) Restricted cash in foreign banks should be reported as a receivable (current or noncurrent), but unrestricted deposits are classified as cash.

4. Compensating Balances

a. As part of an agreement regarding either an existing loan or the provision of future credit, a borrower may keep an average or minimum amount on deposit with the lender. This compensating balance increases the effective rate of interest paid by the borrower. It also creates a disclosure issue because the full amount reported as cash might not be available to meet general obligations. The SEC's recommended solution depends on the duration of the lending arrangement and the nature of the restriction.

    1) If the balance relates to a short-term agreement and is legally restricted, it is separately reported among the cash and cash equivalents as a current asset.

    2) If the agreement is long-term, the legally restricted balance is noncurrent. It should be treated as an investment or other asset.

    3) If the use of the compensating balance is not restricted, full disclosure is required. Separate classification is not.

5. Cash Equivalents

a. Cash equivalents are short-term, highly liquid investments. Common examples are Treasury bills, money market funds, and commercial paper.

b. Cash equivalents are

    1) Readily convertible to known amounts of cash

    2) So near maturity that interest rate risk is insignificant.

        a) Only investments with an original maturity to the holder of 3 months or less qualify.

EXAMPLE

Debtor issues a note with a 2-year maturity to Creditor. After 1 year and 10 months, Creditor sells the note to Holder. The original maturity to Holder is 2 months. If the note is highly liquid, it may be a cash equivalent. The note would not have been a cash equivalent to Creditor at the date of sale.

6. **Noncash Items**

   a. **Nonsufficient funds (NSF) checks**, postdated checks, and IOUs should be treated as receivables. Advances for expenses to employees may be classified as receivables (if expected to be paid by employees) or as prepaid expenses.

   b. An **overdraft** is a current liability unless the entity has sufficient funds in another account at the same bank to cover it.

      1) If an entity has separate accounts in one bank, an overdraft will usually be subject to a right of offset: The funds in another account may be legally transferred by the bank to cover the shortage.

      2) This right does not exist when the accounts are in different institutions. Thus, the overdraft must be reported as a liability, not netted.

   c. **Noncash short-term investments** are usually substantially restricted and thus not readily available for use by the entity. They should be classified as current or temporary investments, not cash. However, they may qualify as cash equivalents.

      1) Money market funds are essentially mutual funds that have portfolios of commercial paper and Treasury bills. However, a money market fund with a usable checking feature might be better classified as cash.

      2) Commercial paper (also known as negotiable instruments) consists of short-term (no more than 270 days) corporate obligations.

      3) Treasury bills are short-term, guaranteed U.S. government obligations. In contrast, an obligation of a federal agency is guaranteed only by the agency, not by the U.S. government.

      4) Certificates of deposit are formal debt instruments issued by a bank or other financial institution and are subject to penalties for withdrawal before maturity.

7. **Recording Cash**

   a. Cash may be recorded in a general ledger control account, with a subsidiary ledger for each bank account. An alternative is a series of general ledger accounts.

      1) On the balance sheet, one account is presented. It reflects all unrestricted cash.

      2) Each transfer of cash from one account to another requires an entry.

      3) At the end of each period, a schedule of transfers should be prepared and reviewed to make certain all cash transfers are counted only once.

Cash	$100,000	
Revenues		$100,000

8. **Bank Reconciliation**

> The AICPA has released a number of bank reconciliation problems that test cash reporting on the exam. CPA candidates may see a bank reconciliation problem on the CPA exam.

   a. A bank reconciliation is a schedule comparing the cash balance per books with the balance per bank statement (usually received monthly). The common approach is to reconcile the bank balance to the book balance to reach the true balance.

      1) The bank and book balances usually vary. Thus, the reconciliation permits the entity to determine whether the difference is attributable to normal conditions, error, or fraud. It is also a basis for entries to adjust the books to reflect unrecorded items.

      2) The bank and the entity inevitably record many transactions at different times. Both also may make errors.

b.   **Items Known to Entity but Not Known to Bank**

   1)   **Outstanding checks.** The books may reflect checks written by the entity that have not yet cleared the bank. These amounts are subtracted from the bank balance to arrive at the true balance.

   2)   **Deposits in transit.** A time lag may occur between deposit of receipts and the bank's recording of the transaction. Thus, receipts placed in a night depository on the last day of the month are reflected only in the next month's bank statement. These receipts are added to the bank balance to arrive at the true balance.

   3)   **Errors.** If the bank has wrongly charged or credited the entity's account (or failed to record a transaction at all), the error will be detected in the process of preparing the reconciliation.

c.   **Items Known to Bank but Not Known to Entity**

   1)   **Amounts added by the bank.** Interest income added to an account may not be included in the book balance. Banks may act as collection agents, for example, for notes on which the depositor is the payee. If the depositor has not learned of a collection, it will not be reflected in its records.

      a)   These amounts are added to the book balance to arrive at the true balance.

      b)   They should be recorded on the entity's books, after which they are not reconciling items.

   2)   **Amounts subtracted (or not added) by the bank.** These amounts generally include service charges and customer checks returned for insufficient funds (NSF checks). Service charges cannot be recorded in the books until the bank statement is received. Customer checks returned for insufficient funds are not added to the bank balance but are still included in the book balance.

      a)   These amounts are subtracted from the book balance to arrive at the true balance.

      b)   They should be recorded on the entity's books, after which they are not reconciling items.

   3)   **Errors.** Bookkeeping errors made by the entity will likewise be discovered.

d.   **Common Reconciliation Items**

	To Book Balance	To Bank Balance
Additions	Interest earned Deposits collected Errors	Deposits in transit Errors
Subtractions	Service charges NSF checks Errors	Outstanding checks Errors

EXAMPLE

Raughley Company's bank statement on March 31 indicated a balance of $6,420. The book balance on that date was $7,812. The bank balance did not include $3,229 of receipts for March 31 that were deposited on that day but were not recorded until April 1 by the bank. It also did not include $450 of checks written in March that did not clear until April. The March bank statement revealed that (1) the bank had collected $1,500 in March on a note owed to Raughley, (2) a $160 customer check had been returned for insufficient funds, and (3) service charges totaled $7. Finally, a check for $60 written by Raughley cleared the bank for $6.

Bank Reconciliation

Book balance – March 31		$7,812
Add items on bank statement not on books:		
Note proceeds	$1,500	1,500
Subtract items on bank statement not on books:		
Service charges	$ (7)	
Deposited check returned NSF	(160)	(167)
True cash balance – March 31		**$9,145**
Bank balance – March 31		$6,420
Add items on books not on bank statement:		
Bank error: $60 check cleared for $6	$ (54)	
Deposits in transit	3,229	3,175
Subtract items on books not on bank statement:		
Outstanding checks	$ (450)	(450)
True cash balance – March 31		**$9,145**

Stop and review! You have completed the outline for this subunit. Study multiple-choice questions 1 through 3 beginning on page 214.

6.2 FAIR VALUE OPTION (FVO)

Background

In 2007, the FASB granted preparers of financial statements the choice of reporting most financial assets and liabilities at fair value (the fair value option). This permits reporting entities to avoid the cost and complexity of hedge accounting. Current GAAP are in FASB ASC 825. Under IFRS, certain financial assets or liabilities that do not otherwise qualify may be designated at fair value through profit or loss when they are initially recognized if fair value is reliably measurable. However, the FVO under IFRS is more limited in scope. The nature of these limitations (e.g., qualifying criteria) is beyond the scope of this text.

1. **Scope**

   a. The FVO allows entities to measure most recognized financial assets and liabilities at **fair value**.

      1) Unrealized gains and losses are reported in earnings at each subsequent reporting date.

   b. An entity **may elect** the **FVO** for most recognized financial assets and liabilities. It also may be elected for certain other items that are beyond the scope of this text.

   c. The FVO **may not be elected** for the following:

      1) An investment that must be consolidated

         a) The FVO is not an alternative to consolidation.

         b) Consolidation is required for subsidiaries and variable interest entities (covered in detail in Study Unit 16).

2) Postretirement employee benefit obligations, employee stock option and purchase plans, and deferred compensation obligations
3) Most financial assets and liabilities under leases
4) Demand deposit liabilities
5) Financial instruments at least partly classified in equity

2. **Election of the FVO**

a. The decision whether to elect the FVO is **made irrevocably at an election date** (unless a new election date occurs).

1) With certain exceptions, the decision is made **instrument by instrument** and only for an **entire instrument**.

a) One such exception exists for an investment otherwise accounted for under the **equity method**. If the FVO is applied to the investment, it also must be applied to other financial interests in the investee (e.g., debt and other equity interests).

2) Thus, the FVO generally need **not be applied to all instruments** in a single transaction. For example, it might be applied only to some of the shares or bonds issued or acquired in a transaction.

3) But an instrument that constitutes one legal contract is indivisible for FVO purposes.

b. The following are **election dates**:

1) Initial recognition of an eligible item
2) Making an eligible firm commitment
3) A change in accounting for an investment in another entity because it becomes subject to the equity method
4) Deconsolidation of a subsidiary or a variable interest entity (with retention of an interest)
5) An event that causes financial assets previously measured at fair value through earnings because of a specialized accounting principle to no longer qualify
6) An event requiring fair value measurement when it occurs but not at subsequent reporting dates (excluding recognition of nontemporary impairment, e.g., of inventory or long-lived assets)

c. **Examples of events** requiring either remeasurement at fair value or initial recognition (or both) of eligible items and that result in an election date are a

1) Business combination,
2) Consolidation or deconsolidation, or
3) Significant modification of debt.

3. **Financial Statement Presentation**

a. **Balance Sheet**

1) Assets and liabilities measured using the FVO are reported by separating their reported fair values from the carrying amounts of similar items. One of the following presentations must be made:

a) Two separate line items

b) One combined line item (with the amount measured at fair value indicated in parentheses)

b. **Income Statement**

    1) Unrealized gains and losses on items measured using the FVO are recognized at subsequent reporting dates.

        a) Upfront costs and fees related to those items are recognized as incurred.

c. **Cash Flow Statement**

    1) Cash flows related to items measured at fair value are classified according to their nature and purpose.

Stop and review! You have completed the outline for this subunit. Study multiple-choice questions 4 through 7 beginning on page 215.

6.3 CLASSIFICATION OF INVESTMENTS

Background
Beginning in 1975, the FASB only required securities held as investments to be classified as debt or equity. However, there was dissatisfaction among regulators that reporting debt securities at amortized cost did not provide investors with optimum decision-making information. As a result, in 1993 the FASB established the current three-way classification system, which takes cognizance of the entity's intent regarding its investment securities. Current GAAP are found in FASB ASC 320.

1. **Investments in Debt and Equity Securities**

    a. A **debt security** represents a **creditor** relationship with the issuer.

        1) This category includes mandatorily redeemable preferred stock and collateralized mortgage obligations. It excludes leases, options, financial futures contracts, and forward contracts.

    b. An **equity security** is an **ownership** interest in an entity or a right to acquire or dispose of such an interest.

        1) When equity securities do not have readily determinable fair values, i.e., when quoted market prices are unavailable, they are measured using the **cost method**.

            a) Such equity securities are reported at historical cost until sold, at which time realized gains and losses are recognized.

        2) Convertible debt securities do not represent an equity interest in the issuer.

2. **Applicability**

    a. This subunit applies to the following investments:

        1) All investments in debt securities
        2) Equity securities with readily determinable fair values

    b. The securities to which this subunit applies are classified at acquisition into one of **three categories**. The classification is reassessed at each reporting date.

Category	Criteria
Held-to-maturity	Debt securities that the reporting entity has the positive intent and ability to hold to maturity
Trading	Intended to be sold in the near term
Available-for-sale	Not classified as held-to-maturity or trading

c.   This subunit does **not** apply to the following:

1)   Investments for which the entity has elected the FVO
2)   Investments in equity securities accounted for using the equity method
3)   Investments in consolidated subsidiaries
4)   Not-for-profit entities
5)   Most derivative instruments

The AICPA has heavily tested the classification of investments and related topics. Both conceptual and calculation questions have been used.

3.   **Held-to-Maturity Securities -- Amortized Cost**

a.   An investment in a debt security is classified as held-to-maturity when the holder has both the **positive intent** and the **ability** to hold the security until its maturity date.

1)   The investor may intend to hold the security for an indefinite period. Also, the possibility may exist that it will be sold before maturity to supply needed cash, avoid interest rate risk, etc. In these cases, the security cannot be classified as held-to-maturity.

2)   If a sale before maturity takes place, the security can still be deemed to have been held-to-maturity if

a)   Sale is near enough to the maturity or call date (e.g., within 3 months) so that interest rate risk (change in the market rate) does not have a significant effect on fair value, or

b)   Sale is after collection of 85% or more of the principal.

b.   A security is not held-to-maturity if it can be settled under terms that prevent the holder from substantially recovering its investment.

1)   Such a security may therefore need to be reclassified and measured as an available-for-sale or trading security.

c.   Held-to-maturity securities are reported at amortized cost.

1)   The purchase of held-to-maturity securities is recorded as follows:

Held-to-maturity securities	$XXX	
Cash		$XXX

d.   **Presentation -- balance sheet.** Held-to-maturity securities are presented net of any unamortized premium or discount. No valuation account is used.

1)   Amortization of any discount (premium) is reported by a debit (credit) to held-to-maturity securities and a credit (debit) to interest income.

2)   Individual securities are presented as current or noncurrent.

e.   **Presentation -- income statement.** Realized gains and losses and interest income (including amortization of premium or discount) are included in earnings.

f.   **Presentation -- cash flow statement.** Cash flows are from investing activities.

4.   **Trading Securities -- Fair Value**

a.   Trading securities are bought and held primarily for sale in the near term. They are purchased and sold frequently.

1)   Each trading security is initially recorded at **cost** (including brokerage commissions and taxes).

Trading securities	$XXX	
Cash		$XXX

2) At each balance sheet date, trading securities are **remeasured at fair value**. (The fair value measurement framework was discussed in Study Unit 4, Subunit 7.)

b. **Unrealized holding gains and losses** on trading securities are included in **earnings**. A holding gain or loss is the net change in fair value during the period, not including recognized dividends or interest not received.

1) To retain historical cost in the accounts while reporting changes in the carrying amount from changes in fair value, a valuation allowance may be established. For example, the entry below debits an allowance for an increase in the fair value of trading securities.

> Securities fair value adjustment (trading) $XXX
> Unrealized holding gain -- earnings $XXX

c. **Presentation -- balance sheet.** The balances of the securities and valuation allowances are netted. One amount is displayed for fair value.

1) Assets similar to those classified as trading that are not measured subsequently at fair value are reported separately.

2) Individual securities are presented as current or noncurrent.

d. **Presentation -- income statement.** Unrealized and realized holding gains and losses, dividends, and interest income (including premium or discount amortization) are included in earnings.

e. **Presentation -- cash flow statement.** Classification of cash flows depends on the nature of the securities and the purpose of their acquisition. They are typically considered to be from operating activities.

5. **Available-for-Sale Securities -- Fair Value**

a. Securities that are not classified as held-to-maturity or trading are considered available-for-sale. The initial acquisition is recorded at **cost** by a debit to available-for-sale securities and a credit to cash.

> Available-for-sale securities $XXX
> Cash $XXX

1) Amortization of any discount (premium) is reported by a debit (credit) to available-for-sale securities or an allowance and a credit (debit) to interest income.

2) Receipt of cash dividends is recorded by a debit to cash and a credit to dividend income.

b. **Unrealized holding gains and losses** are reported in **other comprehensive income** (OCI).

> Unrealized holding loss -- OCI $XXX
> Securities fair value adjustment
>   (available-for-sale) $XXX

1) Tax effects are debited or credited directly to OCI.

2) All or part of unrealized gains and losses for an available-for-sale security designated and qualifying as the hedged item in a fair value hedge are recognized in earnings.

c. **Presentation -- balance sheet.** The balances of the securities and valuation allowances are netted. One amount is displayed for fair value.

1) Assets similar to those classified as available-for-sale that are not measured subsequently at fair value are reported separately.

2) Individual securities are presented as current or noncurrent.

3) In the equity section, unrealized holding gains and losses are reported in accumulated OCI (the real account to which OCI is closed).

d.   **Presentation -- income statement.** Realized gains and losses, dividends, and interest income (including premium or discount amortization) are included in earnings.

e.   **Presentation -- statement of comprehensive income.** Unrealized holding gains and losses are included in comprehensive income.

   1)   Reclassification adjustments also must be made for each component of OCI. Their purpose is to avoid double counting when an item included in net income also was included in OCI for the same or a prior period. For example, if a gain on available-for-sale securities is realized in the current period, the prior-period recognition of an unrealized holding gain must be eliminated by debiting OCI and crediting a gain.

f.   **Presentation -- cash flow statement.** Cash flows are from investing activities.

6.   **Transfers between Categories**

a.   Transfers between categories are accounted for at transfer-date fair value. The following describes the treatment of **unrealized holding gains and losses** at that date:

   1)   **From trading to any category.** Amounts already recognized in earnings are not reversed.

   2)   **To trading from any category.** Amounts not already recognized in earnings are recognized in earnings.

   3)   **To available-for-sale from held-to-maturity.** Amounts are recognized in OCI.

   4)   **To held-to-maturity from available-for-sale.** Amounts recognized in OCI are not reversed but are amortized in the same way as premium or discount.

      a)   This amortization at least partly offsets the earnings effect of the amortization of the premium or discount. Fair value accounting may result in recognition of a premium or discount when a debt security is transferred to the held-to-maturity category.

   5)   Transfers **from held-to-maturity** or **into or from trading** should be rare.

b.   **Summary of Transfers**

From	To	Earnings Recognition
Trading	Any category	Already recognized, not reversed
Any category	Trading	If not already recognized
Held-to-maturity	Available-for-sale	Unrealized gain (loss) recognized in OCI
Available-for-sale	Held-to-maturity	Amounts in OCI not reversed but are amortized in same way as premium (discount)

7.   **Dividends and Interest Income**

a.   The guidance in this subunit does not change the recognition and measurement principles for dividends and interest, such as amortization of premium or discount using the effective interest method.

8.   **Impairment**

a.   Unrealized changes in fair value are recognized if they represent nontemporary declines. The **amortized cost basis** is used to calculate any impairment. It differs from fair value, which equals the cost basis plus or minus the net unrealized holding gain or loss.

    b.   If a decline in fair value of an individual **held-to-maturity or available-for-sale** security below its amortized cost basis is other than temporary, the amortized cost basis is **written down to fair value** as a new cost basis.

        1)   However, if a security has been the hedged item in a fair value hedge, its amortized cost basis will reflect adjustments in its carrying amount for changes in fair value attributable to the hedged risk.

    c.   The impairment is a **realized loss** included in **earnings**.

        1)   The new cost basis is not affected by recoveries in fair value.

        2)   Subsequent changes in fair value of available-for-sale securities, except for other-than-temporary declines, are included in OCI.

9.   **Summary of Investments in Securities**

    a.   The following table summarizes GAAP applicable when the FVO has not been elected:

Category	Held-to-maturity		Trading		Available-for-sale	
Definition	Debt that the entity has the positive ability and intent to hold to maturity		Bought and held for near-term sale		All securities not in the other two categories	
Type of security	Debt	Equity	Debt	Equity	Debt	Equity
Recognize holding G/L?	No	--	Yes	Yes	Yes	Yes
Recognize unrealized holding G/L in	--	--	Earnings	Earnings	OCI	OCI
Measured at	Amortized cost	--	Fair value	Fair value	Fair value	Fair value

---

IFRS Difference

A financial asset not at fair value through profit or loss is measured initially at fair value plus transaction costs. Other financial assets are measured at fair value.

Unless the fair value option has been elected, financial assets must be classified as subsequently measured at either (1) amortized cost or (2) fair value. This determination is made on the basis of the business model test and the contractual cash flow test.

A financial asset is subsequently measured at amortized cost if it meets the business model test (objective: collect the contractual cash flows) and the cash flow test (contract provides for specific dates for cash flows that are principal and interest payments only).

Equity investments are measured at fair value through profit or loss unless the entity has elected at initial recognition to recognize holding gains or losses in other comprehensive income. This irrevocable election may be made for an equity investment not held for trading. But dividend income is still recognized in profit or loss.

Financial assets are **reclassified** only if the entity changes its business model for managing them.

Stop and review! You have completed the outline for this subunit. Study multiple-choice questions 8 through 15 beginning on page 216.

6.4 EQUITY METHOD

1.   **Significant Influence**

    a.   An investment in voting stock that enables the investor to exercise significant influence over the investee should be accounted for by the equity method (assuming no FVO election).

IFRS Difference

In assessing the investor's influence, the entity also considers **potential voting rights** (share call options, share warrants, or other instruments convertible into ordinary shares). These must be currently exercisable or convertible and must be considered even if held by other entities.

---

b. The accounting method used by the investor depends on its presumed influence based on the ownership interest held. This diagram depicts the three possibilities:

% Ownership	Presumed Influence	Accounting Method
100% 50%	Control	Consolidation
50% 20%	Significant	Equity Method or FVO
20% 0%	Little or none	Fair Value Method

1) The **FVO**, which may be elected when the investor does not have control, was discussed in Subunit 6.2. The fair value method, used when the investor has not elected the FVO and does not have significant influence, was discussed in Subunit 6.3.

2) The **equity method**, used when the investor has significant influence and has not elected the FVO, is discussed in this subunit.

3) **Consolidation**, required when the investor owns more than 50% of the outstanding voting interests, will be discussed in Study Unit 16. (Consolidation is not required if control **does not rest with the majority owner**.)

IFRS Difference

When the investor has significant influence, the equity method must be applied unless (1) the investment is classified as held for sale, or (2) conditions exist similar to those that would exempt a parent from preparing consolidated statements.

 CPA candidates should expect to see questions on applying the equity method to investments. Past exam questions have most often used calculations to test candidates' understanding of this topic.

---

2. **Applying the Equity Method**

a. Under the equity method, the investor's **share of the investee's earnings or losses** is adjusted to eliminate intra-entity profits and losses not realized in third-party transactions.

1) It is also reduced by any dividends on cumulative preferred stock, whether or not declared. The adjusted share of the investee's earnings is a debit (losses and dividends are credits) to the carrying amount of the investment.

2) A cash dividend from the investee is a return of an investment. It is credited to the investment but does not affect equity-based earnings.

b.   The investor's share of the investee's earnings or losses is recognized only for the portion of the year that the investment was held under the equity method.

EXAMPLE

On March 1, Byrd company purchased, at the market price, 40% of the outstanding common stock of Dowland Corporation. On March 1, Dowland had 50,000 shares of $1 par value common stock outstanding, and the market price was $12 per share.

Investment in Dowland Corp. (50,000 × $12 × .40)	$240,000	
Cash		$240,000

On September 13, Dowland declared and paid a $15,000 cash dividend.

Cash ($15,000 × .40)	$6,000	
Investment in Dowland Corp.		$6,000

For the year ending December 31, Dowland reported net income of $60,000, earned at a constant rate throughout the year. Byrd had held its equity-method investment in Dowland for 10 months of the year.

Investment in Dowland Corp. [$60,000 × .40 × (10 ÷ 12)]	$20,000	
Income -- equity-method investee		$20,000

---

c.   The difference between the cost of the investment and the underlying equity in the investee's net assets is treated as if the investee were a consolidated subsidiary. The difference also affects the investor's share of the investee's earnings or losses.

1)   This difference may be related wholly or in part to specific accounts, such as assets not recorded at fair value.

2)   For example, if the investee's depreciable assets are understated, amortization of the excess of the fair value over the carrying amount must be recognized by the following entry:

Revenue -- equity in X Co. earnings	$XXX	
Investment in X Co.		$XXX

3)   Similarly, the investee's sale of land or inventory with a fair value in excess of the carrying amount requires an adjustment to prevent double-counting. The excess fair value is already reflected in the investment balance. It should not be counted when the investor's share of the investee's earnings is debited to the investment. The entry is the following:

Revenue -- equity in X Co. earnings (excess profit)	$XXX	
Investment in X Co.		$XXX

d.   The difference between cost and the underlying equity in the investee's net assets that is not attributable to specific accounts is treated as **goodwill**.

1)   This amount is not amortized. The equity method investment (but not the equity method goodwill itself, which is inseparable from the investment) is **tested for impairment**.

e.   The investor's shares of the investee's extraordinary items and prior-period adjustments are classified similarly by the investor if material.

f.   Use of the equity method is discontinued when the investment is reduced to zero by investee losses unless the investor has committed to provide additional financial support to the investee.

g.   Disclosures should include (1) the difference, if any, between the carrying amount of the investment and the underlying equity in the net assets of the investee and (2) the accounting method applied to the difference.

3.   **Change to the Equity Method**

a.   When ownership of the voting stock of an investee **rises to the level of significant influence**, the investor must adopt the equity method or the FVO. A 20% or greater ownership interest is presumed to permit such influence absent strong contrary evidence.

b.   The investor must **retroactively adjust** (1) the carrying amount of the investment, (2) results of operations for current and prior periods presented, and (3) retained earnings. The adjustments are made as if the equity method had been in effect during all of the previous periods in which any percentage was held.

c.   When the change is **from the fair value method**, the entity must eliminate the effects of recognition of unrealized holding gains and losses on available-for-sale securities: (1) their classification as available for sale, (2) accumulated OCI, and (3) the amount included in the allowance account.

d.   When the investor no longer has control of the investee but retains significant influence, it may choose the FVO or the equity method. The new method is applied only from the deconsolidation date.

4.   **Change from the Equity Method**

a.   If an investor can **no longer be presumed** to exert significant influence, it ceases to recognize its share of the undistributed earnings or losses of the investee. This change from the equity method is **not** a basis for

1)   The FVO election or
2)   Any retroactive adjustment.

b.   The shares retained ordinarily will be accounted for as available-for-sale or trading securities.

1)   A fair-value adjustment is made at the next balance sheet date (assuming the fair value is readily determinable).

IFRS Difference

When significant influence is lost, any retained investment is measured at fair value.

---

c.   Subsequent dividends are accounted for as dividend income. However, if they are liquidating dividends, they reduce the investment balance.

d.   Amortization of the excess of the fair value over the carrying amount of depreciable assets is no longer recognized.

IFRS Difference

Under the equity method, the investor's statements must use uniform accounting policies. Thus, adjustments must be made to conform the investee's policies to the investor's.

---

5.   **Cost Method**

a.   Under the fair value method, equity securities are accounted for based on fair values if the equity method is not appropriate. However, if such equity securities do **not have readily determinable fair values**, they are accounted for after acquisition using the cost method.

1)   Under the cost method, an investment in stock is initially recorded at cost, but subsequent unrealized changes in fair value are not recognized unless they are nontemporary declines.

2)   Under the cost and fair-value methods,

a)   Dividends are accounted for by the investor as dividend income. But a liquidating dividend reduces the investment balance.

b)   Interentity transactions should be accounted for separately and in full.

Stop and review! You have completed the outline for this subunit. Study multiple-choice questions 16 through 23 beginning on page 219.

6.5 INVESTMENTS IN BONDS

1. **Definition and Classification**

   a. A bond is a formal contractual agreement by an issuer to pay an amount of money (face amount) at the maturity date plus interest at the stated rate at specific intervals. All terms are stated in a document called an indenture.

      1) An investment in a bond is a financial asset. Thus, the investor may elect the FVO.

      2) Absent this election (or proper classification as a trading security), a bond is classified as held-to-maturity or available for sale.

      3) For a description of the various types of bonds, see Study Unit 13, Subunit 1.

2. **Purchase Price**

   a. An investment in a bond is recorded on the purchaser's books at the present value of the bond's two cash flows, discounted at the interest rate prevailing in the market at the time of the purchase. (For a thorough discussion of the time value of money, see Study Unit 13, Subunit 2.)

      1) The face amount (also called the maturity amount) is received on the bond's maturity date, e.g., 20 years after the initial purchase.

      2) The annual cash interest equals the bond's face amount times the stated (or coupon) rate, e.g., $1,000 face amount × 4% stated rate = $400 annual cash interest.

   b. If the bond's stated (coupon) rate differs from the market rate at the time of the purchase, the price paid will not equal the face amount.

      1) If the bond's stated rate is greater than the current market rate, the purchase price is higher than the face amount and the bond is purchased at a premium.

         a) An investor in bonds rarely uses a separate premium or discount account, instead recording the investment at historical cost.

EXAMPLE

An investor purchases an 8%, 5-year, $5,000 bond when the prevailing interest rate in the market is 6%. The present value of the face amount and interest payments, discounted at 6%, is $5,421. The premium as of the date of purchase (unrecorded) is thus $421 ($5,000 face amount – $5,421 present value). The investor records the following entry:

Investment in bond	$5,421	
Cash		$5,421

---

      2) If the bond's stated rate is less than the current market rate, the purchase price is lower than the face amount and the bond is purchased at a discount.

EXAMPLE

An investor purchases a 6%, 5-year, $5,000 bond at 92 (meaning 92% of par). The present value of the face amount and interest payments must be $4,600 ($5,000 × .92). This reflects a market rate of 8%. The discount at the date of purchase (unrecorded) is $400 ($5,000 face amount – $4,600 present value). The investor records the following entry:

Investment in bond	$4,600	
Cash		$4,600

---

   c. When a bond is purchased between interest dates, the investor generally pays to the issuer the amount of interest that has accrued since the last interest payment. On the next payment date, the investor receives a full interest payment.

      1) The purchaser of the bond, in effect, "buys" the amount of interest that has accrued since the last payment.

3.   **Amortizing a Premium or Discount**

a.   Any premium or discount is amortized over the life of the bond using the effective-interest method.

1)   The effective rate is the interest rate prevailing in the market at the time of the initial purchase (also called the yield).

2)   The essence of the effective rate method is application of a constant interest rate. The total amount of interest revenue recognized changes every period.

3)   Amortization results in the carrying amount of the asset (liability) being adjusted over time, reaching the face amount at maturity.

4)   The straight-line method is used only if its results are not materially different from those of the effective-interest method.

EXAMPLE

The entries recorded by the two investors in the examples on the previous page of premium and discount are shown here:

Amortization of Premium			Amortization of Discount		

End of Year 1:

Cash	$400		Cash	$300	
Investment in bond		$ 75	Investment in bond	68	
Interest revenue		325	Interest revenue		$368

End of Year 2:

Cash	$400		Cash	$300	
Investment in bond		$ 79	Investment in bond	73	
Interest revenue		321	Interest revenue		$373

End of Year 3:

Cash	$400		Cash	$300	
Investment in bond		$ 84	Investment in bond	79	
Interest revenue		316	Interest revenue		$379

End of Year 4:

Cash	$400		Cash	$300	
Investment in bond		$ 89	Investment in bond	86	
Interest revenue		311	Interest revenue		$386

End of Year 5:

Cash	$400		Cash	$300	
Investment in bond		$ 94	Investment in bond	93	
Interest revenue		306	Interest revenue		$393

The premium and discount have been fully amortized. The premium was $421 ($75 + $79 + $84 + $89 + $94), and the discount was $400 ($68 + $73 + $79 + $86 + $93 with $1 rounding error). The bond's carrying amount equals its face amount when redeemed.

End of Year 5:

Cash	$5,000		Cash	$5,000	
Investment in bond		$5,000	Investment in bond		$5,000

---

4.   **Balance Sheet Presentation**

a.   Investments in bonds are reported at carrying amount, i.e., amortized cost, and classified as held-to-maturity, available-for-sale, or trading.

b.   Any unrealized holding gains or losses are debited or credited to a valuation allowance.

1)   The adjusted face amount (amortized cost) remains the basis for calculating amortization of premium or discount using the effective interest method.

5.   **Other Aspects**

    a.   When a **bond is sold** to another investor subsequent to original issue, the price of the bond must move inversely with the market rate because the nominal interest rate is fixed. In other words, each time a bond is sold, the effective rate must be adjusted to the new market rate.

        1)   For example, as described on the previous page, bonds selling at a premium have a nominal rate in excess of the market rate. If the market rate subsequently increases, the price of the bonds must decrease to provide a yield equal to the new market rate.

    b.   When debt securities with **detachable stock warrants** are purchased, the price should be allocated between the warrants and the securities based upon their relative fair values at issuance.

        1)   The amount debited to investment in stock warrants relative to the total amount paid increases the discount or decreases the premium on the investment.

Stop and review! You have completed the outline for this subunit. Study multiple-choice questions 24 through 27 on page 222.

6.6 CASH SURRENDER VALUE

1.   **Definition**

    a.   The cash surrender value of **life insurance** policies on **key executives** is reported in the noncurrent asset section of the balance sheet. A policy typically contains a schedule specifying the cash surrender value and loan value for each year.

2.   **Accounting Treatment**

    a.   The annual premium is allocated between expense and the cash surrender value.

        1)   The life insurance expense recognized equals the difference between the (a) premiums paid (cash) and (b) the sum of the cash surrender value and dividends received on the policy.

        2)   Thus, an increase in the policy's cash surrender value decreases insurance expense.

Cash surrender value	$XXX	
Insurance expense	XXX	
Cash		$XXX

    b.   If the entity is the **beneficiary**, the premiums are not deductible on its tax return, and the proceeds of the policy are not taxable.

    c.   When **proceeds** from the policy are received, the entry is

Cash	$XXX	
Cash surrender value		$XXX
Insurance income		XXX

Stop and review! You have completed the outline for this subunit. Study multiple-choice questions 28 through 30 on page 223.

QUESTIONS

6.1 Cash

1. Burr Company had the following account balances at December 31, Year 1:

Cash in banks	$2,250,000
Cash on hand	125,000
Cash legally restricted for additions to plant (expected to be disbursed in Year 2)	1,600,000

Cash in banks includes $600,000 of compensating balances related to short-term borrowing arrangements. The compensating balances are not legally restricted as to withdrawal by Burr. In the current assets section of Burr's December 31, Year 1, balance sheet, total cash should be reported at

A. $1,775,000

B. $2,250,000

C. $2,375,000

D. $3,975,000

Answer (C) is correct.
REQUIRED: The total cash reported in current assets given legal restrictions and compensating balance requirements.
DISCUSSION: Legally restricted amounts related to long-term arrangements should be classified separately as noncurrent. Thus, the amount restricted for additions should be classified as noncurrent because it relates to a plant asset. Compensating balances against short-term borrowing arrangements that are legally restricted should be reported separately among the cash and cash equivalents in the current assets section. Total cash reported as current assets therefore equals $2,375,000 ($2,250,000 + $125,000).
Answer (A) is incorrect. The amount of $1,775,000 results from subtracting the $600,000 of compensating balances from cash in banks. Answer (B) is incorrect. Cash on hand should be included in total cash. Answer (D) is incorrect. The legally restricted cash related to a long-term arrangement should be classified as noncurrent.

2. Ral Corp.'s checkbook balance on December 31, Year 7, was $5,000. In addition, Ral held the following items in its safe on that date:

Check payable to Ral Corp., dated January 2, Year 8, in payment of a sale made in December Year 7, not included in December 31 checkbook balance	$2,000
Check payable to Ral Corp., deposited December 15 and included in December 31 checkbook balance but returned by Bank on December 30 stamped "NSF." The check was redeposited on January 2, Year 8, and cleared on January 9	500
Check drawn on Ral Corp.'s account, payable to a vendor, dated and recorded in Ral's books on December 31, but not mailed until January 10, Year 8	300

The proper amount to be shown as cash on Ral's balance sheet at December 31, Year 7, is

A. $4,800

B. $5,300

C. $6,500

D. $6,800

Answer (A) is correct.
REQUIRED: The amount to be recorded as cash on the year-end balance sheet.
DISCUSSION: The December 31 checkbook balance is $5,000. The $2,000 check dated January 2, Year 8, is properly not included in this balance because it is not negotiable at year end. The $500 NSF check should not be included in cash because it is a receivable. The $300 check that was not mailed until January 10 should be added to the balance. This predated check is still within the control of the company and should not decrease the cash account. Consequently, the cash balance to be reported on the December 31, Year 7, balance sheet is $4,800.

Balance per checkbook	$5,000
Add: Predated check	300
Deduct: NSF check	(500)
Cash balance 12/31/Year 7	$4,800

Answer (B) is incorrect. The amount of $5,300 does not include the NSF check. Answer (C) is incorrect. The amount of $6,500 includes the postdated check but not the predated check. Answer (D) is incorrect. The amount of $6,800 includes the postdated check.

3. The following information pertains to Grey Co. at December 31, Year 4:

Checkbook balance	$12,000
Bank statement balance	16,000
Check drawn on Grey's account, payable to a vendor, dated and recorded 12/31/Yr 4 but not mailed until 1/10/Yr 5	1,800

On Grey's December 31, Year 4, balance sheet, what amount should be reported as cash?

A. $12,000

B. $13,800

C. $14,200

D. $16,000

Answer (B) is correct.

REQUIRED: The amount of cash that should be reported on the balance sheet.

DISCUSSION: The cash account on the balance sheet should consist of (1) coin and currency on hand, (2) demand deposits (checking accounts), (3) time deposits (savings accounts), and (4) near-cash assets (e.g., deposits in transit or checks written to creditors but not yet mailed). Thus, the cash balance should be $13,800 ($12,000 checkbook balance + $1,800 check drawn but not mailed). The checkbook balance is used instead of the bank balance in the calculation. It more closely reflects the amount of cash that is unrestricted at the balance sheet date.

Answer (A) is incorrect. The amount of $12,000 excludes the check that was recorded but not mailed. Answer (C) is incorrect. The amount of $14,200 equals the bank statement balance minus the check not mailed. Answer (D) is incorrect. The amount of $16,000 is the bank statement balance.

6.2 Fair Value Option (FVO)

4. Election of the fair value option (FVO)

A. Permits only for-profit entities to measure eligible items at fair value.

B. Results in recognition of unrealized gains and losses in earnings of a business entity.

C. Requires deferral of related upfront costs.

D. Results in recognition of unrealized gains and losses in other comprehensive income of a business entity.

Answer (B) is correct.

REQUIRED: The accounting for the FVO.

DISCUSSION: A business measures at fair value the eligible items for which the FVO election was made at a specified election date. The unrealized gains and losses on those items are reported in earnings at each subsequent reporting date.

Answer (A) is incorrect. The FVO may be elected by all entities. Answer (C) is incorrect. Upfront costs and fees are recognized in earnings of a business as they are incurred if they relate to eligible items for which the FVO election was made. Answer (D) is incorrect. The unrealized gains and losses are recognized in earnings, not OCI.

5. The decision to elect the fair value option (FVO)

A. Is irrevocable until the next election date, if any.

B. May be applied to a portion of a financial instrument.

C. Must be applied only to classes of financial instruments.

D. Must be applied to all instruments issued in a single transaction.

Answer (A) is correct.

REQUIRED: The scope of the decision to elect the FVO.

DISCUSSION: The decision to elect the FVO is final and cannot be revoked unless a new election date occurs. For example, an election date occurs when an entity recognizes an investment in equity securities with readily determinable fair values issued by another entity. A second election date occurs when the accounting changes because the investment later becomes subject to equity-method accounting. An original decision to classify the equity securities as available-for-sale may then be revoked at the second election date by choosing the FVO instead of the equity method.

Answer (B) is incorrect. The decision to elect the FVO applies "only to an entire instrument and not to only specified risks, specific cash flows, or portions of that instrument." Answer (C) is incorrect. The decision to elect the FVO ordinarily may be applied to individual eligible items. Answer (D) is incorrect. With certain exceptions, the FVO need not be applied to all eligible items acquired or issued in the same transaction. For example, an acquirer of registered bonds may apply the FVO to only some of the bonds.

6. Which of the following is an election date for the purpose of determining whether to elect the fair value option (FVO)?

A. The accounting treatment of an equity investment changes because the entity no longer has significant influence.

B. The entity enters into a firm commitment to purchase soybeans in 3 months.

C. The accounting for an equity investment changes because the entity no longer consolidates a subsidiary.

D. The accounting treatment of an equity investment changes because the entity must consolidate the investee.

Answer (C) is correct.
REQUIRED: The election date.
DISCUSSION: An entity may choose the FVO only on an election date. For example, an election date occurs when the accounting for an equity investment in another entity changes because the investor retains an interest but no longer consolidates a subsidiary or a variable interest entity.
Answer (A) is incorrect. An election date occurs when the accounting changes because the investment becomes subject to equity-method accounting. Loss of significant influence does not result in an election date. Answer (B) is incorrect. A firm commitment is not an eligible item unless it involves financial instruments only. Answer (D) is incorrect. The FVO is not an alternative to consolidation.

7. The reporting entity may elect the fair value option (FVO) for

A. An investment consisting of more than 50% of the outstanding voting interests of another entity.

B. An interest in a variable interest entity (VIE) if the reporting entity is the primary beneficiary.

C. Its obligation for pension and other postretirement employee benefits.

D. Most financial assets and liabilities.

Answer (D) is correct.
REQUIRED: The item eligible for the FVO election.
DISCUSSION: An entity may elect the FVO for most recognized financial assets and liabilities. For example, the FVO may be elected for most held-to-maturity and available-for-sale securities.
Answer (A) is incorrect. An investment in a subsidiary required to be consolidated is not an eligible item. Answer (B) is incorrect. The primary beneficiary must consolidate the VIE. Thus, the interest in the VIE is not an eligible item. Answer (C) is incorrect. Items eligible for the FVO election do not include employers' and plans' obligations for (1) employee pension benefits, (2) other postretirement employee benefits, (3) postemployment benefits, (4) employee stock option and stock purchase plans, or (5) other deferred compensation.

6.3 Classification of Investments

8. The following pertains to Smoke, Inc.'s investment in equity securities:

- On December 31, Year 3, Smoke reclassified a security acquired during the year for $70,000. It had a $50,000 fair value when it was reclassified from trading to available-for-sale.
- An available-for-sale security costing $75,000, written down to $30,000 in Year 2 because of an other-than-temporary impairment of fair value, had a $60,000 fair value on December 31, Year 3.

What is the net effect of the above items on Smoke's net income for the year ended December 31, Year 3?

A. No effect.

B. $10,000 increase.

C. $20,000 decrease.

D. $30,000 increase.

Answer (C) is correct.
REQUIRED: The effect on net income of a reclassification and a recovery in value of an impaired security.
DISCUSSION: Unrealized holding gains and losses on trading securities are included in earnings, and reclassification is at fair value. Furthermore, "for a security transferred from the trading category, the unrealized holding gain or loss at the date of transfer will have already been recognized in earnings and shall not be reversed." Hence, Smoke should include a $20,000 ($70,000 cost – $50,000 fair value at 12/31/Yr 3) unrealized holding loss in the determination of net income. After an available-for-sale security has been written down to reflect an other-than-temporary decline in fair value, with the loss included in earnings, subsequent increases in its fair value are included in OCI (assuming it is not designated as being hedged in a fair value hedge). Thus, the appreciation of this security has no effect on Year 3 net income.

9. Kale Co. purchased bonds at a discount on the open market as an investment and has the intent and ability to hold these bonds to maturity. Absent an election of the fair value option, Kale should account for these bonds at

A. Cost.

B. Amortized cost.

C. Fair value.

D. Lower of cost or market.

Answer (B) is correct.
REQUIRED: The proper recording of held-to-maturity securities.
DISCUSSION: Absent an election of the fair value option, investments in debt securities must be classified as held-to-maturity and measured at amortized cost in the balance sheet if the reporting entity has the positive intent and ability to hold them to maturity.
Answer (A) is incorrect. The discount will be amortized over the term of the bonds. Answer (C) is incorrect. Trading and available-for-sale securities are accounted for at fair value absent an election of the FVO. Answer (D) is incorrect. Inventory is accounted for at lower of cost or market.

10. On December 31, Ott Co. had investments in trading securities as follows:

	Cost	Fair Value
Man Co.	$10,000	$ 8,000
Kemo, Inc.	9,000	11,000
Fenn Corp.	11,000	9,000
	$30,000	$28,000

Ott's December 31 balance sheet should report the trading securities as

A. $26,000

B. $28,000

C. $29,000

D. $30,000

Answer (B) is correct.
REQUIRED: The amount at which the trading securities should be reported.
DISCUSSION: Trading securities are reported at fair value, and unrealized holding gains and losses are included in earnings. Consequently, the securities should be reported as $28,000.
Answer (A) is incorrect. The amount of $26,000 is the lower of cost or fair value determined on an individual security basis. Answer (C) is incorrect. The amount of $29,000 is the average of the aggregate cost and aggregate fair value. Answer (D) is incorrect. The aggregate cost is $30,000.

11. On July 2, Year 4, Wynn, Inc., purchased as a short-term investment a $1 million face-value Kean Co. 8% bond for $910,000 plus accrued interest to yield 10%. The bonds mature on January 1, Year 11, and pay interest annually on January 1. On December 31, Year 4, the bonds had a fair value of $945,000. On February 13, Year 5, Wynn sold the bonds for $920,000. In its December 31, Year 4, balance sheet, what amount should Wynn report for the bond if it is classified as an available-for-sale security?

A. $910,000

B. $920,000

C. $945,000

D. $950,000

Answer (C) is correct.
REQUIRED: The amount to be reported for a bond classified as an available-for-sale security.
DISCUSSION: Available-for-sale securities should be measured at fair value in the balance sheet. Hence, the bond should be reported at its fair value of $945,000 to reflect the unrealized holding gain (change in fair value).
Answer (A) is incorrect. The amount of $910,000 is the cost (accrued interest is not recorded as part of the cost but as an adjustment of interest income). Answer (B) is incorrect. The sale price is $920,000. Answer (D) is incorrect. The amount of $950,000 equals the cost plus accrued interest (the total price paid) on July 2, Year 4.

12. The following information pertains to Lark Corp.'s available-for-sale securities:

	December 31	
	Year 2	Year 3
Cost	$100,000	$100,000
Fair value	90,000	120,000

Differences between cost and fair values are considered to be temporary. The decline in fair value was properly accounted for at December 31, Year 2. Ignoring tax effects, by what amount should other comprehensive income (OCI) be credited at December 31, Year 3?

A. $0

B. $10,000

C. $20,000

D. $30,000

Answer (D) is correct.

REQUIRED: The credit to OCI if fair value exceeds cost.

DISCUSSION: Unrealized holding gains and losses on available-for-sale securities, including those classified as current assets, are not included in earnings but ordinarily are reported in OCI, net of tax effects (ignored in this question). At December 31, Year 2 (assuming the securities are not designated as being hedged in a fair value hedge), OCI should have been debited for $10,000 for the excess of cost over fair value to reflect an unrealized holding loss. At December 31, Year 3, OCI should be credited to reflect a $30,000 unrealized holding gain ($120,000 fair value at 12/31/Year 3 – $90,000 fair value at 12/31/Year 2).

Answer (A) is incorrect. Unrealized holding gains on available-for-sale securities are recognized. Answer (B) is incorrect. This figure is merely the recovery of the previously recognized unrealized holding loss. The recognition of gain is not limited to that amount. Answer (C) is incorrect. The excess of fair value over cost is $20,000.

13. The following information was extracted from Gil Co.'s December 31 balance sheet:

Noncurrent assets:
    Available-for-sale securities
        (carried at fair value) $96,450
Equity:
    Accumulated other comprehensive
        income (OCI)
        Unrealized gains and losses on
            available-for-sale securities   (19,800)

Historical cost of the available-for-sale securities was

A. $63,595

B. $76,650

C. $96,450

D. $116,250

Answer (D) is correct.

REQUIRED: The historical cost of the available-for-sale securities.

DISCUSSION: The existence of an equity account with a debit balance signifies that the available-for-sale securities are reported at fair value that is less than historical cost. The difference is the net unrealized loss balance. Hence, historical cost must have been $116,250 ($96,450 available-for-sale securities at fair value + $19,800 net unrealized loss).

Answer (A) is incorrect. The amount of $63,595 is a nonsense figure. Answer (B) is incorrect. The amount of $76,650 results from subtracting the unrealized loss instead of adding. Answer (C) is incorrect. The amount of $96,450 ignores the unrealized loss balance.

14. During Year 6, Wall Co. purchased 2,000 shares of Hemp Corp. common stock for $31,500 that are classified as trading securities. The fair value of this investment was $29,500 at December 31, Year 6. Wall sold all of the Hemp common stock for $14 per share on December 15, Year 7, incurring $1,400 in brokerage commissions and taxes. In its income statement for the year ended December 31, Year 7, Wall should report a recognized loss of

A. $4,900

B. $3,500

C. $2,900

D. $1,500

Answer (C) is correct.

REQUIRED: The realized loss on the sale of trading securities.

DISCUSSION: A realized loss or gain is recognized when an individual security is sold or otherwise disposed of. Wall would have included the $2,000 ($31,500 – $29,500) decline in the fair value of the trading securities (an unrealized holding loss) in earnings at 12/31/Yr 6. Consequently, the realized loss on disposal at 12/15/Yr 7 is $2,900 {$29,500 carrying amount – [(2,000 shares × $14) – $1,400]}.

Answer (A) is incorrect. The sum of the recognized losses for Year 6 and Year 7 is $4,900. Answer (B) is incorrect. The sum of the recognized losses for Year 6 and Year 7 without regard to the commissions and taxes is $3,500. Answer (D) is incorrect. Ignoring the commissions and taxes results in $1,500.

15. When the fair value of an investment in debt securities exceeds its amortized cost, how should each of the following debt securities be reported at the end of the year, given no election of the fair value option?

	Debt Securities Classified As	
	Held-to-Maturity	Available-for-Sale
A.	Amortized cost	Amortized cost
B.	Amortized cost	Fair value
C.	Fair value	Fair value
D.	Fair value	Amortized cost

Answer (B) is correct.
REQUIRED: The reporting of debt securities classified as held-to-maturity and available-for-sale.
DISCUSSION: Investments in debt securities must be classified as held-to-maturity and measured at amortized cost in the balance sheet if the reporting entity has the positive intent and ability to hold them to maturity. Investments in equity securities are classified as either trading or available-for-sale. Equity securities that are not expected to be sold in the near term should be classified as available-for-sale. These securities should be reported at fair value, with unrealized holding gains and losses (except those on securities designated as being hedged in a fair value hedge) excluded from earnings and reported in OCI.

6.4 Equity Method

16. Birk Co. purchased 30% of Sled Co.'s outstanding common stock on December 31 for $200,000. On that date, Sled's equity was $500,000, and the fair value of its net assets was $600,000. On December 31, what amount of goodwill should Birk attribute to this acquisition?

A. $0

B. $20,000

C. $30,000

D. $50,000

Answer (B) is correct.
REQUIRED: The amount of goodwill attributable to a purchase of 30% of the investee's common stock.
DISCUSSION: When an investment in voting interests enables the investor to exercise significant influence over the investee, even when the amount held is 50% or less of such interests, the investment should be accounted for under the equity method. Significant influence is presumed when the investment, whether direct or indirect, is at least 20% of the voting interests. Moreover, if the carrying amount of the investment ($200,000) differs from the underlying equity in net assets ($150,000) of the investee, and the difference cannot be related to specific accounts of the investee, the difference is equity method goodwill. Because the fair value of the net assets was $100,000 ($600,000 – $500,000) greater than their carrying amount, $30,000 [($600,000 – $500,000) × 30%] of the acquisition differential was attributable to specific accounts. Accordingly, on the date of purchase, equity method goodwill was $20,000 ($200,000 purchase price – $150,000 – $30,000).
Answer (A) is incorrect. Equity method goodwill exists if the cost of the investment exceeds the fair value of the underlying equity in net assets acquired. Answer (C) is incorrect. The amount of $30,000 equals 30% of the difference between the carrying amount of the investee's equity and the fair value of the underlying equity in net assets. Answer (D) is incorrect. The amount of $50,000 is the difference between 30% of the equity and the investment cost.

17. On January 2, Well Co. purchased 10% of Rea, Inc.'s outstanding common shares for $400,000, which equaled the carrying amount and the fair value of the interest purchased in Rea's net assets. Well did not elect the fair value option. Well is the largest single shareholder in Rea, and Well's officers are a majority on Rea's board of directors. Rea reported net income of $500,000 for the year and paid dividends of $150,000. In its December 31 balance sheet, what amount should Well report as investment in Rea?

A. $450,000

B. $435,000

C. $400,000

D. $385,000

Answer (B) is correct.
REQUIRED: The amount reported in the investment account.
DISCUSSION: The equity method should be used because Well Co. exercises significant influence over Rea. The investment in Rea equals $435,000 [$400,000 investment + ($500,000 net income × 10%) – ($150,000 of dividends × 10%)].
Answer (A) is incorrect. The amount of $450,000 does not subtract Well's dividends. Answer (C) is incorrect. The amount of $400,000 does not include Well's share of net income or deduct Well's dividends. Answer (D) is incorrect. The amount of $385,000 does not include Well's share of net income.

Questions 18 through 20 are based on the following information. Grant, Inc., acquired 30% of South Co.'s voting stock for $200,000 on January 2, Year 1, and did not elect the fair value option. The price equaled the carrying amount and the fair value of the interest purchased in South's net assets. Grant's 30% interest in South gave Grant the ability to exercise significant influence over South's operating and financial policies. During Year 1, South earned $80,000 and paid dividends of $50,000. South reported earnings of $100,000 for the 6 months ended June 30, Year 2, and $200,000 for the year ended December 31, Year 2. On July 1, Year 2, Grant sold half of its stock in South for $150,000 cash. South paid dividends of $60,000 on October 1, Year 2.

18. Before income taxes, what amount should Grant include in its Year 1 income statement as a result of the investment?

A. $15,000

B. $24,000

C. $50,000

D. $80,000

Answer (B) is correct.

REQUIRED: The income statement amount derived from an equity-based investment.

DISCUSSION: Under the equity method, Grant's share of South's revenue reported in the income statement is $24,000 ($80,000 × 30%). The cash dividends received are recorded as a decrease in the investment's carrying amount.

Answer (A) is incorrect. Grant's share of the cash dividends equals $15,000. Answer (C) is incorrect. The amount of cash dividends South paid is $50,000. Answer (D) is incorrect. The amount of South's Year 1 earnings is $80,000.

19. In Grant's December 31, Year 1, balance sheet, what should be the carrying amount of this investment?

A. $200,000

B. $209,000

C. $224,000

D. $230,000

Answer (B) is correct.

REQUIRED: The carrying amount of an equity-based investment.

DISCUSSION: Grant acquired the investment for $200,000. The investment was debited for Grant's share of South's Year 1 earnings ($80,000 × 30% = $24,000) and credited for Grant's share of Year 1 cash dividends ($50,000 × 30% = $15,000). Grant's December 31, Year 1, carrying amount for its investment in South is therefore $209,000 ($200,000 + $24,000 – $15,000).

Answer (A) is incorrect. The original carrying amount was $200,000. Answer (C) is incorrect. The amount of $224,000 does not reflect cash dividends received. Answer (D) is incorrect. The amount of $230,000 equals $200,000 plus the difference between South's Year 1 earnings and the cash dividends it paid.

20. In its Year 2 income statement, what amount should Grant report as gain from the sale of half of its investment?

A. $24,500

B. $30,500

C. $35,000

D. $45,500

Answer (B) is correct.

REQUIRED: The gain reported from the sale of half of the investment.

DISCUSSION: At December 31, Year 1, the carrying amount of the investment is $209,000 ($200,000 original investment + $24,000 share of Year 1 earnings – $15,000 share of Year 1 dividends). At June 30, Year 2, the investment is increased to $239,000 by the $30,000 share of South's earnings. Half of the new carrying amount is $119,500. Grant received $150,000, so the gain is $30,500 ($150,000 – $119,500).

Answer (A) is incorrect. The amount of $24,500 is based on a carrying amount of $251,000. Answer (C) is incorrect. The amount of $35,000 is based on a carrying amount of $230,000. Answer (D) is incorrect. The amount of $45,500 is based on a carrying amount of $209,000, which does not include the $30,000 of Year 2 income.

21. Park Co. uses the equity method to account for its January 1 purchase of Tun, Inc.'s common stock. On January 1, the fair values of Tun's FIFO inventory and land exceeded their carrying amounts. How do these excesses of fair values over carrying amounts affect Park's reported equity in Tun's earnings for the year?

	Inventory Excess	Land Excess
A.	Decrease	Decrease
B.	Decrease	No effect
C.	Increase	Increase
D.	Increase	No effect

Answer (B) is correct.
    REQUIRED: The effect on equity in investee earnings of the excess of the fair values of the investee's FIFO inventory and land over their carrying amounts.
    DISCUSSION: The equity method of accounting requires the investor's proportionate share of the investee's reported net income to be adjusted for acquisition differentials. Thus, the difference at the date of acquisition of the investee's stock between the fair value and carrying amount of inventory is such an adjustment when the inventory is sold. A similar adjustment for land is required when the land is sold. Assuming that the FIFO inventory was sold during the year and the land was not, Park's proportionate share of Tun's reported net income is decreased by the inventory differential allocated at the date of acquisition.

22. Plack Co. purchased 10,000 shares (2% ownership) of Ty Corp. on February 14 and did not elect the fair value option. Plack received a stock dividend of 2,000 shares on April 30, when the market value per share was $35. Ty paid a cash dividend of $2 per share on December 15. In its income statement for the year, what amount should Plack report as dividend income?

A. $20,000

B. $24,000

C. $90,000

D. $94,000

Answer (B) is correct.
    REQUIRED: The amount of dividend income to be reported.
    DISCUSSION: Plack Co. owns 2% of the stock of Ty Corp. Accordingly, this investment should be accounted for using the fair value method. If the fair value of the stock is not readily determinable, the cost method is used. Under either method, dividends from an investee are accounted for by the investor as dividend income unless a liquidating dividend is received. The recipient of a stock dividend does not recognize income. Thus, Plack should report dividend income of $24,000 [(10,000 shares + 2,000 shares received as a stock dividend on April 30) × $2 per share dividend].
    Answer (A) is incorrect. The amount of $20,000 does not include the dividends received on the 2,000 shares from the April 30 stock dividend. Answer (C) is incorrect. The amount of $90,000 equals the sum of the $2 per share cash dividend on 10,000 shares and the April 30 market value of the 2,000-share stock dividend. However, the recipient of a stock dividend does not recognize income. Answer (D) is incorrect. The amount of $94,000 equals the sum of the $2 per share cash dividend on 12,000 shares and the April 30 market value of the 2,000-share stock dividend. However, the recipient of a stock dividend does not recognize income.

23. In its financial statements, Prak, Inc., uses the cost method of accounting for its 15% ownership of Sabe Co. because the fair value of the shares is not readily determinable. At December 31, Prak has a receivable from Sabe. How should the receivable be reported in Prak's December 31 balance sheet?

A. The total receivable should be reported separately.

B. The total receivable should be included as part of the investment in Sabe without separate disclosure.

C. Eighty-five percent of the receivable should be reported separately with the balance offset against Sabe's payable to Prak.

D. The total receivable should be offset against Sabe's payable to Prak without separate disclosure.

Answer (A) is correct.
    REQUIRED: The amount of a receivable from an investee to be reported on the balance sheet.
    DISCUSSION: No presumption of an ability to exercise significant influence over the investee arises when the investor holds less than 20% of the outstanding voting stock of the investee. Thus, the equity method should not be used to account for the investment. Furthermore, the fair-value method is not used when equity securities do not have readily determinable fair values. Accordingly, the cost method is appropriate. Under this method, intra-entity receivables should be accounted for separately and in full.

6.5 Investments in Bonds

24. An investor purchased a bond as a long-term investment between interest dates at a premium. At the purchase date, the cash paid to the seller is

A. The same as the face amount of the bond.

B. The same as the face amount of the bond plus accrued interest.

C. More than the face amount of the bond.

D. Less than the face amount of the bond.

Answer (C) is correct.
REQUIRED: The cash paid for a bond issued at a premium.
DISCUSSION: At the date of purchase, the cash paid to the seller is equal to interest accrued since the last interest date, plus the face amount of the bonds, plus the premium. The carrying amount of the bonds (face amount plus the premium) is equal to the present value of the cash flows associated with the bond discounted at the market rate of interest (yield).

25. An investor purchased a bond classified as a long-term investment between interest dates at a discount. At the purchase date, the carrying amount of the bond is more than the

	Cash Paid to Seller	Face Amount of Bond
A.	No	Yes
B.	No	No
C.	Yes	No
D.	Yes	Yes

Answer (B) is correct.
REQUIRED: The carrying amount of a bond purchased at a discount between interest dates.
DISCUSSION: At the date of purchase, the carrying amount of the bond equals its face amount minus the discount. The cash paid equals the initial carrying amount plus accrued interest. Hence, the initial carrying amount is less than the cash paid by the amount of the accrued interest.

26. Jent Corp. purchased bonds at a discount of $10,000. Subsequently, Jent sold these bonds at a premium of $14,000. During the period that Jent held this investment, amortization of the discount amounted to $2,000. What amount should Jent report as gain on the sale of bonds?

A. $12,000

B. $22,000

C. $24,000

D. $26,000

Answer (B) is correct.
REQUIRED: The amount reported as gain on the sale of bonds.
DISCUSSION: The gain equals the sale price (face amount + $14,000 premium) minus the carrying amount [face amount – ($10,000 original discount – $2,000 amortization)]. Consequently, the gain is $22,000 [(face amount + $14,000) – (face amount – $8,000)].
Answer (A) is incorrect. The amount of $12,000 assumes a carrying amount equal to face amount plus the amortization. Answer (C) is incorrect. The amount of $24,000 ignores the amortization. Answer (D) is incorrect. The amount of $26,000 results from increasing the discount by the amortization.

27. On July 1, Year 4, Pell Co. purchased Green Corp. 10-year, 8% bonds with a face amount of $500,000 for $420,000. The bonds are classified as held-to-maturity, mature on June 30, Year 14, and pay interest semiannually on June 30 and December 31. Using the interest method, Pell recorded bond discount amortization of $1,800 for the 6 months ended December 31, Year 4. From this long-term investment, Pell should report Year 4 revenue of

A. $16,800

B. $18,200

C. $20,000

D. $21,800

Answer (D) is correct.
REQUIRED: The interest revenue when amortization of bond discount is known.
DISCUSSION: Interest income for a bond issued at a discount is equal to the sum of the periodic cash flows and the amount of bond discount amortized during the interest period. The periodic cash flows are equal to $20,000 ($500,000 face amount × 8% coupon rate × 1/2 year). The discount amortization is given as $1,800. Thus, revenue for the 6-month period from July 1 to December 31, Year 4, is $21,800 ($20,000 + $1,800).
Answer (A) is incorrect. The amount of $16,800 is 50% of 8% of $420,000. Answer (B) is incorrect. The amount of $18,200 equals the cash flow minus discount amortization. Answer (C) is incorrect. The amount of $20,000 equals the cash flow.

6.6 Cash Surrender Value

28. Upon the death of an officer, Jung Co. received the proceeds of a life insurance policy held by Jung on the officer. The proceeds were not taxable. The policy's cash surrender value had been recorded on Jung's books at the time of payment. What amount of revenue should Jung report in its statements?

A. Proceeds received.

B. Proceeds received minus cash surrender value.

C. Proceeds received plus cash surrender value.

D. None.

Answer (B) is correct.
REQUIRED: The revenue reported from life insurance proceeds.
DISCUSSION: When life insurance proceeds are received, cash is debited for the amount received. Cash surrender value is credited for the amount of the asset on the books, and the balancing credit is to insurance income (a revenue account).

29. On January 2, Year 4, Beal, Inc., acquired a $70,000 whole-life insurance policy on its president. The annual premium is $2,000. The company is the owner and beneficiary. Beal charged officer's life insurance expense as follows:

Year 4	$2,000
Year 5	1,800
Year 6	1,500
Year 7	1,100
Total	$6,400

In Beal's December 31, Year 7, balance sheet, the investment in cash surrender value should be

A. $0

B. $1,600

C. $6,400

D. $8,000

Answer (B) is correct.
REQUIRED: The investment in cash surrender value.
DISCUSSION: Cash surrender value is the loan value or surrender value of a whole-life insurance policy. It is equal to the difference between the premiums paid and the life insurance expense recognized. Because the total of premiums paid is $8,000 ($2,000 × 4 years) and the total life insurance expense is $6,400, the investment in cash surrender value is $1,600. This amount is classified as a noncurrent asset on a classified balance sheet because management purchases life insurance policies for the life insurance aspect rather than as a short-term investment.
Answer (A) is incorrect. The excess of the premiums over the expenses is the cash surrender value. Answer (C) is incorrect. The total insurance expense for 4 years is $6,400. Answer (D) is incorrect. The sum of the premiums for 4 years is $8,000.

30. In Year 1, Chain, Inc., purchased a $1 million life insurance policy on its president, of which Chain is the beneficiary. Information regarding the policy for the year ended December 31, Year 6, follows:

Cash surrender value, 1/1/Yr 6	$ 87,000
Cash surrender value, 12/31/Yr 6	108,000
Annual advance premium paid 1/1/Yr 6	40,000

During Year 6, dividends of $6,000 were applied to increase the cash surrender value of the policy. What amount should Chain report as life insurance expense for Year 6?

A. $40,000

B. $21,000

C. $19,000

D. $13,000

Answer (C) is correct.
REQUIRED: The life insurance expense to be reported.
DISCUSSION: Life insurance expense is equal to the excess of the premiums paid over the increase in the sum of cash surrender value and dividends received. However, the dividends were applied to increase the cash surrender value and were therefore not received. Hence, Chain's life insurance expense is $19,000.

Premium	$40,000
Minus:	
Increase in cash surrender value ($108,000 – $87,000)	(21,000)
Dividends received	0
Life insurance expense	$19,000

Answer (A) is incorrect. The premium paid is $40,000. Answer (B) is incorrect. The change in the cash surrender value is $21,000. Answer (D) is incorrect. The amount of $13,000 results from subtracting the dividends applied.

Use the additional questions in Gleim **CPA Test Prep Online** to create Test Sessions that emulate Prometric!

6.7 PRACTICE SIMULATION

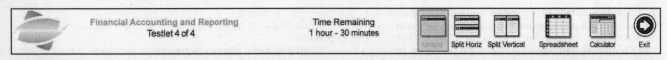

| Financial Accounting and Reporting | Time Remaining | Unsplit | Split Horiz | Split Vertical | Spreadsheet | Calculator | Exit |
| Testlet 4 of 4 | 1 hour - 30 minutes | | | | | | |

DIRECTIONS

Note: If you believe you have encountered a software malfunction, report it to the test center staff immediately.

Navigation

To navigate from task to task, use the controls at the bottom of the screen. Click on the **Next** button to advance to the next task, or the **Previous** button to go to the previous task. To go directly to any task, click on its number.

If you would like a reminder to revisit a task, or want to indicate that you are finished with it, click on the reminder flag below the task number. To clear the flag, click on it again. Reminder flags are for your use only – they do not contribute to your score.

Tabs

In this part of the examination, you will be asked to complete various tasks. Every task has one or more **Work Tabs**. Some tasks have one or more **Information Tabs**, others may have none. Every task has a **Help** tab.

If a task has **Information Tabs**, you may use the information in them to complete your responses in the **Work Tabs**.

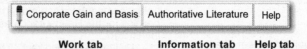

Work tab   Information tab   Help tab

Work Tabs:
- **Work Tabs** are identified with a pencil icon. This is where your responses are expected.
- Each task has one or more **Work Tabs**.
- **Work Tabs** contain directions for completing the task – be sure to read these directions carefully.
- The **Work Tab** name in the example above is for illustration only – yours will differ.
- You must complete all of the **Work Tabs** in each task to receive full credit.

Information Tabs:
- The Authoritative Literature will be provided in all tasks in the AUD, FAR, and REG sections for your reference.
- Your simulation may have one or more additional **Information Tabs**. Like the Authoritative Literature tabs, **Information Tabs** do not have a pencil icon.
- If your task has additional **Information Tabs**, go through each to familiarize yourself with the task content.

Help Tab:
- The **Help Tab** provides assistance with the exam software that is used in this task. For example, if the task is to compose a memorandum, **Help** will provide information about the word processor.

The Toolbar

The toolbar at the top of the screen shows the amount of time remaining for you to complete the tasks. In addition, the following tools are available. Note that only the **Exit** button is displayed when Directions are visible - the others will appear when you begin the tasks.

Click on these buttons to split or unsplit the screen. You can split the screen vertically or horizontally.

Click on this button to display the calculator; click on it again to hide the calculator. To move the calculator, click on the calculator title bar and drag the calculator to the desired location.

Click on this button to use the spreadsheet; click on it again to hide the spreadsheet. To move the spreadsheet, click on the the spreadsheet title bar and drag the spreadsheet to the desired location.

Click on this button to go on to the next part of the examination. You must complete all of the tasks to receive full credit. Once you click on **Exit** and confirm the action, you will NOT be able to return to this testlet.

⚐ = Reminder   Directions   1 2 3 4 5 6   ◀ Previous   Next ▶

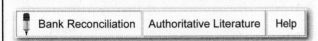

Bank Reconciliation | Authoritative Literature | Help

The following information pertains to Company A's December 31, Year 1, bank reconciliation:

- Check #217 for $4,000 was drawn on the company's account, payable to a vendor, dated and recorded in the company's books on December 31, Year 1, but not mailed until January 9, Year 2.
- Deposits in transit are $5,200.
- Outstanding checks are $8,980.
- On December 31, Year 1, the bank charged the company $500 for service fees. The company received a notice about this charge during Year 2.
- The balance per bank statement received shows that a customer check for $4,600 had been returned due to insufficient funds.
- Check #221 for $800, written by the company, was erroneously cleared by the bank on December 31, Year 1, for $80.
- On November 1, Year 1, one of the company's customers deposited $700 directly to the company's bank account. The bookkeeper recorded this transaction as follows:

Accounts receivable	$700	
Bank account		$700

Using the information above, prepare Company A's December 31, Year 1, bank reconciliation. Enter the correct amounts in the shaded cells below. If the answer is zero, leave the cell blank.

	Bank	Books
Balance per Bank Statement / Books (December 31, Year 1)	$32,400	$27,600
1. Check #217		
2. Deposits in transit		
3. Outstanding checks		
4. Service fees charged by the bank		
5. Nonsufficient funds checks		
6. Check #221		
7. Deposit on November 1, Year 1		
8. **Correct cash balance**		

This set of questions has a matching format. Select from the list provided the appropriate category for each item below. Each choice may be used once, more than once, or not at all.

Explanation	Answer	Category
1. Holding gains or losses are not recognized.		A) Cash
2. Holding gains or losses are recognized in earnings.		B) Restricted cash
3. Holding gains or losses are recognized in a separate component of equity.		C) Held-to-maturity securities
4. Common examples are Treasury bills and money market funds.		D) Available-for-sale securities
5. Assets set aside to retire long-term debt.		E) Trading securities
6. The customary medium of exchange and unit of measurement.		F) Cash equivalents

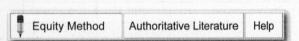

On January 1, Year 1, Company A purchased 25% of Company B's 100,000 outstanding shares of common stock for $10 per share. Company A applies the equity method for its investment in Company B. Company B reported a net profit of $400,000 for Year 1.

For each of the following independent situations that occurred during Year 2, select the Year 2 effect on the carrying amount of Company A's investment in Company B. Each choice may be used once, more than once, or not at all.

Situations	Answer	Choices
1. On December 1, Year 2, Company B declared and paid a dividend of $1 per share.		A) Increase
2. The market price of one share of company B's common stock on December 31, Year 2, is $27.		B) Decrease
3. Company B reported a net profit of $50,000 for Year 2.		C) No effect
4. On December 15, Year 2, Company B declared a dividend of $1 per share. The dividend will be paid on January 31, Year 3.		
5. On November 30, Year 2, Company B sold inventory to Company A for $29,000. The cost of this inventory was $25,000. Company A sold this inventory to third parties during Year 3.		
6. On March 1, Year 2, Company B declared and distributed a stock dividend of one share of common stock for every 10 shares of common stock owned. The market price of Company B's common stock on that date was $24 per share.		

Indicate by checking the appropriate box the correct category for each investment below based upon the description. Make only one choice for each item.

Investment	Held-to-Maturity	Available-for-Sale	Trading
1. Debt securities bought and held for the purpose of selling in the near future			
2. U.S. Treasury bonds that the entity has both the positive intent and ability to hold until maturity			
3. $3 million debt security bought and held for the purpose of selling in 3 years to finance payment of $2 million long-term note payable when it matures			
4. Convertible preferred stock with a readily determinable fair value that the entity does not intend to sell in the near term			

A company classifies its investments in long-term bonds as held-to-maturity. For each of the following independent situations, select the appropriate answer from the list of choices provided. Each choice may be used once, more than once, or not at all.

Situations	Answer		Choices
1. A company purchased a bond on its issue date. On that date, the bond's stated rate is equal to the current market rate. The purchase price of the bond is		A)	The same as the face amount of the bond
2. A company purchased a bond between interest dates. On that date, the bond's stated rate is equal to the current market rate. The purchase price of the bond is		B)	More than the face amount of the bond
3. On January 1, Year 1, a company purchased a 10-year bond at a discount. The carrying amount of the bond in the company's December 31, Year 9, balance sheet is		C)	Less than the face amount of the bond
4. On January 1, Year 1, a company purchased a 5-year bond for its face amount. The stated rate on the bond is 10%. At the end of Year 3, the market interest rate has unexpectedly decreased to 3%. The carrying amount of the bond in the company's December 31, Year 3, balance sheet is			
5. A company purchased a bond between interest dates at a discount. At the purchase date, the carrying amount of the bond is			

| Research | Authoritative Literature | Help |

At the end of 2012, Speculative Financial had the following short- and long-term investments:

90-day certificate of deposit	$20,000
180-day certificate of deposit	30,000
Bond, purchased 11/1/12, matures 1/31/13	15,000
Bond, purchased 5/1/12, matures 2/28/13	70,000
Commercial paper	24,000
Stock	68,000
U.S. Treasury bill, purchased 12/1/12, matures 2/28/13	45,000
U.S. Treasury bill, purchased 3/1/12, matures 2/28/13	80,000

The controller is unsure which of these investments, if any, should be treated as cash equivalents. Which section of the authoritative guidance defines cash equivalents?

Enter your response in the answer fields below. Unless specifically requested, your response should not cite implementation guidance.

FASB ASC [   ] - [   ] - [   ] - [   ]

▼ = Reminder   Directions   1 2 3 4 5 [6]   ◀ Previous   Next ▶

Unofficial Answers

1. Bank Reconciliation (8 Gradable Items)

1. Books: $4,000. The $4,000 check that was not mailed until January 9, Year 2, should be added back to the balance. This predated check is still within the control of the company and should not decrease the cash account.

2. Bank: $5,200. Deposits in transit are items known to the company but not known to the bank. A time lag may occur between deposit of receipts and the bank's recording of the transaction. In the bank reconciliation procedure, these receipts are added to the bank balance to arrive at the true balance.

3. Bank: $(8,980). Outstanding checks are checks written by the company that have not yet cleared the bank. These amounts are subtracted from the bank balance to arrive at the true balance.

4. Books: $(500). Items known to the bank but not known to the company generally include service charges. Service charges cannot be recorded in the books until the bank statement is received. These amounts are subtracted from the book balance to arrive at the true balance.

5. Books: $(4,600). Customer checks returned for insufficient funds are items known to the bank but not always known to the company until the bank statement is received. These amounts are subtracted from the book balance to arrive at the true balance.

6. Bank: $(720). The bank has wrongly charged the company for $720 ($800 – $80) less than it should have. This amount is subtracted from the bank balance to arrive at the true balance.

7. Books: $1,400. The bookkeeper erroneously credited, instead of debited, the bank account for $700. Thus, to arrive at the true balance, $1,400 must be added (debited) to the book balance.

8. Correct cash balance: $27,900. The correct cash balance is the outcome of the bank reconciliation. [$27,900 = $32,400 + $5,200 – $8,980 – $720 = $27,600 + $4,000 – $500 – $4,600 + $1,400.]

2. Accounting Methods (6 Gradable Items)

1. <u>C) Held-to-maturity securities.</u> Unrealized holding gains or losses are not recognized on held-to-maturity securities.

2. <u>E) Trading securities.</u> Unrealized holding gains or losses on trading securities are included in earnings.

3. <u>D) Available-for-sale securities.</u> Unrealized holding gains or losses are recognized for available-for-sale securities in other comprehensive income, a separate component of equity.

4. <u>F) Cash equivalents.</u> These are short-term, highly liquid investments that are both readily convertible to cash and so near their maturity date that they do not present a significant risk of changes in interest rates.

5. <u>B) Restricted cash.</u> Assets set aside for the retirement of long-term debt should be separately presented. An example is a bond sinking fund.

6. <u>A) Cash.</u> Cash is ready money, the most liquid of assets. As the customary medium of exchange, it also provides the standard of value (the unit of measurement) of the transactions that are reported in the financial statements.

3. Equity Method (6 Gradable Items)

1. <u>B) Decrease.</u> A cash dividend from an equity-method investee is a return of an investment. It is credited to the investment on the dividend declaration date.

2. <u>C) No effect.</u> Under the equity method, the investment in an equity-method investee is not affected by increases in the market value of the investee's stock. Thus, the change in the fair value of an investment has no effect on the carrying amount of the equity-method investee.

3. <u>A) Increase.</u> The investor's share of the net profit of an equity-method investee is recognized as an income. The journal entry is

Investment in Company B ($50,000 × 25%)	$12,500	
Income -- share of net profit of Company B		$12,500

4. <u>B) Decrease.</u> A cash dividend from an equity-method investee is a return of an investment. It is credited to the investment account on the dividend declaration date. The journal entry is

Dividend receivable	$25,000	
Investment in B		$25,000

5. <u>B) Decrease.</u> According to the equity method, in upstream transactions (sales by an investee to an investor), the investor's share of the investee's net profit and loss is adjusted to eliminate intra-entity profits not realized in third-party transactions. Thus, the unrealized profit is equal to Company B's net profit from the transaction times Company A's percentage interest in Company B. The journal entry is

Share of net profit of Company B		
[($29,000 – $25,000) × 25%]	$1,000	
Investment in Company B		$1,000

6. <u>C) No effect.</u> A stock dividend does not change the percentage of ownership in Company B and does not change Company A's share in Company B's net assets. Thus, it has no effect on the investment in Company B's carrying amount.

4. Classification of Investments (4 Gradable Items)

1. <u>Trading securities.</u> Trading securities are held with the intention of selling them in the near term. Both debt and equity instruments may qualify as trading securities.

2. <u>Held-to-maturity.</u> Debt securities are classified as held-to-maturity and measured at amortized cost only if the holder has the positive intent and ability to hold the securities to maturity.

3. <u>Available-for-sale.</u> The holder intends to sell this debt security in the future. Thus, it should not be classified as held-to-maturity. Because the holder intends to sell in 3 years, it should be classified as available-for-sale, not trading.

4. <u>Available-for-sale.</u> Available-for-sale securities include equity securities with readily determinable fair values (e.g., preferred stock) that are not classified as trading securities (e.g., because they are not to be sold in the near term).

5. Investments in Bonds (5 Gradable Items)

1. A) The same as the face amount of the bond. When the bond's stated rate is the same as the interest rate prevailing in the market at the time of the purchase (called the market rate or yield rate), the purchase price of the bond is equal to the face amount of the bond.

2. B) More than the face amount of the bond. At the date of purchase, the cash paid to the seller equals the face amount of the bond, plus any premium or minus any discount, plus interest accrued since the last interest date. Since, on the purchase date, the stated rate is the same as the market rate, no premium or discount arose. Thus, the purchase price of the bond must be more than its face amount since it must include the accrued interest.

3. C) Less than the face amount of the bond. When the bond is purchased at a discount, the amount paid for the bond is lower than its face amount. The bond's carrying amount will be equal to its face amount only on the bond's maturity date. Thus, 1 year before its maturity, the bond's carrying amount is less than its face amount.

4. A) The same as the face amount of the bond. When a bond was purchased at its face amount, the stated rate was equal to the market rate on the purchase date, and no premium or discount on the bond was recognized. The decrease in the market interest rate increases the fair value of the bond. Because the bond is classified as held-to-maturity, the increase in its fair value does not increase its carrying amount. The bond's carrying amount continues to equal its face amount.

5. C) Less than the face amount of the bond. At the date of purchase, the cash paid equals the initial carrying amount plus accrued interest. The carrying amount of the bond equals its face amount minus the discount.

6. Research (1 Gradable Item)

Answer: FASB ASC 230-10-20

For purposes of the statement, cash equivalents are short-term, highly liquid investments that are both:

A) Readily convertible to known amounts of cash.

B) So near their maturity that they present insignificant risk of changes in value because of changes in interest rates.

Generally, only investments with original maturities of 3 months or less qualify under that definition. (NOTE: Original maturity means original maturity to the holder.)

Gleim Simulation Grading

Task	Correct Responses		Gradable Items		Score per Task
1	____	÷	8	=	____
2	____	÷	6	=	____
3	____	÷	6	=	____
4	____	÷	4	=	____
5	____	÷	5	=	____
Research	____	÷	1	=	____

Total of Scores per Task ____

÷ Total Number of Tasks 6

Total Score ____%

Use **CPA Gleim Online** and **Simulation Wizard** to practice more task-based simulations in a realistic environment.

STUDY UNIT SEVEN
RECEIVABLES

(15 pages of outline)

7.1	Accounts Receivable -- Fundamentals	231
7.2	Accounts Receivable -- Measurement	234
7.3	Transfers of Receivables and Other Financial Assets	237
7.4	Notes Receivable -- Recognition	242
7.5	Notes Receivable -- Discounting	244
7.6	Practice Simulation	254

This study unit primarily covers **accounts and notes receivable**, assets that rank in liquidity below available-for-sale securities but above inventories. **Accounts receivable** are often short-term, unsecured, and informal credit arrangements (open accounts). **Notes receivable** are evidenced by a formal instrument, such as a promissory note. A formal document provides its holder with a stronger legal status than does an account receivable. Current receivables are measured at **net realizable value**, and noncurrent receivables are measured at the **net present value** of the future cash flows.

7.1 ACCOUNTS RECEIVABLE -- FUNDAMENTALS

1. **Definition**

    a. A receivable is an asset recognized to reflect a claim against another party for the receipt of money, goods, or services. For most accounting purposes, the claim is expected to be settled in cash.

    b. The recording of a receivable, which often coincides with revenue recognition, is consistent with accrual accounting.

2. **Current vs. Noncurrent Receivables**

    a. A receivable is a **current** asset if it is reasonably expected to be collected within the longer of 1 year or the entity's normal operating cycle.

    1) Otherwise, it should be classified as **noncurrent**. Noncurrent receivables are measured at present value.

3. **Trade vs. Nontrade Receivables**

    a. **Trade receivables**, the majority of receivables, are current assets arising from credit sales to customers in the normal course of business and due in customary trade terms. They result in contracts evidenced by sales orders, invoices, or delivery contracts.

    1) They are normally unsecured and noninterest-bearing, but charges are added to revolving charge accounts and installment receivables.

    2) Forfeiture of a cash discount because of delayed payment is an implicit means of charging interest on trade receivables.

    b. **Nontrade receivables** are all other receivables. They may include

    1) Lease receivables
    2) Deposits to guarantee payment or to cover possible loss
    3) Advances to shareholders, directors, officers, etc.
    4) Subscriptions for the entity's securities
    5) Tax refunds
    6) Claims for insurance proceeds or amounts arising from litigation
    7) Interest, dividends, rent, or royalties accrued

4. **Trade Discounts**

  a. Trade discounts adjust the **gross (list) price** for different buyers, quantities, and costs. **Net price after the trade discount** is the basis for recognition.

EXAMPLE

An item with a list price of $1,000 may be subject to a 40% trade discount in sales to wholesalers. Thus, $400 is subtracted from the list price in arriving at the actual selling price of $600. Only the $600 is recorded. The accounts do not reflect trade discounts.

---

  b. Some sellers offer **chain-trade discounts** such as 40%, 10%, which means certain buyers receive both a 40% discount and a 10% discount.

EXAMPLE

In the previous example, an additional discount of $60 reduces the actual selling price to $540. All journal entries by the buyer and seller are for $540, with no recognition of the list price or the discount. The two discounts are not added but are calculated sequentially.

---

  c. Trade discounts are solely a means of calculating the sales price. They are not recorded.

5. **Cash Discounts**

  a. Cash discounts (sales discounts) accelerate cash collection by rewarding customers for early payment.

  b. The **gross method** accounts for receivables at their **face amount**. It is used when customers are not expected to pay soon enough to take the discount. If the customer pays within the discount period, the discount is recognized as an item contra to sales in the income statement.

  c. The **net method** records receivables **net of the cash discount** for early payment. It is used when customers are expected to pay within the discount period. If the payment is not received during the discount period, a miscellaneous revenue, such as sales discounts forfeited, is credited when the payment is received.

EXAMPLE

An item is sold with terms of 2/10, n/30 (2% discount if paid within 10 days, entire balance due in 30 days).

	Gross Method		Net Method	
Accounts receivable	$1,000		$980	
Sales		$1,000		$980

Payment is received **within the discount period**.

	Gross Method		Net Method	
Cash	$ 980		$980	
Sales discounts	20			
Accounts receivable		$1,000		$980

Payment is received **after the discount period**.

	Gross Method		Net Method	
Cash	$1,000		$980	
Accounts receivable		$1,000		$980
Cash			$ 20	
Sales discounts forfeited				$ 20

---

6. **Sales Returns**

   a.   A provision must be made for the return of merchandise because of product defects, customer dissatisfaction, etc.

   b.   If returns are **immaterial**, the accounting is straightforward. The sales are simply removed from the books when the merchandise is returned. The journal entry to record this transaction is as follows:

Sales	XXX	
Accounts receivable		XXX

       1)   This method is not allowed for tax purposes.

   c.   If returns are **material**, the method described above is inconsistent with the matching principle when the sale and the return occur in different periods.

       1)   Accordingly, an **allowance** for sales returns should be established.

EXAMPLE

A company has $500,000 of sales in July, its first month of operations. Management estimates that total returns will be 1% of sales.

Sales returns (contra revenue)	$5,000	
Allowance for sales returns (contra asset)		$5,000

---

7. **Financial Statement Presentation**

   a.   On the face of the balance sheet, accounts receivable is reported net of any allowance and adjustments. The amounts of the allowance and adjustments should be indicated within the text.

      Balance sheet:

Accounts receivable, net of allowance for uncollectible accounts and billing adjustments of $XXX	$X,XXX

   b.   **Material receivables** should be segregated. Among the usual categories are

       1)   Notes receivable (with disclosure of the effective interest rates)
       2)   Trade receivables
       3)   Installment receivables
       4)   Nontrade receivables

   c.   Receivables should be separated into **current and noncurrent** portions.

   d.   **Discount or premium** resulting from a present value measurement directly decreases or increases the face amount of a note. Thus, notes receivable are reported at present value without a separate allowance.

   e.   A receivable from a **related party** should be **separately and fully disclosed**. Related parties include affiliates, which are parties "that, directly or indirectly, through one or more intermediaries, control, are controlled by, or are under common control with, an entity."

   f.   **Disclosure** should be made of

       1)   Related party receivables, e.g., those arising from loans to employees or affiliates
       2)   Loss contingencies, such as those from transfers with recourse

          a)   When a transfer with recourse is made in a sales transaction, disclosure should be made, if possible, of proceeds and of amounts uncollected for each income statement and balance sheet, respectively.

       3)   Pledged or assigned receivables
       4)   Concentrations of credit risk (described in Study Unit 5, Subunit 8)

Stop and review! You have completed the outline for this subunit. Study multiple-choice questions 1 through 8 beginning on page 245.

7.2 ACCOUNTS RECEIVABLE -- MEASUREMENT

1. **Overview**

   a. These current, noninterest-bearing assets are reported at **net realizable value**. Thus, interest recognition (except for late payment) and present value calculations are not relevant.

   b. The principal measurement issue for accounts receivable is the estimation of net realizable value for balance sheet reporting and the related **uncollectible accounts expense** (a loss contingency).

      1) The two approaches to accounting for bad debts are the direct write-off method and the allowance method. Both approaches have the goal of measuring accounts receivable at net realizable value.

2. **Direct Write-Off Method**

   a. The direct write-off method expenses bad debts when they are determined to be uncollectible. It is **not acceptable under GAAP** because

      1) The direct write-off method is subject to manipulation. Timing is at the discretion of management.

      2) It does not match revenue and expense when the receivable and the write-off are recorded in different periods.

      3) It does not state receivables at net realizable value.

Background

Note that the treatment of bad debt expense under GAAP is directly opposed to that for income tax purposes. GAAP prohibit the direct write-off method; tax law requires it. Under the Internal Revenue Code, only a debt that can be proven to be uncollectible can be written off; the matching principle is only relevant for financial reporting.

---

3. **Allowance Method**

   a. The allowance method attempts to **match bad debt expense with the related revenue**. This method systematically records bad debt expense as a percentage of either sales or the level of accounts receivable on an annual basis. The allowance method is **required under GAAP**.

      1) The periodic journal entry to record bad debt expense is

Bad debt expense	$XXX	
Allowance for uncollectible accounts		$XXX

      2) As specific accounts receivable are written off, they are charged to the allowance account.

Allowance for uncollectible accounts	$XXX	
Accounts receivable		$XXX

      3) Thus, the write-off of a particular bad debt has no effect on expenses.

         a) Write-offs do not affect the carrying amount of net accounts receivable because the reductions of gross accounts receivable and the allowance are the same. Thus, they also have no effect on working capital.

   b. Two approaches to calculating the amount charged to bad debt expense are the income-statement approach and the balance-sheet approach.

4. **Income-Statement Approach (Percentage of Sales)**

a. The income-statement approach embodies the **matching principle**. It treats bad debts as a function of sales on account. Periodic bad debt expense is a percentage of sales.

EXAMPLE

Midburg Co. has the following account balances at year end:

Cash	$ 85,000 Dr.
Accounts receivable	100,000 Dr.
Allowance for uncollectible accounts	1,600 Dr.
Sales on credit	500,000 Cr.

Based on its experience, Midburg expects bad debts to average 2% of credit sales. Hence, the estimated expense is $10,000 ($500,000 × 2%). The year-end adjusting entry is

Bad debt expense	$10,000	
Allowance for uncollectible accounts		$10,000

Because the allowance previously had a debit balance, the new credit balance is $8,400.

Balance sheet presentation
Accounts receivable, net of allowance
  for uncollectible accounts of $8,400
  and billing adjustments of $1,200 $90,400

---

5. **Balance-Sheet Approach (Percentage of Receivables)**

a. Under this approach, bad debt expense is a function of both **sales and collections**. The allowance is periodically adjusted to reflect a percentage of accounts receivable.

b. An entity rarely experiences a single rate of uncollectibility on all its accounts. For this reason, entities using the balance-sheet approach to estimate bad debt expense generally prepare an **aging schedule** of accounts receivable.

EXAMPLE

Midburg prepares the following aging schedule of its accounts receivable:

Balance Range	Less than 30 Days	31 – 60 Days	61 – 90 Days	Over 90 Days	Total Balances
$0 - $100	$ 5,000	$ 200	$ 100	$ 100	$ 5,400
$100 - $1,000	8,000	3,800			11,800
$1,000 - $5,000	20,000	2,000	1,900		23,900
$5,000 - $10,000	38,000		8,000	900	46,900
Over $10,000		12,000			12,000
Totals	$71,000	$18,000	$10,000	$1,000	$100,000

Midburg then applies an appropriate percentage to each stratum based on experience.

Aging Intervals	Balance	Estimated Uncollectible	Ending Allowance
Less than 30 days	$ 71,000	2%	$1,420
30 - 60 days	18,000	12%	2,160
61 - 90 days	10,000	15%	1,500
Over 90 days	1,000	20%	200
Total	$100,000		$5,280

Because the allowance currently has a debit balance of $1,600, the following journal entry is required to establish the proper measurement:

Bad debt expense	$6,880	
Allowance for uncollectible accounts		$6,880

Balance sheet presentation
Accounts receivable, net of
  allowance for uncollectible accounts of $5,280
  and billing adjustments of $1,410 $93,310

6.   **Accounts Previously Written Off**

  a.   Occasionally, a customer will pay on an account previously written off.

   1)   The first entry is to **reestablish the account** for the amount the customer has
        agreed to pay (any remainder remains written off).

Accounts receivable	$XXX	
Allowance for uncollectible accounts		$XXX

   2)   The second entry records the receipt of cash.

Cash	$XXX	
Accounts receivable		$XXX

  b.   Bad debt expense is not affected when (1) an account receivable is written off or
       (2) an account previously written off becomes collectible.

Expect to see questions regarding accounts receivable measurement. The AICPA has tested this area
using both conceptual and calculation questions. In the calculation questions, candidates may be asked to
determine the balance of one or more of the following accounts: accounts receivable, allowance for
uncollectible accounts, and uncollectible accounts expense.

COMPREHENSIVE EXAMPLE of Accounts Receivable

A retailer had the following beginning account balances for the year just ended:

Cash	$85,000 Dr.
Accounts receivable	66,000 Dr.
Allowance for uncollectible accounts	3,000 Cr.

Past experience indicates that 0.75% of each year's credit sales will prove to be uncollectible. The retailer recorded the
following transactions during the year:

Sales on credit:
(A)	Accounts receivable	$520,000	
	Sales		$520,000

Collections on credit sales:
(B)	Cash	$495,000	
	Accounts receivable		$495,000

Bad debt expense recognized:
(C)	Bad debt expense ($520,000 × 0.75%)	$3,900	
	Allowance for uncollectible accounts		$3,900

Account previously written off collected:
(D1)	Accounts receivable	$420	
	Allowance for uncollectible accounts		$420
(D2)	Cash	$420	
	Accounts receivable		$420

Accounts considered uncollectible written off:
(E)	Allowance for uncollectible accounts	$600	
	Accounts receivable		$600

Permanent Accounts				Nominal Accounts	
Cash	Accounts Receivable		Allowance for Uncoll. Accounts	Sales	Bad Debt Expense
$ 85,000	$ 66,000			$ -0-	$ -0-
(B) 495,000	(A) 520,000	$495,000 (B)	$3,000	520,000 (A)	(C) 3,900
(D2) 420	(D1) 420	420 (D2)	3,900 (C)		
		600 (E)	(E) US $600 420 (D1)		
	$ 90,400		$6,720		

Figure 7-1

The retailer reports net accounts receivable of $83,680 ($90,400 gross − $6,720 allowance).

Stop and review! You have completed the outline for this subunit. Study multiple-choice questions 9 through 11 beginning on page 248.

7.3 TRANSFERS OF RECEIVABLES AND OTHER FINANCIAL ASSETS

1. **Factoring**

    a. Factoring is a transfer of receivables to a third party (a factor) who assumes the responsibility of collection.

    b. Factoring discounts receivables on a **nonrecourse, notification basis**. Thus, payments by the debtors on the transferred assets are made to the factor. If the transferor (seller) surrenders control, the transaction is a sale.

        1) If a sale is **with recourse**, the transferor (seller) may be required to make payments to the transferee or to buy back receivables in specified circumstances. For example, the seller may become liable for defaults up to a given percentage of the transferred receivables.

            a) The sale proceeds are reduced by the fair value of the recourse obligation.

            b) If the transfer with recourse does not qualify as a sale, the parties account for the transaction as a secured borrowing with a pledge of noncash collateral.

        2) If a sale is **without recourse**, the transferee (the credit agency) assumes the risks and receives the rewards of collection.

    c. The transferor receives money that can be immediately reinvested. The entity can offset the fee charged by eliminating its bad debts, credit department, and receivables staff.

    d. A factor usually receives a high financing fee plus a fee for collection. Furthermore, the factor often operates more efficiently than its clients because of the specialized nature of its services.

EXAMPLE

A factor charges a 2% fee plus an interest rate of 18% on all cash advanced to a transferor of accounts receivable. Monthly sales are $100,000, and the factor advances 90% of the receivables submitted after deducting the 2% fee and the interest. Credit terms are net 60 days. What is the cost to the transferor of this arrangement?

Amount of receivables submitted	$100,000
Minus: 10% reserve	(10,000)
Minus: 2% factor's fee	(2,000)
Amount accruing to the transferor	$ 88,000
Minus: 18% interest for 60 days	(2,640)
Amount to be received immediately	$ 85,360

The transferor also will receive the $10,000 reserve at the end of the 60-day period if it has not been absorbed by sales returns and allowances. Thus, the total cost to the transferor to factor the receivables for the month is $4,640 ($2,000 factor fee + interest of $2,640). Assuming that the factor has approved the customers' credit in advance (the sale is without recourse), the transferor will not absorb any bad debts.

The journal entry to record the preceding transaction is

Cash	$85,360	
Due from factor	10,000	
Loss on sale of receivables	2,000	
Prepaid interest	2,640	
Accounts receivable		$100,000

e. **Credit card sales** are a common form of factoring. The retailer benefits by prompt receipt of cash and avoidance of bad debts and other costs. In return, the credit card company charges a fee.

1) Two methods of accounting for credit card sales may be necessary depending upon the reimbursement method used.

a) If payment is after submission of credit card receipts, the retailer initially records a receivable. After payment, the entry is

Cash	$XXX	
Service charge expense	XXX	
Receivable		$XXX

b) If the retailer's checking account is increased by the direct deposit of credit card receipts, no receivable is recognized. The entry is to credit sales instead of a receivable.

Cash	$XXX	
Service charge expense	XXX	
Sales		$XXX

2. Pledging

a. A pledge (a general assignment) is the use of receivables as collateral (security) for a loan. The borrower agrees to use collections of receivables to repay the loan.

1) Upon default, the lender can sell the receivables to recover the loan proceeds.

b. Because a pledge is a relatively informal arrangement, it is not reflected in the accounts. A transfer of financial assets is a sale only when the transferor relinquishes control.

1) If the transfer (e.g., a pledge) of accounts receivable is not a sale, the transaction is a secured borrowing. The transferor becomes a debtor, and the transferee becomes a creditor in possession of collateral.

a) However, absent default, the collateral remains an asset of the transferor.

3. Secured Borrowings

a. A secured borrowing is a formal borrowing arrangement. The borrower signs a promissory note and financing agreement, and specific receivables are pledged as **collateral**.

1) The loan is at a specified percentage of the face amount of the collateral, and interest and service fees are charged to the borrower.

b. The collateral may be segregated from other receivables on the balance sheet.

Accounts receivable assigned	$XXX	
Accounts receivable		$XXX

1) The note payable is reported as a **liability**.

Cash	$XXX	
Notes payable		$XXX

4. Securitization

a. Securitization is the process of transforming financial assets into securities. It involves (1) the transfer of a portfolio of financial assets (e.g., trade receivables, mortgage loans, automobile loans, or credit card receivables) to a trust or other entity and (2) the sale of beneficial interests in that entity to investors.

1) The proceeds are paid to the transferor. Interest and principal collected on the securitized assets are paid to the investors in accordance with the legal agreement that established the entity.

5. **Transfers of Financial Assets -- Objectives and Control**

  a. The accounting for transfers of financial assets is based on a **financial-components approach** focused on control.

  b. The objective is for each party to

    1) Recognize the assets it controls and the liabilities it has incurred,
    2) Derecognize assets when control has been given up, and
    3) Derecognize liabilities when they have been extinguished.

  c. Whether **control** exists depends, among other things, on the transferor's continuing involvement. **Continuing involvement** is the right to receive benefits from the assets or an obligation to provide additional assets to a party related to the transfer. Examples are

    1) Servicing agreements,
    2) Options written or held,
    3) Recourse provisions,
    4) A beneficial interest in a trust that holds the assets, or
    5) A pledge of collateral.

6. **Transfers of Financial Assets -- Sales**

  a. Transfers of financial assets include transfers of (1) an entire financial asset, (2) a group of entire financial assets, and (3) a participating interest in an entire financial asset.

    1) A **participating interest** exists if

      a) It is a proportionate ownership interest,
      b) Cash receipts are proportionate to shares of ownership,
      c) Each holder has the same priority, and
      d) The entire asset cannot be pledged or exchanged without the agreement of all holders.

  b. A transfer of financial assets is a **sale** when the transferor **relinquishes control**. The transferor relinquishes control only if certain conditions are met:

    1) The transferred assets are beyond the reach of the transferor and its creditors;
    2) Transferees may pledge or exchange the assets or interests received; and
    3) The transferor does not maintain effective control through, for example,

      a) An agreement to reacquire the assets before maturity,
      b) The unilateral ability to benefit from causing the holder to return specific assets, or
      c) An agreement making it probable that the transferee will require repurchase.

  c. If the transfer of an **entire financial asset** (or a group) qualifies as a sale, the financial components approach is applied. The transferor

    1) Derecognizes the financial assets transferred
    2) Recognizes and initially measures at fair value the assets obtained and liabilities incurred

      a) These include servicing assets and liabilities.

    3) Recognizes any gain or loss in earnings

EXAMPLE

A company transfers its entire financial interest in its notes receivable for $60,000. The receivable has a carrying amount of $62,500. The journal entry to record this transfer is

Cash	$60,000	
Loss on transfer	2,500	
Notes receivable		$62,500

d. The **transfer of a participating interest** may qualify as a sale. In that case, the carrying amount of the entire financial asset is **allocated** based on relative fair values between the interests sold and retained.

   1) Transferor accounting is the same as for the sale of an entire financial asset (but with allocation).

EXAMPLE

A company transfers a 90% participating interest in its notes receivable for $54,000. Future benefits and costs of servicing the notes are not material. The receivables have a carrying amount of $62,500. The journal entry to record this transfer is

Cash	$54,000	
Loss on transfer	2,250	
Notes receivable		
($62,500 × 90%)		$56,250

7. **Transfers of Financial Assets -- Secured Borrowings**

   a. If the transfer is not a sale, the transaction is a secured borrowing. The transferor becomes a debtor, and the transferee becomes a creditor in possession of collateral.

      1) If the transferee may sell or repledge the collateral, the transferor reclassifies and separately reports that asset.

      2) If the transferee sells the collateral, it recognizes the proceeds (debits assets) and credits a liability to return the collateral (now in the form of proceeds).

Asset	$XXX
Liability -- collateral (proceeds)	$XXX

      3) If the transferor defaults and no longer has the right of redemption, it derecognizes (credits) the pledged asset. The transferee initially recognizes (debits) an asset at fair value or derecognizes (debits) the liability to return the collateral.

      4) Thus, absent default, the collateral is an asset of the transferor.

8. **Servicing Assets and Liabilities**

   a. A servicing asset is a **contract** under which future revenues from servicing fees, late charges, etc., are expected to more than adequately **compensate the servicer**. A servicing liability arises when such compensation is inadequate.

      1) Agreements by transferors to service transferred mortgage loans, credit card receivables, and other financial assets are common.

   b. Servicing assets and liabilities always are measured initially at fair value.

      1) For subsequent measurement of each class of separately recognized servicing assets or liabilities, the entity may elect (a) the amortization method or (b) the fair value method.

9. The following summarizes transferor accounting:

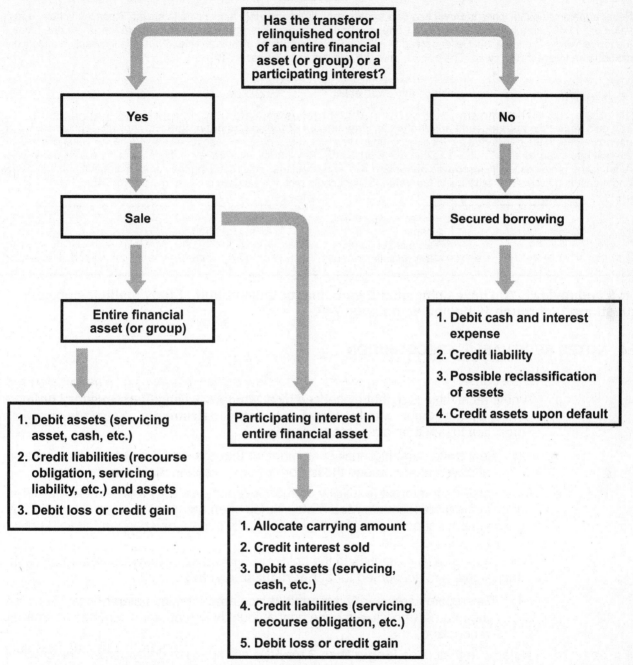

Figure 7-2

EXAMPLE

Seller transferred entire loans to Buyer in a sale transaction. It did not retain a servicing interest. These loans have a fair value of $1,650 and a carrying amount of $1,500. Seller also undertook to **repurchase delinquent loans**. Furthermore, the loans have a fixed rate, but Seller agreed to provide Buyer a return at a variable rate. Thus, the transaction effectively included an **interest rate swap**. The following are the relevant **fair values**:

Cash received	$1,575
Interest rate swap asset	60
Recourse obligation	90

The gain equals the **net proceeds minus the carrying amount of the assets derecognized**. Any asset obtained that is not an interest in the transferred assets is included in the proceeds. Thus, the cash received and the fair value of the interest rate swap asset are debited as part of the proceeds. Any liability incurred, even if related to the assets transferred, reduces the proceeds, so the **recourse obligation** should be credited. After crediting the carrying amount of the loans sold and measuring assets and liabilities at **fair value**, Seller should recognize a **gain** on sale (a credit) of $45.

Cash	$1,575	
Interest rate swap asset	60	
Loans		$1,500
Recourse obligation		90
Gain on sale		45

Stop and review! You have completed the outline for this subunit. Study multiple-choice questions 12 through 16 beginning on page 249.

7.4 NOTES RECEIVABLE -- RECOGNITION

1. **Definition**

   a. A note receivable is a debt evidenced by a two-party writing (a **promissory note**). Thus, it must comply with the law of **negotiable instruments**. Notes are more formal promises to pay than accounts receivable.

      1) New customers, high-risk customers, or those needing an extension for the time of payment are among those from whom a vendor might require a note.

   b. Most notes bear interest (explicitly or implicitly) because they represent longer-term borrowings than accounts receivable. Notes often are given when an extension of the payment period for an account receivable is sought or when the fair value of what is sold is relatively high.

   c. Notes with original maturities to the holder of **3 months or less** are treated as cash equivalents and accounted for at **net realizable value**.

      1) These notes are usually recorded at face amount minus allowances. Because the interest implicit in the maturity amount is immaterial, no interest revenue is recognized.

   d. Notes with maturities **longer than 3 months** are not cash equivalents. The creditor must recognize interest revenue unless an exception applies.

      1) Receivables are recorded at the **present value of the expected future cash flows**. Any difference between the proceeds and the face amount, if material, must be recognized as a premium or discount and amortized.

   e. When the note's stated interest rate is a reasonable rate (e.g., the market rate), the note is issued at its face amount, and no discount or premium is recognized.

2. **Noninterest-Bearing Notes**

   a. Sometimes notes are issued with no stated rate and an **unknown effective rate**. In these cases, the rate must be **imputed** from other facts surrounding the transaction. Such facts include the marketability of the note and the debtor's creditworthiness.

      1) Thus, the interest is **implicit**.

b. Certain notes differ from the customary instruments that explicitly bear interest at a reasonable rate. They are discussed in the following outline.

c. A note may bear no explicit interest because interest is included in the amount to be paid at maturity. The proper accounting treatment is to debit notes receivable for its face (maturity) amount, credit cash (or other appropriate account), and credit a discount account. The discount is amortized to interest revenue.

1) The entry for initial recognition is

Notes receivable	$XXX	
Cash		$XXX
Discount on note		XXX

2) At the end of the period, the discount is amortized to interest revenue. The entry for recognition of interest is

Discount on note	$XXX	
Interest revenue		$XXX

3) When the note arises in the ordinary course of business and is "due in customary trade terms not exceeding approximately 1 year," the interest element need not be recognized.

4) The amortization of a premium or discount using the effective interest method is explained in Study Unit 13, Subunit 4.

3. **Unreasonable Interest**

a. The term "noninterest-bearing" is confusing. It is used not only when a note bears implicit interest but also when no actual interest is charged (the cash proceeds equal the face amount).

1) When a note is noninterest-bearing in the second sense or bears interest at a rate that is unreasonable in the circumstances, interest must be **imputed (estimated)**. A note with imputed interest also results in amortization of discount or premium.

b. When a **note is exchanged solely for cash**, and no other right or privilege is exchanged, the proceeds are assumed to reflect the present value of the note. The effective interest rate is therefore the interest rate implicit in that present value.

c. When a **note is exchanged for property, goods, or services**, the interest rate determined by the parties in an arm's-length transaction is presumed to be fair.

1) That presumption is overcome when (a) no interest is stated, (b) the stated rate is unreasonable, or (c) the nominal amount of the note materially differs from the cash sales price of the item or the market value of the note.

a) In these circumstances, the transaction should be recorded at the more clearly determinable of

i) The fair value of the property, goods, or services or
ii) A reasonable approximation of the market value of the note.

b) Absent established exchange prices or evidence of the note's market value, the present value of a note with no stated rate or an unreasonable rate should be determined by discounting future payments using an imputed rate. The prevailing rate for similar instruments of issuers with similar credit ratings normally helps determine the appropriate rate. The purpose is to approximate the rate in a similar transaction between independent parties.

    d.   The stated interest rate may be less than the effective rate applicable in the circumstances because the lender has received other stated (or unstated) rights and privileges as part of the bargain.

        1)   The difference between the respective present values of the note computed at the stated rate and at the effective rate should be accounted for as the cost of the rights or privileges obtained.

Stop and review! You have completed the outline for this subunit. Study multiple-choice questions 17 through 22 beginning on page 251.

7.5 NOTES RECEIVABLE -- DISCOUNTING

1.   **Nature of Discounting**

    a.   When a note receivable is discounted (sold, usually at a bank), the **gain or loss** on disposition of the note must be calculated.

    b.   The holder of the note receives the maturity amount (principal + interest at maturity) of the note minus the bank's discount. The bank usually collects the maturity amount from the maker of the note.

2.   **Process of Discounting**

    a.   The steps in discounting are to compute the

        1)   Total interest receivable on the note (face amount × stated rate × note term)
        2)   Maturity amount (face amount + total interest receivable)
        3)   Accrued interest receivable (face amount × stated rate × note term elapsed)
        4)   Bank's discount (maturity amount × bank's discount rate × note term remaining)
        5)   Cash proceeds (maturity amount – bank's discount)
        6)   Carrying amount of the note (face amount + accrued interest receivable)
        7)   Gain or loss (proceeds – carrying amount)

           a)   If a gain results, the entry is

Cash	$XXX	
Gain on sale of note receivable		$XXX
Note receivable		XXX
Interest receivable		XXX

           b)   If a loss results, the entry is

Cash	$XXX	
Loss on sale of note receivable	XXX	
Note receivable		$XXX
Interest receivable		XXX

EXAMPLE

A company has a 1-year, $100,000 note with a stated annual interest rate of 8%. After holding the note for 3 months, it decides to discount it at a local bank at an effective interest rate of 10%. The gain or loss on discounting the note is calculated as follows:

Total interest receivable	$100,000 × 8% = $8,000
Maturity amount	100,000 + $8,000 = $108,000
Accrued interest receivable	100,000 × 8% × (3 ÷ 12) = $2,000
Bank's discount	108,000 × 10% × (9 ÷ 12) = $8,100
Cash proceeds	108,000 – $8,100 = $99,900
Carrying amount of the note	100,000 + $2,000 = $102,000
Gain or loss	99,900 – $102,000 = ($2,100)

The journal entry to record this transaction is

Cash	$99,900	
Loss on sale of note receivable	2,100	
Note receivable		$100,000
Interest receivable		2,000

b. If a note is discounted **with recourse**, the note must be disclosed as a **contingent liability**.

1) If the maker dishonors the note, the bank will collect from the entity that discounted the note.

a) The credit in the previous entry is sometimes made to notes receivable discounted, a contra-asset account.

c. When computing yearly interest, the day the note is received, made, etc., is not included, but its maturity date is counted.

EXAMPLE

A 30-day note dated January 17 matures on February 16. Because 14 days (31 – 17) remain in January, 16 days must be counted in February.

Stop and review! You have completed the outline for this subunit. Study multiple-choice questions 23 through 25 on page 253.

QUESTIONS

7.1 Accounts Receivable -- Fundamentals

1. The following information relates to Jay Co.'s accounts receivable for the year just ended:

Accounts receivable, 1/1	$ 650,000
Credit sales for the year	2,700,000
Sales returns for the year	75,000
Accounts written off during the year	40,000
Collections from customers during the year	2,150,000
Estimated future sales returns at 12/31	50,000
Estimated uncollectible accounts at 12/31	110,000

What amount should Jay report for accounts receivable, before allowances for sales returns and uncollectible accounts, at December 31?

A. $1,200,000

B. $1,125,000

C. $1,085,000

D. $925,000

Answer (C) is correct.

REQUIRED: The year-end balance in accounts receivable.

DISCUSSION: The ending balance in accounts receivable consists of the $650,000 beginning debit balance, plus debits for $2,700,000 of credit sales, minus credits for $2,150,000 of collections, $40,000 of accounts written off, and $75,000 of sales returns.

Accounts Receivable (in 000s)

1/1	$ 650	$ 75	Sales returns
Credit sales	2,700	2,150	Collections
		40	Write-offs
12/31	$1,085		

The $110,000 of estimated uncollectible receivables and the $50,000 of estimated sales returns are not relevant because they affect the allowance accounts but not gross accounts receivable.

Answer (A) is incorrect. The amount of $1,200,000 does not subtract write-offs and sales returns from accounts receivable. Answer (B) is incorrect. The amount of $1,125,000 does not subtract sales returns from accounts receivable. Answer (D) is incorrect. Estimated future sales returns and uncollectible accounts affect their respective allowance accounts, not gross accounts receivable.

2. Which one of the following is **false** in regard to the balance sheet presentation?

A. Disclosures are never made of related party transactions or contingencies.

B. Valuation accounts should be separated into current and noncurrent sections.

C. Receivables should be separated into current and noncurrent sections.

D. Material receivables should be segregated.

Answer (A) is correct.

REQUIRED: The false statement regarding balance sheet presentation.

DISCUSSION: Disclosures should be made of related party transactions, such as loans to employees or affiliates. In addition, disclosures should be made for loss contingencies, such as from transfers with recourse.

3. In its December 31 balance sheet, Butler Co. reported trade accounts receivable of $250,000 and related allowance for uncollectible accounts of $20,000. What is the total amount of risk of accounting loss related to Butler's trade accounts receivable, and what amount of that risk is off-balance-sheet risk?

	Risk of Accounting Loss	Off-Balance-Sheet Risk
A.	$0	$0
B.	$230,000	$0
C.	$230,000	$20,000
D.	$250,000	$20,000

Answer (B) is correct.
REQUIRED: The total amount of risk of accounting loss related to trade accounts receivable and the amount that is off-balance-sheet risk.
DISCUSSION: Butler's risk of accounting loss is measured by the net receivables balance ($250,000 accounts receivable – $20,000 allowance for uncollectible accounts = $230,000). Accounting loss is the loss that may have to be recognized due to credit and market risk as a direct result of the rights and obligations of a financial instrument. However, assuming that the carrying amount of these trade receivables approximates their fair value, the accounting loss cannot exceed the amount recognized as an asset. No off-balance-sheet risk of accounting loss results from reported accounts or notes receivable. Off-balance-sheet risk arises because of the existence of conditional rights and obligations that may expose the entity to a risk of accounting loss exceeding the amount recognized in the balance sheet, for example, recourse obligations on receivables sold.

4. On June 1, Pitt Corp. sold merchandise with a list price of $5,000 to Burr on account. Pitt allowed trade discounts of 30% and 20%. Credit terms were 2/15, n/40, and the sale was made FOB shipping point. Pitt prepaid $200 of delivery costs for Burr as an accommodation. On June 12, Pitt received from Burr a remittance in full payment amounting to

A. $2,744

B. $2,912

C. $2,944

D. $3,112

Answer (C) is correct.
REQUIRED: The amount of the full payment.
DISCUSSION: A trade discount is a means of establishing a price for a certain quantity or for a particular class of customers. Neither the buyer nor the seller reflects trade discounts in the accounts. Assuming that the 30% discount is applied first, the initial discount is $1,500 ($5,000 × 30%), and the second discount is $700 [($5,000 – $1,500) × 20%]. Hence, the base price is $2,800. (If both discounts apply, it makes no difference which is taken first.) Because the buyer paid within the discount period, the cash equivalent price is $2,744 ($2,800 × 98%). Given that the goods were shipped FOB shipping point, title passed when they were put in the possession of the carrier, and the buyer is responsible for payment of delivery costs. Accordingly, the full amount owed by the buyer was $2,944 ($2,744 + $200 delivery costs).
Answer (A) is incorrect. The amount of $2,744 does not include the delivery costs. Answer (B) is incorrect. The amount of $2,912 assumes that the delivery costs are part of the list price. It also ignores the cash discount. Answer (D) is incorrect. The amount of $3,112 assumes that the delivery costs are part of the list price. It also ignores the cash discount but adds back the delivery costs.

5. Delta, Inc., sells to wholesalers on terms of 2/15, n/30. Delta has no cash sales, but 50% of Delta's customers take advantage of the discount. Delta uses the gross method of recording sales and trade receivables. An analysis of Delta's trade receivables balances at December 31 revealed the following:

Age	Amount	Collectible
0-15 days	$100,000	100%
16-30 days	60,000	95%
31-60 days	5,000	90%
Over 60 days	2,500	20%
	$167,500	

In its December 31 balance sheet, what amount should Delta report for allowance for discounts?

A. $1,000

B. $1,620

C. $1,675

D. $2,000

Answer (A) is correct.
REQUIRED: The amount to be reported as an allowance for discounts.
DISCUSSION: The allowance for discounts should include an estimate of the expected discount based on the eligible receivables. According to the analysis, receivables equal to $100,000 are still eligible. Based on past experience, 50% of the customers take advantage of the discount. Thus, the allowance should be $1,000 [$100,000 × 50% × 2% (the discount percentage)].
Answer (B) is incorrect. The amount of $1,620 assumes that 50% of all collectible amounts are eligible for the discount. Answer (C) is incorrect. The amount of $1,675 assumes that 50% of the total gross receivables are eligible for the discount. Answer (D) is incorrect. The amount of $2,000 assumes 100% of eligible customers will take the discount.

Questions 6 and 7 are based on the following information. ECG Company recorded two sales on March 1 of $20,000 and $30,000 under credit terms of 3/10, n/30. Payment for the $20,000 sale was received March 10. Payment for the $30,000 sale was received on March 25.

6. Under the gross method and the net method, net sales in ECG's March income statement are reported at which amounts?

	Gross Method	Net Method
A.	$48,500	$48,500
B.	$48,500	$49,400
C.	$49,400	$48,500
D.	$49,400	$49,400

Answer (C) is correct.
REQUIRED: The amounts of net sales under the gross and the net methods.
DISCUSSION: The gross method accounts for receivables at their face amount. If a discount is taken, a sales discount is recorded and classified as an offset to sales in the income statement to yield net sales.
The expression "3/10, n/30" means that a 3% discount can be taken if payment is made within 10 days of the invoice. The $20,000 payment was received during this period. The $30,000 payment was not. Under the gross method, a $600 sales discount offsets the $50,000 of gross sales to give net sales of $49,400.
The net method records receivables net of the applicable discount. If the payment is not received during the discount period, an interest revenue account, such as sales discounts forfeited, is credited at the end of the discount period or when the payment is received. Consequently, both sales are recorded net of discount ($48,500), and $900 ($30,000 × 3%) is recorded as interest income.
The income effect of both methods is the same. The difference is in how the items are presented in the income statement.

7. At what amounts are ECG's gross sales reported for the month of March under the gross method and the net method?

	Gross Method	Net Method
A.	$50,000	$50,000
B.	$50,000	$48,500
C.	$49,400	$48,500
D.	$48,500	$50,000

Answer (B) is correct.
REQUIRED: The gross sales for the month.
DISCUSSION: The gross method records March sales at the gross amount ($50,000). Because the $20,000 receivable was paid within the discount period, sales discount is debited for $600 at the payment date. The net method records March sales at the net amount [$50,000 × (1.0 − .03) = $48,500]. The $30,000 receivable was not paid within the discount period, and the following entry also must be made:

Accounts receivable	$900	
Sales discounts forfeited		$900

8. In its financial statements, Pulham Corp. uses the equity method of accounting for its 30% ownership of Angles Corp. At December 31, Year 4, Pulham has a receivable from Angles. How should the receivable be reported in Pulham's Year 4 financial statements?

A. None of the receivable should be reported, but the entire receivable should be offset against Angles's payment to Pulham.

B. 70% of the receivable should be separately reported, with the balance offset against 30% of Angles's payment to Pulham.

C. The total receivable should be disclosed separately.

D. The total receivable should be included as part of the investment in Angles, without separate disclosure.

Answer (C) is correct.
REQUIRED: The method of reporting a receivable from a related party.
DISCUSSION: Related parties include an entity and its equity-based investees. A receivable from a related party should be separately and fully disclosed. Indeed, nontrade receivables generally are subject to separate treatment.
Answer (A) is incorrect. Elimination of interentity transactions is inappropriate except in the case of combined or consolidated statements. Answer (B) is incorrect. None of the receivable should be separately reported or offset. Answer (D) is incorrect. The investment balance equals cost plus the investor's share of earnings and losses, minus any return of the investment. Also, adjustments may be necessary for acquisition differentials. Furthermore, separate disclosure is required.

7.2 Accounts Receivable -- Measurement

9. In its December 31, Year 3, balance sheet, Fleet Co. reported accounts receivable of $100,000 before allowance for uncollectible accounts of $10,000. Credit sales during Year 4 were $611,000, and collections from customers, excluding recoveries, totaled $591,000. During Year 4, accounts receivable of $45,000 were written off and $17,000 were recovered. Fleet estimated that $15,000 of the accounts receivable at December 31, Year 4, were uncollectible. In its December 31, Year 4, balance sheet, what amount should Fleet report as accounts receivable before allowance for uncollectible accounts?

A. $58,000

B. $67,000

C. $75,000

D. $82,000

Answer (C) is correct.
REQUIRED: The balance of accounts receivable.
DISCUSSION: The ending balance in accounts receivable consists of the beginning balance, plus credit sales, minus collections, minus write-offs and a net $0 effect of accounts written off that were recovered.

Accounts Receivable (in 000s)

1/1/Yr 4	$100	$591	Collections
Sales	611	45	Write-offs
Recoveries	17	17	Recoveries
12/31/Yr 4	$ 75		

Answer (A) is incorrect. Subtracting the recovered accounts results in $58,000. The collection of written-off accounts has no effect on the ending balance of accounts receivable. Answer (B) is incorrect. The amount of $67,000 equals the ending accounts receivable balance, plus the amount recovered, minus the beginning balance of the allowance for uncollectible accounts, minus the estimated uncollectible accounts at year end. Answer (D) is incorrect. The amount of $82,000 is calculated by adding the recovered accounts and subtracting the allowance for uncollectible accounts from Year 3.

10. An internal auditor is deriving cash flow data based on an incomplete set of facts. Bad debt expense was $2,000. Additional data for this period follows:

Credit sales	$100,000
Gross accounts receivable -- beginning balance	5,000
Allowance for bad debts -- beginning balance	(500)
Accounts receivable written off	1,000
Increase in net accounts receivable (after subtraction of allowance for bad debts)	30,000

How much cash was collected this period on credit sales?

A. $64,000

B. $68,000

C. $68,500

D. $70,000

Answer (B) is correct.
REQUIRED: The cash collected on credit sales.
DISCUSSION: The beginning balance of gross accounts receivable (A/R) was $5,000 (debit). Thus, net beginning A/R was $4,500 ($5,000 – $500 credit in the allowance for bad debts). The allowance was credited for the $2,000 bad debt expense. Accordingly, the ending allowance (credit) was $1,500 ($500 – $1,000 write-off + $2,000). Given a $30,000 increase in net A/R, ending net A/R must have been $34,500 ($4,500 beginning net A/R + $30,000), with ending gross A/R of $36,000 ($34,500 + $1,500). Collections were therefore $68,000 ($5,000 beginning gross A/R – $1,000 write-off + $100,000 credit sales – $36,000 ending gross A/R).

Gross A/R

$ 5,000	Beg. Bal.	$ 1,000	Write-off
100,000	Cr. Sales	68,000	Collections
$ 36,000	End. Bal.		

Answer (A) is incorrect. Credit sales minus the ending gross accounts receivable equals $64,000. Answer (C) is incorrect. The amount of $68,500 equals credit sales, minus the increase in net accounts receivable, minus the ending allowance. Answer (D) is incorrect. Credit sales minus the increase in net accounts receivable equals $70,000.

11. Wren Company had the following account balances at December 31:

Accounts receivable	$ 900,000
Allowance for uncollectible accounts (before any provision for the year uncollectible accounts expense)	16,000
Credit sales for the year	1,750,000

Wren is considering the following methods of estimating uncollectible accounts expense for the year:

● Based on credit sales at 2%
● Based on accounts receivable at 5%

What amount should Wren charge to uncollectible accounts expense under each method?

	Percentage of Credit Sales	Percentage of Accounts Receivable
A.	$51,000	$45,000
B.	$51,000	$29,000
C.	$35,000	$45,000
D.	$35,000	$29,000

Answer (D) is correct.
REQUIRED: The amount charged to uncollectible accounts expense under each method.
DISCUSSION: Uncollectible accounts expense is estimated in two ways. One emphasizes asset valuation, while the other emphasizes income measurement. The first is based on an aging of the receivables to determine the balance in the allowance for uncollectible accounts. Bad debt expense is the amount necessary to adjust the allowance account to this estimated balance. The second recognizes bad debt expense as a percentage of sales. The corresponding credit is to the allowance for uncollectible accounts. Under the first method, if uncollectible accounts are estimated to be 5% of gross accounts receivable, the allowance account should have a balance of $45,000 ($900,000 × 5%), and the entry is to debit uncollectible accounts expense and credit the allowance for $29,000 ($45,000 – $16,000 existing balance). Under the second method, bad debt expense is $35,000 ($1,750,000 × 2%).
Answer (A) is incorrect. The amount of $51,000 equals 2% of credit sales plus the balance of the allowance account, and $45,000 equals 5% of gross accounts receivable. Answer (B) is incorrect. The amount of $51,000 equals 2% of credit sales plus the balance of the allowance account. Answer (C) is incorrect. The amount of $45,000 equals 5% of gross accounts receivable.

7.3 Transfers of Receivables and Other Financial Assets

12. Gar Co. factored its receivables without recourse with Ross Bank. Gar received cash as a result of this transaction, which is best described as a

A. Loan from Ross collateralized by Gar's accounts receivable.

B. Loan from Ross to be repaid by the proceeds from Gar's accounts receivable.

C. Sale of Gar's accounts receivable to Ross, with the risk of uncollectible accounts retained by Gar.

D. Sale of Gar's accounts receivable to Ross, with the risk of uncollectible accounts transferred to Ross.

Answer (D) is correct.
REQUIRED: The effect of factoring receivables without recourse.
DISCUSSION: When receivables are factored without recourse, the transaction is treated as a sale and the buyer accepts the risk of collectibility. The seller bears no responsibility for credit losses. A sale without recourse is not a loan. In a sale without recourse, the buyer assumes the risk of uncollectible accounts.

13. A transfer of financial assets may be treated as a sale if the transferor surrenders control of the assets. Which of the following is one of the criteria that must be met before control is deemed to be surrendered?

A. The transferred assets are isolated from the transferor and its creditors except in bankruptcy.

B. The transferee cannot pledge or exchange the transferred assets.

C. The transferor is not a party to an agreement that both entitles and obligates it to repurchase or redeem the securities prior to maturity.

D. An entire financial asset is transferred.

Answer (C) is correct.
REQUIRED: The criterion that must be met before control over transferred financial assets is deemed to be surrendered.
DISCUSSION: Three criteria must be met: (1) The transferred assets are beyond the reach of the transferor and its creditors; (2) transferees may pledge or exchange the assets or interests; and (3) the transferor does not maintain effective control through, for example, (a) an agreement to repurchase or redeem the assets prior to maturity, (b) an ability unilaterally to benefit from causing the holder to return specific assets, or (c) an agreement making it probable that the transferee will require repurchase.
Answer (A) is incorrect. Control is not surrendered if the transferor's creditors can reach the assets in bankruptcy. Answer (B) is incorrect. The transferee is able to pledge or exchange the assets if control is surrendered. Answer (D) is incorrect. A transfer may be accounted for as a sale if it involves a participating interest in an entire financial asset.

14. Red Co. had $3 million in accounts receivable recorded on its books. Red wanted to convert the $3 million in receivables to cash in a more timely manner than waiting the 45 days for payment as indicated on its invoices. Which of the following would alter the timing of Red's cash flows for the $3 million in receivables already recorded on its books?

A. Change the due date of the invoice.

B. Factor the receivables outstanding.

C. Discount the receivables outstanding.

D. Demand payment from customers before the due date.

Answer (B) is correct.
REQUIRED: The action that alters the timing of cash flows from receivables.
DISCUSSION: Factoring transfers accounts receivable to a finance company or bank (the factor) on a nonrecourse, notification (to debtors) basis. The arrangement is an outright sale. If it meets certain criteria, it is accounted for as a sale of financial assets. The seller therefore accelerates cash inflows in exchange for the factor's fee.
Answer (A) is incorrect. Red and its customers have entered into contracts that establish the due date. It cannot be changed without a new agreement. Answer (C) is incorrect. Calculating the present value of the future amounts to be received does not result in cash flows. Answer (D) is incorrect. Customers are not contractually obligated to pay before the due date.

15. The amount of cash received from the transfer of receivables with recourse is most likely to be reported as a liability under which of the following conditions?

A. The transferor is not required to repurchase the receivables except in accordance with limited recourse provisions.

B. A reasonable estimate can be made of the fair value of the obligation of the transferor under the recourse provisions.

C. The transferor is entitled and obligated to repurchase the receivables at a later date.

D. Control of the future economic benefits embodied in the receivables has been surrendered by the transferor.

Answer (C) is correct.
REQUIRED: The proper recognition of the transfer of receivables with recourse.
DISCUSSION: A transfer of financial assets with recourse is accounted for as a sale if the transferor surrenders control. An example of effective control is an agreement that entitles and obligates the transferor to repurchase or redeem the transferred assets prior to maturity. If the control criteria are not met, the transferor and transferee account for a transfer with recourse as a secured borrowing with a pledge of collateral.
Answer (A) is incorrect. If the transferor is not required to repurchase the receivables, and the recourse provisions are limited, control is most likely surrendered, and a liability does not need to be recorded. Answer (B) is incorrect. A determination of the fair value of a recourse obligation does not preclude treatment of the transfer as a sale. If the control criteria are met, a transfer with recourse is treated as a sale, and the proceeds are reduced by the fair value of the recourse obligation. Answer (D) is incorrect. If control has been surrendered, the transfer is treated as a sale.

16. Under IFRS, which of the following is a criterion that permits the derecognition of a financial asset?

A. The asset represents a proportionate ownership interest.

B. Rights to the asset's cash flows have expired.

C. The transfer resulting in the derecognition was on a nonrecourse, notification basis.

D. The asset arose from a secured borrowing.

Answer (B) is correct.
REQUIRED: The condition for derecognition of a financial interest.
DISCUSSION: A financial asset is derecognized if the rights to its cash flows have expired. If they have not, one of the conditions for derecognition is transfer of the contract rights to the cash flows from the financial asset. If, in addition, substantially all risks and rewards of ownership have been transferred, the asset is derecognized. If the entity neither transfers nor retains all of the risks and rewards of ownership, the entity derecognizes the asset if it does not retain control. If control is retained, the asset is recognized to the extent of the entity's continuing involvement.
Answer (A) is incorrect. A proportionate ownership interest is one of the criteria for a participating interest. Answer (C) is incorrect. A nonrecourse, notification basis is one of the aspects of factoring receivables. Answer (D) is incorrect. A secured borrowing is not relevant to the IFRS criteria for derecognition.

7.4 Notes Receivable -- Recognition

17. On August 15, Benet Co. sold goods for which it received a note bearing the market rate of interest on that date. The 4-month note was dated July 15. Note principal, together with all interest, is due November 15. When the note was recorded on August 15, which of the following accounts increased?

A. Unearned discount.

B. Interest receivable.

C. Prepaid interest.

D. Interest revenue.

Answer (B) is correct.
REQUIRED: The account that increased when the note was recorded.
DISCUSSION: Because the note bears interest at a reasonable rate (in this case, the market rate), its present value at the date of issuance is the face amount. Hence, the note should be recorded at this amount. Interest receivable also may be debited, and unearned interest revenue may be credited. The simple alternative is to debit cash and credit interest revenue when payment is received. If the reporting period ends prior to November 15, the period-end entry is to debit interest receivable and credit accrued interest revenue.
Answer (A) is incorrect. The note bears interest at the market rate. Thus, no discount from its face amount is recorded. Answer (C) is incorrect. No prepayment of interest has been made. Answer (D) is incorrect. Interest revenue has not yet been earned.

18. On December 1, Year 4, Tigg Mortgage Co. gave Pod Corp. a $200,000, 12% loan. Pod received proceeds of $194,000 after the deduction of a $6,000 nonrefundable loan origination fee. Principal and interest are due in 60 monthly installments of $4,450, beginning January 1, Year 5. The repayments yield an effective interest rate of 12% at a present value of $200,000 and 13.4% at a present value of $194,000. What amount of accrued interest receivable should Tigg include in its December 31, Year 4, balance sheet?

A. $4,450

B. $2,166

C. $2,000

D. $0

Answer (C) is correct.
REQUIRED: The accrued interest receivable at year end.
DISCUSSION: Accrued interest receivable is always equal to the face amount times the nominal rate for the period of the accrual. Hence, the accrued interest receivable is $2,000 [$200,000 × 12% × (1 ÷ 12)].
Answer (A) is incorrect. The monthly installment is $4,450. It includes principal as well as interest. Answer (B) is incorrect. The amount of $2,166 is based on a present value of $194,000 and an effective rate of 13.4%. It is the interest revenue from the loan. Answer (D) is incorrect. One month's interest should be accrued.

19. On January 1, Year 3, Mill Co. exchanged equipment for a $200,000, noninterest-bearing note due on January 1, Year 6. The prevailing rate of interest for a note of this type at January 1, Year 3, was 10%. The present value of $1 at 10% for three periods is 0.75. What amount of interest revenue should be included in Mill's Year 4 income statement?

A. $0

B. $15,000

C. $16,500

D. $20,000

Answer (C) is correct.
REQUIRED: The interest income from a noninterest-bearing note received for property.
DISCUSSION: When a noninterest-bearing note is exchanged for property, and neither the note nor the property has a clearly determinable exchange price, the present value of the note should be determined by discounting all future payments using an appropriately imputed interest rate. Mill Company will receive $200,000 cash in 3 years. Assuming that 10% is the appropriate imputed rate of interest, the present value (initial carrying amount) of the note at January 1, Year 3, was $150,000 ($200,000 × 0.75). Interest revenue for Year 3 was $15,000 ($150,000 × 10%), and the entry was to debit the discount and credit interest revenue for that amount. Thus, the carrying amount of the note at January 1, Year 4, was $165,000 ($200,000 face amount – $35,000 unamortized discount). Interest revenue for Year 4 is therefore $16,500 ($165,000 carrying amount × 10% interest rate).
Answer (A) is incorrect. Interest should be recognized equal to the imputed rate times the carrying amount of the note. Answer (B) is incorrect. Interest income for Year 3 was $15,000. Answer (D) is incorrect. This figure is 10% of the face amount of the note.

20. On December 1, Year 4, Money Co. gave Home Co. a $200,000, 11% loan. Money paid proceeds of $194,000 after the deduction of a $6,000 nonrefundable loan origination fee. Principal and interest are due in 60 monthly installments of $4,310, beginning January 1, Year 5. The repayments yield an effective interest rate of 11% at a present value of $200,000 and 12.4% at a present value of $194,000. What amount of income from this loan should Money report in its Year 4 income statement?

A. $0

B. $1,833

C. $2,005

D. $7,833

Answer (C) is correct.
REQUIRED: The amount of income from the loan at year end.
DISCUSSION: Under the effective-interest method, the effective rate of interest is applied to the net carrying amount of the receivable to determine periodic interest revenue. Thus, interest revenue from the loan for the month of December equals $2,005 [$194,000 × 12.4% × (1 ÷ 12)].
Answer (A) is incorrect. One month's interest should be accrued. Answer (B) is incorrect. The amount of $1,833 is the accrued interest receivable, which equals the face amount times the nominal rate for the period [$200,000 × 11% × (1 ÷ 12)]. Answer (D) is incorrect. The amount of $7,833 equals the $6,000 origination fee plus the accrued interest receivable of $1,833.

Questions 21 and 22 are based on the following information. On January 2, Year 3, Emme Co. sold equipment with a carrying amount of $480,000 in exchange for a $600,000 noninterest-bearing note due January 2, Year 6. There was no established exchange price for the equipment, and the market value of the note cannot be reasonably approximated. The prevailing rate of interest for a note of this type at January 2, Year 3, was 10%. The present value of 1 at 10% for three periods is 0.75.

21. In Emme's Year 3 income statement, what amount should be reported as interest income?

A. $15,000

B. $45,000

C. $48,000

D. $60,000

Answer (B) is correct.
REQUIRED: The interest income from a noninterest-bearing note received for property.
DISCUSSION: When a noninterest-bearing note is exchanged for property, and neither the note nor the property has a clearly determinable exchange price, the present value of the note should be the basis for recording the transaction. The present value is determined by discounting all future payments using an appropriately imputed interest rate. Emme Co. will receive $600,000 cash in 3 years. Assuming that 10% is the appropriate imputed rate of interest, the present value (initial carrying amount) of the note at January 2, Year 3, was $450,000 ($600,000 × 0.75). Under the interest method, interest income for Year 3 was $45,000 ($450,000 × 10%), and the entry is to debit the discount and credit interest income for that amount.
Answer (A) is incorrect. The amount of $15,000 is the difference between 10% of the face amount and 10% of the carrying amount. Answer (C) is incorrect. Interest income is based on the present value of the note, not the carrying amount of the equipment. Answer (D) is incorrect. Interest income is based on the carrying amount of the note, not the face amount.

22. In Emme's Year 3 income statement, what amount should be reported as gain (loss) on sale of equipment?

A. $(30,000)

B. $30,000

C. $120,000

D. $150,000

Answer (A) is correct.
REQUIRED: The amount reported as gain (loss) on the sale of machinery.
DISCUSSION: Emme Co. sold equipment with a carrying amount of $480,000 and received a note with a present value of $450,000 ($600,000 × .75). Thus, Emme should report a $30,000 loss ($480,000 – $450,000).
Answer (B) is incorrect. The present value of the note is $30,000 less than the carrying amount surrendered. Answer (C) is incorrect. The amount of $120,000 is the difference between the face amount of the note and the carrying amount of the equipment. Answer (D) is incorrect. The amount of $150,000 is the discount (face amount – present value).

7.5 Notes Receivable -- Discounting

23. Leaf Co. purchased from Oak Co. a $20,000, 8%, 5-year note that required five equal, annual year-end payments of $5,009. The note was discounted to yield a 9% rate to Leaf. At the date of purchase, Leaf recorded the note at its present value of $19,485. What should be the total interest revenue earned by Leaf over the life of this note?

A. $5,045

B. $5,560

C. $8,000

D. $9,000

Answer (B) is correct.
REQUIRED: The total interest revenue earned on a discounted note receivable.
DISCUSSION: Leaf Co. will receive cash of $25,045 ($5,009 × 5). Hence, interest revenue is $5,560 ($25,045 – $19,485 present value).
Answer (A) is incorrect. The amount of $5,045 does not include the discount amortization. Answer (C) is incorrect. The amount of $8,000 equals $20,000 times 8% nominal interest for 5 years. Answer (D) is incorrect. The amount of $9,000 equals $20,000 times the 9% yield rate for 5 years.

24. On July 1, Year 3, Kay Corp. sold equipment to Mando Co. for $100,000. Kay accepted a 10% note receivable for the entire sales price. This note is payable in two equal installments of $50,000 plus accrued interest on December 31, Year 3, and December 31, Year 4. On July 1, Year 4, Kay discounted the note at a bank at an interest rate of 12%. Kay's proceeds from the discounted note were

A. $48,400

B. $52,640

C. $52,250

D. $51,700

Answer (D) is correct.
REQUIRED: The proceeds from a discounted note.
DISCUSSION: Following the receipt of $50,000 plus accrued interest on December 31, Year 3, the remaining balance was $50,000. Because the second installment is due 1 year after the first, the interest attributable to this balance is $5,000 ($50,000 principal × 10% × 1 year). On July 1, Year 4, the $55,000 maturity value ($50,000 note + $5,000 interest) is discounted at 12% for the remaining 6 months of the term of the note. The discount fee charged would be $3,300 [$55,000 maturity amount × 12% × (6 ÷ 12)]. The net proceeds are equal to the $55,000 maturity value minus the $3,300 discount fee, or $51,700.

$50,000 × 10% × 1 year = $5,000 interest
$55,000 × 12% × (6 ÷ 12) = $3,300 discount fee

Answer (A) is incorrect. The amount of $48,400 results from charging a discount fee for a full year. Answer (B) is incorrect. This figure assumes the nominal interest rate is also 12%. Answer (C) is incorrect. The amount of $52,250 assumes the discount rate is also 10%.

25. Roth, Inc., received from a customer a 1-year, $500,000 note bearing annual interest of 8%. After holding the note for 6 months, Roth discounted the note at Regional Bank at an effective interest rate of 10%. What amount of cash did Roth receive from the bank?

A. $540,000

B. $528,400

C. $513,000

D. $486,000

Answer (C) is correct.
REQUIRED: The amount of cash received when a note is discounted.
DISCUSSION: The maturity amount of the note is $540,000 [$500,000 face value + ($500,000 × 8%)]. The discount is $27,000 [$540,000 × 10% × (6 ÷ 12)]. Consequently, the proceeds equal $513,000 ($540,000 – $27,000).
Answer (A) is incorrect. The maturity value is $540,000. Answer (B) is incorrect. The amount of $528,400 assumes a nominal rate of 10% and a discount rate of 8%. Answer (D) is incorrect. Discounting the note for 1 year results in $486,000.

Use the additional questions in Gleim **CPA Test Prep Online** to create Test Sessions that emulate Prometric!

7.6 PRACTICE SIMULATION

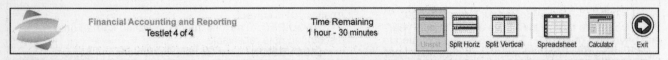

Financial Accounting and Reporting
Testlet 4 of 4

Time Remaining
1 hour - 30 minutes

Unsplit | Split Horiz | Split Vertical | Spreadsheet | Calculator | Exit

---

DIRECTIONS

Note: If you believe you have encountered a software malfunction, report it to the test center staff immediately.

Navigation

To navigate from task to task, use the controls at the bottom of the screen. Click on the **Next** button to advance to the next task, or the **Previous** button to go to the previous task. To go directly to any task, click on its number.

▼ = Reminder   Directions   1 2 3 4 5 6 7   ◄ Previous   Next ►

If you would like a reminder to revisit a task, or want to indicate that you are finished with it, click on the reminder flag below the task number. To clear the flag, click on it again. Reminder flags are for your use only – they do not contribute to your score.

Tabs

In this part of the examination, you will be asked to complete various tasks. Every task has one or more **Work Tabs**. Some tasks have one or more **Information Tabs**, others may have none. Every task has a **Help** tab.

If a task has **Information Tabs**, you may use the information in them to complete your responses in the **Work Tabs**.

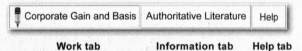

Corporate Gain and Basis | Authoritative Literature | Help

Work tab   Information tab   Help tab

Work Tabs:

- **Work Tabs** are identified with a pencil icon. This is where your responses are expected.
- Each task has one or more **Work Tabs**.
- **Work Tabs** contain directions for completing the task – be sure to read these directions carefully.
- The **Work Tab** name in the example above is for illustration only – yours will differ.
- You must complete all of the **Work Tabs** in each task to receive full credit.

Information Tabs:

- The Authoritative Literature will be provided in all tasks in the AUD, FAR, and REG sections for your reference.
- Your simulation may have one or more additional **Information Tabs**. Like the Authoritative Literature tabs, **Information Tabs** do not have a pencil icon.
- If your task has additional **Information Tabs**, go through each to familiarize yourself with the task content.

Help Tab:

- The **Help Tab** provides assistance with the exam software that is used in this task. For example, if the task is to compose a memorandum, **Help** will provide information about the word processor.

The Toolbar

The toolbar at the top of the screen shows the amount of time remaining for you to complete the tasks. In addition, the following tools are available. Note that only the **Exit** button is displayed when Directions are visible - the others will appear when you begin the tasks.

Unsplit   Split Horiz   Split Vertical

Click on these buttons to split or unsplit the screen. You can split the screen vertically or horizontally.

Calculator

Click on this button to display the calculator; click on it again to hide the calculator. To move the calculator, click on the calculator title bar and drag the calculator to the desired location.

Spreadsheet

Click on this button to use the spreadsheet; click on it again to hide the spreadsheet. To move the spreadsheet, click on the the spreadsheet title bar and drag the spreadsheet to the desired location.

Exit

Click on this button to go on to the next part of the examination. You must complete all of the tasks to receive full credit. Once you click on **Exit** and confirm the action, you will NOT be able to return to this testlet.

▼ = Reminder   Directions   1 2 3 4 5 6   ◄ Previous   Next ►

| Noncurrent Receivables | Authoritative Literature | Help |

Kern, Inc., which is not a public company (an issuer under federal securities laws), had the following noncurrent receivable account balances at December 31, Year 4:

Note receivable from the sale of an idle building	$750,000
Note receivable from an officer	200,000

Transactions during Year 5 and other information relating to Kern's receivables follow:

- The $750,000 note receivable is dated May 1, Year 4, bears interest at 9%, and represents the balance of the consideration Kern received from the sale of its idle building to Able Co. Principal payments of $250,000 plus interest are due annually beginning May 1, Year 5. Able made its first principal and interest payment on May 1, Year 5. Collection of the remaining note installments is reasonably assured.

- The $200,000 note receivable is dated December 31, Year 2, bears interest at 8%, and is due on December 31, Year 7. The note is due from Frank Black, president of Kern, Inc., and is collateralized by 5,000 shares of Kern's common stock. Interest is payable annually on December 31, and all interest payments were made through December 31, Year 5. The quoted market price of Kern's common stock was $45 per share on December 31, Year 5.

- On April 1, Year 5, Kern sold a patent to Frey Corp. in exchange for a $100,000 noninterest-bearing note due on April 1, Year 7. The patent had no established exchange price, and the note had no ready market. The prevailing interest rate for this type of note was 10% at April 1, Year 5. The present value of $1 for two periods at 10% is 0.826. The patent had a carrying amount of $40,000 at January 1, Year 5, and the amortization for the year ended December 31, Year 5, was $8,000. Kern is reasonably assured of collecting the note receivable from Frey.

- On July 1, Year 5, Kern sold a parcel of land to Barr Co. for $400,000 under an installment sale contract. Barr made a $120,000 cash down payment on July 1, Year 5, and signed a 4-year, 10% note for the balance. The equal annual payments of principal and interest on the note will be $88,332, payable on July 1 of each year from Year 6 through Year 9. The fair value of the land at the date of sale was $400,000. The cost of the land to Kern was $300,000. Collection of the remaining note installments is reasonably assured.

Enter in the shaded cells the noncurrent receivables that should be reported on Kern's December 31, Year 5, balance sheet.

Noncurrent portion of installment contract receivable at 12/31/Year 5:	*Amount*
Contract selling price, 7/1/Year 5	
Minus cash down payment	
Balance, 12/31/Year 5	
Minus installment due 7/1/Year 6	
Noncurrent portion, 12/31/Year 5	
Noncurrent 8% note receivable due 12/31/Year 7	

Select from the list provided the most clearly evident additional classification for each of the following items. Select the answers for 1. and 2. from choices A) and B), for 3. through 6. from C) and D), and for 7. through 10. from E) and F). Each choice may be used once, more than once, or not at all.

Item	Answer	Classification
1. Trade account receivable due within 11 months		A) Current asset
2. Nontrade note receivable due within 2 years		B) Noncurrent asset
3. Noncurrent notes receivable for advances to shareholders, directors, and officers		C) Trade receivable
4. Current note receivable for insurance proceeds		D) Nontrade receivable
5. Current account receivable from credit sales		
6. Current note receivable for rent		
7. Unsecured current trade receivable not evidenced by a formal instrument		E) Note receivable
8. Long-term, interest-bearing receivable payable in a single sum		F) Accounts receivable
9. Noncurrent trade receivable evidenced by a formal instrument		
10. Current trade open accounts		

Select from the list provided the best match for each item about transfers of financial assets below. Each choice may be used once, more than once, or not at all.

Item	Answer	Choices
1. Transfer of a participating interest in an entire financial asset.		A) Criterion for surrender of control
2. A recourse provision.		B) Characteristic of a participating interest
3. A beneficial interest in a trust holding transferred assets.		
4. Transferees may pledge the assets received.		C) Example of continuing involvement
5. The transferor has made no agreement to reacquire assets before maturity.		D) Example of transfer of financial assets
		E) Accounting for transfer of a participating interest
		F) None of the above

Select from the list provided the best match for each item about transfers of financial assets below. Each choice may be used once, more than once, or not at all.

Item	Answer		Choices
1. Transferor may be required to repurchase assets.			A) Servicing asset
2. Transfer of receivables to a factor.			B) Servicing liability
3. Sale of beneficial interests in a portfolio of mortgages.			C) Securitization
4. Formal pledge of collateral.			D) Secured borrowing
5. Retailer benefits from prompt cash inflow and avoidance of bad debts.			E) Credit card sale
6. Future revenues from fees, late charges, etc., are inadequate.			F) Sale with recourse
7. Collateral is asset of the transferor.			G) Nonrecourse basis transaction
			H) None of the above

Entries   Authoritative Literature   Help

Fern Company has significant amounts of trade accounts receivable. In March of Year 5, Fern assigned specific trade accounts receivable to Herb Finance Company on a with-recourse, nonnotification basis as collateral for a loan. Fern signed a note and received 70% of the amount assigned. Fern was charged a 5% finance fee and agreed to pay interest at 12% on the unpaid balance. Some specific accounts of the assigned receivables were written off as uncollectible. The remainder of the trade accounts receivable assigned were collected by Fern in March and April. Fern paid Herb Finance in full at the end of April of Year 5.

Fern also sold some special order merchandise and received a 90-day, 15% interest-bearing note receivable on July 1 of Year 5. On July 31, the note was discounted with recourse at 18% at a bank. The transaction was treated as a borrowing, and the bank has the right to sell the collateral.

Based on the information provided, indicate by checking the appropriate box whether each account should be debited or credited by Fern to account for the transaction listed.

	Debit	Credit
Transaction: Assignment of trade accounts receivable		
1. Trade accounts receivable assigned		
2. Trade accounts receivable		
Transaction: Giving a note payable with the assigned receivables as collateral		
3. Notes payable		
4. Finance fee expense		
5. Cash		
Transaction: Subsequent collections on the trade accounts receivable assigned		
6. Cash		
7. Trade accounts receivable assigned		

Research | Authoritative Literature | Help

Daugherty Company owned a participating interest in an oil and gas business. In a transaction that qualifies as a sale, Daugherty transferred the entire interest to a third party. Daugherty received both cash and a forward commitment from the third party to deliver additional receivables to Daugherty over the course of the next 6 months. The CFO has asked if the forward commitment should be recognized as part of the proceeds of the sale. Which section of the authoritative guidance best outlines the accounting for a transfer of a participating interest in a financial asset that satisfies the conditions for treatment as a sale?

Enter your response in the answer fields below. Unless specifically requested, your response should not cite implementation guidance.

FASB ASC ☐ - ☐ - ☐ - ☐

▼ = Reminder   Directions 1 2 3 4 5 [6]   ◀ Previous   Next ▶

Unofficial Answers

1. Noncurrent Receivables (6 Gradable Items)

Noncurrent portion of installment contract receivable at 12/31/Year 5:	
Contract selling price, 7/1/Year 5	$400,000
Minus cash down payment	120,000
Balance, 12/31/Year 5	$280,000
Minus installment due 7/1/Year 6 [$88,332 − ($280,000 × 10%)]	60,332
Noncurrent portion, 12/31/Year 5	$219,668
Noncurrent 8% note receivable due 12/31/Year 7	$200,000

2. Asset Classification (10 Gradable Items)

1. A) Current asset. A receivable is a current asset if it is reasonably expected to be collected within the longer of 1 year or the entity's normal operating cycle. Otherwise, it should be classified as noncurrent.
2. B) Noncurrent asset. A receivable is a current asset if it is reasonably expected to be collected within the longer of 1 year or the entity's normal operating cycle. Otherwise, it should be classified as noncurrent.
3. D) Nontrade receivables. Typical nontrade receivables are reported for advances to shareholders, directors, officers, other employees, affiliates, or customers.
4. D) Nontrade receivable. Nontrade receivables may include claims for insurance proceeds or amounts arising from litigation.
5. C) Trade receivables. Most receivables arise from credit sales to customers as part of the ordinary revenue-producing activities of an entity. These trade receivables represent contractual undertakings usually evidenced by sales orders, invoices, or delivery contracts.
6. D) Nontrade receivable. Nontrade receivables may include interest, dividends, rent, or royalties accrued.
7. F) Accounts receivable. Accounts receivable are often current, unsecured, and informal credit arrangements (open accounts). They constitute the largest portion of trade receivables.
8. E) Note receivable. In a note, the maker (debtor) usually promises to pay to the order of a second party (creditor) a fixed amount of money at a definite time. This item also is not an installment account because payment is in a lump sum.
9. E) Note receivable. Notes receivable are evidenced by a formal instrument, such as a promissory note. A formal document provides its holder with a stronger legal status than does an account receivable.
10. F) Accounts receivable. Accounts receivable are often current, unsecured, and informal credit arrangements (open accounts). They constitute the largest portion of trade receivables.

3. Financial Assets I (5 Gradable Items)

1. D) Example of transfer of financial assets. Transfers of financial assets include transfers of (a) an entire financial asset, (b) a group of entire financial assets, and (c) a participating interest in an entire financial asset.

2. C) Example of continuing involvement. Control depends, among other things, on the transferor's continuing involvement with such assets. Examples of continuing involvement are (a) servicing agreements, (b) options written or held, (c) recourse provisions, (d) a beneficial interest in a trust that holds the assets, and (e) a pledge of collateral.

3. C) Example of continuing involvement. Control depends, among other things, on the transferor's continuing involvement with such assets. Examples of continuing involvement are (a) servicing agreements, (b) options written or held, (c) recourse provisions, (d) a beneficial interest in a trust that holds the assets, and (e) a pledge of collateral.

4. A) Criterion for surrender of control. A transfer of financial assets over which the transferor relinquishes control is a sale. Surrendering control occurs when the transferred assets are beyond the reach of the transferor and its creditors; transferees may pledge or exchange the assets or interest received; and the transferor does not maintain effective control through, for example, an agreement to reacquire the assets before maturity.

5. A) Criterion for surrender of control. A transfer of financial assets over which the transferor relinquishes control is a sale. Surrendering control occurs when the transferred assets are beyond the reach of the transferor and its creditors; transferees may pledge or exchange the assets or interest received; and the transferor does not maintain effective control through, for example, an agreement to reacquire the assets before maturity.

4. Financial Assets II (7 Gradable Items)

1. F) Sale with recourse. If a sale is with recourse, the transferor (seller) may be required to make payments to the transferee or to buy back receivables in specified circumstances.

2. G) Nonrecourse basis transaction. Factoring discounts receivables on a nonrecourse, notification basis.

3. C) Securitization. Securitization is the transfer of a portfolio of financial assets to a trust or other entity and the sale of beneficial interests in that entity to investors.

4. D) Secured borrowing. A secured borrowing is a formal borrowing arrangement. The borrower signs a promissory note and financing agreement, and specific receivables are pledged as collateral.

5. E) Credit card sale. One common form of factoring is the credit card sale. The retailer benefits by prompt receipt of cash and avoidance of bad debts and other costs.

6. B) Servicing liability. A servicing asset is a contract under which the future revenues from servicing fees, late charges, etc., are expected to more than adequately compensate the servicer. A servicing liability arises when such compensation is inadequate.

7. D) Secured borrowing. A secured borrowing is a formal borrowing arrangement. The borrower signs a promissory note and financing agreement, and specific receivables are pledged as collateral.

5. Entries (7 Gradable Items)

1. Debit. Assigned accounts receivable should be segregated.

2. Credit. Assigned accounts receivable should be segregated.

3. Credit. The loan is reported as a liability.

4. Debit. These finance fees are charged to the assignor-debtor as a reduction of the loan proceeds.

5. Debit. The assignor-debtor receives the cash it borrowed.

6. Debit. The assignor-debtor receives the cash collected because the assignment was on a nonnotification basis.

7. Credit. The assigned receivables are derecognized when completed.

6. Research (1 Gradable Item)

Answer: FASB ASC 860-20-25-1

860-20-25-1 Upon completion of a transfer of financial assets that satisfies the conditions to be accounted for as a sale in paragraph 860-10-40-5, the transferor (seller) shall apply the related derecognition guidance in this Subtopic and shall do both of the following:

 a. Recognize all assets obtained and liabilities incurred in consideration as proceeds of the sale, including all of the following:

  1. Cash

  2. Put or call options held or written (for example, guarantee or recourse obligations)

  3. Forward commitments (for example, commitments to deliver additional receivables during the revolving periods of some securitizations)

  4. Swaps (for example, provisions that convert interest rates from fixed to variable)

 b. Recognize in earnings any gain or loss on the sale.

Gleim Simulation Grading

Task	Correct Responses		Gradable Items		Score per Task
1	___	÷	6	=	___
2	___	÷	10	=	___
3	___	÷	5	=	___
4	___	÷	7	=	___
5	___	÷	7	=	___
Research	___	÷	1	=	___

Total of Scores per Task ___

÷ Total Number of Tasks 6

Total Score ___ %

Use **CPA Gleim Online** and **Simulation Wizard** to practice more task-based simulations in a realistic environment.

STUDY UNIT EIGHT
INVENTORIES

(25 pages of outline)

8.1	Inventory Fundamentals	261
8.2	Consignment Accounting	267
8.3	Cost Flow Methods -- Application	268
8.4	Cost Flow Methods -- Comparison	274
8.5	Dollar-Value LIFO	274
8.6	Lower of Cost or Market (LCM)	277
8.7	Special Topics in Inventory Accounting	279
8.8	Estimating Inventory	281
8.9	Practice Simulation	297

Inventory consists of the tangible goods intended to be sold to produce revenue. The cost of inventory is a deferral because it is not included in earnings until the reporting period in which the inventory is sold (produces revenue). Many methods of costing inventory are acceptable. Inventory and related concepts are always tested on the CPA exam.

8.1 INVENTORY FUNDAMENTALS

Background

Inventory accounting is a crucial task for any manufacturer. Trends in the three classes of inventory (materials, work-in-process, finished goods) reveal much to investors about the firm's short-term financial prospects and to analysts about the economy as a whole. For example, increases in materials and work-in-process may indicate the firm is selling all it can produce, but increases in finished goods may indicate overproduction or a slowdown in the economy.

1. **Definition**

   a. Inventory is the total of tangible personal property

      1) Held for sale in the ordinary course of business,

      2) In the form of work-in-process to be completed and sold in the ordinary course of business, or

      3) To be used up currently in producing goods or services for sale.

   b. Inventory does not include long-term assets subject to depreciation.

2. **Sources of Inventories**

   a. **Retailing**

      1) A trading (retailing) entity purchases merchandise to be resold without substantial modification. Such entities may also have supplies inventories.

      2) For a retailer, **cost of goods sold** essentially equals beginning merchandise inventory, plus purchases for the period, minus ending merchandise inventory (purchases adjusted for the change in inventory).

Cost of Goods Sold for a Retailer

Beginning inventory		$ XXX,XXX
Purchases	$X,XXX,XXX	
Purchase returns and discounts	(XX,XXX)	
Freight-in	XX,XXX	
Net purchases		X,XXX,XXX
Goods available for sale		$X,XXX,XXX
Ending inventory		**(XXX,XXX)**
Cost of goods sold		$X,XXX,XXX

b. Manufacturing

1) An entity that acquires goods for conversion into substantially different products has inventories of goods consumed directly or indirectly in production (direct materials and supplies), goods in the course of production (work-in-process), and goods awaiting sale (finished goods).

2) For a manufacturer, **cost of goods sold** essentially equals beginning finished goods inventory, plus the cost of goods manufactured, minus ending finished goods inventory.

3) **Cost of goods manufactured** equals beginning work-in-process, plus current manufacturing costs (direct materials + direct labor + production overhead), minus ending work-in-process (current manufacturing costs adjusted for the change in work-in-process).

Cost of Goods Sold for a Manufacturer

Beginning materials inventory			$ XXX, XXX
Purchases	$X,XXX,XXX		
Purchase returns and discounts	(XX,XXX)		
Freight-in	XX,XXX		
Net purchases		X,XXX,XXX	
Materials available for use		$X,XXX,XXX	
Ending materials inventory		**(XXX,XXX)**	
Direct materials used in production			$X,XXX,XXX
Direct labor costs			X,XXX,XXX
Manufacturing overhead costs			XXX,XXX
Total manufacturing costs for the period			$X,XXX,XXX
Beginning work-in-process inventory			XXX,XXX
Ending work-in-process inventory			**(XXX,XXX)**
Cost of goods manufactured			$X,XXX,XXX
Beginning finished goods inventory			XXX,XXX
Goods available for sale			$X,XXX,XXX
Ending finished goods inventory			**(XXX,XXX)**
Cost of goods sold			$X,XXX,XXX

3. Inventory Accounting Systems

a. Entities that require continuous monitoring of inventory use a perpetual system. Entities that have no need to monitor continuously use a periodic system.

b. Perpetual System

1) In a perpetual system, purchases, purchase returns and allowances, purchase discounts, and freight-in (transportation in) are charged directly to inventory.

   a) Inventory and cost of goods sold are adjusted as sales occur.

   b) A physical count is needed to detect material misstatements in the records.

   c) **Inventory over-and-short** is debited (credited) when the physical count is less (greater) than the balance in the perpetual records.

      i) This account is either closed to cost of goods sold or reported separately under (a) other revenues and gains or (b) other expenses and losses.

Journal Entries in a Perpetual Inventory System

<u>Acquisition and Returns</u>

Inventory	$X,XXX	
Accounts payable		$X,XXX

<u>Sale</u>

Accounts receivable	$X,XXX	
Sales		$X,XXX
Cost of goods sold	X,XXX	
Inventory		X,XXX

<u>Closing</u>

Inventory over-and-short (Dr, Cr)	$XX	
Inventory (correction) (Cr, Dr)		$XX
Cost of goods sold (other expenses and losses)	XX	
Inventory over-and-short		XX

or

Inventory over-and-short	XX	
Cost of goods sold (other revenues and gains)		XX

c. **Periodic System**

1) In a periodic system, inventory is updated at specific intervals, such as quarterly or annually, based on the results of a physical count.

   a) The beginning inventory balance remains unchanged during the accounting period.

   b) Goods bought from suppliers and adjustments usually are tracked in separate temporary accounts (purchases, freight-in, etc.). The adjustments are added to or subtracted from purchases to determine net purchases.

   c) Changes in inventory and cost of goods sold are recorded only at the end of the period based on the physical count.

   d) After the physical count,

      i) The inventory balance is adjusted to match the physical count, and
      ii) Cost of goods sold is calculated.

Journal Entries in a Periodic Inventory System

<u>Acquisition and Returns</u>

Purchases	$X,XXX	
Accounts payable		$X,XXX
Freight-in	XXX	
Cash		XXX
Accounts payable	XXX	
Purchase returns		XXX

<u>Sale</u>

Accounts receivable	$X,XXX	
Sales		$X,XXX

<u>Closing</u>

Inventory (physical count)	$X,XXX	
Cost of goods sold	X,XXX	
Purchase returns	XXX	
Purchases (total for period)		$X,XXX
Inventory (beginning balance)		X,XXX
Freight-in		XXX

4.   **Items Counted in Inventory**

    a.   **Items in Transit**

        1)   Not all inventory is on hand. Most sales are recorded by the seller at the time of shipment and the buyer at the time of receipt. However, this procedure may misstate inventory, receivables, payables, and earnings at the end of the period.

        2)   Proper cut-off is observed by determining when legal title has passed under the FOB (free on board) terms of the contract.

            a)   **FOB shipping point** means title and risk of loss pass to the buyer when the seller makes a proper tender of delivery of the goods to the carrier. The buyer then includes the goods in inventory.

            b)   **FOB destination** means title and risk of loss pass to the buyer when the seller makes a proper tender of delivery of the goods at the destination. The seller should include the goods in inventory until that time.

    b.   **Installment Sales**

        1)   Because of the greater risk of loss in these transactions, the seller often retains title to the goods until full payment has been made. Nevertheless, these items should not be counted in the seller's inventory if uncollectible accounts expense can be reasonably estimated.

        2)   Despite retention of title by the seller, the substance of the transaction is that control of the goods has passed to the buyer, assuming a reasonable expectation of payment in the ordinary course of business.

    c.   **Right of Return**

        1)   When sales are made with the understanding that unsatisfactory goods may be returned, and these returns are expected to be material, revenue and cost of goods sold may be recognized and inventory may be credited when all of the following conditions exist:

            a)   The seller's price is substantially fixed or determinable.

            b)   The buyer has paid or is obligated to pay, and the obligation is not contingent on resale.

            c)   The buyer's obligation is not changed if the product is stolen, damaged, or destroyed.

            d)   The buyer has economic substance apart from the seller.

            e)   The seller is not substantially obligated to directly bring about resale.

            f)   The amount of future returns can be reasonably estimated.

        2)   If the conditions are met, a sale is recorded in the usual way. In addition, the following entry is made:

Estimated sales returns (contra to revenue)	$XXX	
Cost of goods sold		$XXX
Deferred gross profit related to estimated returns		
(contra to accounts receivable)		XXX

3) When returns are made, the entry is

Inventory	$XXX	
Deferred gross profit	XXX	
Accounts receivable (or cash)		$XXX

a) The entry above assumes returns equal the estimate. If returns are lower, the entry to recognize additional sales is

Inventory	$XXX	
Cost of goods sold	XXX	
Deferred gross profit	XXX	
Accounts receivable (or cash)		$XXX
Sales		XXX

4) If the **six conditions are not met**, revenue and cost of goods sold are not recognized until the right of return expires.

a) The initial entry is to debit accounts receivable (or cash) and to credit inventory and deferred gross profit. Returns result in a reversal of this entry.

d. **Goods Out on Consignment** (discussed in detail in the next subunit)

CPA candidates have been asked to calculate amounts for inventory and cost of goods sold using information given in the question, such as shipping terms and consignment sales.

5. **Cost Basis**

a. Inventory is primarily accounted for at cost, which is "the price paid or consideration given to acquire an asset. As applied to inventories, cost means in principle the sum of the applicable expenditures and charges directly or indirectly incurred in bringing an article to its existing condition and location" (FASB Codification).

b. **Product (inventoriable) costs** are incurred to produce or acquire units of inventory and are deferred to the extent they are not sold.

1) Inventoriable costs are expensed in the period the product is sold. They include direct materials, direct labor, and production overhead. The price and the other costs of acquisition, such as freight-in, are inventoried.

c. **Period costs** are charged to expense as incurred and not to a particular product.

1) Period costs are revenue expenditures or capital expenditures.

a) Revenue (income) expenditures, e.g., advertising and officers' salaries, are expensed when incurred. They usually do not benefit future periods.

b) Capital expenditures, e.g., depreciation, are initially recorded as assets and then expensed as they are consumed, used, or disposed of.

2) A period cost cannot feasibly be related to acquisition or production of inventory. The costs of establishing the relationship would exceed the benefit.

d. Interest is ordinarily not capitalized as part of inventory because its incurrence is relatively remote from the purchase or manufacture of products.

e. R&D costs are customarily not inventoried.

6. **Purchases, Freight Costs, and Returns**

    a. Purchased inventory is measured at **invoice cost**.

        1) **Trade discounts** are usually subtracted prior to invoicing. They allow sellers to change prices without reprinting catalogs or to charge different prices to different customers.

            a) A chain discount applies more than one trade discount. The first discount is applied to the list price, the second is applied to the resulting amount, etc.

    b. The buyer's **transportation (freight) costs** for purchased goods are inventoried.

        1) In a perpetual system, these costs can be assigned to specified purchases.
        2) In a periodic system, transportation costs are usually debited to freight-in. Ordinarily, this balance is closed to cost of goods sold when attribution to specific goods is not feasible. However, allocation to cost of goods sold and ending inventory is preferable in such cases.

    c. In a periodic system, **purchase returns and allowances** are debited to accounts payable or a receivable and credited to a contra-asset. In a perpetual system, they are credited to inventory.

        1) A return is recognized for goods returned to the seller.
        2) Purchase returns and allowances is a nominal account closed at year end.

7. **Cash Discounts**

    a. Cash discounts are offered to induce early payment and improve cash flow. Two methods of accounting for them are in general use.

        1) The **net method** is theoretically correct. It records the cash price at the date of sale.

            a) Purchase discounts lost (a financing expense) is debited when payment is not made within the discount period.

                i) This treatment applies in a periodic or perpetual system.

        2) The **gross method** ignores cash discounts. It is more popular than the net method because of its simplicity (no adjusting entries are needed).

            a) Discounts not taken are not recognized.
            b) If payment is made within the discount period, purchase discounts are credited in a periodic system. Inventory is credited in a perpetual system.

EXAMPLE

Inventory accounted for using the perpetual system is purchased with terms of 2/10, n/30 (2% discount within 10 days, entire balance due in 30 days).

	Gross Method		Net Method	
Inventory	$1,000		$980	
Accounts payable		$1,000		$980

Payment is made **within the discount period**.

	Gross Method		Net Method	
Accounts payable	$1,000		$980	
Cash		$980		$980
Inventory		20		

Payment is made **after the discount period**.

	Gross Method		Net Method	
Accounts payable	$1,000		$980	
Purchase discounts lost			20	
Cash		$1,000		$1,000

b. If a **periodic system** is used with the **gross method**, cost of goods sold is calculated as follows:

Goods available for sale:		
Beginning inventory	$XXX	
Purchases (net of trade discounts)	XXX	
Purchase discounts	(XXX)	
Purchase returns and allowances	(XXX)	
Freight-in	XXX	$XXX
Ending inventory		(XXX)
Cost of goods sold		$XXX

Stop and review! You have completed the outline for this subunit. Study multiple-choice questions 1 through 4 beginning on page 285.

8.2 CONSIGNMENT ACCOUNTING

1. **Overview**

   a. A consignment sale is an arrangement between the owner of goods and a sales agent. Consigned goods are not sold but rather transferred to an agent for possible sale. The consignor (owner) records sales only when the goods are sold to third parties by the consignee (agent).

      1) Goods out on consignment are **included in inventory** at cost. Costs of transporting the goods to the consignee are inventoriable costs, not selling expenses.

2. **Consignor's Accounting**

   a. The **consignor** records the initial shipment by a debit to **consigned goods out** (a separate inventory account) and a credit to inventory at cost.

      1) Receipts and expenses incurred by the consignee are recorded by debits to cash, commission expense, consigned goods out, and cost of goods sold. Credits are to sales and consigned goods out.

   b. Consigned goods out is used in a perpetual or periodic inventory system when consignments are recorded in separate accounts.

      1) If the consignor uses a perpetual system, the credit on shipment is to inventory.

      2) If a periodic system is used, the credit is to consignment shipments, a contra cost of goods sold account. Its balance is then closed at the end of the period when the inventory adjustments are made.

3. **Consignee's Accounting**

   a. The **consignee** never records the consigned goods as an asset.

      1) The basic account used in consignee accounting is **consignment-in**, a receivable/payable. Its balance is the amount payable to the consignor (a credit) or the amount receivable from the consignor (a debit).

         a) Before consigned goods are sold, expenses chargeable to the consignor (e.g., freight-in or service costs) are recorded in the consignment-in account as a receivable. After the consigned goods are sold, the credit balance reflects the consignee's net liability to the consignor.

         b) Sales are recorded with a debit to cash (or accounts receivable) and credits to consignment-in (a payable) and commission income.

         c) Payments to the consignor result in a debit to consignment-in and a credit to cash.

4.   Comparative Journal Entries

EXAMPLE

The consignor ships 100 units, costing $50 each, to the consignee.

Consignor			**Consignee**		
Consigned goods out	$5,000		Only a memorandum entry		
Inventory		$5,000			

The consignee pays $120 for freight-in.

Consignor		**Consignee**		
No entry at this time		Consignment-in	$120	
		Cash		$120

The consignee sells 80 units at $80 each. The consignee is to receive a 15% commission on all sales.

Consignor		**Consignee**		
No entry at this time		Cash	$6,400	
		Consignment-in		$5,440
		Commission income		960

The consignee sends a monthly statement to the consignor with the balance owed. The cost of shipping goods to the consignee, including the $120 payment by the consignee, is debited as a cost of consigned inventory.

Consignor		**Consignee**	
Cash	$5,320	Consignment-in	$5,320 ($5,440 – $120)
Commission expense	960	Cash	$5,320
Consigned goods out	120		
Cost of goods sold	4,096 [($5,000 + $120) × 80%]		
Sales	$6,400		
Consigned goods out	4,096		

---

   a.   The consignee may use consignment-in rather than payable to consignor. Consignment-in is a receivable/payable account.

Stop and review! You have completed the outline for this subunit. Study multiple-choice questions 5 through 8 beginning on page 287.

8.3 COST FLOW METHODS -- APPLICATION

Background

The use of full (absorption) costing by manufacturers is required by GAAP. Unfortunately, it results in a perverse incentive known as producing for inventory. Because a portion of fixed costs is included in ending inventory, a firm can inflate its net income by increasing its finished goods inventory whether or not demand for the product exists. This is another reason analysts carefully monitor a manufacturer's inventory policies and trends.

The AICPA has asked candidates to solve calculation questions concerning average-cost, FIFO, and LIFO inventory. Candidates may also see questions that ask for adjusting year-end entries.

---

1.   Specific Identification

   a.   Specific identification requires determining which specific items are sold and therefore reflects the actual physical flow of goods. It can be used for blocks of investment securities or special inventory items, such as automobiles or heavy equipment.

   b.   A practical weakness of specific identification is the need for detailed records.

2. **Average Cost**

    a.   The assumption in an average cost system is that goods are indistinguishable and are therefore measured at an average of the costs incurred.

    b.   The **moving-average** method requires determination of a new weighted-average cost after each purchase and thus is used only in a **perpetual system**.

EXAMPLE

A new average cost is calculated after each purchase. This cost is used for every sale until the next purchase and recalculation.

	Units	Times: Price	Equals: Additions	Equals: Reductions	Inventory Balance	Divided By: Total Units	Equals: Per Unit Cost
Mar. 31 inventory	1,000	$12.50	$12,500		$12,500	1,000	$12.50
Apr. 14 purchase	2,000	12.20	24,400		36,900	3,000	12.30
Apr. 20 sale	(1,800)	12.30		$(22,140)	14,760	1,200	12.30
Apr. 24 purchase	3,200	12.60	40,320		55,080	4,400	12.52
Apr. 28 sale	(800)	12.52		(10,016)	45,064	3,600	12.52
Total available			$77,220				

Cost of goods sold is calculated as follows:

Goods available for sale	$77,220
Minus: ending inventory	(45,065)
Cost of goods sold	**$32,155**

---

    c.   The **weighted-average** method determines an average cost only once (at the end of the period) and is therefore applicable in a **periodic system**.

        1)   It may be used in a perpetual system that records only inventory quantities.

EXAMPLE

Because perpetual records are not kept, purchases and sales for the period are aggregated.

	Units	Times: Price	Equals: On Hand
Mar. 31 inventory	1,000	$12.50	$12,500
Apr. 14 purchase	2,000	12.20	24,400
Apr. 24 purchase	3,200	12.60	40,320
Total available	6,200		$77,220
Apr. 20 sale	(1,800)		
Apr. 28 sale	(800)		
Ending inventory	3,600		

A single per-unit cost is calculated for the entire period.

$$\text{Average per unit cost} = \$77,220 \div 6,200 = \$12.4548$$

Cost of goods sold can then be calculated.

Goods available for sale	$77,220
Minus: ending inventory (3,600 units × $12.4548)	(44,837)
Cost of goods sold	**$32,383**

---

3. **First-in, First-out (FIFO)**

   a. This method assumes that the first goods purchased are the first sold. Thus, ending inventory consists of the latest purchases.

   b. Cost of goods sold includes goods purchased at the beginning of the current period and in prior periods.

   c. Ending inventory is measured at the cost of the latest purchases.

   d. The measurement will be the same regardless of whether the inventory is recorded at the end of the period (a periodic system) or on a perpetual basis.

EXAMPLE

	Units	Times: Price	Equals: Purchases		Inventory Consists of: Units	Per-Unit Cost	Balance
Mar. 31 inventory	1,000	$12.50	$12,500	Beg. layer	1,000	$12.50	$12,500
				Beg. layer	1,000	$12.50	12,500
Apr. 14 purchase	2,000	$12.20	$24,400	Apr. 14 layer	2,000	12.20	24,400
				Inventory bal.	3,000		$36,900
From Mar. 31 layer	(1,000)			Beg. layer	0	$12.50	0
From Apr. 14 layer	(800)			Apr. 14 layer	1,200	12.20	14,640
Apr. 20 sale	(1,800)			Inventory bal.	1,200		$14,640
				Apr. 14 layer	1,200	$12.20	$14,640
Apr. 24 purchase	3,200	$12.60	$40,320	Apr. 24 layer	3,200	12.60	40,320
				Inventory bal.	4,400		$54,960
From Apr. 14 layer	(800)			Apr. 14 layer	400	$12.20	$ 4,880
From Apr. 24 layer	(0)			Apr. 24 layer	3,200	12.60	40,320
Apr. 28 sale	(800)			Inventory bal.	3,600		$45,200
Total available			$77,220				

Cost of goods sold is calculated as follows:

Goods available for sale	$77,220
Minus: ending inventory	(45,200)
Cost of goods sold	**$32,020**

---

   e. **Advantages and Disadvantages of FIFO**

   1) One advantage is that FIFO somewhat approximates the specific identification method's matching of cost flow and physical flow.

      a) A disadvantage for the reporting entity is that it does not have the same potential for manipulation.

   2) Another advantage is that ending inventory approximates current replacement cost.

      a) A disadvantage is that current revenues are matched with older costs.

4. **Last-in, First-out (LIFO)**

   a. **LIFO Fundamentals**

   1) In a time of inflation, this method results in the highest cost of goods sold. LIFO reduces income, defers income tax, and improves cash flow, thereby **reducing net income and tax liability**.

      a) It also defers or avoids the recognition of holding gains or losses arising from specific price changes.

   2) Increasing inventory results in the creation of **LIFO layers**.

EXAMPLE

	Units	Times: Price	Equals: Extended
Year 5 layer	1,600	$74.25	$118,800
Year 4 layer	1,500	59.40	89,100
Year 3 layer	1,350	49.50	66,825
Year 2 layer	1,200	45.00	54,000
Year 1 (base) layer	1,000	40.00	40,000
Year 6 beg. inventory	6,650		$368,725

    a)   Whenever sales exceed purchases, older layers are partially or fully liquidated. Management can manipulate earnings through inventory purchases.

b. **LIFO Perpetual**

    1)   LIFO cost of goods sold may vary with the system chosen.

    2)   In a perpetual system, purchases are directly recorded in the inventory account, and cost of goods sold is determined as the goods are sold.

EXAMPLE

	Units	Times: Price	Equals: Purchases		Units	Per-Unit Cost	Balance
Mar. 31 inventory	1,000	$12.50	$12,500	Beg. layer	1,000	$12.50	$12,500
				Beg. layer	1,000	$12.50	$12,500
Apr. 14 purchase	2,000	$12.20	$24,400	Apr. 14 layer	2,000	12.20	24,400
				Inventory bal.	3,000		$36,900
From Apr. 14 layer	(1,800)			Beg. layer	1,000	$12.50	$12,500
From beg. layer	(0)			Apr. 14 layer	200	12.20	2,440
Apr. 20 sale	(1,800)			Inventory bal.	1,200		$14,940
				Beg. layer	1,000	$12.50	$12,500
				Apr. 14 layer	200	12.20	2,440
Apr. 24 purchase	3,200	$12.60	$40,320	Apr. 24 layer	3,200	12.60	40,320
				Inventory bal.	4,400		$55,260
From Apr. 24 layer	(800)						
From Apr. 14 layer	(0)			Beg. layer	1,000	$12.50	$12,500
From beg. layer	(0)			Apr. 14 layer	200	12.20	2,440
Apr. 28 sale	(800)			Apr. 24 layer	2,400	12.60	30,240
				Inventory bal.	3,600		$45,180
Total available			$77,220				

Cost of goods sold is calculated as follows:

Goods available for sale	$77,220
Minus: ending inventory	(45,180)
Cost of goods sold	**$32,040**

c.   **LIFO Periodic**

1)   In a periodic system, a purchases account is used, and the beginning inventory remains unchanged during the accounting period.

a)   Cost of goods sold is determined only at year end. It equals goods available for sale (beginning inventory + purchases) minus ending inventory.

EXAMPLE

Goods available for sale for the period is calculated.

	Units	Times: Price	Equals: Purchases
Mar. 31 inventory	1,000	$12.50	$12,500
Apr. 14 purchase	2,000	12.20	24,400
Apr. 24 purchase	3,200	12.60	40,320
Total available	6,200		$77,220

The period's unit sales are determined.

Apr. 20 sale	(1,800)
Apr. 28 sale	(800)
Sales for month	(2,600)

Sales are removed from the various layers.

	Units in Layer	Units Sold	End. Units	Per-Unit Cost	Balance
Apr. 24 layer	3,200	(2,600)	600	$12.60	$ 7,560
Apr. 14 layer	2,000	0	2,000	12.20	24,400
Mar. 31 layer	1,000	0	1,000	12.50	12,500
Totals	6,200	(2,600)	3,600		$44,460

Cost of goods sold is calculated as follows:

Goods available for sale	$77,220
Minus: ending inventory	(44,460)
Cost of goods sold	**$32,760**

---

d.   **Initial Adoption**

1)   Unless an entity applies LIFO when it begins operations, initial adoption requires a **change in accounting principle**. With certain exceptions, the new principle is retrospectively applied to all prior periods. Only the direct effects of the change are included in the adjustments. The effects of changes in accounting principle are discussed in Study Unit 4, Subunit 3.

e.   **LIFO Liquidation**

1)   Distortions of net income may result from matching current revenues with older, lower costs. When sales exceed purchases or production, older layers are reduced (a LIFO liquidation).

2)   To offset LIFO liquidation (and simplify the accounting), an entity may treat substantially identical items of inventory as a single accounting unit called a **pool** (explained in item 1. in Subunit 8.5).

    f.   **LIFO Conformity Rule**

        1)   An IRS regulation requires LIFO to be used for financial reporting if it is used in the tax return.

        2)   LIFO must be used to report "income, profit, or loss" in the income statement. It need not be used to report inventory amounts in the balance sheet if a **LIFO valuation allowance** is shown.

        3)   Entities may make supplemental disclosures about net income computed on a basis other than LIFO but not on the income statement.

    g.   **LIFO Valuation Allowance**

        1)   Entities that use a different inventory costing method for internal purposes must convert to LIFO for reporting purposes.

        2)   To adjust the inventory to LIFO, an allowance, sometimes called the **LIFO reserve**, is created. This account is contra to inventory. It is the difference between

            a)   Lower of LIFO cost or market and
            b)   Replacement cost **or** the lower of

                i)   Cost determined under an acceptable method (e.g., FIFO) or
                ii)   Market.

        3)   The accounting profession disapproves of the term "reserve" because no reserve is actually created.

        4)   At period end, this allowance is adjusted to reflect the difference between LIFO and the internal costing method.

Cost of goods sold	$XXX	
Allowance to reduce inventory to LIFO		$XXX

    h.   **LIFO and Interim Reporting**

        1)   Interim accounting ordinarily should be based on the principles used in preparing annual statements.

            a)   Certain principles and practices used for annual reporting, however, may require modification at interim dates so interim reports may relate more closely to the results of operations for the annual period.

        2)   A **temporary LIFO liquidation** need not be given effect in the interim statements.

            a)   The cost of goods sold for the interim period should include the expected cost of replacement of the liquidated base.

            b)   The entry to record cost of goods sold is

Cost of goods sold (replacement cost)	$XXX	
Inventory (liquidated layer)		$XXX
Liability		XXX

                i)   This liability does not appear in the annual statements because, by year end, the true inventory position will be known.

IFRS Difference

    LIFO is not permitted.

Stop and review! You have completed the outline for this subunit. Study multiple-choice questions 9 through 12 beginning on page 288.

8.4 COST FLOW METHODS -- COMPARISON

1. **Varying Results under the Five Methods**

EXAMPLE

	Goods Available for Sale	Ending Inventory	Cost of Goods Sold
Weighted average	$77,220	$(44,837)	$32,383
Moving average	77,220	(45,065)	32,155
FIFO	77,220	(45,200)	32,020
LIFO periodic	77,220	(44,460)	32,760
LIFO perpetual	77,220	(45,180)	32,040

   a. The cost flow model selected should be the one that most clearly reflects periodic income.

2. **FIFO vs. LIFO**

   a. Under LIFO, if fewer units are purchased than sold,

      1) The beginning inventory is partially or fully liquidated,

      2) Old costs are matched against current revenues in the year's income statement, and

      3) LIFO income will usually exceed that for FIFO or average cost (assuming rising prices).

   b. Another consequence is that management can affect net income with an end-of-period purchase that immediately alters cost of goods sold.

      1) A last-minute FIFO purchase included in the ending inventory has no such effect.

Stop and review! You have completed the outline for this subunit. Study multiple-choice questions 13 through 16 beginning on page 290.

8.5 DOLLAR-VALUE LIFO

1. **Pools of Specific Goods**

   a. The previous discussion of LIFO has assumed that the method is applied to specific units of inventory with specific unit costs. However, LIFO may be applied to groups (pools) of inventory items that are substantially identical.

   b. Recordkeeping is simplified because all goods in a beginning inventory pool are presumed to have been acquired on the same date and at the same cost.

      1) Using the pooling method, beginning inventory is costed at a weighted-average unit price (total cost ÷ unit quantity).

      2) Usually, purchases of goods in a pool also are recorded at a weighted-average cost (total cost ÷ unit quantity). If the quantity of units in the pool increases during the year, a new LIFO layer will be formed at the new weighted-average cost.

      3) Because a pool consists of more than one kind of item, erosion of LIFO layers is less likely than if the specific-goods approach is used. An increase in the quantity of one item may offset a decrease of another item.

   c. If an entity discontinues sales of one product and adds another, inventory pools may change if the new product is not substantially identical.

      1) The result may be the liquidation of base layers of inventory.

    d.   Dollar-value LIFO accumulates inventoriable costs of similar (not identical) items. These items should be similar in the sense of

        1)   Being interchangeable,
        2)   Having similar uses,
        3)   Belonging to the same product line, and
        4)   Constituting the raw materials for a given product.

2.   **Deriving a Price Index**

    a.   Under dollar-value LIFO, changes in inventory are measured in terms of dollars of **constant purchasing power** rather than units of physical inventory. This calculation uses a specific price index for each year.

    b.   Selecting an appropriate price index is crucial to dollar-value LIFO accounting.

        1)   An entity may choose to use published indexes. Examples are the Consumer Price Index for All Urban Consumers (CPI-U) and indexes published by trade associations.

        2)   Most often, an index is generated internally for each year.

    c.   The **double-extension method** is the most common technique for internally generating a price index.

        1)   "Extending" inventory is the process of multiplying the quantity of each good on hand by the unit cost to arrive at a total amount for inventory.

        2)   To enable the calculation of price indexes, this operation must be performed twice: once using current-year cost and once using base-year cost.

EXAMPLE

A retailer has the following extended inventory cost data. Note that LIFO liquidation occurred in Year 3.

	At Base-Year Cost	At Current-Year Cost
1/1/Year 1	$250,000	$250,000
Year 1 layer	50,000	50,000
Year 2 layer	40,000	74,000
Year 3 layer	(20,000)	10,000
Year 4 layer	30,000	71,000

---

    d.   A price index can be computed for each year with the following ratio:

$$\text{Price index} = \frac{\text{Ending inventory at current-year cost}}{\text{Ending inventory at base-year cost}}$$

EXAMPLE

The price indexes for computing dollar-value LIFO inventory are calculated as follows:

Year 1 price index = ($250,000 + $50,000) ÷ ($250,000 + 50,000)
                = $300,000 ÷ $300,000
                = 1.00
Year 2 price index = ($250,000 + $50,000 + $74,000) ÷ ($250,000 + $50,000 + $40,000)
                = $374,000 ÷ $340,000
                = 1.10
Year 3 price index = ($250,000 + $50,000 + $74,000 + $10,000) ÷ ($250,000 + $50,000 + $40,000 – $20,000)
                = $384,000 ÷ $320,000
                = 1.20
Year 4 price index = ($250,000 + $50,000 + $74,000 + $10,000 + $71,000) ÷
                   ($250,000 + $50,000 + $40,000 – $20,000 + $30,000)
                = $455,000 ÷ $350,000
                = 1.30

3. **Dollar-Value LIFO Calculations**

    a. To arrive at dollar-value LIFO ending inventory, each layer must be inflated by the relevant price index.

    EXAMPLE

Year 1 Calculation:	At Base-Year Cost		Price Index		At Dollar-Value LIFO Cost
1/1/Year 1	$250,000	×	1.00	=	$250,000
Year 1 layer	50,000	×	1.00	=	50,000
12/31/Year 1	$300,000				$300,000

Year 2 Calculation:	At Base-Year Cost		Price Index		At Dollar-Value LIFO Cost
1/1/Year 1	$250,000	×	1.00	=	$250,000
Year 1 layer	50,000	×	1.00	=	50,000
Year 2 layer	40,000	×	1.10	=	44,000
12/31/Year 2	$340,000				$344,000

    b. In any year when the balance declines, a portion of the most recent year's layer must be removed.

    EXAMPLE

Year 3 Calculation:	At Base-Year Cost		Price Index		At Dollar-Value LIFO Cost
1/1/Year 1	$250,000	×	1.00	=	$250,000
Year 1 layer	50,000	×	1.00	=	50,000
Year 2 layer	40,000	×	1.10	=	44,000
Year 2 liquidation	(20,000)	×	1.10	=	(22,000)
12/31/Year 3	$320,000				$322,000

    c. Once liquidated, layers cannot be replaced.

    EXAMPLE

Year 4 Calculation:	At Base-Year Cost		Price Index		At Dollar-Value LIFO Cost
1/1/Year 1	$250,000	×	1.00	=	$250,000
Year 1 layer	50,000	×	1.00	=	50,000
Year 2 layer	40,000	×	1.10	=	44,000
Year 2 liquidation	(20,000)	×	1.10	=	(22,000)
Year 4 layer	30,000	×	1.30	=	39,000
12/31/Year 4	$350,000				$361,000

4. **Dollar-value LIFO retail** is discussed later in this study unit.

Stop and review! You have completed the outline for this subunit. Study multiple-choice questions 17 through 20 beginning on page 291.

8.6 LOWER OF COST OR MARKET (LCM)

1. **Statement of Rule**

   a. Inventory must be written down to market subsequent to acquisition if its utility is no longer as great as its cost. The difference should be **recognized as a nonreversible loss** of the current period.

      1) Thus, a loss should be recognized whenever **the utility of goods is impaired** by damage, deterioration, obsolescence, changes in price levels, changes in demand, style changes, or other causes.

   b. But the LCM rule is applicable only to goods that will be sold in the ordinary course of business.

      1) Damaged or deteriorated goods are usually carried at net realizable value in a separate account.

2. **Market**

   a. Market is the current cost to replace inventory, subject to certain limitations. Market should not exceed a **ceiling** equal to **net realizable value (NRV)**.

      1) NRV is the estimated selling price in the ordinary course of business minus reasonably predictable costs of completion and disposal.

      2) **Replacement cost** does not accurately measure utility if it exceeds NRV. In that case, the NRV more appropriately measures utility.

         a) Reporting inventory above NRV overstates its utility and will result in a loss at the time of sale.

   b. Market should not be less than a **floor** equal to NRV reduced by an allowance for an approximately **normal profit margin**.

      1) If the inventory were written down to a replacement cost below this amount, an abnormal profit margin (NRV – normal profit – replacement cost) would be included in revenue at the time of sale.

      2) If cost will be recovered with an approximately normal profit upon sale in the ordinary course of business, no loss should be recognized even though replacement or production costs are lower.

   c. Thus, current replacement cost (CRC) is not to be greater than NRV or less than NRV minus a normal profit (NRV – P).

MARKET (M)

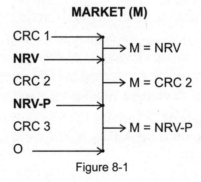

Figure 8-1

EXAMPLE

Replacement cost	$22
Cost	23
Selling price	38
Disposal (selling) costs	4
Normal profit	15

Market is the replacement cost of $22 subject to a ceiling of NRV ($38 selling price – $4 disposal costs = $34) and a floor of NRV minus normal profit ($34 – $15 = $19). Because replacement cost of $22 is within this range ($34 to $19), it equals market. Market is therefore lower than the $23 cost, and LCM is $22.

3. **Applying LCM**

   a. Depending on the nature of the inventory, the LCM rule may be applied either directly to **each item** or to the **total** of the inventory (or, in some cases, to the total of each major category). The method should be the one that most clearly reflects periodic income.

      1) Once inventory is written down, the reduced amount is the **new cost basis**, and a write-up ordinarily will not be permitted if prices increase.

   b. LCM by item always will be equal to or less than the other LCM measurements, and LCM in total always will be equal to or greater than the other LCM measurements.

      1) Most entities use LCM by item. This method is required for **tax purposes**.

         a) If **dollar-value LIFO** is used, LCM should be applied to pools of items.
         b) An entity may not use LCM with LIFO for tax purposes.

EXAMPLE

	Historical Cost	Replacement Cost	NRV	NRV – Normal Profit	Market	LCM
Dowel screws	**$12.45**	$13.60	$14.40	$14.00	$14.00	$12.45
Drywall screws	15.15	12.00	**11.55**	11.35	**11.55**	11.55
Machine screws	16.00	**14.10**	15.00	13.80	**14.10**	14.10
Metal screws	10.30	**8.75**	9.20	8.45	**8.75**	8.75
Wood screws	8.90	**7.85**	8.20	7.65	**7.85**	7.85

4. **Recording LCM**

   a. **Direct reduction.** If inventory is written down to market, the unrealized holding loss can be directly credited to inventory and debited to cost of goods sold.

      1) This method has the theoretical drawback of debiting a holding loss to an account that includes the costs of selling goods.

      2) Also, inventory will be presented at LCM rather than at cost net of write-downs.

   b. **Allowance method.** Debiting a holding loss and crediting an allowance (contra-asset) is preferred.

      1) The unit costs in the subsidiary ledger need not be changed to agree with the control account.

5. **LCM at Interim Dates**

    a. **Nontemporary** market declines are recognized in the interim periods when they occur.

        1) **Recoveries** of these losses on the same inventory later in the fiscal year are recognized as gains (but only to the extent of the previously recognized losses).

        2) If market declines can reasonably be expected to be restored by year end, they are not recognized.

IFRS Difference

Inventories are measured at the lower of cost or net realizable value (NRV). NRV is assessed each period. Accordingly, a write-down may be reversed but not above original cost. The write-down and reversal are recognized in profit or loss.

For an interim period, an inventory loss from a market decline must be recognized even if no loss is reasonably expected for the year.

Stop and review! You have completed the outline for this subunit. Study multiple-choice questions 21 through 24 beginning on page 292.

8.7 SPECIAL TOPICS IN INVENTORY ACCOUNTING

1. **Purchase Commitments**

    a. A commitment to acquire goods in the future is not recorded at the time of the agreement, e.g., by debiting an asset and crediting a liability.

        1) But a **loss** is recognized on a firm, noncancelable, and unhedged purchase commitment if the current market price of the goods is less than the commitment price.

        2) The reason for current loss recognition is the same as that for inventory. A decrease (not an increase) in its future benefits should be recognized when it occurs even if the contract is unperformed on both sides.

        3) Material losses expected on purchase commitments are measured in the same way as inventory losses, recognized, and separately disclosed.

    b. The entry is

Unrealized holding loss -- earnings	$XXX	
Liability -- purchase commitment		$XXX

EXAMPLE

During the year, the Lisbon Company signed a noncancelable contract to purchase 2,000 pounds of a raw material at $64 per pound during the forthcoming year. On December 31, the market price of the raw material is $52 per pound, and the selling price of the finished product is expected to decline accordingly. The financial statements prepared for the year should report a loss of $24,000 in the income statement.

GAAP require recognition in the income statement of a material loss on a purchase commitment as if the inventory were already owned. Losses on firm purchase commitments are measured in the same way as inventory losses. If the cost is $128,000 and the market price is $104,000, a $24,000 loss should be disclosed.

---

    c. When a previously unrecognized firm commitment is designated as a hedged item, an asset or liability is recognized related to the recognition of the gain or loss on the commitment.

2. **Inventory Errors**

 a. These errors may have a material effect on current assets, working capital (current assets – current liabilities), cost of goods sold, net income, and equity. A common error is inappropriate timing of the recognition of transactions.

 b. If a purchase on account is not recorded and the goods are not included in ending inventory, cost of goods sold (BI + purchases – EI) and net income are unaffected. But current assets and current liabilities are understated.

 c. If purchases and beginning inventory are properly recorded but items are excluded from ending inventory, cost of goods sold is overstated. Net income, inventory, retained earnings, working capital, and the current ratio are understated.

 d. If the goods are properly included in ending inventory but the purchase is not recorded, net income is overstated because cost of goods sold is understated. Also, current liabilities are understated and working capital overstated.

 e. Errors arising from recording transactions in the wrong period may reverse in the subsequent period.

 1) If ending inventory is overstated, the overstatement of net income will be offset by the understatement in the following year that results from the overstatement of beginning inventory.

 f. An **overstatement error in year-end inventory** of the current year affects the financial statements of 2 different years.

 1) The **first year's** effects may be depicted as follows:

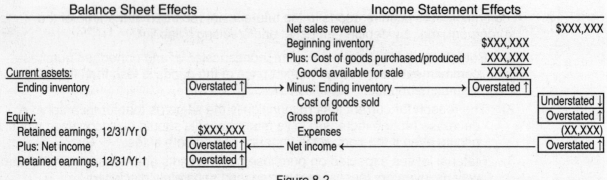

Figure 8-2

 2) At the end of the **second year**, retained earnings is correctly stated:

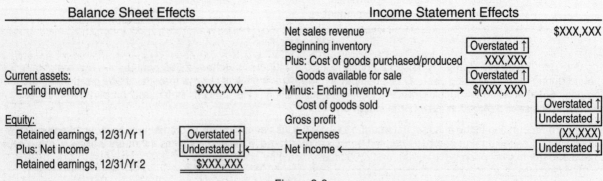

Figure 8-3

Stop and review! You have completed the outline for this subunit. Study multiple-choice questions 25 through 28 beginning on page 294.

8.8 ESTIMATING INVENTORY

1. **Gross Profit Method**

   a. The estimated gross profit method is used to determine inventory for **interim statements**. Adequate disclosure is required of (1) the method used and (2) any significant adjustments that result from reconciliations with the annual physical inventory at year end.

   b. Because of its imprecision, GAAP and federal tax law **do not permit** use of the gross profit method **at year end**. But other applications are possible.

      1) If inventory is destroyed, the method may be used to estimate the loss.
      2) External auditors apply the gross profit method as an analytical procedure to determine the fairness of the ending inventory balance.
      3) The method may be used internally to generate estimates of inventory throughout the year, e.g., as a verification of perpetual records.

   c. The gross profit method calculates ending inventory at a given time by subtracting an estimated cost of goods sold from the sum of beginning inventory and purchases (or cost of goods manufactured).

      1) The estimated cost of goods sold equals sales minus the gross profit.
      2) The gross profit equals sales multiplied by the gross profit percentage, an amount ordinarily computed on a historical basis.

EXAMPLE

Beginning inventory		$60,000
Purchases		20,000
Goods available for sale		$80,000
Sales (at selling price)	$50,000	
Gross profit (20% of sales)	(10,000)	
Sales (at cost)		(40,000)
Approximate inventory at cost		$40,000

---

      3) A simple way to apply this method is to prepare the cost of goods sold section of an income statement and solve algebraically for the amounts not known.

2. **Retail Method**

   a. Some entities, such as major retailers, have a high volume of transactions in relatively low-cost merchandise. They often use the retail method because it is applied to the dollar amounts of goods, not quantities. The result is **easier and less expensive estimates** of ending inventory and cost of goods sold.

   b. Records of the beginning inventory and net purchases are maintained at both cost and retail. Sales at retail and any other appropriate items are subtracted from goods available for sale at retail (the sum of beginning inventory and net purchases at retail) to provide ending inventory at retail.

      1) This amount is adjusted to determine estimated ending inventory at cost using a **cost-retail ratio**.

	Cost	Retail
Beginning inventory (known)	$XX,XXX	$XX,XXX
Add: Purchases (known)	XX,XXX	XX,XXX
Goods available for sale (GAS)	$XX,XXX	$XX,XXX
Sales (at retail)		(XX,XXX)
Ending inventory at retail		$XX,XXX

Cost-retail ratio = GAS at cost ÷ GAS at retail

Ending inventory at cost = Ending inventory at retail × Cost-retail ratio

  c. The following **records** must be available to implement the retail method:

    1) Beginning inventory at cost and retail
    2) Purchases at cost and retail
    3) Markups, markdowns, cancelations, and employee discounts
    4) Other adjustments, such as sales returns and allowances; transportation-in (freight-in); purchase discounts; purchase returns and allowances; and losses on damaged, stolen, obsolete, or deteriorated goods
    5) Sales

  d. **Uses** of the retail inventory method include:

    1) Interim and annual financial reporting in accordance with GAAP
    2) Federal income tax reporting
    3) Verifying year-end inventory and cost of goods sold data, e.g., as an analytical procedure by an independent auditor
    4) Simplifying the physical count at year end

      a) Goods may be marked with sales prices only, and time is saved by not referring to specific purchase records.

    5) Estimating inventory to determine insurance settlements after a casualty

  e. Retail Terminology

    1) Markup: an increase in the original retail price
    2) Net markup: additional markups minus markup cancelations
    3) Markdown: amount subtracted from original retail price
    4) Net markdown: markdowns minus markdown cancelations

3. **Other Factors in Applying the Retail Method**

  a. Transportation-in (freight-in) is an addition to the cost of purchases but does not directly affect the retail measure used in the calculation.

    1) Initial sales prices consider these costs. An addition to the retail measure would therefore overstate goods available at retail.

  b. Purchase allowances are price reductions agreed to by a supplier because goods are nonconforming, e.g., as a result of slight damage incurred in shipment.

    1) Purchase allowances are subtracted from purchases stated at cost but not at retail. The reasons for the allowances ordinarily are considered in setting initial retail prices.

  c. Purchase discounts taken are recognized when purchases are recorded at gross amounts, and early payment is made to take advantage of cash discounts.

    1) These reduce cost of purchases but ordinarily do not affect purchases at retail.

  d. Purchase returns require reductions of the cost and retail measures of purchases. They decrease goods available for sale.

  e. Sales returns and allowances decrease gross sales, which in turn reduce goods available at retail.

  f. Sales discounts offered for early payment ordinarily are not subtracted from gross sales for retail inventory method purposes.

    1) The reason is that sales discounts taken by customers are a financing expense incurred to obtain early payment, not an adjustment of the original markup.

      a) Sales discounts are subtracted from gross sales on the income statement.

g. Employee and special customer discounts are subtracted from goods available for sale at retail after the cost-retail ratio is calculated.

   1) These discounts do not reflect declines in fair value and thus differ from markdowns.

h. Normal shortage (spoilage, breakage, etc.) is anticipated in setting retail prices.

   1) Hence, it is not considered in the calculation of the cost-retail ratio.

   2) However, normal shortage reduces goods available for sale. It is therefore subtracted from the retail measure in the same manner as sales.

i. Abnormal shortage (spoilage, breakage, etc.) is neither a cost of the good units nor anticipated in setting retail prices.

   1) It decreases cost and retail in arriving at goods available for sale. This treatment is justified because

      a) The goods are not available for sale.

      b) The cost-retail ratio will not reflect the normal relationship if the costs and prices of abnormal shortage are included in its computation.

j. Transferred-in goods from other departments are treated as if they were purchases.

4. **FIFO Cost**

a. FIFO cost is the most straightforward of the retail inventory methods.

b. The cost-retail ratio is computed for adjusted purchases, not goods available for sale. Ending inventory is assumed to include only goods from current purchases. Beginning inventory is assumed to be sold first.

   1) To approximate cost, net markups are added to, and net markdowns are subtracted from, purchases at retail to determine the ratio.

   2) Cost-retail ratio: (cost measure of net purchases) ÷ (retail measures of net purchases + net markups – net markdowns).

5. **FIFO to Approximate Lower of Cost or Market**

a. By including net markups but not net markdowns in adjusted purchases at retail, a lower cost-retail ratio is derived. Excluding markdowns results in a greater denominator.

b. Because markdowns reflect a decline in the utility of goods, they should be treated as if they were losses in the current period.

   1) The lower ratio used in the LCM calculation gives a lower inventory cost that effectively includes the loss.

   2) Cost-retail ratio: (cost measure of net purchases) ÷ (retail measures of net purchases + net markups).

6. **Average Cost**

a. This is a straightforward method. The only difference between average cost and FIFO cost is that the cost-retail ratio for average cost is based on goods available for sale (beginning inventory + purchases), not adjusted purchases.

   1) The assumption is that beginning inventory and purchases have been combined and are indistinguishable for purposes of determining cost of goods sold and ending inventory.

   2) Cost-retail ratio: (cost measures of beginning inventory + net purchases) ÷ (retail measures of beginning inventory + net purchases + net markups – net markdowns).

7. **Lower of Average Cost or Market (LACM)**

    a. This is a popular method also known as the conventional retail inventory method.

    b. LACM uses the LCM feature (inclusion of markups but not markdowns in the cost-retail ratio). However, it also achieves the weighted-average effect by including the beginning inventories at cost and retail in the ratio.

        1) Cost-retail ratio: (cost measures of beginning inventory + net purchases) ÷ (retail measures of beginning inventory + net purchases + net markups).

8. **LIFO Retail**

    a. This method is used to obtain tax benefits as well as to match current costs with current revenues. The computation begins in the same way as FIFO cost.

        1) Beginning inventory is excluded from the cost-retail ratio. The current-year ratio is applied only to the layer of inventory added in that year.

            a) However, LIFO retail varies from FIFO cost because a different ratio is used for each annual layer. Thus, only adjusted purchases at cost and retail are used to determine the year's ratio.

            b) LCM may not be used in any of the LIFO retail methods. Net markups and markdowns are considered in computing the ratio.

            c) Cost-retail ratio: (cost measure of net purchases) ÷ (retail measures of net purchases + net markups – net markdowns).

    b. LIFO retail in this form also assumes no adjustment for changes in the unit of measure. The general price level is assumed to be stable, and any increase in the dollar measure of inventory is attributable to an increase in quantity.

9. **Dollar-Value LIFO Retail**

    a. This variant of the retail inventory method is essentially the dollar-value LIFO method with an adjustment from retail to cost. Dollar-value LIFO retail is a cost (not an average-cost or LCM) method.

        1) It excludes beginning inventory from, but includes net markups and markdowns in, the calculation of the cost-retail ratio.

    b. The key feature is that inventory layers are adjusted for changes in price levels to determine whether actual changes in quantities have occurred.

        1) Ending inventory at retail is divided by the current year's price index for restatement at base-date prices.

            a) This computation reveals whether a new layer has been added or old layers have been wholly or partially eliminated.

            b) The index may be a quotient of price indexes. For example, the base-date price index might be 1.25 and the current-date price index 1.50, yielding an index (or conversion factor) of 1.20 (1.50 ÷ 1.25).

        2) Each layer stated at retail in base-date prices is inflated to the price level in effect when it was added. It is multiplied by the price index in effect for that year.

3) The final step is to multiply each layer by the cost-retail ratio for the year it was added, which reduces it to an estimate of cost.

EXAMPLE

	Cost	Retail	Cost Ratio
Beginning inventory	$12,000	$ 16,800	$12,000 ÷ $ 16,800 = 71.43%
Purchases	70,000	100,000	$70,000 ÷ $100,000 = 70%
Sales		90,000	
Ending inventory		$ 26,800	

The beginning price index was 100%. The year-end index is 134%.

The year-end inventory at base-date prices is $20,000 ($26,800 ÷ 1.34).

The increment is $3,200 ($20,000 – $16,800).

Each layer is inflated to the relevant price level, retail prices are converted to cost, and the layers are added.

$16,800 × 1.00 (price index) × 71.43% (cost ratio) = $12,000.24
$3,200 × 1.34 (price index) × 70.00% (cost ratio) = 3,001.60
$15,001.84

COMPARATIVE EXAMPLE

	Cost	Retail
Beginning inventory	$ 90,000	$130,000
Purchases	330,000	460,000
Markups		10,000
Markdowns		40,000
Sales		480,000

Ending inventory at retail is $80,000 ($130,000 + $460,000 + $10,000 – $40,000 – $480,000).

The cost-retail ratio for the **average cost** retail method is $420,000 ÷ $560,000. Markups and markdowns are included in goods available at retail.

The cost-retail ratio for the **FIFO cost** retail method is $330,000 ÷ $430,000. The assumptions are that (1) all markups and markdowns applied to goods purchased this period and (2) all inventory is from current-period purchases.

The cost-retail ratio for the **LACM** retail method is $420,000 ÷ $600,000. Markups, but not markdowns, are included in goods available at retail. This method is typically used if LIFO is not used.

The cost-retail ratio for the **LIFO** retail method (given stable prices) is $90,000 ÷ $130,000 (the prior year's ratio) because ending inventory of $80,000 retail is less than beginning inventory of $130,000. If an increase in inventory had occurred, the increment would be measured using a cost-retail ratio of $330,000 ÷ $430,000.

Stop and review! You have completed the outline for this subunit. Study multiple-choice questions 29 through 32 beginning on page 295.

QUESTIONS

8.1 Inventory Fundamentals

1. In a periodic inventory system that uses the weighted-average cost flow method, the beginning inventory is the

A. Net purchases minus the ending inventory.

B. Net purchases minus the cost of goods sold.

C. Total goods available for sale minus the net purchases.

D. Total goods available for sale minus the cost of goods sold.

Answer (C) is correct.
 REQUIRED: The beginning inventory in a periodic system using weighted average cost.
 DISCUSSION: In a periodic inventory system, the beginning inventory is equal to the total goods available for sale minus the net purchases, regardless of the cost flow method used.
 Answer (A) is incorrect. It states the difference between the beginning inventory and the cost of goods sold. Answer (B) is incorrect. This difference is the change in inventory valuation during the period. Answer (D) is incorrect. Goods available minus cost of sales equals ending inventory.

2. Herc Co.'s inventory at December 31, Year 1, was $1.5 million based on a physical count priced at cost, and before any necessary adjustment for the following:

- Merchandise costing $90,000 was shipped FOB shipping point from a vendor on December 30, Year 1, and was received and recorded on January 5, Year 2.
- Goods in the shipping area were excluded from inventory although shipment was not made until January 4, Year 2. The goods, billed to the customer FOB shipping point on December 30, Year 1, had a cost of $120,000.

What amount should Herc report as inventory in its December 31, Year 1, balance sheet?

A. $1,500,000

B. $1,590,000

C. $1,620,000

D. $1,710,000

Answer (D) is correct.
REQUIRED: The year-end inventory.
DISCUSSION: The inventory balance prior to adjustments was $1.5 million. The merchandise shipped FOB shipping point to Herc should be included because title passed when the goods were shipped. The goods in the shipping area should be included because title did not pass until the goods were shipped in Year 2. Thus, inventory reported at December 31, Year 1, should be $1,710,000 ($1,500,000 + $90,000 + $120,000).
Answer (A) is incorrect. The amount of $1,500,000 excludes the $90,000 of goods shipped by a vendor and the $120,000 of goods not shipped until January 4. Answer (B) is incorrect. The amount of $1,590,000 results from failing to include the $120,000 of goods not shipped until January 4. Answer (C) is incorrect. The amount of $1,620,000 does not include the $90,000 of goods shipped by a vendor FOB shipping point.

3. How should the following costs affect a retailer's inventory?

	Freight-in	Interest on Inventory Loan
A.	Increase	No Effect
B.	Increase	Increase
C.	No effect	Increase
D.	No effect	No effect

Answer (A) is correct.
REQUIRED: The effect of certain costs on inventory.
DISCUSSION: Cost is "the sum of the applicable expenditures and charges directly or indirectly incurred in bringing an article to its existing condition and location." Freight costs are therefore an inventoriable cost to the extent they are not abnormal. However, interest cost for inventories is not capitalized. Interest cost is capitalized only for assets produced for an enterprise's own use or for sale or lease as discrete projects.

4. The following information applied to Fenn, Inc., for the year just ended:

Merchandise purchased for resale	$400,000
Freight-in	10,000
Freight-out	5,000
Purchase returns	2,000

Fenn's inventoriable cost for the year was

A. $400,000

B. $403,000

C. $408,000

D. $413,000

Answer (C) is correct.
REQUIRED: The amount of inventoriable cost for the year.
DISCUSSION: Inventoriable cost is the sum of the applicable expenditures and charges directly or indirectly incurred in bringing all items of inventory to their existing condition and location. Thus, inventoriable cost includes the $400,000 cost of the merchandise purchased, plus the $10,000 of freight-in, minus the $2,000 of purchase returns. Freight-out is not a cost incurred in bringing the inventory to a salable condition. Consequently, the inventoriable cost for Fenn was $408,000 ($400,000 + $10,000 – $2,000). NOTE: The assumption is that purchases, freight-in, etc., are tracked in separate accounts.
Answer (A) is incorrect. The amount of $400,000 excludes freight-in and purchase returns. Answer (B) is incorrect. The amount of $403,000 excludes freight-in. Answer (D) is incorrect. The amount of $413,000 includes freight-out.

8.2 Consignment Accounting

5. Shipping costs incurred by a consignor on transfer of goods to a consignee should be considered as

    A. Expense to the consignee.

    B. Expense to the consignor.

    C. Inventory cost to the consignee.

    D. Inventory cost to the consignor.

Answer (D) is correct.
    REQUIRED: The nature of shipping costs incurred in the transfer of goods from a consignor to a consignee.
    DISCUSSION: Inventoriable costs include all costs of making the inventory ready for sale. Costs incurred by a consignor on the transfer of goods to a consignee are costs necessary to prepare the inventory for sale. Consequently, they are inventoriable. Because goods on consignment remain in the inventory of the consignor, the shipping costs should be debited to consignment-out (the account in which the consignor records consignment-related transactions).

6. The following items were included in Opal Co.'s inventory account at December 31:

Merchandise out on consignment, at sales price, including 40% markup on selling price	$40,000
Goods purchased, in transit, shipped FOB shipping point	36,000
Goods held on consignment by Opal	27,000

By what amount should Opal's inventory balance at December 31 be reduced?

    A. $103,000

    B. $67,000

    C. $51,000

    D. $43,000

Answer (D) is correct.
    REQUIRED: The recognition of inventory for consignment sales and goods in transit.
    DISCUSSION: Consigned goods are in the possession of the consignee but remain the property of the consignor and are included in the consignor's inventory count at cost, not selling price. Thus, Opal should reduce inventory by $16,000 ($40,000 selling price × 40%). Opal should also reduce inventory by $27,000 for the goods held on consignment. The goods in transit are properly included in inventory because title and risk of loss pass to the buyer at the shipping point when the shipping term is FOB shipping point. Consequently, inventory should be reduced by a total of $43,000 ($16,000 + $27,000).
    Answer (A) is incorrect. The cost of goods on consignment and the cost of the goods in transit are included in inventory. Answer (B) is incorrect. The cost of goods on consignment is included in inventory. Answer (C) is incorrect. The amount of $51,000 is the result of deducting the cost, not the markup, of the goods on consignment.

7. On October 20, Grimm Co. consigned 40 freezers to Holden Co. for sale at $1,000 each and paid $800 in transportation costs. On December 30, Holden reported the sale of 10 freezers and remitted $8,500. The remittance was net of the agreed 15% commission. What amount should Grimm recognize as consignment sales revenue for the year?

    A. $7,700

    B. $8,500

    C. $9,800

    D. $10,000

Answer (D) is correct.
    REQUIRED: The amount of consignment sales revenue to be recognized.
    DISCUSSION: Under a consignment sales agreement, the consignor ships merchandise to the consignee, who acts as agent for the consignor in selling the goods. The goods are in the physical possession of the consignee but remain the property of the consignor and are included in the consignor's inventory account. Accordingly, sales revenue from these consigned goods should be recognized by the consignor when the merchandise is sold (delivered to the ultimate customer). Grimm should recognize sales revenue of $10,000 ($1,000 sales price × 10 units). Transportation costs and commissions are consignor inventory costs and selling expenses, respectively, and are not used to compute sales revenue.
    Answer (A) is incorrect. The amount of $7,700 is the amount received from the consignee minus $800 of transportation costs. Answer (B) is incorrect. The amount of $8,500 is the amount received from the consignee. Answer (C) is incorrect. The amount of $9,800 equals the sales price of 10 freezers minus 25% (10 ÷ 40) of the transportation costs.

8. Lia Co.'s December 31 balance sheet reported the following current assets:

Cash	$ 35,000
Accounts receivable	60,000
Inventories	30,000
Total	$125,000

An analysis of the accounts disclosed that accounts receivable comprised the following:

Trade accounts	$48,000
Allowance for uncollectible accounts	(1,000)
Selling price of Lia's unsold goods sent to Jax Co. on consignment at 130% of cost and **not** included in Lia's ending inventory	13,000
Total	$60,000

At December 31, the correct total of Lia's current assets is

A. $112,000

B. $115,000

C. $122,000

D. $135,000

Answer (C) is correct.

REQUIRED: The correct total of current assets.

DISCUSSION: Under a consignment sales agreement, the consignor ships merchandise to the consignee, who acts as agent for the consignor in selling the goods. The goods are in the physical possession of the consignee but remain the property of the consignor and are included in the consignor's inventory account. Accordingly, sales revenue from these consigned goods should be recognized by the consignor when the merchandise is sold (delivered to the ultimate customer). Thus, the unsold consigned goods should be included in inventory at cost ($13,000 ÷ 130% = $10,000), not in receivables at their sales price. Current assets should therefore be $122,000 ($35,000 cash + $47,000 net receivables + $40,000 inventory).

Answer (A) is incorrect. This figure omits the sales price of the consigned goods. Answer (B) is incorrect. This figure results from subtracting the cost of the consigned goods. Answer (D) is incorrect. This figure results from adding the cost of the consigned goods.

8.3 Cost Flow Methods -- Application

Questions 9 and 10 are based on the following information. During January, Metro Co., which maintains a perpetual inventory system, recorded the following information pertaining to its inventory:

	Units	Unit Cost	Total Cost	Units On Hand
Balance on 1/1	1,000	$1	$1,000	1,000
Purchased on 1/7	600	3	1,800	1,600
Sold on 1/20	900			700
Purchased on 1/25	400	5	2,000	1,100

9. Under the moving-average method, what amount should Metro report as inventory at January 31?

A. $2,640

B. $3,225

C. $3,300

D. $3,900

Answer (B) is correct.

REQUIRED: The ending inventory using the moving-average method.

DISCUSSION: The moving-average system is only applicable to perpetual inventories. It requires that a new weighted average be computed after every purchase. This moving average is based on remaining inventory held and the new inventory purchased. Based on the calculations below, the moving-average cost per unit for the 1/20 sale is $1.75, and the cost of goods sold (COGS) for January is $1,575 (900 units sold × $1.75). Thus, ending inventory is $3,225 ($1,000 beginning balance + $1,800 purchase on 1/7 – $1,575 COGS on 1/20 + $2,000 purchase on 1/25).

	Units	Moving-Average Cost/Unit	Total Cost
Balance 1/1	1,000	$1.00	$1,000
Purchase 1/7	600	3.00	1,800
	1,600	$1.75	$2,800

Answer (A) is incorrect. The amount of $2,640 is based on the weighted-average method. Answer (C) is incorrect. The amount of $3,300 is based on a cost of $3 being assigned to each unit in ending inventory. Answer (D) is incorrect. The amount of $3,900 is based on the FIFO method.

10. Under the LIFO method, what amount should Metro report as inventory at January 31?

A. $1,300

B. $2,700

C. $3,900

D. $4,100

Answer (B) is correct.

REQUIRED: The value of ending inventory using a perpetual LIFO system.

DISCUSSION: In a perpetual inventory system, purchases are directly recorded in the inventory account, and cost of goods sold (COGS) is determined as the goods are sold. Under LIFO, the latest goods purchased are assumed to be the first to be sold. Using LIFO perpetual, 600 of the 900 units sold on 1/20 are assumed to have come from the last purchase. Their cost was $1,800 (600 × $3). The remaining 300 came from the beginning balance at a cost of $300 (300 × $1). Hence, the total COGS for January was $2,100, and ending inventory must equal $2,700 ($1,000 beginning inventory + $1,800 purchase on 1/7 + $2,000 purchase on 1/25 – $2,100 COGS).

Answer (A) is incorrect. The amount of $1,300 is based on the periodic LIFO method. Answer (C) is incorrect. The amount of $3,900 is based on the periodic FIFO method. Answer (D) is incorrect. The amount of $4,100 is based on an ending inventory of 400 units at $5 per unit and 700 units at $3 per unit.

11. Trans Co. uses a periodic inventory system. The following are inventory transactions for the month of January:

1/1	Beginning inventory	10,000 units at $3
1/5	Purchase	5,000 units at $4
1/15	Purchase	5,000 units at $5
1/20	Sales at $10 per unit	10,000 units

Trans uses the average pricing method to determine the value of its inventory. What amount should Trans report as cost of goods sold on its income statement for the month of January?

A. $30,000

B. $37,500

C. $40,000

D. $100,000

Answer (B) is correct.

REQUIRED: The cost of goods sold using the average pricing method.

DISCUSSION: The total cost of beginning inventory and purchases is $75,000 ($30,000 + $20,000 + $25,000), and the total number units of beginning inventory and purchases is 20,000. The average price of the beginning inventory and purchases is $3.75 ($75,000 cost ÷ 20,000 units). The total cost of goods sold equals $37,500 (10,000 units sold × $3.75).

Answer (A) is incorrect. The amount of $30,000 is based on FIFO (10,000 units in beginning inventory × $3). Answer (C) is incorrect. The amount of $40,000 is based on the January 5 price. Answer (D) is incorrect. The amount of $100,000 is based on the selling price of the 10,000 units.

12. Drew Co. uses the average cost inventory method for internal reporting purposes and LIFO for financial statement and income tax reporting. At December 31, the inventory was $375,000 using average cost and $320,000 using LIFO. The unadjusted credit balance in the LIFO reserve account on December 31 was $35,000. What adjusting entry should Drew record to adjust from average cost to LIFO at December 31?

		Debit	Credit
A.	Cost of goods sold	$55,000	
	Inventory		$55,000
B.	Cost of goods sold	$55,000	
	LIFO reserve		$55,000
C.	Cost of goods sold	$20,000	
	Inventory		$20,000
D.	Cost of goods sold	$20,000	
	LIFO reserve		$20,000

Answer (D) is correct.

REQUIRED: The journal entry to adjust from average cost to LIFO.

DISCUSSION: The LIFO reserve account is an allowance that adjusts the inventory balance stated according to the method used for internal reporting purposes to the LIFO amount appropriate for external reporting. If the LIFO effect is $55,000 ($375,000 average cost – $320,000 LIFO cost) and the account has a $35,000 credit balance, it must be credited for $20,000, with a corresponding debit to cost of goods sold.

Answer (A) is incorrect. The balance in the reserve account should equal $55,000, and inventory should not be adjusted. Answer (B) is incorrect. The balance in the reserve account should be $55,000. Answer (C) is incorrect. Inventory should not be adjusted.

8.4 Cost Flow Methods -- Comparison

13. The UNO Company was formed on January 2, Year 1, to sell a single product. Over a 2-year period, UNO's costs increased steadily. Inventory quantities equaled 3 months' sales at December 31, Year 1, and zero at December 31, Year 2. Assuming the periodic system and no accounting changes, the inventory cost method that reports the highest amount for each of the following is

	Inventory 12/31/Year 1	Cost of Sales Year 2
A.	LIFO	FIFO
B.	LIFO	LIFO
C.	FIFO	FIFO
D.	FIFO	LIFO

Answer (C) is correct.
REQUIRED: The method resulting in the highest beginning inventory and cost of sales given zero ending inventory.
DISCUSSION: In a period of rising prices, FIFO inventory will be higher than LIFO inventory. FIFO assumes that the latest and therefore the highest priced goods purchased are in inventory, whereas LIFO assumes that these goods were the first to be sold. Accordingly, the inventory valuation at December 31, Year 1 (beginning inventory for Year 2), would be higher for FIFO than LIFO. Given zero inventory at December 31, Year 2, the units sold in Year 2 must have equaled the sum of Year 2 purchases and beginning inventory. Because beginning inventory for Year 2 would be reported at a higher amount under FIFO than LIFO, the result is a higher cost of goods sold under FIFO.

14. Generally, which inventory costing method most closely approximates the current cost for each of the following?

	Cost of Goods Sold	Ending Inventory
A.	LIFO	FIFO
B.	LIFO	LIFO
C.	FIFO	FIFO
D.	FIFO	LIFO

Answer (A) is correct.
REQUIRED: The appropriate inventory costing method.
DISCUSSION: The LIFO basis assumes that the most recently purchased items are the first to be sold. Thus, LIFO is a better approximation of current cost of goods sold than FIFO. Assuming that turnover is rapid and material amounts of depreciation are not allocated to inventory, LIFO cost of goods sold may be an acceptable alternative to cost of goods sold measured at current cost. However, the effect of any LIFO inventory liquidations (decreases in earlier years' LIFO layers) must be excluded. Nevertheless, the FIFO basis more closely approximates the current cost of ending inventory because it assumes the most recent purchases are the last to be sold.

15. Which of the following is **not** valid as it applies to inventory costing methods?

A. If inventory quantities are to be maintained, part of the earnings must be invested (plowed back) in inventories when FIFO is used during a period of rising prices.

B. LIFO tends to smooth out the net income pattern since it matches current cost of goods sold with current revenue when inventories remain at constant quantities.

C. When a firm using the LIFO method fails to maintain its usual inventory position (reduces stock on hand below customary levels), there may be a matching of old costs with current revenue.

D. The use of FIFO permits some control by management over the amount of net income for a period through controlled purchases, which is **not** true with LIFO.

Answer (D) is correct.
REQUIRED: The invalid statement concerning inventory valuation.
DISCUSSION: Under LIFO, the most recent purchases are included in cost of goods sold. Management could affect net income with an end-of-period purchase that would immediately alter cost of goods sold. A last-minute FIFO purchase included in the ending inventory would have no such effect.
Answer (A) is incorrect. Maintenance of inventory quantities results in an increased dollar investment in inventory when FIFO is used during inflationary times. Answer (B) is incorrect. LIFO smooths income in a period of rising prices. The inflated current costs are matched with current sales prices. Answer (C) is incorrect. LIFO results in matching old, lower costs with current revenues when inventory is liquidated. If sales exceed purchases, a firm liquidates earlier, lower-priced LIFO layers.

16. The Hastings Company began operations on January 1 of the year before last and uses the FIFO method in costing its raw material inventory. Management is contemplating a change to the LIFO method and is interested in determining what effect such a change will have on net income. Accordingly, the following information has been developed:

Final Inventory	Year 1	Year 2
FIFO	$240,000	$270,000
LIFO	200,000	210,000
Net income per FIFO	$120,000	$170,000

Based upon the above information, a change to the LIFO method in Year 2 results in net income for Year 2 of

- A. $110,000
- B. $150,000
- C. $170,000
- D. $230,000

Answer (B) is correct.

REQUIRED: The second-year net income after a change from FIFO to LIFO in the second year of operations.

DISCUSSION: A change in accounting principle requires retrospective application. All periods reported must be individually adjusted for the period specific effects of applying the new principle. The difference in income in the second year is equal to the $20,000 difference between the FIFO inventory change and the LIFO inventory change (FIFO: $270,000 – $240,000 = $30,000 change; LIFO: $210,000 – $200,000 = $10,000 change; $30,000 – $10,000 = $20,000 difference). The $170,000 FIFO net income will decrease by $20,000. Net LIFO income will therefore be $150,000 ($170,000 – $20,000).

Answer (A) is incorrect. The amount of $110,000 incorrectly subtracts the difference from Year 1 from the net income under LIFO for Year 2. Answer (C) is incorrect. The amount of $170,000 is the income for Year 2 under FIFO. Answer (D) is incorrect. The amount of $230,000 incorrectly adds the cumulative difference between LIFO and FIFO to FIFO net income instead of subtracting the difference from FIFO net income.

8.5 Dollar-Value LIFO

17. Estimates of price-level changes for specific inventories are required for which of the following inventory methods?

- A. Conventional retail.
- B. Dollar-value LIFO.
- C. Weighted-average cost.
- D. Average cost retail.

Answer (B) is correct.

REQUIRED: The inventory method for which estimates of price-level changes for specific inventories are required.

DISCUSSION: Dollar-value LIFO accumulates inventoriable costs of similar (not identical) items. These items should be similar in the sense of being interchangeable, having similar uses, belonging to the same product line, or constituting the raw materials for a given product. Dollar value LIFO determines changes in ending inventory in terms of dollars of constant purchasing power rather than units of physical inventory. This calculation uses a specific price index for each year.

Answer (A) is incorrect. The conventional retail method calculates ending inventory at retail and then adjusts it to cost by applying a cost-retail ratio. Answer (C) is incorrect. The weighted-average method determines an average cost that is not adjusted for general price-level changes. Answer (D) is incorrect. The average cost retail method calculates ending inventory at retail and then adjusts it to cost by applying a cost-retail ratio.

18. Bach Co. adopted the dollar-value LIFO inventory method as of January 1, Year 4. A single inventory pool and an internally computed price index are used to compute Bach's LIFO inventory layers. Information about Bach's dollar-value inventory follows:

Date	Inventory: At Base-Year Cost	At Current-Year Cost
1/1/Year 4	$90,000	$90,000
Year 4 layer	20,000	30,000
Year 5 layer	40,000	80,000

What was the price index used to compute Bach's Year 5 dollar-value LIFO inventory layer?

- A. 1.09
- B. 1.25
- C. 1.33
- D. 2.00

Answer (C) is correct.

REQUIRED: The price index used to compute the current year dollar-value LIFO inventory layer.

DISCUSSION: To compute the ending inventory under dollar-value LIFO, the ending inventory stated in year-end or current-year cost must be restated at base-year cost. The layers at base-year cost are computed using a LIFO flow assumption and then weighted (multiplied) by the relevant indexes to price the ending inventory. A price index for the current year may be calculated by dividing the ending inventory at current-year cost by the ending inventory at base-year cost. This index is then applied to the current-year inventory layer stated at base-year cost. Thus, the Year 5 index (rounded) is 1.33 {[($90,000 + $30,000 + $80,000) EI at current-year cost] ÷ [($90,000 + $20,000 + $40,000) EI at base-year cost]}.

Answer (A) is incorrect. This figure is the price index for Year 4. Answer (B) is incorrect. This figure is calculated by dividing the difference in the current-year cost of inventory layers for Year 4 and Year 5 by the Year 5 base-year cost. Answer (D) is incorrect. This figure equals the current year cost of the Year 5 layer divided by its base-year.

19. Walt Co. adopted the dollar-value LIFO inventory method as of January 1, when its inventory was valued at $500,000. Walt's entire inventory constitutes a single pool. Using a relevant price index of 1.10, Walt determined that its December 31 inventory was $577,500 at current-year cost and $525,000 at base-year cost. What was Walt's dollar-value LIFO inventory at December 31?

A. $525,000

B. $527,500

C. $552,500

D. $577,500

Answer (B) is correct.

REQUIRED: The dollar-value LIFO inventory cost reported in the balance sheet.

DISCUSSION: A price index for the current year may be calculated by dividing the ending inventory at current-year cost by the ending inventory at base-year cost. This index is then applied to the current-year inventory layer stated at base-year cost. Consequently, the index is 1.10 ($577,500 ÷ $525,000), and the dollar-value LIFO cost at December 31 is $527,500 {$500,000 base layer + [($525,000 − $500,000) × 1.10]}.

Answer (A) is incorrect. The base-year cost is $525,000. Answer (C) is incorrect. The amount of $552,500 results from using $525,000 as the base layer. Answer (D) is incorrect. The amount of $577,500 is the year-end inventory at current cost.

20. On January 1, Year 7, Poe Company adopted the dollar-value LIFO inventory method. Poe's entire inventory constitutes a single pool. Inventory data for Year 7 and Year 8 are as follows:

Date	Inventory at Current-Year Cost	Inventory at Base-Year Cost	Relevant Price Index
01/01/Yr 7	$150,000	$150,000	1.00
12/31/Yr 7	220,000	200,000	1.10
12/31/Yr 8	276,000	230,000	1.20

Poe's dollar-value LIFO inventory at December 31, Year 8, is

A. $230,000

B. $236,000

C. $241,000

D. $246,000

Answer (C) is correct.

REQUIRED: The ending inventory under the dollar-value LIFO method.

DISCUSSION: By using price indexes, dollar-value LIFO implements LIFO without the necessity of monitoring the prices of individual items. To compute the ending inventory under dollar-value LIFO, the ending inventory stated in year-end or current-year cost must be restated at base-year cost. The layers at base-year cost are computed using a LIFO flow assumption and then weighted (multiplied) by the relevant indexes to price the ending inventory. The inventory at the end of Year 8 in base-year cost is $230,000. This inventory is composed of a $150,000 base layer, a $50,000 ($200,000 − $150,000) Year 7 layer, and a $30,000 ($230,000 − $200,000) Year 8 layer. Each of these layers, as indicated below, is multiplied by the relevant price index to translate from base-year cost to the price in effect when the layer was added. The result is a December 31, Year 8, inventory value of $241,000.

Base layer	$150,000	×	1.0	=	$150,000
Year 7 layer	50,000	×	1.1	=	55,000
Year 8 layer	30,000	×	1.2	=	36,000
	$230,000				$241,000

Answer (A) is incorrect. The inventory at base-year cost is $230,000. Answer (B) is incorrect. The amount of $236,000 does not correctly restate the Year 7 layer. Answer (D) is incorrect. The amount of $246,000 assumes an $80,000 layer was added in Year 8 and none in Year 7.

8.6 Lower of Cost or Market (LCM)

21. Which of the following statements are correct when a company applying the lower-of-cost-or-market method reports its inventory at replacement cost?

I. The original cost is less than replacement cost.

II. The net realizable value is greater than replacement cost.

A. I only.

B. II only.

C. Both I and II.

D. Neither I nor II.

Answer (B) is correct.

REQUIRED: The measure(s) of inventory under the lower-of-cost-or-market rule.

DISCUSSION: Market equals current replacement cost subject to a maximum and a minimum. The maximum is net realizable value, and the minimum is net realizable value minus normal profit. When replacement cost is within this range, it is used as market. Consequently, only statement II is correct.

22. Based on a physical inventory taken on December 31, Chewy Co. determined its chocolate inventory on a FIFO basis at $26,000 with a replacement cost of $20,000. Chewy estimated that, after further processing costs of $12,000, the chocolate could be sold as finished candy bars for $40,000. Chewy's normal profit margin is 10% of sales. Under the lower-of-cost-or-market rule, what amount should Chewy report as chocolate inventory in its December 31 balance sheet?

A. $28,000

B. $26,000

C. $24,000

D. $20,000

Answer (C) is correct.
REQUIRED: The LCM value of inventory.
DISCUSSION: Market equals current replacement cost subject to maximum and minimum values. The maximum is NRV, and the minimum is NRV minus normal profit. When replacement cost is within this range, it is used as market. Cost is given as $26,000. NRV is $28,000 ($40,000 selling price – $12,000 additional processing costs), and NRV minus a normal profit equals $24,000 [$28,000 – ($40,000 × 10%)]. Because the lowest amount in the range ($24,000) exceeds replacement cost ($20,000), it is used as market. Because market value ($24,000) is less than cost ($26,000), it is also the inventory amount.
Answer (A) is incorrect. The NRV is $28,000. Answer (B) is incorrect. The cost is $26,000. Answer (D) is incorrect. The replacement cost is $20,000.

23. The lower-of-cost-or-market rule for inventories may be applied to total inventory, to groups of similar items, or to each item. Which application generally results in the lowest inventory amount?

A. All applications result in the same amount.

B. Total inventory.

C. Groups of similar items.

D. Separately to each item.

Answer (D) is correct.
REQUIRED: The application of the LCM rule that usually results in the lowest amount.
DISCUSSION: Applying the LCM rule to each item of inventory produces the lowest amount for each item and therefore the lowest and most conservative measurement for the total inventory. The reason is that aggregating items results in the inclusion of some items at amounts greater than LCM. For example, if item A (cost $2, market $1) and item B (cost $3, market $4) are aggregated for LCM purposes, the inventory measurement is $5. If the rule is applied separately to A and B, the LCM measurement is $4.

24. Rose Co. sells one product and uses the last-in, first-out method to determine inventory cost. Information for the month of January follows:

	Total Units	Unit Cost
Beginning inventory, 1/1	8,000	$8.20
Purchases, 1/5	12,000	7.90
Sales	10,000	

Rose has determined that at January 31, the replacement cost of its inventory was $8 per unit, and the net realizable value was $8.80 per unit. Rose's normal profit margin is $1 per unit. Rose applies the lower-of-cost-or-market rule to total inventory and records any resulting loss. At January 31, what should be the net carrying amount of Rose's inventory?

A. $79,000

B. $78,000

C. $80,000

D. $81,400

Answer (C) is correct.
REQUIRED: The net carrying amount of LIFO-based inventory.
DISCUSSION: Subject to certain restrictions, inventory is valued at the lower of cost or market. Because Rose uses the LIFO method to determine inventory cost, the 10,000 units sold are treated as coming from the purchases made on 1/5. Thus, 2,000 units remain from the purchase, and 8,000 units remain from beginning inventory. The average cost of the remaining 10,000 units is $8.14 {[(8,000 × $8.20) + (2,000 × $7.90)] ÷ 10,000}. The replacement cost of $8, which exceeds NRV minus a normal profit ($8.80 – $1.00 = $7.80) but is lower than NRV ($8.80), is lower than the average cost of $8.14. Consequently, ending inventory on a LIFO-LCM basis is $80,000 (10,000 units × $8 replacement cost).
Answer (A) is incorrect. The FIFO-LCM amount is $79,000. Answer (B) is incorrect. The amount of $78,000 equals 10,000 units times $7.80 (NRV – a normal profit). Answer (D) is incorrect. The amount of $81,400 is based on the assumption that average unit cost is below the unit replacement cost.

8.7 Special Topics in Inventory Accounting

25. On January 1, Year 4, Card Corp. signed a 3-year, noncancelable purchase contract that allows Card to purchase up to 500,000 units of a computer part annually from Hart Supply Co. The price is $.10 per unit, and the contract guarantees a minimum annual purchase of 100,000 units. During Year 4, the part unexpectedly became obsolete. Card had 250,000 units of this inventory at December 31, Year 4, and believes these parts can be sold as scrap for $.02 per unit. What amount of probable loss from the purchase commitment should Card report in its Year 4 income statement?

    A. $24,000

    B. $20,000

    C. $16,000

    D. $8,000

Answer (C) is correct.
    REQUIRED: The amount of probable loss from the purchase commitment.
    DISCUSSION: The entity must accrue a loss in the current year on goods subject to a firm purchase commitment if their market price declines below the commitment price. This loss should be measured in the same manner as inventory losses. Disclosure of the loss is also required. Consequently, given that 200,000 units must be purchased over the next 2 years for $20,000 (200,000 × $.10), and the parts can be sold as scrap for $4,000 (200,000 × $.02), the amount of probable loss for Year 4 is $16,000 ($20,000 – $4,000).
    Answer (A) is incorrect. The amount of $24,000 includes the purchase commitment for the current year. Answer (B) is incorrect. The amount of $20,000 excludes the net realizable value of the parts from the calculation. Answer (D) is incorrect. The amount of $8,000 excludes the probable loss expected in the last year of the purchase commitment.

26. During Year 4, R Corp., a manufacturer of chocolate candies, contracted to purchase 100,000 pounds of cocoa beans at $1.00 per pound, with delivery to be made in the spring of Year 5. Because a record harvest is predicted for Year 5, the price per pound for cocoa beans had fallen to $.80 by December 31, Year 4. Of the following journal entries, the one that would properly reflect in Year 4 the effect of the commitment of R Corp. to purchase the 100,000 pounds of cocoa is

    A.
| Cocoa inventory | $100,000 | |
| Accounts payable | | $100,000 |

    B.
Cocoa inventory	$80,000	
Loss on purchase commitments	$20,000	
Accounts payable		$100,000

    C.
| Loss on purchase commitments | $20,000 | |
| Accrued loss on purchase commitments | | $20,000 |

    D. No entry is necessary in Year 4.

Answer (C) is correct.
    REQUIRED: The journal entries to reflect the purchase commitment.
    DISCUSSION: Recognition of the loss in the income statement and accrual of a liability in Year 4 are required (assuming the purchase commitment is noncancelable). The loss on purchase commitments is an expense. Accrued loss on purchase commitments is a liability.
    Answer (A) is incorrect. The entry does not recognize a loss and improperly records an asset. Answer (B) is incorrect. The entry prematurely records the cocoa as an asset prior to acquisition. The loss on purchase commitments is an expense account. Answer (D) is incorrect. An entry is needed to recognize the loss.

27. Bren Co.'s beginning inventory at January 1 was understated by $26,000, and its ending inventory was overstated by $52,000. As a result, Bren's cost of goods sold for the year was

    A. Understated by $26,000.

    B. Overstated by $26,000.

    C. Understated by $78,000.

    D. Overstated by $78,000.

Answer (C) is correct.
    REQUIRED: The misstatement of cost of goods sold.
    DISCUSSION: When beginning inventory is understated, cost of goods sold will be understated. When ending inventory is overstated, cost of goods sold will be understated. Thus, Bren Co.'s cost of goods sold is understated by $78,000 ($26,000 + $52,000).
    Answer (A) is incorrect. The overstatement of ending inventory also understates cost of goods sold. Answer (B) is incorrect. COGS was understated in the current year by the amounts of both the beginning inventory error and the ending inventory error. Answer (D) is incorrect. Both errors understate cost of goods sold.

28. On December 30, Year 1, Astor Corp. sold merchandise for $75,000 to Day Co. The terms of the sale were net 30, FOB shipping point. The merchandise was shipped on December 31, Year 1, and arrived at Day on January 5, Year 2. Due to a clerical error, the sale was not recorded until January Year 2, and the merchandise, sold at a 25% markup, was included in Astor's inventory at December 31, Year 1. As a result, Astor's cost of goods sold for the year ended December 31, Year 1, was

A. Understated by $75,000.

B. Understated by $60,000.

C. Understated by $15,000.

D. Correctly stated.

Answer (B) is correct.
  REQUIRED: The cost of goods sold given delayed recording of a sale.
  DISCUSSION: Astor should have debited a receivable and credited sales for $75,000, the net amount, on the date of shipment. Astor also should have debited cost of sales and credited inventory at cost on the same date. Under the shipping terms, the sale should have been recognized on December 31, Year 1, because title and risk of loss passed to the buyer on that date; that is, an earning process was complete. The error therefore understated cost sales by $60,000 ($75,000 sales price ÷ 125% of cost).
  Answer (A) is incorrect. The selling price is $75,000. Answer (C) is incorrect. The amount of the markup is $15,000. Answer (D) is incorrect. Cost of goods was understated by $60,000.

8.8 Estimating Inventory

29. The following information was obtained from Smith Co.:

Sales	$275,000
Beginning inventory	30,000
Ending inventory	18,000

Smith's gross margin is 20%. What amount represents Smith purchases?

A. $202,000

B. $208,000

C. $220,000

D. $232,000

Answer (B) is correct.
  REQUIRED: The amount of purchases given the gross margin.
  DISCUSSION: Gross margin equals sales minus cost of goods sold. If it is 20% of sales, cost of goods sold equals $220,000 [$275,000 × (1.0 – .20)]. Cost of goods sold equals beginning inventory, plus purchases, minus ending inventory. Thus, purchases equals $208,000 ($220,000 COGS – $30,000 BI + $18,000 EI).
  Answer (A) is incorrect. Cost of goods sold minus ending inventory equals $202,000. Answer (C) is incorrect. Cost of goods sold equals $220,000. Answer (D) is incorrect. The amount of $232,000 equals cost of goods sold plus beginning inventory, minus ending inventory.

30. Union Corp. uses the first-in, first-out retail method of inventory valuation. The following information is available:

	Cost	Retail
Beginning inventory	$12,000	$ 30,000
Purchases	60,000	110,000
Net additional markups		10,000
Net markdowns		20,000
Sales revenue		90,000

If the lower-of-cost-or-market rule is disregarded, what would be the estimated cost of the ending inventory?

A. $24,000

B. $20,000

C. $19,200

D. $18,000

Answer (A) is correct.
  REQUIRED: The ending inventory using the FIFO version of the retail inventory method.
  DISCUSSION: Under FIFO, ending inventory consists of purchases because beginning inventory is assumed to be sold first. Both markdowns and markups are used to calculate the cost-retail ratio because LCM is not being approximated.

	Cost	Retail
Purchases	$60,000	$110,000
Markups		10,000
Markdowns		(20,000)
Adjusted purchases	$60,000	$100,000
Beg. inv. 1/1	12,000	30,000
Goods available	$72,000	$130,000
Sales		(90,000)
Ending inventory -- retail		$ 40,000
Cost-retail ratio ($60,000 ÷ $100,000)		× .6
Ending inventory -- FIFO		$ 24,000

Answer (B) is incorrect. The amount of $20,000 results from applying the LCM rule (not deducting markdowns in determining the cost-retail ratio) and using the FIFO version of the retail method. Answer (C) is incorrect. The amount of $19,200 results from applying the approximate LCM (conventional) retail method. Answer (D) is incorrect. The amount of $18,000 results from applying the LIFO retail method (assuming stable prices).

31. Which of the following methods of inventory valuation is allowable at interim dates but **not** at year end?

A. Weighted average.

B. Estimated gross profit.

C. Retail method.

D. Specific identification.

Answer (B) is correct.
 REQUIRED: The inventory valuation method permitted at interim dates but not at year end.
 DISCUSSION: The estimated gross profit method may be used to determine inventory for interim statements provided that adequate disclosure is made of reconciliations with the annual physical inventory at year end. Any other method allowable at year end is also allowable at an interim date.

32. At December 31, the following information was available from Huff Co.'s accounting records:

	Cost	Retail
Inventory, 1/1	$147,000	$ 203,000
Purchases	833,000	1,155,000
Additional markups	--	42,000
Available for sale	$980,000	$1,400,000

Sales for the year totaled $1,106,000. Markdowns amounted to $14,000. Under the approximate lower-of-average-cost-or-market retail method, Huff's inventory at December 31 was

A. $280,000

B. $197,160

C. $196,000

D. $194,854

Answer (C) is correct.
 REQUIRED: The estimated inventory using the approximate lower-of-average-cost-or-market retail method.
 DISCUSSION: The LACM retail method includes net markups but not net markdowns in the determination of goods available for sale. The approximate LACM (conventional) retail method is a weighted-average method. Accordingly, the numerator of the cost-retail ratio is the sum of the beginning inventory at cost plus purchases at cost, and the denominator is the sum of beginning inventory at retail, purchases at retail, and net markups.

	Cost	Retail
Beginning inventory	$147,000	$ 203,000
Purchases	833,000	1,155,000
Markups, net		42,000
Goods available	$980,000	$1,400,000
Sales		(1,106,000)
Markdowns, net		(14,000)
Ending inventory -- retail		$ 280,000
Cost-retail ratio ($980 ÷ $1,400)		× .7
Ending inventory at cost		$ 196,000

 Answer (A) is incorrect. The ending inventory at retail is $280,000. Answer (B) is incorrect. The amount of $197,160 (rounded) is the ending inventory using the FIFO version of the retail method without regard to the LCM rule. Answer (D) is incorrect. The amount of $194,854 (rounded) is the ending inventory using the LCM rule and the FIFO version of the retail method.

Use the additional questions in Gleim **CPA Test Prep Online** to create Test Sessions that emulate Prometric!

8.9 PRACTICE SIMULATION

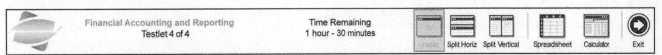

Financial Accounting and Reporting
Testlet 4 of 4

Time Remaining
1 hour - 30 minutes

Unsplit   Split Horiz   Split Vertical   Spreadsheet   Calculator   Exit

DIRECTIONS

Note: If you believe you have encountered a software malfunction, report it to the test center staff immediately.

Navigation

To navigate from task to task, use the controls at the bottom of the screen. Click on the **Next** button to advance to the next task, or the **Previous** button to go to the previous task. To go directly to any task, click on its number.

If you would like a reminder to revisit a task, or want to indicate that you are finished with it, click on the reminder flag below the task number. To clear the flag, click on it again. Reminder flags are for your use only – they do not contribute to your score.

Tabs

In this part of the examination, you will be asked to complete various tasks. Every task has one or more **Work Tabs**. Some tasks have one or more **Information Tabs**, others may have none. Every task has a **Help** tab.

If a task has **Information Tabs**, you may use the information in them to complete your responses in the **Work Tabs**.

Work tab   Information tab   Help tab

Work Tabs:

- **Work Tabs** are identified with a pencil icon. This is where your responses are expected.
- Each task has one or more **Work Tabs**.
- **Work Tabs** contain directions for completing the task – be sure to read these directions carefully.
- The **Work Tab** name in the example above is for illustration only – yours will differ.
- You must complete all of the **Work Tabs** in each task to receive full credit.

Information Tabs:

- The Authoritative Literature will be provided in all tasks in the AUD, FAR, and REG sections for your reference.
- Your simulation may have one or more additional **Information Tabs**. Like the Authoritative Literature tabs, **Information Tabs** do not have a pencil icon.
- If your task has additional **Information Tabs**, go through each to familiarize yourself with the task content.

Help Tab:

- The **Help Tab** provides assistance with the exam software that is used in this task. For example, if the task is to compose a memorandum, **Help** will provide information about the word processor.

The Toolbar

The toolbar at the top of the screen shows the amount of time remaining for you to complete the tasks. In addition, the following tools are available. Note that only the **Exit** button is displayed when Directions are visible - the others will appear when you begin the tasks.

Unsplit   Split Horiz   Split Vertical

Click on these buttons to split or unsplit the screen. You can split the screen vertically or horizontally.

Calculator

Click on this button to display the calculator; click on it again to hide the calculator. To move the calculator, click on the calculator title bar and drag the calculator to the desired location.

Spreadsheet

Click on this button to use the spreadsheet; click on it again to hide the spreadsheet. To move the spreadsheet, click on the the spreadsheet title bar and drag the spreadsheet to the desired location.

Exit

Click on this button to go on to the next part of the examination. You must complete all of the tasks to receive full credit. Once you click on **Exit** and confirm the action, you will NOT be able to return to this testlet.

▼ = Reminder   Directions   1 2 3 4 5 6   ◀ Previous   Next ▶

| Cost Flow Assumptions | Authoritative Literature | Help |

Select from the list of inventory cost flow assumptions the best match for each item. Each choice may be used once, more than once, or not at all.

Item	Answer
1. Method that expenses the most recent purchases first, records them directly in inventory, and determines cost of goods sold as goods are sold.	
2. Recalculates unit cost after each purchase.	
3. Applies to groups of similar inventory items.	
4. Ending inventory approximates current replacement cost.	

Choices
A) LIFO
B) LIFO periodic
C) LIFO perpetual
D) Moving average cost
E) FIFO
F) Weighted-average cost
G) Specific identification
H) Dollar-value LIFO

▼ = Reminder   Directions   1 2 3 4 5 6   ◀ Previous   Next ▶

| Inventory Schedule | Authoritative Literature | Help |

Bristol Co. uses the LIFO periodic inventory flow assumption. Its inventory purchases for Year 5 were as follows:

	Units	Cost per Unit
Beginning inventory, January 1	8,000	$8.20
Purchases, quarter ended March 31	12,000	8.25
Purchases, quarter ended June 30	15,000	7.90
Purchases, quarter ended September 30	13,000	7.50
Purchases, quarter ended December 31	7,000	7.70
	55,000	

Bristol Co. sold 33,000 units in Year 5.

Prepare a schedule of ending inventory by entering the correct response in each of the shaded cells below.

Bristol Co.
Supporting Schedule of Ending Inventory
December 31, Year 5

Inventory at Cost (LIFO)	(a)	(b)	(c)
Inventory Layer	Units	Cost Per Unit	Total Cost
1. Beginning inventory, January 1			
2. Purchases, quarter ended March 31			
3. Purchases, quarter ended June 30			
4. Purchases, quarter ended September 30			
5. Purchases, quarter ended December 31			

▼ = Reminder   Directions   1 2 3 4 5 6   ◀ Previous   Next ▶

| Cost of Goods Sold Schedule | Authoritative Literature | Help |

Bristol Co. sells one product it purchased from various suppliers. Bristol's accounting policy is to report inventory using LIFO periodic and the lower-of-cost-or-market method applied to total inventory. Cash discounts are recorded using the gross method. At December 31, Year 5, the replacement cost of the inventory was $8 per unit, and the net realizable value was $8.80 per unit. The normal profit margin is $1.05 per unit. Bristol uses the direct method of reporting losses from write-downs of inventory to market. The trial balance at December 31, Year 5, included the following accounts:

Sales (33,000 units × $16)	$528,000
Sales discounts	7,500
Purchases	368,900
Purchase discounts	18,000
Freight-in	5,000
Freight-out	11,000

Bristol's inventory purchases during Year 5 were as follows:

	Units	Cost per Unit
Beginning inventory, January 1	8,000	$8.20
Purchases, quarter ended March 31	12,000	8.25
Purchases, quarter ended June 30	15,000	7.90
Purchases, quarter ended September 30	13,000	7.50
Purchases, quarter ended December 31	7,000	7.70
	55,000	

Select from the list provided the correct amount for each item on the schedule of cost of goods sold below. Each choice may be used once, more than once, or not at all.

Bristol Co.
Schedule of Cost of Goods Sold
For the Year Ended December 31, Year 5

Account	Amount
1. Beginning inventory	
2. Purchases	
3. Purchase discounts	
4. Freight in	
5. Goods available for sale	
6. Ending inventory	
7. Cost of goods sold	

Choices	
A)	$ 528,000
B)	$ 368,900
C)	$ 5,000
D)	$ 421,500
E)	$ 515,000
F)	$ (5,000)
G)	$ 18,000
H)	$ (18,000)
I)	$ 11,000
J)	$ (11,000)
K)	$ 65,600
L)	$ 176,000
M)	$(176,000)
N)	$ 245,500
O)	$ 317,000

Bristol uses a FIFO costing system for internal reporting purposes. Ending FIFO inventory is $225,000, and ending LIFO (for this question only) is assumed to be $176,000. Enter in the shaded cells below the journal entry to recognize the difference between Bristol's internal inventory costing method and LIFO.

Account Title	Type of Account	Debit/Credit	Amount
1. Cost of goods sold			
2. Allowance to adjust inventory to LIFO			

▼ = Reminder   Directions   1 2 3 [4] 5 6   ◀ Previous   Next ▶

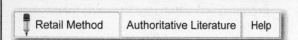

Select from the list provided the version of the retail inventory method that best matches each statement below.

Statement	Answer
1. A cost method that adjusts inventory layers for price level changes.	
2. Cost-retail ratio based on goods available for sale that includes markups and markdowns.	
3. Cost-retail ratio includes inventories and markups but not markdowns.	
4. Cost-retail ratio includes markups but excludes inventories and markdowns.	
5. Cost-retail ratio based on adjusted purchases and calculated for each annual layer.	

Version
A) FIFO cost
B) FIFO lower of cost or market
C) Average cost
D) Lower of average cost or market
E) LIFO retail
F) Dollar-value LIFO retail

▼ = Reminder   Directions   1 2 3 4 [5] 6   ◀ Previous   Next ▶

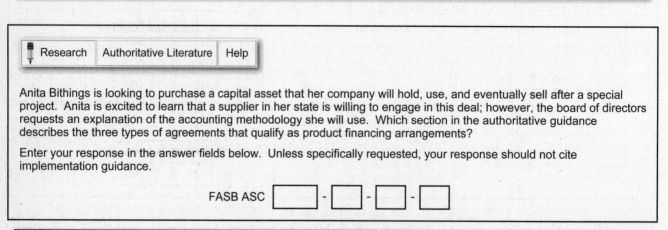

Anita Bithings is looking to purchase a capital asset that her company will hold, use, and eventually sell after a special project. Anita is excited to learn that a supplier in her state is willing to engage in this deal; however, the board of directors requests an explanation of the accounting methodology she will use. Which section in the authoritative guidance describes the three types of agreements that qualify as product financing arrangements?

Enter your response in the answer fields below. Unless specifically requested, your response should not cite implementation guidance.

FASB ASC ☐ - ☐ - ☐ - ☐

▼ = Reminder   Directions   1 2 3 4 5 [6]   ◀ Previous   Next ▶

Unofficial Answers

1. Cost Flow Assumptions (4 Gradable Items)

1. <u>C) LIFO perpetual.</u> The LIFO perpetual method expenses the most recent purchases first, records them directly in inventory, and determines cost of goods sold as goods are sold.

2. <u>D) Moving average cost.</u> The moving average cost method recalculates unit cost after each purchase.

3. <u>H) Dollar-value LIFO.</u> Dollar-value LIFO applies to groups of similar inventory items.

4. <u>E) FIFO.</u> When using the FIFO method, ending inventory approximates current replacement cost.

2. Inventory Schedule (15 Gradable Items)

1. <u>(a) 8,000.</u>   Based on a LIFO periodic assumption, ending inventory consists of 22,000 units (55,000 purchased – 33,000 sold) with no liquidation of the 8,000 units in beginning inventory.
    <u>(b) 8.20.</u>   Given.
    <u>(c) 65,600.</u> The total cost of this layer is $65,600 (8,000 × $8.20).

2. <u>(a) 12,000.</u> Based on a LIFO periodic assumption, ending inventory consists of 22,000 units (55,000 purchased – 33,000 sold) with no liquidation of the 12,000 units in the first quarter layer.
    <u>(b) 8.25.</u>   Given.
    <u>(c) 99,000.</u> The total cost of this layer is $99,000 (12,000 × $8.25).

3. <u>(a) 2,000.</u>   Based on a LIFO periodic assumption, the ending inventory consists of 22,000 units (55,000 purchased – 33,000 sold) or (8,000 BI + 12,000 first quarter + 2,000 second quarter).
    <u>(b) 7.90.</u>   Given.
    <u>(c) 15,800.</u> The total cost of this layer is $15,800 (2,000 × $7.90).

4. <u>(a) 0.</u>   Based on a LIFO periodic assumption, the third quarter layer was completely liquidated.
    <u>(b) 7.50.</u>   Given.
    <u>(c) 0.</u>   The total cost of this layer is $0.

5. <u>(a) 0.</u>   Based on a LIFO periodic assumption, the fourth quarter layer was completely liquidated.
    <u>(b) 7.70.</u>   Given.
    <u>(c) 0.</u>   The total cost of this layer is $0.

3. Cost of Goods Sold Schedule (7 Gradable Items)

1. <u>K) $65,600.</u> The beginning inventory was $65,600 (8,000 × $8.20).

2. <u>B) $368,900.</u> Given. Bristol records purchases at gross amounts.

3. <u>H) $(18,000).</u> Given. In a periodic system used in conjunction with the gross method, the amount of purchase (cash) discounts is subtracted to determine goods available for sale.

4. <u>C) $5,000.</u> Given. In a periodic system, freight-in is an addition to goods available for sale. Ordinarily, it is not allocated to cost of goods sold and ending inventory.

5. <u>D) $421,500.</u> Goods available for sale is the sum of beginning inventory, net purchases, and freight-in.

6. <u>M) $(176,000).</u> Bristol applies the LCM method to total inventory. Per-unit replacement cost ($8) is the per-unit market amount because it is less than NRV ($8.80) and greater than NRV minus a normal profit margin ($8.80 – $1.05 = $7.75). Total inventory at market is therefore $176,000 [(55,000 units purchased – 33,000 units sold) × $8]. Because the ending inventory is assumed to consist of 8,000 units from beginning inventory, 12,000 units from the first quarter layer, and 2,000 units from the second quarter layer, total inventory at cost is therefore $180,400 [($8,000 × $8.20) + (12,000 × $8.25) + (2,000 × $7.90)]. Under the direct method, the $4,400 loss ($176,000 – $180,400) is debited to COGS and credited to inventory.

7. <u>N) $245,500.</u> Cost of goods sold equals goods available for sale minus ending inventory adjusted for the direct writedown to market

4. Journal Entry (6 Gradable Items)

1. <u>Expense; Debit; $49,000.</u> Companies often use LIFO for external reporting purposes to increase cost of goods sold and reduce net income, thereby reducing (or delaying) income taxes. Thus, when another costing method is used for internal reporting, its cost of goods sold is usually lower than that calculated under LIFO. This is the case with Bristol. To equate the internal FIFO cost of goods sold with the amount calculated for external reporting under LIFO, cost of goods sold must be debited for the difference of $49,000 ($225,000 FIFO – $176,000 LIFO).

2. <u>Contra-asset; Credit; $49,000.</u> The credit is to a valuation allowance that reduces the carrying amount of ending inventory.

5. Retail Method (5 Gradable Items)

1. <u>F) Dollar-value LIFO retail.</u> Dollar-value LIFO retail adjusts inventory layers for price level changes.

2. <u>C) Average cost.</u> The cost-retail ratio for average cost is based on goods available for sale that includes markups and markdowns.

3. <u>D) Lower of average cost or market.</u> The cost-retail ratio for lower of average cost or market includes inventories and markups, but not markdowns.

4. <u>B) FIFO lower of cost or market.</u> The cost-retail ratio for FIFO lower of cost or market includes markups, but excludes inventories and markdowns.

5. <u>E) LIFO retail.</u> The cost-retail ratio for LIFO retail is based on adjusted purchases and calculated for each annual layer.

6. Research (1 Gradable Item)

Answer: FASB ASC 470-40-05-2

Applicability and Scope

470-40-05-2 Product financing arrangements include agreements in which a sponsor (the entity seeking to finance product pending its future use or resale) does any of the following:

1. Sells the product to another entity (the entity through which the financing flows) and in a related transaction, agrees to repurchase the product (or a substantially identical product);

2. Arranges for another entity to purchase the product on the sponsor's behalf and, in a related transaction, agrees to purchase the product from the other entity; or

3. Controls the disposition of the product that has been purchased by another entity in accordance with the arrangements described in either (1) or (2).

Gleim Simulation Grading

Task	Correct Responses		Gradable Items		Score per Task
1	____	÷	4	=	____
2	____	÷	15	=	____
3	____	÷	7	=	____
4	____	÷	6	=	____
5	____	÷	5	=	____
Research	____	÷	1	=	____

	Total of Scores per Task	____
÷	Total Number of Tasks	6
	Total Score	____ %

Use **CPA Gleim Online** and **Simulation Wizard** to practice more task-based simulations in a realistic environment.

STUDY UNIT NINE
PROPERTY, PLANT, EQUIPMENT, AND DEPLETABLE RESOURCES

(22 pages of outline)

9.1	Initial Measurement of Property, Plant, and Equipment (PPE)	303
9.2	Special Measurement Issue -- Internally Constructed Assets (ICAs)	307
9.3	Subsequent Expenditures for PPE	310
9.4	Depreciation Methods -- Calculations	312
9.5	Depreciation Methods -- Changes and Comparison	316
9.6	Exchanges of Nonmonetary Assets	317
9.7	Disposals Other than by Exchange	319
9.8	Impairment of Long-Lived Assets	320
9.9	Depletion	323
9.10	Practice Simulation	337

This study unit covers tangible fixed assets. The next study unit addresses intangible assets. Depreciation and depletion are included in this study unit because income statement accounts are traditionally discussed together with the related balance sheet accounts.

9.1 INITIAL MEASUREMENT OF PROPERTY, PLANT, AND EQUIPMENT (PPE)

1. **Definition**

   a. These assets are called property, plant, and equipment; fixed assets; or plant assets. They provide benefits from their use in the production of goods and services, not from their consumption.

      1) PPE are tangible. They have physical existence.

      2) PPE may be either **personal property** (something movable, e.g., equipment) or **real property** (such as land or a building).

      3) PPE are used in the **ordinary operations** of an entity and are not held primarily for investment, resale, or inclusion in another product. But they are often sold.

         a) Land held for development may be classified as an investment or inventory.

         b) Intangible assets and natural resources also are operating assets.

      4) PPE are **noncurrent**. They are not expected to be used up within 1 year or the normal operating cycle of the business, whichever is longer.

         a) The cost of using up the service potential of PPE (except land) is systematically and rationally allocated by means of depreciation (explained in detail later in this study unit).

            i) However, land may sustain a material loss in fair value, e.g., through soil erosion of agricultural property or a natural disaster (flood or earthquake).

         b) Intangible assets and natural resources also are wasting assets. Allocation of their costs is amortization and depletion, respectively.

2. **Types of PPE**

   a. **Land**

   b. **Buildings**

   c. **Land improvements**, such as landscaping, drainage, streets, street lighting, sewers, sidewalks, parking lots, driveways, and fences

   d. **Machinery and equipment**, such as furniture, fixtures (personal property permanently attached to real property, such as a central heating system), and vehicles

   e. **Leasehold improvements**, such as buildings constructed on, and other modifications made to, the leased property by a lessee

   f. **Internally constructed assets**

   g. **Miscellaneous items**, e.g., tools, patterns and dies, and returnable containers

3. **Relevant Accounting Principles**

   a. PPE are initially measured at **historical cost**, which consists of

      1) The amount of cash paid to acquire the asset and

      2) The costs needed to bring the asset to the condition and location necessary for its intended use, e.g., shipping and installation costs.

         a) Historical cost is adjusted for changes in utility over the life of the asset, e.g., depreciation and impairment.

   b. **Capital (asset) expenditures** for acquisition or subsequent enhancement of service potential are those that benefit more than one period. They are added to historical cost.

      1) **Revenue expenditures** (e.g., for repairs) are those that benefit only the period in which they are made. They are expensed (matched with revenue).

   c. As noted in 3.a.2) above, the price bargained for by the buyer and seller is not the only component of historical cost. Under the full-cost principle, the initial measurement embraces all other costs to acquire PPE, transport them to the sites of their intended use, and prepare them for operations.

      1) Freight-in (transportation-in), installation charges, renovation or reconditioning costs, expenses of tests or trial runs, and insurance and taxes during the preoperations period are capitalizable.

         a) Depreciation is not recognized until PPE are placed in operation and begin to contribute economic benefits, that is, to participate in generating the revenues with which such costs should be matched.

   d. In general, **expenses** should be recognized at the time related revenues are earned.

      1) However, no direct relationship ordinarily exists between the consumption of service potential and specific revenues. Thus, the expense (depreciation) must be **systematically and rationally allocated** to periods expected to be benefited.

   e. Initial measurement and subsequent determination of the carrying amount of PPE inevitably require the use of judgment.

   f. Under GAAP, PPE are not revalued upward to reflect appraisal, market, current, or fair values that are above historical cost.

The AICPA often tests candidates' knowledge of the initial measurement of PPE, both by conceptual and calculation questions. A common format for calculation questions gives information about the noncurrent asset and asks for the amount at which the asset should be initially recorded.

4. **Initial Costs -- Land**

   a. The costs of acquiring and preparing land for its expected use are capitalized.

   b. The price should include not only the cash price but also any **encumbrances assumed** (such as mortgages or tax liens).

   c. The cost of land also includes **transaction costs**, e.g., surveying costs, legal fees, brokers' commissions, title insurance, and escrow fees.

   d. The cost of an option to buy land that is subsequently purchased is capitalized.

      1) But the costs of options, surveys, and other items related to land not purchased should be expensed.

   e. **Site preparation costs** [clearing, draining, filling, leveling the property, and razing existing buildings, minus any proceeds (such as timber sales)] are costs of the land, not of the building to be constructed on the land.

   f. Certain **permanent improvements** made by the entity, such as landscaping, have indefinite lives and are debited to the land account.

   g. Other improvements (sidewalks, roads, street lights, and sewers) may be paid for through **special assessments** imposed by local governments, which undertake to maintain and replace them. These assessments should be debited to land cost because depreciation will not be recognized.

   h. Taxes, insurance costs, etc., incurred while holding land for investment should be capitalized if the asset is not generating revenue and expensed if it is.

   i. Land has an indefinite useful life and therefore cannot be depreciated.

5. **Initial Costs -- Land Improvements**

   a. Land improvements with limited useful lives that must be maintained and replaced by the reporting entity are capitalized and depreciated.

6. **Initial Costs -- Buildings**

   a. The costs that are necessary to the purchase or construction of a building and that will result in future economic benefits should be capitalized. These include

      1) The **purchase price**, including any liens assumed by the purchaser, etc.

      2) Costs of **renovating and preparing the structure** for its expected use

      3) Costs of **building permits** for renovation or construction

      4) The expenses of **excavating the site** to build the foundation (but not site preparation costs)

         a) The **costs of razing an old building** are either debited to the land account or treated as an adjustment of a gain or loss on disposal. The accounting depends on whether the land was purchased as a site for the new structure or the old building was previously used in the entity's operations.

         b) The **carrying amount of an existing building** previously used in the entity's operations is not included in the cost of the new structure. It will not produce future benefits.

      5) The materials, labor, and overhead **costs of construction**

7. **Initial Costs -- Machinery and Equipment**

   a. **Costs** include

      1) Purchase price (including sales taxes)

      2) Freight-in, handling, insurance, and storage until use begins

      3) Preparation, installation, and start-up costs, such as testing and trial runs

      4) Reconditioning used assets

    b.   Proper categorization of these assets is important because of differences in depreciation methods and useful lives (especially for federal tax purposes).

        1)   For example, a common error is to include fixtures in the building account rather than the equipment account.

8.   **Initial Costs -- Leasehold Improvements**

    a.   Leasehold improvements, such as buildings constructed on leased land, are accounted for by the lessee in the same way as property to which title is held. However, the term of the lease may limit the depreciation period.

    b.   If the useful life of the asset extends beyond the lease term and lease renewal is likely, the amortization period may include all or part of the renewal period. If renewal is uncertain, the useful life is the remaining term.

9.   **Other Factors Affecting Initial Measurement**

    a.   **Cash discounts.** The issue is whether the discount should be considered in recording the cost, that is, whether the transaction should be recorded at its net or gross amount. The net method is preferable because cost will reflect the cash price. A discount not taken will be charged to discounts lost. Under the gross method, discounts taken (but not lost) will be recorded.

    b.   **Acquisition in exchange for a noncurrent obligation.** If an item of PPE is acquired in exchange for a noncurrent note, its cost is the present value of the consideration paid (the note). But the note's interest rate may be unstated or unreasonable, or the face amount may differ materially from the cash price of the PPE or the market value of the note. In these cases, the cost of the PPE should be the more clearly determinable of the cash price of the PPE or the market value of the note.

    c.   **Basket (lump-sum) purchases.** When two or more assets with varying estimated useful lives are acquired for a single price, allocation of the cost is required.

        1)   Only the common cost is allocated. Capital expenditures related to a particular asset should be debited to that asset.

            a)   For example, if inventory and equipment are purchased, the start-up costs for the equipment should not be allocated to the inventory.

        2)   The basis of allocation is relative fair value.

    d.   **Issuance of an entity's own securities for PPE.** The usual basis for measurement of this transaction is the fair value of the stock or other securities.

    e.   **Donated assets.** In general, contributions received should be recognized as (1) revenues or gains in the period of receipt and (2) assets, or decreases in liabilities or expenses. They are measured at fair value.

PPE	$XXX	
Contribution revenue		$XXX

        1)   Contributions made are recognized as expenses and as increases of liabilities or decreases in assets. Contributions made also are measured at fair value.

        2)   But this guidance does not apply to (a) contributions by governmental units to businesses or (b) tax exemptions, incentives, or abatements. Accordingly, a business may credit a contribution from a governmental unit to donated capital.

            a)   However, treating contributions by governmental units as revenues or gains is not prohibited. Such treatment is consistent with the accounting for contributions by nongovernmental entities. It is also consistent with the definition of comprehensive income: all changes in equity during a period except those from investments by owners and distributions to owners.

IFRS Difference

An entity may choose either the cost model or the revaluation model as its accounting policy. It must apply that policy to an entire class of PPE. A class is a grouping of assets of similar nature and use in an entity's operations, for example, land, office equipment, or motor vehicles.

An item of PPE whose fair value can be reliably measured may be carried at a **revalued amount** equal to fair value at the revaluation date (minus subsequent accumulated depreciation and impairment losses).

Revaluation is needed whenever fair value and the asset's carrying amount differ materially. Accumulated depreciation is restated proportionately or eliminated.

A revaluation increase must be recognized in other comprehensive income and accumulated in equity as revaluation surplus. But the increase must be recognized in profit or loss to the extent it reverses a decrease of the same asset that was recognized in profit or loss.

A revaluation decrease must be recognized in profit or loss. But the decrease must be recognized in other comprehensive income to the extent of any credit in revaluation surplus for the same asset.

IFRS Difference

Under **IAS 40**, *Investment Property*, **investment property** is property (land, building, part of a building, or both) held by the owner or by the lessee under a finance lease to earn rental income or for capital appreciation or both. Investment property may be accounted for according to (1) the **cost model** and carried at historical cost minus accumulated depreciation and impairment losses or (2) the **fair value model**. If the fair value model is chosen as the accounting policy, all of the entity's investment property must be measured at **fair value** at the end of the reporting period. A **gain or loss** arising from a change in the fair value of investment property must be recognized in profit or loss for the period in which it arises. Investment property that is accounted for according to the fair value model is not depreciated.

Stop and review! You have completed the outline for this subunit. Study multiple-choice questions 1 through 7 beginning on page 324.

9.2 SPECIAL MEASUREMENT ISSUE -- INTERNALLY CONSTRUCTED ASSETS (ICAs)

1. **Initial Costs of an ICA**

   a. The costs capitalized when productive assets are internally constructed may be both **direct** (direct materials and direct labor) **and indirect** (overhead items, e.g., utilities, depreciation, insurance, taxes, and supplies).

   b. Disagreement exists about **allocation of overhead**, especially those costs that are unaffected by production of an ICA. Widely used methods are to (1) capitalize the incremental increase in variable overhead associated with the construction or (2) allocate total overhead based on cost drivers in the same manner as in other manufacturing processes.

   c. An ICA should be capitalized at the **lower of its fair value or its cost**.

      1) No gain is recognized in the year of construction because the acquisition of assets is ordinarily not considered the result of an earning process.

      2) If cost exceeds fair value, however, the excess is expensed immediately to avoid overstating the asset.

2. **Capitalization of Interest**

   a. The costs necessary to bring an asset to the condition and location of its intended use are part of the historical cost. **Interest incurred during construction** is such a cost and must be debited to the ICA. An imputed cost of equity capital is not recognized.

3. **Qualifying Assets**

   a. Assets produced by the entity for its own use.

   b. Assets produced for the entity by others for which deposits or progress payments have been made.

   c. Assets produced for sale or lease as separate projects, such as real estate developments or ships.

   d. Equity-based investments. The investor may capitalize interest on the investment if the investee (1) has activities in progress necessary to commence its planned principal operations and (2) is expending funds to obtain qualifying assets for its operations.

4. **Nonqualifying Assets**

   a. Inventories routinely produced in large quantities on a repetitive basis

   b. Assets in use or ready for their intended use in earning activities

   c. Assets not being used in earning activities that are not undergoing the activities necessary to ready them for use

   d. Idle land

5. **Capitalization (Acquisition) Period**

   a. This period is the time required to carry out the activities necessary to bring a qualifying asset to the condition and location necessary for its intended use.

   b. **The period begins and continues** as long as

      1) Expenditures for a qualifying asset are being made,

      2) Activities necessary to make the asset ready for its intended use are in progress, and

      3) Interest cost is being incurred.

   c. **Capitalization ends** when the asset is substantially complete and ready for its intended use. Also, interest capitalization must cease if substantially all asset-related activities are suspended.

   d. Interest capitalization does not end merely because the asset must be measured at less than acquisition cost, e.g., because of recognition of an impairment loss.

6. **Limitation on Capitalized Interest**

   a. Interest cost includes interest (1) on obligations with explicit interest rates (including amortization of issue costs and discount or premium), (2) imputed on certain payables, and (3) on a capital lease.

   b. Capitalizable interest is limited to the **amount theoretically avoidable** if expenditures for ICAs had not been made. For example, if the entity had not incurred costs for ICAs, it might have used the funds to repay debt or to avoid issuing new debts.

   c. Interest capitalized may not exceed the actual total incurred during the period.

   d. Interest earned on borrowed funds is ordinarily not offset against interest cost to determine either capitalization rates or limitations on interest costs to be capitalized. Such income relates to investment, not acquisition, decisions.

7. **Amount of Interest to be Capitalized**

   a. Capitalized interest equals the weighted **average accumulated expenditures (AAE)** for the qualifying asset during the capitalization period times the interest rate(s). The weighting is based on the time expenditures incurred interest.

b. If a specific new borrowing outstanding during the period can be identified with the asset, the rate on that obligation may be applied to the extent that the AAE do not exceed the amount borrowed.

c. To the extent that AAE exceed the amount of specific new borrowings, a weighted-average rate must be applied that is based on other borrowings outstanding during the period.

EXAMPLE

Lyssa Co. constructed a building for its own use. The capitalization period began on 10/1/Year 1 and ended on 9/30/Year 2. The AAE are based on the following construction-related expenditures and the amounts of time they incurred interest:

Quarter Beginning		AAE
10/1/Year 1:	$500,000 × (12 ÷ 12) =	$ 500,000
1/1/Year 2:	$400,000 × (9 ÷ 12) =	300,000
4/1/Year 2:	$600,000 × (6 ÷ 12) =	300,000
7/1/Year 2:	$400,000 × (3 ÷ 12) =	100,000
9/30/Year 2:	$900,000 × (0 ÷ 12) =	0
		$1,200,000

On 10/1/Year 1, Lyssa specifically borrowed $1,000,000 at a rate of 10% to finance the construction. Its other borrowings outstanding during the entire construction period consisted of a $2,000,000 bond issue bearing 8% interest and a $6,000,000 bond issue bearing 9%. All interest is paid at fiscal year end. Accordingly, the weighted-average rate on other borrowings is 8.75%.

		Interest	Principal	Rate
$2,000,000 × 8%	=	$160,000	$2,000,000	
$6,000,000 × 9%	=	540,000	6,000,000	
		$700,000	÷ $8,000,000	= 8.75%

Total actual interest cost for the fiscal year is $800,000.

$1,000,000 × 10%	=	$100,000
$2,000,000 × 8%	=	160,000
$6,000,000 × 9%	=	540,000
		$800,000

Avoidable interest is $117,500.

$1,000,000 × 10%		=	$100,000
($1,200,000 − $1,000,000) × 8.75%		=	17,500
			$117,500

This amount is capitalized because it is less than actual interest.

Interest expense is $682,500 ($800,000 − $117,500).

---

8. **Disposition of Capitalized Interest**

   a. Subsequent to capitalization, interest is not treated differently from other component costs of an ICA. For example, it is not amortized over a period different from that used to depreciate the ICA.

9. **Disclosures**

   a. If no interest cost is capitalized, the amount incurred and expensed during the period should be reported. If some interest cost is capitalized, the total incurred and the amount capitalized should be disclosed.

Stop and review! You have completed the outline for this subunit. Study multiple-choice questions 8 through 11 beginning on page 327.

9.3 SUBSEQUENT EXPENDITURES FOR PPE

1. **Accounting Issues**

   a. The issues are to determine whether subsequent expenditures should be capitalized or expensed and to determine the accounting methods to be used.

   b. **Capital expenditures** provide additional benefits by improving the quality of services rendered by the asset, extending its useful life, or increasing its output.

      1) These expenditures are matched through changes in depreciation schedules with revenues of the future periods expected to be benefited.

   c. **Revenue expenditures** (expenses) maintain an asset's normal service capacity.

      1) These costs are recurring, are not expected to benefit future periods, and are expensed when incurred.

      2) An entity usually specifies a materiality threshold below which all costs are expensed, thereby avoiding the burden of depreciating immaterial amounts.

2. **Additions**

   a. Substantial expenditures for extensions or expansions of existing assets are **capitalized**. An example is an additional floor for a building.

   b. If the addition is essentially a separate asset, it is recorded in a separate account and depreciated over its own useful life.

      1) Otherwise, the addition should be debited to the original asset account and depreciated over the life of that asset.

   c. If the original asset was constructed in anticipation of the addition, the costs related to changes in that asset should be capitalized.

      1) However, costs of alterations in the original asset should be expensed if they could have been avoided by proper planning at an earlier time.

   d. The basic entry is

Asset (new or old)	$XXX	
Cash, etc.		$XXX

3. **Replacements and Improvements (Betterments)**

   a. A **replacement** substitutes a new component of an asset for a similar one, for example, a tile roof for a tile roof. But an **improvement** substitutes a better component, such as a more efficient heating system.

   b. **Substitution method.** If the old component was recorded separately, e.g., recording a central air conditioning system separately from the building, the procedure is to remove it from the ledger, along with accumulated depreciation, and to **substitute the cost of the new component**. A gain or loss may be recognized.

      1) The new component will be depreciated over the shorter of its useful life or that of the entire asset.

      2) The basic entry is

New asset	$XXX	
Accumulated depreciation	XXX	
Old asset		$XXX
Gain (or debit a loss)		XXX
Cash, etc.		XXX

    c.   If (1) the component replaced or improved has not been separately accounted for or (2) the old component has been modified, the substitution method is not used.

        1) If the replacement or improvement increases the asset's service potential but does not extend its estimated useful life, the asset is debited.

            a) The carrying amount of the old component is not removed. However, this amount ordinarily is not material because the transaction will most often occur when the component is almost fully depreciated.

        2) If the replacement or improvement primarily extends the useful life without enhancing service potential, the entry is to debit accumulated depreciation. The expenditure is a recovery of depreciation, not an increase in the quality of service.

            Accumulated depreciation $XXX
                Cash, etc. $XXX

4.   **Rearrangements, Reinstallations, Relocations**

    a.   Rearranging the configuration of plant assets, reinstalling such assets, or relocating operations may require material outlays that are separable from recurring expenses and provide probable future benefits.

    b.   The **substitution method** of accounting for these costs may be used if the original installation costs and accumulated depreciation **are known**.

    c.   Otherwise, if these costs are material, they should be debited to a new account and amortized over the (usually brief) period benefited.

    d.   Relocation (moving) costs often are expensed as incurred.

        1) But if these costs are incurred because of an unusual and infrequent event, such as a natural disaster, they may be included in an extraordinary loss.

5.   **Repairs and Maintenance**

    a.   Routine, **minor expenditures** made to maintain the operating efficiency of PPE are **ordinarily expensed as incurred**. However, as the amounts involved become more significant and the benefits to future periods increase, treatment of a **major repair as an addition, etc.**, may be more appropriate.

    b.   Although a repair or maintenance cost ordinarily should be allocated to a single annual period only, its full recognition at the interim date when incurred may distort the interim statements.

        1) Accordingly, a repair or maintenance cost may be accounted for using an allowance method for interim reporting. This method involves

            a) Estimating the annual cost

            b) Allocating an amount to each interim period

               Repairs and maintenance expense $XXX
                  Allowance $XXX

            c) Recording amounts actually expended

               Allowance $XXX
                  Cash, etc. $XXX

            d) Making an adjustment in the final interim period to reduce the year-end allowance to zero

            e) Presenting the allowance in the interim statements as an addition to or subtraction from the related asset, i.e., as a valuation account

6.   Summary

Action	Accounting Treatment	
Additions	Debit separate asset or debit old asset	
Replacements/Improvements – Carrying Amount Known	Substitution method	
Replacements/Improvements – Carrying Amount Not Known	Increase service potential only: debit asset	Extend useful life only: debit accum. depreciation
Rearrangements/Reinstallations	Cost known: substitution method	Otherwise, material costs debited to new asset
Repairs	Minor: expense	Major: treatment as addition, etc.

Stop and review! You have completed the outline for this subunit. Study multiple-choice questions 12 through 16 beginning on page 328.

9.4 DEPRECIATION METHODS -- CALCULATIONS

CPA candidates can expect to answer questions that test depreciation concepts. CPA exam questions often ask for depreciation calculations, but not in the manner of simply calculating the depreciation amount using a depreciation method. The question may state that the useful life of the asset has increased/decreased and ask for the amount of accumulated depreciation.

1.   **Definition**

   a.   Depreciation systematically and rationally **allocates the historical cost** of the productive capacity of a tangible capital asset to the periods benefited.

      1)   It is not a process of valuation.

   b.   The periodic charge to depreciation expense is offset by a credit to accumulated depreciation, a contra-asset. This account is not a reserve because it does not set aside assets.

   c.   An asset's **depreciable base** is the total amount that is to be systematically and rationally allocated.

Depreciable base = Historical cost – Salvage value – Recognized impairment loss

---

EXAMPLE

Jayhawk Co. recently acquired a robot to be used in its fully automated factory for a purchase price of $850,000. Jayhawk spent another $150,000 installing and testing the robot. The company estimates that the robot will have a 5-year useful life and can be sold at the end of that time for $100,000.

The depreciable base for this asset is calculated as follows:

Purchase price	$ 850,000
Installation and testing	150,000
Historical cost	$1,000,000
Estimated salvage value	(100,000)
Depreciable base	$ 900,000

---

2.   **Depreciation Methods -- Straight-Line**

   a.   Straight-line depreciation is the simplest method to use because an equal amount of depreciation is charged to each period of the asset's useful life.

      1)   The easiest way to calculate straight-line depreciation is to divide the depreciable base by the estimated useful life.

Periodic expense = Depreciable base ÷ Estimated useful life

    2) The straight-line percentage is 100% divided by the number of years in the asset's estimated useful life.

EXAMPLE

If Jayhawk applies the straight-line method, depreciation expense over the life of the asset will be calculated as follows:

	Depreciable Base	Divided: Estimated Useful Life	Equals: Depreciation Expense	Accumulated Depreciation	Carrying Amount, End of Year
Year 1:	$900,000	5	$180,000	$180,000	$820,000
Year 2:	900,000	5	180,000	360,000	640,000
Year 3:	900,000	5	180,000	540,000	460,000
Year 4:	900,000	5	180,000	720,000	280,000
Year 5:	900,000	5	180,000	900,000	100,000
Total			$900,000		

The straight-line percentage for Jayhawk's new robot is 20% (100% ÷ 5-year estimated useful life).

---

3. **Depreciation Methods -- Declining Balance**

    a. **Accelerated methods** were popularized when they became allowable on tax returns. But the same method need not be used for tax and financial statement purposes.

        1) Accelerated methods are time-based. They result in decreasing depreciation charges over the life of the asset. The two major time-based methods are declining balance and sum-of-the-years'-digits.

    b. Declining balance determines depreciation expense by multiplying the carrying amount (not the depreciable base equal to cost minus salvage value) at the beginning of each period by some percentage (e.g., 200% or 150%) of the straight-line rate of depreciation.

Periodic expense = Carrying amount × Declining-balance percentage

        1) The carrying amount decreases by the depreciation recognized. The result is the use of a constant rate against a declining balance.

        2) Salvage value is ignored in determining the carrying amount, but the asset is not depreciated below salvage value.

EXAMPLE

If Jayhawk applies double-declining-balance (DDB) depreciation to the robot, the declining-balance percentage will be 40% (20% straight-line rate × 2). Depreciation expense over the life of the asset will be calculated as follows:

	Carrying Amount, First of Year	Times: DDB Rate	Equals: Depreciation Expense	Accumulated Depreciation	Carrying Amount, End of Year
Year 1:	$1,000,000	40%	$400,000	$400,000	$600,000
Year 2:	600,000	40%	240,000	640,000	360,000
Year 3:	360,000	40%	144,000	784,000	216,000
Year 4:	216,000	40%	86,400	870,400	129,600
Year 5:	129,600	40%	29,600*	900,000	100,000
			$900,000		

    *Year 5 depreciation expense is $29,600 because the carrying amount cannot be less than salvage value.

4.   **Depreciation Methods -- Sum-of-the-Years'-Digits**

   a.   Sum-of-the-years'-digits (SYD) multiplies not the carrying amount but the constant depreciable base (cost minus salvage value) by a declining fraction. It is a declining-rate, declining-charge method.

$$Periodic\ expense = Depreciable\ base \times \frac{Remaining\ years\ in\ useful\ life}{\Sigma\ of\ all\ years\ in\ useful\ life}$$

EXAMPLE

If Jayhawk applies sum-of-the-years'-digits depreciation, the denominator of the SYD fraction is 15 (1 + 2 + 3 + 4 + 5). Depreciation expense over the life of the asset will be calculated as follows:

	Depreciable Base	SYD Fraction	Depreciation Expense	Accumulated Depreciation	Carrying Amount, Year End
Year 1:	$900,000	(5 ÷ 15)	$300,000	$300,000	$700,000
Year 2:	900,000	(4 ÷ 15)	240,000	540,000	460,000
Year 3:	900,000	(3 ÷ 15)	180,000	720,000	280,000
Year 4:	900,000	(2 ÷ 15)	120,000	840,000	160,000
Year 5:	900,000	(1 ÷ 15)	60,000	900,000	100,000

---

5.   **Depreciation Methods -- Usage-Centered**

   a.   Usage-centered activity methods calculate depreciation as a function of an asset's use rather than the time it has been held.

   b.   The **units-of-output method** allocates cost based on production. As production varies, so will the credit to accumulated depreciation.

$$Periodic\ expense = Depreciable\ base \times \frac{Units\ produced\ during\ current\ period}{Estimated\ total\ lifetime\ units}$$

EXAMPLE

On the date of purchase, Jayhawk anticipated that the robot would produce 8,000 units of product over its 5-year life. In actuality, the robot produced the following:

Year 1	Year 2	Year 3	Year 4	Year 5	Total
2,300 units	2,000 units	1,800 units	1,200 units	700 units	8,000 units

Depreciation expense over the life of the asset will be calculated as follows:

	Depreciable Base	Times: Units-of-Production Fraction	Equals: Depreciation Expense	Accumulated Depreciation	Carrying Amount, Year End
Year 1:	$900,000	(2,300 ÷ 8,000)	$258,750	$258,750	$741,250
Year 2:	900,000	(2,000 ÷ 8,000)	225,000	483,750	516,250
Year 3:	900,000	(1,800 ÷ 8,000)	202,500	686,250	313,750
Year 4:	900,000	(1,200 ÷ 8,000)	135,000	821,250	178,750
Year 5:	900,000	(700 ÷ 8,000)	78,750	900,000	100,000
Total			$900,000		

6. **Group and Composite Depreciation**

    a. These methods apply **straight-line** accounting to a collection of assets depreciated as if they were a single asset. The composite method applies to groups of **dissimilar assets** with varying useful lives, and the group method applies to **similar assets**. They provide an efficient way to account for large numbers of depreciable assets. They also result in the offsetting of under- and overstated depreciation estimates.

    b. Each method calculates (1) the total depreciable cost (total acquisition cost − salvage value) for all the assets debited to a control account, (2) the weighted-average estimated useful life (total depreciable cost ÷ total annual straight-line depreciation), and (3) the weighted-average depreciation rate based on cost (total annual straight-line depreciation ÷ total acquisition cost). One accumulated depreciation account also is maintained.

    c. **Early and late retirements** are expected to offset each other. Thus, gains and losses on retirements of single assets are not recognized but are treated as adjustments of accumulated depreciation. The entry is

Cash (proceeds)	$XXX	
Asset (cost)		$XXX
Accumulated depreciation (dr. or cr.)		XXX

    d. **Periodic depreciation** equals the weighted-average rate times the beginning balance of the asset account for the period. Thus, depreciation is calculated based on the cost of assets in use during the period. Prior-period retirements are reflected in this balance.

EXAMPLE

For its first year of operations, Argent Co. used the composite method of depreciation and prepared the following schedule of machinery owned:

	Total Cost	Estimated Salvage Value	Estimated Life in Years
Machine X	$550,000	$50,000	20
Machine Y	200,000	20,000	15
Machine Z	40,000	--	5

Argent computes depreciation on the straight-line method. Based upon the information presented, the composite life of these assets (in years) should be 16.0. The composite or average useful life of the assets is essentially a weighted average. As illustrated below, the annual straight-line depreciation for each asset should be calculated. The total cost, estimated salvage value, and depreciable base of the assets should then be computed. Dividing the composite depreciable base ($720) by the total annual straight-line depreciation ($45) gives the composite life (16 years) of these assets.

	Total Cost	Salvage Value	Dep. Base	Est. Life	Annual S-L Dep.
X	$550	$50	$500	20	$25
Y	200	20	180	15	12
Z	40	0	40	5	8
	$790	$70	$720		$45

---

7. **Depreciation for a Fractional Period**

    a. Because an asset is most likely to be acquired or disposed of at a time other than the beginning or end of a fiscal year, depreciation may need to be computed for a fraction of a period. Time-based methods most often compute depreciation to the nearest month of a partial year, but other conventions also are permitted.

        1) A full year's depreciation may be recognized in the year of acquisition and none in the year of disposal or vice versa.

        2) Depreciation may be recognized to the nearest full year or the nearest half-year.

        3) A half-year's depreciation may be recognized in both the year of acquisition and the year of disposal.

8.   **Disclosure**

a.   Full disclosure should be made of depreciation methods and practices, including

1)   Depreciation expense for the period
2)   Balances of major classes of depreciable assets by nature or function
3)   Accumulated depreciation either by major class or in total
4)   Description of depreciation methods for each major class of assets

---

IFRS Difference

Each part of an item with a cost significant to the total cost must be depreciated separately. But an entity may separately depreciate parts that are not significant.

Stop and review! You have completed the outline for this subunit. Study multiple-choice questions 17 through 20 beginning on page 330.

9.5 DEPRECIATION METHODS -- CHANGES AND COMPARISON

1.   **Effects on Net Income**

a.   Because the accelerated methods charge higher amounts to depreciation expense in the earlier years of an asset's economic life, those methods result in lower net income than the straight-line method in those years.

2.   **Effects of Accounting Changes**

a.   A change in the estimates for depreciation is accounted for prospectively. The new estimates are used in the year of the change, and no "catch-up" amounts are recorded.

EXAMPLE

On January 2, Year 1, a company purchased a machine for $500,000 and depreciated it by the straight-line method using an estimated useful life of 10 years with no salvage value. On January 2, Year 4, the company determined that the machine had a useful life of 6 years from the date of acquisition and will have a salvage value of $20,000. An accounting change was made in Year 4 to reflect the additional data.

For Years 1 through 3, the amount of depreciation was $50,000 per year ($500,000 depreciable base ÷ 10 years estimated useful life), resulting in a balance of accumulated depreciation at December 31, Year 3, of $150,000 ($50,000 × 3 years). The company calculates the new depreciable base as follows:

Historical cost	$500,000
Revised salvage value	(20,000)
Revised depreciable base	$480,000
Balance of accumulated depreciation, 1/2/Year 4	(150,000)
Remaining depreciable base, 1/2/Year 4	$330,000

Annual depreciation for the remaining years of the machine's estimated life is $110,000 ($330,000 depreciable base ÷ 3 years estimated remaining useful life).

Stop and review! You have completed the outline for this subunit. Study multiple-choice questions 21 through 23 beginning on page 331.

9.6 EXCHANGES OF NONMONETARY ASSETS

1. **Exchanges Measured at Fair Value**

   a. Nonmonetary exchanges are reciprocal transfers of nonmonetary assets that leave the transferor with no substantial continuing involvement in the assets given up. Thus, the usual risks and rewards of ownership are transferred.

   b. Accounting for exchanges of monetary assets (receivables, financial instruments, etc.) is straightforward because they are stated in terms of units of money.

      1) Monetary exchanges are measured at the fair value of the assets involved, with gain or loss recognized immediately.

         a) The fair value of the assets given up generally is used to measure the cost of the assets acquired unless the fair value of the assets received is more clearly evident.

   c. When the fair value of both assets in a nonmonetary exchange is determinable, the transaction is treated as a monetary exchange; i.e., it is measured at the fair value of the assets given up, and any gain or loss is recognized immediately.

EXAMPLE

Jayhawk Co. and Wildcat Corp. agree to exchange pieces of machinery. No exception to fair-value accounting applies. The following information is gathered from the two companies' books:

	Jayhawk Co.	Wildcat Corp.
Historical cost	$ 280,000	$ 300,000
Accumulated depreciation	(150,000)	(160,000)
Fair value	250,000	275,000

The journal entries to record the exchange are as follows:

Jayhawk's entry

Machinery and equipment (total fair value given up)	$250,000	
Accumulated depreciation (balance in account)	150,000	
Machinery and equipment (historical cost of old machine)		$280,000
Gain on exchange of machinery (difference)		120,000

Wildcat's entry

Machinery and equipment (total fair value given up)	$275,000	
Accumulated depreciation (balance in account)	160,000	
Machinery and equipment (historical cost of old machine)		$300,000
Gain on exchange of machinery (difference)		135,000

---

   d. Occasionally, one of the parties to a nonmonetary exchange pays the other a monetary incentive, called boot. The party paying boot includes this amount in the total fair value of assets given up in the exchange.

EXAMPLE

The same facts apply from the previous example, but Jayhawk also pays Wildcat $25,000. The journal entries to record the exchange are as follows:

Jayhawk's entry

Machinery and equipment (total fair value given up)	$275,000	
Accumulated depreciation (balance in account)	150,000	
Machinery and equipment (historical cost of old machine)		$280,000
Gain on exchange of machinery (difference)		120,000
Cash (boot given)		25,000

Wildcat's entry

Machinery and equipment (total fair value given up)	$275,000	
Accumulated depreciation (balance in account)	160,000	
Cash (boot received)	25,000	
Machinery and equipment (historical cost of old machine)		$300,000
Gain on exchange of machinery (difference)		160,000

2.   **Exchanges Measured at Carrying Amount**

a.   When certain exceptions apply, the accounting for a nonmonetary exchange is based on the carrying amount of the assets given up. Unless boot is received, no gain is recognized. The following are the exceptions:

   1)   Neither the fair value of the assets given up nor the fair value of the assets received is reasonably determinable,

   2)   The exchange involves inventory sold in the same line of business that facilitates sales to customers not parties to the exchange, or

   3)   The exchange lacks **commercial substance** because it is not expected to change the entity's cash flows significantly.

b.   If boot is given as part of an exchange measured at carrying amount, the recipient of the boot must recognize a proportionate amount of any potential gain. The amount of gain is calculated in the following steps:

   1)   Calculate the total potential gain on the exchange.

   Fair value of other assets received
   + Boot received
   − Carrying amount of assets given up
   Total potential gain

   2)   Calculate the proportion of assets received represented by boot.

   $$\frac{Boot\ received}{Fair\ value\ of\ other\ assets\ received\ +\ Boot\ received}$$

   3)   Determine the amount of gain to be recognized.

   Total potential gain × Proportion represented by boot

c.   If a loss is indicated in an exchange (with or without boot) measured at the carrying amount of the assets given up, the entire loss is recognized.

EXAMPLE

The same facts apply from the previous example, but the transaction lacks commercial substance.

Jayhawk's entry

Machinery and equipment (total carrying amount given up)	$155,000	
Accumulated depreciation (balance in account)	150,000	
Machinery and equipment (historical cost of old machine)		$280,000
Cash (boot given)		25,000

Wildcat's proportional gain

Fair value of other assets received	$250,000
Boot received	25,000
Carrying amount of assets given up	(140,000)
Total potential gain	$135,000

Proportion represented by boot = $25,000 ÷ ($250,000 + $25,000)
                    = 9.091% (< 25% of total)

Gain recognized = $135,000 × 9.091%
               = $12,272

Wildcat's entry

Machinery and equipment (total carrying amount given up)	$127,272	
Accumulated depreciation (balance in account)	160,000	
Cash (boot received)	25,000	
Machinery and equipment (historical cost of old machine)		$300,000
Gain (calculated above)		12,272

    d.   If boot constitutes 25% or more of the fair value of the exchange, the exchange is treated as a monetary exchange. Both parties record the transaction at fair value and recognize any gain or loss in full.

3.   **Summary**

Measure of Exchange	Gain	Loss
Fair value	Full	Full
Carrying amount -- no boot received	None	Full
Carrying amount -- boot received	Partial	Full

Stop and review! You have completed the outline for this subunit. Study multiple-choice questions 24 through 27 beginning on page 332.

9.7 DISPOSALS OTHER THAN BY EXCHANGE

1.   **Procedures**

    a.   Depreciation is recorded up to the time of disposal so that periodic depreciation expense is not understated and the carrying amount of the asset is not overstated.

    b.   The asset's carrying amount is removed from the accounts by eliminating the asset, its accumulated depreciation, and any other valuation account.

    c.   Any consideration (proceeds) received is debited appropriately.

    d.   Gain or loss is usually included in the results of continuing operations as an ordinary item unless the disposal is reported in discontinued operations.

2.   **Sale**

    a.   Accounting for a cash sale of PPE (including a scrap sale) is straightforward.

        1)   Depreciation, if any, is recognized to the date of sale, the carrying amount is removed from the books, the proceeds are recorded, and any gain or loss is recognized.

3.   **Abandonment**

    a.   An asset to be abandoned is disposed of when it is no longer used.

    b.   If the asset to be abandoned is still in use, it is normally not immediately written down to zero. Continued use indicates that the asset has service potential. However, depreciation estimates should be revised to account for the reduced service period.

        1)   A noncurrent asset that is temporarily idled is not treated as abandoned.

    c.   An abandonment may sometimes involve receipt of scrap value.

4.   **Contributions**

    a.   Contributions made do not involve an exchange. They are recorded at fair value, and an expense and a gain or loss are recognized.

```
Expense                    $XXX
    Asset                           $XXX
    Gain (cr.) or loss (dr.)         XXX
```

5.   **Nonreciprocal Transfers to Owners**

    a.   The accounting is based on the recorded amount (after recognition of impairment loss) in a distribution of nonmonetary assets to owners in a spinoff or other similar transaction.

6.   **Involuntary Conversion**

   a.   An item of PPE is involuntarily converted when it is (1) lost through a casualty (flood, earthquake, fire, etc.), (2) expropriated (seized by a foreign government), or (3) condemned (through the governmental power of eminent domain).

   1)   The accounting is the same as for other nonexchange dispositions.

   2)   The **gain or loss** on an involuntary conversion is reported as an ordinary item unless the criteria for treatment as an extraordinary item are met.

   3)   A nonmonetary asset may be involuntarily converted to monetary assets (e.g., insurance proceeds). Tax law may treat the gain as an adjustment of the basis of replacement property, not a currently taxable amount.

   4)   Gain or loss recognition is required even though the entity reinvests or is required to reinvest the proceeds in replacement nonmonetary assets.

   a)   Hence, the replacement property should be recorded at its cost. The involuntary conversion and replacement are not equivalent to a single exchange transaction between entities.

EXAMPLE

A state government condemned Owner Co.'s parcel of real estate. Owner will receive $1,500,000 for this property, which has a carrying amount of $1,150,000. Owner incurred the following costs as a result of the condemnation:

Appraisal fees to support a $1,500,000 fair value	$5,000
Attorney fees for the closing with the state	7,000
Attorney fees to review contract to acquire replacement property	6,000
Title insurance on replacement property	8,000

Gain or loss must be recognized even if the entity reinvests or is required to reinvest the monetary assets in replacement nonmonetary assets. The gain equals the consideration received ($1,500,000) minus the sum of the carrying amount ($1,150,000) and the direct costs of condemnation ($5,000 attorney fees + $7,000 appraisal fees = $12,000). The gain is therefore $338,000 ($1,500,000 – $1,162,000). The costs of acquiring the replacement property (attorney fees and title insurance) are included in its carrying amount.

Stop and review! You have completed the outline for this subunit. Study multiple-choice questions 28 through 31 beginning on page 333.

9.8 IMPAIRMENT OF LONG-LIVED ASSETS

1.   **Overview**

   a.   A long-lived asset may become permanently impaired. An entity may choose to keep and use such impaired assets or dispose of them.

   b.   The guidance in this subunit also applies to long-lived assets included in a group with other assets and liabilities not subject to such guidance. The unit of accounting for such a long-lived asset is the group.

   1)   If a long-lived asset is to be held and used, the **asset group** is the lowest level at which identifiable cash flows are largely independent of those of other groups.

   2)   If a long-lived asset is to be disposed of, the **disposal group** consists of assets to be disposed of together in one transaction and directly associated liabilities to be transferred in the same transaction (for example, warranties associated with an acquired customer base).

2. **Long-Lived Assets to Be Held and Used**

   a. **Measurement of impairment.** A long-lived asset (asset group) is impaired when its carrying amount is greater than its fair value. However, a loss equal to this excess is recognized for the impairment only when the carrying amount is not recoverable.

   b. **Recoverability test.** The carrying amount is not recoverable when it exceeds the sum of the undiscounted cash flows expected from the use and disposition of the asset (asset group).

   c. The assessment is based on the carrying amount at the time of the recoverability test.

      1) Testing should occur when events or changes in circumstances indicate that the carrying amount may not be recoverable, for example, when

         a) Market price has decreased significantly, or

         b) The use or physical condition of the asset (asset group) has changed significantly and adversely.

      2) The entry for an impairment of a depreciable asset is

Impairment loss	$XXX	
Accumulated depreciation		$XXX

      3)

Determination of an Impairment Loss
1. Events or changes in circumstances indicate a possible loss
2. Carrying amount > Sum of undiscounted cash flows
3. Loss = Carrying amount – Fair value

   d. An **impairment loss** decreases only the carrying amounts of the long-lived assets in the group on a pro rata basis according to their relative carrying amounts. However, the carrying amount of a given long-lived asset is not reduced below fair value if it is determinable without undue cost and effort.

   e. The carrying amount of a long-lived asset adjusted for an impairment loss is its new cost basis. A previously recognized impairment loss **must not be reversed**.

   f. **Fair value.** If a long-lived asset (asset group) has uncertainties about the timing and amounts of cash flows, an expected present value technique is often an appropriate estimator of fair value.

   g. **Reporting.** An impairment loss is reported in income from continuing operations. If a subtotal for "income from operations" is reported, the impairment loss is included.

3. **Long-Lived Assets to Be Disposed of**

   a. An asset (disposal group) is classified as **held for sale** when six conditions are met:

      1) Management has committed to a **plan to sell**.

      2) The asset is **available for immediate sale** in its current condition on usual and customary terms.

      3) Actions (such as actively seeking a buyer) have begun to complete the plan.

      4) Completion of sale **within 1 year is probable**.

         a) This condition need not be met if certain events or circumstances occur that the entity cannot control, e.g., when circumstances arise that previously were deemed to be unlikely, the entity takes steps to respond on a timely basis, and a favorable resolution is anticipated.

      5) The asset is **actively marketed** at a price reasonably related to current fair value.

      6) The likelihood is low of significant change in, or withdrawal of, the plan.

   b. Whenever the conditions are not met, the asset or disposal group must be reclassified as held and used.

c. When the recognition criteria for held-for-sale assets are met only after the balance sheet date, a long-lived asset is classified as held and used. However, disclosures about the expected disposal are still required.

1) Any recoverability test should be on a held-and-used basis as of the balance sheet date. Thus, the estimates of future cash flows and an impairment loss, if any, are determined as of the balance sheet date.

d. If disposition is to be **other than by sale**, for example, by abandonment, exchange, or a distribution to owners in a spinoff, the asset is classified as **held and used** until disposal. It will continue to be depreciated or amortized.

e. **Measurement.** Assets held for sale are measured at the **lower of carrying amount or fair value minus cost to sell**. If the asset (disposal group) is newly acquired, the carrying amount is the fair value minus cost to sell at the acquisition date.

1) An asset classified as held for sale is **not depreciated or amortized**, but expenses related to the liabilities of a disposal group are accrued.

2) Costs to sell are the incremental direct costs. Examples are brokers' commissions, legal and title transfer fees, and closing costs (but not future operating losses expected to be incurred).

a) The cost to sell is discounted when the sale will occur in more than 1 year in the circumstances described for the 1-year condition.

3) A **loss** is recognized for a write-down to fair value minus cost to sell. A **gain** is recognized for any subsequent increase but only to the extent of previously recognized losses for write-downs.

a) The loss or gain adjusts only the carrying amount of a long-lived asset even if it is included in a disposal group.

4) A gain or loss from the sale is recognized at the date of sale.

f. **A plan of sale may change** because of circumstances (previously unlikely) that result in a decision not to sell. The asset (disposal group) then must be reclassified as held and used.

1) A reclassified long-lived asset is measured individually at the lower of

a) Carrying amount before the asset (disposal group) was classified as held for sale, minus any depreciation (amortization) that would have been recognized if it had always been classified as held and used, or

b) Fair value at the date of the decision not to sell.

g. **Reporting.** A **reclassification adjustment** of the carrying amount is included in **income from continuing operations** in the period of a decision not to sell. It is reported in the same income statement caption used to report a disposal loss, if any, recognized for an asset (disposal group) classified as held for sale that is **not** a component of an entity.

1) When a component of an entity is reclassified as held and used, its results of operations previously reported in discontinued operations are reclassified and included in income from continuing operations for all periods presented.

2) If a long-lived asset is held for sale, it is reported separately.

a) If a disposal group is held for sale, its assets and liabilities are reported separately in the balance sheet and are not presented as one amount.

i) The major classes of assets and liabilities held for sale are separately disclosed on the face of the balance sheet or in the notes.

IFRS Difference

An asset is impaired when its carrying amount exceeds its recoverable amount. The entity assesses at each reporting date whether an indication of impairment exists. Given such an indication, the recoverable amount must be estimated. Moreover, intangible assets with indefinite useful lives or those not yet available for use and goodwill are tested for impairment at least annually.

The recoverable amount of an asset is the greater of its fair value minus costs to sell or value in use. Value in use is the present value of the asset's expected cash flows. The recognized impairment loss is the excess of the asset's carrying amount over its recoverable amount.

An impairment loss on an asset (except goodwill) may be reversed if a change in the estimates used to measure the recoverable amount has occurred.

Stop and review! You have completed the outline for this subunit. Study multiple-choice questions 32 through 36 beginning on page 335.

9.9 DEPLETION

Background

Firms operating in the extractive industries are unlike those in most other fields where the inflow of revenue is fairly steady. A company searching for an oil or gas deposit may sink many unsuccessful wells before finding one that will be profitable. It would thus be extremely disadvantageous to require all extractive firms to recognize expenses during a period when there are few revenues. For this reason, GAAP permits the use of either of two methods. Large firms that both explore and extract minerals tend to favor the successful-efforts method, while smaller firms that only explore prefer the full-cost method. The focus of the CPA exam tends to be on calculating the proper depletion base and depletion expense for the year.

1.   **Overview**

   a.   **Natural resources** (wasting assets) are held for direct resale or consumption in other products. Examples are petroleum, gold, silver, timber, iron ore, gravel, and coal.

   b.   Natural resources differ from depreciable assets because they

      1)   Lose their separate character during extraction and consumption
      2)   Are produced only by natural processes
      3)   Are recorded as inventory after extraction

         a)   The entry to record the inventory and the depletion of the natural resource is

Inventory	$XXX	
Accumulated depletion (a contra account)		$XXX

         b)   But some entities credit the natural resource account directly.

   c.   Depletion is similar to depreciation. It is an accounting process of allocating the historical cost of a tangible asset to the periods benefited by its uses.

2.   **Components of the Depletion Base**

   a.   **Acquisition costs** of land (but not the costs of extractive machinery, which are depreciated)

   b.   **Development costs** to prepare the site for extraction

   c.   **Restoration costs** required by law to return the land to its original condition

   d.   The **residual value** of the property

3. **Calculating Periodic Depletion**

   a. Depletion is similar to usage-centered depreciation because it is most often determined by applying the units-of-output (production) method.

   b. The depletion base (capitalized costs of acquisition, exploration, and development minus residual value adjusted for restoration costs) is divided by the units estimated to be economically recoverable to determine the **per-unit depletion rate**.

   Per-unit depletion rate = (Acquisition costs + Exploration costs + Development costs − Residual value + Restoration costs) ÷ Units estimated to be economically recoverable

   c. Units extracted times the depletion rate equals periodic depletion.

      1) To the extent that extracted units are sold, cost of goods sold is debited.
      2) Unsold units remain in inventory.

EXAMPLE

Mullinax Mining acquired a mine in Idaho for $3.2 million. The company estimates that the mine contains 1,125 recoverable grams of a particular rare earth. Mullinax further estimates that it will eventually be able to sell the mine for $600,000 after spending $200,000 on restoration. The company must spend $800,000 to prepare the site for mining. The depletion base for this mine is calculated as follows:

Purchase price	$3,200,000
Add: preparation costs	800,000
Add: restoration costs	200,000
Minus: residual value	(600,000)
Depletion base	$3,600,000

The depletion charge for this mine will therefore be $3,200 per gram ($3,600,000 depletion base ÷ 1,125 total recoverable grams). During the first year of operations, the mine produced 200 grams of ore. The depletion charge for the first year was thus $640,000 (200 grams × $3,200 per gram).

Stop and review! You have completed the outline for this subunit. Study multiple-choice questions 37 and 38 on page 336.

QUESTIONS

9.1 Initial Measurement of Property, Plant, and Equipment (PPE)

1. On July 1, Casa Development Co. purchased a tract of land for $1.2 million. Casa incurred additional costs of $300,000 during the remainder of the year in preparing the land for sale. The tract was subdivided into residential lots as follows:

Lot Class	Number of Lots	Sales Price per Lot
A	100	$24,000
B	100	16,000
C	200	10,000

Using the relative sales value method, what amount of costs should be allocated to the Class A lots?

A. $300,000

B. $375,000

C. $600,000

D. $720,000

Answer (C) is correct.

REQUIRED: The amount of costs allocated using the relative sales value method.

DISCUSSION: The relative sales value method allocates cost based on the relative value of assets in a group. The total sales value of the lots is $6,000,000 [(100 × $24,000) + (100 × $16,000) + (200 × $10,000)]. Class A represents 40% of the total value ($2,400,000 ÷ $6,000,000). Total costs equal $1,500,000 ($1,200,000 + $300,000). Thus, the amount of costs allocated to Class A is $600,000 ($1,500,000 × .40).

Answer (A) is incorrect. The amount of $300,000 equals the additional costs incurred. Answer (B) is incorrect. The amount of $375,000 equals 25% of the total cost. Class A represents 25% of the lots but 40% of the total value. Answer (D) is incorrect. The amount of $720,000 equals 48% of the total cost. Class A's sales price per lot is 48% of the sum of the unit sales prices of Classes A, B, and C.

2. Land was purchased to be used as the site for the construction of a plant. A building on the property was sold and removed by the buyer so that construction on the plant could begin. The proceeds from the sale of the building should be

A. Classified as other income.

B. Deducted from the cost of the land.

C. Netted against the costs to clear the land and expensed as incurred.

D. Netted against the costs to clear the land and amortized over the life of the plant.

Answer (B) is correct.
REQUIRED: The treatment of proceeds from the sale of a building removed to prepare for construction.
DISCUSSION: Land obtained as a plant site should be recorded at its acquisition cost. This cost includes the purchase price of the land and any additional expenses such as legal fees, title insurance, recording fees, assumption of encumbrances on the property, and any other costs incurred in preparing the property for its intended use. Because the intended use of the land was as a site for the construction of a plant, the proceeds from the sale of the building removed to prepare the land for construction should be deducted from the cost of the land.

3. Merry Co. purchased a machine costing $125,000 for its manufacturing operations and paid shipping costs of $20,000. Merry spent an additional $10,000 testing and preparing the machine for use. What amount should Merry record as the cost of the machine?

A. $155,000

B. $145,000

C. $135,000

D. $125,000

Answer (A) is correct.
REQUIRED: The amount to be recorded as the acquisition cost.
DISCUSSION: The amount to be recorded as the acquisition cost of a machine includes all costs necessary to prepare it for its intended use. Thus, the cost of a machine used in the manufacturing operations of a company includes the cost of testing and preparing the machine for use and the shipping costs. The acquisition cost is $155,000 ($125,000 + $20,000 + $10,000).
Answer (B) is incorrect. The amount of $145,000 does not include the $10,000 cost of testing and preparation. Answer (C) is incorrect. The amount of $135,000 does not include the shipping costs. Answer (D) is incorrect. The amount of $125,000 does not include the shipping, testing, and preparation costs.

4. During the year just ended, Burr Co. had the following transactions pertaining to its new office building:

Purchase price of land	$ 60,000
Legal fees for contracts to purchase land	2,000
Architects' fees	8,000
Demolition of the old building on site	5,000
Sale of scrap from old building	3,000
Construction cost of new building (fully completed)	350,000

In Burr's December 31 balance sheet, what amounts should be reported as the cost of land and cost of building?

	Land	Building
A.	$60,000	$360,000
B.	$62,000	$360,000
C.	$64,000	$358,000
D.	$65,000	$362,000

Answer (C) is correct.
REQUIRED: The amounts reported as the cost of land and cost of building.
DISCUSSION: The cost of the land should include the purchase price of the land and such additional expenses as legal fees, title insurance, recording fees, subsequent assumption of encumbrances on the property, and the costs incurred in preparing the property for its intended use. Because the land was purchased as the site of an office building, the cost of razing the old building, minus any proceeds received from the sale of salvaged materials, should be capitalized as part of the land account. Thus, land should be reported as $64,000 ($60,000 + $2,000 + $5,000 – $3,000). The architect's fees are included in the cost of the building, which should be reported as $358,000 ($350,000 + $8,000).
Answer (A) is incorrect. A $60,000 land cost omits the legal fees and the net demolition cost, and a $360,000 building cost improperly includes the legal fees. Answer (B) is incorrect. A $62,000 land cost omits the legal fees or the net demolition cost, and a $360,000 building cost improperly includes the legal fees. Answer (D) is incorrect. A $65,000 land cost includes the gross demolition cost but not the legal fees. A $362,000 building cost includes the legal fees and the net demolition cost.

5. During January, Yana Co. incurred landscaping costs of $120,000 to improve leased property. The estimated useful life of the landscaping is 15 years. The remaining term of the lease is 8 years, with an option to renew for an additional 4 years. However, Yana has not reached a decision with regard to the renewal option. In Yana's December 31 balance sheet, what should be the net carrying amount of landscaping costs?

A. $0

B. $105,000

C. $110,000

D. $112,000

Answer (B) is correct.
    REQUIRED: The net amount of leasehold improvements reported in the balance sheet.
    DISCUSSION: General improvements to leased property should be capitalized as leasehold improvements and amortized in accordance with the straight-line method over the shorter of their expected useful life or the lease term. However, if the useful life of the asset extends beyond the lease term and renewal of the lease is likely, the amortization period may include all or part of the renewal period. If renewal is uncertain, the useful life is the remaining term, and the salvage value is the amount, if any, to be paid by the lessor to the lessee at the expiration of the lease. Consequently, the amortization period is the 8-year lease term, and the net carrying amount at December 31 of the landscaping costs incurred in January is $105,000 [$120,000 × (7 years ÷ 8 years)].
    Answer (A) is incorrect. Land improvements with limited lives should be capitalized. Answer (C) is incorrect. The amount of $110,000 assumes that renewal for 4 years is likely. Answer (D) is incorrect. The amount of $112,000 assumes amortization over 15 years.

6. Star Co. leases a building for its product showroom. The 10-year nonrenewable lease will expire on December 31, Year 6. In January Year 1, Star redecorated its showroom and made leasehold improvements of $48,000. The estimated useful life of the improvements is 8 years. Star uses the straight-line method of amortization. What amount of leasehold improvements, net of amortization, should Star report in its June 30, Year 1, balance sheet?

A. $45,600

B. $45,000

C. $44,000

D. $43,200

Answer (C) is correct.
    REQUIRED: The net amount of leasehold improvements reported in the balance sheet.
    DISCUSSION: General improvements to leased property should be capitalized as leasehold improvements and amortized in accordance with the straight-line method over the shorter of their expected useful life or the lease term. Because the remaining lease term is less than the estimated life of the improvements, the cost should be amortized equally over 6 years. On 6/30/Year 1, $44,000 {$48,000 – [($48,000 ÷ 6 years) × 1/2 year]} should be reported for net leasehold improvements.
    Answer (A) is incorrect. The amount of $45,600 assumes the amortization period is 10 years. Answer (B) is incorrect. The amount of $45,000 assumes the amortization period is 8 years. Answer (D) is incorrect. The amount of $43,200 assumes that 1 year's amortization has been recorded and that the amortization period is 10 years.

7. Under IFRS, when an entity chooses the revaluation model as its accounting policy for measuring property, plant, and equipment, which of the following statements is correct?

A. When an asset is revalued, the entire class of property, plant, and equipment to which that asset belongs must be revalued.

B. When an asset is revalued, individual assets within a class of property, plant, and equipment to which that asset belongs can be revalued.

C. Revaluations of property, plant, and equipment must be made at least every 3 years.

D. Increases in an asset's carrying amount as a result of the first revaluation must be recognized as a component of profit or loss.

Answer (A) is correct.
    REQUIRED: The true statement about revaluation of PPE.
    DISCUSSION: Under IFRS, measurement of PPE subsequent to initial recognition may be at fair value at the revaluation date (minus subsequent depreciation and impairment losses). The assumption is that the PPE can be reliably measured. If an item of PPE is revalued, every item in its class also should be revalued.
    Answer (B) is incorrect. If an item of PPE is revalued, every item in its class also should be revalued. Answer (C) is incorrect. Revaluation is needed whenever an asset's fair value and carrying amount differ materially. Answer (D) is incorrect. A revaluation increase (surplus) is credited directly to equity.

9.2 Special Measurement Issue -- Internally Constructed Assets (ICAs)

8. On January 2, Year 1, Cruises, Inc., borrowed $3 million at a rate of 10% for 3 years and began construction of a cruise ship. The note states that annual payments of principal and interest in the amount of $1.3 million are due every December 31. Cruises used all proceeds as a down payment for construction of a new cruise ship that is to be delivered 2 years after start of construction. What should Cruises report as interest expense related to the note in its income statement for Year 2?

A. $0

B. $300,000

C. $600,000

D. $900,000

Answer (A) is correct.

REQUIRED: The interest reported in Year 2.

DISCUSSION: An asset produced by an entity for its own use qualifies for interest capitalization. Capitalized interest is limited to the amount theoretically avoidable if expenditures for the asset had not been made. It is also limited to the interest incurred for the period. Interest capitalized equals average accumulated expenditures (AAE) for the qualifying asset times the appropriate interest rate(s). The capitalization period (e.g., 2 years for the cruise ship beginning January 2 of Year 1) is the time required to carry out the activities necessary to bring the asset to the condition and location necessary for its intended use. Accordingly, no interest expense related to the note is recognized in the second year. The 10% interest rate on the note, a specific new borrowing outstanding during the capitalization period and identified with the qualifying asset, may be used as the capitalization rate to the extent that AAE do not exceed the amount of the new borrowing. Given that the $3 million of proceeds were used as a down payment, the total interest on the note (the carrying amount of the note for Year 2 × 10%) qualifies for capitalization. Thus, the AAE are at least equal to the carrying amount of the note for the second year. A weighted-average rate must be applied to the amount exceeding the specified new borrowings.

9. Cole Co. began constructing a building for its own use in January. During the year, Cole incurred interest of $50,000 on specific construction debt and $20,000 on other borrowings. Interest computed on the weighted-average amount of accumulated expenditures for the building during the year was $40,000. What amount of interest cost should Cole capitalize?

A. $20,000

B. $40,000

C. $50,000

D. $70,000

Answer (B) is correct.

REQUIRED: The amount of interest capitalized.

DISCUSSION: Material interest costs incurred for the construction of certain assets for internal use are capitalized. The interest to be capitalized is determined by applying an appropriate rate to the average qualifying expenditures accumulated during a given period. However, the interest capitalized may not exceed the amount incurred during the period. Thus, $40,000 of the interest incurred on the construction is capitalized.

Answer (A) is incorrect. The amount of $20,000 equals interest on other borrowings. Answer (C) is incorrect. The amount of $50,000 equals the total interest on specific construction debt. Answer (D) is incorrect. The amount of $70,000 equals the sum of interest on other borrowings and the total interest on specific construction debt.

10. A company is constructing an asset for its own use. Construction began in Year 3. The asset is being financed entirely with a specific new borrowing. Construction expenditures were made in Year 3 and Year 4 at the end of each quarter. The total amount of interest cost capitalized in Year 4 should be determined by applying the interest rate on the specific new borrowing to the

A. Total accumulated expenditures for the asset in Year 3 and Year 4.

B. Average accumulated expenditures for the asset in Year 3 and Year 4.

C. Average expenditures for the asset in Year 4.

D. Total expenditures for the asset in Year 4.

Answer (B) is correct.

REQUIRED: The expenditures used in determining the capitalizable interest.

DISCUSSION: An asset constructed for an entity's own use qualifies for capitalization of interest if (1) relevant expenditures have been made, (2) activities necessary to prepare the asset for its intended use are in progress, and (3) interest is being incurred. The capitalized amount is determined by applying an interest rate to the average qualifying expenditures accumulated during the period. These expenditures in any given period include those incurred in that period plus those incurred in the construction of the asset in all previous periods. Thus, the total interest cost capitalized in Year 4 equals the interest rate on the specific new borrowing times the average accumulated expenditures for the asset in Year 3 and Year 4.

Answer (A) is incorrect. The basis is an average for Year 3 and Year 4, not the total. Answer (C) is incorrect. The basis includes expenditures during the entire construction period. Answer (D) is incorrect. The basis is an average for Year 3 and Year 4.

11. Clay Company started construction of a new office building on January 1, Year 8, and moved into the finished building on July 1, Year 9. Of the building's $2.5 million total cost, $2 million was incurred in Year 8 evenly throughout the year. Clay's incremental borrowing rate was 12% throughout Year 8, and the total amount of interest incurred by Clay during Year 8 was $102,000. What amount should Clay report as capitalized interest at December 31, Year 8?

    A. $102,000

    B. $120,000

    C. $150,000

    D. $240,000

Answer (A) is correct.
    REQUIRED: The amount of interest to be capitalized as a cost of an asset.
    DISCUSSION: The new office building qualifies for capitalization of interest cost because (1) the asset is being constructed for the entity's own use, (2) expenditures relative to the qualifying asset have been made, (3) activities necessary to prepare the asset for its intended use are in progress, and (4) interest cost is being incurred. The amount capitalized is determined by applying an interest rate to the average accumulated expenditures (AAE) for the period. The AAE equals the simple average of any cost that is incurred evenly throughout the year. Here, the AAE are $1,000,000 ($2,000,000 × .5). The amount of interest to be capitalized is the $1,000,000 AAE times the rate of interest paid during Year 8, which is given as 12%. Because the $120,000 result ($1,000,000 × 12%) exceeds the $102,000 total amount of interest incurred, $102,000 is the maximum amount of interest that can be capitalized during the period ending 12/31/Year 8.

9.3 Subsequent Expenditures for PPE

12. An expenditure to install an improved electrical system is a

	Capital Expenditure	Revenue Expenditure
A.	No	Yes
B.	No	No
C.	Yes	No
D.	Yes	Yes

Answer (C) is correct.
    REQUIRED: The nature of an expenditure to install an improved electrical system.
    DISCUSSION: A betterment (improvement) occurs when a replacement asset is substituted for an existing asset, and the result is increased productivity, capacity, or expected useful life. If the improvement benefits future periods, it should be capitalized.

13. A building suffered uninsured fire damage. The damaged portion of the building was refurbished with higher-quality materials. The cost and related accumulated depreciation of the damaged portion are identifiable. The owner should

    A. Reduce accumulated depreciation equal to the cost of refurbishing.

    B. Record a loss in the current period equal to the sum of the cost of refurbishing and the carrying amount of the damaged part of the building.

    C. Capitalize the cost of refurbishing and record a loss in the current period equal to the carrying amount of the damaged part of the building.

    D. Capitalize the cost of refurbishing by adding the cost to the carrying amount of the building.

Answer (C) is correct.
    REQUIRED: The proper accounting for a substitution.
    DISCUSSION: When a substantial portion of a productive asset is replaced and the cost and related accumulated depreciation associated with the old component are identifiable, the substitution method of accounting is used. Under this approach, the asset account and accumulated depreciation should be reduced by the appropriate amounts, and a gain or loss should be recognized. In this instance, the damages were uninsured, and a loss equal to the carrying amount of the damaged portion of the building should be recognized. In addition, the cost of refurbishing should be capitalized in the asset account.

14. On June 18, Dell Printing Co. incurred the following costs for one of its printing presses:

Purchase of collating and stapling attachment	$84,000
Installation of attachment	36,000
Replacement parts for overhaul of press	26,000
Labor and overhead in connection with overhaul	14,000

The overhaul resulted in a significant increase in production. Neither the attachment nor the overhaul increased the estimated useful life of the press. What amount of the above costs should be capitalized?

A. $0

B. $84,000

C. $120,000

D. $160,000

Answer (D) is correct.
REQUIRED: The amount of costs to be capitalized.
DISCUSSION: Expenditures that increase the quality or quantity of a machine's output should be capitalized whether or not its useful life is extended. Thus, the amount of the cost to be capitalized equals $160,000 ($84,000 + $36,000 + $26,000 + $14,000).
Answer (A) is incorrect. Zero omits all of the listed capital expenditures. Answer (B) is incorrect. The installation and overhaul costs are capitalized. Answer (C) is incorrect. The amount of $120,000 excludes the overhaul costs.

15. Tomson Co. installed new assembly line production equipment at a cost of $175,000. Tomson had to rearrange the assembly line and remove a wall to install the equipment. The rearrangement cost $12,000, and the wall removal cost $3,000. The rearrangement did not increase the life of the assembly line, but it did make it more efficient. What amount of these costs should be capitalized by Tomson?

A. $175,000

B. $178,000

C. $187,000

D. $190,000

Answer (D) is correct.
REQUIRED: The capitalized cost of a new assembly line.
DISCUSSION: The initial measurement equals the sum of the cost to acquire the equipment and the costs necessarily incurred to bring it to the condition and location necessary for its intended use. A rearrangement is the movement of existing assets to provide greater efficiency or to reduce production costs. If the rearrangement expenditure benefits future periods, it should be capitalized. If the wall removal costs likewise improve future service potential, they too should be capitalized. Thus, the capitalized cost is $190,000 ($175,000 + $12,000 + $3,000).
Answer (A) is incorrect. The amount capitalized must include all costs incurred to bring the equipment to use. Answer (B) is incorrect. The rearrangement cost must be included in the amount capitalized. If this cost was incurred for the benefit of existing equipment, different rules apply. Answer (C) is incorrect. Cost of removal of the wall is capitalized.

16. During the year just ended, Fox Company made the following expenditures relating to plant machinery and equipment:

- Renovation of a group of machines at a cost of $50,000 to secure greater efficiency in production over their remaining 5-year useful lives. The project was completed on December 31.
- Continuing, frequent, and low-cost repairs at a cost of $35,000.
- A broken gear on a machine was replaced at a cost of $5,000.

What total amount should be charged to repairs and maintenance?

A. $35,000

B. $40,000

C. $85,000

D. $90,000

Answer (B) is correct.
REQUIRED: The amount to be charged to repair and maintenance expense.
DISCUSSION: Repair and maintenance costs are incurred to maintain plant assets in operating condition. The continuing, frequent, and low-cost repairs and the replacement of a broken gear meet the definition of repairs and maintenance expense. Accordingly, the amount that should be charged to repairs and maintenance is $40,000 ($35,000 + $5,000). The renovation cost increased the quality of production during the expected useful life of the group of machines. Hence, this $50,000 cost should be capitalized.
Answer (A) is incorrect. The amount of $35,000 excludes the gear replacement. Answer (C) is incorrect. The amount of $85,000 includes the renovation cost but not the gear replacement. Answer (D) is incorrect. The amount of $90,000 includes the renovation cost.

9.4 Depreciation Methods -- Calculations

17. Ichor Co. reported equipment with an original cost of $379,000 and $344,000 and accumulated depreciation of $153,000 and $128,000, respectively, in its comparative financial statements for the years ended December 31, Year 2 and Year 1. During Year 2, Ichor purchased equipment costing $50,000 and sold equipment with a carrying amount of $9,000. What amount should Ichor report as depreciation expense for Year 2?

A. $19,000

B. $25,000

C. $31,000

D. $34,000

Answer (C) is correct.

REQUIRED: The depreciation given comparative information and a purchase and a sale of equipment.

DISCUSSION: The reported equipment cost increased by $35,000 ($379,000 – $344,000), and the reported accumulated depreciation increased by $25,000 ($153,000 – $128,000) from December 31, Year 1, to December 31, Year 2. Given that the equipment purchased had a cost of $50,000, the cost of the equipment sold must have been $15,000 ($50,000 – $35,000 increase in the equipment cost balance). Given also that the equipment sold had a carrying amount of $9,000, the accumulated depreciation removed from the books must have been $6,000 ($15,000 cost – $9,000). Accordingly, the depreciation expense for Year 2 must have been $31,000 ($25,000 net increase in accumulated depreciation + $6,000).

Answer (A) is incorrect. The amount of $19,000 equals the $10,000 increase in the net equipment balance ($35,000 increase in cost – $25,000 increase in accumulated depreciation) plus $9,000. Answer (B) is incorrect. The amount of $25,000 is the increase in accumulated depreciation. Answer (D) is incorrect. The amount of $34,000 equals the increase in accumulated depreciation plus $9,000.

18. Rye Co. purchased a machine with a 4-year estimated useful life and an estimated 10% salvage value for $80,000 on January 1, Year 6. In its income statement, what should Rye report as the depreciation expense for Year 8 using the double-declining-balance (DDB) method?

A. $9,000

B. $10,000

C. $18,000

D. $20,000

Answer (B) is correct.

REQUIRED: The DDB depreciation expense.

DISCUSSION: Under the DDB method, a constant rate is applied to a declining carrying amount of an asset. Salvage value is ignored except that the asset is not depreciated below salvage value. Because the straight-line rate for this machine is 25% (100% ÷ 4 years), the DDB rate is 50% (25% × 2).

	Carrying Amount		DDB %		Depreciation Expense
Year 6:	$80,000	×	.50	=	$40,000
Year 7:	$40,000	×	.50	=	$20,000
Year 8:	$20,000	×	.50	=	$10,000

Answer (A) is incorrect. The amount of $9,000 includes the $8,000 residual value in the calculation. Answer (C) is incorrect. The amount of $18,000 is the Year 7 depreciation expense if the residual value is included in the calculation. Answer (D) is incorrect. The amount of $20,000 is the depreciation expense for Year 7.

19. Which of the following uses the straight-line depreciation method?

	Group Depreciation	Composite Depreciation
A.	No	No
B.	Yes	No
C.	Yes	Yes
D.	No	Yes

Answer (C) is correct.

REQUIRED: The method(s) using straight-line depreciation.

DISCUSSION: Both composite and group depreciation use the straight-line method. Both methods aggregate groups of assets. The composite method is used for a collection of dissimilar assets with varying useful lives, whereas the group method deals with similar assets. Each method involves the calculation of a total depreciable cost for all the assets included in one account and of a weighted-average estimated useful life.

20. A company using the composite depreciation method for its fleet of trucks, cars, and campers retired one of its trucks and received cash from a salvage company. The net carrying amount of these composite asset accounts was decreased by the

A. Cash proceeds received and original cost of the truck.

B. Cash proceeds received.

C. Original cost of the truck minus the cash proceeds.

D. Original cost of the truck.

Answer (B) is correct.

REQUIRED: The effect of a retirement on the net carrying amount of a composite asset account.

DISCUSSION: Because both composite and group methods use weighted averages of useful lives and depreciation rates, early and late retirements are expected to offset each other. Consequently, gains and losses on retirements of single assets are treated as adjustments of accumulated depreciation. The entry is to credit the asset at cost, debit cash for any proceeds received, and debit accumulated depreciation for the difference. Thus, the net carrying amount of the composite asset accounts is decreased by the amount of cash received. The net carrying amount of total assets is unchanged.

9.5 Depreciation Methods -- Changes and Comparison

21. On January 1, Year 5, Crater, Inc., purchased equipment having an estimated salvage value equal to 20% of its original cost at the end of a 10-year life. The equipment was sold December 31, Year 9, for 50% of its original cost. If the equipment's disposition resulted in a reported loss, which of the following depreciation methods did Crater use?

A. Double-declining balance.

B. Sum-of-the-years'-digits.

C. Straight-line.

D. Composite.

Answer (C) is correct.

REQUIRED: The method that would result in a reported loss upon disposition.

DISCUSSION: The straight-line method of depreciation is the only one of the generally accepted methods that is not an accelerated method. It thus yields the lowest amount of depreciation for the early part of the depreciable life of the asset. Because only 50% of the original cost was received and straight-line accumulated depreciation equaled 40% of cost {[(100% − 20%) ÷ 10 years] × 5 years} at the time of sale, a 10% loss [50% − (100% − 40%)] results.

Answer (A) is incorrect. The DDB method results in 5-year accumulated depreciation that is greater than 50% of cost. Answer (B) is incorrect. The SYD method results in 5-year accumulated depreciation that is greater than 50% of cost. Answer (D) is incorrect. The composite method of depreciation applies to the weighted average of multiple useful lives of assets, whereas only one asset is mentioned in this question. Moreover, it recognizes no gain or loss on disposition.

22. On January 2, Year 1, Union Co. purchased a machine for $264,000 and depreciated it by the straight-line method using an estimated useful life of 8 years with no salvage value. On January 2, Year 4, Union determined that the machine had a useful life of 6 years from the date of acquisition and will have a salvage value of $24,000. An accounting change was made in Year 4 to reflect the additional data. The accumulated depreciation for this machine should have a balance at December 31, Year 4, of

A. $179,000

B. $160,000

C. $154,000

D. $146,000

Answer (D) is correct.

REQUIRED: The accumulated depreciation for a machine given changes in estimates.

DISCUSSION: A change in the estimates for depreciation is accounted for prospectively. The new estimates are used in the year of the change, and no "catch-up" amounts are recorded. For Years 1 through 3, the amount of depreciation was $33,000 per year ($264,000 old depreciable base ÷ 8 old estimate of useful life), resulting in a balance of accumulated depreciation at December 31, Year 3, of $99,000 ($33,000 × 3 years). On January 2, Year 4, Union estimates the machine's original depreciable base to be $240,000 ($264,000 historical cost − $24,000 revised salvage value). The remaining depreciable base at January 2, Year 4, is thus $141,000 ($240,000 revised depreciable base − $99,000 accumulated depreciation), resulting in a new annual depreciation expense of $47,000 ($141,000 ÷ 3 years revised estimated life remaining). Thus, accumulated depreciation at December 31, Year 4, is $146,000 ($99,000 + $47,000).

Answer (A) is incorrect. The amount of $179,000 does not reflect subtraction of prior depreciation in calculating depreciation for Year 4. Answer (B) is incorrect. The amount of $160,000 would be the accumulated depreciation if the revised estimates had been used from the beginning. Answer (C) is incorrect. The amount of $154,000 does not reflect subtraction of the salvage value in calculating depreciation for Year 4.

23. In which of the following situations is the units-of-production method of depreciation most appropriate?

A. An asset's service potential declines with use.

B. An asset's service potential declines with the passage of time.

C. An asset is subject to rapid obsolescence.

D. An asset incurs increasing repairs and maintenance with use.

Answer (A) is correct.
   REQUIRED: The situation in which the units-of-production method of depreciation is most appropriate.
   DISCUSSION: The units-of-production depreciation method allocates asset cost based on the level of production. As production varies, so will the credit to accumulated depreciation. Consequently, when an asset's service potential declines with use, the units-of-production method is the most appropriate method.
   Answer (B) is incorrect. The straight-line method is appropriate when an asset's service potential declines with the passage of time. Answer (C) is incorrect. An accelerated method is best when an asset is subject to rapid obsolescence. Answer (D) is incorrect. The units-of-production method does not allow for increasing repairs and maintenance.

9.6 Exchanges of Nonmonetary Assets

24. Iona Co. and Siena Co. exchanged goods held for resale with equal fair values. Each will use the other's goods to promote its own products. The retail price of the wickets that Iona gave up is less than the retail price of the wombles received. What gain should Iona recognize on the nonmonetary exchange?

A. A gain is not recognized.

B. A gain equal to the difference between the retail prices of the wombles received and the wickets.

C. A gain equal to the difference between the retail price and the cost of the wickets.

D. A gain equal to the difference between the fair value and the cost of the wickets.

Answer (D) is correct.
   REQUIRED: The gain to be recognized on a nonmonetary exchange of inventory.
   DISCUSSION: The accounting for a nonmonetary transaction should be based on the carrying amount of the asset given up in an exchange of goods held for sale in the ordinary course of business for goods to be sold in the same line of business. The exchange also must be designed to facilitate sales to customers other than the parties to the exchange. Because Iona will use the wombles to promote its own product, the requirement that the product be used to facilitate sales to customers other than Iona or Siena is not met. Facilitation entails, for example, meeting immediate inventory needs or reducing transportation costs. Hence, Iona should record a gain equal to the difference between the fair value (the same for both assets) and the cost (carrying amount) of the asset surrendered.
   Answer (A) is incorrect. A gain should be recognized. Answer (B) is incorrect. Fair value, not retail prices, is the appropriate basis at which the asset received should be recognized. Answer (C) is incorrect. Fair value, not retail prices, is the appropriate basis at which the asset received should be recognized.

25. Amble, Inc., exchanged a truck with a carrying amount of $12,000 and a fair value of $20,000 for another truck and $5,000 cash. The fair value of the truck received was $15,000. The exchange was not considered to have commercial substance. At what amount should Amble record the truck received in the exchange?

A. $7,000

B. $9,000

C. $12,000

D. $15,000

Answer (D) is correct.
   REQUIRED: The amount at which a nonmonetary asset should be recorded in a transaction involving boot.
   DISCUSSION: A transaction involving nonmonetary assets and boot is monetary if the boot equals or exceeds 25% of the fair value of the exchange. In this exchange, the $5,000 of boot equals 25% of the $20,000 ($5,000 + $15,000) fair value of the exchange. Thus, the exchange is monetary. Accounting for monetary transactions should be based on the fair value of the assets involved, with gain or loss recognized immediately. Amble should record the truck received at its $15,000 fair value. It also should record an $8,000 gain equal to the difference between the $20,000 fair value received and the $12,000 carrying amount of the truck given up.
   Answer (A) is incorrect. The amount of $7,000 is equal to the $12,000 carrying amount of the asset given up minus the $5,000 boot received. Answer (B) is incorrect. The amount of $9,000 is equal to the $12,000 carrying amount of the truck given up, minus the $5,000 boot received, plus the $2,000 ($8,000 × 25%) proportionate gain that would have been recognized had the transaction been nonmonetary. Answer (C) is incorrect. The amount of $12,000 is equal to the carrying amount of the truck given up.

26. Minor Baseball Company had a player contract with Doe that was recorded in its accounting records at $145,000. Better Baseball Company had a player contract with Smith that was recorded in its accounting records at $140,000. Minor traded Doe to Better for Smith by exchanging player contracts. The fair value of each contract was $150,000. Evidence suggested that the contract exchange lacked commercial substance. At what amount should the contracts be valued in accordance with generally accepted accounting principles at the time of the exchange of the player contracts?

	Minor	Better
A.	$140,000	$140,000
B.	$140,000	$145,000
C.	$145,000	$140,000
D.	$150,000	$150,000

Answer (C) is correct.
REQUIRED: The amount at which to record an asset received in a nonmonetary exchange transaction that lacked commercial substance.
DISCUSSION: The accounting for a nonmonetary transaction should be based on the carrying amount of the asset(s) given up when the exchange lacks commercial substance. An exchange lacks commercial substance when an entity's cash flows are not expected to change significantly. Thus, Minor should record its contract with Smith at $145,000, and Better should record its contract with Doe at $140,000.
Answer (A) is incorrect. Minor should record its contract with Smith at $145,000, its previously recorded (carryover) amount for its contract with Doe. Answer (B) is incorrect. Minor should record its contract with Smith at $145,000, and Better should record its contract with Doe at $140,000. Answer (D) is incorrect. The amount of $150,000, the fair value of each contract, should be recorded if the exchange has commercial substance.

27. UVW Broadcast Co. entered into a contract to exchange unsold advertising time for travel and lodging services with Hotel Co. As of June 30, advertising commercials of $10,000 were used. However, travel and lodging services were not provided. How should UVW account for advertising in its June 30 financial statements?

A. Revenue and expense is recognized when the agreement is complete.

B. An asset and revenue for $10,000 is recognized.

C. Both the revenue and expense of $10,000 are recognized.

D. Not reported.

Answer (B) is correct.
REQUIRED: The accounting for advertising broadcast in exchange for services not yet received.
DISCUSSION: Broadcasters frequently barter unsold advertising time for products or services. Barter revenue should be recognized in appropriate amounts when the commercials are broadcast. The amounts should be reported at the estimated fair value of the product or service received. Revenue is not earned until the commercials are broadcast. The merchandise or services need not be resold for revenue to be recognized. An asset should be recognized if the commercials are broadcast before the merchandise or services are received. A liability should be recognized if the merchandise or services are received before the commercials are broadcast. The measurement of the asset and revenue may be based on the fair value ($10,000) of commercials broadcast if that amount is more clearly determinable than the fair value of the services to which the entity has become entitled.
Answer (A) is incorrect. The agreement is complete when a contract has been formed. In this type of arrangement, the contract is formed prior to performance by either party. An executory contract (one not performed by either party) does not (1) complete an earning process (revenue) or (2) use up economic benefits (expense). Answer (C) is incorrect. The expense should not be recognized until the prepaid services are used. Answer (D) is incorrect. Revenue is realizable and has been earned, and an asset should be debited.

9.7 Disposals Other than by Exchange

28. An entity disposes of a nonmonetary asset in a nonreciprocal transfer. A gain or loss should be recognized on the disposition of the asset when the fair value of the asset transferred is determinable and the nonreciprocal transfer is to

	Another Entity	A Shareholder of the Entity
A.	No	Yes
B.	No	No
C.	Yes	No
D.	Yes	Yes

Answer (D) is correct.
REQUIRED: The circumstances under which gain or loss should be recorded in a nonreciprocal transfer.
DISCUSSION: A nonreciprocal transfer is a transfer of assets or services in one direction. A nonreciprocal transfer of a nonmonetary asset to a shareholder or to another entity should be recorded at the fair value of the asset transferred. A gain or loss should be recognized on the transfer. However, an exception to this general rule is provided for distributions of nonmonetary assets to owners in (1) a spin-off or other form of reorganization or liquidation or (2) a plan that is in substance the rescission of a prior business combination.

29. A state government condemned Cory Co.'s parcel of real estate. Cory will receive $750,000 for this property, which has a carrying amount of $575,000. Cory incurred the following costs as a result of the condemnation:

Appraisal fees to support a $750,000 value	$2,500
Attorney fees for the closing with the state	3,500
Attorney fees to review contract to acquire replacement property	3,000
Title insurance on replacement property	4,000

What amount of cost should Cory use to determine the gain on the condemnation?

A. $581,000

B. $582,000

C. $584,000

D. $588,000

Answer (A) is correct.
REQUIRED: The amount of cost used to determine the gain on the condemnation.
DISCUSSION: A gain or loss must be recognized on an involuntary conversion. The determination of the gain is based on the carrying amount ($575,000) and the costs incurred as a direct result of the condemnation ($2,500 appraisal fees and $3,500 attorney fees), a total of $581,000. Because the recipient is not obligated to reinvest the condemnation proceeds in other nonmonetary assets, the costs associated with the acquisition of the replacement property (attorney fees and title insurance) should be treated as part of the consideration paid for that property.
Answer (B) is incorrect. The amount of $582,000 includes the costs associated with the replacement property but not the costs incurred as a direct result of the condemnation.
Answer (C) is incorrect. The amount of $584,000 includes the attorney fees associated with the replacement property.
Answer (D) is incorrect. The amount of $588,000 includes the costs associated with the replacement property.

30. On July 1, one of Rudd Co.'s delivery vans was destroyed in an accident. On that date, the van's carrying value was $2,500. On July 15, Rudd received and recorded a $700 invoice for a new engine installed in the van in May and another $500 invoice for various repairs. In August, Rudd received $3,500 under its insurance policy on the van, which it plans to use to replace the van. What amount should Rudd report as gain (loss) on disposal of the van in its income statement for the year?

A. $1,000

B. $300

C. $0

D. $(200)

Answer (B) is correct.
REQUIRED: The gain (loss) on disposal of the van.
DISCUSSION: Gain (loss) is recognized on an involuntary conversion equal to the difference between the proceeds and the carrying amount. The carrying amount includes the carrying value at July 1 ($2,500) plus the capitalizable cost ($700) of the engine installed in May. This cost increased the carrying amount because it improved the future service potential of the asset. Ordinary repairs, however, are expensed. Consequently, the gain is $300 [$3,500 – ($2,500 + $700)].
Answer (A) is incorrect. The amount of $1,000 results from expensing the cost of the engine. Answer (C) is incorrect. Gain (loss) is recognized on an involuntary conversion. Answer (D) is incorrect. The amount of $(200) assumes the cost of repairs increased the carrying amount.

31. Ocean Corp.'s comprehensive insurance policy allows its assets to be replaced at current value. The policy has a $50,000 deductible clause. One of Ocean's waterfront warehouses was destroyed in a winter storm. Such storms occur approximately every 4 years. Ocean incurred $20,000 of costs in dismantling the warehouse and plans to replace it. The following data relate to the warehouse:

Current carrying amount	$ 300,000
Replacement cost	1,100,000

The gain Ocean should report as a separate component of income before extraordinary items is

A. $1,030,000

B. $780,000

C. $730,000

D. $0

Answer (C) is correct.
REQUIRED: The gain reported as a separate component of income before extraordinary items.
DISCUSSION: To be classified as an extraordinary item, a transaction must be both unusual in nature and infrequent in occurrence within the environment in which the business operates. If an item meets one but not both of these criteria, it should be presented separately as a component of income from continuing operations. The gain is presumably infrequent but is not unusual in the entity's operating environment. The gain does not possess a high degree of abnormality and is not clearly unrelated to, or only incidentally related to, the entity's ordinary and typical activities. Hence, Ocean should separately recognize a gain from continuing operations equal to $730,000 ($1,100,000 current value – $50,000 deductible – $300,000 carrying amount – $20,000 costs of dismantling).
Answer (A) is incorrect. The amount of $1,030,000 disregards the $300,000 carrying amount. Answer (B) is incorrect. The amount of $780,000 omits the deductible. Answer (D) is incorrect. A gain (loss) should be recognized for an involuntary conversion.

9.8 Impairment of Long-Lived Assets

32. Testing for possible impairment of a long-lived asset (asset group) that an entity expects to hold and use is required

A. At each interim and annual balance sheet date.

B. At annual balance sheet dates only.

C. Periodically.

D. Whenever events or changes in circumstances indicate that its carrying amount may not be recoverable.

Answer (D) is correct.
 REQUIRED: The appropriate time for testing impairment of a long-lived asset (asset group) to be held and used.
 DISCUSSION: A long-lived asset (asset group) is tested for recoverability whenever events or changes in circumstances indicate that its carrying amount may not be recoverable. The carrying amount is not recoverable when it exceeds the sum of the undiscounted cash flows expected to result from the use and disposition of the asset (asset group). If the carrying amount is not recoverable, an impairment loss is recognized equal to the excess of the carrying amount over the fair value.

33. Which of the following conditions must exist in order for an impairment loss to be recognized?

I. The carrying amount of the long-lived asset is less than its fair value.

II. The carrying amount of the long-lived asset is not recoverable.

A. I only.

B. II only.

C. Both I and II.

D. Neither I nor II.

Answer (B) is correct.
 REQUIRED: The condition(s), if any, for recognition of an impairment loss.
 DISCUSSION: A long-lived asset (or asset group) to which the guidance for impairment or disposal applies is tested for recoverability whenever events or changes in circumstances indicate that its carrying amount may not be recoverable. The carrying amount is not recoverable when it exceeds the sum of the undiscounted cash flows expected to result from the use and disposition of the asset (or asset group). If the carrying amount is not recoverable, an impairment loss is recognized equal to the excess of the carrying amount over the fair value.

34. A company has a long-lived asset with a carrying value of $120,000, expected future cash flows of $130,000, present value of expected future cash flows of $100,000, and a market value of $105,000. What amount of impairment loss should be reported?

A. $0

B. $5,000

C. $15,000

D. $20,000

Answer (A) is correct.
 REQUIRED: The impairment loss.
 DISCUSSION: An impairment loss is recognized when a long-lived asset's carrying amount exceeds the sum of its undiscounted cash flows. Because the sum of the undiscounted cash flows ($130,000) exceeds the carrying amount ($120,000), the carrying amount is recoverable. Thus, no impairment is recognized.
 Answer (B) is incorrect. The difference between the fair value of the asset and the present value of the expected future cash flows is $5,000. Answer (C) is incorrect. The excess of the carrying amount over the fair value of the asset is $15,000. This unrealized holding loss is not recognized because the recoverability test has not been met. Answer (D) is incorrect. The difference between the carrying amount and the present value of the future cash flows is $20,000.

35. An impairment loss on a long-lived asset (asset group) to be held and used is reported by a business enterprise in

A. Discontinued operations.

B. Extraordinary items.

C. Other comprehensive income.

D. Income from continuing operations.

Answer (D) is correct.
 REQUIRED: The reporting of an impairment loss on a long-lived asset (asset group) to be held and used.
 DISCUSSION: An impairment loss is included in income from continuing operations before income taxes by a business enterprise (income from continuing operations in the statement of activities by a not-for-profit organization). When a subtotal for "income from operations" is reported, the impairment loss is included.
 Answer (A) is incorrect. A long-lived asset (asset group) to be held and used is not a discontinued operation. Answer (B) is incorrect. An impairment loss does not meet the criteria for an extraordinary item (unusual in nature and infrequent in the environment in which the entity operates). Answer (C) is incorrect. An impairment loss is reported in the income statement. Items reported in OCI have bypassed the income statement.

36. If a long-lived asset satisfies the criteria for classification as held for sale,

A. Its carrying amount is the cost at the acquisition date if the asset is newly acquired.

B. It is not depreciated.

C. Interest attributable to liabilities of a disposal group to which the asset belongs is not accrued.

D. It is classified as held for sale even if the criteria are not met until after the balance sheet date but before issuance of the financial statements.

Answer (B) is correct.
    REQUIRED: The treatment of a long-lived asset that meets the criteria for classification as held for sale.
    DISCUSSION: A long-lived asset is not depreciated (amortized) while it is classified as held for sale and measured at the lower of carrying amount or fair value minus cost to sell. The reason is that depreciation (amortization) would reduce the carrying amount below fair value minus cost to sell. Furthermore, fair value minus cost to sell must be evaluated each period, so any future decline will be recognized in the period of decline.
    Answer (A) is incorrect. The carrying amount of a newly acquired long-lived asset classified as held for sale is its fair value minus cost to sell at the acquisition date. Answer (C) is incorrect. Interest and other expenses attributable to liabilities of a disposal group to which the asset belongs are accrued. Answer (D) is incorrect. If the criteria are not met until after the balance sheet date but before issuance of the financial statements, the long-lived asset continues to be classified as held and used in those statements.

9.9 Depletion

37. In January, Vorst Co. purchased a mineral mine with removable ore estimated at 1.2 million tons for $2,640,000. After it has extracted all the ore, Vorst will be required by law to restore the land to its original condition at an estimated cost of $180,000. Vorst believes it will be able to sell the property afterwards for $300,000. During the year, Vorst incurred $360,000 of development costs preparing the mine for production and removed and sold 60,000 tons of ore. In its income statement for the year, what amount should Vorst report as depletion?

A. $135,000

B. $144,000

C. $150,000

D. $159,000

Answer (B) is correct.
    REQUIRED: The amount of depletion to be reported.
    DISCUSSION: Vorst's per-ton depletion charge is calculated as follows:

Purchase price	$2,640,000
Add: restoration costs	180,000
Minus: residual value	(300,000)
Add: preparation costs	360,000
Depletion base	$2,880,000
Divided by: estimated removable tons	÷1,200,000
Depletion charge per ton	$ 2.40

Accordingly, Vorst should report $144,000 (60,000 tons sold × $2.40 per ton) as depletion in its income statement for the year.
    Answer (A) is incorrect. The amount of $135,000 does not include the $180,000 restoration costs. Answer (C) is incorrect. The amount of $150,000 does not consider the restoration costs and the residual value of the land. Answer (D) is incorrect. The amount of $159,000 adds the $180,000 restoration cost instead of deducting the $120,000 net residual value of the land.

38. WD Mining Company purchased a section of land for $600,000 in Year 1 to develop a zinc mine. The mine began operations in Year 9. At that time, management estimated that the mine would produce 200,000 tons of quality ore. A total of 100,000 tons of ore were mined and processed from Year 9 through December 31, Year 16. During January Year 17, a very promising vein was discovered. The revised estimate of ore still to be mined was 250,000 tons. Estimated salvage value for the mine land was $100,000 in both Year 9 and Year 17. Assuming that 10,000 tons of ore were mined in Year 17, what amount should WD Mining Company report as depletion in Year 17?

A. $14,286

B. $11,111

C. $10,000

D. $7,142

Answer (C) is correct.
    REQUIRED: The depletion recorded after allowing for a change of estimate.
    DISCUSSION: The original cost of the land was $600,000. The estimated salvage value in both Year 9 and Year 17 was $100,000. The depletion base in Year 9 was therefore $500,000 ($600,000 – $100,000). Half of the estimated 200,000 tons of quality ore were mined in the period Year 9 through Year 16. Thus, $250,000 would have been allocated to the 100,000 tons mined, and the depletion base in January Year 17 would have been $250,000 ($600,000 – $100,000 – $250,000) before the change in estimate. This amount should be allocated over the 250,000-ton revised estimate of available ore. Multiplying by the 10,000 tons actually mined in Year 17 gives the amount of depletion to record of $10,000.
    Answer (A) is incorrect. The revised estimate of 250,000 tons of ore is not included, and the amount of the depletion base already depleted is not included. Answer (B) is incorrect. The $250,000 allocated to the 100,000 tons mined is not subtracted from the numerator, and the denominator should equal the 250,000-ton revised estimate. Answer (D) is incorrect. The denominator should equal the 250,000-ton revised estimate.

Use the additional questions in Gleim **CPA Test Prep Online** to create Test Sessions that emulate Prometric!

9.10 PRACTICE SIMULATION

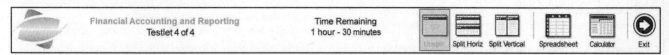

Financial Accounting and Reporting	Time Remaining	Unsplit	Split Horiz	Split Vertical	Spreadsheet	Calculator	Exit
Testlet 4 of 4	1 hour - 30 minutes						

DIRECTIONS

Note: If you believe you have encountered a software malfunction, report it to the test center staff immediately.

Navigation

To navigate from task to task, use the controls at the bottom of the screen. Click on the **Next** button to advance to the next task, or the **Previous** button to go to the previous task. To go directly to any task, click on its number.

If you would like a reminder to revisit a task, or want to indicate that you are finished with it, click on the reminder flag below the task number. To clear the flag, click on it again. Reminder flags are for your use only – they do not contribute to your score.

Tabs

In this part of the examination, you will be asked to complete various tasks. Every task has one or more **Work Tabs**. Some tasks have one or more **Information Tabs**, others may have none. Every task has a **Help** tab.

If a task has **Information Tabs**, you may use the information in them to complete your responses in the **Work Tabs**.

Work tab	Information tab	Help tab

Work Tabs:

- **Work Tabs** are identified with a pencil icon. This is where your responses are expected.
- Each task has one or more **Work Tabs**.
- **Work Tabs** contain directions for completing the task – be sure to read these directions carefully.
- The **Work Tab** name in the example above is for illustration only – yours will differ.
- You must complete all of the **Work Tabs** in each task to receive full credit.

Information Tabs:

- The Authoritative Literature will be provided in all tasks in the AUD, FAR, and REG sections for your reference.
- Your simulation may have one or more additional **Information Tabs**. Like the Authoritative Literature tabs, **Information Tabs** do not have a pencil icon.
- If your task has additional **Information Tabs**, go through each to familiarize yourself with the task content.

Help Tab:

- The **Help Tab** provides assistance with the exam software that is used in this task. For example, if the task is to compose a memorandum, **Help** will provide information about the word processor.

The Toolbar

The toolbar at the top of the screen shows the amount of time remaining for you to complete the tasks. In addition, the following tools are available. Note that only the **Exit** button is displayed when Directions are visible - the others will appear when you begin the tasks.

Click on these buttons to split or unsplit the screen. You can split the screen vertically or horizontally.

Click on this button to display the calculator; click on it again to hide the calculator. To move the calculator, click on the calculator title bar and drag the calculator to the desired location.

Click on this button to use the spreadsheet; click on it again to hide the spreadsheet. To move the spreadsheet, click on the the spreadsheet title bar and drag the spreadsheet to the desired location.

Click on this button to go on to the next part of the examination. You must complete all of the tasks to receive full credit. Once you click on **Exit** and confirm the action, you will NOT be able to return to this testlet.

Yankee Co.'s property, plant, and equipment and accumulated depreciation and amortization balances at December 31, Year 4, are

Asset	Cost	Accumulated Depreciation
Land	$ 275,000	--
Buildings	2,800,000	$ 672,900
Machinery and equipment	1,380,000	367,500
Automobiles and trucks	210,000	114,326
Leasehold improvements	432,000	108,000
Totals	$5,097,000	$1,262,726

Depreciation and amortization methods and useful lives

Buildings	150% declining balance; 25 years
Machinery and equipment	Straight-line; 10 years
Automobiles and trucks	150% declining balance; 5 years, all acquired after 1999
Leasehold improvements	Straight-line

- Depreciation is computed to the nearest month.
- Salvage values of depreciable assets are immaterial except for automobiles and trucks, which have estimated salvage values equal to 15% of cost.

Additional information

- Yankee entered into a 12-year operating lease starting January 1, Year 2. The leasehold improvements were completed on December 31, Year 1, and the facility was occupied on January 1, Year 2.
- On January 6, Year 5, Yankee completed its self-construction of a building on its own land. Direct costs of construction were $1,095,000. Construction of the building required 15,000 direct labor hours. Yankee's construction department has an overhead allocation system for outside jobs based on an activity denominator of 100,000 direct labor hours, budgeted fixed costs of $2.5 million, and budgeted variable costs of $27 per direct labor hour.
- On July 1, Year 5, machinery and equipment were purchased at a total invoice cost of $325,000. Additional costs of $23,000 to repair damage on delivery and $18,000 for concrete embedding of machinery were incurred. A wall had to be demolished for a large machine to be moved into the plant. The wall demolition cost $7,000, and rebuilding the wall cost $19,000.
- On August 30, Year 5, Yankee purchased a new automobile for $25,000.
- On September 30, Year 5, a truck with a cost of $48,000 and a carrying amount of $30,000 on December 31, Year 4, was sold for $23,500.
- On November 4, Year 5, Yankee purchased a tract of land for investment purposes for $700,000. Yankee may use the land as a future building site.
- On December 20, Year 5, a machine with a cost of $17,000, a carrying amount of $2,975 on the date of disposition, and a fair value of $4,000 was given to a corporate officer in partial liquidation of a debt.

Enter the appropriate monetary values in the Increase, Decrease, and Balance columns. If there is no increase or decrease, leave those columns empty. Answers are based on calculations required to draft a schedule of depreciation and amortization expense.

Yankee Co.
ANALYSIS OF CHANGES IN
ACCUMULATED DEPRECIATION AND AMORTIZATION
For the Year Ended December 31, Year 5

Item	Balance 12/31/Year 4	Increase	Decrease	Balance 12/31/Year 5
1. Buildings				
2. Machinery and equipment				
3. Automobiles and trucks				
4. Leasehold improvements				

| PPE Changes | Authoritative Literature | Help |

Yankee Co.'s property, plant, and equipment and accumulated depreciation and amortization balances at December 31, Year 4, are

Asset	Cost	Accumulated Depreciation
Land	$ 275,000	--
Buildings	2,800,000	$ 672,900
Machinery and equipment	1,380,000	367,500
Automobiles and trucks	210,000	114,326
Leasehold improvements	432,000	108,000
Totals	$5,097,000	$1,262,726

Additional information

- Yankee entered into a 12-year operating lease starting January 1, Year 2. The leasehold improvements were completed on December 31, Year 1, and the facility was occupied on January 1, Year 2.

- On January 6, Year 5, Yankee completed its self-construction of a building on its own land. Direct costs of construction were $1,095,000. Construction of the building required 15,000 direct labor hours. Yankee's construction department has an overhead allocation system for outside jobs based on an activity denominator of 100,000 direct labor hours, budgeted fixed costs of $2.5 million, and budgeted variable costs of $27 per direct labor hour.

- On July 1, Year 5, machinery and equipment were purchased at a total invoice cost of $325,000. Additional costs of $23,000 to repair damage on delivery and $18,000 for concrete embedding of machinery were incurred. A wall had to be demolished for a large machine to be moved into the plant. The wall demolition cost $7,000, and rebuilding the wall cost $19,000.

- On August 30, Year 5, Yankee purchased a new automobile for $25,000.

- On September 30, Year 5, a truck with a cost of $48,000 and a carrying amount of $30,000 on December 31, Year 4, was sold for $23,500.

- On November 4, Year 5, Yankee purchased a tract of land for investment purposes for $700,000. Yankee may use the land as a future building site.

- On December 20, Year 5, a machine with a cost of $17,000, a carrying amount of $2,975 on the date of disposition, and a fair value of $4,000 was given to a corporate officer in partial liquidation of a debt.

Enter the appropriate monetary amounts in the Increase, Decrease, and Balance columns for items properly classified as PPE. Do not consider accumulated depreciation. If there is no increase or decrease, leave those columns empty.

Yankee Co.
**ANALYSIS OF CHANGES IN
PROPERTY, PLANT, AND EQUIPMENT**
For the Year Ended December 31, Year 5

Item	Balance 12/31/Year 4	Increase	Decrease	Balance 12/31/Year 5
1. Land				
2. Buildings				
3. Machinery and equipment				
4. Automobiles and trucks				
5. Leasehold improvements				

Depreciation and amortization methods and useful lives

Buildings	150% declining balance; 25 years
Machinery and equipment	Straight-line; 10 years
Automobiles and trucks	150% declining balance; 5 years, all acquired after 1999
Leasehold improvements	Straight-line

- Depreciation is computed to the nearest month.
- Salvage values of depreciable assets are immaterial except for automobiles and trucks, which have estimated salvage values equal to 15% of cost.

Additional information

- On September 30, Year 5, a truck with a cost of $48,000 and a carrying amount of $30,000 on December 31, Year 4, was sold for $23,500.
- On December 20, Year 5, a machine with a cost of $17,000, a carrying amount of $2,975 on the date of disposition, and a fair value of $4,000 was given to a corporate officer in partial liquidation of a debt.

Enter the appropriate monetary amounts in the shaded cells below.

Yankee Co.
**GAIN ON DISPOSITION OF
PROPERTY, PLANT, AND EQUIPMENT**
For the Year Ended December 31, Year 5

Item	*Selling Price*	*Carrying Amount*	*Gain*
1. Sale of truck			
2. Machine exchanged for debt			
3. Totals			

Capitalize vs. Expense   Authoritative Literature   Help

The following items represent expenditures for goods held for resale and equipment. Determine whether the expenditure for each item should be capitalized or expensed as a period cost and check the box to the right of each item that should be capitalized.

Expenditure	*Capitalize*
1. Freight charges paid for goods held for resale	
2. In-transit insurance on goods held for resale purchased FOB shipping point	
3. Interest on note payable for goods held for resale	
4. Installation of equipment	
5. Testing of newly purchased equipment	
6. Cost of current-year service contract on equipment	

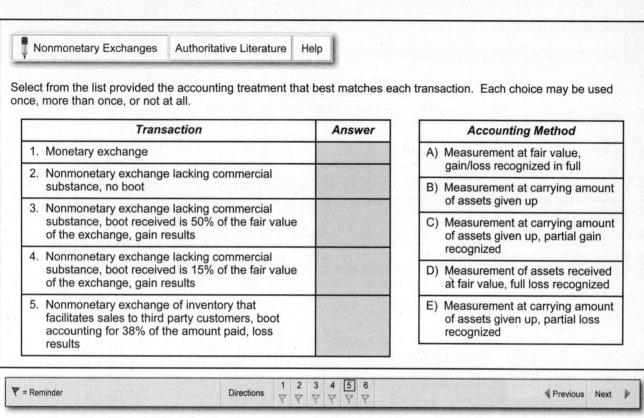

Nonmonetary Exchanges | Authoritative Literature | Help

Select from the list provided the accounting treatment that best matches each transaction. Each choice may be used once, more than once, or not at all.

Transaction	Answer	Accounting Method
1. Monetary exchange		A) Measurement at fair value, gain/loss recognized in full
2. Nonmonetary exchange lacking commercial substance, no boot		B) Measurement at carrying amount of assets given up
3. Nonmonetary exchange lacking commercial substance, boot received is 50% of the fair value of the exchange, gain results		C) Measurement at carrying amount of assets given up, partial gain recognized
4. Nonmonetary exchange lacking commercial substance, boot received is 15% of the fair value of the exchange, gain results		D) Measurement of assets received at fair value, full loss recognized
5. Nonmonetary exchange of inventory that facilitates sales to third party customers, boot accounting for 38% of the amount paid, loss results		E) Measurement at carrying amount of assets given up, partial loss recognized

▼ = Reminder   Directions   1 2 3 4 [5] 6   ◀ Previous   Next ▶

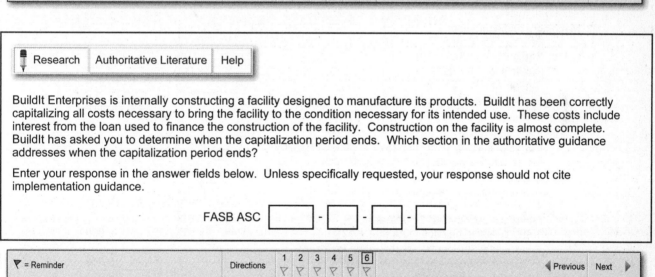

Research | Authoritative Literature | Help

BuildIt Enterprises is internally constructing a facility designed to manufacture its products. BuildIt has been correctly capitalizing all costs necessary to bring the facility to the condition necessary for its intended use. These costs include interest from the loan used to finance the construction of the facility. Construction on the facility is almost complete. BuildIt has asked you to determine when the capitalization period ends. Which section in the authoritative guidance addresses when the capitalization period ends?

Enter your response in the answer fields below. Unless specifically requested, your response should not cite implementation guidance.

FASB ASC [   ] - [   ] - [   ] - [   ]

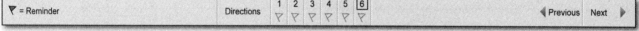

▼ = Reminder   Directions   1 2 3 4 5 [6]   ◀ Previous   Next ▶

Unofficial Answers

1. Depreciation/Amortization (14 Gradable Items)

Yankee Co.
ANALYSIS OF CHANGES IN
ACCUMULATED DEPRECIATION AND AMORTIZATION
For the Year Ended December 31, Year 5

Item	Balance 12/31/Year 4	Increase	Decrease	Balance 12/31/Year 5
1. Buildings	$672,900	$240,126 [a]	$	$913,025
2. Machinery and equipment	367,500	156,450 [b]	14,025 [e]	509,925
3. Automobiles and trucks	114,326	28,952 [c]	24,750 [f]	118,528
4. Leasehold improvements	108,000	36,000 [d]		144,000

Explanation of Amounts:

Increases

[a]   Buildings
          Carrying amount, 1/1/Year 5 ($2,800,000 – $672,900) $2,127,100
          Building completed 1/6/Year 5   1,875,000
          Total subject to depreciation $4,002,100
          150% declining balance [(100% ÷ 25) × 1.5]   ×   6%
               Depreciation for Year 5 $ 240,126

[b]   Machinery and equipment
          Balance, 1/1/Year 5 $1,380,000
          Straight-line (100% ÷ 10)   ×   10% $ 138,000
          Purchased 7/1/Year 5 $ 369,000
          Straight-line [10% × (6 ÷ 12)]   ×   5%   18,450
               Depreciation for Year 5 $ 156,450

[c]   Automobiles and trucks
          Carrying amount, 1/1/Year 5 ($210,000 – $114,326) $ 95,674
          Minus carrying amount, 1/1/Year 5 on truck
               sold 9/30/Year 5   (30,000)
          Amount subject to depreciation $ 65,674
          150% declining balance [(100% ÷ 5) × 1.5]   ×   30% $ 19,702
          Automobile purchased 8/30/Year 5 $ 25,000
          150% declining balance [30% × (4 ÷ 12)]   ×   10%   2,500
          Truck sold 9/30/Year 5 -- depreciation for Year 5
               (1/1 to 9/30/Year 5) [$30,000 × 30% × (9 ÷ 12)]   6,750
               Depreciation for Year 5 $ 28,952

[d]   Leasehold improvements
          Amortization for Year 5 ($432,000 ÷ 12 years) $ 36,000

Decreases

[e]   Machinery and equipment
          Cost $ 17,000
          Carrying amount   (2,975)
          Accumulated depreciation $ 14,025

[f]   Automobiles and trucks
          Cost $ 48,000
          Carrying amount ($30,000 – $6,750)   (23,250)
          Accumulated depreciation $ 24,750

2. PPE Changes (15 Gradable Items)

Yankee Co.
**ANALYSIS OF CHANGES IN
PROPERTY, PLANT, AND EQUIPMENT**
For the Year Ended December 31, Year 5

Item	Balance 12/31/Year 4	Increase	Decrease	Balance 12/31/Year 5
1. Land	$ 275,000	$	$	$ 275,000 [c]
2. Buildings	2,800,000	1,875,000 [a]		4,675,000
3. Machinery and equipment	1,380,000	369,000 [b]	17,000	1,732,000
4. Automobiles and trucks	210,000	25,000	48,000	187,000
5. Leasehold improvements	432,000			432,000

Explanation of Amounts:

[a] Construction cost of building

Direct costs			$1,095,000
Overhead costs			
Fixed [15,000 hours × ($2,500.00 ÷ 100,000 DLH)]		$375,000	
Variable (15,000 hours × $27)		405,000	780,000
			$1,875,000

[b] Machinery and equipment purchased

Invoice cost	$ 325,000
Installation cost (concrete embedding)	18,000
Cost of gaining access to factory ($19,000 + $7,000)	26,000
Total acquisition cost	$ 369,000

[c] The land purchased as an investment should be reported in an investment account, not PPE, because it is not used in the entity's ordinary operations.

3. Gain/Loss (9 Gradable Items)

Yankee Co.
**GAIN ON DISPOSITION OF
PROPERTY, PLANT, AND EQUIPMENT**
For the Year Ended December 31, Year 5

Item	Selling Price	Carrying Amount	Gain
1. Sale of truck	$23,500	$23,250	$ 250
2. Machine given to extinguish debt	4,000	2,975	1,025
3. Totals	$27,500	$26,225	$1,275

4. Capitalize vs. Expense (6 Gradable Items)

1. <u>Capitalize.</u> Expenditures may be capitalized as inventory if they are directly or indirectly incurred in bringing items of inventory to their existing condition and location. Freight charges are therefore an inventoriable cost and should be capitalized.

2. <u>Capitalize.</u> Expenditures are inventoriable and should be capitalized if they are incurred directly or indirectly in bringing items of inventory to their existing condition and location. The cost of insurance for in-transit goods held for resale is an inventoriable cost because the goods were purchased FOB shipping point. Because title and risk of loss pass at the point of shipment, shipping costs are the responsibility of the purchaser.

3. <u>Expense.</u> Interest cost is capitalized only for assets produced for an enterprise's own use or for sale or lease as discrete projects. Interest cost for inventories is not capitalized. Hence, the interest on the note for goods held for resale should be expensed.

4. <u>Capitalize.</u> The initial measurement of property, plant, and equipment includes all costs to acquire these assets, transport them to the sites of their intended use, and prepare them for operations. The installation of equipment should therefore be capitalized.

5. <u>Capitalize.</u> The initial measurement of property, plant, and equipment includes all costs to acquire these assets, transport them to the sites of their intended use, and prepare them for operations. Hence, the costs of testing newly purchased equipment should be capitalized.

6. <u>Expense.</u> The cost of a current-year service contract on equipment should be expensed. Routine expenditures that maintain the normal service capacity of an asset do not benefit future periods and are not capitalized.

5. Nonmonetary Exchanges (5 Gradable Items)

1. <u>A) Measurement at fair value, gain/loss recognized in full.</u> Monetary exchanges are measured at the fair value of the assets involved, with gain or loss recognized immediately.

2. <u>B) Measurement at carrying amount of assets given up.</u> If an exchange lacks commercial substance, that is, when an entity's cash flows are not expected to change significantly, the exchange is a nonmonetary exchange and is based on the carrying amount of the assets given up.

3. <u>A) Measurement at fair value, gain/loss recognized in full.</u> If boot constitutes 25% or more of the fair value of the exchange, the exchange is treated as a monetary exchange. Both parties record the transaction at fair value and recognize any gain or loss in full.

4. <u>C) Measurement at carrying amount of assets given up, partial gain recognized.</u> If boot is given as part of an exchange measured at carrying amount, the recipient of the boot must recognize some gain.

5. <u>D) Measurement of assets received at fair value, full loss recognized.</u> If boot constitutes 25% or more of the fair value of the exchange, the exchange is treated as a monetary exchange. Both parties record the transaction at fair value and recognize any gain or loss in full.

6. Research (1 Gradable Item)

Answer: FASB ASC 835-20-25-5

835-20-25-5 The capitalization period shall end when the asset is substantially complete and ready for its intended use. Consider the capitalization period that is appropriate in each of the following examples:

a. Some assets are completed in parts, and each part is capable of being used independently while work is continuing on other parts. An example is a condominium. For such assets, interest capitalization shall stop on each part when it is substantially complete and ready for use.

b. Some assets must be completed in their entirety before any part of the asset can be used. An example is a facility designed to manufacture products by sequential processes. For such assets, interest capitalization shall continue until the entire asset is substantially complete and ready for use.

c. Some assets cannot be used effectively until a separate facility has been completed. Examples are the oil wells drilled in Alaska before completion of the pipeline. For such assets, interest capitalization shall continue until the separate facility is substantially complete and ready for use.

Gleim Simulation Grading

Task	Correct Responses		Gradable Items		Score per Task
1	____	÷	14	=	____
2	____	÷	15	=	____
3	____	÷	9	=	____
4	____	÷	6	=	____
5	____	÷	5	=	____
Research	____	÷	1	=	____

Total of Scores per Task   ____

÷ Total Number of Tasks   6

Total Score   ____%

Use **CPA Gleim Online** and **Simulation Wizard** to practice more task-based simulations in a realistic environment.

STUDY UNIT TEN
INTANGIBLE ASSETS AND
OTHER CAPITALIZATION ISSUES

(16 pages of outline)

10.1 Intangible Assets Distinct from Goodwill -- Initial Recognition 347
10.2 Intangible Assets Distinct from Goodwill -- Accounting Subsequent to Acquisition 348
10.3 Franchise Accounting 352
10.4 Goodwill 353
10.5 Research and Development 356
10.6 Prepayments 359
10.7 Computer Software 359
10.8 Special Issues 361
10.9 Practice Simulation 373

Intangible assets can take many forms. The FASB has defined six categories of intangibles: marketing-related (e.g., trademarks), customer-related (e.g., customer lists), artistic-related (e.g., copyrights), contract-related (e.g., franchise rights), technology-related (e.g., computer software) and goodwill (which arises only in business combinations).

10.1 INTANGIBLE ASSETS DISTINCT FROM GOODWILL -- INITIAL RECOGNITION

1. **Definition**
   a. They **lack physical substance**.
      1) In general, intangible assets convey to the holder a contractual or legal right to receive future economic benefits.
      2) Common examples are patents, trademarks, copyrights, and franchise arrangements.
   b. They **are not financial assets**.
      1) Intangible assets thus do not include such items as cash, equity investments, accounts and notes receivable, bonds receivable, or prepaid expenses.
   c. Because the accounting treatment of goodwill is different from that of other intangible assets, goodwill is discussed later in this study unit.

2. **Initial Recognition**
   a. **Externally acquired** intangibles other than goodwill are initially recorded at acquisition cost plus any incidentals such as legal fees.
      1) If the intangible was acquired for cash, the asset is initially recorded at the amount of cash paid.
      2) If the intangible was acquired in an exchange involving noncash assets, initial recognition is at the fair value of the more clearly evident of (a) the consideration given or (b) the intangible asset received.
   b. **Internally developed** intangibles other than goodwill are most often initially recorded at the amount of the incidental costs (e.g., legal fees) only.
      1) Most of the costs of an internally generated intangible asset consist of research and development (R&D), which must be expensed as incurred.

IFRS Difference

An intangible asset must be recognized only if (1) it is **probable** that the entity will receive the asset's expected economic benefits and (2) the cost is reliably **measurable**.

---

3.   **Organization and Start-up Costs**

   a.   Organization costs are those incurred in the formation of a business entity. They include payments to promoters, legal and accounting fees, and costs of registering with the state of incorporation.

      1)   Under the federal tax code, organization and start-up costs must be capitalized and amortized over a period of not less than 15 years.

      2)   However, for financial accounting purposes, nongovernmental entities must expense all start-up and organization costs as incurred.

Stop and review! You have completed the outline for this subunit. Study multiple-choice questions 1 through 4 beginning on page 362.

10.2 INTANGIBLE ASSETS DISTINCT FROM GOODWILL -- ACCOUNTING SUBSEQUENT TO ACQUISITION

1.   **Useful Life and Amortization**

   a.   The useful life of an asset is the period during which it is expected to contribute either directly or indirectly to the future cash flows of the reporting entity.

   b.   An intangible asset with a **finite useful life** to the reporting entity is **amortized** over that useful life.

      1)   If the useful life is finite but not precisely known, the amortization period is the best estimate of the useful life.

      2)   The useful life should be reevaluated each reporting period. A change in the estimate results in a prospective change in amortization.

   c.   Amortization is based on the pattern of consumption of economic benefits, if reliably determinable. Otherwise, the straight-line method must be used.

      1)   The **amortizable amount** equals the amount initially assigned minus the residual value. The **residual value** is the estimated fair value to the entity at the end of the asset's useful life minus disposal costs. This amount is zero unless

         a)   A third party has committed to purchase the asset, or

         b)   It can be determined from an exchange transaction in an existing market for the asset that is expected to exist at the end of the useful life.

      2)   An intangible asset is not written down in the period of acquisition unless it becomes impaired during that period.

IFRS Difference

The **revaluation model** may be used for intangible assets if they are traded in active markets (this is described on page 307 in Study Unit 9).

EXAMPLE

An intangible asset was purchased on the first day of the fiscal year for $1,000,000. Its useful life is 5 years, and it has a residual value of $100,000. However, its pattern of consumption of economic benefits is not reliably determinable. The year-end amortization entry is

Intangible asset amortization	$180,000	
Accumulated amortization		$180,000

[($1,000,000 – $100,000) ÷ 5 years = $180,000 straight-line amortization]

---

   d.   An intangible asset with an **indefinite useful life** is **not amortized**.

2. **Patents**

     a.   Patents may be purchased or developed internally.

         1)   The initial capitalized cost of a **purchased patent** is normally the fair value of the consideration given, that is, its purchase price plus incidental costs, such as registration and attorneys' fees.

         2)   **Internally developed patents** are less likely to be capitalized because related R&D costs must be expensed when incurred.

             a)   Thus, only relatively minor costs can be capitalized, for example, patent registration fees and legal fees.

     b.   The **amortization period** for a patent is the shorter of its useful life or the legal life remaining after acquisition.

         1)   The useful life may be substantially shorter than the legal life because of changes in consumer tastes, delays in marketing the product or service, and development of substitutes or improvements.

     c.   Patents may be sold outright or temporarily licensed.

         1)   Patent fee revenue should be recognized when an earning process has been completed. Royalty revenue must be recognized as it is earned.

     d.   The accounting treatment of the costs of the **legal defense of a patent** depends upon the outcome of the litigation.

         1)   The unrecovered costs of successful litigation are capitalized because they will benefit future periods.

             a)   They are amortized over the shorter of the remaining legal life or the estimated useful life of the patent.

         2)   The costs of unsuccessful litigation (damages, attorneys' fees) are expensed.

             a)   An unsuccessful suit also indicates that the unamortized cost of the patent has no value and should be recognized as a loss.

3. **Copyrights**

     a.   The Copyright Act provides broad rights to intellectual property consisting of "original works of authorship in any tangible medium of expression, now known or later developed."

         1)   An **author's copyright** is for life plus 70 years.

         2)   A **publisher's copyright** is for the earlier to expire of 95 years from publication or 120 years from creation.

     b.   The Copyright Act is based on specific authority granted in the Constitution.

     c.   Among the works protected are literary, musical, and dramatic works; sound recordings; motion pictures and other audiovisual works; and computer software.

     d.   The copyright holder has **exclusive rights** to reproduce, distribute, perform, display, and prepare derivative works from copyrighted material.

     e.   **Limited exceptions** are allowed for library or archive reproduction and fair use for purposes of comment, criticism, news coverage, teaching, scholarship, or research.

     f.   The Copyright Act does not protect ideas, processes, discoveries, principles, etc.

     g.   A copyright provides automatic protection once it is in tangible form.

         1)   Registration with the federal Copyright Office is necessary only to give a copyright owner standing to sue in federal court for infringement.

         2)   Furthermore, a notice of copyright is not required to be placed on the work.

    h.   Ordinarily, the **estimated useful life** of a copyright is substantially less than its legal life. However, some exceptions are well-known, e.g., classic films.

    i.   Copyrights are similar to patents in that they can be sold.

        1)   Moreover, rights under copyrights and patents can be licensed.

        2)   Another similarity to patents is that legal fees, registration fees, litigation costs, and the purchase price can be capitalized. But internal R&D costs cannot.

4. **Trademarks and Similar Property**

    a.   Trademarks and related property are **not as readily transferable** as patents and copyrights.

        1)   Their use with goods or services having qualities other than those with which they are commonly associated may be confusing to consumers.

           a)   Hence, uncontrolled licensing is contrary to the spirit of the law.

        2)   A trademark or similar intangible asset may be sold only in connection with the goodwill of the entity it represents.

    b.   **Capitalizable costs** include attorneys' fees, registration fees, design costs, and the costs of successfully defending the intangible asset. These costs do not include advertising and R&D expenditures.

5. **Testing for Impairment**

    a.   If an amortized intangible asset is later determined to have an **indefinite useful life**, it (1) must no longer be amortized and (2) must be tested for impairment.

    b.   An **amortized** intangible asset is reviewed for impairment when events or changes in circumstances indicate that its carrying amount may not be recoverable.

        1)   An impairment loss is recognized only if the carrying amount is not recoverable and is greater than the asset's fair value. Reversal of a recognized impairment loss is prohibited.

           a)   The impairment test is met if the sum of the undiscounted expected future cash flows from the asset is less than the carrying amount.

               i)   The loss recognized is the excess of that carrying amount over the fair value.

               ii)   This loss is nonreversible, so the adjusted carrying amount is the new accounting basis.

Determination of an Impairment Loss
1. Events or changes in circumstances indicate a possible loss.
2. Carrying amount > Sum of undiscounted cash flows
3. Loss = Carrying amount – Fair value

IFRS Difference

An impairment loss for an asset (except goodwill) may be reversed if a change in the estimates used to measure the recoverable amount has occurred. The test for impairment of assets other than goodwill has one step: determine whether an asset's carrying amount is greater than its recoverable amount (greater of fair value minus costs to sell or value in use).

EXAMPLE

A patent was purchased on the first day of the fiscal year for $900,000. Its useful life is 5 years with no residual value. At the end of Year 3, an event occurred indicating that the asset may be impaired. The patent's fair value is $350,000, and its undiscounted future net cash inflows are $355,000.

The carrying amount of $360,000 {$900,000 – [($900,000 ÷ 5 years) × 3 years]} exceeds the undiscounted future net cash flows of $355,000. The impairment loss is $10,000 ($360,000 carrying amount – $350,000 fair value).

The journal entry to record the impairment is

Loss due to impairment	$10,000	
Patent		$10,000

---

c. A **nonamortized** intangible asset must be reviewed for impairment at least annually. It is tested more often if events or changes in circumstances suggest that the asset may be impaired. An entity may first perform a **qualitative assessment** to determine whether it is necessary to perform the **quantitative impairment test**.

1) After the assessment of qualitative factors, the entity may determine that it is more likely than not (probability > 50%) that an indefinite-lived intangible asset is not impaired. In this case, the quantitative impairment test is not required.

2) If potential impairment is found, the quantitative impairment test needs to be performed. This impairment test does not consider recoverability.

a) If the carrying amount exceeds the fair value, the asset is impaired, and the excess is the recognized loss. This loss also is nonreversible, so the adjusted carrying amount is the new accounting basis.

Determination of an Impairment Loss
1. Review for impairment
2. Loss = Carrying amount – Fair value

b) The asset is then amortized prospectively and otherwise accounted for as an amortized asset.

EXAMPLE

A company has a trademark with a carrying amount of $750,000 and an indefinite useful life. At the end of Year 4, an event occurred indicating that the asset may be impaired. The trademark's fair value is $700,000, and its undiscounted future net cash inflows are $790,000.

The impairment loss is $50,000 ($750,000 carrying amount – $700,000 fair value).

The journal entry to record the impairment is

Loss due to impairment	$50,000	
Trademark		$50,000

NOTE: The undiscounted future net cash inflows are not considered when testing an intangible asset with an indefinite life. The cash flows could continue for many years.

Stop and review! You have completed the outline for this subunit. Study multiple-choice questions 5 through 10 beginning on page 364.

10.3 FRANCHISE ACCOUNTING

> Franchise accounting has been a well-tested topic on recent exams, from the points of view of both the franchisor and the franchisee. Be able to calculate amounts for franchise capitalization, amortization, and revenue recognition.

1. **Franchises**

   a. A franchise is a contractual agreement by a **franchisor** (grantor of the franchise) to permit a **franchisee** (purchaser) to operate a certain business.

      1) Thus, an exclusive right may be granted to sell a specified product or service in a given geographical area and to use trademarks, patents, trade secrets, etc.

2. **Franchisee Accounting**

   a. The franchisee should capitalize the costs of acquiring the franchise. The **capitalizable amount** includes the initial fee and other expenditures, e.g., legal fees, necessary to acquire the franchise that will provide future benefits.

      1) Future payments based on a percentage of revenues or for franchisor services are expensed as incurred. They benefit only the period of payment.

   b. Franchise costs are **amortized** over their **estimated useful life** if such life is **finite**.

3. **Franchisor Accounting**

   a. **Franchise fee revenue** ordinarily should be recognized with a provision for uncollectible amounts. **Recognition** is at the earliest time when the franchisor has substantially performed.

   b. The earliest time usually is the beginning of operations by the franchisee unless substantial performance of all obligations occurred previously.

   c. Substantial performance occurs when

      1) The franchisor has no remaining obligation or intent to refund any cash or to forgive any debt,

      2) The franchisor has performed substantially all of the initial contracted services, and

      3) No other relevant material obligations or conditions exist.

   d. The **installment and cost recovery methods** are appropriate only when the franchise fees are to be collected over an extended period and collectibility cannot be reasonably estimated.

   e. **Initial fees are deferred** if they are large in relation to subsequent continuing fees or if future related services are promised, e.g., if bargain purchase prices exist for supplies.

      1) Deferral is indicated when it is probable that continuing fees will not cover the cost of continuing services and provide a reasonable profit. The deferral should cover those amounts.

      2) Continuing fees are recognized as revenue when they are earned and receivable.

      3) The portion of the initial franchise fee applicable to any **tangible assets** provided to the franchisee is recognized based on the fair values.

   f. Repossession of the franchise or refund of the franchise fee is a reduction of revenue in the current period.

      1) If a refund is made to the franchisee, previously recognized revenue is a contra revenue in the current period.

      2) If no refund is made, bad debt and other expenses are recognized, and associated deferred revenues should be recognized in the current period.

EXAMPLE

On December 31, Year 1, Sigrid Corp. authorized Vortigern to operate as a franchisee for an initial franchise fee of $300,000. Of this amount, $120,000 was received upon signing the agreement, and the balance, represented by a note, is due in three annual payments of $60,000 each, beginning December 31, Year 2. The present value on December 31, Year 1, of the three annual payments appropriately discounted is $144,000. According to the agreement, the nonrefundable down payment is a fair measure of the services already performed by Sigrid. However, substantial future services are required of Sigrid. Collectibility of the note is reasonably certain. Accordingly, Sigrid's entry is

Note receivable	$180,000	
Cash	120,000	
Unearned revenue		$144,000
Franchise fee revenue		120,000
Discount on note receivable		36,000

Because the down payment is the agreed amount paid for services already performed, Sigrid should recognize $120,000 of revenue. The note is a long-term receivable that should be reported at its present value. However, this amount ($144,000) should be recorded as unearned revenue because the franchisor has not substantially performed (completed the earning process).

Stop and review! You have completed the outline for this subunit. Study multiple-choice questions 11 and 12 on page 366.

10.4 GOODWILL

1. **Definition**

   a. Goodwill is recognized only in a business combination. It is "an asset representing the future economic benefits arising from other assets acquired in a business combination that are not individually identified and separately recognized."

      1) Study Unit 16 covers the accounting for the initial recognition of goodwill.

2. **Accounting for Goodwill Subsequent to Recognition**

   a. Goodwill is not amortized. Instead, goodwill of a reporting unit is tested for impairment each year at the same time.

      1) Different reporting units may be tested at different times. Furthermore, additional testing also may be indicated.

   b. A reporting unit is an operating segment or one of its components. An entity must identify its operating segments (the process used to identity operating segments is described in Study Unit 5, Subunit 2).

      1) A component is a reporting unit if (a) it is a business for which discrete financial information is available and (b) segment management regularly reviews its operating results. Similar components must be aggregated.

   c. As part of testing goodwill for impairment, acquired assets and assumed liabilities must be assigned to reporting units. Also, assets and liabilities considered by the reporting entity to be part of its corporate assets and liabilities are assigned.

      1) The assignment is made at the acquisition date to the reporting unit if the assets and liabilities relate to its operations and are included in its fair value.

      2) The amounts of assets relating to multiple reporting units are assigned based on a reasonable, supportable, and consistently applied method.

Background

Goodwill is only recognized as the result of a business combination. For years, U.S. GAAP required that goodwill be amortized over a period not to exceed 40 years. Recognizing that this requirement did not produce useful information, in 2001, the FASB eliminated this provision and replaced it with an annual test for impairment. The FASB reasoned that the consolidated entity receives the benefit of goodwill for the term of its economic life and that any recognized reduction in the balance of goodwill should be the result of identifiable events and circumstances, not an arbitrary time period.

3.   **Assignment of Goodwill to Reporting Units**

    a.   All goodwill is **assigned to the reporting units that will benefit** from the business combination. The method used should be reasonable, supportable, consistently applied, and consistent with the objectives of the assignment.

        1)   The assignment, in principle, should be done in the same manner as the determination of goodwill in a business combination. Thus, the fair value of the acquired business included in the reporting unit is determined.

            a)   An excess of this amount over the fair value of the net assets assigned to the reporting unit is the goodwill assigned.

            b)   If no assets or liabilities are assigned to a reporting unit, the goodwill to be assigned equals the increase in the fair value of the reporting unit as a result of the combination.

Goodwill Assigned to a Reporting Unit
FV of reporting unit – FV of net assets assigned

4.   **Measuring Fair Value of a Reporting Unit**

    a.   The **best evidence of fair value** is a quoted market price in an active market. Such prices should be used if available.

        1)   However, the market capitalization of a reporting unit may not reflect its fair value. Because of the synergies and other benefits of control, an investor may be willing to pay a control premium.

        2)   Another valuation method is estimation of fair value based on multiples of a performance measure, such as earnings or revenue. This method may be appropriate when information (observable fair value and multiples) about an entity comparable to the reporting unit is known.

5.   **Potential Impairment of Goodwill**

    a.   Potential impairment of goodwill exists only if the carrying amount (including goodwill) of a reporting unit is greater than its fair value. The accounting for goodwill is based on the units of the combined entity into which the acquiree was absorbed. The goodwill impairment test includes an optional qualitative test and a two-step quantitative test.

    b.   **Goodwill Impairment Test**

        1)   **Qualitative test.** Prior to performing the quantitative goodwill impairment test, the entity may elect to make a **qualitative assessment**.

            a)   Thus, the entity may choose to assess whether qualitative factors indicate that it is more likely than not (probability > 50%) that the fair value of the reporting unit is less than its carrying amount.

            b)   The qualitative assessment considers relevant events and circumstances. Among many others, they may include (1) macroeconomic, industry, and market conditions; (2) cost increases; (3) overall financial performance; (4) other entity-specific events; and (5) events affecting the reporting unit.

        2)   **Quantitative test.** The quantitative test need not be performed if the qualitative assessment does not indicate impairment. **If a potential impairment is found**, the following two-step quantitative test is performed to determine any goodwill impairment.

            a)   **Step 1**: Calculate the fair value of the reporting unit and compare with its carrying amount including goodwill. If the fair value is greater than the carrying amount, no impairment loss is recognized. However, if the fair value is less than the carrying amount, perform step 2.

b) **Step 2**: Calculate and compare the implied fair value of the reporting-unit goodwill with the carrying amount of that goodwill. An impairment loss not exceeding the carrying amount of goodwill is then recognized equal to any excess of that carrying amount over the implied fair value. This loss is **nonreversible**.

   i) The **implied fair value** of reporting-unit goodwill is estimated by assigning the fair value of the reporting unit to its assets and liabilities. The excess of reporting-unit fair value over the sum of the amounts assigned equals the implied fair value.

Determination of Impairment Loss
1.   Carrying amount of reporting unit > Its fair value
2.   Estimate implied fair value of reporting-unit goodwill
3.   Carrying amount of reporting-unit goodwill > Its implied fair value
4.   Loss = Excess in 3.

EXAMPLE

On January 1, Year 1, Apogee Co. purchased Perigee Co. for $200,000,000 and recognized $20,000,000 of goodwill. It properly classifies Perigee as a reporting unit. On December 31, Year 2, Apogee's fiscal year end, the following information is available about Perigee:

Carrying amount of net assets (including goodwill)	$190,000,000
Fair value	150,000,000
Fair value of net assets (excluding goodwill)	135,000,000

Apogee elected not to make a preliminary qualitative assessment of the potential impairment of goodwill. Instead, it performed the quantitative test. The carrying amount ($190,000,000) exceeds the fair value ($150,000,000). Thus, goodwill may be impaired.

The implied fair value of goodwill is $15,000,000 ($150,000,000 – $135,000,000). The impairment loss is $5,000,000 ($20,000,000 carrying amount of goodwill – $15,000,000 implied fair value).

---

6.   **Disposal of a Reporting Unit**

   a.   In the calculation of the gain or loss on disposal of a reporting unit, goodwill is included as part of its carrying amount.

   b.   If only part of the reporting unit is to be disposed of and that part constitutes a business, the goodwill related to the business is included in the carrying amount. The included goodwill of the business and the portion retained by the reporting unit are determined based on relative fair values.

      1)   When a partial assignment of goodwill is made to a business to be disposed of, the remaining reporting-unit goodwill is tested for impairment.

      2)   An acquired business may not have been integrated with the other activities of the reporting unit. Thus, the total carrying amount of the goodwill acquired with the business should be included in the carrying amount of the business.

7.   **Equity Method Goodwill**

   a.   The difference between the cost of an investment and the investor's underlying equity in the net assets of the investee (stated at its carrying amount) is allocated between two elements: **goodwill** and the difference between the carrying amounts and fair values that can be related to **specific accounts** at the acquisition date.

   b.   Equity method investments are reviewed for impairment. However, equity method goodwill itself is not reviewed for impairment because it is not separable from the investment. Furthermore, it is not amortized.

8. **Presentation in the Financial Statements**

   a. In the **balance sheet**, intangible assets are required to be presented, at a minimum, as a single aggregated line item. But individual intangible assets or classes of these assets may be separately presented.

      1) Goodwill is presented in the aggregate as a separate line item.

   b. In the **income statement**, amortization expense and impairment losses related to intangible assets are presented as line items under continuing operations.

      1) The aggregate goodwill impairment loss is presented as the last separate line item before the subtotal income from continuing operations.

      2) However, if a discontinued operation is reported, a loss related to impairment of goodwill associated with that operation is presented net of tax within the discontinued operations caption.

IFRS Difference

For the purpose of impairment testing, **goodwill** is allocated to the entity's **cash-generating units (CGUs)** that will benefit from the business combination. A CGU is the lowest level at which goodwill is monitored and must not be larger than an operating segment. The test for impairment of a CGU to which goodwill has been allocated is whether the carrying amount of the CGU (including allocated goodwill) exceeds its **recoverable amount** (greater of fair value minus costs to sell or value in use). Thus, the test has one step. An impairment loss for a CGU is allocated first to reduce allocated goodwill to zero and then pro rata to other assets of the CGU.

Stop and review! You have completed the outline for this subunit. Study multiple-choice questions 13 and 14 beginning on page 366.

10.5 RESEARCH AND DEVELOPMENT

Background

The appropriate treatment of R&D costs was one of the first topics tackled by the newly formed FASB and was the subject of its *Statement No. 2* issued in 1974. Previously, there had been a wide variety of treatments used in practice, and it was clear that a single method was needed to improve comparability. Citing the uncertainty of future benefits and the extreme difficulty of matching benefits to costs, the FASB required all R&D costs to be expensed as incurred.

---

1. **Overview**

   a. Research and development (R&D) costs must be **expensed as incurred**.

      1) This rule does not apply to R&D activities conducted for others.

      2) This rule also does not apply to assets (tangible or intangible) acquired in a business combination that are used in R&D activities. Such assets are initially recognized and measured at fair value even if they have no alternative use.

IFRS Difference

Development results in **recognition of an intangible asset** if the entity can demonstrate the (1) technical feasibility of completion of the asset, (2) intent to complete, (3) ability to use or sell the asset, (4) way in which it will generate probable future economic benefits, (5) availability of resources to complete and use or sell the asset, and (6) ability to measure reliably expenditures attributable to the asset.

---

   b. **Research** is planned search or critical investigation aimed at discovery of new knowledge with the hope that it will be useful in developing a new (or significantly improving an existing) product, service, process, or technique (product or process).

   c. **Development** is translation of research findings or other knowledge into a plan or design for a new or improved product or process.

      1) It includes conceptual formulation, design, and testing of product alternatives; prototype construction; and operation of pilot plants.

      2) Development does **not** include routine alterations to existing products, production lines, processes, and other ongoing operations.

         a) Market research or testing also is excluded.

The AICPA has used both theoretical and calculation questions to test candidates' knowledge of expensing research and development costs. Calculation questions may list several items and ask for the amount of research and development expense to be reported on the income statement.

---

2. **R&D Activities**

   a. The following are examples of activities typically included in R&D unless conducted for others under a contract (reimbursable costs are not expensed):

      1) Laboratory research aimed at discovery of new knowledge

      2) Searching for applications of new research findings or other knowledge

      3) Conceptual formulation and design of possible product or process alternatives

      4) Testing in search for, or evaluation of, product or process alternatives

      5) Modification of the formulation or design of a product or process

      6) Design, construction, and testing of preproduction prototypes and models

      7) Design of tools, jigs, molds, and dies involving new technology

      8) Design, construction, and operation of a pilot plant that is not of a scale economically feasible to the entity for commercial production

      9) Engineering activity required to advance the design of a product until it meets specific functional and economic requirements and is ready for manufacture

3. **Activities Not Classified as R&D**

   a. The following are examples of activities that typically are not classified as R&D:

      1) Engineering follow-through in an early phase of commercial production

      2) Quality control during commercial production, including routine testing of products

      3) Troubleshooting in connection with breakdowns during commercial production

      4) Routine, ongoing efforts to refine, enrich, or otherwise improve upon the qualities of an existing product

      5) Adaptation of an existing capability to a particular requirement or customer's need as part of a continuing commercial activity

      6) Seasonal or other periodic design changes to existing products

      7) Routine design of tools, jigs, molds, and dies

      8) Activity, including design and construction engineering, related to the construction, relocation, rearrangement, or start-up of facilities or equipment other than pilot plants and facilities or equipment whose sole use is for a particular R&D project

      9) Legal work in connection with patent applications or litigation and the sale or licensing of patents

4. **Elements of R&D Costs**

    a. **Materials, equipment, and facilities.** The costs of such items acquired or constructed for R&D and having alternative future uses are capitalized as tangible assets and depreciated accordingly.

        1) The costs of materials consumed in R&D and the depreciation of equipment or facilities used in R&D are R&D costs and are expensed when incurred.

        2) The costs of materials, equipment, or facilities acquired (but not in a business combination) or constructed for a particular project and having no alternative future uses (and no separate economic values) are R&D costs and are expensed when incurred.

    b. **Personnel.** Salaries, wages, and other related costs of personnel engaged in R&D are included in R&D costs and are expensed when incurred.

    c. **Intangible assets purchased from others.** These costs of R&D assets having alternative future uses are capitalized as intangible assets. They are amortized if their useful lives are finite.

        1) The amortization of those intangible assets is an R&D cost.

        2) The costs of intangible assets purchased from others (but not in a business combination) for a particular project and having no alternative future uses (and no separate economic values) are R&D costs and are expensed when incurred.

    d. **Contract services.** The costs of services performed by others in connection with the R&D activities of an entity, including R&D conducted by others on behalf of the entity, are R&D costs and are expensed when incurred.

    e. **Indirect costs.** R&D costs include a reasonable allocation of indirect costs, which also are expensed.

        1) General and administrative costs not clearly related to R&D are excluded.

    f. **Disclosure** is made in the financial statements of the total R&D costs charged to expense in each period for which an income statement is presented.

5. **R&D Funded by Others**

    a. Sometimes an entity's R&D is funded wholly or partly by others.

        1) If the entity is **obligated to repay** any of the funds provided by the other party regardless of the outcome of the project, it recognizes a **liability**.

        2) If repayment depends solely on the results of the R&D having future economic benefit, the entity accounts for its obligation as a contract to perform R&D for others.

    b. Repayment of a loan or advance to others may depend on whether the R&D will have future economic benefits. In this case, the loan or advance is debited to R&D expense unless it relates to another activity.

CPA candidates should expect to be tested on research and development costs. Common questions have focused on what activities are classified as R&D activities, and both theoretical and calculation formats have been utilized.

Stop and review! You have completed the outline for this subunit. **Study multiple-choice questions 15 through 18 beginning on page 367.**

10.6 PREPAYMENTS

1. **Prepayments**

    a. An asset provides future economic benefits. If a cash payment is made in one period and the recognition of the related expense (receipt of the benefit) is not appropriate until a later period, the **deferred cost** is recorded as an **asset**.

    1) Examples include prepaid insurance, rent, interest, and income taxes.

    2) The amount of the prepaid expense that will be used up within the longer of 1 year or the next operating cycle of the entity is classified as a current asset.

    3) If the payment is initially recorded as an asset, the year-end adjusting entry will credit the asset and debit an expense for the expired portion.

    a) If the payment is initially recorded as an expense, the year-end adjusting entry will debit an asset and credit expense for the unexpired portion.

Stop and review! You have completed the outline for this subunit. Study multiple-choice questions 19 through 21 beginning on page 368.

10.7 COMPUTER SOFTWARE

1. **Overview**

    a. Accounting for the costs of developing or obtaining computer software depends on whether the software will be sold to external customers or used strictly internally.

    1) Costs of software may be (a) expensed as incurred, (b) capitalized as computer software costs, or (c) included in inventory.

    2) Costs of software to be used internally are either expensed or capitalized.

2. **Software to Be Marketed**

    a. **Costs Expensed**

    1) Costs incurred before technological feasibility is established (coding, testing, etc.) are expensed as incurred. Thus, they are treated as R&D costs.

    2) Technological feasibility is established when either a detailed program design is complete or the entity has created a working model.

    b. **Costs Capitalized**

    1) Costs incurred after technological feasibility is established (coding, testing, producing product masters) are capitalized as computer software costs.

    2) Amortization begins and capitalization ends when the product is available for general release.

    3) If purchased software to be marketed has **no alternative future use**, the entity accounts for its cost as if it had been developed internally to be marketed. If purchased software to be marketed **has an alternative future use**, the entity **capitalizes** the costs when it purchases the software and accounts for it according to use.

    c. **Costs Included in Inventory**

    1) Costs incurred to prepare the product for sale (duplication of software, training materials, packaging) are capitalized as inventory.

Costs of Software to Be Marketed

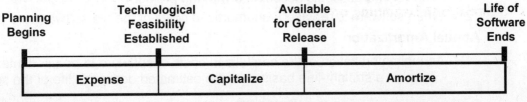

Figure 10-1

EXAMPLE

During Year 1, TriloByte, Inc., incurred and properly classified the following costs to prepare a software package for the market:

	Costs	Expensed	Capitalized	Inventory
Work on detail program design	$93,000	$ 93,000		
Coding to establish technological feasibility	58,000	58,000		
Testing to establish technological feasibility	64,000	64,000		
Coding after establishment of technological feasibility	60,000		$ 60,000	
Testing after establishment of technological feasibility	45,000		45,000	
Production of product masters	20,000		20,000	
Duplication of software	80,000			$ 80,000
Preparation of training materials	15,000			15,000
Packaging	27,000			27,000
Totals		$215,000	$125,000	$122,000

    d.   **Annual Amortization**

        1)   Annual amortization is the greater of

            a)   Total capitalized cost times the revenue ratio (annual gross software revenue divided by total projected gross revenue) or

            b)   Total capitalized cost divided by the estimated economic life of the software (i.e., straight-line).

    e.   **Balance Sheet Measurement**

        1)   Capitalized software costs are reported at the lower of unamortized cost or net realizable value (NRV).

EXAMPLE

TriloByte, Inc., expected its software package to have an economic life of 6 years. Sales during Year 2 were 20% of the projected total revenues expected over the life of the software. The net realizable value of the software at December 31, Year 2, was $90,000. TriloByte calculates annual amortization of software costs as follows:

            Revenue ratio: $125,000 × 20% = $25,000
            Straight-line: $125,000 ÷ 6 = $20,833

Because the amount derived using the revenue ratio is the greater of the two, it equals amortization for the year. Unamortized software costs at December 31, Year 2, are therefore $100,000 ($125,000 – $25,000). However, NRV is lower ($90,000 < $100,000), so NRV is the new carrying amount.

    3.   **Software to Be Used Internally**

        a.   **Costs Expensed**

            1)   Costs incurred during the preliminary project stage (planning, evaluation) are expensed as incurred.

            2)   Costs incurred for training and maintenance are also expensed.

        b.   **Costs Capitalized**

            1)   Costs incurred during the application development stage (coding, testing) are capitalized as computer software costs. They include (a) external direct costs of materials and services, (b) payroll costs directly associated with the project, and (c) interest costs associated with the project.

            2)   When software is replaced, unamortized costs of the old software are expensed.

        c.   **Annual Amortization**

            1)   Annual amortization of the capitalized costs of software to be used internally is done on a straight-line basis over the estimated economic life of the software.

EXAMPLE

Dancy Corp. spent $22,000,000 during the current year developing a new software package that will only be used internally. Of this amount, $6,000,000 was spent before the project reached the application development stage. The package was completed during the year and is expected to have a 4-year useful life. Dancy's policy is to take a full year's amortization in the first year. After the application development stage, Dancy spent $125,000 on training materials and sessions. Dancy will calculate expense associated with this software package for the current year as follows:

Costs incurred during preliminary project stage	$ 6,000,000
Amortization expense [($22,000,000 – $6,000,000) ÷ 4]	4,000,000
Costs incurred for training	125,000
Current-year expense	$10,125,000

---

    d.   **Subsequent Sale**

        1)   Occasionally, software developed for internal use will be sold to outside parties.

            a)   The net proceeds from these sales reduce the carrying amount of capitalized software costs.

            b)   Once software costs reach $0, any further net proceeds are recognized as revenue.

Stop and review! You have completed the outline for this subunit. Study multiple-choice questions 22 through 25 beginning on page 369.

10.8 SPECIAL ISSUES

    1.   **Deferred Charges**

        a.   Deferred charges (other assets) is a catchall category. It includes long-term prepayments and any noncurrent assets not classified elsewhere.

        b.   Such a classification has been criticized because many assets (e.g., PPE) are deferred charges. Thus, they are noncurrent prepayments that will be depreciated or amortized.

    2.   **Development Stage Entities (DSEs)**

        a.   DSEs (1) are devoting substantially all of their efforts to establishing the business and (2) have not begun principal operations or have not earned significant revenues from those operations.

            1)   Financial statements of DSEs must be presented in accordance with the same GAAP applicable to established operating entities.

        b.   The following additional information must be disclosed:

            1)   The **deficit accumulated** during the development stage should be presented in the equity section of the balance sheet. The income statement and statement of cash flows should include not only amounts for each period for which an income statement is presented but also **cumulative amounts from the entity's inception**.

               a)   These disclosures are accomplished by placing a cumulative amount column to the right of the current period's amounts.

            2)   During the development stage, the financial statements are identified as those of a DSE, and the nature of the development stage activities should be disclosed.

            3)   When the development stage is complete, the statements for the next year must disclose that, in prior years, the entity was in the development stage. No other disclosure is required.

        c.   The **development stage is complete when significant revenue** is generated from the planned principal operations.

        d.   Cost deferral is permitted to DSEs only to the same extent as to established operating entities under GAAP.

3.   **Advertising Costs**

a.   Advertising costs should be **expensed** either **as incurred** or **when advertising first occurs**. The primary costs are production and communication. Production includes idea development, copywriting, artwork, printing, hiring personnel (e.g., audio and video crews and actors), etc. Communication requires use of the Internet, newspapers, magazines, radio, television, billboards, etc.

b.   However, certain **direct response advertising** costs should be **capitalized** (deferred).

1)   Capitalization is appropriate if

a)   The primary purpose is to generate sales from customers who respond specifically to the advertising and

b)   Probable future economic benefits result.

2)   An entity that wishes to capitalize the costs of direct response advertising must document that customers have specifically responded to the advertising. It also must document the benefits from prior direct response advertising.

3)   The deferral of advertising costs is appropriate for both interim and year-end financial reporting if their benefits clearly apply to more than one period.

a)   Moreover, if a cost that would be fully expensed in an annual report benefits more than one interim period, it may be allocated to those interim reports.

IFRS Difference

Advertising costs generally are expensed as incurred.

Stop and review! You have completed the outline for this subunit. Study multiple-choice questions 26 through 29 beginning on page 371.

QUESTIONS

10.1 Intangible Assets Distinct from Goodwill -- Initial Recognition

1. On June 30, Year 5, Finn, Inc., exchanged 2,000 shares of Edlow Corp. $30 par-value common stock for a patent owned by Bisk Co. The Edlow stock was acquired in Year 1 at a cost of $50,000. At the exchange date, Edlow common stock had a fair value of $40 per share, and the patent had a net carrying amount of $100,000 on Bisk's books. Finn should record the patent at

A. $50,000

B. $60,000

C. $80,000

D. $100,000

Answer (C) is correct.
    REQUIRED: The amount at which a patent should be recorded.
    DISCUSSION: When an intangible asset is acquired in an exchange transaction, initial recognition is at the fair value of the more clearly evident of the consideration given or the asset acquired. The fair value of the assets given in return for the patent was $80,000 (2,000 shares of stock × $40 per share fair value).
    Answer (A) is incorrect. The acquisition cost of the stock is $50,000. Answer (B) is incorrect. The par value of the stock is $60,000. Answer (D) is incorrect. The net carrying amount of the patent is $100,000.

2. An entity purchases a trademark and incurs the following costs in connection with the trademark:

One-time trademark purchase price	$100,000
Nonrefundable VAT taxes	5,000
Training sales personnel on the use of the new trademark	7,000
Research expenditures associated with the purchase of the new trademark	24,000
Legal costs incurred to register the trademark	10,500
Salaries of the administrative personnel	12,000

Applying IFRS and assuming that the trademark meets all of the applicable initial asset recognition criteria, the entity should recognize an asset in the amount of

A. $100,000

B. $115,500

C. $146,500

D. $158,500

Answer (B) is correct.

REQUIRED: The initial amount recognized for an intangible asset.

DISCUSSION: Cost includes the purchase price (including purchase taxes and import duties) and any directly attributable costs to prepare the asset for its intended use, such as legal fees. Thus, the intangible asset is initially recognized at $115,500 ($100,000 price + $5,000 value-added taxes + $10,500 of legal costs).

Answer (A) is incorrect. Purchase taxes and legal fees for registration also are capitalized. Answer (C) is incorrect. Training and research costs are expensed as incurred. Answer (D) is incorrect. Training and research costs and administrative salaries and other overhead costs are not directly attributable costs.

3. Under IFRS, which of the following is a criterion that must be met in order for an item to be recognized as an intangible asset other than goodwill?

A. The item's fair value can be measured reliably.

B. The item is part of the entity's activities aimed at gaining new scientific or technical knowledge.

C. The item is expected to be used in the production or supply of goods and services.

D. The item is identifiable and lacks physical substance.

Answer (D) is correct.

REQUIRED: The criterion for recognizing an intangible asset other than goodwill.

DISCUSSION: IAS 38, *Intangible Assets*, defines an intangible asset as an identifiable nonmonetary asset without physical substance.

Answer (A) is incorrect. Initial recognition of an intangible asset is at cost. Recognition is permitted only when it is probable that the entity will receive the expected economic benefits, and the cost is reliably measurable. Answer (B) is incorrect. Research is undertaken to gain new scientific or technical knowledge and understanding. Answer (C) is incorrect. Property, plant, and equipment are expected to be used in the production or supply of goods or services.

4. Neue Co., a developmental stage enterprise, incurred the following costs during its first year of operations:

Legal fees for incorporation and other related matters	$55,000
Underwriters' fees for initial stock offering	40,000
Exploration costs and purchases of mineral rights	60,000

Neue had no revenue during its first year of operation. What amount must Neue expense as organizational costs?

A. $155,000

B. $100,000

C. $95,000

D. $55,000

Answer (D) is correct.

REQUIRED: The organizational costs to be expensed.

DISCUSSION: Organization costs are those incurred in the formation of a business entity. For financial accounting purposes, nongovernmental entities must expense all start-up and organization costs as incurred. Thus, the legal fees should be expensed because they are organization costs. Fees for an initial stock offering are customarily treated as a reduction in the proceeds rather than as organization costs, and exploration costs and purchases of mineral rights are capitalizable items that are not organization costs.

10.2 Intangible Assets Distinct from Goodwill -- Accounting Subsequent to Acquisition

5. Tech Co. bought a trademark 2 years ago on January 2. Tech accounted for the trademark as instructed under the provisions of the Accounting Standards Codification during the current year. The intangible was being amortized over 40 years. The carrying amount at the beginning of the year was $38,000. It was determined that the cash flow will be generated indefinitely at the current level for the trademark. What amount should Tech report as amortization expense for the current year?

A. $0

B. $922

C. $1,000

D. $38,000

Answer (A) is correct.
REQUIRED: The amortization expense for a purchased trademark.
DISCUSSION: An intangible asset with an indefinite useful life to the reporting entity is not amortized.

6. During the year just ended, Jase Co. incurred research and development costs of $136,000 in its laboratories relating to a patent that was granted on July 1. Costs of registering the patent equaled $34,000. The patent's legal life is 20 years, and its estimated economic life is 10 years. In its December 31 balance sheet, what amount should Jase report for the patent, net of accumulated amortization?

A. $32,300

B. $33,150

C. $161,500

D. $165,000

Answer (A) is correct.
REQUIRED: The amount reported for the patent, net of accumulated amortization.
DISCUSSION: R&D costs are expensed as incurred. However, legal work in connection with patent applications or litigation and the sale or licensing of patents are specifically excluded from the definition of R&D. Hence, the legal costs of filing a patent should be capitalized. The patent should be amortized over its estimated economic life of 10 years. Amortization for the year equals $1,700 [($34,000 ÷ 10) × (6 ÷ 12)]. Thus, the reported amount of the patent at year end equals $32,300 ($34,000 – $1,700).
Answer (B) is incorrect. The amount of $33,150 results from using the 20-year legal life of the patent. Answer (C) is incorrect. The $136,000 of R&D costs should not be capitalized. Answer (D) is incorrect. The R&D costs should not be capitalized, and the useful life, not the legal life, should be used.

7. Wall Company bought a trademark from Black Corporation on January 1 for $112,000. An independent consultant retained by Wall estimated that the remaining useful life is 50 years. Its unamortized cost on Black's accounting records was $56,000. Wall decided to write off the trademark over the maximum period allowed. However, the pattern of consumption of the economic benefits of the trademark is not reliably determinable. How much should be amortized for the year ended December 31?

A. $1,120

B. $1,400

C. $2,240

D. $2,800

Answer (C) is correct.
REQUIRED: The amount of amortization of a trademark for the first year.
DISCUSSION: If the consideration given is cash, an exchange transaction is measured by the amount of cash paid. If the consideration given is not cash, measurement is based on the more reliably measurable of the fair value of the consideration given or the fair value of the assets (or net assets) acquired. The foregoing guidance should be followed when initially measuring the "cost" of an intangible asset at its fair value. When the useful life of a recognized intangible asset to the reporting entity is finite, the asset is amortized over that useful life. The amortization method should reflect the pattern in which the economic benefits of the intangible asset are consumed. If the pattern is not reliably determinable, the straight-line method is used. Consequently, annual amortization is $2,240 ($112,000 ÷ 50 years).
Answer (A) is incorrect. The amount of $1,120 results from amortizing the unamortized cost on Black's books over 50 years. Answer (B) is incorrect. The amount of $1,400 results from amortizing the unamortized cost on Black's books over 40 years. Answer (D) is incorrect. The amount of $2,800 is based on a 40-year useful life.

8. Under IFRS, an entity that acquires an intangible asset may use the revaluation model for subsequent measurement only if

A. The useful life of the intangible asset can be reliably determined.

B. An active market exists for the intangible asset.

C. The cost of the intangible asset can be measured reliably.

D. The intangible asset is a monetary asset.

Answer (B) is correct.
REQUIRED: The condition for use of the revaluation model for subsequent measurement of an intangible asset.
DISCUSSION: An intangible asset is carried at cost minus any accumulated amortization and impairment losses, or at a revalued amount. The revaluation model is similar to that for items of PPE (initial recognition of an asset at cost). However, fair value must be determined based on an active market.
Answer (A) is incorrect. An intangible asset may have an indefinite life. Answer (C) is incorrect. Initial recognition of an intangible asset is at cost. Recognition is permitted only when it is probable that the entity will receive the expected economic benefits, and the cost is reliably measurable. Answer (D) is incorrect. An intangible asset is nonmonetary.

9. Gray Co. was granted a patent on January 2, Year 5, and appropriately capitalized $45,000 of related costs. Gray was amortizing the patent over its estimated useful life of 15 years. During Year 8, Gray paid $15,000 in legal costs in successfully defending an attempted infringement of the patent. After the legal action was completed, Gray sold the patent to the plaintiff for $75,000. Gray's policy is to take no amortization in the year of disposal. In its Year 8 income statement, what amount should Gray report as gain from sale of patent?

A. $15,000

B. $24,000

C. $27,000

D. $39,000

Answer (B) is correct.
REQUIRED: The amount reported as gain from the sale of a patent.
DISCUSSION: The patent was capitalized at $45,000 in Year 5. Annual amortization of $3,000 ($45,000 ÷ 15 years) for Year 5, Year 6, and Year 7 reduced the carrying amount to $36,000. The $15,000 in legal costs for successfully defending an attempted infringement may be capitalized, which increases the carrying amount of the patent to $51,000 ($36,000 + $15,000). Accordingly, the gain from the sale is $24,000 ($75,000 – $51,000).
Answer (A) is incorrect. The amount of legal costs for defending the patent is $15,000. Answer (C) is incorrect. The amount of $27,000 assumes amortization in the year of disposal. Answer (D) is incorrect. The amount of $39,000 results from not capitalizing the $15,000 in legal costs.

10. After an impairment loss is recognized, the adjusted carrying amount of the intangible asset shall be its new accounting basis. Which of the following statements about subsequent reversal of a previously recognized impairment loss is correct?

A. It is prohibited.

B. It is required when the reversal is considered permanent.

C. It must be disclosed in the notes to the financial statements.

D. It is encouraged but **not** required.

Answer (A) is correct.
REQUIRED: Treatment of previously recognized impairment losses.
DISCUSSION: When an impairment of an intangible asset is recognized, the previous carrying amount of the asset is reduced by the impairment loss. The adjusted carrying amount is the new accounting basis. Thus, it cannot be increased subsequently for a change in fair value. This rule applies whether the intangible asset has a finite or an indefinite useful life.
Answer (B) is incorrect. Recognition of an impairment loss is required when it is considered permanent, that is, when the applicable impairment test is met. Any increase in the fair value of an intangible asset related to the previous impairment loss is not recognized. Answer (C) is incorrect. Reversal is prohibited, so disclosure is not necessary. Answer (D) is incorrect. It is not encouraged, required, or even permitted to make an adjustment to the accounting of an intangible asset for a reversal of a previously recognized impairment loss.

10.3 Franchise Accounting

11. Baker Co. has a franchise restaurant business. On January 15 of the current year, Baker charged an investor a franchise fee of $65,000 for the right to operate as a franchisee of one of Baker's restaurants. A cash payment of $25,000 towards the fee was required to be paid to Baker during the current year. Four subsequent annual payments of $10,000 with a present value of $34,000 at the current market interest rate represent the balance of the fee, which is expected to be collected in full. The initial cash payment is nonrefundable and no future services are required by Baker. Thus, Baker should report franchise revenue for the current year of

A. $0

B. $25,000

C. $59,000

D. $65,000

Answer (C) is correct.
REQUIRED: The franchise revenue reported.
DISCUSSION: Franchise fee revenue ordinarily should be recognized, with a provision for uncollectible amounts, at the earliest time when the franchisor has substantially performed or satisfied all material services or conditions relating to the franchise sale. Given that (1) the initial cash payment is nonrefundable, (2) the franchisor is not required to perform future services, and (3) no amounts are uncollectible, Baker should report current franchise revenue of $59,000 ($25,000 current payment + $34,000 present value of future payments). Furthermore, the long-term receivable in principle should be measured at its $34,000 present value.
Answer (A) is incorrect. Baker has earned revenue in the current year. Answer (B) is incorrect. The present value of payments receivable should be recorded as revenue in the current period. Answer (D) is incorrect. The payments receivable should be discounted.

12. Helsing Co. bought a franchise from Anya Co. on January 1 for $204,000. An independent consultant retained by Helsing estimated that the remaining useful life of the franchise was a finite period of 50 years and that the pattern of consumption of benefits of the franchise is not reliably determinable. Its unamortized cost on Anya's books on January 1 was $68,000. What amount should be amortized for the year ended December 31, assuming no residual value?

A. $5,100

B. $4,080

C. $3,400

D. $1,700

Answer (B) is correct.
REQUIRED: The first-year amortization expense of the cost of a franchise.
DISCUSSION: A franchise is an intangible asset. The initial measurement of an intangible asset acquired other than in a business combination is at fair value. Thus, the "cost" to be amortized should be based on the more reliably measurable of the fair value of the consideration given or the fair value of the assets acquired. If the useful life is finite, the intangible asset is amortized over that period. Moreover, if the consumption pattern of benefits of the intangible asset is not reliably determinable, the straight-line method of amortization is used. Accordingly, given no residual value, the amortization expense is $4,080 ($204,000 consideration given ÷ 50-year finite useful life).
Answer (A) is incorrect. The amount of $5,100 is based on a 40-year period. Answer (C) is incorrect. The amount of $3,400 is the difference between the $204,000 franchise price and Anya's $68,000 unamortized cost, divided by 40 years. Answer (D) is incorrect. The amount of $1,700 equals the unamortized cost on Anya's books amortized over 40 years.

10.4 Goodwill

13. On January 2, Paye Co. acquired Shef Co. in a business combination that resulted in recognition of goodwill of $200,000 having an expected benefit period of 10 years. Shef is treated as a reporting unit, and the entire amount of the recognized goodwill is assigned to it. During the first quarter of the year, Shef spent an additional $80,000 on expenditures designed to maintain goodwill. Due to these expenditures, at December 31, Shef estimated that the benefit period of goodwill was 40 years. In its consolidated December 31 balance sheet, what amount should Paye report as goodwill?

A. $180,000

B. $200,000

C. $252,000

D. $280,000

Answer (B) is correct.
REQUIRED: The amount of goodwill in the balance sheet.
DISCUSSION: Goodwill is not recorded except in a business combination. Thus, only the $200,000 recognized at the acquisition date should be recorded as goodwill. It should not be amortized but should be tested for impairment at the reporting-unit level. The facts given suggest that the fair value of the reporting unit (Shef) is not less than its carrying amount. Hence, no impairment of goodwill has occurred, and goodwill is unchanged at $200,000. Moreover, the cost of internally developing, maintaining, or restoring intangible assets (including goodwill) that are not specifically identifiable, have indeterminate useful lives, or are inherent in a continuing business and related to an entity as a whole should be expensed as incurred.
Answer (A) is incorrect. The amount of $180,000 results when goodwill is amortized on the straight-line basis over 10 years. Answer (C) is incorrect. The amount of $252,000 results from amortizing an additional $80,000 of expenditures to maintain goodwill over 10 years. Answer (D) is incorrect. The amount of $280,000 results from adding $80,000 of expenditures for the maintenance of goodwill.

14. Which of the following costs of goodwill should be capitalized and amortized?

	Maintaining Goodwill	Developing Goodwill
A.	Yes	No
B.	No	No
C.	Yes	Yes
D.	No	Yes

Answer (B) is correct.
　　REQUIRED: The cost(s) of goodwill, if any, that should be capitalized and amortized.
　　DISCUSSION: Goodwill arising from a business combination must be capitalized. However, amortization of goodwill is prohibited. Moreover, the cost of developing, maintaining, or restoring intangible assets (including goodwill) that (1) are not specifically identifiable, (2) have indeterminate useful lives, or (3) are inherent in a continuing business and related to an entity as a whole are expensed as incurred.

10.5 Research and Development

15. During the year just ended, Orr Co. incurred the following costs:

Research and development services performed by Key Corp. for Orr	$150,000
Design, construction, and testing of preproduction prototypes and models	200,000
Testing in search for new products or process alternatives	175,000

In its income statement for the year, what should Orr report as research and development expense?

A. $150,000
B. $200,000
C. $350,000
D. $525,000

Answer (D) is correct.
　　REQUIRED: The R&D expense.
　　DISCUSSION: Research is planned search or critical investigation aimed at discovery of new knowledge useful in developing a new product, service, process, or technique or in bringing about a significant improvement to an existing product, etc. Development is translation of research findings or other knowledge into a plan or design for a new or improved product or process. R&D expenses include R&D performed under contract by others; design, construction, and testing of prototypes; and testing in search for new products.
　　Answer (A) is incorrect. The amount of $150,000 does not include design, construction, and testing of preproduction prototypes or testing in search of new products. Answer (B) is incorrect. The amount of $200,000 does not include R&D performed under contract by others or testing in search for new products. Answer (C) is incorrect. The amount of $350,000 does not include testing in search for new products.

16. West, Inc., made the following expenditures relating to Product Y:

- Legal costs to file a patent on Product Y -- $10,000. Production of the finished product would not have been undertaken without the patent.
- Special equipment to be used solely for development of Product Y -- $60,000. The equipment has no other use and has an estimated useful life of 4 years.
- Labor and material costs incurred in producing a prototype model -- $200,000.
- Cost of testing the prototype -- $80,000.

What is the total amount of costs that will be expensed when incurred?

A. $280,000
B. $295,000
C. $340,000
D. $350,000

Answer (C) is correct.
　　REQUIRED: The total amount of costs that will be expensed when incurred.
　　DISCUSSION: R&D costs are expensed as incurred. However, legal work in connection with patent applications or litigation and the sale or licensing of patents are specifically excluded from the definition of R&D. The legal costs of filing a patent should be capitalized. West's R&D costs include those incurred for the design, construction, and testing of preproduction prototypes. Moreover, the cost of equipment used solely for a specific project is also expensed immediately. Thus, the total amount of costs that will be expensed when incurred is $340,000.
　　Answer (A) is incorrect. The amount of $280,000 omits the cost of the special equipment. Answer (B) is incorrect. The amount of $295,000 includes 1 year's straight-line depreciation on the special equipment instead of the full cost. Answer (D) is incorrect. The amount of $350,000 includes the legal costs of filing a patent.

17. In the year just ended, Ball Labs incurred the following costs:

Direct costs of doing contract R&D work for the government to be reimbursed by governmental unit	$400,000

R&D costs not included above were

Depreciation	$300,000
Salaries	700,000
Indirect costs appropriately allocated	200,000
Materials	180,000

What was Ball's total R&D expense for the year?

A. $1,080,000

B. $1,380,000

C. $1,580,000

D. $1,780,000

Answer (B) is correct.

REQUIRED: The total R&D expense.

DISCUSSION: Materials used in R&D, compensation costs of personnel, and indirect costs appropriately allocated are R&D costs that should be expensed immediately. The costs of equipment and facilities that are used for R&D activities and have alternative future uses, whether for other R&D projects or otherwise, are to be capitalized as tangible assets when acquired or constructed. Thus, the depreciation is also expensed immediately. However, this guidance does not apply to R&D activities conducted for others. Hence, the reimbursable costs are not expensed. Ball's total R&D expense is therefore $1,380,000 ($300,000 + $700,000 + $200,000 + $180,000).

Answer (A) is incorrect. The amount of $1,080,000 omits depreciation. Answer (C) is incorrect. The amount of $1,580,000 includes the reimbursable costs of R&D conducted for others but omits the indirect costs. Answer (D) is incorrect. The amount of $1,780,000 includes the reimbursable costs of R&D conducted for others.

18. Ward Company incurred research and development costs in Year 1 as follows:

Equipment acquired for use in various research and development projects	$975,000
Depreciation on the above equipment	135,000
Materials used	200,000
Compensation costs of personnel	500,000
Outside consulting fees	150,000
Indirect costs appropriately allocated	250,000

The total research and development costs charged in Ward's Year 1 income statement should be

A. $850,000

B. $1,085,000

C. $1,235,000

D. $1,825,000

Answer (C) is correct.

REQUIRED: The total research and development costs for the year.

DISCUSSION: Materials used in R&D ($200,000), compensation costs of personnel ($500,000), outside consulting fees ($150,000), and indirect costs appropriately allocated ($250,000) are R&D costs that should be expensed immediately. The cost of equipment having an alternative future use should be capitalized and depreciated. Alternative use includes other R&D projects as well as non-R&D use. The depreciation, in this case $135,000, is included in R&D cost. Total R&D expense was thus $1,235,000 ($200,000 + $500,000 + $150,000 + $250,000 + $135,000).

Answer (A) is incorrect. This amount results from not including depreciation and indirect costs as part of R&D expense. Answer (B) is incorrect. This amount results from not including outside consulting fees. Answer (D) is incorrect. This amount results from not including depreciation and indirect costs and including the cost of the equipment.

10.6 Prepayments

19. On January 1, Sip Co. signed a 5-year contract enabling it to use a patented manufacturing process beginning in the year just ended. A royalty is payable for each product produced, subject to a minimum annual fee. Any royalties in excess of the minimum will be paid annually. On the contract date, Sip prepaid a sum equal to 2 years' minimum annual fees. During the year, only minimum fees were incurred. The royalty prepayment should be reported in Sip's December 31 financial statements as a(n)

A. Expense only.

B. Current asset and an expense.

C. Current asset and noncurrent asset.

D. Noncurrent asset.

Answer (B) is correct.

REQUIRED: The proper reporting of a royalty prepayment.

DISCUSSION: Current assets include prepaid expenses, such as royalty prepayments, that are expected to be realized in cash, sold, or consumed within the longer of 1 year or the normal operating cycle of the business. At December 31, the entity should therefore recognize an expense for the first year's royalties and a current asset (a deferred cost) for the second year's royalties.

Answer (A) is incorrect. An asset should be recognized for the unexpired portion of the prepayment. Answer (C) is incorrect. The company should recognize an expense for the expired portion of the prepayment. Answer (D) is incorrect. The unexpired portion of the prepayment will be consumed within 1 year. Thus, it should be classified as current.

20. An analysis of Thrift Corp.'s unadjusted prepaid expense account at December 31, Year 4, revealed the following:

- An opening balance at $1,500 for Thrift's comprehensive insurance policy. Thrift had paid an annual premium of $3,000 on July 1, Year 3.
- A $3,200 annual insurance premium payment made July 1, Year 4.
- A $2,000 advance rental payment for a warehouse Thrift leased for 1 year beginning January 1, Year 5.

In its December 31, Year 4, balance sheet, what amount should Thrift report as prepaid expenses?

A. $5,200

B. $3,600

C. $2,000

D. $1,600

Answer (B) is correct.
REQUIRED: The amount reported for prepaid expenses.
DISCUSSION: The $1,500 beginning balance of prepaid insurance expired on 6/30/Yr 4, leaving a $0 balance. The $3,200 annual insurance premium paid on 7/1/Yr 4 should be allocated equally to Year 4 and Year 5, leaving a $1,600 prepaid insurance balance. The $2,000 advance rental payment is an expense that is wholly deferred until Year 5. Consequently, the total of prepaid expenses at year end is $3,600 ($1,600 + $2,000).
Answer (A) is incorrect. Half of the $3,200 of prepaid insurance should be expensed in Year 4. Answer (C) is incorrect. Only half of the $3,200 of prepaid insurance should be expensed in Year 4. Answer (D) is incorrect. The prepaid rent is deferred until Year 5.

21. Roro, Inc., paid $7,200 to renew its only insurance policy for 3 years on March 1, Year 4, the effective date of the policy. At March 31, Year 4, Roro's unadjusted trial balance showed a balance of $300 for prepaid insurance and $7,200 for insurance expense. What amounts should be reported for prepaid insurance and insurance expense in Roro's financial statements for the 3 months ended March 31, Year 4?

	Prepaid Insurance	Insurance Expense
A.	$7,000	$300
B.	$7,000	$500
C.	$7,200	$300
D.	$7,300	$200

Answer (B) is correct.
REQUIRED: The amounts reported for prepaid insurance and insurance expense.
DISCUSSION: The entry to record the insurance renewal included a debit to insurance expense for $7,200, and the balance in prepaid insurance has expired. At year end, the expense and prepaid insurance accounts should be adjusted to reflect the expired amounts. The 3-year prepayment is amortized at $200 per month ($7,200 ÷ 36 months). Consequently, insurance expense for the period should be $500 ($300 prepaid insurance balance + $200 amortization of the renewal amount). The $7,000 unexpired amount should be debited to prepaid insurance.
Answer (A) is incorrect. The amount of $300 does not include the $200 expense for March. Answer (C) is incorrect. Neither the prepaid insurance nor the insurance expense amounts have been adjusted for the $200 expense for March. Answer (D) is incorrect. Prepaid insurance includes $300 that should be expensed.

10.7 Computer Software

22. On December 31, Year 7, Byte Co. had capitalized software costs of $600,000 with an economic life of 4 years. Sales for Year 8 were 10% of expected total sales of the software. At December 31, Year 8, the software had a net realizable value of $480,000. In its December 31, Year 8, balance sheet, what amount should Byte report as net capitalized cost of computer software?

A. $432,000

B. $450,000

C. $480,000

D. $540,000

Answer (B) is correct.
REQUIRED: The net capitalized cost of computer software at year end.
DISCUSSION: The annual amortization is the greater of the amount determined using (1) the ratio of current gross revenues to the sum of current gross revenues and anticipated future gross revenues, or (2) the straight-line method over the remaining estimated economic life, including the current reporting period. At year end, the unamortized cost of each software product must be compared with the net realizable value (NRV) of that software product. Any excess of unamortized cost over NRV must be written off. The amount of amortization under the straight-line method is used because it is greater than the amount determined using the 10% ratio of current sales to expected total sales. Thus, Byte Co. had an unamortized cost of software of $450,000 [$600,000 capitalized cost – ($600,000 ÷ 4)] at December 31, Year 8. The $450,000 unamortized cost is lower than the $480,000 NRV, so $450,000 is the amount reported in the year-end balance sheet.
Answer (A) is incorrect. The amount of $432,000 equals the NRV at December 31, Year 8, minus amortization calculated as 10% of NRV. Answer (C) is incorrect. The NRV at December 31, Year 8, is $480,000. Answer (D) is incorrect. The amount of $540,000 assumes amortization at 10% with no adjustment for NRV.

Questions 23 and 24 are based on the following information. During the year just ended, Pitt Corp. incurred costs to develop and produce a routine, low-risk computer software product as follows:

Completion of detail program design	$13,000
Costs incurred for coding and testing to establish technological feasibility	10,000
Other coding costs after establishment of technological feasibility	24,000
Other testing costs after establishment of technological feasibility	20,000
Costs of producing product masters for training materials	15,000
Duplication of computer software and training materials from product masters (1,000 units)	25,000
Packaging product (500 units)	9,000

The guidance pertaining to accounting for the costs of computer software to be sold, leased, or otherwise marketed applies.

23. In Pitt's December 31 balance sheet, what amount should be capitalized as software cost subject to amortization?

A. $54,000

B. $57,000

C. $59,000

D. $69,000

Answer (C) is correct.

REQUIRED: The amount capitalized as software cost subject to amortization.

DISCUSSION: Costs incurred internally in creating a computer software product are expensed when incurred as research and development until technological feasibility has been established for the product. Afterward, all software production costs incurred until the product is available for general release to customers are capitalized and amortized separately for each product. Subsequently, the lower of unamortized cost or net realizable value at the end of the period is reported in the balance sheet. Hence, (1) the costs of completing the detail program design and establishing technological feasibility are expensed; (2) the costs of duplicating software, documentation, and training materials and packaging the product are inventoried; and (3) the costs of coding and other testing after establishing technological feasibility and the costs of producing product masters are capitalized and amortized. The amount capitalized as software cost subject to amortization is therefore $59,000 ($24,000 + $20,000 + $15,000).

Answer (A) is incorrect. Inventoriable costs plus the other testing costs equals $54,000. Answer (B) is incorrect. The sum of the costs expensed and the costs inventoried is $57,000. Answer (D) is incorrect. This figure assumes the costs of coding and testing to establish feasibility are capitalized and amortized.

24. In Pitt's December 31 balance sheet, what amount should be reported in inventory?

A. $25,000

B. $34,000

C. $40,000

D. $49,000

Answer (B) is correct.

REQUIRED: The amount reported in inventory.

DISCUSSION: Costs incurred internally in creating a computer software product are expensed when incurred as R&D until technological feasibility has been established. Afterward, all software production costs incurred until the product is available for general release to customers shall be capitalized and amortized. The costs of (1) duplicating the software, documentation, and training materials from the product masters and (2) physically packaging the product for distribution are capitalized as inventory. Hence, inventory should be reported at $34,000 ($25,000 duplication costs + $9,000 packaging costs).

Answer (A) is incorrect. The amount of $25,000 excludes packaging costs. Answer (C) is incorrect. The amount of $40,000 excludes packaging costs but includes costs of producing product masters. Answer (D) is incorrect. The amount of $49,000 includes costs of producing product masters.

25. Yellow Co. spent $12,000,000 during the current year developing its new software package. Of this amount, $4,000,000 was spent before it was at the application development stage and the package was only to be used internally. The package was completed during the year and is expected to have a four-year useful life. Yellow has a policy of taking a full-year's amortization in the first year. After the development stage, $50,000 was spent on training employees to use the program. What amount should Yellow report as an expense for the current year?

- A. $1,600,000
- B. $2,000,000
- C. $6,012,500
- D. $6,050,000

Answer (D) is correct.

REQUIRED: The first year expense for new software developed to be used internally.

DISCUSSION: Costs incurred in the preliminary project stage for computer software to be used internally are expensed as incurred. During the application development stage, costs are capitalized. However, training costs are expensed. Accordingly, $8,000,000 ($12,000,000 total – $4,000,000 spent before application development) of the development cost was capitalized. Amortization is on a straight-line basis over the four-year useful life of the software. Thus, given that a full-year's amortization is recognized in year one, the expense for the year is $6,050,000 [$4,000,000 preliminary project expense + ($8,000,000 ÷ 4) amortization + $50,000 training cost].

Answer (A) is incorrect. This figure results from using a five-year useful life for the software. Answer (B) is incorrect. This figure results from failing to include the costs incurred before the application development stage and the costs of training. Answer (C) is incorrect. This figure results from improperly capitalizing training costs.

10.8 Special Issues

26. A development stage entity (DSE) should use the same generally accepted accounting principles that apply to established operating enterprises for

	Revenue Recognition	Deferral of Expenses
A.	Yes	Yes
B.	Yes	No
C.	No	No
D.	No	Yes

Answer (A) is correct.

REQUIRED: The item(s), if any, for which DSEs should use standard GAAP.

DISCUSSION: DSEs are required to use the same GAAP that apply to established operating entities. Thus, the accounting treatment of revenues and expenses should be governed by the same principles whether or not the reporting entity is a DSE.

27. Direct response advertising costs are capitalized (deferred) to provide an appropriate expense in each period for

	Interim Financial Reporting	Year-End Financial Reporting
A.	Yes	No
B.	Yes	Yes
C.	No	No
D.	No	Yes

Answer (B) is correct.

REQUIRED: The type(s) of reporting, if any, in which direct response advertising costs may be accrued or deferred.

DISCUSSION: Direct response advertising costs are capitalized (deferred) if the primary purpose is to make sales to customers who respond specifically to the advertising and probable future economic benefits result. An entity that capitalizes these costs must document that customers have specifically responded to the advertising. It also must document the benefits from prior direct response advertising. The deferral of advertising costs is appropriate for both interim and year-end financial reporting if their benefits clearly apply to more than one period. Moreover, if a cost that would be fully expensed in an annual report benefits more than one interim period, it may be allocated to those interim periods.

28. Lex Corp. was a development stage entity (DSE) from October 10, Year 2, (inception) through December 31, Year 3. The year ended December 31, Year 4, was the first year in which Lex qualified as an established operating entity. The following are among the costs incurred by Lex:

	For the Period 10/10/Yr 2-12/31/Yr 3	For the Year Ended 12/31/Yr 4
Leasehold improvements, equipment, and furniture	$1,000,000	$ 300,000
Security deposits	60,000	30,000
Research and development	750,000	900,000
Laboratory operations	175,000	550,000
General and administrative	225,000	685,000
Depreciation	25,000	115,000
	$2,235,000	$2,580,000

From its inception through the period ended December 31, Year 4, what is the total amount of costs incurred by Lex that should be charged to operations?

A. $3,425,000

B. $2,250,000

C. $1,775,000

D. $1,350,000

Answer (A) is correct.
    REQUIRED: The total amount of costs that a DSE should charge to operations.
    DISCUSSION: DSEs are required to use the same GAAP as established operating entities. An established operating entity would have capitalized the entire $1.3 million of leasehold improvements, equipment, and furniture, as well as the $90,000 of security deposits. Consequently, Lex Corp., a DSE, should also capitalize these costs. An established operating entity would have expensed the $1,650,000 of research and development costs, the $725,000 of laboratory operations costs, the $910,000 of general and administrative costs, and the $140,000 of depreciation. Lex Corp. also should expense these costs. The total to be expensed by Lex therefore equals $3,425,000 ($1,650,000 + $725,000 + $910,000 + $140,000).
    Answer (B) is incorrect. The amount of $2,250,000 equals costs incurred in Year 4 minus security deposits and leasehold improvements, equipment, and furniture. Answer (C) is incorrect. The amount of $1,775,000 excludes R&D costs. Answer (D) is incorrect. The amount of $1,350,000 equals costs incurred during the development stage, minus leasehold improvements, equipment, and furniture, plus Year 4 depreciation.

29. A statement of cash flows for a development stage entity

A. Is the same as that of an established operating entity and, in addition, shows cumulative amounts from the entity's inception.

B. Shows only cumulative amounts from the entity's inception.

C. Is the same as that of an established operating entity but does **not** show cumulative amounts from the entity's inception.

D. Is **not** presented.

Answer (A) is correct.
    REQUIRED: The true statement about a statement of cash flows for a DSE.
    DISCUSSION: A DSE must present financial statements in conformity with GAAP together with certain additional information accumulated since its inception. Cumulative net losses must be disclosed in the equity section of the balance sheet, cumulative amounts of revenue and expense in the income statement, cumulative amounts of cash inflows and outflows in the statement of cash flows, and information about each issuance of stock in the statement of equity.
    Answer (B) is incorrect. The statement of cash flows also must conform with GAAP. Answer (C) is incorrect. The statement of cash flows also must show cumulative amounts from the enterprise's inception. Answer (D) is incorrect. A statement of cash flows is required as part of a full set of financial statements.

Use the additional questions in Gleim **CPA Test Prep Online** to create Test Sessions that emulate Prometric!

10.9 PRACTICE SIMULATION

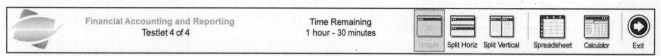

| Financial Accounting and Reporting | Time Remaining | | | | | | |
| Testlet 4 of 4 | 1 hour - 30 minutes | Unsplit | Split Horiz | Split Vertical | Spreadsheet | Calculator | Exit |

DIRECTIONS

Note: If you believe you have encountered a software malfunction, report it to the test center staff immediately.

Navigation

To navigate from task to task, use the controls at the bottom of the screen. Click on the **Next** button to advance to the next task, or the **Previous** button to go to the previous task. To go directly to any task, click on its number.

| ▼ = Reminder | | Directions | 1 | 2 | 3 | 4 | 5 | 6 | 7 | | ◀ Previous | Next ▶ |

If you would like a reminder to revisit a task, or want to indicate that you are finished with it, click on the reminder flag below the task number. To clear the flag, click on it again. Reminder flags are for your use only – they do not contribute to your score.

Tabs

In this part of the examination, you will be asked to complete various tasks. Every task has one or more **Work Tabs**. Some tasks have one or more **Information Tabs**, others may have none. Every task has a **Help** tab.

If a task has **Information Tabs**, you may use the information in them to complete your responses in the **Work Tabs**.

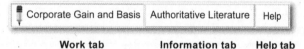

| Corporate Gain and Basis | Authoritative Literature | Help |

| Work tab | Information tab | Help tab |

Work Tabs:

- **Work Tabs** are identified with a pencil icon. This is where your responses are expected.
- Each task has one or more **Work Tabs**.
- **Work Tabs** contain directions for completing the task – be sure to read these directions carefully.
- The **Work Tab** name in the example above is for illustration only – yours will differ.
- You must complete all of the **Work Tabs** in each task to receive full credit.

Information Tabs:

- The Authoritative Literature will be provided in all tasks in the AUD, FAR, and REG sections for your reference.
- Your simulation may have one or more additional **Information Tabs**. Like the Authoritative Literature tabs, **Information Tabs** do not have a pencil icon.
- If your task has additional **Information Tabs**, go through each to familiarize yourself with the task content.

Help Tab:

- The **Help Tab** provides assistance with the exam software that is used in this task. For example, if the task is to compose a memorandum, **Help** will provide information about the word processor.

The Toolbar

The toolbar at the top of the screen shows the amount of time remaining for you to complete the tasks. In addition, the following tools are available. Note that only the **Exit** button is displayed when Directions are visible - the others will appear when you begin the tasks.

Click on these buttons to split or unsplit the screen. You can split the screen vertically or horizontally.

Click on this button to display the calculator; click on it again to hide the calculator. To move the calculator, click on the calculator title bar and drag the calculator to the desired location.

Click on this button to use the spreadsheet; click on it again to hide the spreadsheet. To move the spreadsheet, click on the the spreadsheet title bar and drag the spreadsheet to the desired location.

Click on this button to go on to the next part of the examination. You must complete all of the tasks to receive full credit. Once you click on **Exit** and confirm the action, you will NOT be able to return to this testlet.

| ▼ = Reminder | | Directions | 1 | 2 | 3 | 4 | 5 | 6 | | ◀ Previous | Next ▶ |

| Intangibles | Authoritative Literature | Help |

Select from the list provided the intangible asset that best matches each of the following characteristics. Each choice may be used once, more than once, or not at all.

Characteristic	Answer	Choices
1. Grants an exclusive right given to the holder to use, produce, and sell a product or process for a period specified by law without interference or infringement by others		A) Copyright
2. Only arises from a business combination		B) Goodwill
3. Granted for the life of the author plus 70 years		C) Franchise
4. Can be renewed for 10-year periods indefinitely		D) Patent
5. Permits an entity to use rights owned by others		E) Trademark
6. Grants the right to sell certain products or services within a designated area using a certain trademark or trade name		F) Organization costs
7. May include underwriter's fees, legal fees, and incorporation fees		G) Licensing agreement
		H) Leaseholds

▼ = Reminder   Directions   1 2 3 4 5 6   ◀ Previous   Next ▶

| Software Costs | Authoritative Literature | Help |

This question addresses the costs of software to be (1) marketed as a separate product or as part of a product or process or (2) used internally. Check the appropriate box to indicate whether each item should be capitalized or expensed.

Item	Capitalize	Expense
1. Costs of software for internal use incurred in the preliminary project stage.		
2. Costs of producing product masters for software to be marketed.		
3. R&D costs of software to be marketed.		
4. Unamortized costs of replaced software for internal use.		
5. Costs of purchased software to be marketed having an alternative use.		
6. The excess of amortized cost over net realizable value of software to be marketed.		
7. Costs of software for internal use incurred in the application development stage.		
8. Costs of software to be marketed incurred when the product is available for general release.		

▼ = Reminder   Directions   1 2 3 4 5 6   ◀ Previous   Next ▶

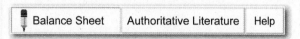

During Year 5, Broca Co. had the following transactions:

- On January 2, Broca acquired 100% of the voting interests of Amp Co. for $360,000. The acquisition-date fair value of Amp's acquired net assets (the net of the amounts assigned to assets acquired and liabilities assumed) was $172,000. Broca believes that, due to the popularity of Amp's consumer products, the life of the resulting goodwill is 15 years.

- On February 1, Broca purchased a franchise to operate a ferry service from the state government for $60,000 and an annual fee of 1% of ferry revenues. The franchise expires after 5 years. Ferry revenues were $20,000 during Year 5. Broca projects future revenues of $40,000 in Year 6 and $60,000 per annum for the following 3 years.

- On April 5, Broca was granted a patent that had been applied for by Amp. During Year 5, Broca incurred legal costs of $51,000 to register the patent and an additional $85,000 to successfully prosecute a patent infringement suit against a competitor. Broca estimates the patent's economic life to be 10 years. When Broca purchased Amp's net assets, it properly did not assign an amount to the possible grant of a patent.

- Broca incurred organization costs of $98,000 for incorporation, state and local licensing fees and permits, training of new employees, feasibility studies, and attorneys' and accountants' fees.

- At December 31, Year 5, Broca had prepaid rent (1 year) and insurance (2 years) balances of $60,000 and $24,000, respectively.

Broca's accounting policy is to amortize all intangible assets on the straight-line basis over the maximum period permitted by generally accepted accounting principles, taking a full year's amortization in the year of acquisition.

Using the information above, enter in the shaded cells the amounts to be recorded on the intangible assets section of the balance sheet for Broca Co.

Balance Sheet Item	Calculated Amounts
Goodwill:	
Cash paid	
Fair value of net assets	
Goodwill	
Amortization	
Balance 12/31/Year 5	
Franchise:	
Franchise	
Amortization	
Balance 12/31/Year 5	
Patent:	
Legal costs	
Amortization	
Balance 12/31/Year 5	

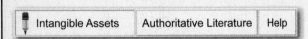

For each of the following independent situations described below, select from the list of choices provided the appropriate effect, if any, on Company A's December 31, Year 5, financial statements. Each choice may be used once, more than once, or not at all.

Characteristic	Answer
1. On December 31, Year 5, Company A paid $30,000 in legal fees for a successful defense of the patent.	
2. During Year 3, the company recognized an impairment loss on goodwill. On December 31, Year 5, the company estimates that the fair value of goodwill is greater than its carrying amount.	
3. During Year 5, the company incurred a cost of $60,000 on development activities for the internally developed patent.	
4. The company applies IFRS. During Year 3, the company recognized an impairment loss on a franchise with a useful life of 20 years. On December 31, Year 5, the company estimates that the recoverable amount of the franchise is greater than its carrying amount.	
5. On December 31, Year 5, the company purchased for $50,000 on credit a machine that can be used for the company's current R&D project and also for other alternative future projects.	
6. On December 31, Year 5, Company A paid $45,000 in legal fees for an unsuccessful defense of the patent.	
7. The company applies IFRS and accounts for its intangible assets in accordance with the revaluation model. The company's policy is to revalue its assets at the end of each year. On December 31, Year 5, the fair value of a franchise that can be traded in active markets is greater than its carrying amount.	
8. On December 31, Year 5, the company purchased for $55,000 on credit a machine that can be used for the company's current R&D project only.	

Choices
A) Increase the amount of expenses recognized
B) No effect
C) Increase the amount of intangible assets
D) Increase the amount of income recognized
E) Increase the amount of tangible assets

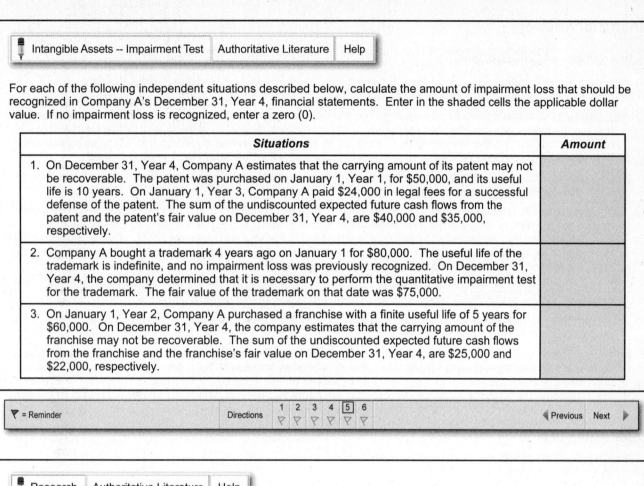

Intangible Assets -- Impairment Test | Authoritative Literature | Help

For each of the following independent situations described below, calculate the amount of impairment loss that should be recognized in Company A's December 31, Year 4, financial statements. Enter in the shaded cells the applicable dollar value. If no impairment loss is recognized, enter a zero (0).

Situations	Amount
1. On December 31, Year 4, Company A estimates that the carrying amount of its patent may not be recoverable. The patent was purchased on January 1, Year 1, for $50,000, and its useful life is 10 years. On January 1, Year 3, Company A paid $24,000 in legal fees for a successful defense of the patent. The sum of the undiscounted expected future cash flows from the patent and the patent's fair value on December 31, Year 4, are $40,000 and $35,000, respectively.	
2. Company A bought a trademark 4 years ago on January 1 for $80,000. The useful life of the trademark is indefinite, and no impairment loss was previously recognized. On December 31, Year 4, the company determined that it is necessary to perform the quantitative impairment test for the trademark. The fair value of the trademark on that date was $75,000.	
3. On January 1, Year 2, Company A purchased a franchise with a finite useful life of 5 years for $60,000. On December 31, Year 4, the company estimates that the carrying amount of the franchise may not be recoverable. The sum of the undiscounted expected future cash flows from the franchise and the franchise's fair value on December 31, Year 4, are $25,000 and $22,000, respectively.	

▼ = Reminder   Directions   1 2 3 4 [5] 6   ◀ Previous   Next ▶

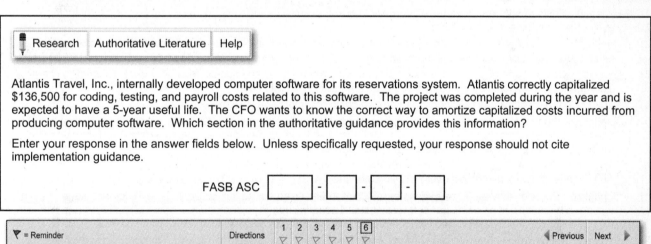

Research | Authoritative Literature | Help

Atlantis Travel, Inc., internally developed computer software for its reservations system. Atlantis correctly capitalized $136,500 for coding, testing, and payroll costs related to this software. The project was completed during the year and is expected to have a 5-year useful life. The CFO wants to know the correct way to amortize capitalized costs incurred from producing computer software. Which section in the authoritative guidance provides this information?

Enter your response in the answer fields below. Unless specifically requested, your response should not cite implementation guidance.

FASB ASC [   ] - [   ] - [   ] - [   ]

▼ = Reminder   Directions   1 2 3 4 5 [6]   ◀ Previous   Next ▶

Unofficial Answers

1. Intangibles (7 Gradable Items)

1. <u>D) Patent.</u> Utility patents granted by the U.S. have a legal life of 20 years. A patent is an exclusive right to use, manufacture, and sell a product or process.

2. <u>B) Goodwill.</u> Goodwill reflects future economic benefits arising from other assets acquired in a business combination that are not individually identified and separately recognized. Thus, it consists of the favorable characteristics of a business entity that are that are intangible and cannot be separately identified and measured. Such characteristics include a superior management team, high standing in the community, and good labor relations.

3. <u>A) Copyright.</u> A copyright is the exclusive right to reproduce and sell an artistic or literary work. The U.S. grants author copyrights for life plus 70 years.

4. <u>E) Trademark.</u> Trademarks are words, symbols, or other devices that identify particular products. The common law recognizes the right to exclusive use of a trademark or similar property as long as it is used by the original holder. A trademark also may be protected by registration with the U.S. Patent and Trademark Office. This registration can be renewed for an indefinite number of 10-year periods (with the initial renewal made between the 5th and 6th years after initial registration) as long as the trademark is used continuously.

5. <u>G) Licensing agreement.</u> Licensing agreements are contractual agreements that permit an enterprise (the licensee) to engage in a given activity, such as selling a well-known product, or to use rights (e.g., a patent) owned by others.

6. <u>C) Franchise.</u> A franchise is an agreement in which one party provides another party with the exclusive right to market a product or service within a designated territory.

7. <u>F) Organization costs.</u> Organization costs are costs incurred in the formation of a business entity before operations commence and during their early stages. They include legal fees, accounting fees, underwriter's fees, incorporation fees, taxes, and promotional costs. They must be expensed when incurred by nongovernmental entities. However, for federal income tax purposes, organization costs that are not deductible may be amortized over not less than 15 years.

2. Software Costs (8 Gradable Items)

1) <u>Expense.</u> Costs of software to be used internally that are incurred during the preliminary project stage (planning, evaluation) are expensed as incurred.

2) <u>Capitalize.</u> Costs of software to be marketed that are incurred after technological feasibility is established (coding, testing, producing product masters) are capitalized as computer software costs.

3) <u>Expense.</u> Costs of software to be marketed that are incurred before technological feasibility is established (coding, testing, etc.) are expensed as incurred; i.e., they are treated as R&D costs.

4) <u>Expense.</u> When software is replaced, unamortized costs of the old software are expensed.

5) <u>Capitalize.</u> If purchased software to be marketed has no alternative future use, the entity accounts for its cost as if it had been developed internally to be marketed. If purchased software to be marketed has an alternative future use, the entity capitalizes the costs when it purchases the software and accounts for it according to use.

6) <u>Expense.</u> At year end, the total cost of each software product to be marketed is compared with its net realizable value. Any excess of unamortized cost over NRV is expensed.

7) <u>Capitalize.</u> Costs of software to be used internally that are incurred during the application development stage (coding, testing) are capitalized as computer software costs. These include (a) external direct costs of materials and services, (b) payroll costs directly associated with the project, and (c) interest costs associated with the project.

8) <u>Expense.</u> Amortization of capitalized software costs begins and capitalization ends when the product is available for general release.

3. Balance Sheet (11 Gradable Items)

Balance Sheet Item	Calculated Amounts
Goodwill:	
Cash paid	$ 360,000
Fair value of net assets	(172,000)
Goodwill	188,000
Amortization	0
Balance 12/31/Year 5	$ 188,000
Franchise:	
Franchise	$ 60,000
Amortization	(12,000)
Balance 12/31/Year 5	$ 48,000
Patent:	
Legal costs	$ 136,000
Amortization	(13,600)
Balance 12/31/Year 5	$ 122,400

4. Intangible Assets (8 Gradable Items)

1) C) Increase the amount of intangible assets. Legal costs incurred to successfully defend an internally developed patent should be capitalized and amortized over the patent's remaining useful life. No amortization of legal costs should be recognized in Year 5 since the costs were incurred on the last day of the year.

2) B) No effect. The impairment loss recognized is nonreversible. Thus, it has no effect on the financial statements.

3) A) Increase the amount of expenses recognized. Research and development costs must be expensed as incurred.

4) D) Increase the amount of income recognized. Under IFRS, an impairment loss for an asset (except goodwill) may be reversed if a change in the estimates used to measure the recoverable amount has occurred. The reversal of an impairment loss is recognized as current-period income.

5) E) Increase the amount of tangible assets. The equipment purchased with alternative future uses is capitalized (recognized as a tangible asset) and depreciated. No depreciation expense is recognized in Year 5 since the machine was purchased on the last day of the year.

6) B) Increase the amount of expenses recognized. Legal fees incurred in an unsuccessful defense should be expensed as incurred.

7) C) Increase the amount of intangible assets. Under IFRS, the revaluation model may be used for intangible assets if they are traded in active markets. According to the revaluation model, on the revaluation day, the asset is measured at its fair value. An increase in an asset's carrying amount as a result of revaluation is recognized in other comprehensive income and has no effect on profit or loss.

8) B) Increase the amount of expenses recognized. The cost of the equipment with no alternative future uses besides current R&D activities is recognized as an R&D expense.

5. Intangible Assets -- Impairment Test (3 Gradable Items)

1) $13,000. Legal fees incurred in the successful defense of a patent should be capitalized as part of the cost of the patent and then amortized over its remaining useful life. Thus, the carrying amount of the patent on December 31, Year 4, is $48,000 [($50,000 ÷ 10) × 6 + ($24,000 ÷ 8) × 6]. An amortized intangible asset is reviewed for impairment when events or changes in circumstances indicate that its carrying amount may not be recoverable. An impairment loss is recognized only if the carrying amount is not recoverable and is greater than the patent's fair value. Thus, the impairment test has two steps. First, the carrying amount of the patent ($48,000) exceeds the undiscounted cash flows expected from the patent ($40,000). Second, the impairment loss equals the difference between the carrying amount of the patent and its fair value [($48,000 – $35,000) = $13,000].

2) $5,000. An intangible asset with an indefinite useful life must not be amortized. The impairment test for an intangible asset that is not subject to amortization consists of a comparison of its fair value with its carrying amount. Thus, the impairment loss recognized is $5,000 ($80,000 – $75,000).

3) $0. The carrying amount of the franchise on December 31, Year 4, is $24,000 [$60,000 – ($60,000 ÷ 5) × 3]. The carrying amount of the franchise ($24,000) is lower than the undiscounted expected future cash flows from the franchise ($25,000). Thus, the carrying amount is recoverable, and no impairment loss is recognized.

6. Research (1 Gradable Item)

Answer: FASB ASC 350-40-35-4

Amortization of Capitalized Costs

43. The costs of computer software developed or obtained for internal use shall be amortized on a straight-line basis unless another systematic and rational basis is more representative of the software's use.

Gleim Simulation Grading

Task	Correct Responses		Gradable Items		Score per Task
1	___	÷	7	=	___
2	___	÷	8	=	___
3	___	÷	11	=	___
4	___	÷	8	=	___
5	___	÷	3	=	___
Research	___	÷	1	=	___

Total of Scores per Task   ___

÷ Total Number of Tasks   6

Total Score   ___%

Use **CPA Gleim Online** and **Simulation Wizard** to practice more task-based simulations in a realistic environment.

STUDY UNIT ELEVEN
PAYABLES AND TAXES

(17 pages of outline)

11.1	Accounts Payable	381
11.2	Accrued Expenses	382
11.3	Certain Taxes Payable	384
11.4	Deposits and Other Advances	384
11.5	Coupons and Premiums	385
11.6	Warranties	386
11.7	Income Tax Accounting -- Overview	387
11.8	Income Tax Accounting -- Temporary and Permanent Differences	389
11.9	Income Tax Accounting -- Applicable Tax Rate	392
11.10	Income Tax Accounting -- Recognition of Tax Expense	392
11.11	Income Tax Accounting -- Other Issues	394
11.12	Practice Simulation	410

This study unit is the first of four dealing with liabilities. The first six subunits apply basic accrual accounting procedures to the recognition and reporting of liabilities in the balance sheet. The next five subunits address the financial statement implications of the differences between accounting under GAAP and accounting under the federal tax code.

11.1 ACCOUNTS PAYABLE

1. **Definition**

    a. Accounts payable (trade payables) are **liabilities**. They are obligations to sellers incurred when an entity purchases inventory, supplies, or services on credit.

    b. Accounts payable should be recorded at **net settlement value**. Thus, they are measured at the undiscounted amounts of cash (or the equivalent) expected to be paid to liquidate an obligation in the due course of business.

    c. Accounts payable are usually **noninterest-bearing** unless they are not settled when due or payable.

    1) They also are usually **not** secured by collateral.

2. **Current Liabilities**

    a. A current liability is an obligation that will be either paid using current assets or replaced by another current liability.

    b. The following are also current liabilities: (1) Obligations that, by their terms, are **due on demand** within 1 year (or the operating cycle if longer), and (2) obligations that are **callable** by the creditor within 1 year because of a violation of a debt agreement.

    1) But noncurrent debt need not be reclassified if

        a) It is probable that a violation at the balance sheet date will be remedied within a specified period,

        b) The creditor formally waives the right to demand repayment for a period of more than a year from the balance sheet date, or

        c) The debtor expects and has the ability to refinance on a noncurrent basis.

    c. **Checks** written before the end of the period but not mailed to creditors should not be accounted for as cash payments for the period. The amounts remain current liabilities until control of the checks has been surrendered.

3. **Gross Method vs. Net Method**

    a.   Purchases and related accounts payable may be recorded using the gross method or the net method.

    b.   The **gross method** accounts for payables at their face amount. It is used when the purchaser does not expect to pay soon enough to take the discount.

        1)   In a **periodic system**, inventory purchases are initially debited to a **purchases** account that is closed at the end of the period.

            a)   **Purchase discounts taken** are credited to a contra purchases account and closed to cost of goods sold.

        2)   In a **perpetual system**, entries are made directly to inventory.

    c.   The **net method** records payables net of the cash (sales) discount for early payment. It is used when the purchaser expects to pay within the discount period.

        1)   Its advantage is that it isolates **purchase discounts lost**, which are treated as financing charges.

    d.   The journal entries are similar to those recorded for the gross and net methods of treating accounts receivable discussed in Study Unit 8, Subunit 1.

4. **Shipping Terms**

    a.   The timing of recognition of accounts payable may depend on the shipping terms.

    b.   When goods are shipped **FOB shipping point**, the buyer records inventory and a payable at the time of shipment.

    c.   When goods are shipped **FOB destination**, the buyer records inventory and a payable when the goods are tendered at the destination.

EXAMPLE

Kew Co.'s accounts payable balance at December 31, Year 3, was $2.2 million before considering the following:

- Goods shipped to Kew **FOB shipping point** on December 22, Year 3, were lost in transit. The invoice cost of $40,000 was not recorded by Kew. On January 7, Year 4, Kew filed a $40,000 claim against the common carrier.

- On December 27, Year 3, a vendor authorized Kew to return, for full credit, goods shipped and billed at $70,000 on December 3, Year 3. The returned goods were shipped by Kew on December 28, Year 3. A $70,000 credit memo was received and recorded by Kew on January 5, Year 4.

- Goods shipped to Kew **FOB destination** on December 20, Year 3, were received on January 6, Year 4. The invoice cost was $50,000.

When goods are shipped FOB shipping point, inventory and a payable are recognized at the time of shipment. Hence, Kew should currently recognize a $40,000 payable for the goods lost in transit. The $70,000 purchase return should be recognized currently because the seller authorized the credit on December 27. However, the goods shipped FOB destination and not received until January should be excluded. Kew should not recognize inventory and a payable until the goods are tendered at the destination. Accordingly, the ending accounts payable balance is $2,170,000 ($2,200,000 + $40,000 – $70,000).

Stop and review! You have completed the outline for this subunit. Study multiple-choice questions 1 and 2 on page 398.

11.2 ACCRUED EXPENSES

1. **Accrual Entries**

    a.   Ordinarily, accrued expenses meet **recognition criteria** in the current period but have **not been paid** as of year end. They are accounted for using basic accrual entries.

    b.   Accruals may be used to facilitate accounting for accrued expenses in the next period. For example, if wages payable are accrued at year end, the **accrual entry** is

Wages expense	$XXX	
Wages payable		$XXX

2. **Reversing Entries**

    a.   The reversing entry at the beginning of the next period is

            Wages payable $XXX

                Wages expense $XXX

    b.   No allocation between the liability and wages expense is needed when wages are paid in the subsequent period. All expenses paid in the next period can be charged to expense. The entry will simply be

            Wages expense $XXX

                Cash $XXX

3. **No Reversing Entries**

    a.   If **reversing entries are not made**, one of two methods is used in the next period:

        1)   The **liability is debited** when the accrued expense is actually paid. For example, the entry for the first wages payment of the year is

                Wages expense $XXX

                    Wages payable   XXX

                    Cash $XXX

            a)   This entry will differ from subsequent entries recording payment.

        2)   Payments are recorded by **debiting expense for the full amounts** paid. At year end, the liability is adjusted to the balance owed at that date. For example, if the liability for accrued wages has decreased, the adjusting entry is

                Wages payable $XXX

                    Wages expense $XXX

4. **Effects of Nonaccrual**

    a.   If an entity fails to accrue expenses at year end, **income** is overstated in that period and understated in the next period (when they are paid and presumably expensed).

        1)   Moreover, expenses incurred but unpaid and not recorded result in understated **accrued liabilities** and possibly understated assets (for example, if the amounts should be inventoried).

            a)   In addition, working capital (current assets – current liabilities) will be overstated, but cash flows will not be affected.

EXAMPLE

Windy Co. must determine the December 31, Year 2, year-end accruals for advertising and rent expenses. A $500 advertising bill was received January 7, Year 3. It related to costs of $375 for advertisements in December Year 2 and $125 for advertisements in January Year 3. A lease, effective December 16, Year 1, calls for fixed rent of $1,200 per month, payable beginning 1 month from the effective date. In addition, rent equal to 5% of net sales over $300,000 per calendar year is payable on January 31 of the following year. Net sales for Year 2 were $550,000.

The $375 of advertising expense should be accrued in Year 2 because this amount can be directly related to events in that period. The $125 amount is related to events in Year 3 and should not be accrued in Year 2.

The fixed rental is due at mid-month. Thus, the fixed rental for the last half month of Year 2 ($1,200 ÷ 2 = $600) and the rental based on annual sales [($550,000 – $300,000) × 5% = $12,500] also should be accrued.

In its December 31, Year 2, balance sheet, Windy should report accrued liabilities of $13,475 ($375 + $600 + $12,500).

Stop and review! You have completed the outline for this subunit. Study multiple-choice questions 3 through 5 beginning on page 398.

11.3 CERTAIN TAXES PAYABLE

1. **Federal**

   a. **Federal unemployment tax** and the employer's share of **FICA taxes** are expenses incurred as employees earn wages. But they are only paid on a periodic basis to the federal government.

      1) Accordingly, liabilities should be accrued for both expenses, as well as for wages earned but not paid.

Payroll tax expense	$X,XXX	
Employer FICA taxes payable		$XXX
Federal unemployment taxes payable		XXX

   b. Income taxes withheld and the employees' share of FICA taxes are accrued as **withholding taxes** (payroll deductions), not as employer payroll taxes.

Wages expense	$XX,XXX	
Withholding taxes payable		$X,XXX
Employee FICA taxes payable		XXX
Cash		X,XXX

2. **State**

   a. Most states impose **sales taxes** on certain types of merchandise. Ordinarily, the tax is paid by the buyer but is collected and remitted by the seller.

   b. Most states require quarterly or monthly filing of sales tax returns and remittance of taxes collected.

3. **Local**

   a. **Property taxes** are usually expensed by monthly accrual over the fiscal period of the taxing authority.

Stop and review! You have completed the outline for this subunit. Study multiple-choice questions 6 through 9 beginning on page 399.

11.4 DEPOSITS AND OTHER ADVANCES

The AICPA has used questions to test CPA candidates' knowledge of deposits and advances that have often asked for the calculation of the liability amount. Use your scratch paper to write out the appropriate T-accounts or journal entries showing the flow of the transactions. This may be helpful in answering these types of questions.

1. **Definition**

   a. A deposit or other advance is a **liability**. It does not qualify for revenue recognition because the earning process is not substantially complete.

2. **Accounting Treatment**

   a. An issue is whether deposits/advances are classified as **current or noncurrent**.

   b. For the sale of a **gift certificate**, the seller debits cash and credits a liability.

Cash	$XXX	
Deferred revenue		$XXX

   c. Cash received from customers for **magazine subscriptions** creates a liability for unearned subscription revenue

---

EXAMPLE

Nepal Co. requires advance payments with special orders for machinery constructed to customer specifications. These advances are nonrefundable. Information for Year 2 is as follows:

Customer advances -- balance 12/31/Year 1	$236,000
Advances received with orders in Year 2	368,000
Advances applied to orders shipped in Year 2	328,000
Advances applicable to orders canceled in Year 2	100,000

In Nepal's December 31, Year 2, balance sheet, the amount reported as a current liability is $176,000 ($236,000 beginning balance + $368,000 advances received – $328,000 advances credited to revenue after shipment of orders – $100,000 for canceled orders) for customer advances. Deposits or other advance payments are liabilities because they involve a probable future sacrifice of economic benefits arising from a current obligation. The advances applicable to canceled orders are not refundable. Thus, no future sacrifice of economic benefits is necessary. The nonrefundable advances applicable to canceled orders qualify for revenue recognition (debit the liability, credit revenue) because the entity's earning process is complete.

Stop and review! You have completed the outline for this subunit. Study multiple-choice questions 10 through 12 on page 401.

11.5 COUPONS AND PREMIUMS

1. **Definition**

    a. Many sellers include stamps, coupons, special labels, etc., with merchandise that can be redeemed for premiums (cash or goods). The purpose is to increase sales.

2. **Accounting Treatment**

    a. In accordance with the **matching principle**, the expense associated with premium offers is recognized in the same period as the related revenue. Moreover,

    1) The premiums must be purchased and recorded as inventory,
    2) The expense of redemptions must be debited, and
    3) A liability for estimated redemptions must be credited at the end of the accounting period.

    b. The following are **typical entries** to account for an offer to provide a toy in exchange for a sum of cash and a label from a box of the seller's primary product:

    1) To record inventory

Inventory of toys	$XXX	
Cash or accounts payable		$XXX

    2) To record sales of the primary product

Cash	$XXX	
Sales		$XXX

    3) To record redemptions when cash is received

Cash	$XXX	
Premium expense	XXX	
Inventory of toys		$XXX

    4) To record the estimated liability at the end of the period

Premium expense	$XXX	
Estimated liability		$XXX

EXAMPLE

In packages of its products, the Lilac Company includes coupons that may be presented to grocers for discounts of certain products on or before a stated expiration date. The grocers are reimbursed when they send the coupons to Lilac. In Lilac's experience, 40% of such coupons are redeemed, and 1 month usually elapses between the date a grocer receives a coupon from a consumer and the date Lilac receives it. During Year 1, Lilac issued two series of coupons as follows:

Date Issued	Total Face Amount	Consumer Expiration Date	Amount Disbursed as of 12/31/Year 1
1/1/Year 1	$100,000	6/30/Year 1	$34,000
7/1/Year 1	120,000	12/31/Year 1	40,000

No liability should be reported for unredeemed coupons at December 31 with regard to the coupons issued on 1/1/Year 1 because more than 1 month has elapsed since their expiration date. The total estimated liability for the coupons issued on 7/1/Year 1 is $48,000 ($120,000 total face amount of coupons issued × 40%) minus the $40,000 disbursed as of 12/31/Year 1. Consequently, the liability at December 31 is $8,000 ($48,000 – $40,000).

Stop and review! You have completed the outline for this subunit. Study multiple-choice questions 13 and 14 on page 402.

11.6 WARRANTIES

1. **Definition**

    a. A warranty is a **written guarantee** of the integrity of a product or service. The seller also agrees to repair or replace a product, refund all or part of the price, or provide additional service.

        1) A warranty is customarily offered for a limited time, such as 90 days.
        2) It **may or may not be separable** from the product or service.

2. **Accounting Treatment**

    a. A warranty creates a **loss contingency**. Thus, if incurrence of warranty expense is probable, the amount can be reasonably estimated, and the amount is material, **accrual accounting** should be used.

    b. If these criteria are not met, warranty expense should be recorded as incurred, that is, on the **cash basis**. This basis must be used for **tax purposes**.

3. **Inseparable Warranties**

    a. The following are **accrual-basis** entries for warranty expense estimated as a percentage of sales when the **warranty is not separable**:

        1) To record a sale of product

Cash or accounts receivable	$XXX	
Sales revenue		$XXX

        2) To record related warranty expense accrued and incurred for the current period

Warranty expense	$XXX	
Estimated warranty liability		$XXX
Cash, inventory, wages payable, etc.		XXX

        3) To record the costs incurred for prior period sales

Estimated warranty liability	$XXX	
Cash, inventory, wages payable, etc.		$XXX

4. **Separable Warranties**

    a. The accounting for separately extended warranty and product maintenance contracts applies when the contract is separately priced. **Revenue is deferred** and is ordinarily recognized on the **straight-line basis** over the term of the contract.

        1) **Costs** are deferred and amortized only when they are directly related to, and vary with, the sale of the warranty. The primary example of such a cost is a commission.

            a) Furthermore, if service costs are **not incurred on a straight-line basis**, revenue recognition over the contract's term should be proportionate to the estimated service costs.

Stop and review! You have completed the outline for this subunit. Study multiple-choice questions 15 through 17 beginning on page 402.

11.7 INCOME TAX ACCOUNTING -- OVERVIEW

Background
Until 1954, business income reported to the IRS and income reported on financial statements were essentially the same. In that year, accelerated depreciation for tax purposes was permitted for the first time. Since then, more and more provisions of the tax code have diverged from GAAP. The procedures necessary to calculate the amount owed for taxes and current-year tax expense are the subject of the next four subunits.

1. **Objectives**

    a. The objectives of accounting for income taxes are to recognize

        1) The amount of taxes currently payable or refundable

        2) Deferred tax liabilities and assets for the future tax consequences of events that have been recognized in the financial statements or tax returns

2. **Asset-and-Liability Approach**

    a. The asset-and-liability approach is used to account for income taxes. It establishes standards for income taxes currently payable and for the tax consequences of

        1) Items included in **taxable income (loss)** of an earlier or later year than the year in which they are recognized in earnings

        2) Other events that create differences between the **tax bases** of assets and liabilities and their **financial statement amounts**

        3) Operating loss or tax credit carrybacks for refunds of taxes paid in prior years and carryforwards to reduce taxes payable in future years

3. **Interperiod Tax Allocation**

    a. Amounts in the entity's income tax return for a year include the tax consequences of most items recognized in the financial statements for the same year.

        1) But **significant exceptions** exist. Thus, the **tax consequences** of some items may be recognized in tax returns for a year different from that in which their **financial-statement effects** are recognized.

        2) Moreover, some items may have tax consequences or financial-statement effects but never both.

    b. When tax consequences and financial-statement effects differ, income taxes currently payable or refundable also **may differ from** income tax expense or benefit.

        1) The accounting for these differences is **interperiod tax allocation**.

4. **Basic Definitions**

    a. **Income tax expense or benefit** is the sum of (1) current tax expense or benefit and (2) deferred tax expense or benefit.

    b. **Current tax expense or benefit** is the amount of taxes paid or payable (or refundable) for the year as determined by applying the enacted tax law to the taxable income or excess of deductions over revenues for that year.

    c. **Current tax liability** is equal to taxable income times the applicable tax rate.

    d. **Deferred tax expense or benefit** is the net change during the year in an entity's deferred tax amounts.

    e. A **deferred tax liability** records the deferred tax consequences of taxable temporary differences. It is measured using the enacted tax rate and tax laws.

    f. A **deferred tax asset** records the deferred tax consequences of deductible temporary differences and carryforwards. It is measured using the enacted tax rate and tax law.

    g. A **temporary difference (TD)** results when the GAAP basis and the tax basis of an asset or liability differ.

        1) Differences in the two bases arise when items of income and expense are recognized in different periods under GAAP and under the tax code.

        2) The effect is that a taxable or deductible amount will occur in future years when the asset is recovered or the liability is settled.

            a) But some TDs are not related to an asset or liability for financial reporting.

    h. A **permanent difference** is an event that is recognized either in pretax financial income or in taxable income but never in both. It does not result in a deferred tax amount.

5. **Basic Principles of Income Tax Accounting**

    a. A **current tax liability or asset** is recognized for the estimated taxes payable or refundable on current-year tax returns.

    b. A **deferred tax liability or asset** is recognized for the estimated future tax effects of temporary differences and carryforwards.

    c. **Measurement** of tax liabilities and assets is based on **enacted tax law**. The effects of future changes in that law are not anticipated.

IFRS Difference

Deferred tax amounts are measured based on the enacted tax rates or the substantively enacted tax rates at the end of the reporting period.

---

    d. A deferred tax asset is reduced by a **valuation allowance** if it is more likely than not that some portion will not be realized.

Stop and review! You have completed the outline for this subunit. Study multiple-choice questions 18 through 20 beginning on page 403.

11.8 INCOME TAX ACCOUNTING -- TEMPORARY AND PERMANENT DIFFERENCES

 Be prepared to answer questions about income tax accounting, as the AICPA has consistently tested this topic. Candidates must understand and be able to identify both temporary and permanent differences in conceptual aspects.

1. **Asset-and-Liability Approach**

   a. Income reported under **GAAP** (accrual basis) differs from income reported for **tax purposes** (modified cash basis).

      1) The asset-and-liability approach accounts for the resulting temporary (but not permanent) differences.

   b. This approach recognizes the deferred tax consequences for balance sheet measurements and related income statement amounts.

      1) Taxable TDs give rise to future taxable amounts and deferred tax liabilities.

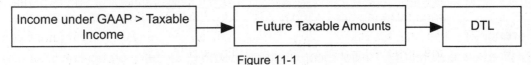

Figure 11-1

      2) Deductible TDs give rise to future deductible amounts and deferred tax assets.

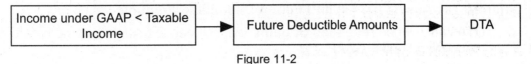

Figure 11-2

2. **Deferred Tax Liabilities (DTLs) and Future Taxable Amounts**

   a. DTLs arise when **revenues or gains** are recognized under GAAP before they are included in taxable income. Examples include

      1) Income recognized under the equity method for financial statement purposes and at the time of distribution in taxable income

      2) Sales revenue accrued for financial reporting and recognized on the installment basis for tax purposes

      3) Gains on involuntary conversion

$$DTL = Future\ taxable\ amount \times Enacted\ tax\ rate$$

EXAMPLE

In Year 1, Luxite Corp. recognizes $800,000 of sales on the accrual basis. These sales will be recognized under the installment method for tax purposes in Years 2 through 5 in the amounts of $300,000, $200,000, $200,000, and $100,000, respectively. These are amounts by which taxable income in Years 2 through 5 will exceed GAAP income. Accordingly, they are future taxable amounts. The enacted tax rate is 40%.

Year 1 excess of GAAP income over taxable income	$800,000
Future taxable amount in Year 2	$300,000
Future taxable amount in Year 3	200,000
Future taxable amount in Year 4	200,000
Future taxable amount in Year 5	100,000
Total future taxable amount	$800,000
Enacted tax rate	× 40%
Year 1 DTL	$320,000

The total future taxable amount, i.e., the amount that will reverse, must equal the current-period difference between GAAP income and taxable income.

b. DTLs also arise when **expenses or losses** are deductible for tax purposes before they are recognized under GAAP.

1) An example is accelerated tax depreciation of property.

EXAMPLE

In Year 1, Luxite buys a piece of equipment for $100,000. It will be depreciated over its 5-year useful life on the straight-line basis for financial reporting (20% per year), and the following accelerated percentages will be used for tax purposes: 59%, 16.5%, 9.5%, 8%, 7%.

Year 1 excess of GAAP income over taxable income (59% – 20%)	$39,000
Future taxable amount in Year 2 (16.5% – 20%)	$ 3,500
Future taxable amount in Year 3 (9.5% – 20%)	10,500
Future taxable amount in Year 4 (8% – 20%)	12,000
Future taxable amount in Year 5 (7% – 20%)	13,000
Total future taxable amount	$39,000
Enacted tax rate	× 40%
Year 1 DTL	$15,600

IFRS Difference

With limited exceptions (e.g., initial recognition of goodwill), all deferred tax liabilities must be recognized.

---

3. **Deferred Tax Assets (DTAs) and Future Deductible Amounts**

a. DTAs arise when **revenues or gains** are included in taxable income before they are recognized under GAAP.

1) Examples are unearned revenues such as rent and subscriptions received in advance.

$$DTA = Future\ deductible\ amount \times Enacted\ tax\ rate$$

EXAMPLE

In Year 1, Luxite sold 5-year subscriptions to its industry journal for $50,000 in cash. It will recognize revenue from these subscriptions on the straight-line basis for financial reporting purposes.

Year 1 excess of taxable income over GAAP income	$40,000
Future deductible amount in Year 2	$10,000
Future deductible amount in Year 3	10,000
Future deductible amount in Year 4	10,000
Future deductible amount in Year 5	10,000
Total future deductible amount	$40,000
Enacted tax rate	× 40%
Year 1 DTA	$16,000

The total future deductible amount, i.e., the amount that will reverse, must equal the current-period difference between GAAP income and taxable income.

---

b. DTAs also arise when **expenses or losses** are recognized under GAAP before they are deductible for tax purposes. Examples include

1) Bad debt expense recognized under the allowance method
2) Warranty costs
3) Startup and organizational costs

EXAMPLE

In Year 1, Luxite accrued $70,000 of warranty costs for financial reporting purposes. From past experience, it expects these costs to be incurred in Years 2 through 5 as follows: $5,000, $15,000, $40,000, $10,000.

Year 1 excess of taxable income over GAAP income	$70,000
Future deductible amount in Year 2	$ 5,000
Future deductible amount in Year 3	15,000
Future deductible amount in Year 4	40,000
Future deductible amount in Year 5	10,000
Total future deductible amount	$70,000
Enacted tax rate	× 40%
Year 1 DTA	$28,000

---

4. **Goodwill**

   a. A deferred tax **liability must be recognized** for the taxable TD arising from tax deductions for goodwill, which is not amortizable for financial statement purposes.

      1) This treatment is required even though the deferred tax liability will not be settled until some indefinite future period when goodwill is impaired, sold, or otherwise disposed of.

      2) The same treatment applies to **other intangible assets** that are not amortizable because their useful lives are indefinite.

5. **Permanent Differences -- No Deferred Tax Consequences**

   a. One category of permanent differences consists of income items included in **net income** but not taxable income. Examples include

      1) State and municipal bond interest
      2) Proceeds from life insurance on key employees

   b. Another category of permanent differences consists of items subtracted in calculating net income but **not taxable income**. Examples include

      1) Premiums paid for life insurance on key employees
      2) Fines resulting from a violation of law

   c. A third category of permanent differences consists of items subtracted in calculating taxable income but not net income. Examples include

      1) Percentage depletion of natural resources
      2) The dividends-received deduction

6. **Valuation Allowance**

   a. A valuation allowance reduces a **deferred tax asset**. It is recognized if, based on the weight of all available evidence, it is **more likely than not** (probability > 50%) that some portion of the asset will not be realized. The allowance should reduce the deferred tax asset to the amount that is more likely than not to be realized.

Income tax expense	$X,XXX	
Deferred tax asset -- valuation allowance		$X,XXX

      1) A new judgment about realizability may require a change in the beginning balance. This revision ordinarily is an item of **income from continuing operations**.

IFRS Difference

A deferred tax asset is recognized for most deductible TDs and for the carryforward of unused tax losses and credits, but only to the extent it is probable that taxable profit will be available. Thus, no valuation allowance is recognized. Moreover, IFRS do not define "probable."

Stop and review! You have completed the outline for this subunit. Study multiple-choice questions 21 through 24 beginning on page 404.

11.9 INCOME TAX ACCOUNTING -- APPLICABLE TAX RATE

1. **Applicable Tax Rates**

    a. A deferred tax amount is measured using the **enacted tax rate(s)** expected to apply when the liability or asset is expected to be settled or realized. In the U.S., the **applicable tax rate** is the **regular rate**.

        1) The tax rate used in the measurement of deferred tax amounts is, in essence, a flat rate if graduated rates are **not** significant to the entity. Otherwise, an **average** of the applicable graduated rates is used.

2. **Enacted Changes in Law or Rates**

    a. Such changes require an adjustment of a deferred tax amount in the period of the enactment. The effect is included in the amount of income tax expense or benefit allocated to continuing operations.

EXAMPLE

The income tax rate is 30% for Years 4 and 5. Under the previous enacted rate, Luxite's deferred tax liability and asset balances were $320,800 ($320,000 installment sales + $800 excess depreciation) and $44,000 ($16,000 subscription revenue + $28,000 warranty costs), respectively. The company recalculates its deferred tax liabilities and assets as follows:

	Future Taxable Amounts				Expected Tax Rate		Deferred Tax Liabilities
	Installment Sales	Excess Tax Depreciation	Totals				
Year 2	$300,000	$ 3,500	$303,500	×	40%	=	$121,400
Year 3	200,000	10,500	210,500	×	40%	=	84,200
Year 4	200,000	12,000	212,000	×	30%	=	63,600
Year 5	100,000	13,000	113,000	×	30%	=	33,900
Total							$303,100

	Future Deductible Amounts				Expected Tax Rate		Deferred Tax Assets
	Subscription Revenue	Warranty Costs	Totals				
Year 2	$10,000	$ 5,000	$15,000	×	40%	=	$ 6,000
Year 3	10,000	15,000	25,000	×	40%	=	10,000
Year 4	10,000	40,000	50,000	×	30%	=	15,000
Year 5	10,000	10,000	20,000	×	30%	=	6,000
Total							$37,000

Stop and review! You have completed the outline for this subunit. Study multiple-choice questions 25 and 26 on page 406.

11.10 INCOME TAX ACCOUNTING -- RECOGNITION OF TAX EXPENSE

 The AICPA has frequently tested candidates' knowledge of the recognition and measurement of deferred income taxes. The AICPA has released a number of former CPA questions that require calculations of deferred tax assets or deferred tax liabilities.

1. **Determination of Deferred Taxes**

    a. The process below is followed for each taxpaying entity in each tax jurisdiction:

        1) Identify TDs (types and amounts) and operating loss and tax credit carryforwards for tax purposes (nature and amounts of each type and the remaining carryforward period).

        2) Measure the total deferred tax liability for taxable TDs using the applicable tax rate.

3) Measure the total deferred tax asset for deductible TDs and operating loss carryforwards using the applicable tax rate.

4) Measure deferred tax assets for each type of tax credit carryforward.

5) Recognize a valuation allowance if necessary.

2. **Calculating Taxable Income**

   a. Taxable income (or excess of deductions over revenue) equals pretax accounting income (or loss) adjusted for permanent and temporary differences.

`Pretax accounting income`		`$xxx,xxx`
Temporary differences:		
<u>`Subtract revenues recognized first under GAAP:`</u>		
`  Accrual sales (installment method for tax)`	`$(x,xxx)`	
`  Equity method income`	`(x,xxx)`	
`  Gain on involuntary conversion`	`(x,xxx)`	`(xx,xxx)`
<u>`Subtract expenses recognized first on tax return:`</u>		
`  Excess tax depreciation`	`$(x,xxx)`	`(xx,xxx)`
<u>`Add revenues recognized first on tax return:`</u>		
`  Unearned revenues (subscriptions, rent, etc.)`	`$ x,xxx`	`xx,xxx`
<u>`Add expenses recognized first under GAAP:`</u>		
`  Excess financial statement depreciation`	`$ x,xxx`	
`  Warranty costs`	`x,xxx`	
`  Startup and organizational costs`	`x,xxx`	
`  Bad debt expense using allowance method`		
`    (direct write-off for tax)`	`x,xxx`	`xxx,xxx`
Permanent differences:		
<u>`Subtract GAAP revenues that are not taxed:`</u>		
`  State and municipal bond interest`	`$(x,xxx)`	
`  Proceeds from key officer life insurance`	`(x,xxx)`	`$(xx,xxx)`
<u>`Subtract deductible expenses not recognized under GAAP:`</u>		
`  Percentage depletion of natural resources`	`$(x,xxx)`	
`  Dividends-received deduction`	`(x,xxx)`	`(xx,xxx)`
<u>`Add GAAP expenses that are not deductible:`</u>		
`  Premiums on key officer life insurance`	`$ x,xxx`	
`  Fines resulting from violation of law`	`x,xxx`	`xx,xxx`
`Taxable income`		`$xxx,xxx`

3. **Calculating Tax Expense or Benefit**

   a. Income tax expense or benefit reported on the income statement is the sum of the current component and the deferred component.

      1) **Current tax expense or benefit** is the amount of taxes paid or payable (or refundable) for the year based on the enacted tax law.

         <u>Current tax expense or benefit:</u>

         `Taxable income (or excess of deductions over revenue) × Enacted rate`

      2) **Deferred tax expense or benefit** is the net change during the year in an entity's deferred tax amounts.

         <u>Deferred tax expense or benefit:</u>

         `Changes in DTL balances ± Changes in DTA balances`

4.   Basic Journal Entries

<u>If the DTL balance increased during the year:</u>

Income tax expense	$xx,xxx	
Deferred tax liability		$x,xxx
Income tax payable		x,xxx

<u>If the DTA balance increased during the year:</u>

Income tax expense	$x,xxx	
Deferred tax asset	x,xxx	
Income tax payable		$xx,xxx

<u>If the DTL balance decreased during the year:</u>

Income tax expense	$x,xxx	
Deferred tax liability	x,xxx	
Income tax payable		$xx,xxx

<u>If the DTA balance decreased during the year:</u>

Income tax expense	$xx,xxx	
Deferred tax asset		$x,xxx
Income tax payable		x,xxx

EXAMPLE

Lucas Company had the following deferred tax balances for the year just ended. The deferred tax asset is fully realizable. The company's taxable income was $1,000,000 for the year. The enacted tax rate is 40%.

	Beginning Balance	Ending Balance
Deferred tax asset	$ 9,000	$17,000
Deferred tax liability	13,000	23,000

Lucas calculates income tax expense for the year as follows:

- Current tax expense is $400,000 ($1,000,000 × 40%).
- Deferred tax expense is the net change in the deferred tax liability and asset balances for the year. The DTL balance increased by $10,000 ($23,000 − $13,000), and the DTA balance increased by $8,000 ($17,000 − $9,000). Thus, the net DTL increase is $2,000 ($10,000 − $8,000).

Lucas records the following entry:

Income tax expense	$402,000	
Deferred tax asset	8,000	
Income tax payable		$400,000
Deferred tax liability		10,000

Stop and review! You have completed the outline for this subunit. Study multiple-choice questions 27 through 30 beginning on page 407.

11.11 INCOME TAX ACCOUNTING -- OTHER ISSUES

1.   Net Operating Losses

a.   Entities that incur net operating losses have two options for obtaining the tax benefit of the loss:

1)   Carry the loss back 2 years and forward 20 years, or
2)   Carry the loss forward 20 years.

b.   **Loss carryback and carryforward**

1)   Under this option, the entity files an amended tax return that carries the loss back to the second prior year, offsetting some or all of that year's tax expense.

a)   If any of the current-year loss remains after exhausting the taxable income of the second prior year, the entity files an amended return offsetting some or all of the prior year's tax expense.

2)   The prior-year financial statements are not restated. The effect is recognized in the current-period statements only.

a)   Both the balance sheet and income statement are affected.

Income tax refund receivable (tax offset by carryback)	$xx,xxx	
Income tax benefit from loss carryback		$xx,xxx

3) Carryforwards are deductions or credits that cannot be used in the current year but may be carried forward to reduce taxable income or taxes payable in a future year.

    a) A carryforward gives rise to a **future deductible amount**, requiring recognition of a deferred tax asset.

    b) Thus, if any of the current-year loss remains after the 2-year carryback, the FASB allows the entity to assume it will be profitable at some time in the next 20 years.

Deferred tax asset (remaining tax expense after carryback)	$xx,xxx	
Income tax benefit from loss carryforward		$xx,xxx

EXAMPLE

Putnam Horn, Inc., incurred a $600,000 net operating loss in Year 5. The enacted tax rate for Year 5 is 30%, resulting in a tax benefit of $180,000 ($600,000 × 30%) available for offsetting. The company has the following historical income tax information:

	Taxable Income (Loss)		Enacted Tax Rate		Income Tax Paid
Year 1	$100,000	×	40%	=	$ 40,000
Year 2	300,000	×	40%	=	120,000
Year 3	200,000	×	40%	=	80,000
Year 4	100,000	×	35%	=	35,000

Putnam Horn has elected to carry the loss both back and forward. The company records the following entries:

Income tax refund receivable ($80,000 + $35,000)	$115,000	
Income tax benefit from loss carryback		$115,000
Deferred tax asset ($180,000 − $115,000)	$65,000	
Income tax benefit from loss carryforward		$65,000

---

  c. **Loss carryforward only**

    1) Under this option, the entity carries the entire loss forward 20 years.

EXAMPLE

MacBeth Seal Corp. incurred a $90,000 net operating loss in Year 5. The enacted tax rate for Year 5 is 30%, resulting in a tax benefit of $27,000 ($90,000 × 30%). The company has the following historical income tax information:

	Taxable Income (Loss)		Enacted Tax Rate		Income Tax Paid
Year 1	$10,000	×	40%	=	$ 4,000
Year 2	40,000	×	40%	=	16,000
Year 3	(10,000)	×	40%	=	--
Year 4	(20,000)	×	35%	=	--

Carrying the loss back will not result in a tax benefit. MacBeth Seal therefore elects to carry the loss forward only. The company records the following journal entry:

Deferred tax asset	$27,000	
Income tax benefit from loss carryforward		$27,000

---

2. **Financial Statement Presentation**

  a. Deferred tax amounts must be classified as **current or noncurrent** based on the classification of the related asset or liability.

    1) If a deferred tax item is not related to an asset or liability for financial reporting, it is classified based on the **expected reversal date** of the TD.

      a) An example of an item not related to a particular asset or liability for financial reporting is a net operating loss carryforward.

2)   A **valuation allowance** for a particular tax jurisdiction is allocated pro rata between current and noncurrent deferred tax assets.

3)   For a given tax-paying entity and within a specific jurisdiction, current deferred tax amounts are **netted**. Noncurrent deferred tax amounts also are offset and presented as a single amount.

EXAMPLE

Luxite is preparing its financial statements for the year just ended and has the following deferred tax balances:

    Deferred tax liabilities: $320,000 installment sales
                                15,600 excess depreciation

    Deferred tax assets: $16,000 subscription revenue
                                28,000 warranty costs

The company prepares the following analysis:

- The installment sales are related to accounts receivable, a current asset.
- The excess depreciation is related to property, plant, and equipment, a noncurrent asset.
- The subscription revenue is related to unearned revenue, a current liability.
- The warranty costs are related accrued expenses, a current liability.

	Current	Noncurrent
Installment sales	$320,000 Cr.	
Excess depreciation		$15,600 Cr.
Subscription revenue	16,000 Dr.	
Warranty costs	28,000 Dr.	
Totals	$276,000 Cr.	$15,600 Cr.

Luxite presents the following items on its balance sheet for the year just ended:

    Current liabilities:
        Deferred tax liability $276,000

    Noncurrent liabilities:
        Deferred tax liability $15,600

IFRS Difference

All deferred tax amounts are noncurrent.

---

3.   **Disclosures**

a.   The following are required disclosures:

1)   Total deferred tax liabilities and total deferred tax assets

2)   Total DTA valuation allowance and the net annual change in it

3)   Tax effect of each TD or carryforward resulting in a significant deferred tax amount **(by public entities only)**

a)   A nonpublic entity must disclose only the types of significant TDs and carryforwards.

4)   The significant components of income tax expense related to continuing operations

b.   No disclosures about permanent differences are required.

4.   **Intraperiod Tax Allocation**

a.   Intraperiod tax allocation **is required**. Income tax expense (benefit) is allocated to

1)   Continuing operations,
2)   Discontinued operations,
3)   Extraordinary items,
4)   Other comprehensive income, and
5)   Items debited or credited directly to equity.

      b.   The tax benefits of most operating loss carryforwards and carrybacks are reported in the same manner as the source of the income or loss in the current year.

5.   **Accounting for Uncertainty in Income Taxes**

      a.   A **tax position** is one taken or to be taken in a **tax return**. It is reflected in financial statement measurements of tax assets and liabilities, whether current or deferred.

           1)   For example, tax positions may include

                a)   Decisions not to file,
                b)   Income exclusions,
                c)   Transaction exemptions,
                d)   Income characterizations, or
                e)   Shifts of income among jurisdictions.

      b.   The evaluation of a tax position is a two-stage procedure:

           1)   **Recognition threshold.** The financial statement effects are initially recognized if it is **more likely than not** (probability > 50%) that the position will be sustained upon examination based on its technical merits. It also may be recognized if **effective settlement** has occurred.

           2)   **Measurement.** The entity recognizes the largest benefit that is **more than 50% likely** to be realized.

      c.   Applying this guidance may result in recognition of a tax benefit different from the amount in the current tax return. Thus, **unrecognized tax benefits** are differences between a tax position in a tax return and the benefits recognized under GAAP.

           1)   The result is a **contingent liability** (or reduction of a loss carryforward or refund). This result reflects the entity's possible future tax obligation because of a tax position not recognized in the financial statements.

           2)   The entity ordinarily recognizes one or both of the following:

                a)   An increased liability for taxes payable or a reduced refund receivable
                b)   A decreased deferred tax asset or increased deferred tax liability

           3)   A tax position recognized under this guidance may affect the **tax bases** of assets or liabilities and change (or create) **temporary differences**.

EXAMPLE

In Year 1, Luxite Corp. took a deduction on its tax return for $15,000. The effective tax rate was 40%, resulting in a tax benefit of $6,000. Luxite believes that it is more likely than not that this deduction will be sustained upon examination. However, Luxite prefers not to litigate the matter and would accept a settlement offer. Luxite has considered the amounts and probabilities of the possible estimated outcomes as follows:

Possible Estimated Outcome	Individual Probability of Occurring (%)	Cumulative Probability of Occurring (%)
$6,000	5	5
5,000	25	30
4,000	25	55
3,000	20	75
2,000	10	85
1,000	10	95
0	5	100

Because $4,000 is the largest benefit that is more likely than not to be realized upon settlement, the entity recognizes a tax benefit of $4,000 in the financial statements.

Stop and review! You have completed the outline for this subunit. **Study multiple-choice questions 31 through 33 beginning on page 408.**

QUESTIONS

11.1 Accounts Payable

1. Which of the following is usually associated with payables classified as accounts payable?

	Periodic Payment of Interest	Secured by Collateral
A.	No	No
B.	No	Yes
C.	Yes	No
D.	Yes	Yes

Answer (A) is correct.

REQUIRED: The characteristic(s) usually associated with accounts payable.

DISCUSSION: Accounts payable, commonly termed trade accounts payable, are liabilities reflecting the obligations to sellers that are incurred when an entity purchases inventory, supplies, or services on credit. Accounts payable should be recorded at their settlement value. Short-term liabilities, such as accounts payable, do not usually provide for a periodic payment of interest unless the accounts are not settled when due or payable. They also are usually not secured by collateral.

2. Lyle, Inc., is preparing its financial statements for the year ended December 31, Year 3. Accounts payable amounted to $360,000 before any necessary year-end adjustment related to the following:

- At December 31, Year 3, Lyle has a $50,000 debit balance in its accounts payable to Ross, a supplier, resulting from a $50,000 advance payment for goods to be manufactured to Lyle's specifications.
- Checks in the amount of $100,000 were written to vendors and recorded on December 29, Year 3. The checks were mailed on January 5, Year 4.

What amount should Lyle report as accounts payable in its December 31, Year 3, balance sheet?

A. $510,000

B. $410,000

C. $310,000

D. $210,000

Answer (A) is correct.

REQUIRED: The amount of accounts payable reported after year-end adjustments.

DISCUSSION: The ending accounts payable balance should include amounts owed as of December 31, Year 3, on trade payables. Although Lyle wrote checks for $100,000 to various vendors, that amount should still be included in the accounts payable balance because the company had not surrendered control of the checks at year end. The advance to the supplier was erroneously recorded as a reduction of (debit to) accounts payable. This amount should be recorded as a prepaid asset, and accounts payable should be credited (increased) by $50,000. Thus, accounts payable should be reported as $510,000 ($360,000 + $50,000 + $100,000).

Answer (B) is incorrect. The amount of $410,000 does not include the $100,000 in checks not yet mailed at year end. Answer (C) is incorrect. The amount of $310,000 does not include the $100,000 in checks, and it reflects the subtraction, not the addition, of the $50,000 advance. Answer (D) is incorrect. The amount of $210,000 results from subtracting the advance payment and the checks.

11.2 Accrued Expenses

3. Ross Co. pays all salaried employees on a Monday for the 5-day workweek ended the previous Friday. The last payroll recorded for the year ended December 31, Year 4, was for the week ended December 25, Year 4. The payroll for the week ended January 1, Year 5, included regular weekly salaries of $80,000 and vacation pay of $25,000 for vacation time earned in Year 4 not taken by December 31, Year 4. Ross had accrued a liability of $20,000 for vacation pay at December 31, Year 3. In its December 31, Year 4, balance sheet, what amount should Ross report as accrued salary and vacation pay?

A. $64,000

B. $68,000

C. $69,000

D. $89,000

Answer (D) is correct.

REQUIRED: The accrued salary and vacation pay.

DISCUSSION: The salary accrual at December 31, Year 4, was for a 4-day period (December 28-31). Thus, the accrued salary (amount earned in Year 4 but not paid until Year 5) should be $64,000 [$80,000 in salaries for a 5-day week × (4 days ÷ 5 days)]. Vacation pay ($25,000) for time earned but not taken in Year 4 was not paid until Year 5. Hence, $25,000, not $20,000, should have been accrued at year end. The total accrual is $89,000 ($64,000 + $25,000).

Answer (A) is incorrect. The amount of $64,000 does not include vacation pay. Answer (B) is incorrect. The amount of $68,000 equals the accrued Year 4 salary for a 3-day, rather than a 4-day, period, and the erroneous deduction of $20,000 for accrued Year 4 vacation time. Answer (C) is incorrect. The amount of $69,000 results from erroneously deducting $20,000.

4. In its Year 4 financial statements, Cris Co. reported interest expense of $85,000 in its income statement and cash paid for interest of $68,000 in its cash flow statement. There was no prepaid interest or interest capitalization at either the beginning or the end of Year 4. Accrued interest at December 31, Year 3, was $15,000. What amount should Cris report as accrued interest payable in its December 31, Year 4, balance sheet?

A. $2,000

B. $15,000

C. $17,000

D. $32,000

Answer (D) is correct.
REQUIRED: The accrued interest payable at year end.
DISCUSSION: The cash paid for interest was $68,000, including $15,000 of interest paid for Year 3. Consequently, $53,000 ($68,000 – $15,000) of the cash paid for interest related to Year 4. Interest payable is therefore $32,000 ($85,000 – $53,000).
Answer (A) is incorrect. The amount of $2,000 results from adding the $15,000 to $68,000 and subtracting that sum from the $85,000 interest expense. Answer (B) is incorrect. The interest paid for Year 3 is $15,000. Answer (C) is incorrect. The difference between the interest expense and cash paid out is $17,000.

5. On December 31, Year 4, Deal, Inc., failed to accrue the December Year 4 sales salaries that were payable on January 6, Year 5. What is the effect of the failure to accrue sales salaries on working capital and cash flows from operating activities in Deal's Year 4 financial statements?

	Working Capital	Cash Flows from Operating Activities
A.	Overstated	No effect
B.	Overstated	Overstated
C.	No effect	Overstated
D.	No effect	No effect

Answer (A) is correct.
REQUIRED: The effect of the failure to accrue sales salaries on working capital and cash flows from operating activities.
DISCUSSION: The effect is to overstate working capital (current assets – current liabilities) because of the failure to accrue a current liability by a debit to salaries expense and a credit to salaries payable. The error has no effect on cash flows because an accrual does not involve a cash payment or receipt.
Answer (B) is incorrect. Cash flows are unaffected. Answer (C) is incorrect. Cash flows are unaffected, but working capital is overstated. Answer (D) is incorrect. Working capital is overstated.

11.3 Certain Taxes Payable

6. Bloy Corp.'s payroll for the pay period ended October 31, Year 4, is summarized as follows:

Depart-ment Payroll	Total Wages	Federal Income Tax Withheld	FICA	Unemploy-ment
Factory	$ 60,000	$ 7,000	$56,000	$18,000
Sales	22,000	3,000	16,000	2,000
Office	18,000	2,000	8,000	--
	$100,000	$12,000	$80,000	$20,000

Assume the following payroll tax rates:

FICA for employer and employee	7% each
Unemployment	3%

What amount should Bloy accrue as its share of payroll taxes in its October 31, Year 4, balance sheet?

A. $18,200

B. $12,600

C. $11,800

D. $6,200

Answer (D) is correct.
REQUIRED: The amount to be accrued for payroll taxes.
DISCUSSION: The amount of wages subject to payroll taxes for FICA purposes is $80,000. At a 7% rate, the employer's share of FICA taxes equals $5,600 ($80,000 × 7%). Wages subject to unemployment payroll taxes are $20,000. At a 3% rate, unemployment payroll taxes equal $600 ($20,000 × 3%). Consequently, the total of payroll taxes is $6,200 ($5,600 + $600). A 7% employee rate also applies to the wages subject to FICA taxes. This amount ($80,000 × 7% = $5,600) should be withheld from the employee's wages and remitted directly to the federal government by the employer, along with the $6,200 in employer payroll taxes. The employee's share, however, should be accrued as a withholding tax (an employee payroll deduction) and not as an employer payroll tax.
Answer (A) is incorrect. The amount of $18,200 includes the federal income tax withheld. Answer (B) is incorrect. The amount of $12,600 is the sum of the federal income tax withheld and the unemployment tax. Answer (C) is incorrect. The amount of $11,800 includes the FICA employee taxes.

7. Lime Co.'s payroll for the month ended January 31, Year 4, is summarized as follows:

Total wages	$10,000
Federal income tax withheld	1,200

All wages paid were subject to FICA. FICA tax rates were 7% each for employee and employer. Lime remits payroll taxes on the 15th of the following month. In its financial statements for the month ended January 31, Year 4, what amounts should Lime report as total payroll tax liability and as payroll tax expense?

	Liability	Expense
A.	$1,200	$1,400
B.	$1,900	$1,400
C.	$1,900	$700
D.	$2,600	$700

Answer (D) is correct.
   REQUIRED: The amounts reported as total payroll tax liability and as payroll tax expense.
   DISCUSSION: The payroll liability is $2,600 ($1,200 federal income tax withheld + $700 employer's FICA + $700 employees' FICA). The payroll tax expense consists of the employer's share of FICA. The employees' share is considered a withholding, not an expense.
   Answer (A) is incorrect. The amount of $1,200 does not include employer and employee shares of current FICA taxes, and $1,400 includes the employees' share of FICA taxes. Answer (B) is incorrect. The amount of $1,900 does not include $700 of FICA taxes, and $1,400 includes the employees' share of FICA taxes. Answer (C) is incorrect. The amount of $1,900 does not include $700 of FICA taxes.

8. Under state law, Acme may pay 3% of eligible gross wages or it may reimburse the state directly for actual unemployment claims. Acme believes that actual unemployment claims will be 2% of eligible gross wages and has chosen to reimburse the state. Eligible gross wages are defined as the first $10,000 of gross wages paid to each employee. Acme had five employees, each of whom earned $20,000 during Year 4. In its December 31, Year 4, balance sheet, what amount should Acme report as accrued liability for unemployment claims?

A. $1,000

B. $1,500

C. $2,000

D. $3,000

Answer (A) is correct.
   REQUIRED: The accrued liability for unemployment claims.
   DISCUSSION: A contingent liability should be accrued when it is probable that a liability has been incurred and the amount can be reasonably estimated. Thus, Acme should accrue a liability for $1,000 [(5 employees × $10,000) eligible wages × 2%].
   Answer (B) is incorrect. The amount of $1,500 is based on a 3% rate. Answer (C) is incorrect. The amount of $2,000 is based on the total wages paid to the employees. Answer (D) is incorrect. The amount of $3,000 is based on a 3% rate and the total wages paid to the employees.

9. On July 1, Year 4, Ran County issued realty tax assessments for its fiscal year ended June 30, Year 5. The assessments are to be paid in two equal installments. On September 1, Year 4, Day Co. purchased a warehouse in Ran County. The purchase price was reduced by a credit for accrued realty taxes. Day did not record the entire year's real estate tax obligation, but instead records tax expenses at the end of each month by adjusting prepaid real estate taxes or real estate taxes payable, as appropriate. On November 1, Year 4, Day paid the first installment of $12,000 for realty taxes. What amount of this payment should Day record as a debit to real estate taxes payable?

A. $4,000

B. $8,000

C. $10,000

D. $12,000

Answer (B) is correct.
   REQUIRED: The amount to be debited to real estate taxes payable.
   DISCUSSION: The credit balance in real estate taxes payable at November 1, Year 4, is $8,000. This amount reflects accrued real estate taxes of $2,000 a month [(2 × $12,000) ÷ 12 months] for 4 months (July through October). This payable should be debited for $8,000 when the real estate taxes are paid.
   Answer (A) is incorrect. The amount of $4,000 includes real estate taxes for September and October only. Answer (C) is incorrect. The amount of $10,000 includes real estate taxes for November. Answer (D) is incorrect. The amount of $12,000 equals 6 months of real estate taxes.

11.4 Deposits and Other Advances

10. Barnel Corp. owns and manages 19 apartment complexes. On signing a lease, each tenant must pay the first and last months' rent and a $500 refundable security deposit. The security deposits are rarely refunded in total because cleaning costs of $150 per apartment are almost always deducted. About 30% of the time, the tenants are also charged for damages to the apartment, which typically cost $100 to repair. If a 1-year lease is signed on a $900 per month apartment, what amount would Barnel report as refundable security deposit?

A. $1,400

B. $500

C. $350

D. $320

11. Buc Co. receives deposits from its customers to protect itself against nonpayments for future services. These deposits should be classified by Buc as

A. A liability.

B. Revenue.

C. A deferred credit deducted from accounts receivable.

D. A contra account.

12. Marr Co. sells its products in reusable containers. The customer is charged a deposit for each container delivered and receives a refund for each container returned within 2 years after the year of delivery. Marr accounts for the containers not returned within the time limit as being retired by sale at the deposit amount. The information for Year 4 is as follows:

Container deposits at December 31, Year 3, from deliveries in

| Year 2 | $150,000 | |
| Year 3 | 430,000 | $580,000 |

Deposits for containers delivered in
Year 4 .... $780,000

Deposits for containers returned in Year 4 from deliveries in

Year 2	$ 90,000	
Year 3	250,000	
Year 4	286,000	$626,000

In Marr's December 31, Year 4, balance sheet, the liability for deposits on returnable containers should be

A. $494,000

B. $584,000

C. $674,000

D. $734,000

Answer (B) is correct.
REQUIRED: The amount of the refundable security deposit.
DISCUSSION: The refundable security deposit is a liability because it involves a probable future sacrifice of economic benefits arising from a current obligation of a particular entity to transfer assets or provide services to another entity in the future as a result of a past transaction. The reported amount of the liability for the refundable security deposit should be $500 because that is the probable future sacrifice of economic benefits, whether in the form of (1) a $500 refund or (2) the sum of an estimated $320 refund, $150 of cleaning costs, and $30 of damages.
Answer (A) is incorrect. The amount of $1,400 equals the deposit plus the last month's rent, an amount that is not refundable. Answer (C) is incorrect. The amount of $350 does not reflect the expected value of cleaning costs. Answer (D) is incorrect. The amount of $320 does not reflect the expected value of cleaning costs or damages.

Answer (A) is correct.
REQUIRED: The nature of customer deposits.
DISCUSSION: A customer deposit is a liability because it involves a probable future sacrifice of economic benefits arising from a current obligation of a particular entity to transfer assets or provide services to another entity in the future as a result of a past transaction.
Answer (B) is incorrect. A revenue is not recognized until it is earned. Answer (C) is incorrect. GAAP ordinarily prohibit offsetting assets and liabilities. Most deferred credits are liabilities. Answer (D) is incorrect. A contra account is a valuation account.

Answer (C) is correct.
REQUIRED: The liability for deposits on returnable containers at year end.
DISCUSSION: At the beginning of Year 4, the liability for returnable containers is given as $580,000. This liability is increased by the $780,000 attributable to containers delivered in Year 4. The liability is decreased by the $626,000 attributable to containers returned in Year 4. Moreover, the 2-year refund period for Year 2 deliveries has expired. Accordingly, the liability should also be decreased for $60,000 ($150,000 – $90,000) worth of containers deemed to be retired. As indicated below, the liability for returnable containers at December 31, Year 4, is $674,000.

Deposits on Returnable Containers

Containers		$580,000	12/31/Yr 3
returned	$626,000	780,000	Year 4 Containers
Year 2 retired	60,000		delivered
		$674,000	12/31/Yr 4

Answer (A) is incorrect. The amount of $494,000 is the difference between total deposits for containers delivered in Year 4 and Year 4 deposits returned. Answer (B) is incorrect. The amount of $584,000 assumes that all Year 2 containers were retired. Answer (D) is incorrect. The amount of $734,000 omits the Year 2 containers retired by sale from the calculation.

11.5 Coupons and Premiums

13. In December Year 4, Mill Co. began including one coupon in each package of candy that it sells and offering a toy in exchange for $.50 and five coupons. The toys cost Mill $.80 each. Eventually, 60% of the coupons will be redeemed. During December, Mill sold 110,000 packages of candy, and no coupons were redeemed. In its December 31, Year 4, balance sheet, what amount should Mill report as estimated liability for coupons?

   A. $3,960

   B. $10,560

   C. $19,800

   D. $52,800

Answer (A) is correct.
   REQUIRED: The amount to be reported as a liability for unredeemed coupons at year end.
   DISCUSSION: The liability for coupon redemptions is $3,960 {[(110,000 coupons issued ÷ 5 per toy) × 60% redemption rate] × ($.80 – $.50) set cost per toy}.
   Answer (B) is incorrect. The amount of $10,560 does not include the $.50 paid by customers for the toy. Answer (C) is incorrect. The amount of $19,800 assumes one coupon can be redeemed for a toy. Answer (D) is incorrect. The amount of $52,800 assumes one coupon can be redeemed for a toy, and it excludes the $.50 that customers must pay per toy.

14. Dunn Trading Stamp Company records stamp service revenue and provides for the cost of redemptions in the year stamps are sold to licensees. Dunn's past experience indicates that only 80% of the stamps sold to licensees will be redeemed. Dunn's liability for stamp redemptions was $6 million at December 31, Year 3. Additional information for Year 4 is as follows:

Stamp service revenue from stamps sold to licensees	$4,000,000
Cost of redemptions (stamps sold prior to 1/1/Yr 4)	2,750,000

If all the stamps sold in Year 4 were presented for redemption in Year 5, the redemption cost would be $2,250,000. What amount should Dunn report as a liability for stamp redemptions at December 31, Year 4?

   A. $7,250,000

   B. $5,500,000

   C. $5,050,000

   D. $3,250,000

Answer (C) is correct.
   REQUIRED: The reported liability for stamp redemptions at year end.
   DISCUSSION: The liability for stamp redemptions at the beginning of Year 4 is given as $6 million. This liability would be increased in Year 4 by $2,250,000 if all stamps sold in Year 4 were presented for redemption. However, because only 80% are expected to be redeemed, the liability should be increased by $1,800,000 ($2,250,000 × 80%). The liability was decreased by the $2,750,000 attributable to the costs of redemptions. Thus, the liability for stamp redemptions at December 31, Year 4, is $5,050,000 ($6,000,000 + $1,800,000 – $2,750,000).
   Answer (A) is incorrect. The amount of $7,250,000 equals the beginning balance, plus stamp service revenue, minus redemptions of stamps sold before Year 4. Answer (B) is incorrect. The amount of $5,500,000 is based on an expected 100% redemption rate. Answer (D) is incorrect. The amount of $3,250,000 assumes that no stamps were sold in Year 4.

11.6 Warranties

15. Vadis Co. sells appliances that include a 3-year warranty. Service calls under the warranty are performed by an independent mechanic under a contract with Vadis. Based on experience, warranty costs are estimated at $30 for each machine sold. When should Vadis recognize these warranty costs?

   A. Evenly over the life of the warranty.

   B. When the service calls are performed.

   C. When payments are made to the mechanic.

   D. When the machines are sold.

Answer (D) is correct.
   REQUIRED: The proper recording of warranty costs.
   DISCUSSION: Under the accrual method, a provision for warranty costs is made when the related revenue is recognized.
   Answer (A) is incorrect. The accrual method matches the costs and the related revenues. Answer (B) is incorrect. When the warranty costs can be reasonably estimated, the accrual method should be used. Recognizing the costs when the service calls are performed is the cash basis. Answer (C) is incorrect. Recognizing costs when paid is the cash basis.

16. During Year 3, Rex Co. introduced a new product carrying a 2-year warranty against defects. The estimated warranty costs related to dollar sales are 2% within 12 months following sale and 4% in the second 12 months following sale. Sales and actual warranty expenditures for the years ended December 31, Year 3 and Year 4, are as follows:

	Sales	Actual Warranty Expenditures
Year 3	$ 600,000	$ 9,000
Year 4	1,000,000	30,000
	$1,600,000	$39,000

At December 31, Year 4, Rex should report an estimated warranty liability of

A. $0

B. $39,000

C. $57,000

D. $96,000

Answer (C) is correct.
  REQUIRED: The estimated warranty liability at the end of the second year.
  DISCUSSION: Because this product is new, the beginning balance in the estimated warranty liability account at the beginning of Year 3 is $0. For Year 3, the estimated warranty costs related to dollar sales are 6% (2% + 4%) of sales or $36,000 ($600,000 × 6%). For Year 4, the estimated warranty costs are $60,000 ($1,000,000 sales × 6%). These amounts are charged to warranty expense and credited to the estimated warranty liability account. This liability account is debited for expenditures of $9,000 and $30,000 in Year 3 and Year 4, respectively. Hence, the estimated warranty liability at 12/31/Yr 4 is $57,000.

Estimated Warranty Liability

		$ 0 1/1/Yr 3
Year 3 expenditures	$ 9,000	36,000 Year 3 expense
Year 4 expenditures	30,000	60,000 Year 4 expense
		$57,000 12/31/Yr 4

  Answer (A) is incorrect. All warranties have not expired. Answer (B) is incorrect. The total warranty expenditures to date equals $39,000. Answer (D) is incorrect. The total warranty expense to date equals $96,000.

17. Oak Co. offers a 3-year warranty on its products. Oak previously estimated warranty costs to be 2% of sales. Due to a technological advance in production at the beginning of Year 4, Oak now believes 1% of sales to be a better estimate of warranty costs. Warranty costs of $80,000 and $96,000 were reported in Year 2 and Year 3, respectively. Sales for Year 4 were $5 million. What amount should be disclosed in Oak's Year 4 financial statements as warranty expense?

A. $ 50,000

B. $ 88,000

C. $100,000

D. $138,000

Answer (A) is correct.
  REQUIRED: The amount of warranty expense reported.
  DISCUSSION: The change affects only Year 4 sales. No change in the previously recorded estimates is necessary. Thus, the debit to warranty expense is $50,000 ($5,000,000 sales × 1%). Estimated liability under warranties is credited for $50,000.
  Answer (B) is incorrect. The amount of $88,000 is the average of Year 2 and Year 3 costs. Answer (C) is incorrect. The amount of $100,000 results from using 2% instead of 1%. Answer (D) is incorrect. The amount of $138,000 includes $88,000, which is the average of Year 2 and Year 3 costs.

11.7 Income Tax Accounting -- Overview

18. Intraperiod income tax allocation arises because

A. Items included in the determination of taxable income may be presented in different sections of the financial statements.

B. Income taxes must be allocated between current and future periods.

C. Certain revenues and expenses appear in the financial statements either before or after they are included in taxable income.

D. Certain revenues and expenses appear in the financial statements but are excluded from taxable income.

Answer (A) is correct.
  REQUIRED: The accounting reason for intraperiod allocation of income taxes.
  DISCUSSION: To provide a fair presentation, GAAP require that income tax expense for the period be allocated among continuing operations, discontinued operations, extraordinary items, other comprehensive income, and items debited or credited directly to equity.
  Answer (B) is incorrect. Allocation among periods is interperiod tax allocation. Answer (C) is incorrect. Differences in the timing of revenues and expenses for financial statement and tax return purposes create the need for interperiod income tax allocation. Answer (D) is incorrect. Permanent differences do not create a need for tax allocation.

19. Under current generally accepted accounting principles, which approach is used to determine income tax expense?

    A. Asset-and-liability approach.

    B. "With and without" approach.

    C. Net-of-tax approach.

    D. Deferred approach.

Answer (A) is correct.
    REQUIRED: The current approach used to determine income tax expense.
    DISCUSSION: The asset-and-liability approach accrues liabilities or assets (taxes payable or refundable) for the current year. It also recognizes deferred tax amounts for the future tax consequences of events previously recognized in the financial statements or tax returns. These liabilities and assets recognize the effects of temporary differences measured using the tax rate(s) expected to apply when the liabilities and assets are expected to be settled or realized. Accordingly, deferred tax expense (benefit) is determined by the change during the period in the deferred tax assets and liabilities. Income tax expense (benefit) is the sum of current tax expense (benefit), that is, the amount paid or payable, and the deferred tax expense (benefit).
    Answer (B) is incorrect. The "with and without" approach was an element of the deferred approach. This guidance stated that the tax effect of a timing difference should "be measured by the differential between income taxes computed with and without inclusion of the transaction creating the difference between taxable income and pretax accounting income." Answer (C) is incorrect. The net-of-tax approach accounts for the effects of taxability or deductibility on assets and liabilities as reductions in their reported amounts. Answer (D) is incorrect. The deferred method determined income tax expense by multiplying pretax financial income by the current tax rate. The difference between taxes payable (refundable) and income tax expense (benefit) was recorded as a deferred credit or charge.

20. Temporary differences arise when expenses are deductible for tax purposes

	After They Are Recognized in Financial Income	Before They Are Recognized in Financial Income
A.	No	No
B.	No	Yes
C.	Yes	Yes
D.	Yes	No

Answer (C) is correct.
    REQUIRED: The situations in which temporary differences arise.
    DISCUSSION: A temporary difference exists when (1) the reported amount of an asset or liability in the financial statements differs from the tax basis of that asset or liability, and (2) the difference will result in taxable or deductible amounts in future years when the asset is recovered or the liability is settled at its reported amount. A temporary difference may also exist although it cannot be identified with a specific asset or liability recognized for financial reporting purposes. Temporary differences most commonly arise when either expenses or revenues are recognized for tax purposes either earlier or later than in the determination of financial income.

11.8 Income Tax Accounting -- Temporary and Permanent Differences

21. Orlean Co., a cash-basis taxpayer, prepares accrual-basis financial statements. In its current-year balance sheet, Orlean's deferred income tax liabilities increased compared with those reported for the prior year. Which of the following changes would cause this increase in deferred income tax liabilities?

I. An increase in prepaid insurance
II. An increase in rent receivable
III. An increase in warranty obligations

    A. I only.

    B. I and II only.

    C. II and III only.

    D. III only.

Answer (B) is correct.
    REQUIRED: The change(s) causing an increase in deferred income tax liabilities.
    DISCUSSION: An increase in prepaid insurance signifies the recognition of a deduction on the tax return of a cash-basis taxpayer but not in the accrual-basis financial statements. The result is a temporary difference giving rise to taxable amounts in future years when the reported amount of the asset is recovered. An increase in rent receivable involves recognition of revenue in the accrual-basis financial statements but not in the tax return of a cash-basis taxpayer. This temporary difference also will result in future taxable amounts when the asset is recovered.
A deferred tax liability records the tax consequences of taxable temporary differences. Hence, these transactions increase deferred tax liabilities. An increase in warranty obligations is a noncash expense recognized in accrual-basis financial statements but not on a modified-cash-basis tax return. The result is a deductible temporary difference and an increase in a deferred tax asset.

22. Under IFRS, a deferred tax asset is

A. Required to be reduced by a valuation allowance if it is more likely than not that some portion will not be realized.

B. Measured by applying the tax rates effective when the asset is realized.

C. Recognized to the extent that realization is probable.

D. Recognized to reflect the deferred tax consequences of a taxable temporary difference.

Answer (C) is correct.
REQUIRED: The amount recorded for a deferred tax asset.
DISCUSSION: Under IFRS, a deferred tax asset is recognized for most deductible temporary differences and for the carryforward of unused tax losses and credits, but only to the extent it is probable that taxable profit will be available to permit the use of those amounts. Probable means more likely than not. Thus, no valuation allowance is separately recognized under IFRS.
Answer (A) is incorrect. Under U.S. GAAP, a deferred tax asset is reduced by a credit to a separate valuation allowance. This credit equals the amount needed to reduce the asset to the amount more likely than not (the probability exceeds 50%) to be realized. Under IFRS, the presentation of a separate allowance is not necessary. Instead, the deferred tax asset is recognized to the extent it is probable that taxable profit will be available against which tax deductions may be taken. Answer (B) is incorrect. According to IAS 12, deferred tax assets and liabilities ordinarily are measured using the tax rates that (1) have been enacted or substantively enacted as of the end of the reporting period and (2) apply when the asset is realized or the liability is settled. Thus, a tax rate effective when the asset is realized may not have been enacted or substantively enacted as of the end of the reporting period. Answer (D) is incorrect. A deferred tax liability is recognized to reflect the deferred tax consequences of a taxable temporary difference.

23. Miro Co. began business on January 2, Year 1. Miro used the double-declining balance method of depreciation for financial statement purposes for its building and the straight-line method for income taxes. On January 16, Year 3, Miro elected to switch to the straight-line method for both financial statement and tax purposes. The building cost $240,000 in Year 1, which has an estimated useful life of 15 years and no salvage value. Information related to the building is as follows:

Year	Double-declining balance depreciation	Straight-line depreciation
1	$30,000	$16,000
2	20,000	16,000

Miro's tax rate is 40%.

Which of the following statements is correct?

A. There should be no reduction in Miro's deferred tax liabilities or deferred tax assets in Year 3.

B. Miro's deferred tax liability should be reduced by $7,200 in Year 3.

C. Miro's deferred tax asset should be reduced by $554 in Year 3.

D. Miro's deferred tax asset should be reduced by $7,200 in Year 3.

Answer (C) is correct.
REQUIRED: The accounting for deferred taxes.
DISCUSSION: The difference between the tax basis and the carrying amount of a depreciable asset is a temporary difference. This temporary difference will result in future deductible amounts after Year 2 because more depreciation was recognized in Year 1 and Year 2 for financial-statement purposes than for tax purposes. Thus, after Year 2, the tax basis of the building was $208,000 ($240,000 − $16,000 − $16,000), and its carrying amount was $190,000 ($240,000 − $30,000 − $20,000), a difference of $18,000. The result was a deferred tax asset of $7,200 ($18,000 future deductible amount × 40% tax rate). However, Miro changed to the straight-line depreciation method for tax and financial statements purposes at the beginning of Year 3. A change in a method of depreciation is accounted for prospectively as a change in estimate because the change in principle is inseparable from the change in estimate. Hence, Miro will recognize $190,000 of depreciation in its financial statements for the remainder of the building's estimated useful life (13 years, starting in Year 3). During the same period, Miro will deduct $208,000 on its tax return (assuming sufficient taxable income). Miro's depreciation expense for Year 3 is $14,615 ($190,000 ÷ 13 years). The excess tax deduction (assuming sufficient taxable income) is $1,385 ($16,000 − $14,615), so the reduction in the deferred tax asset is $554 ($1,385 × 40%).
Answer (A) is incorrect. Use of prospective accounting for the change in depreciation method means that depreciation expense will be less than the tax deduction (assuming sufficient taxable income) for each remaining year of the estimated useful life. The effect in Year 3 is a partial reversal of the deductible temporary difference and a reduction in the deferred tax asset. Answer (B) is incorrect. Miro recognized a deferred tax asset. Answer (D) is incorrect. Under prior guidance, a change in depreciation methods would have been accounted for by a cumulative-effect adjustment recognized through the income statement (debit accumulated depreciation for $18,000, credit deferred tax asset for $7,200, and credit cumulative-effect adjustment for $10,800). Under current guidance, however, the carrying amount of the building is not adjusted, and the deferred tax asset is not eliminated.

24. West Corp. leased a building and received the $36,000 annual rental payment on June 15, Year 4. The beginning of the lease was July 1, Year 4. Rental income is taxable when received. West's tax rates are 30% for Year 4 and 40% thereafter. West had no other permanent or temporary differences. West determined that no valuation allowance was needed. What amount of deferred tax asset should West report in its December 31, Year 4, balance sheet?

    A. $5,400

    B. $7,200

    C. $10,800

    D. $14,400

Answer (B) is correct.
    REQUIRED: The amount of deferred tax asset reported at year end.
    DISCUSSION: The $36,000 rental payment is taxable in full when received in Year 4, but only $18,000 [$36,000 × (6 ÷ 12)] should be recognized in financial accounting income for the year. The result is a deductible temporary difference (deferred tax asset) arising from the difference between the tax basis ($0) of the liability for unearned rent and its reported amount in the year-end balance sheet ($36,000 – $18,000 = $18,000). The income tax payable for Year 4 based on the rental payment is $10,800 ($36,000 × 30% tax rate for Year 4), the deferred tax asset is $7,200 ($18,000 future deductible amount × 40% enacted tax rate applicable after Year 4 when the asset will be realized), and the income tax expense is $3,600 ($10,800 current tax expense – $7,200 deferred tax benefit). The deferred tax benefit equals the net change during the year in the entity's deferred tax liabilities and assets ($7,200 deferred tax asset recognized in Year 4 – $0).
    Answer (A) is incorrect. The amount of $5,400 is based on a 30% tax rate. Answer (C) is incorrect. The income tax payable is $10,800. Answer (D) is incorrect. The amount of $14,400 would be the income tax payable if the 40% tax rate applied in Year 4.

11.9 Income Tax Accounting -- Applicable Tax Rate

25. Scott Corp. received cash of $20,000 that was included in revenues in its Year 1 financial statements, of which $12,000 will not be taxable until Year 2. Scott's enacted tax rate is 30% for Year 1, and 25% for Year 2. What amount should Scott report in its Year 1 balance sheet for deferred income tax liability?

    A. $2,000

    B. $2,400

    C. $3,000

    D. $3,600

Answer (C) is correct.
    REQUIRED: The amount reported for deferred income tax liability.
    DISCUSSION: This transaction gives rise to a taxable temporary difference. The resulting deferred tax liability should be measured using the enacted rate expected to apply to taxable income in the period in which the deferred tax liability is expected to be settled. Hence, the deferred tax liability is $3,000 ($12,000 taxable amounts × 25% rate applicable in Year 2).
    Answer (A) is incorrect. The amount of $2,000 is 25% of $8,000, the amount taxable in Year 2. Answer (B) is incorrect. The amount of $2,400 is 30% of $8,000, the amount taxable in Year 1. Answer (D) is incorrect. The amount of $3,600 results from applying a 30% tax rate.

26. As a result of differences between depreciation for financial reporting purposes and tax purposes, the financial reporting basis of Noor Co.'s sole depreciable asset acquired in the current year exceeded its tax basis by $250,000 at December 31. This difference will reverse in future years. The enacted tax rate is 30% for the current year and 40% for future years. Noor has no other temporary differences. In its December 31 balance sheet, how should Noor report the deferred tax effect of this difference?

    A. As an asset of $75,000.

    B. As an asset of $100,000.

    C. As a liability of $75,000.

    D. As a liability of $100,000.

Answer (D) is correct.
    REQUIRED: The deferred tax effect of the difference between the financial reporting basis and the tax basis.
    DISCUSSION: The temporary difference arises because the excess of the reported amount of the depreciable asset over its tax basis will result in taxable amounts in future years when the reported amount is recovered. A taxable temporary difference results in a deferred tax liability. Because the enacted tax rate for future years is 40%, the deferred income tax liability is $100,000 ($250,000 × 40%).
    Answer (A) is incorrect. The deferred income tax effect should be calculated using the 40% rate, and it is a liability. Answer (B) is incorrect. The deferred income tax effect is a liability. The temporary difference results in taxable, not deductible, amounts. Answer (C) is incorrect. The amount of $75,000 is based on the current-year tax rate.

11.10 Income Tax Accounting -- Recognition of Tax Expense

27. For the year ended December 31, Tyre Co. reported pretax financial statement income of $750,000. Its taxable income was $650,000. The difference is due to accelerated depreciation for income tax purposes. Tyre's effective income tax rate is 30%, and Tyre made estimated tax payments during the year of $90,000. What amount should Tyre report as current income tax expense for the year?

A. $105,000

B. $135,000

C. $195,000

D. $225,000

Answer (C) is correct.

REQUIRED: The current income tax expense for Year 1.

DISCUSSION: Current income tax expense equals taxable income for the year times the applicable enacted rate, or $195,000 ($650,000 × 30%).

Answer (A) is incorrect. The amount of $105,000 results when the estimated tax payments are subtracted from the current income tax expense. Answer (B) is incorrect. The amount of $135,000 results when the financial statement income is used and the estimated tax payments are subtracted. Answer (D) is incorrect. The amount of $225,000 results when the financial statement income is used.

28. Pine Corp.'s books showed pretax income of $800,000 for the year ended December 31. In the computation of federal income taxes, the following data were considered:

Gain on an involuntary conversion (Pine has elected to replace the property within the statutory period using the total proceeds.)	$350,000
Depreciation deducted for tax purposes in excess of depreciation deducted for book purposes	50,000
Federal estimated tax payments	70,000
Enacted federal tax rates	30%

What amount should Pine report as its current federal income tax liability on its December 31 balance sheet?

A. $50,000

B. $65,000

C. $120,000

D. $135,000

Answer (A) is correct.

REQUIRED: The amount to be reported as the current federal income tax liability.

DISCUSSION: Current income tax expense equals taxable income times the enacted tax rate. Taxable income equals pretax accounting income adjusted for the items that are treated differently on the tax return and in the accounting records.

Pretax accounting income	$ 800,000
Untaxed gain on involuntary conversion	(350,000)
Excess of tax depreciation	(50,000)
Taxable income	$ 400,000
Enacted tax rate	× 30%
Current tax expense	$ 120,000

Because $70,000 has already been paid to the federal government in the form of estimated tax payments, the current federal income tax liability is $50,000 ($120,000 current income tax expense – $70,000 estimated tax payments).

Answer (B) is incorrect. The amount of $65,000 results from omitting the excess tax depreciation from the calculation. Answer (C) is incorrect. The current portion of income tax expense is $120,000. Answer (D) is incorrect. The amount of $135,000 results from omitting the excess tax depreciation and the estimated payments from the calculation.

29. Quinn Co. reported a net deferred tax asset of $9,000 in its December 31, Year 1, balance sheet. For Year 2, Quinn reported pretax financial statement income of $300,000. Temporary differences of $100,000 resulted in taxable income of $200,000 for Year 2. At December 31, Year 2, Quinn had cumulative taxable temporary differences of $70,000. Quinn's effective income tax rate is 30%. In its December 31, Year 2, income statement, what should Quinn report as deferred income tax expense?

A. $12,000

B. $21,000

C. $30,000

D. $60,000

Answer (C) is correct.

REQUIRED: The deferred income tax expense.

DISCUSSION: Deferred tax expense or benefit is the net change during the year in the entity's deferred tax liabilities and assets. Quinn had a net deferred tax asset of $9,000 at the beginning of Year 2 and a net deferred tax liability of $21,000 ($70,000 × 30%) at the end of Year 2. The net change (a deferred tax expense in this case) is $30,000 ($9,000 reduction in the deferred tax asset + $21,000 increase in deferred tax liabilities).

Answer (A) is incorrect. This amount results from offsetting the deferred tax liability and the deferred tax asset. Answer (B) is incorrect. The deferred tax liability is $21,000. Answer (D) is incorrect. The amount of $60,000 is the income tax expense for the year ($200,000 × 30%).

30. In its Year 4 income statement, Cere Co. reported income before income taxes of $300,000. Cere estimated that, because of permanent differences, taxable income for Year 4 would be $280,000. During Year 4, Cere made estimated tax payments of $50,000, which were debited to income tax expense. Cere is subject to a 30% tax rate. What amount should Cere report as income tax expense?

A. $34,000

B. $50,000

C. $84,000

D. $90,000

Answer (C) is correct.
    REQUIRED: The amount to be reported for income tax expense.
    DISCUSSION: A permanent difference does not result in a change in a deferred tax asset or liability, that is, in a deferred tax expense or benefit. Thus, total income tax expense equals current income tax expense, which is the amount of taxes paid or payable for the year. Income taxes payable for Year 4 equal $84,000 ($280,000 taxable income × 30%).
    Answer (A) is incorrect. The amount of $34,000 equals the $84,000 of income taxes payable minus the $50,000 of income taxes paid. Answer (B) is incorrect. The amount of $50,000 equals income taxes paid, not the total current income tax expense. Answer (D) is incorrect. The amount of $90,000 is equal to the reported income of $300,000 times the tax rate.

11.11 Income Tax Accounting -- Other Issues

31. At the end of Year 4, the tax effects of Thorn Co.'s temporary differences were as follows:

	Deferred Tax Assets (Liabilities)	Related Asset Classification
Accelerated tax depreciation	$(75,000)	Noncurrent asset
Additional costs in inventory for tax purposes	25,000	Current asset
	$(50,000)	

A valuation allowance was not considered necessary. Thorn anticipates that $10,000 of the deferred tax liability will reverse in Year 5. In Thorn's December 31, Year 4, balance sheet, what amount should Thorn report as noncurrent deferred tax liability?

A. $40,000

B. $50,000

C. $65,000

D. $75,000

Answer (D) is correct.
    REQUIRED: The noncurrent deferred tax liability.
    DISCUSSION: In a classified balance sheet, deferred tax assets and liabilities are separated into current and noncurrent amounts. Classification as current or noncurrent is based on the classification of the related asset or liability. Because the $75,000 deferred tax liability is related to a noncurrent asset, it should be classified as noncurrent.
    Answer (A) is incorrect. The amount of $40,000 equals the $50,000 net deferred tax liability minus the $10,000 expected to reverse in Year 5. Answer (B) is incorrect. The amount of $50,000 equals the net deferred tax liability. Answer (C) is incorrect. The amount of $65,000 equals the $75,000 noncurrent deferred tax liability minus the $10,000 expected to reverse in Year 5.

32. Because Jab Co. uses different methods to depreciate equipment for financial statement and income tax purposes, Jab has temporary differences that will reverse during the next year and add to taxable income. Deferred income taxes that are based on these temporary differences should be classified in Jab's balance sheet as a

A. Contra account to current assets.

B. Contra account to noncurrent assets.

C. Current liability.

D. Noncurrent liability.

Answer (D) is correct.
    REQUIRED: The classification of deferred income taxes based on temporary differences.
    DISCUSSION: These temporary differences arise from use of an accelerated depreciation method for tax purposes. Future taxable amounts reflecting the difference between the tax basis and the reported amount of the asset will result when the reported amount is recovered. Accordingly, Jab must recognize a deferred tax liability to record the tax consequences of these temporary differences. This liability is noncurrent because the related asset (equipment) is noncurrent.
    Answer (A) is incorrect. A liability is not shown as an offset to assets and it is not current. Answer (B) is incorrect. A liability is not shown as an offset to assets. Answer (C) is incorrect. The classification of a deferred tax liability should not be determined by the reversal date of the temporary differences unless it is not related to an asset or liability for financial reporting.

33. Mobe Co. reported the following amounts of taxable income (operating loss) for its first 3 years of operations:

Year 2	$ 300,000
Year 3	(700,000)
Year 4	1,200,000

For each year, Mobe had no temporary differences, and its effective income tax rate was 30% at all relevant times. In its Year 3 income tax return, Mobe elected to carry back the maximum amount of loss possible. Furthermore, Mobe determined that it was more likely than not that the full benefit of any loss carryforward would be realized. In its Year 4 income statement, what amount should Mobe report as total income tax expense?

A. $120,000

B. $150,000

C. $240,000

D. $360,000

Answer (D) is correct.

REQUIRED: The total income tax expense.

DISCUSSION: A net operating loss (NOL) may be carried back 2 years (earlier year first) and forward 20 years. The taxpayer also may elect to carry the NOL forward only. Mobe's first year of operations was Year 2, and it elected to carry the NOL back. Thus, it applied $300,000 of the loss (equal to the taxable income for Year 2) to Year 2 and the remaining $400,000 to Year 4. As a result, a deferred tax asset was recognized for the future tax benefit of the NOL. But no valuation allowance was necessary because it was more likely than not that all of the tax benefit would be realized. Accordingly, in Year 3, Mobe recognized a deferred tax asset (a debit) of $120,000 [($700,000 – $300,000 NOL carryback) NOL carryforward × 30%], a tax refund receivable (a debit) of $90,000 ($300,000 NOL carryback × 30%), and a tax benefit (a credit) of $210,000 ($120,000 + $90,000).

Income tax refund receivable	$90,000	
Income tax benefit from loss carryback		$90,000
Deferred tax asset	$120,000	
Income tax benefit from loss carryforward		$120,000

In Year 4, Mobe's income tax payable equals $240,000 [($1,200,000 – $400,000 NOL carryforward) × 30%]. Because the benefit of the deferred tax asset is fully realized in Year 4, it is credited for $120,000. Consequently, total income tax expense for the year is $360,000 ($240,000 current portion + $120,000 deferred portion).

Answer (A) is incorrect. The amount of $120,000 is the tax benefit (the credit to the deferred tax asset). Answer (B) is incorrect. The amount of $150,000 is the income tax payable if the loss is carried forward only. Answer (C) is incorrect. The income tax payable is $240,000.

Use the additional questions in Gleim **CPA Test Prep Online** to create Test Sessions that emulate Prometric!

11.12 PRACTICE SIMULATION

 Financial Accounting and Reporting Testlet 4 of 4 | **Time Remaining** 1 hour - 30 minutes |

DIRECTIONS

Note: If you believe you have encountered a software malfunction, report it to the test center staff immediately.

Navigation

To navigate from task to task, use the controls at the bottom of the screen. Click on the **Next** button to advance to the next task, or the **Previous** button to go to the previous task. To go directly to any task, click on its number.

| ▼ = Reminder | | Directions | 1 2 3 4 5 6 7 | | ◀ Previous | Next ▶ |

If you would like a reminder to revisit a task, or want to indicate that you are finished with it, click on the reminder flag below the task number. To clear the flag, click on it again. Reminder flags are for your use only – they do not contribute to your score.

Tabs

In this part of the examination, you will be asked to complete various tasks. Every task has one or more **Work Tabs**. Some tasks have one or more **Information Tabs**, others may have none. Every task has a **Help** tab.

If a task has **Information Tabs**, you may use the information in them to complete your responses in the **Work Tabs**.

    Work tab   Information tab   Help tab

Work Tabs:

- **Work Tabs** are identified with a pencil icon. This is where your responses are expected.
- Each task has one or more **Work Tabs**.
- **Work Tabs** contain directions for completing the task – be sure to read these directions carefully.
- The **Work Tab** name in the example above is for illustration only – yours will differ.
- You must complete all of the **Work Tabs** in each task to receive full credit.

Information Tabs:

- The Authoritative Literature will be provided in all tasks in the AUD, FAR, and REG sections for your reference.
- Your simulation may have one or more additional **Information Tabs**. Like the Authoritative Literature tabs, **Information Tabs** do not have a pencil icon.
- If your task has additional **Information Tabs**, go through each to familiarize yourself with the task content.

Help Tab:

- The **Help Tab** provides assistance with the exam software that is used in this task. For example, if the task is to compose a memorandum, **Help** will provide information about the word processor.

The Toolbar

The toolbar at the top of the screen shows the amount of time remaining for you to complete the tasks. In addition, the following tools are available. Note that only the **Exit** button is displayed when Directions are visible - the others will appear when you begin the tasks.

 Click on these buttons to split or unsplit the screen. You can split the screen vertically or horizontally.

 Click on this button to display the calculator; click on it again to hide the calculator. To move the calculator, click on the calculator title bar and drag the calculator to the desired location.

 Click on this button to use the spreadsheet; click on it again to hide the spreadsheet. To move the spreadsheet, click on the the spreadsheet title bar and drag the spreadsheet to the desired location.

 Click on this button to go on to the next part of the examination. You must complete all of the tasks to receive full credit. Once you click on **Exit** and confirm the action, you will NOT be able to return to this testlet.

| ▼ = Reminder | | Directions | 1 2 3 4 5 6 | | ◀ Previous | Next ▶ |

| Temporary and Permanent Differences | Authoritative Literature | Help |

Indicate by checking the appropriate box whether each situation below results in a temporary or permanent difference for the purpose of accounting for income taxes.

	Difference	
Situation	Temporary	Permanent
1. A warranty liability recognized as an expense in financial income when a product is sold and recognized in taxable income when the expenditures are made in a future period.		
2. A receivable from a nondealer installment sale recognized at the time of sale in financial income and at the time of collection in taxable income.		
3. An asset depreciates more quickly for tax purposes than for financial reporting purposes.		
4. Percentage depletion of certain natural resources.		
5. The insurance premiums paid by a beneficiary entity on policies covering its corporate officers.		
6. Subscriptions revenue received in advance that is recognized in taxable income when received and in financial income when earned in a later period.		

▼ = Reminder   Directions   1 2 3 4 5 6   ◀ Previous   Next ▶

| Income Tax Issues | Authoritative Literature | Help |

Select from the list provided the best match(es) for each issue below. More than one item may be selected for each issue.

Issue	Answer(s)		Choices
1. Entity changes to nontaxable status.		A)	Interperiod tax allocation
2. Classification of deferred tax amount arising from accelerated tax depreciation.		B)	Intraperiod tax allocation
		C)	Valuation allowance
3. Presentation of current deferred tax amounts for a specific jurisdiction.		D)	Elimination of a deferred tax amount
4. Classification of deferred tax amount arising from recognition of organization costs.		E)	Effect included in income from continuing operations
5. Allocation of tax expense to continuing operations and discontinued operations.		F)	Determined by related asset or liability
		G)	Determined by expected reversal date
6. Enactment of a change in tax rates.		H)	Reported as one amount
		I)	Reported as separate amounts

▼ = Reminder   Directions   1 2 3 4 5 6   ◀ Previous   Next ▶

Presented below is the unaudited balance sheet as of December 31, Year 2, as prepared by the bookkeeper of Zed Manufacturing Corp., a firm not required to report under federal securities law.

Zed Manufacturing Corp.
BALANCE SHEET
For the Year Ended December 31, Year 2

Assets		Liabilities and Equity	
Cash	$ 225,000	Accounts payable	$ 133,800
Accounts receivable (net)	345,700	Mortgage payable	900,000
Inventories	560,000	Notes payable	500,000
Prepaid income taxes	40,000	Lawsuit liability	80,000
Investments	57,700	Income taxes payable	61,200
Land	450,000	Deferred tax liability	28,000
Building	1,750,000	Accumulated depreciation	420,000
Machinery and equipment	1,964,000	Total liabilities	$2,123,000
Goodwill	37,000	Common stock, $50 par;	
Total assets	$5,429,400	40,000 shares issued	2,231,000
		Retained earnings	1,075,400
		Total equity	$3,306,400
		Total liabilities and equity	$5,429,400

Your firm has been engaged to perform an audit, during which the following data are found:

- Checks totaling $14,000 in payment of accounts payable were mailed on December 30, Year 2, but were not recorded until Year 3. Late in December Year 2, the bank returned a customer's $2,000 check, marked "NSF," but no entry was made. Cash includes $100,000 restricted for building purposes.
- Included in accounts receivable is a $30,000 note due on December 31, Year 5, from Zed's president.
- During Year 2, Zed purchased 500 shares of common stock of a major corporation that supplies Zed with raw materials. Total cost of this stock was $51,300, and fair value on December 31, Year 2, was $47,000. The decline in fair value is considered temporary. Zed plans to hold these shares indefinitely.
- Treasury stock was recorded at cost when Zed purchased 200 of its own shares for $32 per share in May Year 2. This amount is included in investments.
- On December 30, Year 2, Zed borrowed $500,000 from a bank in exchange for a 10% note payable, maturing December 30, Year 7. Equal principal payments are due December 30 of each year, beginning in Year 3. This note is collateralized by a $250,000 tract of land acquired for speculative purposes. This tract is included in the land account.
- The mortgage payable requires $50,000 principal payments, plus interest, at the end of each month. Payments were made on January 31 and February 28, Year 3. The balance of this mortgage was due June 30, Year 3. On March 1, Year 3, prior to issuance of the audited financial statements, Zed consummated a noncancelable agreement with the lender to refinance this mortgage. The new terms require $100,000 annual principal payments, plus interest, on February 28 of each year, beginning in Year 4. The final payment is due February 28, Year 11.
- The lawsuit liability will be paid in Year 3.
- The following is an analysis of the deferred tax liability at December 31, Year 2:

Deferred tax liability -- depreciation	$48,000
Deferred tax asset -- lawsuit liability	(20,000)
Net deferred tax liability	$28,000

  $25,000 of the deferred taxes related to depreciation will reverse in Year 3.
- The current income tax expense reported in Zed's Year 2 income statement was $61,200.
- The company was authorized to issue 100,000 shares of $50 par value common stock.

Additional Information:

One of Zed's manufacturing plants is located in a foreign country. This plant is threatened with expropriation. Expropriation is deemed to be reasonably possible. Any compensation from the foreign government would be less than the carrying amount of the plant.

-- Continued on next page --

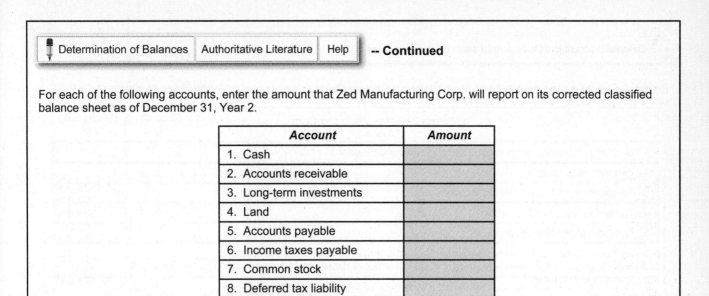

| Determination of Balances | Authoritative Literature | Help | -- **Continued** |

For each of the following accounts, enter the amount that Zed Manufacturing Corp. will report on its corrected classified balance sheet as of December 31, Year 2.

Account	Amount
1. Cash	
2. Accounts receivable	
3. Long-term investments	
4. Land	
5. Accounts payable	
6. Income taxes payable	
7. Common stock	
8. Deferred tax liability	
9. Cost of treasury stock	

▼ = Reminder   Directions   1 2 3 4 5 6   ◀ Previous   Next ▶

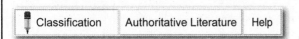

| Classification | Authoritative Literature | Help |

Select from the list provided to indicate whether each of the following is a current liability, noncurrent liability, or other item. Each choice may be used once, more than once, or not at all.

Item	Answer		Choices
1. An appropriation of retained earnings			A) Current liability
2. Current maturity of a long-term debt			B) Noncurrent liability
3. Short-term obligations to be refinanced, given an ability to consummate the refinancing			C) Other item
4. An accommodation endorsement on a demand note issued by an affiliated entity			
5. Unfunded past service costs of a pension plan to the extent that the benefits have not vested and the costs have not been charted to operations			

▼ = Reminder   Directions   1 2 3 4 5 6   ◀ Previous   Next ▶

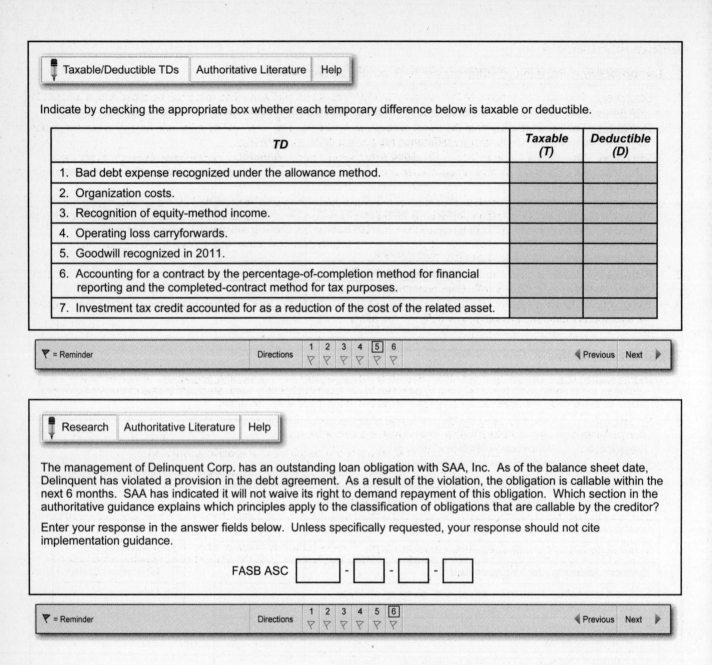

1 2 3 4 5 6

The management of Delinquent Corp. has an outstanding loan obligation with SAA, Inc. As of the balance sheet date, Delinquent has violated a provision in the debt agreement. As a result of the violation, the obligation is callable within the next 6 months. SAA has indicated it will not waive its right to demand repayment of this obligation. Which section in the authoritative guidance explains which principles apply to the classification of obligations that are callable by the creditor?

Enter your response in the answer fields below. Unless specifically requested, your response should not cite implementation guidance.

FASB ASC ☐ - ☐ - ☐ - ☐

Unofficial Answers

1. Temporary and Permanent Differences (6 Gradable Items)

1. <u>Temporary.</u> The reported amount of the warranty liability exceeds its tax basis. The result will be a deductible amount in the future when the liability is settled. This deductible temporary difference results in a deferred tax asset.

2. <u>Temporary.</u> The reported amount of the asset exceeds its tax basis. The result will be a taxable amount when the asset is recovered. This taxable temporary difference results in a deferred tax liability.

3. <u>Temporary.</u> The reported amount of a depreciable asset subject to accelerated tax depreciation exceeds its tax basis. The result will be a future taxable amount when the asset is recovered. This taxable temporary difference results in a deferred tax liability.

4. <u>Permanent.</u> Cost depletion, which is a function of the cost basis of the asset, is permitted on the tax return and the financial statements. Percentage depletion is an additional deduction that is a function of the gross income from the property. It is recognized in the determination of taxable income but is never recognized in the determination of financial income. Because percentage depletion has no deferred tax consequences, it results in a permanent difference, and no deferred tax asset or liability arises.

5. <u>Permanent.</u> Insurance premiums paid by a beneficiary entity on policies covering its corporate officers are not deductible for tax purposes. Hence, the difference is permanent.

6. <u>Temporary.</u> A future deductible amount relating to a revenue or gain that is taxable before it is recognized in net income is a temporary difference resulting in a deferred tax asset.

2. Income Tax Issues (6 Gradable Items)

1. <u>D) Elimination of a deferred tax amount, E) Effect included in income from continuing operations.</u> When an entity changes to nontaxable status, any existing deferred tax amount is ordinarily eliminated at the date of the change. The effect of eliminating the deferred tax amount is included in the income tax expense.

2. <u>F) Determined by related asset or liability.</u> Deferred tax amounts should be separated into current and noncurrent components based on the classification of the related asset or liability.

3. <u>H) Reported as one amount.</u> Current deferred tax amounts are netted within a specific jurisdiction.

4. <u>G) Determined by expected reversal date.</u> If a deferred tax item is not related to an asset or liability for financial reporting, it is classified based on the expected reversal date of the deferred taxes.

5. <u>B) Intraperiod tax allocation.</u> Intraperiod tax allocation is required. Income tax expense (benefit) is allocated to continuing operations, discontinued operations, extraordinary items, other comprehensive income, and items debited or credited directly to equity.

6. <u>E) Effect included in income from continuing operations.</u> Enacted changes in law or rates require an adjustment of a deferred tax amount in the period of the enactment. The effect is included in the amount of income tax expense or benefit allocated to continuing operations.

3. Determination of Balances (9 Gradable Items)

1. **$109,000.**

Cash (unaudited)	$ 225,000
Unrecorded checks in payment of accounts payable	(14,000)
NSF check not recorded	(2,000)
Cash restricted for building purposes (should be reported in other assets)	(100,000)
Corrected balance	$ 109,000

2. **$317,700.**

Net accounts receivable (unaudited)	$345,000
Charge-back for NSF check	2,000
Officer's note receivable (should be reported in other assets)	(30,000)
Corrected balance	$317,700

3. **$297,000.**

Investments (unaudited)	$ 57,700
Land acquired for speculation	250,000
Treasury stock (should be reported as a deduction from total equity)	(6,400)
Unrealized holding loss ($51,300 – $47,000) (erroneously reported in accumulated other comprehensive income)	(4,300)
Corrected balance	$297,000

4. **$200,000.**

Land (unaudited)	$ 450,000
Land acquired for speculation (should be reported in investments)	(250,000)
Corrected balance	$ 200,000

5. **$119,800.**

Accounts payable (unaudited)	$133,800
Unrecorded payments (checks mailed 12/30/Year 2)	(14,000)
Corrected balance	$119,800

6. **$21,200.**

Income taxes payable (unaudited)	$ 61,200
Prepaid income taxes	(40,000)
Corrected balance	$ 21,200

7. **$2,000,000.**

Common stock (unaudited)	$2,231,000
Additional paid-in capital in excess of par value	(231,000)
Corrected balance	$2,000,000

8. **$48,000.** The deferred tax liability is noncurrent because it relates to a depreciable (noncurrent) asset. Current and noncurrent deferred tax amounts are not offset.

9. **$(6,400).** Treasury stock (properly reported as a reduction of total equity).

4. Classification (5 Gradable Items)

1. **C) Other Item.** An appropriation of retained earnings is presented in an equity account. Its sole purpose is disclosure. The account is established with a credit, and retained earnings is debited. The effect is to reduce retained earnings available for dividend payments.

2. **A) Current liability.** Current maturity of a long-term debt customarily requires expenditure of current assets. Thus, it is treated as a current liability with certain exceptions; e.g., it is to be retired using assets accumulated for that purpose that are not classified as current, or it is to be refinanced.

3. **B) Noncurrent liability.** The portion of debt scheduled to mature in the following fiscal year ordinarily should be classified as a current liability. However, if an enterprise intends to refinance short-term obligations on a long-term basis and demonstrates an ability to consummate the refinancing, the obligation should be excluded from current liabilities and classified as noncurrent.

4. **C) Other Item.** An endorsement would not give rise to a liability until the maker of the note defaulted.

5. **C) Other Item.** Such pension costs are not expensed or otherwise recorded as liabilities. As they are expensed, they become liabilities that are usually noncurrent.

5. Taxable/Deductible TDs (7 Gradable Items)

1. (D) Bad debt expense recognized under the allowance method is deductible.

2. (D) Organization costs are deductible.

3. (T) Recognition of equity-method income is taxable.

4. (D) Operating loss carryforwards is deductible.

5. (T) Goodwill recognized in 2011 is taxable.

6. (T) The temporary difference from accounting for a contract by the percentage-of-completion method for financial reporting and the completed-contract method for tax purposes is taxable.

7. (D) An investment tax credit accounted for as a reduction of the cost of the related asset is deductible.

6. Research (1 Gradable Item)

Answer: FASB ASC 470-10-45-11

470-10-45-11 Current liabilities shall include long-term obligations that are or will be callable by the creditor either because the debtor's **violation of a provision** of the debt agreement at the balance sheet date makes the **obligation callable** or because the violation, if not cured within a specified grace period, will make the obligation callable. Accordingly, such callable obligations shall be classified as current liabilities unless either of the following conditions is met:

a. The creditor has waived or subsequently lost (for example, the debtor has cured the violation after the balance sheet date and the obligation is not callable at the time the financial statements are issued or are available to be issued [as discussed in Section 855-10-25]) the right to demand repayment for more than one year (or operating cycle, if longer) from the balance sheet date. If the obligation is callable because of violations of certain provisions of the debt agreement, the creditor needs to waive its right with regard only to those violations.

b. For long-term obligations containing a grace period within which the debtor may cure the violation, it is **probable** that the violation will be cured within that period, thus preventing the obligation from becoming callable.

Gleim Simulation Grading

Task	Correct Responses		Gradable Items		Score per Task
1	____	÷	6	=	____
2	____	÷	6	=	____
3	____	÷	9	=	____
4	____	÷	5	=	____
5	____	÷	7	=	____
Research	____	÷	1	=	____

Total of Scores per Task   ____

÷ Total Number of Tasks   6

Total Score   ____%

Use **CPA Gleim Online** and **Simulation Wizard** to practice more task-based simulations in a realistic environment.

STUDY UNIT TWELVE
EMPLOYEE BENEFITS

(20 pages of outline)

12.1	Components of Pension Expense	419
12.2	Funded Status of Pension Plans	426
12.3	Pension Disclosures and Other Issues	429
12.4	Postretirement Benefits Other than Pensions	430
12.5	Compensated Absences and Postemployment Benefits	432
12.6	Share-Based Payment	434
12.7	Practice Simulation	449

The beginning of this study unit emphasizes accounting for defined benefit pensions. Postretirement benefits other than pensions are accounted for similarly. The remainder of the study unit covers other forms of employee compensation.

12.1 COMPONENTS OF PENSION EXPENSE

Background

The major victory for the defined benefit pension plan was the so-called Treaty of Detroit, agreed to in 1950 between the United Auto Workers union and the three largest American automobile manufacturers. Management discovered that it was much easier to promise money in the future (i.e., increased pension benefits) than to pay higher salaries today. As life expectancies increased, however, Americans' retirement periods lasted longer and longer, and increased foreign competition ended the Detroit automakers' historic profits. These changes have put tremendous pressure on traditional defined benefit plans.

A historic change occurred on January 1, 1980, when the 401(k) account became available to all employees. Under this provision, workers could set aside pretax income and choose their own investments. However, many defined benefit plans that were entered into during years of prosperity are still in force. The employer accounting for the noncurrent liabilities associated with these plans has been addressed by five major FASB pronouncements. Current guidance is in FASB ASC 715.

1. **Types of Plans**

    a. A **pension plan** is a **separate accounting entity** to which a sponsoring employer makes contributions. It invests the assets and makes payments to beneficiaries (but the assets and liabilities are the employer's). The following are the two basic types of pension plans:

        1) In a **defined contribution plan**, the employer makes no guarantee as to the amount of benefits the employee will receive during retirement. The employer's only obligation is to make periodic deposits of the amounts defined by the plan's formula in return for services rendered by employees. Accordingly, employees bear the investment risk (the benefit of gain or risk of loss from assets contributed to the plan). The accounting is relatively easy.

            a) The employer's **annual pension expense** is the amount of the contribution determined by the plan's formula.

                i) The employer reports an **asset** only if the contribution is greater than the defined, required contribution.

                ii) The employer reports a **liability** only if the contribution is less than the required amount.

EXAMPLE

According to the pension agreement of a defined contribution plan, an employer must contribute $100,000 to the plan each year. The following are the employer's journal entries for different contributions:

a) The employer deposits $100,000 in the pension plan.

Pension expense	$100,000	
Cash		$100,000

b) The employer deposits $110,000 in the pension plan.

Pension expense	$100,000	
Prepaid expenses	10,000	
Cash		$110,000

c) The employer deposits $90,000 in the pension plan.

Pension expense	$100,000	
Cash		$90,000
Pension payable		10,000

---

2) In a **defined benefit plan**, the employer guarantees to all qualifying employees upon retirement a certain periodic payment and, therefore, bears actuarial risk and investment risk.

   a) The accounting is **complex**. The exact amounts of future payouts are unknown and must be estimated.

      i) Each year, entities with defined benefit plans must recognize pension expense, the funding provided, and the funded status of the plan.

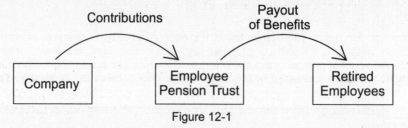

Figure 12-1

2. **Employers' Accounting for Defined Benefit Plans**

   a. The assumption is that a pension plan is part of an **employee's compensation** incurred when his/her services are rendered.

   b. The defined pension benefit is in the form of **deferred payments** that are not precisely determinable.

Background

The employer accounting for a defined benefit pension plan is based on uncertain future events. These include (1) years of service rendered by employees, (2) the life expectancies of employees and their survivors, (3) future compensation levels, (4) expected rates of return on assets, (5) plan amendments, (6) vesting considerations, and (7) various other assumptions. Challenges arise because of the use of estimates and assumptions to determine the current period effects on the financial statements. Thus, the entity must employ actuaries to determine the probabilities and effects of relevant events and the various measures related to financial reporting, such as the benefit obligation and annual service cost.

3. **Projected Benefit Obligation (PBO)**

    a. The PBO at a certain date is the actuarial present value of all benefits attributed by the **pension benefit formula** to employee services rendered prior to that date.

       1) The **measurement date** for benefit obligations and plan assets is generally the **balance sheet date**.
       2) The PBO is measured using assumptions about **future** as well as past and current compensation.

    b. Assumptions about **discount (interest) rates** must be made to calculate the PBO.

       1) They reflect the rates at which benefit obligations can be settled, e.g., current prices of **annuity contracts** and rates on high-quality fixed investments.

4. **Fair Value of Plan Assets**

    a. These assets are invested by a trustee. They are segregated and restricted, generally in a trust, to provide for pension benefits.

    b. Plan assets change as a result of

       1) The return on investments (decrease or increase plan assets)
       2) Benefit payments (decrease plan assets)
       3) Contributions from the employer (increase plan assets)

5. **Income Statement -- Pension Expense**

    a. The **required minimum** pension expense consists of the following elements:

    <pre>
    + Service cost
    + Interest cost
    − Expected return on plan assets
    ± Amortization of net gain or loss
    ± Amortization of prior service cost or credit
      Pension expense
    </pre>

       1) The following is the entry to record annual service cost, interest cost, and expected return on plan assets (assuming service cost and interest cost are unfunded and their sum is greater than the expected return):

Pension expense	$XXX	
Pension liability		$XXX

    b. **Service cost** is the actuarial present value of benefits attributed by the pension benefit formula to services rendered by employees during the current period. It is calculated by the plan's actuary.

       1) Service cost increases the PBO.

          a) Service cost increases pension expense and is unaffected by the funded status of the plan.

    c. **Interest cost** is the increase in the PBO resulting from the passage of time. It equals the PBO at the beginning of the period times the **current discount rate**.

       1) The PBO and the discount rate are provided by the plan's actuary.
       2) Interest cost increases pension expense.

EXAMPLE

The beginning PBO is $100,000, and the discount rate is 4%. The interest cost component of current-year pension expense is $4,000 ($100,000 × 4%). It increases the PBO and is recognized in the income statement as a component of pension expense.

d. The **expected return on plan assets** is the **market-related value of plan assets (MRV)** at the beginning of the period multiplied by the **expected long-term rate of return.**

$$Expected\ return\ =\ MRV\ \times\ Long\text{-}term\ rate$$

1) MRV may be either **fair value or a calculated value** that recognizes changes in fair value systematically and rationally. In this text, MRV is assumed to be fair value.

2) The return on plan assets (if positive) decreases pension expense.

e. **Amortization of Net Gain or Loss**

1) Gains and losses arise from changes in the PBO (what actuaries call **liability gains and losses**) or changes in plan assets (**asset gains and losses**) that result from experience different from that assumed or from a change in an actuarial assumption.

a) A liability gain or loss can be derived from the following PBO equation:

    Beginning PBO
+ Service cost
+ Interest cost
+ Prior service cost
− Prior service credit
− Benefit paid
+/−**Liability gain or loss**
    Ending PBO

EXAMPLE

The following data relate to Entity A's Year 1 PBO:

PBO -- January 1, Year 1	$250,000
PBO -- December 31, Year 1	400,000
Benefits paid (on December 30, Year 1)	20,000
Discount rate	5%
Service cost recognized in Year 1	$35,000
Prior service cost recognized in Year 1	67,500

The liability loss for Year 1 can be derived from the following Year 1 PBO equation:

January 1, Year 1, PBO	$250,000
Service cost	35,000
Interest cost ($250,000 × 5%)	12,500
Prior service cost	67,500
Benefits paid in Year 1	(20,000)
Liability loss	**55,000**
December 31, Year 1, PBO	$400,000

---

b) The **actual return on plan assets** is based on the **fair value of the plan assets** at the beginning and end of the accounting period, adjusted for contributions and payments.

+ Fair value – End of period
− Fair value – Beginning of period
− Contributions to plan assets
+ Benefits paid
    Actual return on plan assets

> i) An **asset loss** occurs when the expected return on plan assets is greater than the actual return on plan assets for the period.
>
> ii) An **asset gain** occurs when the actual return on plan assets is greater than the expected return.

EXAMPLE

The following data relate to Entity A's Year 1 plan assets:

Beginning fair value of plan assets	$150,000
Ending fair value of plan assets	170,000
Benefit payments made at year end	20,000
Expected long-term rate of return on plan assets	8%
Contributions to plan assets made at year end	$ 15,000

1)	Fair value -- end of period	$170,000
	Less: fair value -- beginning of period	(150,000)
	Less: contributions to plan assets	(15,000)
	Benefits paid	20,000
	Actual return on plan assets	**$ 25,000**

2) The expected return on plan assets is $12,000 ($150,000 × 8%).

3) The actual return on plan assets is greater than the expected return on plan assets. Thus, the **asset gain** is $13,000 ($25,000 – $12,000).

> c) Using the results of the two previous examples, Entity A's Year 1 net loss is $42,000 ($55,000 liability loss – $13,000 asset gain).

IFRS Difference

Interest income on plan assets for the period is a component of the return on plan assets. It is recognized in profit or loss. It equals the fair value of plan assets at the beginning of the year (adjusted for contributions and benefits paid during the year) times the same rate used to discount the defined benefit obligation. Under U.S. GAAP, different interest rates may be used to calculate interest cost and the expected return on plan assets.

The remeasurement of plan assets for the period is the return on plan assets, excluding the interest income on plan assets.

The following is an example of the calculation of the remeasurement of plan assets:

Fair value of plan assets end of the year	$ 1,200
Fair value of plan assets beginning of the year	(1,000)
Interest income (included in profit or loss)	(100)
Contributions	(200)
Benefit payments	150
Remeasurement of plan assets	$ 50

> 2) Gains and losses not recognized in pension expense must be recognized in **other comprehensive income (OCI)**, net of tax, when they occur.
>
> a) OCI is a nominal account that is closed to accumulated OCI, a real account, at the end of the period.
>
> b) The entry for a loss not recognized in pension expense is

OCI	$XXX	
Pension liability		$XXX

3) A **corridor approach** may be used to reduce the volatility of the pension expense caused by gains and losses.

a) The **net gain or loss included in accumulated OCI** (excluding asset gains and losses not reflected in MRV) is subject to **required amortization** in pension expense.

　　i) However, only the amount that exceeds (at the beginning of the year) 10% of the greater of the PBO or the MRV must be amortized.

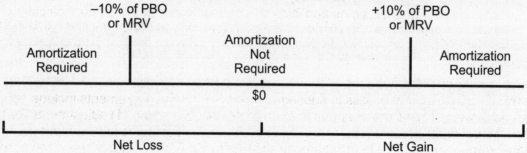

Figure 12-2

b) The minimum required amortization equals the excess described above divided by the **average remaining service period** of active employees expected to receive benefits.

c) Amortization of a net gain (loss) decreases (increases) pension expense.

d) OCI is debited (credited), net of tax, each period for required amortization of net gain (loss) arising in prior periods. The entry for **amortization of a net loss** from a prior period is

Pension expense	$XXX
OCI	XXX

　　i) This entry reclassifies the amortized amount from OCI to net income.

EXAMPLE

The following data relate to Entity A's defined benefit pension plan:

	PBO	Fair Value of Plan Assets	Net Loss Included in Accumulated OCI
January 1, Year 1	$200,000	$180,000	$19,000
December 31, Year 1	260,000	240,000	
December 31, Year 2	250,000	245,000	

Entity A recognized a net loss of $21,000 in Year 1 and a net gain of $8,600 in Year 2. Entity A uses the corridor method of accounting for net gain or loss included in accumulated OCI. The average remaining service period for Years 1-3 is 10 years.

Year 1. No amortization of net loss included in accumulated OCI is required. The net loss at the beginning of the year ($19,000) is lower than the corridor amount of $20,000 ($200,000 × 10%).

Year 2. The beginning net loss included in accumulated OCI is $40,000 ($19,000 + $21,000). This exceeds the corridor amount of $26,000 ($260,000 × 10%). Required amortization of net loss in Year 2 is $1,400 [($40,000 – $26,000) ÷ 10]. This amount is reclassified from accumulated OCI to pension expense in Year 2.

Year 3. The beginning net loss included in accumulated OCI is $30,000 ($40,000 – $1,400 – $8,600). The corridor amount is $25,000 ($250,000 × 10%). Required amortization of net loss in Year 3 is $500 [($30,000 – $25,000) ÷ 10]. This amount is reclassified from accumulated OCI to pension expense.

e) The two other acceptable treatments for net gains or losses (instead of the corridor approach) are as follows:

    i) Net gains or losses can be recognized immediately in the income statement as a component of pension expense. This method is permitted if it is applied consistently to all gains and losses on plan assets and obligations.

    ii) Any systematic method of amortizing net gains or losses included in accumulated OCI may be used if the minimum amortization of net gains and losses is at least equal to the amount calculated under the corridor approach and the method is applied consistently.

IFRS Difference

Remeasurements of the net defined benefit liability (asset) are recognized in OCI. They are never reclassified to profit or loss in subsequent periods. Remeasurements include actuarial gains and losses. These are changes in the benefit obligation from (1) adjustments for the differences between assumptions and actual results and (2) changes in assumptions. Remeasurements also include the remeasurement of plan assets. Accordingly, the corridor approach is not used.

---

f) **Amortization of prior service cost.** Prior service cost is recognized when a plan is amended or initiated to grant **additional benefits** for services already rendered by employees.

    i) This cost is allocated to the future periods of service of employees active at the date of the amendment who are expected to receive benefits.

    ii) Prior service cost increases the PBO. The entry at the amendment date is

OCI	$XXX	
Pension liability		$XXX

    iii) **Required amortization** of prior service cost assigns an equal amount to each future period of service of each qualifying employee. The entry is

Pension expense	$XXX	
OCI		$XXX

IFRS Difference

Past service cost is recognized as an expense at the earlier of (1) when the plan amendment or curtailment occurs and (2) when an entity recognizes related restructuring costs or termination benefits. Thus, past service cost is never included in OCI and never reclassified to profit or loss as it is amortized.

---

iv) To reduce the burden of allocation computations, any **alternative approach** (e.g., straight-line) that more rapidly amortizes the cost is acceptable. This alternative must be applied consistently.

EXAMPLE

At the start of its current fiscal year, Cannon Co. amended its defined benefit pension plan, resulting in an increase of $200,000 in the PBO. Cannon had 20 employees on the date of the amendment. Five employees are expected to leave at the end of each of the next 4 years (including the current year). Hence, the total service years expected to be rendered during the 4-year period equal 50 (20 + 15 + 10 + 5). The amortization fraction for the first year is therefore 20 ÷ 50. The minimum amortization equals the amount of the increase in the PBO multiplied by the amortization fraction. Accordingly, Cannon's minimum amortization for the first year is $80,000 [$200,000 × (20 ÷ 50)].

---

v) A plan amendment that retroactively reduces benefits decreases the PBO. This decrease (**prior service credit**) is **credited to OCI**, net of tax.

- First, it is used to reduce any prior service cost in accumulated OCI.
- Second, any remaining prior service credit is amortized as part of pension expense on the same basis as prior service cost.

vi) Amortization of prior service cost (credit) increases (decreases) pension expense.

Stop and review! You have completed the outline for this subunit. Study multiple-choice questions 1 through 4 beginning on page 438.

12.2 FUNDED STATUS OF PENSION PLANS

1. **Recognition of Funded Status**

   a. The statement of financial position must report the full under- or overfunded status of the pension plan as a liability or asset. OCI (presented in equity) must report unamortized gains or losses, prior service cost, and prior service credit.

   b. The funded status of a pension plan is the difference between the PBO and the fair value of plan assets at the reporting date.

      1) The **PBO** at the end of a period is calculated as follows:

         + Beginning PBO
         + Service cost
         + Interest cost
         + Prior service cost
         − Prior service credit
         − Benefits paid
         ± Changes in the PBO resulting from
             (a) experience different from that assumed
             (b) changes in assumptions
         ────────────────────────
         Ending PBO
         ════════════════════════

      2) The **fair value of the plan assets** at the end of a period is calculated as follows:

         + Fair value -- beginning of period
         + Contributions
         − Benefits paid
         ± Actual return on plan assets
         ────────────────────────
         Fair value -- end of period

2. **Pension Liability or Asset**

    a.   If the **pension is underfunded**, i.e., the PBO exceeds the fair value of the plan assets at the reporting date, the deficit must be recognized in the statement of financial position as a **liability**.

```
Pension liability = PBO - Fair value of plan assets
```

    b.   If the **pension is overfunded**, i.e., the fair value of the plan assets at the reporting date exceeds the PBO, the excess must be recognized in the statement of financial position as an **asset**.

```
Pension asset = Fair value of plan assets - PBO
```

EXAMPLE

On December 31, Year 1, Entity A determines the following information regarding its defined benefit plan:

PBO	$400,000
Fair value of plan assets	170,000

Entity A reports a $230,000 ($400,000 – $170,000) pension liability in its December 31, Year 1, financial statements.

---

3. **Other Considerations**

    a.   If the employer has **multiple plans**, the aggregate overfunding for the **overfunded plans** is recognized as a noncurrent asset.

        1)   The aggregate underfunding for all **underfunded plans** is recognized as a liability as follows:

            a)   A **current liability** is recognized for the amount by which the benefits payable by an underfunded plan over the next 12 months (or longer operating cycle) exceed the fair value of plan assets.

            b)   The remainder is a **noncurrent liability**.

    b.   A **temporary difference** may arise from recognition of an asset or liability reflecting the funded status of a plan. Any **deferred tax effects** are recognized in income tax expense (benefit) and allocated to OCI and other financial statement components.

    c.   The balances of net gains (losses) and prior service costs (credits) in **accumulated OCI** are adjusted and reported in **OCI** when

        1)   The net gains (losses), etc., are amortized as part of pension expense or

        2)   A new determination of funded status of the plan is made.

When testing candidates' knowledge of pensions, the AICPA has often presented questions requiring the determination of the pension's funded status amount through the calculations of both the projected benefit obligation and pension expense. Knowing the journal entries for pension accounting can be vital to a candidate's success.

Pension Accounting

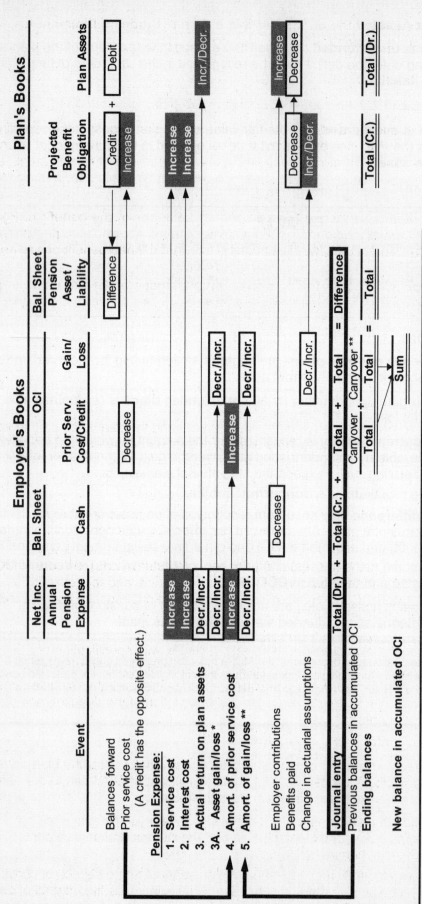

Figure 12-3

Stop and review! You have completed the outline for this subunit. Study multiple-choice questions 5 through 10 beginning on page 439.

12.3 PENSION DISCLOSURES AND OTHER ISSUES

1. **Required Disclosures**

   a. An employer that sponsors one or more defined benefit plans must make certain disclosures. However, **nonpublic entities** are allowed to make reduced disclosures. Disclosure must be separate for pension plans and other postretirement plans, but amounts within each category are normally totaled. The following are among the required disclosures for **public entities**:

      1) A **reconciliation of beginning and ending balances of the benefit obligation** [the PBO for defined benefit pension plans and the accumulated postretirement benefit obligation (see the next subunit) for other defined benefit postretirement plans]

      2) A **reconciliation of beginning and ending balances of the fair value of plan assets**

      3) The **funded status** of the plans and the amounts recognized in the balance sheet, with separate display of (a) assets and (b) current and noncurrent liabilities

      4) Information about **plan assets**

      5) The **accumulated benefit obligation** (the PBO with no assumption about future compensation) of a defined benefit pension plan

      6) **Benefits** to be paid in each of the next 5 years and the total to be paid in years 6-10 based on the assumptions used to determine the benefit obligation at the current year end. Future employee service is considered in the calculation

      7) The best estimate of **contributions** in the next year (the aggregate of legal mandates, discretionary amounts, and noncash items)

      8) **Net periodic benefit cost** recognized, showing separately each of its components and gain or loss recognized due to a settlement or curtailment

      9) Separate amounts for (a) net gain (loss) and prior service cost (credit) recognized in **OCI for the period**, (b) **reclassification adjustments** of OCI recognized in net periodic benefit cost for the period, and (c) items still in **accumulated OCI** (net gain or loss, unamortized prior service cost or credit, and **the transition amount**)

      10) Weighted-average **assumptions** about the discount rate, rate of compensation increase, and expected long-term rate of return, with specification of assumptions for calculating the benefit obligation and net benefit cost

      11) Assumed **healthcare cost trend rate(s)** used to measure the expected cost of benefits for the next year and a general description of the direction and pattern of change thereafter

2. **Curtailments, Settlements, and Terminations**

   a. A **settlement** is an irrevocable action that relieves the employer (or the plan) of the primary responsibility for a PBO. It eliminates significant risks related to the pension obligation and the assets used to effect the settlement.

      1) Recognition of a settlement gain or loss is mandatory if the cost of all settlements in a year exceeds the sum of the interest and service cost components of pension expense.

   b. A **curtailment** significantly reduces the expected years of future service of current employees. An event also may be a curtailment if it eliminates the accrual of defined benefits for some or all future service for a significant number of employees.

c.   Termination benefits are provided to employees in connection with their termination of employment.

   1) **Special** termination benefits are offered only for a short period.

      a) The liability and loss are recognized when the employees **accept the offer** and the amount can be reasonably estimated.

   2) **Contractual** termination benefits are required by the terms of a pension plan only if a specified event occurs.

      a) The liability and loss are recognized when it is probable that employees will be **entitled to benefits** and the amount can be reasonably estimated.

   3) The amount includes any lump-sum payments and the present value of any future payments.

Stop and review! You have completed the outline for this subunit. Study multiple-choice questions 11 through 13 beginning on page 441.

12.4 POSTRETIREMENT BENEFITS OTHER THAN PENSIONS

1. The accounting for **other postretirement employee benefits (OPEB)** is similar to pension accounting.

   a. Benefits depend on such factors as the

      1) Benefit formula,
      2) Life expectancy of the retiree and any beneficiaries and covered dependents, and
      3) Frequency and significance of events (e.g., illnesses) requiring payments.

   b. **Measurements** of plan assets and benefit obligations are generally made as of the balance sheet date.

   c. The costs are expensed during **the attribution period**, which begins on the **date of hire** unless the plan's benefit formula grants credit for service only from a later date.

      1) The end of the period is the **full eligibility date**.

EXAMPLE

An employer provides postretirement health insurance benefits to employees who have completed 20 years of service and have attained age 55 when they retire. The plan specifies that the attribution start date is the later of an employee's 35th birthday or his/her start date.

An employee is hired on August 5, Year 1, and turns 35 on January 9, Year 2. The employee's attribution period begins on January 9, Year 2.

---

2. **Benefit Obligations**

   a. The **expected postretirement benefit obligation (EPBO)** equals the **accumulated postretirement benefit obligation (APBO)** after the full eligibility date.

   b. The **EPBO** for an employee is the actuarial present value at a given date of the OPEB expected to be paid. Its measurement depends on the

      1) Anticipated amounts and timing of future benefits,
      2) Costs to be incurred to provide those benefits, and
      3) Extent the costs are shared by the employee and others (such as governmental programs).

c. The **APBO** for an employee is the actuarial present value at a given date of the OPEB attributable to the employee's service as of that date.

1) The APBO (as well as the EPBO and service cost) implicitly includes the consideration of **future salary progression**.

2) An employer's obligation for OPEB must be **fully accrued** by the full eligibility date for all benefits even if the employee is expected to render additional service.

a) The **full eligibility date** is reached when the employee has rendered all the services necessary to earn all of the expected benefits.

b) Prior to that date, the EPBO exceeds the APBO.

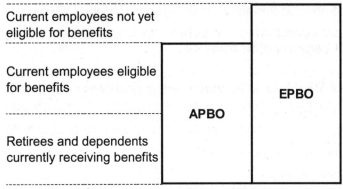

Figure 12-4

3. Funded Status

a. The funded status of the plan must be recognized in the statement of financial position as the difference between the **fair value of plan assets and the APBO**. An employer must apply the guidance on income tax accounting to determine the **tax effects** of recognizing the following:

1) Funded status of the plan

2) Gains (losses) and prior service costs (credits) arising in the current period but included in OCI

3) Reclassification adjustments for gains (losses), prior service costs (credits), and any transition amount included in accumulated OCI but amortized in the current period

4. Net Periodic Postretirement Benefit Cost (NPPBC)

a. The possible components of the NPPBC of an employer sponsoring a defined benefit postretirement plan are

1) Service cost

2) Interest on the APBO

3) Actual return on plan assets

a) However, gains and losses normally are **not** required to be recognized in NPPBC when they are incurred. Thus, the amount that must be included in this component of NPPBC is the **expected return** for the period.

4) Amortization of any prior service cost or credit included in accumulated OCI

5) Amortization of any transition obligation or asset included in accumulated OCI

6) Gain or loss **component**

b. **Service cost** increases NPPBC. It is the part of the **EPBO** attributed to services by employees during the period and is not affected by the level of funding.

c. **Interest cost** increases NPPBC. It is the change in the **APBO** during the period resulting solely from the passage of time.

1) It equals the APBO at the beginning of the period times the **assumed discount rate** used in determining the present value of cash outflows currently expected to be required to satisfy the obligation.

$$APBO \times Discount\ rate$$

d. **Prior service cost** is an increase in the APBO. It is incurred due to a **plan amendment** that provides improved benefits for prior service.

1) The entry at the amendment date is to debit OCI net of tax.

OCI	$XXX	
OPEB liability		$XXX

2) Prior service cost generally should be recognized in NPPBC by assigning an equal amount to each remaining year of service to the full eligibility date of each participant active at the amendment date who was not yet fully eligible.

a) The entry for inclusion of prior service cost in NPPBC is

NPPBC	$XXX	
OCI		$XXX

e. A **prior service credit** retroactively reduces benefits and the APBO.

1) The credit to OCI, net of tax, first reduces any prior service cost still in accumulated OCI. It then reduces any transition obligation in accumulated OCI.

2) The remainder is amortized as part of NPPBC on the same basis as prior service cost.

3) The remaining prior service credit must not be recognized in full immediately.

f. The **gain or loss component** equals any gain (loss) immediately recognized in NPPBC or the amortization of the net gain (loss) from prior periods that was recognized in OCI.

1) Moreover, the employer may use a systematic method of amortizing net gain or loss included in accumulated OCI **other than the corridor approach** that may be used in pension accounting.

a) The alternative is allowable if it results in amortization at least equal to the minimum determined using the corridor approach.

2) If an entity consistently recognizes gains and losses immediately, gains (losses) that do not offset previously recognized losses (gains) must first reduce any transition obligation (asset) included in accumulated OCI.

Stop and review! You have completed the outline for this subunit. Study multiple-choice questions 14 through 18 beginning on page 442.

12.5 COMPENSATED ABSENCES AND POSTEMPLOYMENT BENEFITS

1. **Compensated Absences**

a. The accounting for compensated absences applies to employees' rights to receive compensation for future absences, such as vacations. It requires an accrual of a liability when four criteria are met:

1) The payment of compensation is **probable**.

2) The amount can be **reasonably estimated**.

3) The benefits either **vest** or **accumulate**.

    a) Rights **vest** if they do not depend on future service.

    b) Rights **accumulate** if earned but, if unused, may be carried forward to subsequent periods.

4) The compensation relates to employees' **services** that have **already** been **rendered**.

b. However, **sick pay benefits** that meet the criteria above are accrued only if the rights **vest**.

c. The common way to **measure the liability** for compensated absences at the end of the reporting period is to multiply current employees' daily average wage rate by the number of vacation days earned and expected to be used in subsequent periods.

1) In future periods, the wage rate may change. Thus, the amount paid for compensated absences may differ from the liability recognized. The difference is accounted for as a change in estimate and recognized in income.

2) The liability should be classified as (a) a **current liability** for the amount expected to be paid within 12 months after the end of the fiscal year and (b) a **noncurrent liability** for the remaining amount.

EXAMPLE

Entity A provides each of its 500 employees 15 days of paid vacation a year. The unused annual leave may be rolled over for an unlimited time and is payable even upon termination. The employees' daily average wage rate is $150. During Year 1, each employee used an average of 12 vacation days. Entity A expects that 80% of unused accumulated vacation days will be used in Year 2 and the rest in Year 3.

On December 31, Year 1, Entity A must recognize a liability for paid vacation earned and not yet used by the employees. The amount of liability recognized is $225,000 [500 employees × (15 days accrued annually – 12 average days used annually) × $150 daily average wage]. The current portion is $180,000 ($225,000 × 80%), and the noncurrent portion is $45,000 ($225,000 – $180,000). The following is the journal entry:

Vacation pay expense	$225,000	
Compensated absences payable -- current liability		$180,000
Compensated absences payable -- noncurrent liability		45,000

IFRS Difference

Short term employee benefits are employee benefits (other than termination benefits), such as paid annual leave, sick leave, and wages, that are expected to be **settled wholly** before 12 months after the annual reporting period in which employees render the related services.

Using the data from the previous example, the entire liability for outstanding annual leave must be recognized at the end of Year 1 as a **long-term** liability because it is not expected to be settled wholly in Year 2. The long-term liability should be measured at the present value of the projected future cash flow.

---

2. **Postemployment Benefits**

a. The accounting for postemployment benefits applies to employers who provide benefits to former or inactive employees after employment but before retirement.

b. **Postemployment benefits** are all benefits provided to former or inactive employees, their beneficiaries, and covered dependents. Examples are

    1) Salary continuation,
    2) Supplemental unemployment benefits,
    3) Severance benefits,
    4) Disability-related benefits (including workers' compensation),
    5) Job training and counseling, and
    6) Continuation of such benefits as healthcare and life insurance coverage.

    c.   However, the accounting for postemployment benefits does not apply to

        1)   Pensions,
        2)   Postretirement benefit plans,
        3)   Certain deferred compensation arrangements,
        4)   Special or contractual termination agreements, and
        5)   Share-based compensation plans.

    d.   An employer should accrue a liability for postemployment benefits if all four criteria stated in the guidance on compensated absences are met.

EXAMPLE

Papina Co. developed reasonable estimates of its obligations for $450,000 in severance pay and $150,000 in job training benefits. Payment is probable, and the benefits relate to employees' services previously rendered. The job training benefits vest, and the severance pay benefits accumulate. Because all the criteria are met, Papina should accrue a liability of $600,000 for postretirement benefits.

---

    e.   Postemployment benefits may be within the scope of the accounting for postemployment benefits but not meet the criteria stated above.

        1)   In this case, they are accounted for in accordance with the principles governing **loss contingencies**, which will be discussed thoroughly in Study Unit 14.

    f.   If an obligation for postemployment benefits is not accrued solely because the amount cannot be reasonably estimated, the statements should disclose that fact.

Stop and review! You have completed the outline for this subunit. Study multiple-choice questions 19 through 23 beginning on page 444.

12.6 SHARE-BASED PAYMENT

Background

During the so-called Tech Boom of the 1990s, many technology firms used stock options to attract and retain skilled people. The proper accounting treatment for this form of deferred stock compensation was controversial. Until the 1990s, the relevant guidance required that compensatory stock options be measured using intrinsic value (fair value of an underlying share at the measurement date minus its exercise price). Thus, no compensation expense was recognized unless an option was in the money.

During the 1990s, the FASB proposed to expense stock options based on their fair value, not intrinsic value. The opposition to this proposal compelled the FASB to issue a pronouncement in which it recommended but did not require the fair value method. But in December 2004, the FASB issued a comprehensive pronouncement in which it required fair value accounting unless fair value could not be reasonably estimated.

NOTE: The FASB now uses the term "share option" instead of "stock option."

---

1.   **Basic Accounting**

    a.   This guidance applies to **share-based payments** (stock compensation) involving receipt by the entity of **goods or services** in return for the following:

        1)   Its **equity instruments**, e.g., shares or share options
        2)   Incurrence of **liabilities** to suppliers that

            a)   Are based on the **price** of the entity's equity instruments or
            b)   May require **share settlement**.

    b.   **Initial recognition** of **goods or services** occurs when they are received.

        1)   The **credit** is to equity or a liability depending on which **classification criteria** are met.
        2)   **Cost** is recognized upon disposal or consumption of the goods or services.

3) In a transaction with **nonemployees**, the **more reliably measurable** of the fair value of the equity instruments issued or the consideration received is used to measure the transaction.

4) In a transaction with **employees**, the fair value of the **equity** instruments issued ordinarily is the basis for measurement.

    a) The fair value of the **services** they render ordinarily is not readily determinable.

2. **Equity Awards**

    a. **Employee compensation cost** for an award classified as **equity** is recognized over the **requisite service period**. The **credit** is usually to **paid-in capital**. The following are typical **entries**:

Recognition of expense:

Compensation expense	$XXX	
Paid-in capital -- equity award		$XXX

Issuance of shares:

Cash	$XXX	
Paid-in capital -- equity award	XXX	
Common stock		$XXX
Paid-in capital in excess of par		XXX

Forfeitures, expiration of options, etc.:

Paid-in capital -- equity award	$XXX	
Paid-in capital -- forfeitures		$XXX

1) The requisite service period is the period during which employees must perform services. It is most often the **vesting period**.

    a) The beginning of the requisite service period is usually the grant date. The **grant date** is when

        i) A mutual understanding of key terms of the award has been reached, and

        ii) The employer is obligated if the employee renders the requisite service.

2) **Vesting conditions** may be performance conditions or service conditions or both.

    a) **Performance conditions** relate to rendering services for a specified period and reaching objectives that relate solely to the employer's activities (e.g., achieving a stated rate of growth).

    b) **Service conditions** pertain solely to rendering services for the designated period.

    c) **Market conditions** (e.g., attaining a specified share price) do not affect vesting.

        i) Hence, an entity must **not** remeasure previously recognized compensation cost solely because a market condition is unsatisfied.

3) **Total compensation cost** at the end of the requisite service period is based on the **number of equity instruments** for which the requisite service was completed.

    a) The entity must estimate this number when **initial accruals** are made.

        i) **Changes in the estimate** result in recognition of the **cumulative effect** on prior and current periods in the calculation of compensation cost for the **period of change**.

3. **Measurement**

    a. The cost of **employee services** performed in exchange for awards of share-based compensation normally is measured at the

        1) **Grant-date fair value** of the equity instruments issued or
        2) **Fair value of the liabilities** incurred.

            a) Such liabilities are remeasured at each reporting date.

4. **Share Options**

    a. The fair value of an **equity share option** (i.e., one with **time value**) is determined using an observable market price of an option with similar terms if available.

        1) In other cases, a valuation method, such as an **option-pricing model** (for example, the **Black-Scholes-Merton model** or a binomial model), may be used.

    b. When an entity **cannot reasonably estimate** the fair value of equity instruments at the grant date, the accounting is based on **intrinsic value**.

        Fair value of an underlying share – Exercise price of an option

        1) **Remeasurement** is required at each reporting date and on final settlement. Periodic compensation cost is based on the change in intrinsic value.

        2) The **final measure** of compensation cost is the intrinsic value on the settlement date.

5. **Liabilities**

    a. An award may meet the criteria for classification as a **liability**.

        1) The **measurement date** for liabilities is the **settlement date**. Thus, after initial recognition, liabilities are remeasured at each reporting date.

            a) A **public entity** remeasures liabilities based on their **fair values**.

                i) Periodic compensation cost depends on the change (or part of the change, depending on the requisite service performed to date) in fair value.

            b) A **nonpublic entity** may **elect** to measure all such liabilities at **fair value** or **intrinsic value**.

            c) The percentage of fair value or intrinsic value accrued as compensation cost equals the **percentage of required service rendered to date**.

EXAMPLE -- Share Option

On January 1, Year 1, an entity grants five executives options to purchase 10,000 shares each of its $1 par value common stock at $40 per share. The executives must work for 2 more years for the options to be vested. They must be exercised within 10 years of the grant date.

On the grant date, an option pricing model determines that the total fair value of the options is $620,000. The market price of the shares on that day is $50. Because no time has passed, no services associated with the options have been performed, and no compensation cost is recognized.

> January 1, Year 1:
> No entry

At the end of each of the first 2 years, 1 year of compensation cost associated with the options must be recognized. (Ignore tax effects.)

> December 31, Year 1:
> Compensation cost ($620,000 ÷ 2) $310,000
>   Paid-in capital -- share options $310,000

-- continued on the next page --

EXAMPLE -- Share Option -- continued

After 1 year, one of the executives left the entity. The effect is that the estimated total compensation cost has changed because 20% (1 ÷ 5 executives) of the options have been forfeited. Thus, the new estimated total compensation cost is $496,000 [($620,000 × (4 ÷ 5)], and the cost for Year 1 would have been $248,000 ($496,000 ÷ 2). Assuming the Year 1 books were closed before the forfeiture (and ignoring tax effects), no restatement of the Year 1 statements is appropriate for this change of estimate. Accordingly, the compensation cost to be recognized in Year 2 is $186,000 ($496,000 revised cumulative amount – $310,000 recognized in Year 1).

December 31, Year 2:

Compensation cost	$186,000	
Paid-in capital -- share options		$186,000

Two and a half years after the grant date, two of the executives (50% of those remaining) choose to exercise their options. Total compensation cost is unaffected, and the market price of the stock is irrelevant. (It is assumed to be higher than the exercise price.) Moreover, the balance in paid-in capital -- share options is reduced to $248,000 to reflect a reclassification.

Cash (10,000 shares × 2 executives × $40)	$800,000	
Paid-in capital -- share options ($496,000 × 50%)	248,000	
Common stock (20,000 shares × $1 par value)		$ 20,000
Additional paid-in capital -- common stock		1,028,000

After 10 years, the other two executives still have not exercised their options. The expiration is recorded as follows:

December 31, Year 10:

Paid-in capital -- share options	$248,000	
Paid-in capital -- expired share options ($496,000 × 50%)		$248,000

---

6. **Other Types of Compensation Plans**

   a. A **share award plan** is a compensatory plan in which employees are granted shares of the entity to sell on their own behalf.

      1) Shares granted under the stock award plan are usually **restricted** by the issuer.

         a) The employees are vested in the shares but are prohibited from selling them before rendering services for a specified period.

   b. **Share appreciation rights (SARs)** allow employees to receive the increase in the fair value of the shares directly from the employer.

      1) The covered employee receives compensation equal to the **appreciation of the market price** on the exercise date over the option price.

         a) The award may be distributed in **cash** or **shares** of the entity's stock.

      2) If the employer has the right to settle the award in shares, an **equity transaction** is reported.

         a) The fair value of the SARs is measured at the grant date in the same way as share options, and the compensation cost is recognized over the service period.

      3) If the employee may elect to **receive cash** on the exercise date, the SARs are considered to be a **liability**.

         a) The liability is estimated at the grant date but continually adjusted to recognize the fair value of the liability at the balance sheet date.

      4) Compensation cost is recognized every year of the service period as a fraction of total compensation cost.

         a) The estimate of total compensation cost changes every year, so the accounting for a change in estimate must be applied.

EXAMPLE

On January 1, Year 1, Sistina Corp., a nonpublic entity, grants its chief executive officer 5,000 share appreciation rights. The SARs entitle the CEO to cash for the difference between (1) the market price of its stock on December 31, Year 2, and (2) a predetermined price of $50. Sistina Corp. measures share-based payment liabilities at their intrinsic value. On December 31, Year 1, the market price of Sistina's stock was $65. Sistina must recognize a liability of $37,500 for compensation expense [5,000 shares × ($65 – $50) × (1 yr. ÷ 2 yrs.)]. On December 31, Year 2, the stock price is $58. Sistina must recognize an additional liability of $2,500 for compensation expense {[5,000 shares × ($58 – $50) × (2 yrs. ÷ 2 yrs.)] – $37,500}.

Stop and review! You have completed the outline for this subunit. Study multiple-choice questions 24 through 31 beginning on page 445.

QUESTIONS

12.1 Components of Pension Expense

1. Visor Co. maintains a defined benefit pension plan for its employees. The service cost component of Visor's pension expense is measured using the

A. Unfunded accumulated benefit obligation.

B. Unfunded vested benefit obligation.

C. Projected benefit obligation.

D. Expected return on plan assets.

Answer (C) is correct.
REQUIRED: The item that is used to measure the service cost component of the pension expense.
DISCUSSION: Service cost is the actuarial present value of benefits attributed by the pension benefit formula to services rendered during the accounting period. It is a component of the projected benefit obligation (PBO). The PBO as of a date is equal to the actuarial present value of all benefits attributed by the pension benefit formula to employee service rendered prior to that date. The PBO is measured using assumptions as to future salary levels.
Answer (A) is incorrect. The accumulated benefit obligation is based on current salaries without assumptions about future salaries. Answer (B) is incorrect. Service cost includes nonvested benefits. Answer (D) is incorrect. The expected return on plan assets is not a cost.

2. Which of the following components must be included in the calculation of pension expense recognized for a period by an employer sponsoring a defined benefit pension plan?

	Interest Cost	Expected Return on Plan Assets
A.	Yes	No
B.	Yes	Yes
C.	No	Yes
D.	No	No

Answer (B) is correct.
REQUIRED: The component(s), if any, to be included in pension expense.
DISCUSSION: The required minimum pension expense consists of the following elements:

+	Service cost
+	Interest cost
–	Expected return on plan assets
±	Amortization of net gain or loss
±	Amortization of prior service cost of credit
	Pension expense

Thus, both interest cost and expected return on plan assets are components of pension expense.

3. On July 31, Year 1, Tern Co. amended its single employee defined benefit pension plan by granting increased benefits for services provided prior to Year 1. This prior service cost will be reflected in the financial statement(s) for

A. Years before Year 1 only.

B. Year 1 only.

C. Year 1 and years before and following Year 1.

D. Year 1 and following years only.

Answer (D) is correct.
REQUIRED: The year(s) in which prior service cost will be reflected in the financial statement(s).
DISCUSSION: Prior service cost is recognized when a plan is amended to grant additional benefits for services already rendered by employees. The amortization of prior service cost should be recognized as a component of pension expense during the future service periods of those employees active at the date of the plan amendment and who are expected to receive benefits under the plan. Thus, prior service cost is reflected in the Year 1 financial statements when the plan was amended and in the following years as it is amortized.

4. The following information pertains to Gali Co.'s defined benefit pension plan for Year 1:

Fair value of plan assets, beginning of year	$350,000
Fair value of plan assets, end of year	525,000
Employer contributions	110,000
Benefits paid	85,000

In computing pension expense, what amount should Gali use as actual return on plan assets?

A. $65,000

B. $150,000

C. $175,000

D. $260,000

Answer (B) is correct.
REQUIRED: The actual return on plan assets.
DISCUSSION: The actual return on plan assets is based on the fair value of plan assets at the beginning and end of the accounting period adjusted for contributions and payments during the period. The actual return for Gali is $150,000 ($525,000 – $350,000 – $110,000 + $85,000).
Answer (A) is incorrect. The amount of $65,000 results when benefits paid to employees are not included. Answer (C) is incorrect. The amount of $175,000 is the change in the fair value of plan assets without adjustment for contributions or benefits paid. Answer (D) is incorrect. The amount of $260,000 does not deduct employer contributions.

12.2 Funded Status of Pension Plans

5. The following information pertains to Seda Co.'s pension plan:

Actuarial estimate of projected benefit obligation (PBO) at 1/1/Year 1	$72,000
Assumed discount rate	10%
Service cost for Year 1	18,000
Pension benefits paid during Year 1	15,000

If no change in actuarial estimates occurred during Year 1, Seda's PBO at December 31, Year 1, was

A. $67,800

B. $75,000

C. $79,200

D. $82,200

Answer (D) is correct.
REQUIRED: The projected benefit obligation at the end of the year.
DISCUSSION: Seda's ending PBO balance can be calculated as follows:

Beginning PBO balance	$ 72,000
Service cost	18,000
Interest cost ($72,000 × 10%)	7,200
Less: benefits paid	(15,000)
Ending PBO balance	$ 82,200

Answer (A) is incorrect. The amount of $67,800 results from subtracting interest cost. Answer (B) is incorrect. The amount of $75,000 excludes interest cost. Answer (C) is incorrect. The amount of $79,200 ignores service costs and benefits paid.

6. The following is the only information pertaining to Kane Co.'s defined benefit pension plan:

Pension asset, January 1, Year 1	$ 2,000
Service cost	19,000
Interest cost	38,000
Actual and expected return on plan assets	22,000
Amortization of prior service cost arising in a prior period	52,000
Employer contributions	40,000

In its December 31, Year 1, balance sheet, what amount should Kane report as the unfunded or overfunded projected benefit obligation (PBO)?

A. $7,000 overfunded.

B. $15,000 underfunded.

C. $45,000 underfunded.

D. $52,000 underfunded.

Answer (A) is correct.
REQUIRED: The unfunded or overfunded PBO.
DISCUSSION: The employer must recognize the funded status of the plan as the difference between the fair value of plan assets and the PBO at year end. That amount is an asset or a liability. Current service cost and interest cost increase the PBO. The return on plan assets and contributions increase plan assets. Amortization of prior service cost arising in a prior period and recognized in accumulated OCI has no additional effect on the PBO or plan assets. However, it is a component of pension expense. The PBO was overfunded by $2,000 on January 1. It increased during the year by $57,000 ($19,000 + $38,000). Plan assets increased by $62,000 ($22,000 + $40,000). Accordingly, the plan is overfunded by $7,000 [$2,000 + ($62,000 – $57,000)] at year end. Kane should recognize a pension asset of $7,000 at year end.
Answer (B) is incorrect. The return on plan assets should be added to plan assets. Answer (C) is incorrect. The $45,000 underfunded includes prior service cost amortization. Prior service cost that arose in a prior period was reflected in the asset or liability recognized for the funded status of the plan at the beginning of the year. When prior service cost arises, the entry is to debit OCI, net of tax, and credit pension liability. Answer (D) is incorrect. The $52,000 underfunded is the prior service cost amortization.

7. On January 2, Year 1, Loch Co. established a noncontributory defined-benefit pension plan covering all employees and contributed $400,000 to the plan. At December 31, Year 1, Loch determined that the Year 1 service and interest costs on the plan were $720,000. The expected and the actual rate of return on plan assets for Year 1 was 10%. Loch's pension expense has no other components. What amount should Loch report in its December 31, Year 1, balance sheet as liability for pension benefits?

A. $280,000

B. $320,000

C. $360,000

D. $720,000

Answer (A) is correct.
REQUIRED: The accrued pension liability.
DISCUSSION: Service and interest costs and the expected return on plan assets are the entity's only components of pension expense in the plan's first year. The return on plan assets for Year 1 is $40,000 ($400,000 contributed to the plan × 10%). Because the actual and expected returns were the same, no gain or loss occurred in Year 1. The funded status of the plan is the difference between year-end plan assets at fair value ($400,000 + $40,000 = $440,000) and the projected benefit obligation ($720,000 service and interest costs, given no prior service cost or credit). Consequently, the liability recognized to record the unfunded status of the plan at year end is $280,000 ($720,000 – $440,000).
Answer (B) is incorrect. The amount of $320,000 is the result if the return on plan assets is not added to plan assets at year end. Answer (C) is incorrect. The amount of $360,000 results when the return on plan assets is subtracted from plan assets at year end. Answer (D) is incorrect. The amount of $720,000 is the sum of service and interest costs.

8. Payne, Inc., implemented a defined benefit pension plan for its employees on January 2. The following data are provided for the year ended December 31:

Projected benefit obligation (PBO)	$108,000
Accumulated benefit obligation (ABO)	103,000
Plan assets at fair value	78,000
Pension expense	90,000
Employer's contribution	70,000

What amount should Payne record as the liability for pension benefits at December 31?

A. $0

B. $30,000

C. $20,000

D. $45,000

Answer (B) is correct.
REQUIRED: The additional minimum pension liability.
DISCUSSION: A pension liability must be recognized for any excess of the PBO over the fair value of plan assets at year end. Thus, the liability for pension benefits is $30,000 ($108,000 PBO – $78,000 FV of plan assets).
Answer (A) is incorrect. The PBO has not been fully funded. Answer (C) is incorrect. This figure is the difference between the pension expense and the contribution. Answer (D) is incorrect. The amount of $45,000 equals the unfunded ABO plus the difference between the pension expense and the contribution.

9. Webb Co. implemented a defined benefit pension plan for its employees on January 1, Year 1. During Year 1 and Year 2, Webb's contributions fully funded the plan. The following data are provided for Year 4 and Year 3:

	Year 4 Estimated	Year 3 Actual
Projected benefit obligation, December 31	$750,000	$700,000
Accumulated benefit obligation, December 31	520,000	500,000
Plan assets at fair value, December 31	675,000	600,000
Projected benefit obligation in excess of plan assets	75,000	100,000
Pension expense	90,000	75,000
Employer's contribution	?	50,000

What amount should Webb contribute to report a pension liability of $15,000 in its December 31, Year 4, balance sheet?

A. $50,000

B. $60,000

C. $75,000

D. $100,000

Answer (B) is correct.
REQUIRED: The amount contributed to report an accrued pension liability.
DISCUSSION: A reported pension liability reflects an excess of the PBO over the fair value of the plan assets at the balance sheet date. If Webb projects this excess to be $75,000 ($750,000 – $675,000) at the end of Year 4 and wishes to report a liability of $15,000, a contribution of $60,000 ($75,000 – $15,000) will have to be made.
Answer (A) is incorrect. The Year 3 contribution is $50,000. Answer (C) is incorrect. The excess of the PBO over the plan assets is $75,000. Answer (D) is incorrect. The excess of the PBO for Year 3 is $100,000.

10. An entity sponsors a defined benefit pension plan that is underfunded by $800,000. A $500,000 increase in the fair value of plan assets would have which of the following effects on the financial statements of the entity?

A. An increase in the assets of the entity.

B. An increase in accumulated other comprehensive income of the entity for the full amount of the increase in the value of the assets.

C. A decrease in accumulated other comprehensive income of the entity for the full amount of the increase in the value of the assets.

D. A decrease in the liabilities of the entity.

Answer (D) is correct.
REQUIRED: The effects of an increase in the fair value of plan assets that is less than the underfunded amount.
DISCUSSION: If a projected benefit obligation exceeds the fair value of plan assets, the amount of the underfunding must be recognized as a liability. If the pension plan is underfunded by $800,000, an increase in the fair value of plan assets of $500,000 reduces the underfunding to $300,000. Thus, the increase in the fair value of plan assets decreases but does not eliminate the pension liability.
Answer (A) is incorrect. Given that the projected benefit obligation is underfunded by $800,000, the fair value of plan assets would have to increase by more than $800,000 to increase the assets of the entity. For example, if the fair value of the plan assets, which are not assets of the sponsor, had increased by $900,000, the entity would recognize an asset of $100,000 for the overfunding. Answer (B) is incorrect. The full over- or underfunded status of the plan is reported as an asset or liability, respectively. Unamortized gains or losses, prior service cost, and prior service credit are reported in OCI. The total OCI for the period is transferred to accumulated OCI (a component of equity in the statement of financial position). Thus, the funded status of the plan does not affect accumulated OCI. Answer (C) is incorrect. The funded status of the plan does not affect accumulated OCI.

12.3 Pension Disclosures and Other Issues

11. A public entity that sponsors a defined benefit pension plan must disclose in the notes to its financial statements a reconciliation of

A. The vested and nonvested benefit obligation of its pension plan with the accumulated benefit obligation.

B. The accrued or prepaid pension cost reported in its balance sheet with the pension expense reported in its income statement.

C. The accumulated benefit obligation of its pension plan with its projected benefit obligation.

D. The beginning and ending balances of the projected benefit obligation.

Answer (D) is correct.
REQUIRED: The employer disclosures required for a defined benefit pension plan.
DISCUSSION: One of the required disclosures by a public entity with a defined benefit pension plan is a reconciliation of the beginning and ending balances of the PBO. It should display separately the effects during the period of (1) service cost, (2) interest cost, (3) participants' contributions, (4) actuarial gains and losses, (5) foreign currency exchange rate changes, (6) benefits paid, (7) plan amendments, (8) business combinations, (9) divestitures, (10) curtailments, (11) settlements, and (12) special termination benefits.
Answer (A) is incorrect. Vested and nonvested amounts need not be disclosed. Answer (B) is incorrect. The employer must disclose the full funded status of the plan. Accrued/prepaid pension cost measures the extent of the funding of net period pension cost. Answer (C) is incorrect. The ABO must be disclosed but not with the PBO.

12. Note section disclosures in the financial statements of a public entity that sponsors a defined benefit pension plan for its employees are **not** required to include

A. The components of periodic pension cost.

B. The funded status of the plan.

C. Reclassification adjustments of other comprehensive income for the period.

D. A detailed description of the plan, including employee groups covered.

Answer (D) is correct.
REQUIRED: The note section disclosures by a public entity for a defined benefit pension plan that are not required.
DISCUSSION: The guidance on pension accounting originally required disclosure of a detailed description of the plan, including employee groups covered. However, the currently effective disclosure requirements do not require this disclosure.
Answer (A) is incorrect. Required disclosures by a public (not a nonpublic) entity include the net periodic benefit cost, showing separately each of its components and gain or loss recognized due to a settlement or curtailment. Answer (B) is incorrect. Required disclosures by a public (not a nonpublic) entity include the funded status of the plan and the amounts recognized in the balance sheet, with separate display of assets and current and noncurrent liabilities. Answer (C) is incorrect. Required disclosures by a public entity include reclassification adjustments of other comprehensive income as they are recognized in pension expense.

13. On September 1, Year 1, Howe Corp. offered special termination benefits to employees who had reached the early retirement age specified in the company's pension plan. The termination benefits consisted of lump-sum and periodic future payments. Additionally, the employees accepting the company offer receive the usual early retirement pension benefits. The offer expired on November 30, Year 1. Actual or reasonably estimated amounts at December 31, Year 1, relating to the employees accepting the offer are as follows:

- Lump-sum payments totaling $475,000 were made on January 1, Year 2.
- Periodic payments of $60,000 annually for 3 years will begin January 1, Year 3. The present value at December 31, Year 1, of these payments was $155,000.
- Reduction of accrued pension costs at December 31, Year 1, for the terminating employees was $45,000.

At December 31, Year 1, Howe should report a total liability for special termination benefits of

A. $475,000

B. $585,000

C. $630,000

D. $655,000

Answer (C) is correct.
REQUIRED: The total liability for special termination benefits.
DISCUSSION: The liability and expense arising from special termination benefits should be recognized by an employer when the employees accept the offer and the amount can be reasonably estimated. The amount should include the lump-sum payments and the present value of any future payments. Thus, Howe should report a total liability for special termination benefits of $630,000 ($475,000 lump-sum payments + $155,000 present value of future payments) in its 12/31/Year 1 balance sheet. The reduction of accrued pension costs is recognized by a debit for $45,000. After crediting the liability for $630,000, the debit to a loss account will be $585,000.
Answer (A) is incorrect. The amount of $475,000 omits the present value of the future benefits. Answer (B) is incorrect. The amount of $585,000 is the loss, not the liability. Answer (D) is incorrect. The amount of $655,000 is the undiscounted amount of the payments for termination benefits.

12.4 Postretirement Benefits Other than Pensions

14. Bounty Co. provides postretirement healthcare benefits to employees who have completed at least 10 years service and are aged 55 years or older when retiring. Employees retiring from Bounty have a median age of 62, and no one has worked beyond age 65. Fletcher is hired at 48 years old. The attribution period for accruing Bounty's expected postretirement healthcare benefit obligation to Fletcher is during the period when Fletcher is aged

A. 48 to 65.

B. 48 to 58.

C. 55 to 65.

D. 55 to 62.

Answer (B) is correct.
REQUIRED: The attribution period for accruing the expected postretirement healthcare benefit obligation to an employee.
DISCUSSION: The attribution period begins on the date of hire unless the plan's benefit formula grants credit for service only from a later date. The end of the period is the full eligibility date. If the exception does not apply, Fletcher's attribution period is from age 48, the date of hire, to age 58, the date of full eligibility.

15. An employer's obligation for postretirement health benefits that are expected to be fully provided to or for an employee must be fully accrued by the date the

A. Benefits are paid.

B. Benefits are utilized.

C. Employee retires.

D. Employee is fully eligible for benefits.

Answer (D) is correct.
REQUIRED: The full accrual date for postretirement health benefits that are expected to be fully paid.
DISCUSSION: Costs are expensed over the attribution period. It begins on the date of hire unless the plan's benefit formula states otherwise. It ends on the full eligibility date of the employee. This rule applies even if the employee is expected to render additional service. The full eligibility date is reached when the employee has rendered all the services necessary to earn all of the expected benefits.

16. Postretirement employee benefits other than pensions (OPEB) may be defined in terms of monetary amounts (e.g., a given dollar value of life insurance) or benefit coverage (e.g., amounts per day for hospitalization). The amount of benefits depends on such factors as the benefit formula, the life expectancy of the retiree and any beneficiaries and covered dependents, and the frequency and significance of events (e.g., illnesses) requiring payments. The basic elements of accounting for OPEB include

A. The expected postretirement benefit obligation (EPBO), which equals the accumulated postretirement benefit obligation (APBO) after the full eligibility date.

B. The APBO, which is the actuarial present value at a given date of the benefits projected to be earned after the full eligibility date.

C. Required recognition of a minimum liability for any excess of the EPBO over the APBO.

D. The projected benefit obligation (PBO) and the vested benefit obligation (VBO).

Answer (A) is correct.
REQUIRED: The true statement about the elements of accounting for OPEB.
DISCUSSION: The EPBO for an employee is the actuarial present value at a given date of the OPEB expected to be paid. Its measurement depends on the anticipated amounts and timing of future benefits, the costs to be incurred to provide those benefits, and the extent the costs are shared by the employee and others (such as governmental programs). The APBO for an employee is the actuarial present value at a given date of the future benefits attributable to the employee's service as of that date. The determination of the APBO (as well as of the EPBO and service cost) implicitly includes the consideration of future salary progression to the extent the benefit formula defines benefits as a function of future compensation levels. The full eligibility date is reached when the employee has rendered all the services necessary to earn all of the benefits expected to be received by that employee. After the full eligibility date, the EPBO and APBO are equal. Prior to that date, the EPBO exceeds the APBO.
Answer (B) is incorrect. The APBO for an employee is the actuarial present value at a given date of the future benefits attributable to the employee's service as of that date, not as of the full eligibility date. Answer (C) is incorrect. The full funded status must be recognized in the balance sheet. Answer (D) is incorrect. These terms relate to pension accounting only.

17. The service cost component of the net periodic postretirement benefit cost is

A. Included in the APBO but not in the EPBO.

B. Defined as the portion of the EPBO attributed to employee service for a period.

C. Included in the EPBO but not the APBO.

D. Measured using implicit and explicit actuarial assumptions and present value techniques.

Answer (B) is correct.
REQUIRED: The definition of the service cost component of the NPPBC.
DISCUSSION: Service cost is defined as the actuarial present value of benefits attributed to services rendered by employees during the period. It is the portion of the EPBO attributed to service in the period and is not affected by the level of funding.
Answer (A) is incorrect. The service cost for the most recently completed period is included in the EPBO as well as the APBO. Answer (C) is incorrect. The service cost for the most recently completed period is included in the APBO as well as the EPBO. Answer (D) is incorrect. GAAP require the use of explicit (not implicit) assumptions, each of which is the best estimate of a particular event.

18. An employer sponsors a single-employer plan that defines postretirement employee benefits other than pensions. The employer may use a systematic method of amortizing net gain or loss included in accumulated OCI other than the corridor approach. The alternative is allowable if it results in amortization at least equal to the minimum determined using that approach. However, if the employer consistently recognizes gains and losses immediately,

A. Any net loss in excess of a net gain previously recognized first offsets any prior service cost remaining in accumulated OCI.

B. Any net gain in excess of a net loss previously recognized first offsets any transition asset remaining in accumulated OCI.

C. Any net loss in excess of a net gain previously recognized first offsets any transition obligation remaining in accumulated OCI.

D. Any net gain in excess of a net loss previously recognized first offsets any transition obligation remaining in accumulated OCI.

Answer (D) is correct.
REQUIRED: The proper treatment of gains or losses recognized immediately.
DISCUSSION: Immediately recognized gains (losses) that do not offset previously recognized losses (gains) must first reduce any transition obligation (asset) remaining in accumulated OCI. The transition obligation (asset) represents an underlying unfunded (overfunded) APBO. The FASB believes that gains (losses) should not be recognized until the unfunded (overfunded) APBO is recognized.

12.5 Compensated Absences and Postemployment Benefits

19. If the payment of employees' compensation for future absences is probable, the amount can be reasonably estimated, and the obligation relates to rights that vest, the compensation should be

A. Recognized when paid.

B. Accrued if attributable to employees' services whether or not already rendered.

C. Accrued if attributable to employees' services already rendered.

D. Accrued if attributable to employees' services not already rendered.

Answer (C) is correct.
REQUIRED: The additional criterion to be met to accrue an expense for compensated absences.
DISCUSSION: GAAP require an accrual when four criteria are met: (1) The payment of compensation is probable, (2) the amount can be reasonably estimated, (3) the benefits either vest or accumulate, and (4) the compensation relates to employees' services that have already been rendered.

20. Gavin Co. grants all employees 2 weeks of paid vacation for each full year of employment. Unused vacation time can be accumulated and carried forward to succeeding years and will be paid at the salaries in effect when vacations are taken or when employment is terminated. There was no employee turnover in Year 4. Additional information relating to the year ended December 31, Year 4, is as follows:

Liability for accumulated vacations at
  12/31/Year 3 $35,000
Pre-Year 4 accrued vacations taken from
  1/1/Year 4 to 9/30/Year 4
  (the authorized period for vacations)   20,000
Vacations earned for work in Year 4
  (adjusted to current rates)   30,000

Gavin granted a 10% salary increase to all employees on October 1, Year 4, its annual salary increase date. For the year ended December 31, Year 4, Gavin should report vacation pay expense of

A. $45,000

B. $34,500

C. $31,500

D. $30,000

Answer (C) is correct.
REQUIRED: The amount of vacation pay expense.
DISCUSSION: GAAP require an accrual for vacation pay when the compensation relates to services previously provided, the benefits either vest or accumulate, and payment is both probable and reasonably estimable. Gavin Co. pays salaries at the amount in effect when the vacations are taken, and the amount estimated should be based on this provision. At 9/30/Year 4, the liability for accumulated vacations is equal to $15,000 ($35,000 beginning balance – $20,000 attributable to vacations taken). This balance must be adjusted by $1,500 to reflect the 10% salary increase. Consequently, vacation pay expense to be reported in Year 4 is equal to the $30,000 attributable to vacations earned for work in Year 4 (adjusted to current rates) plus the $1,500 attributable to the adjustment of the pre-Year 4 liability, a total of $31,500.
Answer (A) is incorrect. The amount of $45,000 equals vacation pay earned in Year 4 plus the liability at 9/30/Year 4 before adjustment for the salary increase. Answer (B) is incorrect. The amount of $34,500 assumes the vacation pay earned in Year 4 has not been adjusted to current rates. Answer (D) is incorrect. The amount of $30,000 omits the adjustment of the remaining liability for pre-Year 4 accrued vacation pay.

21. The following information relating to compensated absences was available from Graf Company's accounting records at December 31, Year 4:

- Employees' rights to vacation pay vest and are attributable to services already rendered. Payment is probable, and Graf's obligation was reasonably estimated at $110,000.
- Employees' rights to sick pay benefits do not vest but accumulate for possible future use. The rights are attributable to services already rendered, and the total accumulated sick pay was reasonably estimated at $50,000.

What amount is Graf required to report as the liability for compensated absences in its December 31, Year 4, balance sheet?

A. $160,000

B. $110,000

C. $50,000

D. $0

Answer (B) is correct.
REQUIRED: The amount to be reported as a liability for compensated absences at year end.
DISCUSSION: In general, GAAP require an accrual for compensated services when the compensation relates to services previously provided, the benefits either vest or accumulate, and payment is both probable and reasonably estimable. An exception is made for sick pay benefits, which must be accrued only if the rights vest. Because Graf's obligation for sick pay benefits relates to benefits that do not vest, no accrual for the $50,000 in accumulated sick pay should be recognized. Consequently, only the $110,000 obligation for employee rights to vacation pay should be recognized as part of the liability for compensated absences in the year-end balance sheet.
Answer (A) is incorrect. The amount of $160,000 includes the nonvesting sick pay benefits. Answer (C) is incorrect. The amount of $50,000 includes the nonvesting sick pay benefits but excludes the vacation pay. Answer (D) is incorrect. Zero excludes the vacation pay.

22. At December 31, Year 2, Taos Co. estimates that its employees have earned vacation pay of $100,000. Employees will receive their vacation pay in Year 3. Should Taos accrue a liability at December 31, Year 2, if the rights to this compensation accumulated over time or if the rights are vested?

	Accumulated	Vested
A.	Yes	No
B.	No	No
C.	Yes	Yes
D.	No	Yes

Answer (C) is correct.
REQUIRED: The effect of accumulation and vesting on accrual of a liability for vacation pay.
DISCUSSION: GAAP require an accrual for compensated services when the compensation relates to services previously provided, the benefits either vest or accumulate, and payment is both probable and reasonably estimable. The single exception is for sick pay benefits, which must be accrued only if the rights vest.
Answer (A) is incorrect. Vesting meets one of the criteria for accrual of a liability. Answer (B) is incorrect. Either vesting or accumulation meets one of the criteria for accrual of a liability. Answer (D) is incorrect. Accumulation meets one of the criteria for accrual of a liability.

23. The following information pertains to Rik Co.'s two employees:

Name	Weekly Salary	Number of Weeks Worked in Year	Vacation Rights Vest or Accumulate
Ryan	$800	52	Yes
Todd	600	52	No

Neither Ryan nor Todd took the usual 2-week vacation during the year. In Rik's December 31 financial statements, what amount of vacation expense and liability should be reported?

A. $2,800
B. $1,600
C. $1,400
D. $0

Answer (B) is correct.
REQUIRED: The amount of vacation expense and liability.
DISCUSSION: An accrual is required when four criteria are met: (1) The payment of compensation is probable, (2) the amount can be reasonably estimated, (3) the benefits either vest or accumulate, and (4) the compensation relates to employees' services that have already been rendered. Hence, no accrual is made of Todd's vacation rights because they do not vest or accumulate. The liability reported should therefore be $1,600 ($800 weekly salary earned by Ryan × 2 weeks).
Answer (A) is incorrect. The amount of $2,800 includes Todd's vacation rights. Answer (C) is incorrect. The amount of $1,400 equals 1 week's salary for both Ryan and Todd. Answer (D) is incorrect. Zero excludes Ryan's vacation rights.

12.6 Share-Based Payment

24. Pine Corp. is required to contribute, to an employee stock ownership plan (ESOP), 10% of its income after deduction for this contribution but before income tax. Pine's income before charges for the contribution and income tax was $75,000. The income tax rate is 30%. What amount should be accrued as a contribution to the ESOP?

A. $7,500
B. $6,818
C. $5,250
D. $4,907

Answer (B) is correct.
REQUIRED: The amount that should be accrued as a contribution to the ESOP.
DISCUSSION: The contribution equals 10% of pretax income after deduction of the contribution. Hence, the contribution is $6,818.

$$C = .10\% \times (\$75,000 - C)$$
$$C = \$7,500 - .1C$$
$$1.1C = \$7,500$$
$$C = \$6,818$$

Questions 25 through 28 are based on the following information. On December 21, Year 1, the board of directors of Oak Corporation approved a plan to award 600,000 share options to 20 key employees as additional compensation. Effective January 1, Year 2, each employee was granted the right to purchase 30,000 shares of the company's $2 par value stock at an exercise price of $36 per share. The market price on that date was $32 per share. All share options vest at December 31, Year 4, the end of the 3-year requisite service period. They expire on December 31, Year 11. Based on an appropriate option-pricing formula, the fair value of the options on the grant date was estimated at $12 per option.

25. What amount of compensation expense should Oak Corporation recognize in its annual income statement for the year ended December 31, Year 2?

A. $7,200,000

B. $6,400,000

C. $2,400,000

D. $1,200,700

Answer (C) is correct.

REQUIRED: The compensation expense recognized in Year 2.

DISCUSSION: Total compensation cost recognized during the requisite service period should equal the grant-date fair value of all share options for which the requisite service is rendered. GAAP require an entity to (1) estimate the number of share options for which the requisite service is expected to be rendered, (2) measure the cost of employee services received in exchange for those options at their fair value on the grant date, and (3) allocate that cost to the requisite service period. Given that all options vest at the same time (known as cliff vesting), the $7,200,000 (600,000 shares × $12 estimated fair value) total compensation cost should be allocated proportionately to the 3-year requisite service period. Thus, $2,400,000 ($7,200,000 ÷ 3) should be expensed in the annual income statement for the year ended December 31, Year 2.

Answer (A) is incorrect. The amount of $7,200,000 is the total estimated compensation cost for the entire requisite service period. Answer (B) is incorrect. The amount of $6,400,000 is total compensation expense based on the $32 market price. Answer (D) is incorrect. The amount of $1,200,000 is 600,000 shares times the $2 par value.

26. On January 1, Year 3, five key employees left Oak Corporation. What amount of compensation expense should Oak report in the income statement for the year ended December 31, Year 3?

A. $5,400,000

B. $3,600,000

C. $2,400,000

D. $1,200,000

Answer (D) is correct.

REQUIRED: The compensation expense recognized in Year 3 after a change in estimate.

DISCUSSION: Given that all options vest at the same time (known as cliff vesting), the $7,200,000 (600,000 shares × $12 estimated fair value) total compensation cost should be allocated proportionately to the 3-year requisite service period. Thus, $2,400,000 ($7,200,000 ÷ 3) should be expensed in the annual income statement for the year ended December 31, Year 2. However, only 15 key employees are covered in Year 3. The total compensation expense for these employees is $5,400,000 [(30,000 options × 15 employees) × $12 fair value]. The amount to be recognized each year of the requisite service period is $1,800,000 ($5,400 ÷ 3). The revised cumulative amount to be recognized at the end of Year 3 is therefore $3,600,000 ($1,800,000 × 2 years). Because $2,400,000 was expensed in Year 2, Year 3 expense is $1,200,000 ($3,600,000 revised cumulative expense − $2,400,000).

Answer (A) is incorrect. The total compensation expense for the entire requisite service period is $5,400,000. Answer (B) is incorrect. The total compensation expense that should be recognized in Years 2 and 3 combined is $3,600,000. Answer (C) is incorrect. The amount of $2,400,000 is based on the assumption that all 20 key employees remain employed.

27. On January 1, Year 3, five key employees left Oak Corporation. During the period from January 1, Year 5, through December 31, Year 11, 400,000 of the share options that vested were exercised. At the end of this period, the cumulative amount that should have been credited to additional paid-in capital is

A. $19,200,000

B. $18,400,000

C. $13,600,000

D. $4,000,000

Answer (B) is correct.

REQUIRED: The credit to additional paid-in capital at the end of the period.

DISCUSSION: Additional paid-in capital–share options was credited for $5,400,000 (450,000 × $12) as compensation expense was recognized during the requisite service period. During the period from January 1, Year 5, through December 31, Year 11, 400,000 options were exercised. Hence, additional paid-in capital should be credited for $18,400,000 [400,000 shares × ($36 exercise price + $12 previously credited to additional paid-in capital–stock options – $2 par value allocated to common stock)].

Answer (A) is incorrect. The amount of $19,200,000 includes the $2 par value allocated to the common stock account. Answer (C) is incorrect. The amount of $13,600,000 does not include the $12 fair value of the options determined at the grant date. Answer (D) is incorrect. The amount of $4,000,000 does not include the $36 exercise price.

28. On January 1, Year 3, five key employees left Oak Corporation. During the period from January 1, Year 5, through December 31, Year 11, 400,000 of the share options that vested were exercised. The remaining options were not exercised. What amount of the previously recognized compensation expense should be adjusted upon expiration of the share options?

A. $2,400,000

B. $2,300,000

C. $100,000

D. $0

Answer (D) is correct.

REQUIRED: The adjustment to previously recognized compensation expense when share options are not exercised.

DISCUSSION: Total compensation expense for the requisite service period is not adjusted for expired options.

Answer (A) is incorrect. This amount is the annual compensation expense recognized during each of the years of the requisite service period assuming no forfeitures. Answer (B) is incorrect. This amount is the additional amount that would have been credited to additional paid-in capital if the 50,000 expired options had been exercised. Answer (C) is incorrect. This amount is the additional amount that would have been credited to common stock if the 50,000 expired options had been exercised.

29. The measurement date for shares issued to employees in share option plans accounted for using the fair-value method is

A. The date on which options are granted to specified employees.

B. The earliest date on which both the number of shares to be issued and the option price are known.

C. The date on which the options are exercised by the employees.

D. The date the corporation forgoes alternative use of the shares to be sold under option.

Answer (A) is correct.

REQUIRED: The measurement date for shares issued after exercise of options if the accounting is in accordance with the fair-value method.

DISCUSSION: Under the fair-value method, compensation cost is measured at the grant date, which is when any needed approvals have been received, and the employer and employee "reach a mutual understanding of the key terms and conditions of a share-based payment award." This expense is based on the fair value of the award at that date and recognized over the requisite service period. This period is most often the period over which the vesting conditions are expected to be satisfied.

Answer (B) is incorrect. The earliest date on which the number of shares to be issued and the option price are known may coincide with, but does not define, the measurement date. Answer (C) is incorrect. The date on which the options are exercised by employees may coincide with, but does not define, the measurement date. Answer (D) is incorrect. The date the entity forgoes alternative use of the shares to be sold under option may coincide with, but does not define, the measurement date.

30. On January 1, Year 2, an employer tells an executive whose substantive employment began on August 1, Year 1, that she will receive 500 fully vested share options on January 1, Year 3. The exercise price is the share price on the latter date. Required approvals, which were not mere formalities, were received on December 10, Year 1. If the executive is still an employee on January 1, Year 3, and receives the options, the grant date for the award is

A. August 1, Year 1.

B. December 10, Year 1.

C. January 1, Year 2.

D. January 1, Year 3.

Answer (D) is correct.
REQUIRED: The grant date for an award of fully vested share options.
DISCUSSION: On the grant date, the employer and employee have a mutual understanding of the key terms and conditions of the share-based payment arrangement, necessary approvals have been received, and (in the case of equity instruments) the employee has begun to benefit from (or be adversely affected by) changes in the share price. Accordingly, the grant date is January 1, Year 3, the post-approval date when (1) the employee will potentially benefit or not benefit from changes in the share price, and (2) a sufficient basis exists to understand the equity and compensatory relationship created by the award.
Answer (A) is incorrect. August 1, Year 1, precedes the service inception date and the grant date. Answer (B) is incorrect. December 10, Year 1, precedes the service inception date and the grant date. Answer (C) is incorrect. January 1, Year 2, is the service inception date. The requisite service period is from January 1, Year 2, to January 1, Year 3, the period during which the employee must perform service to receive the awards.

31. On January 2, Year 1, Kine Co. granted Morgan, its president, fully vested share options to buy 1,000 shares of Kine's $10 par common stock. The options have an exercise price of $20 per share and are exercisable for 3 years following the grant date. Morgan exercised the options on December 31, Year 1. The market price of the shares was $50 on January 2, Year 1, and $70 on the following December 31. If the fair value of the options is not reasonably estimable at the grant date, by what net amount will equity increase as a result of the grant and exercise of the options? (Ignore tax considerations.)

A. $20,000

B. $30,000

C. $50,000

D. $70,000

Answer (A) is correct.
REQUIRED: The amount equity increases as a result of the grant and exercise of share options.
DISCUSSION: In the rare cases in which an entity cannot reasonably estimate the fair value of equity instruments at the grant date, the measurement is based on intrinsic value (market price of an underlying share – exercise price of an option). Remeasurement is required at each reporting date and on final settlement. The initial measurement date is January 2, Year 1. At that date, the intrinsic value of the fully vested options is $30,000 [1,000 shares × ($50 market price – $20 option price)]. The entry is

Compensation expense	$30,000	
Additional paid-in		
capital (share options)		$30,000

When the options are exercised, compensation expense will be debited and additional paid-in capital (share options) will be credited for $20,000 [1,000 shares × ($70 – $50)] to reflect the final measure of intrinsic value.

Compensation expense	$20,000	
Additional paid-in		
capital (share options)		$20,000

The final entry records the receipt of payment and the issuance of shares.

Cash	$20,000	
Additional paid-in capital		
(share options)	50,000	
Common stock		
(1,000 shares × $10 par)		$10,000
Additional paid-in capital		60,000

The net effect on equity is an increase of $20,000 ($10,000 common stock + $60,000 additional paid-in capital – $50,000 compensation expense).
Answer (B) is incorrect. The amount of the initial debit to compensation expense and credit to additional paid-in capital is $30,000. Answer (C) is incorrect. The final measure of intrinsic value is $50,000. Answer (D) is incorrect. The market price of the shares issued on the settlement date is $70,000.

Use the additional questions in Gleim **CPA Test Prep Online** to create Test Sessions that emulate Prometric!

12.7 PRACTICE SIMULATION

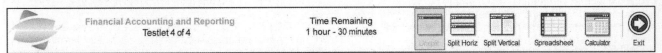

Financial Accounting and Reporting
Testlet 4 of 4

Time Remaining
1 hour - 30 minutes

Unsplit | Split Horiz | Split Vertical | Spreadsheet | Calculator | Exit

DIRECTIONS

Note: If you believe you have encountered a software malfunction, report it to the test center staff immediately.

Navigation

To navigate from task to task, use the controls at the bottom of the screen. Click on the **Next** button to advance to the next task, or the **Previous** button to go to the previous task. To go directly to any task, click on its number.

If you would like a reminder to revisit a task, or want to indicate that you are finished with it, click on the reminder flag below the task number. To clear the flag, click on it again. Reminder flags are for your use only – they do not contribute to your score.

Tabs

In this part of the examination, you will be asked to complete various tasks. Every task has one or more **Work Tabs**. Some tasks have one or more **Information Tabs**, others may have none. Every task has a **Help** tab.

If a task has **Information Tabs**, you may use the information in them to complete your responses in the **Work Tabs**.

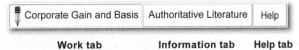

Work tab   Information tab   Help tab

Work Tabs:

- **Work Tabs** are identified with a pencil icon. This is where your responses are expected.
- Each task has one or more **Work Tabs**.
- **Work Tabs** contain directions for completing the task – be sure to read these directions carefully.
- The **Work Tab** name in the example above is for illustration only – yours will differ.
- You must complete all of the **Work Tabs** in each task to receive full credit.

Information Tabs:

- The Authoritative Literature will be provided in all tasks in the AUD, FAR, and REG sections for your reference.
- Your simulation may have one or more additional **Information Tabs**. Like the Authoritative Literature tabs, **Information Tabs** do not have a pencil icon.
- If your task has additional **Information Tabs**, go through each to familiarize yourself with the task content.

Help Tab:

- The **Help Tab** provides assistance with the exam software that is used in this task. For example, if the task is to compose a memorandum, **Help** will provide information about the word processor.

The Toolbar

The toolbar at the top of the screen shows the amount of time remaining for you to complete the tasks. In addition, the following tools are available. Note that only the **Exit** button is displayed when Directions are visible - the others will appear when you begin the tasks.

Click on these buttons to split or unsplit the screen. You can split the screen vertically or horizontally.

Click on this button to display the calculator; click on it again to hide the calculator. To move the calculator, click on the calculator title bar and drag the calculator to the desired location.

Click on this button to use the spreadsheet; click on it again to hide the spreadsheet. To move the spreadsheet, click on the the spreadsheet title bar and drag the spreadsheet to the desired location.

Click on this button to go on to the next part of the examination. You must complete all of the tasks to receive full credit. Once you click on **Exit** and confirm the action, you will NOT be able to return to this testlet.

| Equity Section | Authoritative Literature | Help |

Field Co.'s equity account balances at December 31, Year 2, were as follows:

Common stock	$ 800,000
Additional paid-in capital	1,600,000
Retained earnings	1,845,000

The following Year 3 transactions and other information relate to the equity accounts:

- Field had 400,000 authorized shares of $5 par common stock, of which 160,000 shares were issued and outstanding.
- On March 5, Year 3, Field acquired 5,000 shares of its common stock for $10 per share to hold as treasury stock. The shares were originally issued at $15 per share. Field uses the cost method to account for treasury stock. Treasury stock is permitted in Field's state of incorporation.
- On July 15, Year 3, Field declared and distributed a property dividend of inventory. The inventory had a $75,000 carrying amount and a $60,000 fair value.
- On January 2, Year 1, Field granted share options to employees to purchase 20,000 shares of Field's common stock at $18 per share, the market price on that date. The options have a grant-date fair value of $10 per option and a 2-year requisite service period. They may be exercised within a 3-year period beginning January 2, Year 3. No forfeitures were expected, and tax effects should be ignored. On October 1, Year 3, employees exercised all 20,000 options. Field issued new shares to settle the transaction.
- Field's net income for Year 3 was $240,000. It included $50,000 of unrealized holding gains on trading securities.
- Field intends to issue new share options to key employees in Year 4. Field's management is aware that FASB guidance discusses both the "intrinsic value" method and the "fair value" method of accounting for share options. Field's management is unsure of the application of the two methods.

Enter in the shaded cells the amounts to be listed on the equity section of Field's December 31, Year 3, balance sheet.

Field Co.
**EQUITY SECTION OF
BALANCE SHEET**
December 31, Year 3

Common stock		
Additional paid-in capital		
Retained earnings:		
Beginning balance		
Add: Net Income		
Minus: Property dividend distributed		
Minus: Common stock in treasury		
Total equity		

Pension Accounting | Authoritative Literature | Help

The following information pertains to Field Co.'s defined benefit pension plan at December 31, Year 3:

Projected benefit obligation	$150,000
Service cost	6,000
Amortization of prior service cost in accumulated OCI	2,000
Fair value of plan assets	160,000
Unamortized prior service cost	12,000
Expected return on plan assets	5,000
Amortization of net gain in accumulated OCI	8,000
Interest cost	10,000

Select the correct answer for each item from the choices provided.

Item	Answer	Choices
1. At December 31, Year 3, what amount should Field record as a pension asset or liability?		A) $8,000 B) $12,000 C) $10,000
2. In its December 31, Year 3, statement of income, what amount should Field report as the required minimum pension expense?		A) $5,000 B) $10,000 C) $18,000
3. Field Co. must disclose in the notes to its financial statements a reconciliation of		A) The beginning and ending balances of the projected benefit obligation. B) The accumulated benefit obligation of its pension plan with its projected benefit obligation. C) The vested and nonvested benefit obligation of its pension plan with the accumulated benefit obligation.
4. GAAP applicable to accounting for contractual termination benefits provides that		A) A liability and a loss when the employees accept the offer. B) The cost of a participation right reduces the maximum gain or loss subject to recognition. C) A liability and a loss when it is probable that employees will be entitled to benefits.

Identify by checking the appropriate box whether each of the following is a factor in calculating the minimum required pension expense:

Factor	Element of Pension Expense	Non-Element
1. Asset gain or loss occurring in current period		
2. Amortization of gain or loss consisting of the difference between the actual and expected return on plan assets		
3. Interest cost		
4. Underfunded projected benefit obligation		
5. Service cost		
6. Cost of termination benefits		
7. Amortization of unrecognized prior service cost		
8. Market-related value of plan assets		

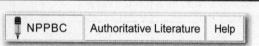

Identify by checking the appropriate box whether each of the following elements increases, decreases, or has no effect on net periodic postretirement benefit cost:

Element	Increase	Decrease	No Effect
1. Service cost			
2. Gain from a temporary deviation from the substantive plan			
3. Expected return on plan assets			
4. Interest cost			
5. Amortization of prior service credit included in accumulated OCI			
6. Interest on the EPBO			

SU 12: Employee Benefits

Defined Benefit Plan | Authoritative Literature | Help

The following information pertains to Company A's Year 5 defined benefit pension plan:

January 1, Year 5, fair value of plan assets	$100,000
January 1, Year 5, projected benefit obligation (PBO)	200,000
Contribution to the plan (made on December 31, Year 5)	10,000
Benefits paid to employees (made on December 31, Year 5)	15,000
December 31, Year 5, fair value of plan assets	106,000
December 31, Year 5, projected benefit obligation (PBO)	340,000
Discount rate	5%
Expected long-term rate of return on plan assets	8%
Service cost recognized in Year 5	40,000
Prior service cost recognized in Year 5	70,000

Additional information

- On December 31, Year 5, the company amended its defined benefit plan, resulting in an increase of $70,000 in the PBO.
- Neither net gain or loss in relation to the company's defined benefit plan nor prior service cost were recognized in prior years.
- The company applies the corridor approach to account for its net gains or losses in relation to the defined benefit plan.
- Assume that the market-related value of plan assets is equal to the fair value of plan assets.

Using the information above, for each of the items below, enter in the shaded cells the applicable dollar value. If the amount is zero, enter a zero (0).

Items	Amount
1. Year 5 interest cost	
2. Year 5 actual return on plan assets	
3. Year 5 expected return on plan assets	
4. Year 5 required minimum net pension expense	
5. Year 5 net gain or loss in relation to the defined benefit pension plan	
6. Pension liability as presented in December 31, Year 5, financial statements	

▼ = Reminder | Directions | 1 2 3 4 [5] 6 | ◀ Previous Next ▶

Research | Authoritative Literature | Help

During the annual audit of JDV, Inc., a publicly traded company, the independent auditor noticed that the company's current-year expected return on plan assets is much greater than the actual return on plan assets.

The auditor asked the company's controller and actuary to explain the difference. The actuary's answer was that one of the reasons for this situation is that the expected long-term rate of return on plan assets reflects the expected return on current and future years' contributions to the pension plan; since future contributions are expected to be greater in the following years, the expected long-term rate of return is greater. Which section in the authoritative guidance addresses whether the expected long-term rate of return on plan assets should reflect the long-term expected earnings on future years' contributions to the pension plan?

Enter your response in the answer fields below. Unless specifically requested, your response should not cite implementation guidance.

FASB ASC ☐ - ☐ - ☐ - ☐

▼ = Reminder | Directions | 1 2 3 4 5 [6] | ◀ Previous Next ▶

Unofficial Answers

1. Equity Section (8 Gradable Items)

Field Co.
**EQUITY SECTION OF
BALANCE SHEET**
December 31, Year 3

Common stock		$ 900,000 [1]
Additional paid-in capital		2,060,000 [2]
Retained earnings:		
Beginning balance	$1,845,000 [3]	
Add: Net Income	240,000 [4]	
Minus: Property dividend distributed	(60,000) [5]	2,025,000 [6]
		4,985,000 [7]
Minus: Common stock in treasury		(50,000) [8]
Total equity		$4,935,000

[1] [(160,000 + 20,000) shares issued × $5] = $900,000

[2] Additional paid-in capital: $1,600,000 + [20,000 × ($18 + $10 − $5)] = $1,600,000 + $460,000 = $2,060,000

[3] Provided in situation

[4] Provided in situation

[5] $60,000 was the fair value of the property distributed on July 15, Year 3.

[6] Current year retained earnings adjustments: $1,845,000 + $240,000 − $60,000 = $2,025,000

[7] [6] above + Common stock of $900,000 + Additional paid in capital of $2,060,000 = $4,985,000

[8] 5,000 shares re-acquired in Year 5 at a cost of $10 per share: 5,000 × $10 = $50,000

2. Pension Accounting (4 Gradable Items)

1. C) $10,000. The PBO is overfunded by $10,000 ($160,000 fair value of plan assets − $150,000 PBO).

2. A) $5,000. The required minimum pension expense equals $5,000 ($6,000 service cost + $2,000 amortization of prior service cost in accumulated OCI + $10,000 interest cost − $5,000 expected return on plan assets − $8,000 amortization of net gain in accumulated OCI).

3. A) The beginning and ending balances of the projected benefit obligation. One of the required disclosures by a company with a defined benefit pension plan is a reconciliation of the beginning and ending balances of the PBO. It should display separately the effects during the period of service cost, interest cost, participants' contributions, actuarial gains and losses, foreign currency exchange rate changes, benefits paid, plan amendments, business combinations, divestitures, curtailments, settlements, and special termination benefits.

4. C) A liability and a loss when it is probable that employees will be entitled to benefits. Contractual termination benefits are required by a plan only if a given event occurs, e.g., the closing of a factory.

3. Pension Expenses (8 Gradable Items)

1. Non-element. Asset gains and losses are differences between the actual and expected returns. They are included in the gain or loss component of pension expense. Gains and losses (including asset gains and losses) are not required to be recognized in pension expense of the period in which they occur. Thus, the required minimum pension expense reflects the amount of the expected, not the actual, return on plan assets. The current asset gain or loss, that is, the difference between the actual and expected returns, may be deferred.

2. Element of pension expense. The cumulative unrecognized net gain or loss at the beginning of the year (excluding the asset gains and losses not reflected in market-related value) is subject to required amortization in pension expense. However, only the amount exceeding 10% of the greater of the PBO or the market-related value of plan assets must be amortized.

3. <u>Element of pension expense.</u> Interest cost is the increase in the projected benefit obligation (PBO) determined by multiplying the PBO at the beginning of the year by the current discount rate (e.g., the interest rate at which annuities could be purchased to settle pension obligations).

4. <u>Non-element.</u> An underfunded PBO is recognized as a liability, not as an element of pension expense.

5. <u>Element of pension expense.</u> Service cost is the present value of the future benefits earned by the employees in the current period (as calculated according to the plan's benefit formula). This amount is a portion of the PBO and is calculated by the plan's actuary. It is unaffected by the funded status of the plan.

6. <u>Non-element.</u> Termination benefits are provided to employees in connection with their termination of employment. Special termination benefits are offered for a short period. Contractual termination benefits are required by the terms of a pension plan only if a specified event occurs.

7. <u>Element of pension expense.</u> If a plan is amended to grant additional benefits for past service, the cost is allocated to future periods of service.

8. <u>Element of pension expense.</u> The expected return on plan assets is the market-related value of the plan assets at the beginning of the period multiplied by the expected long-term rate of return. The expected return (given that it is positive) decreases pension expense. Market-related value may be either fair value or a calculated value that recognizes changes in fair value systematically and rationally over not more than 5 years, such as a 5-year moving average.

4. NPPBC (6 Gradable Items)

1. <u>Increase.</u> Service cost increases NPPBC. It is the part of the EPBO attributed to services by employees during the period and is not affected by the level of funding.

2. <u>Decrease.</u> The NPPBC gain or loss component equals any gain (loss) immediately recognized in NPPBC or the amortization of the net gain (loss) from prior periods that was recognized in OCI.

3. <u>Decrease.</u> The expected return on plan assets is the market-related value of plan assets (MRV) at the beginning of the period multiplied by the expected long-term rate of return.

4. <u>Increase.</u> Interest cost increases NPPBC. It is the part of the EPBO attributed to services by employees during the period and is not affected by the level of funding.

5. <u>Decrease.</u> A prior service credit retroactively reduces benefits and the APBO. The credit to OCI, net of tax, first reduces any prior service cost still in accumulated OCI. It then reduces any transition obligation in accumulated OCI.

6. <u>No effect.</u> Service interest is an incidental cost having no effect on the NPPBC.

5. Defined Benefit Pension Plan (6 Gradable Items)

1. <u>$10,000.</u> Interest cost is calculated as beginning PBO ($200,000) multiplied by the discount rate (5%).

2. <u>$11,000.</u> The actual return on plan assets can be derived from the Year 5 plan assets equation:

Fair value of plan assets, December 31, Year 5	$106,000
Less: fair value of plan assets, January 1, Year 5	(100,000)
Less: contribution to the plan	(10,000)
Benefits paid	15,000
Actual return on plan assets	$ 11,000

3. <u>$8,000.</u> The expected return on plan assets is calculated as beginning fair value of plan assets times the expected long-term rate of return ($100,000 × 8%).

4. <u>$42,000.</u> The required minimum annual pension expense is calculated as follows:

Current-year service cost	$40,000
Interest cost	10,000
Less: expected return on plan assets	(8,000)
Net periodic pension expense	$42,000

Since no net gain or loss and no prior service cost were previously recognized, no amortization of these elements is recognized in Year 5.

5. **$32,000.** Net gains and losses in relation to the defined benefit plan arise from changes in the PBO or plan assets that result from changes in actuarial assumptions and experience different from that expected (liability gains and losses + asset gains and losses). (a) The actual return on plan assets is greater than the expected return on plan assets. Thus, asset gain of $3,000 ($11,000 – $8,000) is recognized for the difference. (b) Liability gains and losses can be derived from the Year 5 PBO equation:

December 31, Year 5 PBO	$340,000
Less: January 1, Year 5, PBO	(200,000)
Less: interest cost	(10,000)
Less: prior service cost	(70,000)
Less: current-year service cost	(40,000)
Benefits paid	15,000
Liability loss	$ 35,000

Thus, the total net loss is $32,000 ($35,000 liability loss – $3,000 asset gain).

6. **$234,000.** The year-end PBO ($340,000) is greater than the year-end fair value of plan assets ($106,000). Thus, a pension liability of $234,000 ($340,000 – $106,000) is presented in the financial statements.

6. Research (1 Gradable Item)

Answer: FASB ASC 715-30-35-49

715-30-35-49 However, the expected return on future years' contributions to a pension plan shall not be considered in determining the expected long-term rate of return on plan assets. The expected long-term rate of return on plan assets shall reflect long-term earnings expectations only on existing plan assets and those contributions expected to be received during the current year.

Gleim Simulation Grading

Task	Correct Responses		Gradable Items		Score per Task
1	_____	÷	8	=	_____
2	_____	÷	4	=	_____
3	_____	÷	8	=	_____
4	_____	÷	6	=	_____
5	_____	÷	6	=	_____
Research	_____	÷	1	=	_____

Total of Scores per Task	_____
÷ Total Number of Tasks	6
Total Score	_____ %

Use **CPA Gleim Online** and **Simulation Wizard** to practice more task-based simulations in a realistic environment.

STUDY UNIT THIRTEEN
NONCURRENT LIABILITIES

(18 pages of outline)

13.1	Types of Bond Liabilities	457
13.2	Time Value of Money	458
13.3	Bonds Payable -- Initial Measurement	460
13.4	Bonds Payable -- Subsequent Measurement	462
13.5	Debt Issue Costs	463
13.6	Securities with Characteristics of Liabilities and Equity	464
13.7	Extinguishment of Debt	466
13.8	Refinancing of Current Obligations	467
13.9	Noncurrent Notes Payable	468
13.10	Troubled Debt Restructurings	469
13.11	Asset Retirement Obligations	472
13.12	Costs Associated with Exit or Disposal Activities	473
13.13	Practice Simulation	488

This study unit covers traditional noncurrent liabilities (bonds and notes), including some securities that have characteristics of debt and equity. Unless the **fair value option** (see Study Unit 6) is elected, they are measured and accounted for in accordance with the guidance for interest on receivables and payables. The topics in this study unit are frequently tested.

13.1 TYPES OF BOND LIABILITIES

1. **Classification of Bonds**

    a. A bond is a formal contract to pay an amount of money (face amount) at the maturity date plus interest at the stated rate at specific intervals.

    1) All of the terms of the agreement are stated in an **indenture**.

    b. Bonds may be classified as follows:

    1) Nature of security

        a) **Mortgage bonds** are backed by specific assets, usually real estate.
        b) **Debentures** are backed only by the borrower's general credit.
        c) **Collateral trust bonds** are backed by specific securities.
        d) **Guaranty bonds** are guaranteed by a third party, e.g., the parent of the subsidiary that issued the bonds.

    2) Maturity pattern

        a) A **term bond** has a single maturity date at the end of its term.
        b) A **serial bond** matures in stated amounts at regular intervals.

    3) Ownership

        a) **Registered bonds** are issued in the name of the owner, who receives interest payments directly.

            i) When the owner sells the bonds, the certificates must be surrendered and new certificates issued.

        b) **Bearer bonds** (coupon bonds) are bearer instruments.

            i) Whoever presents the interest coupons is entitled to payment.

    4) Priority

        a) **Subordinated debentures** and **second mortgage bonds** are junior securities with claims inferior to those of senior bonds.

     5)   Repayment provisions

        a)   **Income bonds** pay interest contingent on the debtor's profitability.

        b)   **Revenue bonds** are issued by governments and are payable from specific revenue sources.

        c)   **Participating bonds** share in excess earnings of the debtor.

     6)   Valuation

        a)   **Variable rate bonds** pay interest that is dependent on market conditions.

        b)   **Zero-coupon** or **deep-discount bonds** are noninterest-bearing.

           i)   Because they are sold at less than their face amount, an interest rate is imputed.

        c)   **Commodity-backed bonds** are payable at prices related to a commodity, such as gold.

     7)   Redemption provisions

        a)   **Callable bonds** may be repurchased by the issuer before maturity.

        b)   **Redeemable bonds** may be presented for payment by the creditor prior to the maturity date. The bonds usually are redeemable only after a specified period.

        c)   **Convertible bonds** may be converted into equity securities of the issuer at the option of the holder (buyer) under specified conditions.

  c.   A bond indenture may require a **bond sinking fund** (a long-term investment).

     1)   Payments into the fund plus the revenue earned on its investments provide the assets to settle bond liabilities.

Stop and review! You have completed the outline for this subunit. Study multiple-choice questions 1 through 3 on page 475.

13.2 TIME VALUE OF MONEY

1. **Overview**

  a.   Time value of money concepts are important in financial accounting. They affect the accounting for noncurrent receivables and payables (bonds and notes), leases, and certain employee benefits.

  b.   A quantity of money to be received or paid in the future is worth less than the same amount now. The difference is measured in terms of interest calculated using the appropriate **discount rate**. Interest is the payment received by an owner of money from the current consumer to forgo current consumption.

  c.   Standard tables have been developed to facilitate the calculation of present and future values. Each entry in one of these tables represents the factor by which any monetary amount can be modified to obtain its present or future value.

2. **Present Value (PV) of a Single Amount**

  a.   The present value of a single amount is the value today of some future payment.

  b.   It equals the future payment times the present value of 1 (a factor found in a standard table) for the given number of periods and interest rate.

EXAMPLE

No. of Periods	Present Value		
	6%	8%	10%
1	0.943	0.926	0.909
2	0.890	0.857	0.826
3	0.840	0.794	0.751
4	0.792	0.735	0.683
5	0.747	0.681	0.621

The present value of $1,000, to be received in 3 years and discounted at 8%, is $794 ($1,000 × 0.794).

3.   **Future Value (FV) of a Single Amount**

   a.   The future value of a single amount is the amount available at a specified time in the future based on a single investment (deposit) today. The FV is the amount to be computed if one knows the present value and the appropriate discount rate.

   b.   It equals the current payment times the future value of 1 (a factor found in a standard table) for the given number of periods and interest rate.

EXAMPLE

	Future Value		
No. of Periods	6%	8%	10%
1	1.0600	1.0800	1.1000
2	1.1236	1.1664	1.2100
3	1.1910	1.2597	1.3310
4	1.2625	1.3605	1.4641
5	1.3382	1.4693	1.6105

The future value of $1,000 invested today for 4 years at 10% interest will be $1,464 ($1,000 × 1.464).

---

4.   **Annuities**

   a.   An annuity is usually a series of equal payments at equal intervals of time, e.g., $1,000 at the end of every year for 10 years.

      1)   An **ordinary annuity (annuity in arrears)** is a series of payments occurring at the end of each period. In an **annuity due (annuity in advance)**, the payments are made (received) at the beginning of each period.

         a)   **Present value.** The first payment of an ordinary annuity is discounted. The first payment of an annuity due is not discounted.

         b)   **Future value.** Interest is not earned for the first period of an ordinary annuity. Interest is earned on the first payment of an annuity due.

      2)   The **PV of an annuity.** A typical present value table is for an ordinary annuity, but the factor for an annuity due can be easily derived. Select the factor for an ordinary annuity for one less period ($n - 1$) and add 1.000 to it to include the initial payment (which is not discounted).

EXAMPLE

	Present Value		
No. of Periods	6%	8%	10%
1	0.943	0.926	0.909
2	1.833	1.783	1.736
3	2.673	2.577	2.487
4	3.465	3.312	3.170
5	4.212	3.993	3.791

To calculate the present value of an **ordinary annuity** of four payments of $1,000 each discounted at 10%, multiply $1,000 by the appropriate factor ($1,000 × 3.170 = $3,170).

Using the same table, the present value of an **annuity due** of four payments of $1,000 each also may be calculated. This value equals $1,000 times the factor for one less period (4 – 1 = 3), increased by 1.0. Thus, the present value of the annuity due for four periods at 10% is $3,487 [$1,000 × (2.487 + 1.0)].

The present value of the annuity due ($3,487) is greater than the present value of the ordinary annuity ($3,170) because the payments occur 1 year sooner.

---

      3)   The **FV of an annuity** is the value that a series of equal payments will have at a certain moment in the future if interest is earned at a given rate.

EXAMPLE

| | Future Value | | |
No. of Periods	6%	8%	10%
1	1.0000	1.0000	1.0000
2	2.0600	2.0800	2.1000
3	3.1836	3.2464	3.3100
4	4.3746	4.5061	4.6410
5	5.6371	5.8667	6.1051

To calculate the FV of a 3-year **ordinary annuity** with payments of $1,000 each at 6% interest, multiply $1,000 by the appropriate factor ($1,000 × 3.184 = $3,184).

The FV of an **annuity due** also may be determined from the same table. Multiply the $1,000 payment by the factor for one additional period (3 + 1 = 4) decreased by 1.0 (4.375 – 1.0 = 3.375) to arrive at a FV of $3,375 ($1,000 × 3.375).

The future value of the annuity due ($3,375) is greater than the future value of an ordinary annuity ($3,184). The deposits are made earlier.

Time value of money has been tested on the CPA exam, but many of the questions testing this topic are from older exams, including questions from the 1970s. People employed in the accounting field are assumed to understand time value of money concepts. If this area challenges you, please use this subunit to re-strengthen your knowledge level. Successful CPA candidates understand how to calculate present and future values as well as annuities.

Stop and review! You have completed the outline for this subunit. Study multiple-choice questions 4 through 6 on page 476.

13.3 BONDS PAYABLE -- INITIAL MEASUREMENT

1. **Calculation of Proceeds**

    a. Of primary concern to an entity issuing bonds is the amount of cash that it will receive from investors on the day the bonds are sold.

    1) This amount is equal to the sum of the **present value of the cash flows** associated with the bonds discounted at the interest rate prevailing in the market at the time (called the market rate or effective rate).

        a) The cash flows associated with bonds are

           i)   Face amount (present value of a single amount)
           ii) Interest payments (present value of an annuity)

    2) Using the effective rate as the discount rate ensures that the bonds' **yield to maturity** (that is, their ultimate rate of return to the investor) is equal to the rate of return prevailing in the market at the time of the sale.

    b. This present value calculation can result in cash proceeds equal to, less than, or greater than the face amount of the bonds, depending on the relationship of the bonds' stated rate of interest to the market rate.

    1) If the bonds' stated rate equals the market rate at the time of sale, the present value of the bonds will exactly equal their face amount, and the bonds are said to be sold "at par." It is rare, however, for the coupon rate to precisely match the market rate at the time the bonds are ready for sale.

2. **Issuance at a Premium**

    a. If the bonds' stated rate is greater than the current market rate, the cash proceeds are greater than the face amount, and the bonds are sold at a premium.

    1) Sometimes the issue price is an exact percentage of the face amount. In these cases, the bonds are said to be sold, for example, "at 101" or "at 102."

EXAMPLE

Pritzker, Inc., issues 200 8%, 5-year, $5,000 bonds when the prevailing interest rate in the market is 6%. The total face amount of bonds issued is therefore $1,000,000 ($5,000 face amount × 200 bonds). Annual cash interest payments of $80,000 ($1,000,000 face amount × 8% stated rate) will be made at the end of each year. The present value of the cash flows associated with this bond issue, discounted at the market rate of 6%, is calculated as follows:

Present value of face amount ($1,000,000 × 0.74726)	$ 747,260
Present value of cash interest ($80,000 × 4.21236)	336,987 (rounded)
Cash proceeds from bond issue	$1,084,247

Because the bonds are issued at a premium, the cash proceeds exceed the face amount. Pritzker records the following entry:

Cash (present value of cash flows)	$1,084,247	
Bonds payable (face amount)		$1,000,000
Premium on bonds payable (difference)		84,247

---

3.   **Issuance at a Discount**

a.   If the bonds' stated rate is less than the current market rate, the cash proceeds are less than the face amount, and the bonds are sold at a discount.

1)   Sometimes the issue price is an exact percentage of the face amount. In these cases, the bonds are said to be sold, for example, "at 97" or "at 98."

EXAMPLE

Disler Co. issues 200 6%, 5-year, $5,000 bonds when the prevailing interest rate in the market is 8%. The total face amount of bonds issued is therefore $1,000,000 ($5,000 face amount × 200 bonds). Annual cash interest payments of $60,000 ($1,000,000 face amount × 6% stated rate) will be made at the end of each year. The present value of the cash flows associated with this bond issue, discounted at the market rate of 8%, is calculated as follows:

Present value of face amount ($1,000,000 × 0.68058)	$680,580
Present value of cash interest ($60,000 × 3.99271)	239,566 (rounded)
Cash proceeds from bond issue	$920,146

Because the bonds are issued at a discount, the cash proceeds are less than the face amount. Disler records the following entry:

Cash (present value of cash flows)	$920,146	
Discount on bonds payable (difference)	79,854	
Bonds payable (face amount)		$1,000,000

---

4.   **Bonds Sold between Interest Dates**

a.   When bonds are sold between interest payment dates, the buyer pays the issuer the amount of interest that has accrued since the last payment date.

EXAMPLE

On November 1, Year 1, Bland Co. issues, at par, a 15-year bond with a face amount of $100,000 bearing a coupon rate of 9%, payable semiannually on January 1 and July 1.

Annual interest on the bond is $9,000 ($100,000 face amount × 9% coupon rate). On the next payment date, Bland will pay the full semiannual interest of $4,500 [$9,000 × (6 ÷ 12)] to the buyer. The buyer must therefore pay Bland for the time during the most recent interest period that (s)he will not hold the bond (July 1 – November 1). The buyer will thus include accrued interest of $3,000 [$9,000 × (4 ÷ 12)] in the purchase price of the bond.

Stop and review! You have completed the outline for this subunit. Study multiple-choice questions 7 through 9 on page 477.

13.4 BONDS PAYABLE -- SUBSEQUENT MEASUREMENT

1.   **Effective Interest Method of Amortization**

> CPA candidates should understand the effective interest method and expect to see a question asking for the calculation of interest expense. Remembering the associated journal entries will allow you to handle any question regarding the effective interest method with confidence.

a.   Bond discount or premium must be amortized using the effective interest method (unless the results of another method are not materially different).

1)   Under this method, interest expense changes every period, but the interest rate remains constant.

   Annual interest expense = Carrying amount × Effective interest rate

2)   The cash paid for periodic interest also remains constant over the life of the bonds.

   Cash paid = Face amount × Stated rate

b.   The difference between interest expense and cash interest paid is the discount or premium amortization.

1)   At the maturity date, the discount or premium is fully amortized, and the carrying amount of the bonds equals the face amount.

2.   **Amortization Schedules**

a.   Premium amortized, total interest expense, and the carrying amount of the bonds decrease each period when amortizing a premium. The entry is

Interest expense	$XXX	
Premium on bonds payable	XXX	
Cash		$XXX

EXAMPLE

Pritzker, which issued bonds at a premium, uses the following amortization schedule:

Year	Beginning Carrying Amount	Times: Effective Rate	Equals: Interest Expense	Minus: Cash Paid	Equals: Premium Amortized	Ending Carrying Amount
1	$1,084,247	6%	$65,055	$80,000	$(14,945)	$1,069,302
2	1,069,302	6%	64,158	80,000	(15,842)	1,053,460
3	1,053,460	6%	63,208	80,000	(16,792)	1,036,668
4	1,036,668	6%	62,200	80,000	(17,800)	1,018,868
5	1,018,868	6%	61,132	80,000	(18,868)	1,000,000
					$(84,247)	

b.   Discount amortized, total interest expense, and the carrying amount of the bonds increase each period when amortizing a discount. The entry is

Interest expense	$XXX	
Discount on bonds payable		$XXX
Cash		XXX

EXAMPLE

Disler, which issued bonds at a discount, uses the following amortization schedule:

Year	Beginning Carrying Amount	Times: Effective Rate	Equals: Interest Expense	Minus: Cash Paid	Equals: Discount Amortized	Ending Carrying Amount
1	$920,146	8%	$73,612	$60,000	$13,612	$ 933,758
2	933,758	8%	74,701	60,000	14,701	948,458
3	948,458	8%	75,877	60,000	15,877	964,335
4	964,335	8%	77,147	60,000	17,147	981,482
5	981,482	8%	78,519	60,000	18,519	1,000,000
					$79,854	

3. **Reporting**

    a.   The face amount of the bonds payable is reported net of unamortized discount or premium in the balance sheet.

EXAMPLE

Pritzker reports the ending Year 1 carrying amount on its balance sheet as follows:

Bonds payable $1,069,302

Disler reports the ending Year 1 carrying amount on its balance sheet as follows:

Bonds payable $ 933,758

Stop and review! You have completed the outline for this subunit. Study multiple-choice questions 10 through 12 on page 478.

13.5 DEBT ISSUE COSTS

Background

As described below, debt issue costs must be capitalized and amortized over the life of the debt. This treatment is inconsistent with SFAC 6, *Elements of Financial Statements*. It states that debt issue costs are either an expense or a reduction of the related debt liability. They do not satisfy the definition of an asset because they do not provide a future economic benefit. However, SFAC 6 is not authoritative guidance.

1. **Costs Included**

    a.   Issue costs are incurred to bring debt to market. They include

        1) Printing and engraving costs,
        2) Legal fees,
        3) Accountants' fees,
        4) Underwriters' commissions,
        5) Registration fees, and
        6) Promotion costs.

2. **Accounting Treatment**

    a.   Under GAAP, issue costs should be reported in the balance sheet as **deferred charges** and **amortized over the life of the debt**, not combined with premium or discount.

Cash	$9,225,000	
Discount on debt payable	500,000	
Unamortized debt issue costs	275,000	
Debt payable		$10,000,000

b.   Issue costs should be amortized using the interest method, but the straight-line method may be applied if the results are not materially different.

Debt issue expense ($275,000 ÷ 10 years)	$27,500	
Unamortized debt issue costs		$27,500

Stop and review! You have completed the outline for this subunit. Study multiple-choice questions 13 through 15 on page 479.

13.6 SECURITIES WITH CHARACTERISTICS OF LIABILITIES AND EQUITY

1.   **Classification**

a.   A liability results from a current obligation to transfer assets or provide services. Equity is the residual interest in the assets of an entity after subtraction of liabilities.

b.   Common stock or preferred stock that is not redeemable is treated as equity.

1)   Each confers a residual interest in entity assets, and no obligation exists to pay dividends or redeem the stock.

c.   Bonds are treated as liabilities.

1)   They represent an obligation to make interest and principal payments, with no residual interest in entity assets.

d.   However, the classification of the securities covered in the following outline is more complex because they have liability and equity components.

2.   **Convertible Debt**

a.   Convertible debt may be exchanged for common stock of the issuer.

1)   Convertible debt is more attractive to issuers than nonconvertible debt because it is usually issued at a lower interest rate.

b.   Under GAAP, the debt and equity elements of convertible debt are treated as inseparable. The entire proceeds, typically cash, should be accounted for and reported as a liability until conversion.

1)   However, the issue price (fair value) is affected by the conversion feature.

Cash	$XXX	
Premium on bonds payable		$XXX
Bonds payable		XXX

IFRS Difference

A compound financial instrument (e.g., bonds convertible into stock) has liability and equity components. The issuer allocates to the liability component its fair value. The equity component is allocated the residual amount of the initial carrying amount of the instrument.

---

3.   **Conversion of Debt**

a.   The conversion of debt into common stock ordinarily is accounted for using the book-value method. Bonds payable and unamortized premium (discount) are eliminated, common stock and additional paid-in capital (carrying amount of bonds minus par or stated value of stock) are credited, and **no gain (loss)** is recognized.

Bonds payable	$XXX	
Unamortized premium (discount) on bonds payable	XXX	
Common stock		$XXX
Additional paid-in capital		XXX

4. **Carrying Amount**

    a.   The carrying amount of convertible debt is affected by all related accounts.

        1)   Unamortized premium or discount, unamortized issue costs, and conversion costs all affect the carrying amount.

        2)   Consequently, these items are adjustments of additional paid-in capital when the book-value method is used for the conversion.

5. **Induced Conversion**

    a.   To reduce interest costs or total debt, an issuer of convertible debt may induce conversion. This is accomplished by offering cash, additional securities, or other consideration as an incentive.

        1)   The additional consideration given is reported as an ordinary expense.

    b.   The amount equals the fair value of the consideration transferred in excess of the fair value of the securities that would have been issued under the original conversion privilege.

Bonds payable	$XXX	
Debt conversion expense	XXX	
Common stock		$XXX
Additional paid-in capital		XXX
Cash		XXX

    c.   The treatment of gains or losses from early extinguishment of convertible debt is the same as for the retirement of ordinary debt.

6. **Detachable vs. Nondetachable Warrants**

    a.   Like convertible debt, warrants allow a debtholder to obtain common shares.

        1)   Unlike convertible debt, warrants require the debtholder to pay an additional amount to receive the shares.

    b.   When warrants are **nondetachable**, their conversion feature is considered to be inseparable from the underlying debt, and the entire proceeds are attributed to debt.

    c.   When debt is issued with **detachable** warrants, the proceeds must be allocated between the underlying debt and the warrants pro rata based on their relative fair values at the time of issuance.

        1)   Allocate the proceeds pro rata to the debt.

$$Cash\ proceeds\ received \times \left(\frac{FV\ of\ debt}{FV\ of\ debt\ +\ Warrants} \right)$$

        2)   Record the issuance of the debt.

Cash (calculated above)	$XXX	
Discount on bonds payable	XXX	
Bonds payable		$XXX

        3)   Allocate the proceeds pro rata to the warrants.

$$Cash\ proceeds\ received \times \left(\frac{FV\ of\ warrants}{FV\ of\ debt\ +\ Warrants} \right)$$

        4)   Record the issuance of the warrants.

Cash (calculated above)	$XXX	
Paid-in capital -- warrants		$XXX

        5)   When the fair value of the warrants but not the debt is known, paid-in capital from warrants should be credited (increased) for the fair value of the warrants.

           a)   The remainder is credited to the debt.

d.   When the warrants are exercised, the journal entry is

Cash	$XXX	
Paid-in capital -- warrants	XXX	
Common stock		$XXX
Additional paid-in capital		XXX

EXAMPLE

On January 2, Matrix Co. issued $1,000,000 of 9% bonds for $1,040,000. Each $1,000 bond had 20 detachable warrants. Each warrant was redeemable for one share of Matrix $10 par-value stock at a price of $30. Directly after the issuance, the warrants were trading for $5 each.

The fair value of the 20,000 warrants [($1,000,000 ÷ $1,000) bonds × 20] was $100,000 (20,000 warrants × $5). Given that the fair value of the bonds is not known, the warrants are credited for $100,000. The remainder of the proceeds ($1,040,000 – $100,000 = $940,000) is assigned to the bonds.

To record the issuance of the bonds:

Cash	$940,000	
Discount on bonds payable	60,000	
Bonds payable		$1,000,000

To record the issuance of the warrants:

Cash	$100,000	
Paid-in capital -- warrants		$100,000

To record the exercise of the warrants:

Cash (20,000 × $30)	$600,000	
Paid-in capital -- warrants	100,000	
Common stock (20,000 × $10)		$200,000
Additional paid-in capital		500,000

Stop and review! You have completed the outline for this subunit. Study multiple-choice questions 16 through 18 on page 480.

13.7 EXTINGUISHMENT OF DEBT

1.   **Early Extinguishment**

    a.   Issuers sometimes retire debt before maturity, for example, to eliminate high-interest debt when rates are declining or to improve debt ratios.

    b.   All extinguishments of debt before scheduled maturities are fundamentally alike and should be accounted for similarly.

    c.   The carrying amount is the amount due at maturity, adjusted for unamortized premium or discount and unamortized issue costs.

    d.   The reacquisition price is the amount paid on extinguishment, including any call premium and miscellaneous costs of reacquisition.

        1)   An extinguishment may be done by exchanging new securities for the old (a refunding). The reacquisition price equals the total present value of the new securities.

2.   **Gains or Losses**

    a.   Gains or losses are recognized in earnings in the period of extinguishment. They are presumed to be ordinary.

        1)   The gain or loss is measured by the difference between the reacquisition price (including any call premium and miscellaneous costs of reacquisition) and the carrying amount of the debt.

EXAMPLE

Debtor has a noncurrent note payable outstanding with a face amount of $1,000,000. When Debtor decides to extinguish the note at a cost of $1,050,000, the unamortized premium and debt issue costs are $20,000 and $12,500, respectively. Accordingly, the loss on extinguishment is $42,500 [$1,050,000 cost – ($1,000,000 face amount + $20,000 unamortized premium – $12,500 unamortized issue costs)].

Noncurrent note payable	$1,000,000	
Loss on extinguishment	42,500	
Unamortized premium	20,000	
Cash		$1,050,000
Unamortized debt issue costs		12,500

---

3. **Derecognition**

   a. A debtor derecognizes a liability only if it has been extinguished. Extinguishment results only if the debtor

      1) Pays the creditor and is relieved of its obligation with respect to the liability or

      2) Is legally released from being the primary obligor, either judicially or by the creditor.

Stop and review! You have completed the outline for this subunit. Study multiple-choice questions 19 through 21 on page 481.

13.8 REFINANCING OF CURRENT OBLIGATIONS

1. **Ability to Refinance**

   a. An obligation may be reclassified from current liabilities to noncurrent when an entity

      1) **Intends to refinance** it on a noncurrent basis and
      2) Demonstrates an ability to consummate the refinancing.

   b. The **ability to consummate** the refinancing may be demonstrated by a post-balance-sheet-date issuance of a noncurrent obligation or equity securities prior to the issuance of the balance sheet.

      1) It also may be demonstrated by a financing agreement prior to the issuance of the balance sheet that meets the following criteria:

         a) The agreement does not expire within the longer of 1 year or the operating cycle.

         b) It is noncancelable by the lender.

         c) No violation of the agreement exists at the balance sheet date.

         d) The lender is financially capable of honoring the agreement.

2. **Balance Sheet Classification**

   a. The amount excluded from current liabilities must not exceed the proceeds from the new obligation or equity securities issued.

      1) The amount excluded may be further reduced by the amount of proceeds not expected to be available for refinancing.

   b. Sometimes a current liability is repaid after year end and refinanced by noncurrent debt before the balance sheet is issued.

      1) Because this retirement requires the use of current assets, the liability must be classified as current in the balance sheet.

    c.   Noncurrent obligations that are callable by the creditor because of the debtor's violation of the debt agreement at the balance sheet date are classified as current liabilities.

    d.   Notes to the financial statements should include a general description of the financing agreement and the terms of any new obligation incurred or securities issued.

Stop and review! You have completed the outline for this subunit. Study multiple-choice questions 22 through 24 on page 482.

13.9 NONCURRENT NOTES PAYABLE

1.   Notes payable are essentially the same as bonds. However,

    a.   A note is payable to a single creditor, while bonds are payable to many creditors.
    b.   Notes are usually of shorter duration than bonds.

2.   Noncurrent notes that are payable in installments are classified as current to the extent of any payments due in the coming year.

    a.   Payments not due in the current year are classified as noncurrent.

3.   Any material premium or discount is amortized using the effective-interest method, as described in Subunit 13.4.

EXAMPLE

An entity agrees to give, in return for merchandise, a 3-year, $100,000 note bearing 8% interest paid annually. The effective interest rate is 6%. Because the note's stated rate exceeds the effective rate, the note will be issued at a premium.

The entity records the note at the present value of (1) a single payment of $100,000 in 3 years and (2) three interest payments of $8,000 each. These payments are discounted at the effective rate (five decimal places are used for increased accuracy).

Present value of principal ($100,000 × 0.83962)	$ 83,962
Present value of interest ($8,000 × 2.67301)	21,384
Present value of note	$105,346

The entry to record the note is

Inventory	$105,346	
Premium on note payable		$ 5,346
Note payable		100,000

---

4.   **Discount or Premium**

    a.   Discount or premium, loan origination fees, etc., are amortized in accordance with the effective-interest method.

        1)   The result is periodic interest expense that reflects a constant rate when applied to the beginning balance.

    b.   Discount or premium is not an asset or liability separable from the related note.

        1)   A discount or premium is therefore reported in the balance sheet as a direct subtraction from, or addition to, the face amount of the note.

Stop and review! You have completed the outline for this subunit. Study multiple-choice questions 25 through 27 on page 483.

13.10 TROUBLED DEBT RESTRUCTURINGS

1.   **Overview**

   a.   A troubled debt restructuring (TDR) occurs when "the creditor for economic or legal reasons related to the debtor's financial difficulties grants a concession to the debtor that it would not otherwise consider."

   b.   A TDR can consist of either a settlement of the debt in full or a continuation of the debt with a modification in terms. TDRs almost always involve a loss to the creditor and a gain to the debtor.

2.   **Settlement in Full with a Transfer of Assets**

   a.   The **creditor recognizes a loss** equal to the difference between the fair value of the assets received and the carrying amount of the receivable.

      1)   Thus, if the allowance method is used for recording bad debts, the loss is net of the previously recognized bad debt expense related to the debt.

EXAMPLE

Debtor gave a mortgage on its building to Creditor. The principal amount of Creditor's mortgage receivable is $5,000,000 (the recorded investment), and it has credited the related allowance for uncollectible accounts for $200,000. Thus, the carrying amount of the receivable is $4,800,000. Assume (for computational simplicity) that the carrying amount of Debtor's mortgage is $5,000,000. The building's fair value is $4,500,000, and its carrying amount on Debtor's balance sheet is $6,000,000. Debtor transfers the building to Creditor in full settlement of the debt.

Creditor's entry:

Building (fair value)	$4,500,000	
Loss on receivable (difference)	300,000	
Allowance for uncollectible accounts (related amount)	200,000	
Mortgage receivable (principal)		$5,000,000

---

      2)   If the creditor receives long-lived assets to be sold in full satisfaction, the assets are recorded at fair value minus cost to sell.

   b.   The **debtor recognizes a gain** when the carrying amount of the debt exceeds the fair value of the asset(s) given.

EXAMPLE

Debtor also recognizes a **gain (loss)** equal to the difference between the fair value of the assets given and their carrying amount.

Debtor's entry:

Mortgage payable (carrying amount)	$5,000,000	
Loss on disposition of building (carrying amount – fair value)	1,500,000	
Building (carrying amount)		$6,000,000
Gain on restructuring (debt settled – fair value of building)		500,000

---

   c.   The creditor's total loss (bad debt expense previously recognized + current loss) equals the debtor's gain on restructuring.

3.   **Settlement in Full with a Transfer of an Equity Interest**

   a.   The creditor again recognizes a current loss equal to the difference between the assets received and the carrying amount of the receivable.

      1)   The **debtor** recognizes a **gain** only on the restructuring.

EXAMPLE

In the previous example, assume that Creditor receives Debtor common stock (100,000 shares at $10 par) with a fair value of $4,800,000. Because the fair value received ($4,800,000) equals the carrying amount ($5,000,000 – $200,000 allowance), Creditor recognizes no current loss.

<u>Creditor's entry:</u>

Investment in debtor (fair value)	$4,800,000	
Allowance for uncollectible accounts (related amount)	200,000	
Mortgage receivable (principal)		$5,000,000

<u>Debtor's entry:</u>

Mortgage payable (carrying amount)	$5,000,000	
Common stock (100,000 shares at $10 par)		$1,000,000
Additional paid-in capital (fair value of stock – total par value)		3,800,000
Gain on restructuring (debt settled – fair value of stock)		200,000

---

    2) As in the previous case, the creditor's total loss equals the debtor's gain on restructuring.

4. **Modification of Terms When Future Cash Flows Exceed the Carrying Amount**

    a. Three changes in the terms of the loan are common:

        1) A reduction in the principal
        2) An extension of the maturity date
        3) A lowering of the interest rate

    b. The debtor will recognize a gain if the total of the cash flows associated with the modified terms is less than the carrying amount of the troubled debt.

        1) The recording of this event **does not consider the time value of money**.

    c. When a TDR involves a modification of terms and the undiscounted total future cash flows (UCF) that the debtor has committed to pay are greater than the carrying amount of the debt, the debtor recognizes no gain.

EXAMPLE

Instead of a full settlement as illustrated in the example above, Creditor agrees that (1) the mortgage principal will be reduced from $5,000,000 to $4,000,000, (2) the final maturity will be extended from 1 year to 5 years, and (3) the interest rate will be reduced from 8% to 6%. Interest continues to be paid at year end.

The new principal of $4,000,000 plus interest of $1,200,000 ($4,000,000 × 6% × 5 years) yields a UCF of $5,200,000. Because the UCF exceeds the carrying amount of the debt ($5,200,000 > $5,000,000), Debtor recognizes no gain. It continues making journal entries to record periodic interest payments and retirement of debt.

---

    d. The creditor must recognize the impairment of a loan when it is probable that the debtor will not be able to pay all the amounts (principal and interest) due in accordance with the original terms of the loan.

        1) The total impairment recognized is based on the recorded investment in the loan, not the carrying amount.

        2) In this circumstance, the current impairment loss is the difference between

            a) The discounted expected cash flows (DCF) reflecting an effective rate based on the original contractual rate and

            b) The carrying amount of the receivable.

EXAMPLE

The present value of the new principal, discounted at 8% for 5 years, is $2,722,320 ($4,000,000 × .68058). The present value of the new annual interest payments, discounted at 8% for 5 years, is $958,250 ($4,000,000 × 6% × 3.99271).

Mortgage receivable (principal)	$5,000,000
Minus: discounted principal	(2,722,320)
Minus: discounted interest payments	(958,250)
Total impairment of receivable	$1,319,430

Given an existing credit in the allowance account of $200,000, Creditor records the current impairment loss as follows:

Bad debt expense ($1,319,430 – $200,000)	$1,119,430	
Allowance for uncollectible accounts		$1,119,430

---

3) Because the creditor uses the time value of money in this calculation, its impairment loss does not equal the debtor's gain (the debtor can have no gain).

4) An alternative measure of impairment is the loan's observable market price or the fair value of the collateral if the loan is collateral dependent.

   a) If foreclosure is probable, impairment is based on the fair value of the collateral.

5. **Modification of Terms when Future Cash Flows Are Less than the Carrying Amount**

   a. When a TDR involves a modification of terms and the UCF are less than the carrying amount of the debt, the debtor recognizes a gain.

EXAMPLE

Instead of reducing the principal to $4,000,000, Creditor agrees to reduce the principal to $3,000,000. The principal of $3,000,000 plus interest of $900,000 ($3,000,000 × 6% × 5 years) yields UCF of $3,900,000.

Because the UCF are less than the carrying amount of the debt ($3,900,000 < $5,000,000), Debtor recognizes a gain equal to the difference.

Debtor's entry:

Mortgage payable	$1,100,000	
Gain on restructuring		$1,100,000

---

b. In the second version of the revised example, the creditor's current impairment loss is the difference between the DCF and the carrying amount of the receivable.

EXAMPLE

The present value of the principal, discounted at 8% for 5 years, is $2,041,740 ($3,000,000 × .68058). The present value of the new annual interest payments, discounted at 8% for 5 years, is $718,688 ($3,000,000 × 6% × 3.99271).

Mortgage receivable (carrying amount)	$5,000,000
Minus: discounted principal	(2,041,740)
Minus: discounted interest payments	(718,688)
Total impairment of receivable	$2,239,572

Given an existing credit in the allowance account of $200,000, Creditor records the current impairment loss as follows:

Creditor's entry:

Bad debt expense ($2,239,572 – $200,000)	$2,039,572	
Allowance for uncollectible accounts		$2,039,572

---

c. The creditor's impairment loss does not equal the debtor's gain (if any).

d. GAAP for accounting by creditors for impairment of a loan do not address the issues of recognition, measurement, or display of interest income derived from an impaired loan.

e. Costs of debt restructuring are expensed as incurred, except by debtors issuing equity securities (restructuring expenses reduce paid-in capital from these securities).

IFRS Difference

Derecognition of a financial liability (or a part) occurs only by extinguishment. This condition is satisfied only when the debtor pays the creditor or is legally released from primary responsibility either by the creditor or through the legal process.

- An extinguishment of the old debt and recognition of new debt occurs when the borrower and lender exchange debt instruments with substantially different terms.

- A substantial modification of terms of any part of an existing financial liability must be accounted for as an extinguishment of the original financial liability and recognition of a new one.

- The difference between the carrying amount of a liability (or a part) that has been extinguished or transferred and the amount paid is included in profit or loss.

Stop and review! You have completed the outline for this subunit. Study multiple-choice questions 28 through 30 on page 484.

13.11 ASSET RETIREMENT OBLIGATIONS

1. **Overview**

   a. Certain long-lived tangible assets, such as mines or nuclear power plants, incur significant costs after the end of their productive lives.

   b. An asset retirement obligation (ARO) reflects a legal obligation arising from acquisition, construction, development, or normal operation of an asset.

      1) A legal obligation is one arising from an existing or enacted law, statute, ordinance, or contract.

2. **Accounting Treatment**

   a. The ARO is recognized at **fair value** when incurred if it can be reasonably estimated.

      1) An expected present value technique ordinarily should be used to estimate the fair value of an ARO.

         a) A credit-adjusted risk-free (CARF) rate is the appropriate discount rate.

      2) The liability is adjusted periodically for the passage of time and revisions in the original estimates.

   b. When the ARO is initially recognized, the debit is to the related long-lived tangible asset.

      1) This debit is termed the asset retirement cost (ARC). It must be expensed systematically and rationally over the asset's useful life.

   c. An ARO may be conditional, e.g., because a governmental unit has the right to decide in the future whether to require an asset retirement activity.

      1) Nevertheless, the entity has a legal obligation to be ready to perform.

EXAMPLE

A mining entity is required by law to restore land used in its operations. The entity estimates that a new mine will be productive for 12 years. The adjusted expected cash flows for reclamation costs equal $4,000,000. The entity's CARF rate is 8%. The expected present value of the reclamation costs, discounted at 8% for 12 years, is $1,588,455 ($4,000,000 × .3971138).

The ARC is added to the carrying amount of the long-lived asset, and the ARO is credited.

Mine	$1,588,455	
Asset retirement obligation		$1,588,455

The entity expenses this initial ARC over the life of the mine using the straight-line method.

Depreciation expense ($1,588,455 ÷ 12)	$132,371	
Accumulated depreciation		$132,371

The entity amortizes the difference between the maturity amount and the carrying amount of the ARO by annual recognition of accretion expense.

Year	Beginning Net Carrying Amount	Times: Discount Rate	Equals: Dr Accretion Expense, Cr ARO	Ending Net Carrying Amount
1	$1,588,455	8%	$127,076	$1,715,531
2	1,715,531	8%	137,243	1,852,774
3	1,852,774	8%	148,222	2,000,996
4	2,000,996	8%	160,080	2,161,075
5	2,161,075	8%	172,886	2,333,962
6	2,333,962	8%	186,717	2,520,678
7	2,520,678	8%	201,652	2,722,333
8	2,722,333	8%	217,787	2,940,119
9	2,940,119	8%	235,210	3,175,329
10	3,175,329	8%	254,026	3,429,355
11	3,429,355	8%	274,348	3,703,704
12	3,703,704	8%	296,296	4,000,000

The first-year journal entry is

Accretion expense	$127,076	
Asset retirement obligation		$127,076

At the end of the mine's service life, the entity may incur costs to reclaim the land exceeding the initial estimate. The journal entry is

Asset retirement obligation	$4,000,000	
Loss on settlement of ARO	125,000	
Cash		$4,125,000

Stop and review! You have completed the outline for this subunit. Study multiple-choice questions 31 through 33 on page 485.

13.12 COSTS ASSOCIATED WITH EXIT OR DISPOSAL ACTIVITIES

1. **Overview**

    a. A **liability** for exit or disposal costs is ordinarily recognized and measured at **fair value** when the liability is incurred.

        1) The liability is incurred when a present obligation to others exists.

            a) A present obligation exists when the entity has little discretion to avoid a future transfer of assets in settlement.

            b) The commitment to an exit or disposal plan does not, by itself, create the required present obligation.

b.   An exit activity includes an activity involving any entity recently acquired through a business combination.

   1)   Among the activities included in the definition are restructurings, which are programs planned and controlled by management that materially alter either the scope of the business or how it is conducted.

c.   Costs subject to the guidance in this subunit include

   1)   Certain one-time termination benefits;
   2)   Contract termination costs other than those for a capital lease; and
   3)   Other costs, such as facilities consolidation and employee relocation costs.

d.   Changes in the liability are recorded using the CARF rate on which the initial measurement was based.

2.   **One-Time Termination Benefits**

a.   One-time termination benefits are paid under a one-time benefit arrangement based on a plan of termination for a specified termination event or future period.

   1)   The arrangement exists when the plan has been communicated to employees and certain other requirements are met.

b.   Timing of recognition and the fair value (FV) measurement of the liability depend on whether employees must provide services until terminated.

   1)   If so, a second issue is whether employees will be retained beyond a minimum retention period (MRP), which cannot exceed 60 days.

   a)   No required service to termination or no retention beyond MRP

   i)   Recognition: On communication date (CD)
   ii)   Measurement: At FV on the CD

   b)   Required service to termination and retention beyond MRP

   i)   Recognition: Proportionately over the future service period
   ii)   Measurement: On CD at FV on termination date

3.   **Contract Termination Costs**

a.   Such costs (other than those for a capital lease) are of two types:

   1)   Costs to terminate prior to completion of the contract's term and
   2)   Contract costs that will continue to be incurred without economic benefit (continuing costs).

   a)   If the contract is an operating lease, the fair value of the liability at the date use ends must be determined based on the remaining lease rentals. This amount is reduced by estimated sublease rentals that could be reasonably obtained even if the entity does not intend to sublease the property.

   i)   The remaining lease rentals must not be reduced below zero.

4.   **Reporting**

a.   Costs covered by exit or disposal activities are included in income from continuing operations (before income taxes for a business entity).

   1)   If these costs involve a discontinued operation, they are included in the results of discontinued operations.

Stop and review! You have completed the outline for this subunit. Study multiple-choice questions 34 through 36 beginning on page 486.

QUESTIONS

13.1 Types of Bond Liabilities

1. Bonds payable issued with scheduled maturities at various dates are called

	Serial Bonds	Term Bonds
A.	No	Yes
B.	No	No
C.	Yes	No
D.	Yes	Yes

Answer (C) is correct.
  REQUIRED: The name(s) for bonds issued with scheduled maturities at various dates.
  DISCUSSION: Serial bonds are bond issues that mature in installments at various dates. Term bonds mature on a single date.

2. Hancock Co.'s December 31, Year 4, balance sheet contained the following items in the long-term liabilities section:

Unsecured
9.375% registered bonds ($25,000
  maturing annually beginning in Year 8) $275,000
11.5% convertible bonds, callable
  beginning in Year 13, due Year 24   125,000

Secured
9.875% guaranty security bonds, due
  Year 24 $250,000
10.0% commodity backed bonds ($50,000
  maturing annually beginning in Year 8)   200,000

What are the total amounts of serial bonds and debenture bonds?

	Serial Bonds	Debenture Bonds
A.	$475,000	$400,000
B.	$475,000	$125,000
C.	$450,000	$400,000
D.	$200,000	$650,000

Answer (A) is correct.
  REQUIRED: The total amounts of serial bonds and debenture bonds.
  DISCUSSION: Serial bonds mature in installments at various dates. Debentures are unsecured bonds. The commodity-backed bonds and the registered bonds are serial bonds. They total $475,000 ($275,000 + $200,000). The registered bonds and the convertible bonds are debentures. They total $400,000 ($275,000 + $125,000).
  Answer (B) is incorrect. The registered bonds are also debentures. Answer (C) is incorrect. The registered bonds, not the guaranty security bonds, are serial bonds. Answer (D) is incorrect. The registered bonds are serial bonds, and the guaranty security bonds are not debentures.

3. Blue Corp.'s December 31, Year 4, balance sheet contained the following items in the long-term liabilities section:

9.75% registered debentures, callable in
  Year 15, due in Year 20 $700,000
9.50% collateral trust bonds, convertible
  into common stock beginning in Year 13,
  due in Year 23   600,000
10% subordinated debentures ($30,000
  maturing annually beginning in Year 10)   300,000

What is the total amount of Blue's term bonds?

A. $600,000

B. $700,000

C. $1,000,000

D. $1,300,000

Answer (D) is correct.
  REQUIRED: The total amount of term bonds.
  DISCUSSION: Term bonds mature on a single date. Hence, the registered bonds and the collateral trust bonds are term bonds, a total of $1,300,000 ($700,000 + $600,000).
  Answer (A) is incorrect. The registered bonds are also term bonds. Answer (B) is incorrect. The collateral trust bonds are also term bonds. Answer (C) is incorrect. The collateral trust bonds, not the subordinated debentures, are term bonds.

13.2 Time Value of Money

4. On December 30, Chang Co. sold a machine to Door Co. in exchange for a noninterest-bearing note requiring 10 annual payments of $10,000. Door made the first payment on December 30. The market interest rate for similar notes at date of issuance was 8%. Information on present value factors is as follows:

Number of Periods	Present Value of $1 at 8%	Present Value of Ordinary Annuity of $1 at 8%
9	0.50	6.25
10	0.46	6.71

In its December 31 balance sheet, what amount should Chang report as note receivable?

A. $45,000

B. $46,000

C. $62,500

D. $67,100

Answer (C) is correct.
REQUIRED: The carrying amount of a noninterest-bearing note receivable at the date of issuance.
DISCUSSION: The purchase agreement calls for a $10,000 initial payment and equal payments of $10,000 to be received at the end of each of the next 9 years. The amount reported for the receivable should consist of the present value of the nine future payments. The present value factor to be used is the present value of an ordinary annuity for nine periods at 8%, or 6.25. The note receivable should be recorded at $62,500 ($10,000 × 6.25).
Answer (A) is incorrect. The amount of $45,000 results from multiplying $90,000 ($10,000 payments × 9 years) by 0.50. Answer (B) is incorrect. The amount of $46,000 results from multiplying the $100,000 total by 0.46. Answer (D) is incorrect. The amount of $67,100 results from using the present value of an ordinary annuity of $1 at 8% for 10 years instead of 9 years.

5. On September 1, Year 1, an entity purchased a new machine that it does not have to pay for until September 1, Year 3. The total payment on September 1, Year 3, will include both principal and interest. Assuming interest at a 10% rate, the cost of the machine will be the total payment multiplied by what time value of money factor?

A. Present value of annuity of $1.

B. Present value of $1.

C. Future amount of annuity of $1.

D. Future amount of $1.

Answer (B) is correct.
REQUIRED: The time value of money factor to compute current cost when payment is to be made in a lump sum at a future date.
DISCUSSION: The cost of the machine on 9/1/Year 1 is the present value of the payment to be made on 9/1/Year 3. To obtain the present value, i.e., today's price, the future payment is multiplied by the present value of $1 for two periods at 10%.
Answer (A) is incorrect. The present value of an annuity is the value today of a series of future payments, not merely one payment. Answer (C) is incorrect. The future value of an annuity is the amount available at a specified time in the future after a series of deposits (investments). Answer (D) is incorrect. The future value of a dollar is the amount that will be available at a specified time in the future based on a single investment (deposit) today.

6. For which of the following transactions would the use of the present value of an annuity due concept be appropriate in calculating the present value of the asset obtained or liability owed at the date of incurrence?

A. A capital lease is entered into with the initial lease payment due 1 month subsequent to the signing of the lease agreement.

B. A capital lease is entered into with the initial lease payment due upon the signing of the lease agreement.

C. A 10-year, 8% bond is issued on January 2 with interest payable semiannually on July 1 and January 1, yielding 7%.

D. A 10-year, 8% bond is issued on January 2 with interest payable semiannually on July 1 and January 1, yielding 9%.

Answer (B) is correct.
REQUIRED: The transaction for which the present value of an annuity due concept would be appropriate.
DISCUSSION: In an annuity due, the first payment is made at the beginning of the first period and is therefore not discounted. In an ordinary annuity, the first payment is made at the end of the first period and therefore is discounted. For annuities due, the first payment is included in the computation at its face value.
Answer (A) is incorrect. Given that the first payment is due 1 month from signing and not on the day of signing, an ordinary annuity, not an annuity due, is the relevant model. Answer (C) is incorrect. The bonds have just passed an interest payment (coupon) date. The next one is not for another 6 months. Given no immediate payment, the annuity is ordinary. Furthermore, the yield percentage is irrelevant to annuity. Answer (D) is incorrect. The initial payment is not due immediately.

13.3 Bonds Payable -- Initial Measurement

7. The market price of a bond issued at a discount is the present value of its principal amount at the market (effective) rate of interest

   A. Less the present value of all future interest payments at the market (effective) rate of interest.

   B. Less the present value of all future interest payments at the rate of interest stated on the bond.

   C. Plus the present value of all future interest payments at the market (effective) rate of interest.

   D. Plus the present value of all future interest payments at the rate of interest stated on the bond.

Answer (C) is correct.
   REQUIRED: The market price of a bond issued at a discount.
   DISCUSSION: The market price of a bond is the sum of the present value of the amount due at the end of the bond's term (its face amount) plus the present value of the periodic interest payments, both discounted at the prevailing market rate.

8. The following information pertains to Camp Corp.'s issuance of bonds on July 1, Year 4:

Face amount	$800,000
Term	10 years
Stated interest rate	6%
Interest payment dates	Annually on July 1
Yield	9%

	At 6%	At 9%
Present value of 1 for 10 periods	0.558	0.422
Future value of 1 for 10 periods	1.791	2.367
Present value of ordinary annuity of 1 for 10 periods	7.360	6.418

What should the issue price be for each $1,000 bond?

   A. $1,000

   B. $943

   C. $864

   D. $807

Answer (D) is correct.
   REQUIRED: The issue price for each bond.
   DISCUSSION: The issue price of a bond equals the sum of the present values of the future cash flows (principal + interest). This amount is $807 [($1,000 face amount × .422 PV of 1 for 10 periods at 9%) principal + ($1,000 face amount × 6% stated rate × 6.418 PV of an ordinary annuity for 10 periods at 9%) interest].
   Answer (A) is incorrect. The face amount is $1,000. Answer (B) is incorrect. The amount of $943 is the result of discounting the interest payments at 9% and the face amount at 6%. Answer (C) is incorrect. The amount of $864 is the result of discounting the interest payments at 6% and the face amount at 9%.

9. On January 31, Year 4, Beau Corp. issued $300,000 maturity value, 12% bonds for $300,000 cash. The bonds are dated December 31, Year 3, and mature on December 31, Year 13. Interest will be paid semiannually on June 30 and December 31. What amount of accrued interest payable should Beau report in its September 30, Year 4, balance sheet?

   A. $27,000

   B. $24,000

   C. $18,000

   D. $9,000

Answer (D) is correct.
   REQUIRED: The amount of accrued interest payable that should be reported in the balance sheet.
   DISCUSSION: Because interest is paid semiannually on June 30 and December 31, the amount of each payment is $18,000 [($300,000 face amount × 12% stated rate) × (6 ÷ 12)]. On June 30, $18,000 was paid (because the bonds were issued at par, periodic interest expense consists entirely of the cash interest payment). From July 1 to September 30, Year 4 (3 months), interest accrued for the December 31, Year 4, payment. Thus, $9,000 [$18,000 × (3 ÷ 6)] of accrued interest payable should be reported.
   Answer (A) is incorrect. The amount of $27,000 includes the $18,000 already paid on June 30. Answer (B) is incorrect. The amount of $24,000 includes the $18,000 already paid on June 30 and erroneously records $6,000, which is the accrued interest for 2 months. Answer (C) is incorrect. This figure is the amount of the semiannual interest payable.

13.4 Bonds Payable -- Subsequent Measurement

10. How is the carrying amount of a bond payable affected by amortization of the following?

	Discount	Premium
A.	Increase	Increase
B.	Decrease	Decrease
C.	Increase	Decrease
D.	Decrease	Increase

11. On January 1, Year 2, Oak Co. issued 400 of its 8%, $1,000 bonds at 97 plus accrued interest. The bonds are dated October 1, Year 1, and mature on October 1, Year 11. Interest is payable semiannually on April 1 and October 1. Accrued interest for the period October 1, Year 1, to January 1, Year 2, amounted to $8,000. On January 1, Year 2, what amount should Oak report as bonds payable, net of discount?

A. $380,300

B. $388,000

C. $388,300

D. $392,000

12. On December 31, Year 1, Arnold, Inc., issued $200,000, 8% serial bonds, to be repaid in the amount of $40,000 each year. Interest is payable annually on December 31. The bonds were issued to yield 10% per year. The bond proceeds were $190,280 based on the present values at December 31, Year 1, of the five annual payments:

Due Date	Amounts Due Principal	Interest	Present Value at 12/31/Yr 1
12/31/Yr 2	$40,000	$16,000	$ 50,900
12/31/Yr 3	40,000	12,800	43,610
12/31/Yr 4	40,000	9,600	37,250
12/31/Yr 5	40,000	6,400	31,690
12/31/Yr 6	40,000	3,200	26,830
			$190,280

Arnold amortizes the bond discount by the interest method. In its December 31, Year 2, balance sheet, at what amount should Arnold report the carrying amount of the bonds?

A. $139,380

B. $149,100

C. $150,280

D. $153,308

Answer (C) is correct.
REQUIRED: The effect of discount and premium amortization on the carrying value of a bond payable.
DISCUSSION: The carrying amount of a bond payable is equal to its maturity (face) amount plus any unamortized premium or minus any unamortized discount. Amortization results in a reduction of the discount or premium. Consequently, the carrying amount of a bond is increased when discount is amortized and decreased when premium is amortized.

Answer (B) is correct.
REQUIRED: The bonds payable, net of discount.
DISCUSSION: A bond issued "at 97" is issued at a price equal to 97% of its face amount (400 bonds × $1,000 face amount × .97 = $388,000). At the issue date, no time has passed, so no amortization has occurred, and the accrued interest is credited to either interest payable or interest expense. The reported amount is therefore $388,000 ($400,000 – $12,000).
Answer (A) is incorrect. The amount of $380,300 deducts the accrued interest from the net bonds payable and adds 3 months of discount amortization. Answer (C) is incorrect. The amount of $388,300 includes 3 months of discount amortization. Answer (D) is incorrect. The amount of $392,000 equals face amount minus accrued interest.

Answer (D) is correct.
REQUIRED: The carrying amount after year one of bonds issued at a discount.
DISCUSSION: The carrying amount of the bonds at the end of Year 1 equals the proceeds of $190,280. Interest expense for Year 2 at the 10% effective rate is thus $19,028. Actual interest paid is $16,000, discount amortization is $3,028 ($19,028 – $16,000), and the discount remaining at year end is $6,692 [($200,000 face amount – $190,280 issue proceeds) – $3,028 discount amortization]. Given that $40,000 in principal is paid at year end, the December 31, Year 2, carrying amount is $153,308 ($160,000 face amount – $6,692 unamortized discount).
Answer (A) is incorrect. The amount of $139,380 is the carrying amount of the bonds at December 31, Year 2, less the total amount due in Year 3. Answer (B) is incorrect. The amount of $149,100 is the difference between the face amount of the bonds and the total payment in Year 3. Answer (C) is incorrect. The amount of $150,280 results from reducing the carrying amount at December 31, Year 2, by the payment of principal during Year 3.

13.5 Debt Issue Costs

13. On June 30, Year 4, Huff Corp. issued 1,000 of its 8%, $1,000 bonds at 99. The bonds were issued through an underwriter to whom Huff paid bond issue costs of $35,000. On June 30, Year 4, Huff should report the bond liability at

A. $955,000

B. $990,000

C. $1,000,000

D. $1,025,000

Answer (B) is correct.
  REQUIRED: The amount of the bond liability at the issue date.
  DISCUSSION: A bond issued "at 99" is issued at a price equal to 99% of its face amount (1,000 bonds × $1,000 face amount × .99 = $990,000). Debt issue costs are capitalized and amortized separately.
  Answer (A) is incorrect. The amount of $955,000 equals the net proceeds (assuming no accrued interest was received). Answer (C) is incorrect. The amount of $1,000,000 is the face amount. Answer (D) is incorrect. The amount of $1,025,000 is the sum of the net liability and the issue costs.

14. During Year 4, Eddy Corp. incurred the following costs in connection with the issuance of bonds:

Printing and engraving	$ 30,000
Legal fees	160,000
Fees paid to independent accountants for registration information	20,000
Commissions paid to underwriter	300,000

What amount should be recorded as a deferred charge to be amortized over the term of the bonds?

A. $510,000

B. $480,000

C. $300,000

D. $210,000

Answer (A) is correct.
  REQUIRED: The amount to be recorded as a deferred charge.
  DISCUSSION: Issue costs should be reported in the balance sheet as deferred charges to be amortized over the life of the bonds. They should not be combined with bond premium or discount. Issue costs are incurred to bring a bond to market. They include (1) lawyers', accountants', and underwriters' fees; (2) engraving and printing costs; (3) registration costs; and (4) promotion costs. In this case, they include the $30,000 of printing and engraving costs, the $160,000 of legal fees, the $20,000 of accountants' fees, and the $300,000 of underwriter's commissions. Hence, the amount that should be recorded as a deferred charge to be amortized over the term of the bonds is equal to $510,000.
  Answer (B) is incorrect. The amount of $480,000 omits the printing and engraving costs. Answer (C) is incorrect. The amount of $300,000 includes the commissions only. Answer (D) is incorrect. The amount of $210,000 excludes the commissions.

15. On January 2, Year 3, Gill Co. issued $2 million of 10-year, 8% bonds at par. The bonds, dated January 1, Year 3, pay interest semiannually on January 1 and July 1. Bond issue costs were $250,000. What amount of bond issue costs are unamortized at June 30, Year 4?

A. $237,500

B. $225,000

C. $220,800

D. $212,500

Answer (D) is correct.
  REQUIRED: The amount to be recorded as unamortized bond issue costs.
  DISCUSSION: Bond issue costs are customarily amortized using the straight-line method over the term of the bonds. The amortization is $25,000 per year ($250,000 ÷ 10 years). Because the bond has been held for 18 months, $37,500 ($25,000 + $12,500) of issue costs have been amortized by June 30, Year 4. The unamortized issue costs are $212,500 ($250,000 – $37,500).
  Answer (A) is incorrect. An additional full year of amortization should have been claimed. Answer (B) is incorrect. Six more months of issue costs should have been amortized for the time between January 1 and June 30, Year 4. Answer (C) is incorrect. The amount of $220,800 results from amortization using the interest method. Although the interest method is theoretically superior, issue costs are customarily amortized using the straight-line method.

13.6 Securities with Characteristics of Liabilities and Equity

16. Which of the following statements characterizes convertible debt?

A. The holder of the debt must be repaid with shares of the issuer's stock.

B. No value is assigned to the conversion feature when convertible debt is issued.

C. The transaction should be recorded as the issuance of stock.

D. The issuer's stock price is **less** than market value when the debt is converted.

Answer (B) is correct.
    REQUIRED: The characteristic of convertible debt.
    DISCUSSION: The debt and equity elements of convertible debt are inseparable. The entire proceeds should be accounted for as debt until conversion.
    Answer (A) is incorrect. The holder of the debt has an option to receive (1) the face or redemption amount of the security or (2) common shares. Answer (C) is incorrect. The entire proceeds should be accounted for as debt until conversion. Answer (D) is incorrect. Conversion is favorable to the holder when the market value of the issuer's common stock is greater than the conversion price. (The conversion price exceeds market value upon initial issuance.)

17. On March 31, Year 4, Ashley, Inc.'s bondholders exchanged their convertible bonds for common stock. The carrying amount of these bonds on Ashley's books was less than the market value but greater than the par value of the common stock issued. If Ashley used the book-value method of accounting for the conversion, which of the following statements accurately states an effect of this conversion?

A. Equity is increased.

B. Additional paid-in capital is decreased.

C. Retained earnings is increased.

D. An extraordinary loss is recognized.

Answer (A) is correct.
    REQUIRED: The effect of converting bonds to common stock when using the book-value method.
    DISCUSSION: Under the book-value method for recognizing the conversion of outstanding bonds payable to common stock, the stock issued is recorded at the carrying amount of the bonds with no recognition of gain or loss. Because the carrying amount of the bonds is greater than the par value of the common stock, the conversion will record common stock at par value and additional paid-in capital for the remainder of the carrying amount of the bonds. Ashley will decrease its liabilities (debit bonds payable) and increase its equity (credit common stock and additional paid-in capital).
    Answer (B) is incorrect. Additional paid-in capital will increase. Answer (C) is incorrect. Retained earnings is not directly affected. Answer (D) is incorrect. No loss is associated with the conversion.

18. On December 30, Year 4, Fort, Inc., issued 1,000 of its 8%, 10-year, $1,000 face value bonds with detachable stock warrants at par. Each bond carried a detachable warrant for one share of Fort's common stock at a specified option price of $25 per share. Immediately after issuance, the market value of the bonds without the warrants was $1,080,000, and the market value of the warrants was $120,000. In its December 31, Year 4, balance sheet, what amount should Fort report as bonds payable?

A. $1,000,000

B. $975,000

C. $900,000

D. $880,000

Answer (C) is correct.
    REQUIRED: The amount reported for bonds payable with detachable stock warrants.
    DISCUSSION: The issue price of the bonds is allocated between the bonds and the detachable stock warrants based on their relative fair values. The market price of bonds without the warrants is $1,080,000, which is 90% [$1,080,000 ÷ ($1,080,000 + $120,000)] of the total fair value. Consequently, 90% of the issue price should be allocated to the bonds, and they should be reported at $900,000 ($1,000,000 × 90%) in the balance sheet.
    Answer (A) is incorrect. The total proceeds equals $1,000,000. Answer (B) is incorrect. The amount of $975,000 is the result of deducting the option price of the stock from the issue price. Answer (D) is incorrect. The amount of $880,000 is the result of deducting the fair value of the warrants from the issue price.

13.7 Extinguishment of Debt

19. On March 1, Year 1, Somar Co. issued 20-year bonds at a discount. By September 1, Year 6, the bonds were quoted at 106 when Somar exercised its right to retire the bonds at 105. How should Somar report the bond retirement on its Year 6 income statement?

    A. A gain in continuing operations.

    B. A loss in continuing operations.

    C. An extraordinary gain.

    D. An extraordinary loss.

Answer (B) is correct.
    REQUIRED: The proper accounting for the retirement of a bond.
    DISCUSSION: All extinguishments of debt before scheduled maturities are fundamentally alike and should be accounted for similarly. Gains or losses from early extinguishment should be recognized in income of the period of extinguishment. Because the bonds were issued at a discount and were retired early for more than the carrying amount, a loss was incurred. An event or transaction is perceived to be ordinary and usual absent clear evidence to the contrary. No such evidence is presented, and Somar should recognize an ordinary loss.
    Answer (A) is incorrect. The amount paid exceeded the carrying amount. Thus, an ordinary loss is recognized. Answer (C) is incorrect. The bond retirement resulted in a loss that, absent contrary evidence, should be classified as ordinary. Answer (D) is incorrect. The loss is presumptively ordinary absent contrary evidence.

20. A 15-year bond was issued in Year 1 at a discount. During Year 10, a 10-year bond was issued at face amount with the proceeds used to retire the 15-year bond at its face amount. The net effect of the Year 10 bond transactions was to increase long-term liabilities by the excess of the 10-year bond's face amount over the 15-year bond's

    A. Face amount.

    B. Carrying amount.

    C. Face amount minus the deferred loss on bond retirement.

    D. Carrying amount minus the deferred loss on bond retirement.

Answer (B) is correct.
    REQUIRED: The net effect of the bond transactions.
    DISCUSSION: The 10-year bond was issued at its face amount, that is, at neither a premium nor a discount. Its face amount, therefore, equaled its proceeds, which were used to retire the 15-year bond at its face amount. The 15-year bond was carried at a discount (face amount – unamortized discount). Consequently, net long-term liabilities must have increased by the amount of the unamortized discount on the 15-year bond, which is the excess of the 10-year bond's face amount over the carrying amount of the 15-year bond.
    Answer (A) is incorrect. The face amount of the 10-year bond equaled the face amount of the 15-year bond. Answer (C) is incorrect. The carrying amount of the 15-year bond should be used, and the loss is not deferred. Answer (D) is incorrect. The loss on early extinguishment is not deferred.

21. On July 31, Year 4, Dome Co. issued $1,000,000 of 10%, 15-year bonds at par and used a portion of the proceeds to call its 600 outstanding 11%, $1,000 face amount bonds due on July 31, Year 14, at 102. On that date, unamortized bond premium relating to the 11% bonds was $65,000. In its Year 4 income statement, what amount should Dome report as gain or loss, before income taxes, from retirement of bonds?

    A. $53,000 gain.

    B. $0

    C. $(65,000) loss.

    D. $(77,000) loss.

Answer (A) is correct.
    REQUIRED: The amount to be reported for the retirement of bonds.
    DISCUSSION: The excess of the net carrying amount of the bonds over the reacquisition price is a gain from extinguishment. The carrying amount of the bonds equals $665,000 ($600,000 face amount + $65,000 unamortized premium). The reacquisition price is $612,000 (600 bonds × $1,000 face amount × 1.02). Thus, the gain from extinguishment is $53,000 ($665,000 – $612,000).
    Answer (B) is incorrect. The excess of the carrying amount over the reacquisition cost is a gain. Answer (C) is incorrect. The unamortized premium is $65,000. Answer (D) is incorrect. The amount of $77,000 equals the reacquisition price of $612,000, minus the face amount of $600,000, plus $65,000 unamortized premium.

13.8   Refinancing of Current Obligations

22. Verona Co. had $500,000 in current liabilities at the end of the current year. Verona issued $400,000 of common stock subsequent to the end of the year but before the financial statements were issued. The proceeds from the stock issue were intended to be used to pay the current debt. What amount should Verona report as a current liability on its balance sheet at the end of the current year?

A. $0

B. $100,000

C. $400,000

D. $500,000

Answer (B) is correct.
REQUIRED: The amount of the current liability.
DISCUSSION: The portion of debt scheduled to mature in the following fiscal year ordinarily should be classified as a current liability. However, if an entity intends to refinance current obligations on a noncurrent basis and demonstrates an ability to consummate the refinancing, the obligation should be excluded from current liabilities and classified as noncurrent. One method of demonstrating the ability to refinance is to issue noncurrent obligations or equity securities after the balance sheet date but before the financial statements are issued. Verona demonstrated an ability to refinance $400,000 of the current liabilities by issuing common stock. Hence, it should report a current liability of $100,000 ($500,000 – $400,000).
Answer (A) is incorrect. Verona did not demonstrate an ability to refinance the full amount of the current liabilities. Answer (C) is incorrect. The amount of $400,000 equals the proceeds from the issuance of stock. Answer (D) is incorrect. The amount of $500,000 is based on the assumption that the entity's intent to refinance has not been demonstrated.

23. On December 31, Year 4, Largo, Inc., had a $750,000 note payable outstanding due July 31, Year 5. Largo borrowed the money to finance construction of a new plant. Largo planned to refinance the note by issuing noncurrent bonds. Because Largo temporarily had excess cash, it prepaid $250,000 of the note on January 12, Year 5. In February Year 5, Largo completed a $1.5 million bond offering. Largo will use the bond offering proceeds to repay the note payable at its maturity and to pay construction costs during Year 5. On March 3, Year 5, Largo issued its Year 4 financial statements. What amount of the note payable should Largo include in the current liabilities section of its December 31, Year 4, balance sheet?

A. $750,000

B. $500,000

C. $250,000

D. $0

Answer (C) is correct.
REQUIRED: The amount that should be classified as current obligations.
DISCUSSION: The portion of debt scheduled to mature in the following fiscal year ordinarily should be classified as a current liability. However, if an entity intends to refinance current obligations on a noncurrent basis and demonstrates an ability to consummate the refinancing, the obligation should be excluded from current liabilities and classified as noncurrent. One method of demonstrating the ability to refinance is to issue noncurrent obligations or equity securities after the balance sheet date but before the financial statements are issued. Largo demonstrated an intention to refinance $500,000 of the note payable. Thus, the portion prepaid ($250,000) is a current liability, and the remaining $500,000 should be classified as noncurrent.
Answer (A) is incorrect. The amount of $750,000 includes the $500,000 that was refinanced. Answer (B) is incorrect. The amount of $500,000 is the amount that should be reclassified as noncurrent. Answer (D) is incorrect. A portion of the debt should be classified as a current liability.

24. Cali, Inc., had a $4 million note payable due on March 15, Year 2. On January 28, Year 2, before the issuance of its Year 1 financial statements, Cali issued long-term bonds in the amount of $4.5 million. Proceeds from the bonds were used to repay the note when it came due. How should Cali classify the note in its December 31, Year 1, financial statements?

A. As a current liability, with separate disclosure of the note refinancing.

B. As a current liability, with no separate disclosure required.

C. As a noncurrent liability, with separate disclosure of the note refinancing.

D. As a noncurrent liability, with no separate disclosure required.

Answer (C) is correct.
REQUIRED: The appropriate reporting of a refinancing of notes payable.
DISCUSSION: If an entity intends to refinance short-term obligations on a long-term basis and demonstrates an ability to consummate the refinancing, the obligation should be excluded from current liabilities and reclassified as noncurrent. One way to demonstrate this ability is to issue, after the date of the balance sheet but before its issuance, a long-term obligation or equity securities for the purpose of refinancing the short-term obligation on a long-term basis. Because the proceeds exceeded the note payable, the entity has demonstrated an ability to refinance 100% of the short-term obligation. Thus, the entire $4 million note should be classified as a noncurrent liability.
Answer (A) is incorrect. If an entity has an intent and ability to refinance the obligation, it should be reported as noncurrent. Answer (B) is incorrect. The note should be classified as noncurrent and requires separate disclosure. Answer (D) is incorrect. The notes to the financial statements should include a general description of the financing agreement and the terms of any new obligation incurred or equity securities issued.

13.9 Noncurrent Notes Payable

25. On December 31, Year 4, Roth Co. issued a $10,000 note payable to Wake Co. in exchange for services rendered to Roth. The transaction was not in the normal course of business. The note, made at usual trade terms, is due in 9 months and bears interest, payable at maturity, at the annual rate of 3%, a rate that is unreasonable in the circumstances. The market interest rate is 8%, the prevailing rate for similar instruments of issuers with similar credit ratings. The compound interest factor of $1 due in 9 months at 8% is .944. At what amount should the note payable be credited in Roth's December 31, Year 4, balance sheet?

   A. $10,300

   B. $10,000

   C. $9,652

   D. $9,440

Answer (C) is correct.
   REQUIRED: The amount credited for a note payable.
   DISCUSSION: The transaction was not in the ordinary course of business. Thus, the payable is measured at present value. Moreover, absent evidence of the market value of the note or an established exchange price for the services, the present value of a note with an interest rate that is clearly unreasonable is determined by discounting the payments at an imputed rate. The prevailing rate for issuers with similar credit ratings normally helps determine the appropriate rate. Assuming that 8% is the best approximation of the rate that would have resulted in a similar transaction between independent parties, the note payable should be credited at its present value of $9,652 {($10,000 × .944) + [$10,000 × 3% × .944 × (9 ÷ 12)]}.
   Answer (A) is incorrect. The amount of $10,300 is the sum of the face amount of the note and annual 3% interest. Answer (B) is incorrect. The face amount of the note is $10,000. Answer (D) is incorrect. The present value of the principal of the note is $9,440.

Questions 26 and 27 are based on the following information. House Publishers offered a contest in which the winner would receive $1 million, payable over 20 years. On December 31, Year 4, House announced the winner of the contest and signed a note payable to the winner for $1 million, payable in $50,000 installments every January 2. Also on December 31, Year 4, House purchased an annuity for $418,250 to provide the $950,000 prize monies remaining after the first $50,000 installment, which was paid on January 2, Year 5.

---

26. In its December 31, Year 4, balance sheet, at what amount should House measure the note payable, net of current portion?

   A. $368,250

   B. $418,250

   C. $900,000

   D. $950,000

Answer (B) is correct.
   REQUIRED: The amount at which the note payable should be measured.
   DISCUSSION: Noninterest-bearing notes payable should be measured at their present value rather than their face amount. Thus, the measure of the note payable, net of the current portion, which has a nominal amount equal to its present value at December 31, Year 4, of $50,000, is its present value of $418,250 (debit annuity cost $418,250, debit discount $531,750, credit note payable $950,000). The present value of the noncurrent portion of the note is assumed to be the cash given for the annuity ($418,250) because no other right or privilege was exchanged.
   Answer (A) is incorrect. The amount of $368,250 includes a reduction of $50,000 for the first installment. Answer (C) is incorrect. The amount of $900,000 equals the face amount of the note payable minus two installments. Answer (D) is incorrect. The amount of $950,000 equals the face amount of the note payable minus the first installment.

27. In its Year 4 income statement, what should House report as contest prize expense?

   A. $0

   B. $418,250

   C. $468,250

   D. $1,000,000

Answer (C) is correct.
   REQUIRED: The contest prize expense.
   DISCUSSION: The contest prize expense equals $468,250 ($418,250 cost of the annuity + $50,000 first installment).
   Answer (A) is incorrect. The sum of the cost of the annuity and the first installment must be recognized as an expense in Year 4. Answer (B) is incorrect. The amount of $418,250 does not include the $50,000 installment due in Year 5. Answer (D) is incorrect. The face amount of the note is $1,000,000.

13.10 Troubled Debt Restructurings

28. For a troubled debt restructuring involving only a modification of terms, which of the following items specified by the new terms would be compared with the carrying amount of the debt to determine whether the debtor should report a gain on restructuring?

A. The total future cash payments.

B. The present value of the debt at the original interest rate.

C. The present value of the debt at the modified interest rate.

D. The amount of future cash payments designated as principal repayments.

Answer (A) is correct.
 REQUIRED: The item used to determine the debtor's gain on a troubled debt restructuring.
 DISCUSSION: When a troubled debt restructuring includes a modification of terms that results in future undiscounted cash flows less than the carrying amount of the debt, the debtor recognizes a gain equal to the difference. If the future undiscounted cash flows are greater than the carrying amount of the debt, the difference is recognized as interest using a new effective interest rate that equates the future cash payments with the carrying amount.

29. Ace Corp. entered into a troubled debt restructuring agreement with National Bank. National agreed to accept land with a carrying amount of $75,000 and a fair value of $100,000 in exchange for a note with a carrying amount of $150,000. Disregarding income taxes, what amount should Ace report as extraordinary gain in its income statement?

A. $0

B. $25,000

C. $50,000

D. $75,000

Answer (A) is correct.
 REQUIRED: The amount reported by the debtor as an extraordinary gain in a troubled debt restructuring.
 DISCUSSION: The debtor must recognize a gain as a result of the extinguishment of debt because the creditor settled the debt by accepting assets with a fair value less than the carrying amount of the debt. However, no extraordinary gain is recognized. An event or transaction is presumed to be ordinary and usual absent clear evidence to the contrary. Accordingly, Ace should recognize an ordinary gain of $75,000 attributable to the $25,000 appreciation of the land ($100,000 fair value – $75,000 carrying amount) and the $50,000 excess of the carrying amount of the debt over the fair value of the land ($150,000 – $100,000).

30. Under IFRS, an entity most likely may derecognize a financial liability if it

A. Transfers amounts to a trust to be used to repay the obligation.

B. Exchanges debt instruments with the lender that have substantially similar terms.

C. Exchanges debt instruments with the lender that have substantially different terms.

D. Transfers amounts in a transaction that meets the requirements of an in-substance defeasance.

Answer (C) is correct.
 REQUIRED: The circumstances in which an entity may derecognize a financial liability.
 DISCUSSION: Derecognition of a financial liability (or a part) occurs only by means of extinguishment. This condition is satisfied only when the debtor pays the creditor or is legally released from primary responsibility either by the creditor or through the legal process. An extinguishment and derecognition of the old debt and recognition of new debt occurs when the borrower and lender exchange debt instruments with substantially different terms, that is, when the respective discounted cash flows differ by at least 10%.
 Answer (A) is incorrect. Payment to a third party such as a trust (also known as an in-substance defeasance) does not by itself extinguish the obligation absent a legal release. Answer (B) is incorrect. The terms should be substantially different. Answer (D) is incorrect. Payment to a third party such as a trust (also known as an in-substance defeasance) does not by itself extinguish the obligation absent a legal release.

13.11 Asset Retirement Obligations

31. The guidance for asset retirement obligations prescribes the accounting for obligations related to the retirement of long-lived tangible assets. A liability for an asset retirement obligation (ARO) within the scope of this guidance may arise solely from

A. A plan to sell a long-lived asset.

B. The improper operation of a long-lived asset.

C. The temporary idling of a long-lived asset.

D. The acquisition, construction, development, or normal operation of a long-lived asset.

Answer (D) is correct.
    REQUIRED: The source of a liability for an ARO.
    DISCUSSION: An ARO is recognized for a legal obligation relating to the retirement of a long-lived tangible asset. This obligation results from the acquisition, construction, development, or normal operation of such an asset.
    Answer (A) is incorrect. The scope of the guidance for asset retirement obligations does not extend to obligations arising solely from a plan to sell or otherwise dispose of any long-lived asset. Answer (B) is incorrect. The scope of the guidance for asset retirement obligations does not extend to obligations arising from the improper operation of an asset. Answer (C) is incorrect. Retirement is the nontemporary removal of the asset from service, for example, by sale, abandonment, or recycling.

32. An entity is most likely to account for an asset retirement obligation (ARO) by

A. Recognizing the fair value of the liability using an expected present value technique.

B. Recognizing a liability equal to the sum of the net undiscounted future cash flows associated with the ARO.

C. Decreasing the carrying amount of the related long-lived asset.

D. Decreasing the liability for the ARO to reflect the accretion expense.

Answer (A) is correct.
    REQUIRED: The proper accounting for an ARO.
    DISCUSSION: The fair value of the ARO liability is recognized when incurred. If a reasonable estimate of the fair value cannot be made at that time, the ARO will be recognized when such an estimate can be made. An expected present value technique ordinarily should be used to estimate the fair value. A credit-adjusted risk-free rate is the appropriate discount rate.
    Answer (B) is incorrect. A present value method may be used to estimate fair value. Probability-weighted present values, not undiscounted amounts, are ordinarily used to measure the ARO. Answer (C) is incorrect. The associated asset retirement cost (ARC) is debited to the carrying amount of the long-lived tangible asset when the ARO is recognized (credited). Answer (D) is incorrect. Accretion expense is debited when the ARO is credited to reflect its increase due to passage of time.

33. On January 1, 10 years ago, Andrew Co. created a subsidiary for the purpose of buying an oil tanker depot at a cost of $1,500,000. Andrew expected to operate the depot for 10 years, at which time it is legally required to dismantle the depot and remove underground storage tanks. It was estimated that it would cost $150,000 to dismantle the depot and remove the tanks at the end of the depot's useful life. However, the actual cost to demolish and dismantle the depot and remove the tanks in the 10th year is $155,000. What amount of loss should Andrew recognize in its financial statements in Year 10?

A. None.

B. $5,000

C. $150,000

D. $155,000

Answer (B) is correct.
    REQUIRED: The settlement loss for an asset retirement obligation.
    DISCUSSION: The asset retirement obligation (ARO) is recognized at fair value when incurred. An expected present value technique ordinarily is used to estimate the fair value. An amount equal to the ARO is the associated asset retirement cost (ARC). It is debited to the long-lived asset when the ARO is credited. The ARC is allocated to expense using the straight-line method over the life of the underlying asset (debit depreciation expense, credit accumulated depreciation). Furthermore, the entity recognizes accretion expense as an allocation of the difference between the maturity amount and the carrying amount of the ARO. Accretion expense for a period equals the beginning carrying amount of the ARO times the credit-adjusted risk-free interest rate. This amount is debited to accretion expense and credited to the ARO. At the end of the useful life of the underlying asset (the depot), the ARO should equal its maturity amount ($150,000). Moreover, the carrying amount of the ARC is zero. The total credits to accumulated depreciation equal the initial debit to record the ARC. Accordingly, given that the ARO liability after 10 years is $150,000, and the settlement cost is $155,000, the entry to record the settlement is to debit the ARO for $150,000, debit a loss for $5,000, and credit cash (or other accounts) for $155,000.
    Answer (A) is incorrect. The actual settlement cost exceeded the ARO. Answer (C) is incorrect. The amount of $150,000 is the maturity amount of the ARO. Answer (D) is incorrect. The actual settlement cost equals $155,000.

13.12 Costs Associated with Exit or Disposal Activities

Questions 34 and 35 are based on the following information. Employer plans to close a plant in 18 months. All of the employees of the plant will be terminated at the time of closing. Because of its need to retain employees until closing, Employer defines a one-time benefit arrangement in a plan of termination that meets the criteria established by GAAP, including communication to employees. Under the plan, each employee who provides services for the entire 18-month period will receive a bonus of $5,000 payable 6 months after termination. An employee who leaves voluntarily prior to closing will receive no part of the bonus. The expected value of the cash outflow for this one-time termination benefit is $2,000,000. Employer's credit-adjusted risk-free (CARF) rate is 3% semiannually. Potentially relevant interest factors for the present value of $1 include the following:

3% for	1 period	.971
	2 periods	.943
	3 periods	.915
	4 periods	.888

34. What is the amount of the liability recognized by Employer in the first month of the future service period?

A. $98,667

B. $107,889

C. $1,776,000

D. $1,942,000

Answer (B) is correct.

REQUIRED: The liability recognized in the first month of the future service period.

DISCUSSION: Employees may be required to provide services until terminated and be retained beyond the minimum retention period. Hence, an exchange transaction (promise of one-time benefits for rendition of services beyond a minimum period) is involved, and no present obligation exists at the communication date. In these circumstances, initial measurement of the liability is at the communication date in an amount equal to the fair value on the termination date. The liability is recognized proportionately over the future service period, that is, as employees provide services over the future service period. The termination date is 18 months after the communication date and 6 months before payment must be made. Using expected present value to estimate fair value, the initial measurement of the fair value at the termination date equals $2,000,000 discounted at the CARF rate of 3% for one semiannual period, or $1,942,000 ($2,000,000 × .971). Accordingly, the monthly liability recognized ratably over the future service period is $107,889 ($1,942,000 ÷ 18 months).

Answer (A) is incorrect. The amount of $98,667 results from using the present value at the communication date. Answer (C) is incorrect. The amount of $1,776,000 is the present value at the communication date. Answer (D) is incorrect. The amount of $1,942,000 is the present value at the termination date calculated at the measurement date.

35. Assume that, after 6 months, Employer revises its expected value of the cash outflow for the bonus to $1,600,000 because fewer employees are likely to remain for the full service period. What is the amount of the cumulative-effect change, if any, required to reflect this revised estimate?

A. $86,311

B. $129,467

C. $517,867

D. $647,334

Answer (B) is correct.

REQUIRED: The amount of the cumulative effect change.

DISCUSSION: The timing or amount of estimated cash flows may be revised. Any revisions must be measured using the CARF rate on which the initial measurement was based. The cumulative effect of this accounting change adjusts the liability in the period of change. The new expected present value estimate of the fair value of the one-time termination benefit at the termination date is $1,553,600 ($1,600,000 × .971 interest factor for 3% and one semiannual period). The liability that should have been recognized for the first 6 months is $517,867 [($1,553,600 ÷ 18 months) × 6 months]. The liability recognized would have been $647,334 ($107,889 recognized per month under the original estimate × 6 months). Thus, the reduction in the liability (the cumulative-effect change) is $129,467 ($647,334 − $517,867).

Answer (A) is incorrect. The amount of $86,311 is the monthly amount of the liability that should be recognized given the new estimate. Answer (C) is incorrect. The amount of $517,867 is the liability that should have been recognized for the first 6 months given the new estimate. Answer (D) is incorrect. The amount of $647,334 is the liability recognized for the first 6 months under the initial estimate.

36. Grand Corporation has decided to close its plant in Littleville. Accordingly, it will terminate the 50 employees who work at the plant. Grand gives the employees 60 days' notice on March 1 that it will close the plant on April 30. It will pay each employee $3,000 at the time (s)he stops providing services during the retention period. This one-time benefit arrangement is defined in a plan of termination that meets the criteria established by GAAP, including communication to employees. Grand should account for the one-time termination benefits by recognizing a liability

A. At the communication date at either fair value on that date or $150,000.

B. At the termination date for $150,000.

C. At the communication date at fair value on the termination date.

D. Ratably over the future service period.

Answer (A) is correct.
REQUIRED: The accounting for one-time termination benefits payable if employees will receive those benefits whenever they stop providing services.
DISCUSSION: One-time termination benefits are paid under a one-time benefit arrangement based on a plan of termination for a specified termination event or future period. If employees need not provide services until terminated to receive the benefits, or if they will not be retained beyond the minimum retention period, the liability is recognized at the communication date. The reason is that a present obligation exists at that time. Measurement is at fair value on the communication date. However, use of estimates and computational shortcuts consistent with measurement at fair value is permitted. Thus, given the brevity of the discount period, the total of the undiscounted cash payments of $150,000 (50 employees × $3,000) is a reasonable estimate of the fair value.
Answer (B) is incorrect. The liability is recognized at the communication date if employees need not provide services until they are terminated to qualify for the benefits or if they will not be retained beyond the minimum retention period. No exchange of benefits for future services exists in this case. Answer (C) is incorrect. Recognition and measurement are at fair value (or $150,000) on the communication date. Answer (D) is incorrect. If employees must provide services until terminated and will be retained beyond the minimum retention period, the liability is recognized ratably over the future service period.

Use the additional questions in Gleim **CPA Test Prep Online** to create Test Sessions that emulate Prometric!

13.13 PRACTICE SIMULATION

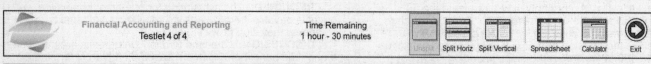

Financial Accounting and Reporting	Time Remaining						
Testlet 4 of 4	1 hour - 30 minutes						
		Unsplit	Split Horiz	Split Vertical	Spreadsheet	Calculator	Exit

DIRECTIONS

Note: If you believe you have encountered a software malfunction, report it to the test center staff immediately.

Navigation

To navigate from task to task, use the controls at the bottom of the screen. Click on the **Next** button to advance to the next task, or the **Previous** button to go to the previous task. To go directly to any task, click on its number.

If you would like a reminder to revisit a task, or want to indicate that you are finished with it, click on the reminder flag below the task number. To clear the flag, click on it again. Reminder flags are for your use only – they do not contribute to your score.

Tabs

In this part of the examination, you will be asked to complete various tasks. Every task has one or more **Work Tabs**. Some tasks have one or more **Information Tabs**, others may have none. Every task has a **Help** tab.

If a task has **Information Tabs**, you may use the information in them to complete your responses in the **Work Tabs**.

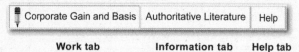

| Work tab | Information tab | Help tab |

Work Tabs:

- **Work Tabs** are identified with a pencil icon. This is where your responses are expected.
- Each task has one or more **Work Tabs**.
- **Work Tabs** contain directions for completing the task – be sure to read these directions carefully.
- The **Work Tab** name in the example above is for illustration only – yours will differ.
- You must complete all of the **Work Tabs** in each task to receive full credit.

Information Tabs:

- The Authoritative Literature will be provided in all tasks in the AUD, FAR, and REG sections for your reference.
- Your simulation may have one or more additional **Information Tabs**. Like the Authoritative Literature tabs, **Information Tabs** do not have a pencil icon.
- If your task has additional **Information Tabs**, go through each to familiarize yourself with the task content.

Help Tab:

- The **Help Tab** provides assistance with the exam software that is used in this task. For example, if the task is to compose a memorandum, **Help** will provide information about the word processor.

The Toolbar

The toolbar at the top of the screen shows the amount of time remaining for you to complete the tasks. In addition, the following tools are available. Note that only the **Exit** button is displayed when Directions are visible - the others will appear when you begin the tasks.

Click on these buttons to split or unsplit the screen. You can split the screen vertically or horizontally.

Click on this button to display the calculator; click on it again to hide the calculator. To move the calculator, click on the calculator title bar and drag the calculator to the desired location.

Click on this button to use the spreadsheet; click on it again to hide the spreadsheet. To move the spreadsheet, click on the the spreadsheet title bar and drag the spreadsheet to the desired location.

Click on this button to go on to the next part of the examination. You must complete all of the tasks to receive full credit. Once you click on **Exit** and confirm the action, you will NOT be able to return to this testlet.

| ▽ = Reminder | | Directions | 1 | 2 | 3 | 4 | 5 | 6 | | ◀ Previous | Next ▶ |

Indicate by selecting from the list provided whether each transaction increased, decreased, or had no effect on the balances of bond discount, bond premium, and bonds payable. Each choice may be used once, more than once, or not at all.

Transaction	Bond Discount	Bond Premium	Bonds Payable
1. Dru issued bonds payable with a nominal rate of interest that was less than the market rate of interest.			
2. Dru issued bonds convertible to common stock for an amount in excess of the bonds' face amount.			
3. Dru issued common stock when the convertible bonds described in item 2 were submitted for conversion. Each $1,000 bond was converted into 20 common shares. The book-value method was used for the early conversion.			
4. Dru issued bonds with detachable stock warrants for a total amount equal to the face amount of the bonds. The stock warrants have a determinable value.			
5. Dru declared and issued a 2% stock dividend.			

Choices
Increased
Decreased
No effect

Interest Method | Authoritative Literature | Help

On January 2, Year 1, Dru, Inc., issued bonds payable with a face amount of $480,000 at a discount. The bonds are due in 10 years, and interest is payable semiannually every June 30 and December 31. On June 30, Year 1, and on December 31, Year 1, its fiscal year end, Dru made the semiannual interest payments due and recorded interest expense and amortization of bond discount.

Dru, Inc.'s $50 par-value common stock has always traded above par.

On December 31, Year 1, Dru had short-term obligations that it intends to refinance on a long-term basis, including $100,000 of commercial paper and a $200,000 construction loan. To refinance the commercial paper, Dru issued equity securities on January 10, Year 1. To refinance the construction loan, Dru entered into a financing agreement on January 15, Year 1, that will expire on December 31, Year 2.

Given the information above, enter in the shaded cells the appropriate amounts or rates.

	Cash	Interest Expense	Amortization	Discount	Carrying Amount
1/2/Year 1					[1]
6/30/Year 1	[3]	$18,000	$3,600	[2]	$363,600
12/31/Year 1	$14,400	[6]	[7]		

Interest Rates	
Stated	[4]
Effective	[5]

Select from the list provided the type of bond described in each item below. Each choice may be used once, more than once, or not at all.

Description	Answer		Choices
1. Backed by the borrower's general credit only		A)	Debentures
2. Usually backed by real estate		B)	Mortgage bonds
3. Usually bearer instruments		C)	Term bonds
4. May be retired before maturity		D)	Coupon bonds
5. Payable at prices related to gold		E)	Income bonds
6. Issued by governmental units		F)	Deep discount bonds
7. Pays interest only at maturity		G)	Commodity-backed bonds
		H)	Revenue bonds
		I)	Callable bonds
		J)	Collateral trust bonds
		K)	Convertible bonds
		L)	Serial bonds

Bonds and Extinguishment   Authoritative Literature   Help

On January 2, Year 7, Drew Company issued 9% term bonds dated January 2, Year 7, at an effective annual interest rate (yield) of 10%. Drew uses the effective interest method of amortization. On July 1, Year 9, the bonds were extinguished early when Drew acquired them in the open market for a price greater than their face amount.

On September 1, Year 9, Drew issued for cash 7% nonconvertible bonds dated September 1, Year 9, with detachable stock purchase warrants. Immediately after issuance, both the bonds and the warrants had separately determined market values.

Check the appropriate box to indicate which answer best completes each statement below.

Statement	Answer	
1. The bonds were issued at a	☐ Premium	☐ Discount
2. The amount of interest expense was higher in	☐ Year 7	☐ Year 8
3. The extinguishment resulted in a	☐ Gain	☐ Loss
4. The gain/loss on extinguishment is a component of	☐ Operating income	☐ Net income
5. The portion of the proceeds allocable to the stock warrants is accounted for as	☐ Stock warrants outstanding	☐ Paid-in capital

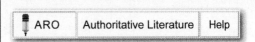

A business acquired a long-lived tangible asset on January 1, Year 1. It recorded a liability for an asset retirement obligation (ARO), and it depreciates the asset retirement cost (ARC), using the straight-line method. The estimated useful life of the long-lived tangible asset is 5 years, the credit-adjusted risk-free (CARF) rate is 10%, the market rate is 12%, the undiscounted estimated cash flows are $402,627.50, and no changes occur in those cash flows. The entity settles the ARO on December 31, Year 5, for $420,000. The present values of 1 for 5 years at 12% and 10% are .567430 and .620921, respectively.

Based on this information, enter in the shaded cells the (rounded) amounts for each item below.

Item	Amount
1. Beginning ARO	
2. Periodic depreciation of the ARC	
3. Year 2 accretion expense	
4. ARO balance at end of Year 3	
5. Settlement gain (loss)	

▼ = Reminder   Directions   1 2 3 4 [5] 6   ◀ Previous   Next ▶

Research | Authoritative Literature | Help

On January 1, Year 1, Negate Industries issued $1,000,000 of 12%, 20-year bonds. In Year 10, interest rates dropped to 8%. Negate decides to take advantage of the lower interest rates by extinguishing the entire outstanding bond issue and replacing it with new bonds bearing a lower rate. Which section in the authoritative guidance explains how any gains or losses from this extinguishment should be recognized?

Enter your response in the answer fields below. Unless specifically requested, your response should not cite implementation guidance.

FASB ASC [   ] - [   ] - [   ] - [   ]

▼ = Reminder   Directions   1 2 3 4 5 [6]   ◀ Previous   Next ▶

Unofficial Answers

1. Bond Transactions (15 Gradable Items)

	Bond Discount	Bond Premium	Bonds Payable
1. Dru issued bonds payable with a nominal rate of interest that was less than the market rate of interest.	Increased	No effect	Increased
2. Dru issued bonds convertible to common stock for an amount in excess of the bonds' face amount.	No effect	Increased	Increased
3. Dru issued common stock when the convertible bonds described in item 2 were submitted for conversion. Each $1,000 bond was converted into 20 common shares. The book-value method was used for the early conversion.	No effect	Decreased	Decreased
4. Dru issued bonds with detachable stock warrants for a total amount equal to the face amount of the bonds. The stock warrants have a determinable value.	Increased	No effect	Increased
5. Dru declared and issued a 2% stock dividend.	No effect	No effect	No effect

1.   Bonds are sold at a discount when they sell for less than their face amount, that is, when the contract (stated) interest rate is less than the market (effective) interest rate. The entry is to debit cash and a discount and to credit bonds payable.

2.   The debt and equity aspects of convertible debt are inseparable. The entire proceeds (usually cash) should be accounted for as debt (a liability) until conversion. Because the proceeds exceeded the face amount, the entry is to debit cash and credit a premium and bonds payable.

3.   Under the book-value method for recognizing the conversion of outstanding bonds payable to common stock, the stock issued is recorded at the carrying amount of the bonds (credit common stock and additional paid-in capital, debit the payable) at the time of issuance, with no recognition of gain or loss. This method is the most common and is deemed to be the generally accepted approach. The entry is to debit the premium and bonds payable and to credit common stock and additional paid-in capital.

4.   The proceeds from debt securities issued with detachable warrants are allocated between the debt securities and the warrants based on their relative fair values at the time of issuance. The bonds are then recorded in the customary way (debit cash, credit bonds payable at face amount, and debit discount or credit premium). Because the bonds and warrants were issued at the face amount of the bonds, and the warrants have a determinable value, the entry is to debit cash and a discount and to credit bonds payable and paid-in capital from warrants.

5.   The entry is to debit retained earnings and credit common stock and additional paid-in capital for the fair value of the shares.

2. Interest Method (7 Gradable Items)

1. $360,000. The original carrying amount was $360,000 ($363,600 carrying amount on 6/30/Year 1 – $3,600 discount amortization on 6/30/Year 1).

2. $116,400. The original discount was $120,000 ($480,000 face amount – $360,000 original carrying amount). Thus, the discount at 6/30/Year 1 was $116,400 ($120,000 – $3,600 amortization).

3. $14,400. The semiannual credit to cash for interest paid does not change. The amount paid on 12/31/Year 1 ($14,400) is the same as that paid on 6/30/Year 1.

4.   6%. The stated annual interest rate equals cash paid ($14,400 × 2 = $28,800) divided by the face amount ($480,000), or 6%.

5.   10%. The semiannual effective interest rate equals interest expense ($18,000) divided by the carrying amount ($360,000), or 5%. Hence, the annual rate is 10% (2 × 5%).

6. $18,180. Interest expense equals the semiannual effective interest rate (5%) times the carrying amount at the beginning of the period ($363,600), or $18,180.

7. $3,780. The amortization equals the difference between interest expense ($18,180) and cash paid ($14,400), or $3,780.

3. Bond Classifications (7 Gradable Items)

1. A) Debentures are backed by the borrower's general credit but not by specific collateral.

2. B) Mortgage bonds are backed by specific assets, usually real estate.

3. D) Coupon bonds are usually bearer instruments. Whoever presents the periodic interest coupons is entitled to payment.

4. I) Callable bonds may be redeemed by the issuer and retired before maturity.

5. G) Commodity-backed bonds are payable at prices related to a commodity, such as gold. They are also known as asset-linked bonds.

6. H) Revenue bonds are issued by governmental units and are payable from specific revenue sources.

7. F) Deep discount bonds (zero-interest debentures or zero-coupon bonds) provide capital appreciation, not periodic interest income.

4. Bonds and Extinguishment (5 Gradable Items)

1. Discount. The stated (coupon) rate of the bonds was less than the yield (effective) rate.

2. Year 8. As the discount is amortized, the carrying amount of the bonds increases. The (constant) effective interest rate applied to an increasing balance results in higher interest expense each year.

3. Loss. The bonds were redeemed for more than their face amount. Because they had been originally issued at a discount, a loss resulted.

4. Operating income. Extinguishments of debt are not treated as extraordinary items.

5. Paid-in capital. When debt is issued with stock purchase warrants, the portion of the proceeds allocable to the warrants is accounted for as paid-in capital.

5. ARO (5 Gradable Items)

1. $250,000. $402,627.50 × .620921 = $250,000.

2. $50,000. $250,000 ÷ 5 = $50,000.

3. $27,500. The beginning ARO balance for Year 2 is $275,000 [$250,000 + ($250,000 × 10%)]. The accretion adjustment is therefore $27,500 ($275,000 × 10%).

4. $332,750.

Year	Beginning Balance	Accretion Adjustment	Ending Balance
1	$250,000	$25,000	$275,000
2	275,000	27,500	302,500
3	302,500	30,250	332,750
4	332,750	33,275	366,025
5	366,025	36,602.5	402,627.5

5. $(17,372). The settlement loss is $17,372 (rounded) ($420,000 − $402,627.50).

6. Research (1 Gradable Item)

Answer: FASB ASC 470-50-40-2

470-50-40-2 A difference between the reacquisition price and the net carrying amount of the extinguished debt shall be recognized currently in income of the period of extinguishment as losses or gains and identified as a separate item. Gains and losses shall not be amortized to future periods. If upon extinguishment of debt the parties also exchange unstated (or stated) rights or privileges, the portion of the consideration exchanged allocable to such unstated (or stated) rights or privileges shall be given appropriate accounting recognition. Moreover, extinguishment transactions between related entities may be in essence capital transactions.

Gleim Simulation Grading

Task	Correct Responses		Gradable Items		Score per Task
1	_____	÷	15	=	_____
2	_____	÷	7	=	_____
3	_____	÷	7	=	_____
4	_____	÷	5	=	_____
5	_____	÷	5	=	_____
Research	_____	÷	1	=	_____

Total of Scores per Task	_____
÷ Total Number of Tasks	6
Total Score	_____ %

Use **CPA Gleim Online** and **Simulation Wizard** to practice more task-based simulations in a realistic environment.

STUDY UNIT FOURTEEN
LEASES AND CONTINGENCIES

(14 pages of outline)

14.1	Lease Classification	495
14.2	Lessee Accounting for Capital Leases -- Initial Measurement	496
14.3	Lessee Accounting for Capital Leases -- Subsequent Measurement	498
14.4	Lessee Accounting for Capital Leases -- Other Considerations	499
14.5	Lessor Accounting for Capital Leases	500
14.6	Operating Leases	504
14.7	Sale-Leaseback Transactions	504
14.8	Contingencies -- Recognition and Reporting	506
14.9	Contingencies -- Amounts Recognized	508
14.10	Practice Simulation	519

A **lease** is a long-term, contractual agreement in which the **lessor** (owner) conveys to the **lessee** the right to use **specific property** for a stated period in exchange for a stated payment. The complex accounting rules for leases attempt to remove subjectivity from the classification of the transactions. The fundamental issue is whether a lease is a long-term rental contract or a purchase-and-financing agreement. **Lessees** have an incentive to avoid capitalizing leases because such contracts require recognition of debt on the balance sheet. However, **lessors** may benefit, although the matter is more complex. For example, the lessee, not the lessor, depreciates a leased asset for financial statement purposes. Also, the financing aspect of the transaction may be at a favorable rate.

14.1 LEASE CLASSIFICATION

Background

An old accountant's joke is, "The basic needs of humans are few: food, shelter, clothing, and keeping debt off the balance sheet." The spirit behind that remark is clear in the struggles over the appropriate treatment of leases. Leasing rather than buying gives an entity two distinct advantages. One is built-in protection against obsolescence. The lease agreement is usually structured to allow the lessee to trade up to a newer model periodically. The second is that not purchasing a major asset avoids recognition of a liability. Because an adequate report of an entity's debt is crucial to assessing its financial health, the FASB has issued a set of criteria intended to keep what are in substance purchases from being disguised as rental agreements.

1. **Classification**

   a. Leases are classified in one of two ways.

      1) Substantially all of the benefits and risks of ownership remain with the lessor under an **operating lease**. Such a lease is a simple rental arrangement.

      2) Substantially all of the benefits and risks of ownership are transferred to the lessee under a **capital lease**. Such a lease is a purchase-and-financing arrangement.

2. **Capital Leases**

   a. A lease is **classified as a capital lease by the lessee** if, at its inception, one or more of four criteria is satisfied.

   b. The presence of **any of the following** indicates that substantially all of the benefits and risks of ownership have been transferred:

      1) The lease provides for the transfer of **ownership**.

      2) The lease contains a **bargain purchase option** (BPO).

3) The lease term is 75% or more of the estimated **economic life** of the leased property.

   a) This criterion is inapplicable if the beginning of the lease term falls within the last 25% of the property's total estimated economic life.

4) The present value of the minimum lease payments (excluding executory costs) is at least 90% of the **fair value** of the leased property to the lessor at the inception of the lease.

   a) This criterion is inapplicable if the beginning of the lease term falls within the last 25% of the property's total estimated economic life.

   Memory aid: **Owners bargain** for **life** and **fair value**.

IFRS Difference

A lease is classified as a finance lease if it transfers substantially all the risks and rewards of ownership to the lessee. Whether the lease is a **finance lease** (a capital lease under U.S. GAAP) or an operating lease depends on the substance of the transaction. IFRS provide examples and indicators of situations that individually or together can result in classification as a finance lease but are not always conclusive. Thus, a lease is classified at its inception as a finance lease if, for example, (1) it provides for the transfer of ownership of the leased asset by the end of the lease term, (2) it contains a bargain purchase option, (3) the lease term is for the major part of the economic life of the leased asset, (4) the present value of the minimum lease payments is at least substantially all of the fair value of the leased asset at the inception of the lease, and (5) the leased asset is such that it can be used only by the lessee without major modification. Other factors also may indicate classification as a finance lease: (1) lessor losses from cancelation of the lease are borne by the lessee, (2) the lessee bears the risk of fluctuations in the fair value of the residual value, and (3) the lessee may renew the lease at a rent substantially below the market rent.

---

c. If a lease covers **only land** and it provides for either a transfer of ownership at the end of its term or a BPO, the lessee capitalizes the lease. Otherwise, it is accounted for as an operating lease.

Stop and review! You have completed the outline for this subunit. Study multiple-choice questions 1 through 3 beginning on page 508.

14.2 LESSEE ACCOUNTING FOR CAPITAL LEASES -- INITIAL MEASUREMENT

1. **Components of Lessee's Minimum Lease Payments**

   a. **Minimum rental payments** are the periodic amounts owed by the lessee, minus any executory costs (such as insurance, maintenance, or taxes) to be paid by the lessor.

   b. A **BPO** gives the lessee the right to purchase the leased property for a price lower than its expected fair value at the date the BPO becomes exercisable. To qualify as a BPO, the option price must be sufficiently low that exercise "appears, at the inception of the lease, to be reasonably assured."

   c. **Guaranteed residual value.** The residual value is generally the estimated fair value of the leased property upon expiration of the lease. All or part of this amount may be guaranteed by the lessee (or by an unrelated third party). Any amount guaranteed by the lessee is, in effect, a final payment to the lessor.

      1) The amount of guaranteed residual value to be included in the lessee's minimum lease payments is the maximum amount the lessee is obligated to pay.

        2) A guarantee of residual value may be obtained by the lessee from an unrelated third party for the benefit of the lessor. This **third-party guarantee** is specifically excluded from the lessee's minimum lease payments if the lessor explicitly releases the lessee from liability on a residual value deficiency.

            a) Furthermore, amounts paid as consideration for this third-party guarantee are treated as executory costs and also are excluded.

    d. A **nonrenewal penalty** is a required payment by the lessee upon failure to renew or extend the lease at the end of the lease term.

        1) Minimum lease payments do not include contingent rentals.

2. **Capital Lease Liability**

    a. The lessee must record a capital lease as an asset and as an obligation at an amount equal to the **present value of the minimum lease payments**.

Leased property	$XXX	
Lease obligation		$XXX

        1) The discount rate used in calculating the present value of the minimum lease payments is the **lower** of

            a) The **lessor's implicit rate** if it is known to the lessee or
            b) The **lessee's incremental borrowing rate**.

        2) If the lessor's implicit rate is unknown to the lessee, the lessor and the lessee may use different rates.

            a) The higher the rate used, the lower the present value of the minimum lease payments and the less likely that the fourth capitalization criterion will be met.

            b) Thus, if the lessee and lessor use different rates, one might recognize an operating lease and the other might recognize a capital lease.

    b. Given a BPO, the minimum lease payments have two components: (1) minimum rental payments (excluding executory costs) and (2) the amount of the BPO.

EXAMPLE

On January 2, Year 1, Cottle, Inc., leased a machine from Crimson, LLC. Cottle must pay Crimson $100,000 on January 2 of each of the next 3 years. The machine's useful life is 4 years, and the estimated residual value at the end of 3 years is $50,000. The lease allows Cottle to purchase the machine at the end of the lease for $10,000. Cottle's incremental borrowing rate is 15%, but the rate implicit in the lease is 10%, which is known to Cottle. The present value factor for an ordinary annuity at 10% for 3 periods is 2.4869, and the present value of $1 at 10% for 3 periods is .7513.

PV of minimum rental payments ($100,000 × 2.4869)	$248,690	
PV of BPO ($10,000 × .7513)	7,513	
PV of minimum lease payments	$256,203	
Leased machine	$256,203	
Lease obligation		$256,203

---

    c. If no BPO exists, the minimum lease payments have three components: (1) the minimum rental payments, (2) the amount of residual value guaranteed by the lessee, and (3) any nonrenewal penalty imposed.

EXAMPLE

In the previous example, Cottle does not agree to a BPO but does guarantee that the residual value of the machine will be $50,000.

PV of minimum rental payments ($100,000 × 2.4869)	$248,690
PV of guaranteed residual value ($50,000 × .7513)	37,565
PV of minimum lease payments	$286,255
Leased machine	$286,255
Lease obligation	$286,255

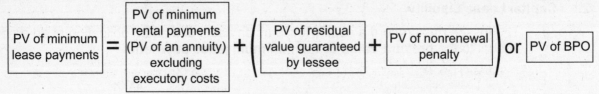

Figure 14-1

d.   The amount recorded for the leased asset and related liability **cannot exceed the fair value** of the leased property at the inception of the lease.

Stop and review! You have completed the outline for this subunit. Study multiple-choice questions 4 through 6 beginning on page 509.

14.3 LESSEE ACCOUNTING FOR CAPITAL LEASES -- SUBSEQUENT MEASUREMENT

1.   **Amortization of Lease Obligation and Balance Sheet Presentation**

    a.   Each periodic lease payment made by the lessee has two components: interest and the reduction of the lease obligation.

    b.   The **effective-interest method** (also known as the effective rate method or the interest method) is required. It applies the appropriate interest rate to the carrying amount of the lease obligation at the beginning of each period to calculate interest expense. The result is a constant periodic rate of interest on the remaining balance.

        1)   The portion of the minimum lease payment in excess of interest expense reduces the lease liability.

    c.   In a classified balance sheet, the lease liability must be allocated between current and noncurrent portions. The current portion at a balance sheet date is the reduction of the lease liability in the forthcoming year.

EXAMPLE

Cottle prepares the following amortization schedule and records the following journal entries:

Date	Beginning Lease Obligation	Times: Effective Rate	Equals: Interest Expense	Minus: Cash Payment	Difference: Reduction of Lease Obligation	Ending Lease Obligation
1/2/Yr 1						$286,255
12/31/Yr 1	$286,255	10%	$28,626	$100,000	$(71,374)	214,881
12/31/Yr 2	214,881	10%	21,488	100,000	(78,512)	136,369
12/31/Yr 3	136,369	10%	13,637	100,000	(86,363)	50,005

-- Continued on next page --

EXAMPLE -- Continued

12/31/Yr 1

Journal entry:	Interest expense	$28,626	
	Interest payable		$28,626

In its December 31, Year 1, balance sheet, Cottle reports a current lease obligation of $71,374, interest payable of $28,626, and a noncurrent lease obligation of $214,881.

1/2/Yr 2

Journal entry:	Lease obligation	$71,374	
	Interest payable	28,626	
	Cash		$100,000

The AICPA has heavily tested candidates' knowledge of lessee accounting for capital leases. Numerous questions have asked for calculations of such items as minimum lease liability and interest expense.

Stop and review! You have completed the outline for this subunit. Study multiple-choice questions 7 through 10 beginning on page 510.

14.4 LESSEE ACCOUNTING FOR CAPITAL LEASES -- OTHER CONSIDERATIONS

1. **Depreciation of Leased Assets**

   a. An asset recorded under a capital lease by the lessee must be depreciated in a manner consistent with the lessee's normal depreciation policy.

      1) Thus, the lease obligation is accounted for under lease accounting. However, the depreciation of the asset is the same as if the lessee owned the asset.

EXAMPLE

Using the information in the example in Subunit 14.3 (above and on the previous page), Cottle will depreciate the machine using the same method (straight-line) that Cottle uses for other machines.

Depreciation expense [($286,255 − $50,000) ÷ 3]	$78,752	
Accumulated depreciation		$78,752

---

   b. If the lease is capitalized because the lease either transfers ownership to the lessee by the end of the lease term (criterion 1) or contains a BPO (criterion 2), the depreciation of the asset is over its entire estimated **economic life**.

EXAMPLE

On January 1, Year 4, Nori Mining Co. (lessee) entered into a 5-year lease for drilling equipment. Nori accounted for the acquisition as a capital lease for $120,000, which includes a $5,000 bargain purchase option (BPO). At the end of the lease, Nori expects to exercise the BPO. Nori estimates that the equipment's fair value will be $10,000 at the end of its 8-year life. For the year ended December 31, Year 4, Nori recognizes $13,750 of depreciation expense on the leased asset. When a lease is capitalized because it contains a BPO, the depreciation period is the estimated economic life of the asset. The asset should be depreciated in accordance with the lessee's normal depreciation policy for owned assets. Nori regularly uses the straight-line method. Hence, depreciation expense is $13,750 [($120,000 leased asset − $10,000 salvage value) ÷ 8-year economic life]. The BPO is a component of minimum lease payments. (See item 3.e. on page 502.) Its present value is therefore included in the calculation of the recognized amount of the capital lease ($120,000). It is not explicitly recognized in the calculation of depreciation.

---

c. The lessee may capitalize the lease based on the third criterion (lease term) or the fourth criterion (PV of minimum lease payments). In these cases, the asset is depreciated over the **lease term** to its expected value to the lessee, if any, at the end of that term.

1) For example, if the lessee has guaranteed a residual value and has no interest in any excess that might be realized, the maximum expected value to the lessee is the amount of the guarantee.

Capitalization Criterion Satisfied	Depreciation Period
1	Economic Life
2	Economic Life
3	Lease Term
4	Lease Term

d. A lessee does not recognize depreciation for an operating lease.

1) However, general improvements to leased property should be capitalized as leasehold improvements and amortized in accordance with the straight-line method over the shorter of their expected useful life or the lease term.

2. **Disclosures**

a. Future minimum lease payments as of the latest balance sheet presented must be disclosed in the aggregate and for each of the 5 succeeding fiscal years. This disclosure is required whether the lease is a capital or an operating lease.

Stop and review! You have completed the outline for this subunit. Study multiple-choice questions 11 and 12 beginning on page 511.

14.5 LESSOR ACCOUNTING FOR CAPITAL LEASES

1. **Classification**

a. Lease classification is more complex for the lessor. A lessor can capitalize a lease if it meets one of the four criteria described in item 2.b. of Subunit 14.1 and **two additional criteria**:

1) Collectibility of the remaining payments is reasonably predictable, **and**
2) No material uncertainties exist regarding unreimbursable costs to be incurred by the lessor.

b. If the lease is to be capitalized, the lessor also must determine whether it is a direct financing or sales-type lease.

2. **Direct Financing Leases**

a. In a direct financing lease, the lessor's economic interest is in financing the purchase, not promoting the sale of its product. The lessor will recognize no manufacturer's or dealer's profit or loss in connection with the lease.

1) Upon inception, the lessor debits a lease receivable and credits the asset leased.

b. The fair value of the leased property and its cost or carrying amount are the same at the inception of the lease.

1) The difference between the **gross investment** (minimum lease payments + unguaranteed residual value) and the cost or carrying amount is recorded as **unearned interest income**.

c. **Initial direct costs** include the lessor's costs to originate a lease incurred in dealings with independent third parties that directly result from, and are essential to, the acquisition of the lease.

1) They also include certain costs directly related to specified activities performed for that lease, e.g., (a) evaluating lessee financial condition and security arrangements, (b) negotiating terms, (c) preparing documents, and (d) closing.

d. The lease should produce a **constant rate of return on the net investment** (gross investment + unamortized initial direct costs − unearned interest income).

1) To accomplish this, the unearned interest income and the initial direct costs of a direct financing lease are amortized to income over the lease term using the **interest method**.

EXAMPLE

On January 2, Year 1, Crimson, LLC, leased a machine to Cottle, Inc. Crimson will receive $100,000 on January 2 of each of the next 3 years. The machine has zero residual value after 3 years. The rate implicit in the lease is 10%. The lease is appropriately accounted for as a direct financing lease. The present value factor for an ordinary annuity at 10% for 3 periods is 2.4869, and the present value of $1 at 10% for 3 periods is .7513.

$$\text{PV of minimum rental payments} = \text{PV of minimum lease payments}$$
$$= \$100,000 \times 2.4869$$
$$= \$248,690$$

Crimson's journal entry on January 2, Year 1:

Gross method
Lease receivable	$300,000	
Asset		$248,690
Unearned interest income		51,310

Net method
| Lease receivable | $248,690 | |
| Asset | | $248,690 |

Crimson prepares the following amortization schedule:

Date	Beginning Net Investment	Times: Effective Rate	Equals: Interest Income	Minus: Cash Receipt	Difference: Reduction of Net Investment	Ending Net Investment
1/2/Yr 1						$248,690
12/31/Yr 1	$248,690	10%	$24,869	$100,000	$(75,131)	173,559
12/31/Yr 2	173,559	10%	17,356	100,000	(82,644)	90,915
12/31/Yr 3	90,915	10%	9,091	100,000	(90,915)	0

Crimson's journal entries on December 31, Year 1:

Gross method
| Cash | $100,000 | |
| Lease payments receivable | | $100,000 |

| Unearned interest income | $24,869 | |
| Interest income | | $24,869 |

Net method
Cash	$100,000	
Lease receivable		$75,131
Interest income		24,869

---

3. **Sales-Type Leases**

a. In a sales-type lease, the lessor recognizes a **manufacturer's or dealer's profit (loss)**. The fair value of the leased property at the lease's inception differs from its cost or carrying amount.

b. In the entry for a sales-type lease,

1) Cost of goods sold is debited for the cost or carrying amount, plus any initial direct costs, minus the present value of any unguaranteed residual value (a continuing investment of the lessor).

2) Lease payments receivable is debited for the gross or net investment depending on whether unearned interest income is separately recognized.

3)   The asset is credited for its cost or carrying amount.

4)   Sales revenue (price) is credited for the present value of the minimum lease payments.

5)   Under the gross method, unearned interest income is credited for the difference between the gross investment (lease payments receivable) and the sum of the present values of its components discounted at the rate implicit in the lease.

Gross investment
(PV of minimum lease payments)
(PV of unguaranteed residual value)
Unearned interest income

c.   Assuming no initial direct costs, the **gross profit** on the sale will equal the sales revenue minus cost of goods sold.

d.   Profit is not affected if **residual value is unguaranteed**. In that case, the present value of the residual value is not included in the present value of the minimum lease payments. As a result, both cost of goods sold and sales revenue are lower. Minimum lease payments include any residual value guaranteed by the lessee.

e.   The **minimum lease payments** calculated by the **lessor** are the same as those for the lessee except that they include any residual value or rental payments beyond the lease term guaranteed by a financially capable third party unrelated to the lessor or the lessee.

$$\text{Lessor's PV of minimum lease payments} = \text{Lessee's PV of minimum lease payments} + \text{Amounts guaranteed by independent third party}$$

1)   The effect of this difference may be that the fourth capitalization criterion is met by the lessor but not the lessee.

EXAMPLE

Assume a leased asset with a guaranteed residual value of $20,000 and a fair value of $15,000 at the end of the lease term. The lessor's entry at this time is

Leased asset	$15,000	
Cash	5,000	
Lease receivable		$20,000

---

f.   The **unearned interest income** must be amortized to income over the lease term using the interest method. The purpose is to produce a constant rate of return on the net investment. In the case of a sales-type lease, it equals the gross investment minus unearned interest income.

EXAMPLE

In the continuing example, assume that Crimson produced the machine, which has a carrying amount of $200,000. No direct costs were associated with the lease of the machine to Cottle.

Crimson's journal entry on January 2, Year 1:

Cost of goods sold	$200,000	
Lease payments receivable	300,000	
Leased asset		$200,000
Sales revenue		248,690
Unearned interest income		51,310

Crimson's journal entry on December 31, Year 1:

Cash	$100,000	
Lease payments receivable		$100,000
Unearned interest income	$24,869	
Interest income		$24,869

g. The estimate of residual value is reviewed at least annually. A nontemporary decrease results in revision of the accounting for the transaction and recognition of a irreversible loss because of the reduction in the net investment.

EXAMPLE

In the continuing example, assume that Cottle guarantees a residual value of $20,000.

PV of minimum rental payments ($100,000 × 2.4869)		$248,690
PV of guaranteed residual value ($20,000 × .7513)		15,026
PV of minimum lease payments		$263,716
Cost of goods sold	$200,000	
Lease payments receivable	320,000	
Leased asset		$200,000
Sales revenue		263,716
Unearned interest income		56,284

Crimson's journal entry on December 31, Year 1:

Cash	$100,000	
Lease payments receivable		$100,000
Unearned interest income	$26,372	
Interest income		$26,372

---

h. The following are calculations by a lessor:

Sales - Type Lease

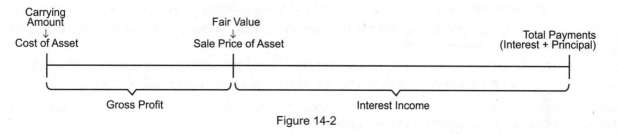

Figure 14-2

Direct Financing Lease

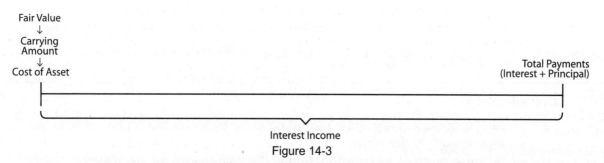

Figure 14-3

i. Selling or assigning a sales-type or financing lease or property subject to such a lease does not change the original accounting. Moreover, any transfer of minimum lease payments under, or residual values guaranteed at the inception of, such a lease is governed by the guidance on transfers of financial assets.

Stop and review! You have completed the outline for this subunit. Study multiple-choice questions 13 through 15 beginning on page 512.

14.6 OPERATING LEASES

1. **Lessee Accounting**

   a. Rent is reported as an expense by the lessee in accordance with the lease agreement.

   b. If rental payments vary from a straight-line basis, e.g., if the first month is free, rent expense must be recognized over the full lease term on the straight-line basis. However, another systematic and rational basis may be used if it is more representative of the time pattern in which the benefit of the property is reduced.

2. **Lessor Accounting**

   a. Operating leases do not meet the criteria for capitalization. They are transactions in which lessees rent the right to use lessor assets without acquiring a substantial portion of the benefits and risks of ownership. Thus, the lessor does not record a sale or financing.

   b. **Rent** is reported as **revenue** by the lessor in accordance with the lease agreement.

      1) If rental payments vary from a straight-line basis, e.g., if the first month is free, rental revenue should be recognized over the full lease term on the straight-line basis. However, another systematic and rational basis may be used if it is more representative of the time pattern in which the use benefit from the property is reduced.

      2) Nonrefundable lease bonuses also should be recognized as rental revenue on a straight-line basis over the lease term.

   c. The lessor must report the leased property near property, plant, and equipment in the balance sheet.

      1) It must depreciate the property according to its normal depreciation policy for owned assets.

   d. Initial direct costs, such as realtor fees, must be deferred and amortized by the lessor over the lease term in proportion to the recognition of rental income.

Stop and review! You have completed the outline for this subunit. Study multiple-choice questions 16 through 18 beginning on page 513.

14.7 SALE-LEASEBACK TRANSACTIONS

Background
A sale-leaseback is similar to a homeowner giving a lender a mortgage on an otherwise unencumbered house. If the homeowner needs cash, (s)he can in effect sell the property while retaining its use in exchange for lease payments.

1. **Classification**

   a. A sale-leaseback involves the sale of property by the owner and a lease of the property back to the seller.

   b. If the lease qualifies as a **capital lease**, the gain or loss on the sale is normally deferred and amortized by the seller-lessee in proportion to the amortization of the leased asset, that is, at the same rate at which the leased asset is depreciated.

      1) The gain deferred may be reported as an asset valuation allowance (a contra asset with a credit balance).

      2) A loss occurs when the carrying amount is greater than the fair value. In this instance, the full loss is recognized immediately.

      3) However, if the carrying amount is greater than the sale price but the fair value exceeds the carrying amount, the loss is deferred and amortized as prepaid rent.

    c.   If the lease qualifies as an **operating lease**, a gain or loss on the sale normally should be deferred and amortized in proportion to the gross rental payments expensed over the lease term.

        1)   When the seller-lessee classifies the lease as an operating lease, no asset is reported on the balance sheet. Thus, the deferral cannot be presented as a contra asset. Accordingly, the usual practice is to report the gain (loss) as a deferred credit (debit).

2.   **Exceptions**

    a.   One exception applies when the seller-lessee retains **more than a minor part** (more than 10%) but **less than substantially all** (less than 90%) of the use of the property through the leaseback.

        1)   The excess profit must be recognized at the date of the sale if the seller-lessee in this situation realizes a profit on the sale in excess of either

            a)   The present value of the minimum lease payments over the lease term if the leaseback is an operating lease or

            b)   The recorded amount of the leased asset if the leaseback is classified as a capital lease.

        2)   "Substantially all" has essentially the same meaning as the "90% test" used in determining whether a lease is a capital or operating lease (the present value of the lease payments is 90% or more of the fair value of the leased property). "Minor" refers to a transfer of 10% or less of the use of the property in the lease.

            a)   If a leaseback of the entire property sold qualifies as a capital lease, the seller-lessee is presumed to retain substantially all of the remaining use of the property.

    b.   Another exception applies when the seller-lessee **relinquishes the right to substantially all** of the remaining use of the property sold and retains only a minor portion of such use.

        1)   This exception is indicated if the present value of a reasonable amount of rentals for the leaseback represents a minor part of the use of the property (10% or less of the fair value of the asset sold). In this case, the seller-lessee must account for the sale and the leaseback as separate transactions based upon their respective terms.

    c.   The third exception applies when the undepreciated cost of the asset exceeds its fair value. In this case, a **loss** must be recognized immediately.

3.   **Purchaser-Lessor Accounting**

    a.   The purchaser-lessor accounts for a sale-leaseback transaction as a purchase and a direct financing lease if the capitalization criteria are satisfied. If these criteria are not met, the lessor records a purchase and an operating lease.

IFRS Difference

If a sale and leaseback transaction results in an operating lease and the transaction is at fair value, any profit or loss must be recognized immediately.

Stop and review! You have completed the outline for this subunit. Study multiple-choice questions 19 through 21 beginning on page 514.

14.8 CONTINGENCIES -- RECOGNITION AND REPORTING

1. **Definition**

   a. A contingency is "an existing condition, situation, or set of circumstances **involving uncertainty** as to possible gain (a gain contingency) or loss (a loss contingency) to an enterprise that will ultimately be resolved when one or more future events occur or fail to occur."

      1) A contingency should not be confused with an estimate. Thus, the estimated depreciation for the period is not consistent with the definition of a contingency because it is certain that the utility of a depreciable asset will expire.

   b. A contingency may be

      1) Probable. Future events are likely to occur.
      2) Reasonably possible. The chance of occurrence is more than remote but less than probable.
      3) Remote. The chance of occurrence is slight.

2. **Probable Loss Contingencies**

   a. A material **contingent loss** must be accrued (debit loss, credit liability or asset valuation allowance) when two conditions are met. Based on information available prior to the issuance (or availability for issuance) of the financial statements, accrual is required if

      1) It is **probable** that, at a balance sheet date, an asset has been impaired or a liability has been incurred, and
      2) The amount of the loss can be **reasonably estimated**.

   b. If the estimate is stated within a **range** and no amount within that range appears to be a better estimate than any other, the minimum should be accrued.

   c. Disclosure of the nature of the accrual and, in some cases, the amount or the range of loss may be required to prevent the financial statements from being misleading.

3. **Reasonably Possible Loss Contingencies**

   a. If one or both conditions are not met but the probability of the loss is at least reasonably possible, the nature of the contingency must be described. Also, an estimate of the amount or the range of loss must be disclosed, or a statement must be included indicating that an estimate cannot be made.

4. **Remote Loss Contingencies**

   a. These loss contingencies ordinarily are not disclosed.

   b. However, a **guarantee** (e.g., of the indebtedness of another or to repurchase receivables) must be disclosed even if the probability of loss is remote. The disclosure should include the nature and amount of the guarantee.

      1) This disclosure is required whether the guarantee is direct or indirect.
      2) A guarantee is a **noncontingent obligation** to perform after the occurrence of a triggering event or condition. It is coupled with a **contingent** obligation to make payments if such an event or condition occurs. Thus, **recognition of a liability** at the inception of a guarantee is required even when it is not probable that payments will be made.
      3) The **initial measurement** of a noncontingent obligation ordinarily is at **fair value**. If a contingent loss and liability also are required to be recognized, the liability recognized by the guarantor is the greater of the fair value measurement or the contingent liability amount.

        4)   Examples of a noncontingent obligation are

            a)   A standalone guarantee given for a premium (debit cash or a receivable),

            b)   A standalone guarantee to an unrelated party without consideration (debit expense), or

            c)   An operating lessee's guarantee of residual value (debit prepaid rent).

  c.   Other remote loss contingencies that should be disclosed are obligations of commercial banks under standby letters of credit and guarantees to repurchase receivables (or the related property) that were sold or assigned.

  d.   No accrual is permitted for general or unspecified business risks, for example, those related to national and international economic conditions. No disclosure is required.

GLEIM SUCCESS TIPS

> Historically, the AICPA has asked conceptual questions involving contingencies. Successful candidates will know how to ascertain if situations are probable or remote loss contingencies.

5.   **Gain Contingencies**

  a.   Gain contingencies are **recognized only when realized**. For example, an award of damages in a lawsuit is not realized if it is being appealed.

  b.   A gain contingency must be adequately disclosed, but misleading implications about realization must be avoided.

IFRS Difference

Provisions are liabilities of uncertain timing or amount except (1) those resulting from unperformed contracts (unless their unavoidable costs exceed their expected benefits) or (2) those covered by other IFRS. Examples are liabilities for violations of environmental law, nuclear plant decommissioning costs, warranties, and restructurings.

- Provisions differ from trade payables and accruals because of their greater uncertainty. They differ from contingent liabilities because they are present obligations that meet the recognition criteria.

- Recognition of provisions is appropriate when (a) the entity has a legal or constructive present obligation resulting from a past event (called an obligating event), (b) it is probable that an outflow of economic benefits will be necessary to settle the obligation, and (c) its amount can be reliably estimated.

- If the estimate of a provision is stated within a continuous range of possible outcomes, and each point in the range is as likely as any other, the midpoint is used.

A contingent liability is a possible obligation arising from past events. Its existence will be confirmed only by uncertain future events not wholly within the entity's control. A liability also is contingent if it is a present obligation that arises from past events but does not meet the recognition criteria. For example, if the entity and other parties are jointly and severally liable on an obligation, the amount expected to be paid by the other parties is a contingent liability. A contingent liability must not be recognized. However, it should be disclosed unless the possibility of resource outflows is remote.

A contingent asset is a possible asset arising from past events, the existence of which will be confirmed only by uncertain future events not wholly within the entity's control. An example is a potential recovery on a legal claim with an uncertain outcome. A contingent asset must not be recognized, but it is disclosed if an inflow of economic benefits is probable.

Stop and review! You have completed the outline for this subunit. Study multiple-choice questions 22 through 26 beginning on page 515.

14.9 CONTINGENCIES -- AMOUNTS RECOGNIZED

Many questions concerning contingencies ask for the amount to be reported in the balance sheet. This subunit consists entirely of such questions. Please review Subunit 14.8 before answering the questions.

Stop and review! You have completed the outline for this subunit. Study multiple-choice questions 27 through 29 beginning on page 517.

QUESTIONS

14.1 Lease Classification

1. Crane Mfg. leases a machine from Frank Leasing. Ownership of the machine returns to Frank after the 15-year lease expires. The machine is expected to have an economic life of 17 years. At this time, Frank is unable to predict the collectibility of the lease payments to be received from Crane. The present value of the minimum lease payments exceeds 90% of the fair value of the machine. What is the appropriate classification of this lease for Crane?

A. Operating.

B. Leveraged.

C. Capital.

D. Installment.

Answer (C) is correct.
   REQUIRED: The criteria for properly classifying leases.
   DISCUSSION: A lease is classified as a capital lease by the lessee if, at its inception, any of the following four criteria are satisfied: (1) the lease provides for the transfer of ownership of the leased property, (2) the lease contains a bargain purchase option, (3) the lease term is 75% or more of the estimated economic life of the leased property, or (4) the present value of the minimum lease payments (excluding executory costs) is at least 90% of the fair value of the leased property to the lessor. Because the lease is for 75% or more of the estimated economic life of the leased property, Crane must capitalize the lease. Note that payment collectibility is an issue only for the lessor.
   Answer (A) is incorrect. The lease is for 75% or more of the estimated economic life of the leased property. It must be capitalized. Answer (B) is incorrect. A lessee accounts for leveraged and nonleveraged leases in the same manner. Furthermore, a leveraged lease involves at least three parties (lessee, long-term creditor, and lessor), financing provided by the creditor that is nonrecourse with respect to the general credit of the lessor, and a substantial degree of leverage. Absent a third party, this transaction cannot be recorded as a leveraged lease even by the lessor. Answer (D) is incorrect. An installment lease is a lease contract that authorizes or requires the delivery of goods in separate lots to be separately accepted.

2. Which of the following factors most likely indicates that a lease should be accounted for as a finance lease under IFRS?

A. The present value (PV) of the minimum lease payments is at least equal to the majority of the fair value of the leased property.

B. The lease agreement provides for the transfer of ownership of the leased property.

C. The lease term equals at least 50% the remaining estimated useful life of the leased property.

D. The lessee guarantees the residual value of the leased property.

Answer (B) is correct.
   REQUIRED: The factor indicative of a finance lease under IFRS.
   DISCUSSION: For a lease accounted for under IFRS to be classified as a finance lease, it must transfer substantially all of the risks and rewards of ownership. Otherwise, the lease will be classified as an operating lease. The following are examples of situations that, singly or together, indicate that a lease should be classified as a finance lease: (1) The lease provides for the transfer of ownership of the leased asset by the end of the lease term; (2) the lease contains a bargain purchase option, and it is reasonably certain that the option will be exercisable; (3) the lease term is for the major part of the economic life of the leased asset; (4) the present value of the minimum lease payments is at least equal to substantially all of the fair value of the leased asset at the inception of the lease; or (5) the leased asset is such that it can be used only by the lessee without major modification.
   Answer (A) is incorrect. The present value of the minimum lease payments should be at least equal to substantially all of the fair value of the leased asset at the inception of the lease. Answer (C) is incorrect. The lease term should be for the major part of the economic life of the asset. Answer (D) is incorrect. No guarantees need to be made about the residual value of the leased property.

3. On January 1, Year 4, Mollat Co. signed a 7-year lease for equipment having a 10-year economic life. The present value of the monthly lease payments equaled 80% of the equipment's fair value. The lease agreement provides for neither a transfer of title to Mollat nor a bargain purchase option. In its Year 4 income statement, Mollat should report

A. Rent expense equal to the Year 4 lease payments.

B. Rent expense equal to the Year 4 lease payments less interest expense.

C. Lease amortization equal to one-tenth of the equipment's fair value.

D. Lease amortization equal to one-seventh of 80% of the equipment's fair value.

Answer (A) is correct.
REQUIRED: The income statement effect of the lease.
DISCUSSION: A lease must be classified as a capital lease by a lessee if, at its inception, any of the following four criteria are satisfied: (1) the lease provides for the transfer of ownership of the leased property, (2) the lease contains a bargain purchase option, (3) the lease term is 75% or more of the estimated economic life of the leased property, or (4) the present value of the minimum lease payments (excluding executory costs) is at least 90% of the fair value of the leased property to the lessor. None of these criteria are satisfied, and the lease can therefore be treated as an operating lease. Under an operating lease, the lessee recognizes periodic rental expense but records neither an asset nor a liability (except for accrued rental expense at the end of a period). Mollat should not recognize interest expense on an operating lease.

14.2 Lessee Accounting for Capital Leases -- Initial Measurement

4. Beal, Inc., intends to lease a machine from Paul Corp. Beal's incremental borrowing rate is 14%. The prime rate of interest is 8%. Paul's implicit rate in the lease is 10%, which is known to Beal. Beal computes the present value of the minimum lease payments using

A. 8%

B. 10%

C. 12%

D. 14%

Answer (B) is correct.
REQUIRED: The discount rate used by the lessee in determining the present value of minimum lease payments.
DISCUSSION: A lessee should compute the present value of the minimum lease payments using its incremental borrowing rate unless

1. The lessee knows the lessor's implicit rate, and
2. The lessor's implicit rate is less than the lessee's incremental borrowing rate.

If both conditions are met, the lessee must use the lessor's implicit rate. The 10% implicit rate is less than Beal's 14% incremental borrowing rate, and Beal has this information, so the rate to be used is 10%.
Answer (A) is incorrect. The prime rate (8%) is irrelevant. Answer (C) is incorrect. This percentage is merely the average of the implicit rate and the incremental rate. Answer (D) is incorrect. The implicit rate is known and is lower than the incremental rate (14%).

5. At the inception of a capital lease, the guaranteed residual value should be

A. Included as part of minimum lease payments at present value.

B. Included as part of minimum lease payments at future value.

C. Included as part of minimum lease payments only to the extent that guaranteed residual value is expected to exceed estimated residual value.

D. Excluded from minimum lease payments.

Answer (A) is correct.
REQUIRED: The treatment of guaranteed residual value at the inception of a capital lease.
DISCUSSION: A capital lease is recorded at the present value of the minimum lease payments. Minimum lease payments from the lessee's perspective include the minimum rental payments (excluding executory costs) required during the lease term and the amount of a bargain purchase option. If no such option exists, the minimum lease payments equal the sum of (1) the minimum rental payments, (2) the amount of residual value guaranteed by the lessee, and (3) any nonrenewal penalty imposed. From the lessor's perspective, minimum lease payments also include residual value guaranteed by a financially capable third party unrelated to the lessee or lessor.
Answer (B) is incorrect. Minimum lease payments are recorded at present value. Answer (C) is incorrect. The full guaranteed residual value is included in the minimum lease payments. At the end of the lease, any difference between the guaranteed residual value and the fair value is recognized as a gain or loss. Answer (D) is incorrect. Minimum lease payments include guaranteed residual value.

6. Neal Corp. entered into a 9-year capital lease on a warehouse on December 31, Year 4. The land and building are capitalized as a single unit. Lease payments of $52,000, which include real estate taxes of $2,000, are due annually, beginning on December 31, Year 5, and every December 31 thereafter. Neal does not know the interest rate implicit in the lease; Neal's incremental borrowing rate is 9%. The rounded present value of an ordinary annuity for 9 years at 9% is 5.6. What amount should Neal report as capitalized lease liability at December 31, Year 4?

A. $280,000

B. $291,200

C. $450,000

D. $468,000

Answer (A) is correct.
REQUIRED: The amount reported as capitalized lease liability.
DISCUSSION: For a capital lease, the present value of the minimum lease payments should be recorded at the inception date. The minimum lease payments exclude executory costs, such as insurance, maintenance, and taxes. The capitalized lease liability is therefore $280,000 [($52,000 – $2,000) × 5.6].
Answer (B) is incorrect. The amount of $291,200 is based on a $52,000 annual payment. Answer (C) is incorrect. The amount of $450,000 is the total undiscounted amount of the minimum lease payments. Answer (D) is incorrect. The amount of $468,000 is the total undiscounted amount of the minimum lease payments plus real estate taxes.

14.3 Lessee Accounting for Capital Leases -- Subsequent Measurement

7. A 6-year capital lease entered into on December 31, Year 4, specified equal minimum annual lease payments due on December 31 of each year. The first minimum annual lease payment, paid on December 31, Year 4, consists of which of the following?

	Interest Expense	Lease Liability
A.	Yes	Yes
B.	Yes	No
C.	No	Yes
D.	No	No

Answer (C) is correct.
REQUIRED: The item(s) included in a lease payment made at the inception of the lease.
DISCUSSION: Under the effective-interest method, interest is recognized to account for a change in value due to the passage of time. Given that the first payment is made at the inception of the lease, no time has passed. Thus, the first payment reduces the lease liability, but no interest is recognized.

8. On January 1, Year 4, Day Corp. entered into a 10-year lease agreement with Ward, Inc., for industrial equipment. Annual lease payments of $10,000 are payable at the end of each year. Day knows that the lessor expects a 10% return on the lease. Day has a 12% incremental borrowing rate. The equipment is expected to have an estimated useful life of 10 years. In addition, a third party has guaranteed to pay Ward a residual value of $5,000 at the end of the lease.

The present value of an ordinary annuity of $1 at

    12% for 10 years is 5.6502
    10% for 10 years is 6.1446

The present value of $1 at

    12% for 10 years is .3220
    10% for 10 years is .3855

In Day's October 31, Year 4, balance sheet, the principal amount of the lease obligation was

A. $63,374

B. $61,446

C. $58,112

D. $56,502

Answer (B) is correct.
REQUIRED: The amount of the lease obligation recorded at the end of the fiscal year.
DISCUSSION: This lease qualifies as a capital lease because the 10-year lease term is greater than 75% of the 10-year estimated useful life of the equipment. The lessee should record the present value of the minimum lease payments at the lower of the lessee's incremental borrowing rate or the lessor's implicit rate if known to the lessee. Because the 10% implicit rate (the lessor's expected return on the lease) is less than the 12% incremental borrowing rate, the lease obligation should be recorded on 1/1/Year 4 at $61,446 ($10,000 periodic payment × 6.1446). The end of the fiscal year (10/31/Year 4) is 10 months after the inception of the lease, but the annual lease payments are payable at the end of the calendar year. Hence, the lease obligation recorded at the inception of the lease has not yet been reduced by the first payment. Moreover, given that the residual value of $5,000 is guaranteed by a third party, it is not included in the minimum lease payments by the lessee.
Answer (A) is incorrect. The amount of $63,374 includes the PV of $1 calculated at 10% for 10 years of the residual value guaranteed by a third party. Answer (C) is incorrect. The amount of $58,112 is based on the interest factor for the PV of an ordinary annuity of $1 at 12% for 10 years. It also includes the PV of $1 calculated at 12% for 10 years of the residual value guaranteed by a third party. Answer (D) is incorrect. The amount of $56,502 is based on the interest factor for the PV of an ordinary annuity of $1 at 12% for 10 years.

9. On January 1, Year 4, Harrow Co., as lessee, signed a 5-year noncancelable equipment lease with annual payments of $100,000 beginning December 31, Year 4. Harrow treated this transaction as a capital lease. The five lease payments have a present value of $379,000 at January 1, Year 4, based on interest of 10%. What amount should Harrow report as interest expense for the year ended December 31, Year 4?

A. $37,900

B. $27,900

C. $24,200

D. $0

Answer (A) is correct.
REQUIRED: The interest to be recognized in the first year of a capital lease.
DISCUSSION: Under the effective-interest method, interest expense for the first year is $37,900 ($379,000 lease obligation × 10% effective interest rate).
Answer (B) is incorrect. The amount of $27,900 assumes the initial payment was made immediately. Answer (C) is incorrect. The amount of $24,200 is one-fifth of the total interest ($500,000 – $379,000 PV). Answer (D) is incorrect. Interest must be accrued.

10. In the long-term liabilities section of its balance sheet at December 31, Year 3, Mene Co. reported a capital lease obligation of $75,000, net of current portion of $1,364. Payments of $9,000 were made on both January 2, Year 4, and January 2, Year 5. Mene's incremental borrowing rate on the date of the lease was 11%, and the lessor's implicit rate, which was known to Mene, was 10%. In its December 31, Year 4, balance sheet, what amount should Mene report as capital lease obligation, net of current portion?

A. $66,000

B. $73,500

C. $73,636

D. $74,250

Answer (B) is correct.
REQUIRED: The capital lease obligation, net of current portion.
DISCUSSION: The total lease obligation on 12/31/Yr 3 was $76,364 ($75,000 noncurrent portion + $1,364 current portion). After the Year 4 payment, which included the current portion, the lease obligation was $75,000. Consequently, the Year 5 payment included interest of $7,500 ($75,000 carrying amount during Year 4 × 10% lessor's implicit rate, which is both known to the lessee and lower than the lessee's incremental borrowing rate) and a principal component of $1,500 ($9,000 cash – $7,500 interest). The latter is the current portion of the lease obligation on 12/31/Year 4. The capital lease obligation at December 31, Year 4, net of current portion, is therefore $73,500 ($75,000 – $1,500).
Answer (A) is incorrect. The amount of $66,000 results from treating the full $9,000 payment made in Year 5 as principal. Answer (C) is incorrect. The amount of $73,636 assumes the current portion is the same as the previous years'. Answer (D) is incorrect. The amount of $74,250 is based on an 11% rate.

14.4 Lessee Accounting for Capital Leases -- Other Considerations

11. On January 1 of the current year, Tell Co. leased equipment from Swill Co. under a 9-year sales-type lease. The equipment had a cost of $400,000 and an estimated useful life of 15 years. Semiannual lease payments of $44,000 are due every January 1 and July 1. The present value of lease payments at 12% was $505,000, which equals the sales price of the equipment. Using the straight-line method, what amount should Tell recognize as depreciation expense on the equipment in the current year?

A. $26,667

B. $33,667

C. $44,444

D. $56,111

Answer (D) is correct.
REQUIRED: The depreciation expense for a lease.
DISCUSSION: The lessee capitalizes the lease because the present value of the minimum lease payments (excluding executory costs) is at least equal to 90% of the excess of the fair value of the leased property to the lessor. The fair value to the lessor is presumably the sales price. Given that the sale price equals the present value of the minimum lease payments, the latter amount equals 100% of the lessor's fair value. Thus, the lessee records an asset and an obligation for $505,000. The lessee should depreciate the asset in a manner consistent with its normal depreciation policy. Given straight-line depreciation, annual depreciation expense is $56,111 ($505,000 ÷ 9 years). The estimated useful life is used only if a bargain purchase option exists and most likely will be exercised.
Answer (A) is incorrect. The amount of $26,667 is based on the equipment's cost and estimated useful life. Answer (B) is incorrect. The amount of $33,667 is based on the lease term, not the estimated useful life. Answer (C) is incorrect. The amount of $44,444 is based on the equipment's cost.

12. On July 1, Year 3, South Co. entered into a 10-year operating lease for a warehouse facility. The annual minimum lease payments are $100,000. In addition to the base rent, South pays a monthly allocation of the building's operating expenses, which amounted to $20,000 for the year ended June 30, Year 4. In the notes to South's June 30, Year 4, financial statements, what amounts of subsequent years' lease payments should be disclosed?

A. $100,000 per annum for each of the next 5 years and $500,000 in the aggregate.

B. $120,000 per annum for each of the next 5 years and $600,000 in the aggregate.

C. $100,000 per annum for each of the next 5 years and $900,000 in the aggregate.

D. $120,000 per annum for each of the next 5 years and $1,080,000 in the aggregate.

Answer (C) is correct.
REQUIRED: The amounts of subsequent years' lease payments to be disclosed.
DISCUSSION: The future minimum lease payments as of the date of the latest balance sheet presented are disclosed in the aggregate and for each of the 5 succeeding fiscal years. This disclosure is required whether the lease is classified as a capital lease or as an operating lease. Thus, South should disclose that annual minimum lease payments are $100,000 for each of the next 5 years and that the aggregate of the remaining minimum lease payments is $900,000. The operating expenses are executory costs and are not included in the minimum lease payments.
Answer (A) is incorrect. The aggregate includes the entire length of the term of the lease, not just the next 5 years. Answer (B) is incorrect. The operating expenses should not be added to the amount of the minimum lease payments, and the aggregate amount is for the remaining portion of the lease. Answer (D) is incorrect. The operating expenses should not be added to the amount of the minimum lease payments.

14.5 Lessor Accounting for Capital Leases

13. Glade Co. leases computer equipment to customers under direct-financing leases. The equipment has no residual value at the end of the lease, and the leases do not contain bargain purchase options. Glade wishes to earn 8% interest on a 5-year lease of equipment with a fair value of $323,400. The present value of an annuity due of $1 at 8% for 5 years is 4.312. What is the total amount of interest revenue that Glade will earn over the life of the lease?

A. $51,600

B. $75,000

C. $129,360

D. $139,450

Answer (A) is correct.
REQUIRED: The interest revenue earned over the life of a lease.
DISCUSSION: To earn 8% interest over the lease term, the annual payment must be $75,000 ($323,400 fair value at the inception of the lease ÷ 4.312 annuity factor). Given no residual value and no bargain purchase option, total lease payments will be $375,000 ($75,000 payment × 5 years). Because this is a direct-financing lease, the fair value is presumably equal to the carrying amount, so no dealer's profit will be recognized. The entire difference between the gross lease payments received and their present value is treated as interest revenue ($375,000 − $323,400 = $51,600).

14. Farm Co. leased equipment to Union Co. on July 1, Year 4, and properly recorded the sales-type lease at $135,000, the present value of the lease payments discounted at 10%. The first of eight annual lease payments of $20,000 due at the beginning of each year of the lease term was received and recorded on July 3, Year 4. Farm had purchased the equipment for $110,000. What amount of interest revenue from the lease should Farm report in its Year 4 income statement?

A. $0

B. $5,500

C. $5,750

D. $6,750

Answer (C) is correct.
REQUIRED: The interest income recognized by the lessor in the first year of a sales-type lease.
DISCUSSION: Under the effective-interest method, interest revenue equals the carrying amount of the net investment in the lease at the beginning of the interest period multiplied by the interest rate used to calculate the present value of the lease payments. The present value of $135,000 is reduced by the $20,000 payment made at the inception of the lease, leaving a carrying amount of $115,000. Interest revenue for Year 4 is therefore $5,750 ($115,000 × 10% × 6/12).
Answer (A) is incorrect. Interest income for Year 2 is $5,750. Answer (B) is incorrect. The amount of $5,500 equals ($110,000 × 10% × 6/12). Answer (D) is incorrect. The amount of $6,750 equals ($135,000 × 10% × 6/12).

15. Le Chat Co. made the following entry at the inception of a lease:

Lease payments receivable	$XXX	
Asset		$XXX
Unearned interest revenue		XXX

This entry reflects recognition of

A. An operating lease by a lessor.

B. A sale-leaseback transaction by a seller-lessee.

C. A sales-type lease by a lessee.

D. A direct-financing lease by a lessor.

Answer (D) is correct.
 REQUIRED: The nature of the entry recording a lease.
 DISCUSSION: The lease is a capital lease recorded by a lessor (owner). Le Chat has removed an asset from the statement of financial position and replaced it with a receivable to reflect the transfer of substantially all the benefits and risks of ownership. Moreover, the lease is a direct-financing lease because no net profit or loss is recognized.
 Answer (A) is incorrect. An operating lease is not capitalized. Answer (B) is incorrect. The entry was made by a lessor. Answer (C) is incorrect. A sales-type lease requires recognition of a profit or loss.

14.6 Operating Leases

16. Kew Apparel, Inc., leases and operates a retail store. The following information relates to the lease for the year ended December 31, Year 4:

- The store lease, an operating lease, calls for a base monthly rent of $1,500 due the first day of each month.
- Additional rent is computed at 6% of net sales over $300,000 up to $600,000 and 5% of net sales over $600,000, per calendar year.
- Net sales for Year 4 were $900,000.
- Kew paid executory costs to the lessor for property taxes of $12,000 and insurance of $5,000.

For Year 4, Kew's expenses relating to the store lease are

A. $71,000

B. $68,000

C. $54,000

D. $35,000

Answer (B) is correct.
 REQUIRED: The lessee's expenses relating to a store lease.
 DISCUSSION: This lease is properly classified as an operating lease. The expenses for Year 4 relating to this lease should include the fixed monthly rental payment, the contingent rental payments, and the executory costs. The Year 4 expenses, as indicated below, amount to $68,000.

Monthly rent ($1,500 × 12 months)	$18,000
Additional rent [($600,000 − $300,000) × 6%]	18,000
[($900,000 − $600,000) × 5%]	15,000
Executory costs (property taxes)	12,000
(insurance)	5,000
Total expenses	$68,000

Answer (A) is incorrect. The amount of $71,000 assumes additional rent is 6% of all net sales over $300,000. Answer (C) is incorrect. The amount of $54,000 assumes additional rent is 6% of all net sales over $300,000 but omits the executory costs. Answer (D) is incorrect. The amount of $35,000 omits the additional rent.

17. As an inducement to enter a lease, Arts, Inc., a lessor, grants Hompson Corp., a lessee, 9 months of free rent under a 5-year operating lease. The lease is effective on July 1, Year 3, and provides for monthly rent payments of $1,000 to begin on April 1, Year 4. In Hompson's income statement for the year ended June 30, Year 4, rent expense should be reported as

A. $10,200

B. $9,000

C. $3,000

D. $2,550

Answer (A) is correct.
 REQUIRED: The rent expense for a year when a free-month inducement is included in the rent agreement.
 DISCUSSION: Rent expense for an operating lease is recognized on a straight-line basis unless another systematic or rational basis is more appropriate. This requirement holds regardless of whether the lease payments are made on a straight-line basis. The total lease payments for this operating lease are $51,000 [$1,000 monthly rent × (60 total months in the lease term − 9 months' free rent)]. Allocating this $51,000 on the straight-line basis to the 5 years of the operating lease results in rent expense of $10,200 ($51,000 ÷ 5 years) per year. The amount of $12,000 would be the rent expense if 9 months of free rent had not been granted.
 Answer (B) is incorrect. The figure of $9,000 is the amount of rent not required to be paid during the fiscal year. Answer (C) is incorrect. The figure of $3,000 is the amount paid during the fiscal year. Answer (D) is incorrect. The amount of $2,550 is the rent expense from April 1, Year 4, to June 30, Year 4.

18. On January 1, Year 4, Wren Co. leased a building to Brill under an operating lease for 10 years at $50,000 per year, payable the first day of each lease year. Wren paid $15,000 to a real estate broker as a finder's fee. The building is depreciated $12,000 per year. For Year 4, Wren incurred insurance and property tax expenses totaling $9,000. Wren's net rental income for Year 4 should be

A. $27,500

B. $29,000

C. $35,000

D. $36,500

Answer (A) is correct.
REQUIRED: The net rental income in the first year.
DISCUSSION: The net rental income equals the annual payment minus expenses. The finder's fee is an initial direct cost that should be deferred and allocated over the lease term in proportion to the recognition of rental income. It should therefore be recorded as a deferred charge and amortized using the straight-line method over the 10-year lease term. Accordingly, the net rental income for Year 4 is $27,500 [$50,000 annual rental − $12,000 depreciation − $9,000 insurance and taxes − ($15,000 ÷ 10 years) amortization of the finder's fee].
Answer (B) is incorrect. The amount of $29,000 omits amortization of the finder's fee. Answer (C) is incorrect. The amount of $35,000 equals rental income minus the full finder's fee. Answer (D) is incorrect. The amount of $36,500 excludes insurance and property taxes from the computation.

14.7 Sale-Leaseback Transactions

19. On December 31, Year 4, Bain Corp. sold a machine to Ryan and simultaneously leased it back for 1 year. Pertinent information at this date follows:

Sales price	$360,000
Carrying amount	330,000
Present value of reasonable lease rentals ($3,000 for 12 months at 12%)	34,100
Estimated remaining useful life	12 years

In Bain's December 31, Year 4, balance sheet, the deferred revenue from the sale of this machine should be

A. $34,100

B. $30,000

C. $4,100

D. $0

Answer (D) is correct.
REQUIRED: The deferred revenue to be reported from a sale-leaseback transaction.
DISCUSSION: The general rule is that profit or loss on the sale in a sale-leaseback transaction is deferred and amortized over the life of the lease. However, certain exceptions exist. One exception applies when the seller-lessee relinquishes the right to substantially all of the remaining use of the property sold and retains only a minor portion of such use. This exception is indicated if the present value of a reasonable amount of rentals for the leaseback represents 10% or less of the fair value of the asset sold. In this case, the seller-lessee should account for the sale and the leaseback as separate transactions based upon their respective terms. Because the $34,100 present value of the reasonable lease rentals is less than 10% of the $360,000 sales price (the fair value), Bain should recognize the entire $30,000 difference between the $360,000 sales price and the $330,000 carrying amount as a gain from the sale. The leaseback should then be accounted for as if it were unrelated to the sale because the leaseback is considered to be minor.
Answer (A) is incorrect. The amount of $34,100 is the present value of reasonable lease rentals. Answer (B) is incorrect. The amount of $30,000 is the profit recognized. Answer (C) is incorrect. The amount of $4,100 is the excess of the present value of reasonable lease rentals over the profit recognized.

20. On January 1, Year 4, Hook Oil Co. sold equipment with a carrying amount of $100,000 and a remaining useful life of 10 years to Maco Drilling for $150,000. Hook immediately leased the equipment back under a 10-year capital lease with a present value of $150,000. It will depreciate the equipment using the straight-line method. Hook made the first annual lease payment of $24,412 in December Year 4. In Hook's December 31, Year 4, balance sheet, the unearned gain on the equipment sale should be

A. $50,000

B. $45,000

C. $25,588

D. $0

Answer (B) is correct.
REQUIRED: The unearned gain on the equipment sale 1 year after a sale-leaseback transaction.
DISCUSSION: A profit or loss on the sale in a sale-leaseback transaction is ordinarily deferred and amortized in proportion to the amortization of the leased asset if the leaseback is classified as a capital lease. At 12/31/Year 4, a gain proportionate to the lease amortization will be recognized [($150,000 − $100,000) ÷ 10 years = $5,000]. Hence, the deferred gain will be $45,000 ($50,000 − $5,000).
Answer (A) is incorrect. The amount of $50,000 is the total deferred gain at the inception of the lease. Answer (C) is incorrect. The amount of $25,588 is the difference between the total deferred gain and the periodic lease payment. Answer (D) is incorrect. The seller-lessee has retained substantially all of the use of the property and should therefore defer gain.

21. On December 31, Year 4, Dirk Corp. sold Smith Co. two airplanes and simultaneously leased them back. Additional information pertaining to the sale-leasebacks follows:

	Plane #1	Plane #2
Sales price	$600,000	$1,000,000
Carrying amount, 12/31/Yr 4	$100,000	$ 550,000
Remaining useful life, 12/31/Yr 4	10 years	35 years
Lease term	8 years	3 years
Annual lease payments	$100,000	$ 200,000

In its December 31, Year 4, balance sheet, what amount should Dirk report as deferred gain on these transactions?

A. $950,000

B. $500,000

C. $450,000

D. $0

Answer (A) is correct.
REQUIRED: The amount to be recorded as deferred gain in a sale and leaseback.
DISCUSSION: The lease of Plane #1 is a capital lease. Its 8-year term exceeds 75% of the 10-year estimated remaining useful life of the plane. In a sale and leaseback, any gain or loss on the sale ordinarily is deferred and amortized in proportion to the amortization of the leased asset if the lease is a capital lease. If a leaseback of the entire property sold (e.g., Plane #1) qualifies as a capital lease, the seller-lessee is presumed to retain substantially all of the remaining use of the property. Thus, no exception to deferral of gain or loss applies. At the inception of this lease, the $500,000 gain ($600,000 sales price –$100,000 carrying amount) should be deferred.
The lease of Plane #2 is an operating lease that may be subject to an exception. The seller-lessee has agreed to make undiscounted lease payments of $600,000 ($200,000 × 3 years). No bargain purchase option or transfer of ownership is stated, the lease term is less than 75% of the useful life, and the present value of the lease payments is less than 90% of the fair value of the property (presumably $1,000,000). Thus, no capital lease criterion is met.
When the seller-lessee retains less than substantially all of the remaining use of the property sold (the present value of the lease payments is less than 90% of the fair value) but more than a minor portion (the present value of the lease payments is more than 10% of the fair value), the seller-lessee should recognize any excess gain (for an operating lease, in excess of the present value of the minimum lease payments). The present value of the $600,000 of payments under the leaseback of Plane #2 is clearly less than 90% of the $1,000,000 fair value of the leased property and clearly more than 10% ($1,000,000 × 10% = $100,000) of that fair value. However, the present value of the lease payments will exceed the gain ($1,000,000 – $550,000 = $450,000) unless the discount rate is very high (about 16%). Accordingly, the gain on the sale of Plane #2 also is deferred (assuming the applicable interest rate is less than 16%). The total deferred gain is therefore $950,000 ($500,000 + $450,000). The gain on Plane #2 also is recognized.
Answer (B) is incorrect. The gain on Plane #2 also is recognized. Answer (C) is incorrect. The gain on Plane #1 also is recognized. Answer (D) is incorrect. The gain on both planes is recognized.

14.8 Contingencies -- Recognition and Reporting

22. Invern, Inc., has a self-insurance plan. Each year, retained earnings is appropriated for contingencies in an amount equal to insurance premiums saved less recognized losses from lawsuits and other claims. As a result of a Year 4 accident, Invern is a defendant in a lawsuit in which it will probably have to pay damages of $190,000. What are the effects of this lawsuit's probable outcome on Invern's Year 4 financial statements?

A. An increase in expenses and **no** effect on liabilities.

B. An increase in both expenses and liabilities.

C. No effect on expenses and an increase in liabilities.

D. No effect on either expenses or liabilities.

Answer (B) is correct.
REQUIRED: The effect on the financial statements of litigation with a probable unfavorable outcome.
DISCUSSION: A loss contingency is an existing condition, situation, or set of circumstances involving uncertainty as to the impairment of an asset's value or the incurrence of a liability as of the balance sheet date. Resolution of the uncertainty depends on the occurrence or nonoccurrence of one or more future events. A loss should be debited and either an asset valuation allowance or a liability credited when the loss contingency is both probable and reasonably estimable. Thus, the company should accrue a loss and a liability.

23. Wyatt Co. has a probable loss that can only be reasonably estimated within a range of outcomes. No single amount within the range is a better estimate than any other amount. The loss accrual should be

A. Zero.

B. The maximum of the range.

C. The mean of the range.

D. The minimum of the range.

Answer (D) is correct.
REQUIRED: The contingent loss that should be accrued when a range of estimates is provided.
DISCUSSION: Because the loss is probable and can be reasonably estimated, it should be accrued if the amount is material. If the estimate is stated within a given range and no amount within that range appears to be a better estimate than any other, the minimum of the range should be accrued.

24. In Year 4, hail damaged several of Toncan Co.'s vans. Hailstorms had frequently inflicted similar damage to Toncan's vans. Over the years, Toncan had saved money by not buying hail insurance and either paying for repairs or selling damaged vans and then replacing them. In Year 4, the damaged vans were sold for less than their carrying amount. How should the hail damage cost be reported in Toncan's Year 4 financial statements?

A. The actual Year 4 hail damage loss as an extraordinary loss, net of income taxes.

B. The actual Year 4 hail damage loss in continuing operations, with **no** separate disclosure.

C. The expected average hail damage loss in continuing operations, with **no** separate disclosure.

D. The expected average hail damage loss in continuing operations, with separate disclosure.

Answer (B) is correct.
REQUIRED: The reporting of hail damage costs when a company is uninsured and sells the damaged item for a loss.
DISCUSSION: Because Toncan sold its damaged vans for less than their carrying amount, the company suffered a loss. The actual loss should be reported even though the company is uninsured against future hail damage and a contingency exists. With respect to future hailstorms, no asset has been impaired and no contingent loss should be recorded. Furthermore, this occurrence is not unusual or infrequent, and a separate disclosure is not needed.
Answer (A) is incorrect. Hail damage is a frequent occurrence and does not meet the definition of an extraordinary item. Answer (C) is incorrect. Toncan should report the actual loss incurred in Year 4. Answer (D) is incorrect. Toncan should report the actual loss, and a separate disclosure is not needed.

25. An entity has been sued for $100 million for producing and selling an unsafe product. Attorneys for the entity cannot reliably predict the outcome of the litigation. In its IFRS-based financial statements, the entity should

A. Make the following journal entry and disclose the existence of the lawsuit in a note.

Estimated loss
  from litigation $100,000,000
    Estimated provision
      for litigation loss $100,000,000

B. Disclose the existence of the lawsuit in a note without making a journal entry.

C. Neither make a journal entry nor disclose the lawsuits in a note because bad publicity will hurt the entity.

D. Make the following journal entry and disclose the existence of the lawsuit in a note.

Cost of goods sold $100,000,000
    Estimated provision
      for litigation loss $100,000,000

Answer (B) is correct.
REQUIRED: The financial statement treatment of a loss from pending litigation.
DISCUSSION: When a reliable estimate of an obligation that otherwise qualifies for treatment as a provision cannot be determined, no liability is recognized. Instead, the existing liability is disclosed as a contingent liability (unless the possibility of any outflow in settlement is remote).
Answer (A) is incorrect. A journal entry is made when the outflow in settlement is probable and can be reliably estimated. Answer (C) is incorrect. A disclosure must be made of a contingent liability. Answer (D) is incorrect. A journal entry is made when the outflow in settlement is probable and can be reliably estimated.

26. Because of a defect discovered in its seat belts in December Year 1, an automobile manufacturer believes it is probable that it will be required to recall its products. The final decision on the recall is expected to be made in March Year 2. The cost of the recall is reliably estimated to be $2.5 million. Under IFRS, how should this information be reported in the December 31, Year 1, financial statements?

A. As a loss of $2.5 million and a provision of $2.5 million.

B. As an adjustment of the opening balance of retained earnings equal to $2.5 million.

C. As an appropriation of retained earnings of $2.5 million.

D. It should not be disclosed because it has not yet happened.

Answer (A) is correct.
    REQUIRED: The IFRS reporting of a probable loss from a product recall.
    DISCUSSION: A provision is a liability of uncertain timing or amount. Recognition of provisions is appropriate when (1) the entity has a legal or constructive present obligation resulting from a past event (called an obligating event), (2) it is probable that an outflow of economic benefits will be necessary to settle the obligation, and (3) its amount can be reliably estimated. Consequently, the entity must recognize a loss and a liability for $2.5 million.
    Answer (B) is incorrect. An adjustment of beginning retained earnings is not appropriate. A loss should be recognized because it is probable and can be reliably estimated. Answer (C) is incorrect. An appropriation of retained earnings is permissible although not required, but the entity must still recognize a loss and a provision. Moreover, no part of the appropriation may be transferred to income, and no loss may be charged to an appropriation of retained earnings. Answer (D) is incorrect. If the loss is probable and can be reliably estimated, it should be recognized by a charge to income.

14.9 Contingencies -- Amounts Recognized

27. Bell Co. is a defendant in a lawsuit that could result in a large payment to the plaintiff. Bell's attorney believes that there is a 90% chance that Bell will lose the suit and estimates that the loss will be anywhere from $5,000,000 to $20,000,000 and possibly as much as $30,000,000. None of the estimates are better than the others. What amount of liability should Bell report on its balance sheet related to the lawsuit?

A. $0

B. $5,000,000

C. $20,000,000

D. $30,000,000

Answer (B) is correct.
    REQUIRED: The liability of a defendant in a lawsuit.
    DISCUSSION: A loss contingency is accrued by a debit to expense and a credit to a liability if it is probable that a loss will occur and the loss can be reasonably estimated. The $5,000,000 estimated loss is reported on the balance sheet, and the range of the contingent loss is disclosed in the notes. The loss is probable (likely to occur) given expert opinion that the chance of loss is 90%. When no amount within a reasonable estimated range is a better estimate than any other, the minimum is accrued.

28. Seller-Guarantor sold an asset with a carrying amount at the time of sale of $500,000 to Buyer for $650,000 in cash. Seller also provided a guarantee to Guarantee Bank of the $600,000 loan that Guarantee made to Buyer to finance the sale. The probability that Seller will become liable under the guarantee is remote. In a stand-alone arm's-length transaction with an unrelated party, the premium required by Seller to provide the same guarantee would have been $40,000. The entry made by Seller at the time of the sale should include a

A. Gain of $150,000.

B. Noncontingent liability of $40,000.

C. Contingent liability of $600,000.

D. Loss of $450,000.

Answer (B) is correct.
    REQUIRED: The entry made to reflect sale of an asset and the seller's guarantee of the buyer's debt.
    DISCUSSION: No contingent liability results because the likelihood of payment by the guarantor is remote. However, a noncontingent liability is recognized at the inception of the seller's obligation to stand ready to perform during the term of the guarantee. This liability is initially measured at fair value. In a multiple-element transaction with an unrelated party, the fair value is estimated, for example, as the premium required by the guarantor to provide the same guarantee in a stand-alone arm's-length transaction with an unrelated party. The amount of that premium is given as $40,000. Hence, Seller debits cash for the total received ($650,000), credits the asset sold for its carrying amount ($500,000), credits the noncontingent liability for its estimated fair value ($40,000), and credits a gain for $110,000 ($650,000 – $500,000 – $40,000).
    Answer (A) is incorrect. A gain of $150,000 assumes neither a noncontingent nor a contingent liability is recognized. Answer (C) is incorrect. No contingent liability is recognized. The likelihood of payment is remote, not probable. Answer (D) is incorrect. A loss of $450,000 assumes recognition of a contingent liability of $600,000.

29. An entity introduced a new product that carries a 2-year warranty against defects. It estimates that warranty costs will be 2% of sales in the year of sale and 3% of those sales in the following year. Sales in Year 1 and Year 2 were $5 million and $7 million, respectively. Actual costs of servicing the warranty in Year 1 and Year 2 were $110,000 and $260,000, respectively. What warranty expense must the entity recognize for Year 2?

- A. $260,000
- B. $290,000
- C. $350,000
- D. $370,000

30. On February 5, Year 2, an employee filed a $2 million lawsuit against Steel Co. for damages suffered when one of Steel's plants exploded on December 29, Year 1. Steel's legal counsel expects the company will lose the lawsuit and estimates the loss to be between $500,000 and $1 million. The employee has offered to settle the lawsuit out of court for $900,000, but Steel will not agree to the settlement. In its December 31, Year 1, balance sheet, what amount should Steel report as liability from lawsuit?

- A. $2,000,000
- B. $1,000,000
- C. $900,000
- D. $500,000

Answer (C) is correct.
REQUIRED: The warranty expense.
DISCUSSION: The warranty expense must be matched with revenue in the year of sale. Thus, the expense related to Year 2 sales must be recognized in Year 2 even if actual expenditures will not occur until Year 3. The expense related to Year 2 sales equals $350,000 [$7,000,000 × (2% for the year of sale + 3% for the year after the year of sale)].
Answer (A) is incorrect. The actual cost of servicing the warranty in Year 2 is $260,000. Answer (B) is incorrect. The amount of $290,000 equals the sum of 2% of Year 2 sales and 3% of Year 1 sales. Answer (D) is incorrect. The actual cost of servicing the warranty in Year 1 and Year 2 equals $370,000.

Answer (D) is correct.
REQUIRED: The contingent loss that should be accrued when a range of estimates is provided.
DISCUSSION: Because the loss is probable and can be reasonably estimated, it should be accrued if the amount is material. If the estimate is stated within a given range, and no amount within that range appears to be a better estimate than any other, the minimum of the range should be accrued. Thus, Steel should report a $500,000 contingent liability.
Answers (A) and (B) are incorrect. The minimum of the range should be accrued. Answer (C) is incorrect. The amount of $900,000 is the proposed settlement amount.

Use the additional questions in Gleim **CPA Test Prep Online** to create Test Sessions that emulate Prometric!

14.10 PRACTICE SIMULATION

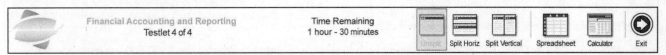

DIRECTIONS

Note: If you believe you have encountered a software malfunction, report it to the test center staff immediately.

Navigation

To navigate from task to task, use the controls at the bottom of the screen. Click on the **Next** button to advance to the next task, or the **Previous** button to go to the previous task. To go directly to any task, click on its number.

If you would like a reminder to revisit a task, or want to indicate that you are finished with it, click on the reminder flag below the task number. To clear the flag, click on it again. Reminder flags are for your use only – they do not contribute to your score.

Tabs

In this part of the examination, you will be asked to complete various tasks. Every task has one or more **Work Tabs**. Some tasks have one or more **Information Tabs**, others may have none. Every task has a **Help** tab.

If a task has **Information Tabs**, you may use the information in them to complete your responses in the **Work Tabs**.

Work tab   Information tab   Help tab

Work Tabs:

- **Work Tabs** are identified with a pencil icon. This is where your responses are expected.
- Each task has one or more **Work Tabs**.
- **Work Tabs** contain directions for completing the task – be sure to read these directions carefully.
- The **Work Tab** name in the example above is for illustration only – yours will differ.
- You must complete all of the **Work Tabs** in each task to receive full credit.

Information Tabs:

- The Authoritative Literature will be provided in all tasks in the AUD, FAR, and REG sections for your reference.
- Your simulation may have one or more additional **Information Tabs**. Like the Authoritative Literature tabs, **Information Tabs** do not have a pencil icon.
- If your task has additional **Information Tabs**, go through each to familiarize yourself with the task content.

Help Tab:

- The **Help Tab** provides assistance with the exam software that is used in this task. For example, if the task is to compose a memorandum, **Help** will provide information about the word processor.

The Toolbar

The toolbar at the top of the screen shows the amount of time remaining for you to complete the tasks. In addition, the following tools are available. Note that only the **Exit** button is displayed when Directions are visible - the others will appear when you begin the tasks.

Click on these buttons to split or unsplit the screen. You can split the screen vertically or horizontally.

Click on this button to display the calculator; click on it again to hide the calculator. To move the calculator, click on the calculator title bar and drag the calculator to the desired location.

Click on this button to use the spreadsheet; click on it again to hide the spreadsheet. To move the spreadsheet, click on the the spreadsheet title bar and drag the spreadsheet to the desired location.

Click on this button to go on to the next part of the examination. You must complete all of the tasks to receive full credit. Once you click on **Exit** and confirm the action, you will NOT be able to return to this testlet.

On January 2, Year 4, Drake Co. leased equipment from Brewer, Inc. Lease payments are $100,000, payable annually every December 31 for 20 years. Title to the equipment passes to Drake at the end of the lease term. The lease is noncancelable.

Additional Facts:

- The equipment has a $750,000 carrying amount on Brewer's books. Its estimated economic life was 25 years on January 2, Year 4.
- The rate implicit in the lease, which is known to Drake, is 10%. Drake's incremental borrowing rate is 12%.
- Drake normally uses the straight-line method of depreciation for equipment.

The rounded present value factors of an ordinary annuity for 20 years are as follows:

12%	7.5
10%	8.5

Enter in the shaded cells the amounts for the necessary journal entries to be recorded by Drake.

	Debits	Credits
1. January 2, Year 4		
Leased equipment		
Capital lease liability		
2. December 31, Year 4		
Capital lease liability		
Cash		
3. December 31, Year 4		
Depreciation expense		
Accumulated depreciation		
4. December 31, Year 4		
Interest expense		
Capital lease liability		

Indicate by checking the appropriate box whether each item that should be disclosed in an entity's financial statements relates to capital leases of a lessor or bonds payable.

Disclosure Information	Capital Leases	Bonds Payable
1. The face amount		
2. The gross amount		
3. A general description of the arrangements, including certain clauses and restrictions		
4. Significant concentrations of credit risk		
5. The fair value and method used to estimate their fair value		
6. Future minimum payments as of the balance sheet date		

Contingencies - Adjustments I | Authoritative Literature | Help

On January 2, Year 4, Drake Co. leased equipment from Brewer, Inc. Lease payments are $100,000, payable annually every December 31 for 20 years. Title to the equipment passes to Drake at the end of the lease term. The lease is noncancelable.

Additional Facts:

- The equipment has a $750,000 carrying amount on Brewer's books. Its estimated economic life was 25 years on January 2, Year 4.
- The rate implicit in the lease, which is known to Drake, is 10%. Drake's incremental borrowing rate is 12%.
- Drake normally uses the straight-line method of depreciation for equipment.

The rounded present value factors of an ordinary annuity for 20 years are as follows:

    12%   7.5
    10%   8.5

Each item below describes an amount(s) not reflected in the financial statements. Select from the list provided the amount, if any, required to be recognized in Drake's financial statements based on a calendar year for Year 4. Each choice may be used once, more than once, or not at all.

Description	Answer	Choices
1. Drake owns a small warehouse located on the banks of a river in which it stores inventory worth approximately $500,000. Drake is not insured against flood losses. The river last overflowed its banks 20 years ago.		A) No adjustment is required
2. During Year 4, Drake began offering certain healthcare benefits to its eligible retired employees. Drake's net periodic postretirement benefit cost (NPPBC) is $150,000.		B) $100,000
3. Drake offers an unconditional warranty on its toys. Based on past experience, Drake estimates its warranty expenses to be 1% of sales. Sales during Year 4 were $10 million.		C) $150,000
4. On October 20, Year 4, a safety hazard related to one of Drake's toy products was discovered. It is probable that Drake will be liable for an amount in the range of $100,000 to $500,000. No amount in the range is a better estimate than any other.		D) $250,000
5. On November 22, Year 4, Drake initiated a lawsuit seeking $250,000 in damages from patent infringement.		E) $400,000
6. On December 17, Year 4, a former employee filed a lawsuit seeking $100,000 for unlawful dismissal. Drake's attorneys believe the suit is without merit. No court date has been set.		F) $500,000

▼ = Reminder   Directions   1 2 3 4 5 6   ◀ Previous   Next ▶

| Contingencies - Adjustments II | Authoritative Literature | Help |

On January 2, Year 4, Drake Co. leased equipment from Brewer, Inc. Lease payments are $100,000, payable annually every December 31 for 20 years. Title to the equipment passes to Drake at the end of the lease term. The lease is noncancelable.

Additional Facts:

- The equipment has a $750,000 carrying amount on Brewer's books. Its estimated economic life was 25 years on January 2, Year 4.
- The rate implicit in the lease, which is known to Drake, is 10%. Drake's incremental borrowing rate is 12%.
- Drake normally uses the straight-line method of depreciation for equipment.

The rounded present value factors of an ordinary annuity for 20 years are as follows:

    12%   7.5
    10%   8.5

Each numbered item describes an amount(s) not reflected in the financial statements. Select from the list provided the amount, if any, required to be recognized in Drake's financial statements based on a calendar year for Year 4. Each choice may be used once, more than once, or not at all.

Description	Answer
1. On December 15, Year 4, Drake guaranteed a bank loan to a related entity for $1,000,000. It is not likely that payments will be made. The fair value of the guarantee is $250,000.	
2. On December 31, Year 4, Drake's board of directors voted to sell its computer games division, which qualifies as a component of an entity held for sale. The division was sold on February 15, Year 5. On December 31, Year 4, Drake estimated that losses from operations, net of tax, for the period January 1, Year 5, through February 15, Year 5, would be $400,000 and that the gain from the sale of the division's assets, net of tax, would be $250,000. These estimates were materially correct.	
3. On January 5, Year 5, a warehouse containing a substantial portion of Drake's inventory was destroyed by fire. Drake expects to recover the entire loss, except for a $250,000 deductible, from insurance.	
4. On January 4, Year 5, inventory purchased FOB shipping point on December 30, Year 4, from a foreign country was detained at that country's border because of political unrest. The shipment is valued at $150,000. Drake's attorneys have stated that it is probable that Drake will be able to obtain the shipment.	
5. On January 30, Year 5, Drake issued $10 million of bonds at a premium of $500,000.	

Choices
A) No adjustment is required
B) $100,000
C) $150,000
D) $250,000
E) $400,000
F) $500,000

| ▼ = Reminder | | Directions | 1 2 3 [4] 5 6 | | ◀ Previous   Next ▶ |

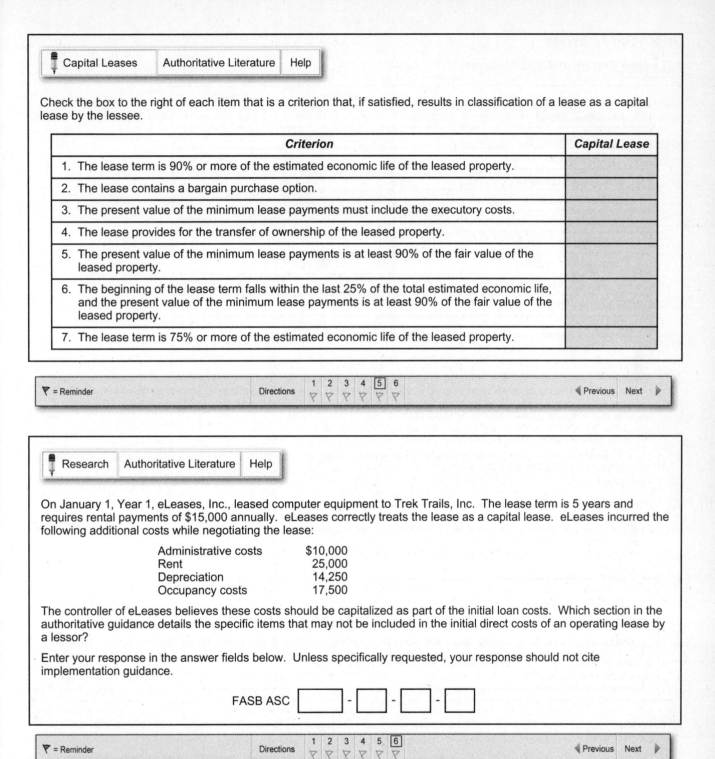

Capital Leases | Authoritative Literature | Help

Check the box to the right of each item that is a criterion that, if satisfied, results in classification of a lease as a capital lease by the lessee.

Criterion	Capital Lease
1. The lease term is 90% or more of the estimated economic life of the leased property.	
2. The lease contains a bargain purchase option.	
3. The present value of the minimum lease payments must include the executory costs.	
4. The lease provides for the transfer of ownership of the leased property.	
5. The present value of the minimum lease payments is at least 90% of the fair value of the leased property.	
6. The beginning of the lease term falls within the last 25% of the total estimated economic life, and the present value of the minimum lease payments is at least 90% of the fair value of the leased property.	
7. The lease term is 75% or more of the estimated economic life of the leased property.	

▼ = Reminder   Directions   1 2 3 4 [5] 6   ◀ Previous   Next ▶

Research | Authoritative Literature | Help

On January 1, Year 1, eLeases, Inc., leased computer equipment to Trek Trails, Inc. The lease term is 5 years and requires rental payments of $15,000 annually. eLeases correctly treats the lease as a capital lease. eLeases incurred the following additional costs while negotiating the lease:

Administrative costs	$10,000
Rent	25,000
Depreciation	14,250
Occupancy costs	17,500

The controller of eLeases believes these costs should be capitalized as part of the initial loan costs. Which section in the authoritative guidance details the specific items that may not be included in the initial direct costs of an operating lease by a lessor?

Enter your response in the answer fields below. Unless specifically requested, your response should not cite implementation guidance.

FASB ASC [   ] - [   ] - [   ] - [   ]

▼ = Reminder   Directions   1 2 3 4 5 [6]   ◀ Previous   Next ▶

Unofficial Answers

1. Lessee Entries (8 Gradable Items)

	Debits		Credits	
1. January 2, Year 4				
Leased equipment	[1]	850,000		
Capital lease liability			[1]	850,000
2. December 31, Year 4				
Capital lease liability	[2]	100,000		
Cash			[2]	100,000
3. December 31, Year 4				
Depreciation expense	[3]	34,000		
Accumulated depreciation			[3]	34,000
4. December 31, Year 4				
Interest expense	[4]	85,000		
Capital lease liability			[4]	85,000

1.   The lessee capitalizes the lease because the lease transfers ownership. Also, the lease term is 75% or more (20 years ÷ 25 years = 80%) of the estimated economic life of the leased asset. The capitalized amount is $850,000 ($100,000 annual payment × 8.5 PV factor for an ordinary 20-year annuity and an interest rate of 10%, the lower of the implicit rate or the lessee's incremental borrowing rate).

2.   The annual lease payment is $100,000.

3.   The lease transfers ownership, so the leased asset is depreciated over its 25-year estimated economic life using the lessee's normal depreciation policy (straight-line). Accordingly, depreciation expense is $34,000 ($850,000 ÷ 25 years).

4.   The appropriate interest rate is 10%. Thus, interest expense for the lease's first year is $85,000 ($850,000 balance at the beginning of the period × 10%), and the net decrease in the liability is $15,000 ($100,000 annual payment – $85,000 interest expense), which is the result of combining entries 2. and 4.

2. Disclosure (6 Gradable Items)

1.   Bonds payable. A lease does not have a face amount.

2.   Capital leases. Accounting for a capital lease by a lessor includes debiting an asset for the gross investment.

3.   Capital leases. A lessee must disclose restrictions (e.g., on debt, further leasing, and dividends) and certain clauses (e.g., escalator clauses and purchase options).

4.   Bonds payable. Credit risk is the risk of accounting loss from an instrument because of the possible failure of another party to perform. With certain exceptions, an entity must disclose all significant concentrations of credit risk arising from instruments, whether from one counterparty or groups.

5.   Bonds payable. An entity must disclose the fair value and method used to estimate their fair value of financial instruments.

6.   Capital leases. Future minimum lease payments as of the latest balance sheet presented must be disclosed in the aggregate and for each of the 5 succeeding fiscal years. This disclosure is required whether the lease is a capital or an operating lease.

3. Contingencies – Adjustments I (6 Gradable Items)

1. A) No adjustment is required. Contingent losses for which occurrence of the future event is not probable require no accrual. The river last overflowed 20 years ago. The possibility of a flood is no more than reasonably possible.

2. C) $150,000. The NPPBC should be recognized.

3. B) $100,000. If incurrence of warranty expense is probable and the amount can be reasonably estimated, accrual of the liability is appropriate. The estimate for warranties of 1% of sales is reasonable.

4. B) $100,000. If a loss contingency is considered probable and can be reasonably estimated, the loss should be accrued. When a range is estimated, the minimum amount of loss should be accrued if no other amount is a better estimate.

5. A) No adjustment is required. A gain contingency should not be recognized until it is realized.

6. A) No adjustment is required. When a loss contingency is not probable, no accrual is required.

4. Contingencies – Adjustments II (5 Gradable Items)

1. D) $250,000. Assuming the loss contingency arising from the guarantee of the loan is considered either reasonably possible or remote, no accrual is required. However, Drake must recognize the $250,000 fair value of the noncontingent guarantee obligation.

2. A) No adjustment is required. When a component is classified as held for sale, its operating results are reported in discontinued operations in the period(s) in which they occur.

3. A) No adjustment is required. A subsequent event providing evidence about conditions not existing at the balance sheet date may require disclosure but not adjustment of the statements. Examples of subsequent events requiring disclosure only are sale of a bond or stock issue and loss of a plant or inventories due to fire or flood.

4. A) No adjustment is required. Because the receipt of the shipment is probable, no accrual is necessary.

5. A) No adjustment is required. A subsequent event providing evidence about conditions not existing at the balance sheet date may require disclosure but not adjustment of the statements. Examples of subsequent events requiring disclosure only are sale of a bond or stock issue and loss of a plant or inventories due to fire or flood.

5. Capital Leases (7 Gradable Items)

1. Not for a capital lease. A lessee classifies a lease as a capital lease if the lease term is 75% or more of the estimated economic life of the leased property.

2. For a capital lease. A lessee classifies a lease as a capital lease if the lease contains a bargain purchase option (BPO).

3. Not for a capital lease. A lessee classifies a lease as a capital lease if the present value of the minimum lease payments (excluding executory costs) is at least 90% of the fair value of the leased property to the lessor at the inception of the lease.

4. For a capital lease. A lessee classifies a lease as a capital lease if the lease provides for the transfer of ownership.

5. For a capital lease. A lessee classifies a lease as a capital lease if the present value of the minimum lease payments (excluding executory costs) is at least 90% of the fair value of the leased property to the lessor at the inception of the lease.

6. Not for a capital lease. The lease-term and present-value criteria do not apply when the lease term begins within the last 25% of the economic life of the property.

7. For a capital lease. A lessee classifies a lease as a capital lease if the lease term is 75% or more of the estimated economic life of the leased property.

6. Research (1 Gradable Item)

Answer: ASC 840-20-25-19

840-20-25-19 Further, initial direct costs shall not include any of the following:

a. Administrative costs
b. Rent
c. Depreciation
d. Any other occupancy and equipment costs
e. Employees' compensation and fringe benefits related to activities described in the preceding paragraph
f. Unsuccessful origination efforts
g. Idle time

Gleim Simulation Grading

Task	Correct Responses		Gradable Items		Score per Task
1	____	÷	8	=	____
2	____	÷	6	=	____
3	____	÷	6	=	____
4	____	÷	5	=	____
5	____	÷	7	=	____
Research	____	÷	1	=	____

	Total of Scores per Task	____
÷	Total Number of Tasks	6
	Total Score	____ %

Use **CPA Gleim Online** and **Simulation Wizard** to practice more task-based simulations in a realistic environment.

Success story!

I passed all 4 sections with scores greatly exceeding 75. The main thing I liked about Gleim Review Systems for passing the CPA exam was how the information was broken down into 20 separate study units. Each unit covered a small selection of material at a time which made it easier to study it. I felt my personal counselor was a useful asset. There was one instance when I do not think I would have been able to get past my issue without my counselor's guidance. I have already recommended Gleim to others.

- Kyle Boehnlein, CPA

STUDY UNIT FIFTEEN
EQUITY

(24 pages of outline)

15.1	Classes of Equity	527
15.2	Issuance of Stock	530
15.3	Stock Warrants and Stock Rights	533
15.4	Treasury Stock -- Acquisition	534
15.5	Treasury Stock -- Reissue	535
15.6	Retirement of Stock	536
15.7	Cash Dividends	537
15.8	Property Dividends and Liquidating Dividends	538
15.9	Stock Dividends and Stock Splits	539
15.10	Partnerships -- Formation and Allocation	540
15.11	Partnerships -- Changes and Liquidation	543
15.12	Quasi-Reorganization	549
15.13	Practice Simulation	563

Corporate equity is more complex than partner or proprietor equity. Its major components are contributed capital, retained earnings, and accumulated other comprehensive income.

15.1 CLASSES OF EQUITY

1. **Reporting**

    a. Equity is reported on the face of the balance sheet.

EXAMPLE

Capital stock:
Preferred stock, $50 par value, 6% cumulative, 10,000 shares authorized, issued, and outstanding	$ 500,000	
Preferred stock, $40 par value, 7% cumulative, 5,000 shares authorized, issued, and outstanding, each convertible to 1 share of no-par common stock	200,000	
Common stock, no par, stated value $1 per share, 50,000 shares authorized, 45,000 issued and outstanding	50,000	
Common stock subscribed, 10,000 shares	10,000	
Common stock dividend distributable, 4,500 shares	4,500	
Stock warrants outstanding	1,500	
Total capital stock		$ 766,000

Additional paid-in capital:
Excess over par -- preferred	$ 464,000	
Excess over par -- common	800,000	1,264,000
Total paid-in capital		$2,030,000

Retained earnings:
Retained earnings -- unappropriated	$5,800,000	
Retained earnings -- appropriated for expansion	1,520,000	
Total retained earnings		7,320,000

Total paid-in capital and retained earnings		$9,350,000
Accumulated other comprehensive income		611,000
Minus: receivable from stock subscription		(84,000)
Minus: cost of treasury stock (5,000 common shares)		(100,000)
Total shareholders' equity		$9,777,000

2. **Common Stock**

    a. The most widely used classes of stock are common and preferred. Common shareholders are entitled to receive **liquidating distributions** only after all other claims have been satisfied, including those of preferred shareholders.

    b. Common shareholders are not entitled to **dividends**.

        1) A corporation may choose not to declare dividends. Among the reasons are insufficient retained earnings to meet a legal requirement or the need to use cash for some other purpose.

    c. State statutes typically permit different classes of common stock with different rights or privileges, e.g., class A common with voting rights and class B common with no voting rights.

    d. If only one class of stock is issued, it is treated as common, and each shareholder must be treated equally.

    e. Common shareholders elect directors to the board.

3. **Preferred Stock**

    a. Preferred shareholders have the right to receive (1) dividends at a specified rate (before common shareholders may receive any) and (2) distributions before common shareholders (but after creditors) upon liquidation. But they tend not to have voting rights or to enjoy the same capital gains as the common shareholders.

Background

In the equity section, preferred stock is generally reported before common stock because it is a hybrid of debt and equity. This position reminds readers that, in liquidation, the claims of the preferred shareholders must be satisfied before the common shareholders can be paid.

---

    b. If a board issues preferred stock, it may establish different classes or series. Each may be assigned independent rights, dividend rates, and redemption prices.

    c. Holders of **convertible preferred stock** have the right to convert the stock into shares of another class (usually common stock) at a predetermined ratio set forth in the articles or bylaws.

        1) The potential for acquiring the voting rights inherent in common stock makes convertible preferred stock more desirable to investors.

    d. **Callable preferred stock** is issued with the condition that it may be called (redeemed or repurchased) by the issuer at a stated price and time. Issuers may establish a sinking fund for this purpose.

    e. Holders of preferred stock may also have a right to compel redemption.

        1) The SEC prohibits the combining of common and preferred stock or of redeemable and nonredeemable preferred stock in financial statements.

        2) Moreover, equity may not include redeemable preferred stock.

        3) Accordingly, redeemable preferred stock, especially **transient preferred stock** (redeemable within a relatively short period, such as 5 to 10 years), may be similar to debt.

    f. **Mandatorily redeemable financial instruments (MRFIs)** are redeemable shares that embody an unconditional obligation to transfer assets at a fixed or determinable time or upon an event certain to occur.

        1) MRFIs must be accounted for as liabilities unless the redemption is required only upon the liquidation or termination of the entity.

4.   **Equity Accounts**

   a.   **Contributed capital** (paid-in capital) represents amounts invested by owners in exchange for stock (common or preferred).

   1)   The **capital stock** (stated capital) shows the par or stated value of all shares issued and outstanding. If stock has no par or stated value, the amount received is presented.

   a)   Amounts for common and preferred stock are separately listed. Absent treasury stock, the number of shares may be determined by dividing these amounts by the related par or stated value per share.

   b)   Stated capital can be affected by treasury stock transactions.

   2)   **Additional paid-in capital** (paid-in capital in excess of par or stated value) consists of amounts in excess of stated capital. Sources include

   a)   Amounts in excess of par or stated value received for the entity's stock.

   b)   A debit item for receipts that are less than par or stated value, for example, discount on common stock.

   c)   Transfers at fair value from retained earnings upon the declaration of stock dividends.

   d)   Stock subscriptions defaults (if forfeiture is allowed by law and corporate policy).

   e)   Amounts attributable to treasury stock transactions.

   b.   **Retained earnings** is increased by net income and quasi-reorganization and decreased by (1) net losses, (2) cash or property dividends, (3) stock dividends, (4) split-ups effected in the form of a dividend, and (5) certain treasury stock transactions.

   1)   Prior-period adjustments (error corrections) also are made to retained earnings.

   2)   A change in accounting principle is applied retrospectively. The cumulative effect on all prior periods is reflected in the opening balances of assets, liabilities, and retained earnings (or other appropriate components of equity) for the first period presented.

   c.   Amounts may be **appropriated** (restricted) to disclose that earnings are to be used for purposes other than dividends. An appropriation must be clearly displayed within equity.

   1)   Purposes include (a) compliance with a bond indenture (bond contract), (b) retention of assets for internally financed expansion, (c) anticipation of losses, or (d) adherence to legal restrictions. For example, a state law may restrict retained earnings by an amount equal to the cost of treasury stock.

   2)   The appropriation **does not set aside assets**. It limits the availability of dividends. A formal entry (debit retained earnings, credit retained earnings appropriated) or disclosure in a note may be made.

   3)   Transfers to and from an appropriation do not affect net income.

   a)   Costs and losses are not debited to an appropriation, and no amount is transferred to income.

   d.   **Treasury stock** is the entity's own stock reacquired to, e.g., (1) effect mergers, (2) issue share options, (3) issue stock dividends, (4) obtain tax advantages (favorable capital gains rates) for shareholders, (5) improve EPS and other ratios, (6) avoid a hostile takeover, or (7) eliminate an ownership interest.

   1)   Treasury stock reduces the shares outstanding, not the shares authorized.
   2)   It is commonly accounted for at cost (discussed later in this study unit).
   3)   Treasury stock is not an asset, and dividends are never paid to these shares.

e.   **Accumulated other comprehensive income** is a separate component of equity that includes items excluded from net income. Items in that component should be classified according to their nature. For a list of items reported as other comprehensive income, see Study Unit 2, Subunit 3.

Stop and review! You have completed the outline for this subunit. Study multiple-choice questions 1 and 2 beginning on page 550.

15.2 ISSUANCE OF STOCK

1.   **Par or Stated Value**

a.   The par value of stock is an arbitrary amount assigned by the issuer. Most states treat par value as **legal capital**, an amount unavailable for dividends.

1)   When **no-par stock** is issued, most states require it to have a stated value equivalent to par value.

2.   **Issuance of Stock**

a.   Cash is debited, the appropriate stock account is credited for the total par value, and additional paid-in capital (paid-in capital in excess of par) is credited for the difference.

EXAMPLE

Parvenu Corp. issued 50,000 shares of no-par common stock with a stated value of $1. The market price of the stock was $17 per share on the day of issue.

Cash (50,000 shares × $17 market price)	$850,000	
Common stock (50,000 shares × $1 stated value)		$ 50,000
Additional paid-in capital -- common (difference)		800,000

Parvenu also issued 10,000 shares of $50 par value, 6% preferred stock. The market price at the time was $62 per share.

Cash (10,000 shares × $62 market price)	$620,000	
6% preferred stock (10,000 shares × $50 par value)		$500,000
Additional paid-in capital -- preferred (difference)		120,000

---

1)   Requiring no-par stock to have a stated value prevents an entity from crediting the entire proceeds of an issuance to additional paid-in capital.

3.   **Costs of Issuance**

a.   **Direct costs of issuing stock** (underwriting, legal, accounting, tax, registration, etc.) reduce the net proceeds received and additional paid-in capital. Equity interests and the issue costs inherent to them are permanent. Thus, they are not expensed.

EXAMPLE

In the common stock issue illustrated above, Parvenu incurred direct issue costs of $1.35 per share, resulting in net per-share proceeds of $15.65. The entry is the following:

Cash (50,000 shares × $15.65 net proceeds)	$782,500	
Common stock (50,000 shares × $1 stated value)		$ 50,000
Additional paid-in capital -- common (difference)		732,500

---

1)   In contrast, **debt issue costs** are capitalized and amortized. They benefit the entity only for the life of the debt, and the cost therefore must be systematically and rationally allocated over that life.

4.   **Stock Subscriptions**

a.   A stock subscription is a contractual arrangement to sell a specified number of shares at a specified price at some future date.

    1) If payment is reasonably assured, the corporation recognizes an obligation to issue stock, and the subscriber undertakes to pay for the shares subscribed.

    2) A down payment is usually made. The shareholder cannot resell the stock or exercise voting rights until the subscription is paid in full.

EXAMPLE

Parvenu has issued 10,000 shares of its no-par, $1 stated value common stock on a subscription basis when the market price is $14 per share. The subscribers are required to make a 40% down payment, with the remainder due in 6 months.

Cash (10,000 shares × $14 market price × 40%)	$56,000	
Receivable from stock subscription (10,000 shares × $14 market price × 60%)	84,000	
Common stock subscribed (10,000 shares × $1 stated value)		$ 10,000
Additional paid-in capital -- common (difference)		130,000

---

    3) The SEC requires that **stock subscriptions receivable** be reported as a **contra-equity account** unless collection has occurred before issuance of the financial statements. In that case, the account may be reported as an asset.

  b. When the subscription price is paid and the stock is issued, common stock subscribed is replaced with common stock.

EXAMPLE

In the example above, the subscribers later make full payment. The entry is the following:

Cash	$84,000	
Common stock subscribed (balance)	10,000	
Receivable for stock subscription (balance)		$84,000
Common stock (10,000 shares × $1 stated value)		10,000

---

    1) Thus, additional paid-in capital is increased when the stock is subscribed and is not affected when the stock is subsequently issued.

  c. When a subscriber defaults, the entry to record the subscription must be reversed.

    1) State laws and corporate policies vary with regard to defaults. The possibilities range from complete refund to complete forfeiture.

    2) To the extent that payment has been received and is forfeited, additional paid-in capital from stock subscription default is credited for the amount forfeited.

5. **Issuance for Property or Services**

  a. Occasionally, stock is issued for property received or services rendered.

    1) The transaction should be recorded at the more clearly determinable of the **fair values** of the stock issued or the property or services received.

    2) The fair value used is that in effect at the date of the agreement.

EXAMPLE

Consultant agreed to perform an internal control study in return for 500 shares of Parvenu common stock. On the day the contract was signed, Parvenu common stock was trading at $12.50 per share. Consultant spent 39 hours on the study, and its normal billing rate is $160 per hour. At the time Consultant submitted the completed study to Parvenu's management, the stock was trading at $13.50 per share.

Parvenu records the transaction at the market price of the stock because its fair value is more clearly determinable than the value of the services.

Consulting expense (500 shares × $12.50 price at time of contract)	$6,250	
Common stock (500 shares × $1 stated value)		$ 500
Additional paid-in capital -- common (difference)		5,750

6. **Donated Capital**

    a. In general, contributions received must be recognized as revenues or gains in the period of receipt. They should be measured at fair value.

    b. Thus, the receipt of a contribution of an **entity's own stock** is recorded at fair value as increases in both contributed capital and treasury stock.

        1) Because these accounts offset, the transaction has no net effect on equity. Also, transactions in an entity's own stock cannot result in a gain or loss.

7. **Conversion of Convertible Preferred Stock**

    a. When conversion occurs, all related amounts are removed from the books and replaced with amounts related to the new security.

        1) Transactions in an entity's own stock may not result in a gain or loss. Thus, the conversion is reported using the **book value method**. The new shares are recorded at the carrying amount of the converted shares.

EXAMPLE

Parvenu issued 5,000 shares of $40 par value, 7% preferred stock, each share convertible into five shares of its no-par, $1 stated value common stock beginning 6 months after issue. The market price on the day of issue was $68 per share.

Cash (5,000 shares × $68 market price)	$340,000	
7% convertible preferred stock (5,000 shares × $40 par value)		$200,000
Additional paid-in capital -- preferred (difference)		140,000

Six months after the convertible preferred stock was issued, all the shareholders exercised their conversion privilege.

7% convertible preferred stock (balance)	$200,000	
Additional paid-in capital -- preferred (balance)	140,000	
Common stock (5,000 shares × 5 × $1 stated value)		$ 25,000
Additional paid-in capital -- common (difference)		315,000

---

8. **Combined Issuance**

    a. The proceeds of the combined issuance of different classes of securities are allocated based on the relative fair values of the securities.

EXAMPLE

Parvenu issued 2,000 shares of its no-par, $1 stated value common stock and 1,000 shares of its $50 par value, 6% preferred stock for a lump sum of $99,000. At the time, the common stock was trading at $15 per share, and the preferred stock was trading at $60 per share.

Fair value of common stock (2,000 shares × $15 market price)	$30,000
Fair value of preferred stock (1,000 shares × $60 market price)	60,000
Total fair value issued	$90,000

Common stock is 33.3333% of the total ($30,000 ÷ $90,000), and preferred stock is 66.6667% ($60,000 ÷ $90,000). The proceeds are therefore assigned as $33,000 to common stock ($99,000 × 33.3333%) and $66,000 to preferred stock ($99,000 × 66.6667%). The sale is recorded as follows:

Cash (lump sum)	$99,000	
Common stock (2,000 shares × $1 stated value)		$ 2,000
Additional paid-in capital -- common ($33,000 – $2,000)		31,000
6% preferred stock (1,000 shares × $50 par value)		50,000
Additional paid-in capital -- preferred ($66,000 – $50,000)		16,000

b. If the fair value of one class of securities is not known, the **incremental method** is used. The other securities are recorded at their fair values. The remaining proceeds are credited to the securities for which fair value is not determinable.

EXAMPLE

Simdyne, Inc., a closely held corporation, issued 5,000 shares of $2 par value common stock and 8% bonds with a face amount of $100,000 for a lump sum of $120,000. Because no active market exists for Simdyne's stock, its fair value cannot be determined. If the bonds had been issued separately, they would have resulted in proceeds of $80,000.

Lump sum received	$120,000	
Fair value of bonds	(80,000)	
Remainder assigned to common stock	$ 40,000	

The sale is recorded as follows:

Cash (lump sum)	$120,000	
Discount on bonds payable (difference)	20,000	
Bonds payable (face amount)		$100,000
Common stock (5,000 shares × $2 par value)		10,000
Additional paid-in capital -- common ($40,000 – $10,000)		30,000

Stop and review! You have completed the outline for this subunit. Study multiple-choice questions 3 through 6 beginning on page 551.

15.3 STOCK WARRANTS AND STOCK RIGHTS

1. **Stock Warrants**

   a. A warrant is a certificate representing **a right to purchase shares** at a specified price within a specified period. Thus, it is an equity security. Warrants are usually attached to other securities.

2. **Preemptive Right**

   a. The preemptive right safeguards a shareholder's proportionate ownership. It is the **right to purchase a pro rata amount** of a new issuance of the same class of stock. However, many entities have eliminated the preemptive right because it may inhibit the large issuances of stock that are often needed in business combinations.

3. **Issuer's Accounting**

   a. In a rights offering, each shareholder is issued a warrant that is an option to buy a certain number of shares at a fixed price.

      1) When rights are issued for no consideration, the issuer makes only a memorandum entry.

         a) If rights previously issued without consideration are allowed to lapse, contributed capital is unaffected.

      2) Rights issued for consideration constitute share-based payment, discussed in detail in Study Unit 12, Subunit 6.

   b. From the announcement of the rights offering to the issue date, the stock trades **rights-on**. After the issue date, it trades **ex-rights** because the rights can be sold separately.

      1) If the **rights are exercised** and stock is issued, the issuer will reflect the proceeds received as a credit to (an increase in) common (preferred) stock at par value, with any remainder credited to additional paid-in capital.

   c. Transaction costs associated with the redemption of stock rights reduce equity.

4.   **Recipient's Accounting**

a.   The recipient of stock rights must **allocate the carrying amount of the shares owned** between the shares and rights based on their relative fair values at the time the rights are received. The recipient then has three options:

1)   If the rights are exercised, the amount allocated to them becomes part of the carrying amount of the acquired shares.

2)   If the rights are sold, their carrying amount is credited, cash is debited, and a gain (loss) is credited (debited).

3)   If the rights expire, a loss is recorded.

b.   Stock rights with readily determinable fair values are equity securities that are classified as available-for-sale or trading.

Stop and review! You have completed the outline for this subunit. Study multiple-choice questions 7 and 8 beginning on page 552.

15.4 TREASURY STOCK -- ACQUISITION

The AICPA has released multiple CPA questions involving treasury stock calculations under both the cost and par-value methods. Successful candidates need to know the journal entries used by each method to be able to identify the correct debits and credits.

1.   **Cost Method vs. Par-Value Method**

a.   Under the **cost method**, treasury shares are reported at their reacquisition price, and the journal entry is a debit to treasury stock and a credit to cash.

1)   On the balance sheet, treasury stock is reported separately as a reduction from the other shareholder equity accounts.

2)   The cost method is much more common in practice.

b.   Under the **par-value method**, the acquisition is treated as a constructive retirement. All related amounts are removed from the books.

c.   Donated stock may be accounted for using either method.

2.   **Acquisition Price > Original Issue Price**

a.   Under the par-value method, if the acquisition price is greater than par (stated) value and the original issue price, the difference is a reduction of retained earnings or a credit balance in paid-in capital (PiC) from treasury stock transactions.

EXAMPLE

Parvenu reacquired 5,000 shares of its no-par, $1 stated value common stock for $20 per share. This stock had originally been issued at $17 per share. Parvenu had no prior treasury stock transactions.

Cost Method:

Treasury stock (5,000 shares × $20 market price)	$100,000	
Cash (payment)		$100,000

Par-Value Method:

Treasury stock (5,000 shares × $1 stated value)	$ 5,000	
Additional paid-in capital -- common (5,000 shares × $16 original issue excess)	80,000	
Retained earnings (difference)	15,000	
Cash (payment)		$100,000

3. **Acquisition Price < Par (Stated) Value**

   a. Under the par-value method, if the acquisition price is less than par (stated) value and the original issue price, the difference is an increase in PiC from treasury stock transactions. (Gains and losses are not recognized on transactions in an entity's own stock.)

EXAMPLE

Parvenu reacquired 5,000 shares of its no-par, $1 stated value common stock for $0.90 per share.

Cost Method:

Treasury stock (5,000 shares × $0.90 market price)	$4,500	
Cash (payment)		$4,500

Par-Value Method:

Treasury stock (5,000 shares × $1 stated value)	$5,000	
PiC from treasury stock transactions (5,000 shares × $0.10 reacquisition excess)		$ 500
Cash (payment)		4,500

---

4. **Presentation**

   a. Treasury stock is not an asset. It is reported as a contra-equity account.

Stop and review! You have completed the outline for this subunit. Study multiple-choice questions 9 through 12 beginning on page 553.

15.5 TREASURY STOCK -- REISSUE

1. **Reissue Price > Cost**

   a. The excess is credited to paid-in capital from treasury stock transactions.

EXAMPLE

Parvenu reissued 1,000 shares of its treasury stock that had been acquired for $20 per share. At the time of reissue, the market price was $22 per share.

Cost Method:

Cash (1,000 shares × $22 market price)	$22,000	
Treasury stock (1,000 shares × $20 cost)		$20,000
PiC from treasury stock transactions (difference)		2,000

Par-Value Method:

Cash (1,000 shares × $22 market price)	$22,000	
Treasury stock (1,000 shares × $1 stated value)		$ 1,000
PiC from treasury stock transactions (difference)		21,000

---

2. **Reissue Price < Cost**

   a. Under the cost method, the difference is debited to paid-in capital from treasury stock transactions to the extent of any credit balance. Otherwise, the debit is to retained earnings.

   b. Under the par-value method, the difference is credited to paid-in capital from treasury stock transactions.

EXAMPLE

Parvenu reissued 1,000 shares of its treasury stock that had been acquired for $20 per share. At the time of reissue, the market price was $18 per share. Parvenu had no prior reissuance of treasury stock. Thus, the accounting under the cost method includes a debit to retained earnings for the entire difference between the cost and the price of the reissued shares.

Cost Method:

Cash (1,000 shares × $18 market price)	$18,000	
Retained earnings (difference)	2,000	
Treasury stock (1,000 shares × $20 cost)		$20,000

Par-Value Method:

Cash (1,000 shares × $18 market price)	$18,000	
Treasury stock (1,000 shares × $1 stated value)		$ 1,000
PiC from treasury stock transactions (difference)		17,000

The AICPA has also released a number of CPA questions addressing the reissue price and associated journal entries used when a corporation reissues previously purchased treasury stock.

Stop and review! You have completed the outline for this subunit. Study multiple-choice questions 13 through 16 beginning on page 554.

15.6 RETIREMENT OF STOCK

1. Occasionally, a company decides to retire its own stock. The company may retire treasury stock it already owns or non-treasury stock it purchases. The journal entry to record this retirement includes the following:

    a. When treasury stock is retired, the treasury stock account is credited. When non-treasury stock is retired, cash or other consideration given is credited.

    b. The stock account is debited for the par or stated value.

    c. Additional paid-in capital is debited to the extent it exists from the original issuance.

    d. Any remainder is debited to retained earnings or credited to paid-in capital from stock retirement.

EXAMPLE

Maincat Co. reacquired 10,000 shares of its only class of common stock (par value $1 per share) for $50,000. The shares were issued at $10 per share. Maincat uses the cost method to account for treasury stock transactions but has no current balances related to them. The following is the entry to record retirement of the shares:

Common stock	$10,000	
Additional paid-in capital -- common	90,000	
Treasury stock		$50,000
PiC from retirement of treasury stock		50,000

---

2. No gain or loss is reported on transactions involving an entity's own stock.

    a. However, the transfer of nonmonetary assets in exchange for stock requires recognition of any holding gain or loss on the nonmonetary assets.

3. A retirement of treasury stock does not change the number of shares authorized.

4. Preferred stock may be subject to a call provision, that is, mandatory redemption at the option of the issuer at a specified price.

Stop and review! You have completed the outline for this subunit. Study multiple-choice questions 17 and 18 on page 556.

15.7 CASH DIVIDENDS

1. Dividends may be distributed in the form of cash or property. (Stock dividends, discussed later in this study unit, are not a form of return on investment.)

   a. Dividends are paid on outstanding shares only, not on treasury stock.

2. **Relevant Dates**

   a. On the **date of declaration**, the board of directors formally approves a dividend.

      1) Unlike a stock dividend, a cash or property dividend cannot be withdrawn once declared. Thus, a cash or property dividend becomes a legal liability of the corporation on the date of declaration.

      2) The dividend is recorded by reclassifying a portion of retained earnings as a payable.

         a) In most states, a corporation may not declare a dividend in excess of its balance of retained earnings.

   b. All holders of the stock on the **date of record** are legally entitled to receive the dividend.

      1) The gap between the date of declaration and the date of record allows investors to acquire or dispose of shares in response to the announcement of the dividend.

   c. The **date of payment** is the date on which the dividend is paid.

EXAMPLE

On September 12, Parvenu's board of directors declared a $4 per share dividend to be paid on October 15 to all holders of common stock as of October 1. On the date of declaration, Parvenu held 5,000 of its common shares in the treasury, and 45,000 shares were outstanding.

September 12:

Retained earnings (45,000 shares outstanding × $4 per share)	$180,000	
Dividend payable		$180,000

October 1:
Memorandum entry only

October 15:

Dividend payable	$180,000	
Cash		$180,000

---

3. **Dividends on Preferred Stock**

   a. Most preferred shares are issued with a **stated dividend rate**.

   b. Unlike interest on debt, dividends on preferred stock are not a legal obligation of the corporation until the board chooses to declare them. Common shareholders may not receive a dividend unless the current-year preferred dividend has been paid.

   c. When a corporation has outstanding **cumulative preferred stock**, common shareholders may not receive a dividend until all preferred dividends in arrears have been paid.

      1) **Dividends in arrears** are preferred dividends that were not declared in prior years.

      2) Although they are not legal liabilities of the corporation, dividends in arrears must be disclosed either on the face of the balance sheet or in the notes, both in the aggregate and per share.

EXAMPLE

On January 10 of the current year, Parvenu's board declared a $3 per share dividend to all holders of common stock. Parvenu has not paid dividends on its 10,000 outstanding shares of $50 par value, 6% cumulative preferred stock for the previous 2 years. Parvenu had 45,000 shares of common stock outstanding. On the date of declaration, Parvenu makes the following calculation:

Preferred dividends -- arrears (10,000 shares × $50 par value × 6% × 2 years)	$ 60,000
Preferred dividends -- current (10,000 shares × $50 par value × 6%)	30,000
Common dividends (45,000 shares × $3 per share)	135,000
Debit to retained earnings	$225,000

    d.   Preferred stock may be fully participating. It may share equally in a cash dividend after a basic return has been paid to holders of both common and preferred stock at the preference rate for the preferred.

        1)   Participation may be limited, for example, up to a ceiling rate or only after a specified higher rate has been paid to the common shareholders.

Stop and review! You have completed the outline for this subunit. Study multiple-choice questions 19 through 22 beginning on page 556.

15.8 PROPERTY DIVIDENDS AND LIQUIDATING DIVIDENDS

    1.   **Property Dividends**

        a.   When a corporation declares a dividend consisting of tangible property, the property is first remeasured to fair value as of the date of declaration.

EXAMPLE

Parvenu's board of directors resolved to distribute obsolete inventory from its warehouse to holders of common stock. The inventory had a carrying amount of $40,000 and a fair value of $10,000.

Date of declaration:

Loss on inventory revaluation (carrying amount – fair value)	$30,000	
Inventory		$30,000
Retained earnings (fair value)	$10,000	
Property dividend payable		$10,000

Date of distribution:

Property dividend payable	$10,000	
Inventory		$10,000

    2.   **Liquidating Dividends**

        a.   Dividends in excess of a corporation's retained earnings are liquidating dividends. They are not considered dividends but are treated as a return of capital.

        1)   The effect of a liquidating dividend is to decrease contributed capital.

        2)   Additional paid-in capital is debited first to the extent available before other contributed capital accounts are charged.

Stop and review! You have completed the outline for this subunit. Study multiple-choice questions 23 and 24 beginning on page 557.

15.9 STOCK DIVIDENDS AND STOCK SPLITS

1. **Definitions**

   a. Stock dividends and stock splits are distributions of stock to current shareholders in return for no consideration.

      1) In a **stock dividend**, a portion of retained earnings is capitalized as part of paid-in capital.

         a) The **par or stated value** of the shares is unchanged.

         b) An issuance of shares **less than 20% to 25%** of the previously outstanding common shares should be recognized as a **stock dividend**.

            i) The **SEC requires** an issuance of less than 25% by a public entity to be treated as a stock dividend.

         c) An issuance of **more than 20% to 25%** of the previously outstanding common shares (25% or more for public entities) more closely resembles a **stock split** than a dividend.

            i) An entity may be legally required to capitalize the par (or stated) value of the additional shares issued. In this case, the term **stock split in the form of a dividend** should be used.

      2) In a **stock split**, no journal entry is made other than a memorandum entry.

         a) The **par or stated value** of the shares is reduced.

   b. Stock dividends and stock splits do not affect the fair value of a shareholder's interest or the proportionate amount of that interest. Thus, the effect is simply a reclassification of equity.

      1) However, because more shares are outstanding, the fair value (and market price) of a share is reduced.

2. **Stock Dividends**

   a. The **primary purpose** is to provide shareholders with additional evidence of their interests in the retained earnings of the business without distribution of cash or other assets.

   b. In accounting for a stock dividend, the fair value of the additional shares issued is reclassified from retained earnings to capital stock (at par or stated value) and the difference to additional paid-in capital.

EXAMPLE

Parvenu's board of directors declared a 10% stock dividend on the 45,000 shares of common stock outstanding ($1 stated value). The stock was trading for $15 per share at the declaration date.

Date of declaration:

Retained earnings [(45,000 shares × 10%) × $15 market price]	$67,500	
Common stock dividend distributable [(45,000 shares × 10%) × $1]		$ 4,500
Additional paid-in capital -- common (difference)		63,000

Date of distribution:

Common stock dividend distributable	$ 4,500	
Common stock		$ 4,500

---

   c. Unlike cash and property dividends, stock dividends are revocable. However, undistributed stock dividends normally are reported in the equity section.

3.   **Stock Split in the Form of a Dividend**

a.   The state of incorporation may require capitalization of retained earnings for a **stock split in the form of a dividend**, usually in an amount based on **par or stated value**.

EXAMPLE

In the preceding example, assume that a 40% stock split in the form of a dividend was declared.

Date of declaration:

Retained earnings [(45,000 shares × 40%) × $1 stated value]	$18,000	
Common stock dividend distributable [(45,000 shares × 40%) × $1]		$18,000

Date of distribution:

Common stock dividend distributable	$18,000	
Common stock		$18,000

---

4.   **Stock Splits**

a.   The **primary purpose of** a stock split is to improve the stock's marketability by reducing its market price and proportionally increasing the number of shares outstanding.

b.   A stock split does not require an adjustment to retained earnings or paid-in capital and **does not affect total equity**.

EXAMPLE

Parvenu's board of directors declared a 2-for-1 common stock split. The laws of Parvenu's state of incorporation protect treasury stock from dilution. Thus, Parvenu reduces the stated value of its common stock to $0.50 per share and issues 100,000 new shares: 90,000 to shareholders (45,000 × 2) and 10,000 to the treasury (5,000 × 2). Total equity remains unchanged.

100,000 shares × $0.50 (new) = 50,000 shares × $1 (old)

---

c.   A **reverse stock split** reduces the number of shares outstanding, which serves to increase the fair value per share of those shares still outstanding.

5.   **Other Issues**

a.   The **recipient** of a stock dividend or stock split should **not recognize income**. After receipt, the shareholder has the same proportionate interest in the corporation and the same total carrying amount as before the declaration.

b.   **Treasury stock** may be adjusted for stock dividends and splits to protect it from dilution. However, **some states prohibit** the payment of stock dividends on treasury stock.

Stop and review! You have completed the outline for this subunit. Study multiple-choice questions 25 through 28 beginning on page 558.

15.10 PARTNERSHIPS -- FORMATION AND ALLOCATION

1.   **Sole Proprietorships**

a.   Sole proprietorships are business entities **owned by individuals**.

1)   A sole proprietorship is not a separate legal entity. It is an extension of the owner. Thus, a sole proprietor has **unlimited liability** for business debts.

b.   A single capital (equity) account is customarily used to account for all equity transactions of a sole proprietorship.

c.   A sole proprietorship does not pay income taxes. Rather, any profit or loss flows through to the owner, who reports the amounts in his/her individual tax return.

d.   Relevant GAAP ordinarily apply regardless of the form of business organization.

2. **Partnerships Defined**

    a. A partnership is an association of two or more persons to carry on, as co-owners, a business for profit.

    b. Unlike corporations, general partnerships do not insulate a partner from liability to creditors. **Each general partner has unlimited liability** for partnership debts.

3. **Partnership Formation**

    a. Partners **contribute cash and other property** as the basis of their equity in a partnership. Cash is recorded at its nominal amount, and property at its **fair value**.

EXAMPLE

Gilda Rosecrans, Bill Bragg, and Tim Thomas agree to form Chickamauga Partners. Besides cash, each partner contributes tangible property consisting of a building, inventory, and equipment, respectively. Rosecrans's building is subject to a $45,000 mortgage. The values of the contributions on the date of formation are as follows:

Partner	Cash	Property at Carrying Amount	Property at Fair Value
Rosecrans	$20,000	$80,000	$110,000
Bragg	55,000	18,000	15,000
Thomas	40,000	30,000	20,000

The journal entry to record the formation of the partnership is

Cash ($20,000 + $55,000 + $40,000)	$115,000	
Inventory	15,000	
Equipment	20,000	
Building	110,000	
Mortgage payable		$45,000
Bragg, capital ($55,000 + $15,000)		70,000
Rosecrans, capital ($20,000 + $110,000 – $45,000)		85,000
Thomas, capital ($40,000 + $20,000)		60,000

---

    b. The equity section of the partnership balance sheet includes only the partners' capital accounts.

    c. The partners may decide that a partner's contribution exceeds the fair value of cash and tangible property contributed, e.g., because (s)he has special expertise or an established customer list. Two accounting treatments are available.

        1) Under the **bonus method**, only the fair values of cash and tangible property contributed are recorded on the partnership's books. The partners then apportion the capital accounts to reflect a partner's special contribution.

EXAMPLE

Dick McPherson and Josh Logan contribute $90,000 and $10,000, respectively, to their new partnership. Under normal circumstances, the journal entry is

Cash	$100,000	
McPherson, capital		$90,000
Logan, capital		10,000

However, the two partners agree that Logan's extensive contacts in the field in which the partnership will do business are worth more than the cash he is contributing. Their agreement results in a 60:40 apportionment.

Cash	$100,000	
McPherson, capital		$60,000
Logan, capital		40,000

---

        2) Under the **goodwill method**, the partners record an asset account for the perceived fair value of the intangible benefit contributed by a given partner. In practice, no objective basis is needed for this measure of the goodwill.

EXAMPLE

McPherson and Logan acknowledge the worth of Logan's professional contacts by creating a goodwill account. Their 60:40 apportionment of equity results in the following journal entry:

Cash	$100,000	
Goodwill	30,000	
McPherson, capital		$78,000
Logan, capital		52,000

---

4. **Additions and Withdrawals of Capital**

   a. Existing partners may make **additional contributions** to the partnership.

      1) The appropriate asset is debited for the nominal amount of cash or fair value of property, and that partner's capital account is credited. No reapportionment of equity among the partners is performed.

   b. Partners' withdrawals are recorded in **distribution accounts**.

EXAMPLE

Rosecrans and Thomas make a withdrawal of cash from Chickamauga Partners:

Rosecrans, distributions	$10,000	
Thomas, distributions	5,000	
Cash		$15,000

Distribution accounts are nominal accounts that are closed to partnership capital at the end of each period.

Rosecrans, capital	$10,000	
Thomas, capital	5,000	
Rosecrans, distributions		$10,000
Thomas, distributions		5,000

---

5. **Partnership Income and Loss -- Simple**

   a. Profit and loss are distributed equally among partners unless the partnership agreement provides otherwise.

      1) The equal distribution is based on the number of partners, not capital balances.

      2) If the partnership agreement specifies how profits are to be shared but is silent with respect to losses, losses are divided in the same manner as profits.

EXAMPLE

Chickamauga Partners' agreement is that net income will be distributed 50% to Rosecrans and 25% each to Bragg and Thomas. The partnership's net income for the period is $60,000.

Income summary	$60,000	
Bragg, capital		$15,000
Rosecrans, capital		30,000
Thomas, capital		15,000

The distribution of profit and loss is not based on the relative proportions of the partners' capital balances, but only on the contractual agreement entered into by the partners at the time of formation. Had Chickamauga Partners lacked such an agreement, profits and losses would have been distributed equally. Given three partners, each would have received 33 1/3% of the net income.

The statement of partners' capital can be prepared once the books are closed.

	Bragg	Rosecrans	Thomas	Totals
Capital balances, beginning of year	$70,000	$ 85,000	$60,000	$215,000
Add: Allocation of net income	15,000	30,000	15,000	60,000
Minus: Distributions	0	(10,000)	(5,000)	(15,000)
Capital balances, end of year	$85,000	$105,000	$70,000	$260,000

6. **Partnership Income and Loss -- Complex**

    a. Partners often find that a division of profits based on a simple formula (e.g., 40%:30%:30%) is not adequate to reflect the business dynamics of the partnership.

    b. A typical arrangement calls for either or both of the following provisions:

        1) The accrual of interest on each partner's capital balance
        2) A bonus to one or more of the partners

    c. Any remaining profit is then divided among the partners according to the agreed-upon ratio.

EXAMPLE

The McPherson and Logan partners have agreed to the following provisions for the division of profits:

1) Both partners will be allocated 15% interest on their average monthly capital balances for the year.
2) Logan will receive a bonus of 10% of net income after subtraction of interest.
3) Any remainder will be divided according to the agreed-upon ratio of 60% to McPherson and 40% to Logan.

McPherson's and Logan's average monthly capital balances for the year were $60,000 and $40,000, respectively. The partnership has $50,000 of net income for the year. The three provisions for the division of profit are applied in order as follows:

	McPherson	Logan
Average monthly capital balances	$60,000	$40,000
Times: interest percentage	15%	15%
Interest on capital	$ 9,000	$ 6,000

	Total
Remaining net income ($50,000 – $9,000 – $6,000)	$35,000
Minus: Logan's bonus (10%)	(3,500)
Remaining net income	$31,500

	McPherson	Logan
Remaining net income	$31,500	$31,500
Times: allocation percentages	60%	40%
Residual net income	$18,900	$12,600

The following is the total allocation of the year's net income to the partners:

	McPherson	Logan
Interest on capital	$ 9,000	$ 6,000
Bonus		3,500
Residual net income	18,900	12,600
Allocated total net income	$27,900	$22,100

Total net income of $50,000 was allocated ($27,900 + $22,100).

Stop and review! You have completed the outline for this subunit. Study multiple-choice questions 29 through 32 beginning on page 559.

15.11 PARTNERSHIPS -- CHANGES AND LIQUIDATION

1. **Sale of a Partnership Interest**

    a. When an existing partner sells his/her interest in a partnership to an outside party, the new partner is entitled to share in the partnership's profits and losses. However, (s)he is not allowed to participate in management decisions until the remaining partners agree to admit the new partner to the partnership.

EXAMPLE

Bill Bragg sells his interest in Chickamauga Partners to Jenna Longstreet for $100,000, an amount greater than Bragg's capital balance.

Bragg, capital	$85,000	
Longstreet, capital		$85,000

(The cash exchanged between Bragg and Longstreet is irrelevant to the partnership accounting.) Longstreet now shares in the partnership's profits and losses. She owns Bragg's partnership interest but may not participate in management.

---

2. **Addition of a New Partner**

   a. New partners may contribute cash, property, or services. A partner's tangible and intangible contributions may be recognized using one of four accounting methods.

   b. **Bonus Credited to the Original Partners**

   1) If the fair value of the new partner's contribution exceeds the amount credited to his/her capital account, the excess is a bonus to the existing partners.

EXAMPLE

Instead of buying out Bragg, Longstreet contributes $80,000 in cash to the partnership. The three existing partners agree to assign her a 20% interest in the partnership's capital.

Longstreet's contribution of $80,000 increases the total capital of the partnership to $340,000. Her capital account is credited for the agreed-upon 20% interest in the new partnership's total capital ($68,000). The existing partners split the bonus ($80,000 – $68,000) in proportion to their contractual profit-loss allocation.

Cash	$80,000	
Bragg, capital ($12,000 × 25%)		$ 3,000
Longstreet, capital ($340,000 × 20%)		68,000
Rosecrans, capital ($12,000 × 50%)		6,000
Thomas, capital ($12,000 × 25%)		3,000

---

   c. **Goodwill Credited to the Original Partners**

   1) If the original partners wish to recognize an increase in total partnership capital in excess of the new partner's contribution, the excess is debited to goodwill.

EXAMPLE

The original partners have assigned Longstreet a 20% interest in return for $80,000, implying a fair value of $400,000 for the partnership as a whole ($80,000 ÷ 20%).

Cash	$80,000	
Longstreet, capital		$80,000

Goodwill is calculated, recorded, and allocated among the partners as follows:

Fair value of partnership	$400,000	
Minus: current capital balances	(260,000)	
Minus: allocated to new partner	(80,000)	
Goodwill	$ 60,000	

Goodwill	$60,000	
Bragg, capital ($60,000 × 25%)		$15,000
Rosecrans, capital ($60,000 × 50%)		30,000
Thomas, capital ($60,000 × 25%)		15,000

---

   d. **Revaluation of Current Assets**

   1) The existing partners may recognize changes in the fair values of the partnership assets and any increase as a bonus in their respective capital accounts.

EXAMPLE

Before admitting Longstreet, the partners remeasure their identifiable assets. They determine that the building and equipment are each worth $10,000 more than their carrying amounts. This revaluation is allocated to the existing partners' capital accounts.

Equipment	$10,000	
Building	10,000	
Bragg, capital ($20,000 × 25%)		$ 5,000
Rosecrans, capital ($20,000 × 50%)		10,000
Thomas, capital ($20,000 × 25%)		5,000

The partnership's total capital is now $360,000 ($260,000 + $20,000 + $80,000 cash from Longstreet). Longstreet's capital account is credited for 20% of the new total ($72,000). The bonus ($80,000 – $72,000) is allocated among the existing partners in proportion to their profit-and-loss percentages.

Cash	$80,000	
Bragg, capital ($8,000 × 25%)		$ 2,000
Longstreet, capital ($360,000 × 20%)		72,000
Rosecrans, capital ($8,000 × 50%)		4,000
Thomas, capital ($8,000 × 25%)		2,000

    e.   **Bonus or Goodwill Credited to the New Partner**

        1)   The existing partners acknowledge an intangible benefit brought to the partnership in addition to cash or property.

EXAMPLE

The existing partners wish to recognize the leadership that Longstreet brings to the business by crediting her with a 25% interest in the partnership. A 25% interest in the resulting $340,000 total partnership capital ($260,000 existing + $80,000 contributed by Longstreet) is $85,000. The excess of Longstreet's capital over her cash contribution is a reduction in the existing partners' capital accounts.

Cash	$80,000	
Bragg, capital ($5,000 × 25%)	1,250	
Rosecrans, capital ($5,000 × 50%)	2,500	
Thomas, capital ($5,000 × 25%)	1,250	
Longstreet, capital		$85,000

---

  3. **Withdrawal of a Partner**

    a.   When a partner withdraws, the transaction is in essence a buy-out by the remaining partners. An appraisal determines the fair values of the partnership assets, and the withdrawing partner receives cash or other property equal to his/her capital balance after the appraisal. One of three accounting methods may be used.

        1)   **Bonus Method**

            a)   The results of the appraisal are not formally recognized.

EXAMPLE

Bragg decides that he wants to leave Chickamauga Partners without bringing in another partner to replace him.

An appraisal of the business concludes that the building and equipment are each worth $10,000 more than their carrying amounts and that the partnership has generated $10,000 of goodwill during its time in operation. Bragg is entitled to a distribution that includes his proportionate share of these valuations ($30,000 × 25% = $7,500).

The apportionment of Bragg's share of the revaluation and recognition of the new goodwill is subtracted from the remaining partners' capital accounts, based on the relative profit-and-loss percentages (Rosecrans: 50% ÷ 75% = 66 2/3%, Thomas: 25% ÷ 75% = 33 1/3%).

Bragg, capital	$85,000	
Rosecrans, capital ($7,500 × 66 2/3%)	5,000	
Thomas, capital ($7,500 × 33 1/3%)	2,500	
Cash		$92,500

2) Goodwill Method

    a) Tangible assets are formally remeasured, and any goodwill is recognized.

EXAMPLE

The appraisal results in the asset accounts being adjusted.

Building	$10,000	
Equipment	10,000	
Goodwill	10,000	
Bragg, capital ($30,000 × 25%)		$ 7,500
Rosecrans, capital ($30,000 × 50%)		15,000
Thomas, capital ($30,000 × 25%)		7,500

Bragg's capital account is removed from the books and the appropriate amount of cash is distributed to him.

Bragg, capital	$92,500	
Cash		$92,500

---

3) Hybrid Method

    a) Tangible assets are formally remeasured, but goodwill is not recognized.

EXAMPLE

The appraisal results in the asset accounts being adjusted but not in the recognition of goodwill.

Building	$10,000	
Equipment	10,000	
Bragg, capital ($20,000 × 25%)		$ 5,000
Rosecrans, capital ($20,000 × 50%)		10,000
Thomas, capital ($20,000 × 25%)		5,000

Bragg's capital account is removed from the books, and the appropriate amount of cash is distributed to him.

Bragg, capital	$90,000	
Cash		$90,000

---

4. **Liquidation of a Partnership -- Process**

    a. When the partners dissolve their partnership, the process of liquidating noncash assets and settling liabilities begins. The liquidation process has **four steps**:

        1) First, any gain or loss realized from the actual sale of assets is allocated to the partners' capital accounts in accordance with the profit-and-loss ratio.

        2) Second, remaining noncash assets are assumed to have a fair value of $0, which results in an **assumed loss** equal to their carrying amounts. This amount is allocated to the partners' accounts in accordance with the profit-and-loss ratio.

        3) Third, if at least one of the partners' capital accounts has a deficit balance, the deficit is allocated to the remaining partners' accounts.

        4) Fourth, the final balances in the partnership accounts equal the amounts of cash, if any, that may be distributed to the partners.

    b. Creditors are paid in full before any distributions are made to partners. However, partners who are creditors share equally with nonpartner creditors. In practice, because partners are liable for all partnership debts, partnership creditors are paid first.

c.   After payment of creditors, any **surplus** is paid in cash to the partners. A partner has no right to a distribution in kind and is not required to accept a distribution in kind.

d.   To settle partnership accounts with **credit balances**, each partner receives a distribution equal to the excess of credits over debits to his/her account. Thus, no distinction is made between distributions of capital and of profits.

   1)   **Profits and losses** from liquidation of assets are credits and debits, respectively.

   2)   **Prior credits** to an account include contributions made and the share of profits.

   3)   **Prior debits** include distributions received and the share of losses.

e.   If the account has a debit balance, the partner is liable to contribute the amount of the balance.

   1)   If a partner does not make a required contribution, the other partners must pay the difference in the same proportion in which they share losses.

   2)   A partner making an excess contribution may recover the excess from the other partners.

   3)   Moreover, the representative of creditors of the partnership or of a partner (e.g., a trustee in bankruptcy) may enforce the obligation to contribute.

   4)   One effect of these rules is that, consistent with the federal Bankruptcy Code, partnership creditors

      a)   Have priority in partnership assets and

      b)   Share equally with creditors of a partner in the partner's separate assets.

5.   **Liquidation of a Partnership -- Cash Predistribution Plan**

   a.   This plan (a schedule of possible losses) is prepared at the beginning of the liquidation process. It avoids the need for new schedules after each transaction during the liquidation period.

      1)   The plan consists of a series of maximum incremental losses to be incurred during liquidation. Thus, it indicates the amount of loss that would eliminate each partner's capital balance in sequence.

      2)   The purpose of the cash predistribution plan is to determine the amount of **cash that can safely be distributed** to the partners.

EXAMPLE

After several years of operation, Rosecrans, Bragg, and Thomas decide to dissolve Chickamauga Partners. At the time, the partnership's balance sheet is as follows:

Assets		Liabilities and Equity	
Cash	$ 20,000	Accounts payable	$ 10,000
Inventory	4,000	Loan from Rosecrans	40,000
Equipment	6,000	Bragg, capital	20,000
Building	110,000	Rosecrans, capital	60,000
		Thomas, capital	10,000
Total	$140,000	Total	$140,000

The maximum loss that would eliminate each partner's capital balance is calculated.

	Beginning of Liquidation	Loss Allocation	Maximum Loss
Bragg, capital	$20,000	25%	$ 80,000
Rosecrans, capital	60,000	50%	120,000
Thomas, capital	10,000	25%	40,000

Thomas is the most vulnerable. A loss of $40,000 eliminates Thomas's interest in the partnership.

	Bragg, Capital	Rosecrans, Capital	Thomas, Capital
Beginning balances	$20,000	$60,000	$10,000
Assumed $40,000 loss	(10,000)	(20,000)	(10,000)
Balances after Step 1	$10,000	$40,000	$ 0

The next maximum loss allowable is then calculated. Bragg's share is now 33% (25% ÷ 75%), and Rosecrans's is 67% (50% ÷ 75%).

	Beginning of Step 2	Loss Allocation	Maximum Loss
Bragg, capital	$10,000	33%	$30,303
Rosecrans, capital	40,000	67%	59,701

Bragg is the next most vulnerable. A further loss of $30,303 eliminates Bragg's interest.

	Bragg, Capital	Rosecrans, Capital
Beginning balances	$10,000	$40,000
Assumed $30,303 loss	(10,000)	(20,303)
Balances after Step 2	$ 0	$19,697

Given three partners, only three incremental losses eliminate the partnership's capital.

	Bragg, Capital	Rosecrans, Capital	Thomas, Capital
Beginning balances	$20,000	$60,000	$10,000
Assumed $40,000 loss	(10,000)	(20,000)	(10,000)
Balances after Step 1	$10,000	$40,000	$ 0
Assumed $30,303 loss	(10,000)	(20,303)	
Balances after Step 2	$ 0	$19,697	
Assumed $19,697 loss		(19,697)	
Final balance		$ 0	

If each successive loss in reverse does not occur, that amount of cash may safely be distributed to the partners. As cash becomes available after the partnership's liabilities are settled, it is safe to distribute the first $19,697 to Rosecrans. If a further $30,303 becomes available, it can be distributed as $20,303 to Rosecrans and $10,000 to Bragg. Any additional cash may be distributed to all three partners.

-- Continued on next page --

EXAMPLE -- Continued

The following is the cash predistribution plan:

Outside creditors	$10,000
Liquidation expenses	14,000
First distribution	$24,000
Loan from Rosecrans	$40,000
Second distribution	$40,000
To Rosecrans	$19,697
Third distribution	$19,697
To Bragg	$10,000
To Rosecrans	20,303
Fourth distribution	$30,303

All further distributions:
   Bragg -- 25%
   Rosecrans -- 50%
   Thomas -- 25%

---

6. **Incorporation of a Partnership**

   a. When a partnership incorporates, the transfer of the net assets, including goodwill, should be at fair value. Thus, contributed capital will equal the fair value of the assets transferred minus the fair value of the liabilities assumed.

When testing partnership accounting concepts, the AICPA has used questions asking for calculations of amounts of partner capital balances at partnership formation, income allocation among partners, and amounts of partner capital balances after the addition of a new partner.

Stop and review! You have completed the outline for this subunit. Study multiple-choice questions 33 through 36 beginning on page 561.

15.12 QUASI-REORGANIZATION

1. **Definition**

   a. Quasi-reorganizations are undertaken by corporations with **negative retained earnings**. In many states, such entities are **not permitted to pay dividends**.

      1) Accordingly, a corporation that has begun to be profitable may nevertheless not be able to pay dividends because of accumulated losses.

      2) In this situation, a quasi-reorganization may be permitted to reduce the deficit in retained earnings to zero. However, shareholder approval is required.

2. **Accounting Treatments**

   a. A quasi-reorganization begins by restating assets to fair values and liabilities to present values. This process (an accounting reorganization) usually increases the deficit in retained earnings. But the restatement must not result in a writeup of net assets.

      1) Additional paid-in capital or its equivalent then must be available or be created to provide a source of capital against which the deficit may be written off.

      2) This result is usually accomplished by reducing par or stated value, with a debit to common stock and a credit to additional paid-in capital. The latter is then debited to enable the retained earnings balance to be reduced to zero. However, additional paid-in capital need not be eliminated.

b.   If only a deficit in retained earnings is eliminated, the procedure is called a **deficit reclassification**.

EXAMPLE

The following information is available for the Tabitha Company as of December 31, Year 1:

- Property, plant, and equipment recorded at $1,000,000
- Common stock, par value $30 per share, 50,000 shares outstanding recorded at $1,500,000
- Additional paid-in capital recorded at $500,000
- Retained earnings (deficit) ($100,000)
- Property, plant, and equipment's fair value is $400,000
- The par value of the common stock reduced to $10 per share

The effects of a quasi-reorganization in the form of an accounting reorganization are as follows:

1)   Restate assets to fair value

Retained earnings	$ 600,000	
Property, plant, and equipment		$ 600,000

2)   Adjust common stock

Common stock [50,000 shares × ($30 – $10)]	$1,000,000	
Additional paid-in capital		$1,000,000

3)   Write-off deficit

Additional paid-in capital	$ 700,000	
Retained earnings		$ 700,000

4)   Present the new equity section as follows:

Common stock, par value $10 per share, 50,000 shares outstanding	$ 500,000
Additional paid-in capital ($500,000 – $700,000 + $1,000,000)	800,000
Retained earnings (after quasi-reorganization dated December 31, Year 1)	0
Total equity	$1,300,000

---

c.   After a quasi-reorganization, the retained earnings account must be **dated** for a period of 10 years. Dating discloses the quasi-reorganization and when it occurred.

Stop and review! You have completed the outline for this subunit. Study multiple-choice questions 37 and 38 on page 562.

QUESTIONS

15.1 Classes of Equity

1. Munn Corp.'s records included the following equity accounts:

Preferred stock, par value $15, authorized 20,000 shares	$255,000
Additional paid-in capital, preferred stock	15,000
Common stock, no par, $5 stated value, 100,000 shares authorized	300,000

In Munn's statement of equity, the number of issued and outstanding shares for each class of stock is

	Common Stock	Preferred Stock
A.	60,000	17,000
B.	60,000	18,000
C.	63,000	17,000
D.	63,000	18,000

Answer (A) is correct.
    REQUIRED: The number of issued and outstanding shares of common and preferred stock.
    DISCUSSION: If an entity does not hold any stock as treasury stock, the number of shares of each type of stock may be determined by dividing the amount allocated to each stock account by the related par value or stated value. The number of shares of preferred stock issued and outstanding is therefore 17,000 ($255,000 ÷ $15 par value), and the number of shares of common stock issued and outstanding is 60,000 ($300,000 ÷ $5 stated value).
    Answer (B) is incorrect. The 18,000 shares of preferred would have a par value of $270,000. Answer (C) is incorrect. The 63,000 shares of common would have a stated value of $315,000. Answer (D) is incorrect. The 18,000 shares of preferred would have a par value of $270,000, and 63,000 shares of common would have a stated value of $315,000.

2. A retained earnings appropriation can be used to

A. Absorb a fire loss when a company is self-insured.

B. Provide for a contingent loss that is probable and reasonable.

C. Smooth periodic income.

D. Restrict earnings available for dividends.

Answer (D) is correct.
   REQUIRED: The use of a retained earnings appropriation.
   DISCUSSION: Transfers to and from accounts properly designated as appropriated retained earnings (such as general purpose contingency reserves or provisions for replacement costs of fixed assets) are always excluded from the determination of net income. However, appropriation of retained earnings is permitted if it is displayed within the equity section and is clearly identified. The effect of the appropriation is to restrict the amount of retained earnings available for dividends, not to set aside assets.

15.2 Issuance of Stock

3. On February 1, Hyde Corp., a newly formed company, had the following stock issued and outstanding:

- Common stock, no par, $1 stated value, 10,000 shares originally issued for $15 per share
- Preferred stock, $10 par value, 3,000 shares originally issued for $25 per share

Hyde's February 1 statement of equity should report

	Common Stock	Preferred Stock	Additional Paid-in Capital
A.	$150,000	$30,000	$45,000
B.	$150,000	$75,000	$0
C.	$10,000	$75,000	$140,000
D.	$10,000	$30,000	$185,000

Answer (D) is correct.
   REQUIRED: The amounts of common stock, preferred stock, and additional paid-in capital to be reported in the statement of equity.
   DISCUSSION: The common stock was issued for a total of $150,000 (10,000 shares × $15). Of this amount, $10,000 (10,000 shares × $1 stated value) should be allocated to the common stock, with the remaining $140,000 ($150,000 – $10,000) credited to additional paid-in capital. The preferred stock was issued for $75,000 (3,000 shares × $25), of which $30,000 (3,000 shares × $10 par value) should be allocated to the preferred stock and $45,000 ($75,000 – $30,000) should be allocated to additional paid-in capital. In the statement of equity, Hyde therefore should report $10,000 in the common stock account, $30,000 in the preferred stock account, and $185,000 ($140,000 + $45,000) as additional paid-in capital.

4. During the prior year, Brad Co. issued 5,000 shares of $100 par value convertible preferred stock for $110 per share. One share of preferred stock can be converted into three shares of Brad's $25 par value common stock at the option of the preferred shareholder. On December 31 of the current year, when the market value of the common stock was $40 per share, all of the preferred stock was converted. What amount should Brad credit to common stock and to additional paid-in capital -- common stock as a result of the conversion?

	Common Stock	Additional Paid-in Capital
A.	$375,000	$175,000
B.	$375,000	$225,000
C.	$500,000	$50,000
D.	$600,000	$0

Answer (A) is correct.
   REQUIRED: The amounts credited to common stock and additional paid-in capital.
   DISCUSSION: Brad recorded the issue of the convertible preferred stock with this entry:

Cash (5,000 shares × $110 market value)	$550,000	
Preferred stock (5,000 shares × $100 par value)		$500,000
Additional paid-in capital -- preferred (difference)		50,000

Brad recorded the conversion as follows:

Preferred stock (balance)	$500,000	
Additional paid-in capital -- preferred (balance)	$50,000	
Common stock (5,000 shares × 3 × $25 par value)		$375,000
Additional paid-in capital -- common (difference)		175,000

   Answer (B) is incorrect. The amount of $175,000 is credited to additional paid-in capital ($550,000 – $375,000). Answer (C) is incorrect. The amount of $500,000 is the par value of the preferred stock, not the common stock. Answer (D) is incorrect. The amount of $600,000 equals the fair value of the common stock at the date of conversion.

5. East Co. issued 1,000 shares of its $5 par value common stock to Howe as compensation for 1,000 hours of legal services performed. Howe usually bills $160 per hour for legal services. On the date of issuance, the stock was trading on a public exchange at $140 per share. By what amount should the additional paid-in capital account increase as a result of this transaction?

A. $135,000

B. $140,000

C. $155,000

D. $160,000

Answer (A) is correct.
    REQUIRED: The increase in additional paid-in capital.
    DISCUSSION: When stock is issued in exchange for property or services, the transaction is recorded at the more clearly determinable of the fair values of the stock issued or of the property or services received. In this case, the quoted price of the stock is used because it is based on trading in an active market (a level 1 input). The entry is to debit legal expense for $140,000 (1,000 shares × $140 market price), credit common stock for $5,000 (1,000 shares × $5 par value), and credit additional paid-in capital for the difference ($135,000).
    Answer (B) is incorrect. The amount of $5,000 should be allocated to common stock. Answer (C) is incorrect. The value of the stock should be used to record the transaction. Answer (D) is incorrect. The amount of $5,000 should be allocated to common stock, and the value of the stock should be used to record the transaction.

6. On July 1, Year 4, Cove Corp., a closely held corporation, issued 6% bonds with a maturity value of $60,000 together with 1,000 shares of its $5 par value common stock for a combined cash amount of $110,000. The market value of Cove's stock cannot be ascertained. If the bonds were issued separately, they would have sold for $40,000 on an 8% yield to maturity basis. What amount should Cove record for additional paid-in capital on the issuance of the stock?

A. $75,000

B. $65,000

C. $55,000

D. $45,000

Answer (B) is correct.
    REQUIRED: The amount allocated to additional paid-in capital together with bonds.
    DISCUSSION: The proceeds of the combined issuance of different classes of securities should be allocated based on the relative fair values of the securities. Since the fair value of the stock is not known, the bonds should be recorded at their fair value ($40,000), with the remainder of the proceeds ($110,000 – $40,000 = $70,000) credited to common stock at par value (1,000 shares × $5 = $5,000) and additional paid-in capital ($70,000 – $5,000 par = $65,000).
    Answer (A) is incorrect. The amount of $75,000 results from adding the par value to the total allocable to the stock. Answer (C) is incorrect. The amount of $55,000 is based on an allocation of $60,000 to the stock. Answer (D) is incorrect. The amount of $45,000 is based on an allocation of $60,000 (maturity value) to the bonds.

15.3 Stock Warrants and Stock Rights

7. Blue Co. issued preferred stock with detachable common stock warrants at a price that exceeded both the par value and the fair value of the preferred stock. At the time the warrants are exercised, Blue's total equity is increased by the

	Cash Received upon Exercise of the Warrants	Carrying Amount of the Warrants
A.	Yes	No
B.	Yes	Yes
C.	No	No
D.	No	Yes

Answer (A) is correct.
    REQUIRED: The effect of the exercise of warrants on total equity.
    DISCUSSION: When shares of preferred stock with detachable common stock warrants are issued at a price that exceeds both the par value and the fair value of the preferred stock, the consideration received must be allocated between the preferred stock and the detachable warrants. The amount allocated to the stock warrants outstanding should be recorded in the equity section as contributed capital. At the time the warrants are exercised, contributed capital will reflect both the cash received upon the exercise of the warrants and the carrying amount of the warrants. Total equity, however, will be increased only by the amount of cash received because the carrying amount of the warrants is already included in total equity.

8. An entity issued rights to its existing shareholders without consideration. The rights allowed the recipients to purchase unissued common stock for an amount in excess of par value. When the rights are issued, which of the following accounts will be increased?

	Common Stock	Additional Paid-in Capital
A.	Yes	Yes
B.	Yes	No
C.	No	No
D.	No	Yes

Answer (C) is correct.
REQUIRED: The effect on common stock and additional paid-in capital when rights are issued without consideration.
DISCUSSION: When rights are issued without consideration, only a memorandum entry is made. Common stock and additional paid-in capital are affected only if the rights are exercised.

15.4 Treasury Stock -- Acquisition

9. Grid Corp. acquired some of its own common shares at a price greater than both their par value and original issue price but less than their book value. Grid uses the cost method of accounting for treasury stock. What is the impact of this acquisition on total equity and the book value per common share?

	Total Equity	Book Value per Share
A.	Increase	Increase
B.	Increase	Decrease
C.	Decrease	Increase
D.	Decrease	Decrease

Answer (C) is correct.
REQUIRED: The effect of the acquisition on total equity and the book value per common share.
DISCUSSION: Under the cost method, the acquisition of treasury stock is recorded as a debit to treasury stock and a credit to cash equal to the amount of the purchase price. This transaction results in a decrease in both total assets and total equity because treasury stock is a contra-equity account. Moreover, if the acquisition cost is less than book value, the book value per share will increase. For example, if equity is $100, 10 shares are outstanding, and 5 shares are purchased for $45, the book value per share will increase from $10 ($100 ÷ 10) to $11 [($100 − $45) ÷ 5].
Answer (A) is incorrect. Total equity will decrease.
Answer (B) is incorrect. Total equity will decrease and book value per share will increase. Answer (D) is incorrect. Book value per share will increase.

10. Selected information from the accounts of Row Co. at December 31, Year 4, follows:

Total income since incorporation	$420,000
Total cash dividends paid	130,000
Total value of property dividends distributed	30,000
Excess of proceeds over cost of treasury stock sold, accounted for using the cost method	110,000

In its December 31, Year 4, financial statements, what amount should Row report as retained earnings?

A. $260,000

B. $290,000

C. $370,000

D. $400,000

Answer (A) is correct.
REQUIRED: The amount to be reported as retained earnings.
DISCUSSION: Retained earnings is increased by net income and decreased by net losses, dividends, and certain treasury stock transactions. Thus, retained earnings is $260,000 ($420,000 − $130,000 − $30,000). Because Row uses the cost method to account for treasury stock, the $110,000 excess of proceeds over the cost of treasury stock sold does not affect retained earnings. Under the cost method, the excess should be credited to additional paid-in capital.
Answer (B) is incorrect. The amount of $290,000 fails to subtract the $30,000 in property dividends. Answer (C) is incorrect. The amount of $370,000 includes the $110,000 excess of proceeds over cost of treasury stock. Answer (D) is incorrect. The amount of $400,000 includes the $110,000 excess of proceeds over cost of treasury stock and does not subtract the $30,000 value of property dividends distributed.

11. Posy Corp. acquired treasury shares at an amount greater than their par value but less than their original issue price. Compared with the cost method of accounting for treasury stock, does the par-value method report a greater amount for additional paid-in capital and a greater amount for retained earnings?

	Additional Paid-in Capital	Retained Earnings
A.	Yes	Yes
B.	Yes	No
C.	No	No
D.	No	Yes

Answer (C) is correct.
REQUIRED: The effect of the par-value method on additional paid-in capital and retained earnings compared with that of the cost method.
DISCUSSION: Under the cost method, the purchase of treasury stock (debit treasury stock, credit cash) has no effect on additional paid-in capital and retained earnings. Under the par-value method, given that the acquisition cost is greater than par but less than the original issue price, treasury stock is debited at par, and the additional paid-in capital associated with the original issue is also debited. Cash and paid-in capital from treasury stock transactions are credited. Hence, the par-value method does not report a greater amount for additional paid-in capital or retained earnings.

12. The acquisition of treasury stock will cause the number of shares outstanding to decrease if the treasury stock is accounted for by the

	Cost Method	Par-Value Method
A.	Yes	No
B.	No	No
C.	Yes	Yes
D.	No	Yes

Answer (C) is correct.
REQUIRED: The effect of the acquisition of treasury stock on the number of shares outstanding.
DISCUSSION: When treasury stock is acquired, the effect will be to decrease the number of shares of common stock outstanding whether the treasury stock is accounted for by the cost method or the par-value method.
Answer (A) is incorrect. Outstanding shares also decrease under the cost method. Answer (B) is incorrect. Outstanding shares decrease under the both methods. Answer (D) is incorrect. Outstanding shares also decrease under the par-value method.

15.5 Treasury Stock -- Reissue

13. Murphy Co. had 200,000 shares outstanding of $10 par common stock on March 30 of the current year. Murphy reacquired 30,000 of those shares at a cost of $15 per share and recorded the transaction using the cost method on April 15. Murphy reissued the 30,000 shares at $20 per share and recognized a $50,000 gain on its income statement on May 20. Which of the following statements is correct?

A. Murphy's comprehensive income for the current year is correctly stated.

B. Murphy's net income for the current year is overstated.

C. Murphy's net income for the current year is understated.

D. Murphy should have recognized a $50,000 loss on its income statement for the current year.

Answer (B) is correct.
REQUIRED: The true statement about the accounting for treasury stock transactions.
DISCUSSION: The cost method debits cash and credits treasury stock and paid-in capital from treasury stock transactions when a reissuance of shares is made for an amount in excess of cost. The credit to treasury stock is $450,000 (30,000 shares × $15), and the credit to paid-in capital from treasury stock transactions is $150,000 [$600,000 cash (debit) – $450,000 treasury stock (credit)]. The reason for the latter credit (an equity account) instead of a gain is that the effects of transactions in the entity's own stock are always excluded from net income or the results of operations. Thus, recognizing a gain on the reissuance of treasury stock overstates current net income.
Answer (A) is incorrect. Comprehensive income for the current year includes net income and items of other comprehensive income. Comprehensive income is therefore overstated if a gain is recognized in net income. Answer (C) is incorrect. Net income is overstated. Answer (D) is incorrect. No revenue, expense, gain, or loss is recognized on transactions in the entity's own stock.

14. At December 31, Year 3, Rama Corp. had 20,000 shares of $1 par value treasury stock that had been acquired in Year 3 at $12 per share. In May Year 4, Rama issued 15,000 of these treasury shares at $10 per share. The cost method is used to record treasury stock transactions. Rama is located in a state where laws relating to acquisition of treasury stock restrict the availability of retained earnings for declaration of dividends. At December 31, Year 4, what amount should Rama show in notes to financial statements as a restriction of retained earnings as a result of its treasury stock transactions?

A. $5,000

B. $10,000

C. $60,000

D. $90,000

Answer (C) is correct.
REQUIRED: The amount shown as a restriction of retained earnings as a result of treasury stock transactions.
DISCUSSION: The treasury stock account was initially debited for the cost of the 20,000 shares (20,000 × $12 = $240,000). The reissuance reduced the balance to $60,000 [$240,000 – (15,000 shares × $12)]. In the state where Rama is located, retained earnings are restricted by the amount of the cost of the treasury stock (in this case, $60,000 at December 31, Year 4).
Answer (A) is incorrect. The amount of $5,000 is the par value of the unissued treasury shares. Answer (B) is incorrect. The amount of $10,000 is the difference between the reacquisition cost and the reissuance price multiplied by the unissued treasury shares. Answer (D) is incorrect. The amount of $90,000 is the difference between the cost of the 20,000 shares and the proceeds of the sale of 15,000 shares.

15. Asp Co. was organized on January 2, Year 4, with 30,000 authorized shares of $10 par common stock. During Year 4, the corporation had the following capital transactions:

January 5 -- Issued 20,000 shares at $15 per share
July 14 -- Purchased 5,000 shares at $17 per share
December 27 -- Reissued the 5,000 shares held in treasury at $20 per share

Asp used the par-value method to record the purchase and reissuance of the treasury shares. It had no prior treasury stock transactions. In its December 31, Year 4, balance sheet, what amount should Asp report as additional paid-in capital?

A. $100,000

B. $125,000

C. $140,000

D. $150,000

Answer (B) is correct.
REQUIRED: The additional paid-in capital reported under the par-value method.
DISCUSSION: Under the par-value method, additional paid-in capital is debited for $25,000 (5,000 shares × $5 excess of the issue price over par) when the treasury stock is acquired. Treasury stock is debited for the $50,000 par value (5,000 shares × $10), and retained earnings is debited for $10,000 [5,000 shares × ($17 – $15)]. When the stock is reissued, additional paid-in capital is credited for $50,000 (5,000 shares × $10 excess over par). Thus, ending additional paid-in capital is $125,000 ($100,000 – $25,000 + $50,000).
Answer (A) is incorrect. The amount of $100,000 does not reflect the acquisition and reissuance of treasury stock. Answer (C) is incorrect. The amount of $140,000 does not include the $25,000 debit to additional paid-in capital but does include the $10,000 amount that should be debited to retained earnings. Answer (D) is incorrect. The amount of $150,000 does not reflect the $25,000 debit resulting from the purchase of treasury stock.

16. The par-value method of accounting for treasury stock differs from the cost method because

A. Any gain is recognized upon repurchase of stock, but a loss is treated as an adjustment to retained earnings.

B. No gains or losses are recognized on the issuance of treasury stock using the par-value method.

C. It reverses the original entry to issue the common stock, with any difference between carrying amount and purchase price adjusted through paid-in capital or retained earnings. It treats a subsequent reissuance as a new issuance of common stock.

D. It reverses the original entry to issue the common stock, with any difference between carrying amount and purchase price being shown as an ordinary gain or loss. It does not recognize any gain or loss on a subsequent resale of the stock.

Answer (C) is correct.
REQUIRED: The difference(s) between the par-value and the cost methods of accounting for treasury stock.
DISCUSSION: The par-value method treats the acquisition of treasury stock as a constructive retirement and the resale as a new issuance. Upon acquisition, the entry originally made to issue stock is reversed by offsetting the common stock account with treasury stock at par value and removing the paid-in capital recorded when the stock was originally issued. Any difference between the original issuance price and the reacquisition price is ordinarily adjusted through paid-in capital accounts and retained earnings. The subsequent reissuance removes the treasury stock at par value and reestablishes paid-in capital in excess of par for any excess of par value over the reissuance price. By contrast, the cost method does not treat the acquisition and reissuance of treasury stock as a constructive retirement and new issuance.

15.6 Retirement of Stock

17. In Year 2, Fogg, Inc., issued $10 par value common stock for $25 per share. No other common stock transactions occurred until March 31, Year 4, when Fogg acquired some of the issued shares for $20 per share and retired them. Which of the following statements accurately states an effect of this acquisition and retirement?

A. Year 4 net income is decreased.

B. Year 4 net income is increased.

C. Additional paid-in capital is decreased.

D. Retained earnings is increased.

Answer (C) is correct.
REQUIRED: The effect of the acquisition and retirement of a company's stock for less than the issue price.
DISCUSSION: When shares of common stock are reacquired and retired, contributed capital should be debited for the amount that was credited upon the issuance of the securities. In addition, because the acquisition of a company's own shares is an equity transaction, no gain or loss should be reflected in the determination of income. The entry is to debit common stock at par (number of shares × $10) and additional paid-in capital [number of shares × ($25 – $10)], and to credit additional paid-in capital from retirement of common stock [number of shares × ($25 – $20)] and cash (number of shares × $20). The net effect is to decrease total additional paid-in capital.
Answer (A) is incorrect. Net income is not affected. Answer (B) is incorrect. Net income is not affected. Answer (D) is incorrect. Retained earnings is only affected when a company retires its stock at a higher price than the original issue price.

18. Cross Corp. had 2,000 outstanding shares of 11% preferred stock, $50 par. These shares were not mandatorily redeemable. On August 8, Cross redeemed and retired 25% of these shares for $22,500. On that date, Cross's additional paid-in capital from preferred stock totaled $30,000. To record this transaction, Cross should debit (credit) its capital accounts as follows:

	Preferred Stock	Additional Paid-in Capital	Retained Earnings
A.	$25,000	$7,500	$(10,000)
B.	$25,000	--	$(2,500)
C.	$25,000	$(2,500)	--
D.	$22,500	--	--

Answer (C) is correct.
REQUIRED: The accounting for redemption and retirement of preferred stock.
DISCUSSION: Under the cost method, the entry to record a treasury stock purchase is to debit treasury stock at cost ($22,500) and credit cash. The entry to retire this stock is to debit preferred stock at par [(2,000 shares × 25%) × $50 = $25,000], debit additional paid-in capital from the original issuance ($30,000 × 25% = $7,500), credit treasury stock at cost ($22,500), and credit additional paid-in capital from stock retirement ($10,000). Thus, the net effect on additional paid-in capital is a $2,500 credit ($10,000 credit – $7,500 debit). No entry to retained earnings is necessary.
Answer (A) is incorrect. If the reacquisition price is less than the issuance price, a credit is made to additional paid-in capital, not retained earnings. Answer (B) is incorrect. Additional paid-in capital is debited to the extent it exists from the original issuance ($30,000 × 25% = $7,500), and a credit is made to additional paid-in capital for the stock retirement ($10,000). Retained earnings is not affected by this transaction. Answer (D) is incorrect. Preferred stock must be debited for the par value of the retired shares.

15.7 Cash Dividends

19. On January 15, Year 5, Rico Co. declared its annual cash dividend on common stock for the year ended January 31, Year 5. The dividend was paid on February 9, Year 5, to shareholders of record as of January 28, Year 5. On what date should Rico decrease retained earnings by the amount of the dividend?

A. January 15, Year 5.

B. January 31, Year 5.

C. January 28, Year 5.

D. February 9, Year 5.

Answer (A) is correct.
REQUIRED: The date to decrease retained earnings by the amount of the dividend.
DISCUSSION: On the date of declaration, a cash dividend becomes a legal liability of the corporation (unlike stock dividends, cash dividends cannot be rescinded). Thus, on January 15, a portion of retained earnings was reclassified as dividends payable.

20. Bal Corp. declared a $25,000 cash dividend on May 8 to shareholders of record on May 23, payable on June 3. As a result of this cash dividend, working capital

A. Was **not** affected.

B. Decreased on June 3.

C. Decreased on May 23.

D. Decreased on May 8.

Answer (D) is correct.
   REQUIRED: The effect of a cash dividend on working capital.
   DISCUSSION: On May 8, the date of declaration, retained earnings is debited, and dividends payable is credited. The declaration decreases working capital because a current liability is increased. On May 23, the date of record, no entry is made, and there is no effect on working capital. On June 3, when payment is made, both a current liability (dividends payable) and a current asset (cash) are decreased, which has no net effect on working capital. Thus, the only net effect to working capital took place on May 8.

21. At December 31, Year 3 and Year 4, Apex Co. had 3,000 shares of $100 par, 5% cumulative preferred stock outstanding. No dividends were in arrears as of December 31, Year 2. Apex did not declare a dividend during Year 3. During Year 4, Apex paid a cash dividend of $10,000 on its preferred stock. Apex should report dividends in arrears in its Year 4 financial statements as a(n)

A. Accrued liability of $15,000.

B. Disclosure of $15,000.

C. Accrued liability of $20,000.

D. Disclosure of $20,000.

Answer (D) is correct.
   REQUIRED: The amount and means of reporting preferred dividends in arrears.
   DISCUSSION: Dividends in arrears on preferred stock are not obligations of the company and are not recognized in the financial statements. However, the aggregate and per-share amounts of arrearages in cumulative preferred dividends should be disclosed on the face of the balance sheet or in the notes. The aggregate amount in arrears is $20,000 [(3,000 shares × $100 par × 5% × 2 years) – $10,000 paid in Year 4].
   Answer (A) is incorrect. Dividends in arrears do not meet recognition criteria. Answer (B) is incorrect. The amount of $15,000 is the arrearage for 1 year. Answer (C) is incorrect. Dividends in arrears should be disclosed on the face of the balance sheet or in the notes, not accrued.

22. At December 31, Year 3 and Year 4, Carr Corp. had outstanding 4,000 shares of $100 par value, 6% cumulative preferred stock and 20,000 shares of $10 par value common stock. At December 31, Year 3, dividends in arrears on the preferred stock were $12,000. Cash dividends declared in Year 4 totaled $44,000. What amounts were payable on each class of stock?

	Preferred Stock	Common Stock
A.	$44,000	$0
B.	$36,000	$8,000
C.	$32,000	$12,000
D.	$24,000	$20,000

Answer (B) is correct.
   REQUIRED: The amount of cash dividends payable to preferred and common shareholders.
   DISCUSSION: Given that the preferred stock is cumulative, preferred dividends in arrears and the dividends for the current period must be paid before common shareholders may receive any dividends. The preferred dividends for the year ending December 31, Year 4, are $24,000 (4,000 shares × $100 par value × 6%). Consequently, the preferred shareholders should receive $36,000 ($12,000 Year 3 dividends in arrears + $24,000 Year 4 dividends). The common shareholders will receive the remaining $8,000 ($44,000 – $36,000).
   Answer (A) is incorrect. Common shareholders will receive a portion of the cash dividends. Answer (C) is incorrect. The amount of $36,000 of preferred dividends must be paid prior to paying any dividends on common stock. Answer (D) is incorrect. The amount of $24,000 for preferred stock dividends omits the $12,000 dividends in arrears that must be paid prior to paying dividends on common stock.

15.8 Property Dividends and Liquidating Dividends

23. On December 1, Year 4, Pott Co. declared and distributed a property dividend when the fair value exceeded the carrying amount. As a consequence of the dividend declaration and distribution, what are the accounting effects?

	Property Dividends Recorded at	Retained Earnings
A.	Fair value	Decreased
B.	Fair value	Increased
C.	Cost	Increased
D.	Cost	Decreased

Answer (A) is correct.
   REQUIRED: The effects of a property dividend.
   DISCUSSION: When a corporation declares a dividend consisting of tangible property, the property is first remeasured to fair value as of the date of declaration. The dividend should then be recognized as a decrease in (debit to) retained earnings and a corresponding increase in (credit to) a dividend payable. The distribution of the property dividend is recognized by a debit to property dividend payable and a credit to the property account.
   Answer (B) is incorrect. Retained earnings is decreased. Answer (C) is incorrect. Retained earnings is decreased and the dividends are recorded at fair value. Answer (D) is incorrect. Property dividends are recorded at fair value.

24. A corporation declared a dividend, a portion of which was liquidating. How does this declaration affect each of the following?

	Additional Paid-in Capital	Retained Earnings
A.	Decrease	No effect
B.	Decrease	Decrease
C.	No effect	Decrease
D.	No effect	No effect

Answer (B) is correct.
REQUIRED: The effect of a dividend, a portion of which was liquidating, on additional paid-in capital and retained earnings.
DISCUSSION: The portion of a dividend that is liquidating results in a distribution in excess of the corporation's retained earnings. The effect of a liquidating dividend is to decrease contributed capital. Additional paid-in capital is debited first to the extent available before other contributed capital accounts are charged. Thus, declaration of a cash dividend, a portion of which is liquidating, decreases both additional paid-in capital and retained earnings.
Answer (A) is incorrect. Retained earnings is also decreased. Answer (C) is incorrect. Additional paid-in capital is also decreased. Answer (D) is incorrect. Both additional paid-in capital and retained earnings are decreased.

15.9 Stock Dividends and Stock Splits

25. Universe Co. issued 500,000 shares of common stock in the current year. Universe declared a 30% stock dividend. The market value was $50 per share, the par value was $10, and the average issue price was $30 per share. By what amount will Universe decrease shareholders' equity for the dividend?

A. $0

B. $1,500,000

C. $4,500,000

D. $7,500,000

Answer (A) is correct.
REQUIRED: The decrease in equity after declaration of a stock dividend.
DISCUSSION: When a stock dividend is declared, a portion of retained earnings is reclassified as contributed capital. The net effect on total equity is thus $0.

26. Nest Co. issued 100,000 shares of common stock. Of these, 5,000 were held as treasury stock at December 31, Year 3. During Year 4, transactions involving Nest's common stock were as follows:

May 3	-- 1,000 shares of treasury stock were sold.
August 6	-- 10,000 shares of previously unissued stock were sold.
November 18	-- A 2-for-1 stock split took effect.

Laws in Nest's state of incorporation protect treasury stock from dilution. At December 31, Year 4, how many shares of Nest's common stock were issued and outstanding?

	Shares Issued	Outstanding
A.	220,000	212,000
B.	220,000	216,000
C.	222,000	214,000
D.	222,000	218,000

Answer (A) is correct.
REQUIRED: The number of shares of common stock issued and outstanding.
DISCUSSION: In Nest's state, stock splits and dividends apply to treasury stock. Accordingly, the number of shares issued is 220,000 [(100,000 + 10,000) × 2]. The number of shares outstanding is 212,000 [(95,000 + 1,000 + 10,000) × 2].
Answer (B) is incorrect. The figure 216,000 does not properly account for the stock split on the treasury stock. Answer (C) is incorrect. The figure 222,000 includes 1,000 shares of treasury stock sold on May 3 twice [(100,000 + 1,000 + 10,000) × 2]. Answer (D) is incorrect. The figure 222,000 includes 1,000 shares of treasury stock sold on May 3 twice [(100,000 + 1,000 + 10,000) × 2]. Moreover, 218,000 shares outstanding includes 4,000 treasury stock shares that are not outstanding [(95,000 + 4,000 + 10,000) × 2].

27. Effective April 27, the shareholders of Dorr Corp. approved a 2-for-1 split of its common stock and an increase in authorized common shares from 100,000 shares (par value $20 per share) to 200,000 shares (par value $10 per share). Dorr's equity accounts immediately before issuance of the stock-split shares were as follows:

Common stock, par value $20;
  100,000 shares authorized;
  50,000 shares outstanding $1,000,000
Additional paid-in capital ($3 per share
  on issuance of common stock) 150,000
Retained earnings 1,350,000

The stock-split shares were issued on June 30. In Dorr's June 30 statement of equity, the balances of additional paid-in capital and retained earnings are

	Additional Paid-in Capital	Retained Earnings
A.	$0	$500,000
B.	$150,000	$350,000
C.	$150,000	$1,350,000
D.	$1,150,000	$350,000

Answer (C) is correct.
 REQUIRED: The effect of a 2-for-1 stock split on additional paid-in capital and retained earnings.
 DISCUSSION: A 2-for-1 stock split is a nonreciprocal transfer of an entity's own shares to its common shareholders for the purpose of reducing the unit market price of the shares. The goal is to increase their marketability and broaden their distribution. The transaction described will increase the number of shares outstanding to 100,000 (50,000 shares × 2). The par value will be reduced to $10 ($20 ÷ 2), but the capital accounts will be unaffected. To effect a stock split, no formal entry is necessary because no capitalization of retained earnings occurs. Thus, additional paid-in capital ($150,000) and retained earnings ($1,350,000) will not change.
 Answer (A) is incorrect. Additional paid-in capital and retained earnings will not change. Answer (B) is incorrect. Retained earnings will not change. Answer (D) is incorrect. Additional paid-in capital and retained earnings will not change.

28. Band Co. uses the equity method to account for its investment in Guard, Inc., common stock. How should Band record a 2% stock dividend received from Guard?

A. As dividend revenue at Guard's carrying amount of the stock.

B. As dividend revenue at the market value of the stock.

C. As a reduction in the total cost of Guard stock owned.

D. As a memorandum entry reducing the unit cost of all Guard stock owned.

Answer (D) is correct.
 REQUIRED: The entry to record a stock dividend received from an equity investee.
 DISCUSSION: No entries are made to record the receipt of stock dividends. However, a memorandum entry should be made in the investment account to record additional shares owned. This treatment applies whether the investment is accounted for by the fair-value method, the equity method, or the cost method.
 Answer (A) is incorrect. The receipt of a stock dividend is not a revenue. The shareholder has the same proportionate interest in the investee. Answer (B) is incorrect. The stock dividend does not result in revenue. Answer (C) is incorrect. The cost per share, not the total cost, is reduced.

15.10 Partnerships -- Formation and Allocation

29. Gow and Cubb formed a partnership on March 1 and contributed the following assets:

	Gow	Cubb
Cash	$80,000	
Equipment (fair value)		$50,000

The equipment was subject to a chattel mortgage of $10,000 that was assumed by the partnership. The partners agreed to share profits and losses equally. Cubb's capital balance at March 1 should be

A. $40,000

B. $45,000

C. $50,000

D. $60,000

Answer (A) is correct.
 REQUIRED: The capital account balance of a partner who contributed equipment subject to a mortgage.
 DISCUSSION: Cubb's capital balance should represent the fair value of the assets contributed. The equipment is measured net of the mortgage for this purpose. Thus, Cubb's capital balance should be $40,000 ($50,000 fair value of equipment – $10,000 mortgage assumed by the partnership).
 Answer (B) is incorrect. The amount of $45,000 assumes that half the mortgage is a reduction of Gow's capital. Answer (C) is incorrect. The amount of $50,000 does not consider the mortgage. Answer (D) is incorrect. The amount of $60,000 assumes capital is shared equally.

30. Hayes and Jenkins formed a partnership, each contributing assets to the business. Hayes contributed inventory with a current fair value in excess of its carrying amount. Jenkins contributed real estate with a carrying amount in excess of its current fair value. At what amount should the partnership record each of the following assets?

	Inventory	Real Estate
A.	Fair value	Fair value
B.	Fair value	Carrying amount
C.	Carrying amount	Fair value
D.	Carrying amount	Carrying amount

Answer (A) is correct.
   REQUIRED: The amount at which nonmonetary assets contributed to a partnership should be recorded.
   DISCUSSION: When partners invest nonmonetary assets in the business, those assets should be recorded at their current fair value at the date they are contributed.

31. On January 2, Smith purchased the net assets of Jimmy's Cleaning, a sole proprietorship, for $350,000 and commenced operations of Spiffy Cleaning, a sole proprietorship. The assets had a carrying amount of $375,000 and a market value of $360,000. In Spiffy's cash-basis financial statements for the year ended December 31, Spiffy reported revenues in excess of expenses of $60,000. Smith's distributions during the year were $20,000. In Spiffy's financial statements, what amount should be reported as Capital -- Smith?

A. $390,000

B. $400,000

C. $410,000

D. $415,000

Answer (A) is correct.
   REQUIRED: The amount to be reported as the capital of a sole proprietor.
   DISCUSSION: In accordance with the historical-cost principle, the assets should be recorded at their $350,000 cost. Given that Spiffy had a net cash inflow of $40,000 ($60,000 excess of revenues over expenses – $20,000 of drawings), Smith's capital balance should be reported as $390,000 ($350,000 + $40,000).
   Answer (B) is incorrect. The amount of $400,000 assumes that the assets are recorded at fair value. Answer (C) is incorrect. The amount of $410,000 assumes no distributions. Answer (D) is incorrect. The amount of $415,000 assumes that the assets are recorded at their carrying amount.

32. The partnership agreement of Donn, Eddy, and Farr provides for annual distribution of profit or loss in the following sequence:

- Donn, the managing partner, receives a bonus of 10% of profit.
- Each partner receives 6% interest on average capital investment.
- Residual profit or loss is divided equally.

Average capital investments for the current year were

Donn	$80,000
Eddy	50,000
Farr	30,000

What portion of the $100,000 partnership profit for the year should be allocated to Farr?

A. $28,600

B. $29,800

C. $34,933

D. $41,600

Answer (A) is correct.
   REQUIRED: The share of partnership profits to be distributed to a partner.
   DISCUSSION: The partnership agreement provides for a bonus to one partner and payment of interest on each partner's average capital investment. The bonus and the interest must be allocated and included in the calculation of the residual profit or loss. Donn's bonus is $10,000 ($100,000 × 10%), and total interest is $9,600 ($160,000 total capital × 6%). Hence, the residual profit following the allocation of bonus and interest is $80,400 ($100,000 partnership profits – $10,000 bonus – $9,600 of interest on capital). Sharing the residual profit equally among the partners results in an allocation to Farr of $28,600 [($30,000 × 6%) interest + ($80,400 ÷ 3) residual profit].

	Donn	Eddy	Farr
Bonus	$10,000		
Interest on capital	4,800	$ 3,000	$ 1,800
Residual	26,800	26,800	26,800
Totals	$41,600	$29,800	$28,600

Answer (B) is incorrect. The amount of $29,800 is the profit allocated to Eddy. Answer (C) is incorrect. The amount of $34,933 would be the profit allocated to Donn if no bonus were paid. Answer (D) is incorrect. The amount of $41,600 is the profit allocated to Donn.

15.11 Partnerships -- Changes and Liquidation

33. Max Blau and Harry Rubi are partners who share profits and losses in the ratio of 6:4, respectively. On May 1, their respective capital accounts were as follows:

Blau	$60,000
Rubi	50,000

On that date, Joe Lind was admitted as a partner with a one-third interest in capital and profits for an investment of $40,000. The new partnership began with total capital of $150,000. Immediately after Lind's admission, Blau's capital should be

- A. $46,000
- B. $50,000
- C. $54,000
- D. $60,000

Answer (C) is correct.
   REQUIRED: The capital balance of an existing partner following the admission of a new partner.
   DISCUSSION: Following the entrance of Lind, the partnership began with total capital of $150,000, the sum of the capital balances of Blau and Rubi and Lind's investment. Thus, no goodwill was recognized. Lind received a one-third interest, and his capital balance must be credited for $50,000 ($150,000 × 33 1/3). But Lind contributed only $40,000, so the $10,000 bonus ($50,000 – $40,000) must be allocated to the existing partners in the ratio of 6:4. The result will be debits to the capital accounts of Blau and Rubi of $6,000 ($10,000 × 60%) and $4,000 ($10,000 × 40%), respectively. Consequently, immediately after Lind's admission, Blau's capital is $54,000 ($60,000 – $6,000).
   Answer (A) is incorrect. The amount of $46,000 is Rubi's capital balance after the admission of Lind. Answer (B) is incorrect. The amount of $50,000 is Lind's initial capital balance. Answer (D) is incorrect. The amount of $60,000 is Blau's initial capital balance.

34. The partnership of Metcalf, Petersen, and Russell shared profits and losses equally. When Metcalf withdrew from the partnership, the partners agreed that there was unrecorded goodwill in the partnership. Under the bonus method, the capital balances of Petersen and Russell were

- A. Not affected.
- B. Each reduced by one-half of the total amount of the unrecorded goodwill.
- C. Each reduced by one-third of the total amount of the unrecorded goodwill.
- D. Each reduced by one-half of Metcalf's share of the total amount of the unrecorded goodwill.

Answer (D) is correct.
   REQUIRED: The effect of a retirement under the bonus method.
   DISCUSSION: If the partnership had unrecorded goodwill, Metcalf would have received the balance in her capital account plus one-third of the unrecorded goodwill. Under the bonus method, revaluation of assets to reflect goodwill is not permitted. Hence, given that the partners shared profits and losses equally, the payment to Metcalf of one-third of the unrecorded goodwill would have resulted in equal reductions of the capital balances of the remaining partners, that is, in the payment of a bonus to Metcalf. Thus, one-sixth [(1 ÷ 3) × (1 ÷ 2)] of the unrecorded goodwill would have been subtracted from both Petersen's and Russell's accounts.

35. The following condensed balance sheet is presented for the partnership of Axel, Barr, and Cain, who share profits and losses in the ratio of 4:3:3, respectively:

Cash	$100,000
Other assets	300,000
Total	$400,000
Liabilities	$150,000
Axel, capital	40,000
Barr, capital	180,000
Cain, capital	30,000
Total	$400,000

The partners agreed to dissolve the partnership after selling the other assets for $200,000. Upon dissolution of the partnership, Axel should have received

- A. $0
- B. $40,000
- C. $60,000
- D. $150,000

Answer (A) is correct.
   REQUIRED: The amount Axel should receive upon liquidation.
   DISCUSSION: When the other assets with a carrying amount of $300,000 were sold for $200,000, a loss of $100,000 resulted. When this loss is distributed in the ratio of 4:3:3 to the capital balances, Axel's and Cain's capital balances are eliminated. Thus, upon dissolution of the partnership, neither Axel nor Cain will receive any cash. Of the $300,000 available ($100,000 cash on hand + $200,000 proceeds from the sale of other assets), $150,000 will be distributed to creditors (liabilities) and $150,000 will be distributed to Barr.

	Axel	Barr	Cain
Beginning capital	$ 40,000	$180,000	$ 30,000
Loss on sale	(40,000)	(30,000)	(30,000)
Distribution of cash	$ 0	$150,000	$ 0

   Answer (B) is incorrect. The amount of $40,000 is Axel's capital balance before dissolution. Answer (C) is incorrect. The amount of $60,000 is 40% of the assets remaining after payment of liabilities. Answer (D) is incorrect. This figure is the amount distributed to Barr.

36. Jay & Kay partnership's balance sheet at December 31, Year 3, reported the following:

Total assets	$100,000
Total liabilities	20,000
Jay, capital	40,000
Kay, capital	40,000

On January 2, Year 4, Jay and Kay dissolved their partnership and transferred all assets and liabilities to a newly formed corporation. At the date of incorporation, the fair value of the net assets was $12,000 more than the carrying amount on the partnership's books, of which $7,000 was assigned to tangible assets and $5,000 was assigned to goodwill. Jay and Kay were each issued 5,000 shares of the corporation's $1 par value common stock. Immediately following incorporation, additional paid-in capital in excess of par should be credited for

   A. $68,000

   B. $70,000

   C. $77,000

   D. $82,000

Answer (D) is correct.
   REQUIRED: The additional paid-in capital in excess of par credited after incorporation.
   DISCUSSION: The net assets of the partnership, including goodwill, are transferred at fair value. Hence, the $92,000 fair value of the net assets ($100,000 carrying amount of partnership assets + $12,000 excess of fair value over carrying amount – $20,000 liabilities) measures the amount credited to contributed capital. The credit to common stock is $10,000 (5,000 shares × $1 par × 2), and the credit to additional paid-in capital is $82,000 ($92,000 – $10,000).
   Answer (A) is incorrect. This figure equals carrying amount of total assets minus total liabilities minus $12,000. Answer (B) is incorrect. This figure equals carrying amount of total assets minus total liabilities minus par value of the stock issued. Answer (C) is incorrect. The amount of $77,000 assumes that the goodwill is not recorded.

15.12 Quasi-Reorganization

37. The primary purpose of a quasi-reorganization is to give a corporation the opportunity to

   A. Obtain relief from its creditors.

   B. Revalue understated assets to their fair values.

   C. Eliminate a deficit in retained earnings.

   D. Distribute the stock of a newly created subsidiary to its shareholders in exchange for part of their stock in the corporation.

Answer (C) is correct.
   REQUIRED: The purpose of a quasi-reorganization.
   DISCUSSION: A quasi-reorganization is undertaken to reduce a deficit in retained earnings to zero. The purpose is to permit the corporation to pay dividends in the near future.
   Answer (A) is incorrect. A quasi-reorganization is an accounting adjustment. Answer (B) is incorrect. Assets are usually written down to fair value. Answer (D) is incorrect. A quasi-reorganization does not entail an exchange of stock.

38. The equity section of Brown Co.'s December 31, Year 3, balance sheet consisted of the following:

Common stock, $30 par, 10,000 shares authorized and outstanding	$ 300,000
Additional paid-in capital	150,000
Retained earnings (deficit)	(210,000)

On January 2, Year 4, Brown put into effect a shareholder-approved quasi-reorganization by reducing the par value of the stock to $5 and eliminating the deficit against additional paid-in capital. Immediately after the quasi-reorganization, what amount should Brown report as additional paid-in capital?

   A. $(60,000)

   B. $150,000

   C. $190,000

   D. $400,000

Answer (C) is correct.
   REQUIRED: The amount reported as additional paid-in capital following a quasi-reorganization.
   DISCUSSION: In many states, a corporation with negative retained earnings is not permitted to pay dividends. Thus, when it reverses a negative trend, it may effect a quasi-reorganization to eliminate the deficit. Brown's reduction of the par value results in a credit to additional paid-in capital of $250,000 [10,000 shares × ($30 – $5)]. Hence, additional paid-in capital is $400,000 ($150,000 + $250,000) before a $210,000 debit to eliminate the retained earnings deficit. The ending balance in additional paid-in capital is $190,000 ($400,000 – $210,000).
   Answer (A) is incorrect. The amount of $(60,000) does not reflect the $250,000 credit for the change in par value. Answer (B) is incorrect. The amount of $150,000 is the 12/31/Year 3 balance. Answer (D) is incorrect. The amount of $400,000 does not include the $210,000 debit to eliminate the retained earnings deficit.

Use the additional questions in Gleim **CPA Test Prep Online** to create Test Sessions that emulate Prometric!

15.13 PRACTICE SIMULATION

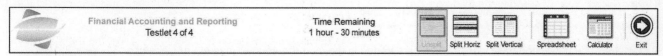

Financial Accounting and Reporting
Testlet 4 of 4

Time Remaining
1 hour - 30 minutes

Unsplit Split Horiz Split Vertical Spreadsheet Calculator Exit

DIRECTIONS

Note: If you believe you have encountered a software malfunction, report it to the test center staff immediately.

Navigation

To navigate from task to task, use the controls at the bottom of the screen. Click on the **Next** button to advance to the next task, or the **Previous** button to go to the previous task. To go directly to any task, click on its number.

▼ = Reminder   Directions   1 2 3 4 5 6 7   ◄ Previous Next ►

If you would like a reminder to revisit a task, or want to indicate that you are finished with it, click on the reminder flag below the task number. To clear the flag, click on it again. Reminder flags are for your use only – they do not contribute to your score.

Tabs

In this part of the examination, you will be asked to complete various tasks. Every task has one or more **Work Tabs**. Some tasks have one or more **Information Tabs**, others may have none. Every task has a **Help** tab.

If a task has **Information Tabs**, you may use the information in them to complete your responses in the **Work Tabs**.

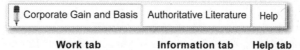

Corporate Gain and Basis   Authoritative Literature   Help

Work tab   Information tab   Help tab

Work Tabs:
- **Work Tabs** are identified with a pencil icon. This is where your responses are expected.
- Each task has one or more **Work Tabs**.
- **Work Tabs** contain directions for completing the task – be sure to read these directions carefully.
- The **Work Tab** name in the example above is for illustration only – yours will differ.
- You must complete all of the **Work Tabs** in each task to receive full credit.

Information Tabs:
- The Authoritative Literature will be provided in all tasks in the AUD, FAR, and REG sections for your reference.
- Your simulation may have one or more additional **Information Tabs**. Like the Authoritative Literature tabs, **Information Tabs** do not have a pencil icon.
- If your task has additional **Information Tabs**, go through each to familiarize yourself with the task content.

Help Tab:
- The **Help Tab** provides assistance with the exam software that is used in this task. For example, if the task is to compose a memorandum, **Help** will provide information about the word processor.

The Toolbar

The toolbar at the top of the screen shows the amount of time remaining for you to complete the tasks. In addition, the following tools are available. Note that only the **Exit** button is displayed when Directions are visible - the others will appear when you begin the tasks.

Unsplit Split Horiz Split Vertical

Click on these buttons to split or unsplit the screen. You can split the screen vertically or horizontally.

Calculator

Click on this button to display the calculator; click on it again to hide the calculator. To move the calculator, click on the calculator title bar and drag the calculator to the desired location.

Spreadsheet

Click on this button to use the spreadsheet; click on it again to hide the spreadsheet. To move the spreadsheet, click on the the spreadsheet title bar and drag the spreadsheet to the desired location.

Exit

Click on this button to go on to the next part of the examination. You must complete all of the tasks to receive full credit. Once you click on **Exit** and confirm the action, you will NOT be able to return to this testlet.

▼ = Reminder   Directions   1 2 3 4 5 6   ◄ Previous Next ►

| Retained Earnings | Authoritative Literature | Help |

Mart, Inc., is a public company whose shares are traded in the over-the-counter market. At December 31, Year 2, Mart had 6 million authorized shares of $5 par value common stock, 2 million shares of which were issued and outstanding. The equity accounts at December 31, Year 2, had the following balances:

Common stock	$10,000,000
Additional paid-in capital	7,500,000
Retained earnings	3,250,000

Transactions during Year 3 and other information relating to Mart's equity accounts were as follows:

- On January 5, Year 3, Mart issued 100,000 shares of $50 par value, 9% cumulative, convertible preferred stock at $54 per share. Each share of preferred stock is convertible, at the option of the holder, into two shares of common stock. Mart had 250,000 authorized shares of preferred stock. The preferred stock has a liquidation value of $55 per share.
- On February 1, Year 3, Mart reacquired 20,000 shares of its common stock for $16 per share. Mart uses the cost method to account for treasury stock.
- On March 15, Year 3, Mart paid $200,000 for 10,000 shares of common stock of Lew, Inc., a public company whose stock is traded on a national stock exchange. This stock was 1% of the outstanding common stock of Lew. It was acquired for long-term investment purposes and had a fair value of $15 per share on December 31, Year 3. This decline in fair value was not considered permanent.
- On April 30, Year 3, Mart had completed an additional public offering of 500,000 shares of its $5 par value common stock. The stock was sold to the public at $12 per share, net of offering costs.
- On June 17, Year 3, Mart declared a cash dividend of $1 per share of common stock, payable on July 10, Year 3, to shareholders of record on July 1, Year 3.
- On November 6, Year 3, Mart sold 10,000 shares of treasury stock for $21 per share.
- On December 7, Year 3, Mart declared the yearly cash dividend on preferred stock, payable on January 7, Year 4, to shareholders of record on December 31, Year 3.
- On January 17, Year 4, before the books were closed for Year 3, Mart became aware that the ending inventories at December 31, Year 2, were overstated by $200,000. The tax rate applicable to Year 2 net income was 30%. The appropriate correcting entry was recorded the same day.
- After correction of the beginning inventories, net income for Year 3 was $2,250,000.

Enter in the shaded cells the amounts to be reported on Mart's statement of retained earnings for the year ended December 31, Year 3.

Mart, Inc.
Statement of Retained Earnings
For the Year Ended December 31, Year 3

Balance on December 31, Year 2		
As originally reported		
Prior-period adjustment from error overstating inventories at December 31, Year 2		
Income tax effect		
Net income for Year 3		
Cash dividends on		
Preferred stock		
Common stock		
Balance on December 31, Year 3		

Partnership Liquidation | Authoritative Literature | Help

Garr and Pat do business as Linden Consulting Associates, a general partnership. On December 31, Year 2, the partners' capital balances and profit sharing percentages were as follows:

	Capital	Profit Sharing %
Garr	$1,020,000	60%
Pat	680,000	40%
	$1,700,000	

On January 1, Year 3, Garr and Pat admitted Scott to the partnership for a cash payment of $340,000 to Linden Consulting Associates. This was the agreed amount of Scott's beginning capital account. In addition, Scott paid a $50,000 cash bonus directly to Garr and Pat. Of this amount, $30,000 was paid to Garr, and $20,000 to Pat. The new profit sharing arrangement is as follows:

Garr	50%
Pat	30%
Scott	20%

On October 1, Year 3, Linden purchased and paid for equipment costing $170,000, including $15,000 for sales tax, delivery, and installation. There were no dispositions of property and equipment during Year 3.

Throughout Year 3, Linden owned 25% of Zach, Inc.'s common stock. As a result of this ownership interest, Linden can exercise significant influence over Zach's operating and financial policies. During Year 3, Zach paid dividends totaling $384,000 and reported net income of $720,000. Linden's amortization of the excess of the cost over the carrying amount of the investment in Zach resulting from the undervaluation of Zach's depreciable assets was $4,000.

Partners' drawings for Year 3 were as follows:

Garr	$280,000
Pat	200,000
Scott	150,000
	$630,000

The books of Linden Consulting Associates reflect the following balances at December 31, Year 3:

Cash	$ 20,000
Inventory	120,000
Plant assets -- net	300,000
Accounts payable	170,000
Garr, capital	100,000
Pat, capital	90,000
Scott, capital	80,000

On January 1 of the next year, the partners decide to liquidate the partnership. They agree that all cash should be distributed as soon as it becomes available during the liquidation process. They also agree that a cash predistribution plan is necessary to facilitate the distribution of cash.

Enter in the shaded cells the correct percentage to determine how much cash should be distributed to the creditors and partners, respectively, as it becomes available.

Cash Distribution	Creditors	Garr	Pat	Scott
1. First $170,000				
2. Next $20,000				
3. Next $50,000				
4. Then				

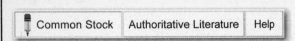

Select from the list provided the effect (increase, decrease, or no effect) each transaction below will have on Mart's common stock account. Each choice may be used once, more than once, or not at all. The state in which Mart is incorporated requires capitalization of retained earnings in the amount of the par value of the shares issued when a stock split in the form of a dividend occurs.

Transaction	Answer		Choices
1. Mart declares and distributes a 10% stock dividend.			A) Increase
2. Mart retires 5,000 of its outstanding shares of common stock.			B) Decrease
3. Mart acquires its own stock to hold as treasury stock using the cost method.			C) No effect
4. Mart issues a 3-for-1 stock split.			
5. Mart issues 1,000 previously unissued common shares at $25 per share.			
6. Mart declares and distributes a 30% stock dividend.			
7. Mart distributes a dividend of $1,200,000. Only $900,000 is in retained earnings to distribute as a cash dividend.			

⛝ = Reminder   Directions   1 2 **3** 4 5 6   ◀ Previous   Next ▶

Select from the list provided the correct order in which each of the following steps must be taken when distributing partnership assets to partners pursuant to a liquidation of the partnership.

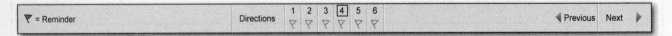

Steps During Liquidation	Answer	Choices
1. Remaining assets are assumed to have a fair value of $0.		A) First
2. Any deficit balance in a partner's account is allocated.		B) Second
3. Any gain or loss realized from the actual sale of assets is allocated.		C) Third
4. Cash is distributed.		D) Fourth

⛝ = Reminder   Directions   1 2 3 **4** 5 6   ◀ Previous   Next ▶

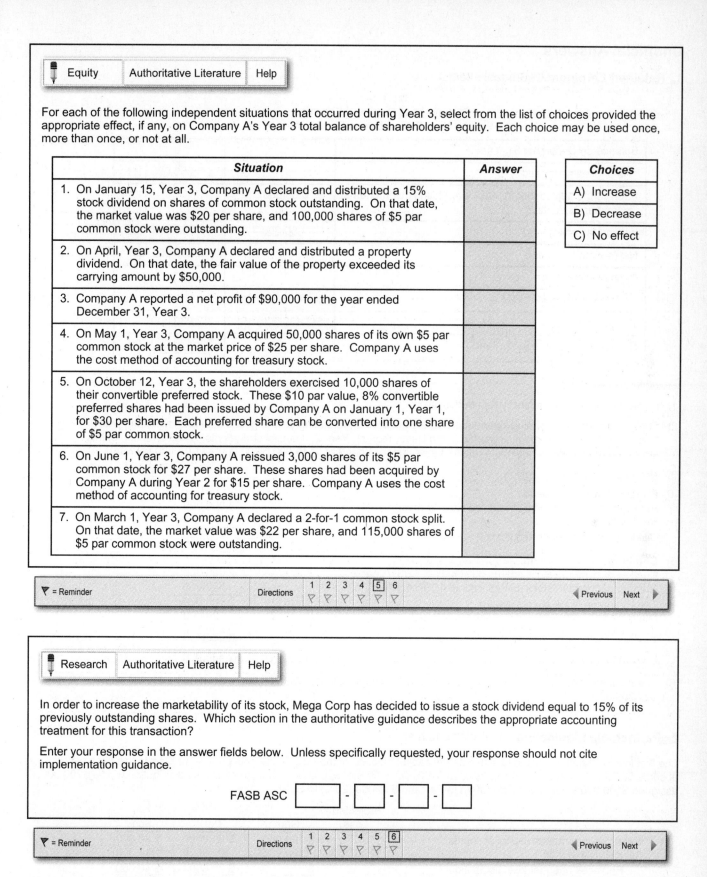

Equity   Authoritative Literature   Help

For each of the following independent situations that occurred during Year 3, select from the list of choices provided the appropriate effect, if any, on Company A's Year 3 total balance of shareholders' equity. Each choice may be used once, more than once, or not at all.

Situation	Answer		Choices
1. On January 15, Year 3, Company A declared and distributed a 15% stock dividend on shares of common stock outstanding. On that date, the market value was $20 per share, and 100,000 shares of $5 par common stock were outstanding.			A) Increase
2. On April, Year 3, Company A declared and distributed a property dividend. On that date, the fair value of the property exceeded its carrying amount by $50,000.			B) Decrease
3. Company A reported a net profit of $90,000 for the year ended December 31, Year 3.			C) No effect
4. On May 1, Year 3, Company A acquired 50,000 shares of its own $5 par common stock at the market price of $25 per share. Company A uses the cost method of accounting for treasury stock.			
5. On October 12, Year 3, the shareholders exercised 10,000 shares of their convertible preferred stock. These $10 par value, 8% convertible preferred shares had been issued by Company A on January 1, Year 1, for $30 per share. Each preferred share can be converted into one share of $5 par common stock.			
6. On June 1, Year 3, Company A reissued 3,000 shares of its $5 par common stock for $27 per share. These shares had been acquired by Company A during Year 2 for $15 per share. Company A uses the cost method of accounting for treasury stock.			
7. On March 1, Year 3, Company A declared a 2-for-1 common stock split. On that date, the market value was $22 per share, and 115,000 shares of $5 par common stock were outstanding.			

▼ = Reminder   Directions   1 2 3 4 [5] 6   ◀ Previous   Next ▶

Research   Authoritative Literature   Help

In order to increase the marketability of its stock, Mega Corp has decided to issue a stock dividend equal to 15% of its previously outstanding shares. Which section in the authoritative guidance describes the appropriate accounting treatment for this transaction?

Enter your response in the answer fields below. Unless specifically requested, your response should not cite implementation guidance.

FASB ASC [ ] - [ ] - [ ] - [ ]

▼ = Reminder   Directions   1 2 3 4 5 [6]   ◀ Previous   Next ▶

Unofficial Answers

1. Retained Earnings (6 Gradable Items)

Mart, Inc.
Statement of Retained Earnings
For the Year Ended December 31, Year 3

Balance on December 31, Year 2		
As originally reported		$ 3,250,000 [1]
Prior-period adjustment for error overstating inventories at December 31, Year 2	$ (200,000)	
Income tax effect	60,000	(140,000) [2]
Net income for Year 3		2,250,000 [3]
Cash dividends on		
Preferred stock	$ (450,000) [4]	
Common stock	$(2,480,000) [5]	(2,930,000)
Balance on December 31, Year 3		$ 2,430,000 [6]

Explanation of Amounts

[1] Retained earnings as originally reported is given.

[2] The overstatement of ending inventories had the effect of understating cost of goods sold and overstating net income and retained earnings reported in the December 31, Year 2, financial statements. The correction of this error requires a debit to beginning retained earnings for Year 3 of $140,000 [$200,000 × (1.0 – .30 tax rate)].

[3] Net income for Year 3 is given.

[4] **Preferred stock dividend:**

Par value of all outstanding preferred stock shares	$5,000,000
Dividend rate	9%
Dividends paid on preferred stock	$ 450,000

[5] **Common stock dividend:**

Number of common stock shares outstanding, 12/31/Year 2	2,000,000
Number of common stock shares issued, 4/30/Year 3	500,000
Total common stock shares issued	2,500,000
Minus treasury stock shares acquired 2/1/Year 3	(20,000)
Shares outstanding, 7/1/Year 3	2,480,000
Dividends paid (2,480,000 × $1)	$2,480,000

[6] The balance of retained earnings on 12/31/Year 3 equals $2,430,000 ($3,250,000 – $140,000 + $2,250,000 – $2,930,000).

2. Partnership Liquidation (4 Gradable Items)

The first loss distribution is used to eliminate the capital balance of the most vulnerable partner, or Garr in this case (who absorbs 50% of all losses). Garr's balance of $100,000 is 50% of $200,000. Thus, the first loss distribution will be $200,000, assigned $100,000 to Garr, $60,000 (30%) to Pat, and $40,000 (20%) to Scott.

	Projected Loss	Garr	Pat	Scott
Balances in partners' capital accounts		$ 100,000	$ 90,000	$ 80,000
1st loss distribution	$200,000	(100,000)	(60,000)	(40,000)
Balances after 1st loss distribution		$ 0	$ 30,000	$ 40,000

Pat and Scott are now in a 60:40 relationship (formerly 30:20). Pat is the next most vulnerable partner; a further $50,000 loss will wipe out Pat's $30,000 balance ($50,000 × 60% = $30,000).

	Projected Loss	Pat	Scott
Balances in partners' capital accounts		$ 30,000	$ 40,000
2nd loss distribution	$50,000	(30,000)	(20,000)
Balances after 2nd loss distribution		$ 0	$ 20,000

The last capital balance remaining is Scott's at $20,000. Thus, an additional $20,000 loss would eliminate the final partner's equity.

A cash predistribution plan is prepared by working backwards through the calculated loss distributions. Since the creditors must be paid first, cash can be distributed as it becomes available in these amounts and proportions:

Cash Distribution	Creditors	Garr	Pat	Scott
1. First $170,000	100%			
2. Next $20,000				100%
3. Next $50,000			60%	40%
4. Then		50%	30%	20%

3. Common Stock (7 Gradable Items)

1. A) Increase. A 10% stock dividend is accounted for at fair value by debiting retained earnings and crediting common stock and additional paid-in capital.

2. B) Decrease. When stock is retired, cash is credited (or treasury stock if separate reacquisition and retirement entries are made). The stock account is debited for the par or stated value. Additional paid-in capital is debited to the extent additional paid-in capital exists from the original stock issuance. Any remainder is debited to retained earnings or credited to additional paid-in capital from stock retirement.

3. C) No effect. The entry is to debit treasury stock and credit cash.

4. C) No effect. A stock split is recognized by a decrease in the par or stated value of each common share, resulting in a proportionate increase in the number of shares outstanding. Thus, a stock split does not change the aggregate par or stated value of shares outstanding.

5. A) Increase. The entry is to debit cash for $25,000, credit the par value of common stock for $5,000, and credit additional paid-in capital for $20,000.

6. A) Increase. According to SEC rules, this distribution is a split-up effected in the form of a dividend. The issuance is of 25% or more of the previously outstanding shares of a public company. Accordingly, Mart capitalizes retained earnings for the par value as required by applicable state law.

7. C) No effect. The entry is to debit retained earnings for $900,000, debit additional paid-in capital for $300,000, and credit cash for $1,200,000.

4. Liquidation (4 Gradable Items)

1. B) Second. The second step in the liquidation of a partnership is to assume that the remaining assets have a fair value of $0, which results in an assumed loss equal to their carrying amount. This assumed loss is allocated to the partners' capital accounts in accordance with the profit and loss ratio.

2. C) Third. The third step in the liquidation of a partnership is, if at least one of the partners' capital accounts has a deficit balance, to allocate the deficit to the remaining partners' accounts.

3. A) First. The first step in the liquidation of a partnership is to allocate any gain or loss realized from the actual sale of assets to the partners' capital accounts in accordance with the profit and loss ratio.

4. D) Fourth. The last step in the liquidation of a partnership is to ensure that the final balances in the partnership accounts equal the amounts of cash, if any, that may be distributed to the partners.

5. Equity (7 Gradable Items)

1. <u>C) No effect.</u> When a stock dividend is declared, a portion of retained earnings is reclassified as contributed capital. The net effect on total equity is thus $0.

2. <u>B) Decrease.</u> When a company declares a dividend consisting of tangible property, the property is first remeasured to fair value as of the date of declaration. The dividend should then be debited to retained earnings and credited to the remeasured property. Thus, the decrease in total equity is equal to the carrying amount of the property before the remeasurement.

3. <u>A) Increase.</u> The retained earnings account increases by the amount of net profit recognized for the period.

4. <u>B) Decrease.</u> Under the cost method, treasury shares are reported at their reacquisition price, and the journal entry is a debit to treasury stock and a credit to cash. Treasury stock is reported separately as a reduction from the other shareholder equity accounts.

5. <u>C) No effect.</u> Both preferred shares and common shares are equity accounts. Thus, conversion of preferred shares into common shares has no effect on total equity.

6. <u>A) Increase.</u> The reissue of treasury shares increases the Year 3 total equity. Since the reissue price per share is greater than the price at which the shares were repurchased, the increase in Year 3 total equity is equal to the amount of cash received from reissuing the shares.

7. <u>C) No effect.</u> A stock split does not require an adjustment to retained earnings or paid-in capital and does not affect total equity.

6. Research (1 Gradable Item)

Answer: FASB ASC 505-20-30-3

505-20-30-3 In accounting for a stock dividend, the corporation shall transfer from retained earnings to the category of capital stock and additional paid-in capital an amount equal to the fair value of the additional shares issued. Unless this is done, the amount of earnings that the shareholder may believe to have been distributed to him or her will be left, except to the extent otherwise dictated by legal requirements, in retained earnings subject to possible further similar stock issuances or cash distributions.

Gleim Simulation Grading

Task	Correct Responses		Gradable Items		Score per Task
1	____	÷	6	=	____
2	____	÷	4	=	____
3	____	÷	7	=	____
4	____	÷	4	=	____
5	____	÷	7	=	____
Research	____	÷	1	=	____

	Total of Scores per Task	____
÷	Total Number of Tasks	6
	Total Score	____ %

Use **CPA Gleim Online** and **Simulation Wizard** to practice more task-based simulations in a realistic environment.

STUDY UNIT SIXTEEN
BUSINESS COMBINATIONS AND CONSOLIDATED FINANCIAL REPORTING

(16 pages of outline)

16.1	Accounting for Business Combinations -- Overview	571
16.2	Consolidated Financial Reporting -- Acquisition Method	575
16.3	Consolidated Financial Reporting -- Acquisition-Date Balance Sheet	577
16.4	Consolidated Financial Reporting -- Net Income and Changes in Equity	579
16.5	Consolidated Financial Reporting -- Intraentity Eliminations	581
16.6	Other Aspects of Business Combinations	584
16.7	Combined Financial Statements	586
16.8	Practice Simulation	598

This study unit addresses the accounting for business combinations, the preparation of consolidated financial statements, the accounting implications of other aspects of business combinations, and the difference between consolidated statements and combined statements.

16.1 ACCOUNTING FOR BUSINESS COMBINATIONS -- OVERVIEW

Background

For many years, GAAP permitted business combinations to be structured as either a pooling of interests or as a purchase of one entity by another. Because a pooling received favorable accounting treatment (among other things, assets and liabilities did not have to be remeasured to fair value), businesses had a strong incentive to structure any combination as a pooling. In 2001, the FASB ended the use of pooling-of-interests accounting for all new combinations.

1. **Definitions**

   a. A **business combination** (hereafter called a combination) is "a transaction or other event in which an acquirer obtains control of one or more businesses."

      1) An acquirer gains control of the acquiree in a combination.

   b. **Control** is a controlling financial interest. This usually means one entity's direct or indirect ownership of more than 50% of the outstanding voting interests of another entity.

      1) However, a controlling financial interest is not deemed to exist when control does not rest with the majority owner, such as when the entity is in bankruptcy, in legal reorganization, or under severe governmentally imposed uncertainties.

      2) Control may be obtained in many ways, such as by (a) transferring assets (such as cash, cash equivalents, or other assets, including a business), (b) issuing equity interests, (c) incurring liabilities, and (d) combining two entities solely by contract.

IFRS Difference

An investor **controls** an investee if and only if the investor has all of the following: (1) power over the investee; (2) exposure, or rights, to variable returns from its involvement with the investee; and (3) the ability to use its power over the investee to affect the amount of the investor's returns. **Potential voting rights** that are currently exercisable must be considered when assessing control.

c.   A **business** consists of integrated activities and assets that can be conducted to provide a return of economic benefits directly to investors or others.

    1)   The essential elements of a business are inputs and processes, but it need not have outputs if it can be managed to provide them.

BUSINESS

| INPUTS | → | PROCESSES | → | POTENTIAL OUTPUTS |

Figure 16-1

    2)   A set of assets and activities that includes goodwill is assumed to be a business absent contrary evidence, but a business need not have goodwill.

2.   **Structure of a Combination**

a.   A combination may be structured in many ways. The following are three possibilities:

    1)   A business(es) may be legally merged with the acquirer. In a **merger**, the assets and liabilities of one combining entity are transferred to the books of the surviving entity. The first entity ceases to have a separate legal existence.

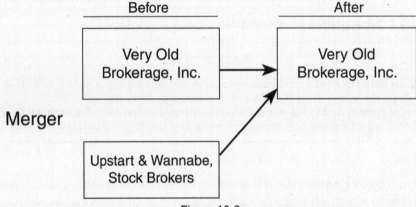

Figure 16-2

      a)   A merger may result from (1) a direct acquisition of the net assets of the acquiree or (2) an acquisition of all of the acquiree's shares followed by transfer of the net assets.

    2)   In a **consolidation**, the combining entities are dissolved, and a new legal entity is created with their assets and liabilities.

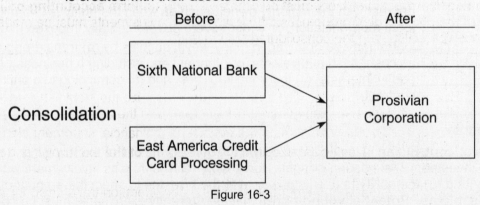

Figure 16-3

      a)   A combination in the form of a consolidation should not be confused with the accounting process to prepare statements for combined entities that are legally separate.

3) **Parent and subsidiary.** The acquirer (parent) and the acquiree (subsidiary) may remain **legally separate**, although the parent has control.

Combination	Surviving Entity(ies)
Merger	Acquirer
Consolidation	New entity
Voting interest > 50%	Acquirer and acquiree

3. **Consolidated Reporting**

   a. When one entity controls another, consolidated financial statements must be issued regardless of the percentage of ownership. Consolidated statements are the general-purpose statements of a parent with one or more subsidiaries.

      1) Consolidated statements present amounts for the parent and subsidiary as if they were a single economic entity.

         a) Separate parent and subsidiary statements may be used for internal purposes, but they are not in conformity with GAAP.

      2) Consolidated reporting is required even when majority ownership is indirect, i.e., when a subsidiary holds a majority interest in another subsidiary.

EXAMPLE

Schoenberg Co. owns 85% of the total outstanding voting interests of Berg Corp. Berg owns 60% of the total outstanding voting interests of Webern, Inc. The consolidated entity includes Schoenberg, Berg, and Webern.

---

   b. A parent and subsidiary may exist separately for an indefinite period, but annual consolidated financial statements must be issued that report them as a single entity.

      1) Consolidation in the accounting sense therefore does not imply that either a merger or consolidation has taken place in the legal sense.

   c. Required consolidated reporting is an example of substance over form. Even if the two entities remain legally separate, the financial statements are more meaningful to users if they see the effects of control by one over the other.

   d. For internal reporting purposes, the parent may choose any accounting method it deems appropriate for its purposes.

IFRS Difference

Consolidated financial statements must be prepared using **uniform accounting policies**. If a member of the consolidated group uses different policies, adjustments must be made to its statements when preparing the consolidated statements.

---

4. **Recognition**

   a. **Recognition principle.** The acquirer must recognize the identifiable assets acquired, liabilities assumed, and noncontrolling interests in the acquiree.

   b. Assets and liabilities must meet the definitions of financial statement elements.

   c. The assets and liabilities recognized must be **part of the exchange** and not the result of separate transactions.

      1) The acquirer must recognize only the consideration transferred for the acquiree.

      2) The acquirer also must identify amounts not part of the exchange and account for them according to their nature and relevant GAAP.

         a) A precombination transaction that primarily benefits the acquirer is most likely to be accounted for separately from the exchange.

EXAMPLE

The acquiree undertakes to make severance payments to certain executives when an expected combination is completed. If the main purpose is to benefit the acquirer, the payments are not part of the exchange. If the main purpose is to benefit the acquiree or its former owners, the payments are included in accounting for the combination.

---

    b)   Other types of **transactions to be accounted for separately** from the combination are

        i)   Compensation to the acquiree's employees or former owners for future services and

        ii)   Reimbursement of the acquiree or former owners for paying acquisition-related costs.

5.   **Costs Associated with Business Combinations**

    a.   **Acquisition-related costs**, such as finder's fees, professional and consulting fees, and general administrative costs, are expensed as incurred.

    b.   Issue costs for securities are accounted for as follows:

        1)   **Direct issue costs of equity** (underwriting, legal, accounting, tax, registration, etc.) reduce additional paid-in capital.

            a)   Indirect costs of issue, records maintenance, and ownership transfers (e.g., a stock transfer agent's fees) are expensed.

        2)   **Debt issue costs** are reported in the balance sheet as deferred charges and amortized over the life of the debt using the interest method.

EXAMPLE

Platonic Corp. incurred the following costs in connection with its acquisition of Socratic Corp.:

Investment bankers' fees	$66,000
Indirect and general expenses	44,000
SEC registration fee	10,000
Printer's fee for stock certificates	6,000

Platonic records the following journal entry in recognition of the costs of the Socratic acquisition:

Business combination expense ($66,000 + $44,000)	$110,000	
Additional paid-in capital ($10,000 + $6,000)	16,000	
Cash		$126,000

---

6.   **Contingencies**

    a.   Assets and liabilities arising from contractual contingencies are recognized and measured at acquisition-date fair values.

    b.   If it is more likely than not at the acquisition date that a noncontractual contingency will result in an asset or liability, the same accounting applies.

EXAMPLE

Acquiree (AE) has been sued by former employees. Subsequent to the filing of the suit, Acquirer (AR) paid cash for all of AE's shares. At the acquisition date, AR will recognize a liability if, given all the relevant facts, it is more likely than not that the suit will be lost. The measure of any liability will depend on the probabilities of outcomes, including settlement.

---

    c.   The asset (liability) is derecognized when the contingency is resolved.

    d.   The acquirer recognizes an **indemnification asset** when the seller contracts to pay for the result of a contingency or uncertainty related to an asset or liability.

EXAMPLE

The seller in a business combination guarantees that the acquirer will not have to pay more than a certain amount to settle an assumed liability (the indemnified item). Because the liability is recognized at the acquisition date, it is measured at its acquisition-date fair value. Accordingly, the indemnification asset also is measured at fair value. No valuation allowance is necessary because fair value includes the effects of the uncertainty of collection.

IFRS Difference

An acquirer must recognize a contingent liability at the acquisition date if (1) it is a present obligation arising from past events and (2) its fair value can be measured reliably. Recognition occurs even if it is not probable that an outflow of economic benefits will be needed to settle the obligation. In circumstances other than a business combination, a liability (called a provision) is recognized only if (1) the outflow of benefits is probable and (2) the other criteria are met.

Stop and review! You have completed the outline for this subunit. Study multiple-choice questions 1 through 5 beginning on page 586.

16.2 CONSOLIDATED FINANCIAL REPORTING -- ACQUISITION METHOD

1. **Summary of the Accounting**

   a. A combination must be accounted for using the **acquisition method**. It

      1) Determines the acquirer and the acquisition date.
      2) Recognizes and measures

         a) Identifiable assets acquired,
         b) Liabilities assumed,
         c) Any noncontrolling interest, and
         d) Goodwill or a gain from a bargain purchase.

   b. **Measurement principle.** The identifiable assets acquired, liabilities assumed, and any noncontrolling interest in the acquiree must be measured at acquisition-date fair value.

EXAMPLE

Platonic Corp. issues 10,000 shares of its common stock to acquire of all of the outstanding common stock of Socratic Corp. (25,000 shares). Platonic's stock is currently trading at $12 per share, and Socratic's stock is trading at $3.80 per share.

Fair value of consideration given (10,000 shares × $12 market price)	$120,000
Market value of acquiree (25,000 shares × $3.80 market price)	95,000

Platonic will record this acquisition at $120,000.

---

2. **Goodwill or Bargain Purchase**

   a. Goodwill is an intangible asset reflecting the future economic benefits arising from other assets acquired in a business combination that are not individually identified and separately recognized.

b. The acquirer may recognize goodwill at the acquisition date. Goodwill equals the excess of 1) over 2):

    1) The sum of the acquisition-date fair values of

        a) The consideration transferred,
        b) Any noncontrolling interest, and
        c) Any previously held equity interest in the acquiree.

    2) The net of the acquisition-date fair values of

        a) Identifiable assets acquired and
        b) Liabilities assumed.

EXAMPLE

Platonic issued stock with a fair value of $120,000 to acquire all the outstanding stock of Socratic Corp. Socratic's inventories and property, plant, and equipment had carrying amounts of $40,000 and $60,000, respectively. These amounts were lower than the fair values of the assets by $4,000 and $10,000, respectively. Given no noncontrolling interest or prior equity interest, goodwill is calculated as follows:

Consideration transferred	$120,000
Acquisition-date fair value of net assets acquired:	
Carrying amount	(100,000)
Holding gain -- inventories	(4,000)
Holding gain -- PP&E	(10,000)
Goodwill	$ 6,000

---

c. If b.2) above exceeds b.1), the entity reports an ordinary gain from a bargain purchase.

EXAMPLE

In the preceding example, assume that the fair value of the PP&E exceeded the carrying amount by $20,000. The result is a gain calculated as follows:

Carrying amount	$100,000
Holding gain -- inventories	4,000
Holding gain -- PP&E	20,000
Acquisition-date fair value of net assets acquired	$124,000
Consideration transferred	(120,000)
Gain from bargain purchase	$ 4,000

---

d. A combination may involve an exchange only of equity interests. If the fair value of the acquiree's equity interests is more reliably measurable than the acquirer's, it is used to determine goodwill.

3. **Basic Aspects of the Acquisition Method**

a. The acquirer is acquiring assets and assuming liabilities only. The acquiree's equity accounts are not relevant.

b. Only the acquiree's identifiable assets acquired and liabilities assumed are recognized. Any goodwill recognized by the acquiree is not an identifiable asset of the acquirer.

    1) However, the acquirer may recognize certain intangible assets that did not qualify for recognition by the acquiree. For example, the acquiree may have internally developed intangible assets and expensed their cost.

c. Because assets and liabilities are recorded at fair value, valuation allowances are not recognized.

4. **Accounting for a Noncontrolling Interest (NCI)**

    a. A noncontrolling interest is the equity in a subsidiary not attributable to the parent. NCI is reported separately in the equity section of the parent's balance sheet.

EXAMPLE

In this version of the example, assume that (1) Platonic transfers $108,000 for a 90% voting interest in Socratic, (2) the holding gain on PP&E is $10,000, and (3) the fair value of the noncontrolling interest (NCI) is $12,000. Platonic performs the following calculation:

Consideration transferred		$108,000
Noncontrolling interest		12,000
Acquisition-date fair value of net assets acquired:		
Carrying amount	$100,000	
Holding gain -- inventories	4,000	
Holding gain -- PP&E	10,000	(114,000)
Goodwill		$ 6,000

IFRS Difference

A noncontrolling interest (NCI) may be measured at (1) fair value or (2) a proportionate share of the fair value of the acquiree's identifiable net assets.

Stop and review! You have completed the outline for this subunit. Study multiple-choice questions 6 through 8 beginning on page 588.

16.3 CONSOLIDATED FINANCIAL REPORTING -- ACQUISITION-DATE BALANCE SHEET

1. **Acquisition-Date Balance Sheet**

    a. A balance sheet should be prepared that reports the financial position of the consolidated entity at the acquisition date.

        1) Step 1 -- Determine the amount of goodwill or gain from bargain purchase recognized on the business combination.

EXAMPLE

On December 31, Year 0, Platonic and Socratic have the following condensed balance sheets:

	Platonic	Socratic		Platonic	Socratic
Current assets	$140,000	$ 40,000	Current liabilities	$ 60,000	$ 20,000
Noncurrent assets	180,000	80,000	Noncurrent liabilities	100,000	0
			Equity	160,000	100,000
Total assets	$320,000	$120,000	Total liabilities and equity	$320,000	$120,000

On January 1, Year 1, Platonic borrowed $120,000 and used the proceeds to purchase 80% of the outstanding common shares of Socratic. Platonic had no prior equity interest in Socratic. Assume that the carrying amounts of Socratic's assets and liabilities equal their fair values except that the fair value of inventory exceeds its carrying amount by $25,000. Also assume that the fair value of the noncontrolling interest (NCI) was $30,000.

Platonic performs the following calculation:

Consideration transferred		$120,000
Acquisition-date fair value of net assets acquired:		
Carrying amount	$(100,000)	
Holding gain -- inventory	(25,000)	(125,000)
Noncontrolling interest		30,000
Goodwill		$ 25,000

2) Step 2 -- Prepare the assets section of the consolidated balance sheet. Assets and liabilities are reported at 100% of their fair value even though an NCI exists.

EXAMPLE

Consolidated assets are calculated as follows:

Current assets of parent	$140,000	Noncurrent assets of parent	$180,000
Current assets of subsidiary	40,000	Noncurrent assets of subsidiary	80,000
Holding gain -- inventory	25,000	Goodwill	25,000
Consolidated current assets	$205,000	Consolidated noncurrent assets	$285,000

---

3) Step 3 -- Classify new debt as current and noncurrent.

EXAMPLE

The new debt issued to effect the acquisition requires 10 equal annual principal and interest payments beginning December 31, Year 1. For the January 1, Year 1, consolidated balance sheet, the principal amount of the first payment must be classified as current and the balance as noncurrent.

Current portion [($120,000 ÷ 10) × 1]	$ 12,000
Noncurrent portion [($120,000 ÷ 10) × 9]	108,000
Total new debt	$120,000

---

4) Step 4 -- Prepare the liabilities section of the consolidated balance sheet.

EXAMPLE

Consolidated liabilities are calculated as follows:

Current liabilities of parent	$60,000	Noncurrent liabilities of parent	$100,000
Current liabilities of subsidiary	20,000	Noncurrent liabilities of subsidiary	0
Current portion of new debt	12,000	New noncurrent debt	108,000
Consolidated current liabilities	$92,000	Consolidated noncurrent liabilities	$208,000

---

5) Step 5 -- Determine the NCI. An NCI is not reported for every asset and liability. The entire NCI is reported as a single component of consolidated equity (the fair value of the NCI was given earlier as $30,000).

6) Step 6 -- Eliminate reciprocal investments. Subsidiary shareholdings in a parent are treated as treasury stock of the consolidated entity. Because no gain or loss on treasury stock transactions is recognized, reciprocal investments have no effect on the net income or retained earnings of the consolidated entity.

EXAMPLE

On the date of acquisition, Socratic held 1,000 shares of Platonic common stock. In preparing the consolidated balance sheet, this holding is eliminated by a debit to treasury stock and a credit to investment in Platonic.

---

7) Step 7 -- Because a combination is an acquisition of net assets, the subsidiary's equity accounts are eliminated. Thus, in the absence of a bargain purchase, the equity of the consolidated entity immediately after acquisition is the equity of the parent just prior to acquisition plus the fair value of the noncontrolling interest.

EXAMPLE

Consolidated equity is calculated as follows:

Platonic's shareholders' equity	$160,000
Noncontrolling interest	30,000
Consolidated total equity	$190,000

---

8)   Step 8 -- Prepare the acquisition-date balance sheet.

EXAMPLE

Platonic's condensed consolidated balance sheet at the acquisition date is as follows:

Consolidated current assets	$205,000	Consolidated current liabilities	$ 92,000
Consolidated noncurrent assets	285,000	Consolidated noncurrent liabilities	208,000
		Platonic's shareholders' equity	160,000
		Noncontrolling interest	30,000
Consolidated total assets	$490,000	Consolidated total equity	$490,000

Stop and review! You have completed the outline for this subunit. Study multiple-choice questions 9 through 14 beginning on page 589.

16.4 CONSOLIDATED FINANCIAL REPORTING -- NET INCOME AND CHANGES IN EQUITY

1.   **Year-End Financial Statements**

a.   After the close of the fiscal year in which the combination occurred, the consolidated entity prepares its first full set of consolidated financial statements.

b.   Year-end consolidated equity is affected by the net income earned, items of other comprehensive income, and the dividends paid by the consolidating entities.

c.   **Consolidation procedures.** The following steps must be performed when preparing consolidated financial statements:

1)   All assets, liabilities, items of income (including revenues and gains), items of expense (including losses), and items of OCI of a subsidiary are added item by item to those of the parent.

2)   The carrying amount of the parent's investment in a subsidiary and all the equity of the subsidiary are eliminated (not presented in the consolidated financial statements).

3)   The periodic net income or loss and OCI of a consolidated subsidiary attributable to NCIs are presented separately from the periodic net income or loss and OCI of the shareholders of the parent.

4)   Goodwill from the acquisition of a subsidiary is presented separately in noncurrent assets.

5)   Intraentity balances, transactions, income, and expenses must be eliminated in full (discussed in Subunit 16.5).

6)   The balance of NCIs is reduced by their share of the subsidiary's dividends declared during the period.

2.   **Consolidated Net Income**

a.   The total consolidated net income for the period must be presented separately for the net income attributable to the

1)   NCIs (NCI's share in the subsidiary's net income) and

2)   Shareholders of the parent (parent's separate net income plus parent's share in the subsidiary's net income).

EXAMPLE

The following are the separate statements of income of the two companies, excluding Platonic's share of income from Socratic, for the year ended December 31, Year 1:

	Platonic	Socratic
Sales	$ 250,000	$120,000
Cost of goods sold	(120,000)	(70,000)
Selling and administrative expenses	(50,000)	(10,000)
Interest costs	(20,000)	0
Income tax expense	(21,000)	(14,000)
Net income	$ 39,000	$ 26,000

Assume that (1) the ownership percentages were not changed from the acquisition date, (2) no items of other comprehensive income were recognized in Year 1, and (3) no intraentity transactions occurred during Year 1. Platonic's Year 1 consolidated statement of income is presented as follows:

Sales	$370,000
Cost of goods sold	(190,000)
Selling and administrative expenses	(60,000)
Interest costs	(20,000)
Income tax expense	(35,000)
Net income	$ 65,000
Net income attributable to NCIs ($26,000 × 20%)	(5,200)
Net income attributable to Platonic shareholders [$39,000 + ($26,000 × 80%)]	$ 59,800

   b.   If an acquisition occurs after the first business day of the year, revenues, expenses, gains, and losses of the subsidiary are included in the financial statements of the consolidated entity only from the date of the acquisition.

3. **Dividends Paid**

   a.   Consolidated dividends are those paid to parties outside the consolidated entity by the parent and the subsidiary.

EXAMPLE

Platonic and Socratic declared and paid $40,000 and $20,000 of dividends, respectively, during the year. Consolidated dividends paid are calculated as follows:

Dividends paid by parent	$40,000
Dividends paid by subsidiary	20,000
Parent's proportionate share of sub's dividends ($20,000 × 80%)	(16,000)
Consolidated dividends paid	$44,000

4. **Retained Earnings**

   a.   Retained earnings of the consolidated entity at the acquisition date consist solely of the retained earnings of the parent. Equity amounts of the subsidiary are eliminated.

   b.   Retained earnings of the consolidated entity at a subsequent reporting date consist of (1) acquisition-date retained earnings, plus (2) the parent's share of consolidated net income (including its proportionate share of the subsidiary's net income included in consolidated net income), minus (3) dividends paid by the parent to entities outside the consolidated entity.

EXAMPLE

Platonic's equity balance of $160,000 just prior to acquisition consisted of common stock of $10,000, additional paid-in capital of $100,000, and retained earnings of $50,000. Consolidated retained earnings is calculated as follows:

Acquisition-date retained earnings of parent	$50,000
Consolidated net income attributable to parent's shareholders	59,800
Parent's dividends paid since acquisition date	(40,000)
Consolidated retained earnings at reporting date	$69,800

5. **Noncontrolling Interest**

    a. The NCI must be adjusted for its proportionate share of (1) the net income of the subsidiary included in consolidated net income, (2) items of consolidated other comprehensive income attributable to the subsidiary, and (3) dividends paid by the subsidiary.

EXAMPLE

Platonic owns 80% of Socratic. At the acquisition date, Platonic recognized $30,000 for the fair value of the NCI. During the current year, the subsidiary's net income and dividends paid were $26,000 and $20,000, respectively. The NCI at the reporting date is calculated as follows:

NCI at acquisition date	$30,000
NCI in subsidiary's net income included in consolidated net income	
($26,000 × 20%)	5,200
NCI in dividends paid by subsidiary ($20,000 × 20%)	(4,000)
Total NCI at reporting date	$31,200

---

6. **Consolidated Statement of Changes in Equity**

    a. This statement satisfies the requirement for a presentation of a reconciliation of the beginning and ending balances of (1) total equity, (2) equity attributable to the parent, and (3) equity attributable to the NCI.

    b. The following is Platonic's Year 1 consolidated statement of changes in equity:

EXAMPLE

		Platonic's Shareholders' Equity				
	Total	Retained Earnings	Accumulated OCI	Common Stock	APIC	NCI
Beginning balance	$190,000	$50,000	–	$10,000	$100,000	$30,000
Net income (loss)	65,000	59,800				5,200
Dividends paid	(44,000)	(40,000)	–	–	–	(4,000)
Ending balance	$211,000	$69,800	–	$10,000	$100,000	$31,200

Stop and review! You have completed the outline for this subunit. Study multiple-choice questions 15 through 18 beginning on page 592.

16.5 CONSOLIDATED FINANCIAL REPORTING -- INTRAENTITY ELIMINATIONS

1. **Year-End Consolidated Financial Statements**

    a. Consolidating entities routinely conduct business with each other. The effects of these intraentity transactions must be eliminated.

    b. Consolidated financial statements report the financial position, results of operations, and cash flows as if the consolidated entities were a single economic entity.

        1) Thus, all line items in the consolidated financial statements must be presented at the amounts that would have been reported if the intraentity transactions had never occurred.

    c. After adding together all the assets, liabilities, and income statement items of a parent and a subsidiary, **eliminating journal entries** for intraentity transactions must be recorded for proper presentation of the consolidated financial statements.

2. **Reciprocal Balances**

    a. In a consolidated balance sheet, reciprocal balances, such as receivables and payables, between a parent and a subsidiary are eliminated in their entirety, regardless of the portion of the subsidiary's stock held by the parent.

EXAMPLE

Platonic's separate balance sheet reports a $12,600 receivable from and an $8,500 payable to Socratic. Socratic's separate balance sheet reports an $8,500 receivable from and a $12,600 payable to Platonic. These balances are not reported on the consolidated balance sheet.

---

3.   **Intraentity Inventory Transactions -- Gross Profit**

    a.   Intraentity transactions that give rise to gross profit require more complex treatment.

          1)   Profit from the sale of inventory between consolidating entities is a component of the net income of the entity that sold the inventory.

          2)   However, the consolidated entity recognizes profit on this exchange only in proportion to the inventory that is sold to outside parties. Accordingly, the gross profit included in the inventory remaining on the purchaser's books must be eliminated from consolidated net income.

          3)   The year-end eliminating journal entry eliminates the gross profit recognized for the inventory remaining on the purchaser's books and reduces the inventory account to the balance it would have had if the intraentity transactions had never occurred.

               a)   The **sales** account is debited (decreased) for the amount recognized by the seller on the intraentity sale.

               b)   The **inventory** account is credited (decreased) for the amount equal to the unrealized intraentity gross profit (seller's gross profit percentage × inventory remaining on purchaser's books).

               c)   The **cost of goods sold** account is credited (decreased) for the difference between a) and b). The total decrease in both the sales account and cost of goods sold account is exactly equal to the amount of gross profit eliminated.

Gross Profit Eliminated:

Inventory remaining on purchaser's books × Seller's gross profit percentage

---

EXAMPLE

During the year, Platonic sold $100,000 of goods to Socratic on the same terms as sales made to third parties. Socratic sold 90% of this inventory to others. Socratic's cost of goods sold in connection with these outside sales was $90,000. Platonic had total sales of $800,000 and total cost of goods sold of $650,000 for the year.

    Seller's gross profit percentage: [($800,000 − $650,000) ÷ $800,000] = 18.75%

Unsold inventory on purchaser's books	$ 10,000
Seller's gross profit percentage	× 18.75%
Unrealized intraentity gross profit	$ 1,875

The eliminating journal entry is as follows:

Sales	$100,000	
Inventory		$ 1,875
Cost of goods sold		98,125

---

4.   **Intraentity Plant Assets Transactions**

    a.   Transfers of plant assets require elimination of any **gain or loss on sale** recognized on the intraentity transaction.

    b.   All the accounts related to the plant asset transferred must be reported in the consolidated financial statements at the amounts that would have been reported if the intraentity transactions had never occurred.

          1)   Thus, the **depreciation expense** recognized in the consolidated financial statements must be the depreciation expense as it would have been recognized in the seller's separate financial statements.

2) If the original useful life and the depreciation method remain the same, the depreciation expense eliminated (added) is equal to the amount of gain (loss) on sale of equipment divided by the years of useful life remaining.

EXAMPLE

On the first day of its fiscal year, Platonic sold equipment to Socratic for $99,000. The equipment was originally purchased by Platonic 3 years ago for $120,000. Platonic depreciated the equipment using the straight-line method over 8 years with no salvage value. Socratic depreciates the equipment using the straight-line method over 5 years with no salvage value. The following steps must be performed to record the eliminating journal entry for proper presentation of the equipment in the year-end consolidated financial statements:

1. Eliminate the gain or loss on sale of the equipment that was recognized. Platonic recognized depreciation expense each year of $15,000 ($120,000 historical cost ÷ 8 years). Thus, the carrying amount of the equipment on the sale date in Platonic's separate financial statements was $75,000 ($120,000 historical cost – $45,000 accumulated depreciation). The gain on the sale was $24,000 ($99,000 transfer price – $75,000 seller's carrying amount). This gain must be eliminated (debited) in the eliminating journal entry.

2. The depreciation expense must be equal to the depreciation expense that would have been recognized by Platonic ($15,000) as if the intraentity transaction had never occurred. Since the equipment is on Socratic's books, the depreciation expense before the eliminating journal entry is $19,800 ($99,000 transfer price ÷ 5 years). Thus, the depreciation expense must be decreased (credited) in the eliminating journal entry by $4,800 ($15,000 – $19,800). Note that this amount is equal to the gain on sale recognized divided by the years of useful life remaining ($24,000 ÷ 5 = $4,800).

3. The cost of the equipment in the consolidated financial statements must be $120,000 (the amount that would have been reported if the intraentity transaction had never occurred). Thus, the equipment account must be increased (debited) in the eliminating journal entry by $21,000 ($120,000 historical cost – $99,000 transfer price).

4. The accumulated depreciation account in the consolidated financial statements must be $60,000 (the amount that would have been reported if the intraentity transaction had never occurred). Thus, the accumulated depreciation account must be increased (credited) in the eliminating journal entry by $40,200 ($60,000 – $19,800).

5. The eliminating journal entry is as follows:

Equipment	$21,000	
Gain on sale of equipment	24,000	
Accumulated depreciation		$40,200
Depreciation expense		4,800

---

5. **Debt**

   a. When one entity holds the debt securities of another entity with which it is consolidated, the elimination is treated as an extinguishment of debt, with recognition of any resulting gain or loss.

      1) The following are accounting issues:

         a) Maturity or face amount of the debt
         b) Interest receivable/payable at period end
         c) Interest income/expense based on maturity amount and stated rate
         d) Discount or premium on the books of the issuer (debtor)
         e) Discount or premium on the books of the purchaser (creditor)

      2) The maturity amount, interest receivable/payable, and interest income/expense are direct eliminations.

EXAMPLE

Wagner, a holder of a $1 million Palmer, Inc., bond, collected the interest due on March 31 and then sold the bond to Seal, Inc., for $975,000. On that date, Palmer, a 75% owner of Seal, had a $1,075,000 carrying amount for this bond. The purchase was in substance a retirement of debt by the consolidated group for less than its carrying amount. The transaction resulted in a gain of $100,000 ($1,075,000 carrying amount – $975,000 price) and therefore a $100,000 increase in consolidated retained earnings.

b.   The premium or discount on the debtor's and creditor's books, and any related amortization, is eliminated and recognized as a gain or loss on extinguishment in the period of purchase.

6.   **Reciprocal Dividends**

a.   When consolidated entities hold reciprocal equity stakes, the portion of dividends paid to each other must be eliminated from the consolidated financial statements.

1)   The portion of the parent's dividends paid to outside parties reduces consolidated retained earnings.

2)   The portion of the subsidiary's dividends paid to outside parties reduces any noncontrolling interest.

Dividends	Consolidated Treatment
Parent's dividends to subsidiary	Eliminated
Subsidiary's dividends to parent	Eliminated
Parent's dividends to third parties	Reduces retained earnings
Subsidiary's dividends to third parties	Reduces NCI

The AICPA has released exam questions asking for the amount of a line item shown on the consolidated financial statements. When intraentity transactions are involved, determining the consolidated amount involves calculating the amount that must be eliminated for any intraentity transactions. Testable items include receivables; payables; property, plant, and equipment; accumulated depreciation; etc.

Stop and review! You have completed the outline for this subunit. Study multiple-choice questions 19 through 24 beginning on page 594.

16.6 OTHER ASPECTS OF BUSINESS COMBINATIONS

1.   **Deconsolidation**

a.   A parent deconsolidates a subsidiary when it no longer has a controlling financial interest.

1)   Typically, this occurs when the parent sells enough of its ownership interest in the subsidiary such that its equity interest falls below 50%.

2)   Deconsolidation is also necessary in the case of a spinoff or other nonreciprocal transfer to owners.

b.   Upon deconsolidation, the parent recognizes a gain or loss in net income. It equals the difference at the deconsolidation date between 1) and 2) below.

1)   The sum of the

a)   Fair value of the consideration received
b)   Fair value of any retained investment
c)   Carrying amount of any NCI (including accumulated OCI attributable to it)

2)   The carrying amount of the subsidiary (including the carrying amount of goodwill).

c.   A parent may deconsolidate a subsidiary during the year while retaining significant influence. The fair value option (FVO) or the equity method must be elected to account for such a retained interest but only from the deconsolidation date.

2.   **Off-Balance-Sheet Arrangements**

a.   **Interests in Unconsolidated Subsidiaries**

1)   An investor with less than a controlling interest reports the investment as an asset.

a)   The investee's debts, for which the investor could be substantially responsible, are not reported as liabilities of the investor.

b. **Operating Leases**

    1) Techniques for keeping the substantial amounts of debt associated with a capital lease off an entity's balance sheet were discussed in Study Unit 14.

c. **Variable Interest Entities (VIEs)**

    1) A VIE is an off-balance-sheet arrangement that may take any legal form (e.g., corporation, partnership, not-for-profit entity, limited liability company, or trust). Moreover, the equity investors

        a) Have insufficient equity at risk (the entity is undercapitalized) or

        b) Lack one of the following characteristics:

            i) The power, through voting (or similar) rights, to direct the most significant economic activities (voting rights)

            ii) An obligation to absorb expected losses (risk of loss)

            iii) The right to receive expected residual returns (rewards of ownership)

    2) **Variable interests** are ownership, contractual, or monetary interests that vary with changes in the fair value of the VIE's net assets (excluding variable interests). Examples are

        a) Common stock in a VIE formed as a corporation,

        b) Subordinated debt issued by the VIE, and

        c) Guarantees of the VIE's assets or liabilities.

    3) An entity **must be consolidated as a VIE** if, by design, the equity investors meet one of the conditions in c.1).

        a) Equity investors as a group also lack the voting rights characteristic and consolidation is required if

            i) Voting rights of some investors are disproportionate to their risk of loss or their rights to expected returns, and

            ii) Substantially all of the VIE's activities involve or are performed for an investor with disproportionately few voting rights.

    4) An entity consolidates a VIE when its variable interest(s) provides a **controlling financial interest**.

        a) This entity is the **primary beneficiary** of the VIE. It must have

            i) The power to direct the activities of the VIE that most significantly affect its economic performance and

            ii) The risk of loss or the right to benefits with potential significance to the VIE.

Background

In late 2001, the national media revealed that Enron Corporation had used special purpose entities (SPEs) to hide a huge amount of debt for which it was responsible by moving it to the balance sheets of SPEs. These SPEs had been deliberately structured so that Enron would not have to consolidate them. The FASB responded by issuing pronouncements on variable interest entities. Moreover, the concept of a qualifying SPE is no longer relevant for accounting purposes. Thus, such entities should be evaluated for consolidation under the applicable guidance.

Stop and review! You have completed the outline for this subunit. Study multiple-choice questions 25 and 26 on page 596.

16.7 COMBINED FINANCIAL STATEMENTS

1.   Consolidated statements should be prepared only when the controlling financial interest is held by one of the consolidated entities.

2.   When consolidated statements are not prepared, combined statements may be more meaningful than the separate statements of commonly controlled entities.

   a.   For example, combined statements are useful when one individual owns a controlling financial interest in several entities with related operations. They also may be used to present the statements of entities under common management.

3.   Combined statements are prepared in the same way as consolidated statements.

   a.   When they are prepared for related entities, e.g., commonly controlled entities, intraentity transactions and gains or losses are eliminated.

   b.   Moreover, consolidation procedures are applied to such matters as (1) noncontrolling interests, (2) foreign operations, (3) different fiscal periods, and (4) income taxes.

EXAMPLE

Fructose Corp. owns 85% of the stock of Sucrose Co., 75% of Lactose Co., and 90% of Maltose Co. Fructose is considering selling its entire interest in all three subsidiaries to one buyer. The subsidiaries do not own each other's stock. Lactose has a $15,000 payable due from Sucrose, and Sucrose has $33,000 in profits and a $28,000 payable from its dealings with Maltose.

Fructose will issue one set of financial statements that reports consolidated information for all four entities. The $15,000 receivable/payable, the $33,000 in profits, and the $28,000 receivable/payable are all eliminated from these statements.

Another set of statements also will be prepared that reports combined information only for Sucrose, Lactose, and Maltose. These statements also will eliminate the mutual receivable/payable and profit amounts. These combined statements contain no asset, liability, equity, revenue, or expense amounts of Fructose.

Stop and review! You have completed the outline for this subunit. Study multiple-choice questions 27 and 28 on page 597.

QUESTIONS

16.1 Accounting for Business Combinations -- Overview

1. Pendragon Co. issues 200,000 shares of $5 par value common stock to acquire Squire Co. in a business combination. The market value of Pendragon's common stock is $12. Legal and consulting fees incurred in relationship to the combination are $110,000. Direct registration and issuance costs for the common stock are $35,000. What should be recorded in Pendragon's additional paid-in capital (APIC) for this business combination?

A. $1,545,000

B. $1,400,000

C. $1,365,000

D. $1,255,000

Answer (C) is correct.

REQUIRED: The effect of the business combination on APIC.

DISCUSSION: Acquisition-related costs, such as finder's fees, professional (e.g., legal) and consulting fees, and general administrative costs (e.g., for an acquisitions department), are expensed as incurred. The one exception is for the issuance costs of debt or equity securities. These are accounted for under other GAAP. Thus, direct issuance costs of equity (underwriting, legal, accounting, tax, registration, etc.) are debited to additional paid-in capital. Accordingly, the amount recorded in APIC for the combination should be $1,365,000 {[200,000 shares × ($12 market value – $5 par value)] – $35,000 direct issuance costs}.

Answer (A) is incorrect. The amount of $1,545,000 equals $1,400,000 [200,000 × ($12 – $5)] plus legal and consulting fees ($110,000) and direct issuance costs ($35,000). Answer (B) is incorrect. APIC without an adjustment for direct issuance costs equals $1,400,000. Answer (D) is incorrect. The amount of $1,255,000 equals $1,400,000 [200,000 × ($12 – $5)], minus legal and consulting fees ($110,000), minus direct issuance costs ($35,000).

2. On August 31, Planar Corp. exchanged 100,000 shares of its $40 par value common stock for all of the net assets of Sistrock Co. The fair value of Planar's common stock on August 31 was $72 per share. Planar paid a fee of $320,000 to the consultant who arranged this acquisition. Direct costs of registering and issuing the equity securities amounted to $160,000. No goodwill or bargain purchase was involved in the acquisition. At what amount should Planar record the acquisition of Sistrock's net assets?

A. $7,200,000

B. $7,360,000

C. $7,520,000

D. $7,680,000

Answer (A) is correct.
REQUIRED: The fair value of the net assets acquired.
DISCUSSION: Acquisition-related costs, such as the $320,000 consultant's fee, are expensed as incurred. But exceptions are made for direct issue costs of securities accounted for under other GAAP. Thus, the direct issue costs of equity ($160,000) are debited to additional paid-in capital. The consideration transferred is measured at its fair value of $7,200,000 (100,000 shares of common stock issued × $72). Given that no goodwill or bargain purchase was involved, neither goodwill nor a gain is recognized. Consequently, the identifiable assets acquired and liabilities assumed are recorded at their net amount of $7,200,000. The journal entries are

Investment in Sistrock (100,000 × $72)	$7,200,000	
Common stock (100,000 × $40)		$4,000,000
Additional paid-in capital (difference)		3,200,000

Business combination expense	$ 320,000	
Additional paid-in capital	160,000	
Cash		$ 480,000

Answer (B) is incorrect. The fair value of the net assets acquired plus the registration and issuance costs equals $7,360,000. Answer (C) is incorrect. The fair value of the net assets acquired plus the consultant's fee equals $7,520,000. Answer (D) is incorrect. The fair value of the net assets acquired plus the registration and issuance costs and the consultant's fee equals $7,680,000.

3. Primor, a manufacturer, owns 75% of the voting interests of Sublette, an investment firm. Sublette owns 60% of the voting interests of Minos, an insurer. In Primor's consolidated financial statements, should consolidation accounting or equity method accounting be used for Sublette and Minos?

A. Consolidation used for Sublette and equity method used for Minos.

B. Consolidation used for both Sublette and Minos.

C. Equity method used for Sublette and consolidation used for Minos.

D. Equity method used for both Sublette and Minos.

Answer (B) is correct.
REQUIRED: The method of accounting used by an entity that has a direct controlling interest in one entity and an indirect interest in another.
DISCUSSION: All entities in which a parent has a controlling financial interest through direct or indirect ownership of a majority voting interest ordinarily must be consolidated. However, a subsidiary is not consolidated when control does not rest with the majority owner. Primor has direct control of Sublette and indirect control of Minos and should consolidate both.
Answer (A) is incorrect. Primor has a controlling interest in Minos as well. Answer (C) is incorrect. Primor has a controlling interest in Sublette as well. Answer (D) is incorrect. Primor should consolidate both Sublette and Minos.

4. Consolidated financial statements are typically prepared when one entity has a majority voting interest in another **unless**

A. The subsidiary is a finance entity.

B. The fiscal year ends of the two entities are more than 3 months apart.

C. Control does **not** rest with the majority owner(s).

D. The two entities are in unrelated industries, such as manufacturing and real estate.

Answer (C) is correct.
REQUIRED: The circumstance in which a majority-owned entity is not consolidated.
DISCUSSION: Consolidated financial reporting is required when one entity owns, directly or indirectly, more than 50% of the outstanding voting interests of another entity. However, a majority-owned subsidiary is not consolidated if control does not rest with the majority owner.
Answer (A) is incorrect. The nature of the subsidiary's business is irrelevant. Answer (B) is incorrect. A difference in fiscal periods is irrelevant. Answer (D) is incorrect. Whether the parent and subsidiary are in related industries is irrelevant.

5. Rolan Corporation issued 10,000 shares of common stock in exchange for all of Sandin Corporation's outstanding stock on September 1. Rolan's common stock had a market price of $60 per share on September 1. The market price of Sandin's stock was not readily ascertainable. Condensed balance sheets of Rolan and Sandin immediately prior to the combination are indicated below.

	Rolan	Sandin
Total assets	$1,000,000	$500,000
Liabilities	$ 300,000	$150,000
Common stock ($10 par)	200,000	100,000
Retained earnings	500,000	250,000
Total liabilities and shareholders' equities	$1,000,000	$500,000

Rolan's investment in Sandin's stock will be stated in Rolan's parent-only balance sheet immediately after the combination in the amount of

A. $100,000

B. $350,000

C. $500,000

D. $600,000

Answer (D) is correct.

REQUIRED: The recorded amount of the acquired entity.

DISCUSSION: In a parent-only balance sheet, the acquirer recognizes only an investment in subsidiary and the issuance of equity. The fair value of the consideration transferred (10,000 shares × $60 = $600,000) is the measure of the investment immediately after the combination. (In a consolidated balance sheet, no investment in the subsidiary would be recognized.)

Answer (A) is incorrect. The par value of the stock issued equals $100,000. Answer (B) is incorrect. The carrying amount of Sandin's net assets equals $350,000. Answer (C) is incorrect. The fair value of the stock issued minus its par value equals $500,000.

16.2 Consolidated Financial Reporting -- Acquisition Method

6. Pellew Corp. paid $600,000 for all of the outstanding common stock of Samos Co. in a business combination initiated and completed in December. At that time, Samos had the following condensed balance sheet:

	Carrying Amounts
Current assets	$ 80,000
Plant and equipment, net	760,000
Liabilities	400,000
Equity	440,000

The acquisition-date fair value of the plant and equipment was $120,000 more than its carrying amount. The acquisition-date fair values and carrying amounts were equal for all other assets and liabilities. What amount of goodwill, related to Samos's acquisition, must Pellew report in its December 31 consolidated balance sheet?

A. $40,000

B. $80,000

C. $120,000

D. $160,000

Answer (A) is correct.

REQUIRED: The amount of goodwill reported in the consolidated balance sheet.

DISCUSSION: A business combination is accounted for as an acquisition. Under the acquisition method, the entry recording the transaction is based on the fair values exchanged. Goodwill is the excess of (1) the sum of the acquisition-date fair values of (a) the consideration transferred, (b) any noncontrolling interest in the acquiree, and (c) the acquirer's previously held equity interest in the acquiree over (2) the net of the acquisition-date fair values of the identifiable assets acquired and liabilities assumed. Pellew's goodwill is therefore calculated as follows:

Consideration transferred	$600,000
Acquisition-date fair value of net assets acquired:	
Current assets	(80,000)
Plant and equipment, fair value ($760,000 + $120,000)	(880,000)
Liabilities	400,000
Goodwill	$ 40,000

Answer (B) is incorrect. The amount of current assets is $80,000. Answer (C) is incorrect. The amount of plant and equipment is undervalued is $120,000. Answer (D) is incorrect. The difference between the $600,000 cost and the $440,000 carrying amount of the net assets is $160,000.

7. Company J acquired all of the outstanding common stock of Company K in exchange for cash. The consideration transferred exceeds the acquisition-date fair value of the net assets acquired. How should Company J determine the amounts to be reported for the plant and equipment and long-term debt acquired from Company K?

	Plant and Equipment	Long-Term Debt
A.	K's carrying amount	K's carrying amount
B.	K's carrying amount	Fair value
C.	Fair value	K's carrying amount
D.	Fair value	Fair value

Answer (D) is correct.
REQUIRED: The correct valuation of assets and liabilities acquired in a business combination accounted for as a purchase.
DISCUSSION: A business combination is accounted for as an acquisition. Under the acquisition method, the entry recording the transaction is based on the fair values exchanged.
Answer (A) is incorrect. The plant and equipment and long-term debt should be recorded at their acquisition-date fair values. Answer (B) is incorrect. The plant and equipment should be recorded at their acquisition-date fair values. Answer (C) is incorrect. The long-term debt should be recorded at acquisition-date fair value.

8. Acquirer Corporation acquired for cash at $10 per share 100,000 shares of the outstanding common stock of Acquiree Company. The total fair value of the identifiable assets acquired minus liabilities assumed of Acquiree was $1.4 million on the acquisition date, including the fair value of its property, plant, and equipment (its only noncurrent asset) of $250,000. The consolidated financial statements of Acquirer Corporation and its wholly owned subsidiary must reflect

A. A deferred credit of $150,000.

B. Goodwill of $150,000.

C. A gain of $150,000.

D. A gain of $400,000.

Answer (D) is correct.
REQUIRED: The accounting for a bargain purchase.
DISCUSSION: When (1) the net of the acquisition-date fair values of the identifiable assets acquired and liabilities assumed exceeds (2) the sum of the acquisition-date fair values of (a) the consideration transferred, (b) any noncontrolling interest in the acquiree, and (c) the acquirer's previously held equity interest in the acquiree, the acquirer recognizes the excess as an ordinary gain.

Acquisition-date fair value of net assets acquired	$ 1,400,000
Consideration transferred (100,000 shares × $10)	(1,000,000)
Gain from bargain purchase	$ 400,000

Answer (A) is incorrect. A deferred credit is never recognized for a bargain purchase. Answer (B) is incorrect. This acquisition results in a gain from bargain purchase, not goodwill. Answer (C) is incorrect. A gain of $150,000 results from reducing the fair value of the PPE to zero.

16.3 Consolidated Financial Reporting -- Acquisition-Date Balance Sheet

9. On December 31, Poe Corporation exchanged 200,000 shares of its $10 par common stock, with a market price of $18 per share, for all of Saxe Corporation's common stock. The equity section of each entity's balance sheet immediately before the combination is presented below:

	Poe	Saxe
Common stock	$3,000,000	$1,500,000
Additional paid-in capital	1,300,000	150,000
Retained earnings	2,500,000	850,000
Totals	$6,800,000	$2,500,000

In the December 31 consolidated balance sheet, additional paid-in capital should be reported at

A. $950,000

B. $1,300,000

C. $1,450,000

D. $2,900,000

Answer (D) is correct.
REQUIRED: The additional paid-in capital to be reported in the consolidated balance sheet.
DISCUSSION: To effect the acquisition, Poe records the following journal entry in its separate books:

Investment in Saxe Corp.		
(200,000 shares × $18 market price)	$3,600,000	
Common stock (200,000 shares ×		
$10 par value)		$2,000,000
Additional paid-in capital (difference)		1,600,000

The additional paid-in capital carried on Poe's (the parent's) books is therefore $2,900,000 ($1,300,000 + $1,600,000). This balance also is reported on the consolidated balance sheet.
Answer (A) is incorrect. The additional paid-in capital reported under the pooling-of-interests method, which is no longer applied to business combinations, is $950,000. Answer (B) is incorrect. The amount reported by Poe immediately before the combination is $1,300,000. Answer (C) is incorrect. The sum of the amounts reported by Poe and Saxe immediately before the combination is $1,450,000.

Questions 10 through 14 are based on the following information. On January 2, Parma borrowed $60,000 and used the proceeds to purchase 90% of the outstanding common shares of Seville. Parma had no prior equity interest in Seville. Ten equal principal and interest payments begin December 30. The excess of the implied fair value of Seville over the carrying amount of its identifiable net assets should be assigned 60% to inventory and 40% to goodwill. Moreover, the fair value of the noncontrolling interest (NCI) is 10% of the implied fair value of the acquiree.

The following are the balance sheets of Parma and Seville on January 1:

	Parma	Seville
Current assets	$ 70,000	$20,000
Noncurrent assets	90,000	40,000
Total assets	$160,000	$60,000
Current liabilities	$ 30,000	$10,000
Noncurrent liabilities	50,000	--
Equity	80,000	50,000
Total liabilities and equity	$160,000	$60,000

10. On Parma's January 2 consolidated balance sheet, current assets equal

A. $100,000

B. $96,000

C. $90,000

D. $80,000

Answer (A) is correct.
  REQUIRED: The consolidated current assets.
  DISCUSSION: The implied fair value of the subsidiary is $66,667 ($60,000 cash paid by the parent ÷ 90%). The excess of this amount over the carrying amount of the subsidiary's identifiable net assets is $16,667 ($66,667 – $50,000). This amount is allocated $10,000 to inventory ($16,667 × 60%) and $6,667 to goodwill ($16,667 × 40%). Thus, the reported amount of the current assets is $100,000.

Current assets of Parma	$ 70,000
Current assets of Seville	20,000
Undervaluation of inventory	10,000
Consolidated current assets	$100,000

  Answer (B) is incorrect. The amount of $96,000 assumes an assignment of $6,000 to inventory. Answer (C) is incorrect. The amount of $90,000 ignores the $10,000 excess of the fair value of inventory over its carrying amount. Answer (D) is incorrect. The amount of $80,000 excludes the carrying amount of Seville's current assets.

11. On Parma's January 2 consolidated balance sheet, noncurrent assets equal

A. $130,000

B. $134,000

C. $136,667

D. $140,000

Answer (C) is correct.
  REQUIRED: The consolidated noncurrent assets.
  DISCUSSION: The implied fair value of the subsidiary is $66,667 ($60,000 cash paid by the parent ÷ 90%). The excess of this amount over the carrying amount of the subsidiary's identifiable net assets is $16,667 ($66,667 – $50,000). This amount is allocated $10,000 to inventory ($16,667 × 60%) and $6,667 to goodwill ($16,667 × 40%). Thus, reported noncurrent assets equal $136,667.

Noncurrent assets of Parma	$ 90,000
Noncurrent assets of Seville	40,000
Goodwill	6,667
Consolidated noncurrent assets	$136,667

  Answer (A) is incorrect. The amount of $130,000 ignores goodwill. Answer (B) is incorrect. The amount of $134,000 assumes that a 100% interest was acquired and that goodwill was therefore $4,000 [($60,000 – $50,000) × 40%]. Answer (D) is incorrect. The amount of $140,000 assumes that a 100% interest was acquired and that goodwill was $10,000.

12. On Parma's January 2 consolidated balance sheet, current liabilities equal

A. $50,000

B. $46,000

C. $40,000

D. $30,000

Answer (B) is correct.
REQUIRED: The consolidated current liabilities.
DISCUSSION: Consolidated current liabilities contain the current portion of the debt issued by Parma to finance the acquisition ($60,000 ÷ 10 equal principal payments = $6,000). Reported current liabilities equal $46,000.

Current liabilities of Parma	$30,000
Current liabilities of Seville	10,000
Current component of new debt	6,000
Consolidated current liabilities	$46,000

Answer (A) is incorrect. The pre-existing noncurrent debt is $50,000. Answer (C) is incorrect. The amount of $40,000 ignores the new borrowing. Answer (D) is incorrect. The amount of Parma's pre-existing current liabilities is $30,000.

13. On Parma's January 2 consolidated balance sheet, the sum of the noncurrent liabilities and the NCI equal

A. $116,667

B. $110,667

C. $104,000

D. $50,000

Answer (B) is correct.
REQUIRED: The sum of the noncurrent liabilities and the NCI.
DISCUSSION: Consolidated noncurrent liabilities include the noncurrent portion of the debt issued by Parma to finance the acquisition ($60,000 – $6,000 = $54,000). Thus, reported noncurrent liabilities equal $104,000.

Noncurrent liabilities of Parma	$ 50,000
Noncurrent component of new debt	54,000
Consolidated noncurrent liabilities	$104,000

The implied fair value of the subsidiary is $66,667 ($60,000 cash paid by the parent ÷ 90%), and the NCI is $6,667 ($66,667 × 10%). The sum of the noncurrent liabilities and the NCI is therefore $110,667 ($104,000 + $6,667).

Answer (A) is incorrect. The amount of $116,667 is the sum of noncurrent liabilities (excluding the new borrowing) and the implied fair value of the subsidiary. Answer (C) is incorrect. The amount of $104,000 omits the NCI. Answer (D) is incorrect. The amount of $50,000 ignores the new borrowing and the NCI.

14. On Parma's January 2 consolidated balance sheet, Parma's shareholders' equity should be

A. $80,000

B. $86,667

C. $90,000

D. $130,000

Answer (A) is correct.
REQUIRED: The equity in the consolidated balance sheet.
DISCUSSION: An NCI is the equity of a subsidiary not directly or indirectly attributable to the parent. Thus, the equity section of the consolidated balance sheet at the acquisition date is not the same as the equity section of the parent's separate balance sheet. Consolidated equity includes any NCI in the fair value of the acquiree's identifiable net assets presented separately from the parent's shareholders' equity. Thus, Parma's shareholders' equity on the consolidated balance sheet is calculated as follows:

Consolidated current assets	$ 100,000
Consolidated noncurrent assets	136,667
Consolidated current liabilities	(46,000)
Consolidated noncurrent liabilities	(104,000)
Noncontrolling interest	(6,667)
Parma's shareholders' equity	$ 80,000

Answer (B) is incorrect. Parma's equity at 1/1 plus the fair value of the noncontrolling interest equals $86,667. Answer (C) is incorrect. The total liabilities of the two entities at 1/1 equal $90,000. Answer (D) is incorrect. The sum of the equity amounts for Parma and Seville at 1/1 is $130,000.

16.4 Consolidated Financial Reporting -- Net Income and Changes in Equity

15. To effect a business combination, Proper Co. acquired all the outstanding common shares of Scapula Co., a business entity, for cash equal to the carrying amount of Scapula's net assets. The carrying amounts of Scapula's assets and liabilities approximated their fair values at the acquisition date, except that the carrying amount of its building was more than fair value. In preparing Proper's year-end consolidated income statement, what is the effect of recording the assets acquired and liabilities assumed at fair value, and should goodwill amortization be recognized?

	Depreciation Expense	Goodwill Amortization
A.	Lower	Yes
B.	Higher	Yes
C.	Lower	No
D.	Higher	No

Answer (C) is correct.
REQUIRED: The effects of the combination on depreciation and goodwill amortization.
DISCUSSION: A business combination is accounted for as an acquisition. Under the acquisition method, the entry recording the transaction is based on the fair values exchanged. Accordingly, the identifiable assets acquired and liabilities assumed ordinarily are recorded at their acquisition-date fair values. The differences between those fair values and carrying amounts will affect net income when related expenses are incurred. The effect of recording the building at fair value in the consolidated balance sheet instead of its higher carrying amount on Scapula's books will be to decrease future depreciation. Goodwill is the excess of (1) the sum of the acquisition-date fair values of (a) the consideration transferred, (b) any noncontrolling interest in the acquiree, and (c) the acquirer's previously held equity interest in the acquiree over (2) the net of the acquisition-date fair values of the identifiable assets acquired and liabilities assumed. Thus, Proper recognizes goodwill for the excess of the cash paid over the fair value of the net assets acquired (given an acquisition of 100% of Scapula's common shares). This amount will be tested for impairment, not amortized.
Answer (A) is incorrect. Goodwill will be recognized but not amortized. Answer (B) is incorrect. Depreciation will decrease, and goodwill will be recognized but not amortized. Answer (D) is incorrect. Depreciation will decrease.

16. On January 1, Year 4, Pane Corp. exchanged 150,000 shares of its $20 par value common stock for all of Sky Corp.'s common stock. At that date, the fair value of Pane's common stock issued was equal to the fair value of the identifiable assets acquired and liabilities assumed. Both corporations continued to operate as separate businesses, maintaining accounting records with years ending December 31. In its separate statements, Pane accounts for the investment using the equity method. Information from separate company operations follows:

	Pane	Sky
Retained earnings – 12/31/Yr 3	$3,200,000	$925,000
Dividends paid – 3/25/Yr 4	750,000	200,000

If consolidated net income was $800,000, what amount of retained earnings should Pane report in its December 31, Year 4, consolidated balance sheet?

A. $4,925,000

B. $4,125,000

C. $3,050,000

D. $3,250,000

Answer (D) is correct.
REQUIRED: The consolidated retained earnings.
DISCUSSION: Retained earnings of the consolidated entity at the acquisition date consist solely of the retained earnings of the parent. The consolidated entry does not report any equity amounts of the subsidiary. Retained earnings of the consolidated entity at the reporting date consist of acquisition-date retained earnings, plus consolidated net income (no NCI exists), minus consolidated dividends paid. Sky's dividends, if any, are paid solely to Pane. Thus, consolidated dividends (those paid outside the entity) consist entirely of those paid by Pane.

Acquisition-date retained earnings of Pane	$3,200,000
Consolidated net income since acquisition date	800,000
Consolidated dividends paid since acquisition date	(750,000)
Consolidated retained earnings at reporting date	$3,250,000

Answer (A) is incorrect. The amount of $4,925,000 includes Sky's retained earnings at 12/31/Yr 3 and does not reflect an adjustment for the dividends paid. Answer (B) is incorrect. The amount of $4,125,000 is the sum of the retained earnings of Pane and Sky at 12/31/Yr 3. Answer (C) is incorrect. The amount of $3,050,000 results from treating Sky's dividends as consolidated dividends.

17. A 70%-owned subsidiary declares and pays a cash dividend. What effect does the dividend have on the retained earnings and noncontrolling interest balances in the consolidated balance sheet?

A. No effect on either retained earnings or the noncontrolling interest.

B. No effect on retained earnings and a decrease in the noncontrolling interest.

C. Decreases in both retained earnings and the noncontrolling interest.

D. A decrease in retained earnings and no effect on the noncontrolling interest.

Answer (B) is correct.
REQUIRED: The effect of payment of a cash dividend by a subsidiary.
DISCUSSION: The parent's investment in subsidiary, intraentity dividends, and the subsidiary's equity accounts, which include retained earnings, are among the eliminations in a consolidation. The equity (net assets) of the subsidiary not directly or indirectly attributable to the parent is reported separately in consolidated equity as the noncontrolling interest. Consolidated retained earnings equals the accumulated earnings of the consolidated group not distributed to the owners of, or capitalized by, the parent. Thus, it equals the parent's retained earnings. Accordingly, the subsidiary's cash dividend reduces retained earnings reported in the subsidiary-only statements and the noncontrolling interest reported in the consolidated statements. But it does not affect consolidated retained earnings.
Answer (A) is incorrect. Cash dividends from a subsidiary decrease the noncontrolling interest. Answer (C) is incorrect. Cash dividends from a subsidiary have no effect on consolidated retained earnings but decrease the noncontrolling interest. Answer (D) is incorrect. Cash dividends from a subsidiary have no effect on consolidated retained earnings.

18. On January 2 of the current year, Peace Co. paid $310,000 to purchase 75% of the voting shares of Surge Co. Surge held no shares in Peace. Peace reported retained earnings of $80,000, and Surge reported contributed capital of $300,000 and retained earnings of $100,000. The purchase differential was attributed to depreciable assets with a remaining useful life of 10 years. Peace used the equity method in accounting for its investment in Surge. Surge reported net income of $20,000 and paid dividends of $8,000 during the current year. Peace reported income, exclusive of its income from Surge, of $30,000 and paid dividends of $15,000 during the current year. What amount will Peace report as dividends declared and paid in its current year's consolidated statement of retained earnings?

A. $8,000

B. $15,000

C. $17,000

D. $23,000

Answer (C) is correct.
REQUIRED: The consolidated dividends declared and paid.
DISCUSSION: Peace acquired a greater than 50% share of the voting interests in Surge. Accordingly, Peace must consolidate Surge unless it does not have control. Moreover, the equity method is not appropriate except in parent-only statements. The consolidated statements should report only dividends paid to parties outside the consolidated entity. Because Peace acquired only 75% of the voting shares of Surge, a 25% noncontrolling interest exists. Thus, 25% of Surge's dividends were paid to parties outside the consolidated entity. Furthermore, all of Peace's dividends were paid to parties outside of the consolidated entity. Accordingly, consolidated dividends paid are calculated as follows:

Dividends paid by parent	$15,000
Dividends paid by subsidiary	8,000
Parent's proportionate share of sub's dividends ($8,000 × 75%)	(6,000)
Consolidated dividends paid	$17,000

Answer (A) is incorrect. The amount of $8,000 equals the dividends declared by Surge. Answer (B) is incorrect. The amount of $15,000 equals the dividends paid by Peace. Answer (D) is incorrect. The amount of $23,000 includes $6,000 of intraentity dividends.

16.5 Consolidated Financial Reporting -- Intraentity Eliminations

19. Wright Corp. has several subsidiaries that are included in its consolidated financial statements. In its December 31 trial balance, Wright had the following intraentity balances before eliminations:

	Debit	Credit
Current receivable due from Main Co.	$ 32,000	
Noncurrent receivable from Main Co.	114,000	
Cash advance to Corn Corp.	6,000	
Cash advance from King Co.		$ 15,000
Payable to King Co.		101,000

In its December 31 consolidated balance sheet, what amount should Wright report as intraentity receivables?

A. $152,000

B. $146,000

C. $36,000

D. $0

Answer (D) is correct.
REQUIRED: The amount reported as intraentity receivables.
DISCUSSION: In a consolidated balance sheet, reciprocal balances, such as receivables and payables, between a parent and a consolidated subsidiary are eliminated in their entirety, regardless of the portion of the subsidiary's stock held by the parent. Thus, Wright should report $0 as intraentity receivables.
    Answer (A) is incorrect. The amount of $152,000 includes intraentity transactions in the consolidated financial statements. Answer (B) is incorrect. The effects of intraentity transactions should be completely eliminated in consolidated financial statements. Answer (C) is incorrect. Intraentity transactions should not be netted out in the consolidated financial statements.

20. During the current year, Park Corp. recorded $500,000 of sales of inventory to Small Co., its wholly owned subsidiary, on the same terms as sales made to third parties. At December 31, Small held one-fifth of these goods in its inventory. The following information pertains to Park's and Small's sales for the year:

	Park	Small
Sales	$2,000,000	$1,400,000
Cost of sales	800,000	700,000
Gross profit	$1,200,000	$ 700,000

In its consolidated income statement, what amount should Park report as cost of goods sold?

A. $1,000,000

B. $1,060,000

C. $1,360,000

D. $1,500,000

Answer (B) is correct.
REQUIRED: The amount to be reported as consolidated cost of sales.
DISCUSSION: The year-end eliminating journal entry must be recorded to prepare consolidated financial statements. This entry eliminates the gross profit recognized for the inventory remaining on the purchaser's books and reduces the inventory account to the balance it would have had if the intraentity transactions had never occurred. Park's gross profit percentage is 60% ($1,200,000 ÷ $2,000,000). The inventory from intraentity sales remaining on Small's books is $100,000 [$500,000 × (1 ÷ 5)]. The sales account is debited (decreased) by $500,000, the amount of intraentity sales recognized by Park. The inventory account is credited (decreased) by $60,000 ($100,000 inventory remaining on purchaser's books × 60% seller's gross profit percentage). The cost of goods sold account is credited (decreased) by $440,000, the difference between eliminated sales of $500,000 and eliminated inventory of $60,000. Thus, the eliminating journal entry recorded is as follows:

Sales	$500,000	
Cost of goods sold		$440,000
Inventory		60,000

Accordingly, consolidated cost of goods should be $1,060,000 ($800,000 + $700,000 – $440,000).
    Answer (A) is incorrect. The amount of $1,000,000 assumes that all inventory purchased from Park was sold. Answer (C) is incorrect. The amount of $1,360,000 results from eliminating 20% of Small's cost of sales. Answer (D) is incorrect. The amount of $1,500,000 does not eliminate the effect of intraentity sales of inventory.

21. Dunn Corp. owns 100% of Grey Corp.'s common stock. On January 2, Year 3, Dunn sold to Grey for $40,000 machinery with a carrying amount of $30,000. Grey is depreciating the acquired machinery over a 5-year life by the straight-line method. The net adjustments to compute Year 3 and Year 4 consolidated income before income tax are an increase (decrease) of

	Year 3	Year 4
A.	$(8,000)	$2,000
B.	$(8,000)	$0
C.	$(10,000)	$2,000
D.	$(10,000)	$0

Answer (A) is correct.
REQUIRED: The net adjustments to pretax 2000 and 2002 consolidated income resulting from an intercompany transaction.
DISCUSSION: In consolidated financial statements, intraentity transactions should be eliminated. Thus, in Year 3 the $10,000 ($40,000 selling price – $30,000 carrying amount) gain and the $2,000 excess depreciation ($10,000 ÷ 5 years) should be eliminated. The $2,000 of excess depreciation should also be eliminated in Year 4. The net adjustment to Year 3 pretax consolidated income is an $8,000 decrease ($2,000 excess depreciation added back – $10,000 gain subtracted). In Year 4, the adjustment is a $2,000 increase resulting from adding back the excess depreciation.
Answer (B) is incorrect. The amount of $2,000 of excess depreciation should be added back in Year 4. Answer (C) is incorrect. The $8,000 net gain should be subtracted in Year 3. Answer (D) is incorrect. The $8,000 net gain should be subtracted in Year 3, and $2,000 of excess depreciation should be added back in Year 4.

22. P Co. purchased term bonds at a premium on the open market. These bonds represented 20% of the outstanding class of bonds issued at a discount by S Co., P's wholly owned subsidiary. P intends to hold the bonds until maturity. In a consolidated balance sheet, the difference between the bond carrying amounts of the two companies is

A. Included as a decrease in retained earnings.

B. Included as an increase in retained earnings.

C. Reported as a deferred debit to be amortized over the remaining life of the bonds.

D. Reported as a deferred credit to be amortized over the remaining life of the bonds.

Answer (A) is correct.
REQUIRED: The effect of an intercompany bond transaction.
DISCUSSION: Because a consolidated financial statement should include both P and S as a single (consolidated) reporting entity, the purchase of the outstanding bonds of S by P at a premium was in substance a retirement of debt for more than the debt's carrying amount. This transaction should be reflected in the consolidated income statement for the year of the purchase as a constructive loss from the retirement of debt. Hence, the effect on the balance sheet is to decrease retained earnings by an amount equal to the premium plus the unamortized discount before the tax effect.

23. Pelota Co. owns 80% of Saginaw Co.'s outstanding common stock. Saginaw, in turn, owns 10% of Pelota's outstanding common stock. What percentage of the common stock cash dividends declared by the individual companies should be reported as dividends declared in the consolidated financial statements?

	Dividends Declared by Pelota	Dividends Declared by Saginaw
A.	90%	0%
B.	90%	20%
C.	100%	0%
D.	100%	20%

Answer (A) is correct.
REQUIRED: The dividends declared by a parent and its subsidiary reported in the consolidated statements.
DISCUSSION: Because the parent owns 80% of the subsidiary and the subsidiary owns 10% of the parent, 80% of the dividends declared by the subsidiary and 10% of the dividends declared by the parent are transferred within the consolidated group. These amounts are eliminated as intraentity transactions. Consequently, 90% of the parent's and 20% of the subsidiary's dividend payments are to third parties. The 90% declared by the parent will be reported as dividends declared. The 20% declared by the subsidiary is treated as a reduction of the noncontrolling interest in the consolidated financial statements, not as consolidated dividends declared.

24. Jane Co. owns 90% of the common stock of Dun Corp. and 100% of the common stock of Beech Corp. On December 30, Dun and Beech each declared a cash dividend of $100,000 for the current year. What is the total amount of dividends that should be reported in the December 31 consolidated financial statements of Jane and its subsidiaries, Dun and Beech?

    A. $10,000

    B. $100,000

    C. $190,000

    D. $200,000

Answer (A) is correct.
    REQUIRED: The total dividends reported in the consolidated financial statements.
    DISCUSSION: The only dividends declared by the subsidiaries that are reported are those paid to noncontrolling interests. Beech has no NCIs because the parent (Jane) owns 100% of its shares. Accordingly, the dividends reported equal $10,000 ($100,000 declared by Dun × 10% noncontrolling ownership interest in Dun).
    Answer (B) is incorrect. The amount of $100,000 is the amount declared by Dun or Beech. Answer (C) is incorrect. The amount of $190,000 is the amount eliminated in the consolidation. Answer (D) is incorrect. The amount of $200,000 is the total declared by Dun and Beech.

16.6 Other Aspects of Business Combinations

25. Acquiree Co. is a 90%-owned subsidiary of Acquirer Co. The carrying amounts of the noncontrolling interest and the subsidiary are $1,000,000 and $10,000,000, respectively. The subsidiary's fair value is $15,000,000. Acquirer transferred part of its interest to Third Co. on December 31 for $12,000,000 in cash but retained a noncontrolling interest equal to 20% of Acquiree's voting interests. The fair value of the retained interest, which gives Acquirer significant influence, is $3,000,000. The fair values and carrying amounts are as of December 31. Acquirer must account for this transaction

    A. By recognizing a gain of $5,000,000.

    B. By recognizing a gain of $6,000,000.

    C. By recognizing a gain of $1,000,000.

    D. By recognizing a loss of $3,000,000.

Answer (B) is correct.
    REQUIRED: The description of the PB.
    DISCUSSION: The parent records a deconsolidation by recognizing a gain or loss in net income attributable to the parent. It equals the difference between (1) the sum of (a) the fair value of consideration received, (b) the fair value of any retained investment at the date of deconsolidation, and (c) the carrying amount of any noncontrolling interest (including accumulated other comprehensive income attributable to the noncontrolling interest at the date of deconsolidation and (2) the carrying amount of the subsidiary. Consequently, the gain is $6,000,000 [($12,000,000 + $3,000,000 + $1,000,000) − $10,000,000].
    Answer (A) is incorrect. The carrying amount of NCIs must be included in the calculation of gain or loss on the deconsolidation. Answer (C) is incorrect. This figure assumes that the carrying amount of the subsidiary is $15,000,000. Answer (D) is incorrect. The amount of $3,000,000 is the difference between the consideration received and the fair value of the subsidiary.

26. According to GAAP relative to consolidation of variable interest entities,

    A. A not-for-profit organization may **not** be treated as a variable interest entity.

    B. A variable interest entity has an equity investment of more than 10% of its total assets.

    C. A variable interest entity is consolidated by its primary beneficiary when the beneficiary becomes involved with the entity.

    D. Corporations may **not** be organized as variable interest entities.

Answer (C) is correct.
    REQUIRED: The true statement about VIEs.
    DISCUSSION: In essence, a variable interest entity (VIE) is any legal structure (including, but not limited to, those previously described as special-purpose entities) with insufficient equity investment or whose equity investors lack one of the essential characteristics of financial control. When an entity becomes involved with a VIE, it must determine whether it is the primary beneficiary and therefore must consolidate the VIE. A primary beneficiary holds a variable interest(s) that will absorb a majority of the VIE's expected losses or receive a majority of its expected residual returns (or both).
    Answer (A) is incorrect. The guidance for VIEs applies to NPOs if they are used to avoid the requirements of GAAP. Answer (B) is incorrect. An entity qualifies as a VIE if the equity at risk does not suffice to finance entity activities without additional subordinated financial support. An equity investment of less than 10% of total assets is usually considered to be insufficient. But a greater investment also may not suffice if, for example, assets or entity activities are high risk. Answer (D) is incorrect. A VIE may take any form.

16.7 Combined Financial Statements

27. Combined statements may be used to present the results of operations of

	Entities under Common Management	Commonly Controlled Entities
A.	No	Yes
B.	Yes	No
C.	No	No
D.	Yes	Yes

Answer (D) is correct.
REQUIRED: The use(s) of combined financial statements.
DISCUSSION: Combined (as distinguished from consolidated) statements of commonly controlled entities may be more meaningful than separate statements. For example, combined statements may be used (1) to combine the statements of several entities with related operations when one individual owns a controlling financial interest in them or (2) to combine the statements of entities under common management.
Answer (A) is incorrect. Common management justifies use of combined statements. Answer (B) is incorrect. Common control justifies use of combined statements. Answer (C) is incorrect. Either common management or common control justifies use of combined statements.

28. At December 31, S Corp. owned 80% of J Corp.'s common stock and 90% of C Corp.'s common stock. J's net income for the year was $200,000 and C's net income was $400,000. C and J had no interentity ownership or transactions during the year. Combined financial statements are being prepared for C and J in contemplation of their sale to an outside party. In the combined income statement, combined net income should be reported at

A. $420,000

B. $520,000

C. $560,000

D. $600,000

Answer (D) is correct.
REQUIRED: The combined net income.
DISCUSSION: Combined financial statements are appropriate when common management or common control exists for two or more entities not subject to consolidation. The calculation of combined net income is similar to the calculation for consolidated net income. Thus, combined net income should be recorded at the total of the net income reported by the combined entities, adjusted for any profits or losses from transactions between the combined entities. In the combined income statement issued for J Corp. and C Corp., net income should be reported at $600,000 ($200,000 + $400,000).
Answer (A) is incorrect. The amount of $420,000 is 70% of the combined net income. Answer (B) is incorrect. The amount of $520,000 equals 80% of the net income of J and 90% of the net income of C. Answer (C) is incorrect. The amount of $560,000 equals 80% of J's net income and 100% of C's net income.

Use the additional questions in Gleim **CPA Test Prep Online** to create Test Sessions that emulate Prometric!

16.8 PRACTICE SIMULATION

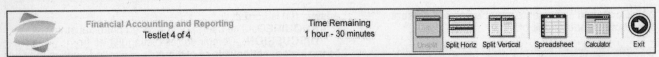

| | Financial Accounting and Reporting
Testlet 4 of 4 | Time Remaining
1 hour - 30 minutes | Unsplit | Split Horiz | Split Vertical | Spreadsheet | Calculator | Exit |

DIRECTIONS

Note: If you believe you have encountered a software malfunction, report it to the test center staff immediately.

Navigation

To navigate from task to task, use the controls at the bottom of the screen. Click on the **Next** button to advance to the next task, or the **Previous** button to go to the previous task. To go directly to any task, click on its number.

| ▽ = Reminder | | Directions | 1 2 3 4 5 6 7 | | ◀ Previous Next ▶ |

If you would like a reminder to revisit a task, or want to indicate that you are finished with it, click on the reminder flag below the task number. To clear the flag, click on it again. Reminder flags are for your use only – they do not contribute to your score.

Tabs

In this part of the examination, you will be asked to complete various tasks. Every task has one or more **Work Tabs**. Some tasks have one or more **Information Tabs**, others may have none. Every task has a **Help** tab.

If a task has **Information Tabs**, you may use the information in them to complete your responses in the **Work Tabs**.

| ✏ Corporate Gain and Basis | Authoritative Literature | Help |
| **Work tab** | **Information tab** | **Help tab** |

Work Tabs:

- **Work Tabs** are identified with a pencil icon. This is where your responses are expected.
- Each task has one or more **Work Tabs**.
- **Work Tabs** contain directions for completing the task – be sure to read these directions carefully.
- The **Work Tab** name in the example above is for illustration only – yours will differ.
- You must complete all of the **Work Tabs** in each task to receive full credit.

Information Tabs:

- The Authoritative Literature will be provided in all tasks in the AUD, FAR, and REG sections for your reference.
- Your simulation may have one or more additional **Information Tabs**. Like the Authoritative Literature tabs, **Information Tabs** do not have a pencil icon.
- If your task has additional **Information Tabs**, go through each to familiarize yourself with the task content.

Help Tab:

- The **Help Tab** provides assistance with the exam software that is used in this task. For example, if the task is to compose a memorandum, **Help** will provide information about the word processor.

The Toolbar

The toolbar at the top of the screen shows the amount of time remaining for you to complete the tasks. In addition, the following tools are available. Note that only the **Exit** button is displayed when Directions are visible - the others will appear when you begin the tasks.

| Unsplit | Split Horiz | Split Vertical |

Click on these buttons to split or unsplit the screen. You can split the screen vertically or horizontally.

Calculator

Click on this button to display the calculator; click on it again to hide the calculator. To move the calculator, click on the calculator title bar and drag the calculator to the desired location.

Spreadsheet

Click on this button to use the spreadsheet; click on it again to hide the spreadsheet. To move the spreadsheet, click on the the spreadsheet title bar and drag the spreadsheet to the desired location.

Exit

Click on this button to go on to the next part of the examination. You must complete all of the tasks to receive full credit. Once you click on **Exit** and confirm the action, you will NOT be able to return to this testlet.

| ▽ = Reminder | | Directions | 1 2 3 4 5 6 | | ◀ Previous Next ▶ |

| Acquisition-Date Balance Sheet | Authoritative Literature | Help |

Presented below are the balance sheets of Prawn Co. and Shell Corp. at December 31, Year 1.

On January 2, Year 2, Prawn paid $300,000 to purchase 80% of Shell's common stock. The fair value of the noncontrolling interest (NCI) equals 20% of the implied fair value of the acquiree. On that date, the fair values of Shell's inventories and plant assets exceeded their carrying amounts by $12,500 and $75,000, respectively. The remaining assets and all liabilities are reported at fair value. The principal of the new debt incurred by Prawn to effect the acquisition must be repaid in 10 equal annual installments.

Assets:	Prawn	Shell
Cash	$ 73,000	$ 4,000
Accounts receivable	40,000	12,000
Inventories	167,000	29,000
Current assets	$280,000	$ 45,000
Property, plant, and equip. (net)	$477,000	$240,000
Intangible assets	23,000	---
Noncurrent assets	$500,000	$240,000
Total assets	**$780,000**	**$285,000**
Liabilities and shareholders' equity:		
Accounts payable	$ 61,000	$ 25,000
Note payable	9,000	---
Current liabilities	$ 70,000	$ 25,000
Bonds payable	$200,000	---
Common stock	$100,000	$ 50,000
Additional paid-in capital	210,000	50,000
Retained earnings	200,000	160,000
Total shareholders' equity	$510,000	$260,000
Total liabilities and shareholders' equity	**$780,000**	**$285,000**

Enter in the shaded cells below the correct balance amount for each consolidated balance sheet line item.

Consolidated Balance Sheet Line Item	Balance Immediately after Acquisition
1. Consolidated current assets	
2. Consolidated noncurrent assets	
3. Consolidated current liabilities	( )
4. Consolidated noncurrent liabilities	( )
5. Noncontrolling interest	( )
6. Prawn's equity (total of above)	

Net Income and Retained Earnings | Authoritative Literature | Help

Presented below are selected items of financial information for Plaster, Inc., and Stucco Co. On January 2, Year 3, Plaster purchased for cash 80% of the common stock of Stucco. The fair value of the noncontrolling interest at the acquisition date was $52,000.

Stucco has no equity interest in Plaster, and consolidated net income for Year 3 was $122,000.

	Plaster	Stucco
Retained earnings at December 31, Year 2	$65,000	$44,000
Net income for Year 3 included in the consolidated financial statements		60,000
Dividends paid in Year 3	30,000	15,000

Enter in the shaded cells below the correct amount for each consolidated line item.

Consolidated Line Item	Amount
1. Net income attributable to Plaster for Year 3	
2. Dividends paid during Year 3	
3. Retained earnings at December 31, Year 3	
4. Noncontrolling interest at December 31, Year 3	

▼ = Reminder   Directions   1 [2] 3 4 5 6   ◀ Previous   Next ▶

Intraentity Eliminations | Authoritative Literature | Help

On January 2, Year 7, a parent with no prior equity interest in the acquiree purchased 90% of its 100,000 outstanding common shares for cash of $155,000. On that date, (1) the subsidiary's equity equaled $150,000, (2) the acquisition-date fair values of the subsidiary's assets and liabilities equaled their carrying amounts, and (3) the fair value of the noncontrolling interest (NCI) was 10% of the implied fair value of the acquiree.

For each of the following transactions, determine the dollar effect on Year 7 consolidated income before considering any noncontrolling interest, and enter the correct amount in the shaded cell below. Ignore income tax considerations.

Transaction	Amount
1. On January 3, Year 7, the subsidiary sold equipment with an original cost of $30,000 and a carrying amount of $15,000 to the parent for $36,000. The equipment had a remaining life of 3 years and was depreciated using the straight-line method by both companies.	
2. During Year 7, the subsidiary sold merchandise to the parent for $60,000, which included a profit of $20,000. At December 31, Year 7, half of this merchandise remained in the parent's inventory.	
3. On December 31, Year 7, the parent paid $91,000 to purchase the outstanding bonds issued by the subsidiary. The bonds mature on December 31, Year 13, and were originally issued at their face amount of $100,000. The bonds pay interest annually on December 31 of each year, and the interest was paid to the prior investor immediately before the parent's purchase of the bonds.	
4. The parent recognized goodwill on January 2, Year 7. It determined on December 31, Year 7, that goodwill was not impaired.	

▼ = Reminder   Directions   1 2 [3] 4 5 6   ◀ Previous   Next ▶

| Consolidated Financial Statements | Authoritative Literature | Help |

On December 31, Year 1, Company A purchased 75% of Company B's outstanding common shares for $150,000 in cash. On that date, the carrying amount of Company B's assets and liabilities approximated their fair value, and the fair value of the noncontrolling interest (NCI) was $12,000. The following is the summarized balance sheet information for the two companies on December 31, Year 1, before the acquisition.

	Company A	Company B
Current assets	$200,000	$ 80,000
Noncurrent assets	320,000	140,000
Current liabilities	70,000	45,000
Noncurrent liabilities	110,000	55,000
Common stock	100,000	30,000
Retained earnings	90,000	70,000
Additional paid-in capital	150,000	20,000

Additional information:

- Company B reported net income of $60,000 for the year ended December 31, Year 2.
- On December 1, Year 2, Company B declared and distributed a cash dividend of $40,000 to its common shareholders.
- On November 15, Year 2, Company A declared and distributed a cash dividend of $25,000 to its common shareholders.
- Company A reported net income of $110,000 in its separate statements for the year ended December 31, Year 2.
- In its separate statements, Company A accounts for its investment in Company B using the equity method.
- During Year 2, no shares of common stock were issued and no items of other comprehensive income were recognized either by Company A or by Company B.
- No intraentity transactions occurred during Year 2.

1. Using the information above, enter in the shaded cell the amount of goodwill or gain from bargain purchase recognized by Company A on the business combination date.

2. Using the information above, prepare Company A's consolidated statement of changes in equity for the year ended December 31, Year 2. Enter in the shaded cells below the correct dollar amounts. Enter a positive amount for an increase in the consolidated equity balance and a negative amount for a decrease in the consolidated equity balance. Note that some of the cells may remain blank.

Company A Consolidated Statement of Changes in Equity for the Year Ended December 31, Year 2

	Total Equity	Retained Earnings	Common Stock	Additional Paid-in Capital	Noncontrolling Interest
January 1, Year 2	$352,000				
Dividends	(35,000)				
Net income (loss)	125,000				
December 31, Year 2	$442,000	$175,000	$100,000	$150,000	$17,000

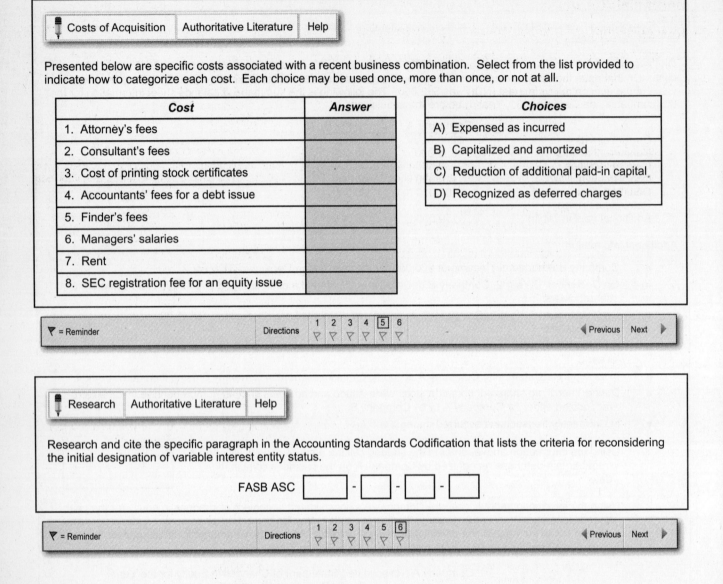

| Costs of Acquisition | Authoritative Literature | Help |

Presented below are specific costs associated with a recent business combination. Select from the list provided to indicate how to categorize each cost. Each choice may be used once, more than once, or not at all.

Cost	Answer
1. Attorney's fees	
2. Consultant's fees	
3. Cost of printing stock certificates	
4. Accountants' fees for a debt issue	
5. Finder's fees	
6. Managers' salaries	
7. Rent	
8. SEC registration fee for an equity issue	

Choices
A) Expensed as incurred
B) Capitalized and amortized
C) Reduction of additional paid-in capital
D) Recognized as deferred charges

▼ = Reminder   Directions   1 2 3 4 5 6   ◀ Previous   Next ▶

| Research | Authoritative Literature | Help |

Research and cite the specific paragraph in the Accounting Standards Codification that lists the criteria for reconsidering the initial designation of variable interest entity status.

FASB ASC [ ] - [ ] - [ ] - [ ]

▼ = Reminder   Directions   1 2 3 4 5 6   ◀ Previous   Next ▶

Unofficial Answers

1. Acquisition-Date Balance Sheet (6 Gradable Items)

1. <u>$337,500.</u> Consolidated current assets are calculated as follows:

Current assets of Prawn	$280,000
Current assets of Shell	45,000
Holding gain -- inventories	12,500
Consolidated current assets	$337,500

2. <u>$842,500.</u> Before calculating noncurrent assets, Prawn must calculate goodwill, the excess of the sum of (1) the acquisition-date fair values of (a) the consideration transferred, (b) any noncontrolling interest, and (c) any acquirer's previous equity interest over (2) the net of the acquisition-date fair value of the identifiable assets acquired and liabilities assumed.

Consideration transferred		$ 300,000
Noncontrolling interest [($300,000 ÷ 80%) implied FV of Shell × 20%]		75,000
Acquisition-date fair value of net assets acquired:		
Carrying amount ($285,000 – $25,000)	$260,000	
Holding gain -- inventories	12,500	
Holding gain -- PP&E	75,000	(347,500)
Goodwill		$ 27,500

Consolidated noncurrent assets are calculated as follows:

Noncurrent assets of Prawn	$500,000
Noncurrent assets of Shell	240,000
Holding gain -- PP&E	75,000
Goodwill	27,500
Consolidated noncurrent assets	$842,500

3. <u>$125,000.</u> The current portion of the new debt must be classified as a current liability ($300,000 ÷ 10 years = $30,000). Consolidated current liabilities are calculated as follows:

Current liabilities of Prawn	$ 70,000
Current liabilities of Shell	25,000
Current portion of new noncurrent debt	30,000
Consolidated current liabilities	$125,000

4. <u>$470,000.</u> The noncurrent portion of the new debt is classified as a noncurrent liability ($300,000 – $30,000 = $270,000). Consolidated noncurrent liabilities are calculated as follows:

Noncurrent liabilities of Prawn	$200,000
Noncurrent liabilities of Shell	--
New noncurrent debt	270,000
Consolidated noncurrent liabilities	$470,000

5. <u>$75,000.</u> The fair value of the NCI is given as 20% of the implied fair value of the acquiree [($300,000 consideration transferred ÷ 80% interest acquired) × 20% = $75,000].

6. <u>$510,000.</u> Prawn's equity in the consolidated entity immediately after acquisition is calculated as follows:

Consolidated current assets	$337,500
Consolidated noncurrent assets	842,500
Consolidated current liabilities	(125,000)
Consolidated noncurrent liabilities	(470,000)
Noncontrolling interest	(75,000)
Prawn's equity	$510,000

2. Net Income and Retained Earnings (4 Gradable Items)

1. Consolidated net income equals the net income attributable to the parent plus the net income attributable to the noncontrolling interest.

Consolidated net income		$122,000
Stucco's net income included in the consolidated statements	$60,000	
Times: NCI's ownership percentage	× 20%	
		(12,000)
Consolidated net income attributable to Plaster		$110,000

2. <u>$33,000.</u> Consolidated dividends are those paid to parties outside the consolidated entity.

Dividends paid by Plaster	$ 30,000
Dividends paid by Stucco	15,000
Plaster's proportionate share of Stucco's dividends ($15,000 × 80%)	(12,000)
Consolidated dividends paid	$ 33,000

3. <u>$145,000.</u> A business combination is an acquisition of net assets only. The subsidiary's equity accounts are not included. Thus, beginning retained earnings of the consolidated entity are the retained earnings of the parent.

Consolidated retained earnings at 1/1/Year 3	$ 65,000
Net income of Plaster included in consolidated net income	110,000
Plaster's dividends paid during year	(30,000)
Consolidated retained earnings at December 31	$145,000

4. <u>$61,000.</u> The noncontrolling interest in Stucco's net assets is adjusted for the subsidiary's net income and dividends.

Noncontrolling interest at January 1	$52,000
Noncontrolling interest in Stucco's net income included in consolidated net income ($60,000 × 20%)	12,000
Noncontrolling interest in Stucco's dividends paid ($15,000 × 20%)	(3,000)
Noncontrolling interest at December 31	$61,000

3. Intraentity Eliminations (4 Gradable Items)

1. <u>$14,000.</u> The intraentity profit to be eliminated is $21,000 ($36,000 sales price − $15,000 carrying amount). Accordingly, the excess depreciation to be eliminated is $7,000 ($21,000 ÷ 3 years). The net adjustment to consolidated net income before considering any noncontrolling interest and taxes is therefore $14,000 ($21,000 − $7,000).

2. <u>$10,000.</u> The profit on the intraentity sale of inventory should be eliminated to the extent that it is unrealized. Thus, the net adjustment to consolidated net income before considering any noncontrolling interest and taxes is $10,000 ($20,000 profit × 50% inventory still held by the parent).

3. <u>$9,000.</u> This transaction is a retirement of debt by the consolidated entity that resulted in a $9,000 gain before taxes and before considering any noncontrolling interest ($100,000 carrying amount on the subsidiary's books − $91,000 paid by the parent).

4. <u>$0.</u> On the date of acquisition, the consolidated entity recognized goodwill. Goodwill is the excess of the sum of (1) the fair value of (a) the consideration transferred ($155,000), (b) the NCI [($155,000 ÷ 90%) × 10% = $17,222], and (c) any prior equity interest ($0) over (2) the fair value of the acquiree's net identifiable assets ($155,000). Thus, goodwill at the acquisition date was $172,222. However, no Year 2 amortization or impairment loss is recognized. Goodwill is not amortized. Moreover, the entity determined at year end that goodwill was not impaired.

4. Consolidated Financial Statements (13 Gradable Items)

1. **$42,000.** The amount of goodwill recognized at the business combination date is calculated as follows:

Consideration transferred	$150,000
Fair value of noncontrolling interest	12,000
(Fair value of identifiable assets acquired)	(220,000)
Fair value of liabilities assumed	100,000
Goodwill	$ 42,000

January 1, Year 2:

2. Retained earnings: $90,000.

3. Common stock: $100,000.

4. Additional paid-in capital: $150,000.

5. Noncontrolling interest: $12,000.

The consolidated shareholders' equity includes only the equity accounts of the parent (Company A). The equity accounts of the subsidiary (Company B) are eliminated in the consolidation process. NCI is initially recognized at its fair value.

Dividends:

6. Retained earnings: $(25,000).

7. Common stock: $0.

8. Additional paid-in capital: $0.

9. Noncontrolling interest: $(10,000).

The journal entry for declaration and payment of cash dividend by Company A is a debit to retained earnings of $25,000 and a credit to cash of $25,000. The NCI account is decreased by the amount of dividend that was declared/distributed by the subsidiary (Company B) to parties outside the consolidated entity ($40,000 × 25% = $10,000).

Net income (loss):

10. Retained earnings: $110,000.

11. Common stock: $0.

12. Additional paid-in capital: $0.

13. Noncontrolling interest: $15,000.

In its separate statements, Company A accounts for its investment in Company B using the equity method. Thus, Company A's share of Company B's net income of $45,000 ($60,000 × 75%) is already included in the net income of $110,000 reported in its separate financial statements. Note: Under the equity method, a dividend received from an equity-method investee is accounted for as a return of an investment and does not affect net income. The balance of NCI increases for their share in the net income of the subsidiary ($60,000 × 25% = $15,000).

The following is the summary of Company A's consolidated statement of income for the year ended December 31, Year 2:

Consolidated net income for the period [$60,000 + ($110,000 – $45,000)]	$125,000
Minus: net income attributable to noncontrolling interest	(15,000)
Net income attributable to Company A's shareholders	$110,000

5. Costs of Acquisition (8 Gradable Items)

1. A) Expensed as incurred. Except for issue costs of securities, acquisition-related costs, such as legal fees, are business combination expenses.

2. A) Expensed as incurred. Except for issue costs of securities, acquisition-related costs, such as consultant's fees, are business combination expenses.

3. C) Reduction of additional paid-in capital. Direct costs of issuing equity securities reduce additional paid-in capital.

4. D) Recognized as deferred charges. Debt issue costs are reported in the balance sheet as deferred charges and amortized over the debt's life using the interest method.

5. A) Expensed as incurred. Except for issue costs of securities, acquisition-related costs, such as finders' fees, are business combination expenses.

6. A) Expensed as incurred. Except for issue costs of securities, acquisition-related costs, such as management salaries, are business combination expenses.

7. A) Expensed as incurred. Except for issue costs of securities, acquisition-related costs, such as rent, are business combination expenses.

8. C) Reduction of additional paid-in capital. Direct costs of issuing equity securities reduce additional paid-in capital.

6. Research (1 Gradable Item)

Answer: FASB ASC 810-10-35-4

810-10-35-4 A legal entity that previously was not subject to the Variable Interest Entities Subsections shall not become subject to them simply because of losses in excess of its expected losses that reduce the equity investment. The initial determination of whether a legal entity is a VIE shall be reconsidered if any of the following occur:

a. The legal entity's governing documents or contractual arrangements are changed in a manner that changes the characteristics or adequacy of the legal entity's equity investment at risk.

b. The equity investment or some part thereof is returned to the equity investors, and other interests become exposed to expected losses of the legal entity.

c. The legal entity undertakes additional activities or acquires additional assets, beyond those that were anticipated at the later of the inception of the entity or the latest reconsideration event, that increase the entity's expected losses.

d. The legal entity receives an additional equity investment that is at risk, or the legal entity curtails or modifies its activities in a way that decreases its expected losses.

Gleim Simulation Grading

Task	Correct Responses		Gradable Items		Score per Task
1	___	÷	6	=	___
2	___	÷	4	=	___
3	___	÷	4	=	___
4	___	÷	13	=	___
5	___	÷	8	=	___
Research	___	÷	1	=	___

Total of Scores per Task   ___

÷ Total Number of Tasks   6

Total Score   ___%

Use **CPA Gleim Online** and **Simulation Wizard** to practice more task-based simulations in a realistic environment.

STUDY UNIT SEVENTEEN
DERIVATIVES, HEDGING, AND OTHER TOPICS

(19 pages of outline)

17.1 Derivatives and Hedging 607
17.2 Foreign Currency Issues 616
17.3 Financial Statement Analysis -- Liquidity 619
17.4 Financial Statement Analysis -- Activity 621
17.5 Financial Statement Analysis -- Solvency, Valuation, and Comparative Analysis 624
17.6 Practice Simulation 636

This is the last study unit covering financial accounting for nongovernmental, for-profit entities. Derivatives and hedge accounting, foreign currency transactions and translation, and financial statement analysis are topics listed in the AICPA's CSO.

17.1 DERIVATIVES AND HEDGING

Background

A derivative is a bet on whether the value of something will go up or down. The purpose is either to speculate (incur risk) or to hedge (avoid risk). The value of a derivative changes as the value of the specified variable changes.

For example, a corn farmer can guarantee the price of his annual corn production using a derivative. In this case, the derivative is a hedge against the changes in the price of corn (to avoid risk).

1. **General Financial Market Terms**

   a. A **call option** is the right to purchase an asset at a fixed price (i.e., the exercise price) on or before a future date (i.e., expiration date).

   b. A **put option** is the right to sell an asset at a fixed price (i.e., the exercise price) on or before a future date (i.e., expiration date).

   c. The **exercise or strike price** is the agreed upon price of exchange in an option contract.

   d. The **expiration date** is the date when the option may no longer be exercised.

   e. **Embedded** means that a derivative is contained within either (1) another derivative or (2) a financial instrument. For example, a mortgage has an embedded option. The mortgagor (the debtor) generally has the option to refinance the mortgage if interest rates decrease.

2. **Characteristics of a Derivative**

   a. A derivative has at least one **underlying** (interest rate, currency exchange rate, price of a specific financial instrument, etc.) and at least one **notional amount** (number of units specified in the contract) or payment provision, or both.

   b. No **initial net investment**, or one smaller than that necessary for contracts with similar responses to the market, is required.

   c. A derivative's terms require or permit net settlement or provide for the equivalent.

      1) **Net settlement** means that the derivative can be readily settled with only a net delivery of assets. Thus, neither party must deliver (a) an asset associated with its underlying or (b) an asset that has a principal, stated amount, etc., equal to the notional amount (possibly adjusted for discount or premium).

3. **Hedging**

   a.   Hedging is not defined formally in the Codification. However, according to *The CPA Letter* (October 2000), "A hedge is used to avoid or reduce risks by creating a relationship by which losses on certain positions are expected to be counterbalanced in whole or in part by gains on separate positions in another market."

   b.   The purchase or sale of a derivative or other instrument is a hedge if it is **expected to neutralize the risk** of (1) a recognized asset or liability, (2) an unrecognized firm commitment, or (3) a forecasted (anticipated) transaction.

      1)   For example, a flour company buys and uses wheat in its product. It may wish to guard against increases in wheat costs when it has committed to sell at a price related to the current cost of wheat. If so, the company will purchase wheat futures contracts that will result in gains if the price of wheat increases (offsetting the actual increased costs).

4. **Typical Derivatives**

   a.   A **call option** allows the purchaser to benefit from an increase in the price of the underlying. The purchaser pays a premium for the opportunity to benefit from this appreciation.

   b.   A **put option** allows the purchaser to benefit from a decrease in the price of the underlying. The gain is the excess of the exercise price over the market price. The purchaser pays a premium for the opportunity to benefit from the depreciation in the underlying.

   c.   A **forward contract** is an agreement for the purchase and sale of a stated amount of a commodity, foreign currency, or financial instrument at a stated price. Delivery or settlement is at a stated future date.

      1)   Forward contracts are usually specifically negotiated agreements and are not traded on regulated exchanges. Accordingly, the parties are subject to **default risk** (i.e., that the other party will not perform).

   d.   A **futures contract** is a forward-based agreement to make or receive delivery or make a cash settlement that involves a specified quantity of a commodity, foreign currency, or financial instrument during a specified time interval.

   e.   An **interest rate swap** is an exchange of one party's interest payments based on a **fixed rate** for another party's interest payments based on a **variable rate**. Moreover, most interest rate swaps permit **net settlement** because they do not require delivery of interest-bearing assets with a principal equal to the contracted amount.

      1)   An interest rate swap is appropriate when one counterparty prefers the payment pattern of the other. For example, a firm with **fixed-rate** debt may have revenues that vary with interest rates. It may prefer variable-rate debt so that its **debt service** will correlate directly with its **revenues**.

   f.   Certain **financial instruments**, e.g., accounts receivable, notes receivable, bonds, preferred stock, and common stock, are not derivatives. However, any of these instruments may be an underlying of a derivative.

5. **Accounting Standards for Derivatives and Hedging**

    a. Derivatives should be recognized as **assets or liabilities**.

    b. **Fair value** is the only relevant measure for derivatives. Moreover, adjustments to the carrying amount of a **hedged item** should reflect any changes in its fair value while the hedge is in effect that are attributable to the hedged risk.

        1) Derivatives usually have **no initial fair value** but result in positive or negative fair value as the price of the underlying changes.

    c. **Designated hedged items** should receive special accounting treatment only if they meet qualifying criteria. An example is the likelihood of effectiveness of the hedge in producing offsetting **fair value or cash flow changes** during the term of the hedge for the risk being hedged.

        1) At all times, the hedge is expected to be **highly effective**. Effectiveness is the percentage of the gain or loss on the hedged item that is offset by the hedging instrument's loss or gain. Thus, these amounts should be highly correlated.

6. **Accounting for Derivatives**

    a. The accounting for changes in fair value of a derivative depends on (1) the **reasons for holding it**, (2) whether the entity has elected to **designate** it as part of a hedging relationship, and (3) whether it meets the **qualifying criteria** for the particular accounting.

        1) All or part of a derivative may be designated as a hedging instrument. The proportion must be expressed as a **percentage of the entire derivative**.

    b. Most qualifying criteria are not reproduced here because they are numerous and complex.

        1) An entity that elects hedge accounting must formally determine at the **hedge's inception** the methods for determining the **effectiveness and ineffectiveness** of the hedge. Thus, an entity must specify whether all of the gain or loss on the hedging instrument will be included in the assessment of effectiveness.

            a) For example, an entity may exclude all or part of the **time value** from the assessment of effectiveness.

        2) **Special hedge accounting** is not permitted when the hedged item (or forecasted transaction) is remeasured, with changes in fair value related to the hedged risk recognized in current earnings.

            a) An example of such a hedged item is a **trading security**.

    c. **Gains and losses** from changes in the **fair value** of most derivatives are **included in earnings** in the period of change. **Exceptions** are certain gains and losses on a derivative designated as a (1) cash flow hedge, (2) foreign currency cash flow hedge, or (3) hedge of a net investment in a foreign operation.

7. **Types of Hedges**

    a. A **fair value hedge** mitigates the risk of changes in the **fair value** of a **recognized asset or liability** or of an **unrecognized firm commitment** with fixed cash flows. These changes must relate to a specified risk.

        1) A firm commitment is an agreement with an unrelated party that is binding on both parties and is usually legally enforceable. It specifies all significant terms, and its performance is probable because of the negative consequences of nonperformance.

b.   A **cash flow hedge** mitigates the risk of variability in the cash flows of a **recognized asset or liability** or of a **forecasted transaction** that relates to a specified risk.

  1)   A forecasted transaction is probable, i.e., expected to occur, although no firm commitment exists. It does not (a) provide current rights or (b) impose a current obligation because no transaction or event has occurred.

    a)   When such a transaction or event occurs, it will be at the prevailing market price.

c.   Certain **foreign currency exposures** also may qualify for hedge accounting.

8.   **Fair Value Hedges**

a.   Examples of hedged items are (1) fixed rate investments and debt and (2) firm commitments to purchase or sell assets or incur liabilities.

b.   The change in fair value of the **hedged item** (the gain or loss) related to the risk being hedged is an adjustment to the carrying amount of the item. It is recognized currently in **earnings**.

  1)   This rule applies even if changes in fair value of the hedged item are normally reported in **other comprehensive income (OCI)**.

    a)   An example is a hedge of an **available-for-sale security**.

  2)   When the hedged item is a **previously unrecognized firm commitment**, the recognition of the gain or loss on the firm commitment includes debiting an asset or crediting a liability, respectively.

    a)   Accordingly, the phrase "asset or liability" includes a firm commitment.

  3)   The change in fair value of the **hedging instrument** (the loss or gain) also is recognized currently in **earnings**.

c.   A **fair value hedge** is permitted for certain types of **foreign currency exposures**. If the hedged item is measured in a foreign currency, an entity may designate a fair value hedge of an **unrecognized firm commitment** or a **recognized asset or liability** (including an available-for-sale security).

  1)   A hedging instrument that may result in a **foreign currency transaction gain or loss** may hedge the changes in fair value of an **unrecognized firm commitment** that are attributable to exchange rates.

    a)   In this case, a **nonderivative** also may be the hedging instrument.

  2)   Only a **derivative** may hedge the changes in fair value of a **recognized asset or liability** for which a **foreign currency transaction gain or loss** is recognized.

EXAMPLE

Fair value hedge of a recognized asset. A company wishes to hedge the fair value of its investment in an inventory of Commodity A. It sells futures contracts on August 1, Year 1, for delivery on February 1, Year 2, the date on which it intends to sell the inventory. The following information is available about spot and futures prices and estimates of changes in the fair value of the inventory (changes in spot rates adjusted for transportation costs, storage costs, etc.):

	Spot Rate	Futures Rate for February 1 Delivery	Change in Fair Value of Inventory
August 1, Year 1	$.51	$.53	
December 31, Year 1	.49	.51	$(21,000)
February 1, Year 2	.52	.52	32,000

-- Continued on next page --

EXAMPLE -- Continued

The company sold futures contracts for 1 million pounds of Commodity A at $.53 per pound. Its inventory had an average cost of $.38 per pound, and it sold the entire inventory of Commodity A on February 1, Year 2, at the spot rate of $.52 per pound. The company also bought offsetting February Year 2 futures contracts on February 1, Year 2, for 1 million pounds of Commodity A at $.52 per pound. This transaction closed out its futures position. The following journal entries should be made (ignoring the margin deposit with the broker):

August 1, Year 1
The fair value of the futures contracts is zero at the inception date. Thus, no entry is made to record their fair value.

December 31, Year 1
The company estimates a loss of $21,000 in the value of its holdings of Commodity A.

Loss	$21,000	
Inventory -- Commodity A		$21,000

The recognized gain on the futures contract is $20,000 [1,000,000 pounds × ($.53 futures rate at August 1, Year 1 – $.51 futures rate at December 31, Year 1, for February 1, Year 2, delivery)].

Receivable from/liability to broker	$20,000	
Gain on the hedge		$20,000

February 1, Year 2
The company estimates a gain of $32,000 in the value of its holdings of Commodity A.

Inventory -- Commodity A	$32,000	
Gain		$32,000

The recognized loss on the futures contract is $10,000 [1,000,000 pounds × ($.52 futures rate at February 1, Year 2 – $.51 futures rate at December 31, Year 1, for February 1, Year 2, delivery)].

Loss on the hedge	$10,000	
Receivable from/liability to broker		$10,000

The company settles the futures contract.

Cash	$10,000	
Receivable from/liability to broker		$10,000

The revenue from the sale equaled $520,000 (1,000,000 pounds × $.52 spot rate). The inventory equaled $391,000 [(1,000,000 pounds × $.38 average cost) – $21,000 fair value loss on December 31, Year 1 + $32,000 fair value gain on February 1, Year 2].

Accounts receivable	$520,000	
Cost of goods sold	391,000	
Sales		$520,000
Inventory -- Commodity A		391,000

---

9. **Cash Flow Hedges**

   a. Examples are (1) all or certain interest payments on variable rate debt (a recognized liability) or (2) an anticipated purchase or sale (a forecasted transaction).

   b. The earnings effect of the hedged item may not occur until a future period.

      1) Thus, the **effective portion** of the loss or gain on the hedging instrument is reported in OCI. It will be recognized in earnings (reclassified from OCI) when the hedged item affects earnings.

         a) The **ineffective portion** is recognized in earnings immediately.

      2) The entity's specified **risk management strategy** may exclude part of the gain or loss (or related cash flows) from the assessment of effectiveness. These excluded amounts are recognized currently in earnings.

    c.   A **nonderivative** may **not** hedge a **foreign currency cash flow hedge**.

    d.   A **derivative** may hedge the foreign currency exposure to variability in the functional-currency-equivalent cash flows of a(n)

        1)   Forecasted transaction,

        2)   Recognized asset or liability,

        3)   Unrecognized firm commitment, or

        4)   Forecasted intraentity transaction (e.g., a forecasted sale to a foreign subsidiary).

    e.   A derivative may hedge the foreign currency exposure of a **net investment in a foreign operation**. Gains and losses on the derivative are reported in the cumulative translation adjustment in **OCI** to the extent the hedge is effective.

        1)   If the hedging instrument is a **nonderivative**, the **foreign currency transaction gain or loss** on the instrument is treated in the same manner. [Recall that a nonderivative also may hedge the foreign currency exposure of an unrecognized firm commitment (a fair value hedge).]

        2)   GAAP applicable to foreign currency translation prescribe accounting rules (other than for hedging) for (a) translation (including remeasurement), (b) transaction gains and losses, and (c) a net investment in a foreign investment (discussed in the next subunit).

EXAMPLE

Cash flow hedge of a forecasted transaction. At January 2, Year 1, a company determines that it will need to purchase 100,000 pounds of Commodity B in June Year 1. The purchase is expected to be at the spot rate. To hedge this forecasted transaction, the company agrees to purchase futures contracts for 100,000 pounds of Commodity B at the June Year 1 futures price of $3.05 per pound. Hedge effectiveness will be determined by comparing the total change in the fair value of the futures contracts with the changes in the cash flows of the anticipated purchase. In June, the company buys 100,000 pounds of Commodity B at the spot rate of $3.20 per pound. Ignoring the margin deposit for the futures contracts, the following are the journal entries for this transaction:

January Year 1

    Because the margin deposit is ignored in this problem, no journal entry is made. The futures contract is not recorded because, at its inception, its fair value is zero.

June Year 1

    The price of the quantity purchased was $320,000 (100,000 pounds × $3.20 spot rate).

Inventory -- Commodity B	$320,000	
Cash		$320,000

    The gain, which will subsequently be reclassified into earnings when the inventory is sold, equals $15,000 [100,000 pounds × ($3.20 spot rate – $3.05 futures contract rate)].

Futures contracts	$15,000	
Other comprehensive income		$15,000

    The company records the net cash settlement. (In practice, futures contracts are settled daily.)

Cash	$15,000	
Futures contracts		$15,000

10. Foreign Currency Hedges

EXAMPLE

Hedge of a net investment in a foreign operation. Parent, Inc., a U.S. company, has a net investment in its Xenadian subsidiary, Subco. The amount is 100 million foreign currency units (FCU), the subsidiary's functional currency. At November 1, Year 1, Parent sells a forward exchange contract for the delivery of 100 million FCU on February 1, Year 2. This contract is designated as a hedge of the net investment in Subco. The contract rate equals the forward rate at November 1, Year 1, of $1.15 per FCU. On that date, the spot rate is $1.17 per FCU. Parent records the premium on the forward contract [100,000,000 FCU × ($1.17 − $1.15) = $2,000,000] as a translation adjustment. Moreover, Parent records the change in fair value of the forward contract at fair value in its balance sheet. The effective portion of the hedge (100% in this case) is recorded in other comprehensive income (OCI). Parent also translates its net investment in Subco into U.S. dollars, and it reports the effects of changes in exchange rates as a cumulative translation adjustment in OCI.

The following table provides information about exchange rates, the forward contract's changes in fair value, and the translation adjustments (change in spot rates × the notional amount). Measuring the fair value of a foreign currency forward contract requires discounting the estimated future cash flows. This estimate of cash flows is based on the changes in the forward rate, not in the spot rate.

	Gain (Loss) – Forward Contract's Change in Fair Value (Discounted)	Gain (Loss) – Cumulative Translation Adjustment	Spot Rates per FCU	Forward Rates per FCU for 2/1 Delivery
November 1, Year 1			$1.17	$1.15
December 31, Year 1	$3,920,000	$(4,000,000)	1.13	1.11
February 1, Year 2	2,080,000	(4,000,000)	1.09	1.09
	$6,000,000	$(8,000,000)		

November 1, Year 1

No entry is made because the forward rate and the contract rate were the same.

December 31, Year 1

The change in fair value of the contract (discounted future cash flows based on changes in the forward rate) is recorded in OCI in the same manner as a translation adjustment. Parent determined that the estimated change in cash flows equaled $4,000,000 [100,000,000 FCU × ($1.15 forward rate at November 1, Year 1 − $1.11 forward rate at December 31, Year 1)]. It then determined that the present value of that change was $3,920,000 (given).

Receivable -- forward contract	$3,920,000	
OCI		$3,920,000

The translation adjustment in accordance with U.S. GAAP is $4,000,000 [100,000,000 FCU × ($1.17 spot rate at November 1, Year 1 − $1.13 spot rate at December 31, Year 1)].

OCI	$4,000,000	
Net investment -- Subco		$4,000,000

February 1, Year 2

The total change in fair value of the contract is a gain of $6,000,000 [100,000,000 FCU × ($1.15 forward rate at November 1, Year 1 − $1.09 forward rate at February 1, Year 2)]. Of this amount, $3,920,000 (discounted) was recognized at December 31, Year 1. Thus, to record the fair value of the contract on the settlement date requires an additional credit to OCI of $2,080,000 ($6,000,000 gain − $3,920,000).

Receivable -- forward contract	$2,080,000	
OCI		$2,080,000

The translation adjustment is a loss of $4,000,000 [100,000,000 FCU × ($1.13 spot rate at December 31, Year 1 − $1.09 spot rate at February 1, Year 2)].

OCI	$4,000,000	
Net investment -- Subco		$4,000,000

The company records the net cash settlement of the foreign currency forward contract.

Cash	$6,000,000	
Receivable -- forward contract		$6,000,000

11. **Embedded Derivatives**

a. A common example is the conversion feature of convertible debt. It is a call option on the issuer's stock. Embedded derivatives must be **accounted for separately** from the host if

1) The economic characteristics and risks of the embedded derivative are **not clearly and closely related** to the economic characteristics of the host;

2) The hybrid instrument is **not remeasured at fair value** under otherwise applicable GAAP, with changes in fair value reported in earnings; and

3) A freestanding instrument with the same terms as the embedded derivative is **subject to the guidance on derivative instruments and hedging**.

b. If an embedded derivative is accounted for separately, the **host contract** is accounted for based on the accounting standards that apply to instruments of its type. The **separated derivative** should be accounted for under the guidance on derivative instruments and hedging.

1) If the embedded derivative to be separated is **not reliably identifiable and measurable**, the entire contract must be measured at **fair value**, with gains and losses recognized in **earnings**.

2) It may not be designated as a hedging instrument because nonderivatives usually do not qualify as hedging instruments.

12. **Not-for-Profit Entities**

a. For a not-for-profit entity not reporting earnings separately, the change in fair value of hedging instruments and nonhedging derivatives is a **change in net assets** (unless the hedge is of a foreign currency exposure of a net investment in a foreign operation).

b. In a **fair value hedge**, the change in fair value of the **hedged item** attributable to the risk being hedged is recognized as a change in net assets.

c. These entities may **not** use cash flow hedge accounting.

13. **Hedging Summary**

	What is it?	Requirements	Initial Recognition	
			Hedged Asset, Liability, Forecasted Transaction, or Firm Commitment	Hedging Instrument
1. Cash flow hedge	The hedging instrument must offset the variability of the cash flows of a recognized asset or liability or a forecasted transaction. In a foreign currency cash flow hedge, the hedged item also may be an unrecognized firm commitment.	The hedging instrument must be designated as part of a hedge and meet the criteria for a cash flow hedge.	Recognize receivable or payable.	No journal entry is made. The contract has no initial fair value because it is unperformed at its inception.
Journal entry			A/R $XXX Sales $XXX	
2. Fair value hedge	A fair value hedge must offset the changes in fair value of a recognized asset or liability or an unrecognized firm commitment.	The hedging instrument must be designated as part of a hedge and meet the criteria for a fair value hedge.	Recognize receivable or payable.	No journal entry is made. The contract has no initial fair value because it is unperformed at its inception.
Journal entry			A/R $XXX Sales $XXX	

14. Hedge Reporting at a Balance Sheet Date

	Hedged Asset, Liability, Forecasted Transaction, or Firm Commitment	Hedging Instrument		Amortization of Discount/Premium
1. Cash flow hedge	Adjusted to fair value. Recognized in earnings.	Adjusted to fair value. An asset/liability is recognized on balance sheet. Offsetting entry is an adjustment to other comprehensive income (OCI).		The discount/premium (forward contract) or the time value (option) must be amortized over the life of the derivative. This amount is recognized in earnings and offset by an entry to OCI.

Journal entry	A/R $XXX
	    Gain $XXX
		OCI $XXX
		    Derivative $XXX
				Discount amortization $XXX
				    OCI $XXX

2. Fair value hedge	Adjusted to fair value. Change is recognized in earnings.	Adjusted to fair value. An asset/liability is recognized on balance sheet. Offsetting entry is gain/loss and is recognized in earnings.		

Journal entry	A/R $XXX
	    Gain $XXX
		Loss on derivative $XXX
		    Derivative $XXX		

15. Hedge Reporting at the Expiration Date

	Hedged Asset, Liability, Forecasted Transaction, or Firm Commitment	Hedging Instrument	OCI Entry	Amortization of Discount/Premium
1. Cash flow hedge	Adjusted to fair value. Recognized in earnings.	Adjusted to fair value. The offsetting entry is to OCI.	The adjustment of OCI is transferred to earnings. This allows the gain/loss on the hedged item to be offset by the change in fair value of the derivative.	The discount/premium (forward contract) or the time value (option) must be amortized over the life of the derivative. This amount is recognized in earnings and offset by an entry to OCI.

Journal entry	Loss $XXX
	    A/R $XXX
		Derivative $XXX
		    OCI $XXX
			OCI $XXX
			    Gain on derivative $XXX
				Discount amortization $XXX
				    OCI $XXX

2. Fair value hedge	Adjusted to fair value. Offsetting entry is to gain/loss recognized in earnings.	Adjusted to fair value. Offsetting entry is to gain/loss recognized in earnings.	N/A	N/A

Journal entry	Loss $XXX
	    A/R $XXX
		Derivative $XXX
		    Gain on derivative $XXX		

Regarding accounting for derivatives, the AICPA has released both conceptual and calculation questions. Successful CPA candidates will know the fundamental accounting concepts for derivatives. Some CPA candidates choose to briefly study this part. Dr. Gleim believes you should understand the functions of derivatives and how to account for them. However, if you are having difficulty answering the calculation questions, move on to other study units where you can use your time more efficiently.

Stop and review! You have completed the outline for this subunit. Study multiple-choice questions 1 through 8 beginning on page 625.

17.2 FOREIGN CURRENCY ISSUES

1. **Definitions**

   a. The **reporting currency** is the currency in which an entity prepares its financial statements.

   b. **Foreign currency translation** expresses in the reporting currency amounts that are (1) denominated in (fixed in units of) a different currency or (2) measured in a different currency. For example, a U.S. entity may have a liability denominated in (fixed in) euros that it measures in U.S. dollars.

   1) A consolidated entity may consist of separate entities operating in different economic and currency environments. Translation is necessary in these circumstances so that consolidated amounts are presented in one currency.

   c. The **functional currency** is the currency of the primary economic environment in which the entity operates. Normally, that environment is the one in which it primarily generates and expends cash.

   1) For example, the functional currency of a foreign subsidiary is more likely to be the parent's currency if its cash flows directly and currently affect the parent's cash flows.

   d. **Foreign currency transactions** are fixed in a currency other than the functional currency. They result when an entity

   1) Buys or sells on credit;
   2) Borrows or lends;
   3) Is a party to a derivative instrument; or,
   4) For other reasons, acquires or disposes of assets, or incurs or settles liabilities, fixed in a foreign currency.

   e. A **foreign currency** is any currency other than the entity's functional currency.

   f. The **current exchange rate** is the rate used for currency conversion.

   g. The **spot rate** is the rate for immediate exchange of currencies.

   h. The **transaction date** is the date when a transaction is recorded under GAAP.

   i. A **transaction gain (loss)** results from a change in exchange rates between the functional currency and the currency in which the transaction is denominated. It is the change in functional currency cash flows

   1) Actually realized on settlement and
   2) Expected on unsettled transactions.

2. **Foreign Currency Transactions**

   a. Transactions are recorded at the spot rate in effect at the transaction date.

   b. Transaction gains and losses are recorded at each balance sheet date and at the date the receivable or payable is settled. The gains or losses ordinarily are included in earnings.

   c. When the amount of the functional currency exchangeable for a unit of the currency in which the transaction is fixed increases, a transaction gain or loss is recognized on a receivable or payable, respectively. The opposite occurs when the exchange rate (functional currency to foreign currency) decreases.

EXAMPLE

JRF Corporation, a U.S. entity, purchases and receives radios from Tokyo Corporation, a Japanese entity, on December 15, Year 1. The transaction is fixed in yen and calls for JRF to pay Tokyo 1.5 million yen on January 15, Year 2. The spot rate for yen is U.S. $.01015 at the time of the transaction. The spot rate is U.S. $.01010 on December 31, Year 1, and U.S. $.01020 on January 15, Year 2. JRF records the transaction as follows:

12/15/Year 1:	Inventory	$15,225	
	Accounts payable		$15,225
	(¥1,500,000 × $0.01015 spot rate)		
12/31/Year 1:	Accounts payable	$75	
	Transaction gain		$75
	[$15,225 − (¥1,500,000 × $.01010) = $75 gain]		
1/15/Year 2:	Accounts payable	$15,150	
	Transaction loss	150	
	Cash		$15,300
	[(¥1,500,000 × $.01020) − $15,150 = $150 loss]		

---

3.   **Translation**

   a.   The method used to convert foreign currency amounts into units of the reporting currency is the **functional currency translation approach**.

   b.   It is appropriate for use in accounting for and reporting the financial results and relationships of foreign subsidiaries in consolidated statements. This method

   1)   Identifies the **functional currency** of the entity (the currency of the primary economic environment in which the foreign entity operates),

   2)   Measures all elements of the statements in the functional currency, and

   3)   Uses a **current exchange rate** for translation from the functional currency to the reporting currency.

   c.   **Assets and liabilities** are translated at the exchange rate at fiscal year end.

   d.   **Revenues, expenses, gains, and losses** are translated at the rates in effect when they were recognized. However, a **weighted-average rate** for the period may be used for these items.

4.   **Translation Adjustments**

   a.   Foreign currency translation adjustments for a foreign operation that is relatively self-contained and integrated within its environment do not affect cash flows of the reporting entity. They should be excluded from earnings. Accordingly, translation adjustments are reported in **other comprehensive income** (OCI).

   b.   When an operation is **relatively self-contained**, the cash generated and expended by the entity is normally in the currency of the foreign country. That currency is the operation's functional currency.

   c.   A **pro rata portion** of the accumulated translation adjustment attributable to an investment in a foreign entity is recognized in measuring the gain or loss on the sale.

   d.   The functional currency may **change to the reporting currency**. After the change, translation adjustments are not removed from equity. Also, the translated amounts of nonmonetary assets become the accounting bases for those assets.

   1)   If the **change is from the reporting currency to a foreign currency**, the adjustment for translation of nonmonetary assets at the date of change is reported in **OCI**.

5. **Remeasurement**

   a. If the books of a foreign entity are maintained in a currency not the functional currency, foreign currency amounts must be remeasured into the functional currency using the **temporal method**. They are then translated into the reporting currency using the **current-rate method**.

   b. **Nonmonetary** balance sheet items and related revenue, expense, gain, and loss amounts are remeasured at the **historical rate**.

       1) Examples are (a) marketable securities carried at cost; (b) inventories carried at cost; (c) cost of goods sold; (d) prepaid expenses; (e) property, plant, and equipment; (f) depreciation; (g) intangible assets; (h) amortization of intangible assets; (i) deferred income; (j) common stock; (k) preferred stock carried at its issuance price; and (l) any noncontrolling interest.

   c. **Monetary** items are remeasured at the **current rate**.

       1) Examples of monetary items are (a) receivables, (b) payables, (c) inventories carried at market, and (d) marketable securities carried at fair value.

   d. Any **gain or loss** on remeasurement of monetary assets and liabilities is recognized in current earnings as part of continuing operations. This accounting treatment was adopted because gains or losses on remeasurement affect functional currency cash flows.

EXAMPLE

A U.S.-based conglomerate has a subsidiary in Norway that keeps its books using the krone (kr) (its local currency). But its primary operations involve Eurozone entities. Accordingly, to prepare the consolidated financial statements, the parent first must remeasure all unsettled transactions of the subsidiary from kroner to euros. It then must translate those remeasured amounts into dollars ($).

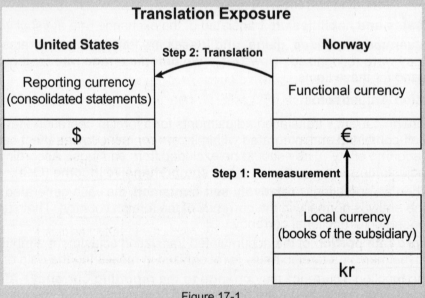

Figure 17-1

e. The financial statements of a foreign entity in a **highly inflationary economy** are remeasured into the reporting currency using the temporal method. Thus, the reporting currency is treated as if it were the functional currency.

   1) A highly inflationary economy has cumulative inflation of approximately **100% or more** over a 3-year period.

f. **Transaction gains and losses** on the following are excluded from earnings and are reported in the same way as translation adjustments, that is, in **OCI**:

   1) Transactions that are designated and effective as economic hedges of a **net investment in a foreign entity**

   2) Transactions that are in effect **long-term investments** in foreign entities to be consolidated, combined, or accounted for by the equity method

6. **Tax Effects of Changes in Exchange Rates**

   a. **Interperiod tax allocation** is necessary when transaction gains and losses result in temporary differences. Moreover, the tax consequences of translation adjustments are accounted for in the same way as temporary differences.

   b. **Intraperiod tax allocation** is also required. For example, taxes related to transaction gains and losses and translation adjustments reported in OCI should be allocated to those items.

Stop and review! You have completed the outline for this subunit. Study multiple-choice questions 9 through 16 beginning on page 628.

17.3 FINANCIAL STATEMENT ANALYSIS -- LIQUIDITY

The most common form of financial statement analysis is ratio analysis, in which two financial statement measures are compared.

1. **Liquidity**

   a. Liquidity is a firm's ability to pay its current obligations as they come due and thus remain in business in the short run. Liquidity measures the ease with which assets can be converted to cash.

   b. Liquidity ratios measure this ability by relating a firm's liquid assets to its current liabilities.

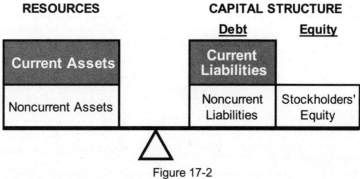

Figure 17-2

EXAMPLE of a Balance Sheet

RESOURCES	Current Year End	Prior Year End	FINANCING	Current Year End	Prior Year End
CURRENT ASSETS:			**CURRENT LIABILITIES:**		
Cash and equivalents	$ 325,000	$ 275,000	Accounts payable	$ 150,000	$ 75,000
Available-for-sale securities	165,000	145,000	Notes payable	50,000	50,000
Accounts receivable (net)	120,000	115,000	Accrued interest on note	5,000	5,000
Notes receivable	55,000	40,000	Current maturities of L.T. debt	100,000	100,000
Inventories	85,000	55,000	Accrued salaries and wages	15,000	10,000
Prepaid expenses	10,000	5,000	Income taxes payable	70,000	35,000
Total current assets	**$ 760,000**	**$ 635,000**	**Total current liabilities**	**$ 390,000**	**$ 275,000**
NONCURRENT ASSETS:			**NONCURRENT LIABILITIES:**		
Equity-method investments	$ 120,000	$ 115,000	Bonds payable	$ 500,000	$ 600,000
Property, plant, and equipment	1,000,000	900,000	Long-term notes payable	90,000	60,000
Less: accum. depreciation	(85,000)	(55,000)	Employee-related obligations	15,000	10,000
Goodwill	5,000	5,000	Deferred income taxes	5,000	5,000
Total noncurrent assets	**$1,040,000**	**$ 965,000**	**Total noncurrent liabilities**	**$ 610,000**	**$ 675,000**
			Total liabilities	**$1,000,000**	**$ 950,000**
			STOCKHOLDERS' EQUITY:		
			Preferred stock, $50 par	$ 120,000	$ 0
			Common stock, $1 par	500,000	500,000
			Additional paid-in capital	110,000	100,000
			Retained earnings	70,000	50,000
			Total stockholders' equity	**$ 800,000**	**$ 650,000**
Total assets	**$1,800,000**	**$1,600,000**	**Total liabilities and stockholders' equity**	**$1,800,000**	**$1,600,000**

Know the formulas and how to calculate the various financial ratios as well as how to analyze the ratio results. Numerous prior CPA exams have included questions on both the calculation and analysis of financial ratios. In ratio calculation, the numbers necessary to calculate a ratio often will not be given directly. You will have to determine these numbers using information given in the question and then calculate the ratio.

2. **Liquidity Ratios**

   a. The **current ratio** is the most common measure of liquidity.

$$\frac{Current\ assets}{Current\ liabilities}$$

EXAMPLE

Current year: $760,000 ÷ $390,000 = 1.95
Prior year: $635,000 ÷ $275,000 = 2.31

Although working capital increased in absolute terms ($10,000), current assets now provide less proportional coverage of current liabilities than in the prior year.

   b. The **quick (acid-test) ratio** excludes inventories and prepaids from the numerator, recognizing that those assets are difficult to liquidate at their stated values. The quick ratio is thus a more conservative measure than the basic current ratio.

$$\frac{Cash\ +\ Short\text{-}term\ investment\ securities\ +\ Net\ receivables}{Current\ liabilities}$$

EXAMPLE

Current year: ($325,000 + $165,000 + $120,000 + $55,000) ÷ $390,000 = 1.71
Prior year: ($275,000 + $145,000 + $115,000 + $40,000) ÷ $275,000 = 2.09

In spite of its increase in total working capital, the company's position in its most liquid assets deteriorated significantly.

---

3. **Effects of Transactions**

   a. If a ratio is less than 1.0, the numerator is lower than the denominator.

      1) A transaction that causes equal changes in the numerator and denominator will thus have a proportionally greater effect on the numerator, resulting in a change in the ratio in the same direction.

   b. If a ratio is equal to 1.0, the numerator and denominator are the same.

      1) A transaction that causes equal changes in the numerator and denominator results in no change in the ratio.

   c. If a ratio is greater than 1.0, the numerator is higher than the denominator.

      1) A transaction that causes equal changes in the numerator and denominator will thus have a proportionally greater effect on the denominator, resulting in a change in the ratio in the opposite direction.

Ratio range	Effect on ratio of equal increase to numerator and denominator	Effect on ratio of equal decrease to numerator and denominator
< 1.0	Increase	Decrease
= 1.0	No effect	No effect
> 1.0	Decrease	Increase

Stop and review! You have completed the outline for this subunit. Study multiple-choice questions 17 through 20 beginning on page 631.

17.4 FINANCIAL STATEMENT ANALYSIS -- ACTIVITY

1. **Receivables Ratios**

EXAMPLE

Excerpt from an income statement:

	Current Year	Prior Year
Net sales	**$1,800,000**	**$1,400,000**
Cost of goods sold	(1,650,000)	(1,330,000)
Gross profit	**$ 150,000**	**$ 70,000**

---

   a. The **accounts receivable turnover ratio** is the number of times in a year the total balance of receivables is converted to cash.

$$Accounts\ receivable\ turnover = \frac{Net\ credit\ sales}{Average\ balance\ in\ receivables}$$

EXAMPLE

All of the company's sales are on credit (see the example of a balance sheet on page 620). Net trade receivables at the balance sheet date of the second prior year were $105,000.

Current year: $1,800,000 ÷ [($120,000 + $115,000) ÷ 2] = 15.3 times
Prior year: $1,400,000 ÷ [($115,000 + $105,000) ÷ 2] = 12.7 times

The company turned over its trade receivables balance 2.6 more times during the current year, even as receivables were growing in absolute terms. Thus, the company's effectiveness at collecting accounts receivable has improved noticeably.

---

b.   The **average collection period** (also called the **days' sales in receivables**) measures the average number of days that pass between the time of a sale and receipt of the invoice amount.

$$Days'\ sales\ in\ receivables = \frac{Days\ in\ year}{Accounts\ receivable\ turnover\ ratio}$$

EXAMPLE

Current year: 365 days ÷ 15.3 times = 23.9 days
Prior year: 365 days ÷ 12.7 times = 28.7 days

Since the denominator (calculated in item a. on the previous page) increased and the numerator is a constant, days' sales will necessarily decrease. In addition to improving its collection practices, the company also may have become better at assessing the creditworthiness of its customers.

---

2.   **Inventory Ratios**

a.   **Inventory turnover** measures the number of times in a year the total balance of inventory is converted to cash or receivables.

1)   Generally, the higher the inventory turnover rate, the more efficient the inventory management of the firm. A high rate may imply that the firm is not carrying excess levels of inventory or inventory that is obsolete.

$$Inventory\ turnover = \frac{Cost\ of\ goods\ sold}{Average\ balance\ in\ inventory}$$

EXAMPLE

The balance in inventories at the balance sheet date of the second prior year was $45,000.

Current year: $1,650,000 ÷ [($85,000 + $55,000) ÷ 2] = 23.6 times
Prior year: $1,330,000 ÷ [($55,000 + $45,000) ÷ 2] = 26.6 times

The company did not turn over its inventories as many times during the current year. This is to be expected during a period of growing sales (and building inventory level) and so is not necessarily a sign of poor inventory management.

---

2)   As with receivables turnover, if a business is highly seasonal, a simple average of beginning and ending balances is inadequate. The monthly balances should be averaged instead.

3)   Since cost of goods sold is in the numerator, higher sales (i.e., higher cost of goods sold) without an increase in inventory balances will result in better turnover.

a)   Since inventory is in the denominator, reducing inventory levels results in a higher turnover ratio.

4)   The ratio of a firm that uses LIFO may not be comparable with that of a firm with a higher inventory valuation.

b.   **Days' sales in inventory** measures the average number of days that pass between the acquisition of inventory and its sale.

$$Days'\ sales\ in\ inventory = \frac{Days\ in\ year}{Inventory\ turnover\ ratio}$$

EXAMPLE

Current year: 365 days ÷ 23.6 times = 15.5 days
Prior year: 365 days ÷ 26.6 times = 13.7 days

Since the numerator is a constant, the decreased inventory turnover calculated meant that days' sales tied up in inventory would increase. This is a common phenomenon during a period of increasing sales.

---

3. **Operating Cycle**

   a. A firm's operating cycle is the amount of time that passes between the acquisition of inventory and the collection of cash on the sale of that inventory.

   Operating cycle = Days' sales in receivables + Days' sales in inventory

EXAMPLE
Current year: 23.9 days + 15.5 days = 39.4 days Prior year: 28.7 days + 13.7 days = 42.4 days
The company has managed to slightly reduce its operating cycle, even while increasing sales and building inventories.

   b. The following diagram depicts the phases of the operating cycle:

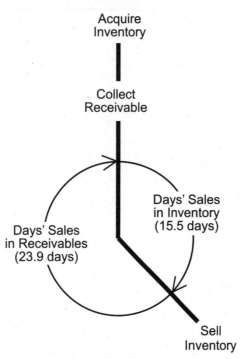

**Operating Cycle
39.4 Days**

Acquire
Inventory

Collect
Receivable

Days' Sales
in Inventory
(15.5 days)

Days' Sales
in Receivables
(23.9 days)

Sell
Inventory

Figure 17-3

4. **Other Turnover Ratios**

   a. The total assets turnover and fixed assets turnover are broader-based ratios that measure the efficiency with which assets are used to generate revenue.

      1) Both cash and credit sales are included in the numerator.

$$Total\ assets\ turnover = \frac{Net\ total\ sales}{Average\ total\ assets}$$

$$Fixed\ assets\ turnover = \frac{Net\ total\ sales}{Average\ net\ fixed\ assets}$$

Stop and review! You have completed the outline for this subunit. Study multiple-choice questions 21 through 25 beginning on page 632.

17.5 FINANCIAL STATEMENT ANALYSIS -- SOLVENCY, VALUATION, AND COMPARATIVE ANALYSIS

1. **Solvency and Leverage**

   a. Solvency is a firm's ability to pay its noncurrent obligations as they come due and thus remain in business in the long run (contrast with liquidity).

      1) Leverage in this context refers to the use of a high level of debt relative to equity in the firm's capital structure.

      2) An overleveraged firm risks insolvency.

$$Debt\text{-}to\text{-}equity\ ratio = \frac{Total\ liabilities}{Total\ equity}$$

   b. The ability to service debt out of current earnings is a key aspect of the successful use of leverage.

$$Times\text{-}interest\text{-}earned\ ratio = \frac{Earnings\ before\ interest\ and\ taxes}{Interest\ expense}$$

2. **Profitability Ratios**

   a. Profitability ratios measure how effectively the firm is deploying its resource base to generate a return.

$$Profit\ margin\ on\ sales = \frac{Net\ income}{Sales}$$

$$Return\ on\ assets = \frac{Net\ income}{Average\ total\ assets}$$

$$Return\ on\ equity = \frac{Net\ income}{Average\ total\ equity}$$

$$Return\ on\ common\ equity = \frac{Net\ income - Preferred\ dividends}{Average\ common\ equity}$$

3. **Corporate Valuation Measures**

   a. These ratios reflect and shape the stock market's assessment of a firm's current standing and future prospects.

$$Basic\ earnings\ per\ share = \frac{Income\ available\ to\ common\ shareholders}{Weighted\text{-}average\ common\ shares\ outstanding}$$

$$Book\ value\ per\ common\ share = \frac{Net\ assets\ available\ to\ common\ shareholders}{Ending\ common\ shares\ outstanding}$$

$$Price\text{-}to\text{-}earnings\ ratio = \frac{Price\ per\ common\ share}{Basic\ EPS}$$

 The AICPA has traditionally tested financial ratios. Gleim materials contain CPA questions dating back to the mid 1980s that test the candidate's knowledge of financial ratios, and the AICPA continues to release new questions on this topic. Successful CPA candidates have memorized the various ratios and are able to correctly answer the majority of financial ratio questions in the Gleim materials.

4. **Comparative Analysis**

   a. Comparative analysis involves both horizontal and vertical analysis. Horizontal (trend) analysis compares analytical data over a period of time. Vertical analysis makes comparisons among a single year's data.

   b. **Common-size financial statements** are used to compare entities of different sizes. Items on common-size financial statements are expressed as percentages of corresponding base amounts. A base amount is assigned the value of 100%.

      1) The **horizontal** form of common-size analysis is useful for evaluating trends. Each amount for subsequent years is stated as a percentage of a **base-year amount**.

      2) **Vertical** common-size analysis presents amounts for a single year expressed as percentages of a base amount on the **balance sheet** (e.g., total assets) and on the **income statement** (e.g., sales). Common-size analysis permits management to compare individual expenses or asset categories with those of other entities and with industry averages.

   c. Comparing an entity's performance with respect to its industry may identify strengths and weaknesses. Horizontal analysis of the industry may identify industrywide trends and practices.

Stop and review! You have completed the outline for this subunit. Study multiple-choice questions 26 through 30 beginning on page 634.

QUESTIONS

17.1 Derivatives and Hedging

1. The effective portion of a gain arising from an increase in the fair value of a derivative is included in earnings in the period of change if the derivative is appropriately designated and qualifies as a hedge of

  A. A foreign currency exposure of a net investment in a foreign operation.

  B. A foreign currency exposure of a forecasted transaction.

  C. A foreign currency exposure of an available-for-sale security.

  D. The variable cash flows of a forecasted transaction.

Answer (C) is correct.

  REQUIRED: The derivative for which the effective portion of a gain is included in earnings in the period in which a change in fair value occurs.

  DISCUSSION: A fair value hedge includes a hedge of an exposure to changes in the fair value of a recognized asset or liability or an unrecognized firm commitment. Such a hedge minimizes the risk associated with fixed cash flows. A foreign currency fair value hedge includes a hedge of a foreign currency exposure of an unrecognized firm commitment. It also includes a hedge of a foreign currency exposure of a recognized asset or liability (including an available-for-sale security) for which a foreign currency transaction gain or loss is recognized in earnings under U.S. GAAP. Gains and losses arising from changes in fair value of a derivative classified as either a fair value or a foreign fair value hedge are included in the determination of earnings in the period of change. They are offset by losses or gains on the hedged item attributable to the risk being hedged. Thus, earnings of the period of change are affected only by the net gain or loss attributable to the ineffective aspect of the hedge.

  Answer (A) is incorrect. The effective portion of gains and losses on this hedge is reported as a component of the cumulative translation adjustment in other comprehensive income. Answer (B) is incorrect. The effective portion of gains and losses on these hedges is included in other comprehensive income until periods in which the forecasted transaction affects earnings. Answer (D) is incorrect. The effective portion of gains and losses on these hedges is included in other comprehensive income until periods in which the forecasted transaction affects earnings.

2. Which of the following risks is (are) inherent in an interest-rate swap agreement?

I.   The risk of exchanging a lower interest rate for a higher interest rate

II.   The risk of nonperformance by the counterparty to the agreement

    A.   I only.

    B.   II only.

    C.   Both I and II.

    D.   Neither I nor II.

Answer (C) is correct.
    REQUIRED: The risk(s) of an interest-rate swap.
    DISCUSSION: An interest-rate swap is an exchange of fixed interest payments for payments based on a floating rate. The risks inherent in an interest-rate swap include both credit risk and market risk. Credit risk is the risk of accounting loss from a financial instrument because of the possibility that a loss may occur from the failure of another party to perform according to the terms of a contract. Market risk arises from the possibility that future changes in market prices may make a financial instrument less valuable or more onerous. Market risk therefore includes the risk that changes in interest rates will make the swap agreement less valuable or more onerous.
    Answer (A) is incorrect. An interest-rate swap also may result in nonperformance by the counterparty. Answer (B) is incorrect. An interest-rate swap also may result in a higher interest rate. Answer (D) is incorrect. An interest-rate swap may result in a higher interest rate or nonperformance by the counterparty.

3. Which of the following financial instruments is **not** considered a derivative financial instrument?

    A.   Interest-rate swaps.

    B.   Currency futures.

    C.   Stock-index options.

    D.   Bank certificates of deposit.

Answer (D) is correct.
    REQUIRED: The financial instrument not a derivative.
    DISCUSSION: A derivative is a financial instrument or other contract that (1) has (a) one or more underlyings and (b) one or more notional amounts or payment provisions, or both; (2) requires either no initial net investment or an immaterial net investment; and (3) requires or permits net settlement. An underlying may be a specified interest rate, security price, commodity price, foreign exchange rate, index of prices or rates, or other variable. A notional amount is a number of currency units, shares, bushels, pounds, or other units specified. Settlement of a derivative is based on the interaction of the notional amount and the underlying. A certificate of deposit is a financial instrument of the issuing bank that is a type of promissory note. It has no underlying and requires a material net investment. Thus, it is not a derivative.
    Answer (A) is incorrect. Interest-rate swaps are derivatives. Answer (B) is incorrect. Currency futures are derivatives. Answer (C) is incorrect. Stock-index options are derivatives.

4. Which of the following is the characteristic of a perfect hedge?

    A.   No possibility of future gain or loss.

    B.   No possibility of future gain only.

    C.   No possibility of future loss only.

    D.   The possibility of future gain and **no** future loss.

Answer (A) is correct.
    REQUIRED: The trait of a perfect hedge.
    DISCUSSION: A hedge is used to avoid or reduce risks by creating a relationship by which losses on certain positions are expected to be counterbalanced in whole or in part by gains on separate positions in another market. A perfect hedge is completely effective. It has a complete negative correlation with the item being hedged and results in no net gain or loss.
    Answer (B) is incorrect. A perfect hedge also has no possibility of future loss. Answer (C) is incorrect. A perfect hedge also has no possibility of future gain. Answer (D) is incorrect. A perfect hedge results in no net gain or loss.

Questions 5 and 6 are based on the following information. As part of its risk management strategy, Copper Monkey Mining sells futures contracts to hedge changes in fair value of its inventory. On March 12, the commodity exchange spot price was $0.81/lb., and the futures price for mid-June was $0.83/lb. On that date, Copper Monkey, which has a March 31 fiscal year end, sold 200 futures contracts on the commodity exchange at $0.83/lb. for delivery in June. Each contract was for 25,000 lb. Copper Monkey designated these contracts as a fair value hedge of 5 million lb. of current inventory for which a mid-June sale is expected. The average cost of this inventory was $0.58/lb. Copper Monkey documented (1) the hedging relationship between the futures contracts and its inventory, (2) its objectives and strategy for undertaking the hedge, and (3) its conclusion that the hedging relationship will be highly effective. On March 31, the mid-June commodity exchange futures price was $0.85/lb.

5. In the March 31 statement of financial position, the company should record the futures contracts as a

A. $100,000 asset.

B. $100,000 liability.

C. $4,250,000 liability.

D. $4,250,000 asset.

Answer (B) is correct.

REQUIRED: The amount at which the futures contracts should be recorded on March 31.

DISCUSSION: GAAP require that derivative instruments be recorded as assets and liabilities and measured at fair value. At the inception of the futures contracts, their fair value was $0 because the contracts were entered into at the futures price at that date. On March 31, the fair value of the futures contracts is equal to the change in the futures price between the inception price and the price on the balance sheet date. Given that the futures contracts created an obligation to deliver 5 million lb. (25,000 lb. × 200 contracts) of copper at $0.83/lb. and that the price had risen to $0.85/lb. at the date of the financial statements, Copper Monkey should record a loss and a liability of $100,000 [5 million lb. × ($0.83 – $0.85)].

6. If, on March 31, the company concluded that the hedge was 100% effective, it should record the hedged copper inventory in the March 31 statement of financial position at

A. $4,350,000

B. $4,250,000

C. $3,000,000

D. $2,900,000

Answer (C) is correct.

REQUIRED: The amount at which the hedged inventory should be recorded on March 31.

DISCUSSION: On March 31, Copper Monkey recognized a loss and liability for the futures contracts of $100,000 [5 million lb. × ($0.83 contract price – $0.85 futures price)]. If the hedge was completely effective, the loss on the hedging derivatives must have been offset by a $100,000 gain on the hedged item. For a fair-value hedge, changes in the fair value of the hedged item attributable to the hedged risk are reflected as adjustments to the carrying amount of the hedged recognized asset or liability or the previously unrecognized firm commitment. The adjustments to carrying amount are accounted for in the same manner as other components of the carrying amount of the asset or liability. Thus, the inventory should be recorded at $3,000,000 [(5 million lb. × $0.58) original cost + $100,000 gain in fair value].

Answer (A) is incorrect. The amount of $4,350,000 equals the fair value of the inventory at the futures price on March 31 plus $100,000. Answer (B) is incorrect. The amount of $4,250,000 equals the fair value of the inventory at the futures price on March 31. Answer (D) is incorrect. The amount of $2,900,000 is the original cost of the inventory.

7. The effective portion of a loss associated with a change in fair value of a derivative instrument should be reported as a component of other comprehensive income only if the derivative is appropriately designated as a

A. Cash flow hedge of the foreign currency exposure of a forecasted transaction.

B. Fair value hedge of the foreign currency exposure of an unrecognized firm commitment.

C. Fair value hedge of the foreign currency exposure of a recognized asset or liability for which a foreign currency transaction gain or loss is recognized in earnings.

D. Speculation in a foreign currency.

Answer (A) is correct.

REQUIRED: The derivative for which the effective portion of a loss associated with its change in fair value is reported as a component of other comprehensive income.

DISCUSSION: The hedge of the foreign currency exposure of a forecasted transaction is designated as a cash flow hedge. The effective portion of gains and losses associated with changes in fair value of a derivative instrument designated and qualifying as a cash flow hedging instrument is reported as a component of other comprehensive income.

Answer (B) is incorrect. A hedge of the foreign currency exposure of an unrecognized firm commitment may be a cash flow hedge or a fair value hedge. Answer (C) is incorrect. A hedge of the foreign currency exposure of a recognized asset or liability for which a foreign currency transaction gain or loss is recognized in earnings may be a cash flow hedge or a fair value hedge. Answer (D) is incorrect. Gains and losses associated with changes in fair value of a derivative used as a speculation in a foreign currency are included in earnings of the period of change.

8. On October 1, Year 3, Weeks Co., a calendar-year-end U.S. company, forecasts that, near the end of March Year 4, Sullivan Corp., a foreign entity, will purchase 50,000 gallons of Weeks's primary product for 500,000 FCU. Sullivan has not firmly committed to the purchase. However, based on Sullivan's purchasing pattern, Weeks believes that the sale is probable. Weeks's risk-management policy includes avoiding foreign currency exposure through the use of foreign currency forward contracts. Thus, on October 1, Weeks enters into a 6-month foreign currency forward contract to sell 500,000 FCU to a dealer on March 31. Weeks designates the contract as a hedge and determines that hedge effectiveness will be based on changes in forward rates. The following information is available:

	Value of 500,000 FCU Based on Spot Rates	Value of 500,000 FCU Based on Forward Rates for 03/31/Yr 4	Incremental Discounted Changes in Value of Forward Contract Based on Changes in Forward Rates
10/01/Yr 3	$570,000	$500,000	$0
12/31/Yr 3	$540,000	$490,000	$9,800
03/31/Yr 4	$475,000	$475,000	$15,200

At what amounts should Weeks record the forward contract on December 31, Year 3, and March 31, Year 4?

	12/31/Yr 3	03/31/Yr 4
A.	$9,800	$25,000
B.	$10,000	$25,000
C.	$540,000	$475,000
D.	$490,000	$475,000

Answer (A) is correct.
REQUIRED: The amounts at which the forward contract should be recognized.
DISCUSSION: Weeks should record the forward contract as a receivable at fair value. Fair value is based on changes in forward rates discounted on a net present value basis. Thus, the receivable should be recorded at $9,800 on December 31, Year 3, and $25,000 ($9,800 + $15,200) on March 31, Year 4. Because a hedge of the foreign currency exposure of a forecasted transaction is a cash flow hedge, Weeks should also credit these amounts to other comprehensive income. On March 31, the sale should be recorded at $500,000 ($475,000 value based on the spot rate at March 31 + $25,000 balance in other comprehensive income). The amount of cash received also is equal to $500,000 ($475,000 + $25,000 balance in the forward contract receivable).
Answer (B) is incorrect. The change in forward rates should be adjusted for the time value of money. Answer (C) is incorrect. The amounts of $540,000 and $475,000 reflect the value of 500,000 FCU at spot rates. Answer (D) is incorrect. The amounts of $490,000 and $475,000 reflect the value of 500,000 FCU at forward rates.

17.2 Foreign Currency Issues

9. Which of the following statements regarding foreign exchange gains and losses is true (where the exchange rate is the ratio of units of the functional currency to units of the foreign currency)?

A. An exchange gain occurs when the exchange rate increases between the date a payable is recorded and the date of cash payment.

B. An exchange gain occurs when the exchange rate increases between the date a receivable is recorded and the date of cash receipt.

C. An exchange loss occurs when the exchange rate decreases between the date a payable is recorded and the date of the cash payment.

D. An exchange loss occurs when the exchange rate increases between the date a receivable is recorded and the date of the cash receipt.

Answer (B) is correct.
REQUIRED: The true statement about foreign exchange gains and losses.
DISCUSSION: A foreign currency transaction gain or loss (commonly known as a foreign exchange gain or loss) is recorded in earnings. When the amount of the functional currency exchangeable for a unit of the currency in which the transaction is fixed increases, a transaction gain or loss is recognized on a receivable or payable, respectively. The opposite occurs when the exchange rate (functional currency to foreign currency) decreases.
Answer (A) is incorrect. The payable will become more expensive in the functional currency, resulting in a loss. Answer (C) is incorrect. The payable will become less expensive in the functional currency, resulting in a gain. Answer (D) is incorrect. An exchange gain occurs.

10. Fogg Co., a U.S. company, contracted to purchase foreign goods. Payment in foreign currency was due 1 month after the goods were received at Fogg's warehouse. Between the receipt of goods and the time of payment, the exchange rates changed in Fogg's favor. The resulting gain should be included in Fogg's financial statements as a(n)

A. Component of income from continuing operations.

B. Extraordinary item.

C. Deferred credit.

D. Item of other comprehensive income.

Answer (A) is correct.

REQUIRED: The accounting treatment of a foreign currency transaction gain.

DISCUSSION: This foreign currency transaction resulted in a payable stated in a foreign currency. The favorable change in the exchange rate between the functional currency and the currency in which the transaction was stated should be included in determining net income for the period in which the exchange rate changed. It should be classified as a component of income from continuing operations because it does not meet the criteria for classification under any other caption in the income statement, for example, as an extraordinary item.

Answer (B) is incorrect. Gains or losses from exchange or translation of foreign currencies are not extraordinary items except in rare situations. They are usual in nature and may be expected to recur in the course of customary and continuing business activities. Answer (C) is incorrect. The gain should not be deferred but should be recognized in the period in which the exchange rate changed. Answer (D) is incorrect. Translation adjustments, not transaction gains and losses, are included in OCI.

11. On October 1, Year 4, Mild Co., a U.S. company, purchased machinery from Grund, a German company, with payment due on April 1, Year 5. If Mild's Year 4 operating income included no foreign currency transaction gain or loss, the transaction could have

A. Resulted in an extraordinary gain.

B. Been denominated in U.S. dollars.

C. Caused a foreign currency gain to be reported as a contra account against machinery.

D. Caused a foreign currency translation gain to be reported in other comprehensive income.

Answer (B) is correct.

REQUIRED: The reason no foreign currency transaction gain or loss occurred.

DISCUSSION: The terms of a foreign currency transaction are stated in a currency other than the functional currency. A fluctuation in the exchange rate between the functional currency and the other currency is a gain or loss that ordinarily should be included in determining net income when the exchange rate changes. If Mild's functional currency is the U.S. dollar and the transaction was stated in U.S. dollars, no foreign currency transaction gain or loss occurred.

Answer (A) is incorrect. Foreign currency transaction gains and losses are ordinarily operating items. Answer (C) is incorrect. Foreign currency transaction gains and losses not included in the determination of net income (certain intraentity transactions and certain hedges) are reported in OCI. Answer (D) is incorrect. Translation expresses in the reporting currency amounts denominated in the functional currency. The U.S. dollar is the reporting and functional currency of Mild, so translation is not required.

12. On September 22, Year 2, Yumi Corp. purchased merchandise from an unaffiliated foreign company for 10,000 units of the foreign company's local currency. On that date, the spot rate was $.55. Yumi paid the bill in full on March 20, Year 3, when the spot rate was $.65. The spot rate was $.70 on December 31, Year 2. What amount should Yumi report as a foreign currency transaction loss in its income statement for the year ended December 31, Year 2?

A. $0

B. $500

C. $1,000

D. $1,500

Answer (D) is correct.

REQUIRED: The amount of foreign currency transaction loss to be reported in the income statement.

DISCUSSION: A receivable or payable stated in a foreign currency is adjusted to its current exchange rate at each balance sheet date. The resulting gain or loss should ordinarily be included in determining net income. It is the difference between the spot rate on the date the transaction originates and the spot rate at year end. Thus, the Year 2 transaction loss for Yumi Corp. is $1,500 [10,000 units × ($0.55 – $0.70)].

Answer (A) is incorrect. A loss resulted when the spot rate increased. Answer (B) is incorrect. The amount of $500 results from using the spot rates at 12/31/Year 2 and 3/20/Year 3. Answer (C) is incorrect. The amount of $1,000 results from using the spot rates at 9/22/Year 2 and 3/20/Year 3.

13. Which of the following is debited to other comprehensive income (OCI)?

A. Discount on convertible bonds that are dilutive potential common stock.

B. Premium on convertible bonds that are dilutive potential common stock.

C. Cumulative foreign currency translation loss.

D. Organizational costs.

Answer (C) is correct.
REQUIRED: The item debited to OCI.
DISCUSSION: When the currency used to prepare a foreign entity's financial statements is its functional currency, the current rate method is used to translate the foreign entity's financial statements into the reporting currency. The translation gains and losses arising from applying this method are reported in OCI in the consolidated statements and are not reflected in income. Accumulated OCI is a component of equity displayed separately from retained earnings and additional paid-in capital in the statement of financial position. Because a cumulative foreign currency translation loss reduces the balance, it is a debit item.
Answer (A) is incorrect. A discount on bonds is a contra account to bonds payable in the liability section of the balance sheet. Answer (B) is incorrect. Premium on bonds is a contra account to bonds payable in the liability section. Answer (D) is incorrect. Organizational costs are expensed when incurred.

14. A wholly owned subsidiary of Ward, Inc., has certain expense accounts for the year ended December 31, Year 4, stated in local currency units (LCU) as follows:

	LCU
Depreciation of equipment (related assets were purchased Jan. 1, Year 2)	120,000
Provision for doubtful accounts	80,000
Rent	200,000

The exchange rates at various dates are as follows:

	Dollar Equivalent of 1 LCU
December 31, Year 4	$.40
Average for year ended 12/31/Yr 4	.44
January 1, Year 2	.50

Assume that the LCU is the subsidiary's functional currency and that the charges to the expense accounts occurred approximately evenly during the year. What total dollar amount should be included in Ward's Year 4 consolidated income statement to reflect these expenses?

A. $160,000
B. $172,000
C. $176,000
D. $200,000

Answer (C) is correct.
REQUIRED: The amount of expenses in the consolidated income statement.
DISCUSSION: When the local currency of the subsidiary is the functional currency, translation into the reporting currency is necessary. Assets and liabilities are translated at the exchange rate at the balance sheet date, and revenues, expenses, gains, and losses are usually translated at average rates for the period. Thus, the 400,000 LCU in total expenses should be translated at the average exchange rate of $.44, resulting in expenses reflected in the consolidated income statement of $176,000 (400,000 LCU × $.44).
Answer (A) is incorrect. The average exchange rate, not the current year-end rate, should be used. Answer (B) is incorrect. The average exchange rate, not a combination of rates, should be used. Answer (D) is incorrect. It values all assets at the January 1, Year 2, rate.

15. In preparing consolidated financial statements of a U.S. parent company with a foreign subsidiary, the foreign subsidiary's functional currency is the currency

A. In which the subsidiary maintains its accounting records.

B. Of the country in which the subsidiary is located.

C. Of the country in which the parent is located.

D. Of the environment in which the subsidiary primarily generates and expends cash.

Answer (D) is correct.
REQUIRED: The foreign subsidiary's functional currency.
DISCUSSION: The method used to convert foreign currency amounts into units of the reporting currency is the functional currency translation approach. It is appropriate for use in accounting for and reporting the financial results and relationships of foreign subsidiaries in consolidated statements. This method (1) identifies the functional currency of the entity (the currency of the primary economic environment in which the foreign entity operates), (2) measures all elements of the financial statements in the functional currency, and (3) uses a current exchange rate for translation from the functional currency to the reporting currency. The currency indicated by the relevant economic indicators, such as cash flows, sales prices, sales markets, expenses, financing, and intraentity transactions, may not be (1) the currency in which the subsidiary maintains its accounting records, (2) the currency of the country in which the subsidiary is located, or (3) the currency of the country in which the parent is located.

16. Gains from remeasuring a foreign subsidiary's financial statements from the local currency into its functional currency should be reported

A. As a deferred foreign currency transaction gain.

B. In other comprehensive income.

C. As an extraordinary item, net of income taxes.

D. In current income.

Answer (D) is correct.
  REQUIRED: The proper reporting of a gain arising from remeasurement.
  DISCUSSION: If the books of record of a foreign entity are maintained in a currency other than the functional currency, the foreign currency amounts first must be remeasured into the functional currency using the temporal method and then translated using the current rate method into the reporting currency. The gain arising from remeasurement should be reported in current income.
  Answer (A) is incorrect. The gain is not deferred. Answer (B) is incorrect. A gain arising from translation, not remeasurement, is reported in other comprehensive income. Answer (C) is incorrect. The criteria for treatment as an extraordinary item have not been met.

17.3 Financial Statement Analysis -- Liquidity

17. North Bank is analyzing Belle Corp.'s financial statements for a possible extension of credit. Belle's quick ratio is significantly better than the industry average. Which of the following factors should North consider as a possible limitation of using this ratio when evaluating Belle's creditworthiness?

A. Fluctuating market prices of short-term investments may adversely affect the ratio.

B. Increasing market prices for Belle's inventory may adversely affect the ratio.

C. Belle may need to sell its available-for-sale investments to meet its current obligations.

D. Belle may need to liquidate its inventory to meet its long-term obligations.

Answer (A) is correct.
  REQUIRED: The possible limitation of using the quick ratio to evaluate creditworthiness.
  DISCUSSION: The quick ratio equals cash plus short-term investment securities plus net receivables, divided by current liabilities. Because short-term investment securities are included in the numerator, fluctuating market prices of these investments may adversely affect the ratio if Belle holds a substantial amount of such current assets.
  Answer (B) is incorrect. Inventory is excluded from the calculation of the quick ratio. Answer (C) is incorrect. If the available-for-sale securities are not current, they are not included in the calculation of the ratio. If they are classified as current, their sale to meet current obligations is consistent with normal current assets management practices. Answer (D) is incorrect. Inventory and noncurrent obligations are excluded from the calculation of the quick ratio.

18. A company's year-end balance sheet is shown below:

Assets

Cash	$ 300,000
Accounts receivable	350,000
Inventory	600,000
Property, plant, and equipment (net)	2,000,000
	$3,250,000

Liabilities and Shareholder Equity

Current liabilities	$ 700,000
Long-term liabilities	600,000
Common stock	800,000
Retained earnings	1,150,000
	$3,250,000

What is the current ratio as of December 31?

A. 1.79

B. 0.93

C. 0.67

D. 0.43

Answer (A) is correct.
  REQUIRED: The current ratio.
  DISCUSSION: The current ratio equals current assets divided by current liabilities [($300,000 + $350,000 + $600,000) ÷ $700,000 = 1.79].
  Answer (B) is incorrect. Inventory is included in current assets. Answer (C) is incorrect. Retained earnings is not included in current liabilities. Answer (D) is incorrect. Accounts receivable and inventory are included in current assets.

19. At December 30, Vida Co. had cash of $200,000, a current ratio of 1.5:1, and a quick ratio of .5:1. On December 31, all cash was used to reduce accounts payable. How did these cash payments affect the ratios?

	Current Ratio	Quick Ratio
A.	Increased	Decreased
B.	Increased	No effect
C.	Decreased	Increased
D.	Decreased	No effect

Answer (A) is correct.
REQUIRED: The effect of the cash payments on the current and quick ratios.
DISCUSSION: The current ratio (1.5) equals current assets (cash, marketable securities, and net accounts receivable) divided by current liabilities (accounts payable, etc.). If a ratio is greater than 1.0, equal decreases in the numerator and denominator (debit accounts payable and credit cash for $200,000) increase the ratio. The quick ratio (.5) equals quick assets (cash, trading securities, net accounts receivable) divided by current liabilities. If a ratio is less than 1.0, equal decreases in the numerator and denominator (debit accounts payable and credit cash for $200,000) decrease the ratio.

20. Zenk Co. wrote off obsolete inventory of $100,000 during the year. What was the effect of this write-off on Zenk's ratio analysis?

A. Decrease in current ratio but **not** in quick ratio.

B. Decrease in quick ratio but **not** in current ratio.

C. Increase in current ratio but **not** in quick ratio.

D. Increase in quick ratio but **not** in current ratio.

Answer (A) is correct.
REQUIRED: The effect of writing off obsolete inventory.
DISCUSSION: Inventory is included in the numerator of the current ratio but not the quick ratio. Hence, an inventory write-off decreases the current ratio but not the quick ratio.

17.4 Financial Statement Analysis -- Activity

21. The following financial ratios and calculations were based on information from Kohl Co.'s financial statements for the current year:

Accounts receivable turnover
Ten times during the year

Total assets turnover
Two times during the year

Average receivables during the year
$200,000

What was Kohl's average total assets for the year?

A. $2,000,000

B. $1,000,000

C. $400,000

D. $200,000

Answer (B) is correct.
REQUIRED: The average total assets.
DISCUSSION: The total assets turnover ratio (given as 2.0) equals net sales divided by average total assets. The accounts receivable turnover ratio (given as 10.0) equals net sales divided by average accounts receivable (it must be assumed that all sales are on credit). Given $200,000 of average accounts receivable, net sales must equal $2,000,000 ($200,000 × 10.0). Accordingly, average total assets equals $1,000,000 ($2,000,000 net revenue ÷ 2.0 total assets turnover).
Answer (A) is incorrect. The amount of $2,000,000 equals net revenue. Answer (C) is incorrect. The amount of $400,000 equals average accounts receivable times total assets turnover. Answer (D) is incorrect. The amount of $200,000 equals average receivables during the year.

22. Selected information for Clay Corp. for the year ended December 31 follows:

Average days' sales in inventories   124
Average days' sales in accounts receivable   48

The average number of days in the operating cycle for the year was

A. 172

B. 124

C. 86

D. 76

Answer (A) is correct.
REQUIRED: The number of days in the operating cycle.
DISCUSSION: The operating cycle is the time needed to turn cash into inventory, inventory into receivables, and receivables back into cash. It is equal to the sum of the number of days' sales in inventory and the number of days' sales in receivables. The number of days in Clay's operating cycle is thus 172 (124 + 48).
Answer (B) is incorrect. The average days' sales in inventories is 124. Answer (C) is incorrect. This figure equals the sum of the average days' sales in inventories and the average days' sales in receivables, divided by 2. Answer (D) is incorrect. This figure is the average days' sales in inventories minus the average days' sales in receivables.

Questions 23 through 25 are based on the following information. Selected data pertaining to Lore Co. for the Year 4 calendar year is as follows:

Net cash sales	$ 3,000
Cost of goods sold	18,000
Inventory at beginning of year	6,000
Purchases	24,000
Accounts receivable at beginning of year	20,000
Accounts receivable at end of year	22,000

23. The accounts receivable turnover for Year 4 was 5.0 times. What were Lore's Year 4 net credit sales?

A. $105,000

B. $107,000

C. $110,000

D. $210,000

Answer (A) is correct.
REQUIRED: The net credit sales.
DISCUSSION: Credit sales may be determined from the accounts receivable turnover formula (credit sales ÷ average accounts receivable). Credit sales are equal to 5.0 times average receivables [($20,000 + $22,000) ÷ 2], or $105,000.
Answer (B) is incorrect. The amount of $107,000 equals ending accounts receivable multiplied by the accounts receivable turnover ratio, minus cash sales. Answer (C) is incorrect. The amount of $110,000 equals ending accounts receivable multiplied by the accounts receivable turnover ratio. Answer (D) is incorrect. The amount of $210,000 equals beginning accounts receivable plus ending accounts receivable, multiplied by the accounts receivable turnover ratio.

24. What was Lore's inventory turnover for Year 4?

A. 1.2 times.

B. 1.5 times.

C. 2.0 times.

D. 3.0 times.

Answer (C) is correct.
REQUIRED: The inventory turnover ratio.
DISCUSSION: Inventory turnover is equal to cost of goods sold divided by average inventory. Ending inventory equals beginning inventory, plus purchases, minus cost of goods sold, or $12,000 ($6,000 + $24,000 – $18,000). Average inventory is $9,000 [($6,000 + $12,000) ÷ 2]. Inventory turnover is 2.0 times ($18,000 cost of goods sold ÷ $9,000 average inventory).
Answer (A) is incorrect. This figure uses the average of beginning inventory and purchases. Answer (B) is incorrect. This figure uses ending inventory instead of average inventory. Answer (D) is incorrect. This figure uses beginning inventory instead of average inventory.

25. Lore would use which of the following to determine the average days' sales in inventory?

	Numerator	Denominator
A.	365	Average inventory
B.	365	Inventory turnover
C.	Average inventory	Sales divided by 365
D.	Sales divided by 365	Inventory turnover

Answer (B) is correct.
REQUIRED: The formula to calculate average day's sales in inventory.
DISCUSSION: The average days' sales in inventory is calculated by dividing the number of days in the year by the inventory turnover.

17.5 Financial Statement Analysis -- Solvency, Valuation, and Comparative Analysis

26. Barr Co. has total debt of $420,000 and equity of $700,000. Barr is seeking capital to fund an expansion. Barr is planning to issue an additional $300,000 in common stock and is negotiating with a bank to borrow additional funds. The bank requires a debt-to-equity ratio of .75. What is the maximum additional amount Barr will be able to borrow?

    A. $225,000

    B. $330,000

    C. $525,000

    D. $750,000

Answer (B) is correct.
    REQUIRED: The maximum additional borrowing allowed to satisfy a specific debt-to-equity ratio.
    DISCUSSION: Barr will have $1,000,000 ($700,000 + $300,000) in total equity. The debt-to-equity restriction allows up to $750,000 ($1,000,000 × .75) in debt. Barr already has $420,000 in debt, so the additional borrowing cannot exceed $330,000 ($750,000 – $420,000).
    Answer (A) is incorrect. The amount of $225,000 results from multiplying the $300,000 of additional common stock by the debt-to-equity ratio. Answer (C) is incorrect. The amount of $525,000 equals the $700,000 of shareholders' equity times the debt-to-equity ratio. Answer (D) is incorrect. The amount of $750,000 is the total debt allowed.

27. The following data pertain to Cowl, Inc., for the year ended December 31, Year 4:

Net sales	$ 600,000
Net income	150,000
Total assets, January 1, Year 4	2,000,000
Total assets, December 31, Year 4	3,000,000

What was Cowl's rate of return on assets for Year 4?

    A. 5%

    B. 6%

    C. 20%

    D. 24%

Answer (B) is correct.
    REQUIRED: The rate of return on assets.
    DISCUSSION: Return on assets equals net income ($150,000) divided by average total assets [($2,000,000 + $3,000,000) ÷ 2 = $2,500,000], or 6%.
    Answer (A) is incorrect. A return of 5% results from using ending total assets instead of the average total assets. Answer (C) is incorrect. A return of 20% results from dividing net sales by ending total assets. Answer (D) is incorrect. A return of 24% results from using net sales rather than net income in the numerator.

28. The following is the equity section of Harbor Co.'s balance sheet at December 31:

Common stock $10 par, 100,000 shares authorized, 50,000 shares issued, of which 5,000 have been reacquired and are held in treasury	$ 450,000
Additional paid-in capital-common stock	1,100,000
Retained earnings	800,000
Subtotal	$2,350,000
Minus: treasury stock (at cost)	(150,000)
Total stockholders' equity	$2,200,000

Harbor has insignificant amounts of convertible securities, stock warrants, and stock options. What is the book value per share of Harbor's common stock?

    A. $31

    B. $44

    C. $46

    D. $49

Answer (D) is correct.
    REQUIRED: The book value per share of common stock.
    DISCUSSION: The book value per share of common stock equals net assets available to common shareholders divided by ending common shares outstanding. Net assets available to common shareholders can also be stated as total equity minus liquidation value of preferred stock. Given no preferred shares, the numerator equals total equity ($2,200,000). Thus, the book value per share of common stock is $49 [$2,200,000 equity ÷ (50,000 shares issued – 5,000 shares held in treasury)].
    Answer (A) is incorrect. The amount of $31 results from not including retained earnings in the numerator. Answer (B) is incorrect. The amount of $44 results from including treasury shares in the denominator. Answer (C) is incorrect. The amount of $46 results from measuring the treasury shares at $10 per share and including those shares in the denominator.

29. In financial statement analysis, expressing all financial statement items as a percentage of base-year amounts is called

- A. Horizontal common-size analysis.
- B. Vertical common-size analysis.
- C. Trend analysis.
- D. Ratio analysis.

Answer (A) is correct.
   REQUIRED: The term for expressing all financial statement items as a percentage of base-year amounts.
   DISCUSSION: Expressing financial statement items as percentages of corresponding base-year figures is a horizontal form of common-size (percentage) analysis that is useful for evaluating trends. The base amount is assigned the value of 100%, and the amounts for other years are denominated in percentages compared to the base year.
   Answer (B) is incorrect. Vertical common-size (percentage) analysis presents figures for a single year expressed as percentages of a base amount on the balance sheet (e.g., total assets) and on the income statement (e.g., sales). Answer (C) is incorrect. The term "trend analysis" is most often applied to the quantitative techniques used in forecasting to fit a curve to given data. Answer (D) is incorrect. It is a general term.

30. In assessing the financial prospects for a firm, financial analysts use various techniques. Which of the following is an example of vertical common-size analysis?

- A. An assessment of the relative stability of a firm's level of vertical integration.
- B. A comparison in financial ratio form between two or more firms in the same industry.
- C. A statement that current advertising expense is 2% greater than in the prior year.
- D. A statement that current advertising expense is 2% of sales.

Answer (D) is correct.
   REQUIRED: The example of vertical common-size analysis.
   DISCUSSION: Vertical common-size analysis compares the components within a set of financial statements. A base amount is assigned a value of 100%. For example, total assets on a common-size balance sheet and net sales on a common-size income statement are valued at 100%. Common-size statements permit evaluation of the efficiency of various aspects of operations. An analyst who states that advertising expense is 2% of sales is using vertical common-size analysis.
   Answer (A) is incorrect. Vertical integration occurs when a corporation owns one or more of its suppliers or customers. Answer (B) is incorrect. Vertical common-size analysis restates financial statement amounts as percentages. Answer (C) is incorrect. A statement that advertising expense is 2% greater than in the previous year results from horizontal analysis.

Use the additional questions in Gleim **CPA Test Prep Online** to create Test Sessions that emulate Prometric!

17.6 PRACTICE SIMULATION

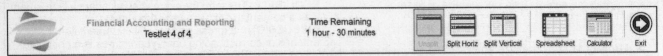

Financial Accounting and Reporting	Time Remaining	Unsplit Split Horiz Split Vertical Spreadsheet Calculator Exit
Testlet 4 of 4	1 hour - 30 minutes	

DIRECTIONS

Note: If you believe you have encountered a software malfunction, report it to the test center staff immediately.

Navigation

To navigate from task to task, use the controls at the bottom of the screen. Click on the **Next** button to advance to the next task, or the **Previous** button to go to the previous task. To go directly to any task, click on its number.

If you would like a reminder to revisit a task, or want to indicate that you are finished with it, click on the reminder flag below the task number. To clear the flag, click on it again. Reminder flags are for your use only – they do not contribute to your score.

Tabs

In this part of the examination, you will be asked to complete various tasks. Every task has one or more **Work Tabs**. Some tasks have one or more **Information Tabs**, others may have none. Every task has a **Help** tab.

If a task has **Information Tabs**, you may use the information in them to complete your responses in the **Work Tabs**.

Work tab   Information tab   Help tab

Work Tabs:
- **Work Tabs** are identified with a pencil icon. This is where your responses are expected.
- Each task has one or more **Work Tabs**.
- **Work Tabs** contain directions for completing the task – be sure to read these directions carefully.
- The **Work Tab** name in the example above is for illustration only – yours will differ.
- You must complete all of the **Work Tabs** in each task to receive full credit.

Information Tabs:
- The Authoritative Literature will be provided in all tasks in the AUD, FAR, and REG sections for your reference.
- Your simulation may have one or more additional **Information Tabs**. Like the Authoritative Literature tabs, **Information Tabs** do not have a pencil icon.
- If your task has additional **Information Tabs**, go through each to familiarize yourself with the task content.

Help Tab:
- The **Help Tab** provides assistance with the exam software that is used in this task. For example, if the task is to compose a memorandum, **Help** will provide information about the word processor.

The Toolbar

The toolbar at the top of the screen shows the amount of time remaining for you to complete the tasks. In addition, the following tools are available. Note that only the **Exit** button is displayed when Directions are visible - the others will appear when you begin the tasks.

Click on these buttons to split or unsplit the screen. You can split the screen vertically or horizontally.

Click on this button to display the calculator; click on it again to hide the calculator. To move the calculator, click on the calculator title bar and drag the calculator to the desired location.

Click on this button to use the spreadsheet; click on it again to hide the spreadsheet. To move the spreadsheet, click on the the spreadsheet title bar and drag the spreadsheet to the desired location.

Click on this button to go on to the next part of the examination. You must complete all of the tasks to receive full credit. Once you click on **Exit** and confirm the action, you will NOT be able to return to this testlet.

Analysis | Authoritative Literature | Help

Parker, Inc., is consistently profitable. Parker's normal financial statement relationships are as follows:

I.	Current ratio	3 to 1
II.	Inventory turnover	4 times
III.	Total debt-total assets ratio	0.5 to 1

Select from the list provided to indicate whether each Year 8 transaction or event increased, decreased, or had no effect on each of the Year 8 ratios given. Each choice may be used once, more than once, or not at all.

Transaction	I.	II.	III.
1. Parker issued a stock dividend.			
2. Parker declared, but did not pay, a cash dividend.			
3. Customers returned invoiced goods for which they had not paid.			
4. Accounts payable were paid on December 31, Year 8.			
5. Parker recorded both a receivable from an insurance company and a loss from fire damage to a factory building.			
6. Early in Year 8, Parker increased the selling price of one of its products that had a demand in excess of capacity. The number of units sold and costs incurred in Year 7 and Year 8 were the same.			

Choices
A) Increase
B) Decrease
C) No effect

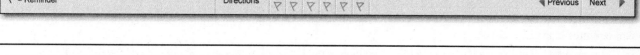

Monetary and Nonmonetary Items | Authoritative Literature | Help

Indicate by checking the appropriate box whether each item is monetary or nonmonetary.

Item	Monetary	Nonmonetary
1. Cash		
2. Patent		
3. Accumulated depreciation		
4. Accounts receivable		
5. Trademark		
6. Accounts payable		
7. Demand bank deposits		
8. Allowance for doubtful accounts		
9. Noncontrolling interest from the consolidated entity's perspective		
10. Deferred revenue from sale of goods		

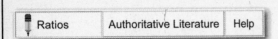

Select from the list provided to indicate whether each ratio below is a liquidity ratio, activity ratio, leverage ratio, or profitability ratio. Each choice may be used once, more than once, or not at all.

Ratio	Answer
1. Current ratio	
2. Inventory turnover ratio	
3. Asset turnover	
4. Quick ratio	
5. Times-interest-earned ratio	
6. Accounts receivable turnover	
7. Profit margin on sales	

Choices
A) Liquidity ratio
B) Activity ratio
C) Leverage ratio
D) Profitability ratio

Jay Co.'s Year 1 consolidated financial statements include two wholly owned subsidiaries, Jay Co. of Australia (Jay A) and Jay Co. of France (Jay F). The currency of the primary economic environment in which Jay A operates is the U.S. dollar, but its books are kept in Australian dollars. The currency of the primary economic environment in which Jay F operates is the euro, the currency in which it keeps its books. The currency of the primary economic environment in which Jay Co. operates is the U.S. dollar.

Select from the list provided the correct response to each of the following statements about consolidated reporting by Jay Co. Each choice may be used once, more than once, or not at all.

Statement	Answer
1. The Australian dollar is this type of currency in relation to Jay A.	
2. A current exchange rate is used for this adjustment to the U.S. dollar from the euro.	
3. If an enterprise consists of separate entities operating in different currency environments, their financial statements must be presented in this manner.	
4. Items stated in different currencies must be restated into this currency.	
5. If Jay F's books are not kept in euros, amounts must be remeasured using this method.	
6. The process described in 5. can result in this effect.	
7. Describes the environment in which the reporting entity operates.	

Choices
A) Reporting currency
B) Functional currency
C) Local currency
D) Translation
E) Consolidated
F) Economic indicators
G) Historical rate
H) Exchange rate
I) Temporal
J) Current
K) Transaction gain or loss

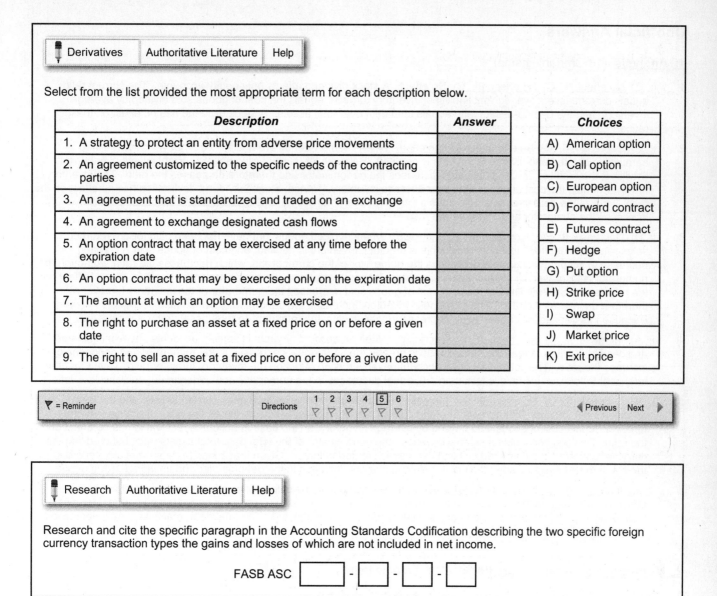

Select from the list provided the most appropriate term for each description below.

Description	Answer
1. A strategy to protect an entity from adverse price movements	
2. An agreement customized to the specific needs of the contracting parties	
3. An agreement that is standardized and traded on an exchange	
4. An agreement to exchange designated cash flows	
5. An option contract that may be exercised at any time before the expiration date	
6. An option contract that may be exercised only on the expiration date	
7. The amount at which an option may be exercised	
8. The right to purchase an asset at a fixed price on or before a given date	
9. The right to sell an asset at a fixed price on or before a given date	

Choices

- A) American option
- B) Call option
- C) European option
- D) Forward contract
- E) Futures contract
- F) Hedge
- G) Put option
- H) Strike price
- I) Swap
- J) Market price
- K) Exit price

Research and cite the specific paragraph in the Accounting Standards Codification describing the two specific foreign currency transaction types the gains and losses of which are not included in net income.

FASB ASC ☐ - ☐ - ☐ - ☐

Unofficial Answers

1. Analysis (18 Gradable Items)

1. <u>I: C) No effect; II: C) No effect; III: C) No effect.</u> A stock dividend affects only equity accounts. The current ratio equals current assets over current liabilities, inventory turnover equals the cost of goods sold divided by average inventory, and the debt-to-assets ratio equals total debt over total assets. A stock dividend has no effect on these ratios.

2. <u>I: B) Decrease; II: C) No effect; III: A) Increase.</u> When cash dividends are declared but not yet paid, retained earnings is debited and dividends payable is credited. Because the current ratio equals current assets over current liabilities, the credit to dividends payable increases the denominator and therefore decreases the ratio. The inventory turnover equals the cost of goods sold over average inventory. Hence, a cash dividend declaration has no effect on the ratio. Finally, the debt-to-assets ratio equals total debt over total assets, and an increase in dividends payable increases the numerator and therefore the ratio.

3. <u>I: B) Decrease; II: B) Decrease; III: A) Increase.</u> When invoiced goods that have not been paid for are returned, sales returns is debited, accounts receivable is credited, inventory is debited, and cost of goods sold is credited. A decrease in accounts receivable decreases the numerator of the current ratio, which decreases the ratio. Although the numerator is increased by the increase in inventory (at cost), assuming the goods are sold at a profit, the net effect on the ratio is a decrease. The decrease in cost of goods sold decreases the numerator of the inventory turnover ratio and therefore decreases the ratio. The increase in inventory increases the denominator, which also decreases the ratio. Because this transaction caused a net decrease in total assets, the total-debt-to-total-assets ratio is increased.

4. <u>I: A) Increase; II: C) No effect; III: B) Decrease.</u> When an account payable is settled, accounts payable is debited and cash is credited. When the current ratio is greater than 1.0, equal decreases in the numerator and denominator increase the ratio. The settlement of an account payable has no effect on the inventory turnover ratio. Given that the total debt to total assets ratio is less than 1.0, equal decreases in the numerator and denominator decrease the ratio.

5. <u>I: A) Increase; II: C) No effect; III: A) Increase.</u> Recording a receivable increases current assets, and the loss decreases net income. The numerator of the current ratio increases, which increases the ratio. Because inventory turnover equals cost of goods sold divided by average inventory, an increase in accounts receivable has no effect on the ratio. Debiting accounts receivable increases the denominator of the total debt-total assets ratio, but crediting the carrying amount of the damaged building decreases the denominator. Given that a loss (a debit) was also recorded, the credit must have exceeded the debit, resulting in a net decrease in the denominator and an increase in the ratio.

6. <u>I: A) Increase; II: C) No effect; III: B) Decrease.</u> An increase in the selling price when sales and costs remain constant increases cash and receivables. Accordingly, the current ratio increases because the numerator increases. Cost of goods sold remains constant and inventory turnover is unaffected. The total debt-total assets ratio decreases because total assets increases.

2. Monetary and Nonmonetary Items (10 Gradable Items)

1. <u>Monetary.</u> A monetary asset is either cash or a claim to receive cash.

2. <u>Nonmonetary.</u> Nonmonetary assets are held primarily for resale or to provide services for the business. They also may be claims to cash that change in relationship to future prices of specific goods and services. A third category consists of residual rights (e.g., goodwill or common stock not accounted for using the equity method). Examples are intellectual property (such as patents, copyrights, and trademarks); most inventories; and property, plant, and equipment (including accumulated depreciation).

3. <u>Nonmonetary.</u> Nonmonetary assets are held primarily for resale or to provide services for the business. They also may be claims to cash that change in relationship to future prices of specific goods and services. A third category consists of residual rights (e.g., goodwill or common stock not accounted for using the equity method). Examples are intellectual property (such as patents, copyrights, and trademarks); most inventories; and property, plant, and equipment (including accumulated depreciation).

4. <u>Monetary.</u> A monetary asset is either cash or a claim to receive cash. The amount is fixed or determinable without regard to future prices of specific goods or services.

5. <u>Nonmonetary.</u> Nonmonetary assets are held primarily for resale or to provide services for the business. They also may be claims to cash that change in relationship to future prices of specific goods and services. A third category consists of residual rights (e.g., goodwill or common stock not accounted for using the equity method). Examples are intellectual property (such as patents, copyrights, and trademarks); most inventories; and property, plant, and equipment (including accumulated depreciation).

6. <u>Monetary.</u> A monetary liability is an obligation to pay cash. The amount is fixed or determinable without regard to future prices of specific goods and services. Examples are accounts and notes payable, bonds payable, and various accrued payables.

7. <u>Monetary</u>. A monetary asset is either cash or a claim to receive cash. The amount is fixed or determinable without regard to future prices of specific goods or services.

8. <u>Monetary</u>. A monetary asset is either cash or a claim to receive cash. The amount is fixed or determinable without regard to future prices of specific goods or services. Examples are accounts and notes receivable (including allowance accounts), bond investments, long-term receivables, and demand bank deposits.

9. <u>Nonmonetary</u>. Nonmonetary liabilities are obligations to provide goods or services in amounts that are fixed or determinable without regard to price changes. They also may be obligations to pay cash amounts dependent on future prices of specific goods or services. From the consolidated entity's perspective, the noncontrolling interest is a residual that varies with earnings of the subsidiary, dividends, and other transactions affecting equity.

10. <u>Nonmonetary</u>. Nonmonetary liabilities are obligations to provide goods or services in amounts that are fixed or determinable without regard to price changes. They also may be obligations to pay cash amounts dependent on future prices of specific goods or services. An example is deferred revenue if the obligation is to provide goods or services.

3. Ratios (7 Gradable Items)

1. <u>A) Liquidity ratio.</u> The current ratio equals current assets divided by current liabilities. Liquidity (solvency) ratios measure the short-term viability of the business, i.e., the firm's ability to continue in the short term by paying its obligations.

2. <u>B) Activity ratio.</u> Inventory turnover equals cost of sales divided by average inventory. Activity ratios measure the entity's ability to generate revenue and income.

3. <u>B) Activity ratio.</u> Asset turnover equals net revenue divided by average total assets. Activity ratios measure the entity's ability to generate revenue and income.

4. <u>A) Liquidity ratio.</u> The acid test or quick ratio equals the quick assets (cash + net receivables + marketable securities) divided by current liabilities. Liquidity (solvency) ratios measure an entity's ability to continue in the short term by paying its obligations.

5. <u>C) Leverage ratio.</u> The times-interest-earned ratio equals the sum of net income, interest expense, and income tax expense, divided by interest expense. Leverage ratios measure an entity's use of debt to finance assets and operations.

6. <u>B) Activity ratio.</u> Accounts receivable turnover equals net credit sales divided by average accounts receivable. Activity ratios measure an entity's ability to generate revenue and income.

7. <u>D) Profitability ratio.</u> The profit margin on sales equals net income divided by sales. Profitability ratios measure income on a relative basis.

4. Foreign Currency (7 Gradable Items)

1. <u>C) Local currency.</u> The functional currency is the currency of the primary economic environment in which the entity operates. The U.S. dollar is the functional currency of the Australian subsidiary. The Australian dollar is its local currency.

2. <u>D) Translation.</u> Translation is the process of expressing amounts stated in the functional currency as amounts stated in the reporting currency. The euro is Jay F's functional currency. Thus, restating euro-based amounts in U.S. dollars is foreign currency translation.

3. <u>E) Consolidated.</u> If an enterprise consists of separate entities operating in different currency environments, their financial statements must be consolidated. A consolidated entity may consist of separate entities operating in different economic and currency environments.

4. <u>A) Reporting currency.</u> Consolidated financial statements must be stated in the reporting currency of the parent.

5. <u>I) Temporal.</u> If the books of a foreign entity are maintained in a currency not the functional currency (euro), these foreign currency amounts must be remeasured into the functional currency using the temporal method.

6. <u>K) Transaction gain or loss.</u> Remeasurement expresses amounts stated in another currency as amounts stated in the functional currency. This process results in gains and losses included in earnings.

7. <u>F) Economic indicators.</u> The functional currency is the currency of the primary economic environment in which the entity operates. The economic indicators are characteristic of that environment.

5. Derivatives (9 Gradable Items)

1. <u>F) Hedge.</u> Hedging is a defensive strategy designed to protect an entity against the risk of adverse price or interest-rate movements on certain of its assets, liabilities, or anticipated transactions.

2. <u>D) Forward contract.</u> A forward contract is a typical contract entered into between two parties who exchange consideration for a promise to perform.

3. <u>E) Futures contract.</u> Futures contracts are convenient hedging tools because they are not individually negotiated. They are standardized and sold on an exchange.

4. <u>I) Swap.</u> Swaps are agreements to exchange designated cash flows.

5. <u>A) American option.</u> An American option is an option contract that can be exercised at any time on or before the expiration date.

6. <u>C) European option.</u> A European option is an option contract that can be exercised only on the expiration date.

7. <u>H) Strike price.</u> Also called the exercise price, this is the price at which the holder of an option can demand to buy (if a call) or sell (if a put) the underlying.

8. <u>B) Call option.</u> A call option gives the holder the right to purchase an item at a fixed price on or before the expiration date.

9. <u>G) Put option.</u> A put option gives the holder the right to sell an item at a fixed price on or before the expiration date.

6. Research (1 Gradable Item)

Answer: FASB ASC 830-20-35-3

Transaction Gains and Losses to Be Excluded from Net Income

830-20-35-3 Gains and losses on the following foreign currency transactions shall not be included in determining net income but shall be reported in the same manner as translation adjustments:

   a. Foreign currency transactions that are designated as, and are effective as, economic hedges of a net investment in a foreign entity, commencing as of the designation date (see Subtopic 815-35)

   b. Intra-entity foreign currency transactions that are of a long-term-investment nature (that is, settlement is not planned or anticipated in the foreseeable future), when the entities to the transaction are consolidated, combined, or accounted for by the equity method in the reporting entity's financial statements.

Gleim Simulation Grading

Task	Correct Responses		Gradable Items		Score per Task
1	_____	÷	18	=	_____
2	_____	÷	10	=	_____
3	_____	÷	7	=	_____
4	_____	÷	7	=	_____
5	_____	÷	9	=	_____
Research	_____	÷	1	=	_____
			Total of Scores per Task		_____
	÷		Total Number of Tasks		6
			Total Score		_____%

Use **CPA Gleim Online** and **Simulation Wizard** to practice more task-based simulations in a realistic environment.

STUDY UNIT EIGHTEEN
GOVERNMENTAL ACCOUNTING

(24 pages of outline)

18.1	Fund Accounting Concepts and Reporting	643
18.2	Budgetary Accounting and Encumbrances	649
18.3	Governmental Sources of Financing	654
18.4	Characteristic Transactions of Governmental Entities	661
18.5	Practice Simulation	678

Study Units 18 and 19 relate to the governmental entities group in the Content Specification Outlines. Study Unit 18 is an overview of (1) the concepts underlying state and local governmental accounting and reporting, (2) budgetary accounting in government, and (3) the recognition rules and journal entries for governmental financing.

18.1 FUND ACCOUNTING CONCEPTS AND REPORTING

Background

In 1984, the Financial Accounting Foundation (FAF), the independent body that oversees the FASB, created the GASB to establish GAAP for state and local governments in the U.S. On November 30, 1989, the trustees of the FAF reaffirmed the GASB as the standard setter for state and local governments. Thus, after November 30, 1989, FASB pronouncements are not effective for state and local governments unless adopted by the GASB.

1. **Standard-Setting for Governmental Accounting**

   a. The **Governmental Accounting Standards Board (GASB)**, established in 1984, is now the primary standard setter for state and local governmental entities.

   b. The **conceptual framework** for state and local governments, including the objectives of financial reporting, was covered in Study Unit 1, Subunit 4.

   c. The following (in descending order of authority) is the GASB's **hierarchy** of accounting principles:

Category (a): Officially established (Most authoritative)	GASB Statements and Interpretations	
Category (b):	GASB Technical Bulletins	Applicable AICPA Industry Audit and Accounting Guides and Statements of Position Cleared by the GASB
Category (c):	Applicable AICPA Practice Bulletins Cleared by the GASB	Consensus Positions of an Accounting Group Organized by the GASB
Category (d):	GASB Implementation Guides ("Qs and As")	Widely Recognized and Prevalent Practices

   1) The entity also may consider **other accounting literature** if the guidance in categories (a)-(d) does not apply. Examples are GASB Concepts Statements and the AICPA pronouncements in (b)-(d) not cleared by the GASB.

2. **Fund Accounting**

   a. The diversity of governmental activities and the need for legal compliance require the use of more than one accounting entity. Thus, independent, distinct fiscal and accounting entities called funds are established.

b. A **fund** is a fiscal and accounting entity with a self-balancing set of accounts. Items in a fund are segregated because they relate to specific activities or certain objectives that are subject to special regulations or limitations. A fund records

1) Financial resources (including cash),
2) Deferred outflows of resources,
3) Liabilities,
4) Deferred inflows of resources,
5) Residual equities or balances, and
6) Changes in them.

c. A fund accounting system must present fairly in **conformity with GAAP** and with full disclosure the financial position and results of operations of the funds. Also, it must determine and demonstrate **compliance** with finance-related legal and contractual provisions.

1) No more than the number of funds required by law and efficient financial administration should be created.

3. **Funds Used in Governmental Accounting**

a. **Governmental funds** account for the nonbusiness activities of a government and its current, expendable, resources (most often **taxes**).

1) The **general fund** accounts for all financial resources except those required to be accounted for in another fund. Only one general fund may be reported.

2) **Special revenue funds** account for **restricted or committed proceeds** of specific revenue sources. Expenditure must be for a specified purpose (but not debt service or a capital project). Thus, the basis of the fund is a substantial inflow from restricted or committed revenue sources.

   a) For example, a government may have a special revenue fund for operation of its municipal auditorium, its zoo, or road maintenance.

   b) Donations provided by benefactors for programs to be administered by the government also are accounted for in special revenue funds.

   c) A special revenue fund is **not** used for the resources of a trust benefiting specific individuals, private organizations, or other governments.

3) **Capital projects funds** account for financial resources **restricted, committed, or assigned** to be expended for capital purposes.

   a) These resources include general obligation bond proceeds dedicated to the construction of major capital facilities, such as schools, bridges, or tunnels.

   b) The capital assets themselves are not accounted for in these funds.

   c) Other capital facilities may be financed through proprietary funds or certain trust funds.

4) **Debt service funds** account for resources **restricted, committed, or assigned** to paying principal and interest. But these funds do not account for the debt itself.

   a) They also account for resources being accumulated for future principal and interest payments.

   b) A debt service fund is used if it is required by law.

5) **Permanent funds** account for resources that are **restricted** to the use of earnings (not principal) for the benefit of the government or its citizens. An example is a perpetual-care fund for a public cemetery.

   a) Private-purpose trust funds are **not** permanent funds.

    b. **Proprietary funds** account for the **business-type activities** of a government. They serve defined customer groups and are generally financed through **fees**.

        1) **Enterprise funds** account for activities that benefit outside parties who are willing to pay for them, such as municipal pools, parking garages, and utilities. They are the funds that most closely resemble private businesses.

        2) **Internal service funds** account for activities performed primarily for the benefit of other agencies, such as a centralized information technology department or motor pool.

    c. **Fiduciary funds** account for resources held by the government in trust or as an agent for specific individuals, private organizations, or other governments. They cannot be used for the reporting entity's purposes.

        1) **Pension (and other employee benefit) trust funds** account for employee benefit programs.

        2) **Investment trust funds** account for resources held for investment on behalf of other governments in an investment pool.

        3) **Private-purpose trust funds** account for all other trust arrangements that benefit individuals, private organizations, or other governments.

        4) **Agency funds** account for resources held temporarily in a purely custodial capacity, such as tolls that will be paid to a private business.

4. **Accountability Objective of Governmental Reporting**

    a. **"Accountability is the paramount objective of governmental financial reporting – the objective from which all other financial reporting objectives flow."**

        1) **Fiscal accountability** is "the responsibility of governments to justify that their actions in the current period have complied with public decisions concerning the raising and spending of public moneys in the **short term**."

        2) **Operational accountability** is "governments' responsibility to report the extent to which they have met their accounting objectives **efficiently and effectively**, using all resources available for that purpose, and whether they can continue to meet their objectives for the **foreseeable future**."

    b. Governmental reporting traditionally has emphasized fiscal accountability for governmental activities and operational accountability for business-type activities and fiduciary funds.

        1) Reporting for governments was fundamentally changed by the requirement that they present both fund and government-wide financial statements.

            a) The financial statements of **governmental funds** emphasize fiscal accountability.

            b) The financial statements of **proprietary funds** and **fiduciary funds** provide information about their operational accountability.

            c) **Government-wide financial statements** provide information about the operational accountability of the **governmental activities** and **business-type activities** of the government as a whole. They are the

                i) Statement of net position and the
                ii) Statement of activities.

    c. **Interperiod equity** is an important component of accountability. **Financial resources** received during a period should suffice to pay for the services provided during that period. Moreover, **debt** should be repaid during the probable period of usefulness of the assets acquired.

        1) Thus, governmental reporting should help users assess whether **future taxpayers** must pay for services already provided.

      2)   Governmental financial reporting also should help users (e.g., citizens and legislative and oversight bodies) to make **economic, political, and social decisions**.

          a)   For example, revenue forecasts may help advocates for or opponents of spending for education or transportation.

5.   **Current Financial Resources Measurement Focus and Modified Accrual Accounting**

    a.   The **measurement focus** of a set of financial statements is what is being measured or tracked by the information provided.

    b.   The **basis of accounting** is the timing of the recognition in the financial records of economic events or transactions.

    c.   The current financial resources measurement focus and the modified accrual basis of accounting are used to report the **governmental fund** financial statements.

      1)   This approach emphasizes **short-term** fiscal accountability for expendable available financial resources. The reporting elements are sources, uses, and balances of current financial resources.

      2)   Under the **modified accrual basis** of accounting, **revenue** or another increase in financial resources (such as bond issue proceeds) is recognized when it is **susceptible to accrual**.

          a)   Revenue is accrued when it is measurable and available to finance expenditures of the current period.

              i)   Available means collectible within the current period or "soon enough thereafter" to be used to pay liabilities of the current period. Ordinarily, material revenues that are otherwise not recorded until received are accrued if receipt is delayed beyond the normal time.

             ii)   For **property tax purposes**, the phrase "soon enough thereafter" means not more than 60 days after the end of the year. But in unusual cases, a longer period may be justified. The government should disclose the period used and the justification for it.

             iii)   Property taxes are **measurable** when assessed property values can be multiplied by the tax rate to obtain the total tax to be levied.

          b)   Operating **expenditures** normally are made when goods or services are acquired.

              i)   Thus, expenditures are usually measurable and should be recognized when the related liability is incurred.

          c)   However, expenditures for **principal and interest** on **general long-term debt** are usually recognized only when those amounts are due.

              i)   The amount of an expenditure is what is normally paid with expendable available financial resources.

6.   **Economic Resources Measurement Focus and Accrual Accounting**

    a.   The economic resources measurement focus and the accrual basis of accounting are used to report the **government-wide, proprietary fund**, and **fiduciary fund** financial statements.

      1)   This approach provides longer-term operational accountability information about economic activity. It measures revenues and expenses in the same way as in for-profit accounting but without necessarily emphasizing net income.

          a)   Instead, the emphasis is on a longer-range measure of revenues earned or levied (and accrued immediately if measurable).

      2)   Furthermore, the economic resources model focuses on **cost of services**.

b. Under the **accrual basis** of accounting, most economic transactions and other events that can be measured are recognized without regard to cash flows. Moreover, an operating expense is recognized when goods or services are used or consumed instead of an expenditure when they are acquired. Acquired but unused goods and services are treated as assets.

    1) Thus, revenues, expenses, gains, losses, assets, and liabilities that arise from **exchange or exchange-like transactions** are accrued when the exchange occurs.

    2) Recognition of **nonexchange transactions** is described in Subunit 18.3.

c. The **cash basis** is not used in governmental accounting except for miscellaneous cash items that are not measurable until cash is received or paid.

d. **Transfers** are recognized in all affected funds when the interfund receivable and payable arise.

7. **Deferred Outflows and Inflows of Resources**

a. Several items that were previously treated as assets and liabilities for non-governmental entities must be reported separately in a statement of financial position for a governmental entity as deferred outflows and inflows of resources.

    1) A **deferred outflow of resources** is a consumption of net assets by the government that is applicable to a future reporting period.

    2) A **deferred inflow of resources** is an acquisition of net assets by the government that is applicable to a future reporting period.

b. Classification as a deferred outflow of resources or a deferred inflow of resources is limited to those items specifically identified in the authoritative literature. The following transactions generally qualify for this treatment:

    1) Service Concession Arrangements (SCA)

        a) An SCA is a partnership in which another entity (private or governmental) is allowed to build, operate, or collect user fees from a public asset, such as a sports arena or toll road.

    2) Derivative Transactions

    3) Refundings of Debt

        a) Refundings of debt involve using the proceeds from new debt to retire old debt. The difference between the reacquisition price and the net carrying amount of the old debt should be reported either as a deferred outflow or deferred inflow and included in interest expense over the shorter of the remaining life of the old debt or the life of the new debt.

    4) Imposed Nonexchange Revenue Transactions

    5) Government-Mandated Nonexchange Transactions and Voluntary Nonexchange Transactions

    6) Sales and Intraentity Transfers of Future Revenues

    7) Certain Leases

        a) Any gain (loss) recognized in a sale-leaseback transaction must be treated as a deferred inflow (outflow) of resources and recognized in a systematic and rational manner over the lease term.

    8) Assets Associated with Unavailable Revenues

8. **General Capital Assets**

a. General capital assets are all capital assets **not** reported in the **proprietary funds** or the **fiduciary funds**. Thus, they usually result from expenditure of governmental fund financial resources.

b. They are reported at **historical cost**, including ancillary charges (freight-in, site preparation, etc.), only in the **governmental activities** column of the government-wide statement of net position.

　　1) In **governmental funds**, the full cost of a capital asset is debited as an expenditure when acquired in accordance with the current financial resources measurement focus.

c. **Donated capital assets** are reported at **fair value** (plus ancillary charges).

9. **General Long-Term Liabilities**

a. General long-term liabilities are all **unmatured long-term liabilities not** directly related to and expected to be paid from proprietary funds and fiduciary funds.

　　1) They should be reported only in the **governmental activities** column of the government-wide statement of net position.

b. General long-term liabilities include

　　1) The **unmatured principal** amounts of general obligation debt (such as bonds, warrants, and notes);

　　2) Lease-purchase agreements and other commitments not recorded as current liabilities in governmental funds; and

　　3) The noncurrent portions of liabilities for

　　　　a) Capital leases,
　　　　b) Operating leases with scheduled rent increases,
　　　　c) Compensated absences,
　　　　d) Claims and judgments,
　　　　e) Pensions,
　　　　f) Special termination benefits, and
　　　　g) Landfill closure and postclosure care.

10. **Accounting for Capital Assets and Long-Term Liabilities in Other Fund Types**

a. In **proprietary funds**, the measurement focus is on economic resources. Capital assets and long-term liabilities specifically related to proprietary fund activities are accounted for in the same manner as in a for-profit business.

　　1) They are reported in those funds and in the government-wide statements.

b. **Fiduciary funds** contain resources held in a trustee or custodial capacity for other governments, private organizations, or individuals. These resources cannot be used to finance the operations of the government.

　　1) Thus, capital assets and long-term liabilities specifically related to fiduciary funds are reported in the fund financial statements but not in the government-wide statements.

11. **Summary**

	Governmental Funds Financial Statements	Proprietary Funds Financial Statements	Fiduciary Funds Financial Statements	Government-Wide Financial Statements
Measurement Focus	Current financial resources	Economic resources	Economic resources	Economic resources
Basis of Accounting	Modified accrual	Accrual	Accrual	Accrual
Capital Assets	No	Yes	Trust funds only	Yes
Long-Term Liabilities	No	Yes	Trust funds only	Yes

Stop and review! You have completed the outline for this subunit. Study multiple-choice questions 1 through 9 beginning on page 666.

18.2 BUDGETARY ACCOUNTING AND ENCUMBRANCES

1. **Budgetary Accounting**

   a. Budgetary accounting is unique to governments. A government's formal budget is an expression of **public policy**.

   b. The budget is a statement of financial intent indicating how the government plans to raise revenue and expend its resources.

      1) For most governments, the budget is **legally enforceable** against the financial managers. By law, they cannot exceed the budget without a formally approved budget amendment.

      2) The budget provides a basis for **evaluating performance**. Actual expenditures and expenses are compared with amounts budgeted for each period.

2. **Budget Integration**

   a. Because the formally adopted budget has legal implications, most governments integrate their budgets into the accounting system. This integration should be done for the following:

      1) The general fund
      2) Special revenue funds
      3) Other governmental funds with numerous transactions

   b. Integration is usually unnecessary in **debt service funds**. Transactions are few, and contractual provisions prescribe receipts and expenditures.

   c. Some degree of budgetary integration may be needed in a **capital projects fund** when many projects are being accounted for in the fund or work is being done by the government itself.

   d. Because flexible rather than fixed budgets are usually prepared for **proprietary funds**, integration of fixed budgetary accounts is normally inappropriate for these funds.

   e. Budget integration is necessary for **fiduciary funds** that are similar to special revenue funds. It is not necessary for agency funds or for fiduciary funds that are budgeted similarly to proprietary funds.

   f. **Common terminology and classifications** must be used consistently throughout the budget, the accounts, and the financial reports of each fund.

      1) The budget(s) should include every fund of the government.
      2) The **basis of accounting** for the budget preferably should correspond to the basis of accounting used by the fund for which the budget is being prepared.
      3) However, if the law requires another basis, governments often keep supplemental records that permit reporting in accordance with GAAP.

3. **Budgetary Accounts**

   a. Despite being formally integrated into the accounting system, the budgetary amounts are **not reported** in the financial statements. The principal accounts used in the entry to record the annual budget are described below:

      1) **Estimated revenues** is an **anticipatory asset** (a debit).

         a) It records the amount expected to be collected from a government's main sources of revenue, such as taxes, fees, and fines.

      2) **Estimated other financing sources** is another **anticipatory asset** that includes the sources of financing other than revenues.

         a) Examples are the face amount of long-term debt, issuance premium, and interfund transfers.

3) **Estimated other financing uses** is an **anticipatory liability** (a credit) used to record an expected flow of resources to another fund.

   a) Issuance discount and interfund transfers for debt service are common examples.

4) **Appropriations** is an **anticipatory liability** recording the total authorized to be spent by the government for the fiscal period.

   a) Unless a balanced budget or deficit is planned, estimated revenues exceeds appropriations. This allows for some flexibility if revenues prove to be lower, or expenditures prove to be higher, than expected.

5) **Fund balance** is a real account. It is the difference (fund equity) between the assets (plus deferred outflows of resources) and liabilities (plus deferred inflows of resources) of a **governmental fund**.

   a) Some accountants prefer to use **budgetary fund balance**, a nominal account, to record the budgeted change in fund equity for the year.

EXAMPLE

A state adopts its budget for the year. The following entries record the budget for the general fund and one of the special revenue funds:

General fund:
Estimated revenues -- sales taxes	$2,400,000,000	
Estimated other financing sources -- face amount of bonds	400,000,000	
Appropriations		$2,100,000,000
Estimated other financing uses -- transfer to debt service fund		600,000,000
Budgetary fund balance		100,000,000

Special revenue fund -- highway maintenance:
Estimated revenues -- vehicle license fees	$130,000,000	
Appropriations -- salaries		$40,000,000
Appropriations -- wages		20,000,000
Appropriations -- road equipment		40,000,000
Appropriations -- construction materials		20,000,000
Budgetary fund balance		10,000,000

---

6) As conditions change during the year, a portion of the fund balance may be moved to appropriations. This is the formal acknowledgment in the budget of new circumstances.

EXAMPLE

The state discovers that it has underestimated the amount of materials needed to maintain its roads. The authorization to spend more on materials must be recognized in the budget.

Special revenue fund -- highway maintenance:
Budgetary fund balance	$5,000,000	
Appropriations -- construction materials		$5,000,000

---

7) In **proprietary-fund accounting**, budget integration is rare. Thus, the classifications above are not used. Instead, restricted net position is reported on the fund balance sheet.

4. **Classification of Fund Balance**

  a. Fund balance is **classified** according to the limits on the specific purposes for which resources may be spent. The following is the hierarchy of classifications:

1) **Nonspendable.** These amounts (a) are in a form (e.g., inventory, prepayments, or long-term loans) that is not spendable or (b) must be kept intact (e.g., the principal of a permanent fund).

   a) But if the proceeds of such an item are restricted, committed, or assigned, they are presented in one of those classifications.

2) **Restricted.** These amounts may be spent only for specific purposes established by (a) a constitutional mandate, (b) enabling legislation, or (c) an external provider.

3) **Committed.** These amounts may be spent only for specific purposes established by a formal act of the entity's highest decision maker.

   a) This decision maker may redirect the resources by following the necessary due process procedures.

4) **Assigned.** These remaining amounts are not properly classifiable as nonspendable, restricted, or committed in a governmental fund other than the general fund.

   a) In the **general fund**, assigned fund balance includes amounts to be used for a specific purpose that are not restricted or committed.

   b) Expenditure is limited only by the entity's **intent** to use such amounts for specific purposes.

   c) An example of an assignment is an **appropriation** of fund balance to offset a budget deficit expected in the next year.

      i) The amount should equal no more than the excess of expected expenditures over expected revenues.

   d) An assignment should **not** create a deficit in fund balance.

5) **Unassigned.** The **general fund** is the only fund that reports a positive balance (the sum of the amounts not classified elsewhere).

   a) In other governmental funds, this classification is used only for a deficit balance.

EXAMPLE

City of Hobbiton
General Fund
Balance Sheet
December 31, 2012

Assets	$X,XXX,XXX
Deferred outflows of resources	X,XXX,XXX
Total assets and deferred outflows of resources	$X,XXX,XXX
Liabilities	$X,XXX,XXX
Deferred inflows of resources	X,XXX,XXX
Fund balance	
Nonspendable:	
Inventory	XX,XXX
Prepayments	XX,XXX
Principal of permanent fund	XXX,XXX
Restricted:	
Federal social services mandate	XXX,XXX
Committed	XXX,XXX
Assigned	XXX,XXX
Unassigned	X,XXX,XXX
Total fund balance	$X,XXX,XXX
Total liabilities, deferred inflows of resources, and fund balance	$X,XXX,XXX

5. **Encumbrances**

    a.   Encumbrance accounting may be used only for internal purposes.

    b.   A government makes a commitment to spend resources when a contract is signed or a purchase order is approved. The amount then may be formally recorded as an **encumbrance**.

        1)   By contrast, a **for-profit** entity does not accrue a payable until the goods are delivered or the service is performed.

        2)   Encumbrance accounting is used only for governmental funds, especially **general and special revenue funds**.

        3)   Significant encumbrances are disclosed in the notes.

            a)   If resources previously have been encumbered and classified as restricted, committed, or assigned, no separate display is needed in those classifications.

            b)   If an encumbered amount has not been restricted, etc., it is **not** classified as unassigned. Instead, it is included in committed or assigned fund balance.

            c)   No separate line item appears on the balance sheet for an encumbrance. The reason is that encumbering an amount does not further limit the specific purposes for which it may be used.

                i)   For example, an encumbered amount is not reported as committed for encumbrances. Rather, it is reported with other such amounts having the same purpose.

    c.   The encumbrance entry is to debit encumbrances and credit reserve for encumbrances.

EXAMPLE

The state has contracted to purchase road maintenance equipment.

    Special revenue fund -- highway maintenance:

Encumbrances	$750,000	
Reserve for encumbrances		$750,000

---

    d.   When the good is delivered or the service performed, two entries are made.

        1)   The encumbrance entry is reversed.

EXAMPLE

The state takes delivery of the equipment.

    Special revenue fund -- highway maintenance:

Reserve for encumbrances	$750,000	
Encumbrances		$750,000

---

        2)   The legal obligation to pay is recognized.

            a)   Governmental funds debit **expenditures** rather than expenses and credit **vouchers payable** rather than accounts payable.

EXAMPLE

The equipment costs less than anticipated.

    Special revenue fund -- highway maintenance:

Expenditures -- road equipment	$745,000	
Vouchers payable		$745,000

3) If the **actual cost** of the good or service is **greater** than the amount of the original encumbrance, the excess is an expenditure of the period in which it is paid.

 When testing the candidate's knowledge of encumbrance accounting, the AICPA has used questions asking for the journal entries made for the different transactions in the encumbrance process. Calculations of the amounts used in these journal entries also have been required.

6. **Year-End Closing**

a. The budgetary entries are reversed.

EXAMPLE

General fund:

Appropriations	$2,100,000,000	
Estimated other financing uses		
-- transfer to debt service fund	600,000,000	
Budgetary fund balance	100,000,000	
Estimated revenues -- sales taxes		$2,400,000,000
Estimated other financing sources -- bond proceeds		400,000,000

The mid-year amendment to the budget for construction materials is reflected in the reversal entry for the special revenue fund.

Special revenue fund -- highway maintenance:

Appropriations -- salaries	$40,000,000	
Appropriations -- wages	20,000,000	
Appropriations -- road equipment	40,000,000	
Appropriations -- construction materials	25,000,000	
Budgetary fund balance	5,000,000	
Estimated revenues -- vehicle license fees		$130,000,000

---

b. Any encumbrances are removed from the books.

1) Standard practice is for appropriations to lapse at year end.

EXAMPLE

At year end, the state has $12,751,000 of outstanding encumbrances.

Special revenue fund -- highway maintenance:

Reserve for encumbrances	$12,751,000	
Encumbrances		$12,751,000

---

2) A government may reclassify fund balance to acknowledge in its financial statements the claim on next period's resources of commitments made during the reporting period.

EXAMPLE

The state reclassifies a portion of fund balance equal to outstanding encumbrances.

Special revenue fund -- highway maintenance:

Fund balance -- assigned	$12,751,000	
Fund balance -- committed		$12,751,000

---

c. Common anticipated liabilities, such as wages payable and payroll taxes payable, need not be encumbered because of the controls in place for such expenditures.

7.   Summary

	Governmental Funds	Proprietary Funds	Fiduciary Funds
Budgetary accounting	General and special revenue funds; other funds with many transactions; rarely in debt service funds	Rarely	If similar to special revenue funds
Outlays encumbered	General and special revenue funds; possibly other funds	No	No

Stop and review! You have completed the outline for this subunit. Study multiple-choice questions 10 through 20 beginning on page 669.

18.3 GOVERNMENTAL SOURCES OF FINANCING

1.   **Overview of Nonexchange Transactions**

   a.   **Revenue recognition** for a government is unlike that for a private entity.

      1)   A government often does not directly exchange something of value, such as goods or services, for its revenues. Thus, the main sources of government revenues are **nonexchange transactions**.

   b.   All nonexchange transactions are classified into four categories.

      1)   **Derived tax revenues** are assessments on **underlying exchange transactions**. The primary examples are income taxes and sales taxes.

         a)   Income is earned or a sale is completed and a tax is levied based on the amount involved.

      2)   **Imposed nonexchange revenues** are assessments on nongovernmental entities, for example, property taxes, forfeitures, or fines. No underlying exchange exists.

         a)   The assessment is on ownership of property (real estate, automobile, etc.) or the commission of an act (speeding, failing to obtain an occupational license, etc.).

      3)   **Government-mandated nonexchange transactions** occur when one government provides resources to a government at another level and requires that they be used for a specific purpose.

         a)   Fulfillment of **eligibility requirements** is essential.

            i)   An example is federal grant money that state governments are required to spend on primary education.

      4)   **Voluntary nonexchange transactions** arise from legislative or contractual agreements entered into willingly by the parties. They are **not** imposed on any party, and fulfillment of **eligibility requirements** is essential. Moreover, one party may be a nongovernmental entity (e.g., an individual).

         a)   Examples of voluntary nonexchange transactions are

            i)   Certain grants,
            ii)   Certain entitlements, and
            iii)   Private donations (such as a gift of an art collection to a municipal museum).

2. **Timing of Recognition**

a. The timing of recognition of assets, deferred inflows/outflows of resources, liabilities, and expenses or expenditures that arise from nonexchange transactions is not affected by the basis of accounting (accrual or modified accrual).

b. **Revenue recognition** on the **modified accrual basis**, however, requires that the criteria for nonexchange transactions be met and that the resources be **available**.

1) Accordingly, the revenue recognition criteria described below are those for accrual-basis accounting, but the availability criterion also may need to be met.

c. The method of accounting for **property taxes** (recognition in the period for which they were levied) is not changed.

3. **Accounting Procedures -- Derived Tax Revenues**

a. **Assets** are recognized when the underlying exchange transaction occurs or resources are received, whichever is earlier.

b. **Revenues** are recognized when the underlying exchange transaction occurs.

1) Resources received before the underlying exchange are **deferred inflows of resources**.

EXAMPLE

Retail establishments most likely report their sales monthly to the state government.

Receivable -- sales taxes	$100,000,000	
Revenue -- sales taxes		$100,000,000

---

c. In the **governmental funds**, resources also must be available to qualify for revenue recognition.

4. **Accounting Procedures -- Imposed Nonexchange Revenues**

a. **Assets** are recognized when (1) a legal claim to the resources has arisen or (2) resources are received, whichever is earlier.

b. **Revenues** are recognized when the resources are required to be used or when their use is first allowed by the **time requirements**.

1) Resources received or recognized as receivable before the time requirements are met are **deferred inflows of resources**.

2) If **no** time requirements have been established, revenue recognition is at the same time as the recognition of the assets.

c. In the **governmental funds**, resources also must be available to qualify for revenue recognition.

d. Revenue from **property taxes** is recognized in the period for which they were **levied**.

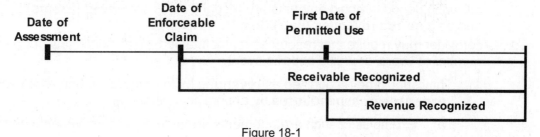

Figure 18-1

EXAMPLE

On November 1, a city levies $110,000,000 of property taxes that are due December 1 and are to be used in the following calendar year.

> November 1:
> No entry

The city offers a discount to taxpayers who pay early and a few property owners take advantage of this provision. Any amounts received before they are legally due (December 1) must be recorded as a liability (deferred revenue).

> November 30:
> | | | |
> |---|---|---|
> | Cash | $1,350,000 | |
> | Deferred property tax revenues | | $1,350,000 |

On the day when the assessment is legally enforceable, the city recognizes a receivable (reduced by an allowance for uncollectibles) and a liability (deferred revenue).

> December 1:
> | | | |
> |---|---|---|
> | Property taxes receivable | $108,000,000 | |
> | Deferred property tax revenues | | $100,000,000 |
> | Allowance for uncollectible taxes | | 8,000,000 |

Once the period when the resources must or may be used begins (the period for which the taxes were levied), the city removes the liability and recognizes the revenue.

> January 1:
> | | | |
> |---|---|---|
> | Deferred property tax revenues | $101,350,000 | |
> | Revenues -- property taxes | | $101,350,000 |

The AICPA has released multiple CPA questions asking for the calculation of the amount of property tax revenue recognized by a governmental entity for a period of time.

---

5. **Accounting Procedures -- Government-Mandated and Voluntary Nonexchange Transactions**

   a. **Assets** are recognized by recipients and **liabilities** by providers when all eligibility requirements are met or resources are received, whichever is earlier.

   b. **Revenues** are recognized by recipients and **expenses or expenditures** by providers when all eligibility requirements are met. Thus, a provider debits an expense or expenditure and credits a liability or an asset.

      1) A recipient debits an asset or a liability and credits revenue.

      2) In the **governmental funds**, resources also must be available to qualify for revenue recognition.

   c. If the provider requires the recipient to use the resources in or beginning in the following period, prepaid amounts are recognized as **advances (assets)** by providers and as **deferred revenues (liabilities)** by recipients.

   d. A provider may require that resources be maintained intact indefinitely, for a specified number of years, or until a specific event.

      1) They should be recognized as **revenues** by the recipient when received and as **expenses or expenditures** by the provider when paid.

         a) Examples of such arrangements are permanent endowments and term endowments.

   e. A provider may share its **derived tax revenues** or **imposed nonexchange revenues** with a recipient.

      1) Both parties account for the sharing as a voluntary or government-mandated nonexchange transaction, as appropriate.

f. **Required characteristics of recipients.** For example, a state may not be able to recognize revenue from a federal law enforcement grant until the state has a certain number of highway patrol officers per mile of highway, as required by the federal legislation establishing the grant.

1) Even if the state already has a sufficient number of patrol officers, it cannot recognize revenue from the grant until the first day specified in the enabling legislation.

g. **Reimbursement.** Some grants are on a reimbursement basis, that is, the recipient spends the money before reimbursement by the grantor. In such cases, the recipient does not recognize revenue until the money has been spent (thereby establishing a receivable).

6. **Summary of Nonexchange Transactions**

Category	Timing of Recognition
Derived tax revenues	**Assets** – Earlier of when underlying exchange has occurred or resources are received. **Revenues** – When underlying exchange has occurred (advance receipts are credited to deferred inflows of resources). Resources also should be **available** if resources are accounted for in a governmental fund.
Imposed nonexchange revenues	**Assets** – Earlier of when an enforceable legal claim has arisen or resources are received. **Revenues** – When resources are required to be used or use is first allowed (for property taxes, the period for which levied). Resources also should be **available** if resources are accounted for in a governmental fund. Absent time requirements, asset and revenue recognition are at the same time.
Government-mandated and voluntary nonexchange transactions	**Assets and liabilities** – Earlier of when all eligibility requirements have been met or (for assets) resources are received. **Revenues and expenses or expenditures** – When all eligibility requirements have been met (advance receipts or payments are recorded as deferred inflows/outflows of resources, respectively). Given **time requirements**, revenues and expenses or expenditures are recorded when the resources are, respectively, received or paid. The resulting net position, equity, or fund balance is restricted. Resources also should be **available** if resources are accounted for in a governmental fund.

7. **Bonds -- Issuance**

a. The proceeds of long-term debt are not revenues but are a major source of funding for governments.

b. The **government-wide financial statements** report all resources and obligations, regardless of whether they are current or noncurrent.

1) The receipt of cash and the related obligation are recognized. The inflow from a financing source is not.

EXAMPLE

The state issues bonds to finance the construction of a new building.

Cash	$200,000,000	
Bonds payable		$200,000,000

---

2) Any **premium received or discount paid** upon issuance is not recognized. Premium and discount do not affect the amount of long-term resources that must be spent to retire the bonds.

c.   In the **governmental fund financial statements**, the treatment is different because they have a short-term focus, and bonds are not repaid with current financial resources.

1)   The fund that will expend the resources recognizes the receipt of cash and the related financing sources. The entry is to (a) debit cash for the proceeds, (b) credit other financing sources for the face amount of the debt, and (c) credit other financing sources or debit other financing uses for issuance premium or discount, respectively.

EXAMPLE

Capital projects fund -- highway patrol headquarters building:

Cash	$202,000,000	
Other financing sources -- bond face amount		$200,000,000
Other financing sources -- bond issue premium		2,000,000

---

2)   The credit to other financing sources indicates that this inflow of resources is not a revenue.

3)   The premium is an inflow of additional resources. It will not be amortized. But a bond indenture or law may require the premium to be applied to debt service.

8.   **Bonds -- Construction**

a.   Payments for the project are made from the bond proceeds.

b.   In the **government-wide financial statements**, the finished building (or construction-in-progress) is reported as a general capital asset.

c.   In the **governmental fund financial statements**, payments to the contractor are recorded as expenditures.

1)   The building itself is not capitalized in the governmental fund financial statements.

EXAMPLE

A progress payment is made for work done during the year.

Capital projects fund -- highway patrol headquarters building:

Expenditures -- capital outlay	$85,000,000	
Cash		$85,000,000

---

9.   **Bonds -- Retirement**

a.   When the bonds are repaid, the entries reflect the same differences in recognition as in the issuance.

b.   The **government-wide financial statements** recognize the reduction in assets and liabilities and interest expense.

1)   Just as the receipt of the bond proceeds was not a revenue in the government-wide statements, so the retirement of the principal is not an expenditure.

EXAMPLE

The current portion of the bond principal is retired.

Bonds payable	$10,000,000	
Interest expense	700,000	
Cash		$10,700,000

---

c. The accounting in the **governmental funds** requires multiple entries.

EXAMPLE

General fund resources are earmarked for debt service.

General fund:		
Other financing uses -- interfund transfer to debt service fund	$10,700,000	
Due to debt service fund		$10,700,000

Debt service fund:		
Due from general fund	$10,700,000	
Other financing sources -- interfund transfer from general fund		$10,700,000

The resources are transferred.

General fund:		
Due to debt service fund	$10,700,000	
Cash		$10,700,000

Debt service fund:		
Cash	$10,700,000	
Due from general fund		$10,700,000

Expenditures are recorded when principal and interest are legally due.

Debt service fund:		
Expenditure -- bond principal	$10,000,000	
Expenditure -- bond interest	700,000	
Bonds payable		$10,000,000
Interest payable		700,000

The current portion of the debt is repaid.

Debt service fund:		
Bonds payable	$10,000,000	
Interest payable	700,000	
Cash		$10,700,000

---

d. The **capital projects fund** records no transactions involving the retirement of debt.

10. **Anticipation Notes**

a. Governments may issue short-term debt because cash is required before the financing is available. In these cases, bond, tax, or revenue anticipation notes are issued.

b. In the **government-wide financial statements**, the notes are reported in two components if average maturities exceed 1 year: (1) amounts due within 1 year and (2) amounts due in more than 1 year.

    1) These liabilities may be reported in either the governmental or business-type activities column.

c. **Proprietary Fund Financial Statements**

    1) Proprietary fund bond, tax, and revenue anticipation notes are reported as long-term liabilities if the enterprise's intent to refinance is supported by an ability to complete the refinancing. The ability to refinance is demonstrated by

        a) Issuance of long-term debt or equity between the date of the balance sheet and the date of its issue, or

        b) Entering into a financing agreement that clearly permits refinancing on readily determinable terms (if certain other conditions are met).

d. **Governmental Fund Financial Statements**

1) **Bond anticipation notes** are reported solely as general long-term liabilities in the governmental activities column of the government-wide financial statements if

a) All legal steps have been taken to refinance the notes, and

b) The intent to refinance is supported by an ability to complete the refinancing on a long-term basis [see the criteria in item 10.c.1) on the previous page].

2) If the criteria above are not met, the bond anticipation notes are reported as liabilities in the

a) Governmental fund receiving the proceeds.
b) Government-wide statement of net position.

3) **Tax and revenue anticipation notes** are reported as liabilities in the governmental fund receiving the proceeds and in the government-wide statement of net position.

11. **Special Assessments**

a. Governments may agree to construct physical improvements that will benefit one or more property owners. The government issues debt, pays for the improvements with the proceeds, then repays the debt with reimbursements from the property owners.

b. In the **government-wide financial statements**, the accounting is straightforward.

EXAMPLE

A city agrees to build roads, install street lights, and lay water and sewer lines for an employer who intends to build a factory. The city is also liable for the special assessment debt. Thus, it recognizes a general long-term liability and a capital asset.

The bonds are issued.

Cash	$10,000,000	
Bonds payable -- special assessment		$10,000,000

The improvements are finished.

Infrastructure assets	$10,000,000	
Cash		$10,000,000

Once the bonds were issued, interest began accruing on them. This amount is added to what the factory owner owes for the improvements.

Special assessment receivable	$10,675,000	
Revenue -- special assessment		$10,675,000

The factory owner pays the assessment.

Cash	$10,675,000	
Special assessment receivable		$10,675,000

The bonds are retired and the portion of the interest that accrued while the project was underway is capitalized.

Bonds payable -- special assessment	$10,000,000	
Infrastructure assets	500,000	
Interest expense	175,000	
Cash		$10,675,000

---

c. In the **governmental fund financial statements**, the accounting is slightly different. Two funds are involved because resources used for the improvements will be reported in one fund, but the repayment of the bonds will be from another.

EXAMPLE

Certain entries are omitted below. These include entries reflecting the reduction of deferred revenue that initially offset the assessment receivable. (Deferred revenue is reduced as resources become available.)

The bonds are issued.

Capital projects fund:
Cash	$10,000,000	
Other financing sources -- bonds payable		$10,000,000

The contractor is paid for building the improvements.

Capital projects fund:
Expenditures -- special assessment	$10,000,000	
Cash		$10,000,000

The factory owner is assessed for the full amount including accrued interest.

Debt service fund:
Special assessment receivable	$10,675,000	
Revenue -- special assessment		$10,675,000

The factory owner pays the assessment.

Debt service fund:
Cash	$10,675,000	
Special assessment receivable		$10,675,000

The bonds are retired.

Debt service fund:
Expenditure -- special assessment bond	$10,000,000	
Expenditure -- interest	675,000	
Cash		$10,675,000

---

12. **Interfund Transactions -- Transfers of Resources**

    a. Transfers from one fund to another are a significant source of financing for governmental units.

    b. For the full outline, see Study Unit 19, Subunit 5.

Stop and review! You have completed the outline for this subunit. Study multiple-choice questions 21 through 30 beginning on page 672.

18.4 CHARACTERISTIC TRANSACTIONS OF GOVERNMENTAL ENTITIES

1. **Outlays for Operations vs. Outlays for Capital Assets**

    a. In the **governmental funds**, whether an expenditure was for services consumed immediately or for a general capital asset is irrelevant.

        1) The focus of governmental-fund reporting is on the disposition of **current period resources**. Such outlays are thus **expenditures** rather than expenses.

EXAMPLE

An entry for the purchase of road maintenance equipment is similar to an entry to pay for extra office space.

General fund:
Expenditures -- rent	$20,000	
Vouchers payable		$20,000

Special revenue fund -- highway maintenance:
Expenditures -- road equipment	$745,000	
Vouchers payable		$745,000

b.   In the **government-wide financial statements**, all economic resources are reported.

1)   The services consumed in the current period are debited to an expense, and the long-lived asset is capitalized.

EXAMPLE

The entries for road maintenance equipment and rental expense are as follows:

Rental expense	$20,000	
Vouchers payable		$20,000
Road equipment	$745,000	
Vouchers payable		$745,000

---

2.   **Supplies and Prepaid Items**

a.   In the **governmental fund financial statements**, inventories of supplies and prepaid items present an accounting challenge.

1)   They are not expendable available financial resources, but they do represent economic benefits retained by the entity.

a)   The **two methods** in common use for accounting for supplies and prepayments are described below.

2)   The **purchases method** is a modified accrual accounting treatment. It is used with a periodic system.

EXAMPLE

Supplies and prepayments are recognized as expenditures in the general fund at the time of purchase.

Expenditures -- supplies	$200,000	
Expenditures -- insurance	400,000	
Vouchers payable		$600,000

Assuming no beginning balances, i.e., increases in inventory and prepaid insurance, the year-end entries are

Inventory of supplies	$ 95,000	
Prepaid insurance	190,000	
Other financing sources -- inventory increase		$ 95,000
Other financing sources -- prepayment increase		190,000
Unassigned fund balance	$285,000	
Fund balance -- nonspendable for increase in supplies inventory		$ 95,000
Fund balance -- nonspendable for increase in prepaid insurance		190,000

---

3)   The **consumption method** is essentially an accrual accounting treatment. It is used with a periodic or perpetual system.

EXAMPLE

Using the perpetual system, supplies and prepayments are recognized as assets in the general fund at the time of purchase.

Inventory of supplies	$200,000	
Prepaid insurance	400,000	
Vouchers payable		$600,000

During the period, issuances of inventory are recognized by debits to expenditures and credits to inventory. At year-end, the following entries recognize an inventory shortage of $5,000 based on a physical count and the expired portion of prepaid insurance ($210,000):

Expenditures	$215,000	
Inventory of supplies		$ 5,000
Prepaid insurance		210,000

---

   b.   In the **government-wide financial statements**, the accrual method is used to account for supplies and prepaid items.

       1)   An asset is recognized at the time of purchase, and an expense (not an expenditure) is recognized with the usage of the asset or the passage of time.

3.   **Capital Leases**

   a.   The GASB adopted the FASB's guidelines for classifying leases as capital or operating (see Study Unit 14 for a discussion). Thus, when any of the four capitalization criteria is met, a governmental unit must recognize a capital lease.

   b.   **Lessee Accounting**

       1)   In the **government-wide financial statements** and in the **fund financial statements of proprietary funds**, a capital lease is recognized in the same way as in an outright purchase.

           a)   The leased asset is capitalized at the present value of the minimum lease payments and a long-term liability is recognized for any remainder after a cash payment at the lease's inception.

EXAMPLE

A government enters into a long-term capital lease for a piece of equipment. The present value of the minimum lease payments is $120,000.

Equipment -- capital lease	$120,000	
Cash		$ 10,000
Capital lease obligation		110,000

At the end of the first year, a portion of the lease is amortized.

Interest expense	$9,000	
Capital lease obligation	1,000	
Cash		$10,000

---

       2)   The **fund financial statements of governmental funds**, with their focus on current financial resources, do not recognize the long-term nature of a leased asset and its related obligation.

EXAMPLE

The initiation of the lease is recorded as follows:

Expenditures -- leased assets	$120,000	
Cash		$ 10,000
Other financing sources -- capital lease		110,000

The payment at the end of the first year is recorded as follows:

Expenditures -- interest	$9,000	
Expenditures -- principal	1,000	
Cash		$10,000

---

   c.   **Lessor Accounting**

       1)   A lease receivable is recognized to the extent it represents another financing source that is measurable and available. The rest is deferred.

       2)   Furthermore, the noncurrent receivable is not a general capital asset. It is therefore reported in the fund accounting for the lease.

4. **Municipal Solid Waste Landfills**

    a. Municipalities that operate solid waste landfills are required to recognize the **long-term liability** for closing landfills using an **expected cash flow** measurement.

        1) The **estimated total current cost** of landfill **closure and postclosure care** includes (a) the cost of equipment expected to be installed and (b) facilities expected to be constructed near or after the date that the landfill stops accepting waste and during the postclosure period.

EXAMPLE

A government estimates that its landfill will eventually require $10,000,000 in total costs for closure and environmental protection. At the end of the first year, the landfill is 15% full.

Government-wide financial statements:		
Expense -- landfill closure	$1,500,000	
Landfill closure liability		$1,500,000

At the end of the first year, a progress payment is made.

Government-wide financial statements:		
Landfill closure liability	$300,000	
Cash		$300,000

---

    b. If the landfill is operated as a **business-type activity** (i.e., it is accounted for in an enterprise fund), the accounting in the fund financial statements is the same as in the government-wide statements.

        1) However, if the landfill is operated as a **governmental activity** (i.e., it is accounted for in the general fund), only the effect on current financial resources is recognized. The long-term liability will be disclosed in the summary reconciliation (discussed in the next study unit).

EXAMPLE

The long-term liability is not recognized. The first year's progress payment is recorded as follows:

General fund:		
Expenditures -- landfill closure	$300,000	
Cash		$300,000

---

5. **Compensated Absences**

    a. When governmental bodies grant their employees paid time off, the salary rate used to calculate the liability should be the rate in effect at the balance sheet date.

        1) In the financial statements of governmental funds, only the portion of compensated absences that employees will use in the upcoming fiscal period is recognized, i.e., the portion that must be paid with current financial resources.

        2) In the government-wide financial statements, the entire liability must be recognized.

EXAMPLE

General fund:		
Expenditures -- compensated absences	$91,000	
Liability -- compensated absences		$91,000

Government-wide financial statements:		
Expenses -- compensated absences	$750,000	
Liability -- compensated absences		$750,000

6.	**Works of Art and Historical Treasures**

    a.	The accounting measurement of a work of art or historic object obtained by a government depends on whether the item is purchased or donated.

        1)	If the object is **purchased**, it is recorded at **historical cost**.

EXAMPLE

A government pays $12,000,000 for an object for its museum. An identical item had recently sold at auction for $14,000,000.

    Government-wide financial statements:
Museum object -- Ming dynasty vase (historical cost)	$12,000,000
    Cash						$12,000,000

---

           a)	If the museum in which the object is displayed is operated as an **enterprise fund**, i.e., an admission fee is charged, the asset generates revenue. The above entry is duplicated in the proprietary fund financial statements.

           b)	If the museum is accounted for in the **general fund**, the current resources focus requires the transaction to be recorded as an expenditure.

EXAMPLE

The government operates its museum as a governmental activity.

    General fund:
Expenditures -- museum object			$12,000,000
    Cash						$12,000,000

---

        2)	If the object is **donated**, it is recorded at **fair value**.

EXAMPLE

If the government accounts for the museum in an enterprise fund, the following entry is recorded in both the government-wide financial statements and the proprietary fund financial statements:

    Museum object -- Ming dynasty vase (fair value)	$14,000,000
    Revenue -- donation				$14,000,000

If the government accounts for the museum in the general fund, the object is not capitalized.

---

    b.	Although the recognition of works of art and historical treasures as assets is encouraged, capitalization is **optional** in some circumstances.

        1)	A government may record the acquisition (whether by purchase or donation) of a work of art or historical treasure as an **expense** if the **collection** to which the object is being added meets these **three criteria**:

           a)	The collection is held for public exhibition, education, or research in furtherance of public service rather than financial gain;

           b)	The collection is protected, kept unencumbered, cared for, and preserved; and

           c)	The collection is subject to an organizational policy that requires the proceeds from sales of collection items to be used to acquire other items for collections.

        2)	A collection or item that is exhaustible is depreciated.

7.   **Infrastructure Assets**

    a.   Infrastructure assets are capital assets that normally are stationary and can be preserved for a longer time than most capital assets. Examples include roads, bridges, tunnels, sidewalks, water and sewer systems, drainage systems, and lighting systems.

    b.   The treatment of public infrastructure assets is similar to that for other capital assets.

        1) In the **government-wide financial statements**, they are reported as assets.

        2) In the **financial statements** of **governmental funds**, they are reported as expenditures (they do not constitute current financial resources).

    c.   The GASB realized that arriving at historical cost information for **older infrastructure assets** (e.g., bridges and dams built in the 1930s) would be very difficult. For this reason, only major assets meeting **one of the following criteria** need be capitalized:

        1) The asset was acquired in a fiscal year ending after June 30, 1980, or

        2) The asset had major renovations, restorations, or improvements after June 30, 1980.

    d.   **Depreciation** of capital assets is required except for (1) land and (2) art and historic objects that have been deemed inexhaustible. Depreciation is recognized in the **government-wide, proprietary fund, and fiduciary fund statements**.

        1) Like works of art and historical treasures, infrastructure assets may have lives so long that they are in effect inexhaustible and therefore nondepreciable. For example, parts of the U.S. Interstate Highway System are already 50 years old, and the system as a whole will last for several generations.

    e.   The following is an alternative to depreciation for very long-lived infrastructure assets.

        1) Under the **modified approach**, infrastructure assets that are part of a network or subsystem of a network (eligible infrastructure assets) need not be depreciated. However, the government must use an asset management system with certain characteristics. It also must document that the assets are being preserved approximately at an established condition level disclosed by the government.

           a) This method allows a government to **expense maintenance costs** instead of recording depreciation expense.

           b) Additions and improvements to infrastructure assets are still **capitalized**.

Stop and review! You have completed the outline for this subunit. Study multiple-choice questions 31 through 36 beginning on page 676.

QUESTIONS

18.1 Fund Accounting Concepts and Reporting

1. Fund accounting is used by governmental units with resources that must be

    A. Composed of cash or cash equivalents.

    B. Incorporated into combined or combining financial statements.

    C. Segregated for the purpose of carrying on specific activities or attaining certain objectives.

    D. Segregated physically according to various objectives.

Answer (C) is correct.
    REQUIRED: The nature of fund accounting.
    DISCUSSION: A fund is a fiscal and accounting entity with a self-balancing set of accounts. It records (1) financial resources (including cash), (2) related liabilities, (3) residual equities or balances, and (4) changes in them. These items are recognized separately because they relate to specific activities or certain objectives that are subject to special regulations or limitations.
    Answer (A) is incorrect. Funds may account for all types of resources, related liabilities, and residuals. Answer (B) is incorrect. The essence of fund accounting is separation of resources into discrete accounting entities. Answer (D) is incorrect. Resources must be accounted for separately but need not be physically separated.

2. The government-wide financial statements report capital assets

A. In the general fixed assets account group.

B. At historical cost, including ancillary charges.

C. Only in the notes if they are donated.

D. At estimated fair value.

Answer (B) is correct.
REQUIRED: The reporting of capital assets in the government-wide financial statements.
DISCUSSION: Capital assets include land, land improvements, easements, buildings, vehicles, machinery, equipment, works of art, historical treasures, infrastructure, and other tangible and intangible operating assets with useful lives greater than one reporting period. They are reported at historical cost, including ancillary charges necessary to put them in their intended location and condition for use. Ancillary charges, e.g., for freight, site preparation, and professional fees, are directly attributable to acquisition of the assets.
Answer (A) is incorrect. Presentation of government-wide financial statements eliminates the need for the general fixed assets account group and the general long-term debt account group. Answer (C) is incorrect. Capital assets are reported at historical cost, including ancillary charges, in the statements. Answer (D) is incorrect. Only donated capital assets are reported at estimated fair value at the time of acquisition plus ancillary charges.

3. Thornton County is required under state law to report its financial statements on a basis that conflicts with generally accepted governmental accounting principles. On which basis of accounting should Thornton County's financial statements be prepared?

A. Generally accepted governmental accounting basis only.

B. State law basis only.

C. State law basis with supplemental disclosure of generally accepted governmental accounting reconciliation schedules.

D. Generally accepted governmental accounting basis with supplemental supporting schedules as necessary to report compliance with state law.

Answer (D) is correct.
REQUIRED: The proper presentation of county financial statements when state law conflicts with GAAP.
DISCUSSION: Certain state laws and regulatory requirements conflict with generally accepted accounting and financial reporting practices. When such a conflict exists, the governmental entity should prepare basic financial statements conforming with GAAP and also present supporting schedules and narrative explanations in the CAFR as necessary to clearly report upon compliance with legal responsibilities.
Answer (A) is incorrect. The financial statements should include supplemental matter to comply with state law. Answer (B) is incorrect. The financial statements should be prepared in accordance with GAAP. Answer (C) is incorrect. The statements should be prepared in accordance with GAAP with supplementary schedules that comply with state law.

4. Kew City received a $15,000,000 federal grant to finance the construction of a center for rehabilitation of drug addicts. The proceeds of this grant should be accounted for in the

A. Special revenue funds.

B. General fund.

C. Capital projects funds.

D. Trust funds.

Answer (C) is correct.
REQUIRED: The fund used to account for a federal grant earmarked to finance the construction of a center for rehabilitation of drug addicts.
DISCUSSION: The capital projects fund is used to account for the receipt and disbursement of resources restricted to acquisition of major capital facilities (other than those financed by proprietary and trust funds) through purchase or construction.
Answer (A) is incorrect. This fund does not record resources to be used for major capital facilities. Answer (B) is incorrect. This fund does not record resources to be used for major capital facilities. Answer (D) is incorrect. A grant for a drug rehabilitation center is not accounted for in a trust fund. A trust fund accounts for assets held by a governmental entity in the capacity of a trustee for individuals, private organizations, or other governments.

5. In governmental accounting, a fund is

I. The basic accounting unit
II. Used to assist in ensuring fiscal compliance

   A. I only.

   B. II only.

   C. Both I and II.

   D. Neither I nor II.

Answer (C) is correct.
REQUIRED: The nature of a fund.
DISCUSSION: Although government-wide financial statements also are reported, the diversity of governmental activities and the need for legal compliance preclude the use of a single accounting entity. Thus, independent, distinct entities called funds are established. A fund is a fiscal and accounting entity with a self-balancing set of accounts. It records (1) financial resources (including cash), (2) related liabilities, (3) residual equities or balances, and (4) changes in them. These items are recognized separately because they relate to specific activities or certain objectives that are subject to special regulations or limitations. A fund accounting system of a governmental reporting entity must be able to present fairly in conformity with GAAP and with full disclosure the financial position and results of operations of the funds. Moreover, it must determine and demonstrate compliance with finance-related legal and contractual provisions.

6. A local governmental unit could use which of the following types of funds?

	Fiduciary	Proprietary
A.	Yes	No
B.	Yes	Yes
C.	No	Yes
D.	No	No

Answer (B) is correct.
REQUIRED: The types of funds that could be used by a local governmental unit.
DISCUSSION: Three broad categories and 11 generic fund types can be used by a state or local governmental unit in its fund financial statements.

1) Governmental – general, special revenue, debt service, capital projects, and permanent funds
2) Proprietary – internal service and enterprise funds
3) Fiduciary – pension (and other employee benefit) trust, investment trust, private-purpose trust, and agency funds

The use of special assessment funds is restricted to internal and compliance reporting. Special assessment funds are not used in the basic financial statements.

7. The focus of accounting and reporting for proprietary funds of governmental units is most likely on

   A. Determination of operating income.

   B. Project completion.

   C. Current financial resources.

   D. Adherence to the budget.

Answer (A) is correct.
REQUIRED: The accounting focus of proprietary funds.
DISCUSSION: The financial statements of proprietary funds focus on determination of operating income, changes in net position (or cost recovery), financial position, and cash flows. A proprietary fund accounts for the business-type functions of a government. Users of the financial statements for proprietary funds may find profitability information to be valuable.
Answer (B) is incorrect. Projects and programs are entities for which information is accumulated, not measurement models. Answer (C) is incorrect. Current financial resources is the measurement focus of governmental funds. Answer (D) is incorrect. Governmental funds have a budgetary orientation.

8. Lake County received the following proceeds that are legally restricted to expenditure for specified purposes:

Levies on affected property owners to install sewers	$500,000
Gasoline taxes to finance road repairs	900,000

What amount most likely will be accounted for in Lake's special revenue funds?

   A. $1,400,000

   B. $900,000

   C. $500,000

   D. $0

Answer (B) is correct.
REQUIRED: The amount to be recorded in special revenue funds.
DISCUSSION: Special assessments for construction activity may be accounted for in a capital projects fund or other appropriate fund. The gasoline taxes are special revenues received from the state government to be expended for a specific purpose and are properly recorded in the special revenue funds. However, special revenue funds need not be used unless they are legally mandated.
Answer (A) is incorrect. The amount of $1,400,000 includes the special assessment for a capital project. Answer (C) is incorrect. This figure is the amount of the special assessment for a capital project. Answer (D) is incorrect. Zero is based on the assumption that neither revenue source is accounted for in special revenue funds.

9. In the fund financial statements of which of the following fund types of a city government are revenues and expenditures recognized on the same basis of accounting as the general fund?

A. Private-purpose trust.

B. Internal service.

C. Enterprise.

D. Debt service.

Answer (D) is correct.
REQUIRED: The fund that recognizes revenues and expenditures in the same manner as the general fund.
DISCUSSION: The debt service fund is the only fund listed that is classified as a governmental fund. The other funds are proprietary or fiduciary. Governmental funds use the modified accrual basis in preparing their fund financial statements, and proprietary and fiduciary funds use the accrual basis.
Answer (A) is incorrect. A private-purpose trust fund is a fiduciary fund. Its financial statements are prepared on the same basis as those of proprietary funds. Answer (B) is incorrect. The internal service fund is a proprietary fund. Its financial statements are prepared using the accrual basis of accounting. Answer (C) is incorrect. The enterprise fund is a proprietary fund. Its financial statements are prepared using the accrual basis of accounting.

18.2 Budgetary Accounting and Encumbrances

Questions 10 and 11 are based on the following information. Ridge Township's governing body adopted its general fund budget for the year ended July 31, Year 1, composed of estimated revenues of $100,000 and appropriations of $80,000. Ridge formally integrates its budget into the accounting records.

10. To record the appropriations of $80,000, Ridge should

A. Credit appropriations control.

B. Debit appropriations control.

C. Credit estimated expenditures control.

D. Debit estimated expenditures control.

Answer (A) is correct.
REQUIRED: The entry to record appropriations.
DISCUSSION: The basic budgetary entry is

Estimated revenues	$x,xxx,xxx	
Estimated other financing sources	x,xxx,xxx	
Appropriations		$xx,xxx,xxx
Estimated other financing uses		x,xxx,xxx
Budgetary fund balance		xxx,xxx

Thus, Ridge should credit appropriations control for $80,000. It is a control account because it is the summation of numerous individual appropriations. Estimated revenues and estimated other financing sources are anticipatory assets. Appropriations and estimated other financing uses are anticipatory liabilities.
Answer (B) is incorrect. Appropriations is credited, not debited. Answer (C) is incorrect. Expenditures is not credited in the budgetary entry. Answer (D) is incorrect. Expenditures is not debited in the budgetary entry.

11. To record the $20,000 budgeted excess of estimated revenues over appropriations, Ridge should

A. Credit estimated excess revenues control.

B. Debit estimated excess revenues control.

C. Credit budgetary fund balance.

D. Debit budgetary fund balance.

Answer (C) is correct.
REQUIRED: The correct entry to record the budgeted excess of estimated revenues over appropriations.
DISCUSSION: The basic budgetary entry is

Estimated revenues	$x,xxx,xxx	
Estimated other financing sources	x,xxx,xxx	
Appropriations		$xx,xxx,xxx
Estimated other financing uses		x,xxx,xxx
Budgetary fund balance		xxx,xxx

Given that estimated revenues exceed appropriations, budgetary fund balance is credited for the $20,000 difference.

12. On what accounting basis does GASB recommend that governmental fund budgets be prepared?

A. Cash.

B. Modified cash.

C. Accrual.

D. Modified accrual.

Answer (D) is correct.
REQUIRED: The basis of accounting for a governmental fund.
DISCUSSION: The basis of accounting for a budget preferably should be the same as that used by the fund for which the budget is being prepared. The modified accrual basis of accounting is used to prepare the fund financial statements for all governmental fund types: general, special revenue, capital projects, debt service, and permanent.
Answer (A) is incorrect. The cash basis is used for miscellaneous cash items that are not practicably measurable until cash is received or paid. Answer (B) is incorrect. The modified cash basis is never used. Answer (C) is incorrect. The accrual basis is used in the government-wide statements and in all fund statements other than governmental fund statements.

13. The estimated revenues control account of a governmental unit is debited when

A. Actual revenues are recorded.

B. Actual revenues are collected.

C. The budget is recorded.

D. The budget is closed at the end of the year.

Answer (C) is correct.
REQUIRED: The circumstance in which the estimated revenues control account of a governmental unit is debited.
DISCUSSION: The budgetary accounts are used to record the budget at the beginning of the fiscal period. The basic budgetary entry is

Estimated revenues	$x,xxx,xxx	
Estimated other financing sources	x,xxx,xxx	
Appropriations		$xx,xxx,xxx
Estimated other financing uses		x,xxx,xxx
Budgetary fund balance		xxx,xxx

No other entries are made in these accounts until the end of the fiscal year, at which time they are closed to fund balance.
Answer (A) is incorrect. Revenues is credited and a receivable is debited when actual revenues are recorded. Answer (B) is incorrect. Cash is debited when actual revenues are collected. Answer (D) is incorrect. Estimated revenues is credited when the budget is closed at the end of the year.

14. During its fiscal year ended June 30, Cliff City issued purchase orders totaling $5 million, which were properly charged to encumbrances at that time. Cliff received goods and related invoices at the encumbered amounts totaling $4.5 million before year end. The remaining goods of $500,000 were not received until after year end. Cliff paid $4.2 million of the invoices received during the year. The amount of Cliff's encumbrances outstanding at June 30 was

A. $0

B. $300,000

C. $500,000

D. $800,000

Answer (C) is correct.
REQUIRED: The amount of encumbrances outstanding.
DISCUSSION: In fund accounting, when a commitment is made to expend monies, an encumbrance is recognized. When the goods are received and the liability is recognized, this entry is reversed and an expenditure is recorded. Because goods totaling $500,000 were not received at year-end, encumbrances outstanding total $500,000 ($5,000,000 – $4,500,000).
Answer (A) is incorrect. Not all of the goods related to the encumbrance amounts were received during the year. Answer (B) is incorrect. The amount of $300,000 is the excess of goods received over the amount actually paid on the invoices during the year. Answer (D) is incorrect. The amount of $800,000 is the excess of total encumbrances over the amount paid on the invoices.

15. A county's balances in the general fund included the following:

Appropriations	$745,000
Encumbrances	37,250
Expenditures	298,000
Vouchers payable	55,875

What is the remaining amount available for use by the county?

A. $353,875

B. $391,125

C. $409,750

D. $447,000

Answer (C) is correct.
REQUIRED: The remaining amount available for use.
DISCUSSION: Appropriations is the account credited in the general fund's budgetary entry. It establishes the total amount available for use during the period. When a commitment is made to expend resources of a governmental unit, the amount of the commitment is recognized by an encumbrance. Comparison of encumbrances, appropriations, and expenditures determines the unencumbered amount of appropriations that may still be expended. Encumbrances will be decreased when previously ordered items have been received. Expenditures and vouchers payable will be increased for the actual amount to be paid for the items. Accordingly, the remaining amount available for use by the county is $409,750 ($745,000 − $37,250 − $298,000).
Answer (A) is incorrect. The amount of $353,875 results from subtracting the vouchers payable balance, the account credited when expenditures is debited. Answer (B) is incorrect. The amount of $391,125 results from subtracting vouchers payable instead of encumbrances. Answer (D) is incorrect. The amount of $447,000 results from not subtracting encumbrances.

16. Park City uses encumbrance accounting and formally integrates its budget into the general fund's accounting records. For the year ending July 31, Year 1, the following budget was adopted:

Estimated revenues	$30,000,000
Appropriations	27,000,000
Estimated transfer to debt service fund	900,000

Park's budgetary fund balance is a

A. $3,000,000 credit balance.

B. $3,000,000 debit balance.

C. $2,100,000 credit balance.

D. $2,100,000 debit balance.

Answer (C) is correct.
REQUIRED: The budgetary fund balance when a budget is adopted and recorded.
DISCUSSION: Park City's budgetary entry for the Year 1 fiscal year:

Estimated revenues	$30,000,000	
Appropriations		$27,000,000
Estimated other financing uses		
-- transfer to debt service fund		900,000
Budgetary fund balance		2,100,000

Answer (A) is incorrect. The $900,000 estimated transfer to debt service fund must be credited. Answer (B) is incorrect. The estimated revenues must be debited and the transfer to debt service must be credited. Answer (D) is incorrect. The estimated revenues should be debited.

17. Which of the following amount(s) is(are) included in a general fund's encumbrances account?

I. Outstanding vouchers payable amounts

II. Outstanding purchase order amounts

III. Excess of the amount of a purchase order over the actual expenditure for that order

A. I only.

B. I and III only.

C. II only.

D. II and III only.

Answer (C) is correct.
REQUIRED: The amounts included in a general fund's encumbrances account.
DISCUSSION: When a purchase order is approved, an encumbrance is recognized. When the contract is complete or virtually complete, the entry is reversed, effectively eliminating the purchase order amount. Thus, encumbrances include only those amounts that represent outstanding purchase orders.
Answer (A) is incorrect. The encumbrance is eliminated when the expenditure and the voucher payable relating to the purchase order are recorded. Answer (B) is incorrect. The encumbrance includes only outstanding purchase order amounts. Answer (D) is incorrect. When the contract is complete or virtually complete, the original encumbrance entry is reversed. The actual amount owed is recorded in the expenditures account, so any excess is not reflected in encumbrances.

18. Which of the following journal entries should be made in the general fund of a city to record $250,000 for salaries and wages incurred during the month of May?

A. Salaries & wages
    expense $250,000
        Appropriations $250,000

B. Salaries & wages
    expense $250,000
        Encumbrances $250,000

C. Encumbrances $250,000
        Salaries payable $250,000

D. Expenditures --
    salaries & wages $250,000
        Salaries payable $250,000

Answer (D) is correct.
    REQUIRED: The entry used by a city to record salaries and wages in the general fund.
    DISCUSSION: An expenditure is recorded when a current liability is to be liquidated with expendable available current resources. Because wages and salaries have been earned by employees, a liability should be recognized, not an encumbrance. The controls in place for such routine outlays as wages and payroll taxes mean that such liabilities are rarely encumbered.

19. For the budgetary year ending December 31, Maple City's general fund expects the following inflows of resources:

Property taxes, licenses, and fines $9,000,000
Proceeds of debt issue   5,000,000
Interfund transfers for debt service   1,000,000

In the budgetary entry, what amount should Maple record for estimated revenues?

A. $9,000,000

B. $10,000,000

C. $14,000,000

D. $15,000,000

Answer (A) is correct.
    REQUIRED: The amount of estimated revenues.
    DISCUSSION: Estimated revenues is an anticipatory asset and is debited for the amount expected to be collected from a governmental body's main source of revenue. In the general fund, the main source of revenue is made up of taxes, fees, penalties, etc. Expected proceeds from the issuance of debt constitute an other financing source. An expected transfer to a different fund is an other financing use.
    Answer (B) is incorrect. The amount of $10,000,000 incorrectly includes the interfund transfers. Answer (C) is incorrect. The amount of $14,000,000 incorrectly includes the debt issue proceeds. Answer (D) is incorrect. The amount of $15,000,000 incorrectly includes the debt issue proceeds and interfund transfers.

20. When a snowplow purchased by a governmental unit is received, it should be recorded in the general fund as a(n)

A. Encumbrance.

B. Expenditure.

C. General capital asset.

D. Appropriation.

Answer (B) is correct.
    REQUIRED: The effect of receipt of equipment.
    DISCUSSION: When previously ordered goods are received, the entry includes a debit to expenditures for the actual amount to be paid. An expenditure is recognized when a liability is incurred, that is, when an executory contract is complete or virtually complete.
    Answer (A) is incorrect. An encumbrance is recorded to account for the purchase commitment. Answer (C) is incorrect. General capital assets are reported only in the governmental activities column of the government-wide statement of net position. Answer (D) is incorrect. Appropriations are accounted for when recording the budget.

18.3 Governmental Sources of Financing

21. Property taxes and fines represent which of the following classes of nonexchange transactions for governmental units?

A. Derived tax revenues.

B. Imposed nonexchange revenues.

C. Government-mandated nonexchange transactions.

D. Voluntary nonexchange transactions.

Answer (B) is correct.
    REQUIRED: The classification of property taxes and fines assessed by a governmental unit.
    DISCUSSION: Imposed nonexchange revenues arise from assessments on nongovernmental entities, including individuals, other than assessments on exchange transactions. Examples are fines, forfeitures, and property taxes.
    Answer (A) is incorrect. Derived tax revenues arise from assessments imposed on exchange transactions. Answer (C) is incorrect. Government-mandated nonexchange transactions occur when one government provides resources to a government at another level and requires that they be used for a specific purpose. Answer (D) is incorrect. Voluntary nonexchange transactions result from legislative or contractual agreements, other than exchanges, entered into willingly.

22. During the current year, Knoxx County levied property taxes of $2,000,000, of which 1% is expected to be uncollectible. The following amounts were collected during the current year:

Prior year taxes collected within the first 60 days of the current year	$ 50,000
Prior year taxes collected between 60 and 90 days into the current year	120,000
Current year taxes collected in the current year	1,800,000
Current year taxes collected within the first 60 days of the subsequent year	80,000

What amount of property tax revenue should Knoxx County report in its government-wide statement of activities?

   A. $1,800,000

   B. $1,970,000

   C. $1,980,000

   D. $2,000,000

Answer (C) is correct.
  REQUIRED: The property tax revenue reported in the government-wide statement of activities.
  DISCUSSION: Revenue from a property tax assessment is recognized in the period for which it was levied, provided the criteria of being available and measurable are met. (Property taxes are accounted for in governmental funds, which use the modified accrual basis.) Property taxes are measurable when assessed property values can be multiplied by a known tax rate. Available means collectible within the current period or expected to be collected soon enough thereafter to pay current liabilities. Such time may not exceed 60 days for a property tax assessment except in unusual circumstances. However, the accrual basis is used to prepare the entity-wide (government-wide) statement of activities. Accrual basis recognition of property tax revenue (imposed nonexchange revenue) also is in the period for which the taxes are levied, but the availability criterion does not apply. Recognition is net of estimated refunds and uncollectible amounts. Because the property tax revenue is to be reported in the government-wide statement of activities, the accrual basis is used. Consequently, current-year property tax revenue recognized on the accrual basis is $1,980,000 [$2,000,000 levied × (100% − 1% estimated to be uncollectible)]. The amounts collected currently but levied for a prior year and the amounts levied for the current year and collected in the subsequent year are accrual basis revenue of the prior year and the current year, respectively.
  Answer (A) is incorrect. This amount ($1,800,000) is the amount of the current-year levy collected in the current year. Answer (B) is incorrect. This amount ($1,970,000) is the amount collected in the current year. Answer (D) is incorrect. One percent of the total levy is expected to be uncollectible.

23. On March 2, Year 4, the city of Finch issued 10-year general obligation bonds at face amount, with interest payable March 1 and September 1. The proceeds were to be used to finance the construction of a civic center over the period April 1, Year 4, to March 31, Year 5. During the fiscal year ended June 30, Year 4, no resources had been provided to the debt service fund for the payment of principal and interest. On June 30, Year 4, Finch should report the construction in progress for the civic center in the

	Capital Projects Fund	Government-Wide Statement of Net Position
A.	Yes	Yes
B.	Yes	No
C.	No	No
D.	No	Yes

Answer (D) is correct.
  REQUIRED: The reporting of construction in progress.
  DISCUSSION: Expenditures for the construction project but not the resulting general capital assets should be reported in the capital projects fund. The construction in progress (a general capital asset if it results from expenditure of governmental fund financial resources and is not related to activities reported in nongovernmental funds) and ultimately the completed civic center should be reported in the government-wide statement of net position at historical cost, including capitalized interest and ancillary charges. They should not be reported in the governmental funds balance sheet.
  Answer (A) is incorrect. Expenditures but not in-progress assets are reported in the capital projects fund. General capital assets are not reported in governmental funds. Answer (B) is incorrect. The completed and in-progress assets are reported in the government-wide statement of net position, not in the capital projects fund. Answer (C) is incorrect. The completed and in-progress assets are reported in the government-wide statement of net position.

24. In which situation(s) should property taxes due to a governmental unit be recorded as deferred inflows of resources?

I. Property taxes receivable are recognized in advance of the year for which they are levied.

II. Property taxes receivable are collected in advance of the year in which they are levied.

   A. I only.

   B. Both I and II.

   C. II only.

   D. Neither I nor II.

Answer (B) is correct.
  REQUIRED: The situation(s) when taxes due should be recorded as deferred inflows of resources.
  DISCUSSION: A property tax assessment is made to finance the budget of a specific period. Hence, the revenue produced should be recognized in the period for which the assessment was levied. When property taxes are recognized or collected in advance, they should be recorded as deferred inflows of resources in a governmental fund. They are not recognized as revenue until the year for which they are levied. A property tax assessment is classified as an imposed nonexchange revenue transaction. In such a transaction, assets should be recognized when an enforceable legal claim arises or when resources are received, whichever is earlier. Thus, recognition of a receivable in a year prior to that for which the property taxes were levied implies that, under the enabling statute, the enforceable legal claim arose in that prior year.

25. In what fund type should the proceeds from special assessment bonds issued to finance construction of sidewalks in a new subdivision be reported?

A. Agency fund.

B. Special revenue fund.

C. Enterprise fund.

D. Capital projects fund.

Answer (D) is correct.
REQUIRED: The fund type that accounts for special assessment bond proceeds used to construct sidewalks.
DISCUSSION: Construction of sidewalks in a new subdivision financed by special assessment bonds is a capital project that results in a general capital asset that will be recognized only in the governmental activities column of the government-wide statement of net position. If the governmental unit is obligated in some manner on the special assessment debt, this capital improvement may be accounted for in the same way as other capital transactions. Hence, the transactions of the construction phase are reported in a capital projects fund. Transactions of the debt service phase are reported in a debt service fund, if one is required. If the government is not obligated, the construction transactions may still be reported in a capital projects fund, but the debt service transactions are recorded in an agency fund.
Answer (A) is incorrect. Agency funds are purely custodial funds. However, an agency fund should report debt service transactions related to special assessment debt if the governmental unit is not obligated in any manner. Answer (B) is incorrect. Bond proceeds are not considered revenues of a governmental unit. They must be repaid. Answer (C) is incorrect. Enterprise funds account for business-type activities.

26. In Year 8, Menton City received $5,000,000 of bond proceeds to be used for capital projects. Of this amount, $1,000,000 was expended in Year 8 with the balance expected to be expended in Year 9. When should the bond proceeds be recorded in a capital projects fund?

A. $5,000,000 in Year 8.

B. $5,000,000 in Year 9.

C. $1,000,000 in Year 8 and $4,000,000 in Year 9.

D. $1,000,000 in Year 8 and in the general fund for $4,000,000 in Year 8.

Answer (A) is correct.
REQUIRED: The date(s) bond proceeds should be recorded in a capital projects fund.
DISCUSSION: The general obligation debt will be reported as a general long-term liability in the governmental activities column of the government-wide statements of net position, and expenditures will be recorded in Year 8 and Year 9. The face amount of long-term debt, issuance premium or discount, certain payments to escrow agents for bond refundings, transfers, and sales of capital assets not qualifying as special items are reported as other financing sources and uses in the governmental funds statement of revenues, expenditures, and changes in fund balances. Thus, the entry in the capital projects fund in Year 8, the year of receipt, to record the bond proceeds is a debit to cash and a credit to other financing sources -- bond issue proceeds for $5,000,000.

27. Wood City, which is legally obligated to maintain a debt service fund, issued the following general obligation bonds on July 1:

Term of bonds	10 years
Face amount	$1,000,000
Issue price	101
Stated interest rate	6%

Interest is payable January 1 and July 1. What amount of bond issuance premium should be amortized in Wood's debt service fund for the year ended December 31?

A. $1,000

B. $500

C. $250

D. $0

Answer (D) is correct.
REQUIRED: The amount of bond premium amortized in the debt service fund.
DISCUSSION: The debt service fund of a governmental unit is a governmental fund used to account for the accumulation of resources for, and the payment of, general long-term debt principal and interest. Bond issuance premium will be accounted for as an other financing source in the fund out of which the proceeds will be spent. Thus, bond issuance premium is not amortized, in the debt service fund or anywhere else.

28. A public school district should recognize revenue from property taxes levied for its debt service fund when

A. Bonds to be retired by the levy are due and payable.

B. Assessed valuations of property subject to the levy are known.

C. Funds from the levy are measurable and available to the district.

D. Proceeds from collection of the levy are deposited in the district's bank account.

Answer (C) is correct.

REQUIRED: The timing of property tax recognition.

DISCUSSION: Debt service funds apply the modified accrual basis of accounting. Thus, revenues are recognized when they are measurable and available. Moreover, assets from imposed nonexchange revenue transactions, such as property tax levies, should be recognized when an enforceable legal claim arises or the resources are received, whichever is earlier. If the legal claim arises in the period after that for which the property taxes are levied, a receivable is recognized when revenues are recognized. Revenues are recognized in the period for which the taxes are levied if the availability criterion is met. For property taxes, this criterion is met if they are collected within the current period or soon enough thereafter (not exceeding 60 days) to pay current liabilities.

Answer (A) is incorrect. Revenues are recognized when property taxes are levied. Answer (B) is incorrect. The assessed valuations are necessary for calculating the amount of tax but do not make the tax revenue available. Answer (D) is incorrect. Revenue recognition is not on the cash basis.

29. The renovation of Fir City's municipal park was accounted for in a capital projects fund. Financing for the renovation, which was begun and completed during the current year, came from the following sources:

Grant from state government	$400,000
Proceeds from general obligation bond issue	500,000
Transfer from Fir's general fund	100,000

In its governmental fund statement of revenues, expenditures, and changes in fund balances for the current year, Fir should report these amounts as

	Revenues	Other Financing Sources
A.	$1,000,000	$0
B.	$900,000	$100,000
C.	$400,000	$600,000
D.	$0	$1,000,000

Answer (C) is correct.

REQUIRED: The amounts to be reported in the governmental fund statement of revenues, expenditures, and changes in fund balances.

DISCUSSION: Governmental fund revenues are increases in fund financial resources other than from interfund transfers, debt issue proceeds, and redemptions of demand bonds. Thus, revenues of a capital projects fund include grants. The grant (a voluntary nonexchange transaction) is recognized when all eligibility requirements, including time requirements, have been met. When modified accrual accounting is used, as in a capital projects fund, the grant must also be "available." Other financing sources include proceeds from bonds and interfund transfers in. Thus, Fir reports revenues of $400,000 and other financing sources of $600,000 ($500,000 + $100,000) in its governmental fund statement of revenues, expenditures, and changes in fund balances.

Answer (A) is incorrect. The proceeds from the bond issue and the transfer from the general fund should be reported under other financing sources. Answer (B) is incorrect. The proceeds from bond issue should be reported under other financing sources. Answer (D) is incorrect. The grant should be reported under revenues.

30. On January 2, City of Walton issued $500,000, 10-year, 7% general obligation bonds. Interest is payable annually, beginning January 2 of the following year. What amount of bond interest is Walton required to report in the statement of revenue, expenditures, and changes in fund balances of its governmental funds at the close of this fiscal year, September 30?

A. $0

B. $17,500

C. $26,250

D. $35,000

Answer (A) is correct.

REQUIRED: The bond interest reported in the governmental funds.

DISCUSSION: The financial statements of governmental funds are prepared using the modified accrual basis of accounting. It recognizes expenditures for principal and interest on general long-term debt only when these amounts are due. Because the fiscal year ends on September 30 and the interest is payable on the following January 2, Walton does not recognize the bond interest.

Answer (B) is incorrect. Walton is not required to report 6 months of interest for the fiscal year, or $17,500 [$500,000 × 7% × (6 ÷ 12)]. Answer (C) is incorrect. Walton is not required to report 9 months of interest for the fiscal year, or $26,500 [$500,000 × 7% × (9 ÷ 12)]. This amount is recognized in the government-wide statement of activities, which is prepared using the accrual basis. Answer (D) is incorrect. Walton is not required to report 12 months of interest for the fiscal year, or $35,000 [$500,000 × 7% × (12 ÷ 12)].

18.4 Characteristic Transactions of Governmental Entities

31. Kingwood Town, at the beginning of the year, paid $22,000 cash for a flatbed trailer to be used in the general operations of the town. The expected useful life of the trailer is 6 years with an estimated $7,000 salvage value. Which of the following amounts should be reported?

A. $15,000 increase in equipment in the general fund.

B. $15,000 increase in general capital assets.

C. $22,000 increase in general capital assets.

D. $22,000 increase in equipment in the general fund.

Answer (C) is correct.
REQUIRED: The recording of the purchase of equipment for general operations.
DISCUSSION: Capital assets related to proprietary funds are accounted for in the government-wide financial statements and in the fund financial statements. Capital assets related to fiduciary funds are reported only in the statement of fiduciary net position. All other capital assets are general capital assets reported only in the governmental activities column in the government-wide statement of net position. Capital assets are recorded at historical cost or at estimated fair value if donated. Thus, general capital assets should be debited for $22,000, the historical cost of the equipment.
Answer (A) is incorrect. Capital assets are not reported in the general fund and the assets are recorded at historical cost. Answer (B) is incorrect. Capital assets are reported at historical cost, not historical cost minus salvage value. Answer (D) is incorrect. Capital assets are not reported in the general fund.

32. Lys City reports a general long-term compensated absences liability in its financial statements. The salary rate used to calculate the liability should normally be the rate in effect

A. When the unpaid compensated absences were earned.

B. When the compensated absences are to be paid.

C. At the balance sheet date.

D. When the compensated absences were earned or are to be paid, or at the balance sheet date, whichever results in the lowest amount.

Answer (C) is correct.
REQUIRED: The salary rate used to calculate the liability for compensated absences.
DISCUSSION: The compensated absences liability should be calculated based on the pay or salary rates in effect at the balance sheet date. However, if the employer pays employees for their compensated absences at other than their pay or salary rates -- for example, at a lower amount as established by contract, regulation, or policy -- that other rate as of the balance sheet date should be used to calculate the liability.

33. Dayne County's general fund had the following disbursements during the year:

Payment of principal on long-term debt $100,000
Payments to vendors   500,000
Purchase of a computer   300,000

What amount should Dayne County report as expenditures in its governmental funds statement of revenues, expenditures, and changes in fund balances?

A. $300,000

B. $500,000

C. $800,000

D. $900,000

Answer (D) is correct.
REQUIRED: The amount classified as expenditures.
DISCUSSION: Expenditures are recognized in the fund financial statements of a governmental fund under the modified accrual basis. They are decreases in (uses of) expendable available financial resources of a governmental fund. Expenditures are usually measurable and should be recognized when the related liability is incurred. However, expenditures for principal and interest on general long-term debt are usually recognized when those amounts are due. The liabilities for payments to vendors and the computer purchase were most likely incurred in the current year. The liability for payment of the principal on long-term debt was most likely due in the current year. Thus, general fund expenditures equaled $900,000 ($100,000 + $500,000 + $300,000).
Answer (A) is incorrect. The purchase of a computer is not the only expenditure. Answer (B) is incorrect. The payments to vendors are not the only expenditures. Answer (C) is incorrect. The payment on long-term debt also should be considered an expenditure.

34. Expenditures of a government for insurance extending over more than one accounting period

A. Must be accounted for as expenditures of the period of acquisition.

B. Must be accounted for as expenditures of the periods subsequent to acquisition.

C. Must be allocated between or among accounting periods.

D. May be allocated among periods or accounted for as expenditures when acquired.

Answer (D) is correct.
REQUIRED: The proper treatment of expenditures extending over more than one period.
DISCUSSION: Under current GAAP, prepaid insurance may be reported by either the purchases method, in which an expenditure is reported when the policy is purchased, or the consumption method, in which an expenditure is reported when the asset is consumed.

35. The City of Bell entered into a capital lease agreement on December 31, Year 4, to acquire a capital asset. Under this agreement, Bell is to make three annual payments of $75,000 each on principal, plus interest of $22,000, $15,000, and $8,000 at the end of Year 5, Year 6, and Year 7, respectively. At the beginning of the lease, what amount should be debited to expenditures control in Bell's general fund?

A. $270,000

B. $225,000

C. $75,000

D. $97,000

Answer (B) is correct.
REQUIRED: The amount that should be debited to expenditures control in the general fund.
DISCUSSION: General capital assets that are acquired by capital lease are recorded in the same manner as those acquired by outright purchase. The asset is reported only in the governmental activities column of the government-wide statement of net position. It is measured in accordance with nongovernmental GAAP. In the general fund, when a capital lease represents the acquisition of a general capital asset, the transaction is reported by debiting an expenditure and crediting an other financing sources -- capital lease at the present value of the minimum lease payments ($75,000 annual principal repayment × 3 years = $225,000).
Answer (A) is incorrect. The amount of $270,000 includes the interest payments. Answer (C) is incorrect. The amount of $75,000 is the amount of one annual payment. Answer (D) is incorrect. The amount of $97,000 is the first annual payment plus the first interest payment.

Use the additional questions in Gleim **CPA Test Prep Online** to create Test Sessions that emulate Prometric!

18.5 PRACTICE SIMULATION

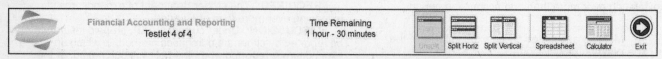

| Financial Accounting and Reporting | Time Remaining | | | | | | |
| Testlet 4 of 4 | 1 hour - 30 minutes | Unsplit | Split Horiz | Split Vertical | Spreadsheet | Calculator | Exit |

DIRECTIONS

Note: If you believe you have encountered a software malfunction, report it to the test center staff immediately.

Navigation

To navigate from task to task, use the controls at the bottom of the screen. Click on the **Next** button to advance to the next task, or the **Previous** button to go to the previous task. To go directly to any task, click on its number.

If you would like a reminder to revisit a task, or want to indicate that you are finished with it, click on the reminder flag below the task number. To clear the flag, click on it again. Reminder flags are for your use only – they do not contribute to your score.

Tabs

In this part of the examination, you will be asked to complete various tasks. Every task has one or more **Work Tabs**. Some tasks have one or more **Information Tabs**, others may have none. Every task has a **Help** tab.

If a task has **Information Tabs**, you may use the information in them to complete your responses in the **Work Tabs**.

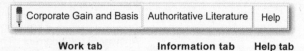

Work tab   Information tab   Help tab

Work Tabs:

- **Work Tabs** are identified with a pencil icon. This is where your responses are expected.
- Each task has one or more **Work Tabs**.
- **Work Tabs** contain directions for completing the task – be sure to read these directions carefully.
- The **Work Tab** name in the example above is for illustration only – yours will differ.
- You must complete all of the **Work Tabs** in each task to receive full credit.

Information Tabs:

- The Authoritative Literature will be provided in all tasks in the AUD, FAR, and REG sections for your reference.
- Your simulation may have one or more additional **Information Tabs**. Like the Authoritative Literature tabs, **Information Tabs** do not have a pencil icon.
- If your task has additional **Information Tabs**, go through each to familiarize yourself with the task content.

Help Tab:

- The **Help Tab** provides assistance with the exam software that is used in this task. For example, if the task is to compose a memorandum, **Help** will provide information about the word processor.

The Toolbar

The toolbar at the top of the screen shows the amount of time remaining for you to complete the tasks. In addition, the following tools are available. Note that only the **Exit** button is displayed when Directions are visible - the others will appear when you begin the tasks.

Click on these buttons to split or unsplit the screen. You can split the screen vertically or horizontally.

Click on this button to display the calculator; click on it again to hide the calculator. To move the calculator, click on the calculator title bar and drag the calculator to the desired location.

Click on this button to use the spreadsheet; click on it again to hide the spreadsheet. To move the spreadsheet, click on the the spreadsheet title bar and drag the spreadsheet to the desired location.

Click on this button to go on to the next part of the examination. You must complete all of the tasks to receive full credit. Once you click on **Exit** and confirm the action, you will NOT be able to return to this testlet.

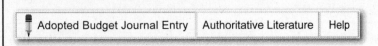

The Wayne City Council approved and adopted its budget for the year just ended. The budget contained the following amounts:

Estimated revenues control	$700,000
Appropriations control	660,000
Authorized interfund transfer to the library debt service fund	30,000

During the year, various transactions and events occurred that affected the general fund.

Property taxes assessed	$800,000
Uncollectible taxes	100,000
Interfund transfer to the debt service fund	30,000
Interfund reimbursement received	40,000
Expenditures	700,000

Determine which accounts are affected when recording the adopted budget in the general fund. Enter the correct amounts in the debit and credit fields by account. If the account is not affected, leave the corresponding boxes blank.

Account	Debit	Credit
1. Estimated revenues		
2. Budgetary fund balance		
3. Appropriations		
4. Estimated other financing uses — interfund transfers		
5. Expenditures		

SU 18: Governmental Accounting

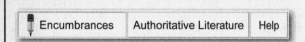

| Encumbrances | Authoritative Literature | Help |

Indicate by checking the appropriate box whether each account listed should be debited, credited, or is not affected.

Recording encumbrances in the general fund at the time purchase orders are issued.

Account	Debited	Credited	Not Affected
1. Encumbrances			
2. Fund balance account			
3. Expenditures			
4. Vouchers payable			
5. Purchases			

| ▼ = Reminder | | Directions | 1 **2** 3 4 5 | | ◀ Previous Next ▶ |

| Closing Entries | Authoritative Literature | Help |

Indicate by checking the appropriate box whether each account below will be debited, credited, or not affected when Wayne City Council records, in the general fund, the closing entries (other than encumbrances) for the year just ended.

Account	Debited	Credited	Not Affected
1. Expenditures			
2. Revenues			
3. Other financing uses — interfund transfers			
4. Bad debt expense			
5. Depreciation expense			
6. Interfund reimbursements			

| ▼ = Reminder | | Directions | 1 2 **3** 4 5 | | ◀ Previous Next ▶ |

| Expenditure and Budget-Closing Journal Entries | Authoritative Literature | Help |

The State of Monongahela adopted a budget for its general fund for the year. The following amounts are relevant:

Estimated total sales taxes to be collected	$100,000,000
Estimated total to be spent	92,000,000
Amount authorized for retirement of debt	1,000,000
Amount authorized to subsidize state agency telecommunications	1,000,000

At the end of the fiscal year, $8.4 million in encumbrances were outstanding.

Enter the correct amounts in the shaded cells below.

Purchase orders in the amount of $15 million are issued in the general fund.	Debit	Credit
1. Encumbrances		
2. Expenditures		
3. Fund balance -- reserve for encumbrances		
4. Purchases		
5. Vouchers payable		

The merchandise for which the purchase orders were issued is received.	Debit	Credit
6. Encumbrances		
7. Expenditures		
8. Fund balance -- reserve for encumbrances		
9. Purchases		
10. Vouchers payable		

The annual budget is closed out at year end.	Debit	Credit
11. Appropriations		
12. Estimated other financing uses -- transfers-out		
13. Budgetary fund balance		
14. Estimated revenues		
15. Expenditures		

Encumbrances are allowed to lapse.	Debit	Credit
16. Encumbrances		
17. Expenditures		
18. Fund balance -- reserve for encumbrances		
19. Unassigned fund balance		
20. Vouchers payable		

| Property Taxes | Authoritative Literature | Help |

The Edward City Council approved and adopted the budget for its general fund for the fiscal year beginning on January 1, Year 2. The budget contained the following amounts:

Estimated revenues $4,900,000
Appropriations   4,780,000

On November 1, Year 1, Edward City levied property taxes of $4,150,000 for the fiscal year beginning January 1, Year 2. It estimated that $25,000 will be uncollectible. Any payment of property taxes received during the discount period receives a 20% discount. During the discount period between the levy (October 15, Year 1) and the date (December 1, Year 1) that the levy became a legally enforceable claim, the city received $120,000 from property owners.

For each date below, select from the list provided the general fund accounts debited and credited the journal entries for this property tax levy. Enter the amounts in the columns for each debit and credit portion of the journal entry. If no entry is required, leave the amount cells blank.

Account	Debit/Credit	Amount
1. November 1, Year 1		
2. November 30, Year 1		
3. December 1, Year 1		
4. January 1, Year 2		

Account Choices
A) Cash
B) Property taxes receivable
C) Bad debt expense
D) Allowance for uncollectible taxes
E) Revenues — property taxes
F) Estimated revenues
G) Deferred property tax revenues
H) No entry required

Unofficial Answers

1. Adopted Budget Journal Entry (5 Gradable Items)

Account	Debit	Credit
1. Estimated revenues	$700,000	
2. Budgetary fund balance		$10,000
3. Appropriations		$660,000
4. Estimated other financing uses — interfund transfers		$30,000
5. Expenditures		

1. Estimated revenues is an anticipatory asset account that is debited in the budgetary entry.

2. Some accountants prefer to use budgetary fund balance, a nominal account, to record the budgeted change in fund equity for the year.

3. The total amount authorized to be expended by the governmental unit for the fiscal period is credited in the budgetary entry. Appropriations control is an anticipatory liability account.

4. Estimated other financing sources (uses) include interfund transfers, the face amount of long-term debt, issuance premium or discount, certain payments to escrow agents for bond refundings, and sales of capital assets not qualifying as special items. The budgetary entry may include estimated other financing sources (a debit) or estimated other financing uses (a credit).

5. Expenditures are not affected by recording the budget. An expenditure is debited when a fund liability is incurred.

2. Encumbrances (5 Gradable Items)

1. Debited. When a commitment is made to expend resources of a governmental unit, appropriations is encumbered. The traditional entry by a government that uses encumbrance accounting is to debit encumbrances and credit a reserve for encumbrances for the amount of the commitment. Comparison of encumbrances, appropriations, and expenditures determines the unencumbered amount of appropriations that may still be expended.

2. Credited. When a commitment is made to expend resources of a governmental unit, appropriations is encumbered. The traditional entry by a government that uses encumbrance accounting is to debit the encumbrances account and credit a reserve for encumbrances for the amount of the commitment. Comparison of encumbrances, appropriations, and expenditures determines the unencumbered amount of appropriations that may still be expended.

3. Not affected. An expenditure is not recognized by a debit until the related liability is incurred.

4. Not affected. Vouchers payable is not recognized by a credit until the related liability is incurred.

5. Not affected. A purchases account is not used to record inventory in a governmental fund.

3. Closing Entries (6 Gradable Items)

1. Credited. Expenditures are debited when liabilities are incurred. Expenditures is therefore credited when operational general-ledger accounts are closed.

2. Debited. Under the modified accrual basis of accounting, revenue is accrued by a credit when it is measurable and available to finance current expenditures. It is therefore debited when operational general-ledger accounts are closed.

3. Credited. Other financing uses – interfund transfer is debited when the interfund transfer is recorded. The account is therefore credited when operational general-ledger accounts are closed.

4. Not affected. Bad debt expense is not recognized in a governmental fund. Revenues are recorded net of estimated bad debts.

5. Not affected. Depreciation expense is not recorded in governmental fund financial statements. Depreciation expense is recorded in proprietary fund financial statements, fiduciary fund financial statements, and the government-wide financial statements.

6. Not affected. Interfund reimbursements are not displayed in the financial statements.

4. Expenditure and Budget-Closing Journal Entries (20 Gradable Items)

1. $15,000,000 Debit.

2.   Blank.

3. $15,000,000 Credit.

4.   Blank.

5.   Blank.

When a government issues a purchase order, it becomes a legal obligation of the government (unlike a business entity). To acknowledge this obligation, the traditional entry for a government that elects to use encumbrance accounting for internal purposes is to debit encumbrances and credit reserve for encumbrances.

6. $15,000,000 Credit.

7. $15,000,000 Debit.

8. $15,000,000 Debit.

9.   Blank.

10. $15,000,000 Credit.

When merchandise is received, the encumbrance and the reserve for encumbrances are reversed. Expenditures is then debited and vouchers payable credited. Purchases is not an account used in the general fund and other governmental funds.

11. $92,000,000 Debit.

12. $2,000,000 Debit.

13. $6,000,000 Debit.

14. $100,000,000 Credit.

15. Blank.

The annual budget entry is closed at year-end by reversing the original entry. Expenditures is not a budgetary account.

16. $8,400,000 Credit.

17. Blank.

18. $8,400,000 Debit.

19. Blank.

20. Blank.

The entry affects only encumbrances and reserve for encumbrances.

5. Property Taxes (4 Gradable Items)

Account	Debit/Credit	Amount
1. November 1, Year 1		
H) No entry required		
2. November 30, Year 1		
A) Cash	Debit	$120,000
G) Deferred property tax revenues	Credit	$120,000
3. December 1, Year 1		
B) Property taxes receivable	Debit	$4,000,000
G) Deferred property tax revenues	Credit	$3,975,000
D) Allowance for uncollectible taxes	Credit	$25,000
4. January 1, Year 2		
G) Deferred property tax revenues	Debit	$4,095,000
E) Revenues – property taxes	Credit	$4,095,000

1. **November 1, Year 1:** H) No entry required. No entry is made on November 1, Year 1, because an enforceable legal claim has not arisen, and no resources have been received.

2. **November 30, Year 1:** A) Cash; G) Deferred property tax revenues.

    Cash $120,000
       Deferred property tax revenues $120,000

    Edward City should record an asset at the earlier of when (a) an enforceable legal claim to the resources has arisen or (b) resources are received. Furthermore, property tax revenues should not be recognized in the general fund until the fiscal period for which the assessment was levied, provided the resources are available (collectible in time to pay liabilities of the current period). Thus, for amounts received during the discount period, the entry is to debit cash and credit deferred property tax revenues. The $120,000 cash received equals $150,000 of property taxes levied [$120,000 ÷ (100% – 20% discount)] minus the prepayment discount ($150,000 × 20%).

3. **December 1, Year 1:** B) Property taxes receivable; G) Deferred property tax revenues; D) Allowance for uncollectible taxes.

    Property taxes receivable $4,000,000
       Deferred property tax revenues $3,975,000
       Allowance for uncollectible taxes   25,000

    Property taxes receivable is debited when the assessment becomes legally enforceable [total property taxes levied – prepaid amount ($4,150,000 – $150,000)]. Allowance for uncollectible taxes is credited for the amount of the tax assessment that is that is estimated to be uncollectible. This amount is recognized when the assessment becomes legally enforceable. If the assessment becomes legally enforceable before the period for which it is levied, the government recognizes a liability (deferred property tax revenues), not revenues.

4. **January 1, Year 2:** G) Deferred property tax revenues; E) Revenues — property taxes.

    Deferred property tax revenues $4,095,000
       Revenues — property taxes $4,095,000

    When the period for which the assessment was made begins, revenues — property taxes is credited for the amount of revenues from property taxes, and deferred property tax revenues is debited for the amount previously credited.

Gleim Simulation Grading

Task	Correct Responses		Gradable Items		Score per Task
1	_____	÷	5	=	_____
2	_____	÷	5	=	_____
3	_____	÷	6	=	_____
4	_____	÷	20	=	_____
5	_____	÷	4	=	_____

Total of Scores per Task   _____

÷   Total Number of Tasks   5

Total Score   _____%

Use **CPA Gleim Online** and **Simulation Wizard** to practice more task-based simulations in a realistic environment.

STUDY UNIT NINETEEN
GOVERNMENTAL REPORTING

(23 pages of outline)

19.1	The Reporting Entity and the CAFR	687
19.2	MD&A and the Government-Wide Financial Statements	691
19.3	Governmental Funds Reporting	697
19.4	Proprietary Funds Reporting	702
19.5	Fiduciary Funds Reporting and Interfund Activity	705
19.6	Practice Simulation	720

This study unit is the second related to the governmental entities group in the Content Specification Outlines. It describes (1) the accounts and journal entries for transactions specific to governmental entities, (2) the governmental reporting entity, (3) the components of the comprehensive annual financial report (CAFR), (4) the reporting requirements for government-wide and fund financial statements, and (5) other required information in the CAFR. The presentation assumes knowledge of the information in Study Unit 18.

19.1 THE REPORTING ENTITY AND THE CAFR

Background

State and local governmental accounting changed substantially in 1999 with the release of GASB Statement No. 34, *Basic Financial Statements – and Management's Discussion and Analysis – for State and Local Governments*. Previously, state and local governments reported detailed fund-level information in their general-purpose financial statements. The typical governmental financial statement therefore contained specialized information for groups of funds in a format that made it difficult for the average user to obtain a comprehensive understanding of how the entity was obtaining and using its resources.

One of the difficulties of the former reporting methods was the use of two account groups. There were free-standing presentations of general fixed assets and general long-term debt. Accordingly, they had no relationship with other elements of the financial statements.

GASB Statement No. 34 clarified state and local government reporting. Governments now produce two separate sets of financial statements: one containing detailed fund information and the other containing an overview of the entity's governmental and business-type activities.

1. **Defining the Reporting Entity**

   a. The variety of activities in which governments engage, the various funds used for accounting for these activities, and the numerous semi-governmental entities with which governments interact complicate reporting.

      1) **Financial accountability** is the primary criterion for defining the reporting entity.

   b. The **overall reporting entity** consists of the primary government and its component units.

      1) The **primary government** is the main portion of the overall reporting entity. It is financially accountable for the entities that make up its legal entity and certain other entities.

         a) Any state or general-purpose local government qualifies as a primary government.

         b) A special-purpose local government (such as a school system) also is considered a primary government if it

            i) Has a separately elected governing body,
            ii) Is legally independent, and
            iii) Is fiscally independent of other state or local governments.

2) **Component units** are legally separate entities for which the primary government is financially accountable. The primary government is also financially accountable when

    a) The separate entity is **fiscally dependent** on the primary government, and

    b) The primary government and the separate entity have a **financial benefit or burden** relationship.

        i) For example, assume that a water district is fiscally dependent because a county must approve the issuance of its bonds. But if the district does not receive a subsidy from, or provide resources to, the county, it is not a component unit of the county. It has no financial benefit or burden relationship with the primary government.

3) A separate entity also must be treated as a component unit if its exclusion would cause the financial statements to be **misleading**.

    a) However, whether the exclusion is misleading ordinarily depends on financial relationships, e.g., a significant, nontemporary financial benefit or burden relationship.

2. **Blended vs. Discretely Presented Component Units**

  a. **Blended component units** are, in substance, the same as the primary government and should be reported as a part of it.

    1) **Blending** is appropriate only if the component unit's governing body is substantively the same as the primary government's, or the component unit exclusively or almost exclusively benefits the primary government.

    2) Moreover, the primary government must have

        a) A financial benefit or burden relationship with the component unit or

        b) At a level below its elected officials, operational responsibility for the component unit's activities.

  b. Blended component-unit **balances and transactions** are reported in a manner similar to the balances and transactions of the primary government.

    1) Thus, blended component units are reported as part of the primary government in the fund financial statements and the government-wide financial statements.

    2) The **funds of the component unit** are blended with those of the primary government in the fund statements and combining statements.

        a) However, the primary government's **general fund** should be the only general fund reported.

            i) The general fund of the blended component unit should be reported as a **special revenue fund** of the primary government.

  c. The financial statements of the reporting entity should **distinguish** between the primary government and its **component units** in a way that does not suggest that they are one legal entity.

    1) For this purpose, the government-wide financial statements should report information about most **discretely (individually) presented component units** in separate rows and columns.

        a) The **equity interest** in a discretely presented component unit must be reported as an **asset**.

    2) Information about discretely presented component units that are **fiduciary** in nature is reported only in the fiduciary fund statements of the primary government.

        a) No other discretely presented component units are reported in the fund financial statements.

      d.   **Discrete presentation** also includes reporting of **major component unit** information in the basic statements. This requirement does not apply to fiduciary component units.

      e.   The financial statements of the reporting entity should include **data from all of its component units**.

          1)   This data from the component units' statements should be the amounts that would be in the **total columns** of those statements if they had been presented.

3.   **Content of the Comprehensive Annual Financial Report (CAFR)**

      a.   The **introductory section** contains the following:

          1)   Letter of transmittal from the appropriate government officials
          2)   Organization chart
          3)   Names of principal officers

      b.   The **financial section** contains the following:

          1)   Independent auditor's report
          2)   Management's discussion and analysis (MD&A)
          3)   Basic financial statements

              a)   **Government-wide financial statements**

                  i)   Statement of net position
                  ii)   Statement of activities

              b)   **Fund financial statements**

                  i)   **Governmental funds financial statements**

- Balance sheet (with reconciliation to government-wide statement of net position)
- Statement of revenues, expenditures, and changes in fund balances (with reconciliation to government-wide statement of activities)

                  ii)   **Proprietary funds financial statements**

- Statement of net position
- Statement of revenues, expenses, and changes in fund net position
- Statement of cash flows

                  iii)   **Fiduciary funds financial statements** (and fiduciary component units)

- Statement of fiduciary net position
- Statement of changes in fiduciary net position

              c)   **Notes to the financial statements**

                  i)   Notes are an integral part of the basic financial statements. They disclose information essential to fair presentation that is not reported on the face of the statements. The focus is on the primary government's

- Governmental activities,
- Business-type activities,
- Major funds, and
- Nonmajor funds in the aggregate.

                  ii)   The notes include a **summary of significant accounting policies**.

4) Required supplementary information (RSI) other than MD&A

   a) **Budgetary comparison schedules (BCSs)** are RSI. They are reported for the following:

      i) General fund
      ii) Each major special revenue fund with a legally adopted annual budget

   b) A BCS includes the following:

      i) The original budgets, that is, the first complete appropriated budgets
      ii) The final appropriated budgets
      iii) The actual inflows, outflows, and balances stated on the **budgetary basis of accounting**

   c) A reconciliation of budgetary and GAAP information should be provided.

   d) If a government has a significant difference between the GAAP fund structure and the fund structure in the legally adopted budget, it must use a different format for the BCS. This format is based on the fund, organization, or program structure used in the legally adopted budget.

5) Combining statements and individual fund statements and schedules

   a) Combining statements are included in the CAFR when the primary government has more than one (1) nonmajor governmental or enterprise fund or (2) internal service or fiduciary fund.

   b) Combining statements also are included when the reporting entity has more than one nonmajor discretely presented component unit.

   c) Individual fund statements are reported when the primary government has just one nonmajor fund of a given type or when prior-year or budgetary comparisons are not included in RSI.

      i) Fund financial statements for individual component units are necessary in the absence of separately issued financial statements of the individual component units.

c. The **statistical section** focuses on the primary government.

   1) It reports information in five categories:

      a) Financial trends indicate changes in financial position over time.

      b) Revenue capacity relates to an entity's ability to produce own-source revenues (e.g., taxes but not shared revenues).

      c) Debt capacity concerns the entity's debt burden and the ability to issue new debt.

      d) Demographic and economic information pertains to the socioeconomic environment.

      e) Operating information furnishes context.

   2) Additional information may be reported.

   3) Sources of information should be identified, and methods and assumptions should be explained.

   4) Narrative explanations should provide analysis of the quantitative data. They address (a) the objectives of the statistical section, (b) the categories of information, (c) unfamiliar concepts, (d) relationships among the data, and (e) unusual trends and data.

4.   **Minimum Elements for General-Purpose External Financial Reporting**

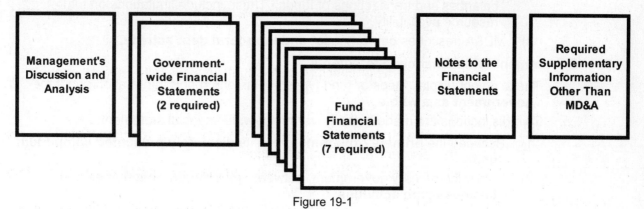

Figure 19-1

5.   **Special-Purpose Governments**

   a.   Special-purpose governments (SPGs) are legally separate entities that are component units or other stand-alone governments. If they have governmental and business-type activities or are engaged in two or more governmental programs, they should be reported as **general-purpose governments**.

   b.   If an SPG is engaged in **one governmental program** (e.g., an assessment or drainage district), it may combine the government-wide and fund statements.

   c.   If an SPG is engaged only in **business-type activities**, it reports the statements for **enterprise funds**. If it is engaged only in **fiduciary activities**, it reports the statements for fiduciary funds.

      1)   **Public colleges and universities** must apply the guidance for special-purpose governments.

Stop and review! You have completed the outline for this subunit. Study multiple-choice questions 1 through 6 beginning on page 709.

19.2 MD&A AND THE GOVERNMENT-WIDE FINANCIAL STATEMENTS

1.   **Management's Discussion and Analysis (MD&A)**

   a.   MD&A is part of required supplementary information (RSI). It precedes the basic financial statements and provides an analytical overview of financial activities. It is based on **currently known** facts, decisions, or conditions expected to affect financial position or results of operations significantly.

      1)   MD&A includes a **comparison** of the current and prior year, with an emphasis on the current year, based on government-wide information. The focus is on the **primary government**, with distinctions between that government and its component units.

      2)   MD&A requirements are stated in general terms to encourage reporting of only the most relevant information.

   b.   MD&A discusses the **basic financial statements**, including (1) their relationships to each other, (2) differences in the information provided, and (3) analyses of relationships of information in the fund and government-wide statements.

      1)   MD&A also analyzes **overall financial position and results of operations** to aid in determining whether the year's activities have resulted in an improvement in that position and those results.

         a)   It should discuss **governmental and business-type activities** and the reasons for significant changes.

    2) Moreover, MD&A analyzes significant **budget variances** and changes in balances and transactions of funds. These include limitations on future resource availability.

    3) MD&A describes **capital asset and long-term debt activity**.

2. **Government-Wide Financial Statements**

    a. These do not display funds or fund types but instead report information about the **government as a whole**.

    b. Two distinctions are made in the government-wide financial statements:

        1) Between the **primary government** and its **discretely presented component units**

        2) Within the primary government, between **governmental activities** and **business-type activities**

            a) Governmental activities are normally financed by nonexchange revenues (taxes, etc.). They are reported in governmental and internal service funds.

            b) Business-type activities are financed at least in part by fees charged to external parties for goods and services. They are usually reported in enterprise funds.

3. **Statement of Net Position**

EXAMPLE

Sample Statement of Net Position
December 31, 20X1

	Primary Government			
ASSETS	**Governmental Activities**	**Business-Type Activities**	**Total**	**Component Units**
Cash and cash equivalents	$ XX,XXX,XXX	$ XX,XXX,XXX	$ XX,XXX,XXX	$ XXX,XXX
Investments	XX,XXX,XXX	--	XX,XXX,XXX	X,XXX,XXX
Derivative instrument -- rate swap	XX,XXX,XXX	X,XXX,XXX	XX,XXX,XXX	X,XXX,XXX
Receivables (net)	XX,XXX,XXX	X,XXX,XXX	XX,XXX,XXX	X,XXX,XXX
Internal balances	XXX,XXX	(XXX,XXX)	--	--
Inventories	XXX,XXX	XXX,XXX	XXX,XXX	XX,XXX
Equity interest in joint venture	XXX,XXX	XXX,XXX	XXX,XXX	XX,XXX
Capital assets, net	XXX,XXX,XXX	XXX,XXX,XXX	XXX,XXX,XXX	XX,XXX,XXX
Total assets	**$XXX,XXX,XXX**	**$XXX,XXX,XXX**	**$XXX,XXX,XXX**	**$ XX,XXX,XXX**
DEFERRED OUTFLOWS OF RESOURCES				
Accumulated decrease in fair value of hedging derivatives	$ X,XXX,XXX	$ XXX,XXX	$ X,XXX,XXX	$ X,XXX,XXX
LIABILITIES				
Accounts payable and accrued expenses	$ X,XXX,XXX	$ XXX,XXX	$ X,XXX,XXX	$ X,XXX,XXX
Advances from grantors	X,XXX,XXX	--	X,XXX,XXX	XX,XXX
Forward contract	X,XXX,XXX	--	X,XXX,XXX	XX,XXX
Long-term liabilities:				
Due within 1 year	X,XXX,XXX	X,XXX,XXX	XX,XXX,XXX	X,XXX,XXX
Due in more than 1 year	XX,XXX,XXX	XX,XXX,XXX	XXX,XXX,XXX	XX,XXX,XXX
Total liabilities	**$XXX,XXX,XXX**	**$ XX,XXX,XXX**	**$XXX,XXX,XXX**	**$XXX,XXX,XXX**

-- Continued on next page --

EXAMPLE -- Continued

DEFERRED INFLOWS OF RESOURCES

Accumulated increase in fair value of hedging derivatives	$ X,XXX,XXX	$ XXX,XXX	$ X,XXX,XXX	$ X,XXX,XXX
Deferred service concession arrangement receipts	$ X,XXX,XXX	$ XXX,XXX	$ X,XXX,XXX	$ X,XXX,XXX
Total deferred inflows of resources	**$XXX,XXX,XXX**	**$XXX,XXX,XXX**	**$XXX,XXX,XXX**	**$ XX,XXX,XXX**

NET POSITION

Net investment in capital assets	$XXX,XXX,XXX	$ XX,XXX,XXX	$XXX,XXX,XXX	$ XX,XXX,XXX
Restricted for:				
Transportation and public works	XX,XXX,XXX	--	XX,XXX,XXX	XXX,XXX
Debt service	X,XXX,XXX	X,XXX,XXX	X,XXX,XXX	--
Housing and community redevelopment	X,XXX,XXX	--	X,XXX,XXX	--
Other purposes	X,XXX,XXX	--	X,XXX,XXX	--
Unrestricted (deficit)	(X,XXX,XXX)	XX,XXX,XXX	X,XXX,XXX	X,XXX,XXX
Total net position	**$XXX,XXX,XXX**	**$ XX,XXX,XXX**	**$XXX,XXX,XXX**	**$ XX,XXX,XXX**

---

a. The statement of net position reports **all financial and capital resources**.

   1) No particular format is required, although the GASB prefers the net position format.

Net Position Format

```
(Assets + Deferred outflows of resources)
- (Liabilities + Deferred inflows of resources)
= Net position
```

Thus, the difference between the sum of assets and deferred outflows of resources and the sum of liabilities and deferred inflows of resources is **net position**, not equity or fund balance.

b. Presentation of assets and liabilities in order of relative liquidity is encouraged. A classified statement of net position is also acceptable.

c. Net position should be displayed as three components:

   1) **Net investment in capital assets** includes unrestricted and restricted capital assets, net of accumulated depreciation and related liabilities for borrowings.

      a) However, **debt** related to significant **unspent proceeds** is classified in the same net position component as those proceeds, such as restricted for capital projects.

   2) **Restricted net position** is subject to constraints imposed by external entities (creditors, grantors, or other governments) or by law (constitutional provisions or **enabling legislation**).

      a) If permanent endowments or permanent fund principal amounts are included, restricted net position should be displayed as two additional components: expendable and nonexpendable. **Nonexpendable** means that the restriction is retained in perpetuity.

   3) **Unrestricted net position** is a residual category. For example, this category includes items that are merely internally **designated** rather than externally restricted or restricted by enabling legislation. Designations are not reported on the face of the financial statements.

EXAMPLE

Statement of Activities

Functions/Programs	Expenses	Program Revenues: Charges for Services	Program Revenues: Operating Grants and Contributions	Program Revenues: Capital Grants and Contributions	Net (Expense) Revenue and Changes in Net Assets — Primary Government: Governmental Activities	Net (Expense) Revenue and Changes in Net Assets — Primary Government: Business-type Activities	Net (Expense) Revenue and Changes in Net Assets — Primary Government: Total	Component Units
Primary government:								
Governmental activities:								
General government	$ X,XXX,XXX	$ X,XXX,XXX	$ XXX,XXX	—	$ (X,XXX,XXX)	—	$ (X,XXX,XXX)	
Public safety	XX,XXX,XXX	X,XXX,XXX	X,XXX,XXX	XX,XXX	(XX,XXX,XXX)	—	(XX,XXX,XXX)	
Public works	XX,XXX,XXX	XXX,XXX	—	X,XXX,XXX	(X,XXX,XXX)	—	(X,XXX,XXX)	
Engineering services	X,XXX,XXX	XXX,XXX	—	—	(XXX,XXX)	—	(XXX,XXX)	
Etc.	XX,XXX,XXX	X,XXX,XXX	X,XXX,XXX	X,XXX,XXX	(XX,XXX,XXX)	—	(XX,XXX,XXX)	
Total governmental activities	$ XXX,XXX,XXX	$ XX,XXX,XXX	$ X,XXX,XXX	$ X,XXX,XXX	$ (XX,XXX,XXX)	—	$ (XX,XXX,XXX)	
Business-type activities:								
Water	$ X,XXX,XXX	$ X,XXX,XXX	$ X,XXX,XXX	$ X,XXX,XXX		$ X,XXX,XXX	$ X,XXX,XXX	
Sewer	X,XXX,XXX	X,XXX,XXX	XXX,XXX	XXX,XXX		X,XXX,XXX	X,XXX,XXX	
Parking facilities	X,XXX,XXX	X,XXX,XXX	—	—		(X,XXX,XXX)	(X,XXX,XXX)	
Total business-type activities	$ XX,XXX,XXX	$ XX,XXX,XXX	$ XX,XXX,XXX	$ XX,XXX,XXX		$ X,XXX,XXX	$ X,XXX,XXX	
Total primary government	$ XXX,XXX,XXX	$ XX,XXX,XXX	$ X,XXX,XXX	$ X,XXX,XXX	$ (XX,XXX,XXX)	$ X,XXX,XXX	$ (XX,XXX,XXX)	
Component units:								
Landfill	$ X,XXX,XXX	$ X,XXX,XXX	$ —	$ XX,XXX				XXX,XXX
Public school system	XX,XXX,XXX	XXX,XXX	X,XXX,XXX	X,XXX,XXX				(XX,XXX,XXX)
Total component units	$ XX,XXX,XXX	$ X,XXX,XXX	$ X,XXX,XXX	$ XX,XXX				$ (XX,XXX,XXX)

General revenues:	Governmental Activities	Business-type Activities	Total	Component Units
Taxes:				
Property taxes levied for general purposes	$ XX,XXX,XXX	—	$ XX,XXX,XXX	$ XX,XXX,XXX
Property taxes levied for debt service	X,XXX,XXX	—	X,XXX,XXX	X,XXX,XXX
Franchise fees	X,XXX,XXX	—	X,XXX,XXX	X,XXX,XXX
Public service taxes	X,XXX,XXX	—	X,XXX,XXX	X,XXX,XXX
Payment from City	—	—	—	$ XX,XXX,XXX
Grants and contributions not restricted to specific programs	X,XXX,XXX	—	X,XXX,XXX	X,XXX,XXX
Investment earnings	X,XXX,XXX	XXX,XXX	X,XXX,XXX	XXX,XXX
Miscellaneous	X,XXX,XXX	XXX,XXX	X,XXX,XXX	XX,XXX
Special item – gain on sale of park land	X,XXX,XXX	—	X,XXX,XXX	—
Transfers	XXX,XXX	(XXX,XXX)	—	—
Total general revenues, special items, and transfers	$ XX,XXX,XXX	$ XXX,XXX	$ XX,XXX,XXX	$ (XX,XXX,XXX)
Change in net assets	(X,XXX,XXX)	X,XXX,XXX	XXX,XXX	XXX,XXX
Net assets – beginning	XX,XXX,XXX	XX,XXX,XXX	XXX,XXX,XXX	XX,XXX,XXX
Net assets – ending	$ XXX,XXX,XXX	$ XX,XXX,XXX	$ XXX,XXX,XXX	$ XX,XXX,XXX

4. **Statement of Activities**

    a.   The statement of activities presents operations in a format that displays **net (expense) revenue** for each function.

       1)   The purpose is to report the relative financial burden to the taxpayers for that function.

       2)   The net (expense) revenue for each governmental or business-type function equals expenses (at a minimum, the **direct expenses** of the function) minus program revenues.

    b.   The minimum levels of detail for activities accounted for in governmental funds and in enterprise funds are by **function** and by **different identifiable activities**, respectively.

       1)   An **identifiable activity** has a specific revenue stream and related expenses, gains, and losses separately accounted for. Whether it is different ordinarily depends on the goods, services, or programs that the activity provides.

    c.   **Direct expenses** must be reported by function. **Indirect expenses** may or may not be allocated. A government may choose to allocate some indirect expenses, to adopt a full-cost allocation approach, or not to allocate.

       1)   If indirect expenses are allocated, direct and indirect expenses should be displayed in separate columns.

       2)   **Depreciation** specifically identifiable with a function is a direct expense. Depreciation of capital assets **shared by functions** is allocated as a direct expense.

          a)   Depreciation of capital assets that **serve all functions** is not required to be included in direct expenses of the functions. It may be displayed on a separate line in the statement of activities or as part of the general government function. It may or may not be allocated.

          b)   Depreciation of infrastructure assets is not allocated to other functions.

       3)   **Interest on general long-term liabilities** is usually an indirect expense.

    d.   **Program revenues** include (1) charges for services, (2) program-specific operating grants and contributions, and (3) program-specific capital grants and contributions.

       1)   They also may include (a) earnings on endowments, (b) permanent fund investments, or (c) other investments if such earnings are specifically restricted to a given program. Multiple columns may be used to report a category.

       2)   **Charges for services** constitute a category of program revenues resulting from charges to customers, applicants, or others who (a) directly benefit from what is provided (goods, services, or privileges) or (b) are otherwise directly affected.

          a)   Thus, **fines and forfeitures** are charges for services because they are paid by persons directly affected by a program or service.

          b)   Charges for services are assigned to a given function if the function generates those revenues.

       3)   Program revenues in the form of **grants and contributions** are assigned to a given function if the revenues are restricted to it.

    e.   **General revenues** are not required to be reported as program revenues. They are reported separately after total net (expense) revenue for all functions. All taxes, including those levied for a special purpose, are general revenues.

       1)   General revenues are reported at the bottom of the statement of activities to determine the change in net position for the period.

    f.   The following are reported separately at the bottom of the statement: (1) contributions to endowments, (2) contributions to permanent fund principal, (3) transfers between governmental and business-type activities, and (4) special and extraordinary items.

        1)   **Extraordinary items** are unusual in nature and infrequent in occurrence.

        2)   **Special items** are significant transactions or other events that are either unusual or infrequent and are **within the control of management**. They are reported separately after extraordinary items.

5.   **Other Reporting Issues**

    a.   Government-wide financial statements are prepared using the **economic resources measurement focus** and the **accrual basis of accounting**. They report all of the government's assets, liabilities, revenues, expenses, gains, and losses.

        1)   Items arising from **exchange or exchange-like transactions** are recognized when the exchange occurs. Items arising from nonexchange transactions are recognized in accordance with the guidance in Study Unit 18, Subunit 3.

        2)   The resources of **fiduciary activities** and similar component units (e.g., some public employee retirement systems) are not available to finance the government's programs. Thus, they are reported only in the fund statements (the statements of fiduciary net position and changes in fiduciary net position).

6.   **Eliminations and Reclassifications**

    a.   **Interfund receivables and payables** reported in fund balance sheets are eliminated in the governmental and business-type activities columns of the statement of net position.

        1)   Exceptions are net residual amounts due (presented as **internal balances** between the two types of activities). Failing to report residual amounts contradicts the principle requiring separate presentation of governmental and business-type activities. However, the total primary government column excludes internal balances.

    b.   Fund receivables from, or payables to, **fiduciary funds** are treated in the statement of net position as amounts arising from transactions with **external parties**, not as internal balances. The reason is that fiduciary funds only report balances held for individuals, private organizations, and other governments.

    c.   The effect of **internal service fund** activity should be eliminated in the statement of activities to avoid double counting. Thus, preparation of this statement essentially requires adjusting the internal service fund's change in net position to zero.

        1)   The result is a decrease or increase in the charges made to the participating funds or functions.

        2)   Moreover, similar internal events (e.g., allocations of accounting staff expenses) that are, in effect, allocations of overhead also result in eliminations. Accordingly, only the function to which they were allocated reports them.

    d.   Eliminations are not made in the statement of activities for the effects of **interfund services provided and used** between functions (e.g., the sale of power by a utility to the general government).

    e.   Flows of resources between **the primary government** and its **blended component units** are reclassified as internal activity based on the requirements for interfund activity.

        1)   Flows between the primary government and its **discretely presented component units** (unless they affect the balance sheet only) are treated as **external transactions** (i.e., as revenues and expenses). The payables and receivables are reported on a separate line.

f.   Any balances of **internal service funds** that are not eliminated are usually reported in the governmental activities column. These funds' activities are ordinarily more governmental than business-type. But this presentation is not appropriate if enterprise funds are the predominant participants in the internal service funds.

Stop and review! You have completed the outline for this subunit. Study multiple-choice questions 7 through 12 beginning on page 711.

19.3 GOVERNMENTAL FUNDS REPORTING

1. **Governmental Funds**

   a.   Governmental funds emphasize sources, uses, and balances of current financial resources.

      1)   Expendable assets are assigned to funds based on their intended use, current liabilities are assigned to funds from which they will be paid, and the difference (fund equity) is the fund balance.

      2)   Thus, the governmental funds are reported using the **current financial resources measurement focus** and the **modified accrual basis of accounting**.

2. **Major vs. Nonmajor Fund Reporting**

   a.   The focus of governmental and enterprise fund financial statements is on **major funds**.

      1)   Each major fund is presented in a separate column.

         a)   The main operating fund (the general fund) is always reported as a major fund.

      2)   Nonmajor funds are aggregated in one column.

      3)   Combining statements are not required for nonmajor funds.

   b.   Any individual governmental or enterprise fund **must be reported as major if both**

      1)   Total assets, liabilities, revenues, or expenditures/expenses (excluding revenues and expenditures/expenses classified as extraordinary) of the fund are **at least 10%** of the corresponding element total (assets, etc.) for all funds of its category or type (i.e., all governmental or all enterprise funds), **and**

      2)   An element that met the 10% standard above is **at least 5%** of the corresponding element total for all governmental and enterprise funds.

   c.   Any governmental or enterprise fund believed to be particularly important to users also may be reported in this way.

   d.   Major fund reporting is **not required** for **internal service funds**.

3. **General Fund**

   a.   The general fund accounts for all resources of the governmental unit not required to be reported elsewhere.

   b.   The reporting entity has **only one** general fund.

4. **Special Revenue Funds**

    a. Special revenue funds account for **restricted or committed** proceeds of specific sources of revenue. Expenditure must be for a **specified purpose** (but not debt service or a capital project). Thus, the basis of the fund is a **substantial inflow** from restricted or committed revenue sources.

        1) Examples of resources accounted for are federal grant monies, revenue-sharing funds, and gasoline taxes.
        2) Examples of a government's uses of special revenue funds are (a) operation of its municipal auditorium, (b) upkeep of its zoo, or (c) road maintenance.

    b. Donations provided by benefactors for programs to be administered by the government also are accounted for in special revenue funds.

    c. A special revenue fund is **not** used for the resources of a trust benefiting specific individuals, private organizations, or other governments.

    d. The general fund of a **blended component unit** is reported as a special revenue fund.

    e. Special revenue funds are not required unless legally mandated.

5. **Capital Projects Funds**

    a. Capital projects funds account for financial resources **restricted, committed, or assigned** to be expended for capital purposes. These resources include general obligation bond proceeds to be used for the acquisition or construction of major capital facilities for general government use (e.g., schools, bridges, or tunnels).

    b. Capital projects financed by proprietary funds or in trust funds for individuals, private organizations, or other governments are accounted for in those funds.

    c. The assets themselves are not accounted for in these funds.

6. **Debt Service Funds**

    a. Debt service funds account for resources **restricted, committed, or assigned** to payment of the principal and interest.

    b. They are required if (1) they are legally mandated or (2) the resources are for payment of principal and interest due in future years.

    c. If the government has no obligation on a **special assessment issue**, the debt service transactions are accounted for in an **agency fund**.

7. **Permanent Funds**

    a. Permanent funds account for resources that are **restricted** to the use of **earnings** for the benefit of the government or its citizens. An example is a perpetual-care fund for a public cemetery.

    b. Permanent funds are **not private-purpose trust funds**, which benefit individuals, private organizations, or other governments. Private-purpose trust funds are reported with the other **fiduciary funds**.

8. **Governmental Funds -- Balance Sheet**

    a. A balance sheet is required for governmental funds. It should be in balance sheet format with a **total column.**

Balance Sheet Format

$$\begin{array}{ccc} & & Liabilities \\ Assets & & + \\ + & = & Deferred\ inflows\ of\ resources \\ Deferred\ outflows\ of\ resources & & + \\ & & Fund\ balances \end{array}$$

    b. **Fund balances** should be classified as nonspendable, restricted, committed, assigned, or unassigned.

EXAMPLE

Governmental Funds Balance Sheet

	General Fund	Major Fund	Major Fund	Major Fund	All Nonmajor Funds	Total Governmental Funds
ASSETS						
Cash	$ XXX,XXX	$ XXX,XXX	$ XXX,XXX	$ XXX,XXX	$ XXX,XXX	$ X,XXX,XXX
Investments	XXX,XXX	XXX,XXX	XXX,XXX	XXX,XXX	XXX,XXX	X,XXX,XXX
Deferred outflows of resources	XXX,XXX	XXX,XXX	XXX,XXX	XXX,XXX	XXX,XXX	X,XXX,XXX
Total assets and deferred outflows of resources	**$X,XXX,XXX**	**$X,XXX,XXX**	**$X,XXX,XXX**	**$X,XXX,XXX**	**$X,XXX,XXX**	**$XX,XXX,XXX**
LIABILITIES AND FUND BALANCES						
Liabilities:						
Accounts payable	$ XXX,XXX	$ XXX,XXX	$ XXX,XXX	$ XXX,XXX	$ XXX,XXX	$ X,XXX,XXX
Due to other funds	XXX,XXX	XXX,XXX	XXX,XXX	XXX,XXX	XXX,XXX	X,XXX,XXX
Deferred inflows of resources	XXX,XXX	XXX,XXX	XXX,XXX	XXX,XXX	XXX,XXX	X,XXX,XXX
Total liabilities and deferred inflows of resources	$X,XXX,XXX	$X,XXX,XXX	$X,XXX,XXX	$X,XXX,XXX	$X,XXX,XXX	$XX,XXX,XXX
Fund balance:						
Nonspendable						
Inventories	$ XXX,XXX	--	--	--	--	$ XXX,XXX
Committed						
Encumbrances	XX,XXX	$ XX,XXX	$ XX,XXX	$ XX,XXX	$ XXX,XXX	XXX,XXX
Debt service	--	--	--	--	XXX,XXX	XXX,XXX
Assigned						
Special revenue funds	--	XXX,XXX	XXX,XXX	--	XXX,XXX	XXX,XXX
Capital projects funds	--	--	--	XXX,XXX	XXX,XXX	XXX,XXX
Unassigned						
General fund	XXX,XXX	--	--	--	--	XXX,XXX
Total fund balances	$X,XXX,XXX	$ XXX,XXX	$ XXX,XXX	$ XXX,XXX	$X,XXX,XXX	$ X,XXX,XXX
Total liabilities, deferred inflows of resources, and fund balances	**$X,XXX,XXX**	**$X,XXX,XXX**	**$X,XXX,XXX**	**$X,XXX,XXX**	**$X,XXX,XXX**	**$XX,XXX,XXX**

9.   **Summary Reconciliation**

   a.   A summary reconciliation of total governmental fund balances to net position of governmental activities in the government-wide statement of net position must be prepared.

   1)   This summary should be presented at the bottom of the statement or in a schedule. Brief explanations on the face of the statement may suffice, but a more detailed explanation in the notes may be necessary.

   b.   **General capital assets and general long-term liabilities** not currently due are reconciling items because they are not reported on the balance sheet. Thus, the **current** financial resources measurement focus of the governmental funds balance sheet is reconciled with the reporting of **all** resources and obligations.

EXAMPLE

Governmental Funds Reconciliation

Total governmental fund balances	$XX,XXX,XXX
Amounts reported for *governmental activities* in the statement of net position are different because:	
Capital assets used in governmental activities are not financial resources and therefore are not reported in the funds.	XX,XXX,XXX
Other long-term assets are not available to pay for current-period expenditures and therefore are deferred in the funds.	X,XXX,XXX
Internal service funds are used by management to charge the costs of certain activities, such as insurance and telecommunications, to individual funds. The assets and liabilities of the internal service funds are included in governmental activities in the statement of net position.	X,XXX,XXX
Long-term liabilities, including bonds payable, are not due and payable in the current period and therefore are not reported in the funds.	(XX,XXX,XXX)
Net position of governmental activities	$XX,XXX,XXX

10. **Governmental Funds -- Statement of Revenues, Expenditures, and Changes in Fund Balances**

   a.   This statement is required. It reports inflows, outflows, and balances of current financial resources. The focus is on major fund reporting.

EXAMPLE
Governmental Funds Statement of Revenues, Expenditures, and Changes in Fund Balances

	General Fund	Major Fund	Major Fund	Major Fund	All Nonmajor Funds	Total Governmental Funds
REVENUES						
Property taxes	$ X,XXX,XXX	--	--	--	$ XXX,XXX	$ X,XXX,XXX
Public service taxes	XXX,XXX	--	--	--	--	XXX,XXX
Fees and fines	XXX,XXX	--	--	--	--	XXX,XXX
Intergovernmental	XXX,XXX	$ XXX,XXX	--	--	XXX,XXX	X,XXX,XXX
Investment earnings	XXX,XXX	XXX,XXX	$ XXX,XXX	$ XXX,XXX	XXX,XXX	X,XXX,XXX
Etc.	XXX,XXX	XXX,XXX	--	XXX,XXX	XXX,XXX	X,XXX,XXX
Total revenues	$ X,XXX,XXX	$X,XXX,XXX	$X,XXX,XXX	$X,XXX,XXX	$ X,XXX,XXX	$ XX,XXX,XXX
EXPENDITURES						
Current:YYYY						
General governmental	$ XXX,XXX	--	$ XXX,XXX	$ XXX,XXX	$ XXX,XXX	$ X,XXX,XXX
Public safety	XXX,XXX	--	--	--	XXX,XXX	X,XXX,XXX
Public works	XXX,XXX	--	--	--	XXX,XXX	X,XXX,XXX
Etc.	XXX,XXX	$ XXX,XXX		--	XXX,XXX	X,XXX,XXX
Debt service:						
Principal	--	--	--	--	XXX,XXX	XXX,XXX
Interest and other charges	--	--	--	--	XXX,XXX	XXX,XXX
Capital outlay	--	--	XXX,XXX	XXX,XXX	XXX,XXX	X,XXX,XXX
Total expenditures	$ X,XXX,XXX	$X,XXX,XXX	$ X,XXX,XXX	$ X,XXX,XXX	$ X,XXX,XXX	$ XX,XXX,XXX
Excess (deficiency) of revenues over expenditures	$(X,XXX,XXX)	$ (XXX,XXX)	$(X,XXX,XXX)	$(X,XXX,XXX)	$(X,XXX,XXX)	$(XX,XXX,XXX)
OTHER FINANCING SOURCES (USES)						
Proceeds of refunding bonds	--	--	--	--	$XX,XXX,XXX	$XX,XXX,XXX
Proceeds of long-term capital-related debt	--	--	$XX,XXX,XXX	--	X,XXX,XXX	XX,XXX,XXX
Payment to bond refunding escrow agent	--	--	--	--	(XX,XXX,XXX)	(XX,XXX,XXX)
Transfers in	$ XXX,XXX	--	--	--	X,XXX,XXX	X,XXX,XXX
Transfers out	(X,XXX,XXX)	$ (XXX,XXX)	(X,XXX,XXX)	--	(XXX,XXX)	(X,XXX,XXX)
Total other financing sources and uses	$X,XXX,XXX	$X,XXX,XXX	$ X,XXX,XXX	--	$X,XXX,XXX	$ XX,XXX,XXX
SPECIAL ITEM						
Proceeds from sale of park land	$ X,XXX,XXX	--	--	--	--	$ X,XXX,XXX
Net changes in fund balances	$(X,XXX,XXX)	$ (XXX,XXX)	$XX,XXX,XXX	$(XX,XXX,XXX)	$ (XXX,XXX)	$ (XXX,XXX)
Fund balances – beginning	X,XXX,XXX	X,XXX,XXX	XX,XXX	XX,XXX,XXX	XX,XXX,XXX	XX,XXX,XXX
Fund balances – ending	$ X,XXX,XXX	$X,XXX,XXX	$XX,XXX,XXX	$ X,XXX,XXX	$ X,XXX,XXX	$ XX,XXX,XXX

---

   b.   **Revenues** are classified in this statement by major source and **expenditures** by, at a minimum, function.

   1) **Debt issue costs** (e.g., underwriter's fees) paid from the proceeds are expenditures. Issue costs (e.g., rating agency fees) paid from existing resources are likewise classified as expenditures (but not until the liability is incurred).

   c.   **Other financing sources and uses** include the face amount of long-term debt, issuance premium or discount, some payments to escrow agents for bond refundings, interfund transfers, and sales of capital assets (unless the sale is a special item).

d. **Special and extraordinary items** are reported separately after other financing sources and uses. A transaction or an event may meet the definition of a special item except that it is **not** within the control of management. Such a transaction or event should be separately identified in the appropriate revenue or expenditure category or disclosed in the notes.

1) **Debt refundings** in governmental funds are not extraordinary items. They result in other financing sources or uses, not gains or losses.

11. **Summary Reconciliation**

a. A summary reconciliation of the net change in governmental fund balances to the change in net position of governmental activities in the government-wide statement of activities must be prepared.

1) This summary should be presented at the bottom of the statement or in a schedule. Brief explanations on the face of the statement may suffice, but a more detailed explanation in the notes may be necessary.

EXAMPLE
Governmental Funds Reconciliation

Net change in fund balances – total governmental funds	$ (XXX,XXX)
Amounts reported for *governmental activities* in the statement of activities are different because:	
Governmental funds report **capital outlays** as expenditures. However, in the statement of activities, the cost of those assets is allocated over their estimated useful lives as depreciation expense. This is the amount by which capital outlays exceeded depreciation in the current period.	XX,XXX,XXX
In the statement of activities, only the **gain on the sale of the park land** is reported. But in the governmental funds, the proceeds from the sale increase financial resources. Thus, the change in net position differs from the change in fund balances by the cost of the land sold.	(XXX,XXX)
Revenues in the statement of activities that do not provide current financial resources are not reported as revenues in the funds.	X,XXX,XXX
Bond proceeds provide current financial resources to governmental funds, but issuing debt increases long-term liabilities in the statement of net position. Repayment of bond principal is an expenditure in the governmental funds, but the repayment reduces long-term liabilities in the statement of net position. This is the amount by which proceeds exceeded repayments.	(XX,XXX,XXX)
Some expenses reported in the statement of activities do not require the use of current financial resources and therefore are not reported as expenditures in governmental funds.	(X,XXX,XXX)
Internal service funds are used by management to charge the costs of certain activities, such as insurance and telecommunications, to individual funds. The net revenue (expense) of the internal service funds is reported with governmental activities.	(XXX,XXX)
Change in net position of governmental activities	**$ (X,XXX,XXX)**

Stop and review! You have completed the outline for this subunit. Study multiple-choice questions 13 and 14 on page 713.

19.4 PROPRIETARY FUNDS REPORTING

1. **Enterprise Funds**

   a. Enterprise funds may be used for any activities for which fees are charged to external users. They need not be used for insignificant activities.

   b. An activity must be reported as an enterprise fund if one of three criteria is met. These are applied in the context of the activity's principal revenue sources. The criteria emphasize **fees charged to external users**.

      1) It is financed with debt, and the only security is a pledge of the activity's net revenues from fees and charges.

      2) Its capital and other costs of providing services are legally required to be recovered from fees and charges, not taxes or similar revenues.

      3) Its pricing policies set fees and charges to recover capital and other costs.

   c. The following are examples of enterprise fund activities:

      1) Public transportation systems
      2) State-run lotteries
      3) Public utilities (water, sewage, electricity)
      4) Unemployment compensation funds
      5) Emergency services
      6) Government-owned healthcare facilities

   d. Journal entries are virtually the same as in any business enterprise. **Major fund reporting** is required for enterprise funds.

2. **Internal Service Funds**

   a. They may be used for activities that provide goods and services to other subunits of the primary government and its component units or to other governments on a **cost-reimbursement basis**.

      1) However, if the reporting government is not the predominant participant, the activity should be reported as an **enterprise fund**.

   b. The following are examples of the uses of an internal service fund:

      1) Information technology
      2) Central purchasing and warehousing
      3) Motor pool maintenance
      4) Photocopying and printing
      5) Self-insurance for payment of claims and judgments

   c. **Billings for goods and services** are recorded as operating revenues. These activities are considered to be interfund services provided and used.

   d. Journal entries are virtually the same as for any business.

      1) The initial allocation of resources may come from an interfund transfer, that is, from an amount not to be repaid or an interfund loan.

         a) To record an interfund transfer from the general fund and an interfund loan from an enterprise fund, the entry might be

Cash	$XXX,XXX	
Interfund transfer from the general fund		$XXX,XXX
Due to enterprise fund		XXX,XXX

   e. **Major fund** reporting is **not** required for internal service funds. Thus, the combined totals for all internal service funds are reported in a separate column (usually labeled as governmental activities) to the right of the total enterprise funds column in each proprietary fund financial statement.

3. **Proprietary Fund Financial Statements**

    a.   The emphasis of proprietary funds is on operating income, changes in net position (or cost recovery), financial position, and cash flows.

        1)   Moreover, these funds customarily do not record a budget and encumbrances.

    b.   The **economic resources measurement focus** and the **accrual basis of accounting** are required in the proprietary fund financial statements.

4. **Proprietary Funds -- Statement of Net Position or Balance Sheet**

    a.   Assets and liabilities must be **classified** as current or noncurrent.

        1)   Either a net position format (see page 693) or a balance sheet format (see page 698) may be used.

    b.   Net position should be reported in three components (net investment in capital assets, restricted, and unrestricted). Moreover, **capital contributions** (such as grants or contributions by developers) should **not** be displayed as a separate component. **Designations** should **not** be shown on the face of the statements.

        1)   **Restricted assets** are subject to use restrictions imposed by external entities or by law that change the nature or normal understanding of the availability of the asset.

        2)   **Capital assets** of proprietary funds and **long-term liabilities** directly related to, and expected to be paid from, proprietary funds are reported in the government-wide statement of net position and in the proprietary fund statement of net position.

5. **Proprietary Funds -- Statement of Revenues, Expenses, and Changes in Fund Net Position (or Fund Equity)**

    a.   **Revenues** are reported by major source either **net** with disclosure of discounts and allowances or **gross** with discounts and allowances reported beneath the revenue amounts.

    b.   **Operating and nonoperating** revenues and expenses are distinguished. Separate subtotals are given for operating revenues, operating expenses, and operating income. The sequence of items in the all-inclusive format shown below must be followed in each column of the statement:

	Operating revenues (detailed)
+	Total operating revenues
	Operating expenses (detailed)
–	Total operating expenses
=	**Operating income (loss)**
+/–	Nonoperating revenues and expenses (detailed)
=	Income before other revenues, expenses, gains, losses, and transfers
+/–	Capital contributions, additions to endowments, special and extraordinary items, and interfund transfers
=	**Change in net position**
+	Net position – beginning
=	**Net position – ending**

    c.   A government should consistently follow appropriate **definitions of operating items**. One consideration in defining these items is the principal purpose of the fund. A second consideration is the presentation of these items in a cash flows statement. Thus, an item not classified as an operating cash flow most likely should be treated as a nonoperating revenue or expense.

    d.   For recognition of **nonexchange revenues**, see Study Unit 18, Subunit 3.

    e.   Restricted net position should be presented in **expendable and nonexpendable components** when additions are made to permanent endowments.

f.   **Reconciliation.** Net position and changes in net position are reported in the proprietary fund statements for total enterprise funds. They will ordinarily be the same as the corresponding amounts for business-type activities in the government-wide statements. Any differences should be reconciled.

1)   For example, although **internal service funds** are proprietary funds, the activities they account for are normally governmental. Thus, they should be included in the governmental activities column in the government-wide statement of activities.

2)   However, if enterprise funds are the **predominant participants** in the internal service funds, this presentation is not appropriate. Accordingly, the reclassification of internal service fund transactions from governmental to business-type activities is an item needed to reconcile the amounts for total enterprise funds to amounts in the government-wide statements.

6.   **Proprietary Funds -- Statement of Cash Flows**

a.   A statement of cash flows is required for (1) proprietary funds and (2) entities engaged in **business-type activities**, e.g., governmental utilities, governmental healthcare providers, and public colleges and universities.

1)   The guidance for preparing the statement is similar to that in Study Unit 3 for nongovernmental entities. Thus, the outlines below emphasize the differences.

b.   Cash flows should be classified as operating, financing, and investing. Moreover, financing cash flows are reported in separate categories.

1)   **Noncapital financing activities** include borrowings (and repayments of debt) for purposes other than acquiring, constructing, or improving capital assets.

a)   Cash flows may include (1) grants and subsidies received or paid, (2) tax receipts, (3) debt proceeds, and (4) cash received from or paid to other funds (excluding flows from interfund services provided or used).

2)   **Capital and related financing activities** include borrowings (and repayments of debt) for (a) acquiring, constructing, or improving capital assets; (b) acquiring and disposing of capital assets used to provide goods or services; and (c) paying for capital assets obtained on credit.

3)   **Operating activities** are those not classified as financing or investing activities. In general, operating activities affect operating income.

a)   They include (1) loan activities not intended as investments (program loans made as part of a government responsibility, e.g., student loans), (2) interfund services provided and used, and (3) providing goods or services.

4)   **Investing activities** include (a) making and collecting loans (other than program loans) and (b) acquiring and disposing of debt and equity instruments.

a)   Cash **interest** received is an inflow from investing activities.

c.   The **direct method** (including a reconciliation of operating income to operating cash flows) should be used to report operating cash flows. It reports major classes of gross operating cash receipts and payments and their sum (net cash flow from operating activities).

1)   The **minimum classes** to be reported are (a) cash receipts from customers, (b) cash receipts from interfund services provided, (c) other operating cash receipts, (d) cash payments to employees for services, (e) cash payments to other suppliers, (f) cash payments for interfund services used, and (g) other operating cash payments.

Successful CPA candidates will remember that a statement of cash flows is required for proprietary funds and entities engaged in business-type activities. The other fund types do not have to present this statement because these two funds function more like a commercial business than a government agency.

Stop and review! You have completed the outline for this subunit. Study multiple-choice questions 15 through 21 beginning on page 714.

19.5 FIDUCIARY FUNDS REPORTING AND INTERFUND ACTIVITY

1. **Fiduciary Funds**

    a. Fiduciary funds emphasize net position and changes in net position. They report assets that cannot be used to support the government's own programs. They are held in trust or in an agency capacity for **specific individuals, private organizations, or other governments**. They are not held for other funds or component units of the reporting entity.

        1) A **trust fund** differs from an **agency fund**. The trust agreement determines how long resources are held and the degree of management involvement. The governmental entity serves as a **fiduciary** of a trust. The role of the government is purely **custodial** for resources held in an agency fund.

        2) The **economic resources measurement focus** and the **accrual basis of accounting** are required in the fiduciary fund financial statements.

2. **Fiduciary Fund Financial Statements**

    a. These statements include information about all fiduciary funds and similar component units. The statements report information in a separate column for each fund type but **not** by major fund. The notes present financial statements for individual defined benefit pension and other postemployment benefit plans unless separate GAAP reports have been issued.

    b. A **statement of fiduciary net position** is required for fiduciary funds. It reports assets (plus deferred outflows of resources), liabilities (plus deferred inflows of resources), and net position for each fiduciary fund type. However, it does not present the three components of net position reported in the government-wide statement of net position or in the proprietary fund statement of net position.

        1) The statement is equivalent to the **statement of plan net assets** required for defined benefit pension and other postemployment benefit plans.

        2) **Capital assets** of fiduciary funds and **long-term liabilities** directly related to, and expected to be paid from, fiduciary funds are reported in the statement of fiduciary net position, **not** in the government-wide statement of net position.

    c. A **statement of changes in fiduciary net position** is required for fiduciary funds. It reports additions to, subtractions from, and the annual net change in net position for each fiduciary fund type.

        1) It is equivalent to the **statement of changes in plan net assets** required for defined benefit pension and other postemployment benefit plans.

3. **Pension (and Other Employee Benefit) Trust Funds**

    a. These funds report resources held for members and beneficiaries of pension plans (defined benefit or contribution), other postemployment benefit plans, or other employee benefit plans.

        1) They (a) report contributions to such plans to be held in a fiduciary capacity by a governmental entity, (b) track investments in the funds, and (c) calculate and disburse benefits due to members and beneficiaries.

b.   A governmental body with a **defined contribution pension plan** should report a plan description, a summary of significant accounting policies, and information about investment concentrations.

   1)   The plan description should identify the plan as a defined contribution plan and disclose in the notes to the financial statements the number of participating employers and other contributing entities.

   2)   The description also should include the classes of employees covered and the total current membership, a brief description of plan provisions and the authority under which they are established (or may be amended), and contribution requirements.

4.   **Investment Trust Funds**

a.   An investment trust fund is used by a sponsoring government to report the external portion of an **external investment pool** (the portion belonging to legally separate entities not part of the sponsor's reporting entity). Moreover, the sponsor should report each external pool as a separate fund.

   1)   The statements required are similar to those for pension trust funds.

   2)   Investments generally are reported at **fair value**.

5.   **Private-Purpose Trust Funds**

a.   These funds are used for all other trust arrangements under which the beneficiaries are specific individuals, private organizations, or other governments. An example is a fund for escheat property. Property escheats when it reverts to a governmental entity in the absence of legal claimants.

6.   **Agency Funds**

a.   These funds report resources held solely in a custodial capacity. They ordinarily account only for the receipt, temporary investment, and payment of resources to specific individuals, private organizations, or other governments.

b.   Agency fund **assets** (plus deferred outflows of resources) should equal **liabilities** (plus deferred inflows of resources) in the statement of fiduciary net position. Agency funds are **not** reported in the statement of changes in fiduciary net position.

   1)   Agency funds may account for **certain grants and other financial assistance** to be transferred to, or spent on behalf of, secondary recipients (individuals, private organizations, or other governments). The agency fund acts purely as a conduit. It receives the resources and passes them through to the ultimate recipients. However, if the recipient has **administrative or direct financial involvement** in the program, the pass-through grant is accounted for in an appropriate governmental, proprietary, or trust fund.

c.   Thus, agency funds record assets (plus deferred outflows of resources) and liabilities (plus deferred inflows of resources) only. Net position (fund equity) does not exist, so **assets (plus deferred outflows of resources) equal liabilities (plus deferred inflows of resources)**.

   1)   Revenues and expenses are not recorded.

d.   **Tax agency funds** are used when a governmental entity is the collection agent of taxes for disbursement to other governmental units, e.g., school districts, city governments, and special taxing districts.

   1)   A governmental unit acting as a collection agent for another government usually subtracts administrative fees for the collection services.

      a)   The agency fund should recognize a liability owed to the general fund for the amount of the administrative fees.

The AICPA has released CPA questions that test candidates' knowledge of the various fiduciary funds and the required financial statements for them. These questions have been mainly conceptual, but a few have required calculations.

7. **Reciprocal Interfund Activity**

    a. **Interfund activity** involves internal events. (A **transaction** is an external event.)

        1) Reciprocal interfund activities are comparable to exchange and exchange-like transactions. They include interfund loans and interfund services.

    b. **Interfund loans** result in interfund receivables and payables, not financing sources and uses. Any amount not expected to be repaid reduces the interfund balances. It is reported as a transfer.

        1) Liabilities arising from interfund activity are not general long-term liabilities. Thus, they may be reported in governmental funds.

    c. **Interfund services provided and used** are activities involving sales and purchases at prices equivalent to external exchange values.

        1) They result in **revenues to seller funds** and **expenditures or expenses to buyer funds**. Unpaid amounts are interfund receivables or payables.

            a) However, when the general fund accounts for **risk-financing activity**, charges to other funds are treated as **reimbursements**.

            b) In the **fund financial statements**, all transactions (those between activities and those within activities) are recognized.

EXAMPLE

A government pays for unemployment benefit coverage and computer processing time.

General fund:

Expenditures -- unemployment compensation	$ 8,500,000	
Expenditures -- information services	15,500,000	
Cash		$24,000,000

Enterprise fund -- unemployment compensation:

Cash	$ 8,500,000	
Revenues		$ 8,500,000

Internal service fund -- information services:

Cash	$15,500,000	
Revenues		$15,500,000

---

            c) In the **government-wide financial statements**, however, only the transactions affecting the enterprise fund are recorded.

EXAMPLE

The transactions affecting the internal service fund are entirely within the governmental activities section.

Governmental activities:

Expenses -- unemployment compensation	$8,500,000	
Cash		$8,500,000

Business-type activities:

Cash	$8,500,000	
Revenues		$8,500,000

---

8. **Nonreciprocal Interfund Activity**

   a. **Interfund transfers** are one-way asset flows with no repayment required. They must be reported in the basic financial statements separately from revenues and expenditures or expenses.

      1) In a **governmental fund**, a transfer is an other financing use (source) in the transferor (transferee) fund. It is reported after excess (deficiency) of revenues over expenditures in the statement of revenues, expenditures, and changes in fund balances.

      2) In a **proprietary fund**, the statement of revenues, expenses, and changes in fund net position reports interfund transfers separately after nonoperating revenues and expenses.

   b. The reporting of transfers is different in the government-wide and the fund financial statements.

      1) Transfers **within the governmental activities section** are not reported in the government-wide statements. These transfers result in no overall change in governmental activities.

      2) Transfers **between governmental activities and business-type activities** are reported in both the government-wide statements and the fund statements.

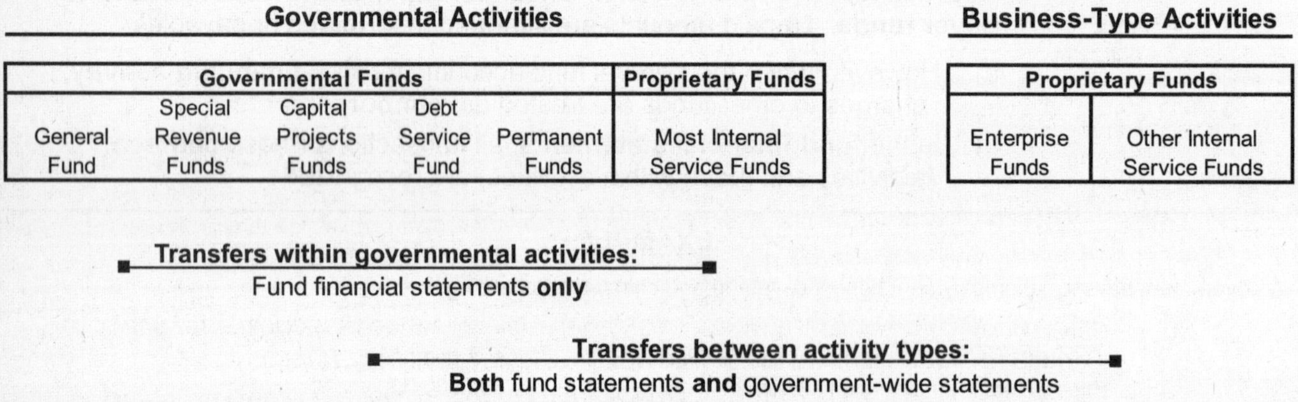

Governmental Activities						Business-Type Activities	
Governmental Funds					**Proprietary Funds**	**Proprietary Funds**	
General Fund	Special Revenue Funds	Capital Projects Funds	Debt Service Fund	Permanent Funds	Most Internal Service Funds	Enterprise Funds	Other Internal Service Funds

Transfers within governmental activities:
Fund financial statements **only**

Transfers between activity types:
Both fund statements **and** government-wide statements
Figure 19-2

   c. **Transfers within Governmental Activities**

EXAMPLE

A common interfund transfer is from the general fund to the debt service fund for the repayment of debts.

Fund financial statements. When the transfer is recognized, the transferor establishes a payable, and the recipient establishes a receivable.

General fund:
| Other financing uses -- transfer to debt service fund | $2,000,000 | |
| Due to debt service fund | | $2,000,000 |

Debt service fund
| Due from general fund | $2,000,000 | |
| Other financing sources -- transfer from general fund | | $2,000,000 |

The following entries are recorded when the transfer is made:

General fund:
| Due to debt service fund | $2,000,000 | |
| Cash | | $2,000,000 |

Debt service fund
| Cash | $2,000,000 | |
| Due from general fund | | $2,000,000 |

Government-wide financial statements. No entries.

---

d.   **Transfers between Activity Types**

EXAMPLE

On occasion, a government transfers resources from the general fund to an enterprise fund for a major upgrade or expansion.

Fund financial statements. When the transfer is recognized, the accounting is identical to that used above.

General fund:

Other financing uses -- transfer to municipal hospital fund	$130,000,000	
Due to municipal hospital fund		$130,000,000

Enterprise fund:

Due from general fund	$130,000,000	
Interfund transfer from general fund		$130,000,000

The movement of cash also is recorded the same way.

General fund:

Due to municipal hospital fund	$130,000,000	
Cash		$130,000,000

Enterprise fund:

Cash	$130,000,000	
Due from general fund		$130,000,000

Government-wide statements. An additional set of entries is made. Resources have passed not only between funds but also between activities.

Governmental activities:

Transfer to municipal hospital fund	$130,000,000	
Cash		$130,000,000

Business-type activities:

Cash	$130,000,000	
Transfer from general fund		$130,000,000

---

e.   **Interfund reimbursements** are repayments by the funds responsible for specific outlays to the payor funds. They are not displayed in the statements.

Stop and review! You have completed the outline for this subunit. Study multiple-choice questions 22 through 30 beginning on page 716.

QUESTIONS

19.1 The Reporting Entity and the CAFR

1. Valley Town's public school system is administered by a separately elected board of education. The board of education is not organized as a separate legal entity and does not have the power to levy taxes or issue bonds. Valley Town's city council approves the school system's budget. How should Valley Town report the public school system's annual financial results?

	Discrete Presentation	Blended
A.	Yes	Yes
B.	Yes	No
C.	No	Yes
D.	No	No

Answer (C) is correct.

REQUIRED: The reporting of a public school system's annual financial results.

DISCUSSION: Most component units should be included in the government-wide financial statements of the reporting entity by discrete presentation, that is, by reporting component-unit financial data in rows and columns separate from the financial data of the primary government. Furthermore, some component units are, in substance, the same as the primary government and should be reported as a part of it, that is, blended. Valley Town's public school system is part of Valley Town's primary government. Although the board of education is separately elected, the school system is not legally separate. Also, Valley Town has a financial benefit or burden relationship with the school system given that the school board cannot levy taxes or issue bonds. Thus, the annual financial results of the school system should be blended with those of Valley Town.

2. The financial statements of the reporting entity of a state or local governmental unit include information about which of the following?

I. The primary government
II. Discretely presented component units
III. Blended component units

    A. I only.

    B. I and II only.

    C. I and III only.

    D. I, II, and III.

Answer (D) is correct.
    REQUIRED: The organization(s) about which information is included in the financial statements of the reporting entity of a state or local governmental unit.
    DISCUSSION: The financial statements of the reporting entity should distinguish between the primary government and its component units in a way that does not suggest that they are one legal entity. For this purpose, the government-wide financial statements should report information about most discretely presented component units in separate rows and columns. Fiduciary component units are reported only in the primary government's fiduciary fund statements. However, the other fund statements report information only for blended (not discretely presented) component units. Discrete presentation also includes reporting of major component unit information in the basic statements. Furthermore, some component units are, in substance, the same as the primary government and should be reported as a part thereof. Blending is appropriate only if the component unit's governing body is substantively the same as the primary government's, or the component unit exclusively or almost exclusively benefits the primary government. Moreover, the primary government must have (1) a financial benefit or burden relationship with the component or (2) operational responsibility for its activities. Blended component-unit balances and transactions are reported in a manner similar to the balances and transactions of the primary government. Thus, blended component units are reported as part of the primary government in the fund financial statements and the government-wide financial statements.

3. What is the basic criterion used to determine the reporting entity for a governmental unit?

    A. Special financing arrangement.

    B. Geographic boundaries.

    C. Scope of public services.

    D. Financial accountability.

Answer (D) is correct.
    REQUIRED: The basic criterion used to determine the reporting entity for a governmental unit.
    DISCUSSION: The financial reporting entity is the primary government, organizations for which the primary government is financially accountable, and other organizations with a relationship with the primary government such that exclusion would cause the reporting entity's basic financial statements to be misleading or incomplete. A separate entity must be included in the reporting entity if (1) it is fiscally dependent on the primary government, and (2) the two entities have a financial benefit or burden relationship. Separate governmental units may be organized based on special financing arrangements, the nature of services provided, and geographic limits and have apparent legal, financial, and administrative autonomy. Nevertheless, their governing bodies are usually appointed by elected officials of a primary government and therefore should be part of that financial reporting entity.

4. What is the correct approach to presentation of the notes to the financial statements?

    A. The notes are essential for fair presentation of the statements.

    B. The notes are required supplementary information.

    C. The notes have the same status as MD&A.

    D. The notes give equal focus to the primary government and its discretely presented component units.

Answer (A) is correct.
    REQUIRED: The approach to presentation of the notes to the financial statements.
    DISCUSSION: Notes to the financial statements are an integral part of the basic financial statements because they disclose information essential to fair presentation that is not reported on the face of the statements. The focus is on the primary government's governmental activities, business-type activities, major funds, and nonmajor funds in the aggregate.
    Answer (B) is incorrect. Notes are not merely RSI. Answer (C) is incorrect. RSI includes MD&A, budgetary comparison schedules for governmental funds, and information about infrastructure assets reported using the modified approach. Answer (D) is incorrect. The notes focus on the primary government.

5. Budgetary comparison schedules must

    A. Be reported for the general fund and each major special revenue fund with a legally adopted budget.

    B. Be presented instead of budgetary comparison statements included in the basic statements.

    C. Convert the appropriated budget information to the GAAP basis for comparison with actual amounts reported on that basis.

    D. Compare only the final appropriated budget with actual amounts.

Answer (A) is correct.
    REQUIRED: The true statement about budgetary comparison schedules.
    DISCUSSION: Certain information must be presented as RSI in addition to MD&A. Budgetary comparison schedules must be reported for the general fund and each major special revenue fund with a legally adopted annual budget. A schedule includes the original budgets, that is, the first complete appropriated budgets; the final appropriated budgets; and the actual inflows, outflows, and balances stated on the budgetary basis of accounting. Thus, budgetary comparison schedules are not required for proprietary funds, fiduciary funds, and governmental funds other than the general fund and major special revenue funds.
    Answer (B) is incorrect. A government may elect to report budgetary comparison information in a statement as part of the basic statements. Answer (C) is incorrect. The budgetary comparison schedules compare the budgets with actual inflows, outflows, and balances stated on the government's budgetary basis. However, a reconciliation to GAAP is required. Answer (D) is incorrect. The original and final appropriated budgets are compared with the actual inflows, outflows, and balances.

6. A state or local government is reported as a special-purpose government if it

    A. Has governmental and business-type activities.

    B. Is engaged in two or more governmental programs.

    C. Is **not** a legally separate entity.

    D. Is engaged in one governmental program.

Answer (D) is correct.
    REQUIRED: The entity that may be reported as a special-purpose government.
    DISCUSSION: Special-purpose governments are legally separate entities that are component units or other stand-alone governments. If they have governmental and business-type activities or are engaged in two or more governmental programs, they should be reported as general-purpose governments. If a special-purpose government is engaged in one governmental program, it may combine the government-wide and fund statements in a format that reconciles individual items of fund data to government-wide data in a separate column.
    Answer (A) is incorrect. A government that has governmental and business-type activities should be reported in the same manner as a general-purpose government. Answer (B) is incorrect. A government that is engaged in two or more governmental programs should be reported in the same manner as a general-purpose government. Answer (C) is incorrect. A special-purpose government is a legally separate entity.

19.2 MD&A and the Government-Wide Financial Statements

7. Government-wide financial statements are prepared using the

	Economic Resources Measure-ment Focus	Current Financial Resources Measure-ment Focus	Accrual Basis	Modified Accrual Basis
A.	Yes	No	Yes	No
B.	No	Yes	No	Yes
C.	Yes	No	No	Yes
D.	No	Yes	Yes	No

Answer (A) is correct.
    REQUIRED: The measurement focus and basis of accounting used in government-wide financial statements.
    DISCUSSION: Government-wide financial statements are prepared using the economic resources measurement focus and the accrual basis of accounting and should report all of the government's assets, liabilities, revenues, expenses, gains, and losses. The economic resources measurement focus differs from the shorter-term flow-of-current-financial-resources approach used in governmental funds. It measures revenues and expenses in the same way as in proprietary funds or commercial accounting but does not necessarily emphasize net income. Instead, the emphasis is on a longer-range measure of revenues earned or levied (and accrued immediately if measurable). Moreover, the economic resources model focuses on cost of services. The accrual basis of accounting recognizes most transactions when they occur, regardless of when cash is received or paid.

8. Financial reporting by general-purpose governments includes presentation of MD&A as

- A. Required supplementary information after the notes to the financial statements.

- B. Part of the basic financial statements.

- C. A description of currently known facts, decisions, or conditions expected to have significant effects on financial activities.

- D. Information that may be limited to highlighting the amounts and percentages of change from the prior to the current year.

Answer (C) is correct.
REQUIRED: The nature of MD&A.
DISCUSSION: Management's discussion and analysis (MD&A) is required supplementary information (RSI) that precedes the basic financial statements and provides an analytical overview of financial activities. It is based on currently known facts, decisions, or conditions and includes comparisons of the current and prior years, with an emphasis on the current year, based on government-wide information. Currently known facts are those of which management is aware at the audit report date.
Answer (A) is incorrect. MD&A precedes the basic financial statements. Answer (B) is incorrect. MD&A is not part of the basic financial statements. Answer (D) is incorrect. MD&A should state the reasons for change from the prior year, not merely the amounts or percentages of change.

9. Government-wide financial statements

- A. Display individual funds.

- B. Display aggregated information about fund types.

- C. Exclude information about discretely presented component units.

- D. Use separate columns to distinguish between governmental and business-type activities.

Answer (D) is correct.
REQUIRED: The focus of government-wide financial statements.
DISCUSSION: The basic financial statements include government-wide financial statements, fund financial statements, and the notes to the financial statements. Government-wide financial statements do not display funds or fund types but instead report information about the overall government. They distinguish between the primary government and its discretely presented component units and between the governmental activities and business-type activities of the primary government by reporting such information in separate rows and columns.

10. The portion of capital improvement special assessment debt maturing in 5 years, to be repaid from general resources of the government, should be reported in the

- A. General fund.

- B. Government-wide statement of net position.

- C. Agency fund.

- D. Capital projects fund.

Answer (B) is correct.
REQUIRED: The reporting of special assessment debt maturing in 5 years.
DISCUSSION: If the government is obligated in some manner for capital improvement special assessment debt, it should be reported as a general long-term liability only in the governmental activities column of the government-wide statement of net position (except for any portion related to, and expected to be paid from, proprietary funds). The public benefit portion (the amount repayable from general resources of the government) is treated in the same manner as other general long-term liabilities.
Answer (A) is incorrect. Governmental funds have a current resources focus. Answer (C) is incorrect. The debt service transactions of special assessment debt for which the government is not obligated in any manner are reported in an agency fund in the statement of fiduciary net position. Answer (D) is incorrect. General long-term liabilities are not reported in governmental funds.

11. In the current year, the city of Beech issued $400,000 of bonds, the proceeds of which were restricted to the financing of a major capital project. The bonds will be paid wholly from special assessments against benefited property owners. However, Beech is obligated to provide a secondary source of funds for repayment of the bonds in the event of default by the assessed property owners. In Beech's basic financial statements, this $400,000 special assessment debt should

- A. Not be reported.

- B. Be reported in the special assessment fund.

- C. Be reported as a general long-term liability.

- D. Be reported in an agency fund.

Answer (C) is correct.
REQUIRED: The proper reporting treatment for special assessment bonds.
DISCUSSION: If the government is obligated in some manner for capital improvement special assessment debt, it should be reported as a general long-term liability only in the governmental activities column of the government-wide statement of net position (except for any portion related to, and expected to be paid from, proprietary funds). The public benefit portion (the amount repayable from general resources of the government) is treated in the same manner as other general long-term liabilities.
Answer (A) is incorrect. All debt of the governmental unit is required to be reported. Answer (B) is incorrect. Special assessment funds are not used for external reporting in the basic financial statements. Answer (D) is incorrect. The debt service transactions of special assessment debt for which the government is not obligated in any manner are reported in an agency fund in the statement of fiduciary net position.

12. In the government-wide statement of net position, restricted capital assets should be included in the

A. Expendable component of restricted net position.

B. Nonexpendable component of restricted net position.

C. Invested in capital assets, net of related debt, component of net position.

D. Designated component of net position.

Answer (C) is correct.
  REQUIRED: The classification of restricted capital assets in the statement of net position.
  DISCUSSION: Invested in capital assets, net of related debt, includes unrestricted and restricted capital assets, net of accumulated depreciation and related liabilities for borrowings. However, debt related to significant unspent proceeds is classified in the same net position component as those proceeds.
  Answer (A) is incorrect. Restricted net position is subject to constraints imposed by external entities (creditors, grantors, or other governments) or by law (constitutional provisions or enabling legislation). If permanent endowments or permanent fund principal amounts are included, restricted net position should be displayed as expendable and nonexpendable. Answer (B) is incorrect. Nonexpendable means that the restriction is retained in perpetuity. However, capital assets must be included in the invested in capital assets, net of related debt, component of net position, even if they are restricted. Answer (D) is incorrect. Designations of net position are not reported on the face of the statement.

19.3 Governmental Funds Reporting

13. The focus of certain fund financial statements of a local government is on major funds. Accordingly,

A. Major internal service funds must be presented separately in the statement of net position for proprietary funds.

B. The main operating fund is always reported as a major fund.

C. Combining statements for nonmajor funds are required.

D. Enterprise funds **not** meeting the quantitative criteria are **not** eligible for presentation as major funds.

Answer (B) is correct.
  REQUIRED: The true statement about major fund reporting.
  DISCUSSION: The focus of governmental and proprietary fund financial statements is on major funds (but major fund reporting is not required for internal service funds). Each major fund is presented in a separate column, and nonmajor funds are aggregated in one column. Combining statements are not required for nonmajor funds. The main operating fund (e.g., the general fund) is always reported as a major fund, and any governmental or enterprise fund believed to be particularly important to users also may be reported in this way. Other individual governmental or enterprise funds must be reported as major if they meet the quantitative thresholds.
  Answer (A) is incorrect. Major fund reporting requirements apply to governmental and enterprise funds but not to internal service funds. Answer (C) is incorrect. Combining statements for nonmajor funds are not required but may be reported as supplementary information. Answer (D) is incorrect.
A government may report any governmental or enterprise individual fund as major if it is believed to be particularly important to users.

14. A capital projects fund of a local government must be reported as major if

A. Total assets of that fund are 5% of the total assets of all governmental funds and 2% of the total assets of all governmental and enterprise funds combined.

B. Total expenditures of that fund are 10% of the total expenditures of all governmental funds and 2% of the total expenditures of all governmental and enterprise funds combined.

C. Total liabilities of that fund are 10% of the total liabilities of all governmental funds and 5% of the total liabilities of all governmental and enterprise funds combined.

D. Total revenues of that fund are 6% of the total revenues of all governmental funds and 3% of the total revenues of all governmental and enterprise funds combined.

Answer (C) is correct.
  REQUIRED: The criteria for requiring major fund reporting.
  DISCUSSION: The main operating fund (e.g., the general fund) is always reported as a major fund, and any governmental or enterprise fund believed to be particularly important to users may also be reported in this way. Moreover, any fund must be reported as major if total revenues, expenditures/expenses, assets, or liabilities (excluding revenues and expenditures/ expenses reported as extraordinary items) of the fund are (1) at least 10% of the corresponding element total (assets, etc.) for all funds of the same category or type, that is, for all governmental or all enterprise funds, and (2) the same element that met the 10% standard is at least 5% of the corresponding element total for all governmental and enterprise funds in the aggregate.

19.4 Proprietary Funds Reporting

15. A state or local government must present which financial statements for proprietary funds?

I. A statement of activities
II. A statement in net position or balance sheet format
III. A statement of cash flows

    A. I only.

    B. I and III only.

    C. II and III only.

    D. I, II, and III.

Answer (C) is correct.
    REQUIRED: The statement(s) required for proprietary funds.
    DISCUSSION: Proprietary funds emphasize determination of operating income, changes in net position (or cost recovery), financial position, and cash flows. A statement of net position or balance sheet is required for proprietary funds, with assets and liabilities classified as current or noncurrent. Either a net position format [(assets + deferred outflows of resources) – (liabilities + deferred inflows of resources) = net position] or a balance sheet format [(assets + deferred outflows of resources) = (liabilities + deferred inflows of resources) + net position] may be used. A statement of revenues, expenses, and changes in fund net position or fund equity (either label may be used) is the required operating statement for proprietary funds. A statement of cash flows also is required for proprietary funds. However, the direct method (including a reconciliation of operating cash flows to operating income) should be used. The direct method reports major classes of gross operating cash receipts and payments and their sum (net cash flow from operating activities).

16. With regard to the statement of cash flows for a governmental unit's proprietary funds, items generally presented as cash equivalents are

	2-month Treasury Bills	3-month Certificates of Deposit
A.	No	No
B.	No	Yes
C.	Yes	Yes
D.	Yes	No

Answer (C) is correct.
    REQUIRED: The items generally presented as cash equivalents.
    DISCUSSION: Cash equivalents are highly liquid investments, readily convertible to known amounts of cash with an original time to maturity at acquisition of 3 months or less. The T-bills and CDs both meet these criteria and are presented as cash equivalents.

17. The statement of revenues, expenses, and changes in fund net position (or fund equity) for proprietary funds

    A. Combines special and extraordinary items in a subtotal presented before nonoperating revenues and expenses.

    B. Must report revenues at gross amounts, with discounts and allowances disclosed parenthetically.

    C. Distinguishes between operating and nonoperating revenues and expenses.

    D. Must define operating items in the same way as in the statement of cash flows.

Answer (C) is correct.
    REQUIRED: The true statement about the statement of revenues, expenses, and changes in fund net position (or fund equity).
    DISCUSSION: A statement of revenues, expenses, and changes in fund net position or fund equity (either label may be used) is the required operating statement for proprietary funds. Operating and nonoperating revenues and expenses should be distinguished with separate subtotals for operating revenues, operating expenses, and operating income.
    Answer (A) is incorrect. Nonoperating revenues and expenses are presented immediately after operating income (loss). Moreover, special and extraordinary items are reported separately. Answer (B) is incorrect. Revenues are reported by major source either net with disclosure of discounts and allowances or gross with discounts and allowances reported beneath the revenue amounts. Answer (D) is incorrect. A government should consistently follow appropriate definitions of operating items. Considerations in defining these items are (1) the principal purpose of the fund and (2) their presentation in a cash flows statement. However, the categorization of items in the statement of cash flows need not control the definitions of operating items in the statement of revenues, expenses, and changes in fund net position.

18. The GASB has established criteria for the required reporting of activities as enterprise funds. Based on these criteria, and assuming the amounts involved are derived from principal revenue sources, enterprise fund reporting is most likely to be optional if

   A. Fees are charged to external users for goods or services.

   B. The activity is financed with debt, and the only security is a pledge of the activity's net revenues from fees and charges.

   C. The activity's costs are legally required to be recovered from fees and charges.

   D. The activity's pricing policies set fees and charges to recover costs.

Answer (A) is correct.
   REQUIRED: The circumstances in which enterprise fund reporting may be optional.
   DISCUSSION: Enterprise funds need not be used to report insignificant activities. They may be used for activities for which fees are charged to external users, but they must be used if one of three criteria (applied in the context of the activity's principal revenue sources) is satisfied. The criteria primarily emphasize fees charged to external users. The activity should be reported as an enterprise fund if it is financed with debt, and the only security is a pledge of the activity's net revenues from fees and charges. If the debt is also secured by the full faith and credit of a related governmental entity, the debt is not payable solely from the activity's net revenues. The activity also should be reported as an enterprise fund if its costs (including capital costs) of providing services are legally required to be recovered from fees and charges, not taxes or similar revenues. Furthermore, the activity should be reported as an enterprise fund if its pricing policies set fees and charges to recover its costs (including capital costs).

19. On January 2, Basketville City purchased equipment with a useful life of 3 years to be used by its water and sewer enterprise fund. Which of the following is the correct treatment for the asset?

   A. Record the purchase of the equipment as an expenditure.

   B. Capitalize; depreciation is optional.

   C. Capitalize; depreciation is required.

   D. Capitalize; depreciation is **not** permitted.

Answer (C) is correct.
   REQUIRED: The accounting for a purchase of equipment to be used by an enterprise fund.
   DISCUSSION: An enterprise fund is a proprietary fund. Thus, the economic resources measurement focus and the accrual basis of accounting are required in its financial statements. Capital assets, such as equipment, are reported in the government-wide statement of net position and in the proprietary fund statement of net position. They must be depreciated over their estimated useful lives unless they are inexhaustible or are infrastructure assets that meet certain requirements.
   Answer (A) is incorrect. Under the modified accrual basis, the entity must record the purchase of the equipment as an expenditure if it is acquired with governmental fund financial resources. Answer (B) is incorrect. Only depreciation is mandatory. Answer (D) is incorrect. Only depreciation of inexhaustible assets, such as land and land improvements, is prohibited.

20. The following transactions were among those reported by Corfe City's electric utility enterprise fund for the year just ended:

Capital contributed by subdividers	$ 900,000
Cash received from customer households	2,700,000
Proceeds from sale of revenue bonds	4,500,000

In the proprietary funds statement of cash flows for the year ended December 31, what amount should be reported as cash flows from the electric utility enterprise fund's capital and related financing activities?

   A. $4,500,000

   B. $5,400,000

   C. $7,200,000

   D. $8,100,000

Answer (B) is correct.
   REQUIRED: The amount reported as cash flows from capital and related financing activities.
   DISCUSSION: Cash flows should be classified as operating, noncapital financing, capital and related financing, or investing. Operating activities include producing and delivering goods and providing services. Thus, cash from customer households is a revenue item reported under cash flows from operating activities. Capital and related financing activities include acquiring and disposing of capital assets, borrowing and repaying money related to capital asset transactions, etc. Assuming the sale of revenue bonds and the capital contributions by subdividers are for the acquisition or improvement of capital assets, the amount to report under capital and related financing activities is $5,400,000 ($900,000 + $4,500,000).
   Answer (A) is incorrect. The amount of $4,500,000 omits the capital contributed by subdividers. Answer (C) is incorrect. The amount of $7,200,000 includes customer fees revenue and omits capital contributed by subdividers. Answer (D) is incorrect. The amount of $8,100,000 includes customer fees.

21. Dogwood City's water enterprise fund received interest of $10,000 on long-term investments. How should this amount be reported on the statement of cash flows?

A. Operating activities.

B. Noncapital financing activities.

C. Capital and related financing activities.

D. Investing activities.

Answer (D) is correct.
REQUIRED: The classification of interest received on long-term investments in the statement of cash flows.
DISCUSSION: Reporting of cash flows of proprietary funds and entities engaged in business-type activities, e.g., governmental utilities, is required. Cash inflows should be classified as operating, financing, and investing. Investing activities include making and collecting loans (other than program loans) and acquiring and disposing of debt and equity instruments. Cash inflows from investing activities include interest and dividends received as returns on loans (not program loans), debt of other entities, equity securities, and cash management or investment pools.
Answer (A) is incorrect. Operating activities are all transactions and other events that are not classified as either financing or investing activities. In general, operating activities involve transactions and other events the effects of which are included in the determination of operating income. Answer (B) is incorrect. Noncapital financing activities include borrowings for purposes other than acquiring, constructing, or improving capital assets and debt. Answer (C) is incorrect. Capital and related financing activities include borrowings and repayments of debt related to (1) acquiring, constructing, or improving capital assets; (2) acquiring and disposing of capital assets used to provide goods or services; and (3) paying for capital assets obtained on credit.

19.5 Fiduciary Funds Reporting and Interfund Activity

22. Fish Road property owners in Sea County are responsible for special assessment debt that arose from a storm sewer project. If the property owners default, Sea has no obligation regarding debt service, although it does bill property owners for assessments and uses the monies it collects to pay debt holders. What fund type should Sea use to account for these collection and servicing activities?

A. Agency.

B. Debt service.

C. Special revenue funds.

D. Capital projects.

Answer (A) is correct.
REQUIRED: The reporting of debt service transactions of a special assessment issue.
DISCUSSION: When capital improvements are financed by special assessment debt, the debt service transactions of a special assessment issue for which the government is not obligated should be reported in an agency fund in the statement of fiduciary net position, not a debt service fund. This reporting reflects the government's limited responsibility to act as an agent for the assessed property owners and the bondholders.

23. Glen County uses governmental fund accounting and is the administrator of a multiple-jurisdiction deferred compensation plan covering both its own employees and those of other governments participating in the plan. This plan is an eligible deferred compensation plan under the U.S. Internal Revenue Code and Income Tax Regulations and meets the criteria for a pension (and other employee benefit) trust fund. Glen has legal access to the plan's $40 million in assets, of which $2 million pertain to Glen and $38 million pertain to the other participating governments. In Glen's balance sheet, what amount should be reported in an agency fund for plan assets and as a corresponding liability?

A. $0

B. $2,000,000

C. $38,000,000

D. $40,000,000

Answer (A) is correct.
REQUIRED: The deferred compensation plan assets and liability to record in an agency fund.
DISCUSSION: The plan should be reported in a pension (and other employee benefit) trust fund in the statements of fiduciary net position and changes in fiduciary net position if it meets the criteria for that fund type. This treatment is in accordance with a tax law amendment that required all assets and income of the plan to be held in trust for the exclusive benefit of participants and their beneficiaries. Consequently, no amounts should be reported in an agency fund.

24. Fiduciary fund financial statements report

    A. Information by major fund.

    B. Three components of net position.

    C. A separate column for each fund type.

    D. No separate statements for individual pension plans.

Answer (C) is correct.
    REQUIRED: The reporting in fiduciary fund financial statements.
    DISCUSSION: Fiduciary fund financial statements include information about all fiduciary funds and similar component units. The statements report information in a separate column for each fund type but not by major fund. The notes present financial statements for individual pension plans and postemployment healthcare plans unless separate GAAP reports have been issued. A statement of fiduciary net position is required for fiduciary funds. It reports assets (plus deferred outflows of resources), liabilities (plus deferred inflows of resources), and net position for each fiduciary fund type but does not present the three components of net position reported in the government-wide statement of net position or in the proprietary fund statement of net position.
    Answer (A) is incorrect. Major funds are reported only in governmental and enterprise fund statements. Answer (B) is incorrect. Three components of net position are reported only in the government-wide statement of net position and in the proprietary fund statement of net position. Answer (D) is incorrect. Separate financial statements for individual pension plans and postemployment healthcare plans are reported in the notes. However, if separate GAAP financial statements have been issued for such plans, information is given in the notes about how those statements may be obtained.

25. River City has a defined contribution pension plan. How should River report the pension plan in its financial statements?

    A. Amortize any transition asset over the estimated number of years of current employees' service.

    B. Disclose in the notes to the financial statements the amount of the pension benefit obligation and the net position available for benefits.

    C. Disclose in the notes to the financial statements the classes of employees covered and the employer's and employees' obligations to contribute to the fund.

    D. Accrue a liability for benefits earned but **not** paid to fund participants.

Answer (C) is correct.
    REQUIRED: The method for reporting a defined contribution pension plan.
    DISCUSSION: A defined contribution pension plan must report a plan description, a summary of significant accounting policies, and information about investment concentrations. The plan description should identify the plan as a defined contribution plan and disclose the number of participating employers and other contributing entities. The description should also include the classes of employees covered and the total current membership, a brief description of plan provisions and the authority under which they are established (or may be amended), and contribution requirements.
    Answer (A) is incorrect. No transition asset arises under a defined contribution plan. Answer (B) is incorrect. A pension benefit obligation arises under a defined benefit pension plan. Answer (D) is incorrect. Under a defined contribution plan, the governmental employer's obligation is for contributions, not benefits.

26. A government may report which fiduciary funds?

    A. Private-purpose trust funds.

    B. Expendable trust funds.

    C. Nonexpendable trust funds.

    D. Permanent funds.

Answer (A) is correct.
    REQUIRED: The fiduciary funds reportable by a government.
    DISCUSSION: Fiduciary funds include pension (and other employee benefit) trust funds, investment trust funds, private-purpose trust funds, and agency funds. Pension (and other employee benefit) trust funds report resources held for members and beneficiaries of pension plans (defined benefit or contribution), other postemployment benefit plans, or other employee benefit plans. Investment trust funds are used by a sponsoring government to report the external portions of external investment pools. Private-purpose trust funds are used for all other trust arrangements, whether the beneficiaries are individuals, private organizations, or other governments.
    Answer (B) is incorrect. Expendable trust funds have been eliminated. Answer (C) is incorrect. Nonexpendable trust funds have been eliminated. Answer (D) is incorrect. Permanent funds are governmental funds.

27. Taxes collected and held by Franklin County for a separate school district are accounted for in which fund?

    A. Special revenue.

    B. Internal service.

    C. Trust.

    D. Agency.

Answer (D) is correct.
    REQUIRED: The fund that collects and holds taxes for a separate school district.
    DISCUSSION: Agency funds report resources held solely in a custodial capacity. These funds ordinarily account only for the receipt, temporary investment, and payment of resources to individuals, private organizations, or other governments. Thus, tax agency funds are used when a governmental entity is the collection agent of taxes for disbursement to other governmental units, e.g., school districts or special taxing districts.
    Answer (A) is incorrect. Special revenue funds are governmental funds. Special revenue funds account for proceeds of specific revenue sources legally restricted to expenditure for specified purposes. However, a special revenue fund is not required unless legally mandated. Answer (B) is incorrect. Internal service funds may be used for activities that provide goods and services to other subunits of the primary government and its component units or to other governments on a cost-reimbursement basis. However, if the reporting government is not the predominant participant, the activity should be reported as an enterprise fund. Answer (C) is incorrect. A trust fund differs from an agency fund because the trust agreement determines how long resources are held and the degree of management involvement.

28. An internal service provided and used by a state or local government

    A. Is the internal counterpart to a nonexchange transaction.

    B. Results in expenditures or expenses to buyer funds and revenues to seller funds.

    C. Normally is displayed in the financial statements as a reimbursement.

    D. Requires recognition of an other financing source by the transferee fund and an other financing use by the transferor fund.

Answer (B) is correct.
    REQUIRED: The treatment of an internal service provided and used.
    DISCUSSION: Interfund services provided and used are reciprocal interfund activities. They are sales and purchases of goods and services at prices equivalent to external exchange values. Hence, they result in revenues to seller funds and expenditures or expenses to buyer funds. Unpaid amounts are interfund receivables or payables.
    Answer (A) is incorrect. An internal service provided and used is a reciprocal interfund activity, which is analogous to an exchange or an exchange-like transaction. Answer (C) is incorrect. Interfund services provided and used normally result in revenues to sellers and expenditures or expenses to buyers. Reimbursements are not displayed in the statements. Answer (D) is incorrect. An interfund transfer (nonreciprocal interfund activity) is an other financing source (use) in a transferee (transferor) governmental fund. An internal service provided and used is reciprocal interfund activity.

29. Which of the following is a reporting requirement for agency funds?

    A. They should be reported in a statement of fiduciary net position and a statement of changes in fiduciary net position.

    B. Agency fund assets (plus deferred outflows of resources) should equal liabilities (plus deferred inflows of resources) in the statement of fiduciary net position.

    C. An agency fund used as a clearing account should report as assets the amounts pertaining to the other funds.

    D. An agency fund should **not** be used as a clearing account.

Answer (B) is correct.
    REQUIRED: The reporting requirement for agency funds.
    DISCUSSION: Agency fund assets (plus deferred outflows of resources) should equal liabilities (plus deferred inflows of resources) in the statement of fiduciary net position, but agency funds are not reported in the statement of changes in fiduciary net position.
    Answer (A) is incorrect. Agency funds are not reported in the statement of changes in fiduciary net position. Answer (C) is incorrect. An agency fund may be used as a clearing account to distribute resources to other funds as well as to other entities, for example, by a county tax collector to distribute taxes to other funds and other governments. Assets pertaining to other funds are reported in those funds, not in the agency fund. Answer (D) is incorrect. An agency fund may be used as a clearing account.

30. During the year, a city's electric utility, which is operated as an enterprise fund, rendered billings for electricity supplied to the general fund. Which of the following accounts should be debited by the general fund?

- A. Appropriations.
- B. Expenditures.
- C. Due to electric utility enterprise fund.
- D. Other financing uses -- interfund transfer.

Answer (B) is correct.
REQUIRED: The account debited by the general fund for receipt of services supplied by an enterprise fund.
DISCUSSION: Enterprise funds are used to account for operations similar to those of private businesses. This rendition of services by the enterprise fund to the general fund is presumably at prices equivalent to external exchange values and is classified as an interfund service provided and used. The result is revenue to the seller and an expenditure to the buyer, a governmental fund. Unpaid amounts are interfund receivables or payables. The entry is to debit expenditures control and credit due to enterprise fund.
Answer (A) is incorrect. Appropriations is debited when the budgetary accounts are closed. Answer (C) is incorrect. Due to enterprise fund should be credited. Answer (D) is incorrect. This transaction is an interfund service provided and used, not an interfund transfer.

Use the additional questions in Gleim **CPA Test Prep Online** to create Test Sessions that emulate Prometric!

19.6 PRACTICE SIMULATION

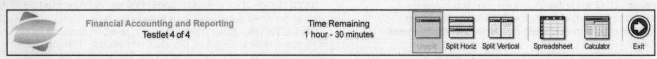

Financial Accounting and Reporting
Testlet 4 of 4

Time Remaining
1 hour - 30 minutes

Unsplit | Split Horiz | Split Vertical | Spreadsheet | Calculator | Exit

DIRECTIONS

Note: If you believe you have encountered a software malfunction, report it to the test center staff immediately.

Navigation

To navigate from task to task, use the controls at the bottom of the screen. Click on the **Next** button to advance to the next task, or the **Previous** button to go to the previous task. To go directly to any task, click on its number.

⚐ = Reminder   Directions 1 2 3 4 5 6 7   ◀ Previous Next ▶

If you would like a reminder to revisit a task, or want to indicate that you are finished with it, click on the reminder flag below the task number. To clear the flag, click on it again. Reminder flags are for your use only – they do not contribute to your score.

Tabs

In this part of the examination, you will be asked to complete various tasks. Every task has one or more **Work Tabs**. Some tasks have one or more **Information Tabs**, others may have none. Every task has a **Help** tab.

If a task has **Information Tabs**, you may use the information in them to complete your responses in the **Work Tabs**.

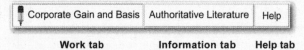

Corporate Gain and Basis | Authoritative Literature | Help

Work tab   Information tab   Help tab

Work Tabs:
- **Work Tabs** are identified with a pencil icon. This is where your responses are expected.
- Each task has one or more **Work Tabs**.
- **Work Tabs** contain directions for completing the task – be sure to read these directions carefully.
- The **Work Tab** name in the example above is for illustration only – yours will differ.
- You must complete all of the **Work Tabs** in each task to receive full credit.

Information Tabs:
- The Authoritative Literature will be provided in all tasks in the AUD, FAR, and REG sections for your reference.
- Your simulation may have one or more additional **Information Tabs**. Like the Authoritative Literature tabs, **Information Tabs** do not have a pencil icon.
- If your task has additional **Information Tabs**, go through each to familiarize yourself with the task content.

Help Tab:
- The **Help Tab** provides assistance with the exam software that is used in this task. For example, if the task is to compose a memorandum, **Help** will provide information about the word processor.

The Toolbar

The toolbar at the top of the screen shows the amount of time remaining for you to complete the tasks. In addition, the following tools are available. Note that only the **Exit** button is displayed when Directions are visible - the others will appear when you begin the tasks.

Unsplit   Split Horiz   Split Vertical

Click on these buttons to split or unsplit the screen. You can split the screen vertically or horizontally.

Calculator

Click on this button to display the calculator; click on it again to hide the calculator. To move the calculator, click on the calculator title bar and drag the calculator to the desired location.

Spreadsheet

Click on this button to use the spreadsheet; click on it again to hide the spreadsheet. To move the spreadsheet, click on the the spreadsheet title bar and drag the spreadsheet to the desired location.

Exit

Click on this button to go on to the next part of the examination. You must complete all of the tasks to receive full credit. Once you click on **Exit** and confirm the action, you will NOT be able to return to this testlet.

⚐ = Reminder   Directions 1 2 3 4 5   ◀ Previous Next ▶

```
┌─────────────────────────────────────────────────────────────────────┐
│  ┌──────────────┐ ┌─────────────────────────┐ ┌──────┐               │
│  │ General Fund │ │ Authoritative Literature │ │ Help │               │
│  └──────────────┘ └─────────────────────────┘ └──────┘               │
└─────────────────────────────────────────────────────────────────────┘
```

The following information relates to Bel City:

1. *General fund:*

    The following selected information is taken from Bel's Year 4 general fund financial records:

	Budget	Actual
Property taxes	$5,000,000	$4,700,000
Other revenues	1,000,000	1,050,000
Total revenues	$6,000,000	$5,750,000
Total expenditures	$5,600,000	$5,700,000
Property taxes receivable – delinquent		$ 420,000
Minus: Allowance for estimated		
uncollectible taxes – delinquent		50,000
		$ 370,000

    - The budget as originally adopted was not amended.
    - No property taxes receivable have been written off, and the allowance for uncollectibles balance (reclassified as uncollectible taxes – delinquent) is unchanged from the initial entry at the time of the original tax levy. Property taxes collectible not more than 90 days after year end are deemed to be measurable and available.
    - The general fund made interfund transfers to the capital projects fund ($500,000) and the water utility enterprise fund ($700,000).
    - No encumbrances were outstanding at December 31, Year 5.
    - Bel issued general obligation bonds with a par value of $1.2 million for $1.23 million. The proceeds are to be used to finance, in part, a new civic center.

Indicate by checking the appropriate box whether the answer to each item relating to Bel's general fund is yes or no.

Item	*Yes*	*No*
1. Assuming a budgetary fund balance account was not used, did recording budgetary accounts at the beginning of Year 4 increase the unreserved fund balance by $50,000?		
2. Should the budgetary accounts for Year 4 include an entry for the expected transfer of funds from the general fund to the capital projects fund?		
3. Should the $700,000 payment from the general fund, which was used to help to establish the water utility fund, be reported as an "other financing use – interfund transfers"?		
4. Did the general fund receive the $30,000 bond premium from the capital projects fund?		
5. Should a payment from the general fund for water received for normal civic center operations be reported as an "other financing use – interfund transfers"?		
6. Does the net property taxes receivable of $370,000 include amounts recognized as revenues expected to be collected after March 1, Year 5?		
7. Would closing only the budgetary accounts cause the fund balance to increase by $400,000?		
8. Would the interaction between budgetary and actual amounts cause the fund balance to decrease by $350,000?		

Other Accounting Issues | Authoritative Literature | Help

The following information relates to Bel City:

1. *Capital projects fund:*

    ● Financing for Bel's new civic center was provided by a combination of general fund transfers, a state grant, and an issue of general obligation bonds. Any bond premium on issuance is to be used for the repayment of the bonds at their $1.2 million par value. At December 31, Year 4, the capital projects fund for the civic center had the following closing entries:

Revenues	$ 800,000	
Other financing sources – bond proceeds	1,230,000	
Other financing sources – interfund transfers from the general fund	500,000	
Expenditures		$1,080,000
Other financing uses – interfund transfers		30,000
Assigned fund balance		1,420,000

    ● Also, at December 31, Year 4, capital projects fund entries reflected Bel's intention to honor the $1.3 million purchase orders and commitments outstanding for the center.

    ● During Year 4, total capital projects fund encumbrances exceeded the related expenditures by $42,000. All expenditures were previously encumbered.

    ● During Year 5, the capital projects fund received no revenues and no other financing sources. The civic center building was completed in early Year 5, and the capital projects fund was closed by a transfer of $27,000 to the general fund.

2. *Water utility enterprise fund:*

    ● Bel issued $4 million of revenue bonds at par. These bonds, together with a $700,000 interfund transfer from the general fund, were used to acquire a water utility. Water utility revenues are to be the sole source of funds to retire these bonds beginning in Year 8.

Indicate by checking the appropriate box whether the answer to each item relating to Bel's general capital assets, general long-term liabilities, and funds other than the general fund is yes or no.

Item	Yes	No
1. Should a debit amount be reported for Year 4 in the government-wide financial statements for the civic center?		
2. Should Bel record depreciation in Year 5 on the civic center?		
3. Should Bel record depreciation on water utility equipment?		
4. Should the capital projects fund be included in Bel's statement of revenues, expenditures, and changes in fund balances?		
5. Should the water utility enterprise fund be included in Bel's governmental funds balance sheet?		

Fund Balances | Authoritative Literature | Help

The following information relates to Bel City:

1.   *General fund:*

The following selected information is taken from Bel's Year 4 general fund financial records:

	Budget	Actual
Property taxes	$5,000,000	$4,700,000
Other revenues	1,000,000	1,050,000
Total revenues	$6,000,000	$5,750,000
Total expenditures	$5,600,000	$5,700,000
Property taxes receivable – delinquent		$ 420,000
Minus: Allowance for estimated uncollectible taxes – delinquent		50,000
		$ 370,000

- The budget as originally adopted was not amended.
- No property taxes receivable have been written off, and the allowance for uncollectibles balance (reclassified as uncollectible taxes – delinquent) is unchanged from the initial entry at the time of the original tax levy. Property taxes collectible not more than 90 days after year end are deemed to be measurable and available.
- The general fund made interfund transfers to the capital projects fund ($500,000) and the water utility enterprise fund ($700,000).
- No encumbrances were outstanding at December 31, Year 5.
- Bel issued general obligation bonds with a par value of $1.2 million for $.23 million. The proceeds are to be used to finance, in part, a new civic center.

Given the information listed above, enter the amounts required in the shaded cells below.

Item	*Amount*
1. What was the amount recorded in the opening entry for appropriations?	
2. What was the total amount debited to property taxes receivable?	
3. What amount should be reported in the government-wide financial statements as a general long-term liability at December 31, Year 4?	

▼ = Reminder   Directions   1 2 3 4 5   ◀ Previous   Next ▶

Other Fund Balances | Authoritative Literature | Help

The following information relates to Bel City:

1. *Capital projects fund:*

    ●   Financing for Bel's new civic center was provided by a combination of general fund transfers, a state grant, and an issue of general obligation bonds. Any bond premium on issuance is to be used for the repayment of the bonds at their $1.2 million par value. At December 31, Year 4, the capital projects fund for the civic center had the following closing entries:

Revenues	$ 800,000	
Other financing sources – bond proceeds	1,230,000	
Other financing sources – interfund transfers from the general fund	500,000	
Expenditures		$1,080,000
Other financing uses – interfund transfers		30,000
Assigned fund balance		1,420,000

    ●   Also, at December 31, Year 4, capital projects fund entries reflected Bel's intention to honor the $1.3 million purchase orders and commitments outstanding for the center.

    ●   During Year 4, total capital projects fund encumbrances exceeded the related expenditures by $42,000. All expenditures were previously encumbered.

    ●   During Year 5, the capital projects fund received no revenues and no other financing sources. The civic center building was completed in early Year 5, and the capital projects fund was closed by a transfer of $27,000 to the general fund.

2. *Water utility enterprise fund:*

    ●   Bel issued $4 million of revenue bonds at par. These bonds, together with a $700,000 interfund transfer from the general fund, were used to acquire a water utility. Water utility revenues are to be the sole source of funds to retire these bonds beginning in Year 8.

Given the information listed above, enter the amounts required in the shaded cells below.

Item	Amount
1. What amount should be reported as a general capital asset in the government-wide financial statements at December 31, Year 4?	
2. What was the completed cost of the civic center?	
3. How much was the state capital grant for the civic center?	
4. In the capital projects fund, what was the amount of the total encumbrances recorded during Year 4?	
5. In the capital projects fund, what was the assigned fund balance reported at December 31, Year 4?	

Funds | Authoritative Literature | Help

For items 1 through 4, select from the first list provided the answer that matches each item description. Each choice may be used once, more than once, or not at all. In items 5 through 8, select from the second list provided to indicate whether each financial statement component is reported in each fund.

Aspect	Governmental Funds	Proprietary Funds	Fiduciary Funds
Government-wide financial statements:			
1. Basis of accounting			
2. Measurement focus			
Fund financial statements:			
3. Basis of accounting			
4. Measurement focus			

Choices
A) Cash
B) Modified cash
C) Accrual
D) Modified accrual
E) Current financial resources
F) Economic resources
G) N/A

Aspect	Governmental Funds	Proprietary Funds	Fiduciary Funds
Government-wide financial statements:			
5. Long-term liabilities			
6. Capital assets			
Fund financial statements:			
7. Long-term liabilities			
8. Capital assets			

Choices
H) Yes
I) No

Unofficial Answers

1. General Fund (8 Gradable Items)

1. **No.** In recording the budget, Bel would have debited estimated revenues control for $6 million and credited appropriations control for $5.6 million. The interfund transfer to the capital projects fund would have been budgeted by crediting estimated other financing uses for $500,000, and the interfund transfer to the water utility would have been budgeted by crediting estimated other financing uses for $700,000. Thus, unassigned fund balance would have been debited for $800,000 [($5,600,000 + $500,000 + $700,000) – $6,000,000].

2. **Yes.** When a budget is recorded, anticipated interfund transfers from the general fund to other funds are credited to the estimated other financing uses account.

3. **Yes.** The purpose of this nonreciprocal interfund activity was to establish the water utility fund. No equivalent asset flow will occur in return, and the amount need not be repaid. Thus, the transaction is debited to other financing use – interfund transfer in the general fund.

4. **No.** Cash equal to the bond premium would have been transferred to the debt service fund. The entry in that fund was to debit cash and to credit other financing sources – interfund transfers.

5. **No.** Such a payment from the general fund to an enterprise fund is for an interfund service provided and used. This type of transaction is reported as an expenditure, an expense, or a revenue of the funds involved. In this case, the general fund records an expenditure.

6. **Yes.** Amounts expected to be collected more than 60 days after year end ordinarily should be reclassified as deferred revenues (because they do not meet the availability criterion) except in unusual circumstances. However, the selected information indicates that management has decided that the facts justify using a period longer than 60 days. Moreover, the uncollectibles balance has not changed. Thus, the net property taxes receivable of $370,000 is deemed by management to be measurable, available, collectible, and recognizable as revenue.

7. **No.** The entry to record the general fund budget included a debit to unassigned fund balance of $800,000 (see item 1). Thus, closing only the budgetary accounts (excluding actual amounts) requires a credit to unassigned fund balance (an increase) of $800,000.

8. **No.** The balancing debit to unassigned fund balance in the budgetary entry was $800,000. Because estimated revenues exceeded actual revenues by $250,000, and expenditures exceeded appropriations by $100,000, the closing of both budgetary and actual accounts requires an additional debit to the unassigned fund balance of $350,000. Thus, the general fund's unassigned fund balance has decreased during the year by $1,150,000 ($800,000 + $350,000). This amount equals the total transfers-out ($700,000 + $500,000 = $1,200,000) minus the excess of actual revenues over actual expenditures ($5,750,000 – $5,700,000).

2. Other Accounting Issues (5 Gradable Items)

1. **Yes.** The construction of the civic center results in a general capital asset because it does not relate to a proprietary fund or a fiduciary fund (Bel has no such funds other than the water utility enterprise fund). General capital assets are reported only in the governmental activities column of the government-wide statement of net position.

2. **Yes.** Capital assets are depreciated unless they are inexhaustible or are infrastructure assets accounted for using the modified approach. Because buildings are not inexhaustible and are not usually infrastructure assets, they should be depreciated over their estimated useful lives. Depreciation expense is reported in the statement of activities, and accumulated depreciation is reported in the government-wide statement of net position. However, depreciation is not reported in the fund statements for the civic center because it is a general capital asset.

3. **Yes.** Capital assets accounted for in a proprietary fund are depreciated unless they are inexhaustible or are infrastructure assets reported using the modified approach. Depreciation expense should be reported in the government-wide statement of activities and in the proprietary fund statement of revenues, expenses, and changes in fund net position (or fund equity).

4. **Yes.** Capital projects fund information is reported in the government-wide statements of net position and activities (but without display of individual funds or fund types) and in the governmental funds balance sheet and statement of revenues, expenditures, and changes in fund balances.

5. **No.** Enterprise fund information is reported in the government-wide statements of net position and activities (but without display of individual funds or fund types) and in the proprietary funds statements of net position (or balance sheet); revenues, expenses, and changes in fund net position (or fund equity); and cash flows.

3. Fund Balances (3 Gradable Items)

1. $5,600,000. In recording a budget, the appropriations account is credited for the total estimated expenditures for the year.

2. $4,750,000. The allowance for estimated uncollectible taxes is a revenue adjustment account. Because Bel City recorded actual tax revenues of $4,700,000, the debit to taxes receivable was $4,750,000 ($4,700,000 actual tax revenue + $50,000 allowance for estimated uncollectible taxes).

3. $1,200,000. The bond issue should be reported at par value as a general long-term liability in the governmental activities column of the government-wide statement of net position. General long-term debt is the unmatured principal of bonds, warrants, notes, and other noncurrent general obligation debt that is not a specific liability of any proprietary fund or trust fund.

4. Other Fund Balances (5 Gradable Items)

1. $1,080,000. The civic center is a general capital asset. Capital assets are reported at historical cost. The cost as of December 31, Year 4, equals the expenditures of $1,080,000 made during Year 4. Encumbrances outstanding at year end do not meet the criteria for expenditures.

2. $2,473,000. The total completed cost of the civic center is represented by the total expenditures recorded, or $2,473,000 ($1,080,000 of Year 4 expenditures + $1,420,000 fund balance at 12/31/Year 4 – $27,000 interfund transfer to the general fund in Year 5).

3. $800,000. Of the fund sources for the civic center, the only one that qualifies as revenue for the capital projects fund is the state grant. Grants from other government entities are government-mandated or voluntary nonexchange transactions. The recipient recognizes revenue when all eligibility requirements are met. The closing entry debits revenues of $800,000.

4. $2,422,000. According to the given information, all expenditures were previously encumbered. To calculate total encumbrances, the outstanding purchase orders and other commitments ($1,300,000), which should have been encumbered, and the excess of encumbrances over related expenditures ($42,000) must be added to total expenditures ($1,080,000). The sum of these amounts is total encumbrances of $2,422,000 ($1,300,000 + $42,000 + $1,080,000).

5. $120,000. The calculation of the assigned fund balance is illustrated in the following statement of revenues, expenditures, and changes in fund balance for the year ended December 31, Year 4:

Revenues:		
State grant		$ 800,000
Expenditures		(1,080,000)
Deficiency of revenues over expenditures		$ (280,000)
Other financing sources (uses):		
Bond proceeds	$1,230,000	
Interfund transfer from general fund	500,000	
Interfund transfer to debt service fund	(30,000)	1,700,000
Net change in fund balance		$ 1,420,000
Fund balance -- beginning		0
		$ 1,420,000
Minus: Reserve for encumbrances		(1,300,000)
Unassigned fund balance, 12/31/Year 4		$ 120,000

5. Funds (24 Gradable Items)

Aspect	Governmental Funds	Proprietary Funds	Fiduciary Funds
Government-wide financial statements:			
1. Basis of accounting	C) Accrual	C) Accrual	G) N/A
2. Measurement focus	F) Economic resources	F) Economic resources	G) N/A
Fund financial statements:			
3. Basis of accounting	D) Modified accrual	C) Accrual	C) Accrual
4. Measurement focus	E) Current financial resources	F) Economic resources	F) Economic resources

Aspect	Governmental Funds	Proprietary Funds	Fiduciary Funds
Government-wide financial statements:			
5. Long-term liabilities	H) Yes	H) Yes	I) No
6. Capital assets	H) Yes	H) Yes	I) No
Fund financial statements:			
7. Long-term liabilities	I) No	H) Yes	H) Yes
8. Capital assets	I) No	H) Yes	H) Yes

Gleim Simulation Grading

Task	Correct Responses		Gradable Items		Score per Task
1	_____	÷	8	=	_____
2	_____	÷	5	=	_____
3	_____	÷	3	=	_____
4	_____	÷	5	=	_____
5	_____	÷	24	=	_____

Total of Scores per Task   _____

÷ Total Number of Tasks   5

Total Score   _____%

Use **CPA Gleim Online** and **Simulation Wizard** to practice more task-based simulations in a realistic environment.

STUDY UNIT TWENTY
NOT-FOR-PROFIT CONCEPTS

(20 pages of outline)

20.1	The Not-for-Profit Environment	729
20.2	Financial Statements of NFPs	731
20.3	Revenues of NFPs	739
20.4	Investments Held by NFPs	744
20.5	Healthcare Entities (HCEs)	745
20.6	Practice Simulation	758

The **operating environments** in which financial reporting occurs are similar for NFPs and business entities. Both use scarce resources to produce and distribute goods and services. Thus, the manner in which resources are obtained is the primary difference between them.

20.1 THE NOT-FOR-PROFIT ENVIRONMENT

1. **Characteristics**

    a. Nonbusiness organizations have three characteristics. They

    1) Have transactions that are infrequent in businesses, such as grants and contributions;

    2) Have no single indicator of performance, such as net income; and

    3) Report net assets rather than equity.

    b. Nongovernmental not-for-profit entities (NFPs) include, among other possibilities, private institutions of higher learning, healthcare entities, and voluntary health and welfare entities (VHWEs).

    c. The accounting profession has established no separate standard-setting body for nongovernmental NFPs. Despite their many similarities to governmental bodies, NFPs follow GAAP issued by the FASB.

    d. An entity may possess **some of the characteristics** of a nonbusiness entity but not others. Examples include private not-for-profit hospitals and schools that receive some contributions but are essentially dependent on debt issues and user fees.

    1) For such entities, the **reporting objectives of business entities** may be more appropriate.

2. **Financial Reporting Model**

    a. A discussion of the objectives of financial reporting for NFPs was discussed in Study Unit 1, Subunit 3.

    b. External financial reporting by NFPs should help external users assess

    1) The **services** an entity provides and its **ability to continue** to provide those services, and

    2) How managers discharge their **stewardship responsibilities** and other aspects of their performance.

c.   Financial accounting and reporting in a **statement of financial position** as of the end of the reporting period is based on a **net assets model**.

1)   Net assets equals the residual interest in the assets of an NFP that remains after subtracting its liabilities. Net assets is divided into the following classes based on the presence or absence of donor restrictions:

a)   Unrestricted
b)   Temporarily restricted
c)   Permanently restricted

2)   Changes in the classes of net assets, including the effects of reclassification, must be reported in a **statement of activities**, and a **statement of cash flows** must be presented.

3)   The net assets model emphasizes combined information for the entity as a whole, not individual funds.

a)   **Fund accounting is not required** for external reporting but may be used for internal purposes. **Separate fund information** may be disclosed in external financial reports if the required combined information is reported.

3.   **Tax Considerations**

a.   NFPs should be aware of relevant tax laws and regulations and their effect on the financial statements. Failure to maintain **tax-exempt status** may have serious tax consequences and affect both the financial statements and related disclosures.

b.   In addition to the tax-exempt entities created by **federal law**, other exemptions may be created by **state law**. NFPs are subject to the laws of the state of incorporation and the laws of states where they conduct significant activities.

c.   The **IRS** may revoke exemptions for any of several reasons. States also have regulatory bodies that can revoke state tax-exempt status without regard to federal tax-exempt status. **Revocation** of an NFP's federal tax-exempt status may be based on, for example,

1)   Material changes in the NFP's character, purpose, or method of operation;
2)   Inappropriate insider transactions;
3)   Private benefit to insiders or outsiders other than incidental benefits;
4)   Commerciality as the NFP's primary purpose; and
5)   Political campaign activities.

d.   Most tax-exempt organizations must file **annual information returns**. States also have registration and filing requirements, some of which include audited financial statements.

e.   **Private foundations** are subject to numerous restrictions, including an excise tax on net investment income, whereas **public charities** are exempt from federal unemployment taxes.

1)   The **IRS considers all** charitable organizations to be **private foundations** unless they qualify as public charities.

f.   Unrelated business income of NFPs is subject to federal corporate taxes on income, including the alternative minimum tax.

Stop and review! You have completed the outline for this subunit. Study multiple-choice questions 1 through 5 beginning on page 748.

20.2 FINANCIAL STATEMENTS OF NFPs

1. **Statement of Financial Position**

EXAMPLE

The American National Red Cross
Consolidated Statement of Financial Position
June 30, 2011 (with comparative information as of June 30, 2010)
(in thousands)

Assets	2011	2010
Current assets:		
Cash and cash equivalents	$ 372,662	$ 407,204
Investments	695,856	798,060
Trade receivables, net of allowance	222,430	81,473
Contributions receivable	66,977	75,955
Inventories, net of allowance	126,382	129,756
Collateral held under securities agreements	110,943	137,749
Other current assets	28,901	16,068
Total current assets	$1,624,151	$1,646,265
Investments	1,309,580	1,076,601
Contributions receivable	14,134	23,944
Land, buildings, and other property, net	1,077,945	1,090,532
Other assets	227,771	161,769
Total assets	**$4,253,581**	**$3,999,111**
Liabilities and net assets		
Current liabilities:		
Accounts payable and accrued expenses	$ 333,223	$ 371,044
Current portion of debt	14,418	39,812
Postretirement benefits	4,147	4,616
Payables under securities agreements	110,943	137,749
Other current liabilities	185,134	26,165
Total current liabilities	$ 647,865	$ 579,386
Debt	558,963	552,245
Pension and postretirement benefits	667,987	757,676
Other liabilities	186,843	150,917
Total liabilities	**$2,061,658**	**$2,040,224**
Net assets:		
Unrestricted net assets	$ 655,029	$ 448,142
Temporarily restricted net assets	871,126	884,910
Permanently restricted net assets	665,768	625,835
Total net assets	**$2,191,923**	**$1,958,887**
Total liabilities and net assets	**$4,253,581**	**$3,999,111**

---

a. **Unrestricted net assets** arise from providing goods and services and from receipts of contributions and dividends or interest, minus expenses. The only limits are the nature of the organization, its environment, its specified purposes, and contractual agreements.

   1) Net assets designated for a particular purpose by the board (i.e., internally designated) are reported as unrestricted net assets.

b. **Temporarily restricted net assets** result from restrictions removable by the passage of time **(time restrictions)** or by the actions of the NFP **(purpose restrictions)**.

   1) **Temporary restrictions** may be for support of operating activities, investment for a specified term **(term endowments)**, use in a specified future period, or acquisition of long-lived assets.

2) For example, a disease-fighting charity may receive a grant specifying that the amount must be used for vaccinations in Africa for 5 years. Any balance remaining at the end of that time may be used for any purpose the board deems appropriate.

c. **Permanently restricted net assets** arise from asset increases and decreases subject to restrictions not removable by passage of time or by the NFP's actions. They may result from reclassifications within the classes of net assets created by donor stipulations.

1) In the example of the disease-fighting charity, the entity may receive a grant that must be invested in AAA-grade bonds in perpetuity, with the income being spent on vaccinations in Africa (i.e., a permanent endowment fund).

d. Information about restrictions (donor-imposed, not self-imposed) on net assets is provided either **on the statement or in the notes**.

e. **Assets and liabilities** must be classified into reasonably homogeneous groups.

1) Assets (including cash) that are **donor-restricted** to long-term use cannot be classified with unrestricted and currently available assets.

2) **Cash and cash equivalents** should be included as a separate item in a statement of financial position.

a) Information about the nature and amount of limitations on the use of cash should be included on the face of the statements or in the notes. Disclosure also should be made of unusual circumstances or of failure to maintain cash balances to meet donor restrictions.

3) NFPs may sell **inventory** obtained in transactions or from contributions. Contributions of inventory are reported when received at fair value.

4) The recognition and measurement of **prepaid expenses, deferred charges, and similar costs** are based on the same principles used by business organizations.

5) **Property and equipment (P&E)** consist of long-lived tangible assets, including the contributed use of facilities and equipment, except collection items and investment assets.

a) The **recognition and measurement** principles for P&E obtained in exchange transactions are similar to those of businesses.

b) P&E used in exchange transactions (for example, federal contracts but not leases) in which the **provider retains title** should be reported as a contribution at fair value only if it is probable that the NFP will keep the assets when the arrangement ends.

c) The amount initially recognized for contributed P&E includes all costs incurred to place the assets in use.

d) NFPs recognize **depreciation** for most P&E. Items not depreciated are land used as a building site and certain individual works of art and historical treasures with very long useful lives.

i) An **artwork** or **historical treasure** is nondepreciable only if verifiable evidence supports the conclusions that (a) it has "cultural, aesthetic, or historical value worth preserving perpetually," and (b) the holder has the means of, and is, preserving its full service potential.

       ii)   Depreciation **decreases unrestricted net assets**. If contributed P&E have donor-imposed restrictions, temporarily restricted net assets should be **reclassified** as unrestricted as the restrictions expire.

- The amount reclassified may not be equal to the related depreciation. It is based on the length of the restrictions, but depreciation is based on the useful economic life.
- Gains and losses on disposal change unrestricted net assets absent a basis for restriction.

       iii)   Guidance related to **asset retirement obligation** also applies to tangible long-lived assets of an NFP (discussed in Study Unit 13, Subunit 11).

6) **Debt and Other Liabilities**

   a)   Obligations of NFPs arising from **tax-exempt financing** arranged by state and local authorities are reported as liabilities.

       i)   NFPs are usually tax-exempt but may be taxed on portions of their income. Thus, **current and deferred tax liabilities (and assets)** also may arise.

   b)   **Deferred revenue** is recognized when resources are received in transactions with service beneficiaries for specific activities that have not yet occurred.

   c)   **Advances from third parties**, e.g., government agencies, are liabilities if they are based on estimated costs of providing services to constituents to the extent such services have not yet been performed.

       i)   Liabilities also are recognized for receipts of resources from third parties for loans to the NFP's constituents.

   d)   An NFP must recognize a liability for an **unconditional promise to give** (discussed in the next subunit) when it is obligated to transfer the promised asset, ordinarily when the donor approves the specific grant or the donee is notified. Payments to be made over several periods are measured at present value.

       i)   The **interest method** is used to amortize discounts on contributions payable measured at present value.

   e)   **Annuity obligations.** Some contributions received by NFPs create obligations to make future payments to others. These annuity obligations are recognized as liabilities and measured at the present value of the actuarially determined obligations.

       i)   Revaluations of these liabilities are reported as changes in the appropriate net asset classes.

   f)   Amounts held under **agency transactions** may be liabilities of an NFP.

   g)   **Loss contingencies** may arise from, for example, failure to comply with donor-imposed restrictions or from uncertainties about the NFP's tax-exempt status.

2.   **Statement of Activities and Changes in Net Assets**

a.   The statement reports the **changes in net assets** and **changes in the categories of net assets**.

1)   Revenues, expenses, gains, and losses increase or decrease net assets.

2)   Other events, e.g., expirations of donor-imposed restrictions, that increase one class of net assets and decrease another (reclassifications) are reported separately as **net assets released from restrictions**.

EXAMPLE

The American National Red Cross
Consolidated Statement of Activities
Year Ended June 30, 2011 (with summarized information for the year ended June 30, 2010)
(in thousands)

	Unrestricted	Temporarily Restricted	Permanently Restricted	Totals 2011	Totals 2010
Operating revenues and gains					
Contributions:					
Corporate, foundation, and individual giving	$ 227,442	$ 458,505	$ --	$ 685,947	$ 813,928
United Way and other federated	36,203	75,070	--	111,273	119,825
Legacies and bequests	51,453	8,063	22,032	81,548	92,496
Services and materials	15,174	20,098	--	35,272	34,888
Products and services:					
Biomedical	2,189,663	--	--	2,189,663	2,200,550
Program materials	139,177	45	--	139,222	145,326
Contracts, including federal government	112,804	--	--	112,804	89,282
Investment income (Note 8)	19,339	30,245	--	49,584	48,595
Other revenues	64,429	793	--	65,222	59,545
Net assets released from restrictions	704,812	(704,812)	--	--	--
Total operating revenues and gains	**$3,560,496**	**$(111,993)**	**$ 22,032**	**$3,470,535**	**$3,604,435**
Operating expenses					
Program services:					
Services to the Armed Forces	$ 57,403	$ --	$ --	$ 57,403	$ 65,300
Biomedical services	2,195,108	--	--	2,195,108	2,194,789
Community services	90,558	--	--	90,558	105,278
Domestic disaster services	282,974	--	--	282,974	268,864
Health and safety services	203,735	--	--	203,735	216,946
International relief and development services	340,106	--	--	340,106	250,993
Total program services	**$3,169,884**	**$ --**	**$ --**	**$3,169,884**	**$3,102,170**
Supporting services:					
Fund raising	127,019	--	--	127,019	130,193
Management and general	142,682	--	--	142,682	138,472
Total supporting services	**$ 269,701**	**$ --**	**$ --**	**$ 269,701**	**$ 268,665**
Total operating expenses	**$3,439,585**	**$ --**	**$ --**	**$3,439,585**	**$3,370,835**
Change in net assets from operations	120,911	(111,993)	22,032	30,950	233,600
Nonoperating gains (losses)	77,047	98,209	17,901	193,157	138,497
Pension-related changes other than net periodic benefit cost	8,929	--	--	8,929	(85,676)
Change in net assets	**$ 206,887**	**$ (13,784)**	**$ 39,933**	**$ 233,036**	**$ 286,421**
Net assets, beginning of year	448,142	884,910	625,835	1,958,887	1,672,466
Net assets, end of year	$ 655,029	$ 871,126	$665,768	$2,191,923	$1,958,887

---

b.   **Revenues** are reported as increases in unrestricted net assets unless the use of the assets received is restricted. All **expenses** are reported as **decreases in unrestricted net assets**.

1)   Absent explicit or implicit restrictions, **contributions** are unrestricted revenues or gains **(unrestricted support)**. They increase unrestricted net assets.

a)   Donor-restricted contributions are restricted revenues or gains **(restricted support)**. They increase temporarily restricted net assets or permanently restricted net assets.

2) **Gains and losses** are changes in unrestricted net assets unless their use is temporarily or permanently restricted explicitly by the donor or by law.

3) The **gross amounts of revenues and expenses** from the entity's ongoing major or central operations are reported. However, **investment revenues** may be reported net of related expenses if those expenses are disclosed.

   a) **Gains and losses** may be reported as **net amounts** if they result from peripheral or incidental transactions or from other events and circumstances largely beyond the control of management.

c. Certain **other categories** of changes in net assets may be useful.

   1) Such **designations** as (a) operating and nonoperating, (b) recurring and nonrecurring, (c) earned and unearned, and (d) expendable or nonexpendable may be employed.

   2) An **intermediate measure of operations**, such as "excess of operating revenues over expenses," may only be used in a statement that reports the change in unrestricted net assets.

d. When expenses are paid out of **restricted** net assets, the following is an additional reporting requirement:

   1) In the subsection of revenues titled "net assets released from restrictions," the amount of the expense is reported as both an **increase in unrestricted revenues** and a **decrease in restricted revenues**.

e. **Exchange transactions** resulting in **revenues and receivables** for NFPs usually involve providing goods or services to beneficiaries for a fee.

   1) An NFP's **recognition, measurement, and display** of revenues and related receivables resulting from exchange transactions are usually consistent with the GAAP applicable to for-profit entities. Revenues from exchange transactions are increases in unrestricted net assets.

   2) **Expenses, gains, and losses** of NFPs are similar to those of for-profit entities.

      a) Some expense recognition issues are unique to NFPs. Thus, expenses are treated as decreases in unrestricted net assets. In addition,

         i) **Fund-raising costs**, including the cost of special events, are expensed as incurred even if they result in contributions in future periods.

         ii) **Reductions in amounts charged for goods or services**, for example, financial aid provided by an educational institution, are expenses if they are given in an exchange transaction. Reductions given **other than in exchange transactions** are expenses to the extent the NFP incurs incremental expense; they are discounts if incremental expense is not incurred.

   3) **Gains and Losses**

      a) How **costs related to sales** are displayed depends on whether the sales constitute a major activity or an incidental activity. For example, a major fundraising activity should report and display separately the revenues from sales and the related cost of sales. If sales relate to a program service, the cost of sales is a program expense. In another case, cost of sales could be reported as a separate supporting service.

         i) If sales relate to an **incidental activity**, gains or losses from those sales, and the receipts and related costs, may be offset. Only the net gains or losses are reported.

3.   **Statement of Functional Expenses**

a.   A statement of activities or the notes must provide information about **expenses reported by functional classification**, e.g., by major classes of program services and supporting services.

EXAMPLE

The American National Red Cross
Statement of Functional Expenses
Year Ended June 30, 2011 (with summarized information for the year ended June 30, 2010)
(in thousands)

	Program Services						
	Service to Armed Forces	Biomedical Services	Community Services	Domestic Disaster Services	Health and Safety Services	Int'l Relief & Development Services	Total Program Services
Salaries and wages	$28,458	$ 953,893	$ 35,974	$ 86,877	$ 96,164	$ 19,422	$1,220,788
Employee benefits	7,284	244,152	9,208	22,236	24,613	4,971	312,464
Subtotal	$35,742	$1,198,045	$ 45,182	$109,113	$120,777	$ 24,393	$1,533,252
Travel	1,708	30,591	1,601	15,778	2,716	2,636	55,030
Equipment maintenance and rental	1,312	74,484	3,647	9,810	4,415	1,549	95,217
Supplies and materials	5,201	507,409	11,775	8,395	24,882	1,374	559,036
Contractual services	9,315	334,496	12,429	50,324	39,114	8,696	454,374
Financial and material assistance	2,646	1,028	12,756	78,753	4,363	300,552	400,098
Depreciation and amortization	1,479	49,055	3,168	10,801	7,468	906	72,877
Total expenses	**$57,403**	**$2,195,108**	**$90,558**	**$282,974**	**$203,735**	**$340,106**	**$3,169,884**

	Supporting Services			Total Expenses	
	Fund Raising	Management and General	Total Supporting Services	2011	2010
Salaries and wages	$ 60,225	$ 71,591	$131,816	$1,352,604	$1,379,677
Employee benefits	15,415	18,324	33,739	346,203	342,179
Subtotal	$ 75,640	$ 89,915	$165,555	$1,698,807	$1,721,856
Travel	3,644	3,124	6,768	61,798	53,795
Equipment maintenance and rental	1,977	2,907	4,884	100,101	93,817
Supplies and materials	9,792	4,452	14,244	573,280	605,747
Contractual services	30,354	33,318	63,672	518,046	535,275
Financial and material assistance	2,199	1,925	4,124	404,222	270,952
Depreciation and amortization	3,413	7,041	10,454	83,331	89,393
Total expenses	**$127,019**	**$142,682**	**$269,701**	**$3,439,585**	**$3,370,835**

b.   **Program services** result in goods and services being distributed to beneficiaries, customers, or members to fulfill the purposes of the entity. Those services are the major purpose and output of the entity. They often relate to several major programs.

c.   **Supporting services** are activities of an NFP that are not program services. They usually include the following:

1)   **Management and General**

a)   Oversight and business management
b)   Budgeting, financing, and related activities
c)   Recordkeeping
d)   Most management and administrative activities

2)   **Fund-Raising**

a)   Publicity and conducting campaigns
b)   Maintenance of donor lists
c)   Conducting special events
d)   Preparing and distributing related materials
e)   Other solicitation activities

3)   **Membership Development**

a)   Soliciting for members and dues
b)   Member relations

d.   Some expenses can be assigned to one major program or service or one supporting activity. Other expenses relate to more than one program or supporting activity or to a combination.

    1)   **Direct identification** (assignment) of specific expenses with programs, services, or support activities is preferable when feasible. Otherwise, these expenses are allocated. A reasonable allocation should be made on an objective basis.

        a)   For example, the cost of a direct-mail solicitation may need to be allocated between fund-raising (a supporting service) and the NFP's educational mission (a program service).

e.   Payments or other support provided to **affiliated organizations** are reported by functional classification, if practicable, even if the entire amount cannot be allocated to functions. Payments that cannot be allocated to functions are considered a separate supporting service and reported separately.

f.   **Federated fund-raising organizations** make grants and awards to other NFPs. Their fund-raising activities, including those related to fund-raising for others, are reported as fund-raising expenses.

g.   The following diagram summarizes the composition of functional expenses for a not-for-profit entity:

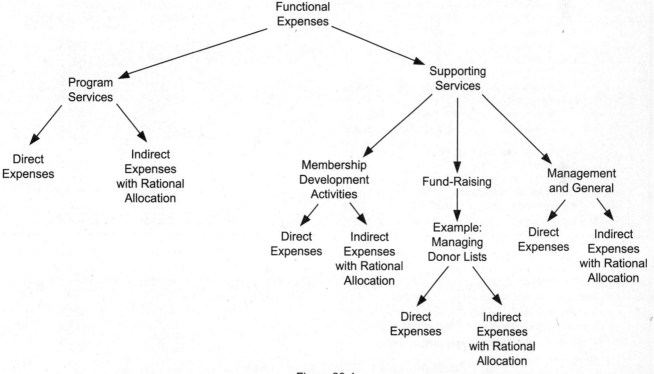

Figure 20-1

h.   **Voluntary health and welfare entities (VHWEs)** are **required** to report a **statement of functional expenses**.

    1)   VHWEs are tax-exempt NFPs organized for the benefit of the public and supported by the public through contributions. Examples are the United Way and the American Cancer Society.

    2)   VHWEs must report information about expenses by **functional classification** and **natural classification** (e.g., salaries, rent, interest, depreciation, electricity, awards to others, grants to subrecipients, and professional fees) in a matrix format.

        a)   Other NFPs are encouraged but not required to provide information about expenses by natural classification.

4.   **Statement of Cash Flows**

    a.   The guidance in Study Unit 3 for reporting a statement of cash flows applies to all business enterprises and NFPs. For example, the terms "income statement" and "net income" apply to "statement of activities" and "change in net assets," respectively.

EXAMPLE

The American National Red Cross
Consolidated Statement of Cash Flows
Year Ended June 30, 2011
(with comparative information for the year ended June 30, 2010)
(in thousands)

	2011	2010
Cash flows from operating activities:		
Change in net assets	$233,036	$ 286,421
Adjustments to reconcile change in net assets to net cash provided by operating activities:		
Depreciation and amortization	83,331	89,393
Provision for doubtful accounts receivable	1,252	4,732
Provision (recovery) for obsolete inventory	(495)	5,024
Net (gain)/loss on sales of property	(2,699)	12,926
Net investment and derivative losses	(192,075)	(124,733)
Pension-related changes other than net periodic benefit cost	(8,929)	85,676
Permanently restricted contributions	(22,032)	(27,121)
Changes in operating assets and liabilities:		
Receivables	(123,257)	43,745
Inventories	3,869	15,116
Other assets	(78,999)	7,624
Accounts payable and accrued expenses	(37,821)	47,454
Other liabilities	192,930	(2,316)
Pension and postretirement benefits	(81,229)	(52,398)
Net cash (used in) provided operating activities	**$ (33,118)**	**$ 391,543**
Cash flows from investing activities:		
Purchases of property	$ (74,452)	$ (55,605)
Proceeds from sales of property	6,407	6,451
Purchases of investments	(158,583)	(467,655)
Proceeds from sales of investments	222,948	312,013
Net cash used in investing activities	**$ (3,680)**	**$(204,796)**
Cash flows from financing activities:		
Permanently restricted contributions	$ 20,932	$ 27,087
Proceeds from borrowings	20,109	225,646
Repayments of debt	(38,785)	(246,882)
Net cash provided financing activities	**$ 2,256**	**$ 5,851**
Net (decrease)/increase in cash and cash equivalents	**$ (34,542)**	**$ 192,598**
Cash and cash equivalents, beginning of year	407,204	214,606
Cash and cash equivalents, end of year	**$ 372,662**	**$ 407,204**
Supplemental disclosures of cash flow information:		
Cash paid during the year for interest	$ 21,342	$ 19,439
Noncash investing and financing transactions:		
Acquisition of equipment under capital lease agreements	--	--
Donated stock and beneficial interest in perpetual trust	1,499	223

---

    b.   **Cash inflows from operating activities** include receipts of unrestricted contributions.

        1)   NFPs and for-profit entities also treat **interest and dividends** on unrestricted investments as operating cash flows.

        2)   Either the **direct or indirect method** of presenting cash flows from operating activities may be used.

        3)   Operating activities may include **agency transactions**.

            a)   In an agency transaction, the NFP receives assets in a voluntary transfer but has little discretion in their use.

c. **Cash inflows from financing activities** include receipts of resources that are donor-restricted for **long-term purposes**.

1) Accordingly, cash donor-restricted to acquiring, constructing, or improving long-lived assets (e.g., a building or equipment) or to establishing or increasing an endowment is a cash inflow from a financing activity.

a) Receipts of investment income (cash interest and dividends) that are donor-restricted for such purposes also are cash inflows from financing activities.

2) The payments to acquire, construct, or improve long-lived assets are cash outflows from **investing activities**.

d. **Noncash** investing and financing activities include receipt of a gift of a building or an investment asset.

5. **Summary of NFP Financial Statements**

	Non-VHWE NFPs	VHWEs
Statement of financial position	x	x
Statement of activities	x	x
Statement of cash flows	x	x
Statement of functional expenses		x

Stop and review! You have completed the outline for this subunit. Study multiple-choice questions 6 through 12 beginning on page 749.

20.3 REVENUES OF NFPs

1. **Definitions**

a. A **contribution** is one entity's **unconditional transfer** of assets to another entity (or a settlement of its liabilities). The transfer must be voluntary and nonreciprocal, and the donor entity must not act as an owner.

1) Assets include cash, securities, land, buildings, use of facilities or utilities, materials and supplies, intangible assets, services, and unconditional promises to give those items in the future.

a) A promise is unconditional if the probability that the promise will not be kept is **remote**.

b. An **unconditional promise to give** is a written or oral agreement to contribute assets to another entity. Sufficient verifiable documentation must exist before the promise may be recognized (i.e., by debiting a receivable and crediting revenue).

c. A **donor-imposed condition** specifies a future and uncertain event. Its occurrence or nonoccurrence gives the donor a right of return or releases the donor from an obligation. Thus, it precludes recognition of a contribution. A **donor-imposed restriction** merely limits the use of contributed assets.

2. **Contributions Received**

a. Contributions received, including gifts in kind, ordinarily are accounted for when received at **fair value** as credits to revenues or gains. Debits are to assets, liabilities, or expenses.

1) The difference between the amount ultimately received and the fair value is recognized as an adjustment to the original contributions.

b.   If **present value** is used to measure the fair value of an unconditional promise to give cash, later **interest accruals** are recorded as contribution income (expense) by donees (donors).

   1)   However, **unconditional promises to give** expected to be collected in less than 1 year may be recognized at **net realizable value** (that is, minus an estimated uncollectible amount).

c.   **Contributions of services** are recognized if they

   1)   Create or enhance nonfinancial assets or

   2)   Require special skills, are provided by those having such skills, and would usually be purchased if not obtained by donations.

d.   A contribution of **utilities**, such as electricity, is a contribution of **other assets**, not services. A simultaneous receipt and use of utilities should be recognized as an unrestricted revenue and an expense in the period of receipt and use.

e.   **Collections** are works of art, historical treasures, etc., that meet the criteria in the relevant GAAP. Upon initial recognition, an NFP may choose to (1) capitalize its collections, including all items not previously capitalized; (2) capitalize only those items acquired afterward; or (3) not capitalize collections. Capitalization of part of the collections is not permitted.

   1)   If an NFP **capitalizes collections**, items acquired in exchange transactions are recognized as assets and measured at cost. Contributed items are recognized as assets and as contributions in the appropriate net asset class and measured at fair value.

   2)   If an NFP does **not capitalize collections**, no assets or contributions are recognized. Contributions need not be capitalized and recognized as revenues if they are

      a)   Held for public exhibition, education, or research in furtherance of public service rather than financial gain;

      b)   Protected, kept unencumbered, cared for, and preserved; and

      c)   Subject to a policy that requires the proceeds of their sale to be used to acquire other collection items.

   3)   If collections are not capitalized,

      a)   The NFP must report on the face of the statement of activities (separately from revenues, expenses, gains, and losses) the costs (proceeds) of the collection items purchased (sold) as a decrease (increase) in the appropriate class of net assets.

      b)   The NFP also must report the proceeds from insurance recoveries of lost or destroyed collection items as an increase in the appropriate class of net assets.

      c)   Furthermore, cash flows from purchases, sales, and insurance recoveries of uncapitalized collection items are reported in the investing activities section of the statement of cash flows.

   4)   **Contributions** by an NFP of previously recognized collection items are expenses and decreases in assets and may be measured at fair value. A gain or loss may be recognized.

      a)   Contributions of previously unrecognized collection items are not recognized; disclosure is made in the notes.

   5)   Works of art, historical treasures, etc., that are not collection items are recognized as assets and disclosed separately.

   6)   If collections are **capitalized prospectively**, proceeds from sales and insurance recoveries of items not previously capitalized are reported separately from revenues, expenses, gains, and losses.

3. **Restrictions**

   a. A **temporary restriction** is donor-imposed. It permits the donee to use up or expend the donation as specified. It is satisfied by the passage of time or by actions of the donee.

   b. A **permanent restriction** is donor-imposed. It requires resources to be maintained permanently. However, it allows the donee to use up or expend the **income** (or other economic benefits) from the donation.

   c. A **permanent endowment** is a donation restricted by the donor to generate investment income in perpetuity (discussed later in this study unit).

   d. Revenues or gains from contributions that increase permanently restricted or temporarily restricted net assets are reported as **restricted support.**

   e. A contribution whose restrictions are met in the same period may be reported as **unrestricted support**. This policy must be disclosed and consistently applied.

   f. Revenues or gains from contributions without restrictions constitute **unrestricted support**. They increase unrestricted net assets.

   g. **Unconditional promises to give**, with amounts due in future periods, are reported as restricted support unless the circumstances clearly indicate that the donor intended support for current activities. Thus, unconditional promises of future cash amounts usually increase temporarily restricted net assets.

   h. **Gifts of long-lived assets** (or other assets required to be used to acquire them) may be received without stipulations about their use. In this case, if the entity's choice of accounting policy is to **imply a time restriction** expiring over their useful life, the gifts are reported as restricted support. Because the implied time restriction will expire, it is temporary.

   i. The **expiration of a restriction** is recognized when it expires. Expiration occurs when the stipulated time has elapsed, the purpose of the restriction has been fulfilled, or both. It is reported **separately as a reclassification** in the statement of activities as net assets released from restrictions. The effect is to increase one class of net assets and decrease another.

      1) For example, an **implied time restriction** on a long-lived depreciable asset expires as the economic benefits are used.

      2) An expense may be incurred for a purpose for which **unrestricted and temporarily restricted** net assets are available. Hence, the use of the unrestricted resources may result in expiration of the donor restriction to the extent of the expense incurred. This result follows even if the restricted resources are not used or are used only in part.

         a) However, this rule does not apply if the expense is for a purpose directly related to **another specific external revenue source**.

   j. **Conditional promises to give** are recognized when the conditions are substantially met.

      1) A conditional promise is considered unconditional if the likelihood is **remote** that the condition will not be met.

      2) A transfer of assets subject to a conditional promise is treated as a refundable advance (debit asset, credit liability) until the conditions are substantially met.

   k. **Recipients of promises to give** must make appropriate disclosures.

4. **Contributions Made**

   a. Contributions made are recognized at **fair value** when made as (1) expenses and (2) decreases of assets or increases in liabilities.

5. **Agency Transactions**

    a.   When an entity voluntarily transfers assets to an NFP, the extent of discretion the NFP has over the use of the assets must be determined.

        1)   If it has little discretion, the transfer is an agency transaction.

        2)   If it has discretion, the transfer is a contribution, an exchange, or combination of the two.

    b.   Amounts received in an **agency transaction** should be reported as increases in assets and liabilities. Distributions should be reported as decreases in those accounts.

        1)   Cash received and paid should be reported in the operating activities section of the statement of cash flows.

6. **Exchange Transactions**

    a.   Exchange transactions are **reciprocal transfers** in which each party receives and sacrifices something of approximately equal value. The issue is to distinguish exchanges from contributions.

        1)   The cost of **premiums** given to potential donors in a mass fund-raising appeal is a fund-raising expense related to exchange transactions.

            a)   The cost of premiums given to acknowledge contributions is also a fund-raising expense, provided the cost is nominal in relation to the contributions.

    b.   **Dues** from members may have elements of both a contribution and an exchange if members receive tangible or intangible benefits from membership.

        1)   **Revenue** from dues in exchange transactions is recognized over the period to which the dues relate.

        2)   **Nonrefundable fees** received in exchange transactions are recognized as revenues when they become receivable if future fees are expected to cover the costs of future services to members.

            a)   If **current fees** are expected to cover those costs, they should be recognized over the average duration of membership, the life expectancy of members, etc.

    c.   **Grants, awards, or sponsorships** are contributions if the resource providers receive no value or if the value is incidental to the potential public benefit.

        1)   The transfers are exchange transactions if the potential public benefit is secondary.

    d.   **Resources received in exchange transactions** are classified as unrestricted revenues and net assets even when resource providers limit the use of the resources.

7. **Donations on Behalf of a Beneficiary**

    a.   A **donor** may make a contribution to an NFP that agrees to use it on behalf of a **third party beneficiary**.

    b.   A recipient NFP that accepts **cash** or other **financial assets** recognizes the **fair value** of the assets as a **liability** to the specified beneficiary when it recognizes the assets received from the donor.

        1)   If the assets are **nonfinancial**, such as materials or supplies, the recipient need not recognize the assets and the liability. The recipient NFP must disclose its accounting policy in this regard and apply it consistently.

        2)   If the donor explicitly grants the recipient NFP **variance power**, the recipient recognizes the fair value of any assets received as a contribution.

            a)   Variance power is the unilateral power to redirect the use of the assets to another beneficiary.

8. **Split-Interest Agreements (SIAs)**

    a. Under trusts or other arrangements, NFPs may share benefits with the donor or third-party beneficiaries.

        1) SIAs may be **revocable or irrevocable**.
        2) The **period covered** may be a specific number of years (or in perpetuity) or the remaining life of a designated individual or individuals.
        3) The assets are invested by the NFP, a trustee, or a fiscal agent. **Distributions** are made to beneficiaries during the term of the agreement.
        4) At the end of the agreement, the remaining assets are distributed to or retained by either the NFP or another beneficiary.
        5) If the NFP has a **lead interest**, it receives distributions during the agreement's term.

            a) If it has a **remainder interest**, the donor (or others designated by the donor) receives those distributions, and the NFP receives all or part of the assets remaining at the end of the agreement.

    b. **Recognition and Measurement**

        1) Assets received under **irrevocable SIAs** are recorded at fair value. The contribution is recognized as a revenue or gain. Liabilities incurred in the exchange portion of an SIA, ordinarily an agreement to pay an annuity to a donor, also are recognized.
        2) In the absence of contrary conditions, **contribution revenue and related assets and liabilities** are recognized when an irrevocable SIA naming the NFP trustee or fiscal agent is executed.

            a) If a third party acts as trustee or fiscal agent, recognition occurs when the NFP is notified of the agreement.
            b) The third party may have **variance power**, or the NFP may have only **conditional rights** to the benefits. In these situations, contribution revenue and related assets and liabilities are not recognized until the NFP has an unconditional right to receive benefits.

        3) A **revocable SIA** is accounted for as an intention to give. If an NFP serves as trustee under a revocable SIA, assets received are recognized at fair value when received and as refundable advances.

            a) **Contribution revenue** is not recognized until the SIA becomes irrevocable or the assets are distributed to the NFP for its unconditional use.
            b) **Income on assets** not available for the NFP's unconditional use and any subsequent adjustments to their carrying amount are treated as adjustments to the assets and as refundable advances.

        4) Upon initial recognition of an unconditional irrevocable SIA, contributions are measured at **fair value**.

            a) **Changes in fair value** of SIAs are recognized in a statement of activities and classified in the appropriate net assets category.

        5) When an SIA **terminates**, related assets and liabilities are closed. Remaining amounts are recognized as changes in the value of SIAs and classified in the appropriate net assets category.

A number of exam questions released by the AICPA have asked for calculations involving contributions to NFPs. The calculations have focused on the contribution classification as unrestricted, temporarily restricted, or permanently restricted.

Stop and review! You have completed the outline for this subunit. Study multiple-choice questions 13 through 18 beginning on page 751.

20.4 INVESTMENTS HELD BY NFPs

1. **Accounting Treatment**

    a. **Equity securities with readily determinable fair values** and **all debt securities** are to be measured at **fair value** in the statement of financial position.

        1) The **total change in fair value** includes the **change in unpaid interest** on debt securities (or unpaid dividends on equity securities until the ex-dividend date) and the **holding gain or loss** (realized or unrealized).

        2) **Purchased investments** are initially recorded at acquisition cost. Those received as contributions or through agency transactions are recorded at fair value.

    b. **Gains and losses** are reported when they occur. They are included in the statement of activities as changes in unrestricted net assets unless a legal or donor restriction exists.

        1) If **unrealized gains and losses** were recognized in prior periods, gains and losses recognized for a current disposition of the same investments exclude the amounts previously recognized.

    c. **Investment income** is reported when earned as increases in unrestricted net assets barring a donor restriction. It is reported as an increase in temporarily restricted or permanently restricted net assets given a donor-imposed restriction.

        1) A statement of activities ordinarily reports gross amounts of revenues and expenses, but investment revenues may be reported net of related expenses if the amount of expenses is disclosed.

    d. **Investment pools**, including investments from contributions with different restrictions, may be created for portfolio management.

        1) Ownership interests (units) are assigned to the pool categories (participants) based on the market value of the cash and securities obtained from each participant.

            a) Current market value also determines the units allocated to additional assets placed in the pool and the value of withdrawals.

        2) Investment income, realized gains and losses, and recognized unrealized gains and losses are allocated based on units assigned.

    e. Realized and unrealized losses may be **netted** against realized and unrealized gains.

        1) An NFP may manage investments on a **total return basis**. The emphasis is on the overall return. A spending-rate formula determines how much of the return to use for current operations.

        2) In addition to other disclosures, NFPs should provide information about financial instruments in accordance with **GAAP**.

    f. Gains and income that are donor-restricted to certain uses may be reported as increases in unrestricted net assets if the **restrictions expire** in the period the gains and income are recognized.

        1) If the entity adopts this policy, it must apply the same policy to contributions, report consistently, and disclose the accounting policy.

2. **Endowments**

   a. A donor may require a gift to be invested permanently or for a specified term. The result is a **donor-restricted endowment fund**. However, absent a legal or donor restriction, gains and losses on investments of a donor-restricted endowment fund are changes in unrestricted net assets.

   b. If a **specific security** is to be held permanently, the gains and losses on that security are assumed to be changes in **permanently restricted net assets** absent a contrary donor instruction.

      1) However, if the donee may **choose investments**, the **gains** are not permanently restricted absent a donor stipulation or legal requirement. Thus, the gains (the net appreciation of the fund investments) are unrestricted or temporarily restricted if the income is unrestricted or temporarily restricted, respectively.

   c. Absent donor stipulations or contrary law, **losses** reduce **temporarily restricted net assets**. This reduction is to the extent that a donor's temporary restriction on net appreciation of the fund has not expired prior to the losses. Any **remaining losses** reduce **unrestricted net assets**.

      1) If losses reduce the fund's assets below the level required by the law or by the donor, gains restoring the fair value to the required level are increases in **unrestricted net assets**.

Stop and review! You have completed the outline for this subunit. Study multiple-choice questions 19 through 24 beginning on page 753.

20.5 HEALTHCARE ENTITIES (HCEs)

1. **Overview**

   a. **Healthcare entities (HCEs)** include such organizations as hospitals, nursing homes, clinics, and medical practices. They may be organized as (1) private for-profit businesses, (2) private not-for-profit entities, or (3) governmental bodies.

      1) Despite the varying requirements of GAAP for the three types of entities, the nature of providing healthcare results in certain common aspects of accounting and reporting.

         a) The guidance for healthcare entities addresses the accounting and reporting issues of **all three types**.

      2) A **private for-profit** (i.e., investor-owned) healthcare entity typically receives **no contributions**.

      3) A **not-for-profit** business-oriented HCE has **no equity**.

      4) **Governmental** HCEs that use enterprise fund accounting must account for uniquely **governmental transactions**.

   b. The typical basic **financial statements** reported by a nongovernmental HCE are

      1) Statement of financial position
      2) Statement of operations (may be combined with the statement of changes)
      3) Statement of changes in net assets (or equity if for-profit)
      4) Statement of cash flows

   c. **Revenues** of an HCE are recognized **at the time a service is provided**.

      1) The **three principal sources of HCE revenue** are patient service revenue, premium revenue, and other revenues.

2. **Patient Service Revenues**

   a. Patient service revenues are recorded on an accrual basis at the provider's established rates, that is, at their **gross amount**.

      1) However, in the statement of operations, a **provision for bad debts** must be presented on a separate line as a deduction from **patient service revenue**. This guidance applies to entities that recognize significant patient service revenue when services are rendered without assessing ability to pay.

   b. A substantial amount of healthcare is paid for by **third-party payors** such as insurance companies and the federal government.

      1) Because the collection practices for the two types of payors are so different, the receivables are **recorded separately** in the accounting records.

EXAMPLE

Accounts receivable -- third-party payors	$1,400,000	
Accounts receivable -- patients	320,000	
Patient service revenues		$1,720,000

---

   c. A certain number of patients will prove unable or unwilling to pay the amounts they have been billed. An HCE establishes an **allowance account** in the same manner as a for-profit entity.

EXAMPLE

Bad debt expense ($320,000 × 5%)	$16,000	
Allowance for uncollectible accounts		$16,000

---

   d. HCEs acknowledge that certain patients cannot be expected to pay.

      1) These **charity care** amounts cannot justifiably be treated as receivables because, at the time the service is rendered, they are not expected to be paid.

      2) Thus, these amounts are treated as **reductions of revenue and receivables**.

EXAMPLE

Patient service revenues ($320,000 × 2%)	$6,400	
Accounts receivable -- patients		$6,400

---

   e. Moreover, HCEs also do not expect to collect the full amount billed to **third-party payors**.

      1) However, the accounting treatment is not the same. These reductions are the result of **contractual arrangements** already agreed to between the HCE and the payor.

      2) The HCE can make a **reasonable estimate** of these write-offs because the terms of the contract are known.

EXAMPLE

Contractual adjustments	$168,000	
Allowance for uncollectible accounts		$168,000

---

3. **Premium Revenues**

   a. Premium revenues are generated by **agreements to provide healthcare** rather than by actually providing services.

   b. For example, an integrated delivery system may contract to provide all health-related services for a certain group within its primary service area for a specified amount per member per month.

4. **Other Revenues**

   a. Donated medicine or supplies

      1) Occasionally a supplier may cancel an invoice billed to an HCE.

EXAMPLE

Accounts payable	$10,000	
Other operating revenue		$10,000

---

   b. Donated labor

      1) Not-for-profit HCEs can recognize revenue from volunteer services if the services either

         a) Create or enhance nonfinancial assets or

         b) Require special skills, are provided by those having such skills, and would usually be purchased if not obtained by donations.

   c. Providing educational programs

   d. Proceeds from the sale of cafeteria meals and guest trays

   e. Gifts and grants, whether restricted to a specific purpose or not

5. **Reporting**

   a. **Revenues are reported** on the statement of operations at their **net amounts**.

EXAMPLE

Unrestricted revenues, gains, and other support:	
Net patient service revenue *	$ 875,400
Premium revenue	168,700
Other revenue	1,200
Net assets released from restrictions used for operations **	550
Total unrestricted revenues, gains, and other support	$1,045,850

* Some entities must present a provision for bad debts on a separate line.
** Not-for-profit HCEs only

---

   b. The **components of net patient service revenue** are **disclosed** in the **notes** to the financial statements.

EXAMPLE

Gross patient service revenue:	
Inpatient	$ 700,000
Outpatient	300,000
Total gross patient service revenue	$1,000,000
Allowances for charity care and contractual adjustments	(124,600)
Net patient service revenue	$ 875,400

---

6. **Expenses**

    a. Expense recognition by for-profit HCEs generally is the same as for other business entities.

    b. A governmental HCE's treatment of expenses resulting from nonexchange transactions depends on the type of transaction (see Study Unit 18, Subunit 3).

7. **Net Assets**

    a. Not-for-profit HCEs must **report three categories of net assets** and the **changes** in them during the reporting period.

The AICPA has tested candidates' knowledge of accounting for healthcare entities. Be prepared to calculate net patient service revenue. Understanding the necessary journal entries should prepare you for possible questions testing this topic on your exam.

Stop and review! You have completed the outline for this subunit. Study multiple-choice questions 25 through 30 beginning on page 755.

QUESTIONS

20.1 The Not-for-Profit Environment

1. Net assets is an element of the financial statements of not-for-profit entities (NFPs). It

A. Is the residual interest in the assets of an NFP after subtracting its liabilities.

B. Is the change in equity during a period from transactions and other events and circumstances not involving resource providers.

C. Differs from equity in business enterprises because it is not a residual interest.

D. Consists of the probable future economic benefits obtained or controlled by a particular entity as a result of past transactions or events.

Answer (A) is correct.
REQUIRED: The definition of the net assets element of the financial statements of not-for-profit entities.
DISCUSSION: Net assets equals the residual interest in the assets of an entity that remains after subtracting its liabilities. In an NFP, which has no ownership interest in the same sense as a business enterprise, the net assets element is divided into three classes based on the presence or absence of donor-imposed restrictions.
Answer (B) is incorrect. Comprehensive income is the change in equity of a business enterprise during a period from transactions and other events and circumstances from nonowner sources. Answer (C) is incorrect. Equity and net assets are residuals. Answer (D) is incorrect. Assets, not net assets, are probable future economic benefits obtained or controlled by a particular entity as a result of past transactions or events.

2. A complete set of general-purpose external financial statements issued by a nongovernmental not-for-profit entity must include

A. Statements of financial position as of the beginning and end of the reporting period, a statement of cash flows, and a statement of activities.

B. A statement of financial position as of the end of the reporting period and a statement of revenues, expenditures, and changes in fund balances.

C. A statement of financial position as of the end of the reporting period, a statement of cash flows, and a statement of activities.

D. Statements of financial position as of the beginning and end of the reporting period, comparative statements of cash flows, and comparative statements of activities.

Answer (C) is correct.
REQUIRED: The statements included in a complete set of financial statements of NFPs.
DISCUSSION: A complete set of financial statements of an NFP must include (1) a statement of financial position as of the end of the reporting period, (2) a statement of activities and a statement of cash flows for the reporting period, and (3) accompanying notes. Furthermore, a voluntary health and welfare entity must report a statement of functional expenses (e.g., major classes of program services and supporting activities).
Answer (A) is incorrect. The statement of financial position must be as of the end of the reporting period. Answer (B) is incorrect. A statement of revenues, expenditures, and changes in fund balances is reported for the governmental funds of a state or local governmental entity. Answer (D) is incorrect. The statement of financial position must be as of the end of the reporting period, and comparative statements are not required.

3. Pharm, a nongovernmental not-for-profit entity, is preparing its year-end financial statements. Which of the following statements is required?

A. Statement of changes in financial position.

B. Statement of cash flows.

C. Statement of changes in fund balances.

D. Statement of revenues, expenses, and changes in fund balances.

Answer (B) is correct.
REQUIRED: The statements required in a complete set of financial statements of NFPs.
DISCUSSION: A complete set of financial statements of an NFP must include a statement of financial position as of the end of the reporting period, a statement of activities and a statement of cash flows for the reporting period, and accompanying notes to financial statements.

4. For external reporting purposes, the not-for-profit reporting model requires information about

A. Individual funds of the entity but not about the entity as a whole.

B. The entity as a whole but not about individual funds.

C. Individual funds of the entity and the entity as a whole.

D. The entity and precludes reporting individual fund information.

Answer (B) is correct.
REQUIRED: The information required by the not-for-profit reporting model.
DISCUSSION: The not-for-profit reporting model emphasizes information about the entity as a whole, not individual funds. Consequently, fund accounting is no longer required for external reporting but is not precluded.

5. The guidance for reporting the financial statements of not-for-profit entities focuses on

A. Basic information for the entity as a whole.

B. Standardization of funds nomenclature.

C. Inherent differences of not-for-profit entities that affect reporting presentations.

D. Distinctions between current fund and noncurrent fund presentations.

Answer (A) is correct.
REQUIRED: The focus of reporting by NFPs.
DISCUSSION: This guidance is intended to promote the relevance, understandability, and comparability of financial statements issued by NFPs by requiring that certain basic information be reported. The focus of the required financial statements is on the entity as a whole. It is also on (1) reporting assets, liabilities, and net assets; (2) changes in net assets; (3) flows of economic resources; (4) cash flows, borrowing and repayment of borrowing, and other factors affecting liquidity; and (5) service efforts.

20.2 Financial Statements of NFPs

6. In its fiscal year ended June 30, Year 4, Barr College, a large private institution, received $100,000 designated by the donor for scholarships for superior students. On July 26, Year 4, Barr selected the students and awarded the scholarships. How should the July 26 transaction be reported in Barr's statement of activities for the year ended June 30, Year 5?

A. As both an increase and a decrease of $100,000 in unrestricted net assets.

B. As a decrease only in unrestricted net assets.

C. By footnote disclosure only.

D. Not reported.

Answer (A) is correct.
REQUIRED: The treatment by a private not-for-profit entity of funds received and used for a designated purpose.
DISCUSSION: When Barr College received the contribution, it should have been classified as temporarily restricted because it was to be used for a specified purpose. Once the purpose has been fulfilled, the temporary restriction expires, and the amount should be reclassified as a decrease in temporarily restricted net assets and an increase in unrestricted net assets. When the scholarships are awarded, unrestricted net assets are decreased.
Answer (B) is incorrect. Unrestricted net assets also must be increased. Answer (C) is incorrect. A donation must be reported on the face of the statement of activities. Answer (D) is incorrect. This donation must be reported as (1) an increase and a decrease in unrestricted net assets and (2) a decrease in temporarily restricted net assets when its purpose is fulfilled and the scholarships are awarded.

7. During the current year, Mill Foundation, a nongovernmental not-for-profit entity, received $100,000 in unrestricted contributions from the general public. Mill's board of directors stipulated that $75,000 of these contributions would be used to create an endowment. At the end of the current year, how should Mill report the $75,000 in the net assets section of the statement of financial position?

A. Permanently restricted.

B. Unrestricted.

C. Temporarily restricted.

D. Donor restricted.

Answer (B) is correct.
REQUIRED: The reporting of unrestricted contributions designated as an endowment.
DISCUSSION: An internal decision to designate a portion of unrestricted net assets as an endowment is not a restriction. If the contributions had been restricted by the donor, the classification of the assets would have been either permanently restricted or temporarily restricted.
Answer (A) is incorrect. The contributions were not restricted by the donors. Answer (C) is incorrect. The contributions were unrestricted because the endowment was designated by the board. Answer (D) is incorrect. The board of directors, not the donors, designated a portion of the contributions as an endowment.

8. In the preparation of the statement of activities for a nongovernmental NFP, all expenses are reported as decreases in which of the following net asset classes?

A. Total net assets.

B. Unrestricted net assets.

C. Temporarily restricted net assets.

D. Permanently restricted net assets.

Answer (B) is correct.
REQUIRED: The net asset class in which expenses are recorded by a nongovernmental NFP.
DISCUSSION: All expenses of an NFP must be reported as decreases in unrestricted net assets. However, revenues, gains, and losses are reported in permanent or temporarily restricted net assets in appropriate cases.
Answer (A) is incorrect. Total net assets is not a category of net assets. Answer (C) is incorrect. Revenues, gains, and losses, not expenses, are reported in temporarily restricted net assets in appropriate cases. Answer (D) is incorrect. Permanently restricted net assets is decreased only by losses.

9. At the beginning of the year, the Baker Fund, a nongovernmental not-for-profit corporation, received a $125,000 contribution restricted to youth activity programs. During the year, youth activities generated revenues of $89,000 and had program expenses of $95,000. What amount should Baker report as net assets released from restrictions for the current year?

A. $0

B. $6,000

C. $95,000

D. $125,000

Answer (C) is correct.
REQUIRED: The net assets released from restrictions for the current year.
DISCUSSION: At the time the contribution was made, net restricted assets increased by $125,000. The restriction stated that the funds were to be used for youth activity programs. The amount of actual program expenses for the year is reported under net assets released from restrictions.
Answer (A) is incorrect. The incurrence of program expenses reduced restricted net assets by fulfilling the purpose of the restriction to the extent the resources were used.
Answer (B) is incorrect. The amount of $6,000 is the excess of program expenses over revenues generated by youth activities.
Answer (D) is incorrect. The purpose of the restriction was fulfilled only to the extent the contribution was used for the stated purpose.

10. A nongovernmental not-for-profit entity borrowed $5,000, which it used to purchase a truck. In which section of the entity's statement of cash flows should the transaction be reported?

A. In cash inflow and cash outflow from investing activities.

B. In cash inflow and cash outflow from financing activities.

C. In cash inflow from financing activities and cash outflow from investing activities.

D. In cash inflow from operating activities and cash outflow from investing activities.

Answer (C) is correct.
REQUIRED: The section of the statement of cash flows in which the purchase of a truck is reported by a nongovernmental NFP.
DISCUSSION: The borrowing is a cash inflow from a financing activity because it arises from issuing debt. The purchase of the truck is a cash outflow from an investing activity because it involves the acquisition of property, plant, or equipment or other productive assets.

11. On January 1, Year 4, a not-for-profit botanical society received a gift of an exhaustible fixed asset with an estimated useful life of 10 years and no salvage value. The donor's cost of this asset was $20,000, and its fair value at the date of the gift was $30,000. What amount of depreciation of this asset should the society recognize in its Year 4 financial statements?

A. $3,000

B. $2,500

C. $2,000

D. $0

12. Functional expenses recorded in the general ledger of ABC, a nongovernmental not-for-profit entity, are as follows:

Soliciting prospective members	$45,000
Printing membership benefits brochures	30,000
Soliciting membership dues	25,000
Maintaining donor list	10,000

What amount should ABC report as fund-raising expenses?

A. $10,000

B. $35,000

C. $70,000

D. $110,000

20.3 Revenues of NFPs

13. During the current year, a voluntary health and welfare entity received $300,000 in unrestricted pledges. Of this amount, $100,000 has been designated by donors for use next year to support operations. If 15% of the unrestricted pledges are expected to be uncollectible, what amount of unrestricted support should the entity recognize in its current-year financial statements?

A. $300,000

B. $270,000

C. $200,000

D. $170,000

14. Janna Association, a nongovernmental not-for-profit entity, received a cash gift with the stipulation that the principal be held for at least 20 years. How should the cash gift be recorded?

A. A temporarily restricted asset.

B. A permanently restricted asset.

C. An unrestricted asset.

D. A temporary liability.

Answer (A) is correct.
REQUIRED: The amount of depreciation to be recognized in the financial statements.
DISCUSSION: GAAP require NFPs to recognize depreciation. Moreover, contributions are recorded at their fair value when received. Assuming the straight-line method is used, the amount of depreciation that the not-for-profit botanical society should recognize is $3,000 [($30,000 fair value – $0 salvage value) ÷ 10 years].
Answer (B) is incorrect. Annual straight-line depreciation for this asset is $3,000. Answer (C) is incorrect. The amount of $2,000 results from using cost as the depreciable basis of the asset. Answer (D) is incorrect. NFPs recognize depreciation on most property and equipment.

Answer (A) is correct.
REQUIRED: The fund-raising expenses.
DISCUSSION: The major functional classes of expenses for an NFP are program services and supporting activities. The latter include management and general, fund-raising, and membership-development activities. Fund-raising expenses include maintaining donor lists ($10,000). Soliciting members and dues and printing membership benefits brochures are membership-development activities.
Answer (B) is incorrect. The amount of $35,000 includes the cost of soliciting dues, a membership-development activity. Answer (C) is incorrect. The amount of $70,000 is the cost of soliciting members and dues. Answer (D) is incorrect. Only the cost of the donor list is an expense of fund-raising.

Answer (D) is correct.
REQUIRED: The current-year unrestricted support to be recognized.
DISCUSSION: Only $200,000 of the pledged total constitutes unrestricted support. These pledges may be recognized at net realizable value (NRV) if their collection is expected in less than 1 year. The NRV of these pledges is $170,000 [$200,000 × (1.0 – .15 estimated uncollectible)].
Answer (A) is incorrect. This figure is the total amount of pledges. Answer (B) is incorrect. The amount of $100,000 of the pledges is restricted until the next year. Answer (C) is incorrect. The amount of $200,000 does not reflect the estimated uncollectible pledges.

Answer (A) is correct.
REQUIRED: The classification of a cash gift with a time restriction.
DISCUSSION: Temporarily restricted net assets result from restrictions removable by the passage of time or by the actions of the NFP. A stipulation that the principal be held for at least 20 years is a temporary time restriction.
Answer (B) is incorrect. Once 20 years pass, the asset is no longer restricted. Answer (C) is incorrect. The asset cash gift is restricted for at least 20 years. Answer (D) is incorrect. Cash is an asset.

15. Stanton College, a not-for-profit entity, received a building with no donor stipulations as to its use. Stanton does not have an accounting policy implying a time restriction on donated assets. What type of net assets should be increased when the building was received?

I.   Unrestricted
II. Temporarily restricted
III. Permanently restricted

    A. I only.

    B. II only.

    C. III only.

    D. II or III.

Answer (A) is correct.
    REQUIRED: The classification of net assets affected by a contribution of a building.
    DISCUSSION: Contributions without donor-imposed restrictions are reported as unrestricted support, which increases unrestricted net assets. If Stanton had an accounting policy to imply a time restriction on gifts of long-lived assets, the gift of the building would be reported as temporarily restricted support even though no donor restrictions were imposed.

16. A storm damaged the roof of a new building owned by K-9 Shelters, a not-for-profit entity. A supporter of K-9, a professional roofer, repaired the roof at no charge. In K-9's statement of activities, the damage and repair of the roof should

    A. Be reported by note disclosure only.

    B. Be reported as an increase in both expenses and contributions.

    C. Be reported as an increase in both net assets and contributions.

    D. Not be reported.

Answer (B) is correct.
    REQUIRED: The treatment of services received at no charge by a not-for-profit entity.
    DISCUSSION: Contributions of services at fair value are recognized if they require special skills, are provided by individuals having those skills, and would have to be purchased if not received by donation. Hence, K-9 should report an expense and contribution revenue for the services received.

17. The Pel Museum, a not-for-profit entity (NFP), received a contribution of historical artifacts. It need **not** recognize the contribution if the artifacts are to be sold and the proceeds used to

    A. Support general museum activities.

    B. Acquire other items for collections.

    C. Repair existing collections.

    D. Purchase buildings to house collections.

Answer (B) is correct.
    REQUIRED: The circumstance under which a contribution of artifacts to be sold need not be recognized.
    DISCUSSION: Contributions of such items as art works and historical treasures need not be capitalized and recognized as revenues if they are added to collections that are (1) held for public exhibition, education, or research for public service purposes rather than financial gain; (2) protected, kept unencumbered, cared for, and preserved; and (3) subject to a policy that requires the proceeds of sale of collection items to be used to acquire other collection items.

18. In July Year 3, Katie irrevocably donated $200,000 cash to be invested and held in trust by a church. Katie stipulated that the revenue generated from this gift be paid to Katie during Katie's lifetime. After Katie dies, the principal is to be used by the church for any purpose chosen by its governing body. The church received interest of $16,000 on the $200,000 for the year ended June 30, Year 4, and the interest was remitted to Katie. In the church's June 30, Year 4, annual financial statements,

    A. $200,000 should be reported as revenue.

    B. $184,000 should be reported as revenue.

    C. $16,000 should be reported as revenue.

    D. The gift and its terms should be disclosed only in notes to the financial statements.

Answer (A) is correct.
    REQUIRED: The proper accounting for a split-interest agreement.
    DISCUSSION: An NFP should report an irrevocable split-interest agreement. Assets under the control of the NFP are recorded at fair value at the time of initial recognition, and the contribution is recognized as revenue. Because the NFP has a remainder interest, it should not recognize revenue from receipt of the income of the trust. Thus, the NFP should recognize revenue of $200,000 (the presumed fair value of the contributed cash).
    Answer (B) is incorrect. The contribution is not reduced by the income paid to the donor. Answer (C) is incorrect. The income paid to the donor is not revenue of the NFP. Answer (D) is incorrect. The contribution should be recognized at fair value.

20.4 Investments Held by NFPs

19. Lane Foundation received a permanent endowment of $500,000 in Year 3 from Gant Enterprises. The endowment assets were invested in publicly traded securities, and Lane is permitted to choose suitable investments. Gant did not specify how gains and losses from dispositions of endowment assets were to be treated. No restrictions were placed on the use of dividends received and interest earned on fund resources. In Year 4, Lane realized gains of $50,000 on sales of fund investments and received total interest and dividends of $40,000 on fund securities. What amount of these capital gains, interest, and dividends increases unrestricted net assets?

A. $0

B. $40,000

C. $50,000

D. $90,000

20. Midtown Church received a donation of equity securities with readily determinable fair values from a church member. The securities had appreciated in value after they were purchased by the donor and continued to appreciate through the end of Midtown's fiscal year. At what amount should Midtown report its investment in donated securities in its year-end balance sheet?

A. Donor's cost.

B. Fair value at the date of receipt.

C. Fair value at the balance sheet date.

D. Fair value at either the date of receipt or the balance sheet date.

21. RST Charities received equity securities valued at $100,000 as an unrestricted gift. During the year, RST received $5,000 in dividends from these securities; at year end, the securities had a fair market value of $110,000. By what amount did these transactions increase RST's net assets?

A. $100,000

B. $105,000

C. $110,000

D. $115,000

Answer (D) is correct.
REQUIRED: The amount of capital gains, interest, and dividends that increases unrestricted net assets.
DISCUSSION: Absent an explicit donor stipulation or law to the contrary and assuming the donee is allowed to choose suitable investments, income and gains or losses on a donor-restricted endowment fund's assets are changes in unrestricted net assets. Thus, the increase in unrestricted net assets is $90,000 ($50,000 gains + $40,000 interest and dividends).
Answer (A) is incorrect. Zero assumes the income and gains are restricted. Answer (B) is incorrect. The amount of $40,000 assumes the gains are restricted. Answer (C) is incorrect. The amount of $50,000 assumes the income is restricted.

Answer (C) is correct.
REQUIRED: The valuation of donated marketable equity securities.
DISCUSSION: In its statement of financial position, an NFP should measure the following investments at fair value: (1) equity securities with readily determinable fair values and (2) debt securities. Thus, the total change in the fair value of the donated securities from the date of receipt to the balance sheet date must be reported in the statement of activities.

Answer (D) is correct.
REQUIRED: The increase in an NFP's net assets from an unrestricted contribution of securities that paid dividends and appreciated after receipt.
DISCUSSION: Contributions received are ordinarily accounted for when received at fair value as credits to revenues or gains. Debits are to assets, liabilities, or expenses. Revenues or gains from contributions without restrictions constitute unrestricted support. They increase unrestricted net assets. Not-for-profit entities must measure investments in equity securities with readily determinable fair values and all investments in debt securities at fair value in the statement of financial position. Unrealized holding gains or losses (changes in fair value) are reported in the statement of activities as changes in unrestricted net assets (barring a legal or donor restriction). Investment income (e.g., dividends) is reported when earned as increases in unrestricted net assets (barring a legal or donor restriction). Accordingly, RST's unrestricted net assets increased by $115,000 [$100,000 fair value of contribution + $5,000 in dividends + $10,000 ($110,000 – $100,000) unrealized holding gain in fair value].
Answer (A) is incorrect. The amount of $100,000 excludes the dividends and the unrealized holding gain. Answer (B) is incorrect. The amount of $105,000 excludes the unrealized holding gain. Answer (C) is incorrect. The amount of $110,000 excludes the dividends.

22. Maple Church has cash available for investments from contributions with different restrictions. Maple's policy is to maximize its financial resources. How may Maple pool its investments?

A. Maple may **not** pool its investments.

B. Maple may pool all investments but must equitably allocate realized and unrealized gains and losses among participants.

C. Maple may pool only unrestricted investments but must equitably allocate realized and unrealized gains and losses among participating funds.

D. Maple may pool only restricted investments but must equitably allocate realized and unrealized gains and losses among participating funds.

23. A voluntary health and welfare entity received a $500,000 permanent endowment. The donor stipulated that the income be used for a mental health program. The endowment fund reported a $60,000 net decrease in fair value and $30,000 of investment income. The entity spent $45,000 on the mental health program during the year. What amount of change in temporarily restricted net assets should the entity report?

A. $75,000 decrease.

B. $15,000 decrease.

C. $0

D. $425,000 increase.

Answer (B) is correct.

REQUIRED: The true statement about pooling of investments by an NFP.

DISCUSSION: Investment pools, including investments from contributions with different restrictions, are created for portfolio management. Ownership interests are assigned (ordinarily in terms of units) to the pool categories (participants) based on the market value of the cash and securities obtained from each participant. Current market value also determines the units allocated to additional assets placed in the pool and to value withdrawals. Investment income, realized gains and losses, and recognized unrealized gains and losses are allocated based on the units assigned.

Answer (A) is incorrect. Pooling of investments is allowed to obtain investment flexibility and reduce risk. Answer (C) is incorrect. Pooling of restricted investments is not prohibited. Answer (D) is incorrect. Pooling of unrestricted investments is not prohibited.

Answer (C) is correct.

REQUIRED: The change in temporarily restricted net assets.

DISCUSSION: The contribution to a permanent endowment is an increase in permanently restricted net assets. Income from a permanent endowment is an increase in restricted support if the donor restricts its use. However, if the restriction is met in the period the income is recognized, it may be reported as an increase in unrestricted net assets if the entity (1) has a similar policy for reporting contributions received, (2) reports consistently, and (3) makes adequate disclosure. The restriction on the $30,000 of investment income expired when it was spent (along with an additional $15,000, presumably from other sources). Absent donor stipulation or contrary law, losses on a permanent endowment reduce temporarily restricted net assets to the extent that a temporary restriction on net appreciation has not expired prior to the losses (any remaining losses reduce unrestricted net assets). Thus, absent such a restriction, the decrease in the fair value of the endowment's investments reduced unrestricted net assets. The effect on temporarily restricted net assets of (1) creation of the endowment, (2) the receipt and expenditure in the same period of income, and (3) the loss on the principal of the endowment (absent a donor restriction) is $0.

Answer (A) is incorrect. The amount of $75,000 is the sum of the fair value decrease and the excess of spending over income. Answer (B) is incorrect. The amount of $15,000 is the excess of the amount spent over the income. Answer (D) is incorrect. The amount of $425,000 equals the contribution (permanent endowment) minus the sum of the fair value decrease and the excess of spending over income.

24. A voluntary health and welfare entity received a $700,000 permanent endowment during the year. The donor stipulated that the income and investment appreciation be used to maintain its senior center. The endowment fund reported a net investment appreciation of $80,000 and investment income of $50,000. The entity spent $60,000 to maintain its senior center during the year. What amount of change in temporarily restricted net assets should the entity report?

A. $50,000

B. $70,000

C. $130,000

D. $770,000

Answer (B) is correct.

REQUIRED: The change in temporarily restricted net assets reported by a VHWE that received a permanent endowment with a use restriction on appreciation and income.

DISCUSSION: The contribution to a permanent endowment is an increase in permanently restricted net assets. Income or appreciation from donor-restricted permanent endowments is an increase in restricted support if the donor restricts its use. However, if the restriction is met in the period the income is recognized, it may be reported as an increase in unrestricted net assets if the entity (1) has a similar policy for reporting contributions received, (2) reports consistently, and (3) makes adequate disclosure. The temporary restriction on the income and appreciation was met and is deemed to have expired only to the extent it was expended during the year. Accordingly, the change in temporarily restricted net assets was $70,000 ($80,000 appreciation + $50,000 income – $60,000 spent).

Answer (A) is incorrect. The amount of $50,000 is the VHWE's investment income. Answer (C) is incorrect. The amount of $130,000 is the sum of appreciation and income. Answer (D) is incorrect. The amount of $770,000 is the sum of the appreciation and the permanent endowment.

20.5 Healthcare Entities (HCEs)

25. Palma Hospital's patient service revenue for services provided in Year 4 at established rates amounted to $8 million on the accrual basis. For internal reporting, Palma uses the discharge method. Under this method, patient service revenue is recognized only when patients are discharged, with no recognition given to revenue accruing for services to patients not yet discharged. Patient service revenue at established rates using the discharge method amounted to $7 million for Year 4. According to generally accepted accounting principles, Palma should report patient service revenue for Year 4 of

A. Either $8,000,000 or $7,000,000, at the option of the hospital.

B. $8,000,000

C. $7,500,000

D. $7,000,000

Answer (B) is correct.

REQUIRED: The amount of patient service revenue to be reported.

DISCUSSION: Revenue is recognized when the service is provided to a patient. Thus, gross patient service revenue is recorded on the accrual basis at the HCE's established rates, regardless of whether it expects to collect the full amount. Contractual and other adjustments are also recorded on the accrual basis and subtracted from gross patient service revenue to arrive at net patient service revenue, which is the amount reported in the statement of operations. Charity care is excluded from patient service revenue for financial reporting purposes. Thus, the discharge method is not acceptable under GAAP. In its general purpose external financial statements, Palma should report $8 million of patient service revenue based on established rates.

Answer (A) is incorrect. The hospital does not have this option. Answer (C) is incorrect. The amount of $7,500,000 is the average of the $8,000,000 accrual basis amount and the $7,000,000 discharge method amount. Answer (D) is incorrect. The $7,000,000 resulting from the discharge method is not acceptable under GAAP.

26. Under Cura Hospital's established rate structure, healthcare services revenues of $9 million would have been earned for the year ended December 31. However, only $6.75 million was collected because of charity allowances of $1.5 million and discounts of $750,000 to third-party payors. For the year ended December 31, what amount should Cura report as healthcare services revenues in the statement of operations?

A. $6,750,000

B. $7,500,000

C. $8,250,000

D. $9,000,000

Answer (A) is correct.

REQUIRED: The healthcare services revenues reported in the statement of operations.

DISCUSSION: Gross healthcare services revenues do not include charity care, which is disclosed separately in the notes to the financial statements. Moreover, such revenues are reported in the financial statements net of contractual and other adjustments. Thus, healthcare services revenues are recorded in the accounting records at the gross amount (excluding charity care) of $7.5 million but reported in the financial statements at the net realizable value of $6.75 million.

Answer (B) is incorrect. Gross revenues equals $7,500,000. Answer (C) is incorrect. The amount of $8,250,000 assumes that charity allowances are included in gross and net revenues. Answer (D) is incorrect. Charity care is excluded from gross revenues, and contractual adjustments are subtracted to arrive at net revenues.

27. Which of the following should normally be considered ongoing or central transactions for a not-for-profit hospital?

I.   Room and board fees from patients
II. Recovery room fees

   A. Neither I nor II.

   B. Both I and II.

   C. II only.

   D. I only.

Answer (B) is correct.
   REQUIRED: The fees, if any, that are ongoing or central transactions for a not-for-profit hospital.
   DISCUSSION: Revenues arise from an entity's ongoing major or central operations. Revenues of an HCE include patient service revenue, premium revenue, resident service revenue, and other revenue. Room and board fees and recovery room fees are patient services revenues.

28. Terry, an auditor, is performing test work for a not-for-profit hospital. Listed below are components of the statement of operations:

Revenue relating to charity care	$100,000
Bad debt expense	70,000
Net assets released from restrictions	
used for operations	50,000
Other revenue	80,000
Net patient service revenue (includes	
revenue related to charity care)	500,000

What amount would be reported as total revenues, gains, and other support on the statement of operations?

   A. $460,000

   B. $530,000

   C. $580,000

   D. $630,000

Answer (B) is correct.
   REQUIRED: The total revenues, gains, and other support reported by a not-for-profit hospital.
   DISCUSSION: The total revenues, gains, and other support subtotal in the statement of operations of a not-for-profit hospital includes net patient service revenue, premium revenue, other revenue, and net assets released from restrictions used for operations. Net patient service revenue is recognized for fees charged for patient care, minus contractual adjustments and discounts. Reported net patient service revenue does not include charity care. Services performed as charity care are not expected to produce cash inflows and thus do not qualify for recognition as revenue or receivables. Bad debt expense is recognized in total expense, not as a reduction to revenue. Other revenue derives from services not involving providing healthcare services or coverage to patients, residents, or enrollees (e.g., of a healthcare delivery plan). Net assets released from restrictions used for operations are reported in the statement of operations when a temporary restriction expires, with a reclassification of net assets to unrestricted net assets. Thus, the total revenues, gains and other support is $530,000 ($500,000 net patient service revenue – $100,000 charity care + $50,000 net assets released from restrictions used for operations + $80,000 other revenue).
   Answer (A) is incorrect. Bad debt expense is not a revenue, gain, or other support and does not decrease any such item in this caption of the statement of operations. Answer (C) is incorrect. The amount of $580,000 includes charity care but excludes net assets released from restrictions for operations. Answer (D) is incorrect. The amount of $630,000 includes charity care.

29. Hospital, Inc., a not-for-profit entity with no governmental affiliation, reported the following in its accounts for the current year ended December 31:

- Gross patient service revenue from all services provided at the established billing rates of the hospital (note that this figure includes charity care of $25,000) $775,000
- Provision for bad debts   15,000
- Difference between established billing rates and fees negotiated with third-party payors (contractual adjustments)   70,000

What amount would the hospital report as net patient service revenue in its statement of operations for the current year ended December 31?

   A. $680,000

   B. $690,000

   C. $705,000

   D. $735,000

Answer (A) is correct.
   REQUIRED: The net patient service revenue.
   DISCUSSION: Total revenues, gains, and other support subtotal in the statement of operations of a not-for-profit healthcare entity includes net patient service revenue, premium revenue, other revenue, and net assets released from restrictions used for operations. Net patient service revenue is recognized for fees charged for patient care, minus contractual adjustments and discounts. Reported net patient service revenue does not include charity care. Services performed as charity care are not expected to produce cash inflows and thus do not qualify for recognition as revenue or receivables. Bad debt expense, however, is recognized in total expenses. Thus, net patient service revenue equals $680,000 ($775,000 gross revenue – $25,000 charity care – $70,000 contractual adjustments).
   Answer (B) is incorrect. The amount of $690,000 includes charity care and subtracts bad debt expense. Answer (C) is incorrect. The amount of $705,000 includes charity care. Answer (D) is incorrect. The amount of $735,000 subtracts bad debt expense but not the contractual adjustments.

30. In April, Delta Hospital purchased medicines from Field Pharmaceutical Co. at a cost of $5,000. However, Field notified Delta that the invoice was being canceled and that the medicines were being donated to Delta. Delta should record this donation of medicines as

A. A memorandum entry only.

B. A $5,000 credit to nonoperating expenses.

C. A $5,000 credit to operating expenses.

D. Other operating revenue of $5,000.

Answer (D) is correct.
REQUIRED: The accounting for a donation of medicine.
DISCUSSION: Contributions of noncash assets that are not long-lived are reported at fair value in the statement of operations. Thus, when a supplier cancels an invoice, the HCE removes the payable and recognizes other operating revenue.

Use the additional questions in Gleim **CPA Test Prep Online** to create Test Sessions that emulate Prometric!

20.6 PRACTICE SIMULATION

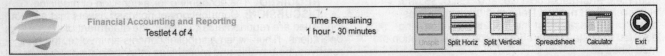

| | Financial Accounting and Reporting
Testlet 4 of 4 | Time Remaining
1 hour - 30 minutes | Unsplit | Split Horiz | Split Vertical | Spreadsheet | Calculator | Exit |

DIRECTIONS

Note: If you believe you have encountered a software malfunction, report it to the test center staff immediately.

Navigation

To navigate from task to task, use the controls at the bottom of the screen. Click on the **Next** button to advance to the next task, or the **Previous** button to go to the previous task. To go directly to any task, click on its number.

| ⚑ = Reminder | | Directions | 1 | 2 | 3 | 4 | 5 | 6 | 7 | | ◄ Previous | Next ► |

If you would like a reminder to revisit a task, or want to indicate that you are finished with it, click on the reminder flag below the task number. To clear the flag, click on it again. Reminder flags are for your use only – they do not contribute to your score.

Tabs

In this part of the examination, you will be asked to complete various tasks. Every task has one or more **Work Tabs**. Some tasks have one or more **Information Tabs**, others may have none. Every task has a **Help** tab.

If a task has **Information Tabs**, you may use the information in them to complete your responses in the **Work Tabs**.

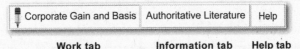

| Corporate Gain and Basis | Authoritative Literature | Help |

| Work tab | Information tab | Help tab |

Work Tabs:
- **Work Tabs** are identified with a pencil icon. This is where your responses are expected.
- Each task has one or more **Work Tabs**.
- **Work Tabs** contain directions for completing the task – be sure to read these directions carefully.
- The **Work Tab** name in the example above is for illustration only – yours will differ.
- You must complete all of the **Work Tabs** in each task to receive full credit.

Information Tabs:
- The Authoritative Literature will be provided in all tasks in the AUD, FAR, and REG sections for your reference.
- Your simulation may have one or more additional **Information Tabs**. Like the Authoritative Literature tabs, **Information Tabs** do not have a pencil icon.
- If your task has additional **Information Tabs**, go through each to familiarize yourself with the task content.

Help Tab:
- The **Help Tab** provides assistance with the exam software that is used in this task. For example, if the task is to compose a memorandum, **Help** will provide information about the word processor.

The Toolbar

The toolbar at the top of the screen shows the amount of time remaining for you to complete the tasks. In addition, the following tools are available. Note that only the **Exit** button is displayed when Directions are visible - the others will appear when you begin the tasks.

Click on these buttons to split or unsplit the screen. You can split the screen vertically or horizontally.

Click on this button to display the calculator; click on it again to hide the calculator. To move the calculator, click on the calculator title bar and drag the calculator to the desired location.

Click on this button to use the spreadsheet; click on it again to hide the spreadsheet. To move the spreadsheet, click on the the spreadsheet title bar and drag the spreadsheet to the desired location.

Click on this button to go on to the next part of the examination. You must complete all of the tasks to receive full credit. Once you click on **Exit** and confirm the action, you will NOT be able to return to this testlet.

| ⚑ = Reminder | | Directions | 1 | 2 | 3 | 4 | 5 | 6 | | ◄ Previous | Next ► |

Net Assets of an NFP | Authoritative Literature | Help

Select from the list provided the most likely classification(s) of net assets, if any, that is(are) affected by each transaction of a not-for-profit entity. Each choice may be used once, more than once, or not at all.

Transaction	Answer
1. Legally restricted gains.	
2. Expenses reported by functional classification.	
3. Contributions of services that do not create or enhance nonfinancial assets or require special skills.	
4. Unrestricted contribution of collection items to be held for financial gain.	
5. Board-designated endowment.	
6. Expenses reported by natural classification.	
7. Conditional promise to give if the likelihood that the condition will not be met is more than remote.	
8. Unconditional promises to give cash with amounts due in future periods.	
9. Receipt of a gift of a long-lived asset for which the entity chooses to imply a time restriction.	
10. Gains and losses on a specific security required by the donor to be held permanently. No donor instruction was made regarding gains and losses.	

Choices
A) Unrestricted net assets
B) Temporarily restricted net assets
C) Permanently restricted net assets
D) No effect on net assets

NFP Accounting Practices | Authoritative Literature | Help

Select from the list provided the appropriate classification for each phenomenon of nongovernmental not-for-profit entities.

Description	Classification
1. Donor stipulations may create limitations on the use of resources, and these limitations are not lifted by the passage of time or an entity's actions.	
2. NFPs base external reporting on this accounting basis.	
3. This is acceptable for internal purposes in an NFP. However, it is not permitted for external reporting.	
4. Reported in lieu of equity.	
5. According to the FASB, one of the purposes for external financial reporting by an NFP.	
6. These arise from providing goods and services.	

Choices
A) Fund accounting
B) GAAP
C) GASB
D) Governmental accounting
E) Net assets
F) Net assets model
G) Permanently restricted net assets
H) Stewardship responsibilities
I) Temporarily restricted net assets
J) Unrestricted net assets
K) IFRS

| ✏ Contributions | Authoritative Literature | Help |

Community Service, Inc., is a nongovernmental, not-for-profit voluntary health and welfare calendar-year entity that began operations on January 1, Year 1. It performs voluntary services and derives its revenue primarily from voluntary contributions from the general public. Community implies a time restriction on all promises to contribute cash in future periods. However, no such policy exists with respect to gifts of long-lived assets.

Selected transactions that occurred during Community's Year 2 calendar year follow:

- Unrestricted written promises to contribute cash--Year 1 and Year 2

Year 1 promises collected in Year 2	$22,000
Year 2 promises collected in Year 2	95,000
Year 2 promises uncollected	28,000

- Written promises to contribute cash restricted to use for community college scholarships--Year 1 and Year 2

Year 1 promises collected and expended in Year 2	10,000
Year 2 promises collected and expended in Year 2	20,000
Year 2 promises uncollected	12,000

- Written promise to contribute $25,000 if matching funds are raised for the capital campaign during Year 2

Cash received in Year 2 from contributor as a good faith advance	25,000
Matching funds received in Year 2	0

- Cash received in Year 1 with donor's only stipulation that a bus be purchased

Expenditure of full amount of donation 7/1/Year 2	37,000

Other selected transactions that occurred during Community's Year 2 calendar year follow:

- Debt security endowment received in Year 2; income to be used for community services

Face amount	$90,000
Fair value at time of receipt	88,000
Fair value at 12/31/Year 2	87,000
Interest earned in Year 2	9,000

- 10 concerned citizens volunteered to serve meals to the homeless

400 hrs. free; FMV of services $5 per hr.	2,000

- Short-term investment in equity securities in Year 2

Cost	10,000
Fair value 12/31/Year 2	12,000
Dividend income	1,000

- Music festival to raise funds for a local hospital

Admission fees	5,000
Sales of food and drinks	14,000
Expenses	4,000

- Reading materials donated to Community and distributed to the children in Year 2

Fair market value	8,000

- Federal youth training fee for service grant

Cash received during Year 2	30,000
Instructor salaries paid	26,000

- Other cash operating expenses

Business manager salary	60,000
General bookkeeper salary	40,000
Director of community activities salary	50,000
Space rental (75% for community activities, 25% for office activities)	20,000
Printing and mailing costs for pledge cards	2,000

- Interest payment on short-term bank loan in Year 2   1,000

- Principal payment on short-term bank loan in Year 2   20,000

-- Continued on next page --

| Contributions | Authoritative Literature | Help | -- **Continued** |

Items 1 through 4 represent the Year 2 amounts that Community reported for selected contribution amounts in its December 31, Year 2, statement of financial position and Year 2 statement of activities. For each item, select from the list provided to indicate whether each amount was overstated, understated, or correctly stated. Each choice may be used once, more than once, or not at all.

Amount	Answer		Choices
1. Community reported $28,000 as contributions receivable.			A) Overstated
2. Community reported $37,000 as net assets released from restrictions (satisfaction of use restrictions).			B) Understated
3. Community reported $22,000 as net assets released from restrictions (due to the lapse of time restrictions).			C) Correctly stated
4. Community reported $97,000 as contributions -- temporarily restricted.			

| Expenses, Services, and Cash Flows | Authoritative Literature | Help |

Select from the list provided the appropriate description of each statement below. Each choice may be used once, more than once, or not at all.

Statement	Answer		Choices
1. Reported as decreases in unrestricted net assets.			A) Voluntary health and welfare entities
2. Reported by functional classification, that is, by major classes of program services and supporting services.			B) Expenses
3. Tax-exempt NFPs organized for the benefit of the public and supported by contributions.			C) Revenues
4. The activities that result in goods and services being distributed to beneficiaries, customers, or members that fulfill the purposes or mission for which the entity exists.			D) Gains and losses
			E) Program services
5. Includes the receipt of a gift of a marketable security.			F) Supporting services
6. Includes the receipt of a gift of unrestricted contributions.			G) Cash inflows from operating activities
7. May include the receipt of resources from an agency transaction.			H) Cash inflows from investing activities
			I) Cash inflows from financing activities

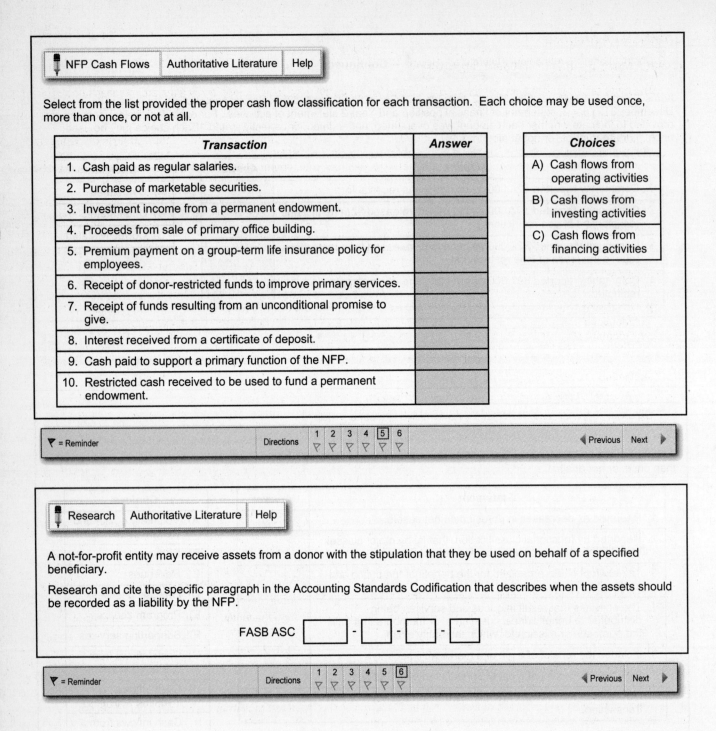

NFP Cash Flows | Authoritative Literature | Help

Select from the list provided the proper cash flow classification for each transaction. Each choice may be used once, more than once, or not at all.

Transaction	Answer
1. Cash paid as regular salaries.	
2. Purchase of marketable securities.	
3. Investment income from a permanent endowment.	
4. Proceeds from sale of primary office building.	
5. Premium payment on a group-term life insurance policy for employees.	
6. Receipt of donor-restricted funds to improve primary services.	
7. Receipt of funds resulting from an unconditional promise to give.	
8. Interest received from a certificate of deposit.	
9. Cash paid to support a primary function of the NFP.	
10. Restricted cash received to be used to fund a permanent endowment.	

Choices

A) Cash flows from operating activities

B) Cash flows from investing activities

C) Cash flows from financing activities

⚐ = Reminder   Directions   1 2 3 4 [5] 6   ◀ Previous   Next ▶

Research | Authoritative Literature | Help

A not-for-profit entity may receive assets from a donor with the stipulation that they be used on behalf of a specified beneficiary.

Research and cite the specific paragraph in the Accounting Standards Codification that describes when the assets should be recorded as a liability by the NFP.

FASB ASC   ☐ - ☐ - ☐ - ☐

⚐ = Reminder   Directions   1 2 3 4 5 [6]   ◀ Previous   Next ▶

Unofficial Answers

1. Net Assets of an NFP (10 Gradable Items)

1. <u>B) Temporarily restricted net assets or C) Permanently restricted net assets.</u> Gains and losses are increases or decreases in unrestricted net assets unless their use is temporarily or permanently restricted by explicit donor stipulations or by law.

2. <u>A) Unrestricted net assets.</u> A statement of activities or the notes should provide information about expenses reported by functional classification, e.g., by major classes of program services and supporting services. However, whether the classification of expenses is functional or natural (e.g., salaries, rent, depreciation, etc.), they are reported as decreases in unrestricted net assets in the statement of activities.

3. <u>D) No effect on net assets.</u> Contributions of services are recognized if they create or enhance nonfinancial assets or if they require special skills, are provided by those having such skills, and would usually be purchased if not obtained by donations.

4. <u>A) Unrestricted net assets.</u> Contributions of collection items, such as art works and historical treasures, need not be capitalized and recognized as revenues if they are (1) held for public exhibition, education, or research in furtherance of public service rather than financial gain; (2) protected, kept unencumbered, cared for, and preserved; and (3) subject to a policy that requires the proceeds of their sale to be used to acquire other collection items.

5. <u>D) No effect on net assets.</u> Unrestricted net assets arise from providing goods and services and from receipts of contributions and dividends or interest, minus expenses. The only limits are the nature of the organization, its environment, its specified purposes, and contractual agreements. Significant contractual limits, including loan covenants, are described in the notes. Self-imposed limits, e.g., voluntary designation of a portion of unrestricted net assets as an endowment (a board-designated endowment), are described in the notes or on the statements. Accordingly, a board-designated endowment does not increase or decrease any component of net assets.

6. <u>A) Unrestricted net assets.</u> Voluntary health and welfare entities (VHWEs) report information about expenses by functional classification and natural classification (salaries, rent, interest, depreciation, etc.) in a matrix format in a separate statement of functional expenses. Other NFPs are encouraged but not required to provide information about expenses by natural classification. However, whether expenses are classified as functional or natural, they are still decreases in unrestricted net assets.

7. <u>D) No effect on net assets.</u> Conditional promises to give are recognized when the conditions are substantially met. A conditional promise is considered unconditional if the likelihood is remote that the condition will not be met. Consequently, this promise should not be recognized.

8. <u>B) Temporarily restricted net assets.</u> Unconditional promises to give with amounts due in future periods are reported as restricted support unless the circumstances clearly indicate that the donor intended support for current activities. Thus, unconditional promises of future cash amounts usually increase temporarily restricted net assets.

9. <u>B) Temporarily restricted net assets.</u> Gifts of long-lived assets (or other assets required to be used to acquire them) may be received without stipulations about their use. In this case, if the entity's choice of accounting policy is to imply a time restriction expiring over their useful life, the gifts are reported as temporarily restricted support.

10. <u>C) Permanently restricted net assets.</u> If a specific security is to be held permanently, the gains and losses on that security are assumed to be changes in permanently restricted net assets absent a contrary donor instruction.

2. NFP Accounting Practices (6 Gradable Items)

1. <u>G) Permanently restricted net assets.</u> These arise from asset increases and decreases subject to restrictions not removable by passage of time or by the organization's actions. They may result from reclassifications within the classes of net assets created by donor stipulations.

2. <u>B) GAAP.</u> The GAAP accounting framework is required for NFP external reporting.

3. <u>A) Fund accounting.</u> Fund accounting is acceptable for internal reporting purposes, but users of the financial statements must be able to interpret the presentation based on GAAP for nongovernmental entities.

4. <u>E) Net assets.</u> Nonbusiness entities report net assets, rather than equity, in conformity with GAAP.

5. <u>H) Stewardship responsibilities.</u> The two purposes for external financial reporting by NFPs are to help external users assess (1) the services an organization provides (and its ability to continue to provide those services) and (2) how managers discharge their stewardship responsibilities and other aspects of their performance.

6. <u>J) Unrestricted net assets.</u> These arise from providing goods and services and from receipts of contributions and dividends or interest, minus expenses. The only limits are the nature of the entity, its environment, its specified purposes, and contractual agreements.

3. Contributions (4 Gradable Items)

1. B) Understated. An unconditional promise to give may be treated as a contribution if it is sufficiently documented. The $28,000 of contributions receivable is understated. It does not include the $12,000 of unconditional but restricted promises made in Year 2 that have not been collected.

2. B) Understated. The $37,000 of net assets released as a result of the satisfaction of use restrictions is understated. It does not include the $30,000 of contributions collected and expended in Year 2 for the stipulated purpose of providing scholarships. Note: Although the restriction on the $37,000 received in Year 1 to purchase a bus expired in Year 2 when the funds were used for the stipulated purpose, the restriction would not have expired if additional donor restrictions on the use of the long-lived asset had been stated or if the entity had a policy of implying a time restriction that expired over the life of the donated asset.

3. C) Correctly stated. The contributions restricted to use for scholarships and purchase of a bus were not time restricted. However, Community implies a time restriction on promises to contribute cash in future periods. Thus, the only net assets released from time restrictions in Year 2 consisted of the $22,000 collected in Year 2 as a result of Year 1 promises. The Year 2 collections on unrestricted promises made in Year 2 were not subject to the implied restriction, and the uncollected amounts related to Year 2 promises.

4. A) Overstated. Restricted contributions include the $28,000 of uncollected Year 2 promises that were not donor restricted but that were subject to an implied time restriction. They also include the $12,000 of uncollected Year 2 promises subject to a donor restriction. The total is therefore only $40,000. The $25,000 of cash received that is conditioned upon the raising of matching funds is treated as arising from a conditional promise to give. It is accounted for as a refundable advance, not a contribution, because the condition has not been substantially met.

4. Expenses, Services, and Cash Flows (7 Gradable Items)

1. B) Expenses. Revenues are reported as increases in unrestricted net assets unless the use of the assets received is restricted. All expenses are reported as decreases in unrestricted net assets. Gains and losses are changes in unrestricted net assets unless their use is temporarily or permanently restricted explicitly by the donor or by law.

2. B) Expenses. A statement of activities or the notes should provide information about expenses reported by functional classification, e.g., by major classes of program services and supporting services.

3. A) Voluntary health and welfare entities. VHWEs are tax-exempt NFPs organized for the benefit of the public and supported by the public through contributions. Examples are the United Way, the Girl Scouts, the Boy Scouts, the American Cancer Society, the YMCA, and the YWCA.

4. E) Program services. Program services are the activities that result in goods and services being distributed to beneficiaries, customers, or members that fulfill the purposes or mission for which the entity exists. Those services are the major purpose for, and the major output of, the entity and often relate to several major programs. Supporting services of a not-for-profit entity are all activities other than program services. Generally, they include management and general, fund-raising, and membership-development activities.

5. H) Cash inflows from investing activities. These include receipt of gifts of investment assets or buildings. However, donations for the purpose of constructing a building are reported as cash inflows from financing activities.

6. G) Cash inflows from operating activities. These include receipts of unrestricted contributions. NFPs and for-profit entities also treat interest and dividends on unrestricted investments as operating cash flows. Either the direct or indirect method of presenting cash flows from operating activities may be used. Operating activities may include agency transactions.

7. G) Cash inflows from operating activities. Operating activities may include agency transactions. In an agency transaction, the NFP receives a voluntary transfer of assets but has little discretion in their use.

5. NFP Cash Flows (10 Gradable Items)

1. A) Cash flows from operating activities. Operating activities include all transactions and other events not classified as investing and financing activities. They usually include producing and selling goods and providing services. In principle, operating cash flows are the cash effects of items included in the determination of the change in net assets of an NFP. Thus, a cash payment for regular salaries is an operating cash outflow.

2. B) Cash flows from investing activities. Investing activities include (1) making and collecting loans and (2) acquiring and disposing of debt or equity instruments and property, plant, and equipment and other productive assets. These assets are held for or used in the production of goods or services (other than the materials held in inventory). Investing activities exclude transactions in cash equivalents and in certain loans or other debt or equity instruments acquired specifically for resale.

3. C) Cash flows from financing activities. Financing activities of an NFP include (1) issuance of debt, (2) repayment or other settlement of debt obligations, and (3) receiving donor-restricted resources that must be used for long-term purposes. For example, contributions and investment income may be donor-restricted to acquiring, constructing, or improving long-lived assets or to establishing or increasing a permanent or term endowment.

4. **B) Cash flows from investing activities.** Investing activities include (1) making and collecting loans and (2) acquiring and disposing of debt or equity instruments and property, plant, and equipment and other productive assets. These assets are held for or used in the production of goods or services (other than the materials held in inventory). Investing activities exclude transactions in cash equivalents and in certain loans or other debt or equity instruments acquired specifically for resale.

5. **A) Cash flows from operating activities.** Operating activities include all transactions and other events not classified as investing and financing activities. They usually include producing and selling goods and providing services. In principle, operating cash flows are the cash effects of items included in the change in net assets of an NFP. Thus, a premium payment for employee benefits is an operating cash outflow.

6. **C) Cash flows from financing activities.** Financing activities of an NFP include (1) issuance of debt, (2) repayment or other settlement of debt obligations, and (3) receiving donor-restricted resources that must be used for long-term purposes. For example, contributions and investment income may be donor-restricted to acquiring, constructing, or improving long-lived assets or to establishing or increasing a permanent or term endowment.

7. **A) Cash flows from operating activities.** Operating activities include all transactions and other events not classified as investing and financing activities. They usually include producing and selling goods and providing services. In principle, operating cash flows are the cash effects of items included in the change in net assets of an NFP. An unconditional promise to give is recognized by debiting an asset and crediting revenue. When the cash inflow is received, the entity therefore classifies it as from an operating activity.

8. **A) Cash flows from operating activities.** Operating activities include all transactions and other events not classified as investing and financing activities. They usually include producing and selling goods and providing services. In principle, operating cash flows are the cash effects of items included in the determination of the change in net assets of an NFP. Thus, a cash receipt of interest is an operating inflow.

9. **A) Cash flows from operating activities.** Operating activities include all transactions and other events not classified as investing and financing activities. They usually include producing and selling goods and providing services. In principle, operating cash flows are the cash effects of items included in the change in net assets. Contributions received are recognized as revenues or gains.

10. **C) Cash flows from financing activities.** Financing activities of an NFP include (1) issuance of debt, (2) repayment or other settlement of debt obligations, and (3) receiving donor-restricted resources that must be used for long-term purposes. For example, contributions and investment income may be donor-restricted to acquiring, constructing, or improving long-lived assets or to establishing or increasing a permanent or term endowment.

6. Research (1 Gradable Item)

Answer: FASB ASC 958-605-25-23

958-605-25-23   If an intermediary receives cash or other financial assets, it shall recognize its liability to the specified beneficiary concurrent with its recognition of the assets received from the donor. If an intermediary receives nonfinancial assets, it is permitted, but not required, to recognize its liability and those assets provided that the intermediary reports consistently from period to period and discloses its accounting policy.

Gleim Simulation Grading

Task	Correct Responses		Gradable Items		Score per Task
1	_____	÷	10	=	_____
2	_____	÷	6	=	_____
3	_____	÷	4	=	_____
4	_____	÷	7	=	_____
5	_____	÷	10	=	_____
Research	_____	÷	1	=	_____

	Total of Scores per Task	_____
÷	Total Number of Tasks	6
	Total Score	_____ %

APPENDIX
IFRS DIFFERENCES

INTERNATIONAL ACCOUNTING STANDARDS (IASs)

IAS 1 - Presentation of Financial Statements

- Financial liabilities due to be settled within 12 months should continue to be classified as current. This treatment applies even if (1) the original term exceeded 12 months and (2) an agreement to refinance or reschedule payments on a noncurrent basis is completed after the reporting period and before the financial statements are authorized for issue.

  62

  - An entity that expects and has discretion to refinance or roll over the liability under an existing loan agreement classifies it as noncurrent.

- The minimum presentation on the face of the statement of financial position includes the following line items (but no particular order or format is prescribed):

  63

  1. Property, plant, and equipment
  2. Investment property
  3. Intangible assets
  4. Financial assets (other than 5., 8., and 9.)
  5. Equity-based investments
  6. Biological assets
  7. Inventories
  8. Trade and other receivables
  9. Cash and cash equivalents
  10. Trade and other payables
  11. Current and deferred tax amounts
  12. Provisions
  13. Financial liabilities (other than 10. and 12.)
  14. Noncontrolling interest
  15. Issued capital and reserves
  16. The total of assets classified as held for sale and assets and liabilities included in disposal groups classified as held for sale

- No items are classified as extraordinary, either on the statement of comprehensive income or in the notes.

  67, 126

- All recognized income and expense items are included in profit or loss unless a   68
  pronouncement requires otherwise. The minimum presentation on the face of the
  statement of comprehensive income includes the following line items:

  1. Revenue

  2. Gains (losses) on (a) derecognition of financial assets measured at amortized
     cost and (b) reclassification of financial assets to fair value

  3. Finance costs

  4. Share of profits and losses of associates and joint ventures accounted for under
     the equity method

  5. Tax expense

  6. One amount for the sum of (a) after-tax profit (loss) on discontinued operations
     and (b) after-tax gain (loss) on the measurement at fair value minus cost to sell
     or on disposal of the assets or disposal groups

  7. Profit or loss

  8. Each component of OCI classified by nature

  9. Share of OCI of associates and joint ventures accounted for under the equity
     method

  10. Total comprehensive income

- An entity must group items of OCI as follows: (1) those that will not be reclassified to   71
  profit or loss (e.g., actuarial gains and losses on defined benefit pension plans) and
  (2) those that may be (e.g., exchange differences arising from foreign operations).

- Personal financial statements are not specifically addressed.   73

IAS 2 - Inventories

- LIFO is not permitted.   273

- Inventories are measured at the lower of cost or net realizable value (NRV). NRV is   279
  assessed each period. Accordingly, a write-down may be reversed but not above
  original cost. The write-down and reversal are recognized in profit or loss.

  For an interim period, an inventory loss from a market decline must be recognized
  even if no loss is reasonably expected for the year.

IAS 7 - Statement of Cash Flows

- Cash flows from interest and dividends should be separately disclosed and   97
  consistently classified. Total interest paid is disclosed whether it was expensed or
  capitalized. A financial institution customarily classifies interest paid or received and
  dividends received as operating items. For entities other than financial institutions,
  the following are the appropriate classifications:

	Operating	Financing	Investing
Interest paid	Yes	Yes	No
Interest received	Yes	No	Yes
Dividends paid	Yes	Yes	No
Dividends received	Yes	No	Yes

Reporting cash flow per share is not prohibited.

An entity must disclose the operating, investing, and financing cash flows of a discontinued operation.

If bank overdrafts that are repayable on demand are part of an entity's cash management program, they are included in cash and cash equivalents, not in cash flows from financing activities.

- An entity must disclose comparative information for the previous period for all amounts reported in the current financial statements.   104

- Net cash flows from operating, investing, and financing activities of a discontinued operation must be disclosed in the notes or the statements.   125

IAS 8 - Accounting Policies, Changes in Accounting Estimates and Errors

- A prior-period error must be corrected by restatement unless it is impracticable to do so. A change in accounting policy must be made only if it (1) is required by a new standard or interpretation or (2) results in reliable and more relevant information about transactions, financial condition, financial performance, and cash flows. The indirect effects of a change in accounting policy are not addressed by IFRS.   129

IAS 11 - Construction Contracts

- The completed-contract method is not used. When the outcome of a long-term construction contract cannot be reliably estimated, revenue recognition is limited to recoverable costs incurred. Contract costs must be recognized as an expense in the period in which they are incurred.   138

IAS 12 - Income Taxes

- Deferred tax amounts are measured based on the enacted tax rates or the substantively enacted tax rates at the end of the reporting period.   388

- With limited exceptions (e.g., initial recognition of goodwill), all deferred tax liabilities must be recognized.   390

- A deferred tax asset is recognized for most deductible TDs and for the carryforward of unused tax losses and credits, but only to the extent it is probable that taxable profit will be available. Thus, no valuation allowance is recognized. Moreover, IFRS do not define "probable."   391

- All deferred tax amounts are noncurrent.   396

IAS 16 - **Property, Plant and Equipment**

- An entity may choose either the cost model or the revaluation model as its accounting   307
  policy. It must apply that policy to an entire class of PPE. A class is a grouping of
  assets of similar nature and use in an entity's operations, for example, land, office
  equipment, or motor vehicles.

  An item of PPE whose fair value can be reliably measured may be carried at a
  revalued amount equal to fair value at the revaluation date (minus subsequent
  accumulated depreciation and impairment losses).

  Revaluation is needed whenever fair value and the asset's carrying amount differ
  materially. Accumulated depreciation is restated proportionately or eliminated.

  A revaluation increase must be recognized in other comprehensive income and
  accumulated in equity as revaluation surplus. But the increase must be recognized
  in profit or loss to the extent it reverses a decrease of the same asset that was
  recognized in profit or loss.

  A revaluation decrease must be recognized in profit or loss. But the decrease must
  be recognized in other comprehensive income to the extent of any credit in
  revaluation surplus for the same asset.

- Each part of the item with a cost significant to the total cost must be depreciated   316
  separately. But an entity may separately depreciate parts that are not significant.

IAS 17 - **Leases**

- A lease is classified as a finance lease if it transfers substantially all the risks and   496
  rewards of ownership to the lessee. Whether the lease is a finance lease (a capital
  lease under U.S. GAAP) or an operating lease depends on the substance of the
  transaction. IFRS provide examples and indicators of situations that individually or
  together can result in classification as a finance lease but are not always conclusive.
  Thus, a lease is classified at its inception as a finance lease if, for example, (1) it
  provides for the transfer of ownership of the leased asset by the end of the lease
  term, (2) it contains a bargain purchase option, (3) the lease term is for the major part
  of the economic life of the leased asset, (4) the present value of the minimum lease
  payments is at least substantially all of the fair value of the leased asset at the
  inception of the lease, and (5) the leased asset is such that it can be used only by the
  lessee without major modification. Other factors also may indicate classification as a
  finance lease: (1) lessor losses from cancelation of the lease are borne by the
  lessee, (2) the lessee bears the risk of fluctuations in the fair value of the residual
  value, and (3) the lessee may renew the lease at a rent substantially below the
  market rent.

- If a sale and leaseback transaction results in an operating lease and the transaction is   505
  at fair value, any profit or loss must be recognized immediately.

IAS 18 - Revenue

- For a sale of goods, revenue is recognized when five conditions are met. (1) The   34
  entity has transferred the significant risks and rewards of ownership, (2) the entity
  has neither continuing managerial involvement to an extent associated with
  ownership nor effective control over the goods, (3) the revenue (measured at the fair
  value of the consideration received or receivable) can be reliably measured, (4) it is
  probable that the economic benefits will flow to the entity, and (5) transaction costs
  can be reliably measured.

  For the rendering of a service, if the outcome can be reliably estimated, revenue
  (measured as described above) is recognized based on the stage of completion (the
  percentage-of-completion method.) The outcome can be reliably estimated when (1)
  revenue can be reliably measured, (2) it is probable that the economic benefits will
  flow to the entity, (3) the stage of completion can be reliably measured, and (4) the
  costs incurred and the costs to complete can be reliably measured.

  Revenue from interest, royalties, and dividends must meet the economic benefits
  and reliability criteria described above. The bases of recognition are (1) the
  effective interest method, (2) the accrual basis in accordance with an agreement,
  and (3) establishment of the right to receive, respectively.

IAS 19 - Employee Benefits

- Interest income on plan assets for the period is a component of the return on plan   423
  assets. It is recognized in profit or loss. It equals the fair value of plan assets at the
  beginning of the year (adjusted for contributions and benefits paid during the year)
  times the same rate used to discount the defined benefit obligation. Under
  U.S. GAAP, different interest rates may be used to calculate interest cost and the
  expected return on plan assets.

  The remeasurement of plan assets for the period is the return on plan assets,
  excluding the interest income on plan assets.

  The following is an example of the calculation of the remeasurement of plan assets:

Fair value of plan assets end of the year	$ 1,200
Fair value of plan assets beginning of the year	(1,000)
Interest income (included in profit or loss)	(100)
Contributions	(200)
Benefit payments	150
Remeasurement of plan assets	$ 50

- Remeasurements of the net defined benefit liability (asset) are recognized in OCI.   425
  They are never reclassified to profit or loss in subsequent periods. Remeasurements
  include actuarial gains and losses. These are changes in the benefit obligation from
  (1) adjustments for the differences between assumptions and actual results and
  (2) changes in assumptions. Remeasurements also include the remeasurement of
  plan assets. Accordingly, the corridor approach is not used.

- Past service cost is recognized as an expense at the earlier of (1) when the plan   425
  amendment or curtailment occurs and (2) when an entity recognizes related
  restructuring costs or termination benefits. Thus, past service cost is never included
  in OCI and never reclassified to profit or loss as it is amortized.

- Short term employee benefits are employee benefits (other than termination benefits),   433
  such as paid annual leave, sick leave, and wages, that are expected to be settled
  wholly before 12 months after the annual reporting period in which employees render
  the related services.

IAS 24 - Related Party Disclosures

- The entity must disclose the compensation of key management personnel in total and   174
by components.

IAS 28 - Investments in Associates and Joint Ventures

- In assessing the investor's influence, the entity also considers potential voting rights   208
(share call options, share warrants, or other instruments convertible into ordinary
shares). These must be currently exercisable or convertible and must be considered
even if held by other entities.

- When the investor has significant influence, the equity method must be applied unless   208
(1) the investment is classified as held for sale, or (2) conditions exist similar to those
that would exempt a parent from preparing consolidated statements.

- When significant influence is lost, any retained investment is measured at fair value.   210

- Under the equity method, the investor's statements must use uniform accounting   210
policies. Thus, adjustments must be made to conform the investee's policies to the
investor's.

IAS 34 - Interim Financial Reporting

- Each interim period is viewed as a discrete reporting period.   168

- An interim financial report must include, at a minimum, condensed financial   168
statements (financial position, comprehensive income, changes in equity, and cash
flows) and notes.

- If the interim financial report contains a complete set of statements, their form and   168
content must conform to those required for annual statements. If the interim financial
report contains condensed statements, they must include, at a minimum, all headings
and subtotals included in the most recent annual statements.

- LIFO liquidation is not an issue in interim (or annual) periods because LIFO is not a   169
permitted accounting policy.

- For an interim period, an inventory loss from a market decline must be recognized   169
even if no loss is reasonably expected for the year.

IAS 36 - Impairment of Assets

- An asset is impaired when its carrying amount exceeds its recoverable amount. The   323
entity assesses at each reporting date whether an indication of impairment exists.
Given such an indication, the recoverable amount must be estimated. Moreover,
intangible assets with indefinite useful lives or those not yet available for use and
goodwill are tested for impairment at least annually.

   The recoverable amount of an asset is the greater of its fair value minus costs to sell
   or value in use. Value in use is the present value of the asset's expected cash
   flows. The recognized impairment loss is the excess of the asset's carrying amount
   over its recoverable amount.

   An impairment loss on an asset (except goodwill) may be reversed if a change in the
   estimates used to measure the recoverable amount has occurred.

IAS 37 - Provisions, Contingent Liabilities and Contingent Assets

- Provisions are liabilities of uncertain timing or amount except (1) those resulting from unperformed contracts (unless their unavoidable costs exceed their expected benefits) or (2) those covered by other IFRS. Examples are liabilities for violations of environmental law, nuclear plant decommissioning costs, warranties, and restructurings.   507

    - Provisions differ from trade payables and accruals because of their greater uncertainty. They differ from contingent liabilities because they are present obligations that meet the recognition criteria.

    - Recognition of provisions is appropriate when (a) the entity has a legal or constructive present obligation resulting from a past event (called an obligating event), (b) it is probable that an outflow of economic benefits will be necessary to settle the obligation, and (c) its amount can be reliably estimated.

    - If the estimate of a provision is stated within a continuous range of possible outcomes, and each point in the range is as likely as any other, the midpoint is used.

    A contingent liability is a possible obligation arising from past events. Its existence will be confirmed only by uncertain future events not wholly within the entity's control. A liability also is contingent if it is a present obligation that arises from past events but does not meet the recognition criteria. For example, if the entity and other parties are jointly and severally liable on an obligation, the amount expected to be paid by the other parties is a contingent liability. A contingent liability must not be recognized. However, it should be disclosed unless the possibility of resource outflows is remote.

    A contingent asset is a possible asset arising from past events, the existence of which will be confirmed only by uncertain future events not wholly within the entity's control. An example is a potential recovery on a legal claim with an uncertain outcome. A contingent asset must not be recognized, but it is disclosed if an inflow of economic benefits is probable.

IAS 38 - Intangible Assets

- An intangible asset must be recognized only if (1) it is probable that the entity will receive the asset's expected economic benefits and (2) the cost is reliably measurable.   347

- The revaluation model may be used for intangible assets if they are traded in active markets.   348

- Development results in recognition of an intangible asset if the entity can demonstrate the (1) technical feasibility of completion of the asset, (2) intent to complete, (3) ability to use or sell the asset, (4) way in which it will generate probable future economic benefits, (5) availability of resources to complete and use or sell the asset, and (6) ability to measure reliably expenditures attributable to the asset.   356

- Advertising costs generally are expensed as incurred.   362

- An impairment loss for an asset (except goodwill) may be reversed if a change in the estimates used to measure the recoverable amount has occurred. The test for impairment of assets other than goodwill has one step: determine whether an asset's carrying amount is greater than its recoverable amount (greater of fair value minus costs to sell or value in use).   350

- For the purpose of impairment testing, goodwill is allocated to the entity's cash-generating units (CGUs) that will benefit from the business combination. A CGU is the lowest level at which goodwill is monitored and must not be larger than an operating segment. The test for impairment of a CGU to which goodwill has been allocated is whether the carrying amount of the CGU (including allocated goodwill) exceeds its recoverable amount (greater of fair value minus costs to sell or value in use). Thus, the test has one step. An impairment loss for a CGU is allocated first to reduce allocated goodwill to zero and then pro rata to other assets of the CGU.   356

IAS 40 - Investment Property

- Under IAS 40, *Investment Property*, investment property is property (land, building, part of a building, or both) held by the owner or by the lessee under a finance lease to earn rental income or for capital appreciation or both. Investment property may be accounted for according to (1) the cost model and carried at historical cost minus accumulated depreciation and impairment losses or (2) the fair value model. If the fair value model is chosen as the accounting policy, all of the entity's investment property must be measured at fair value at the end of the reporting period. A gain or loss arising from a change in the fair value of investment property must be recognized in profit or loss for the period in which it arises. Investment property that is accounted for according to the fair value model is not depreciated.   307

INTERNATIONAL FINANCIAL REPORTING STANDARDS (IFRS)

Page

IASB's Framework

- The elements of financial statements are (1) assets, (2) liabilities, (3) equity, (4) income (including revenues and gains), and (5) expenses (including losses).   31

IFRS 3 - Business Combinations and IFRS 10 - Consolidated Financial Statements

- An investor controls an investee if and only if the investor has all of the following: (1) power over the investee; (2) exposure, or rights, to variable returns from its involvement with the investee; and (3) the ability to use its power over the investee to affect the amount of the investor's returns. Potential voting rights that are currently exercisable must be considered when assessing control.   571

- Consolidated financial statements must be prepared using uniform accounting policies. If a member of the consolidated group uses different policies, adjustments must be made to its statements when preparing the consolidated statements.   573

- An acquirer must recognize a contingent liability at the acquisition date if (1) it is a present obligation arising from past events and (2) its fair value can be measured reliably. Recognition occurs even if it is not probable that an outflow of economic benefits will be needed to settle the obligation. In circumstances other than a business combination, a liability (called a provision) is recognized only if (1) the outflow of benefits is probable and (2) the other criteria are met.   575

- A noncontrolling interest (NCI) may be measured at (1) fair value or (2) a proportionate share of the fair value of the acquiree's identifiable net assets.   577

IFRS 9 - Financial Instruments

- A financial asset not at fair value through profit or loss is measured initially at fair value plus transaction costs. Other financial assets are measured at fair value.

  207

  Unless the fair value option has been elected, financial assets must be classified as subsequently measured at either (1) amortized cost or (2) fair value. This determination is made on the basis of the business model test and the contractual cash flow test.

  A financial asset is subsequently measured at amortized cost if it meets the business model test (objective: collect the contractual cash flows) and the cash flow test (contract provides for specific dates for cash flows that are principal and interest payments only).

  Equity investments are measured at fair value through profit or loss unless the entity has elected at initial recognition to recognize holding gains or losses in other comprehensive income. This irrevocable election may be made for an equity investment not held for trading. But dividend income is still recognized in profit or loss.

  Financial assets are reclassified only if the entity changes its business model for managing them.

- A compound financial instrument (e.g., bonds convertible into stock) has liability and equity components. The issuer allocates to the liability component its fair value. The equity component is allocated the residual amount of the initial carrying amount of the instrument.

  464

- Derecognition of a financial liability (or a part) occurs only by extinguishment. This condition is satisfied only when the debtor pays the creditor or is legally released from primary responsibility either by the creditor or through the legal process.

  472

  - An extinguishment of the old debt and recognition of new debt occurs when the borrower and lender exchange debt instruments with substantially different terms.

  - A substantial modification of terms of any part of an existing financial liability must be accounted for as an extinguishment of the original financial liability and recognition of a new one.

  - The difference between the carrying amount of a liability (or a part) that has been extinguished or transferred and the amount paid is included in profit or loss.

REVIEW CHECKLIST
FINANCIAL

Your objective is to prepare to pass this section of the CPA exam. It is **not** to do a certain amount of work or spend a certain amount of time with this book or other CPA review material/courses. Rather, you **must**

1. Understand the CPA exam thoroughly -- study *CPA Review: A System for Success* and the Introduction in this book.

2. Understand the subject matter in the 20 study units in this book. The list of subunits in each of the 20 study units (presented below and on the following page) should bring to mind core concepts, basic rules, principles, etc.

3. If you have not already done so, prepare a 1- to 2-page summary of each study unit for your final review just before you go to the exam (do not bring notes into the examination room).

Study Unit 1: The Financial Reporting Environment

1.1 Standard Setting for Financial Accounting
1.2 The Objective of General-Purpose Financial Reporting
1.3 Objectives of Financial Reporting -- Not-for-Profit (Nongovernmental) Entities
1.4 Objectives of Financial Reporting -- Governmental Entities
1.5 Assumptions, Principles, and Constraints
1.6 Qualitative Characteristics of Useful Financial Information
1.7 Elements of Financial Statements
1.8 Recognition and Measurement Concepts
1.9 Cash Flow Information and Present Value
1.10 SEC Reporting

Study Unit 2: Financial Statements

2.1 Balance Sheet
2.2 Statements of Income, Retained Earnings, and Changes in Equity
2.3 Comprehensive Income
2.4 Other Financial Statement Presentations
2.5 First-Time Adoption of IFRS

Study Unit 3: Statement of Cash Flows

3.1 Statement of Cash Flows -- Classifications
3.2 Statement of Cash Flows -- Calculations
3.3 Direct and Indirect Methods -- Classifications
3.4 Direct and Indirect Methods -- Calculations

Study Unit 4: Income Statement Items

4.1 Discontinued Operations
4.2 Extraordinary Items
4.3 Accounting Changes and Error Corrections
4.4 Earnings per Share (EPS)
4.5 Long-Term Construction Contracts
4.6 Revenue Recognition after Delivery
4.7 Fair Value Measurements

Study Unit 5: Financial Statement Disclosure

5.1 Significant Accounting Policies
5.2 Segment Reporting
5.3 Interim Financial Reporting
5.4 Related Party Disclosures
5.5 Unconditional Purchase Obligations
5.6 Significant Risks and Uncertainties
5.7 Subsequent Events
5.8 Financial Instrument Disclosures

Study Unit 6: Cash and Investments

6.1 Cash
6.2 Fair Value Option (FVO)
6.3 Classification of Investments
6.4 Equity Method
6.5 Investments in Bonds
6.6 Cash Surrender Value

Study Unit 7: Receivables

7.1 Accounts Receivable -- Fundamentals
7.2 Accounts Receivable -- Measurement
7.3 Transfers of Receivables and Other Financial Assets
7.4 Notes Receivable -- Recognition
7.5 Notes Receivable -- Discounting

Study Unit 8: Inventories

8.1 Inventory Fundamentals
8.2 Consignment Accounting
8.3 Cost Flow Methods -- Application
8.4 Cost Flow Methods -- Comparison
8.5 Dollar-Value LIFO
8.6 Lower of Cost or Market (LCM)
8.7 Special Topics in Inventory Accounting
8.8 Estimating Inventory

Study Unit 9: Property, Plant, Equipment, and Depletable Resources

9.1 Initial Measurement of Property, Plant, and Equipment (PPE)
9.2 Special Measurement Issue -- Internally Constructed Assets (ICAs)
9.3 Subsequent Expenditures for PPE
9.4 Depreciation Methods -- Calculations
9.5 Depreciation Methods -- Changes and Comparison
9.6 Exchanges of Nonmonetary Assets
9.7 Disposals Other than by Exchange
9.8 Impairment of Long-Lived Assets
9.9 Depletion

778

Study Unit 10: Intangible Assets and Other Capitalization Issues

10.1 Intangible Assets Distinct from Goodwill -- Initial Recognition
10.2 Intangible Assets Distinct from Goodwill -- Accounting Subsequent to Acquisition
10.3 Franchise Accounting
10.4 Goodwill
10.5 Research and Development
10.6 Prepayments
10.7 Computer Software
10.8 Special Issues

Study Unit 11: Payables and Taxes

11.1 Accounts Payable
11.2 Accrued Expenses
11.3 Certain Taxes Payable
11.4 Deposits and Other Advances
11.5 Coupons and Premiums
11.6 Warranties
11.7 Income Tax Accounting -- Overview
11.8 Income Tax Accounting -- Temporary and Permanent Differences
11.9 Income Tax Accounting -- Applicable Tax Rate
11.10 Income Tax Accounting -- Recognition of Tax Expense
11.11 Income Tax Accounting -- Other Issues

Study Unit 12: Employee Benefits

12.1 Components of Pension Expense
12.2 Funded Status of Pension Plans
12.3 Pension Disclosures and Other Issues
12.4 Postretirement Benefits Other than Pensions
12.5 Compensated Absences and Postemployment Benefits
12.6 Share-Based Payment

Study Unit 13: Noncurrent Liabilities

13.1 Types of Bond Liabilities
13.2 Time Value of Money
13.3 Bonds Payable -- Initial Measurement
13.4 Bonds Payable -- Subsequent Measurement
13.5 Debt Issue Costs
13.6 Securities with Characteristics of Liabilities and Equity
13.7 Extinguishment of Debt
13.8 Refinancing of Current Obligations
13.9 Noncurrent Notes Payable
13.10 Troubled Debt Restructurings
13.11 Asset Retirement Obligations
13.12 Costs Associated with Exit or Disposal Activities

Study Unit 14: Leases and Contingencies

14.1 Lease Classification
14.2 Lessee Accounting for Capital Leases -- Initial Measurement
14.3 Lessee Accounting for Capital Leases -- Subsequent Measurement
14.4 Lessee Accounting for Capital Leases -- Other Considerations
14.5 Lessor Accounting for Capital Leases
14.6 Operating Leases
14.7 Sale-Leaseback Transactions
14.8 Contingencies -- Recognition and Reporting
14.9 Contingencies -- Amounts Recognized

Study Unit 15: Equity

15.1 Classes of Equity
15.2 Issuance of Stock
15.3 Stock Warrants and Stock Rights
15.4 Treasury Stock -- Acquisition
15.5 Treasury Stock -- Reissue
15.6 Retirement of Stock
15.7 Cash Dividends
15.8 Property Dividends and Liquidating Dividends
15.9 Stock Dividends and Stock Splits
15.10 Partnerships -- Formation and Allocation
15.11 Partnerships -- Changes and Liquidation
15.12 Quasi-Reorganization

Study Unit 16: Business Combinations and Consolidated Financial Reporting

16.1 Accounting for Business Combinations -- Overview
16.2 Consolidated Financial Reporting -- Acquisition Method
16.3 Consolidated Financial Reporting -- Acquisition-Date Balance Sheet
16.4 Consolidated Financial Reporting -- Net Income and Changes in Equity
16.5 Consolidated Financial Reporting -- Intraentity Eliminations
16.6 Other Aspects of Business Combinations
16.7 Combined Financial Statements

Study Unit 17: Derivatives, Hedging, and Other Topics

17.1 Derivatives and Hedging
17.2 Foreign Currency Issues
17.3 Financial Statement Analysis -- Liquidity
17.4 Financial Statement Analysis -- Activity
17.5 Financial Statement Analysis -- Solvency, Valuation, and Comparative Analysis

Study Unit 18: Governmental Accounting

18.1 Fund Accounting Concepts and Reporting
18.2 Budgetary Accounting and Encumbrances
18.3 Governmental Sources of Financing
18.4 Characteristic Transactions of Governmental Entities

Study Unit 19: Governmental Reporting

19.1 The Reporting Entity and the CAFR
19.2 MD&A and the Government-Wide Financial Statements
19.3 Governmental Funds Reporting
19.4 Proprietary Funds Reporting
19.5 Fiduciary Funds Reporting and Interfund Activity

Study Unit 20: Not-for-Profit Concepts

20.1 The Not-for-Profit Environment
20.2 Financial Statements of NFPs
20.3 Revenues of NFPs
20.4 Investments Held by NFPs
20.5 Healthcare Entities (HCEs)

INDEX

Abandonment. 319
Accelerated
   Depreciation. 313
   Filers. 39
Accountability, governmental 25, 645
Accounting
   Budgetary 649
   Changes 126
      Interim. 171
   Consignment 267
   Contributions 739
   Equation 59
   Error 128
   Franchise. 352
   Fund 643
   Governmental standards 643
   Income tax. 387
   Investments 744
   Lessee/lessor. 495
      Governmental. 663
   Pension. 420
   Significant policies 163
   Standards
      Codification (ASC) 20
      Update (ASU). 20
Accounts
   Payable. 381
   Receivable. 231
      Previously written off 236
      Turnover ratio. 621
Accrual 32, 63
   Accounting. 32
Accrued expenses 382
Accumulated
   Depreciation. 312
   Postretirement benefit obligations (APBO) 430
Acid-test ratio 620
Acknowledgments. iv
Acquisition
   (Capitalization) period 308
   Method 575
Additional paid-in capital 529
Administrative (general) expenses. 67
Affiliated company receivables 233
Agency
   Funds. 645
   Transactions 742
Aggregated information, NFPs 730
Aggregation criteria. 164
Aging schedule. 235
All-inclusive approach 64
Allocation. 32, 34
   Interperiod tax 387
   Intraperiod tax 67, 396
Allowance method. 234, 278
Amortizable amount 348
Amortization. 32
   Expense 356
   Premium or discount 462
Annuities 459
Anticipation notes 659

Anticipatory
   Asset. 649
   Liability 650
Appropriations
   Governmental. 650
   Of retained earnings 69, 529
Art and historical treasures. 665
   NFPs. 732
Asset
   And liability approach 387
   Retirement obligation (ARO). 472
Assets 31, 732
   Anticipatory 649
   Capital. 703, 705
      Governmental. 647
   Current 60, 197
   Deferred tax 388
      Interim. 170
   Donated 306, 532
   Group 320
   Infrastructure 666
   Intangible. 60, 356
   Internally constructed (ICAs) 304, 307
   Leased, depreciation. 499
   Long-lived 320
   Net 731
   Noncurrent. 60
   Nonmonetary 317
   Other intangible 347
   Pension plan 421
   Permanently restricted net 745
   Restricted 703
   Servicing 240
   Surrender value 213
   Temporarily restricted net. 745
   Test 164
Assigned fund balance 651
Assumptions 26
Authoritative pronouncements, citations to 18
Available-for-sale securities 205
Average
   Accumulated expenditures (AAE) 308
   Collection period. 622
   Cost 283

Bad debt expense. 234
Balance sheet 31, 59
   Approach. 235
   Governmental funds 698
   Intangible assets. 356
Bank reconciliations 199
Bargain purchase 575
   Option (BPO) 496
Basic
   Earnings per share (BEPS) 129
   Information package (BIP) 38

Basis of accounting
  Cash 72
  Income tax 72
  Modified
    Accrual 646
    Cash 72
  Other comprehensive 72
Basket (lump-sum) purchases 306
Bearer bonds 457
Blending 688
Bond
  Amortizing 212
  As investment 211
  Governmental 657
  Issuance
    Discount 461
    Premium 460
  Types of 457
Book value
  Method 464
  Per common share ratio 624
Books, Gleim i
Boot 318
Budgetary
  Accounting 649
  Comparison schedules (BCSs) 690
  Fund balance 650
Business 572
  Combinations 571
  -Type activities 25, 645, 692

Call option 607, 608
Callable
  Bonds 458
  Preferred stock 528
Capital
  Expenditures 304, 310
  Lease 495
    Governmental 663
  Partnership 542
  Projects funds 644
Capitalization (acquisition) period 308
Cash 197
  Basis of accounting 72
  Discounts (sales discounts) 232, 266
  Dividends 537
  Equivalents 96, 198, 242, 732
  Flows 95, 704
    Direct and indirect presentation 98
    From
      Financing activities 97
      Investing activities 97
      Operating activities 96
    Hedging 180, 610, 611
    Information 36
    Inventory 268
    NFPs 738
  Internal controls 199
  NFPs 732
  Predistribution plan 547
  Restricted 198
  Surrender value 213
Chain discount 266

Change in
  Accounting
    Estimate 127
      Interim 171
    Principle 126
      Interim 171
    Reporting entity 128
Charity care 746
Chief operating decision maker (CODM) 164
Citations to authoritative pronouncements 18
Collateral trust bonds 457
Combined financial statements 71, 586
Committed fund balance 651
Commodity-backed bonds 458
Comparability 29
Comparative analysis 625
Compensated absences 432
  Governmental 664
Compensating balances 198
Completed-contract method 135
Component units 688
  Blended 688
  Discretely presented 688
Composite depreciation 315
Comprehensive
  Annual financial report (CAFR) 689
  Income 31, 69
Computer software 359
Concentrations
  Disclosure 176
  Of credit risk 178
Conceptual framework
  Business entities 22
  Governmental entities 24
  In table format 35
  Not-for-profit entities 23
Condensed income statement 66
Conservatism constraint 27
Consigned goods out 267
Consignment accounting 267
Consolidated financial
  Reporting 573
    Acquisition method 575
    Intraentity eliminations 581
    Noncontrolling interest (NCI) 581
    Year-end financial statements 579
  Statements 71
Consolidation 572
Constant purchasing power accounting 275
Constraints 27
Consumer Price Index 275
Consumption method 662
Content specification outlines (CSOs) 4
Contingencies 506
Contingent
  Liability 245
  Obligation 506
Contract services 358
Contributed capital 529
Contributions 306, 319
  NFPs 739, 741
  To a partnership 542
Contributors and reviewers ii
Control 571

Conversion
Induced 465
Involuntary 320
Convertible
Bonds 458
Debt 464
Preferred stock 528
Securities. 532
Copyrights 349
Corridor approach 424
Cost
Accounting for inventory 265
Advertising. 169, 362
Associated with interim revenue 168
Average. 269, 283
Basis. 265
Constraint 27, 30
Contract termination 474
Current (replacement) 35
Debt issue 463
Governmental. 700
Development 323
Exit or disposal activities 473
FIFO. 283
Flows 268
Historical 27, 35
PPE 304
Indirect 358
Initial
Direct 500
Of Specific PPE 305
Method 210, 534
New basis 321
Of goods
Manufactured. 66, 262
Sold 66, 262
Period 265
Product 265
Recovery method 140
Restoration 323
-Retail ratio 281
Site preparation 305
Transaction 533
Transportation 266
Coupons 385
Credit risk, concentrations 178
Current
Assets. 60, 197
Exchange rate 616
Financial resources. 646
Liabilities 61, 381
Market value (exit value) 35
Obligations. 467
-Rate method 618
Ratio 620
(Replacement) cost 35
Tax liabilities/assets 388

Date of
Declaration 537
Distribution. 537
Record 537

Days' sales in
Inventory 622
Receivables 622
Debentures 457
Debt
Convertible 464
Extinguishment. 466
Issue costs. 463
Governmental. 700
Restructuring 469
Security 203
Service funds 644
-To-equity ratio 624
Declining balance (DB) 313
Deconsolidation 584
Deep-discount bonds 458
Deferrals 32
Deferred
Charges. 61, 361
Inflow of resources 647
Outflow of resources 647
Tax 388, 389, 392
Interim. 170
Defined
Benefit plan 420
Contribution plan 419
Depletion 323
Deposit method 140
Deposits 384
In transit 200
Depreciation. 312
Governmental. 666, 695
Not-for-profit. 732
Derecognition of debt 467
Derivative 179, 607, 609
Embedded 607, 614
Detachable stock warrants 213, 465
Development stage entities (DSEs) 361
Diluted earnings per share (DEPS) 131, 132
Dilution 133
Direct
Expenses. 695
Financing lease 500
Method 704
Operating cash flows. 98, 102
Response advertising 362
Write-off method 234
Disclosures
Defined benefit plans. 429
Depreciation. 316
Fair value. 142
Financial
Instrument 178
Statement 163
ICAs 309
Interim reporting 172
Seasonality 170
Leases 500
Related party 173
Segment reporting 166
Tax 396
Unconditional purchase obligations 175
Discontinued operations 67, 123
Discount, bond issuance 461
Discounting notes receivable 244

Disposal
  Group 320
  Other than by exchange. 319
Distributions to owners 31
Dividends
  Cash. 537
  In arrears. 537
  Liquidating. 538
  Property. 538
  Stock. 539
Dollar-value LIFO 274
  Retail 284
Donor-restricted endowment fund 745
Double-extension method 275

Earnings per share (EPS) 129
Economic-entity assumption. 26
EDGAR. 39
Effective
  Interest method 212, 462
    On lease 498
  Rate method 212
Election dates. 202
Elimination and reclass., governmental 696
Embedded derivatives 607, 614
Encumbrance. 652, 653
Enron Corporation. 585
Enterprise funds 645
Equity 31, 62, 527
  Awards 435
  Interperiod 25, 645
  Method 207
  Security. 203
Error
  Analysis. 128
  Correction 128
  Inventory 280
Estimated
  Other financing
    Sources. 649
    Uses 650
  Revenues 649
Estimates
  Disclosures about 176
  With PPE. 304
Estimating inventory 281
Exchange 317
  Transactions 696, 742
Exercise price. 607
Expected postretirement benefit obligation
  (EPBO) 430
Expenditures 661
Expense
  On income statement 66
  Recognition 34
Expenses. 31
  Accrued. 382
  Governmental. 695
  HCEs 748
Expiration of a restriction 741
External investment pool 706
Extinguishment of debt 466
Extraordinary items 67, 125
  Governmental. 696, 701

Factoring 237
Fair value. 141, 178
  Hedging. 180, 609, 610
  Hierarchy. 142
  Implied 355
  Measurement (FVM) 140, 354
  Method 210
  Of PPE 321
  Option (FVO) 62, 201
Faithful representation. 28
Federal Accounting Standards Advisory
  Board (FASAB). 22
Fiduciary funds. 645, 648, 696, 705
FIFO 270
  Cost 283
  LCM 283
Financial
  Accounting
    Foundation (FAF) 20, 643
    Standards
      Advisory Council (FASAC) 20
      Board (FASB). 20
  Information, summarized at interim 172
  Instrument disclosures. 178
  Reporting
    General purpose external. 691
    Interim. 168
    Releases (FRRs) 37
  Statements 30, 38, 59, 68
    Combined 586
    Common-size. 625
    Consolidated and combined 71
    Disclosure 163
    Fund 689
      Fiduciary 689, 705
      Proprietary. 689
    Government-wide 645
    HCEs 745
    Personal 72
    Presentation. 202
Financing
  Activities 654, 704
  Structure 59
First-time adoption of IFRS. 73
Fiscal accountability 645
FOB (free on board) 264
  Purchases 382
Foreign currency. 616
  Exposures 610
  Transactions 616
  Translation. 616, 617
    Hedging. 612
Form
  8-K 40
  10-K 39
  10-Q 39
  S-1 39
  S-3 39
  S-4 39
Forward contract. 608
Franchises 352
Full-disclosure principle 27
Functional currency. 616

Fund 644
  Agency 645, 705, 706
    Tax 706
  Balance 650
    Classification 650
  Capital projects 644, 698
  Debt service 644, 698
  Enterprise 645, 702
  Fiduciary 645, 648, 696, 705
  Financial statements 645
  General 644, 697
  Governmental 644
  Internal service 645, 696, 702
  Investment trust 645
  Major 697, 702
  Nonmajor 697
  Permanent 644, 698
  Private-purpose trust 645
  Proprietary 645, 648, 702, 703
  Reporting 697
  Special revenue 644, 698
  Trust 645, 705
    Investment 706
    Pension 705
    Private-purpose 706
Fundamental qualitative characteristics 28
Funded status
  OPEB 431
  Pensions 426
Future
  Deductible amount 390
  Value (FV) of an amount 459
Futures contract 608

Gain 31
  Contingency 507
  Transaction 616
GASB Concepts Statement No. 1 24
General
  Capital assets 647
  Fund 644, 697
  Long-term liabilities 648
  Revenues 695
Generally accepted accounting principles (GAAP) . . 20
Gift certificate 384
Gleim, Irvin N. iii
Going-concern (business continuity) assumption . . . 26
Goodwill 353, 575
  Equity method 355
  Impairment 354
Government
  -Mandated nonexchange transactions 654, 656
  -Wide financial statements 645, 688, 692
Governmental
  Accountability 645
  Accounting Standards Board (GASB) 21, 643
  Activities 692
  Concepts 643, 687
  Funds 644, 697
  Transactions 661
  -Type activities 24
Grant, W.T. 95
Grants 695

Gross
  Investment 500
  Method
    Payables 266, 382
    Receivables 232
  Profit
    Method 281
    Percentage 138
    With sales-type lease 502
Group depreciation 315
Guaranteed residual value 496
Guaranty bonds 457

Healthcare entities (HCEs) 745
Hedging 179, 608
  Cash flow 610, 611
  Fair value 609, 610
Held-to-maturity 204
Highest and best use (HBU) 141
Historical cost principle 27
Horizontal (trend) analysis 625

If-converted method 133
IFRS 20
  Accounting changes/error correction 129
  Advertising costs 362
  Balance sheet 63
  Business combinations 571, 575
  Classification of investments 207
  Comparative statements 104
  Compensated absences 433
  Consolidated financial statements 573
  Contingencies 507
  Convertible debt 464
  Current liabilities 62
  Deferred tax
    Asset valuation allowance 391
    Classification 396
    Liabilities 390
    Measurement 388
  Derecognition, liabilities 472
  Discontinued operations 125
  Elements of financial statements 31
  Equity method 208, 210
  Extraordinary items 67, 126
  First-time adoption 73
  Goodwill 356
  Impairment of PPE 316, 323
  Intangible assets 347, 348
    Impairment 350
  Interest income on plan assets 423
  Interim reporting 168, 169
  Lease classification 496
  LIFO 273
  Long-term construction contracts 138
  Lower of cost or market 279
  Measurement of PPE 307
  Noncontrolling interest 577
  Other comprehensive income 71

IFRS (continued)
Past service cost. 425
Pension expense 425
Personal financial statements. 73
Related party disclosures. 174
Reporting, profit or loss 68
Research and development 356
Revenue recognition 34
Sale-leaseback. 505
Statement of cash flows. 97
Immediate recognition 34
Impairment. 206
Long-lived assets 320
Implied
Fair value. 355
Time restriction. 741
Imposed nonexchange revenues 654, 655
Improvements 310
Income 64
Bonds 458
Comprehensive 69
Deferred taxes 392
Investment. 744
Statement 31, 63, 123, 126
Approach. 235
Format 64
Tax. 387
Basis of accounting. 72
Interim. 170
Uncertainty 397
Unearned. 500
Incremental method 533
Indirect
Expenses. 695
Method, operating cash flows 98, 99
Industry practices constraint. 27
Infrastructure assets 666
Initial
Cost of specific PPE 305
Measurement. 506
Installment
Method 138
Sales. 264
Intangible assets. 60, 347
Integrated disclosure system 37
Interest 167, 458
Capitalization 308
Expense 67
Imputed. 242
Income 206
Method 462
With sales-type lease 502
Rate swap 608
Unreasonable. 243
Interfund
Activities 696, 707
Transactions 661
Interim
Financial reporting 168
Inventory estimation 281
Segment reporting 167
Internal service fund 645, 696, 702
Internally constructed assets (ICAs) 307

International
Accounting Standards 20, 767
Board (IASB) 20
Elements of financial statements. 774
Financial Reporting Standards (IFRS) 20, 774
Accounting changes/error correction 129
Advertising costs. 362
Balance sheet 63
Business combinations 571, 575
Classification of investments 207
Comparative statements 104
Compensated absences 433
Consolidated financial statements. 573
Contingencies 507
Convertible debt 464
Current liabilities. 62
Deferred tax
Asset valuation allowance 391
Classification 396
Liabilities 390
Measurement. 388
Derecognition, liabilities 472
Discontinued operations 125
Elements of financial statements. 31
Equity method 208, 210
Extraordinary items. 67, 126
First-time adoption 73
Goodwill 356
Impairment of PPE 316, 323
Intangible assets. 347, 348
Impairment. 350
Interest income on plan assets 423
Interim reporting 168, 169
Lease classification. 496
LIFO 273
Long-term construction contracts 138
Lower of cost or market 279
Measurement of PPE 307
Noncontrolling interest. 577
Other comprehensive income. 71
Past service cost. 425
Pension expense 425
Personal financial statements 73
Related party disclosures. 174
Reporting, profit or loss 68
Research and development 356
Revenue recognition 34
Sale-leaseback. 505
Statement of cash flows. 97
Interperiod equity 645
Intraentity eliminations. 581
Inventory 261
Accounting systems 262
Errors 280
Estimating 281
Pools. 274
Turnover 622
Investing activities. 704
Investments 60
By owners 31
Classification of 203
NFPs. 744
Trust fund 645, 706
Involuntary conversion. 320
Items in transit 264

Journal entries
    Enterprise funds 702
    Internal service funds 702

Land 305
    Improvements 304, 305
Landfills 664
Large accelerated filers 39
Lease 495
    Capital 495
    Governmental 663
    Operating 504
    Payments receivable 501
Leasehold improvements 304, 306
Leverage ratios 624
Liabilities 31
    Contingent 245
    Current 61, 381
    Deferred tax 388, 389
    Long-term 648, 703, 705
    Noncurrent 62, 457
    Share-based payment 436
LIFO 270
    Dollar value 274
    Retail 284
        Dollar value 284
Liquidating dividends 538
Liquidity ratios 619
Long-term construction contracts 135
Loss
    Contingency 506
    Impairment 321, 356
    Recognized 350
    Transaction 616
Losses 31
Lower of
    Average cost or market (LACM) 284
    Cost or market (LCM) 277

Machinery and equipment 304, 305
Magazine subscriptions 384
Major fund 697, 702
Management's discussion and analysis (MD&A) . . . 38
    Governmental 691
Mandatorily redeemable financial
    instruments (MRFIs) 528
Manufacturing, inventories 262
Market 141, 277
    Decline interim 169
Matching 34
    Principle 235, 385
Materiality 28
Maturity date 462

Measurement
    Attributes 35
    Deferred taxes 392
    Fair value 140, 354
    Focus
        Current financial resources 646
        Economic resources 646
    In financial statements 30
    Of impairment 321
    PPE 303
    Purchases 266
    Segment reporting 167
    Share-based 436
Medium of exchange 197
Merger 572
Minimum lease payments 496
Miscellaneous items 304
Modified
    Accrual basis of accounting 646
    Cash basis of accounting 72
Monetary
    Items 618
    -Unit assumption 26
Mortgage
    Bonds 457
    Notes 468
Multiple-step income statement 65

Natural resources 323
Negative retained earnings 549
Net
    Assets 731
        Model 730
    Income 31
    Investment 501
    Method
        Payables 266, 382
        Receivables 232
    Operating losses, deferred tax consequences . . . 394
    Periodic postretirement benefit cost (NPPBC) . . . 431
    Permanently restricted assets 745
    Position 693
        Restricted 693
        Statement of 692, 703
            Fiduciary 705
        Unrestricted 693
    Realizable value (NRV) 35, 235, 277
    Settlement value 381, 607
    Temporarily restricted assets 745
No-par stock 530
Nominal units of money 197
Nonaccelerated filers 39
Nonaccrual 383
Noncash
    Investing and financing activities 97
    Short-term investments 199
Noncontingent obligation 506
Noncontrolling interest (NCI) 577
Noncurrent
    Assets 60
    Liabilities 62, 457
    Notes payable 468
Nonderivative 612
Nonexchange transactions 654, 703

Noninterest-bearing notes 242
Nonmonetary
    Assets 317
    Items 618
Nonspendable fund balance 651
Nontrade receivables 231
Not-for-profit
    Entities (NFPs) 23, 729
        Hedging 614
        Reporting 23
Notes
    Anticipation 659
    Long-term 242
    Noninterest-bearing 242
    Payable 468
    Receivable 242, 244

Operating
    Activities 704
    Cycle 60, 623
    Expenses 66
    Lease 504
    Segment 164
Operational accountability 645
Organization costs 348
Other
    Comprehensive
        Bases of accounting (OCBOA) 72
        Postretirement employee benefits (OPEB) 430
Outstanding checks 200
Overdraft 199

Pacioli, Luca 59
Paid-in capital in excess of par 529
Par value 530
    Method 534
Participating bonds 458
Partnerships 541
    Addition of partner 544
    Cash predistribution plan 547
    Income and loss 542
    Liquidation 546
    Sale of interest 543
    Withdrawal 545
Patents 349
Pension 419, 645
    Benefit obligations 421
    Employer's accounting for 420
Percentage-of-completion method 136
Period cost 265
Periodic system 263
Periodicity assumption 27
Permanent
    Difference 388, 391
    Funds 644
    Restriction 732, 741
Perpetual system 262
Personal financial statements 72
Pledging 238
Position, net 693
Postemployment benefits 433
Postretirement benefits 430
Potential common stock (PCS) 131

Pre-disposal operations 123
Preferred stock 528
    Cumulative 537
Premium, bond issuance 460
Premiums 385
Prepayments 359
Present value (PV) 35
    Expected cash flow (ECF) approach 36
    Of an amount 458
    Traditional approach 36
Primary government 687, 692
Principles 27
Prior-period adjustment 128
    Interim 171
Private-purpose funds 645
Product cost 265
Profit (loss) test 165
Profitability ratios 624
Program
    Revenues 695
    Services 736
Progress billings 137
Projected benefit obligation (PBO) 421
Promissory note 242
Property
    Dividends 538
    Plant, and equipment (PPE) 60, 303
        Expenditures 310
Proprietary funds 645, 648, 702, 703
Proprietorships 540
Purchase commitments 279
Purchases method 662
Put option 607, 608

Qualitative characteristics, enhancing 29
Quasi-reorganization 549
Quick (acid-test) ratio 620

Ratio
    Accounts receivable turnover 621
    Book value per common share 624
    Current 620
    Debt-to-equity 624
    Quick (acid-test) 620
    Times-interest-earned 624
    Working capital 620
Ratios
    Activity 621
    Inventory 622
    Leverage 624
    Liquidity 619
    Profitability 624
    Solvency 624
Realization 33
Rearrangements, reinstallations, relocations 311
Receivables 231
    Affiliated company 233
    Measurement 234
    Ratios 621
Recognition 33
    In financial statements 30

Reconciliations
    Bank 199
    Defined benefit plans. 429
    Governmental. 699, 701
    Proprietary Funds 704
    Segment reporting 167
Recoverability test. 321
Redeemable bonds. 458
Refinancing 467
Registered bonds 457
Regulation
    S-B 37
    S-K 37
    S-X 37
Related party disclosures. 173
Relevance 28
Remeasurement 618
Repairs and maintenance 311
Replacement cost. 277
Replacements 310
Reportable segments 164
Reporting
    Bonds 463
    Currency 616
    Entity, governmental 687
    Exit or disposal costs. 474
    Fiduciary funds. 705
    Governmental. 643
    HCEs 747
    Intangible assets. 356
    Major fund 697
    PPE impairment 321
    Receivables. 233
    Segment 164
    Unit. 353
Required supplementary information (RSI) 690
Requisite service period (RSP) 435
Research and development (R&D) 356
Residual value 348
Resource structure 59
Restatement, segment reporting 167
Restoration costs 323
Restricted
    Cash 198
    Fund balance 651
    Net Position 693
    Support 741
Retail method. 281
Retailing, inventories. 261
Retained earnings. 68, 529
    Negative 549
Retrospective application 127

Revenue
    Bonds 458
    Derived tax 655
    Expenditure 304, 310
    Governmental. 700
    HCEs 745
    Interim. 168
    NFPs. 734
    Nonexchange. 703
    Nonoperating 703
    Operating. 703
    Patient services 746
    Proprietary Funds 703
    Recognition 33
        After delivery 138
        Governmental. 654
    Test 164
Revenues 31
Reverse
    Stock split 540
    Treasury stock method 134
Reversing entries 383
Review checklist. 777
Reviewers and contributors ii
Right of return 264
Rights offering 533
Risk-financing activity 707
Risks and uncertainties 175

Sale-leaseback. 504
Sales
    Returns and allowances. 233
    -Type lease 501
Sarbanes-Oxley Act of 2002
    Personal credit 61
    Real-time disclosure 40
    Related parties 173
Second mortgage bonds 457
Secured borrowings 238
Securities
    Act of 1933 . . . . 37, 39
    And Exchange Commission (SEC) 19, 37
    Exchange Act of 1934 37
Securitization 238
Segment reporting 164
Selling expenses 66
Serial bond 457
Settlement of troubled debt 469
SFAC No.
    4 23
    5 33
    6 30
    7 36
    8 28
Share
    Appreciation rights (SARs) 437
    Award plan. 437
    -Based payment 434
    Options 436
Shelf registration. 40
Significant
    Influence 207
    Risks and uncertainties 175

Simple capital structure 129
    EPS reporting. 134
Simulation questions 16
Single-step income statement. 64
Sinking fund. 458
Skill specification outlines (SSOs) 8
Software to be
    Marketed 359
    Used internally 360
Sole proprietorships 540
Solvency ratios. 624
Special
    Assessments 660
    Items. 696
        Governmental. 701
    -Purpose
        Entity (SPE) 585
        Governments 691
    Revenue funds 644
Specific identification. 268
Spot rate 616
Staff accounting bulletins (SABs) 37
Standardized financial statements 38
Start-up costs. 348
Stated value. 530
Statement of
    Activities 695
        NFPs. 730
    Cash flows. 95
        NFPs. 730, 738
        Proprietary funds 704
    Changes in net worth 73
    Comprehensive income 31
    Earnings 31
    Equity (changes in equity) 68
    Financial
        Condition. 72
        Position 31
    Functional expenses 737
    Income 63, 123, 126
    Investments by and distributions to owners 31
    Net position 692, 703
        Fiduciary 705
    Retained earnings. 68
Statistical section 690
Stock. 528
    Common 528
    Dividends. 539
        In EPS. 131
    Issuance 530
    Preferred 528
        Cumulative. 537
    Retirement. 536
    Rights 533
    Splits. 540
        In EPS. 131
        Reverse. 540
    Subscription 530
    Treasury 63, 529
        Allocation. 534
        Method 133
        Reissue. 535
    Warrants 213, 465, 533
Straight-line method 312, 348
Strike price. 607
Subordinated debentures 457

Subsequent
    Events. 177
    Expenditures, PPE 310
    Measurement 506
Sum-of-the-years'-digits (SYD) 314
Supporting services. 736

Take-or-pay contract 174
Tax
    Accounting. 387
    Applicable rates 392
    Considerations 730
    Deferred
        Asset. 170, 388
        Income 392
        Liability 388, 389
    Derived revenues 655
    Effects of changes in exchange rates 619
    Estimated annual effective rate. 170
    Federal unemployment 384
    FICA 384
    Income 387
        Uncertainty 397
    Interim period 170
    Interperiod allocation 387, 619
    Intraperiod allocation 67, 396, 619
    Payable. 384
    Position 397
    Property. 384
    Sales. 384
Temporal method 618
Temporary
    Difference (TD). 389
    Restriction 731, 741
Term bond 457
Throughput contract 174
Time value of money 458
Timeliness 29
Times-interest-earned ratio 624
Total
    Compensation cost 435
    External revenue 165
Trade
    Discounts. 232, 266
    Receivables 231
Trademarks 350
Trading securities 204
Transaction
    Date 616
    Gains and losses. 619
Transfers 319
    Between categories. 206
    Of financial assets. 239
Translation method 617
Treasury stock 63, 529
    Allocation. 534
    Method 133
    Reissue. 535
Troubled debt restructuring (TDR). 469
Trust fund 645, 705

Unassigned fund balance. 651
Uncertain tax position 397

Unconditional purchase obligations 174
Underlying 607
Understandability 29
Unrealized holding gains and losses 205
Unrestricted support 741
Usage-centered activity, depreciation 314
Users of financial information 22

Valuation 142
    Allowance 391
        Interim 170
Value
    Confirmatory 28
    Predictive 28
Variable
    Interest entities (VIEs) 585
    Rate bonds 458
Variance power 742
Verifiability 29
Vertical analysis 625
Vesting conditions 435
Voluntary
    Health and welfare entities (VHWEs) 737
    Nonexchange transactions 654, 656
Vouchers payable 652

Warranties 386
Weighted-average
    Inventory costing 269
    Rate 617
        For ICAs 309
Working capital ratio 620
WorldCom 173

Yield to maturity 460

Zero-coupon bonds 458

791

Page 1 of 2

GLEIM CPA REVIEW SYSTEM

Includes: Gleim Online, Review Books, Test Prep Online, Simulation Wizard, Audio Review, Practice Exam, CPA Review: A System for Success booklet, plus bonus Book Bag.

$989.95 x _____ = $_____

Also available by exam section (does not include Book Bag).

GLEIM CMA REVIEW SYSTEM

Includes: Gleim Online, Review Books, Test Prep Software Download, Essay Wizard, Audio Review, Practice Exam, CMA Review: A System for Success booklet, plus bonus Book Bag.

$739.95 x _____ = $_____

Also available by exam part (does not include Book Bag).

GLEIM CIA REVIEW SYSTEM

Includes: Gleim Online, Review Books, Test Prep Software Download, Audio Review, Practice Exam, CIA Review: A System for Success booklet, plus bonus Book Bag.

$824.95 x _____ = $_____

Also available by exam part (does not include Book Bag).

GLEIM EA REVIEW SYSTEM

Includes: Gleim Online, Review Books, Test Prep Software Download, Audio Review, Practice Exam, EA Review: A System for Success booklet, plus bonus Book Bag.

$629.95 x _____ = $_____

Also available by exam part (does not include Book Bag).

GLEIM RTRP REVIEW SYSTEM

Includes: Gleim Online, Question Bank Online, Practice Exam, 15 hours of CE.

$139.95 x _____ = $_____

"THE GLEIM EQE SERIES" EXAM QUESTIONS AND EXPLANATIONS

Includes: 5 Books and *Test Prep Software Download*.

$112.25 x _____ = $_____

Also available by part.

GLEIM ONLINE CPE

Try a FREE 4-hour course at gleim.com/cpe
- Easy-to-Complete
- Informative
- Effective

Contact
GLEIM® PUBLICATIONS
for further assistance:

gleim.com
800.874.5346
sales@gleim.com

SUBTOTAL $_____

Complete your order on the next page

Subject to change without notice.

GLEIM® PUBLICATIONS, INC.

P. O. Box 12848   Gainesville, FL 32604

TOLL FREE:	800.874.5346	Customer service is available (Eastern Time):
LOCAL:	352.375.0772	8:00 a.m. - 7:00 p.m., Mon. - Fri.
FAX:	352.375.6940	9:00 a.m. - 2:00 p.m., Saturday
INTERNET:	gleim.com	Please have your credit card ready,
EMAIL:	sales@gleim.com	or save time by ordering online!

SUBTOTAL (from previous page) $_____

Add applicable sales tax for shipments within Florida. _____

Shipping (nonrefundable)   14.00

TOTAL $_____

Email us for prices/instructions on shipments outside the 48 contiguous states, or simply order online.

NAME (please print) _____

ADDRESS _____ Apt. _____
(street address required for UPS/Federal Express)

CITY _____ STATE _____ ZIP _____

____ MC/VISA/DISC/AMEX ____ Check/M.O. Daytime Telephone (_____)

Credit Card No. _____ - _____ - _____ - _____

Exp. _____ / _____ Signature _____
Month / Year

Email address _____

1. We process and ship orders daily, within one business day over 98.8% of the time. Call by 3:00 pm for same day service.

2. Gleim Publications, Inc. guarantees the immediate refund of all resalable texts, unopened and un-downloaded Test Prep Software, and unopened and un-downloaded audios returned within 30 days. Accounting and Academic Test Prep online courses may be canceled within 30 days if no more than the first study unit or lesson has been accessed. In addition, Online CPE courses may be canceled within 30 days if no more than the Introductory Study Questions have been accessed. Accounting Practice Exams may be canceled within 30 days of purchase if the Practice Exam has not been started. Aviation online courses may be canceled within 30 days if no more than two study units have been accessed. This policy applies only to products that are purchased directly from Gleim Publications, Inc. No refunds will be provided on opened or downloaded Test Prep Software or audios, partial returns of package sets, or shipping and handling charges. Any freight charges incurred for returned or refused packages will be the purchaser's responsibility.

3. Please PHOTOCOPY this order form for others.

4. No CODs. Orders from individuals must be prepaid.

Subject to change without notice. 11/12

For updates and other important information, visit our website.

GLEIM
KNOWLEDGE
TRANSFER
SYSTEMS®